Human-Assisted Intelligent Computing

Modeling, simulations and applications

Online at: https://doi.org/10.1088/978-0-7503-4801-0

IOP Series in Next Generation Computing

Series editors

Prateek Agrawal
University of Klagenfurt, Austria and Lovely Professional University, India

Anand Sharma
Mody University of Science and Technology, India

Vishu Madaan
Lovely Professional University, India

About the series

The motivation for this series is to develop a trusted library on advanced computational methods, technologies, and their applications.

This series focuses on the latest developments in next generation computing, and in particular on the synergy between computer science and other disciplines. Books in the series will explore new developments in various disciplines that are relevant for computational perspective including foundations, systems, innovative applications, and other research contributions related to the overall design of computational tools, models, and algorithms that are relevant for the respective domain. It encompasses research and development in artificial intelligence, machine learning, block chain technology, quantum cryptography, quantum computing, nanoscience, bioscience-based sensors, IoT applications, nature inspired algorithms, computer vision, bioinformatics, etc. and their applications in the areas of science, engineering, business, and the social sciences. It covers a broad spectrum of applications in the community, including those in industry, government, and academia.

The aim of the series is to provide an opportunity for prospective researchers and experts to publish works based on next generation computing and its diverse applications. It also provides a data-sharing platform that will bring together international researchers, professionals, and academics. This series brings together thought leaders, researchers, industry practitioners, and potential users of different disciplines to develop new trends and opportunities, exchange ideas and practices related to advanced computational methods, and promote interdisciplinary knowledge.

A full list of titles published in this series can be found here: https://iopscience.iop.org/bookListInfo/iop-series-in-next-generation-computing.

Human-Assisted Intelligent Computing

Modeling, simulations and applications

Edited by

Mukhdeep Singh Manshahia

Punjabi University Patiala, Punjab, India

Igor S Litvinchev

Nuevo Leon State University, Mexico

Gerhard-Wilhelm Weber

Poznan University of Technology, Poznan, Poland

J Joshua Thomas

UOW Malaysia, KDU Penang University College, Malaysia

Pandian Vasant

MERLIN Research Centre, Ton Duc Thang University, Vietnam

IOP Publishing, Bristol, UK

ISBN 978-0-7503-4801-0 (ebook)
ISBN 978-0-7503-4799-0 (print)
ISBN 978-0-7503-4802-7 (myPrint)
ISBN 978-0-7503-4800-3 (mobi)

DOI 10.1088/978-0-7503-4801-0

Version: 20230401

IOP ebooks

British Library Cataloguing-in-Publication Data: A catalogue record for this book is available from the British Library.

Published by IOP Publishing, wholly owned by The Institute of Physics, London

IOP Publishing, No.2 The Distillery, Glassfields, Avon Street, Bristol, BS2 0GR, UK

US Office: IOP Publishing, Inc., 190 North Independence Mall West, Suite 601, Philadelphia, PA 19106, USA

Dedicated to Green Earth

Contents

Preface

During previous decades, the analytical toolbox and the methodological tools of computer science and applied mathematics, of informatics and statistics, of emerging analytics and information technologies has gained the attention of numerous researchers and practitioners worldwide, providing a strong impact also in natural sciences, engineering, economics and finance, the IT sector and, in recent years, the sector of security, e.g., in data storage, data handling, data transfer, in traffic, transportation, supply chains, etc. Here, optimization turns out to be a key technology from an integrated perspective, and it is closely connected with further areas of modern operational research such as development, societal complexity and ethics, in order to appropriately address aspects of living conditions, safety and freedom, in culture and environment with regard to that new and fast growing industry. Big-data-based and security-oriented techniques are more and more well-known and employed in research areas of engineering, science and technology. Current trends on application problems in engineering, science and technology are also expanded into the areas of economy, finance and, especially, into hotels, tourism, travel and urban management across the globe. This edited book delivers the best, high-quality, selected chapters in a rich variety of research topics. Well-known and new methodologies of optimization techniques are used to resolve some of the very complicated and hard problems related to our research subjects.

Contributing authors of this edited book are experienced scientists and practitioners from all over the world; they have used and further refined the deep model-based methods of mathematics and the less model-based, also so-called smart or intelligent algorithms with their roots in the engineering disciplines, in computer science, and informatics. The second type of algorithms are often called heuristics and model-free; they are less rigorous mathematically, released from firm calculus, in order to integrate Nature- and, especially, bio-inspired approaches to efficiently cope with hard problems. The rise of these algorithms from artificial intelligence have happened in parallel to the powerful progress in mathematics that is model-based mainly. Today, labeled by names like statistical learning, machine learning, metaheuristics and matheuristics, and by operational research, model-free and model-based streamlines of traditions and approaches meet and interact in many centers of research, at important congresses, in leading projects and agendas in worldwide to overcome misunderstandings and misperceptions between these two academic avenues, but to gain from synergy effects, to jointly advance scientific progress and to provide a common service to the solution of urgent real-life challenges. Those vast problems exist in every area of the modern world and academics, in engineering, economics, social, life and human sciences, in development and the improvement of living conditions and future perspectives. Among the variety of these subjects and, in fact, including them all, we have selected the fields of human-assisted intelligent computing, modeling, simulations and their applications.

The objective of this edited book is to bring together international experts, scientists, and practitioners in human-assisted intelligent computing, modeling and simulation to share their current research achievements. For this book project, the Editors received over 60 submissions from 30 countries and each chapter was reviewed by at least four expert reviewers. The best 33 chapters were finally selected for inclusion in the book. They represent more than 20 countries, such as India, United Kingdom, Croatia, Latvia, Japan, Republic of Korea, Belarus, Vietnam, Czech Republic, Malaysia, Mexico, Italy, Poland, Russia, USA, Morocco, Thailand, Ukraine, Saudi Arabia and Uganda. This worldwide representation clearly demonstrates the interest of the global research community to this book. The book covers broad aspects of human-assisted intelligent computing in numerical optimization and control, renewable energy and sustainability, artificial intelligence and operations research, language processing and deep learning, smart cities and rural planning, big data and cyber security, block chains and financial engineering, IoTs and Industry 4.0, healthcare and medicine. A brief description of each selected chapter is given below.

In chapter 1, the authors discuss a crop evapotranspiration prediction model to provide scientific foundation for judicious water use, and sustainable increase in agriculture productivity. The water loss from a farmed field is referred to as crop evapotranspiration. Agricultural production will decrease when the crop growth cycle is shortened due to rising temperatures, lack of humidity and soil water scarcity. To resolve complex correlations of non-linear weather conditions with evapotranspiration, IoT-enabled machine learning can be used to predict crop evapotranspiration accurately resulting in designing better and more precise irrigation schedules for farmers to get an insight into the quantity and timing of irrigation and adaptability to change with changing soil type, crop type, weather.

Chapter 2 presents a system of methods which obtains features from iris image and embeds a given secret key there. This yields a combined key, such that the key cannot be extracted unless providing biometric features close to the original ones, i.e. the data of the same person. System processing starts with approximate detection of eye center followed by approximate segmentation of inner and outer borders of iris. Then the borders are refined. Biometric features are binary and are extracted by commonly adopted technique. The embedding method (coder) consists of error-correcting coding of the secret key followed by bit-wise sum modulo 2 with biometric features. The error-correcting coding consists of separate steps, which are executed in sequence: Reed–Solomon, Hadamard, majority coding, and bit hashing. The decoder repeats encoder steps in inverse order. The parameters of error correction codes are selected optimally to provide storing of largest secret key while preserving error rates and fitting in given size of biometric template. Possible size of the secret key is 65 bit. Numerical experiments are conducted with several open-access databases.

In chapter 3, economic load dispatch (ELD) and emission dispatch problems are optimized separately using particle swarm optimization, quantum-inspired particle swarm optimization, and quantum-inspired bat algorithm for the various numbers of units. Later, both objectives are assumed simultaneously as an optimization problem with multiple objectives. The emission dispatch problem is divided into three independent objectives to minimize SO_2, NO_X and CO_2 emissions. Thus, the combined economic emission dispatch (CEED) problem is an optimization problem with four objectives. A unit-wise price penalty factor was assumed to change over all the targets into a single target. The idea is to attain a balanced trade-off between secured and profitable energy choices while maintaining a healthy and sound environment. The quantum computing phenomenon was integrated with swarm intelligence-based particle swarm optimization (PSO) and bat algorithm (BA) to make them computationally more powerful and robust. The results obtained from quantum-inspired bat algorithm (QBA) and quantum particle swarm optimization (QPSO) to solve the CEED problem contrasted with other existing techniques such as Lagrangian relaxation, PSO, and simulated annealing.

Chapter 4 explores the scope of artificial intelligence in cognitive radio (CR)-based scenarios for the internet of things (IoT) networks. The demand for more data rates for internet-connected devices is causing a scarcity in the frequency spectrum. There are some shortcomings of conventional approaches to handle the spectrum scarcity problem that makes them less liable to adoption. To overcome these shortcomings and improve the performance, a novel cooperative spectrum sensing (CSS) scheme based on eigenvalues of the signal covariance matrix and fuzzy C-means (FCM) clustering is proposed. In the proposed approach, multi-input and multi-output (MIMO) based CR technology is adopted for IoTs. The key idea in this chapter is to use an FCM algorithm to train a multidimensional classifier. The proposed approach directly clusters the eigenvalues in multidimensional space; this contrasts with the commonly used schemes, where multiple eigenvalues are used to form a single statistic. An extensive collection of results is provided regarding detection gain, throughput, energy consumption, expected lifetime, and error probability. The reported results are also compared with some of the recent eigenvalue-based approaches.

Chapter 5 considers the general system of ordinary differential equations. This system arises in the theory of gene networks, neuronal and telecommunication networks. The system has a large number of parameters that affect the behavior of solutions. The main group of parameters, describing the interaction of network elements, is written in the so-called regulatory matrix. The evolution of the system (and the described network as well) depends on the attracting sets in the phase space. The chapter contains recently obtained and new results on the structure of the phase space, behavior of solutions, attractors of the system.

Chapter 6 envisions a set of system properties like information privacy research and privacy. Such properties are formalized as technical functionalities in ensuring data subjects' rights in knowing what data is being collected and processed about them. To ensure them, transparency enhancing tools/technologies (TETs) are used to enhance understanding and visibility of procedures, practices and consequences of personal data processing at data processors. As a combination of technological and organizational solutions or methods, their goals can be perceived as privacy, as well as a software engineering prerequisite. By using identification, classification and modeling heuristics of the goal-based requirement analysis method, requirements for effective TETs are systemized across momentous data privacy governance frameworks. The synthesis made of relevant transparency goals can serve as a precondition for computing intelligent privacy organizational environments.

Chapter 7 proposed a smart log-periodic based model of leg-segment regeneration phenomena in multicells. In this model, each cell is assumed to have a value of a log-periodic curve. According to differences between the left–right dimers, a cell is assumed to proliferate, move, and vanish (die). Using this framework, dimers were assumed to be redistributed in a manner of p left + $(1-p)$ right $(0 < p < 1)$, which enables explanation of some leg-regeneration phenomena. It was, however, impossible to explain regeneration across leg segments, namely segment regeneration. In this work, on the other hand, each cell is assumed to have a value of a log-periodic curve, which gives an explanation of segment regeneration.

Chapter 8 attempts to discuss various location-based services available and also to highlight the various anomaly detection techniques available for those services. Mapping and navigation services that provide maps, features, attribute data, positioning information; navigation and route guidance accessible to client applications are discussed. Tracking services that focus on vehicle tracking, traffic prediction and traffic monitoring are reviewed. Finally, several anomaly detection techniques such as route anomalies, user behavior anomalies, and fake check-in anomalies are discussed in the context of location-based services. This chapter also highlights the limitations that exist in location-based services and suggests ways to improve systems using these services.

Chapter 9 presents packing soft ellipses in a minimal convex rectangle domain. The ellipses are soft in the sense that their shapes are not fixed *a priori* and can vary in a certain range subject to their individual areas' conservation. Free translation and rotation of ellipses is permitted. The objective is minimizing the container's height. New mathematical tools to state analytically layout constraints are introduced based on the phi-function approach. Packing soft ellipses is stated as a nonconvex optimization problem, a solution technique is developed, and results of numerical experiment are discussed. Soft packing problems are motivated by modeling porous media under pressure and arise in the oil and gas extracting industry.

Chapter 10 deals with the analysis of phishing emails and modeling of phishing attacks. The introduction explains the definition of phishing, the classification of messages in the content of phishing email, and techniques of phishing email threats and attacks. The research includes some experiments processed during the calendar year. Data collection was made from email accounts of one of the authors in the time interval of one month at the beginning, middle, and end of the period. Data were included in tables, which allow better statistical processing and frequency analysis. Segmentation of emails according to the content of the message results to segment business, fund, transfer, charity, and others are explained, characterized by keywords, and a sample of an email message is introduced. Text analytical SW Tovek is used for analysis and extraction entities (name, email address, phone numbers, geographic data, etc) from the text of emails. This intelligent function of the SW Tovek in the entity's extraction was tested and evaluated.

In chapter 11, authors propose a drought prediction model using remote sensing for design and implementation of the spatiotemporal drought management plan. Overall, They are interested in the interaction between natural vegetation and climate algorithms (ecological modeling or human-assisted intelligent computing), particularly in the development of a drought early warning system that would identify drought risk levels from remote sensing. They are working in particular on Morocco rangelands where access is difficult; in these regions the majority of household income is based on livestock.

Chapter 12 presents a state-of-the-art survey about attention mechanisms in machine vision. A gentle introduction to attention mechanisms is given, followed by a discussion of the popular attention-based deep architectures. Subsequently, the major categories of the intersection of attention mechanisms and deep learning for machine vision (MV) based are discussed. Afterwards, the major algorithms, issues and trends within the scope of the chapter are discussed.

Chapter 13 considers the optimized sparse balance packing. The problem is related to removing burrs by thermal deburring—an intelligent technology of processing parts by combusting gas mixtures. To ensure stable quality, especially when shock waves act, it is desirable to have thermal and pressure characteristics uniformly distributed over the surfaces of the part. The location of parts (objects) should be optimal with respect to themselves as well as to the border of the working volume (chamber or container). The problem can be considered as a two-dimensional optimized sparse layout under balancing restrictions. Applying commercial software ANSYS CFX, numerical modeling of the heat transfer between the objects and the heat field was performed and distributions of temperature and pressure in the chamber were obtained. Two cases are compared: the sparse layout with and without balancing conditions. The balance layout gives the most effective distribution of the heat flows.

Chapter 14 proposes a framework for the implementation of smart manufacturing in small and medium-sized enterprises (SMEs). In recent times, smart industry technology has emerged as the main research issue to increase productivity and efficiency, where smart machines collaborate with each other and with users and customers. Smart industry requires the use of information and communication technology (ICT) convergence for production resources as well as four zero factors, including zero waiting-time/inventory/defect/down-time. Smart manufacturing is the backbone of intelligent manufacturing with the involvement of process automation and automated machine tools, whereas data intelligence is related to data acquisition, storage and analysis for smart decision-making. It is possible with the integration of the latest IoT gadgets, cloud computing and various enterprise resource planning (ERP) packages. The selection varies as per the diversified requirements of the manufacturing units. Quality consultancy is required for the selection of tools and techniques in order to excel the business performance. It is followed by the critical phase of deployment with the requirement of high-level expertize. This framework will be the guiding tool for those SMEs who want to apply smart manufacturing to their units.

Chapter 15 analyzes fractal image compression methods used for medical images. The major goal is to study fractal image compression algorithms to replicate the same information content in the decompressed image as the original image. The reasearchers consider a 3D image to determine spatiotemporal similarity, and find range and domain blocks which are reduced in the matching pool by leveraging self-similarity, to improve the matching speed. By comparing compression reduction time factor and decompression quality assessment, a review of literature demonstrates the importance of each fractal image compression algorithm. They have also looked at how these algorithms exceed other standard techniques in terms of peak signal-to-noise ratio (PNSR), compression time, and quality to avoid information loss about lesions.

Chapter 16 discusses mobile edge computing for an efficient energy management system. Edge computing environment provides an optimal solution for latency and lifetime of a device. Thus edge computing will be considered as the next step in developing applications in the IoT environment, maintaining the benefits. There are overheads that occur with computation at the edges and each of the edge nodes will directly or indirectly influence the battery life, i.e. energy consumption which is maintained by batteries. Apart from the regular constraints, edge computing needs to focus on privacy and data reduction methods, and is then compared with other computational systems. The chapter further addresses the future challenges to be considered in this particular area which will give rise to future research.

Chapter 17 proposes computational models for a class of 3D nanomaterials and nanocomposites. The main aim is to simulate elastic properties of nanostructures with ordered and stochastic distribution of non-classical inclusions. The representative volume elements approach is used. The nanosize cubes are considered as matrices, while conglomerates of spheres with different diameters are used as inclusions. Modeling nanocomposites is reduced to packing one-connected multi-spherical objects in an optimized container. The non-linear programming problem is formulated by the phi-function technique. A multistart solution strategy is proposed and illustrated by numerical examples. Effective mechanical characteristics of 3D nanocomposites for different structural parameters are estimated.

Chapter 18 deals with sentiment analysis for web series during the COVID-19 pandemic. In order to understand the impact and impression the web series makes on the audience, the contents from web platforms were collected and analyzed using the natural language processing (NPL) technique. To analyze the viewer's sentiment, comments and utterances were collected and pre-processed to get generalized vocabulary. The data of 63 578 mentions and reviews were collected and analyzed using Brand24 software. The web series, that are, *Friends*, *Game of Thrones*, *Sherlock Holmes* and *Ragnarok* were found to have constrictive and pragmatic impact on viewers during COVID-19. However, the web series *Cursed* was negatively reviewed by 61% during the same period. Overall, 54.53% of viewers have positive comments on web series.

Chapter 19 proposes new improved blind multi-user detection techniques for both the downlink of the synchronous DS-CDMA wireless communication system and uplink of the asynchronous DS-CDMA wireless communication system. The new techniques make use of an important cross-correlation matrix between the adjacent symbols as a constraint to suppress the effect of interfering users. Two improved blind multi-user generalized receivers are developed based on different optimal criteria with the constraint constructed by the cross-correlation matrix. The proposed generalized receivers can be implemented blindly only with the channel estimation of the desired user. Simulation results show that the proposed improved blind generalized receivers provide a substantial performance gain over the conventional blind detectors.

Chapter 20 discusses a set of critical success factors (CSFs) for smart manufacturing (SM) implementation. For mapping CSF, a research strategy has been applied based on academic literature review and consulting reports. Therefore, interviews were conducted for assessing digital manufacturing CSF influences in automotive assembly factory. The main result is a conceptual framework to assist organizations in developing a strategy for SM implementation, and mapping for that purpose all the required resources and capabilities. This research contributes for updating digital manufacturing CSF discussion in the new context of Industry 4.0 and it provides a guide to checking the organizational readiness for SM.

Chapter 21 devises a prediction model using Streamlit and evaluated it using the benchmarked University of California, Irvine (UCI) repository dataset for heart disease diagnosis which consists of various heart attributes of the patient. Its detects impending heart disease for patients using three novel algorithms: the Genetic Tree based Heart Predictor (GDH), Random Forest Based Heart Predictor (RFH) and Bayesian tree based Heart Predictor (BDH). The results are further evaluated using confusion matrix and cross validation. The study achieved 99% accuracy in decision tree algorithms that correctly predicts the cause of heart disease.

Chapter 22 suggests a mechanism for choosing the optimal risk management strategy for the implementation of cross-border cooperation projects. It includes a step-by-step algorithm covering the identification of factors leading to the occurrence of undesirable events; determination of lost profits under risk conditions; a probabilistic assessment of the proposed strategies to counter project risks; identification of alternative losses of projects; assessment of the economic consequences of the proposed strategies to counter risks. It is proposed to use the criteria of Savage, Wald and Hurwitz as evaluation criteria. The solution of the practical problem of choosing the optimal risk management strategy by Russian companies in cross-border projects involving the use of innovative technologies for the repair of Chinese-made trucks has been obtained. The concept of creating and using information systems to support decision-making of risk management of cross-border cooperation projects of innovation-oriented cluster structures of the Kama agglomeration (Russia) is also proposed.

Chapter 23 documents the various artificial intelligence (AI) usage methods and benefits in a medical imaging system and healthcare surveillance in disease outbreak via the emerging machine intelligence technologies. AI is the adoption of human intelligence processes by computer systems to enable the adaption of theory and development in machine-manned technology. The intuitive system has been largely used in data mining ability combining big-scaled data compiling information into theories to guide scientific innovations in material science fields. The considerable promise of AI has resulted in the improved efficacy of the imaging system development through material science technology adoption. AI systems are now taking center stage in the medical field to conduct tasks such as medical surveillance systems, diagnoses treatment, recommendations to cope with precision management in healthcare, so-called precision medicine. An efficient medical imaging system and healthcare epidemiological data surveillance are essential in the era of precision medicine in ensuring a specific treatment is tailored to patient problems. The colossal data usage and AI software development platforms are taking effect and having impact across medical imaging workhorses.

Chapter 24 explores factors influencing a decision to choose between convenience store chains in the Vietnam market. Data used in the study was collected by the author from highly reliable information sources and primary data collected through a survey of 210 consumers living in Vietnam. The results of exploratory factor analysis with independent and dependent variables all show high convergence of factors in the research model, the tests all give the value to achieve reliability. Factors extracted from the analysis of the independent variables include brand (BD), social influence (SI), quality perception (QP), price perception (PP), distribution density (DD), responsiveness (RE), and promotion perception (PPE). The results of regression analysis showed that factors in the research model could explain 63.73% of the variation in factors affecting shopping decisions at the convenience store chain in the area. A relatively high percentage shows that the suitability of the theoretical model with the actual data is quite good. This study uses the optimal choice by the AIC Algorithm for a decision to choose a convenience store chain in the Vietnam market.

Chapter 25 presents a study of groundwater using hydrodynamic models. Mathematical models as a tool of hydrogeological and ecological forecasting should be a general monitoring subsystem. The influence of water withdrawal destroys the natural process of ground and surface water interaction. The forecast of such a process is especially urgent for such natural ecosystems as swamps, lakes and springs, since their nourishment is ensured by ground waters. The mathematical modeling allows one to forecast the distortion of geoecological equilibrium and to estimate the anthropogenic load on groundwater, including the damage of underground river components.

Chapter 26 envisions an understanding of the fatigue behavior of offshore monopiles under corrosive environment through a numerical simulation framework. The concept of this study can be implemented in all kinds of fixed marine structures. The simulations were carried out using finite element analysis (FEA) to evaluate the dynamic responses of monopile structures employing shell elements. The foundation system consists of soil springs. For estimating the force spectrum, the hydrodynamic force from ocean waves is considered. The long-term sea state of monopile structures is simulated using a wave scatter diagram. The spectral analysis is used to determine the stress spectrum. Experimental *S–N* curves from previous research are used to assess the influence of a corrosive environment. These experimental curves are developed under corrosive environment, i.e., seawater. Three different cases are considered: in the air (ambient temperature), seawater (45 °C), and seawater (45 °C + diffused air). It was observed that higher amounts of diffused air in the seawater provide higher fatigue damage in the structure. The current study can be combined with a decision support intelligent framework to develop a decision support tool for structural integrity assessment in the future.

Chapter 27 discusses an evapotranspiration (ET) based irrigation scheduling to track soil water deficiencies for predicting irrigation volume and frequency, based on a simple water balance principle. A landowner will know the predicted amount of water the crop will require for any given week with ET-based irrigation scheduling, as well as the actual water requirements of the crops. Based on the analysis, it was found that crop water requirement for eggplant ranges up to 800 mm. Based on evapotranspiration data, a total of 44 mm of water usage was reduced at entire crop stages. Furthermore, accurate evapotranspiration data create significant prospects for agricultural applications that eliminate important trade-offs in the energy, water and food sectors.

Chapter 28 focuses on a remote health monitoring system using Internet of Things (IoT). The IoT has a diverse set of applications where the applications get the data within healthcare such as diagnosis reports and type of diseases. The IoT can benefit patients, physicians and hospitals. The IoT applications are implied using wearable types of devices which monitor in the wired and wireless medium. Remote monitoring allows physicians to adjust their medication and treatment of a patient by regularly checking the status of the patient's health. These smart health monitoring devices can determine the health conditions according to the state of health conditions such as body temperature, ECG, EEG (electroencephalogram) and blood pressure. The IoT can connect devices using the internet to attain dynamic access to information and connect people, and it responds to the medical ecosystem structure. Several clinical procedures are performed in an eco-friendly manner using the IoT.

Chapter 29 aims to describe the recent advancements in the smart healthcare system. The smart healthcare system deploys various platforms technologies and devices such as IoT, wearable devices, mobile, and computers. These are connected via internet technologies and are synchronized to work for a specific goal. The breakthrough of smart healthcare systems has brought in reducing medical errors and improving diagnostic capabilities and better patient compliance. The recent connected technologies and medical devices have brought in controlled operation of diagnostic and therapeutic process. The wealth of information generated by smart healthcare systems has also benefited clinical research institutions. A drastic reduction is observed in cost, research time, and redundancy in this connected environment. The application of machine learning (ML) algorithms, artificial intelligence (AI) and other cognitive technologies in medical settings has brought in proactive and predictive care. ML helps in data-driven recommendations and suggestive decisions based on patient health data or research information.

Chapter 30 aims to enhance an enterprise network performance through VLAN implementation by simulating an existing LAN and rectifying LAN using VLAN, in two different scenarios. Therefore, the study had the following objectives: to simulate and compare the new (VLAN) and existing (NO_VLAN) enterprise network performance. Descriptive statistics were used to analyze the first objective while an interview guide was used to generate information from the structured interview in the second objective; and also, OPNET was the tool used to get simulation results, measure and compare the network performance for both scenarios (NO_VLAN and VLAN). Hence, VLAN prohibits the access to the network resources of other departments. Virtual LAN technology can also be used to mitigate vulnerability surface for hackers by reducing the traffic request to servers and network visualization leads to ease of administration.

Chapter 31 proposes an artificial intelligence-based garbage monitoring and management system using integrated sensors. The most essential aim to improving the efficiency of this garbage monitoring system is to identify harmful garbage where the garbage piles at the container. An uncertainty of the system is continuously monitoring garbage level in the garbage container and alerting the authorities for immediate action. To optimize the uncertainties, fuzzy rules are farmed in the suggested system. The proposed system is suitable to be implemented in all cities, residential areas, hospital waste management area, industrial waste management area etc, being useful, reliable and at a reasonable cost.

Chapter 32 focuses on an IOT system that can act as a tele-clinic in itself. The embedded system for health monitoring, along with GSM/GPRS module can enable remote health monitoring. We know that in the severe times of a pandemic, the ratio of doctors to patients considerably reduces and hence, in such critical situations, developing countries like India require the technology of tele-clinics. The design of an IoT based embedded system for monitoring rural health to be used as a real-time monitoring system will help doctors and paramedical staff to get real-time data of health parameters of patients from remote areas.

Chapter 33 gives an overview of data security algorithms in network security and their performance evaluation. AES, RC5 and SHA algorithms have been used for this study. AES (Advanced Encryption Standard) is one of the most widely used security algorithms in network security. Due to the presence of brutal force attack, there is a chance of hacking the data during transmission and reception. It is based on the interleaving technique so as to reduce the logic elements used in encryption and decryption. The total number of logic elements of 38 386 in the existing AES is reduced drastically to 6386. In addition, this study discusses hiding of data in an image after encryption and thus improving data security and performance. The image is processed using MATLAB version R2009b. The software implementation of AES has been made using Verilog HDL and ModelSim 6.3g_p1. The performance factors of throughput, power consumption and operating frequency have been observed using Quartus II software. Implementation of the proposed AES, RC5 and SHA increases the throughput and reduces the power as well.

In conclusion, this edited book deeply inquires, holistically reflects, and comprehensively exposes the current and emerging cutting edge technology in important fields of investigation and facilities for original, innovative, and novel real-world applications of intelligent computing in the modern world related to the emerging areas of big data, data-based cryptography and their emerging applications to individuals, groups, cities and countries.

Mukhdeep Singh Manshahia
Punjabi University Patiala, Punjab, India

Igor S Litvinchev
Nuevo Leon State University, Mexico

Gerhard-Wilhelm Weber
Poznan University of Technology, Poznan, Poland

J Joshua Thomas
UOW Malaysia, KDU Penang University College, Malaysia

Pandian Vasant
MERLIN Research Centre, Ton Duc Thang University, Vietnam

Foreword

While environmental issues and the need for new managerial concepts remain at the forefront of operational research, *renewable energy* has become an all-important area of study today. What is more, while *smart technology* continues to rise, becoming ever refined, its applications broaden and enhance in their potential impact on leading to regime switching and paradigm shifts, and even revolutionize views and entire projects about sustainability. This potential can be fully realized only with a thorough comprehension of the most recent breakthroughs in the fields of renewable energy and smart technology in and of themselves and in their emerging methodolologies from mathematics, statistics, analytics, probability theory and stochastics, operational research (OR) and artificial intelligence. With the present book, the Editors and Authors of chapters even go one step further than renewable energy and smart technology, namely to *human-assisted intelligent computing*.

The objective of this special book is to explore latest developments of mathematical ideas and techniques in modeling and simulation, related with: (i) modeling, including foundations in mathematics and statistics, and further elements of optimization, optimal control and game theory, and (ii) simulation, including its foundations in probability theory and stochastics, numerical and discrete mathematics, algorithms and network theory. They all can be applied in economics, finance and biology, as is illustrated in this book. Chapters on recently evolving topics are especially welcome. The Editors of the book invited researchers, practitioners and experts from all over the world to prepare and send high-quality novel research works and critical review chapters on a diversity of topics.

During previous decades, the algebraical and analytical, statistical and stochastic toolbox, the methods, instruments and programs of computer science and applied mathematics, of informatics and statistics, of emerging OR-analytics and information technologies have gained the attention of many researchers and users worldwide, providing a strong impact and influx also in the natural sciences, engineering, economics and finance, the IT sector and, in recent decades, the security sectors, e.g., in storage, handling and transfer of data, in traffic and transportation, production and supply chains, etc. Big-data-based and safety-oriented techniques are more and more well-known and employed in research areas of engineering, science and technology, of ergonomics, marketing and trade. Today's trends in application problems of engineering, science and technology are also expanded into the areas of economy, finance as well as into hospitality, tourism, travel and urban management, into healthcare, hygiene, education and media, across the globe. This edited book bases and focuses on very interesting and high-level selected chapters in a broad variety of research topics. Well-known and emerging methodologies of optimization, optimal control and simulation are employed to model and solve some of the very complicated, hard and urgent problems related to the considered research subjects.

Authors of contributed and accepted chapters of this edited book are experienced qualified scientists and experts from practice worldwide. They refined further and used the deep model-based methods of mathematics and the less model-based, also so-called intelligent or smart algorithms and codes with their various roots in the engineering fields, in computer science and in informatics. The second type of algorithm are often referred to as heuristics and model-free. Indeed, they are regarded as mathematically less rigorous, relieved from some rigor of firm calculus, in order to integrate and benefit from Nature- and specifically bio-inspired approaches, to efficiently overcome and approximately solve hard problems. The rise of these algorithms from artificial intelligence (AI) occurred at the same time as the powerful progress in mathematics which is widely model-based. In these years, named s*tatistical learning*, *machine learning*, *deep learning* and *AI*, *metaheuristics* and *matheuristic*s, *analytics* and *operational research*, model-free and model-based streamlines of traditions and philosophies are brought together to interact and collaborate in numerous centers of excellence, at leading congresses, in prestigious projects and agendas worldwide to leave behind misunderstandings and misperceptions between these two academic streamlines, and to gain from their joined forces and synergy effects, to jointly advance scientific advancements and to give a common service to the solution of urgent real-world and global challenges. Those immense problems and crises exist in every field of the modern world and academics, in engineering and the environment, in economics and the energy sector, in social, life- or human-sciences and for the ending of conflicts and wars, in development and the improvement of living conditions, in ensuring fairness and giving real chances to the new and following generations. Among the variety of these subjects and, in a sense, encompassing them all, the fields of human-assisted intelligent computing, human resource management, aggregate production planning and logistics, inventory, supply chain and waste management, pension fund systems and disaster relief, including modeling and simulation, deserve an extra mention (cf. [1–5]).

Many problems of our modern society lead to mathematical descriptions and solutions, complex problems being susceptible to mathematical formulations. Modern optimization, optimal control and game theories, both exact and heuristic ones, establish a mathematical framework prepared to address problems with conflicting or cooperating parties, thus playing an important role in many decision-oriented real-world tasks. Some of the objectives of this special book were to explore the latest developments of mathematical and heuristic approaches. concepts and methods in modeling and simulation associated with optimization, optimal control and games, applied in communication and management, operational research and analytics, economics and finance, biology and healthcare, environmental protection and mobility. All of these require new and original ideas which offer fresh insights into emerging problems of the real world, and strategies for solving some of these challenges.

This book *Human-Assisted Intelligent Computing: Modeling, Simulations and Applications* is a worldwide collection innovative research compendium that explores the recent steps forward in the directions of smart applications in sustainable modern and future industries and economies, societies and times. Covering a wide scope of themes which include, e.g., energy assessment and neural control, fuzzy logic and uncertainty modeling, ecology and biogeography, this book is designed and well suited for academicians and researchers, explorers and students, ecomomists and managers, advocates and policy-makers, engineers and educators, implementers and multipliers, designers and artists. This book offers a *'golden opportunity'* to the international research community for familiarizing and deepening, interacting and sharing their newest academic and applied results, inventions and discoveries with their colleagues and friends.

At all of these points, modern *optimization* and *optimal control*, *statistics* and *data science*, *statistical* and *machine learning*, *probability theory* and *stochastics*, *AI* and *OR* come into play as ***key technologies*** of modeling, model regularization and selection, of pre- and post-processing, of simulation, preparation and validating, of guidance, interest and appreciation, of continuous concern, respect and encouragement.

The world population steadily grows while the Earth temperature is increasing, putting on the agenda numerous and hard questions, and so many urgent problems. For example, there is the great need to offer sufficient and clean, human-friendly and healthy air, water, food, clothes, land, housing, infrastructure, security, dignity, services, medical and many further commodities or goods of all kinds, which will not destroy our last natural resources. *Optimization* and *decision-making* have to find and choose, propose and allocate new territories, specifically in the rural countryside, and huge amounts of energy, while all of this should be implemented with not more than a moderate complexity by organizations and governments, within an atmosphere of care and trust, empathy and freedom. In such situations, *Human-Assisted Intelligent Computing* make a big difference and emerge as *key technologies* of the future, as represented in this book in impressive ways.

Having been kindly invited by the precious Guest Editors, *Professor Dr Mukhdeep Singh Manshahia* (Punjabi University, Patiala, India), *Professor Igor S Litvinchev* (Nuevo Leon State University—UANL, Mexico), *Professo Dr Gerhard-Wilhelm Weber* (Poznan University of Technology—PUT, Poznan, Poland), *Professor Dr J Joshua Thomas* (UOW Malaysia, KDU Penang University College, Malaysia), and *Professor Dr Pandian Vasant* (MERLIN Research Centre, Ton Duc Thang University, Vietnam), we *Foreword* authors express our deep gratitude and our hope that the selected subjects in this book represent a core choice of today's international scientific research which copes with the emerging and complex problems of *human-assisted intelligent computing* and their fields in management and environment, trade and economics, finance and energy, engineering and medicine, arts and science, by the results and methods of operational research and analytics, modeling and simulation. We are very thankful to IOP Publishing for the honor of hosting this precious book as a pioneering scientific project. We extend particular thanks to the book's Guest Editors for their dedication and devotion, interest and confidence, support and friendship spent on this book from the many months of its preparation, and to the valuable and kind leadership, management and staff of IOP Publishing. We thank all the authors for their diligent, smart and tasteful work and their readiness to share their state-of-the-art results with our entire community. Finally, we wish from our heart that their research will inspire and initiate cooperation and service at the highest level for humanity and all creation.

References

[1] Babaee Tirkolaee E, Goli A and Weber G-W 2020 Fuzzy mathematical programming and self-adaptive artificial fish Swarm algorithm for just-in-time energy-aware flow shop scheduling problem with outsourcing option *IEEE Trans. Fuzzy Syst.* **28** 2772–83

[2] Babaee Tirkolaee E, Goli A, Gütmen S, Weber G-W and Szwedzka K 2022 A novel formulation for the sustainable periodic waste collection arc-routing problem: pareto-based algorithms *Ann. Oper. Res.*

[3] Graczyk-Kucharska M, Szafranski M, Gütmen S, Golinski M, Spychala M, Wlodarczak Z, Kuter S, Özmen A and Weber G-W 2020 Modeling for human resources management by data mining, analytics and artificial intelligence in the logistics departments *Smart and Sustainable Supply Chain and Logistics–Trends, Challenges, Methods and Best Practices, EcoProduction (Environmental Issues in Logistics and Manufacturing)* (Cham: Springer) pp 291–303

[4] Gütmen S, Weber G-W, Goli A and Babaee Tirkolaee E 2022 Human paradigm and reliability for aggregate production planning under uncertainty *Advances of Artificial Intelligence in a Green Energy Environment* (Amsterdam: Elsevier)

[5] Szafranski M, Gütmen S, Graczyk-Kucharska M, Weber G-W and Modelling 2021 IT specialists competency in the era of Industry 4.0 *Innovations in Mechatronics Engineering, Lecture Notes in Mechanical Engineering* (Cham: Springer)

September 3, 2022,

Dr Alireza Goli *University of Esfahan, Iran*,
Dr Erfan Babaee Tirkolaee *Istinye University, Istanbul, Turkey*,
Professor Gerhard-Wilhelm Weber *Poznan University of Technology, Poland*;
and *IAM, METU, Ankara, Turkey*

Acknowledgments

We would like to sincerely thank all the authors and reviewers for their wonderful job for this book project. The book would not have been completed without the strong support and help from the staff members of IOP Publishing. In particular, we would like to thank Dr John Navas and Dr Phoebe Hooper for their cooperation.

Our deepest regard and appreciation goes to Dr Alireza Goli, Dr Erfan Babaee Tirkolaee and Professor Gerhard-Wilhelm Weber for an excellent foreword.

Finally, many thanks we would like to express to our families and parent organizations for their support during the whole journey of this project.

Mukhdeep Singh Manshahia
Punjabi University Patiala, Punjab, India

Igor S Litvinchev
Nuevo Leon State University, Mexico

Gerhard-Wilhelm Weber
Poznan University of Technology, Poznan, Poland

J Joshua Thomas
UOW Malaysia, KDU Penang University College, Malaysia

Pandian Vasant
MERLIN Research Centre, Ton Duc Thang University, Vietnam

Editor biographies

Mukhdeep Singh Manshahia

Mukhdeep Singh Manshahia is an Assistant Professor at Punjabi University Patiala, Punjab, India. He obtained his PhD in 2016 from Punjabi University Patiala. He is working in sustainable computing, artificial intelligence, wireless sensor networks, Internet of Things (IoT), Nature inspired computing, energy harvesting and renewable energy systems. He has edited two books and published 43 international and national research papers. He has presented 30 research papers in international and national conferences/seminars. He has guided four Master dissertations, 55 undergraduate projects and two PhD dissertations. He has 17 years of working experience at universities. He is a reviewer of many WoS journals. He is a member of Computer Society of India, IEEE and IAENG.

Igor S Litvinchev

Igor Litvinchev received his MSc degree in applied mathematics from Moscow Institute of Physics and Technology (Fizteh), Russia; PhD in systems theory and operations research and Dr. Sci. (Habilitation) in systems modeling and optimization, both from Computing Center, Russian Academy of Sciences (CCAS), Moscow. He is currently a Professor at Nuevo Leon State University (UANL), Mexico and a Leading Mathematician at CCAS. His research is focused on large-scale systems modeling, optimization, and control with applications to interdisciplinary research. He is an author of four books and an editor of seven more. He has published more than 90 research papers in leading international journals and served in program and organizing committees for 48 international conferences. His research was supported by 31 grants from NATO Scientific Affairs Division and European Community; ISF (USA) and RFBR (Russia); CNPq and FAPESP (Brasil); BRFBR (Belarus); CONACYT, PROMEP and PAICYT (Mexico). Litvinchev is a member of Russian Academy of Natural Sciences and Mexican Academy of Sciences.

Gerhard-Wilhelm Weber

Gerhard-Wilhelm Weber is a Professor at Poznan University of Technology, Poznan, Poland, at Faculty of Engineering Management. His research is on mathematics, statistics, operational research, data science, machine learning, finance, economics, optimization, optimal control, management, neuro-, bio- and earth-sciences, medicine, logistics, development, cosmology and generalized space-time research. He is involved in the organization of scientific life internationally. He received Diploma and

Doctorate in Mathematics, and Economics/Business Administration, at RWTH Aachen, and Habilitation at TU Darmstadt (Germany). He replaced Professorships at University of Cologne, and TU Chemnitz, Germany. At Institute of Applied Mathematics, Middle East Technical University, Ankara, Turkey, he was a Professor in Financial Mathematics and Scientific Computing, and Assistant to the Director, and has been a member of five further graduate schools, institutes and departments of METU. G-W Weber has affiliations at Universities of Siegen (Germany), Federation University (Ballarat, Australia), University of Aveiro (Portugal), University of North Sumatra (Medan, Indonesia), Malaysia University of Technology, Chinese University of Hong Kong, KTO Karatay University (Konya, Turkey), Vidyasagar University (Midnapore, India), Mazandaran University of Science and Technology (Babol, Iran), Istinye University (Istanbul, Turkey), Georgian International Academy of Sciences, at EURO (Association of European OR Societies) where he is 'Advisor to EURO Conferences' and IFORS (International Federation of OR Societies), where he is member in many national OR societies, honorary chair of some EURO working groups, subeditor of IFORS Newsletter, member of IFORS Developing Countries Committee, of Pacific Optimization Research Activity Group, etc. G-W Weber has supervised many MSc and PhD students, authored and edited numerous books and articles, and given many presentations from a diversity of areas, in theory, methods and practice. He has been a member of many international editorial, special issue and award boards; he participated at numerous research projects; he has received various recognitions by students, universities, conferences and scientific organizations. G-W Weber is an IFORS Fellow.

J Joshua Thomas

J Joshua Thomas is an Associate Professor at UOW Malaysia KDU Penang University College, Malaysia. He obtained his PhD (Intelligent Systems Techniques) in 2015 from University Sains Malaysia, Penang, and Master's degree in 1999 from Madurai Kamaraj University, India. From July to September 2005, he worked as a research assistant at the Artificial Intelligence Lab in University Sains Malaysia. From March 2008 to March 2010, he worked as a research associate at the same university. He is working with deep learning algorithms, specially targeting on graph convolutional neural networks and bi-directional recurrent neural networks for drug target interaction and image tagging with embedded natural language processing. His work involves experimental research with software prototypes and mathematical modeling and design. He is an editorial board member for the *Journal of Energy Optimization and Engineering* (IJEOE), and special issue journal editor for MDPI (applied sciences, computation, forecasting) and *Mathematical Biosciences and Engineering* (MBE). He was recently invited as a guest with *Computer Methods and Programs in Biomedicine* (Elsevier). He has published more than 40 papers in leading international conference proceedings and peer reviewed journals.

Weblink: https://www.uowmkdu.edu.my/research/our-people/dr-joshua-thomas/
Email: joshua.j.thomas@gmail.com

Pandian Vasant

Pandian Vasant is Research Associate at MERLIN Research Centre, TDTU, HCMC, Vietnam, and Editor-in- Chief of *International Journal of Energy Optimization and Engineering* (IJEOE). He holds a PhD in computational intelligence (UNEM, Costa Rica), MSc (University Malaysia Sabah, Malaysia, engineering mathematics) and BSc (Hons, Second Class Upper) in mathematics (University of Malaya, Malaysia). His research interests include soft computing, hybrid optimization, innovative computing and applications. He has co-authored research articles in journals, conference proceedings, presentations, special issues as a Guest Editor, chapters (300 publications indexed in Research-Gate) and was the General Chair of EAI International Conference on Computer Science and Engineering in Penang, Malaysia (2016) and Bangkok, Thailand (2018). In the years 2009 and 2015, he was awarded top reviewer and outstanding reviewer for the journal *Applied Soft Computing* (Elsevier). He has 32 years of working experience (Teaching, Research and Editorial) in universities. Currently, he is General Chair of International Conference on Intelligent Computing and Optimization (https://www. icico.info/) and Member of AMS (USA), NAVY Research Group (TUO, Czech Republic) and MERLIN Research Centre (TDTU, Vietnam). H-Index Google Scholar = 34; i-10-index = 144.

Weblink: https://www.researchgate.net/profile/Pandian-Vasant;
http://www.igi-global.com/ijeoe

List of contributors

Mohd Nawawi Abdullah
Nuclear Imaging Unit, University Putra Malaysia Teaching Hospital, Serdang, Selangor, Malaysia

A Adaikalam
Department of Electronics and Communication Engineering, UCE, BIT Campus, Anna University, Chennai, Tamil Nadu, India

Sundaram Arun
Jerusalem College of Engineering Chennai, India

Syed Ejaz Shamim Syed Reyaz Uddin Ahmed
Nuclear Imaging Unit, University Putra Malaysia Teaching Hospital, University Putra Malaysia, Serdang, Selangor, Malaysia

Yakubu Makeri Ajiji
Kampala International University Uganda, Kan Sanga, Kampala, Uganda

Marta Alic
Zagreb University of Applied Sciences, Zagreb, Croatia

Pornpong Asavadorndeja
Synterra Co. Ltd, Huai Khwang, Bangkok, Thailand

Vyacheslav Baranov
Russian Presidential Academy of National Economy and Public Administration, Moscow, Russia

Marina Batova
Military University of the Ministry of Defense of the Russian Federation Moscow, Russia

M Amina Begum
Oxford College of Engineering Venmani, Tiruvannamalai, India

V S Bhagavan
Department of Mathematics, Koneru Lakshmaiah Education Foundation, Vaddeswaram, Andhra Pradesh, India

Diptendu Bhattarcharya
NIT Agartala, Chitkara University, Rajpura, Punjab, India

Ladislav Burita
University of Defence, Brno, Czech Republic

Andrei Chugai
A. Pidgorny Institute of Mechanical Engineering Problems of the National Academy of Sciences of Ukraine, Kharkiv, Ukraine

Ahmad Danial
Nuclear Imaging Unit, University Putra Malaysia Teaching Hospital, Serdang, Selangor, Malaysia

Sayan Das
RIMS Imphal, India

R Deepa
SRM Valliammai Engineering College, Kattankulathur, Tamil Nadu, India

Kyril Degtyariov
A. Pidgorny Institute of Mechanical Engineering Problems of the National Academy of Sciences of Ukraine, Kharkiv, Ukraine

Mahendra Deore
Department of Computer Engineering, Cummins College of Engineering for Women, Pune, India

S C Dharmadhikari
PICT Engineering College, Pune, India

Muskan Dixit
Chitkara University Institute of Engineering and Technology, Chitkara University, Rajpura, Punjab, India

Zoia Duryagina
Lviv Polytechnic National University, Lviv, Ukraine

Ugo Fiore
Parthenope University, Italy

Manish Kumar Giri
NIT Raipur, DSP LAB, Department of ECE, NIT Raipur, Raipur, Chhattisgarh, India

Chandran Gomathi
Department of CSE, University College of Engineering, BIT Campus, Anna University, Tiruchairappallai, Tamil Nadu, India

Azeddine Hachmi
University Mohammed V, Rabat, Morocco

Kamil Halouzka
University of Defence, Brno, Czech Republic

Khoi Bui Huy
Industrial University of Ho Chi Minh City, HCM City, Vietnam

Subhashini Sottallu Janakiram
New Horizon College of Engineering, Bangalore, Karnataka, India

G D Anbarasi Jebaselvi
Sathyabama Institute of Science and Technology, Jeppiaar Nagar, Rajiv Gandhi Salai, Chennai, India

Jane Rubel Angelina Jeyaraj
Kalasalingam Academy of Research and Education, Deemed to be University, Krishnankoil, TN, India

U C Jha
Lovely Professional University, Phagwara, Punjab, India

Arfshan Kausar
Department of Computer Science Jazan University (KSA), Saudi Arabia

Thandapani Kavitha
Department of ECE, Veltech University, Chennai, Tamil Nadu, India

Khairul Alif Khairuman
Nuclear Imaging Unit, University Putra Malaysia Teaching Hospital, Serdang, Selangor, Malaysia

Nilofer Shrenik Kittad
Department of Computer Engineering, Cummins College of Engineering for Women, Pune, India

Oleg Korobchenko
Korib Group of Companies, Naberezhnye Chelny, Republic of Tatarstan, Russia

Pavel Kozak
University of Defence, Brno, Czech Republic

Oleg Kravchenko
A. Pidgorny Institute of Mechanical Engineering Problems of the National Academy of Sciences of Ukraine, Kharkiv, Ukraine

Igor S Litvinchev
Federal Research Center 'Computer Science and Control' of Russian Academy of Sciences, Moscow, Russia
and
Nuevo Leon State University, Monterey, Mexico

Ljerka Luic
University North, Koprivnica, Croatia

Pallavi Majumdar
NRS Medical College, Kolkata, India

Parijata Majumdar
NIT Agartala, Chitkara University, Rajpura, Punjab, India

Saikat Majumdar
NIT Raipur, DSP LAB, Department of ECE, NIT Raipur, Raipur, Chhattisgarh, India

Mukhdeep Singh Manshahia
Punjabi University Patiala, Punjab, India

Jose Antonio Marmolejo-Saucedo
Universidad Panamericana, Facultad de Ingenieria, Ciudad de Mexico, Mexico

Ivan Matveev
Federal Research Center 'Computer Science and Control' of Russian Academy of Sciences, Moscow, Russia

Sergey Mayorov
Mechanical Engineering Cluster of the Republic of Tatarstan, Naberezhnye Chelny, Tatarstan Republic, Russia

O Melashenko
A. Pidgorny Institute of Mechanical Engineering Problems of the National Academy of Sciences of Ukraine, Kharkiv, Ukraine

Doreen Hepzibah Miriam
Computational Intelligence Research Foundation, Ayanavaram, Chennai, India

Sanjoy Mitra
TIT Narsingarh, Tripura, India

Abdel Mueed
Department of E&C Engineering, Institute of Technology, University of Kashmir, Srinagar, J&K, India

Rachel Nallathamby
Computational Intelligence Research Foundation, Ayanavaram, Chennai, India

R Narmadha
Sathyabama Institute of Science and Technology, Jeppiaar Nagar, Rajiv Gandhi Salai, Chennai, India

Aleksandr Pankratov
A. Pidgorny Institute of Mechanical Engineering Problems of the National Academy of Sciences of Ukraine, Kharkiv, Ukraine

Sergei Plankovskyy
O.M. Beketov National University of Urban Economy in Kharkiv, Kharkiv, Ukraine

Irina Polshkova
All-Union Institute of Hydrogeology and Engineering Geology, Russia

Wonsiri Punurai
Department of Civil and Environmental Engineering, Mahidol University, Phuttamonthon, Nakhon Pathom, Thailand

Ravi Ramaswamy
Tech Mango, Narayanapuram Madurai, India

Parameswaran Radhika Ravi
Thai Trust, Kochadai, Maduari, India

Krishnamoorthy Ranganathan
Centre for Computational Modeling, Chennai Institute of Technology, Chennai, India

C R Rene Robin
Department of CSE, Sri Sairam Engineering College, Sai Leo Nagar, West Tambaram, Chennai, India

Tatiana Romanova
A. Pidgorny Institute of Mechanical Engineering Problems of the National Academy of Sciences of Ukraine, Kharkiv, Ukraine

Fathinul Fikri Ahmad Saad
Centre for Diagnostic Nuclear Imaging, University Putra Malaysia, Serdang, Selangor, Malaysia

Felix Sadyrbaev
Institute of Mathematics and Informatics, Riga, Latvia

Betty Elezebeth Samuel
Department of Information Technology and Security, Jazan University, Saudi Arabia

Padmanayaki Selvarajan
Department of Information Technology and Security, Jazan University, Saudi Arabia

Abhijeet A Shahade
Lovely Professional University, Phagwara, Punjab, India

Shazreen Shaharuddin
Faculty of Medicine and Defence Health, National Defence University of Malaysia, Kem Sungai Besi, Malaysia

Arvind Kumar Shukla
Department of Computer Applications, IFTM University, Moradabad, Uttar Pradesh, India

Olga Shypul
O.M. Beketov National University of Urban Economy in Kharkiv, Kharkiv, Ukraine

Sherry N Siddiqui
Department of Physics School of Mathematical and Physical Sciences, Dr Harisingh Gour Vishwavidyalaya Sagar, M.P., India

Saravjeet Singh
Chitkara University Institute of Engineering and Technology, Chitkara University, Rajpura, Punjab, India

Chana Sinsabvarodom
Naval Public Works Department, Royal Thai Navy, Wat Arun, Bangkok Yai, Bangkok, Thailand

Yuri Stoyan
A. Pidgorny Institute of Mechanical Engineering Problems of the National Academy of Sciences of Ukraine, Kharkiv, Ukraine

Elena Strelnikova
A. Pidgorny Institute of Mechanical Engineering Problems of the National Academy of Sciences of Ukraine, Kharkiv, Ukraine

M Sumathi
Sathyabama Institute of Science and Technology, Jeppiaar Nagar, Rajiv Gandhi Salai, Chennai, India

Mohd Amirul Tajuddin
Nuclear Imaging Unit, University Putra Malaysia Teaching Hospital, Serdang, Selangor, Malaysia

Ngan Nguyen Thi
Industrial University of Ho Chi Minh City, HCM City, Vietnam

J Joshua Thomas
Department of Computing, School of Engineering, UOW Malaysia, KDU Penang University College, George Town, Malaysia

Yevgen Tsegelnyk
O.M. Beketov National University of Urban Economy in Kharkiv, Kharkiv, Ukraine

Vyacheslav Tuzlukov
Belarusian State Aviation Academy, Minsk, Belarus

Anirban Vanik
National Institute of Technology Agartala, Banikpara, Agartala, Tripura West, India

Pandian Vasant
Faculty of Electrical and Electronics Engineering, Ton Duc Thang University, Ho Chi Minh City, Vietnam

Yegnanarayanan Venkataraman
Kalasalingam Academy of Research and Education, Deemed to be University, Krishnankoil, TN, India

Ashish Verma
Department of Physics School of Mathematical and Physical Sciences, Dr Harisingh Gour Vishwavidyalaya Sagar, M P, India

Jin Wang
Faculty of Engineering and Technology, Liverpool John Moores University, Liverpool, UK

Gerhard-Wilhelm Weber
Poznan University of Technology, Poznan, Poland

B Yamini
Bhaktavatsalam Memorial College for Women, Chennai, India

Gayathri Narayana Yegnanarayanan
Department of Electrical and Computer Engineering, Texas A&M University, TX, USA

Hiroshi Yoshida
Kyushu University, Fukuoka, Japan

Asmae Zbiri
University Mohammed V, Rabat, Morocco

Kai Zhao
Moscow State Technological University 'STANKIN', Moscow, Russia

Chapter 1

Machine learning algorithms to improve crop evapotranspiration prediction covering a broad range of environmental gradients in agriculture 4.0: a review

Parijata Majumdar, Diptendu Bhattacharya, Sanjoy Mitra and Mukhdeep Singh Manshahia

Crop evapotranspiration prediction is beneficial as it provides a scientific foundation for judicious water use, and sustainable increase in agriculture productivity. The water loss from a farmed field is referred to as crop evapotranspiration. Due to lack of rainfall and rising temperature, soil water balance gets disrupted. Agricultural production will decrease when the crop growth cycle is shortened due to rising temperatures, lack of humidity, soil water scarcity. However, the complex correlations of evapotranspiration with dynamically changing weather and soil conditions cannot be captured using traditional methods to estimate evapotranspiration. To resolve complex correlations of non-linear weather conditions with evapotranspiration, machine learning algorithms plays a significant role. IoT-enabled machine learning can be used to predict crop evapotranspiration accurately resulting in designing a better and more precise irrigation schedule for farmers to get an insight into the quantity and timing of irrigation and adaptability to change with changing soil type, crop type, weather.

1.1 Introduction

IoT based modern automation like artificial intelligence (AI) to process big data is used in agriculture to shift towards Agriculture 4.0 practices [1]. It increases the efficiency of irrigation activities by boosting production, enhancing quality, lowering harmful affects and conserving resources such as energy and water. Big data analytics is used to process a large volume of sensor generated data relevant to weather, soil and crop factors to predict irrigation schedules as these agriculture processes are extremely driven and

doi:10.1088/978-0-7503-4801-0ch1

enabled by data. Emerging concepts of IoT oriented wireless sensors enables intelligent and automated irrigation monitoring by real-time weather data collection, intelligent machine learning based processing and storage any time and from anywhere to make it cost effective and labour saving. For effective prediction of evapotranspiration in light of the problem for real-time monitoring of weather parameters, IoT based techniques are utilized in automated monitoring of non-linear weather conditions to schedule irrigation. Evapotranspiration forecasting accuracy can help save irrigation water, especially in dry areas where water is highly consumed and crop development is heavily reliant on water supply [2]. It is therefore critical to precisely anticipate evapotranspiration in order to optimize irrigation water consumption control and crop water use efficiency. It is critical to precisely estimate and anticipate evapotranspiration processes in non-linear weather changes and water scarcity management using controlled irrigation [3]. Evapotranspiration is the water lost due to evaporation and by crop transpiration. Evapotranspiration prediction is an essential component of hydrological systems aimed at conserving water resources, particularly for irrigation. As a result, an evapotranspiration prediction tool can help farmers deal with water scarcity for sustainable agriculture [4, 5]. Actual evapotranspiration can be measured from eddy covariance (EC) [6, 7], but local and lengthy investigations employing EC are hampered by costs, logistics, and measurement scale [8]. As a result, models using widely accessible drivers are needed to estimate evapotranspiration for a wider range of applications. Evapotranspiration simulation research has used a number of data-driven models [9]. Machine learning algorithms that can estimate evapotranspiration using connections of input predictors without using field-based physical characteristics can be used to incorporate information from easily available predictors from ground detection. Non-linear correlations buried in spatial data are extracted using machine learning methods, which are then used to evaluate incoming data. For example, utilising ground observation, Tabari *et al* [11] and Yang *et al* [10] employed support vector prediction to estimate averaged evapotranspiration and reference evapotranspiration. To anticipate weekly reference, Landeras *et al* [12] utilised autoregressive models, and Bodesheim *et al* [13] employed random forest regression (RF) technique. RF can handle multi dimensional regression and displays the interaction between predictors without explicit training [14]. Shiri [15] estimated reference evapotranspiration using wavlet-random forest model, demonstrating the reference evapotranspiration model accuracy. Due to ensemble trees, it prevents overfitting using scarce data and delivering consistent results on both training and test data [16–18]. As of yet, only a small amount of effort has gone into selecting more accurate evapotranspiration prediction models using decision theories that combine a variety of statistical performance measures. The problem of picking the optimal model among a number of evapotranspiration estimation techniques, in particular, demands special attention. As a result, the main contribution of this study is to identify optimum evapotranspiration estimation method in terms of performance metrics.

Figure 1.1 shows the evapotranspiration estimation method using machine learning prediction algorithms. Raw data is collected using IoT sensors and data preprocessing is done where missing data values are removed and outlier if present is detected. Then using reference evapotranspiration and calculated crop coefficient, crop evapotranspiration is calculated. Then the prediction algorithm is tested and validated using performance metrics.

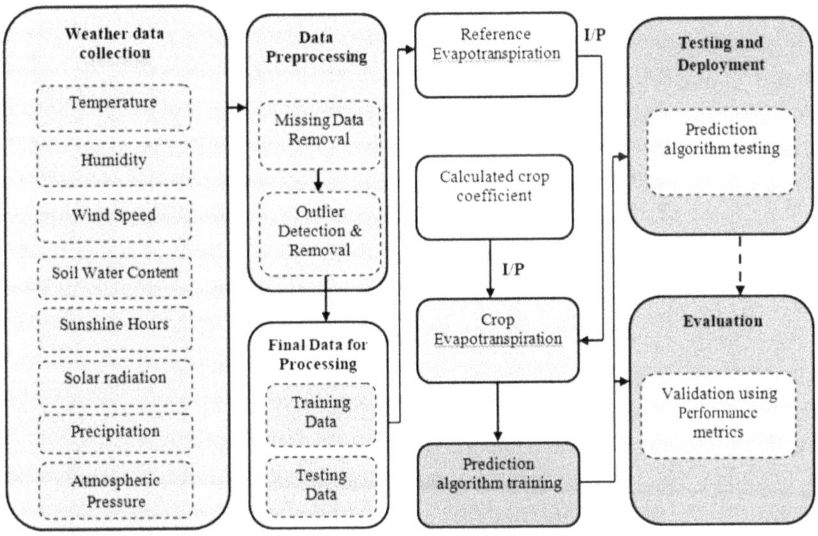

Figure 1.1. Evapotranspiration estimation method using machine learning prediction algorithms.

1.2 Relevant literature

AI-based modeling tools are regarded as the most effective strategies for predicting evapotranspiration in a variety of meteorological conditions around the world. Multiple linear regression (MLR), gradient boost regression (GBR) and random forest (RF) are the algorithms used to estimate evapotranspiration based on minimum temperature, wind speed, soil temperature, maximum temperature, solar radiation humidity. But it is needed to enhance computation speed and memory utilization. Improved mean absolute error of 0.13 and 0.984 is the coefficient of determination for GBR [19]. Fuzzy-genetic algorithm (GA) is used to estimate evapotranspiration based on temperature, sunshine hours, solar radiation, humidity, wind speed. Root mean square error of 0.1160–0.396, mean square error of 0.0134–0.156, coefficient of determination of 0.830–0.99 and accuracy ranging from 94–99 are the performance metrics [20]. Support vector machine (SVM), multi-layer perception (MLP) neural network, RF, K-nearest neighbour (K-NN), are the algorithms used to estimate evapotranspiration using precipitation, humidity, radiation, soil water content, wind speed. Evaluation of evapotranspiration models is needed to understand its requirement under different weather changes as the performance and system needs to be made more robust using various biophysical and meteorological conditions. The performance metric of coefficient of determination ranges from 0.75 to 0.83 and root mean square error range is 18–21 [21]. RF is used to predict evapotranspiration using vapor pressure, temperature, radiation, wind speed. This research has to be extended to tropical and semi-arid locations that necessitate a more thorough examination of additional weather variables. Long short-term memory neural network is outperformed by RF where coefficient of determination is 0.7 with sixteen weather variables and Willmott's skill score is 0.90 [22]. The Bi-directional-Long Term Short Memory (Bi-LSTM) network produced comparatively better results viz., coefficient of determination is 0.999, Willmott's Index of Agreement is 0.999,

Nash–Sutcliffe Efficiency Coefficient is 0.998, Relative Root Mean Square is 0.014, Root Mean Square error is 0.055 mm d^{-1}, a20-index is 1.000, Mean Absolute Error is 0.491 mm d^{-1}, and Mean Absolute Difference is 0.017 mm d^{-1}. The proposed models' prediction performance for multiple-step ahead forecasts must be assessed [23]. Hierarchical Fuzzy System with Particle Swarm Optimization algorithm (PSO–HFS) performed better where 0.93 is coefficient of determination, with entropy weight as 0.93, Root Mean Squared Error is 0.59 mm per day and Willmott's Index of Agreement is 0.94 to estimate evapotranspiration. Sunshine duration, minimum temperature, wind speed, maximum temperature, and humidity are used to predict evapotranspiration. The system has to be made more robust by testing this model in varying climatic zones. Model over- fitting harmed the regression tree a little [24]. Decision tree forest (DTF), tree boost (TB) are used for evapotranspiration prediction using minimum temperature, mean temperature, maximum temperature, wind velocity, and humidity,. The coefficient of determination value is found to be in the range of 0.80 to 0.93 and the Nash–Sutcliffe efficiency coefficient values are approximately found 100% using tree boost. Using this evapotranspiration prediction method, appropriate irrigation scheduling must be designed to aid in water resource management [26]. Artificial neural networks (ANNs) are technologies emulating the electrical activity of human brain and nervous system. These networks emulate a biological neural network but they use a reduced set of ideas generated from a biological neural systems. Processing elements (also called either a neurode or perceptron) are connected to other processing elements. The neurodes are arranged in a layer, with the output of one layer serving as the input to the next layer and subsequent layers. ANNs are used to estimate evapotranspiration using minimum temperature, vapour pressure, sunshine hours, maximum temperature, and wind speed. The root mean square values range from 0.26 to 0.90 and coefficient of determination ranges from 0.83 to 0.98. The application of evapotranspiration in drought indices for prediction has to be applied. Also, machine learning can be used to identify the optimum time lags for model inputs by using time series of nearby stations and finding the best time lags for model inputs [27]. Stacking using RF, gradient boosting method (XGBoost), SVM based ensemble method is used to estimate evapotranspiration using temperature, vapour pressure, humidity, solar radiation and wind speed etc. Root mean square error value is 0.0747 and probability value is 0.1005. The impact of controlled inaccuracies in weather parameters must be investigated. Since, the weather data may change over time it follows different distribution than data models which requires re-training to maintain prediction performance [28]. Weather variables like average sunshine hours, average air pressure, minimum and maximum temperature, mean air temperature etc extracted by the path analysis algorithm of particle swarm optimisation-gradient boosting decision tree (PSO–GBDT) are used to estimate evapotranspiration. The Nash–Sutcliffe efficiency is 22.37%, mean absolute error is 9.05%, coefficient of determination is 2.83%, which is higher than that of PSO–SVM [29]. The performance of deep neural network model is better than gradient boosted tree and RF model with 8%–9.5% of mean absolute error, coefficients of determination ranging from 0.914 to 0.954, 2.6%–2.9% of Nash–Sutcliffe efficiency and root mean squared error. Depending on the characteristics of distinct climatic zones, the order of importance of weather variables influencing evapotranspiration varies. To provide an economical and precise solution for evapotranspiration estimation, a generalised and consistent single input parameter-based evapotranspiration prediction model suited for all sorts of climates is required in the evapotranspiration domain. Here, a unique evapotranspiration model portraying the climatic conditions of a single field zone could not be employed in a worldwide context. Solar radiation, maximum temperature, minimum temperature, and average air temperature, maximum relative humidity, wind speed, and minimum relative humidity, atmospheric pressure are used to estimate evapotranspiration [30]. Back-propagation neural network (BP) model and multiple linear regressions are required to estimate evapotranspiration. The BP that took into account the dynamic change of crop factor was better than BP that took into account the crop coefficient using FAO-56. Also, the precision of the BP that considers changing crop factor as well as the effect of precipitation was much increased. Also, in weather having precipitation, BP outperformed the BP in weather having no humidity. Coefficient of determination is 0.87 and accuracy is 91.44% for BP model [31]. Table 1.1 contains a review of evapotranspiration prediction methods using machine learning. Table 1.2 contains a review of weather parameters used in evapotranspiration prediction methods using machine learning

Table 1.1. Review of evapotranspiration prediction methods using machine learning.

Methods	Algorithm	Drawbacks and Future work	Improved Performance Metrics
Ponraj *et al* 2019 [19]	MLR, RF, GBR.	It is needed to enhance computation speed and memory utilization.	MAE, RMSE, R.
Saggi *et al* 2019 [20]	Fuzzy-GA, RF.	More research should be done to calibrate the evapotranspiration models and improve their performance for more stations. The following literature proposes some of the standard methods for calculating evapotranspiration.	MSE, RMSE, R and accuracy.
Bai *et al* 2020 [21]	K-NN, RF, SVM, and MLP	Existing evapotranspiration models are evaluated; it is necessary to understand its requirement under different climatic factors as the performance and system needs to be made more robust using various biophysical and meteorological conditions.	RMSE, R.

(*Continued*)

Table 1.1. (*Continued*)

Methods	Algorithm	Drawbacks and Future work	Improved Performance Metrics
Talib *et al* 2021 [22]	RF and LSTM.	This research has to be extended to tropical and semi-arid locations that necessitate a more thorough examination of additional weather variables.	R, Willmott's skill score.
Roy *et al* 2021a [23]	LSTM, Bi-directional LSTM	The proposed models' prediction performance for multiple-step ahead forecasts must be assessed.	R, Index of Agreement, and a^{20}-index
Roy *et al* 2021b [24]	PSO–HFS	The system has to be made more robust by testing this model in varying climatic zones. Model over- fitting harmed the regression tree a little.	Entropy Weights, RMSE, MAE, R.
Roy *et al* 2021c [25]	ABC, BA, BBO, Continuous ACOR, CMA-ES, CA, DE, FA, GA, HS, ICA, IWO, PSO, SA and TLBO	Appropriate irrigation scheduling needs to be designed to aid in water resource management using this evapotranspiration prediction method.	Shannon's Entropy, VC and GRA.
Raza *et al* 2019 [26]	SDT, TB, and DTF	Appropriate irrigation scheduling must be created using this evapotranspiration prediction approach for judiciously using water.	R, NSE.
Gocic *et al* 2021 [27]	ANN	Evapotranspiration in drought indices has to be applied to predict drought indices. Also, machine learning can be used to identify the optimum time lags for model inputs by using nearby station's time series to find the optimum time lags.	RMSE and R.
Martin *et al* 2021 [28]	SVM,RF, XGBoost based ensemble method.	The impact of controlled inaccuracies in weather parameters must be investigated. Since, the weather data may change over time it	RMSE, Standard deviation.

		follows different distribution than data models which requires re-training to maintain performance.	
Zhao *et al* 2021 [29]	PSO–GBDT	More prediction algorithms on different subsets of features need to be compared to increase accuracy of evapotranspiration estimation.	MAE, RMSE, R, NSE.
Ravindran *et al* 2021 [30]	RF, and XGBoost	A unique evapotranspiration model portraying the climatic conditions of a single field zone, could not be employed in a worldwide context.	R, MAE, RMSE, and NSE.
Han *et al* 2021 [31]	BP and MLP.	The findings could be used to get an evapotranspiration that is more in line with the crop's real growth status, giving a scientific foundation for better water management during agricultural development.	R and accuracy.

Table 1.2. Review of weather parameters used in evapotranspiration prediction methods using machine learning.

Methods	Weather data used	Observation
Ponraj *et al* 2019 [19]	Humidity, soil temperature, solar radiation, minimum temperature, humidity, maximum temperature, wind speed, soil temperature.	The presence of soil temperature had no favourable impact on daily evapotranspiration prediction.
Saggi *et al* 2019 [20]	Temperature, solar radiation, humidity, wind speed, sunshine hours.	The model performs well when it comes to estimating daily crop factor, evapotranspiration, and accurately anticipating overall water requirements.
Bai *et al* 2020 [21]	Precipitation, humidity, radiation, soil water content, wind speed.	Individual model uncertainty in prediction of daily evapotranspiration must be decreased, and MLP is the most

(Continued)

Table 1.2. *(Continued)*

Methods	Weather data used	Observation
		effective for building evapotranspiration models comparatively.
Talib *et al* 2021 [22]	Vapor pressure, radiation, temperature, Wind speed.	When compared to autoregressive models, RF and LSTM have superior generalisation and can perform well in time and space. Vapor pressure was more important for evapotranspiration prediction.
Roy *et al* 2021a [23]	Humidity, wind speed, minimum temperature, sunshine duration, maximum temperature.	Bi-LSTM is used to accurately forecast one-step ahead evapotranspiration, as per ranking by Shannon's entropy where partial autocorrelation functions are used to give inputs.
Roy *et al* 2021b [24]	Maximum temperature, wind speed, humidity, minimum temperature, and sunshine duration.	With the unknown test dataset the models fared equally well, with the PSO–HFS model providing greater performance and the regression tree providing lowest performance.
Roy *et al* 2021c [25]	Wind speed, minimum temperature, sunshine duration, humidity and maximum temperature.	FA-ANFIS performs well for predicting daily evapotranspiration in areas with similar weather changes as indicated by Shannon's entropy and variation coefficient.
Raza *et al* 2019 [26]	Minimum, maximum and mean temperature, humidity and wind velocity.	Wind velocity and mean temperature are determined to be sufficient for efficient evapotranspiration prediction. It is for estimating evapotranspiration under various environmental conditions. TB outperforms the standard modified Penman–Monteith method.
Gocic *et al* 2021 [27]	Minimum temperature, maximum temperature, vapour pressure, sunshine hours and wind speed.	Using more time lags for monthly evapotranspiration prediction that are picked considering connection to the dataset is comparatively more effective.
Martin *et al* 2021 [28]	Temperature, humidity, wind speed, solar radiation and vapour pressure.	Ensemble approach of stacking performs well in all the feature sets where data comes in a variety of forms and under a variety of circumstances.

Zhao *et al* 2021 [29]	Minimum temperature, average sunshine hours, mean air temperature, average air pressure, maximum temperature,.	The PSO–GBDT prediction model can attain greater accuracy when the weather variables recovered using the PA approach are used as input.
Ravindran *et al* 2021 [30]	Solar radiation, maximum relative humidity, maximum temperature, minimum temperature, average air temperature, wind speed, and minimum relative humidity.	Regardless of dataset, the DNN model beat the XGB and RF models. It is worth mentioning the DNN model's efficacy in evapotranspiration modelling with a single input parameter in various climatic zones.
Han *et al* 2021 [31]	Wind speed, average relative humidity, maximum air temperature, sunshine hours, atmospheric pressure, minimum air temperature, and precipitation.	BP taking into consideration the changes of crop factor performed better compared to BP that used FAO-56 crop coefficient. The accuracy of BP was much improved by taking into consideration the dynamic change of agricultural factors and precipitation.

1.3 Some standard methods to calculate evapotranspiration

Predicting agricultural evapotranspiration in larger areas is difficult due to failure of mapping dynamic changes in crop conditions and weather factor management, as well as our inadequate understanding of evapotranspiration's changing reactions to these changes. By combining unique biophysical concepts with data, various models have been developed that forecast evapotranspiration. Fisher *et al* [32], Long and Singh [34], Mallick *et al* [36], Yao *et al* [35], Tang and Li [38], Bai *et al* [37], Wang *et al* [33], for example, have used vegetation indices (VIs), or diurnal range of TR (DTsR), relative humidity (RH), thermal infrared-retrieved land surface temperature (TR). These models' ability to map evapotranspiration under a wide range of settings is limited due to dependency on a subset of environmental characteristics to confine evapotranspiration. VPD, RH, VIs, WB module, TR, and DTsR to mimic soil moisture using RS-based evapotranspiration models are commonly used, which is a dominant factor in regulating evapotranspiration in dry climates (Mu *et al* [39] Yao *et al* [40]), but with significant drawbacks (Mallick *et al* [36]). Despite the fact that VIs can characterize the vegetation dynamics produced by soil water deficit and estimate the actual stomatal conductance and maximum stomatal conductance (Bai *et al* [37]), vegetation's reaction to soil water deficiency is frequently several days or weeks late (Liu *et al* [41]). An empirical relationship between moisture and DTsR (Yao *et al* [40]) has yet to be confirmed across scales. TR-generated thermal energy balance models (TEBMs) are regarded to be very useful for obtaining ET signals from dehydrated and moist crops due to TR's high reactivity to changes in soil moisture [42]. TR can be used to characterise the biophysical constraints on evapotranspiration with little knowledge of crop-specific characteristics or field management considerations. The discrepancy between TR and aerodynamic temperature (T_0), limit the usage of TEBM [43, 44]. As reactivity of TEBMs to TR errors is high [45] and the problem of accurate estimation of aerodynamic conductance, a single TEBM may not perform well given any conditions (Mallick *et al* [46]; Bhattarai *et al* [47]).

The following proposes some of the standard methods for calculating evapotranspiration.

$$\lambda E = \lambda E_s + \lambda E_c + \lambda E_i \tag{1.1}$$

$$\lambda E_c = \alpha\left(1 - f_{\text{wet}}\right)f_g f_T f_M R_{\text{nc}}\Delta/(\Delta + \gamma)$$

$$\lambda E_s = \alpha\left(f_{\text{wet}} + f_{SM}\left(1 - f_{\text{wet}}\right)\right)(R_{ns} - G)\Delta/(\Delta + \gamma)$$

$$\lambda E_i = \alpha f_{\text{wet}} R_{\text{nc}}\Delta/(\Delta + \gamma)$$

$$f_{\text{wet}} = RH^4, f_{\text{SM}} = \text{RH}^{\text{VPD/10}} f_M = \left(f_{\text{APAR}}/f_{\text{APARmax}}\right), f_{\text{APAR}} = 1.2(1.136\text{SAVI} - 0.04)$$

$$fg = \left(f_{\text{APAR}}/f_{\text{IPAR}}\right), f_{\text{IPAR}} = NDVI - 0.05 \tag{1.2}$$

$$f_T = \exp\left(-\left(\left(T_a - T_{\text{opt}}\right)/T_{\text{opt}}\right)2\right) \tag{1.3}$$

$$T_{\text{opt}} = T_a \text{ at } \max\left\{R_n \cdot f_{\text{APAR}} \cdot T_a/VPD\right\} \tag{1.4}$$

(Fisher *et al* [32]; Vinukollu *et al* [48])

$$\lambda E = \lambda E_s + \lambda E_c + \lambda E_i \tag{1.5}$$

$$\lambda \text{Ec} = \alpha\left(1 - f_{\text{wet}}\right)f_g f_T R_{\text{nc}}\Delta/(\Delta + \gamma)$$

$$\lambda \text{Es} = \alpha\left(f_{\text{wet}} + \left(1 - f_{\text{wet}}\right)f_{SM}\right)(R_{\text{ns}} - G)\Delta/(\Delta + \gamma)$$

$$\lambda \text{Ei} = \alpha f_{\text{wet}} R_{\text{nc}}\Delta/(\Delta + \gamma)$$

$$f_{\text{SM}} = (1/DTsR)^{\text{DTsR/DTsR}_{\text{max}}}, DTsR_{\text{max}} = 60^\circ \text{ C} \tag{1.6}$$

$$f_{\text{wet}} = f_{\text{SM}}^4 \tag{1.7}$$

PT-JPL has to be followed to compute f_{g} and f_{T} (Yao *et al* [35]).

Equations of the state:

$$g_a = (R_n - G)/\left(\rho_a \cdot c_P \cdot ((T_0 - T_a) + (e_0 - e_a)/\gamma)\right) \tag{1.8}$$

$$g_s = g_a \cdot (e_0 - e_a)/(e*_0 - e_0) \tag{1.9}$$

$$T_0 = T_a + (e_0 - e_a)/\gamma \cdot (1 - \Lambda)/\Lambda \tag{1.10}$$

$$\Lambda = 2\alpha \cdot \Delta/(2\Delta + 2\gamma + \gamma \cdot g_a/g_c \cdot (1 + M)) \tag{1.11}$$

The λE can be derived as:

$$\lambda E_{\text{inst}} = \Lambda \cdot (R_n - G)G = R_n \cdot (T_R - 273.15)/\alpha_0 \cdot (0.0038\alpha_0 + 0.007\alpha_0^2) \cdot (1 - 0.98\text{NDVI}^4) \tag{1.12}$$

(Mallick *et al* [36, 43, 44]; Bhattarai *et al* [47]).

1.4 Results and discussions on major findings

Figure 1.2 shows that the most often utilised weather parameter for reference crop evapotranspiration estimation is average temperature, followed by wind speed then solar radiation. Figure 1.3 demonstrates this. In terms of coefficient of determination, the Firefly Algorithm-Adaptive Neuro Fuzzy Inference System outperforms other algorithms, followed by Gradient Boosted Regression Trees and Artificial Neural Network. It is seen from figure 1.4. Bi-directional-Long Term Short Memory outperforms other algorithms in terms of root mean square error followed by stacking (SVM, RF, XGBoost) based ensemble approach and multi-layer perceptron. It is seen from figure 1.5. Fuzzy-Genetic Algorithm followed by Gradient Boosted Regression Trees and Bi-directional-Long Term Short Memory outperform other algorithms using mean absolute error. It is seen from figure 1.6. that in terms of accuracy, Back Propagation Neural Network outperforms Fuzzy-Genetic Algorithm. It is seen from figure 1.7 that in terms of Willmotts' Skill Score, Bi-directional-Long Term Short Memory and FA-ANFIS performs better than other algorithms. Figure 1.8 shows that RF and FA-ANFIS beats other algorithms in

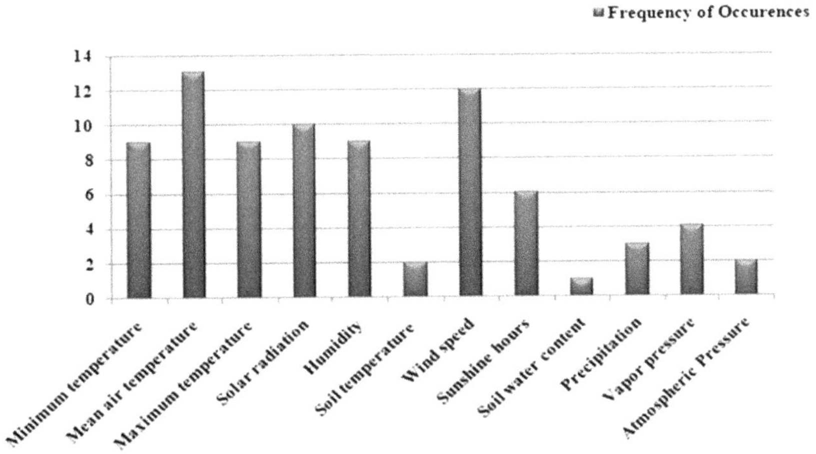

Figure 1.2. Monitored weather parameters for reference crop evapotranspiration methods.

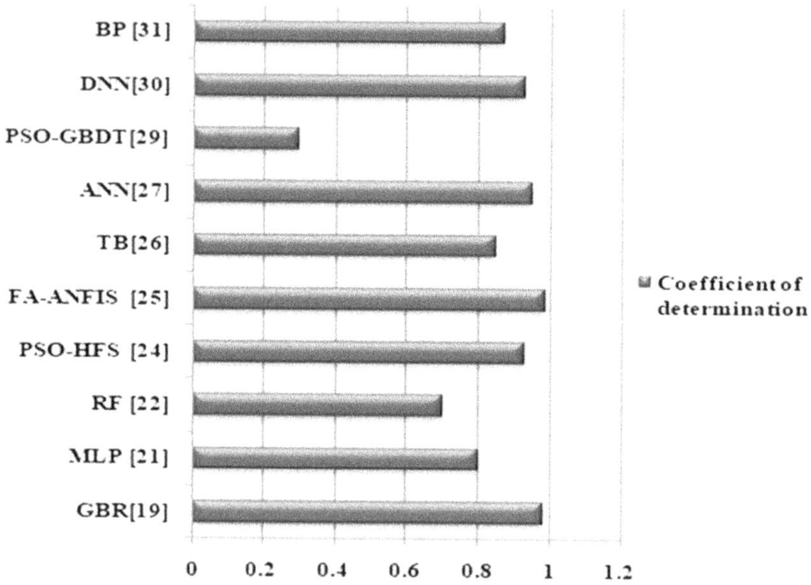

Figure 1.3. Coefficient of determination compared for different algorithms.

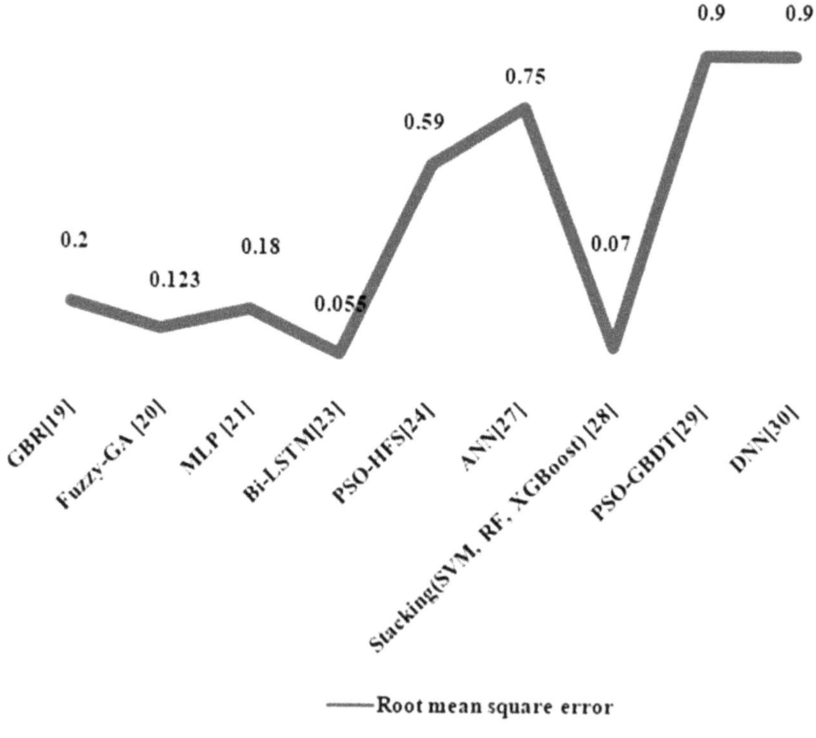

Figure 1.4. Root mean square error values compared for different algorithms.

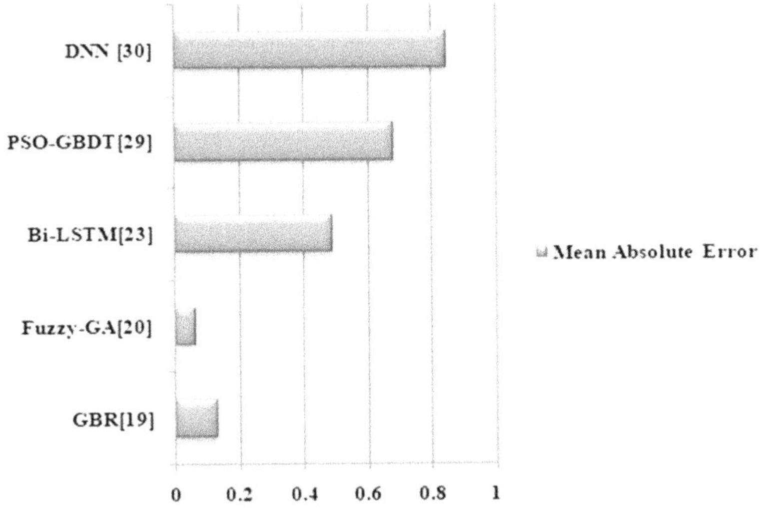

Figure 1.5. Mean absolute error values compared for different algorithms.

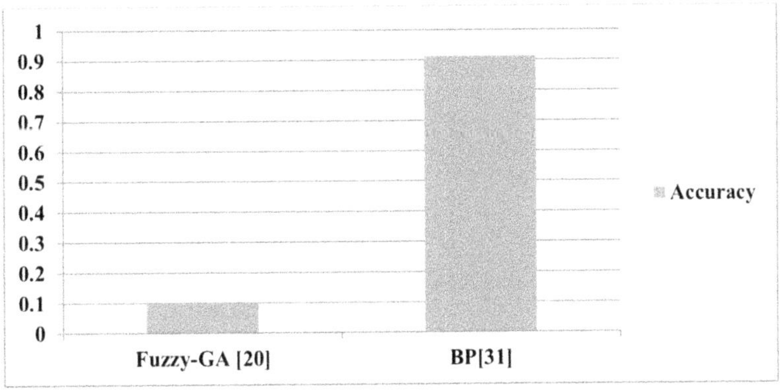

Figure 1.6. Accuracy values compared for different algorithms.

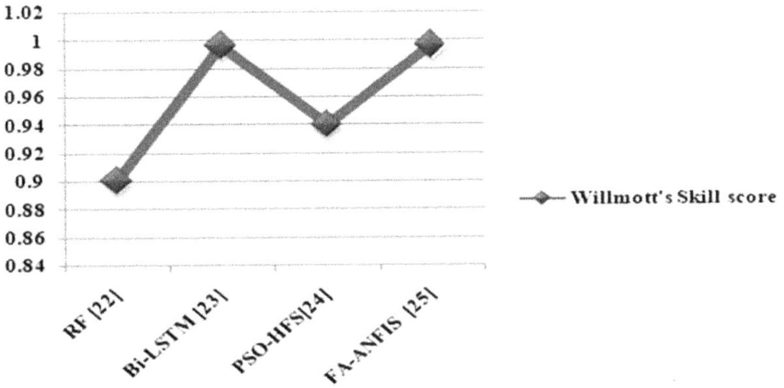

Figure 1.7. Willmotts' Skill Score values compared for different algorithms.

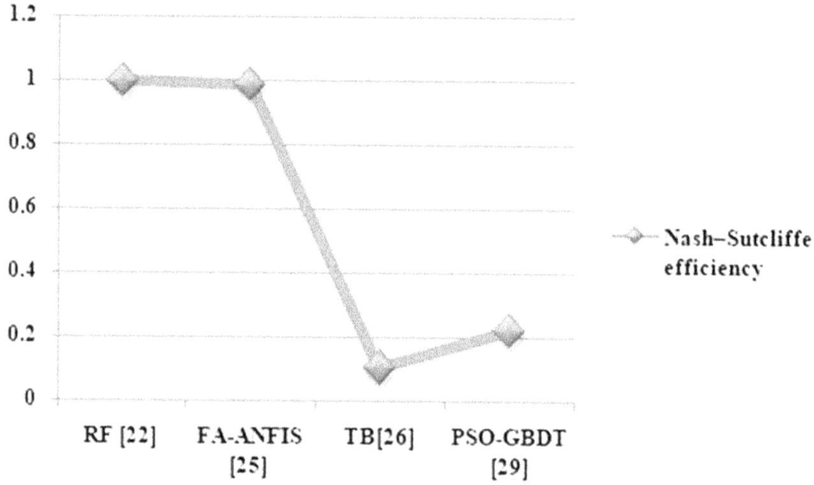

Figure 1.8. Nash–Sutcliffe efficiency values compared for different algorithms.

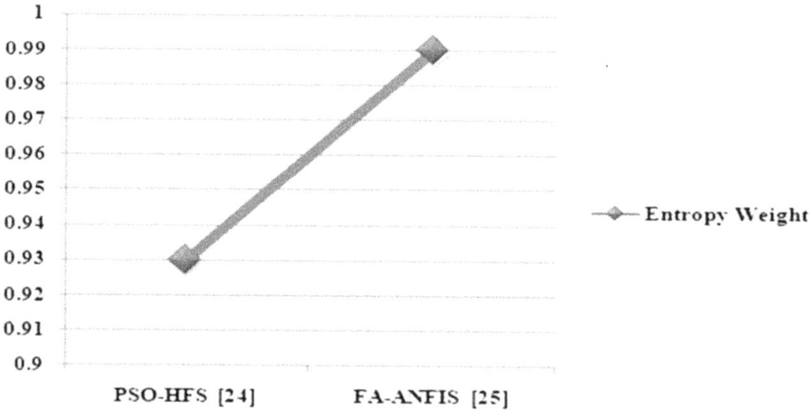

Figure 1.9. Entropy weight values compared for different algorithms.

terms of Nash–Sutcliffe efficiency. In terms of entropy weight, figure 1.9 shows that the FA-ANFIS outperforms Hierarchical Fuzzy System with PSO algorithm.

1.5 Conclusion and future work

We have extensively surveyed machine learning algorithms to estimate of crop evapotranspiration, which is a key component to ascertain soil water retention capacity. Widely monitored weather and soil variables are identified that are pivotal in estimation of crop evapotranspiration. Various performance metrics are also compared to ascertain which algorithm performs better than the rest of the algorithms. Security mechanisms such as making weather and soil data available at the network's edge and machine learning algorithms as well as evapotranspiration estimation using a secured interconnection of IoT devices for precision in designing irrigation schedules, are also not used. Also, parameters obtained from weather using real-time sensors that were not given enough importance in the relevant prior works needs to be identified to understand how its non-linearity strongly affects non-linear changes in soil moisture retention capacity to increase accuracy in evapotranspiration estimation. Accurate estimation of crop evapotranspiration helps farmers designing precise irrigation water supplying decisions to maintain crop growth and productivity of farm land.

References

[1] Zhai Z, Martínez J F, Beltran V and Martínez N L 2020 Decision support systems for agriculture 4.0: survey and challenges *Comput. Electron. Agric.* **620170** 105256

[2] Rana G and Katerji N 2000 Measurement and estimation of actual evapotranspiration in the field under Mediterranean climate: a review *Eur. J. Agron.* **13** 125–53

[3] Allen R G, Pereira L S, Raes D and Smith M 1998 Crop evapotranspiration— guidelines for computing crop water requirements *FAO Irrigation and drainage paper* 56

[4] Djaman K, Smeal D, Koudahe K and Allen S 2020 Hay yield and water use efficiency of alfalfa under different irrigation and fungicide regimes in a semiarid climate *Water (Switzerland)* **12** 1721

[5] Moratiel R, Bravo R, Saa A, Tarquis A M and Almorox J 2020 Estimation of evapotranspiration by the food and agricultural organization of the united nations (FAO) Penman–Monteith temperature (PMT) and Hargreaves-Samani (HS) models under temporal and spatial criteria – a case study in Duero basin (Spain) *Nat. Hazards Earth Syst. Sci.* **20** 859–75

[6] Baldocchi D *et al* 2001 FLUXNET: a new tool to study the temporal and spatial variability of ecosystem- scale carbon dioxide, water vapor, and energy flux densities *Bull. Am. Meteorol. Soc.* **82** 2415–34

[7] Barr A G, van der Kamp G, Black T A, McCaughey J H and Nesic Z 2012 Energy balance closure at the BERMS flux towers in relation to the water balance of the White Gull Creek watershed 1999–2009 *Agric. For. Meteorol.* **153** 3–13

[8] Rosenberry D O, Winter, Thomas C, Buso, Donald C, Likens and Gene E 2007 Comparison of 15 evaporation methods applied to a small mountain lake in the northeastern *USA J. Hydrol.* **340** 149–66

[9] Fang W, Huang S, Huang Q, Huang G, Meng E and Luan J 2018 Reference evapotranspiration forecasting based on local meteorological and global climate information screened by partial mutual information *J. Hydrol.* **561** 764–79

[10] Yang F, White M A, Michaelis A R, Ichii K, Hashimoto H, Votava P, Zhu A-X and Nemani R R 2006 Prediction of continental-scale evapotranspiration by combining MODIS and Ameri flux data through support vector machine *IEEE Trans. Geosci. Remote Sens.* **44** 3452–61

[11] Tabari H, Kisi O, Ezani A and Hosseinzadeh Talaee P 2012 SVM, ANFIS, regression and climate based models for reference evapotranspiration modeling using limited climatic data in a semi-arid highland environment *J. Hydrol.* **444–445** 78–89

[12] Landeras G, Ortiz-Barredo A and L´opez J ’e J 2009 Forecasting weekly evapotranspiration with ARIMA and artificial neural network models *J. Irrig. Drain. Eng.* **135** 323–34

[13] Bodesheim P, Jung M, Gans F, Mahecha M D and Reichstein M 2018 Upscaled diurnal cycles of land-Atmosphere fluxes: a new global half-hourly data product *Earth Syst. Sci. Data.* **10** 1327–65

[14] Auret L and Aldrich C 2012 Interpretation of nonlinear relationships between process variables by use of random forests *Miner. Eng.* **35** 27–42

[15] Shiri J 2018 Improving the performance of the mass transfer-based reference evapotranspiration estimation approaches through a coupled wavelet-random forest methodology *J. Hydrol.* **561** 737–50

[16] Zhang J, Zhu Y, Zhang X, Ye M and Yang J 2018 Developing a long short-term memory (LSTM) based model for predicting water table depth in agricultural areas *J. Hydrol.* **561** 918–29

[17] Chen Z, Zhu Z, Jiang H and Sun S 2020a Estimating daily reference evapotranspiration based on limited meteorological data using deep learning and classical machine learning methods *J. Hydrol.* **591** 125286

[18] Chen Z, Sun S, Wang Y, Wang Q and Zhang X 2020b Temporal convolution-network-based models for modeling maize evapotranspiration under mulched drip irrigation *Comput. Electron. Agric.* **169** 105206

[19] Ponraj A S and Vigneswaran T 2019 Daily evapotranspiration prediction using gradient boost regression model for irrigation planning *The Journal of Supercomputing* **76** 5732–44

[20] Saggi M K and Jain S 2020 Application of fuzzy-genetic and regularization random forest (FG-RRF): estimation of crop evapotranspiration (ETc) for maize and wheat crops *Agric. Water Manage.* **229** 105907

[21] Bai Y, Zhang S, Bhattarai N, Mallick K, Liu Q, Tang L, Im J, Guo L and Zhang J 2021 On the use of machine learning based ensemble approaches to improve evapotranspiration estimates from croplands across a wide environmental gradient *Agric. For. Meteorol.* **298** 108308

[22] Talib A, Desai A R, Huang J, Griffis T J, Reed D E and Chen J 2021 Evaluation of prediction and forecasting models for evapotranspiration of agricultural lands in the Midwest US *J. Hydrol.* **600** 126579

[23] Roy D K 2021 Long short-term memory networks to predict one-step ahead reference evapotranspiration in a subtropical climatic zone *Environmental Processes* **8** 911–41

[24] Roy D K, Saha K K, Kamruzzaman M, Biswas S K and Hossain M A 2021 Hierarchical Fuzzy systems integrated with particle swarm optimization for daily reference evapotranspiration prediction: a novel approach *Water Resour. Manage.* **35** 5383–407

[25] Roy D K, Lal A, Sarker K K, Saha K K and Datta B 2021 Optimization algorithms as training approaches for prediction of reference evapotranspiration using adaptive neuro fuzzy inference system *Agric. Water Manage.* **255** 107003

[26] Raza A, Shoaib M, Khan A, Baig F, Faiz M A and Khan M M 2020 Application of non-conventional soft computing approaches for estimation of reference evapotranspiration in various climatic regions *Theor. Appl. Climatol.* **139** 1459–77

[27] Gocić M and Amiri M A 2021 Reference evapotranspiration prediction using neural networks and optimum time lags *Water Resour. Manage.* **35** 1913–26

[28] Martín J, Sáez J A and Corchado E 2021 On the suitability of stacking-based ensembles in smart agriculture for evapotranspiration prediction *Appl. Soft Comput.* **108** 107509

[29] Zhao L, Zhao X, Zhou H, Wang X and Xing X 2021 Prediction model for daily reference crop evapotranspiration based on hybrid algorithm and principal components analysis in Southwest China *Comput. Electron. Agric.* **190** 106424

[30] Ravindran S M, Bhaskaran S K M and Ambat S K N 2021 A deep neural network architecture to model reference evapotranspiration using a single input meteorological parameter *Environmental Processes* **8** 1567–99

[31] Han X, Wei Z, Zhang B, Li Y, Du T and Chen H 2021 Crop evapotranspiration prediction by considering dynamic change of crop coefficient and the precipitation effect in back-propagation neural network model *J. Hydrol.* **596** 126104

[32] Fisher J B, Tu K P and Baldocchi D D 2008 Global estimates of the land–atmosphere water flux based on monthly AVHRR and ISLSCP-II data, validated at 16 FLUXNET sites *Remote Sens. Environ.* **112** 901–19

[33] Wang K, Dickinson R E and Wild M *et al* 2010 Evidence for decadal variation in global terrestrial evapotranspiration between 1982 and 2002: 1. model development *J. Geophys. Res.* **115** D20112

[34] Long D and Singh V P 2012 A two-source trapezoid model for evapotranspiration (TTME) from satellite imagery *Remote Sens. Environ.* **121** 370–88

[35] Yao Y, Liang S and Cheng J *et al* 2013 MODIS-driven estimation of terrestrial latent heat flux in China based on a modified Priestley–Taylor algorithm *Agr. Forest Meteorol.* **171–172** 187–202

[36] Mallick K, Boegh E and Trebs I *et al* 2015 Reintroducing radiometric surface temperature into the Penman–Monteith formulation *Water Resour. Res.* **51** 6214–43

[37] Bai Y, Zhang J and Zhang S *et al* 2017 Using precipitation, vertical root distribution and satellite-retrieved vegetation information to parameterize water stress in a Penman–Monteith approach to evapotranspiration modelling under Mediterranean climate *J. Adv. Model. Earth Syst.* **9** 168–92

[38] Tang R and Li Z 2017 An end-member-based two-source approach for estimating land surface evapotranspiration from remote sensing data *IEEE Trans. Geosci. Remote Sens.* **55** 5818–32

[39] Mu Q, Zhao M and Running S W 2011 Improvements to a MODIS global terrestrial evapotranspiration algorithm *Remote Sens. Environ.* **115** 1781–800

[40] Yao Y, Liang S and Li X *et al* 2015 A satellite-based hybrid algorithm to determine the Priestley–Taylor parameter for global terrestrial latent heat flux estimation across multiple biomes *Remote Sens. Environ.* **165** 216–33

[41] Liu Q, Zhang S and Zhang H *et al* 2020 Monitoring drought using composite drought indices based on remote sensing *Sci. Tot. Environ.* **711** 134585

[42] Anderson M C, Allen R G and Morse A *et al* 2012 Use of landsat thermal imagery in monitoring evapotranspiration and managing water resources *Remote Sens. Environ.* **122** 50–65

[43] Mallick K, Trebs I and Boegh E *et al* 2016 Canopy-scale biophysical controls of transpiration and evaporation in the Amazon Basin *Hydrol. Earth Syst. Sci.* **20** 4237–64

[44] Mallick K, Toivonen E and Trebs I *et al* 2018a Bridging thermal infrared sensing and physically-based evapotranspiration modeling: from theoretical implementation to validation across an aridity gradient in australian ecosystems *Water Resour. Res.* **54** 3409–35

[45] Wang K and Dickinson R E 2012 A review of global terrestrial evapotranspiration: observation, modeling, climatology, and climatic variability *Rev. Geophys.* **50** RG2005

[46] Mallick K, Wandera L and Bhattarai N *et al* 2018b A critical evaluation on the role of aerodynamic and canopy–surface conductance parameterization in SEB and SVAT models for simulating evapotranspiration: a case study in the upper Biebrza national park Wetland in Poland *Water* **10** 1753

[47] Bhattarai N, Mallick K and Brunsell N A *et al* 2018 Regional evapotranspiration from an image-based implementation of the surface temperature initiated closure (STIC1.2) model and its validation across an aridity gradient in the conterminous US *Hydrol. Earth Syst. Sci.* **22** 2311–41

[48] Vinukollu R K, Wood E F and Ferguson C R *et al* 2011 Global estimates of evapotranspiration for climate studies using multi-sensor remote sensing data: evaluation of three process-based approaches *Remote Sens. Environ.* **115** 801–23

Chapter 2

Iris-based biometric cryptosystem

Ivan A Matveev and Igor S Litvinchev

Most automatic access control systems use cryptography and biometry. Cryptography itself is highly reliable but requires reproduction of quite a long access key. Humans lack the capability to do this, while storage devices may be lost or stolen. Biometric features are always with the person, however, they vary: it is impossible to get precisely same values in two attempts. A system of methods is presented, which obtains features from an iris image and embeds a given secret key there. This yields a combined key, such that the key cannot be extracted unless providing biometric features close to the original ones, i.e. the data of the same person. System processing starts with approximate detection of the eye center followed by approximate segmentation of inner and outer borders of the iris. Then the borders are refined. Biometric features are binary and are extracted by a commonly adopted technique. The embedding method (coder) consists of error-correcting coding of the secret key followed by bit-wise sum modulo 2 with biometric features. The error-correcting coding consists of separate steps, which are executed in sequence: Reed–Solomon, Hadamard, majority coding, and bit hashing. The decoder repeats encoder steps in inverse order. The parameters of error correction codes are selected optimally to provide storing of the largest secret key while preserving error rates and fitting in the given size of the biometric template. Possible size of the secret key is 65 bit. Numerical experiments are conducted with several open-access databases.

2.1 Introduction

Nowadays, information protection based on cryptographic algorithms is widely used. A large number of such algorithms, as well as methods of their application, have been invented [1]. These algorithms and systems are mathematically grounded and reliable. The weak link in their implementation and usage, as usual, is human. Cryptography requires keys, i.e. sequences of digits, which should be reproduced

doi:10.1088/978-0-7503-4801-0ch2

precisely. While a person is able to remember and reproduce a personally invented password (though already here there are difficulties), for an automatically generated sequence of several dozens of pseudorandom symbols it is practically impossible [2]. At the same time, humans have biometric features that are easily retrievable, difficult to emulate, and have a significant amount of information. Biometrics is rarely lost, difficult to forge, and easy to present with special equipment. The disadvantage of biometric traits in this application is their variability: it is impossible to exactly replicate the measurement results, we can only say that two sets of traits obtained from one person are in some sense closer than the sets taken from different people. It is of great interest to combine the two approaches, i.e. to develop methods for exact reproduction (generation) of a cryptographic key from biometric features, or disguised addition of an existing key to such features, or other methods and scenarios for linking strictly defined and statistically relevant data, suitable for use in cryptographic protocols, to sets of volatile biometric features.

The eye iris is the most suitable biometric modality among all non-invasive ones due to its highest information capacity. There is an estimate of 249 degrees of freedom [3] for the iris, which promises to be almost as good as the strongest symmetric cryptography key length of 256 bit, while a fingerprint has 80 uncorrelated parameters [4], and other modalities are around this or worse. In order to design a practically usable system, which goes all the way from source raw biometric data to embedding the cryptographic key to biometric features it is advisable to base on the iris.

Methods, algorithms and applications of iris biometrics have been developing rapidly in recent years. Reviews [5, 6] present more than 100 works concerning this issue and it is only a small share of all the efforts being made. The major focus here is building an identification system, i.e. the system, which can be reduced to a task: take two images of iris and output the probability that the images belong to the same person. Workflow of an iris identification system can be split into three main steps: segmentation, biometric features estimation, and biometric features matching. Here a different problem is solved, thus only primary two stages are usable. The last one is replaced by embedding/extracting the cryptographic key into/from the biometric features.

We start from the segmentation task and present an eye segmentation framework, which stably works across a variety of image databases. The features estimation is taken from [3] with feature raster size of 13 pixels in radial direction and 256 pixels in tangential direction (along a circle). Since each pixel has two bits (convolutions with odd and even functions) the total size of template is 6656 bit [7]. Finally we describe the embedding and extraction methods.

2.2 Eye segmentation framework

The obvious approach to iris segmentation comprises a sequence of operations including initial pupil detection (as a most prominent dark region of the image with pronounced round shape), outlining outer iris border and final refinement of visible iris part by rejecting regions occluded by reflection spots, eyelids and eyelashes. Most researchers and developers follow this way, detection of each iris feature is usually performed only once, then it is considered as being detected with 'final' precision and is not recalculated or refined even after other interrelated features are measured that can be used for refinement. The typical picture here is for pupil parameters. For instance, in [8–11] full cycle of iris detection is proposed, but pupil parameters are detected at one step at the very beginning and are not revised or refined any more.

Only few papers present some broadening of this scheme 'first pupil, then iris, once detected, never revised'. In [12, 13] eye center position is evaluated prior to the pupil which is helpful for robust pupil detection. Refinement of pupil parameters after iris location using information about iris size is done in [14]. In [14, 15] iris features are estimated iteratively, one detection method running several times to refine previous results. In [13, 16] iterations are performed in different scales under multi-scale image processing approach. But none of these works implement more than one method for detecting any of the eye features.

Here we develop a *system of methods* for iris parameter detection in an image. Evaluating each of the parameters is performed in *several steps*. The basic idea of constructing the framework presented here is that at first the most general features of the object should be detected and then gradually refined, forming a more detailed object description. Beginning detection steps should not output precise and final parameters of the object. Instead, the requirement of the beginning steps is to be as much general and robust as possible, accept the widest range of images and conditions and detect the object whenever it exists. On the other hand, ending steps of detection should not be that general but should have the highest possible precision.

Iris pattern in frontal images is bound by two nearly circular contours, inner and outer borders. Hereinafter, the boundary between iris and pupil is referred to as *inner border*, *pupil border* or simply *pupil*, and the boundary between iris and sclera is referred to as *outer border* or *iris*. When meaning pupil or iris region rather than border, it is explicitly defined. As a rule, pupil border is fully visible, but iris border is partially occluded by eyelids and/or eyelashes. One should distinguish visible and real pupil and iris borders. Real iris border shape is close to circumference and at the beginning steps of segmentation visible borders are also modeled as such, while occlusions are treated as noise. At the ending steps detection of occlusions, as more fine peculiarities, is performed.

Pupil and iris contours are almost concentric. Some *eye center* point can roughly approximate both their centres, hence it is the most general feature of an iris image. Therefore, the first step of eye detection in an image is the location of this approximate center. It should be stressed that the goal is only to find the position of the center but not the size of any contour. Omitting size estimation and treating the task as approximate allows involving both borders in center detection. This is especially valuable in images with poor pupil–iris boundary, where traditional iris detection sequence frequently fails. A modification of Hough method for circle detection is used [17].

The next thing to do after center location would seem to be evaluating pupil size. This is the way developed in [12] and other works, where iris segmentation starts from eye center location. However, the authors consider this way is not effective for a wide range of iris images. Since there are two circular contours with approximately the same center, a method trying to detect the radius from a known center will fit to one of them, but then there is no reliable way to tell which contour (pupil or iris) is detected. This hindrance is outlined for instance in [18]. It can easily happen in eye images with high iris–sclera contrast and low pupil–iris contrast. From these consideration authors prefer a method of combined detection of circular approximations of both contours. Hereinafter it is referred to as *base radii* detection, since it determines approximate (base) radii of pupil and iris with respect to a known approximate center. The method relies on circular projections of gradient [19]. Base radii detection produces approximate center coordinates and radii of pupil and iris circles, which satisfy some reasonable limitations. Also, the quality of detection is calculated. The quality should be high enough to pass the image to forward processing.

After approximate evaluation of both iris boundaries they are both refined. Pupil refinement is performed with circular shortest path approach [20, 21]. The method used for iris refinement is for the most part the same as that of base radius. The difference is that the position of pupil is now fixed and only iris center and radius are being searched.

A block scheme of the framework is given in figure 2.1. More details on the framework can be found in [22].

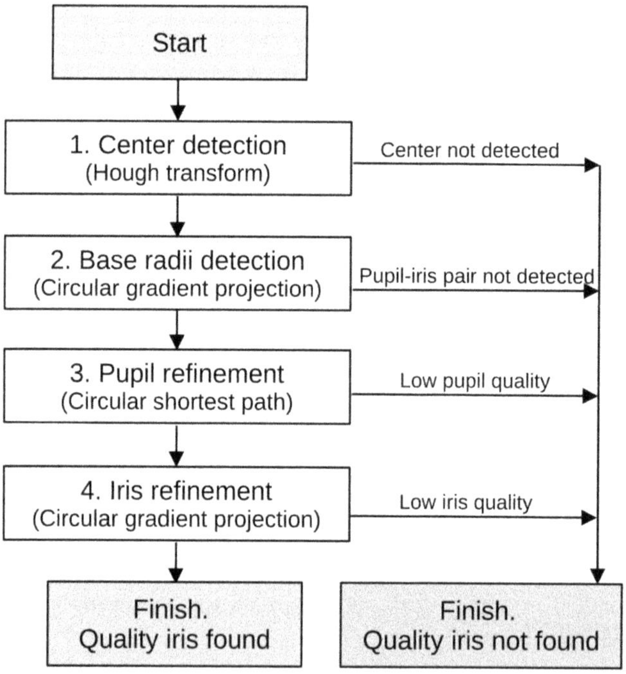

Figure 2.1. Block scheme of the framework.

2.3 Eye segmentation methods

Methods employed for segmentation are briefly presented in this section.

2.3.1 Center detection

The algorithm finds the coordinates $(x_C, y_C) = \vec{c}$ of the eye center, and there is no task of detecting pupil or iris size. Consider rectilinear coordinate system Oxy in an image with center in the left bottom corner and axes Ox and Oy directed horizontally and vertically. The center position is evaluated approximately. Due to such a problem, formulation pixels of both pupil and iris borders may be used in the Hough procedure, since their centers are approximately the same and their differing radii are not required. Also the algorithm has low computational complexity since only two parameters are estimated and thus Hough transform uses only a two-dimensional accumulator, rather than three-dimensional as is done in standard circle detection.

The algorithm is executed as a sequence of steps.

Step 1. Gradient calculation.
Denote brightness $b(\vec{x})$ in image point $\vec{x}$. Brightness gradient $\vec{\nabla} b(\vec{x}) = \vec{g}(\vec{x})$ is calculated by a standard way from smoothed image [23]. It should be noted that the image is a raster and coordinates of pixels and vectors are integer numbers.

Step 2. Selection of pixels with high gradient.
Borders in image are composed of pixels with high brightness gradient. Only they are of interest for the processing. Cumulative distribution of brightness gradient values is constructed: $H(G) = | \{\vec{z}: \|\vec{g}(\vec{z})\| \leqslant G\} |$, where $\|\cdot\|$ is the Euclid norm of vector, $|\cdot|$ is the power of the set. Pixels included in the higher 10% of this distribution are selected:

$$H(\|\vec{g}(\vec{x})\|) \geqslant 0.9N, \tag{2.1}$$

where N is total number of image pixels.

Step 3. Voting to accumulator.
Parameter space (accumulator) in the algorithm is the space of center coordinates $\vec{c} \in A(\vec{x})$, which coincides with source image space. The ray from point $\vec{x}$ in the anti-gradient direction $-\vec{\nabla} b(\vec{x})$ is the locus of all possible dark circles with the border passing through this point. A system of such rays built from pixels selected in step 2 will have thickenings in positions of centers of roundish dark objects. The more circle-like the object is, the more expressed will be the corresponding thickening.

Step 4. Accumulator smoothing.
Parameter space $A(\vec{x})$ is processed by a low-pass filter to outline maxima, denoting the result as $A_B(\vec{x})$.

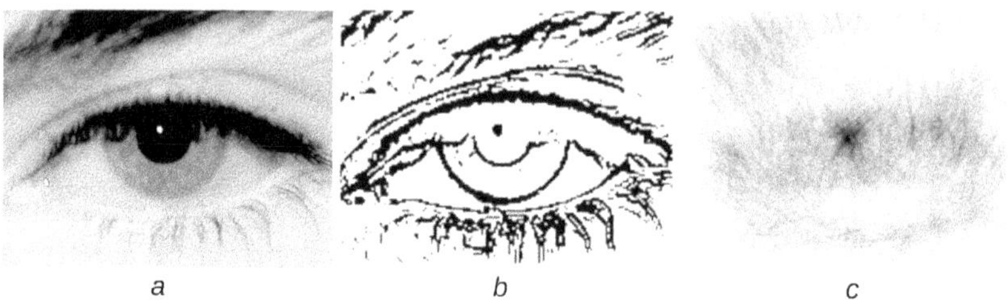

Figure 2.2. Sample of center detection.

Step 5. Maximum detection.
Maximum position in a smoothed accumulator corresponds to the center of the most round object in the image, i.e. eye center $\vec{c} = \text{argmax}_{\vec{x}} A_B(\vec{x})$. If maximum value is below threshold, it is considered that the image does not contain an eye.

A sample of the center detection algorithm is presented in figure 2.2. Subfigure *a* is source image $b(\vec{x})$, *b* depicts points satisfying condition (2.1) and participating in voting, and *c* shows the accumulator $A(\vec{x})$.

2.3.2 Base radii detection

The algorithm locates two approximate circles: pupil (x_P, y_P, r_P) and iris (x_I, y_I, r_I) given the approximate center $\vec{c}$ from the previous step. For simplicity, take the point (x_C, y_C) as the coordinate origin. Since contours of pupil and iris have approximately circular shape, brightness gradient vectors of their pixels lie in lines passing close to the center (i.e. lines making small angle with direction to the center):

$$\phi = \arccos \frac{\vec{g}(\vec{x}) \cdot \vec{x}}{\|\vec{g}(\vec{x})\| \, \|\vec{x}\|} < T_\phi. \tag{2.2}$$

Value T_ϕ is a threshold angle equal to 45°.

Apart, gradient values at borders should be enough big and the condition (2.1) should also hold. Call pixels with gradients satisfying the conditions (2.1) and (2.2) *candidates* meaning that these pixels are candidates for being part of pupil or iris contours. The set of candidates form a binary image (see for instance figure 2.2(b)), denote this set as K. Circular projection of this image with respect to center is calculated:

$$\Pi(r) = \frac{|\{\vec{x}: r - 0.5 \leqslant \|\vec{x}\| < r + 0.5, \vec{x} \in K\}|}{|\{\vec{x}: r - 0.5 \leqslant \|\vec{x}\| < r + 0.5\}|}. \tag{2.3}$$

It means that for each radius a share of candidates among all pixels lying at this distance is calculated. If a dark circle exists in the image with the center close to the eye center, then anti-gradients at its borders will be large and directed approximately towards the eye center, and such border pixels will be marked as candidates. These pixels lie at approximately the same distance from the eye center, hence they all will fall to the same few neighbouring points of projection. Non-circular contours or contours with centers far from the eye center form scattered data without

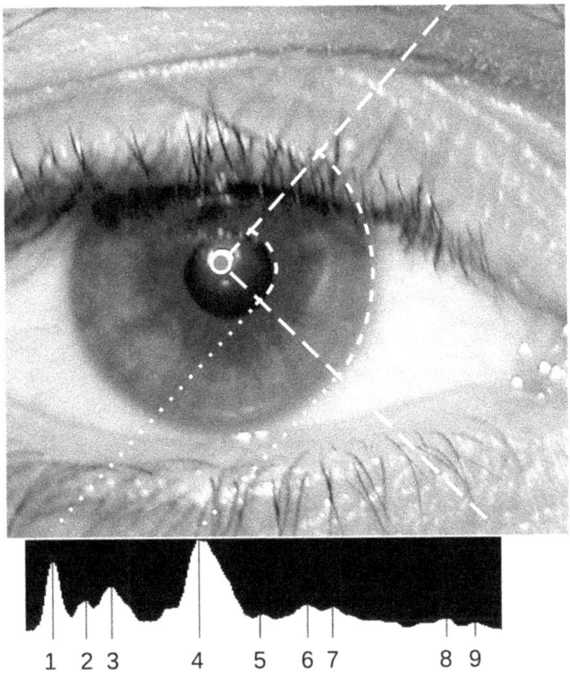

Figure 2.3. Sample of circular projection and local maxima positions.

thickenings. Thus prominent local maxima of circular projections will correspond to concentric contours. Four sub-projections are calculated, separately for left, right, top and bottom quadrants, to which the plane is separated by lines $x = y$ and $x = -y$. Typical sub-projection in the right quadrant $\Pi_R(r)$ is shown in figure 2.3.

By determining the positions of local maxima for all four quadrants, we can obtain the possible distances of the boundaries of hypothetical circles from a center of circular projection in the corresponding direction. The sample histogram in figure 2.3 shows the positions of nine local maxima on the right sub-projection, and we define them as

$$\mu_R(n_R) = \arg \underset{n}{\mathrm{loc}} \, \underset{r}{\max} \, \Pi_R(r), \quad n_R = \overline{1, 9}. \tag{2.4}$$

In this projection the first maximum is produced by the pupil and the fourth is from the iris. The quality of maxima is simply the value of histogram at the point

$$q_R(n) = \Pi_R(\mu_R(n)). \tag{2.5}$$

Analogously μ_L, q_L, n_L stand for positions, qualities and number of local maxima in the right sub-projection, μ_T, q_T, n_T and μ_B, q_B, n_B are for top and bottom sub-projections. Two circular contours (pupil and iris) give a pair of local maxima in each circular sub-projection, if it is not occluded by eyelid, eyelash or something else. Other maxima may appear from reflection spots, eyelids, patterns of the iris pattern itself. Combining local maxima positions (2.4) gives a set of hypothetical pupils:

$$
\begin{aligned}
x_{\mathrm{P}}^{i,j} &= \frac{1}{2}\big(\mu_{\mathrm{R}}(i) - \mu_{\mathrm{L}}(j)\big), \quad i = \overline{1, n_{\mathrm{R}}}, \quad j = \overline{1, n_{\mathrm{L}}}, \\
y_{\mathrm{P}}^{k,l} &= \frac{1}{2}\big(\mu_{\mathrm{T}}(k) - \mu_{\mathrm{B}}(l)\big), \quad k = \overline{1, n_{\mathrm{T}}}, \quad l = \overline{1, n_{\mathrm{B}}}, \\
r_{\mathrm{P}}^{i,j,k,l} &= \frac{1}{4}\big(\mu_{\mathrm{R}}(i) + \mu_{\mathrm{L}}(j) + \mu_{\mathrm{T}}(k) + \mu_{\mathrm{B}}(l)\big),
\end{aligned}
\tag{2.6}
$$

and irises (by a similar formula). Quality of the combination is also defined from values (2.5) as:

$$
q_{\mathrm{P}}^{i,j,k,l} = \frac{1}{4}\big(q_{\mathrm{R}}(i) + q_{\mathrm{L}}(j) + q_{\mathrm{T}}(k) + q_{\mathrm{B}}(l)\big). \tag{2.7}
$$

The problem is to determine combinations corresponding to real positions of pupil and iris circles. The nature of pupil and iris impose certain limitations on their locations and sizes:

$$
\frac{1}{7}r_{\mathrm{I}} < r_{\mathrm{P}} < \frac{3}{4}r_{\mathrm{I}}, \quad d = \|\vec{c}_{\mathrm{P}} - \vec{c}_{\mathrm{I}}\| < r_{\mathrm{P}}, \quad 2(r_{\mathrm{I}} - r_{\mathrm{P}} - d) > r_{\mathrm{I}} - r_{\mathrm{P}} + d, \tag{2.8}
$$

where $\vec{c}_{\mathrm{P}} = (x_{\mathrm{P}}, y_{\mathrm{P}})$, $\vec{c}_{\mathrm{I}} = (x_{\mathrm{I}}, y_{\mathrm{I}})$ are centers of pupil and iris, d is a distance between them. Namely: radius of iris cannot exceed pupil radius more then by seven times; radius of pupil cannot exceed 3/4 of iris radius; center of iris lies inside the pupil; lengths of two segments cut by pupil and iris borders from a line passing through their centers cannot differ more that two times.

From all possible variants of pupil and iris given by (2.6) we select those satisfying conditions (2.8). Typically there are few of them, less than a dozen. The quality of combination is calculated as a sum of pupil and iris qualities (2.7) and a weighted quality of fitting to conditions (2.8):

$$
Q = q_{\mathrm{P}} + q_{\mathrm{I}} + q_{\mathrm{fit}}. \tag{2.9}
$$

The combination with best quality is selected. Also, the variant with absent top and bottom iris local maxima are tested in order to cover the case of occluding iris with upper and lower eyelids/eyelashes. The formulas (2.6) and (2.7) are modified accordingly, iris center vertical position is taken equal to that of pupil: $y_{\mathrm{I}} \equiv y_{\mathrm{P}}$. Other types of occlusion are not treated, the iris images are considered too bad for processing in this case. So, the method is executed in six steps:

Step 1. Gradient calculation.
Same as in center detection.

Step 2. Candidates selection.
Selecting candidate pixels according to conditions (2.1) and (2.2).

Step 3. Circular projecting.
Calculating circular projections (2.3) in four quadrants.

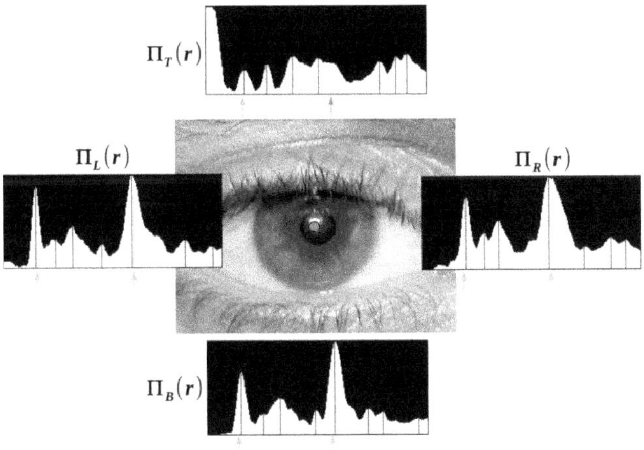

Figure 2.4. Four circular projections, their maxima positions and correct position of borders.

Step 4. Maxima selection.
Estimating local maxima in projections.

Step 5. Combining maxima.
Finding biologically feasible combinations of local maxima.

Step 6. Selecting best of feasible combinations.
If no feasible combination of local maxima is detected, two heuristics are tried: one to detect feasible pupil alone, the other to detect feasible iris alone. If both fail, the result is 'no eye detected'.

Sample of projection combination is presented in figure 2.4. Real positions of pupil and iris borders, taken from expert marking are depicted by arrows. There is no local maxima corresponding to iris border in the top projection $\Pi_T(r)$ since iris border is occluded by eyelid and eyelash. Such minor obstacles do not prevent choosing correct combination.

2.3.3 Pupil border refinement

Circular shortest path (CSP) method builds a closed contour around a given point, optimizing a specific functional. Value of the functional is composed of *inner* and *outer energies* (also referred to as *costs*). Inner energy depends on contour shape, namely its non-smoothness and deviation from circle with the center in a given point. Outer energy is determined by characteristics of the image in points of the contour. For a task of searching the boundary between regions of different brightness, outer energy is set high in points with low brightness gradient (i.e. non-boundary) and is decreased with the growth of the gradient projection in a direction perpendicular to the local contour part. Hence the CSP method locates a near-circular contour passing along the boundary between areas [24].

In the problem of refinement, an approximate circle is given, and the ring surrounding it is considered. To ease calculations, polar transformation is done, which maps the ring to a rectangle. The upper border of the rectangle corresponds to the outer circumference of the ring, the bottom of the rectangle maps to the inner circumference, and two sides of the rectangle conform to the sides of a ray passing from the center of the approximation circle. Typically, the Ox coordinate axis is selected as this ray. Radial and angular coordinates of the ring are mapped to the abscissa and ordinate of the rectangle. The image is transformed from rectilinear Oxy system to polar $O\rho\phi$ system, where it is also represented as a rectilinear raster. Thus the problem of locating CSP is transformed to a problem of detecting optimal path between left and right sides of the rectangle under the condition that starting and ending points have the same ordinate. The contour can be represented as a function $\rho(\phi)$, $\phi \in [0; 2\pi]$, $\rho(0) = \rho(2\pi)$, at which the derivative is limited $d\rho/d\phi < 1$. Accounting for discretization, the contour is represented as a sequence of points in rectilinear raster: $\{(n, \rho_n)\}$, $n \in [0; W - 1]$, $\rho_n \in [0; H - 1]$, where W and H are width and height of polar raster. Limitations to the derivative become $|\rho_{n+1} - \rho_n| \leqslant 1$, edge condition is written as $|\rho_{W-1} - \rho_0| \leqslant 1$.

Consider the cost of transition between points (n, ρ') and $(n + 1, \rho'')$ from adjacent columns of the raster: $C((n, \rho'), (n + 1, \rho'')) \equiv C_n(\rho', \rho'')$. This cost is combined from *inner* and *outer* parts: $C = C^{(\mathrm{I})} + C^{(\mathrm{O})}$, which represent inner and outer energies. The inner part is determined by contour shape and is minimal for horizontal lines in polar raster, which correspond to circles in source image space Oxy:

$$C_n^{(\mathrm{I})}(\rho', \rho'') = \begin{cases} 0, & \rho' = \rho'', \\ T_1, & |\rho' - \rho''| = 1, \\ \infty, & |\rho' - \rho''| > 1. \end{cases} \tag{2.10}$$

Value of $T_1 > 0$ is a parameter defining 'force' compelling the contour to a straight line in the polar raster, and depends on parameters of the polar transform. The outer part is a cost of transition through point (n, ρ'), defined by local image properties so as to be small in candidates and large in other pixels. The cost of transition is set to zero in pixels satisfying conditions (2.1) and (2.2), and is set to T_1 otherwise.

For a given path $S = \{\rho_n\}_{n=1}^{W}$ total cost is:

$$C(S) = C((0, \rho_0), (W, \rho_W)) = \sum_{n=1}^{W} C_n(\rho_n, \rho_{n+1}). \tag{2.11}$$

Optimal contour minimizes the cost: $S^* = \mathrm{argmin}_S C(S)$. This discrete optimization problem can be solved by various methods.

Since the CSP method is applied for refinement, it works in quite a narrow ring. Under this condition the exhaustive search is faster due to small overhead. Figure 2.5 gives a sample image of points satisfying (2.1) and (2.2) and polar transform relative to approximate pupil center.

The algorithm consists of the following steps.

Step 1. Candidates selection.
Calculate gradient and select candidate pixels according to conditions (2.1), (2.2) and $0.9r_P \leqslant \|\vec{x}\| < 1.1r_P$. See figure 2.5(a) for a sample of these data.

Step 2. Polar transform.

Step 3. Optimal path tracking.

Step 4. Restore original coordinates.
Restore the coordinates of the optimal path from $O\rho\phi$ domain back to Oxy domain.

The precise pupil border is not a circle, however, it is possible to define *equivalent circle* which has the same area and mass center. An equivalent circle can also be used as an approximation of pupil border, at which it happens to be a better model. Figure 2.6 shows a sample of refinement of the pupil border by an equivalent circle. The left and central images depict circles located by triangulation method with different initial eye center points. The right image presents an equivalent circle, which is the same and derived from these two different initial approximations.

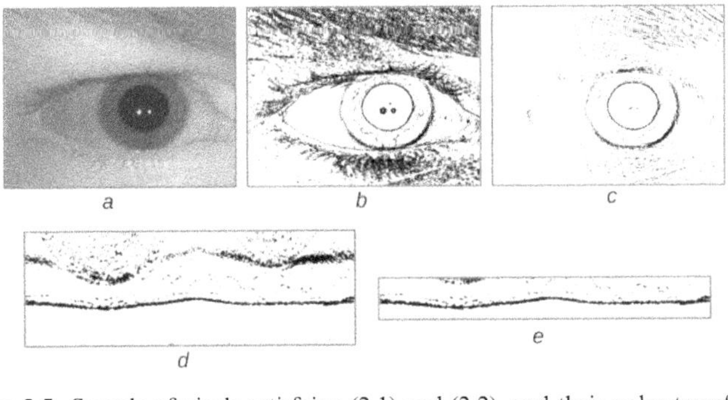

Figure 2.5. Sample of pixels satisfying (2.1) and (2.2), and their polar transform.

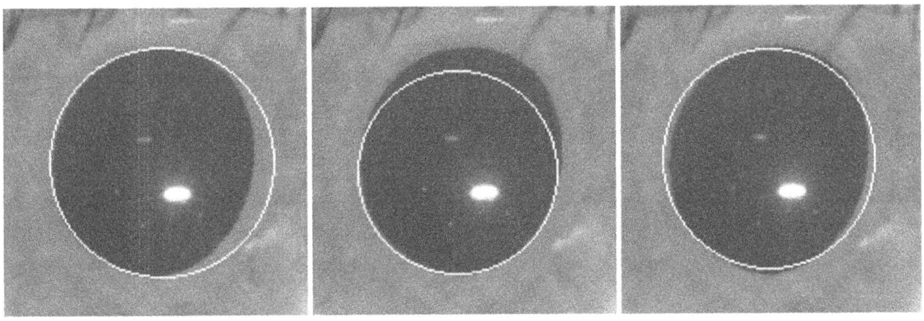

Figure 2.6. Sample of pupil circle refinement.

2.4 Selecting the cryptokey embedding method

In this work, we restrict ourselves to the case of symmetric encryption, in which, at the encoding stage, the *message* M and the secret *key* K are combined into the *code* by the *encoder* function Φ: $C = \Phi(M, K)$, and at the decoding stage the message is reconstructed from code and key by *decoder* functions Ψ: $M = \Psi(C, K)$. It is impossible to get M from C without the key K, so C can be public, not secret. A property of symmetric encryption is that the key K must be repeated exactly; for example, in the case of a binary sequence, all its bits must be reproduced.

Automatic biometrics has been used for quite a long time to identify (search) and authenticate (confirm) a person's identity. The central problem solved by such systems can be formulated as the problem of creating an optimal classifier: it is necessary to construct a distance function between two sets of biometric data $\rho(D_1, D_2)$ and set a threshold θ such that as many pairs D_1 and D_2 belonging to one person as possible gives distance $\rho(D_1, D_2) < \theta$, and as many as possible from different people gives $\rho(D_1, D_2) > \theta$. The function ρ can be represented as a superposition of two stages: the calculation of the biometric template T based on the data $T = T(D)$, i.e., the selection of features that are consistently close for one person and different for different people, and the calculation of the distance itself $\rho(T_1, T_2)$. The template T is a set of data ranging in size from a few hundred bytes to a few kilobytes, although the elements of this data (unlike cryptographic keys) are highly correlated. Nevertheless, the information capacity (entropy) of a biometric template is comparable or exceeds that of currently used cryptographic keys [25]. For example, there is an estimate of 249 degrees of freedom [3] for the iris, and a system has been developed for the fingerprint that allocates 80 uncorrelated parameters [4]. This suggests that it is possible to implement a cryptographic key in biometrics without reducing its robustness.

It should be noted that the main number of works devoted to the application of cryptographic methods in biometrics, develop the scheme of *cancelable biometrics* [26]. Its essence is to convert the biometric data in a format from which they can not be extracted in their original form, but in which they can be compared in the recognition system. Cancelable biometrics is nothing but a kind of fuzzy hashing [26], which can be formally represented as the introduction of an additional step in the calculation of the distance function ρ. This scheme calculates $\rho(H_1, H_2)$ (in some variants $\rho(H_1, T_2)$), where H is the hash function of the biometric template $H = H(T)$. Obviously, the recognition problem is still being solved here.

There are two approaches to how to process volatile biometrics, leading them to an unchanging cryptographic key. The first uses already computed biometric features, which are corrected by different variants of redundant coding with error correction. This work is also done in line with this approach. In the second approach, developed in [27], biometric features are not explicitly calculated, instead, a neural network trained to produce this or that code is trained on <raw> biometric data. The advantage of this approach is said to be less coding redundancy by using continuous data at all stages and quantization only at the end. Disadvantages are unpredictability of neural network training, lack of guaranteed quality of performance, including lack of guarantee that results will retain quality when working with a greater variety of data than used in training.

The task of reproducing a cryptographic key is solved by *biometric cryptosystems* [26], which are divided into two classes implementing different working schemes: *key generation* and *key binding*.

In [28, 29] methods of direct key generation from biometric data without using any additional information were investigated. In this case, during registration and recognition, the same function is calculated, which maps the variety of biometric data into the space of cryptographic keys (usually bit strings): $K(D)$: $D \rightarrow \{0,1\}^n$, where n is the bit length of the key. In this case, the conditions must hold

$$\begin{aligned} &D_1, D_2 \text{ are the data of one person} \Rightarrow K_1 = K_2, \\ &D_1, D_2 \text{ are the data of different persons} \Rightarrow K_1 \neq K_2, \end{aligned} \tag{2.12}$$

where $K_1 = K(D_1)$, $K_2 = K(D_2)$. Failure to meet the first condition is the error of the first kind (false rejection), its probability is denoted FRR (false reject rate), failure to meet the second is the error of the second kind (false acceptance), its probability is denoted FAR (false acceptance rate). Because of the variability of biometric data, this approach gives a large number of errors: FRR = 24% at FAR = 0.07% [29] even on the basis of homogeneous high-quality images CASIA-3-Lamp [30], which makes it of little use in practice.

The best performance is shown by the scheme using its helper code. In this case, during registration, in addition to the cryptographic key $K_1 = K(D_1)$, which is used to encrypt the message M and is immediately destroyed, the auxiliary code $h = \Phi(D_1)$ is calculated using the encoder. It has the following properties: (1) the original data D_1 cannot be recovered from it; (2) upon presentation of the biometrics D_2 using the decoder, it is possible to calculate the key $K_2 = \Psi(D_2, h)$, which satisfies the conditions (2.12). Thus, by presenting the auxiliary code h and genuine biometrics, the user can receive the key $K_1 = K_2$, and hence the message M, encrypted with this key during registration. The intruder, even knowing h, will not be able to get K_1 [31].

If the data $K_1 = D_1$ are used as a key, the original biometrics is restored. This is called a *secure sketch* [32]. Even highly volatile biometric data can be handled with the help code. However, the works available in the press show rather modest results. For example, in [33], an assumption is made about the intraclass variability in 10% of features, although in practice it is more than 20%, which leads to the inoperability of the proposed method.

The key embedding scheme in the above terms looks like a set of functions of the encoder $C = \Phi(K_1, D_1)$ and decoder $K_2 = \Psi(C, D_2)$, satisfying the (2.12) condition. The key K_1 is specified externally, which is an advantage since you do not need to consider the nature of the encryption algorithm. From this point of view, the key K_1 can be perceived as a message M, which is external to the encryption system, which immediately leads to a scenario similar to symmetric encryption. The difference is that in symmetric encryption, the secret key K should not change, and the biometric features (also secret) differ during encoding and decoding: $D_1 \neq D_2$. This is called a

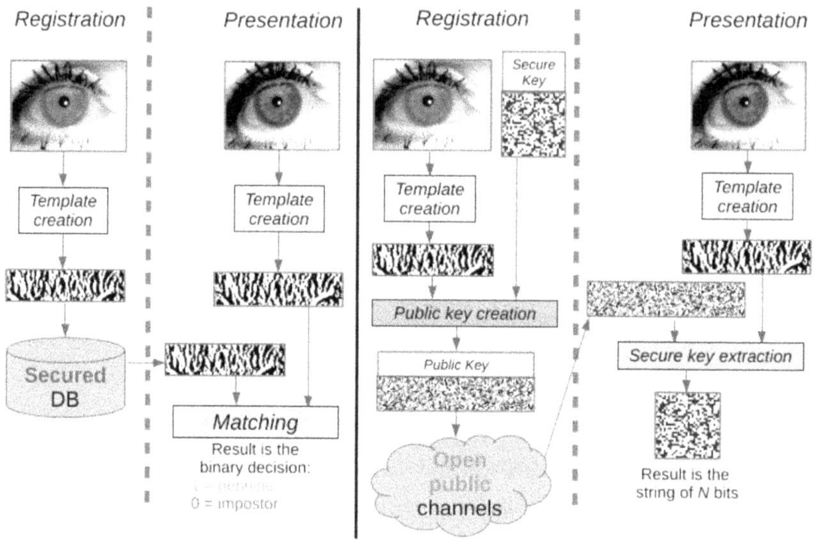

Figure 2.7. Schemes of biometric identification (left) and fuzzy extractor (right).

fuzzy extractor [32]. Biometric identification and fuzzy extractor schemes are shown in figure 2.7.

If the biometric data are the set of real numbers $D \in \mathbb{R}^d$, and the functions Φ and Ψ are inverse of each other: $K = \Psi(\Phi(K, D), D)$, then the resulting scheme is called *shielding functions* [34]. In modern systems of registration and recognition iris features are integers or even bits, so the use of shielding functions is difficult.

A very popular direction of key embedding scheme development is *fuzzy vault* [25]. This approach is essentially an application of Shamir's secret separation scheme [35]. At the same time, rather low, practically meaningful error values are obtained: in [36] at zero FAR, FRR = 0.78% is achieved, in [37] FRR = 4.8%. However, each of these results is shown on one small (less than 1000 images) base.

The *fuzzy commitment* scheme [38] is the most promising for use in iris biometry systems. A simple method described in [39] can be constructed for the iris. The iris template in most recognition systems is a bitmap (raster) of certain dimensions, usually $N = 256*8 = 2048$ bits, each bit is a local feature, usually a convolution sign with a filter at a given point. The basis for comparing such templates is the normalized Hamming distance, i.e. the proportion of mismatched bits:

$$\rho(T_1, T_2) = \frac{1}{N}\sum_{i=1}^{N} T_1(i) \oplus T_2(i), \tag{2.13}$$

where $T(i)$ is the i-th bit of the template T and $\oplus$ is the bit sum modulo 2. If the distance is less than some threshold p, which is set by the developers of the system, the templates T_1 and T_2 are recognized as belonging to one person.

The basic idea of [39] is to use error-correcting code (ECC) [40]. The coding scheme consists of a pair of functions: an encoder $R = \Phi_p(K)$, which maps the key K

into a larger *redundant code* R, and a decoder $K = \Psi_p(R)$, where p is the fraction of errors in the redundant code that can be corrected by the decoder. The secret key K is encoded, and the probability of 'transmission error' is set equal to the classification threshold. The code $R = \Phi_p(K)$ (generally representing pseudorandom numbers) is bit-wise added modulo 2 (exclusive or) to the iris template: $C = R \oplus T$. After C is calculated, the template and the secret message are destroyed. The resulting C data is also random, and neither the iris template T nor the key K can be extracted from it, and it is allowed to be transmitted through unprotected channels. For decoding, the iris is registered and a new template T' is formed, which, of course, does not coincide with the original one. However, if the templates T and T' belong to the same person, they are close in the sense of distance (2.13): $\rho(T, T') \leqslant p$. In this case $R' = C \oplus T' = (R \oplus T) \oplus T'$, hence $R \oplus R' = T \oplus T'$, so $\rho(R, R') \leqslant p$ is valid and the secret key $K = \Psi_p(R')$ can be recovered. The scheme of operation is shown in figure 2.8.

Work [39] uses a cascade of two noise-free coding algorithms: Reed–Solomon [41] and Hadamard [40]. Reed–Solomon coding handles an entire block of data of length L, treating it as a sequence of L/s s-bit characters, and any arbitrary characters (not bits!) can be different as long as their number is not greater than pL. This coding is designed to compensate for group errors arising from the presence of various shading (eyelashes, glare) covering significant areas of the iris. Hadamard coding is executed for small groups of data (a few bits), and corrects no more than 25% of the errors in each group. In other words, errors (differences between the T and T' templates) must be evenly distributed across the template with a density of no more than 25%. This coding is designed to deal with point differences caused by camera noise. The key K is encoded sequentially first by the Reed–Solomon code, then the result—by the Hadamard code.

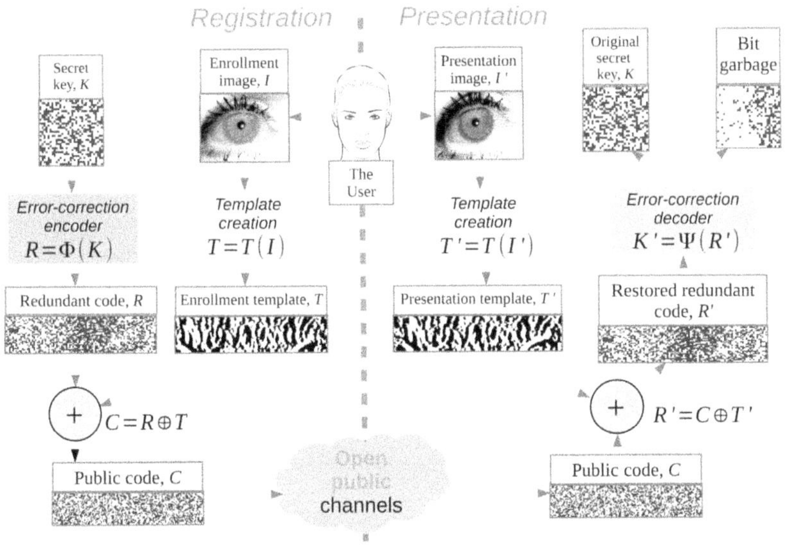

Figure 2.8. Scheme of the method [39].

However, this cascade of algorithms can be used only if the fraction of differing bits in one person's templates does not exceed 25%. This is not the case in real databases and applications, and this limitation leads to an unacceptably high (more than 50%) error of the first kind. To overcome this difficulty, [42] additionally introduces etalon masking: every fourth bit of the iris templates is set to 0. Due to this, the proportion of differing bits in the templates of one person is reduced to 20%. A critique of this method, in terms of resistance to hacking, is given in [27]. The attack is carried out by gradually restoring the original reference (approximation to it).

Here we attempt to refine the [39] scheme in a more reasonable way and build a practically suitable key embedding method. Based on the iris feature extraction system, numerical experiments on several open image bases are carried out, and the threshold Hamming distance is determined. Two additional steps are introduced: simple majority coding and pseudorandom mixing. Parameters of the received four consecutive steps of the coder (and corresponding steps of the decoder) are selected by the solution of a discrete optimization problem.

2.5 Determining the threshold probability

The biometric recognition algorithm can be split into a feature extraction function (construction of a template) $T = T(D)$ and a template matching function $\rho(T_1, T_2)$. Biometric recognition systems have come a long way and achieved very good indicators of classification accuracy (small error values), including the optimization of feature extraction methods. Therefore, the use of features derived from the available methods is justified.

According to a variation of the fuzzy extractor proposed in [39] developed in this paper, the Hamming distance (2.13) is used for comparison. In this scheme, if the biometric template T_1 used in registration and the presented template T_2 are at a distance less than threshold p, then the encrypted message M is recovered, otherwise not. In other words, the threshold p separates 'genuine' and 'intruder'. Figure 2.9 shows a typical distribution by distance $\rho(T_1, T_2)$.

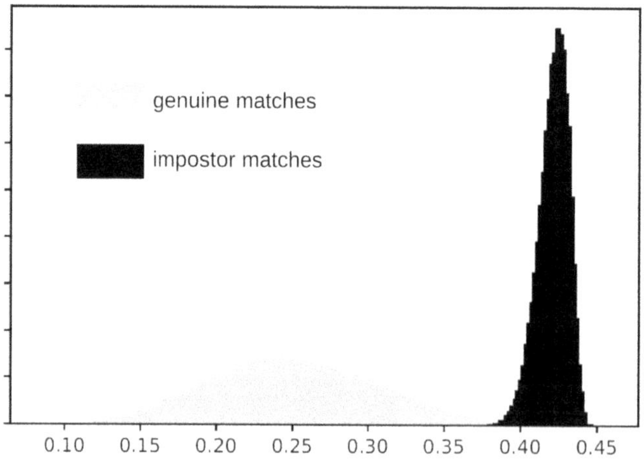

Figure 2.9. An example of the distribution of 'genuines' and 'impostors' by normalized Hamming distance.

Table 2.1. Database characteristics and thresholds.

DB	Number: irises	Number: images	θ at FAR $= 10^{-4}$	FAR at $\theta = 0.35$, $\times 10^{-4}$	FRR at $\theta = 0.35$, $\times 10^{-2}$
BATH	1600	31 988	0.402	0.03	4.46
CASIA	2000	20 000	0.351	0.97	6.71
ICE	242	2953	0.395	0.011	7.13
UBIRIS	240	1207	0.401	0.001	5.18

The left group corresponds to the case when T_1 and T_2 are obtained by registering the same iris ('genuine'). Comparisons of the template with itself (giving zero distance) are excluded, as they do not occur in practice. The right group corresponds to the case where T_1 and T_2 are obtained from different irises (the 'impostors'). It is necessary to determine the value of the threshold.

The following publicly available databases were used for the experiments: CASIA-4-Thousand [30], BATH [43], ICE subset of NDIRIS [44], UBIRIS-1 [45]. Table 2.1 gives a list of databases used with the obtained thresholds. For each database their own parameters (the number of individual irises and the number of images) and the value of the threshold, at which the error of the second kind is 10^{-4}, which corresponds to the probability of guessing a four-digit ATM pin code, are given. From table 2.1 one can see that for the threshold $\theta = 0.35$ the probability of false acceptance is below 10^{-4} in all databases.

Thus, the value $\theta = 0.35$ is further used as the base value, i.e., it is interpreted as the probability of error, which should be corrected by the code. Table 2.1 also shows the values of first- and second-order error probabilities for this threshold. Obviously, the probability of an error of the second kind only decreases at each base, and the stronger the value of the threshold at FAR $= 10^{-4}$ differs from 0.35. In this case, the maximum value of the error of the first kind does not exceed 8%.

2.6 Description of methods

We will describe the applied methods in the sequence of their execution by the decoder, which also corresponds to the transition 'from simple to complex', because in the beginning the data unit is one bit, and at the end the whole message.

So, it is necessary to devise a code reconstructing the original message from a block of data, each bit of which can be changed with average probability no more than $p = 0.35$. Firstly, this value is significantly larger than $p = 0.25$, which is a threshold for the possibility of applying the popular Walsh-Hadamard or Reed–Muller methods [46]. Second, the occurrence of these errors cannot be considered independent. On the contrary, the errors in the close elements are strongly correlated (occur in blocks).

2.6.1 Decorrelation by pseudorandom shuffling

It is much more difficult to design methods correcting correlated errors, and their performance is worse than for the case of uncorrelated errors. Much of the effort in this case is directed precisely at decorrelation. In the system in question, the whole block of data is available (rather than sequentially as in many transmission channel systems) and a simple method of decorrelation can be applied: pseudorandom shuffling of iris template bits. If the same shuffling is applied to all templates, the Hamming distance is unchanged and all constructions based on it are preserved. But the neighboring bits of the sequences used in the codes in the next steps are taken already from the separated pixels of the template, and the errors in them are independent.

2.6.2 Bit-majority coding

The error rate $p = 0.35$ is too high for most correction codes. Practically the only possibility here is majority coding of single bits, which corrects up to 50% of errors. When coding, the bit value is repeated n times, when decoding, the sum of n bits received is counted, and if it is less than $n/2$, then 0 is taken, otherwise 1. If p is the error probability of a single bit and bit distortions are independent, then the error probability at reception is

$$p_D(p) = 1 - \sum_{l=0}^{(n-1)/2} C_n^l p^{n-l}(1-p)^l = 1 - (1-p)^n \sum_{l=0}^{(n-1)/2} C_n^l \left(\frac{p}{1-p}\right)^l, \quad (2.14)$$

where C_n^l is the number of selections of l from n. Figure 2.10 shows graphs of the function (2.14) for some n.

It can be seen that if the error probability of one bit of the code is $p = 0.35$, then by duplicating a bit of the message seven times, we can transmit it with an error

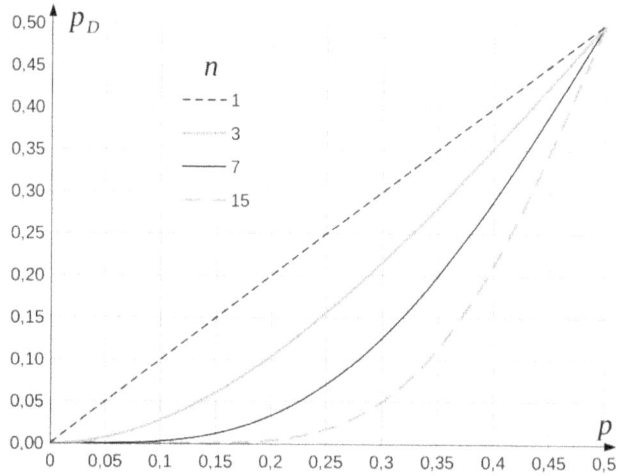

Figure 2.10. Majority coding error graphs for values $n = 1$ (straight line), 3, 7, 13, 25, 101.

probability $p_D = 0.2$, which allows the use of Hadamard codes. A larger multiple of duplication is also acceptable, but results in a larger code size.

The parameter of this method is the bit repetition rate n.

2.6.3 Hadamard block coding

Denote the set of all binary sequences of length l (l-dimensional binary cube) as $\mathbb{B} = \{0, 1\}$, $\mathbb{B}^l = \{(b_1, \dots, b_l): b_i \in \mathbb{B}, i = \overline{1, l}\}$. For any two elements $u, v \in \mathbb{B}^l$ there is a normalized *Hamming distance* (2.13), equal to the ratio of the number of distinct bits in the sequences to their length. Also denote the number of unit bits in the sequence u as $b(u)$.

Let M be the original *message* of length k bits, $M \in \mathbb{B}^k$, that is, the coding unit is a block of several bits. Hadamard coding algorithm maps the message into a redundant *code* of length n bits from some known alphabet $\mathbb{H}$: $C^*(M) \in \mathbb{H} \subset \mathbb{B}^n$, $n > k$. Let $C \in \mathbb{B}^n$ be the distorted code resulting from replacing (inverting) some bits of the original code C^*. The probability of distortion of one bit is p_D (taken from the previous step (2.14)), the distortions are independent. Further in this section for simplicity we re-define $p_D \to p$. We will decode the message assuming that the original code is distorted minimally, i.e. for C we will look for the closest code in terms of Hamming distance from the alphabet $\mathbb{H}$. Let us call it *attractor*. There can be several attractors (several codes can have the same minimal distance to C). If there are several attractors, a random one is chosen. Let us denote the set of attractors C as $A(C)$.

There is a simple and well-known estimation of the probability of Hadamard block coding error, with codeword length n used in the so-called Hamming boundary:

$$p_H \leqslant 1 - P_{\text{corr}} = 1 - (1 - p)^n \sum_{l=0}^{(n-1)/4} C_n^l \left(\frac{p}{1 - p} \right)^l, \tag{2.15}$$

which is the same as (2.14) except for the upper summation limit.

But this is a rather rough estimate, deteriorating as n increases. Let us find the exact formula. Probability of correct decoding is

$$P_{\text{corr}} = \sum_M P(M) \sum_C p(C^*|C) p(C|C^*), \tag{2.16}$$

where $P(M)$ is proportion of messages M in the input stream (probability to encounter message M), $p(C|C^*)$ is probability to get distorted code C while transmitting message M (which is encoded by code C^*), $p(C^*|C)$ is probability to recover message M from distorted code C. Considering all messages as equal probability, we can calculate probability for one of them, for example zero ($M = 0$):

$$P_{\text{corr}} = \sum_C p(C^*|C) p(C|C^*). \tag{2.17}$$

Without loss of generality, due to the symmetry of Hadamard code [40], we can assume that C^* is the zero code, i.e. a sequence of zero bits of appropriate length (it is so in the standard coding). Then the probability of getting a certain code C from zero code is $pb(C)(1 - p)n - b(C)$ and

$$P_{\text{corr}} = \sum_{C} p(0|C)p^{b(C)}(1-p)^{n-b(C)}, \tag{2.18}$$

where $p(0|C)$ is the probability of getting zero code from C:

$$p(0|C) = \begin{cases} 0, & \exists C' \in \mathbb{H},\ C' \neq 0: \rho(C', C) < \rho(0, C) = b(C), \\ 1/|A(C)|, & A(C) = \{C' \in \mathbb{H}: \rho(C', C) = b(C)\}. \end{cases} \tag{2.19}$$

For small values of code length n we can construct a histogram of the distribution of points of code space $\mathbb{B}^n$ depending on the distance to the zero code $b = b(C)$ and the number of attractors $a = |A(C)|$. Assume $a = 0$ if the first condition of (2.19) is satisfied. Then we can write the two-dimensional distribution

$$H(b, a) = |\{C: 0 \in A(C), b = b(C)\}|, \quad b \in [0; n], \quad a \in [1; 2^k], \tag{2.20}$$

get the probability of correct decoding

$$P_{\text{corr}} = \sum_{a \neq 0} \sum_{b} \frac{H(b, a)}{a} p^b (1-p)^{n-b} = \sum_{b} p^b (1-p)^{n-b} \sum_{a \neq 0} \frac{H(b, a)}{a} \tag{2.21}$$

and decoding error

$$p_H = 1 - P_{\text{corr}} = 1 - (1-p)^n \sum_{b} h(b) \left(\frac{p}{1-p}\right)^b, \quad h(b) = \sum_{a \neq 0} \frac{H(b, a)}{a}. \tag{2.22}$$

The formula is the same as (2.15) except for the coefficients and summation limits used (in (2.22) summation is performed on all b). The values of $H(b, a)$ and $h(b)$ for a 5 refilled Hadamard code ($n = 2^5 - 1 = 31$, $k = 5 + 1 = 6$) are given in the table 2.2. The average values of the probability of choosing the correct attractor are also presented:

Table 2.2. Values $H(b, a)$, $h(b)$ and $p_a(b)$ for Hadamard code $k = 6$, $n = 31$.

b	$H(b, 1)$	$H(b, 2)$	$H(b, 3)$	$H(b, 4)$	$H(b, 6)$	$h(b)$	$p_a(b)$
0	1	0	0	0	0	1	1.
1	31	0	0	0	0	31	1.
2	465	0	0	0	0	465	1.
3	4495	0	0	0	0	4495	1.
4	31 465	0	0	0	0	31 465	1.
5	169 911	0	0	0	0	169 911	1.
6	736 281	0	0	0	0	736 281	1.
7	2 629 575	0	0	0	0	2 629 575	1.
8	7 291 200	398 040	0	0	0	7 490 220	0.974
9	11 179 840	5 077 800	238 080	0	0	13 798 100	0.836
10	1 833 216	9 114 000	4 999 680	833 280	5208	8 265 964	0.492
11	0	0	0	624 960	1 630 104	427 924	0.190

$$p_a(b) = \frac{h(b)}{\sum_a H(b, a)}. \tag{2.23}$$

For this code b values vary from 0 to 31, the first 12 are given. The rest of the values are zero; all sequences differing from the zero one by more than 11 bits are 'attracted' to other code vectors. The table shows that up to values $b = 7$ only one attractor is chosen, i.e., at this or less divergence the message is always recovered. This corresponds to the Hamming boundary. However, even with larger divergences, there is a significant probability of correct recovery. This is important because there are many more codes outside the Hamming boundary than inside it. Thus, Hamming estimate of probability of decoding error is greatly overestimated. For example, for the augmented Hadamard code $k = 6$, $n = 31$ and error $p = 0.250$, the estimate by (2.15) gives $p_H = 0.527$, which would seem to prevent using such a code. However, the calculation using the formula (2.22) gives $p_H = 0.261$, which is quite suitable for use in the next step—the Reed–Solomon coding.

The Hadamard coding parameter is the word length k.

2.6.4 Reed–Solomon message coding

The unit of encoding for Reed–Solomon's algorithm is the entire message, which is divided into words of fixed size, s bits each. One such word is a record of an integer in the range $[0; 2^s - 1]$. A sequence of L bits is divided into $k = \lceil L/s \rceil$ words, i.e., numbers. These numbers are treated as coefficients of a polynomial over the Galois field $GF(2^k)$. It turns out that if one extends a polynomial with k coefficients in a certain way to a polynomial with $n > k$ coefficients, then one can arbitrarily distort any $t \leqslant (n - k)/2$ of them among the obtained n coefficients and restore the original coefficients from the resulting entry.

Denote: L—message length (number of encoded bits); s—Reed–Solomon (RS) code word size; k—Number of RS words in the message, $k = \lceil L/s \rceil$; n—number of RS words in the code; N—code length (number of bits in the code obtained by the RS method), $N = ns$; p—the fraction of acceptable error words in the code, at which it is still possible to restore the message. The RS code corrects no more than t of errors, where t equals half of the redundant words in the code added to the original message, i.e. $n = k + 2t$, denoting $p = t/n$, we get

$$p \leqslant \frac{n - k}{2n}. \tag{2.24}$$

The fraction computed in this way can serve as an estimate of the acceptable probability of a code word error. There is also a limit on the maximum number of code words:

$$n \leqslant 2^s - 1. \tag{2.25}$$

Having fixed message length L, having chosen word length s and knowing probability of decoding error of the previous step $p = p_H$, it is possible to construct

RS code. Probability p_H is defined externally, therefore RS code is parameterized by two values: word size s and message length L.

2.6.5 Additional error of code recovery

The Hamming distance specifies a function of the dependence of the first-order error on the second-order error. For some database and a fixed threshold θ, consider the number of different outcomes. There are only four outcomes: true acceptance (denote the number of such events 'true positive' N_{TP}), false rejection ('false positive' N_{FR}), true rejection ('true negative' N_{TN}) and false rejection ('false negative' N_{FN}). The first (false reject) and second (false accept) error probabilities are defined as

$$p_{\mathrm{FR}} = \frac{N_{\mathrm{FN}}}{N_{\mathrm{FN}} + N_{\mathrm{TP}}}, \quad p_{FA} = \frac{N_{\mathrm{FP}}}{N_{\mathrm{FP}} + N_{\mathrm{TN}}}. \tag{2.26}$$

It should be noted that when working with the database, the sum $N_{\mathrm{FN}} + N_{\mathrm{TP}}$ is constant and equal to the number of matches of templates of one person, and the sum $N_{\mathrm{FP}} + N_{\mathrm{TN}}$ is constant and equal to the number of matches of templates of different people.

Restoring a message from the code introduces an additional error, let us estimate it. We denote the probability of recovery error p_{R}. Correspondingly, the probability of correct recovery is $1 - p_{\mathrm{R}}$. The expected number of true positives in the scheme with restoration decreases proportionally to this probability: $N'_{\mathrm{TP}} = N_{\mathrm{TP}}(1 - p_{\mathrm{R}})$. So the number of false negatives increases: $N'_{\mathrm{FN}} = N_{\mathrm{FN}} + N_{\mathrm{TP}}p_{\mathrm{R}}$. Similarly, the number of false positives decreases: $N'_{\mathrm{FP}} = N_{\mathrm{FP}}(1 - p_{\mathrm{R}})$, the number of true negatives increases: $N'_{\mathrm{TN}} = N_{\mathrm{TN}} + N_{\mathrm{FP}}p_{\mathrm{R}}$. Calculating the new first- and second-kind error probabilities, we obtain:

$$\begin{aligned} p'_{\mathrm{FR}} = \frac{N_{\mathrm{FN}} + N_{\mathrm{TP}}p_{\mathrm{R}}}{N_{\mathrm{FN}} + N_{\mathrm{TP}}} &= p_{\mathrm{FR}} + \frac{N_{\mathrm{TP}}}{N_{\mathrm{FN}} + N_{\mathrm{TP}}}p_{\mathrm{R}} \\ &= p_{\mathrm{FR}} + \left(1 - \frac{N_{\mathrm{FN}}}{N_{\mathrm{FN}} + N_{\mathrm{TP}}}\right)p_{\mathrm{R}} = \\ = p_{\mathrm{FR}} + (1 - N_{\mathrm{FR}})p_{\mathrm{R}} &= p_{\mathrm{FR}}(1 - p_{\mathrm{R}}) + p_{\mathrm{R}}, \\ p'_{\mathrm{FA}} = \frac{N_{\mathrm{FP}}}{N_{\mathrm{FP}} + N_{\mathrm{TN}}}(1 - p_{\mathrm{R}}) &= p_{\mathrm{FA}}(1 - p_{\mathrm{R}}). \end{aligned} \tag{2.27}$$

If $p_{\mathrm{R}} \ll 1$, $p_{\mathrm{FR}} \ll 1$, then one can approximate: $p'_{\mathrm{FR}} \approx p_{\mathrm{FR}} + p_{\mathrm{R}}$, $p'_{\mathrm{FA}} \approx p_{\mathrm{FA}}$. Thus, the probability of error of the first kind increases by the value of the probability of recovery error, the probability of error of the second kind can be considered unchanged.

2.7 Selection of coding scheme parameters

The four sequentially executed algorithms described have the following parameters affecting their characteristics: (1) pseudorandom mixing has no such parameters; (2) majority coding is parameterized by the bit repetition multiple n; (3) Hadamard coding—word size k, PC coding—word size s and message length L. Different combinations of (n, k, s, L) values lead to the construction of different codecs having different ratios of code length to message length. One can formally write down the dependences of errors of the first and second kind on these parameters: $FRR(n, k, s, l)$ and $FFR(n, k, s, l)$. In fact, these values were found experimentally. The biometric used has size $Z = 6656$ bits. The code size C cannot be larger, duplication and masking are unacceptable, as they make it trivial to break such a code. Also, it should be taken into account that it is practically meaningful to encode a message of some minimal length Y. Then it is possible to write the problem of search of an optimum code:

$$\begin{aligned} &FRR(n, k, s, L) \to \min, \\ s.t.\quad &FAR \leqslant 10^{-4}, \quad C \leqslant Z, \quad L \geqslant Y. \end{aligned} \tag{2.28}$$

For $Y = 64$ the solution is found: $n = 13$, $k = 5$, $s = 5$, $L = 65$, $FRR = 10.4\%$. This size is considered sufficient for 'common' user keys. For $Y = 128$ and above, no solution to this problem has been obtained. It should be noted that without pseudorandom mixing (not explicitly involved in (2.28)) the problem is not solved even at $Y = 64$.

2.8 Conclusion

A system of methods for detecting iris region in the eye image is presented. Its distinction is detection of iris parameters at several steps (initial approximation followed by refinement), at which algorithms of different nature are exploited. Order of iris parameter detection also differs from that of commonly adopted. In the fuzzy extractor paradigm, a method for introducing a cryptographic key into iris biometrics is constructed. A key of size up to 65 bits is successfully embedded, for larger sizes no solution has been obtained. The use of additional pseudorandom mixing steps and majority bit coding has solved the problems of variability and local correlation of biometric features. The method was tested on several databases of iris images. A study of the cryptography stability of the presented method is required.

References

[1] Paar C and Pelzl J 2010 *Understanding Cryptography: A Textbook for Students and Practitioners* (Berlin: Springer)

[2] Chmora A L 2011 Key masking using biometry *Probl. Inf. Transm.* **47** 201–15

[3] Daugman J 2012 How iris recognition works *Proc. Int. Conf. Image Processing* vol 1 *(Lake Buena Vista, Orlando, FL)* 33–6

[4] Shekar B H, Bharathi R K, Kittler J, Vizilter Y V and Mestestskiy L 2015 Grid structured morphological pattern spectrum for off-line signature verification *Proc. 2015 Int. Conf. Biometrics (Phuket, Thailand)* 430–5

[5] Bowyer K, Hollingsworth K and Flynn P 2008 Image understanding for iris biometrics: a survey *Comput. Vis. Image Underst.* **110** 281–307

[6] Bowyer K, Hollingsworth K and Flynn P 2012 *A Survey of Iris Biometrics Research: 2008–2010. Handbook of Iris Recognition* (Cham: Springer)

[7] Matveev I A, Novik V and Litvinchev I 2018 Influence of degrading factors on the optimal spatial and spectral features of biometric templates *J. Comput. Sci.* **25** 419–24
[8] Cui J, Wang Y and Tan T *et al* 2004 A fast and robust iris localization method based on texture segmentation *Biometric Authentication and Testing* (Beijing: National Laboratory of Pattern Recognition, Chinese Academy of Sciences) pp 401–8
[9] Liu X, Bowyer K W and Flynn P J 2005 Fast and efficient iris image segmentation *Proc. 4th IEEE Workshop on Automatic Identification Advanced Technologies (New York)* 118–23
[10] Dey S and Samanta D 2007 A Novel approach to iris localization for iris biometric processing *Int. J. Biol. Life Sci.* **3** 180–91
[11] Ling L L and de Brito D F 2010 Fast and efficient iris image segmentation *J. Med. Biol. Eng.* **30** 381–92
[12] Yuan W, Lin Z and Xu L 2005 A rapid iris location method based on the structure of human eyes *Proc. 27th Annual Conf. Engineering in Medicine and Biology (Shanghai, China)* 3020–3
[13] Pan L, Xie M and Ma Z 2008 Iris localization based on multiresolution analysis *Proc. 19th Int. Conf. Pattern Recognition (Tampa, FL)* 1–4
[14] He Z, Tan T and Sun Z *et al* 2009 Toward accurate and fast iris segmentation for iris biometrics *IEEE Trans. Pattern Anal. Mach. Intell.* **31** 1670–84
[15] Maenpaa T 2005 An iterative algorithm for fast iris detection *Int. Workshop on Biometric Recognition Systems (Beijing)* p 127
[16] Nabti M, Ghouti L and Bouridane A 2008 An effective and fast iris recognition system based on a combined multiscale feature extraction technique *Pattern Recognit.* **41** 868–79
[17] Matveev I 2012 Iris center location using Hough transform with two-dimensional parameter space *J. Comput. Syst. Sci. Int.* **51** 785–91
[18] Proenca H and Alexandre L A 2006 Iris segmentation methodology for non-cooperative recognition *IEEE Proc. Vision, Image Signal Process.* **153** 199–205
[19] Matveev I 2010 Detection of iris in image by corresponding maxima of gradient projections *Proc. Computer Graphics, Visualization, Computer Vision and Image Processing 2010 (Freiburg)* 17–21
[20] Matveev I 2011 Circular shortest path as a method of detection and refinement of iris borders in eye image *J. Comput. Syst. Sci. Int.* **50** 778–84
[21] Novik V, Matveev I A and Litvinchev I 2020 Enhancing iris template matching with the optimal path method *Wirel. Netw.* **26** 4861–8
[22] Gankin K A, Gneushev A N and Matveev I A 2014 Iris image segmentation based on approximate methods with subsequent refinements *J. Comput. Syst. Sci. Int.* **53** 224–38
[23] Pratt W K 2007 *Digital Image Processing: PIKS Scientific Inside* 4th edn (New York: Wiley-Interscience)
[24] Sun C and Pallottino S 2003 Circular shortest path in images *Pattern Recognit.* **36** 709–19
[25] Juels A and Sudan M 2006 A fuzzy vault scheme *Des. Codes Cryptogr.* **38** 237–57
[26] Rathgeb C and Uhl A 2011 A survey on biometric cryptosystems and cancelable biometrics *EURASIP J. Information Security* **3** 1–25
[27] Akhmetov B S, Ivanov A I and Alimseitova Z K 2018 Training of neural network biometry-code converters *Izvestia NAS RK. A Series of Geology and Technical Sciences* **1** 61
[28] Sutcu Y, Sencar H T and Memon N 2005 A secure biometric authentication scheme based on robust hashing *Proc. 7th Workshop Multimedia and Security (New York)* 111–6
[29] Rathgeb C and Uhl A 2010 *Communications and Multimedia Security* ed B De Decker and I Schaumueller-Bichl (Berlin: Springer) pp 191–200

[30] CASIA Iris Image Database, Institute of Automation, Chinese Academy of Sciences. 2010. http:biometrics.idealtest.org/findTotalDbByMode.do?mode=Iris

[31] Davida G, Frankel Y and Matt B 1999 On the relation of error correction and cryptography to an offline biometric based identification scheme *Proc. Workshop on Coding and Cryptography (France)* 129–38

[32] Dodis Y, Ostrovsky R, Reyzin L and Smith A 2008 Fuzzy extractors: how to generate strong keys from biometrics and other noisy data *SIAM J. Computing* **38** 97–139

[33] Yang S and Verbauwhede I 2007 Secure iris verification *Proc IEEE Int. Conf. Acoustics, Speech and Signal Processing* vol 2 *(Honolulu, HI)* 133–6

[34] Linnartz J-P and Tuyls P 2003 New shielding functions to enhance privacy and prevent misuse of biometric templates *Proc. 4th Int. Conf. Audio- and Video-Based Biometric Person Authentication (Guildford, UK)* 393–402

[35] Shamir A 1979 How to share a secret *Commun. ACM* **22** 612–3

[36] Lee Y J, Bae K, Lee S J, Park K R and Kim J 2007 Biometric key binding: fuzzy vault based on iris images *Proc. 2nd Int. Conf. Biometrics (Seoul)* 800–8

[37] Wu X, Qi N, Wang K and Zhang D 2008 An iris cryptosystem for information security *Proc. Int. Conf. Intelligent Information Hiding and Multimedia Signal Processing (Harbin, China)* 1533–6

[38] Juels A and Wattenberg M 1999 A fuzzy commitment scheme *6th ACM Conf. Computer and Communications Security (Singapore)* 28–36

[39] Hao F, Anderson R and Daugman J 2006 Combining crypto with biometrics effectively *IEEE Trans. Computers* **55** 1081–8

[40] Morelos-Zaragoza R H 2006 *The Art of Error Correcting Coding* (Wiley: New York)

[41] Reed I S and Solomon G 1960 Polynomial codes over certain finite fields *J. Soc. Ind. Appl. Math.* **8** 300–4

[42] Kanade S, Camara D, Krichen E, Petrovska-Delacretaz D and Dorizzi B 2008 Three factor scheme for biometric-based cryptographic key regeneration using iris *Proc. Biometrics Symp. (Tampa, FL)* 59–64

[43] Woodard D L and Ricanek K 2009 Iris databases *Encyclopedia of Biometrics* ed D L Woodard and K Ricanek (Boston MA: Springer)

[44] Phillips P, Scruggs W and O'Toole A *et al* 2010 Frvt2006 and Ice2006 large-scale experimental results *IEEE Trans. Pattern Anal. Mach. Intell.* **5** 831–46

[45] Proenca H and Alexandre L 2005 UBIRIS: a noisy iris image database *13th Int. Conf. Image Analysis and Processing (Cagliari)* 970–7

[46] Reed I S 1954 A class of multiple-error-correcting codes and the decoding scheme *Trans. IRE Prof. Group Inf. Theory* **4** 38–49

IOP Publishing

Human-Assisted Intelligent Computing
Modeling, simulations and applications
Mukhdeep Singh Manshahia, Igor S Litvinchev, Gerhard-Wilhelm Weber, J Joshua Thomas and Pandian Vasant

Chapter 3

Bio-inspired approaches for a combined economic emission dispatch problem

Pandian Vasant, Anirban Banik, J Joshua Thomas, Jose Antonio Marmolejo-Saucedo, Ugo Fiore and Gerhard-Wilhelm Weber

The fast increment in electricity demand followed by supply deficiency of fossil fuels and its related environmental problems makes economic load dispatch (ELD) and emission dispatch issues the primary concerns in the electricity production framework. In this research work, ELD and emission dispatch problems are optimized separately using particle swarm optimization (PSO), quantum-inspired PSO (QPSO), and quantum-inspired bat algorithm (QBA) for the various numbers of units. Later, both objectives are assumed simultaneously as an optimization problem with multiple objectives. The emission dispatch problem is divided into three independent objectives to minimize SO_2, NO_X and CO_2 emissions. Thus, the combined economic emission dispatch (CEED) problem is an optimization problem with four objectives. A unit-wise price penalty factor was assumed to change over all the targets into a single target. The idea is to attain a balanced trade-off between secured and profitable energy choices while maintaining a healthy and sound environment. The quantum computing phenomenon was integrated with swarm intelligence-based PSO and BA to make them computationally more powerful and robust. The results obtained from QBA and QPSO to solve the CEED problem contrasted with other existing techniques such as Lagrangian relaxation, PSO, and simulated annealing.

3.1 Introduction

The present study focuses on addressing the challenging power production framework problem of combined economic emission dispatch (CEED) implementing swarm-based advanced meta-heuristic, and quantum computing (QC) inspired computational intelligence techniques. Electricity production mainly depends on

doi:10.1088/978-0-7503-4801-0ch3

fossil fuel based thermal power plants, which implement coal, oil, and gas to generate electricity. However, different techniques such as hydroelectric power, renewable energy, and nuclear power technology have developed, but fossil fuel is still used as the primary ingredient to produce electricity [1]. For more details on fossil fuel economics and statistics, please refer to [2–7].

Thermal plants are one of the prominent sources of air pollution that release polluted gases and particulates into the atmosphere, such as carbon dioxide (CO_2), sulfur dioxide (SO_2), ozone (O_3), and nitrogen oxides (NO_X). Pollution of the environment due to the emission of many pollutants is one of the significant factors that motivated researchers for the present study to minimize the utilization of fossil fuels in thermal power plants for electricity production. Thus, it is necessary to predict optimum parameters to minimize both the cost and utilization of fuel and emission of pollutants simultaneously. ELD addresses the objective of minimizing fuel cost by finding an optimum combination of power production in each of the power-producing units while fulfilling all equal and inequality constraints. On the other hand, emission dispatch manages the minimization of pollutant emissions from the system. Both the objectives are contradicting each other and it is not possible to optimize them simultaneously. This contradictory nature of the objectives leads to a complex multi-objective optimization problem called the CEED problem. CEED aims to reduce the cost of fuel and emission of pollutants simultaneously while fulfilling all constraints.

3.1.1 Literature review

CEED is an optimization problem with multiple targets in the real-world power generation system. Classical mathematical modeling-based methods first addressed this problem. However, due to the various limitations of classical methods, they were gradually replaced by meta-heuristic methods to solve this problem related to the power generation system. The current research trend demonstrates using hybrid methods rather than standalone methods to solve this problem. More recently, quantum-inspired meta-heuristic algorithms have been used to address this problem. We discuss in detail the use of these techniques to address the CEED problem in this section. These optimization techniques are broadly categorized into three different types as follows: conventional methods, non-conventional techniques, and hybrid techniques. Different types of optimization technique are applied to predict optimal solution of CEED problems by their classification as discussed earlier and given in [8–37].

PSO and its various variants are undoubtedly the most utilized optimization techniques to solve the CEED problem [38]. Thorough investigation shows Kumar *et al* were first to propose PSO to solve the CEED problem [20]. Authors demonstrated results for six generating units and compared their results with traditional methods, RCGA, and hybrid genetic algorithm, which illustrate the superior performance of PSO over other methods. Basu *et al* [39] implemented goal attainment-based PSO to solve CEED problems, where the cost of the fuel and emission are the main objectives. Initially, the goal attainment approach was utilized to change the problem of multiple targets into single targets, and in the next stage, the problem was managed by implementing PSO. Finally, other methods of PSO included modified PSO [40], local search integrated PSO [41], quantum behaved PSO [36], refined PSO [42], fuzzy adaptive modified theta PSO [43], bare-bones multi-objective PSO [44], improved PSO [45], modulated PSO [37], enhanced PSO [38], gravitational enhanced PSO [45]. Self-adaptive PSO [46] was developed and exploited to solve CEED problems.

Ramesh *et al* [47], Nikman *et al* [48] and Azizipanah-Abarghooee [49] used BA for solving the CEED problem. Ramesh *et al* [47] applied BA in two different systems consisting of 3- and 6-units, respectively, and compared the predicted results with refined genetic algorithm (RGA), NSGA-II, and ABC, and hybrid GA–Tabu search (TS). The compared result demonstrates that the BA is an efficient and superior performer to others. An interactive fuzzy-based method had also been implemented to address this multi-objective problem.

Recently, the combination of quantum computing (QC) followed by meta-heuristic techniques is gaining momentum [36]. Quantum inspired techniques are used as a tool to minimize the limitations of other conventional and hybrid methods. One of the advantages of quantum computing based methods is that they can exploit massive quantum parallelism expressed as the superposition principle. In a quantum computation-inspired algorithm, this phenomenon is combined with the existing algorithm. Instead of using a single state, a state of superposition is implemented, resulting in all these states computed in parallel. As a result, the computational speed of the algorithm increases [50]. Below, quantum inspired computational intelligence (QCI) techniques are reviewed for solving the CEED issue.

This method implements a QPSO algorithm followed by differential mutation operation to increase the global search ability. Heuristic methods are used to fulfill the equality constraints, and simultaneously, a feasibility-based selection method utilized to fulfill the reservoir storage volume constraints. The predicted results of studies demonstrate that the method illustrates its superior features as solutions of high-quality and better convergence properties than the other techniques such as differential evolution (DE) or PSO.

The hybrid technique implements several techniques in a single algorithm to utilize their pros and minimize their cons in pronouncing solutions for complex problems. Thus, it is found useful in predicting optimum global solutions for CEED issues with multiple constraints. Gong *et al* [51] demonstrated a hybrid technique that combines PSO with DE and integrates several different methods like coefficients of time-variant acceleration, a method inspired from crowing distance to achieve the optimum solution for the CEED problem. The pronounced outcomes were well distributed, superior, and efficient compared to other existing methods such as linear programming (LP), non-dominated sorting genetic algorithm (NSGA), strength Pareto evolutionary algorithm (SPEA), and fuzzy clustering PSO (FCPSO). A hybrid DE–biogeography-based optimization (BBO) approach to predict a solution for the CEED problem is studied by Bhattacharya *et al* [52] assuming constraints of power demand and operating limit. The approach was first proposed by Gong *et al* [53] to explore and exploit the abilities of DE and BBO techniques, respectively, and earlier utilized for the ELD issue [54].

Two of the most notable optimization strategies, i.e., GA and PSO were fused by Roselyn *et al* [13] to handle the CEED issue. The combination of GA–PSO was to improve the workability of the approach. The elitism approach was implemented before modifying the swarm size in the algorithm, while the particle position and velocity were modified using the mutation approach of GA to achieve the global best solution. The ability of PSO is to converge quickly and has been discovered not to be influenced much by the initial population, though GA is more proficient in fine-tuning, even though it is much influenced by the initial population. Accordingly, to overcome the limitation of both the methods and benefit from their combined advantages, PSO was implemented at the beginning phases. In contrast, GA was implemented at a later phase [55] in hybrid PSO combined with GA algorithm. This illustrated that quality results can be predicted using this hybrid strategy with quick convergence and *k* consumption of minimum memory space.

Hooshmand *et al* [56] studied a novel hybrid bacterial foraging-Nelder–Mead (BF-NM) technique to predict solutions for three objective power-producing systems. The spinning reserve and emission load dispatch issue (ERELD) assumed a broad range of constraints like the constraint of power balance, limits of power generation, limits of ramp rate, the constraint of prohibited operating zones, constraint of spinning reserve, and limit of frequency deviation. Authors discovered this to be one of the neatest and well-developed power-producing framework models to mimic the actual condition. The NM approach's accuracy and BF technique's power to cover a broad area of search were implemented simultaneously to predict the optimum solution for the problem with multiple objectives. Hooshmand *et al* [56] used constraint of frequency in the problem to predict solution for the issue by controlling the frequency inside its permissible limit, which eventually expanded the social welfare for buyers. This proposed crossover strategy's prevalence was evaluated after contrasting it with other conventional GA, BFA, and PSO methods.

Recently, a novel multiple objective crossover evolutionary algorithm has been pioneered by Roy *et al* [57]. In the study, chemical reaction optimization (CRO) is combined with DE to have quick convergence and to abstain from trapping into local optima to predict solutions for dynamic economic emission dispatch (DEED) issues. The developed algorithm shows superior performance in a 10-unit system over the improved bacterial foraging algorithm (IBFA), RCGA, and CRO. The cost of the energy and time of the computation considered was somewhat outperformed by IBFA when emission amount was considered. For a 30-unit system, the algorithm showed superior performance compared to various methods such as IPSO, expectation-propagation (EP), and chaotic DE (CDE) regarding cost function and computational time, yet again marginally outperformed by deterministically guided PSO (DGPSO).

3.1.2 Objective of the study

The study's objective is to pronounce an appropriate method (QCI based method) to predict the power-producing framework's optimum operating parameters to minimize both pollutants emission and fuel cost. The study also searches for a suitable QCI based method to obtain the study's primary objective, i.e., to pronounce the results of the CEED problem efficiently and accurately. The study also investigates the feasibility and effectiveness of a QCI based method using a multi-objective problem developed using the cubic criterion function. Introducing the cubic function illustrates the CEED problem as a means to minimize the nonlinearities in the developed system.

3.2 Problem formulation

The CEED problem is an optimization problem with multiple objectives that minimize fuel cost and pollutant emission while fulfilling total load demand and all other constraints. In the present study, the goals of reducing of SO_2, NO_X and CO_2 emissions are considered as independent objectives. So, in the present research, CEED is treated as a problem with four-objectives.

There are several real life issues such as CEED, where concurrent optimization of multiple objectives is included. Ordinarily, these targets are non-commensurable and regularly conflicting in Nature [58]. This optimization problem is a problem with multiple objectives where the clashing target gives rise to a set of optimum solutions rather than a single optimum solution. It is on the grounds that no single solution can be viewed as better than others concerning all objectives. This pair of optimum solutions is known as Pareto optimum front. ELD is illustrated utilizing cubic function, where total costs *F(P)* can be defined as:

$$F(P) = \sum_{i=1}^{n} a_i P_i^3 + b_i P_i^2 + c_i P_i + d_i \tag{3.1}$$

In equation (3.1) n shows the total number of producing units, P_i denotes actual output power of power producing unit i; a_i, b_i, c_i and d_i illustrates coefficients for cost of the fuel for i generating unit. Cubic criterion is illustrated using the emission dispatch problem. The emission dispatch problem can be defined as;

$$E(P) = \sum_{i=1}^{n} e_i P_i^3 + f_i P_i^2 + g_i P_i + h_i \tag{3.2}$$

In equation (3.2), *E(P)*denotes total emission; e_i, f_i, g_i and h_i illustrate coefficients of emission for i producing unit. P_i and n show the actual power production in MW and total number of power producing units, respectively. In the present research, emission dispatch is segregated into three individual objectives to minimize SO_2, NO_X and CO_2 emission.

The total emission of SO_2 $E_{SO_2}(P)$ due to burning of fossil fuel in a thermal power plant can be defined as,

$$E_{SO_2}(P) = \sum_{i=1}^{n} e_{SO_{2i}} P_i^3 + f_{SO_{2i}} P_i^2 + g_{SO_{2i}} P_i + h_{SO_{2i}} \tag{3.3}$$

Here $e_{SO_{2i}}, f_{SO_{2i}}, g_{SO_{2i}}$ and $h_{SO_{2i}}$ illustrate the coefficients of SO_2 emission for i producing unit. Total NO_X emission from a thermal power plant is denoted by $E_{NO_X}(P)$ and defined as;

$$E_{NO_X}(P) = \sum_{i=1}^{n} e_{NO_{Xi}} P_i^3 + f_{NO_{Xi}} P_i^2 + g_{NO_{Xi}} P_i + h_{NO_{Xi}} \tag{3.4}$$

In the above equation, $e_{NO_{Xi}}, f_{NO_{Xi}}, g_{NO_{Xi}}$ and $h_{NO_{Xi}}$ denote coefficients of NO_X emission for *i*th producing units. The total CO_2 emission due to fossil fuel consumption in thermal power plants is illustrated by $E_{CO2}(P)$ and represented as

$$E_{CO_2}(P) = \sum_{i=1}^{n} e_{CO_{2i}} P_i^3 + f_{CO_{2i}} P_i^2 + g_{CO_{2i}} P_i + h_{CO_{2i}} \tag{3.5}$$

In equation (3.5), $e_{CO_{2i}}, f_{CO_{2i}}, g_{CO_{2i}}$ and $h_{CO_{2i}}$ denotes coefficients of CO_2 emission for *i*th producing units. In a power production system, various equal and inequality constraints are assumed to predict the optimum solution [59]. In the study of concern, the three constraints such as power balance, loss of transmission and constraints for generator limit are primarily assumed. Detailed discussions regarding constraints are reported in the following subsections. Total output power production (P_T) in MW must fulfill the condition of total load. In this way, total output power must be equivalent to the sum of total load demand and total loss of power (in MW). It can be illustrated as

$$P_T = \sum_{i=1}^{n} P_i = P_D + P_L \tag{3.6}$$

In equation (3.6), total demand of load in MW and actual loss of power transmission in MW are illustrated by P_D and P_L, respectively, produced electrical power in a power producing framework experiences loss during its transmission to the grid due to dissipation of energy in conductors, line of transmission, transformer, and magnetic losses in transformers. Such loss is known as loss of transmission, which is one of the significant limitations in CEED issue and can be depicted utilizing Kron's loss formula [60] as:

$$P_L = \sum_{i=1}^{N} \sum_{j=1}^{N} P_{gi} B_{ij} P_{gj} \tag{3.7}$$

In equation (3.7) B_{ij}, denotes a square matrix which is also known as loss coefficient of George's formula. P_{gi} and P_{gj} denote the real power output of *i*th and *j*th generator. For stable activity in the power producing units, output power of each producing unit must exist in its maximum and minimum limit. This constraint is defined as;

$$P_{i,\min} \leqslant P_i \leqslant P_{i,\max} \tag{3.8}$$

In equation (3.8), minimal and maximal output power of *i*th producing unit are denoted by $P_{i,\min}$ and $P_{i,\max}$, respectively.

3.2.1 Combined economic emission dispatch

The goal of minimizing production cost and emissions of CO_2, SO_2, and NO_X can be changed over into a single goal implementing a price penalty factor. A unit-wise max/max penalty factor [9] is assumed in this study to predict optimum parameters for the CEED problem. The objective of the study will be achieved by minimizing the total cost (F_T) and can be illustrated as

$$OF = \min(F_T) \tag{3.9}$$

In the equation (3.9) F_T illustrates the total expense of the power producing framework, which can be defined as

$$F_T = \sum_{i=1}^{n} \{F(P_i) + h_{Si}E_{SO_2}(P_i) + h_{Ni}E_{NO_X}(P_i) + h_{Ci}E_{CO_2}(P_i)\} \tag{3.10}$$

In equation (3.10), h_{Si}, h_{Ni} and h_{Ci} illustrate max/max penalty factors used for emission of SO_2, NO_X and CO_2 for i producing units, respectively. Penalty factors can be defined as

$$h_{Si} = \sum_{i=1}^{n} \frac{F(P_{i,\max})}{E_{SO_2}(P_{i,\max})} \tag{3.11}$$

$$h_{Ni} = \sum_{i=1}^{n} \frac{F(P_{i,\max})}{E_{NO_X}(P_{i,\max})} \tag{3.12}$$

$$h_{Ci} = \sum_{i=1}^{n} \frac{F(P_{i,\max})}{E_{CO_2}(P_{i,\max})} \tag{3.13}$$

Here, $F(P_{i,max})$, $E_{SO_2}(P_{i,\max})$, $E_{NO_X}(P_{i,\max})$ and $E_{CO_2}(P_{i,\max})$ denote total cost of the fuel, total emission SO_2, NO_X and CO_2 for maximum power output for the ith producing unit, respectively.

3.2.2 Particle swarm optimization

The PSO method was pioneered by Kennedy and Eberhart [61] in 1995, drawing its inspiration from animals' social behavior such as the schooling of fish, elephants herding and flocking of birds. PSO gives a populace-based search approach. Individuals are known as particles and can be regarded as a fly or a bird, and modify their position with respect to time to predict optimum solution in a search space with multiple dimensions [62].

The personal best outcome predicted by individuals is known as *p*best. They continue to modify their positions based on their personal experience and the experience of the neighbors. The individual which predicts the overall best solution among all individuals is known as *g*best. The velocity of an individual particle is updated using equation (3.14).

$$v_i^{t+1} = wv_i^t + C_1 rand_1 \times (p\text{best}_i^t - x_i^t) + C_2 rand_2 \times (g\text{best}^t - x_i^t) \tag{3.14}$$

PSO implements weight of inertia (w) to manage the effect of earlier experience of velocities, and subsequently to impact the compromise between global and local search capacities of the particles.

$$w = w_{\max} - \frac{w_{\max} - w_{\min}}{t_{\max}} \times t \tag{3.15}$$

In equation (3.15), $w_{\max}$, $w_{\min}$, and $t_{\max}$ denote minimal weight of inertia, maximal weight of inertia and maximum iteration number, respectively. Once more, particles modify their position in the search space with multiple dimensions by updating the velocities in (3.14) implementing the equation below

$$x_i^{t+1} = x_i^t + v_i^{t+1} \tag{3.16}$$

Particle structures are modified followed by decoding of generations of particle. On the off chance that the conditions are fulfilled, results will be assembled to reflect the proposed strategy's adequacy. Suppose there are further questions on the limitations or the outcomes do not meet certain rules in the given technique. In that case, the particles will be assessed again and further assessed to test for adequacy in the long run. During the process, the algorithm calls the coefficients data and generates different solutions for the objective function. For each step of the iteration, the algorithm updates the solutions and gets *g*best (output). After the algorithm reaches its maximum iteration number, the present *g*best is predicted as the final model outcome. The algorithm of the PSO is provided in table 3.1.

PSO requires parameters that contribute to the overall algorithm performance, much like most evolutionary algorithms [63]. The size of swarms, numbers of steps and number of iterations have no fixed preferable choice. However, the size of the swarms or the population size usually is kept in between 20 and 50 [64, 65]. As discussed earlier in this section, inertia weight $\boldsymbol{w}$ controls the harmony between the global and local

Table 3.1. PSO algorithm.

Algorithm 1

Randomly initialize x_i and v_i
Evaluate fitness function
Set pbest = x_i and select gbest
repeat
    for all particle i do
        update parameter w using equation (3.15)
        update velocities and positions using equations (3.14) *and* (3.16)
        evaluate fitness of updated particles
    set current value as the new pbest
        if the pbest is better than gbest
        set current pbest as the new gbest
        update x_i and v_i
    end for
until stopping criteria met

Table 3.2. Parameter settings of PSO.

Parameters	Values
Swarm size	20–50
Maximum number of steps	100
Acceleration constant 1, C_1	2
Acceleration constant 2, C_2	2
Initial weight of inertia, w_{max}	0.9
Final weight of inertia, w_{min}	0.4
Maximum Iteration number	50–1000

exploration capacity in PSO. Performance of PSO is found to be improved [63] in many applications when the initial weight of inertia is considered as 0.9, and it decreases linearly to the final weight 0.4. ***C1*** and ***C2*** are acceleration constants implemented to ensure convergence in PSO [66]. Recommended values of ***C1*** and ***C2*** are each 2 as reported in [61]. Table 3.2 illustrates the parameter settings of PSO.

3.2.3 Quantum particle swarm optimization

QPSO allows quantum behavior in all particles instead of classical Newtonian dynamics as assumed in perhaps all other versions of PSO. Thus, instead of the position and the velocity, a wave function $\Psi\ (x, s)$ depicts state of individual particles in QPSO. Another attractive feature of QPSO is that it has, strictly speaking, only one control parameter to be tuned.

Application of PSO to quantum space with the aid of DELTA potential well. Wave function $\Psi(x, s)$ is implemented to define the quantum state of a particle in the quantum time-space system instead of position (x) and velocity (v) which is implemented in conventional PSO. Wave function for individual particle in a three dimensional space $\Psi(x, s)$ can be illustrated as:

$$|\Psi|^2 dxdydz = Rdxdydz \tag{3.17}$$

Where $Rdxdydz$ refers to the probability of the estimation that the particle position in time sought to be in the volume component of point (x, y, z) and $|\Psi|^2$ alludes to the probability density function that will fulfill equation (3.19).

$$\int_{-\infty}^{\infty} |\Psi|^2 \mathrm{dxdydz} = \int_{-\infty}^{\infty} R\mathrm{dxdydz} = 1 \tag{3.18}$$

Statistical translation of wave function in equations (3.17) and (3.18), where the time fluctuating wave function $\Psi(x, s)$ follows the below mentioned equation[67]

$$i\hbar\frac{\partial}{\partial t}\Psi(\vec{x}, s) = \widehat{h}\,\Psi(\vec{x}, s) \tag{3.19}$$

In equation (3.19) $\hbar$ denotes Planck's constant and h illustrate Hamiltonian operator. If individual particle having mass m in a potential field (V) is assumed then the equation is represented by below mentioned equation.

$$h = -\frac{\hbar^2}{2m}\nabla^2 + V(x) \tag{3.20}$$

Sun *et al* [67] considered that all individual particles in quantum combined Particle Swarm Optimization as spin-less individuals that are moving with an assigned energy in Hilbert space in a D dimension. Consequently their states can be described by the wave function. Moreover, it is important to make reference to that the wave function just relies upon the particles position.

Presently, on the off chance that considering quantum space with D-dimension that has a populace comprising of k particles, at that point position of ith individual as $Xi = (x_{i1}, x_{i2},..., x_{iD})$. Earlier ideal position that predicts the ideal solution of ith particle which is *pbest* can be defined as $Qi = (Q_{i1}, Q_{i2},..., Q_{iD})$. Likewise, the overall best position among all other particles in the search domain which is known as *gbest* can be defined as $Qg = (Q_{g1}, Q_{g2},..., Q_{gD})$. The particle position in quantum domain after they experience a stochastic simulation of Monte Carlo estimation can be illustrated as [68].

$$x_{\text{id}} = q_{\text{id}} \pm \frac{L}{2}\ln\left(\frac{1}{u}\right) \tag{3.21}$$

In equation (3.21), $i = 1,2, ..., n$ and $d = 1,2, ..., D$; u show randomized number whose value ranges from 0 to1; q_{id} illustrate local attractor of i individuals, it is a random position between *pbest* and *gbest* and illustrated as [69]

$$q_{\text{id}} = \varphi.\ Q_{\text{id}} + (1 - \varphi).\ Q_{\text{gd}} \tag{3.22}$$

Here, φ illustrate uniformly distributed randomized number whose value lies between 0 and1, L denotes mathematical value which can begotten from current particle's position and best particle position and it is demonstrated as $L = 2\beta\mid q_{\text{id}} - x_{\text{id}}\mid$. Equation (3.21) is denoted as,

$$x_{\text{id}} = q_{\text{id}} \pm \beta|q_{\text{id}} - x_{\text{id}}|\ln\left(\frac{1}{u}\right) \tag{3.23}$$

In the equation 3.23, β illustrate the factor of contraction expansion which is the single parameter for QPSO. Selection of β value is critical as it can influence the general performance of QPSO. A huge contraction factor will encourage worldwide investigation and increase the search time, followed by slow convergence property, thus making the algorithm slow. Then again, low value of β will in general encourage local search and hence calibrate the area of search, yet may leads the algorithm into local optima. Research illustrates a high value of β in the initial stage of the search aid to predict a good solution, whereas the low value of β at long last helps fine-tune the search [70]. So, gradual decrease of self-organized contraction factor from 1 to 0.5 is normally proposed in literature to enhance the performance of QPSO. Self-organized contraction factor demonstrated as [69]

$$\beta = (1{-}0.5).\ \frac{t_{\max} - t}{t_{\max}} + 0.5 \tag{3.24}$$

In the equation (3.24), $t_{\max}$ denotes maximum iterations number and t illustrate iteration number. To avoid untimely convergence and to prepare the algorithm more robust Sun *et al* [71] proposed *m*best in QPSO. *m*best denotes average best position of k number of particles and can be defined as

$$mbest = \frac{1}{k}\sum_{i}^{k} Q_i = \left[\frac{1}{k}\sum_{i=1}^{k} Q_{i1}, \frac{1}{k}\sum_{i=1}^{k} Q_{i2}, \ldots, \frac{1}{k}\sum_{i=1}^{k} Q_{iD}\right] \quad (3.25)$$

Where Q_i illustrate the best particle position and in equation (3.23), which demonstrate the individual modifying equation, can be defined utilizing *m*best as

$$x_{\mathrm{id}} = q_{\mathrm{id}} \pm \beta|mbest_d - x_{\mathrm{id}}| \ln\left(\frac{1}{u}\right) \quad (3.26)$$

Mean best position (*m*best) is estimated in this step implementing equation (3.25). Detail description on β has been presented earlier in this section. This parameter exerts significant influence on the convergence of the particles in QPSO. Adaptive contraction factor is considered here in this study to enhance the overall workability of QPSO as discussed earlier. Again, population size and number of iterations vary from application to application. However, QPSO usually requires a larger population than that of PSO [71]. The adaptive contraction expansion factor β can be calculated using equation (3.24). Table 3.3 demonstrates the Quantum inspired PSO algorithm.

3.2.4 Qunatum inspired Bat algorithm

Quantum inspired bat algorithm (QBA) is an upgraded variant of bat algorithm (BA). The characteristics of echolocation of bats influence algorithm. It is generally a new Meta heuristic method inspired from nature that is known for its capacity to effectively combine the advantages of various well established algorithms [72]. A main reason behind its prevalence is that it implements some of the major advantages of GA and PSO in an organized way.

Bat can prey, dodge obstacles, and search food implementing their echolocation ability and adaptive characteristics to compensate Doppler Effect in echoes. In conventional BA, Doppler Effect was not assumed. Additionally, habitat foraging of bats was also not assumed. Rather it was assumed that bats forage single habitat, which doesn't reflect real world condition [73]. In QBA both the characteristics are assumed with rest of the characteristic is of conventional BA. The presentation of quantum conduct in bats differentiates the scavenging environments of bats which add to the broadening of swarm. Moreover, it assists with dodging untimely the premature convergence of BA.

The fundamental BA depends on three rules, (i) echolocation procedure of bats to detect separation and to compute the contrast between their prey (food) and foundation obstructions, (ii) bats modulate their wavelength (λ_0) and loudness (A_0) to scavenge for prey. They additionally regulate frequency and rate of pulse emission, depending on the distance between the prey, (iii) considered that loudness

Table 3.3. Algorithm.

QPSO Algorithm
Begin
Initialize the current position and the pbest positions of all particles along with population size (k), the dimensions of the particles (D), and maximum number of iterations (t_{max});
Set t = 0;
while *the termination condition is not met* ***do***
calculate *the mbest using* equation (3.25);
calculate *the value of* β *using* equation (3.24);
for *i = 1 to swarm size k*
evaluate *the value of the objective function;*
update *pbest* (Q_i) *and gbest* (Q_g);
for *j = 1 to dimension D* ***do***
$\varphi = rand\ (0, 1);$
$u = rand\ (0, 1);$
$P_{ij} = \varphi \bullet Q_{ij} + (1 - \varphi)\ Q_{gj};$
if *rand (0, 1) > 0.5*
$X_{ij} = Q_{ij} + \beta \bullet abs\ (\text{mbest}_j - X_{ij}) \bullet log\ (1/u);$
else
$X_{ij} = Q_{ij} - \beta \bullet abs\ (\text{mbest}_j - X_{ij}) \bullet log\ (1/u);$
end
end
end
set *t = t + 1;*
end
end

is varied from high (A_0) to a low value (A_{min}). The positions (x_i) and velocities (v_i) of the bats are illustrated using following equations,

$$f_i = f_{min} + (f_{max} - f_{min})\alpha \tag{3.27}$$

$$v_i^t = v_i^{t-1} + (x_i^t - g^t)f_i \tag{3.28}$$

$$x_i^t = x_i^{t-1} + v_i^t \tag{3.29}$$

In the above equation, α, f_i, f_{min} and f_{max} denotes random vector whose value range from [0, 1], pulse frequency, minimal and maximal frequency, respectively. Again, v_i^t, v_i^{t-1}, x_i^t, x_i^{t-1} and g^t denotes velocity of bat at t iteration, velocity of bat at $(t-1)$ iteration, position of bat at t iteration, position of bat at $(t-1)$ iteration and current global best position predicted by the bats, respectively.

A local random walk implemented to produce a new position for each bat once an outcome is chosen from the current best outcomes. The new position is defined using equation (3.30)

$$x_{\text{new}} = x_{\text{old}} + \varepsilon A^t \tag{3.30}$$

Here, ε represents random number and its value ranges from [−1, 1] and A^t shows average loudness bats for t iteration. In QBA, new position is updated using below mentioned equation;

$$\begin{aligned} x_{\text{id}}^{t+1} &= g_d^t \times [1 + j(0, \sigma^2)] \\ \sigma^2 &= |A_i^t - A^t| + \varepsilon \end{aligned} \tag{3.31}$$

In the above equation, $j(0, \sigma^2)$ illustrate Gaussian distribution with mean 0 and standard deviation σ^2. x_{id}^{t+1} and g_d^t denotes position of bat at iteration t+1 and current global best location predicted by bats in d dimension. A_i^t denotes loudness of bat at t iteration. ε used to make sure that standard deviation value remain positive.

The loudness A_i and pulse rate emission r_i are modified in each iteration implementing below mentioned equations;

$$A_i^{t+1} = \delta A_i^t \tag{3.32}$$

$$r_i^{t+1} = r_i^0[1 - \exp(-\gamma t)] \tag{3.33}$$

Here, A_i^t, A_i^{t+1}, r_i^0 and r_i^{t+1} denotes loudness of bat at t iteration, loudness of bat at iteration t+1, initial pulse rate emission of bat and pulse rate emission of bat at t +1iteration, respectively. δ and γ represents the constants, value of δ ranges from 0 to 1 whereas value of γ is greater than 0 ($\gamma > 0$), respectively.

To develop an algorithm simulating the real scenario of bats and in this manner make it more efficient, two more best rules are assumed along with three best rules reported in original BA. These are: (1) bats have diverse scavenging living spaces instead of one single scrounging territory that relies upon a stochastic choice; (2) bats adaptive ability to compensate Doppler Effect in echoes. In QBA, bats position is demonstrated implementing equation (3.26);

$$\begin{aligned} x_{\text{id}}^t &= g_d^t + \beta\,|m\text{best}_d - x_{\text{id}}^t|\ \ln\left(\frac{1}{u}\right), \ u(0,1) < 0.5 \\ x_{\text{id}}^t &= g_d^t - \beta\,|m\text{best}_d - x_{\text{id}}^t|\ \ln\left(\frac{1}{u}\right), \ u(0,1) \geqslant 0.5 \end{aligned} \tag{3.34}$$

In the above equation, x_{id}^t denotes position of ith bat in d dimension for t iteration. Assuming self-adaptive characteristics of bats to compensate for Doppler Effect changes the modified formulas as illustrated in equations (3.26) and (3.27). The equations can be defined as;

$$f_{\text{id}} = \frac{(340 + v_i^{t-1})}{(340 + v_g^{t-1})} \times f_{\text{id}} \times \left[1 + C_i \times \frac{(g_d^t - x_{\text{id}}^t)}{|g_d^t - x_{\text{id}}^t| + \varepsilon}\right] \tag{3.35}$$

$$v_{\mathrm{id}}^{t} = \left(w \times v_{\mathrm{id}}^{t-1}\right) + \left(g_{d}^{t} - x_{\mathrm{id}}^{t}\right) f_{\mathrm{id}} \tag{3.36}$$

$$x_{\mathrm{id}}^{t} = x_{\mathrm{id}}^{t-1} + v_{\mathrm{id}}^{t} \tag{3.37}$$

Where f_{id} illustrate frequency of the individual bat in d dimension, v_g^{t-1} shows the velocity corresponding to the global best position at iteration t−1 and C_i represent the positive number of individual bat whose value ranges from 0 to 1. If the value of $C = 0$, it illustrates that the bat cannot compensate for Doppler Effect in echoes. On the off chance that $C = 1$, it implies bat can fully compensate for Doppler Effect in echoes. Weight of the Inertia (w) is acquainted with updated velocity and illustrates qualities similar to the weight of inertia used in PSO. Algorithm of QBA is illustrated in table 3.4.

QBA generates solution by solving the cost function in (3.10). For, various values of P, inside its recommended range, the algorithm predict various solutions. With each progression, the solutions are modified using the formula reported in (3.34)–(3.37). The optimum result predicted by the bats is known as gbest. With every steps of iteration, gbest is modified if the personal best is less than the previous

Table 3.4. Algorithm.

Algorithm 3
Define general parameters of BA: α, γ, $f_{\min}$, $f_{\max}$, A_0 *and* r_0;
Initialize individuals number (N) contained in the swarm, iterations ($t_{\max}$), *probability for selection of the habitat(P), weight of inertia (w), rates of compensation for Doppler Effect in echoes (C), coefficient of contraction/expansion* (β), *frequency of modifying the loudness and pulse rate emission (G);*
Estimation of the value of objective function for each individual
While *iteration*$<t_{\max}$
if *rand(0,1)<P*
generate *new solutions utilizing equations (3.34a) and (3.34b)*
else
generate *new solutions implementing* equations (3.17) and (3.35)–(3.37)
end if
if *rand(0,1)>*r_i
generate *local solution around the chosen best solution applying* equation (3.31)
end if
Evaluate *the value of objective function for each individual.*
update *solutions, loudness and pulse rate emission applying* equations (3.32) and (3.33)
rank *solutions and predicts the current best* g^t
if g^t *does not improve in G time step.*
re-initialize *the loudness* A_i *and set temporary pulse rates* r_i *[0.85–0.9]*
end if
$t = t + 1$;
end while

Table 3.5. Settings of QBA.

Parameters	Values
Maximum iterations	100–1000
swarm size	20–100
maximum and minimum rate of pulse	1 and 0
maximum and minimum frequency (f_{max} and f_{min})	[1, 0]/[2, 0]/[0, 100]
maximum and minimum loudness	2 and 1
Delta, δ	0.9
Gamma, γ	0.9
The frequency for modifying the loudness and pulse rate emission, G	10
Maximal and minimal probability for selection of habitat	0.9 and 0.6
Maximal and minimal rate of compensation for Doppler Effect (C_{max} and C_{min})	0.9 and 0.1
Maximal and minimal coefficient of contraction expansion (β_{max} and β_{min})	1 and 0.5
Maximal and minimal weight of inertia (w_{max} and w_{min})	0.9 and 0.5

best solution. The algorithm ends the iterative process after its maximum iterations number is achieved. Value of the gbest after the maximum iterations number is achieved becomes the final output of the algorithm.

The basic parameters found in BA are maximum number of iterations (t_{max}), population size, dimension, maximum and minimum pulse emission rate, maximum and minimum frequency (f_{max} and f_{min}), maximum and minimum loudness, delta (δ) and gamma (γ). Additional parameters in QBA are frequency for modifying the loudness and pulse rate emission (G), maximal and minimal probability for selection of habitat, maximal and minimal rate of compensation for Doppler Effect (C_{max} and C_{min}), maximal and minimal coefficient of contraction expansion (β_{max} and β_{min}) and the maximal and minimum weight of the inertia (w_{max} and w_{min}).

Population size, the maximum number of iterations and dimension may vary according to the nature of the applications. Most of the researchers set the maximum and minimum pulse emission rate as 1 and 0, respectively [74]. Researchers have considered many sets of minimum and maximum frequency in their respective papers. Some of the most common frequency settings are [0, 1], [0, 2] and [0, 100] as reported in [75]. Most common value of δ and γ is 0.9 [74, 75]. Additional parameters, along with their corresponding values, are presented in table 3.5 with the most common basic BA parameters values.

3.3 Results and discussions

This present section demonstrates predicted results along with a detailed analysis of PSO, QPSO, and QBA for single objective emission dispatch (ED) and ELD problems and CEED issue with multi-objective. All the predictions are made utilizing the same PC, and the configuration of the PC was Operating System: Windows 7 (32-bit), Intel Core i5 Processor, 4 GB of RAM, and using the Matlab 2015a software.

3.3.1 Single objective emission dispatch problem

In this section, two methods, i.e., CI-based PSO and QCI-based QBA are implemented to solve single-objective emission dispatch problems and evaluate separately. Later, both the methods are compared and analyzed with necessary figures and tables. To predict the solution for the single-objective ED problem PSO is utilized, where ED problem is represented implementing cubic function assuming loss of transmission. The emission dispatch problem is mathematically represented as the equation (3.3). PSO is applied to a 3-unit power generation system, where the load condition is 500 MW. The predicted results are contrasted with the SDSM approach. All the data was collected from [10]. Settings of the parameters used in this study for ED problem are: swarm Size = 2000, Maximum step number =100, Acceleration constant 1 and 2, $C_1 = C_2 = 2$, Final weight of inertia (w_{max}) = 0.9, Initial weight of inertia (w_{min}) = 0.4 and Maximum Iteration = 1000. The values of acceleration constants and weighting vectors are borrowed from Shi and Eberhart [76]. Shi and Eberhart [76] claimed that when initial weight of inertia (w_{max}) is 0.9 for 30 runs is able to predict the global optimum. In this research, a total of 30 numbers of runs was also assumed.

The sensible coefficient of transmission loss matrix is considered to fulfill the constraints of transmission capacity. To compare with the SDS method [10] all the data are kept the same, including limit of minimum and maximum power producing units, coefficients of emission and loss. The choice of parameters in PSO is done cautiously as it once in a while is very sensitive to some parameters. Prior to the choice of parameters, the algorithm runs for several times with different parameter setting. From the predicted values, it is concluded that a larger swarm size is better predictor. However, on the other hand, a larger population size increases the computational time.

PSO demonstrate better convergence characteristics for ED problem solved by assuming cubic function. Simulation data shows that the PSO often converges to its best value of the particles to achieve the best position. The maximum, average and minimum values of the trial for total emission, production of power in each unit, loss of transmission and computation time, along with the standard deviation (SD) of total emission, are presented in table 3.6.

Figure 3.1 describes the fluctuation in each run's final result and fluctuation of computational time in each run. Figure 3.1 illustrates that PSO provides a good amount of robustness and reliability in the final results. Simultaneously, the

Table 3.6. Evaluation of PSO for emission dispatch problem.

	Total Emission, E (kg h^{-1})	P_1 (MW)	P_2 (MW)	P_3 (MW)	Transmission Loss, P_L (MW)	Time (s)
Maximum	541.14	158.36	161.74	200.01	11.64	2.87
Average	540.78	153.93	157.61	200.00	11.53	2.53
Minimum	540.7	149.69	153.29	200	11.43	2.15

Standard deviation = 0.11.

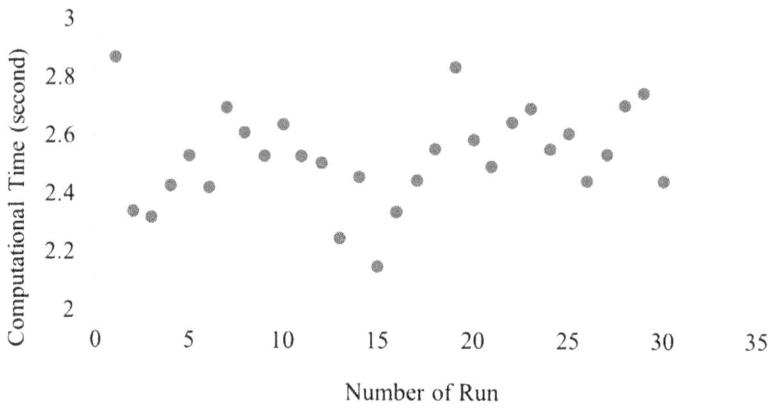

Figure 3.1. Computation time versus number of run for emission dispatch problem utilizing PSO.

Table 3.7. Results of emission dispatch problem for 3-unit system considering transmission loss between PSO and SDSM.

	SDSM [10]	PSO
P_1 (MW)	65	153.93
P_2 (MW)	92	157.61
P_3 (MW)	355.71	200
E (kg h^{-1})	646.06	540.78
P_L (MW)	12.71	11.53

computational time is quite unstable to predict the ED problem assuming the loss of transmission. This experiment ends with table 3.7, which demonstrates that PSO outperforms SDSM regarding giving quality solutions along with a decent measure of robustness and reliability for solving a single-target ED problem assuming the loss of power. Furthermore, PSO also successfully minimizes the transmission loss than SDSM.

3.3.2 Quantum inspired Bat algorithm

To compare the performance between stand-alone CI technique and quantum-behaved CI technique, QBA used to predict a solution for single objective ED problem. Mathematically formulation of emission dispatch problem is given in equation (3.4). All the coefficient values are kept the same for a fair comparison. QBA requires many parameters to be tuned. Based on our investigation, the parameter settings of QBA implemented for solving the ED problem as illustrated in table 3.7.

From table 3.8, it is found that unlike PSO and QPSO, QBA needs few iterations and a smaller population to achieve the ideal solution. Therefore, the computational time of QBA is relatively less (figure 3.2) than PSO for solving the emission dispatch

Table 3.8. Settings of parameter of QBA to solve ED problem.

Parameters	Values
Maximal iterations	100
swarm size	1000
The maximal and minimal rate of pulse	1 and 0, respectively
The maximum and minimum frequency (n_{max} and n_{min})	1.5 and 0, respectively
Maximum and minimum loudness	2 and 1, respectively
Delta, δ	0.99
Gamma, γ	0.9
The frequency of modifying the loudness and emission rate of pulse, G	10
Maximum and minimum probability selection of habitat	0.9 and 0.6, respectively
The maximum and minimum rate for compensation of Doppler Effect (C_{max} and C_{min})	0.9 and 0.1, respectively
Maximum and minimum coefficient of contraction expansion (β_{max} and β_{min})	1 and 0.5, respectively
maximum and minimum weight of inertia (w_{max} and w_{min})	0.9 and 0.5, respectively

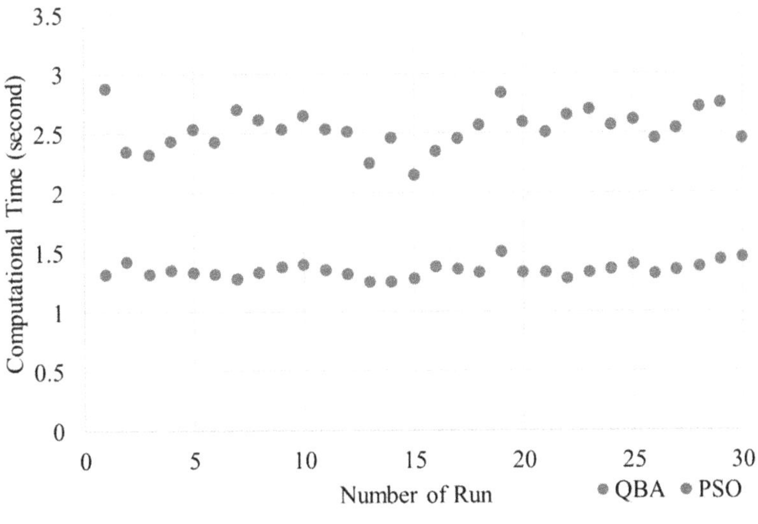

Figure 3.2. Time vs number of runs graph of QBA and PSO for emission dispatch problem considering transmission loss.

problem. The findings in table 3.9 support the research claim. The standard deviation is minimal and omitted from the table. If we compare the results in table 3.6 and table 3.9, it can be concluded that QBA provides far more reliable and robust solutions than PSO. Thus, it also demonstrates and verifies quantum computing power in the CI technique than the stand-alone CI technique.

Table 3.9. Fitness evaluation of QBA for emission dispatch problem.

	Total Emission, E (kg h^{-1})	P_1 (MW)	P_2 (MW)	P_3 (MW)	Transmission Loss, P_L (MW)	Time (s)
Maximum	540.7	155.19	156.41	200.06	11.56	1.5
Average	540.7	155.19	156.37	200	11.56	1.34
Minimum	540.7	155.18	156.34	200	11.56	1.25

Table 3.10. Comparative study of ED problem for 3-unit system considering transmission loss.

	SDSM [10]	PSO	QBA	QPSO
P_1 (MW)	65	153.93	155.19	155.26
P_2 (MW)	92	157.61	156.37	156.31
P_3 (MW)	355.71	200	200	200
E (kg h^{-1})	646.06	540.78	540.7	540.706
P_L (MW)	12.71	11.53	11.56	11.45
Time (s)		2.53	1.34	

The QPSO provides faster and smoother convergence than QBA and PSO. For a lesser number of iterations, PSO and sometimes QPSO also struggle to converge into the optimal point, and the probability is higher regarding its premature convergence. Figure 3.2 verifies the QBA's superiority over PSO. Table 3.10 illustrates a comparative study of the ED problem for a 3-unit system assuming the loss of transmission.

3.3.3 Summary of QBA and PSO

This research aims to verify the use of stand-alone CI and QCI-based techniques to solve a single target ED problem, where formulation of the problem is done by implementing the cubic function. CI-based PSO and QCI-based both performed well for predicting solutions for a single target ED issue. From the obtained results as presented above, the following points can be concluded:

The obtained results confirm that PSO provides a good amount of reliability and robustness in the solution as the deviation in each run's final answer is small. However, QBA provide more reliable, robust, and suitable solutions than PSO and certainly far more superior to classical mathematical modeling-based SDSM. The standard deviation in QBA is minimal and negligible. Thus, it can certainly be said that quantum computing powered BA provides high-quality solutions than their counterparts PSO and SDSM. As PSO shows some fluctuations in its final results, it is better to take as much run as possible and take its average in the final value.

QBA is computationally more powerful than PSO. The results verify the theoretical assumptions. QBA needs less iteration and fewer populations to evolve into the final value and thus is computationally efficient and feasible. PSO takes more iterations and a larger population to evolve to the final value; otherwise, it may trap into the local optima. The comparison of the convergence curves demonstrates that QBA provides better convergence properties with faster convergence than PSO. The solutions are more stable and robust than the other two methods (SDSM and PSO).

The major issue found in QBA is that it requires numerous parameters to set and tune. One must carefully tune all the parameters before getting good results from QBA. A rigorous review of previous literature is carried out to set the parameters. However, individual parameter tuning is also done to get desirable results.

As data regarding emission coefficients for a larger system could not be found, so the present research is limited to a 3-unit power generation system. So, the demonstration of QBA behavior for large systems could not be done.

3.3.4 Single objective economic load dispatch problem

In this section, QPSO is implemented to solve the single target ELD problem. Previously, QPSO was implemented to predict solution for ELD problems, where ELD was illustrated utilizing function of quadratic nature [77]. This research presents QPSO to predict solution of the ELD problem, where cubic criterion function as given in equation (3.1) is implemented to demonstrate ELD issue to minimize the non-linearities of the power producing framework. QPSO is applied to a 3-unit and 5-unit system for 2500 MW and 1800 MW load condition, respectively. All the system data of 3- and 5-unit systems are borrowed from [59, 78]. QPSO is later applied to the 26-unit system, where the loads are 2000 MW and 2200 MW, and all requisite data for 26-unit is borrowed from [8].

3.3.5 Quantum inspired particle Swarm optimization

Table 3.11 shows the parameter settings of QPSO. Swarm size and iteration number is chosen based on our investigation performed to conduct this simulation. An aggregate of 100 runs is viewed as a reasonable trial of robustness, and average results are demonstrated in the present section. The dimensions of 3-, 5-, and 26-unit systems are 3, 5, and 26, respectively.

Table 3.11 illustrate the comparative study for the simulation outcomes for a 3-unit system among PSO, GA, and QPSO without considering power loss. Table 3.11 shows the superior performance of QPSO compared to GA and PSO in terms of

Table 3.11. Settings of the Parameter for QPSO for predicting solution for ELD problem.

Parameters	Values
Swarm Size	2000
Maximum number of Iteration	200
Number of Runs	100
Dimension (3-unit/5-unit/26-unit)	3/5/26

minimizing total cost. The simulation result for a 3-unit system is illustrated in table 3.12 assuming power loss. The minimum standard deviation of total cost demonstrates that the obtained results are highly reliable and robust.

Table 3.11 presents the comparative study between CI-based PSO and GA and QPSO for solving 5-unit ELD problem without considering power loss. Tables 3.13 and 3.14 illustrate that quantum-inspired PSO outperforms the existing methods such as GA and PSO, by minimizing the least amount of cost for 3- and 5-unit systems. QPSO predicts solutions of excellent quality.

Table 3.12. Comparative analysis of total cost for ELD problem in 3-unit system without assuming power loss.

Unit	GA [41]	PSO [41]	QPSO
1	725.02	724.99	726.866
2	910.19	910.15	908.4451
3	864.88	864.85	864.6898
Total Power, P (MW)	2500	2500	2500
Total Cost, F_T (\$ h^{-1})	22 730.14	22 729.35	22 728.52

Table 3.13. Simulation result of ELD for 3-unit framework assuming power loss.

Criteria	QPSO
P_1	742.192
P_2	912.193
P_3	847.965
Total Power, P (MW)	2502.35
Total Cost, F_T (\$ h^{-1})	22 749.277
Standard Deviation	0.0743

Table 3.14. Comparative study of total cost for ELD problem in 5-unit system without assuming power loss.

Unit	GA	PSO	QPSO
1	320.00	320.00	320.51
2	343.74	343.70	346.47
3	472.60	472.60	482.95
4	320.00	320.00	320
5	343.74	343.70	330.08
P (MW)	1800	1800	1800
F_T (\$ h^{-1})	18 611.07	18 610.4	18 610.03

Lastly, QPSO is implemented in a 26-unit large power producing framework to evaluate the workability of QPSO in the actual-world. The parameter settings are kept as before shown in table 3.11. Total 100 numbers of runs are provided, and the average results are considered. The convergence analysis shows that the QPSO's convergence for a large system is smooth and fast. However, for both the load demands, the results get better with the increment of population size and iterations number. However, improvement in the final result comes at the expense of larger computational time.

At the end of this experiment, efforts are laid to enhance the performance of QPSO and compare the predicted results with other techniques such as non-iterative λ-logic-based algorithm and SDSM. The swarm size and iteration number is chosen to be 10 000 and 1500, respectively. The results highlight that with the increase in swarm size and iteration number, QPSO shows better performance than the SDSM and λ-logic-based algorithm for 2000 MW and 2200 MW load conditions. It also enhances the robustness of the system. The standard deviation estimated for the modified parameter is relatively smaller (0.126 for 2000 MW and 0.862 for 2200 MW) than the previous one. However, the Swarm and iteration number's larger size leads to the slow but accurate optimization process. Total 30 numbers of runs have been considered here.

3.3.6 Summary

QPSO is successfully applied on 3-, 5-, and 26-unit frameworks for solving the ELD problem. The obtained results are highly encouraging. QPSO successfully outperforms GA and PSO as far as solution quality, characteristics of the convergence, and efficiency of the computation are considered for 3- and 5- systems and λ-logic-based algorithms SDSM 26-unit system. Thus, the superiority of the QCI-based method over CI-based methods and conventional methods is verified for solving the ELD problem. One problem in handling large systems (26-unit) is that the standard deviation (SD) is quite higher than for small systems (with fewer generating units). SD can be reduced, and more encouraging results can be achieved if we consider higher population size and iteration. With the increased population and number of iteration, QPSO successfully outperforms conventional methods like the λ-logic-based algorithm and SDSM. However, a comparison of QPSO with other Meta-heuristic methods could not be conducted due to a lack of data in the literature. Furthermore, a larger swarm size and iteration number increase the computational time. Thus, a trade-off procedure must be considered in order to ensure optimal results with smaller computational time.

3.3.7 Multi objective CEED problem

In the previous section, the application of QPSO is discussed for solving a single objective ELD problem. This section presents QPSO for predicting solutions for CEED issues with multi-objective. An optimization problem with multiple objectives usually refers to an optimization problem that has more than two objectives. Apart from the ELD problem, CO_2, SO_2, and NO_X emissions are assumed as independent three objectives that lead to CEED issue with multi-objective. All targets are changed over into a single target utilizing unit-wise max/max price penalty factors, as shown in equations (3.10)–(3.12). The equations of ELD and the other three emission objectives are given in equations (3.1)–(3.4). For comparison purposes, only two constraints are considered. Equations of the constraints are given in equations (3.5) and (3.7).

3.3.8 Quantum inspired particle Swarm optimization

QPSO was implemented to predict the CEED issue's optimum solution with multi-objective for four load demands (150 MW, 175 MW, 200 MW, and 225 MW), where cubic criterion functions are shown in equation (1.9) used to formulate the CEED problem. All the goals are changed over into a single goal, and the conclusive outcome, i.e., total cost ($\$ \text{ h}^{-1}$), is introduced to contrast it with other techniques reported in the literature. Table 3.15 illustrates the settings of the parameter for QPSO to predict solution for CEED problem with multi-objective.

QPSO has only one parameter to tune, and this is the contraction expansion factor. In the research, adaptive contraction expansion factor, as shown in table 3.15, has been selected. A total of 100 runs are assumed here as a fair trial of robustness, and the average results of these runs is considered. All requisite data are borrowed from [9], and the penalty factors gathered from equations (3.10)–(3.12).

To demonstrate the effectiveness of QPSO, results obtained from four loads (150 MW, 175 MW, 200 MW, and 225 MW) [9, 41] are contrasted with existing methods reported in the literature. It should be considered that the authors have found only three other methods i.e., LR, PSO, and SA, reported earlier to predict solution for CEED problems with multi-objective, where cubic function is implemented to solve multi-objective CEED issue and solution is achieved assuming unit-wise max/max price penalty factors. Overall pronounced outcomes of QPSO for the 6-unit power producing framework is illustrated using table 3.16 assuming various load demands by introducing the cost of the fuel ($\$ \text{ h}^{-1}$), emission of SO_2, NO_X, and CO_2 and the total cost after implementing unit-wise max/max price penalty factor. Standard deviation illustrated in table 3.16 highlights the dependable and robust results of QPSO for predicting optimum solution for CEED issue with multiple objectives.

Table 3.15. Settings of the parameter for QPSO for CEED problem with multiple objective.

Parameters	Values
Swarm Size	1000
Maximum number of iteration	100
Number of runs	100
Dimension	6
Factor of Contraction expansion	$\beta = (1-0.5).\ \frac{t_{\max} - t}{t_{\max}} + 0.5$

Table 3.16. Results of CEED problem for 6-unit system implementing QPSO.

	150 MW	175 MW	200 MW	225 MW
P_1 (MW)	50	50	50	50
P_2 (MW)	20	23.74	31.1	37.68
P_3 (MW)	15	15	15	17.75
P_4 (MW)	25.25	32.62	38.77	44.77
P_5 (MW)	17.28	23.91	29.47	34.81
P_6 (MW)	22.47	29.72	35.66	40
Fuel Cost	2704.89	3187.93	3727.61	4315.03
SO_2 emission (kg h^{-1})	3146.86	3859.89	4591.38	5340.20
NO_X emission (kg h^{-1})	2406.37	2854.22	3324.62	3820.14
CO_2 emission (kg h^{-1})	2564.82	3129.91	3715.45	4322.77
Total Cost (\$ h^{-1})	10 255.25	12 241.71	14 413.77	16 783.86
Standard Deviation	0.008 15	0.006 14	0.001 93	0.000 20

Table 3.17. Comparative analysis of cost of the fuel for 6-unit system.

Load (MW)	LR [9]	PSO [79]	SA [41]	QPSO
150	2729.349	2734.2	2705.212	2704.89
175	3475.409	3236.3	3220.513	3187.93
200	4210.303	3784.9	3735.730	3727.61
225	5130.534	4402.3	4321.515	4315.03

Table 3.18. Analysis of SO_2 emission for 6-unit system.

Load (MW)	LR [9]	PSO [79]	SA [41]	QPSO
150	3091.648	3193.6	3138.446	3146.86
175	4142.176	3904.9	3763.478	3859.89
200	5053.584	4670.6	4553.972	4591.38
225	6106.498	5426.1	5287.306	5340.20

Table 3.17 compares cost of the fuel (\$ h^{-1}) of a 6-unit framework for different load conditions. Table 3.17 illustrates that QPSO pronounces quality results than other existing methods for all load demands considered in the study.

Tables 3.18–3.20 illustrate a comparative study of SO_2, NO_X, and CO_2 emission assuming various load conditions in a 6-unit power-producing framework. For the emission of SO_2, SA illustrates good performance for all the load conditions followed by QPSO, PSO, and LR, respectively. Then again, regarding the emission

Table 3.19. Comparative analysis of NO_X emission for 6-unit system.

Load (MW)	LR [9]	PSO [79]	SA [41]	QPSO
150	2448.218	2424.6	2379.35	2406.37
175	2604.886	2879.7	2789.92	2854.22
200	3102.077	3373.2	3285.647	3324.62
225	3798.383	3877.6	3781.191	3820.14

Table 3.20. Comparative study for emission of CO_2 for 6-unit system.

Load (MW)	LR [9]	PSO [79]	SA [41]	QPSO
150	2537.122	2607.1	2568.946	2564.82
175	3613.531	3178	3094.688	3129.91
200	4473.369	3771.5	3714.333	3715.45
225	5502.522	4403	4324.3	4322.77

Table 3.21. Results of Comparison for total cost considering 6-unit system.

Load (MW)	LR [9]	PSO [79]	SA [41]	QPSO
150	10 264.566	10 385	10 261.4905	10 255.25
175	13 251.517	12 425	12 280.0437	12 241.71
200	16 077.409	14 642	14 421.3044	14 413.77
225	19 661.328	17 125	16 790.6906	16 783.83

of NO_X, SA also provides good results than the other three methods. However, when it comes to the emission of CO_2, QPSO outperforms for 150 MW and 225 MW loads, while SA predicts quality results for load conditions of 175 MW and 200 MW. At long last, a comparative analysis of minimizing total cost (\$ h^{-1}), presented in table 3.21. QPSO predicts the overall best result for all load conditions in 6-unit power-producing system.

At last, Pareto fronts for various sets of objectives are illustrated in figures 3.3–3.5. Albeit a pair of solutions for various targets in each run is predicted, the important pair of solutions for 225 MW load condition is illustrated. The Pareto optimum front for cost of the fuel and SO_2 emission illustrates great assorted variety qualities for the solutions of non-dominated characteristics, though Pareto-optimum fronts for cost of the fuel and NO_X emission, and fuel cost and CO_2 emission show less assorted variety and will in general focus on a specific area in the center. It is reasonable as more goals increment the likelihood of having any two self-assertive solutions to be non-dominated to one another [80, 81]. There are numerous goals in the problems with

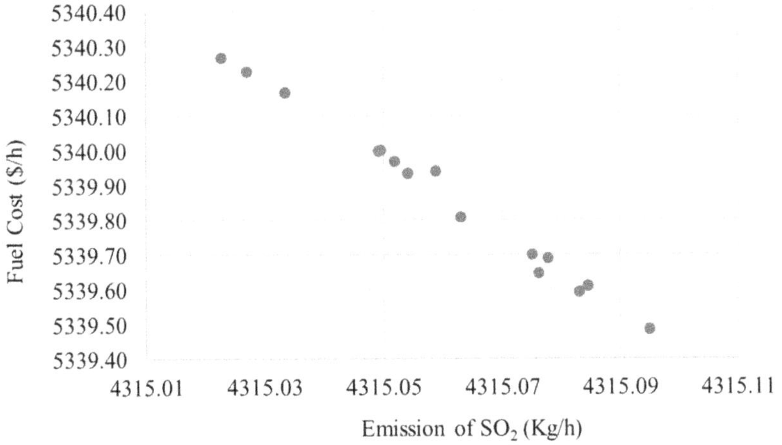

Figure 3.3. Pareto optimum front for cost of the fuel and SO_2 emission for 225 MW load.

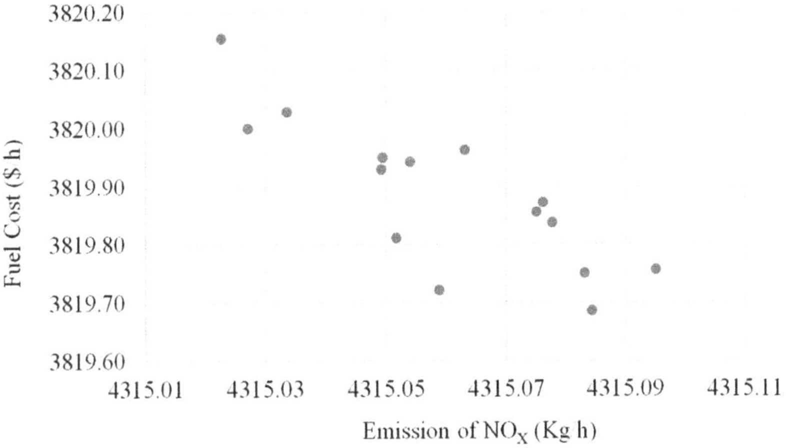

Figure 3.4. Pareto Optimum front for cost of the fuel and NO_X emission for 225 MW load.

multi-targets where a trade-off (one is better in one goal, while more awful in some other goal) can happen. Besides, the extent of the solutions of non-dominated characteristics in the population increments when managing with a finite-sized population inspired method [80, 82]. Notwithstanding, the total cost after implementing a unit-wise price penalty factor among the goals to change over all the targets into a single goal is assumed.

3.3.9 Quantum inspired Bat algorithm

In this section, quantum-behaved BA (QBA) is implemented to predict solution for CEED problem with multiple objectives for four loads (150 MW, 175 MW, 200 MW, and 225 MW), where CEED issue is defined utilizing cubic criterion function

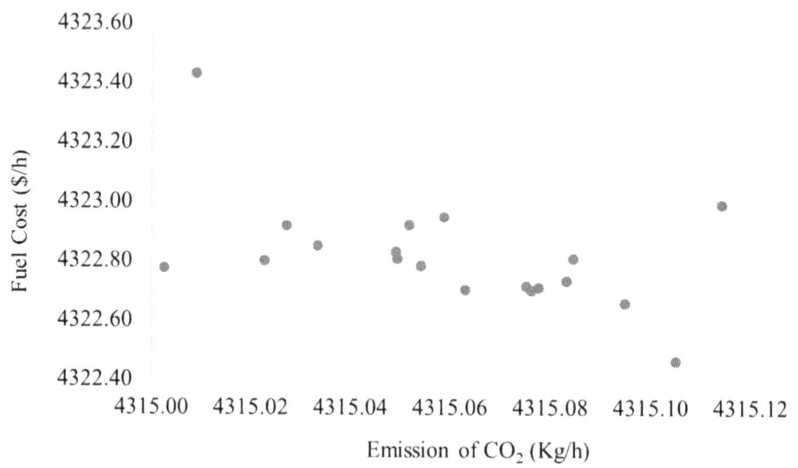

Figure 3.5. Pareto optimum front for cost of the fuel and CO_2 emission for 225 MW load.

Table 3.22. Parameter settings of QBA for multi-objective CEED problem.

Parameters	Values
Maximum number of iteration	200
swarm size	2000
The maximal and minimal rate of pulse	1 and 0, respectively
The maximal and minimal frequency (n_{max} and n_{min})	1.5 and 0, respectively
The maximal and minimal loudness	2 and 1, respectively
Delta, δ	0.9
Gamma, γ	0.9
The frequency of modifying the loudness and pulse rate emission, G	10
The maximum and minimum probability of selection of habitat	0.9 and 0.6, respectively
The maximum and minimum rate of compensation for Doppler Effect (C_{max} and C_{min})	0.9 and 0.1, respectively
The maximum and minimum coefficient of contraction expansion (β_{max} and β_{min})	1 and 0.5, respectively
The maximum and minimum weight of inertia (w_{max} and w_{min})	0.9 and 0.5, respectively

as appeared in condition (9). QBA is executed in a 6-unit power production framework. All the targets are changed over into a solo objective. The total cost ($\$ h^{-1}$), is demonstrated to compare it with other existing techniques reported in the literature, including QPSO. Settings of the parameters for QBA are illustrated in table 3.22 to solve the multi-objective CEED issue.

QBA comprises of numerous parameters to tune. To predict the optimal value the swarm size and iteration number is increased to 2000 and 200, respectively. The research shows that the similar gamma and delta ($\delta = \gamma = 0.9$) value predicts exact and robust outcomes. To test the robustness total 30 numbers of runs are assumed, and average of the predicted results is reported in this section. All the information is collected from [9], and the penalty factors are collected from equations (3.10)–(3.12).

To test and confirm the viability of QBA, the acquired outcomes for four specific loads (150 MW, 175 MW, 200 MW, and 225 MW) contrasted with PSO, LR, QPSO, and SA that were implemented to take care of multi-objective CEED problem. Where multi-objective CEED issue is characterized utilizing cubic criterion function and illuminated assuming unit-wise max/max price penalty factors. Overall outcomes of QBA for the 6-unit power producing system are illustrated in table 3.23. The different load conditions by referencing the fuel cost ($ h^{-1}), emission of SO_2, NO_X, and CO_2, and total cost ($ h^{-1}) in the wake of utilizing unit-wise max/max price penalty factor considered. The standard deviation in table 3.23 illustrate that the results predicted by QBA for CEED problem with multi-objective is quite similar to QPSO, and are a lot of dependable and powerful for various load demands. However, the Quantum inspired bat algorithm needed for larger swarm size and iteration number than Quantum influences Particle Swarm Optimization. The standard deviation is also a little higher than the QPSO.

Table 3.24 shows a comparative study of the fuel's cost ($ h^{-1}) of a 6-unit system for various load conditions. It is highlighted in table 3.24 that QBA predicts superior results than the SA, PSO, and LR techniques for all conditions of loads. However,

Table 3.23. Results of CEED problem for 6-unit system utilized QBA.

	150 MW	175 MW	200 MW	225 MW
P_1 (MW)	50	50	50	50
P_2 (MW)	20	23.79	30.7	37.62
P_3 (MW)	15	15	15	17.63
P_4 (MW)	25.28	32.57	38.89	44.93
P_5 (MW)	17.09	23.94	29.49	34.81
P_6 (MW)	22.63	29.7	35.91	40
Cost of the fuel ($ h^{-1})	2704.97	3188.10	3726.08	4314.63
SO_2 Emission (kg h^{-1})	3147.38	3858.96	4598.20	5344.75
NO_X Emission (kg h^{-1})	2408.10	2853.40	3327.78	3822.53
CO_2 Emission (kg h^{-1})	2565.14	3129.78	3719.64	4323.47
Total Cost ($ h^{-1})	10 255.28	12 241.74	14 413.88	16 783.91
Standard Deviation	0.05393	0.02829	0.10581	0.04982

Table 3.24. Comparison study of fuel cost for 6-unit system for LR, PSO, SA, QPSO and QBA.

Load (MW)	LR [9]	PSO[79]	SA [41]	QPSO
150	2729.35	2734.2	2705.21	2704.89
175	3475.41	3236.3	3220.51	3187.93
200	4210.30	3784.9	3735.73	3727.61
225	5130.53	4402.3	4321.52	4315.03

QPSO provides slightly better results for 150 MW and 175 MW load conditions, while QBA gives good results for 200 MW and 225 MW. Figure 3.3 portrays the comparative graph of various techniques for different loads. It is concluded from table 3.24 and figure 3.3 that QPSO and QBA minimize costs of the fuel, whereas the LR method provides the maximum fuel cost.

Tables 3.25–3.27 illustrate the comparative study of emission for SO_2, NO_X, and CO_2 (kg h^{-1}) assuming different load conditions in a 6-unit power-producing framework. The results show that for SO2 emission, SA predicts the best parameters for all load conditions followed by QPSO, QBA, PSO, and LR, respectively. Then again, for NO_X emission, SA also provides good results than the other three methods. However, when it comes to the emission of CO2, QPSO outperforms for 150 MW and 225 MW loads, while SA shows promising results for 175 MW and 200 MW loads. QBA outperforms QPSO for other emissions in 175 MW load only.

Table 3.25. Results of comparison for SO_2 emission for 6-unit system for LR, PSO, SA, QPSO and QBA.

Load (MW)	LR [9]	PSO[79]	SA [41]	QPSO
150	3091.648	3193.6	3138.446	3146.86
175	4142.176	3904.9	3763.478	3859.89
200	5053.584	4670.6	4553.972	4591.38
225	6106.498	5426.1	5287.306	5340.20

Table 3.26. Comparative study of NO_X emission for 6-unit system for LR, PSO, SA, QPSO and QBA.

Load (MW)	LR [9]	PSO [79]	SA[41]	QPSO
150	2448.218	2424.6	2379.35	2406.37
175	2604.886	2879.7	2789.92	2854.22
200	3102.077	3373.2	3285.647	3324.62
225	3798.383	3877.6	3781.191	3820.14

Table 3.27. Comparison of CO_2 emission for 6-unit system for LR, PSO, SA, QPSO and QBA.

Load (MW)	LR [9]	PSO [79]	SA [41]	QPSO
150	2537.122	2607.1	2568.946	2564.82
175	3613.531	3178	3094.688	3129.91
200	4473.369	3771.5	3714.333	3715.45
225	5502.522	4403	4324.3	4322.77

Table 3.28. Comparative study of total cost for 6-unit system for LR, PSO, SA, QPSO and QBA.

Load (MW)	LR [9]	PSO [79]	SA [41]	QPSO	QBA
150	10 264.57	10 385	10 261.49	10 255.25	10 255.28
175	13 251.52	12 425	12 280.04	12 241.71	12 241.74
200	16 077.41	14 642	14 421.30	14 413.77	14 413.88
225	19 661.33	17 125	16 790.69	16 783.83	16 783.91

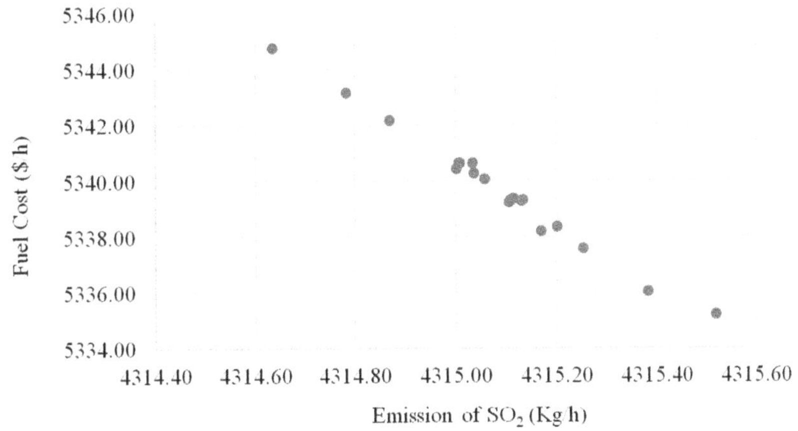

Figure 3.6. Pareto optimum front for cost of the fuel and emission of SO_2 for load demand of 225 MW.

Finally, table 3.28 summarizes the research's main objective, i.e., a comparative illustration of total cost ($ h^{-1}) minimization.

QPSO predicts the best generally speaking results for all load conditions in a 6-unit power-producing framework, and the results obtained from QBA is quite similar. It shows the intensity of quantum processing incorporated CI strategies over conventional stand-alone CI methods.

The convergence curves obtained for all four cases were smooth and reliable, where the curves are converging before 20 iterations, which make it faster than QPSO. QBA also illustrates robust characteristics against catching into the local optima, which are similar to QPSO but superior to LR, SA, and PSO.

Pareto fronts for various sets of objectives have outlined in figures 3.6–3.8. The Pareto-optimal fronts for 225 MW load are only demonstrated in figures 3.6–3.8. The Pareto-optimum front of cost of the fuel and emission of SO_2 demonstrates great a decent variety of attributes of non-commanded solutions, though Pareto fronts of fuel cost and emission of NO_X, and cost of the fuel and emission of CO_2demonstrate less decent variety and tends to focus on a specific territory in the center. The reason explained in the earlier sub-section, and the average of final results is considered.

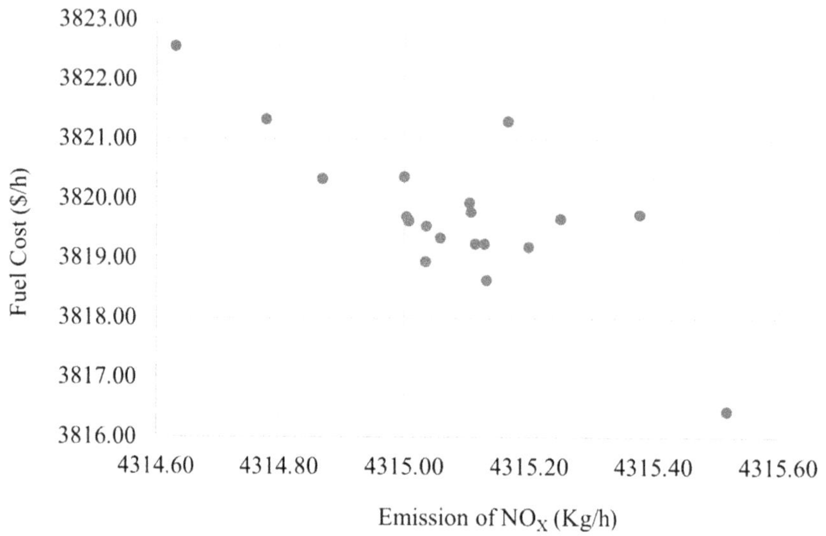

Figure 3.7. Pareto-optimum front for cost of the fuel and emission of NO_X for load demand of 225 MW.

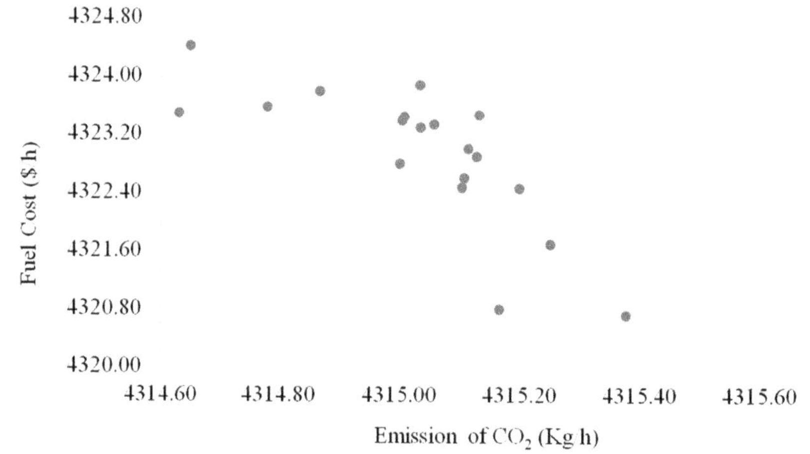

Figure 3.8. Pareto-optimal front for cost of fuel and emission of CO_2 for load demand of 225 MW.

3.3.10 Summary

In this section, QPSO and QBA are implemented to the 6-unit power production system for multi-objective CEED problems. QPSO and QBA are tested for multi-objective CEED problem assumed different load conditions (150 MW, 175 MW, 200 MW, and 225 MW). Cubic criterion function utilized in the research to illustrate CEED problem with multi-objective. According to the literature review, quantum-inspired PSO and BA technique was not reported earlier for CEED problem with multiple objectives. The predicted outcomes of the research for different load demands are contrasted with LR, PSO, SA, QPSO, and QBA, which verifies quantum powered PSO and BA's superior performance over existing techniques in terms of predicting quality, stable and robust solutions. The viability of cubic function combined with QPSO and QBA is established as the outcome of the research. The advantage of QPSO over existing methods is less iteration to achieve the optimum parameters, making it efficient and fast. After executing the algorithm for 100 runs, it demonstrates that the QPSO algorithm able to achieve global optimum. The standard deviation illustrates robust, suitable, and stable results. Even though QPSO predicts the minimum total cost, which is the main objective and for CO2 emission for some load demands other cases such as SO_2, NO_X, and CO_2 emission, it is reported that SA and LR in some cases demonstrate better performance than QPSO and QBA.

Then again, QBA needs a comparatively lesser population size and iteration than LR, SA, and PSO but larger than QPSO. QBA is also found to be successfully avoided local optima. However, the computational time is a little larger than QPSO.

The parallelism characteristics of quantum computing phenomena, along with the qubit's idea, improve the search capability and increase convergence speed. In contrast, the quantum behavior swarms diversify the population and help to avoid premature convergence.

3.4 Conclusions and future research direction

This paper presents three nature-inspired swarm intelligence-based algorithms to address emission dispatch, economic load dispatch (ELD), and combined economic emission dispatch (CEED) issues. Characteristics of the presented algorithms for predicting solution for solo-objective ED, ELD, and CEED problems with multi-objective are summarized, especially their convergence characteristics, computational performance, and ability to provide quality solution are discussed. The highly nonlinear CEED issue is illustrated utilizing the cubic criterion method.

The present research focuses on implementing QCI optimization techniques to solve the CEED issue to mitigate the limitations of existing methods. This research integrates the idea of quantum computing with swarm intelligence-based algorithms to predict the CEED problem's best solution, treating it as a multi-objective problem and separately as two single-objective problems. One SI-based algorithm, i.e., PSO, and two QCI-based algorithms, i.e., QPSO and QBA, have been utilized in this research. Depending on the earlier section's results, their unique characteristics, advantages, and limitations are given below.

The obtained results show that PSO performs better than classical mathematical modeling based on SDSM. PSO is easy to implement and has fewer adjustable parameters. It offers a fair amount of robustness and reliability. The computational performance of PSO is also better than SDSM. However, it may sometimes trap into the local optima if the swarm size and iteration number were not adequate.

QBA is also implemented to solve the single-objective ED problem and CEED issue with multi-objective. The obtained results show that QBA performs better than the classical SDS method and PSO for a single objective emission dispatch problem. On the other hand, like QPSO, QBA outperforms LR, PSO, and SA for solving the

CEED issue with multi-objective. The results of QBA for solving the CEED issue are quite similar to the results found in QPSO. The amount of robustness and reliability is too high in the emission dispatch problem. Simultaneously, it also shows a perfect amount of robustness and reliability for the CEED problem. The standard deviation is also minimal. The convergence characteristics of QBA for both solo objective emission dispatch and CEED issue with multiple objectives are found to be excellent. It verifies the power of quantum computing ideas into CI. Lack of coefficient data for a more extensive system limits our research to the only 3-unit framework for ED issue. However, to solve the multi-objective CEED problem, QBA needs a larger swarm size and iteration number than QPSO to get the optimal result. The most challenging part of QBA is that it has many parameters that need to be adjusted and tuned to get optimal results.

For single objective ELD, it has been tested in 3-, 5- and 26-unit system. The pronounced results are encouraging; it provides excellent robustness in the solutions. The solutions are also highly reliable and suitable. The convergence is also smooth and fast, but for a more extensive system, i.e., 26-unit generating system, convergence is a bit slower. The results are improved in the sizeable 26-unit system by increasing the swarm size and iteration number. However, larger size of the population and iteration number leads to high computational cost and, hence, increases the computational time. QPSO behaves well for multi-objective CEED problem as well. QPSO is tested in four different loads and successfully outperformed SA, LR, PSO, and QBA methods by achieving high quality and robust solutions. It has only one parameter and, thus, easy to implement. Again, the cubic function's consideration to represent the CEED problem to reduce nonlinearities in the system limits us to implement QPSO in a smaller design. The cubic function's necessary data is not available for the more extensive system.

In the future, both QBA and QPSO should be applied to an extensive power production framework to test their effective managing real-world power generation system. For this, it is necessary to gather or find the data required for cubic function (i.e., coefficients of fuel cost and emission). It reduces the nonlinearity and more closely illustrates the power generating system's natural response. The primary concern in QBA is that it consists of various parameters. It should consider appropriate step to minimize the parameters so that the implementation of QBA is easy and useful. Numbers of studies already reported the minimization of parameters and proposed BA without any parameter [81, 82]. Moreover, constraints such as loss of transmission, generator ramp rate limit, prohibited operating zones, and tie-line limit are considered to simulate the actual working conditions.

Furthermore, particular procedure for selection should be assumed along with this study to select the best solution from the sets of best solutions [83–90]. In a CEED problem with multiple objectives, it is difficult for the researchers to choose the best option from numerous Pareto-optimal solutions. Finally, other meta-heuristic techniques such as the CS algorithm might be possible to combine with quantum computing to predict the CEED problem of non-convex nature. A hybrid QCI technique can predict the CEED problem's solution with multiple objectives for an extensive system.

Acknowledgement

The authors thank Dr Fahad Parvez Mahdi at Advanced Medical Engineering Center, Department of Electrical Engineering and Computer Sciences, University of Hyogo, Japan for his support in this research work.

Conflicts of interest

Authors of the paper declare no conflicts of interest.

References

[1] Portal T D 2018 Breakdown of Electricity Generation by Energy Source. The Shift Project Data Portal, Shift Proj. Data Portal http://tsp-data-portal.org/Breakdown-of-Electricity-Generation-by-Energy-Source#tspQvChart Accessed October 21

[2] Dudely B 2015 BP Statistical Review of World Energy

[3] Birol F 2004 World Energy Outlook 2004, *International Energy Agency*http://large.stanford.edu/courses/2018/ph241/lin1/docs/WEO2004.pdf

[4] Agency C I 2015 Comparison: Natural Gas - Proved Reserves www.cia.gov/library/publications/the-world-factbook/rankorder/2253rank.html

[5] Shafiee S and Topal E 2009 When will fossil fuel reserves be diminished? *Energy Policy* **37** 181–9

[6] Walsh J 2000 Projection of cumulative world conventional oil production *Remaining resources and Reserves to* **2050**

[7] Ivanhoe L 1995 Future world oil supplies: there is a finite limit *World Oil.* **216** 77

[8] Nanda J, Kothari D and Lingamurthy K 1988 Economic-emission load dispatch through goal programming techniques *IEEE Trans. Energy Convers.* **3** 26–32

[9] Song Y H, Wang G S, Wang P Y and Johns A T 1997 Environmental/economic dispatch using fuzzy logic controlled genetic algorithms *IEE Proc. Gener. Transm. Distrib.* **144** 377–82

[10] Bhattacharya A and Chattopadhyay P K 2011 Hybrid differential evolution with biogeography-based optimization algorithm for solution of economic emission load dispatch problems *Expert Syst. Appl.* **38** 14001–10

[11] Granelli G P, Montagna M, Pasini G L and Marannino P 1992 Emission constrained dynamic dispatch *Electr. Power Syst. Res.* **24** 55–64

[12] Kumar A I S, Dhanushkodi K, Kumar J J and Paul C K C 2003 Particle swarm optimization solution to emission and economic dispatch problem *IEEE Reg. 10 Annu. Int. Conf. Proc./TENCON.* 1 435–9

[13] Roselyn J P, Devaraj D and Dash S S 2011 Economic emission OPF using hybrid GA-particle swarm optimization, *Swarm, Evol. Memetic Comput. SEMCCO 2011. Lect. Notes Comput. Sci.* **7076** 167–75

[14] Dhillon J S, Parti S C and Kothari D P 1993 Stochastic economic emission load dispatch *Electr. Power Syst. Res.* **26** 179–86

[15] Basu M 2005 A simulated annealing-based goal-attainment method for economic emission load dispatch of fixed head hydrothermal power systems *Int. J. Electr. Power Energy Syst.* **27** 147–53

[16] El-Keib A A and Ding H 1994 Environmentally constrained economic dispatch using linear programming *Electr. Power Syst. Res.* **29** 155–9

[17] Hota P K, Barisal A K and Chakrabarti R 2010 Economic emission load dispatch through fuzzy based bacterial foraging algorithm *Int. J. Electr. Power Energy Syst.* **32** 794–803
[18] Arunachalam S, Saranya R and Sangeetha N 2013 Hybrid artificial bee colony algorithm and simulated annealing algorithm for combined economic and emission dispatch including valve point effect *Lect. Notes Comput. Sci.* **8297** 354–65
[19] Nanda J, Hari L and Kothari M L 1994 Economic emission load dispatch with line flow constraints using a classical technique *IEE Proc. C Gener. Transm. Distrib.* **141** 1–10
[20] Abou El Ela A A, Abido M A and Spea S R 2010 Differential evolution algorithm for emission constrained economic power dispatch problem *Electr. Power Syst. Res.* **80** 1286–92
[21] Sayah S, Hamouda A and Bekrar A 2014 Efficient hybrid optimization approach for emission constrained economic dispatch with nonsmooth cost curves *Int. J. Electr. Power Energy Syst.* **56** 127–39
[22] El-Keib A A, Ma H and Hart J L 1994 Environmentally constrained economic dispatch using the La Grangian relaxation method *IEEE Trans. Power Syst.* **9** 1723–9
[23] Apostolopoulos T and Vlachos A 2011 Application of the Firefly algorithm for solving the economic emissions load dispatch problem *Int. J. Comb.* **2011** 1–23
[24] Radosavljević J 2016 A solution to the combined economic and emission dispatch using hybrid PSOGSA algorithm *Appl. Artif. Intell.* **30** 445–74
[25] Chen J F and Der Chen S 1997 Multiobjective power dispatch with line flow constraints using the fast Newton-Raphson method *IEEE Trans. Energy Convers.* **12** 86–93
[26] Der Chen S and Chen J F 2003 A direct Newton-Raphson economic emission dispatch *Int. J. Electr. Power Energy Syst.* **25** 411–7
[27] Dixit G P, Dubey H M, Pandit M and Panigrahi B K 2011 Artificial bee colony optimization for combined economic load and emission dispatch *IET Conf. Publ.* **2011** 340–5
[28] Younes M, Khodja F and Kherfane R L 2014 Multi-objective economic emission dispatch solution using hybrid FFA (firefly algorithm) and considering wind power penetration *Energy* **67** 595–606
[29] Wong K P 1998 Evolutionary-programming-based algorithm for environmentally-constrained economic dispatch *IEEE Trans. Power Syst.* **13** 301–6
[30] Krishnanand K R, Panigrahi B K, Rout P K and Mohapatra A 2011 Application of multi-objective teaching-learning-based algorithm to an economic load dispatch problem with incommensurable objectives *Lect. Notes Comput. Sci.* **7076** 697–705
[31] Zhang H, Yue D, Xie X, Hu S and Weng S 2015 Multi-elite guide hybrid differential evolution with simulated annealing technique for dynamic economic emission dispatch *Appl. Soft Comput. J.* **34** 312–23
[32] Das D B and Patvardhan C 1998 New multi-objective stochastic search technique for economic load dispatch *IEE Proc., Gener. Transm. Distrib.* **145** 747–52
[33] Arunachalam S, AgnesBhomila T and Ramesh Babu M 2015 Hybrid particle swarm optimization algorithm and firefly algorithm based combined economic and emission dispatch including valve point effect *Lect. Notes Comput. Sci.* **8947** 647–60
[34] Fan J Y and Zhang L 1998 Real-time economic dispatch with line flow and emission constraints using quadratic programming *IEEE Trans. Power Syst.* **13** 320–5
[35] Chandrasekaran K, Simon S P and Padhy N P 2014 Cuckoo search algorithm for emission reliable economic multi-objective dispatch problem *IETE J. Res.* **60** 128–38

[36] Lu S, Sun C and Lu Z 2010 An improved quantum-behaved particle swarm optimization method for short-term combined economic emission hydrothermal scheduling *Energy Convers. Manag.* **51** 561–71

[37] Jadoun V K, Gupta N, Niazi K R and Swarnkar A 2015 Modulated particle swarm optimization for economic emission dispatch *Int. J. Electr. Power Energy Syst.* **73** 80–8

[38] Jadoun V K, Gupta N, Niazi K R, Swarnkar A and Bansal R C 2015 Multi-area environmental economic dispatch with reserve constraints using enhanced particle swarm optimization *Electr. Power Components Syst.* **43** 1667–79

[39] Basu M 2006 Particle swarm optimization based goal-attainment method for dynamic economic emission dispatch *Electr. Power Components Syst.* **34** 1015–25

[40] Wang L and Singh C 2008 Stochastic economic emission load dispatch through a modified particle swarm optimization algorithm *Electr. Power Syst. Res.* **78** 1466–76

[41] Ziane I, Benhamida F and Graa A 2017 Simulated annealing algorithm for combined economic and emission power dispatch using max/max price penalty factor *Neural Comput. Appl.* **28** 197–205

[42] Chen P H and Kuo C C 2011 Economic-Emission load dispatch by refined particle Swarm optimization and interactive Bi-objective programming *Int. Rev. Electr. Eng.* **6** 2584–95

[43] Bahmanifirouzi B, Farjah E and Niknam T 2012 Multi-objective stochastic dynamic economic emission dispatch enhancement by fuzzy adaptive modified theta particle swarm optimization *J. Renew. Sustain. Energy*

[44] Zhang Y, Gong D W and Ding Z 2012 A bare-bones multi-objective particle swarm optimization algorithm for environmental/economic dispatch *Inf. Sci. (Ny).* **192** 213–27

[45] Wang A C, Pan W G and Wang W H 2014 A study of multi-objective load optimal dispatch in thermal power unit based on improved particle swarm optimization algorithm *Adv. Mater. Res.* **860–863** 1425–30

[46] Mandal K K, Mandal S, Bhattacharya B and Chakraborty N 2015 Non-convex emission constrained economic dispatch using a new self-adaptive particle swarm optimization technique *Appl. Soft Comput. J.* **28** 188–95

[47] Ramesh B, Mohan V C J and Eddy V C V 2013 Application of Bat algorithm for combined Economic load and emission *Int. J. Electr. Electron. Eng. Telecommun.* **2** 1–9

[48] Niknam T, Azizipanah-Abarghooee R, Zare M and Bahmani-Firouzi B 2013 Reserve constrained dynamic environmental/economic dispatch: a new multiobjective self-adaptive learning Bat algorithm *IEEE Syst. J.* **7** 763–76

[49] Azizipanah-Abarghooee R and Niknam T 2012 A new improved bat algorithm for fuzzy interactive multi-objective economic/emission dispatch with load and wind power uncertainty *World Sci. Proc. Ser. Comput. Eng. Inf. Sci.* **7** 388–93

[50] Han K H and Kim J H 2002 Quantum-inspired evolutionary algorithm for a class of combinatorial optimization *IEEE Trans. Evol. Comput.* **6** 580–93

[51] wei Gong D, Zhang Y and Liang Qi C 2010 Environmental/economic power dispatch using a hybrid multi-objective optimization algorithm *Int. J. Electr. Power Energy Syst.* **32** 607–14

[52] Bhattacharya A and Chattopadhyay P K 2011 Solving economic emission load dispatch problems using hybrid differential evolution *Appl. Soft Comput. J.* **11** 2526–37

[53] Gong W, Cai Z and Ling C X 2011 DE/BBO: a hybrid differential evolution with biogeography-based optimization for global numerical optimization *Soft Comput.* **15** 645–65

[54] Bhattacharya A and Chattopadhyay P K 2010 Hybrid differential evolution with biogeography-based optimization for solution of economic load dispatch *IEEE Trans. Power Syst.* **25** 1955–64

[55] Jordehi A R 2015 Particle swarm optimisation (PSO) for allocation of FACTS devices in electric transmission systems: a review *Renew. Sustain. Energy Rev.* **52** 1260–7

[56] Hooshmand R A, Parastegari M and Morshed M J 2012 Emission, reserve and economic load dispatch problem with non-smooth and non-convex cost functions using the hybrid bacterial foraging-Nelder–Mead algorithm *Appl. Energy* **89** 443–53

[57] Roy P K and Bhui S 2016 A multi-objective hybrid evolutionary algorithm for dynamic economic emission load dispatch *Int. Trans. Electr. Energy Syst.* **26** 49–78

[58] Abido M A 2006 Multiobjective evolutionary algorithms for electric power dispatch problem *IEEE Trans. Evol. Comput.* **10** 315–29

[59] Wood A J and Wollenberg B F 2013 *Power generation, operation, and control* (New York: *Wiley*) 656

[60] Saadat H 1999 *Power System Analysis* (*New York*: *McGraw-Hill*) 697

[61] Kennedy J and Eberhart R 1995 Particle swarm optimization Proc. IEEE Int. Conf. Neural Networks 4 1942–8

[62] Imran R, Pandian V, Mahinder S B S and Abdullah-Al-Wadud M 2016 Hybrid particle Swarm and gravitational search optimization techniques for charging plug-in hybrid electric vehicles ed V Pandian, W Gerhard-Wilhelm and D V Ngoc *Handb. Res. Mod. Optim. Algorithms Appl. Eng. Econ.* (IGI Global) 471–504

[63] Eberhart R C and Shi Y 2000 Comparing inertia weights and constriction factors in particle swarm optimization *Proc. 2000 Congr. Evol. Comput.* 84–8

[64] Eberhart R C and Shi Y 2001 Tracking and optimizing dynamic systems with particle swarms *Proc. 2001 Congr. Evol. Comput.* 94–100

[65] Abido M 2002 Optimal power flow using particle swarm optimization *Int. J. Electr. Power Energy Syst.* **24** 563–71

[66] Clerc M 1999 The swarm and the queen: towards a deterministic and adaptive particle swarm optimization *Proc. 1999 Congr. Evol. Comput.* **3** 1951–7

[67] Sun J, Fang W, Wu X, Palade V and Xu W 2012 Quantum-behaved particle swarm optimization: analysis of individual particle behavior and parameter selection *Evol. Comput.* **20** 349–93

[68] Yumin D and Li Z 2014 Quantum Behaved particle Swarm optimization algorithm based on artificial fish Swarm *Math. Probl. Eng.*

[69] Sun J, Xu W and Liu J 2005 Parameter selection of quantum-behaved particle swarm optimization *Int. Conf. Nat. Comput.* 543–52

[70] Tian N, Lai C H, Pericleous K, Sun J and Xu W 2011 Contraction-expansion coefficient learning in Quantum-Behaved particle Swarm optimization *10th Int. Symp. Distrib. Comput. Appl. to Business, Eng. Sci.* 303–8

[71] Sun J, Feng B and Xu W 2004 Particle swarm optimization with particles having quantum behavior *Proc. 2004 Congr. Evol. Comput.* 1 325–31

[72] Yang X S and Gandomi A H 2012 Bat algorithm: a novel approach for global engineering optimization *Eng. Comput.* **29** 464–83

[73] Schnitzler H U and Kalko E K V 2001 Echolocation by insect-eating bats *Bioscience.* **51** 557–69

[74] Yang X S 2010 A new metaheuristic Bat-inspired algorithm *Stud. Comput. Intell.* **284** 65–74

[75] Xue F, Cai Y, Cao Y, Cui Z and Li F 2015 Optimal parameter settings for bat algorithm *Int. J. Bio-Inspired Comput.* **7** 125–8
[76] Shi Y and Eberhart R C 1998 Parameter selection in particle swarm optimization *Lect. Notes Comput. Sci.* **1447** 591–600
[77] Meng K, Wang H G, Dong Z Y and Wong K P 2010 Quantum-inspired particle swarm optimization for valve-point economic load dispatch *IEEE Trans. Power Syst.* **25** 215–22
[78] Kumaran G and Mouly V S R K 2001 Using evolutionary computation to solve the economic load dispatch problem *Proc. IEEE Conf. Evol. Comput. ICEC.* 1 296–301
[79] Pitono J, Soepriyanto A and Purnomo M H 2018 Optimization of economic-emission dispatch by particle swarm optimization (PSO) using cubic criterion functions and various price penalty factors *Astra Salvensis.* **6** 749–62
[80] Tozer B, Mazzuchi T and Sarkani S 2017 Many-objective stochastic path finding using reinforcement learning *Expert Syst. Appl.* **72** 371–82
[81] Zou X, Chen Y, Liu M, Kang L and New A 2008 Evolutionary algorithm for solving many-objective optimization problems *IEEE Trans. Syst. Man, Cybern. Part* B*38 1402–12*
[82] Deb K and Saxena D K 2005 On finding Pareto-optimal solutions through dimensionality reduction for certain large-dimensional multi-objective optimization problems EMO for many objectives *Kangal Rep.* **2005011** 3353–60
[83] Ganesan T, Vasant P, Elamvazuthi I and Shaari K Z K 2016 Game-theoretic differential evolution for multiobjective optimization of green sand mould system *Soft Comput.* **20** 3189–200
[84] Ganesan T, Vasant P and Elamvazuthi I 2016 Multiobjective optimization using particle swarm optimization with non-Gaussian random generators *Intell. Decis. Technol.* **10** 93–103
[85] Ganesan T, Vasant P and Elamvazuthi I 2015 Non-Gaussian random generators in Bacteria Foraging algorithm for multiobjective optimization *Ind. Eng. Manag.* **4** 2169–0316
[86] Ganesan T, Aris M S and Elamvazuthi I 2018 Multiobjective strategy for an industrial gas turbine: absorption chiller system *Handb. Res. Emergent Appl. Optim. Algorithms* ed P Vasant, S Z Alparslan-Gok and G W Weber (IGI Global) 531–56
[87] Ganesan T, Vasant P and Elamvazuthi I 2016 *Advances in Meta heuristics: Applications in Engineering Systems* (*Boca Raton*: *CRC Press*) 233
[88] Ganesan T, Vasant P, Sanghvi P, Thomas J and Litvinchev I 2020 Random matrix generators for optimizing a fuzzy biofuel supply Chain system *J. Adv. Eng. Comput.* **4** 33–50
[89] Vasant P, Zelinka I and Weber G-W 2019 *Intelligent Computing & Optimization.* (Berlin: Springer International Publishing) 575
[90] Vasant P, Zelinka I and Weber G-W 2020 Intelligent computing and optimization Proc. of the 2nd Int. Conf. on Intelligent Computing and Optimization 2019 (ICO 2019) (Berlin: Springer International Publishing) 693

Chapter 4

Eigenvalue clustering for spectrum sensing: throughput and energy evaluation for cognitive radio–Internet of Things network

Manish Kumar Giri and Saikat Majumder

Symbols

τ_s	Sensing time
σ_β^2	Variance of primary user signal
σ_n^2	Variance of noise
α_{H_0}	Mean value for hypothesis H_0
α_{H_1}	Mean value for hypothesis H_1
$\sigma_{H_0}^2$	Variance value for hypothesis H_0
$\sigma_{H_1}^2$	Variance value for hypothesis H_1
$\beta_{i,k}$	SNR of the ith CR-IoT user
$\zeta_{i,k}$	Predefined threshold for the ith CR-IoT user
$Q(.)$	Tail distribution function
γ	Eigenvalue of the covariance matrix
ω	Weighting factor
$\hat{\psi}$	Channel status indicator
χ	Trade-off between probability of detection and false alarm
ϵ	Expected lifetime
μ	SNR for transmitter and receiver link

This chapter explores the scope of artificial intelligence in cognitive radio (CR) based scenarios for the Internet of Things (IoT) networks. The demand for more data rate for internet-connected devices is causing a scarcity in the frequency spectrum. There are some shortcomings of conventional approaches to handle the spectrum scarcity problem that makes them less liable to adopt. To overcome these shortcomings and improve the performance, a novel cooperative spectrum sensing (CSS) scheme based on eigenvalues of the signal covariance matrix and fuzzy

doi:10.1088/978-0-7503-4801-0ch4

C-means (FCM) clustering is proposed. In the proposed approach, multi-input and multi-output (MIMO) based CR technology is adopted for IoTs. The key idea in this chapter is to use an FCM algorithm to train a multidimensional classifier. The proposed approach directly clusters the eigenvalues in multidimensional space; this contrasts with the commonly used schemes, where multiple eigenvalues are used to form a single statistic. An extensive collection of results are provided regarding detection gain, throughput, energy consumption, expected lifetime, and error probability. The reported results are also compared with some of the recent eigenvalue-based approaches. Based on the simulation results, it can be said that the proposed approach is suitable for the upcoming CR-IoT technology.

4.1 Introduction

Recently the demand to connect devices to the internet has increased rapidly. The IoT is a popular wireless communication paradigm in which different machines or devices are connected without any outer human interference. The study of IoT technology involves a different set of configurations based on which information is exchanged between devices [22]. The analysis and information exchange are important applications of IoT [4]. The radio spectrum has been getting scarcer due to the increase in IoT devices. This is causing a challenge for properly using the spectrum allocation technique. Moreover, these techniques are fixed and underutilized quite often [34]. The IoT is gaining importance in applications, namely medical services, transportation, weather forecasting, etc. These emerging applications require proper bandwidth allocation, spectrum utilization, and ease of access [1, 21, 47, 48]. The long-standing challenge for IoT communication is efficient utilization of the spectrum, improvement in system throughput, and reduction in total energy consumption. The main concern with IoT devices is that most of the devices do not have the required hardware and energy sources like batteries to perform spectrum sensing (SS) defined over a duration of time [46]. The recently developed SS techniques provide improvement in spectrum access by utilizing the licensed spectrum.

CR is a paradigm that is believed to be a revolution in technology to meet the future spectrum demands of IoT [1, 21]. The ability to adjust dynamically and figure out the vacant band not used by the primary user (PU) makes it more reliable for IoT devices. Some studies have been reported in which CR-assisted IoT devices make a network that exists simultaneously with a PU network [3, 33]. The PUs are licensed users and they have the priority over other users to access the channel. CR-IoT users are unlicensed users and they periodically monitor the spectrum for an opportunity to access it without any interference with the PU. The two primary approaches for CR technology are the overlay approach and the underlay approach [8]. In an overlay approach, the CR-IoT user senses a free licensed spectrum and in the case of availability they access the spectrum opportunistically for transmission of data. In an underlay approach, simultaneous communications are allowed between CR-IoT user and PU. Both can use the same channel at a time of low transmission power. This further displays the ability of the approach to avoid interference in the network. Since CR-IoT users do not interfere in the PU transmission.

Since spectrum sensing (SS) plays a pivotal role for overlay-based CR-IoT networks [43], the study of SS for CR-IoT becomes necessary. Several SS techniques were reported in the literature like energy detection (ED), eigenvalue-based detection, cyclostationary detection, and matched filter detection. ED is a conventional and mostly used technique. It has low complexity and prior knowledge about a PU signal is also not required [11]. However, poor performance in the case of noise uncertainty makes it less durable [38]. The cyclostationary and matched filter approaches require information about the PU features. The added complexity in both techniques makes them less durable to adopt in most cases [24, 36, 41]. Eigenvalue-based approaches are recently developed techniques. The ability to generate the test statistic without having any prior information about the PU signal makes them appropriate to adopt in most cases. The test statistic is formed by calculating the eigenvalues of the received signal covariance matrix [5]. The ED technique is less complex as compared to all these approaches. However, for a single CR-IoT, identification of PU correctly is difficult because of the hidden node problem. To further resolve this issue, a cooperative spectrum sensing (CSS) based multi user (MU) CR-IoT scenario can be adopted. In CSS, a centralized controller is adapted to improve the detection rate further. This controller is called fusion center (FC), as mentioned in past literature. The need for a durable reporting channel is a must for CSS/MU technology to transfer local decisions among CR-IoT devices. Every CR-IoT user will perform the sensing independently and transfer the information to the FC via a reporting channel. All these local decisions are combined at the FC and a global decision will be formed based on some fusion rules. The popular fusion rules are hard decision and soft decision rules [2, 40]. In the hard decision, a one bit decision is formed and transferred to the FC. Some of the examples are AND, OR, and M rule. In the soft decision rule, the CR-IoT user will transfer their entire decision information to FC, which will make a decision by incorporating some logic such as maximum ratio combiner and selection combiner. The performance of the soft decision rule is better in most cases compared to the hard decision rules.

The emergence of multiple-input and multiple-output (MIMO) antennas opened new aspects for SS. Improved performance in terms of spectral efficiency, better achievable bit rate, and multiplexing of antennas has been reported in the literature [10, 18, 27, 29, 32, 45]. The MIMO technology has produced significant interest over recent years for CR research. The ability to reduce the fading and shadowing present in the channel makes it more liable to be adopted for CR areas. Based on these advantages authors in this chapter incorporated MIMO antenna-based technology for the CR-IoT scheme. There are some major advantages of the proposed MIMO-based CR-IoT approach, such as better detection gain as compare to the approach reported in the literature. This research work is motivated by the recent progress of MIMO in the CR area [10, 18, 27, 29, 32, 45]. Inspired by this literature, we propose a novel eigenvalue-base clustering approach for a MIMO-based CR-IoT scenario. The aim is to improve the sensing gain, throughput, energy consumption, expected lifetime, and error probability of the system. The proposed approach incorporates the eigenvalue-based detection approach with fuzzy C-means (FCM) clustering in three-dimensional (3D) vector space.

4.2 Background and motivation

There is a vast amount of literature available for CSS analysis in CR technology. The authors will try to cover the latest background available in the literature. The authors in [31] presented a simple analysis of CSS for the CR network (CRN). The emphasis of the work was to calculate the detection performance for a non-fading environment. However, the analysis for fading scenario and performance of detection in the case of shadowing is not explained. Authors in [35] proposed a different approach based on reinforcement learning. Recently, an extreme learning machine-based CSS approach was proposed by the authors in [12, 13]. It was reported previously that the sensing accuracy is severely affected by the hidden node problem and shadowing [15, 25, 37]. The effect of noisy reporting channels was highlighted by authors in [6, 16, 17, 26]. In a recent development, an eigenvalue-based SS technique utilizing the Gaussian mixture model for uncalibrated multiple antennas was proposed by the author in [28]. Authors in [16] proposed a large-scale MU-MIMO-based approach. But the sensing and throughput analysis was not provided. Authors in [22] highlight the deployment of IoT scenarios for CRN. This further creates an opportunity for a new research area involving the IoT with CRN. An algorithm for multiple-input and single-output (MISO) based on precoding was proposed in [9]. Authors in [7] utilized MIMO technology for IoT to improve the performance in terms of spectral efficiency and data rates. However, the use of MIMO for IoT is an ever-increasing research area. The requirements for making connections are different from other broadband technology. A compressive sensing approach for traffic management was proposed by the authors in [19]. Application-level work was proposed by the authors in [20], in which the channel allocation problem was solved for medical applications. A CSS approach using the ratio of eigenvalues was proposed by the authors in [44], in which maximum to minimum eigenvalues ratio were taken. The authors in [14] proposed an eigenvalue-based technique using Kernel fuzzy C-means clustering to improve the detection performance. Moreover, Kortun *et al* [23] proposed an eigenvalue-based approach for throughput measurement for low signal-to-noise ratio (SNR) conditions under noise uncertainty. The authors incorporated the ratio of maximum to minimum eigenvalues to form test statistic. The authors in [30] proposed a weighted eigenvalue approach for CSS. In this approach, a weighted version of maximum to minimum eigenvalues was utilized to form test statistic. However, in this approach, multiple eigenvalues were represented by a single statistic, thus causing loss of information in the process. Motivated by these observations, we propose an eigenvalue-based approach for CSS in MIMO-based CR-IoT systems. In contrast to the previous approaches, we formed the test statistic by taking maximum, second maximum, and minimum eigenvalues in a 3D vector space. After that, FCM clustering in machine learning is performed on this test statistic.

This chapter has the following major contributions:

1. A technique incorporating the MIMO-based CR-IoT scenario is proposed that forms the feature vector by deploying the eigenvalues of the signal covariance matrix. A feature vector is formed by using the maximum, second

maximum, and minimum eigenvalues. In the proposed approach, important information loss can be prevented, which occurs in the case of reducing the multiple eigenvalues into a single statistic. The multidimensional clustering provides better detection performance compared to the methods available in the literature [23, 30, 44].

2. FCM clustering is utilized as a classifier for the proposed SS technique. The proposed method avoids the complex derivation of the threshold. The performance is measured by evaluating the probability of detection and receiver operating characteristics (ROC) curves.
3. An extensive range of possible simulation results are presented and compared with those of the traditional methods. The comparing metrics were sensing gain, system throughput, energy consumption, expected lifetime, and error probability. The results signify the proposed technique's superiority compared to the existing schemes [30, 39, 44] under a varying number of sample conditions.

The remaining part of this chapter is organized as follows: The background, motivation, and significance of this research are presented in section 4.2. Section 4.3 represents the proposed system model for MIMO-based CR-IoT network. In section 4.4, we discuss the proposed CSS algorithm for the system. This section also provides introductory details about the FCM algorithm. Section 4.5 provides details about the energy and throughput performance of the proposed technique. In section 4.6, simulation results are presented in which the performance of the proposed algorithm is compared with some of the techniques available in the literature. Finally, in section 4.8, we conclude our chapter by providing details about the chapter's contribution with possible future direction.

4.3 Adopted CR-IoT scenario

4.3.1 System model

An MU-MIMO-based system model for the CR-IoT system is illustrated in figure 4.1. It has M multiple-antenna CR-IoT users acting as spectrum sensing units. Each CR-IoT user has A_r receiving and A_t transmitting antennas. The system model consists of a primary network having PU transmitters and receivers only. The sensed information is shared with fusion center (FC) through a dedicated reporting channel. It is assumed that the FC has a single antenna. The FC decides about the spectrum availability and simultaneously communicates this information with all the CR-IoT users whether the licensed spectrum can be accessed. The PU traffic is modelled as a discrete semi-Markov two-state process [30] and represented in figure 4.2. The two states are OFF and ON represented by an exponentially distributed random variable X and Y with duration m_X and m_y, respectively. The probabilities for a PU to remain in ON and OFF state can be given as $P_{\text{on}} = \frac{m_Y}{m_Y + m_X}$, and $P_{\text{off}} = \frac{m_X}{m_X + m_Y}$, respectively. It is worth mentioning here that the primary network

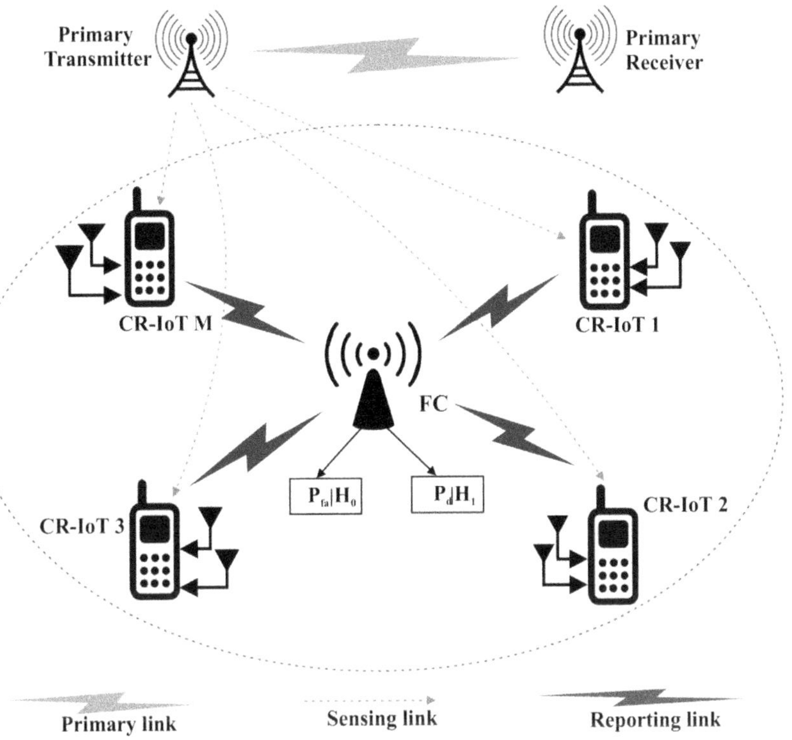

Figure 4.1. Typical multiple-antenna based CR-IoT scenario for CSS.

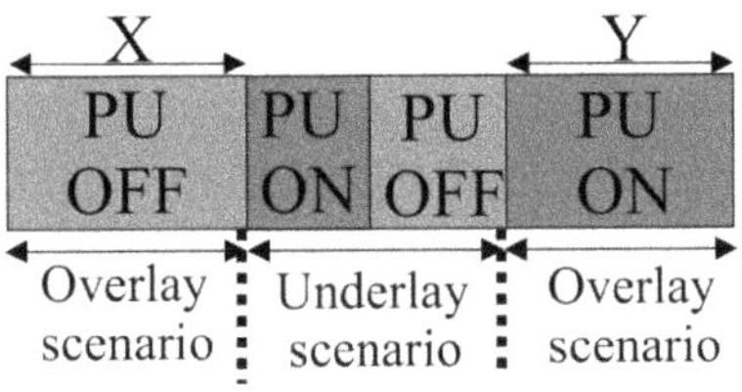

Figure 4.2. Representation of primary user availability by two different states.

and the CR-IoT network are assumed to be perfectly synchronized here. Hence the PU can change its status at the beginning of a time frame.

The local SS is performed by the respective CR-IoT nodes incorporating a link between PU and CR-IoT user. If H_0 and H_1 represent the absence and presence of a PU signal, then the SS problem can be formulated as binary hypothesis:

$$\mathcal{H}_0\colon z_{i,k}(n) = w_{i,k}(n), \tag{4.1}$$

$$\mathcal{H}_1\colon z_{i,k}(n) = h_{i,k}p(n) + w_{i,k}(n) \tag{4.2}$$

where $n = 1, 2, \ldots, N$, and $N = 2\tau_s B$ is the number of sampling points; with τ_s representing the sensing time and B denotes the bandwidth, $k = 1, 2, \ldots, K$ is the number of antennas and the subscript $i = 1, 2, \ldots, M$, where M represents the number of CR-IoT users. A few assumptions are considered for the model, which are stated as follows:

1. $z_{i,k}(n)$ is the signal received at kth antenna of ith CR-IoT node at nth time slot. $p(n)$ is the PU signal with mean and variance value zero and σ_p^2, respectively, i.e. $p(n) \sim \mathbb{CN}(0, \sigma_p^2)$ and $h_{i,k}$ is the channel gain between PU and ith CR-IoT user.
2. Noise $w_{i,k}(n)$ at the ith CR-IoT node, having $k = 1, 2, \ldots, K$ antennas is modelled as circularly symmetric complex Gaussian noise with zero mean and variance σ_n^2.

4.3.2 Conventional CSS techniques

Now we shall briefly enumerate some of the well-known CSS methods, where CR-IoT nodes forward their observations to the FC. The test statistic is computed at FC, and deterministic decision rules are applied to decide whether a PU is present or not.

4.3.2.1 Energy detection

Energy detection (ED) is a widely used conventional technique for the SS. This method is simple to implement without having any prior knowledge about the PU signal. The sensing outcome $z_{i,k}(n)$ represents the received power for ith CR-IoT user in the time domain for a band. The energy at the output of the CR-IoT user is represented as

$$E_i^k = \frac{1}{N}\sum_{n=1}^{N}|z_{i,k}(n)|^2 \tag{4.3}$$

In the case of a large number of samples, expression (4.3) can be represented in form of a Gaussian distribution for both hypothesis H_0 and H_1 with mean value α_{H_0}, α_{H_1} and variance $\sigma_{H_0}^2$, $\sigma_{H_1}^2$, respectively, as:

$$E_i^k = \begin{cases} \alpha_{H_0} = 2\tau_s B, \quad \sigma_{H_0}^2 = 4\tau_s B \\ \alpha_{H_1} = 2\tau_s B(1 + \beta_{i,k}), \quad \sigma_{H_1}^2 = 4\tau_s B(1 + 2\beta_{i,k}) \end{cases} \tag{4.4}$$

where $\beta_{i,k}$ represents the SNR of the ith CR-IoT node, with $k = 1, 2, \ldots, K$ antennas. Assuming the predefined threshold is $\zeta_{i,k}$ for the ith CR-IoT user with $k = 1, 2, \ldots, K$ antennas, then the respective probability of detection (P_D) and probability of false alarm (P_{fa}) can be represented as

$$P_{fa} = P(E_i^k > \zeta_{i,k}|H_0) = Q\left(\frac{\zeta_{i,k} - \alpha_{H_0}}{\sqrt{\sigma_{H_0}^2}}\right) = Q\left(\frac{\zeta_{i,k}}{\sigma_{H_0}^2} - 1\right)\sqrt{N_{i,k}} \tag{4.5}$$

and

$$P_D = P(E_i^k > \zeta_{i,k}|H_1) = Q\left(\frac{\zeta_{i,k} - \alpha_{H_1}}{\sqrt{\sigma_{H_1}^2}}\right) = Q\left(\frac{\zeta_{i,k}}{\sigma_{H_1}^2} - \beta_{i,k} - 1\right)\sqrt{\frac{N_{i,k}}{(1 + 2\beta_{i,k})}} \tag{4.6}$$

here $Q(.)$ denotes the Q function or simply the tail distribution function, which can be represented as $Q(y) = \frac{1}{2\pi}\int_y^{\infty} \exp\left(\frac{-t^2}{2}\right)dt$

4.3.2.2 Eigenvalue-based detection (EVD)

From equation (4.2), considering a set of received signals $z_{i,k}(n)$ for ith CR-IoT device, with $k = 1, 2, \dots, K$ antennas we can write:

$$\begin{bmatrix} z_{i,k}(n) \\ z_{i,k}(n-1) \\ \vdots \\ z_{i,k}(n-f+1) \end{bmatrix} = \begin{bmatrix} w_{i,k}(n) \\ w_{i,k}(n-1) \\ \vdots \\ w_{i,k}(n-f+1) \end{bmatrix} \quad \text{for } \mathcal{H}_0 \tag{4.7}$$

$$\begin{bmatrix} z_{i,k}(n) \\ z_{i,k}(n-1) \\ \vdots \\ z_{i,k}(n-f+1) \end{bmatrix} = h_{i,k}\begin{bmatrix} p(n) \\ p(n-1) \\ \vdots \\ p(n-f+1) \end{bmatrix} + \begin{bmatrix} w_{i,k}(n) \\ w_{i,k}(n-1) \\ \vdots \\ w_{i,k}(n-f+1) \end{bmatrix} \quad \text{for } \mathcal{H}_1 \tag{4.8}$$

Here f denotes the form factor with a positive value. Now the respective covariance of the transmitted signal, noise signal, and the received signal can be represented as:

$$R_p = E\{pp^H\}; \;\; R_w = E\{ww^H\}; \;\; R_z = E\{zz^H\}; \tag{4.9}$$

The covariance matrix of the received signal for both hypotheses is calculated as [44]:

$$R_z = \begin{cases} \sigma_{H_0}^2 I + R_p, & \text{for } \mathcal{H}_1 \\ \sigma_{H_0}^2 I, & \text{for } \mathcal{H}_0 \end{cases} \tag{4.10}$$

where I is an identity matrix. Now equation (4.10) can also be represented as:

$$R_z = U\Gamma U^H; \quad \Gamma = \text{diag}\{\gamma_1, \dots, \gamma_M\} \tag{4.11}$$

where $\gamma_1, \dots, \gamma_M$ are eigenvalues of R_z and are ordered as $\gamma_{\max} = \gamma_1 \geqslant \gamma_2 \geqslant \dots \geqslant \gamma_M = \gamma_{\min}$. U is the eigenvector matrix with dimension $S \times M$ in a network of S transmitting sources. The first S eigenvalues are called *signal space* eigenvalues and are contributed by signal and noise, i.e., for $i = 1, \dots, S$. The test statistic for the eigenvalue-based approach is equal to the ratio of maximum to minimum eigenvalue [44], i.e.

$$T_{\text{EVD}} = \frac{\gamma_{\max}}{\gamma_{\min}} \tag{4.12}$$

The global decision G_d can be calculated as:

$$G_d = \begin{cases} T_{\text{EVD}} \geqslant \zeta_{\text{EVD}}, & \mathcal{H}_1 \\ T_{\text{EVD}} < \zeta_{\text{EVD}}, & \mathcal{H}_0 \end{cases} \tag{4.13}$$

4.3.2.3 Weighted egenvalue detection

Weighted eigenvalue-based detection (WEVD) is proposed by the authors in [30]. Unlike the EVD approach, this method takes account of the weighted average of eigenvalues to form a test statistic. First, the weighting factor is calculated as:

$$\omega = \frac{\gamma_{\max} - \gamma_{\min}}{\gamma_{\max} + \gamma_{\min}} \tag{4.14}$$

After this, the test statistic is formed by multiplying the result of eigenvalue-based method with the weighting factor.

$$T_{\text{WEVD}} = \omega \frac{\gamma_{\max}}{\gamma_{\min}} \tag{4.15}$$

The global decision G_d can be calculated as:

$$G_d = \begin{cases} T_{\text{WEVD}} \geqslant \zeta_{\text{WEVD}}, & \mathcal{H}_1 \\ T_{\text{WEVD}} < \zeta_{\text{WEVD}}, & \mathcal{H}_0 \end{cases} \tag{4.16}$$

It is worth mentioning here that the authors in [30], explained the ability of WEVD technique to a greater number of samples for each CR-IoT user since they are equipped with MIMO antennas. Also, it was highlighted that the CR-IoT user with more antennas would get more samples. The improved frame structure for this scenario is presented in figure 4.3. The frame structure consists of two stages, the first

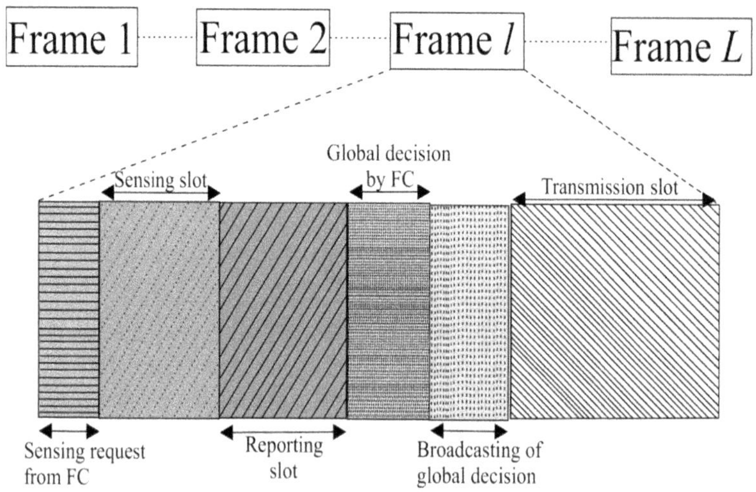

Figure 4.3. Adopted frame structure for the scenario. Adapted from [30], copyright (2020), with permission from Elsevier.

is the setup stage, and the second is the steady state stage. Initially the CR-IoT users will share the necessary information about the location and SNR of the reporting channel with FC. After this, a sensing request will be sent by the FC to the CR-IoT user, while the CR-IoT user will sense the spectrum in between a fixed time slot τ_s. Moreover, the CR-IoT user will make a local decision and transfer the information through a control channel with fixed reporting time slot τ_r. Afterwards, the FC will make a global decision and share this result with the whole network. On the second stage, this global decision will be received by the CR-IoT users. During a fixed transmission slot $T - \tau_s - \tau_r$, the concerned transmitter will send the information to its respective receiver.

4.4 Proposed method for CSS based on eigenvalue clustering

In this section, a novel CSS technique based on FCM clustering is proposed. This technique is based on the generation of test vectors with a combination of signal and noise space eigenvalues of the covariance matrix. The FCM clustering is performed here in 3D space. This approach is in contrast with the existing approaches, as the proposed approach does not convert the calculated eigenvalues into a single test statistic. Here the selected eigenvalues are directly clustered in 3D space. This nominal step reduced the amount of information lost in the process by converting multiple eigenvalues into a single test statistic. We now provide details of the proposed CSS algorithm using FCM clustering.

4.4.1 Maximum—second maximum—minimum eigenvalue clustering

In this proposed approach, we make a 3D test vector by using the eigenvalues of equation (4.11). The test vector can be represented as $\boldsymbol{x}_l = [\gamma_1, \gamma_2, \gamma_M]^T$, and it contains maximum, second maximum, and minimum eigenvalues, respectively. Here in this approach of *maximum—second maximum—minimum eigenvalue clustering* (M2MmEC), the test vectors $\boldsymbol{x}_l$ are clustered into two classes in a 3D space. In contrast to the previous approach of EVD and WEVD, clustering in 3D space is expected to provide improvement in SS performance. It is worth mentioning here that the initial two eigenvalues, γ_1 and γ_2, will represent the changes that occurred in the signal due to the availability of PU. In contrast, the third eigenvalue γ_M will act as a 'mass estimate of cluster' for the $\mathcal{H}_0$ condition. This will further provide a prevalence in making the algorithm completely blind [5]. More details about the proper selection of eigenvalues have been reported previously in [14].

For clustering purposes, the FCM algorithm is used here. FCM is a popular and simple fuzzy clustering approach used for pattern recognition and clustering problems. The training is performed to categorize a data point $\boldsymbol{x}_l$ into D fuzzy clusters by creating different membership values v_{dl}, $d = 1, \ldots, D$. The data point $\boldsymbol{x}_l$ belongs to cluster d with membership value v_{dl} can be represented with the following constraints:

$$v_{dl} \in [0, 1], \ \forall d, l \tag{4.17}$$

$$0 < \sum_{l=1}^{L} v_{dl} < L, \ \forall d \tag{4.18}$$

$$\sum_{d=1}^{D} v_{dl} = 1, \ \forall l \tag{4.19}$$

FCM clustering is an iterative algorithm that minimizes the following objective function

$$F(\boldsymbol{V}, \boldsymbol{W}) = \sum_{l=1}^{L} \sum_{d=1}^{D} v_{dl}^{e} \parallel \boldsymbol{x}_l - \boldsymbol{w}_d \parallel^2 \tag{4.20}$$

where e ($e > 1$) is the fuzzy exponent or fuzzifier and $\boldsymbol{w}_d$ is the dth centroid. In clustering terminology, $\boldsymbol{V} = \{v_{dl}\}$, $d = 1, \dots, D$, $l = 1, \dots, L$ is called partition matrix and $\boldsymbol{W} = [\boldsymbol{w}_1, \dots, \boldsymbol{w}_D]$ is the set of all centroids.

Training in FCM involves iterative learning of $\boldsymbol{W}$ and $\boldsymbol{V}$ to minimize $F(\boldsymbol{V}, \boldsymbol{W})$. At each iteration, centroids are updated as

$$\boldsymbol{w}_d = \frac{\sum_{l=1}^{L} v_{dl}^{e} \boldsymbol{x}_l}{\sum_{l=1}^{L} v_{dl}^{e}}, \tag{4.21}$$

and membership values v_{dl}, $d = 1, \dots, D$, $l = 1, \dots, L$ are updated as follows:

$$v_{dl} = \left\{ \sum_{q=1}^{D} \left(\frac{\parallel \boldsymbol{x}_l - \boldsymbol{w}_d \parallel^2}{\parallel \boldsymbol{x}_l - \boldsymbol{w}_q \parallel^2} \right)^{\frac{1}{e-1}} \right\}^{-1} \tag{4.22}$$

Once the training process is over, a classifier for spectrum sensing is obtained. The classifier will simply predict a point $\mathbf{x}$ to a cluster d for which the corresponding Euclidean distance $\parallel \boldsymbol{x} - \boldsymbol{w}_d \parallel$ is minimum. For SS, status of the channel $\hat{\psi}$ is estimated depending on a new test vector $\mathbf{x}$ as follows

$$\hat{\psi} = \begin{cases} 1, & \dfrac{\parallel \boldsymbol{x} - \boldsymbol{w}_1 \parallel}{\parallel \boldsymbol{x} - \boldsymbol{w}_2 \parallel} > \chi, \\ 0, & \text{otherwise.} \end{cases} \tag{4.23}$$

where parameter χ represents the trade-off between the probability of detection and the probability of false alarm. Figure 4.5 shows a 3D scatter plot for test vectors $\boldsymbol{x}_l = [\gamma_1(l), \gamma_2(l), \gamma_M(l)]^T$, $l = 1, \dots, L$ obtained for a random fading scenario. Based on the PU status, the test vectors can be clustered into two groups and easily identified with different colours. It is clear from figure 4.5 that the data points belonging to $\mathcal{H}_1$ form a spherical cluster, and the data points belonging to $\mathcal{H}_0$ form an oval shape. To obtain the cluster centers, FC incorporates L test vectors

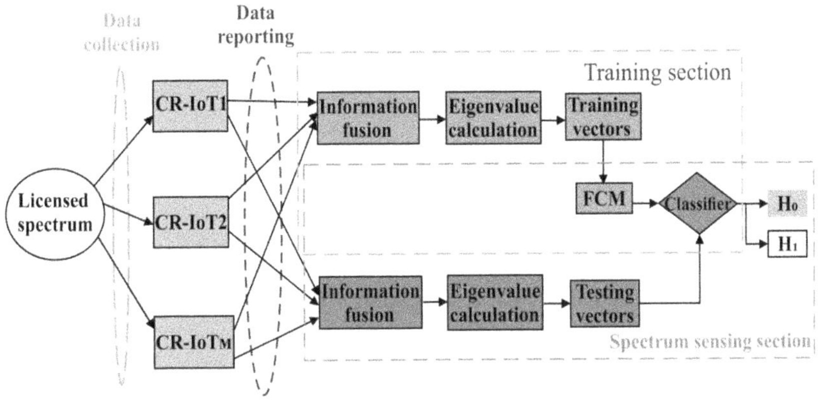

Figure 4.4. Complete steps of the proposed FCM-based technique; blue colour box represents the training part, and the magenta colour box denotes the SS section of the algorithm.

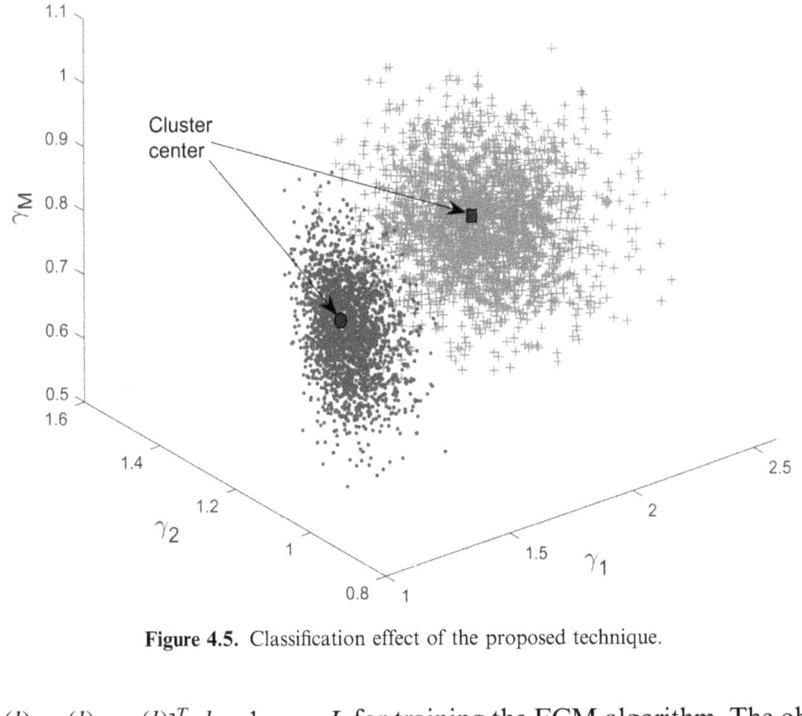

Figure 4.5. Classification effect of the proposed technique.

$\boldsymbol{x}_l = [\gamma_1(l), \gamma_2(l), \gamma_M(l)]^T, l = 1, \ldots, L$ for training the FCM algorithm. The obtained cluster centers can be used for predicting the status of the new test vector $\boldsymbol{x}$ as a channel available or unavailable class using (4.24). The complete process of the proposed method based on FCM clustering is described in figure 4.4.

4.5 Energy and throughput analysis

For the proposed method, the throughput and energy analysis are performed in this section since these are two important constraints for any system. First, the energy analysis is discussed. After that, throughput analysis is performed by highlighting the proposed approach's complexity with the previous methods.

4.5.1 Energy analysis

The total energy consumption for the proposed approach can be calculated using the expression given in [42]

$$\mathcal{E}_g(N) = e_s\tau_s + e_t t_t(1 - G_{d,f})p(H_0) + (1 - G_{d,d})p(H_1) \tag{4.24}$$

where $G_{d,f}$ and $G_{d,d}$ are the global probability of false alarm and detection, respectively, e_s is energy devoured during the sensing interval, t_t is transmission time and $t_t = T - \tau_s - \tau_r$, here T is total slot duration, e_t is energy consumption for transmission duration and $p(H_0)$, $P(H_1)$ are the probability of presence and absence of PU. Continuously the expected lifetime for the proposed approach can be calculated as [42]:

$$\epsilon = \frac{B_c}{\mathcal{E}_g(N)} \tag{4.25}$$

where B_c represents the total battery capacity.

4.5.2 Throughput analysis

The throughput of CR-IoT users can be calculated in the absence of PU. In the transmission slot, the CR-IoT user will send the data assuming that the channel is free to communicate. In other cases, it will wait for the channel to be free if the high-priority PUs are using it. This property is identical to a round-robin rule, where all the CR-IoT users will perform a regular scan to check for the available channel. The information acquired will be reported to the FC next. If the CR-IoT user can detect the channel perfectly, then the spectrum can be accessed by the CR-IoT user with a probability $1 - G_{d,f}$; otherwise $G_{d,d}$ will represent the probability for the no spectrum access. For mentioned scenario, the expression for the average throughput of CR-IoT user over all the PU can be calculated as [30]:

$$\mathcal{T}_{p,\text{avg}}(N) = \frac{T - \tau_s - \tau_r}{T}\left(c_{H_0}(1 - G_{d,f})p(H_0) + c_{H_1}(1 - G_{d,d})p(H_1)\right) \tag{4.26}$$

where c_{H_0} and c_{H_1} represent the channel capacity for the transmitter and receiver link of CR-IoT in the cases of available and busy channel condition. The equation for channel capacity c_{H_0} and c_{H_1} can be represented as:

$$c_{H_0} = \log_2(1 + \mu_{\text{CR-IoT}}) \tag{4.27}$$

$$c_{H_1} = \log_2\left(1 + \frac{\mu_{\mathrm{CR-IoT}}}{1 + \mu_{\mathrm{PU}}}\right) \tag{4.28}$$

where $\mu_{\mathrm{CR-IoT}}$ is SNR for CR-IoT transmitter and receiver link, and μ_{PU} is SNR for PU transmitter and CR-IoT receiver link.

4.5.3 Complexity analysis

The total time complexity required for calculating the EVD approach is CM, here C is a constant, hence by neglecting it, the complexity will be equal to $\mathcal{O}(M)$ [30]. The total complexity for the WEVD approach is C_1M, here C_1 is a constant, hence the final complexity for the WEVD approach will be $\mathcal{O}(M)$ [30]. The proposed approach's complexity primarily depends on two steps, the first is the calculation of eigenvalues, and the second is the clustering process. The first step requires the same number of calculations $\mathcal{O}(M)$ as the approaches mentioned above, whereas the second step requires the calculation of FCM clustering. The total complexity of the proposed approach is $\mathcal{O}(M) + \mathcal{O}(Ncd^2)$ for a single iteration. The clustering process requires extra calculations and makes the proposed approach the most complex among the compared approaches. This added complexity is justified because the proposed approach provides a significant improvement in the detection, throughput performance and also reduces energy consumption.

4.6 Simulation results

In this section, we report the simulation results to evaluate the proposed scheme's performance and compare it with existing schemes in the literature. Here we evaluate the classification performance of our FCM-based approach. The detection performance of the proposed scheme is compared with conventional ED [39], EVD [44], and WEVD [30] techniques. After that, results for energy and throughput analysis are presented.

The simulation setup considered here is similar to that in [30]. A static scenario is considered where the channel between PU and CR-IoT user is Rayleigh flat fading, and it remains unaffected for L frames. For simplicity, an equal number of transmitting and receiving antennas are maintained in figure 4.1. FC stores the eigenvalue statistic from these L frames as $\boldsymbol{X} = [\boldsymbol{x}_1, \ldots, \boldsymbol{x}_L]$ for training the spectrum sensing algorithm. We extracted 4000 signal feature vectors to measure our experiment's correctness based on the technique discussed in the previous section. Among the 4000 feature vectors, 2000 are used for training the classifier, and the remaining 2000 are used for the testing stage. The scatter plot is represented in figure 4.5, and the plot is obtained for 10 CR-IoT users with number of samples fixed at $N = 100$. The probability of PU being in active and idle state is $p(\mathcal{H}_1)$ and $p(\mathcal{H}_0)$, respectively. The remaining simulation parameters are illustrated in table 4.1. The simulations and analysis are performed using the MATLAB® platform on an Intel® Core™ i3 processor with 12 GB RAM.

From figure 4.5, it is clear that the FCM algorithm has an impact on the generated features. The features are clearly distinguished by two different clusters, as

Table 4.1. Simulation parameters used throughout in this article with their values.

Name of the parameters	Parameter value
Probability for PU present $p(H_1)$	0.5
Probability for PU absent $p(H_0)$	0.5
Number of samples	100
Number of PU transmitters	1
Number of PU receivers	1
Number fo CR-IoT users M	10
Sensing duration τ_s	1 ms
Total time slot duration T	10 ms
Bandwidth of channel B	300 kHz
Smoothing factor, f	10
PU signal, $z(n)$	CSCG
SNR of each PU $\mathrm{SNR}_{\mathrm{PU}}$	10 dB
Battery capacity B_c	300 J
energy consumed in sensing e_s	1 J
energy consumed in transmission e_t	3 J

reported in the figure. The red colour points show feature vectors of the signal, and the blue colour dots denote the feature vectors of the signal with noise. The respective cluster centers are denoted by black square and circle, respectively. In figure 4.5 γ_1, γ_2, and γ_M represent the maximum, second maximum, and minimum eigenvalues as a measure to indicate features.

4.6.1 Comparison of ROC performance

The performance comparison of the proposed SS technique is presented in this section. Figure 4.6 compares the detection performance (P_{d}) of the proposed scheme in terms of ROC. ROC is a plot between the probability of false alarm P_{fa} and the probability of detection P_{d}. ROC curves represent a trade-off between different values of P_{d}, which are a result of different choices of P_{fa}. In general, an SS scheme with a larger area under the curve (AUC) of the ROC plot is considered superior to a scheme with less AUC. Figure 4.6 compares the proposed scheme's ROC plot with energy detection, eigenvalue-based method, and weighted eigenvalue-based method, respectively. Among them, algorithms proposed in [30, 44] are based on the computation of signal covariance matrix and hence belong to the same category as the proposed technique. On the other hand, the signal's energy feature is used for classification and spectrum sensing in [39]. From the graphical plot, it can be observed that the proposed scheme provides an improvement in ROC compared to all other schemes. Superior system performance for the proposed technique is indicated by higher P_{d} for low P_{fa} values. When compared in particular to the WEVD method [30], the proposed scheme provides a significant gain in P_{d} in the region $0 < P_{\mathrm{fa}} < 0.2$. The gain in performance is even more pronounced when compared to EVD [44] and ED technique [39]. Table 4.2

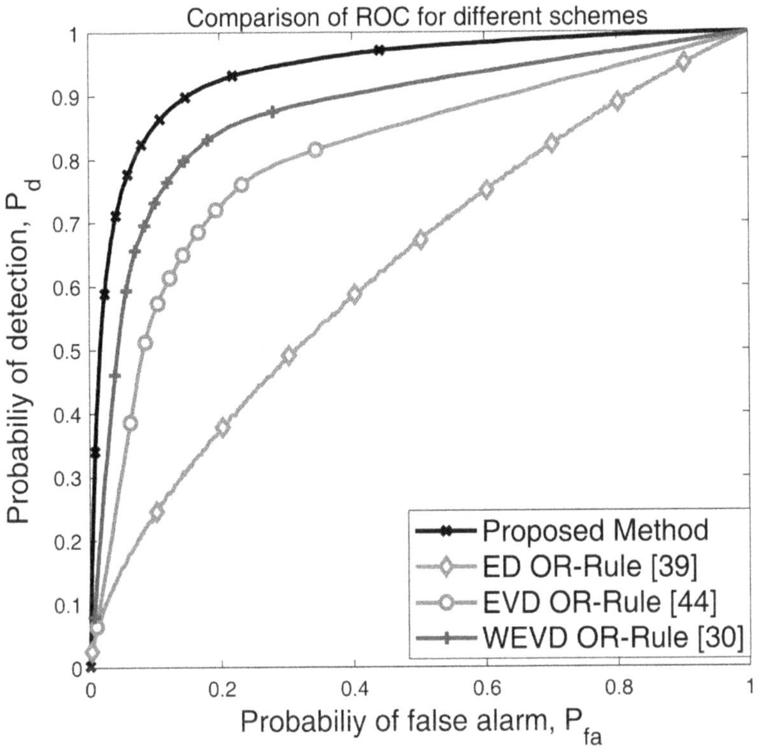

Figure 4.6. Comparison of ROC curves for different schemes with the proposed technique.

Table 4.2. Comparison of detection rate (P_d) obtained by the proposed scheme versus N, with a fixed false alarm of 0.1.

Different techniques	$N = 40$	$N = 50$	$N = 100$
ED with OR rule [39]	0.231 2	0.234 0	0.240 4
EVD with OR rule [44]	0.306 5	0.416 2	0.559 2
WEVD with OR rule [30]	0.438 4	0.586 4	0.729 2
Proposed scheme	0.625 8	0.716 1	0.851 2

presents the results for the probability of detection versus different numbers of samples for a fixed false alarm of value 0.1. From the table, it can be seen that for a varying number of samples, the results are varying. It is obvious that in the case of an increasing number of samples, the detection value will be increasing in nature. The result of table 4.2 demonstrates the superiority of the proposed technique. As we can see, the proposed technique provides a gain in the detection rate of 354%, 152%, and 116.73% in the case of ED [39], EVD [44], and WEVD [30] techniques.

4.6.2 Comparison of throughput performance

Figure 4.7 compares the throughput performance for different schemes with varying values of false alarm. From the figure, we can see that the proposed technique provides a better throughput performance compared to ED, EVD, and WEVD techniques. For example, in the case of $P_{fa} = 0.1$, the proposed technique achieves a throughput value of 3.1 as compared to 1.56, 2.6, and 2.8 of ED [39], EVD [44], and WEVD [30] techniques, respectively.

Table 4.3 presents the result for system throughput achieved in the case of a varying number of samples. The false alarm value was fixed at 0.1. We can see the

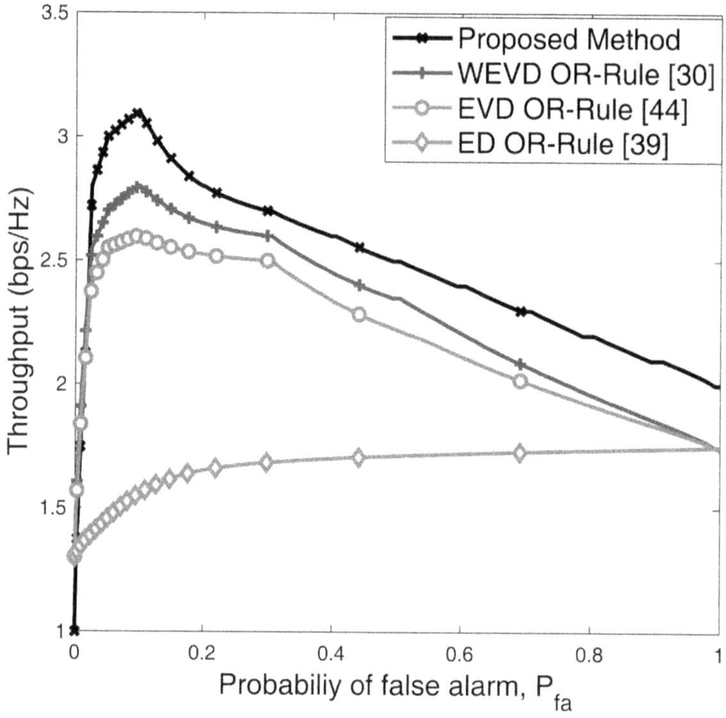

Figure 4.7. Comparison of throughput performance for different schemes with the proposed technique, for varying false alarm.

Table 4.3. Throughput values achieved for different techniques in the case of varying values of N with a fixed false alarm of 0.1.

Different techniques	$N = 40$	$N = 50$	$N = 100$
ED with OR rule [39]	1.23	1.34	1.56
EVD with OR rule [44]	2.30	2.41	2.6
WEVD with OR rule [30]	2.43	2.58	2.8
Proposed scheme	2.62	2.71	3.1

proposed technique outperforms the other competitive techniques by a suitable margin. For example, at $N = 100$, the proposed technique provides a system throughput of 3.1 bps Hz^{-1} as compared to 1.56, 2.6, and 2.8 bps Hz^{-1} of ED [39], EVD [44], and WEVD [30] techniques.

4.6.3 Comparison of energy consumption performance

Figure 4.8 presents the result for energy consumption with varying values of probability of false alarm P_{fa}, where the proposed scheme is compared with ED [39], EVD [44], and WEVD [30] techniques. In the simulation, the number of samples N is set to 40, 50, and 100, respectively. For all the schemes, energy consumption values were obtained corresponding to a false alarm rate of 0.1. It can be seen from the figure that energy consumption decreases with an increase in false alarm for all the schemes, but the proposed scheme provides the lowest value of energy consumption for a given P_{fa}. The proposed technique provides lower energy consumption and is more energy-efficient than schemes in [30] for the entire range of P_{fa}.

Table 4.4 presents the results for energy consumption in the case of a varying number of samples. The false alarm value was fixed at 0.1. We can see the proposed technique shows better results in terms of energy consumption as compared to the other competitive techniques by a suitable margin. For example, at $N = 100$, the proposed technique has an energy consumption value of 1.552 as

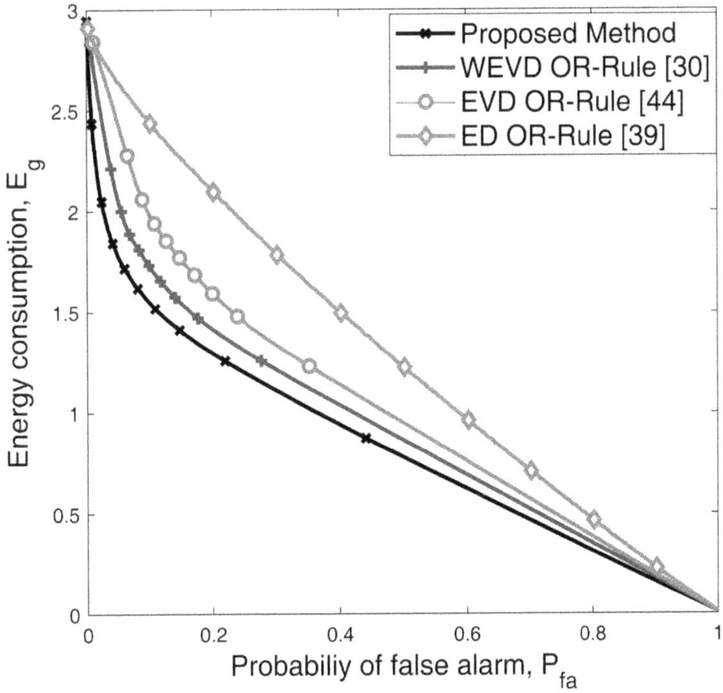

Figure 4.8. Comparison of energy consumption performance for different schemes with the proposed technique, for varying false alarm.

Table 4.4. Comparison of energy consumption for different techniques when the N value is varied with a fixed false alarm of 0.1.

Different techniques	$N = 40$	$N = 50$	$N = 100$
ED with OR rule [39]	2.4	2.44	2.45
EVD with OR rule [44]	2.2	2.1	1.987
WEVD with OR rule [30]	1.9	1.81	1.733
Proposed scheme	1.62	1.61	1.552

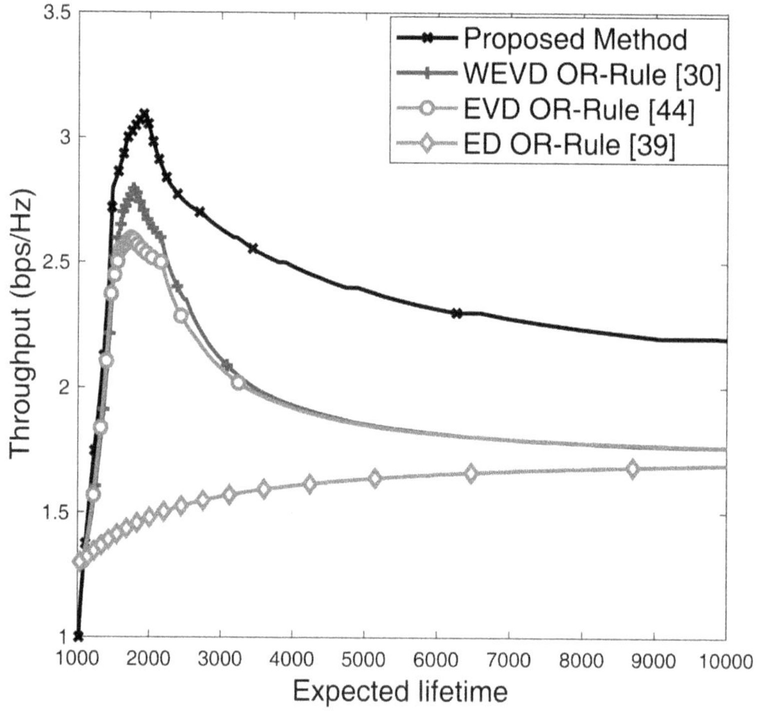

Figure 4.9. Throughput versus expected lifetime performance for different schemes as compared to the proposed technique with varying false alarm.

compared to 2.45, 1.987, 1.733 of ED [39], EVD [44], and WEVD [30] techniques. From these results, we can say that the proposed technique is appropriate for energy-constrained IoT devices.

4.6.4 Comparison of expected lifetime performance

In this section, the throughput performance of the proposed approach is compared with other schemes to highlight its relative improvement as a function of expected lifetime. Figure 4.9 shows this comparison with the number of samples value

$N = 100$. For all the schemes, throughput versus expected lifetime plots were obtained corresponding to a false alarm rate of 0.1. It can be seen from the figure that the proposed scheme provides better energy efficiency as compared to the other schemes. The proposed method achieved a throughput value of 3.1 bps Hz^{-1}, which is an improvement to the competitive approaches of ED [39], EVD [44], and WEVD [30].

Table 4.5 presents the results for throughput versus expected lifetime for different techniques with a varying number of samples. The false alarm value was fixed at 0.1. We can see that the proposed technique shows better results in terms of expected lifetime than the other competitive techniques by a suitable margin. For example, at $N = 100$, the proposed technique has a throughput value of 3.1 bps Hz^{-1} as compared to 1.5, 2.6, and 2.8 of ED [39], EVD [44], and WEVD [30] techniques. From these results, we can say that the proposed technique can be prolonged for a long duration, and it is also more applicable for IoT-based systems, where energy plays a key role.

Figure 4.10 presents the plot of global error probability for different threshold values. The standard form of global error probability at FC can be calculated by the following equation:

$$\mathcal{P}_e = p(H_0)G_{d,f} + (1 - G_{d,d})p(H_1) \tag{4.29}$$

It is clear from figure 4.10 that error probability decreases for an increase in the threshold value. After that, it reaches a minimum point, and then it starts to increase. Once the saturation points arrive, the variation becomes almost constant. This type of curve is a state-of-the-art standard bell curve. We can see that the proposed technique provides a minimum error probability of 0.1226, which is better as compared to the values 0.4061, 0.2385, and 0.173 of ED [39], EVD [44], and WEVD [30] techniques, respectively.

From all the figures and tables demonstrated above, it is appropriate to say that the proposed technique is superior compared to the other competitive techniques in the literature [30, 39, 44]. It provides an improvement in terms of sensing gain, enhanced throughput performance, lower energy consumption with better energy efficiency, better expected lifetime, and less error probability.

Table 4.5. Comparison of throughput versus expected lifetime for different techniques when the N value is varied with a fixed false alarm of 0.1.

Different techniques	$N = 40$	$N = 50$	$N = 100$
ED with OR rule [39]	1.4	1.4	1.5
EVD with OR rule [44]	2.2	2.4	2.6
WEVD with OR rule [30]	2.7	2.71	2.8
Proposed scheme	2.9	2.9	3.1

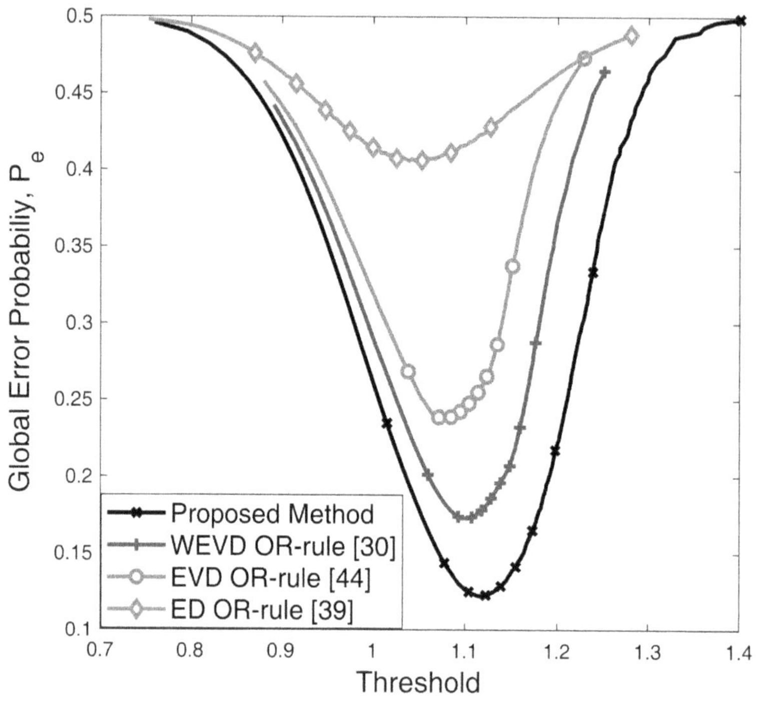

Figure 4.10. Global error probability versus threshold performance for different schemes as compared to the proposed technique.

4.7 Discussion

4.7.1 Major findings of research

A novel technique for the MIMO-based CR-IoT scenario is proposed. In the existing works in literature [23, 30, 44], the clustering used to be done in two dimensions. In contrast, multidimensional clustering is adopted in the proposed method. The classification in higher dimension appears to serve a reasonable advantage. The quantitative gain compared to other competitive techniques in terms of detection performance is provided in figures 4.6 to 4.10 and tables 4.2 to 4.5.

4.7.2 Limitations of research

One notable limitation of this research is regarding the dependence of the FCM algorithm on the fuzzifier value. The cluster shapes may not resemble a circle/sphere, and the clusters are not equidistant from the decision plane. Moreover, the associated uncertainty with the shape, size and density of clusters cannot be modeled by a single fuzzifier value. Since cluster shapes and separation depend on the PU signal type, its power, and SNR, hence choosing a suitable fuzzifier value is a challenging task. Fixing a single fuzzifier value for all channel conditions degrades detection performance.

4.8 Conclusion

In this chapter, a novel CSS technique for MIMO-based CR-IoT network is proposed. This approach adopted the eigenvalues of the signal as a feature vector. More conveniently, the feature vectors are clustered in 3D space to provide better results than the 1D and 2D space. Different simulation analyses are performed to demonstrate the superiority of the proposed technique. The proposed technique demonstrated better sensing gain, enhanced throughput performance, lower energy consumption with better energy efficiency, better expected lifetime, and less error probability. The results were compared with some recent and well-known eigenvalue-based techniques in the literature. Finally, based on the demonstrated results, we can conclude that the proposed technique will be an appropriate choice and apply to future IoT devices. For future work, we will apply a sensor selection approach to this scenario to pick the best performing CR-IoT user to improve the performance.

References

[1] Ali A, Feng L, Bashir A K, El-Sappagh S H A, Ahmed S H, Iqbal M and Raja G 2018 Quality of service provisioning for heterogeneous services in cognitive radio-enabled internet of things *IEEE Trans. on Network Science and Engineering* **7** 328–42

[2] Ali S S, Liu C, Liu J, Jin M and Kim J M 2016 On the eigenvalue based detection for multiantenna cognitive radio system *Mobile Information Systems* **2016** 3848734

[3] Arat F and Demirci S 2019 Analysis of spectrum aware routing algorithms in CR based IoT devices *2019 4th Int. Conf. on Computer Science and Engineering (UBMK) (Piscataway, NJ)* 751–6 IEEE

[4] Atzori L, Iera A and Morabito G 2010 The internet of things: a survey *Comput. Netw.* **54** 2787–805

[5] Awin F, Abdel-Raheem E and Tepe K 2018 Blind spectrum sensing approaches for interweaved cognitive radio system: a tutorial and short course *IEEE Communications Surveys and Tutorials* **21** 238–59

[6] Aysal T C, Kandeepan S and Piesiewicz R 2009 Cooperative spectrum sensing with noisy hard decision transmissions *2009 IEEE Int. Conf. on Communications (Piscataway, NJ)* pp 1–5 IEEE

[7] Bana A-S, Carvalho E De, Soret B, Abrão T, Marinello Jé C, Larsson E G and Popovski P 2019 Massive MIMO for internet of things (IoT) connectivity *Physical Communication* **37** 100859

[8] Chakravarthy V D, Wu Z, Shaw A, Temple M A, Kannan R and Garber F 2007 A general overlay/underlay analytic expression representing cognitive radio waveform *2007 Int. Waveform Diversity and Design Conf.* (Piscataway, NJ: IEEE) pp 69–73

[9] Dai B, Xu W and Zhao C 2011 Multiuser beamforming optimization via maximizing modified SLNR with quantized CSI feedback *2011 7th Int. Conf. on Wireless Communications, Networking and Mobile Computing (Piscataway, NJ)* pp 1–5 IEEE

[10] Deng Z, Li Q, Zhang Q, Yang L and Qin J 2019 Beamforming design for physical layer security in a two-way cognitive radio iot network with swipt *IEEE Internet of Things J.* **6** 10786–98

[11] Gahane L, Sharma P K, Varshney N, Tsiftsis T A and Kumar P 2017 An improved energy detector for mobile cognitive users over generalized fading channels *IEEE Trans. Commun.* **66** 534–45

[12] Giri M K and Majumder S 2020 Extreme learning machine based cooperative spectrum sensing in cognitive radio networks *2020 7th Int. Conf. on Signal Processing and Integrated Networks (SPIN) (IEEE)* pp 636–41 Piscataway, NJ

[13] Giri M K and Majumder S 2021 Cooperative spectrum sensing using extreme learning machines for cognitive radio networks *IETE Tech. Rev.* **39** 698–712

[14] Giri M K and Majumder S 2021 Eigenvalue-based cooperative spectrum sensing using kernel fuzzy c-means clustering *Digit. Signal Process.* **111** 102996

[15] Gupta M, Verma G and Dubey R K 2016 Cooperative spectrum sensing for cognitive radio based on adaptive threshold *2016 Second Int. Conf. on Computational Intelligence and Communication Technology (CICT) (Piscataway, NJ)* pp 444–8 IEEE

[16] Hefnawi M 2016 Large-scale multi-cluster mimo approach for cognitive radio sensor networks *IEEE Sens. J.* **16** 4418–24

[17] Homayounzadeh A and Mahdavi M 2015 Performance analysis of cooperative cognitive radio networks with imperfect sensing *2015 Int. Conf. on Communications, Signal Processing, and their Applications (ICCSPA'15) (Piscataway, NJ)* pp 1–6 IEEE

[18] Islam T, Khan M S and Koo I 2015 Evidence theory-based cooperative spectrum sensing in multi antenna cognitive radio system *2015 2nd Int. Conf. on Electrical Information and Communication Technologies (EICT) (Piscataway, NJ)* pp 278–83 IEEE

[19] Jiang D, Wang W, Shi L and Song H 2018 A compressive sensing-based approach to end-to-end network traffic reconstruction *IEEE Trans. Netw. Sci. Eng.* **7** 507–19

[20] Jiang D, Wang Y, Han Y and Lv H 2017 Maximum connectivity-based channel allocation algorithm in cognitive wireless networks for medical applications *Neurocomputing* **220** 41–51

[21] Khan A A, Rehmani M H and Rachedi A 2016 When cognitive radio meets the internet of things? *2016 Int. Wireless Communications and Mobile Computing Conf. (IWCMC) (Piscataway, NJ)* pp 469–74 IEEE

[22] Khan A A, Rehmani M H and Rachedi A 2017 Cognitive-radio-based internet of things: Applications, architectures, spectrum related functionalities, and future research directions *IEEE Wirel. Commun.* **24** 17–25

[23] Kortun A, Ratnarajah T, Sellathurai M, Liang Y-Chang and Zeng Y 2012 Throughput analysis using eigenvalue based spectrum sensing under noise uncertainty *2012 8th Int. Wireless Communications and Mobile Computing Conf. (IWCMC) (Piscataway, NJ)* pp 395–400 IEEE

[24] Arun Kumar and NandhaKumar P 2019 Ofdm system with cyclostationary feature detection spectrum sensing *ICT Express* **5** 21–5

[25] Kyperountas S, Correal N, Shi Q and Ye Z 2007 Performance analysis of cooperative spectrum sensing in Suzuki fading channels *2007 2nd Int. Conf. on Cognitive Radio Oriented Wireless Networks and Communications (Piscataway, NJ)* pp 428–32 IEEE

[26] Liao Y, Wang T, Song L and Jiao B 2014 Cooperative spectrum sensing for full-duplex cognitive radio networks *2014 IEEE Int. Conf. on Communication Systems (Piscataway, NJ)* pp 56–60 IEEE

[27] Liu C, Li H, Wang J and Jin M 2016 Optimal eigenvalue weighting detection for multi-antenna cognitive radio networks *IEEE Trans. on Wirel. Commun.* **2083–2096**

[28] Saikat Majumder A 2021 Gaussian mixture model method for eigenvalue-based spectrum sensing with uncalibrated multiple antennas *Signal Process.* **192** 108404

[29] Manna S, Saha S, Chatterjee A and De C K 2017 *Spectrum sensing with cooperation of multi antenna based adaptive decode-and-forward relay 2017 8th Int. Conf. on Computing, Communication and Networking Technologies (ICCCNT)* (Piscataway, NJ: IEEE) pp 1–6

[30] Miah M Sipon, Schukat M and Barrett E 2020 Sensing and throughput analysis of a mu-MIMO based cognitive radio scheme for the internet of things *Comput. Commun.*

[31] Mu J, Jing X, Huang H and Gao N 2017 Subspace-based method for spectrum sensing with multiple users over fading channel *IEEE Commun. Lett.* **22** 848–51

[32] Nguyen V-D and Shin O-S 2017 Cooperative prediction-and-sensing-based spectrum sharing in cognitive radio networks *IEEE Trans. Cogn. Commun. Netw.* **4** 108–20

[33] Otermat D T, Kostanic I and Otero C E 2016 Analysis of the FM radio spectrum for secondary licensing of low-power short-range cognitive internet of things devices *IEEE Access* **4** 6681–91

[34] Perera C, Zaslavsky A, Christen P and Georgakopoulos D 2013 Context aware computing for the internet of things: a survey *IEEE Commun. Surveys .Tutor.* **16** 414–54

[35] Rahman M A, Lee Y-D and Koo I 2016 An efficient transmission mode selection based on reinforcement learning for cooperative cognitive radio networks *Human-Centric Comput. Inform. Sci.* **6** 2

[36] Srinu S and Sabat S L 2013 Cooperative wideband sensing based on cyclostationary features with multiple malicious user elimination *EU-Int. J. Electron. Commun.* **67** 702–7

[37] Sun M, Zhao C, Yan S and Li B 2016 A novel spectrum sensing for cognitive radio networks with noise uncertainty *IEEE Trans. Veh. Technol.* **66** 4424–44

[38] Rahul T and Sahai A 2008 Snr walls for signal detection *IEEE Journal of selected topics in Signal Processing* **2** 4–17

[39] Thilina K M, Choi K W, Saquib N and Hossain E 2013 Machine learning techniques for cooperative spectrum sensing in cognitive radio networks *IEEE J. Sel. Areas Commun.* **31** 2209–21

[40] Tian R, Wang Z and Tan X 2018 A new leakage-based precoding scheme in IoT oriented cognitive MIMO-OFDM systems *IEEE Access* **6** 41023–33

[41] Upadhyay S and Deshmukh S 2015 Blind parameter estimation based matched filter detection for cognitive radio networks *2015 Int. Conf. on Communications and Signal Processing (ICCSP) (Piscataway, NJ)* 0904–8 IEEE

[42] Vu V-H and Koo I 2017 Throughput maximization for cognitive radio users with energy constraints in an underlay paradigm *J. Inform. Comm. Converg. Eng.* **15** 79–84

[43] Xing X, Jing T, Cheng W, Huo Y and Cheng X 2013 Spectrum prediction in cognitive radio networks *IEEE Wireless Communications* **20** 90–6

[44] Yonghong Zeng and Liang Y-C 2009 Eigenvalue-based spectrum sensing algorithms for cognitive radio *IEEE Trans. Commun.* **57** 1784–93

[45] Zhang R, Lim T J, Liang Y-C and Zeng Y 2010 Multi-antenna based spectrum sensing for cognitive radios: a GLRT approach *IEEE Trans. Commun.* **58** 84–8

[46] Zhu J, Song Y, Jiang D and Song H 2016 Multi-armed bandit channel access scheme with cognitive radio technology in wireless sensor networks for the internet of things *IEEE Access* **4** 4609–17

[47] Zhu J, Song Y, Jiang D and Song H 2017 A new deep-q-learning-based transmission scheduling mechanism for the cognitive internet of things *IEEE Internet of Things J.* **5** 2375–85

[48] Zikria Y B, Ishmanov F, Afzal M K, Kim S W, Nam S Y and Yu H 2018 Opportunistic channel selection MAC protocol for cognitive radio ad hoc sensor networks in the internet of things *Sust. Comput.: Inform. Syst.* **18** 112–20

Chapter 5

Modeling the evolution of complex networks arising in applications

Felix Sadyrbaev

The general system of ordinary differential equations is considered. This system arises in the theory of gene networks, neuronal and telecommunication networks. The system has a large number of parameters that affect the behavior of solutions. The main group of parameters, describing the interaction of network elements, is written in the so-called regulatory matrix. The evolution of the system (and the described network as well) depends on the attracting sets in the phase space. The chapter contains recently obtained new results on the structure of the phase space, behavior of solutions, attractors of the system. The problems requiring further research, are described. Examples and visualizations are provided, where possible.

5.1 Introduction

In this chapter we consider the problem, that relates to mathematics, biology, neuronal networks, telecommunication networks, and similar topics. All these fields are extremely important, but their combination forms a rapidly developing branch of modern applied science. These scientific directions are united by a universal approach of mathematical modeling.

Following the historical sequence, first the system of ordinary differential equations

$$\begin{cases} \dfrac{dx_1}{dt} = f(-\mu_1(w_{11}x_1 + w_{12}x_2 - \theta_1)) - x_1, \\ \dfrac{dx_2}{dt} = f(-\mu_2(w_{21}x_1 + w_{22}x_2 - \theta_2)) - x_2 \end{cases} \tag{5.1}$$

had appeared in the work [8]. It is known as a Wilson–Cowan system [18], and it models the interaction between subpopulations of excitatory and inhibitory neurons.

doi:10.1088/978-0-7503-4801-0ch5

The function f is a sigmoidal function. It suits best to mathematically describe experimental data obtained as a result of experiments. The properties of a sigmoidal function are: monotonicity, the value range between zero and unity, a single inflection point. There are many sigmoidal functions. The review of those sigmoidal functions, which are often used in models, deserves a separate study. In this chapter we use the logistic function $f(z) = \frac{1}{1+\exp(-\mu z)}$, which is convenient for the analysis.

Studying genetic regulatory networks (GRN in short) is in the center of the whole biomathematics. Huge banks of genetic information were established. Processing this amount of experimental data is a challenging task. The role of suitable mathematical models is increasing and cannot be overestimated.

Ordinary differential equations (ODEs) of the type (5.1) relate also to the theory of telecommunication networks. In articles [13, 14] the problem of managing traffic on a wavelength-routed optical network is studied. For this, the virtual network topology (VNT) should be designed. This task can be accomplished by establishing a set of lightpaths between nodes. Since changes in traffic flows can be rapid and unpredictable, there is a need for control methods, that allow reacting rapidly, reconfiguring VNT accordingly. The authors in [13, 14] have proposed to adopt a suitable biological algorithm, namely, the attractor selection. The mathematical model for this is very similar to what we are studying. The system of differential equations, at least, has the same structure.

In all these interpretations the decisive role is played by attractors of the system.

There are different approaches to the study of the networks models, including graph theory, Bayesian networks, Boolean algebras. The dynamics of the networks and their evolution are better described by systems of ODEs, containing multiple parameters and the regulatory matrices, where the interrelation between nodes of a network is encrypted. The related systems of ODEs can be large, nonlinear, and contain many parameters. The theoretical and numerical analysis of such systems is hard. Attractors in such systems are hard to detect, except for the standard cases of stable equilibria. Our approach is based on the construction of attractors for higher-dimensional systems, using previously obtained information of low-dimensional cases. For this, we consider the hierarchy of attractors, where attractors in higher-dimensional systems are constructed by a combination of attractors observed or found in low-dimensional ones. For example, two stable periodic solutions in different two-dimensional systems produce an attractor for a four-dimensional system. This new attractor can be perturbed and new more complicated attracting sets, exhibiting non-regular behavior, can emerge.

In all constructions and suggestions the computational means are used extensively. Wolfram Mathematica provides enough tools for the investigation, including numerical solving ODEs, visualization of solutions, phase planes and spaces, the impact of the parameters change, etc.

The next section contains information about genetic networks. In section 5.3 the hierarchy of attractors is explained, general mathematical apparatus is introduced and detailed information on the two-dimensional systems is provided. In section 5.4 three-dimensional systems are considered. Section 5.5 contains examples of four-dimensional and six-dimensional systems. The hierarchy approach is shown in action. The elements of reverse engineering in the theory of genetic networks are considered in section 5.6. The construction of a network with a single equilibrium of the desired type is analyzed. Section 5.7 contains a list of topical issues to study. The 'Conclusion' section and the list of references complete the chapter.

5.2 GRN networks

GRN networks are modeled by a number of mathematical tools, among them, Boolean algebras, graph theory, dynamical systems.

Dynamical systems operate with the vector $X(t)$, which usually is multidimensional. Each component of the vector X is understood as a player in a game, where all players can influence each other, and the combined result of this interaction is the network evolution in time. Each x_i can be considered as the protein extraction, which is a message to other genomic network elements. Other factors also can stand behind x_i, for instance, *stress*, *growth signals* [6], etc. The vector $X(t)$ is treated as the system state at a time moment t. The phase space is, therefore, the main object of investigation. Attractors are signs that indicate the future states of the network. Their behavior, location, and properties depend on the parameters of the system and are the objectives of this study.

5.3 Hierarchy of systems

Even low-dimensional systems of ODE, that are met in GRN theory, are not studied fully. The reason is two-fold. First, qualitative research is not easy due to nonlinearity and multiple parameters in a system. Even the two-dimensional (2D for brevity) system is dependent on eight parameters. The number of parameters changes drastically with the increase of dimensionality. In the majority of papers devoted to the qualitative study of GRN systems, simplifying assumptions are usually made. For instance, piece-wise or nearly peace-wise nonlinearities were considered [11, 16].

We wish to focus on the following issues. First, we consider the 2D systems. The main types of interrelations between elements are recalled. The influence of parameters of the system on properties of solutions, possible attracting sets is analyzed. The treatment of 3D systems is more complicated. We focus on the existence of attracting periodic trajectories. Visualizations are provided for more cases. Systems of order four are considered, using decomposition into systems of smaller dimensions. The possibility of studying systems of higher dimensions is discussed. Special attention is paid to the issue of designing systems with specified properties and controlling them.

5.3.1 General

The n-dimensional system of ODE, that is used by many authors to model genetic networks, is of the form

$$\begin{cases} x_1' = \dfrac{1}{1 + e^{-\mu_1(w_{11}x_1 + \cdots + w_{1n}x_n - \theta_1)}} - x_1, \\ x_2' = \dfrac{1}{1 + e^{-\mu_2(w_{21}x_1 + \cdots + w_{2n}x_n - \theta_2)}} - x_2, \\ \cdots \\ x_n' = \dfrac{1}{1 + e^{-\mu_n(w_{n1}x_1 + \cdots + w_{nn}x_n - \theta_n)}} - x_n. \end{cases} \tag{5.2}$$

Recall that $f(z) = \frac{1}{1 + \exp(-\mu z)}$ is a sigmoidal function with the value range (0, 1). The following assertion immediately follows. Systems of the form (5.2) will be referred to as *GRN-type systems.*

Proposition. The n-dimensional unit cube $Qn = \{X \in R^n: 0 < X < 1\}$ is the invariant set of the system (5.2). The vector field $\{(x_1', \dots, x_n')\}$ is directed inward on the border of Qn.

The *nullclines* of the system (5.2) are defined by the equations of the system

$$\begin{cases} x_1 = \dfrac{1}{1 + e^{-\mu_1(w_{11}x_1 + \cdots + w_{1n}x_n - \theta_1)}}, \\ x_2 = \dfrac{1}{1 + e^{-\mu_2(w_{21}x_1 + \cdots + w_{2n}x_n - \theta_2)}}, \\ \cdots \\ x_n = \dfrac{1}{1 + e^{-\mu_n(w_{n1}x_1 + \cdots + w_{nn}x_n - \theta_n)}}. \end{cases} \tag{5.3}$$

Knowledge of isoclines significantly affects the understanding of the properties of the vector field and facilitates the study of the behavior of solutions. The critical points (equilibria) of the system (5.2) are cross-points of nullclines. They (equilibria) can be found solving the system (5.3).

There exists at least one critical point. This follows immediately for 2D systems, since the first nullcline, defined by $x_1 = \frac{1}{1 + e^{-\mu_1(w_{11}x_1 + \cdots + w_{1n}x_n - \theta_1)}}$, is located in the vertical stripe $0 \leqslant x_1 \leqslant 1$ and stretches from $-\infty$ to the $+\infty$. The second nullcline, $x_2 = f(-\mu_2(w_{21}x_1 + w_{22}x_2 - \theta_2))$, behaves similarly, but in a horizontal stripe. The solvability of the system (5.3) can be proved, using the arguments from the degree theory (i.e., rotation of vector fields).

The type of a critical point can be detected by standard process of linearization around the critical point $(x_1^*, \dots, x_n^*)$

$$\begin{cases} u_1' = -u_1 + \mu_1 w_{11} g_1 u_1 + \mu_1 w_{12} g_1 u_2 + \cdots + \mu_1 w_{1n} g_1 u_n, \\ u_2' = -u_2 + \mu_2 w_{21} g_2 u_1 + \mu_2 w_{22} g_2 u_2 + \cdots + \mu_2 w_{2n} g_2 u_n, \\ \cdots \\ u_n' = -u_n + \mu_n w_{n1} g_n u_1 + \mu_n w_{n2} g_n u_2 + \cdots + \mu_n w_{nn} g_n u_n, \end{cases} \tag{5.4}$$

and finding the eigenvalues of the linearized system. Here

$$g_1 = \frac{e^{-\mu_1\left(w_{11}x_1^* + w_{12}x_2^* + \cdots + w_{1n}x_n^* - \theta_1\right)}}{\left[1 + e^{-\mu_1\left(w_{11}x_1^* + w_{12}x_2^* + \cdots + w_{1n}x_n^* - \theta_1\right)}\right]^2}, \tag{5.5}$$

$$g_2 = \frac{e^{-\mu_2\left(w_{21}x_1^* + w_{22}x_2^* + \cdots + w_{2n}x_n^* - \theta_2\right)}}{\left[1 + e^{-\mu_2\left(w_{21}x_1^* + w_{22}x_2^* + \cdots + w_{2n}x_n^* - \theta_2\right)}\right]^2}, \tag{5.6}$$

$$\cdots$$

$$g_n = \frac{e^{-\mu_n\left(w_{n1}x_1^* + w_{n2}x_2^* + \cdots + w_{nn}x_n^* - \theta_n\right)}}{\left[1 + e^{-\mu_n\left(w_{n1}x_1^* + w_{n2}x_2^* + \cdots + w_{nn}x_n^* - \theta_n\right)}\right]^2}. \tag{5.7}$$

The matrix

$$W = \begin{pmatrix} w_{11}w_{12}\cdots w_{1n} \\ w_{21}w_{22}\cdots w_{2n} \\ \cdots \\ w_{n1}w_{n2}\cdots w_{nn} \end{pmatrix}. \tag{5.8}$$

is called the *regulatory matrix*. It plays a significant role in GRN theory, since it determines the type of relationship in the simulated network.

5.3.2 2D systems

These systems first appeared in the paper by Cowan–Vilson [8], where the first variable x_1 meant the population of activatory neurons, and the second one was for inhibitory population. The vector field was studied and a standard analysis of critical points was carried out. For GRN this system can be interpreted as a model of interaction of two elements in a network. The character of interaction is described by the 2 ×2 regulatory matrix

$$W = \begin{pmatrix} w_{11} & w_{12} \\ w_{21} & w_{12} \end{pmatrix}. \tag{5.9}$$

In the *full activation* model all elements are non-negative, but not all zeros. For a simplified version

$$\begin{cases} x_1' &= \dfrac{1}{1 + \exp(-\mu(x_2 - \theta)} - x_1, \\ x_2' &= \dfrac{1}{1 + \exp(-\mu(x_1 - \theta)} - x_2, \end{cases} \tag{5.10}$$

where μ and θ are equal in both equations, the following result was obtained.

Theorem 1. [1] There exists an open region Ω in the (μ, θ)-plane such that:

1. if $(\mu, \theta) \notin \Omega$ then there exists an attractor in the form of a single stable node;
2. if $(\mu, \theta) \in \Omega$ then there exists an attractor in the form of a pair of two stable nodes;

3. if $(\mu, \theta) \in \partial\Omega$ then there exists an attractor in the form of two critical points, of which the first is a stable node, but the second one is a degenerate stable node;

The sketch of the region Ω is depicted in figure 5.1. Later the similar theorem [3] was proved for the n-dimensional system of the form

$$\begin{cases} x_1' = \dfrac{1}{1 + e^{-\mu(x_2+\cdots+x_n-\theta)}}, \\ x_2' = \dfrac{1}{1 + e^{-\mu(x_1+x_3+\cdots+x_n-\theta)}}, \\ \ldots \\ x_n' = \dfrac{1}{1 + e^{-\mu(x_1+x_2+\cdots+x_{n-1}-\theta)}}, \end{cases} \tag{5.11}$$

A less restrictive result was obtained by Brokan and Sadyrbaev in [4]. The main assumption in this result is that the sum of elements in any row of the regulatory matrix W is equal to the same number $a > 0$. What's more, the result is suitable for any sigmoidal function.

5.3.2.1 Nullclines

Especially effective was the method of nullclines. The nullclines for the system are given by the system

$$\begin{cases} x_1 = \dfrac{1}{1 + \exp(-\mu(x_2 - \theta)}, \\ x_2 = \dfrac{1}{1 + \exp(-\mu(x_1 - \theta)}. \end{cases} \tag{5.12}$$

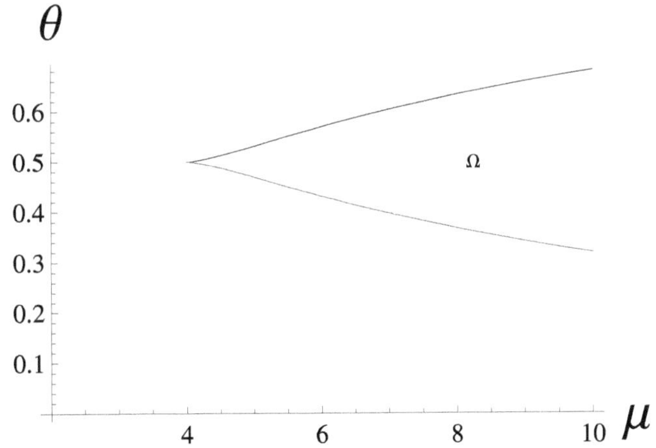

Figure 5.1. Ω-region.

The typical location of nullclines is depicted in figure 5.2. The nullclines intersect at least once. The number of cross-points can vary from one to nine. For the case of nine points, the location of nullclines is depicted in figure 5.3. The matrix W then has to contain non-zero elements on the main diagonal. This issue was considered in the paper [15]. In the five pictures below, the parameters $\mu_i = 6$, $i = 1, 2$.

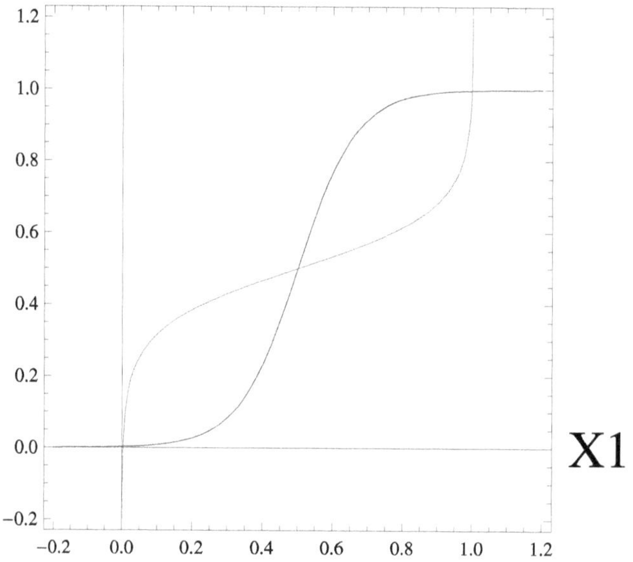

Figure 5.2. Nullclines for 2D equation, $w_{11} = w_{22} = 0$, $w_{12} = w_{21} = 2$, $\theta_1 = \theta_2 = 1$.

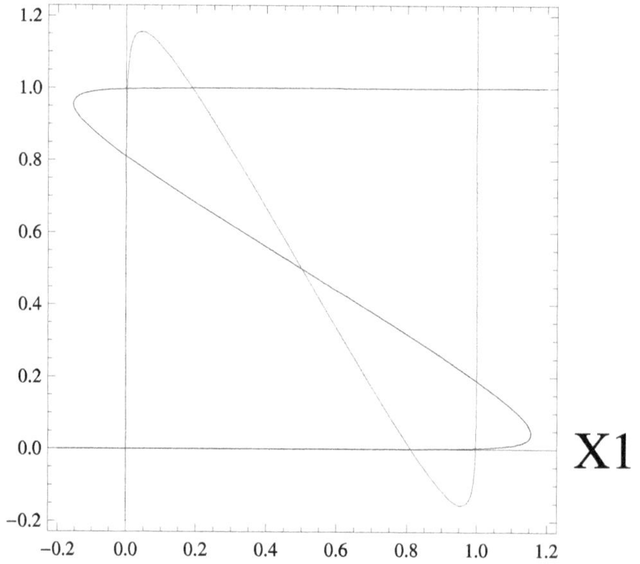

Figure 5.3. Nullclines for 2D equation, $w_{11} = w_{22} = 4$, $w_{12} = w_{21} = 2$, $\theta_1 = \theta_2 = 3$.

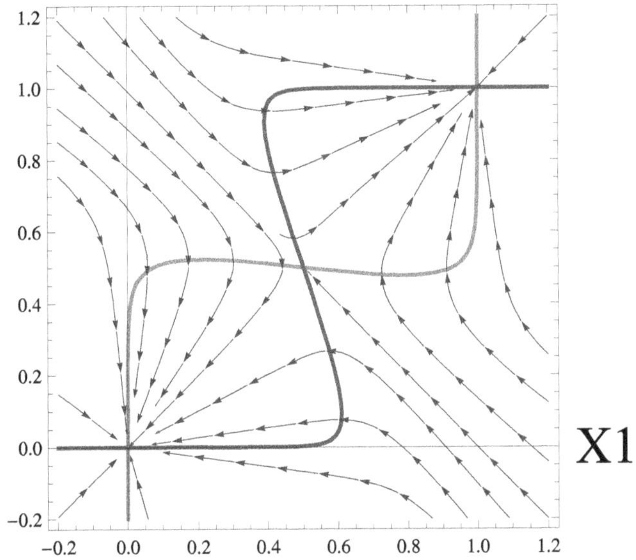

Figure 5.4. Example of activation, $w_{11} = 1$, $w_{22} = 2$, $w_{12} = 3$, $w_{21} = 4$, $\theta_1 = 2$, $\theta_2 = 3$.

Three main types of interaction are met in 2D systems, namely, the activation, the inhibition, and the mixed case.

They are characterized by typical regulatory matrices: $W1 = \{(0, 1), (1, 0)\}$, $W2 = \{(0, -1), (-1, 0)\}$, $W3 = \{(1, -1), (1, 1)\}$.

Inhibition is associated with a special location of nullclines. The attractors are sets of critical points, where their number can vary from one to nine (figure 5.3). The theorem, similar to theorem 1, is valid [9]. The vector field for inhibition is depicted in figure 5.5.

The regulatory matrix W3 is associated with the rotational vector field in the phase plane. It is depicted in figure 5.6. Consequently, the periodic solution of attractive type emerges, through the Andronov–Hopf bifurcation.

5.4 3D systems

The three-dimensional system is of the form

$$\begin{cases} x_1' = \dfrac{1}{1 + e^{-\mu_1(w_{11}x_1 + w_{12}x_2 + w_{13}x_3 - \theta_1)}} - x_1, \\ x_2' = \dfrac{1}{1 + e^{-\mu_2(w_{21}x_1 + w_{22}x_2 + w_{23}x_3 - \theta_2)}} - x_2, \\ x_3' = \dfrac{1}{1 + e^{-\mu_3(w_{31}x + w_{32}x_2 + w_{33}x_3 - \theta_3)}} - x_3. \end{cases} \tag{5.13}$$

Besides the results, following from the above n-dimensional versions, we provide the following observations.

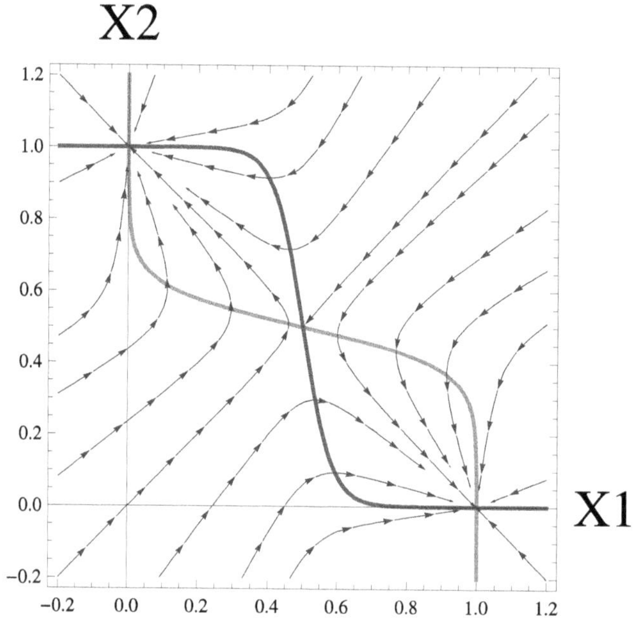

Figure 5.5. Example of inhibition, $w_{11} = w_{22} = 0$, $w_{12} = 3$, $w_{21} = 4$, $\theta_1 = -1.5$, $\theta_2 = -2$.

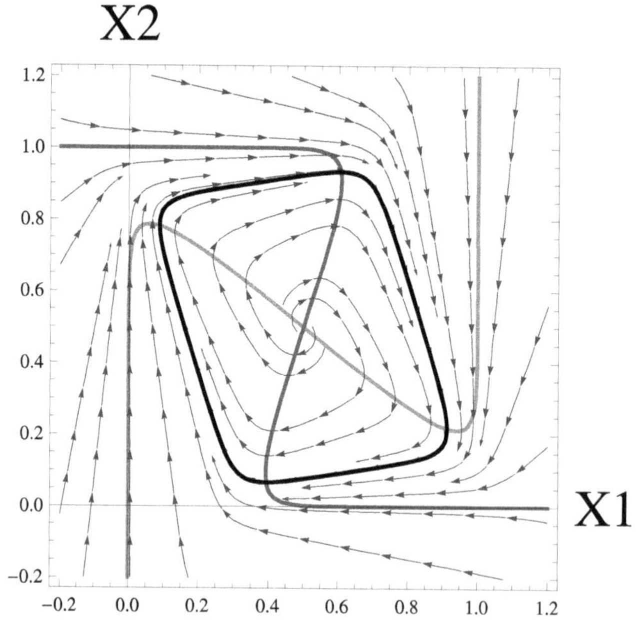

Figure 5.6. Rotational vector field, $w_{11} = 3$, $w_{22} = 2$, $w_{12} = 3$, $w_{21} = -4$, $\theta_1 = 3$, $\theta_2 = -1$, the limit cycle emerges.

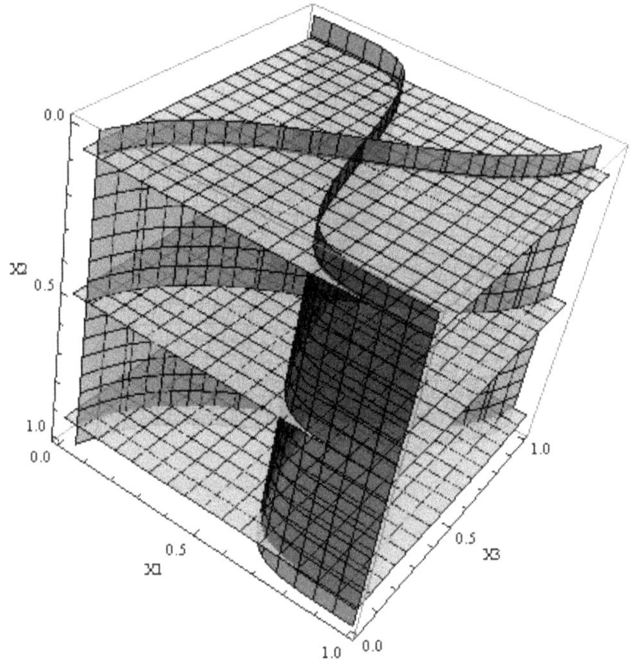

Figure 5.7. Nullclines for the system (5.13); $W = \{0,0,1), (0,1,0), (-3,0,1)\}$, $\theta_1 = \theta_2 = 0.5$, $\theta_3 = -1.0$.

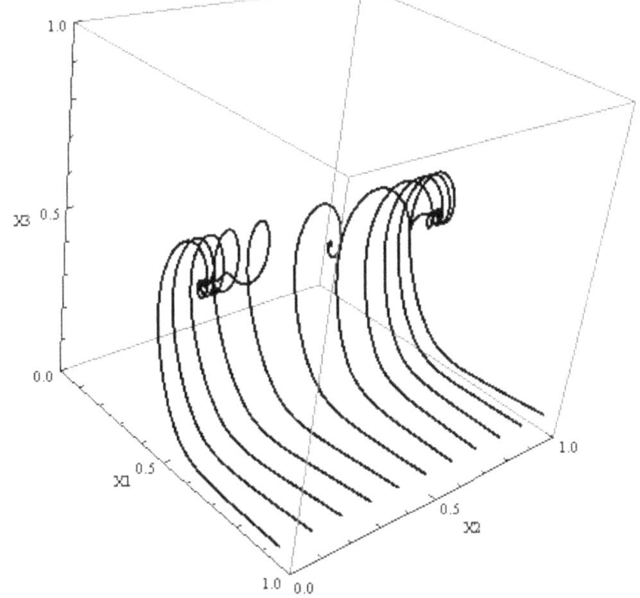

Figure 5.8. Solutions of the same system going to two stable equilibria at (0.07,0.5,0.5), (0.93,0.5,0.5). The middle solution stays at the plane X2 = 0.5.

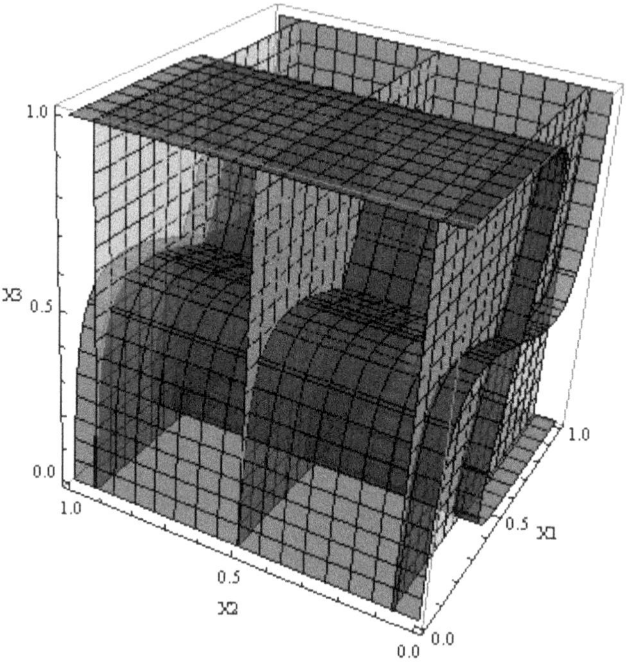

Figure 5.9. Nullclines for the system (5.13), where $W = \{(1,0,1), (0,1,0), (-3,0,2)\}$, $\theta_1 = 1$, $\theta_2 = 0.5$, $\theta_3 = -0.5$.

The nullclines method works well for 3D systems. As an evidence, consider the example of a 3D system, which has several critical points with some of them being attractive. Consider the nullclines, depicted in figure 5.7. Evidently, there are exactly three critical points. Calculations show that two side points are fully attractive (their characteristic numbers have negative real parts).They are depicted together with some trajectories in figure 5.8.

Examples of an attractive periodic trajectory can be found in [5, 19]. We provide an example of three periodic solutions, of which two become attractors under small perturbations. Consider the system (5.13) with the nullclines, depicted in figure 5.9. The three critical points are unstable 3D focuses. Three periodic solutions emerge around these equilibria. A small perturbation of this system leads to the destruction of the middle periodic solution. The two other transform to periodic attractors (figure 5.10). A similar example was published in [2]. The results for the case of large μ, where the middle segment of the graph of sigmoidal functions is 'vertical', were obtained in [11].

There are indications of the existence of attractors of chaotic nature [10, 17]. The solutions of these systems have an irregular form, but tend to a 3D geometrical object (attractor).

5.5 High-dimensional systems

Systems of order greater than three, can be studied also. We will show some 4D examples.

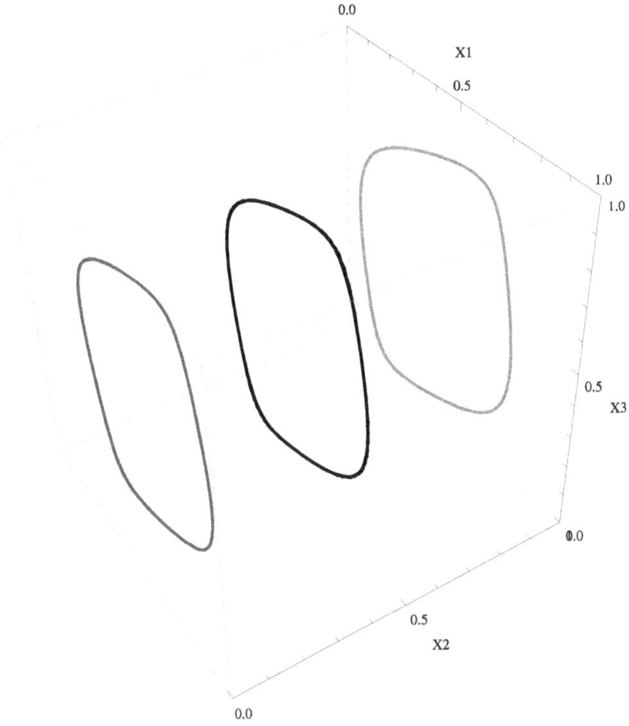

Figure 5.10. Three periodic solutions.

5.5.1 4D system

Consider the 4D system, which is a union of two 2D systems, each of which has a periodic solution. The attractor exists in a 4D phase space, but it can be of different appearance due to the relation between periods. Let the regulatory matrix be

$$W = \begin{pmatrix} 1 & 1 & 0 & 0 \\ -3 & 2 & 0 & 0 \\ 0 & 0 & 1 & 1 \\ 0 & 0 & -3 & 2 \end{pmatrix}. \tag{5.14}$$

Example with two equal periods. Different 2D projections of a periodic attractor with attracted solutions are depicted in figures 5.11, 5.12, 5.13 and 5.14.

Consider an example, where two uncoupled systems have periodic solutions of different periods. Let the regulatory matrix be

$$W = \begin{pmatrix} 1 & 1 & 0 & 0 \\ -3 & 2 & 0 & 0 \\ 0 & 0 & 1 & 2 \\ 0 & 0 & -2 & 1 \end{pmatrix}. \tag{5.15}$$

Projections on 2D subspaces are depicted in figures 5.15, 5.16, 5.17. A solution tends to the periodic attractor. This is illustrated by figure 5.18, where the four components $x_i(t)$ of a solution become periodic.

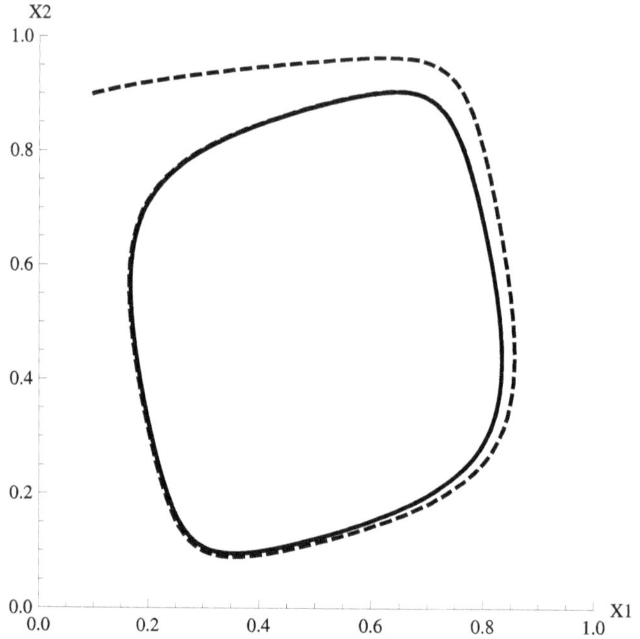

Figure 5.11. Periodic trajectory (solid) and a solution (dashed), projection to (X1, X2).

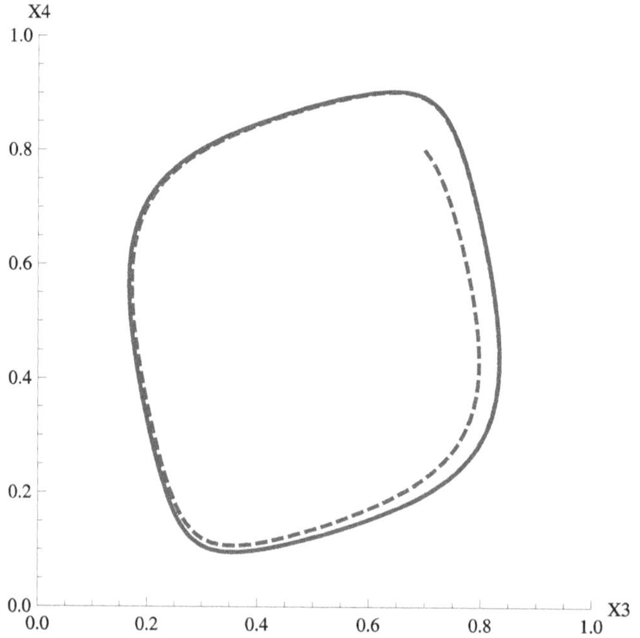

Figure 5.12. Periodic trajectory (solid) and a solution (dashed), projection to (X3, X4).

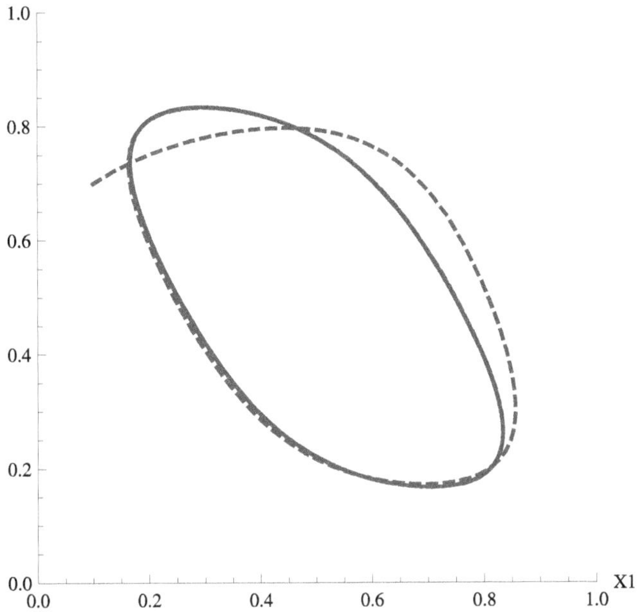

Figure 5.13. Periodic trajectory (solid) and a solution (dashed), projection to (X1, X3).

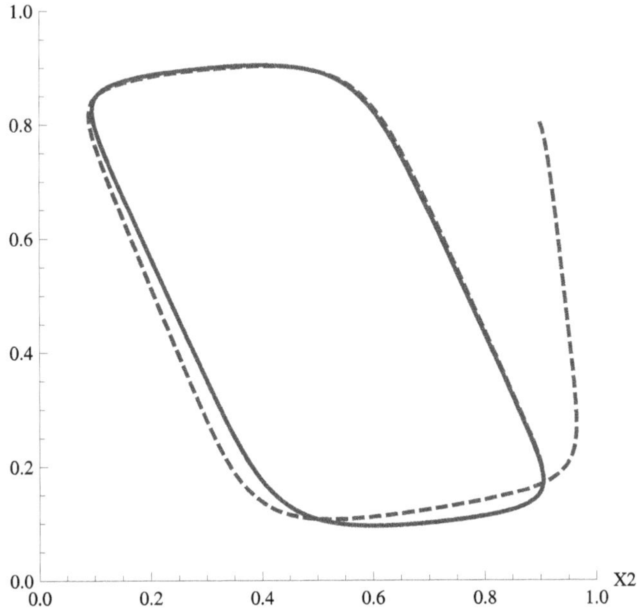

Figure 5.14. Periodic trajectory (solid) and a solution (dashed), projection to (X2, X4).

5.5.2 Examples of 6D systems

Consider the system, that is combined from three 2D systems. Each of these 2D systems has an attractive periodic solution. Let the regulatory matrix be

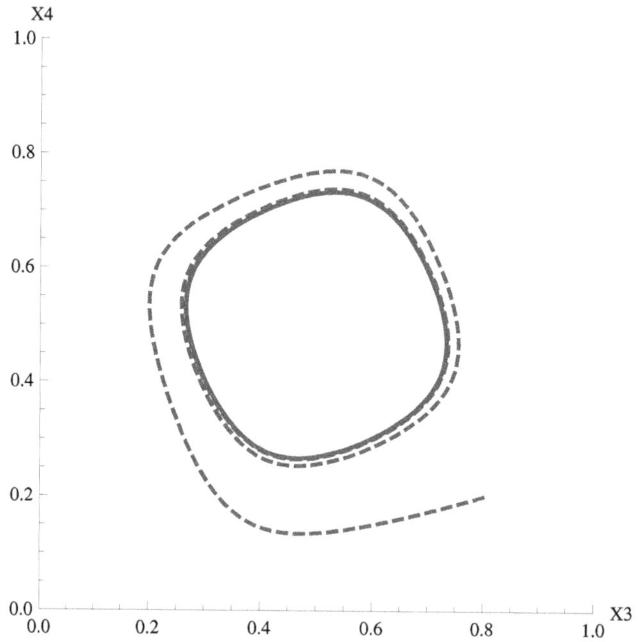

Figure 5.15. 4D system of the form (5.2) with the matrix (5.15). Projection of the periodic attractor onto (X3, X4)-plane.

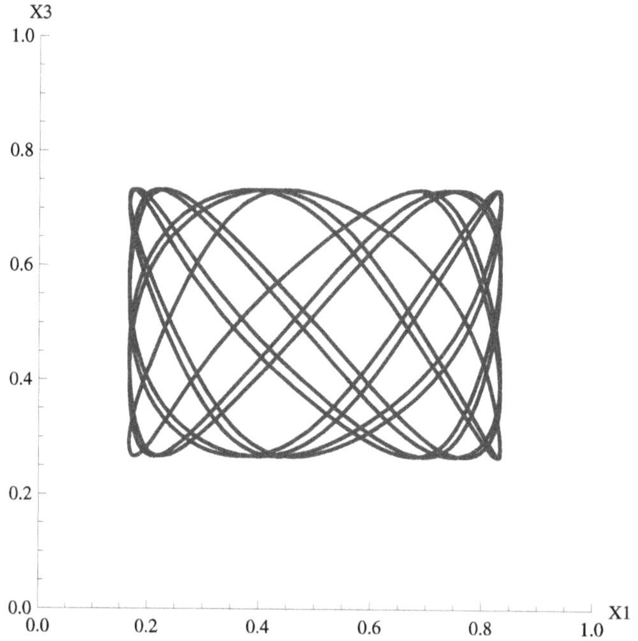

Figure 5.16. Projection of the same periodic attractor onto (X1, X3)-plane.

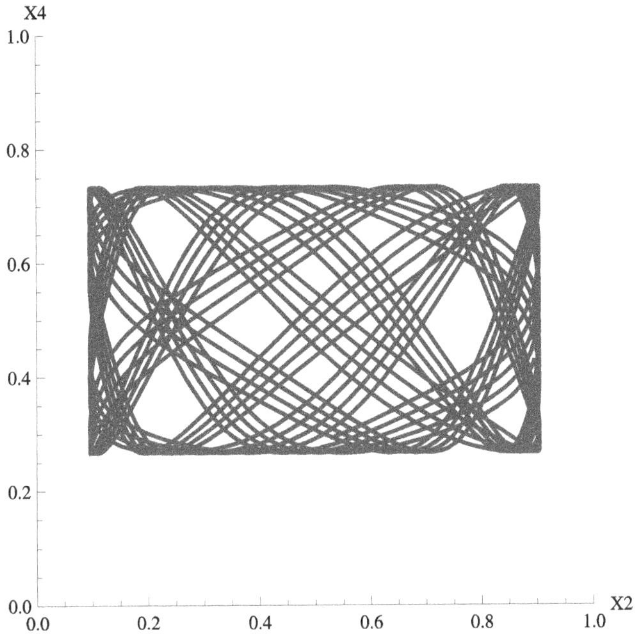

Figure 5.17. Projection of the same periodic attractor onto (X2, X4)-plane.

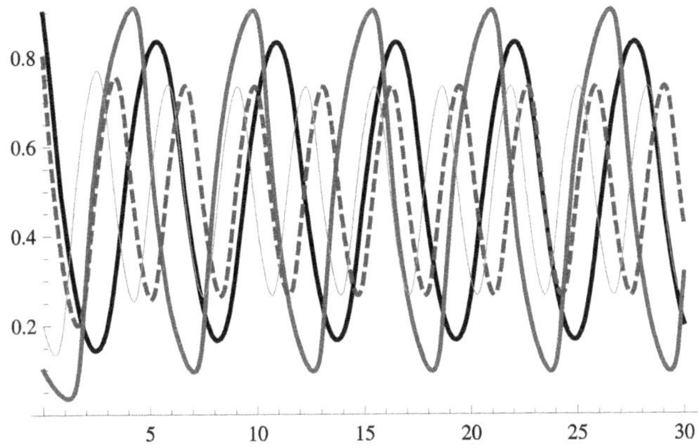

Figure 5.18. Four components of a solution $x(t)$, tending to the same periodic attractor.

$$W = \begin{pmatrix} 0.7 & 2 & 1 & 0 & 0 & 0 \\ -2 & 0.7 & 0 & 0 & 0 & 0 \\ 0 & 0 & 0.9 & 2 & 0 & 0 \\ 0 & 0 & -2 & 0.9 & 0 & 0 \\ 0 & 0 & 0 & 0 & 1.4 & 2 \\ 0 & 0 & 0 & 0 & -2 & 1.4 \end{pmatrix}. \tag{5.16}$$

Other parameters of a 6D system are: $\mu_i = 8,\ \ i = 1, \dots, 8,\ \ \theta_1 = \theta_3 = 1.2$, $\theta_2 = \theta_4 = -0.7$, $\theta_5 = 1.7$, $\theta_6 = -0.3$. The three 2D stable periodic trajectories form a 6D attractive object. The 3D projections of this attractor are depicted in figures 5.19, 5.20.

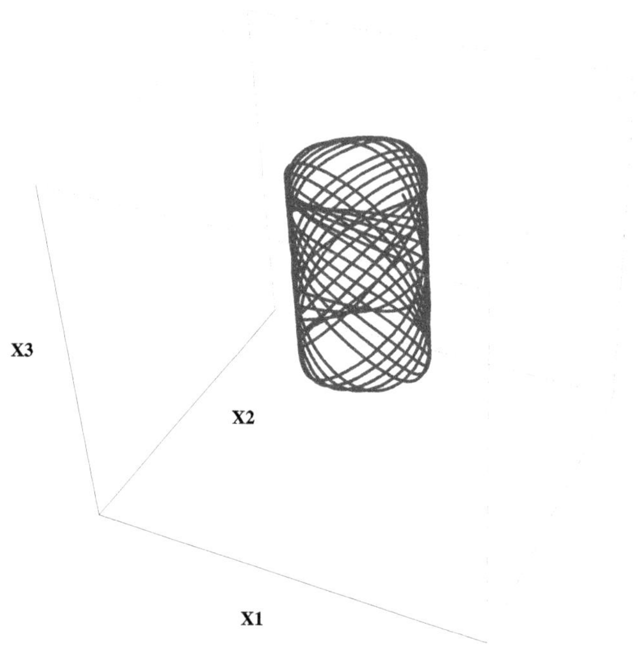

Figure 5.19. 6D system of the form (5.2) with the matrix (5.16). Projection of the periodic attractor onto the (X1, X2, X3)-subspace.

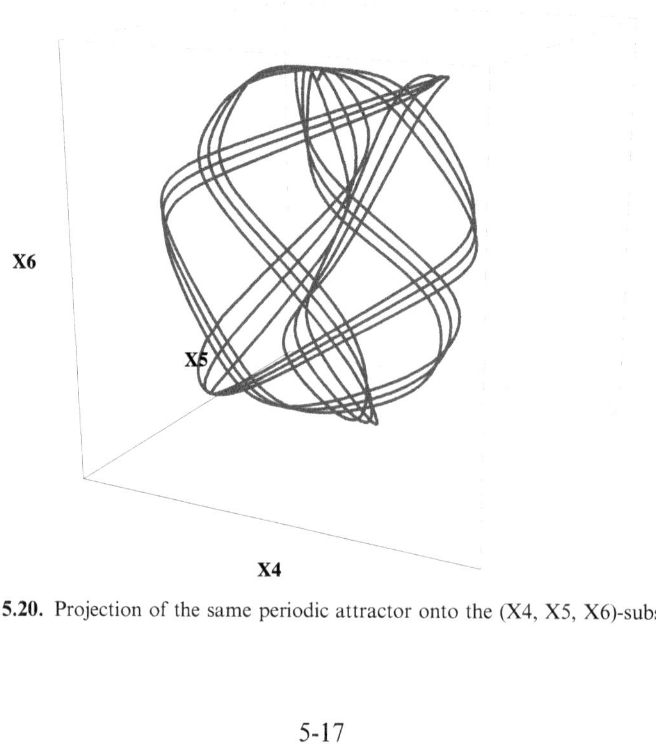

Figure 5.20. Projection of the same periodic attractor onto the (X4, X5, X6)-subspace.

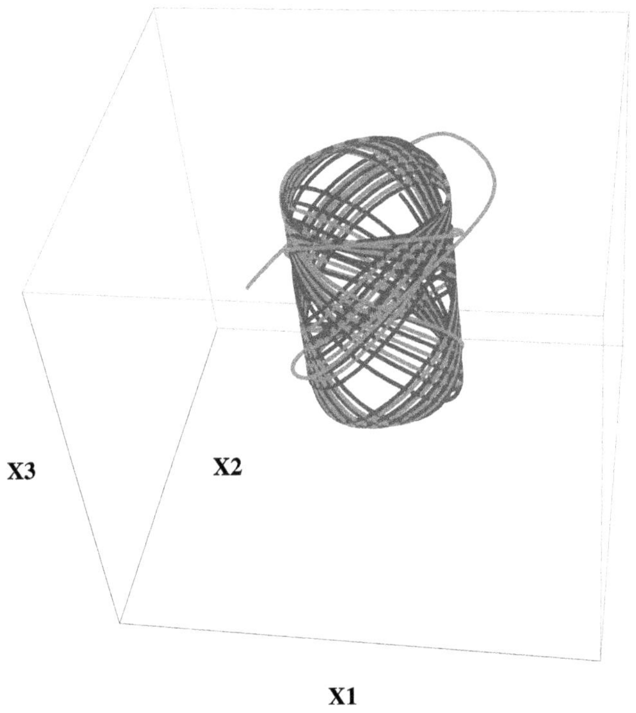

Figure 5.21. Projection of the same periodic attractor onto the (X1, X2, X3)-subspace together with the solution (red) tending to it.

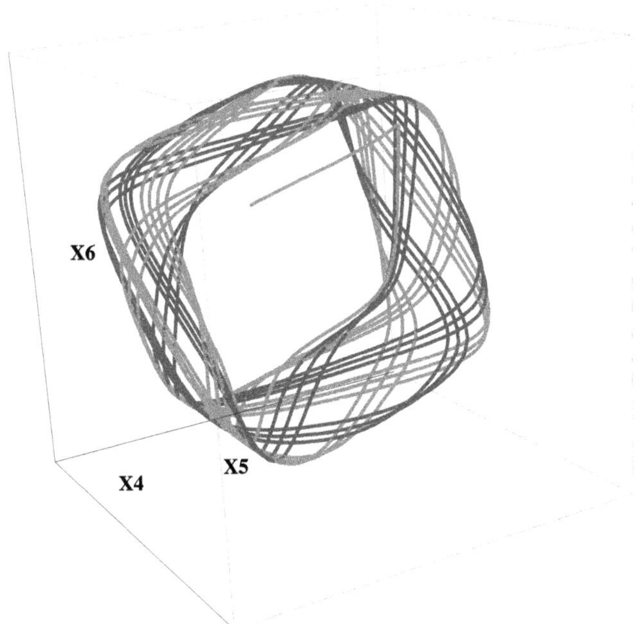

Figure 5.22. Projection of the same periodic attractor onto the (X4, X5, X6)-subspace together with the solution (red) tending to it.

The 3D projections of a 6D attractor together with a solution (in red), tending to it, are depicted in figures 5.21 and 5.22. The initial conditions for a (red) solution are $x_1(0) = 0.2$, $x_2(0) = 0.6$, $x_3(0) = 0.4$, $x_4(0) = 0.6$, $x_5(0) = 0.3$, $x_6(0) = 0.7$.

5.6 Elements of reverse engineering

Up to now we considered a given system and studied its characteristics, such as nullclines, critical points (equilibria), attractors. If the mathematical model is adequately describing a simulated network, the important problems of managing first the model, and then the network, arise. In the works [7, 12] the genomic network of sixty elements was considered. This network was obtained, analyzing the experimental data related to some serious diseases. The current state of the network was interpreted as 60D state vector $X(t)$. The disease was associated with the 'wrong' attractor in a 60D phase space of a mathematical model. The 'normal' attractors were identified also. The mathematical problem, formulated in [12], is to put the 60D trajectory $X(t)$ into the basin of attraction of a 'normal' attractor. The importance of detecting the attractors of a given system and the ability to manage a system is evident in this approach.

In paragraphs below we provide some suggestions, concerning the inverse problems, arising in the study of genomic networks.

5.6.1 Location of a critical point

The GRN-type systems can have multiple equilibria. Sometimes it is important to pay special attention to one of them, or to all of them in a sequence. The simple method of shifting the desired point into the center of an invariant cube in the phase space, is by changing the adjustable parameters θ. Choose θ_i in the system as

$$\theta_i = 0.5\,(w_{i1} + \cdots + w_{in}), \qquad i = 1, \ldots, n. \tag{5.17}$$

Then all the exponents in the system (5.3) are equal to unities and a critical point under studying is moved to a central position (0.5, … , 0.5) without affecting its other characteristics. This operation makes the calculation of critical numbers much easier.

5.6.2 Creating a critical point of the desired type

It was observed, when attempting to construct an attractor of more complicated nature than the stable equilibrium, that the existence of a single critical point with two complex conjugate characteristic numbers $\alpha + \beta\iota$, where $\alpha > 0$, often leads to periodic solutions.

We would like now to show, how the critical point of this kind can be obtained for a 3D system.

Suppose that the 3D system (5.13) is given, and a critical point is in the central position (0.5, 0.5, 0.5). To simplify the calculations, set $\mu_1 = \mu_2 = \mu_3 = 4$. The characteristic equation

$$\begin{aligned}&\Lambda^3 - (w_{11} + w_{22} + w_{33})\Lambda^2\\&- (w_{21}w_{12} - w_{11}w_{22} + w_{31}w_{13} + w_{32}w_{23} - w_{11}w_{33} - w_{22}w_{33})\Lambda\\&- (-w_{31}w_{22}w_{13} + w_{21}w_{32}w_{13} + w_{31}w_{12}w_{23} - w_{11}w_{32}w_{23}\\&- w_{21}w_{12}w_{33} + w_{11}w_{22}w_{33}) = 0\end{aligned} \tag{5.18}$$

with respect to $\Lambda = \lambda + 1$ is expressed in terms of the entries of the regulatory matrix W. Set $\Lambda_1 = 2$, $\Lambda_{2,3} = 2 \pm i$. The cubic equation with those roots is

$$\Lambda^3 - 6\Lambda^2 + 13\Lambda - 10 = 0. \tag{5.19}$$

By comparing these two equations, one can obtain the system for detection of w_{ij}. This system is

$$\begin{cases} -6 = -(w_{11} + w_{22} + w_{33}),\\ 13 = -(w_{21}w_{12} - w_{11}w_{22} + w_{31}w_{13} + w_{32}w_{23} - w_{11}w_{33} - w_{22}w_{33}),\\ -10 = -(-w_{31}w_{22}w_{13} + w_{21}w_{32}w_{13} + w_{31}w_{12}w_{23}\\ \qquad - w_{11}w_{32}w_{23} - w_{21}w_{12}w_{33} + w_{11}w_{22}w_{33}),\end{cases} \tag{5.20}$$

One possible solution is

$$\begin{aligned}w_{11} &= 2, & w_{12} &= 1, & w_{13} &= 0;\\ w_{21} &= -1, & w_{22} &= 2, & w_{23} &= 0;\\ w_{31} &= 1, & w_{32} &= 0, & w_{33} &= 2.\end{aligned} \tag{5.21}$$

Analyzing the system with the obtained values of w_{ij} and θ_i, as in (5.17), we establish that there is a stable periodic solution, depicted together with another trajectory in figure 5.22.

5.7 Miscellaneous

The problems that need to be solved.

Problem 1. Find the algorithmic way of constructing irregular attractors, which are neither sets of stable critical points, nor periodic ones.

Problem 2. Study with block regulatory matrices W. Clarify to which extent zero spaces in these matrices can be filled by non-zero entries to preserve the structure of existing attractors.

Problem 3. Study GRN-type systems with sparse regulatory matrices. Existing examples show that only up to 10 percent of space is filled by non-zero entries.

Problem 4. Construction of GRN-models with desired (mathematical) behavior. For instance, an example of GRN-type system with no stable equilibria should lead to the existence of either attractive periodic solutions, or attractors of a more complicated form. Recall that Lorenz 3D system has three equilibria, two of them are non-attractive focus type points, and one is a 3D saddle point.

Problem 5. In view of the suggestions in [7, 12] the problems of control and management in models of GRN become very important. The problem of redirection of a trajectory from one attractor to another one is of practical value for biomedicine. The control over 2D systems was considered in the work [9].

Problem 6. The problem of control over GRN-system has another side, namely, the influence of stochastic factors to attracting sets and behavior of trajectories.

Problem 7. The interactions in a network can be time-dependent. Therefore, systems with time-dependent regulatory matrices can be in a focus of the investigation. The problem of control over the GRN-system has another side, namely, the influence of stochastic factors to attracting sets and behavior of trajectories.

5.8 Conclusions

The construction and study of dynamic mathematical models of the evolution of genetic and similar networks is an urgent and rather difficult task. To solve this problem, it is necessary to study the structure of phase spaces of the corresponding systems of ordinary differential equations. In these studies, it is important to analyze bifurcations under the change of the parameters of systems. To understand the future states of the network, it is necessary to study attractors and their properties. This information will make it possible to manage the network and change its properties in the right direction. The hierarchy of attractors proposed in the chapter, combined with subsequent perturbations of them, makes it possible to identify possible attractors and study their properties.

References

[1] Atslega S, Finaskins D and Sadyrbaev F 2002 On a planar dynamical system arising in the network control theory *Math. Model. Anal.* **21** 385–98

[2] Atslega S, Sadyrbaev F and Samuilik I 2021 On modelling of complex networks *Proc. 19th Int. Scientific Conf. on Engineering for Rural Development* 1659–65

[3] Brokan E and Sadyrbaev F 2015 An adaptive modular approach to the mining of sensor network data *Int. Conf. on Simulation, Modelling and Mathematical Statistics* (Lancaster, PA: DEStech Publications) pp 135–9

[4] Brokan E and Sadyrbaev F 2018 Attraction in *n*-dimensional differential systems from network regulation theory *Math. Methods Appl. Sci.* **41** 7498–509

[5] Brokan E and Sadyrbaev F 2020 Remarks on GRN-type systems *4open* **3** 1–9

[6] Chong K H, Zhang X and Zheng J 2018 Dynamical analysis of cellular ageing by modeling of gene regulatory network based attractor landscape *PLoS ONE* **13** e0197838

[7] Cornelius S P, Kath W L and Motter A E 2013 Realistic control of network dynamics *Nat. Commun.* **4** 1942

[8] Cowan H R and Vilson J D 1972 Adaptive sampling for sensor networks *Biophys. J.* **12** 1–24

[9] Ogorelova D, Sadyrbaev F and Sengileyev V 2020 Control in inhibitory genetic regulatory network models *Contemp. Math.* **1** 421–8

[10] Das, Pritha A, Das and Roy A B 2002 Chaos in a three-dimensional general model of neural network *Int. J. Bifurc. Chaos* **12** 2271–81

[11] Edwards Ironi L and R 2014 Periodic solutions of gene networks with steep sigmoidal regulatory functions *Physica D: Nonlin. Phenom.* **282** 1–15

[12] Celso Grebogi *et al* 2016 A geometrical approach to control and controllability of nonlinear dynamical networks *Nat. Commun.* **7** 122–73

[13] Koizumi Y *et al* 2010 Adaptive virtual network topology control based on attractor selection *J. Lightwave Technol.* **28** 1720–31

[14] Yuki Koizumi *et al* 2008 Application of attractor selection to adaptive virtual network topology control *Proc. Bionetics* 1–8

[15] Sadyrbaev F, Ogorelova D and Samuilik I 2020 A nullclines approach to the study of 2D artificial network *Contemp. Math.* **1** 1–11

[16] Jong H 2000 Modeling and simulation of genetic regulatory systems : a literature review *HAL Archives* **inria-00072606** 1–47

[17] Mukherjee S, Sanjay Kumar Palit and Bhattacharya D K 2013 Is one dimensional Poincaré map sufficient to describe the chaotic dynamics of a three dimensional system? *Appl. Math. Comput.* **219** 11056–64

[18] Noonburg V W 2019 *Differential Equations: From Calculus to Dynamical Systems* 2nd edn (Providence, RI: AMS)

[19] Sadyrbaev F, Samuilik I and Sengileyev V 2021 On modelling of genetic regulatory networks *WSEAS Trans. Electron.* **12** 73–80

Chapter 6

Computing the intelligent privacy-engineered organization: a metamodel of effective information transparency enhancing tools/technologies

Ljerka Luic and Marta Alic

In information privacy research, privacy is described as a set of system properties. Such properties are formalized as technical functionalities in ensuring data subjects' rights in knowing what data is being collected and processed about them and what they have control over. To ensure this, transparency enhancing tools/technologies (TETs) are used to enhance understanding and visibility of procedures, practices and consequences of personal data processing with data processors. As a combination of technological and organizational solutions or methods their goals can be perceived as privacy, as well as a software engineering prerequisite. Since the principles of data privacy are the subject of numerous international documents from the 1970s, with different levels of abstraction, methods of goal-based reasoning can be applied in their requirement analysis. By using identification, classification and modelling heuristics of the Goal-Based Requirement Analysis Method, requirements for effective TETs are systemized across momentous Data Privacy Governance Frameworks. The synthesis made of relevant transparency goals can serve as a precondition for computing intelligent privacy organizational environments.

6.1 Introduction

In today's age of information abundance, privacy is becoming a luxury. Activities that have been private until recently are now becoming a source of profit by analyzing the interests, characteristics, beliefs, worldviews and intentions of individuals. Using numerous internet services, users, consciously but also unconsciously,

doi:10.1088/978-0-7503-4801-0ch6

share numerous data to various stakeholders: among themselves, to organizations and public authorities.

The issue of privacy is becoming more expressed as is the ability of individuals to control their data in intelligent system environments. Advances in information technology have made the collection and the use of personal data invisible. As a result, individuals rarely have a clear knowledge of what information others have about them or how that information is used and with what consequences.

Although the systems of modern, digital economy are based on an exchange of data for the benefit of all stakeholders as well as society as a whole, the possibilities of data misuse, such as discrimination [1, 2] and manipulation, are alarming, and research shows and considers individuals an important factor in online decision-making [3]. The report of the research project Horizon 2020 of the European Union [4] related to privacy on the platforms of so-called economy sharing shows that service providers mostly express some concern about the misuse of their data as well as the loss of control over their online presentation due to the negative reviews or comments from other users. In fact, the whole concept of so-called impression management, the strategic sharing of personal data to create a more affordable online view, is a source of anxiety for users.

To meet user requirements and design systems according to the Privacy by Design concept, which focuses on system engineering that puts privacy in focus throughout the system design process [5], organizations need to implement high standards of privacy throughout the organizational system and business culture, including visibility and transparency, as a key precondition for ensuring the right of individuals to privacy.

However, in the field of requirement engineering within information systems, transparency is a relatively new topic. The reason is that the concept was approached primarily from the perspective of software engineering and only then the design of the entire information system, in which transparency was usually categorized as a non-functional requirement in relation to software functionality, considered primarily as a 'second-rate' quality issue [6].

The first research in the field of requirement engineering suggested the application of the so-called non-functional requirement (NFR) framework [7] and method of i* modelling [8], allowing for these not to be the final solutions. Further research has led to the definition of aspects of transparency [9], a concept that contains the following five NFRs: accessibility, usability, information, comprehensibility and auditability as conditions for achieving transparency. Furthermore, focused on user requirements are two papers by Dabbish *et al* [10, 11], who cite Github as an example of a transparent software environment, bringing it into relationship with the paradigm of openness of social networks, while [12] at the same time suggesting the application of the so-called argumentation framework in meeting user transparency requirements in software engineering.

Finally, noticing the gap in related literature in the field of transparency requirements from a user or data subject perspective, following their previous research [13, 14], Hosseini *et al* developed a modelling language [15] and, consequently, set up conceptual models [16] in relation to business information systems.

The objective of this chapter is to provide a comprehensive review of requirement engineering goals for effective transparency tools or technology modelling and development, set by the data governance frameworks in the field of privacy. Section 6.2 first provides background material on TETs in the context of privacy management as well as an overview of data privacy governance frameworks and their development. In section 6.3 the selected frameworks are put into an interrelationship, resulting in derived transparency requirements, their entity-relationship metamodel and goal-driven taxonomy. Section 6.4 discusses analysed governance frameworks in the context of their historic development and their relations to current regulatory and standard privacy practices. Section 6.5 refers to the major findings and limitations of the research in reference to the goal-based requirements analysis method. Section 6.6 concludes the chapter, eliciting future scope of the research.

6.2 Transparency enhancing tools/technologies

6.2.1 Right to privacy and information transparency

The right to privacy is a fundamental human right, both international and constitutional, which protects a person from excessive encroachment of state power, the public and other individuals into an individual's spatial and informational intimacy. Different dimensions of privacy, from spatial and physical, privacy of communication to information privacy, can therefore be studied in the so-called vertical relationship to the institutions of the state and society or horizontal relationship to third parties, while their boundaries are constantly reviewed and revised, depending on the context or social and civilizational environment. Accordingly, the right to privacy is not an absolute right, and it is accomplished in addition to the rights of others to know the necessary information about individuals.

Data privacy is a form of material privacy based on the right and ability of an individual to define and live their life in a way determined by themselves [17] in relation to data created by themselves or by others, by observation and analysis, consumption or processing. That kind of data is called personal information (PI). Confidentiality, the ability to choose with whom (or what) to share the information about oneself is one aspect of privacy, while anonymity and de-identification, the separation of information from the subject to which it might otherwise relate [18], are other aspects.

So, the concept of data privacy can be defined as authorized, fair and legitimate processing of personal information where an individual to whom the data applies, or a data subject (who is literally the subject matter of the information) is the ultimate requirement-setting entity. But for the data subject to be able to make informed decisions and have control over his/her privacy, it is necessary for data controllers (the natural or legal persons, public authorities, agencies or other bodies) to provide quality transparency tools, designed to provide insight into data processing practices and their consequences.

In today's human-computer interaction (HCI) environments, the relation between users and services that collect users' information is characterized by high information asymmetry [19]. So, it is a great imperative that people obtain the correct mental models regarding the flow of their personal data. TETs are methods or tools which enhance transparency and can provide users with more control over their PI. TETs can be considered as tools that provide insight into the method the personal data is collected, stored, processed and disclosed in an accurate and comprehensible way [20].

As measures for privacy protection, TETs are generally seen as a combination of technological solutions and legal or procedural frameworks and diverse classifications of TETs can be made based on the degree of interactivity and intervention provided to data subjects [21], their execution environments [22], assertions or declarations by data processors [21] and other parameters. An important distinction for transparency tools is the division into ex-ante (inform before processing), ex-post (inspect after processing) and real-time (inform while processing) TETs [21].

The way data controllers address and implement privacy requirements is an individual decision, as data privacy is a key part of data governance in organisations. In this context, privacy engineering is the construction of data governance into the design and implementation of routines, systems and products that process PI [23]. Privacy frameworks and guidelines can navigate in creating the necessary roles and responsibilities needed to build and maintain privacy-aware enterprises. They are used as tools to recognize and understand privacy policies at meta-use-case requirements for privacy engineering.

6.2.2 Data privacy governance frameworks overview

The Organisation for Economic Co-operation and Development (OECD) Guidelines [24] are one of the better-known privacy governance frameworks as an extension of a series of principles called the Fair Information Practice Principles (FIPPs) [25], developed by the Department of Health, Education, and Welfare in the 1960s in reaction to concerns over implementation of large government databases containing information on citizens of the United States of America. The principles were extended by the OECD in 1980 in a document titled 'The OECD Guidelines on the Protection of Privacy and Transborder Flows of Personal Data'. These principles have become the foundation for the majority of the existing privacy laws and regulations.

It was a regulatory motive for this document in the first place, as OECD Member countries considered it necessary, due to the development of automatic data processing, to develop guidelines which would help to harmonise national privacy legislation and, while upholding human rights on privacy, would at the same time prevent interruptions in international flows of data [24]. As a result, the document represents unanimity on the basic principles which can be integrated into existing national legislation, or serve as a basis for developing legislation in countries which do not have it yet.

The same efforts in the development of effective privacy protection that avoid barriers to information flow and ensure continued trade and economic growth in the Asia-Pacific region were made by the development of The Asia-Pacific Economic Cooperation (APEC) Privacy Framework [26]. It is in line with and also models the core values of the OECD Guidelines on Privacy and Cross-Border Personal Data Flows and reaffirms the value of privacy for individuals and the information society.

The National Institute of Standards and Technology (NIST) Privacy Framework [27] is focused on deriving benefits from the data, while simultaneously managing risks to individuals' privacy. It follows the structure of The Framework for Improving Critical Infrastructure Cybersecurity [28] and is composed of three parts: Core, profiles, and implementation tiers, where each component reinforces privacy risk management through the connection between business and mission drivers, organizational roles and responsibilities, and privacy protection activities. By focusing more on the development of practical privacy engineering requirements, rather than on the general principles recognized in OECD and APEC documents, it sets out a precise overview of activities and outcomes that enable a dialogue on privacy risk management, such as GAPP (Generally Accepted Privacy Principles) [29], developed by the American Institute of Chartered Accountants (AICPA) and the Working Party on Privacy of the Canadian Institute of Chartered Accountants (CICA), to address business perspectives and address significant local, national and international privacy regulations.

GAPP, on the other hand, operationalizes complex privacy requirements into a single privacy objective that is supported by 10 privacy principles. Each principle is supported by an objective, measurable criterion that forms the basis for effective management of privacy risk and compliance in an organization [23].

6.3 Modelling effective transparency enhancing tools/technologies

6.3.1 Aligning privacy frameworks in transparency

The process of requirement engineering consists of determining user needs or expectations in modelling new solutions. In this context, a solution is manifested in an effective TET, characterized by the quantifiable, relevant and detailed requirements. In software engineering such requirements are often called functional specifications and the same development path can be used for requirement gathering and development in privacy engineering. After all, privacy policy creation serves as a critical requirement gathering source or end state upon which to draw certain functional requirements of a system.

For privacy engineers, requirement gathering and development can follow the same development journey as any other functional specifications, but with a variation. The mastery of privacy policy creation for the enterprise is often stated in aspirational or behavioral terms: reasonable, proportional, 'do no harm' options and choices but in TET context policy it serves as a critical requirement-gathering source or end state upon which certain functional requirements for privacy enhancing environments are drawn.

So, to derive the transparency goals related to transparency tools, the description of the privacy principles and their formulations was analysed across all presented privacy frameworks. As transparency is an inevitable part of privacy engineering, all privacy engineering frameworks align with it, albeit with a different terminology (table 6.1).

Table 6.1. Alignment of privacy frameworks in transparency terminology.

NIST Privacy Framework [27]	OECD Guidelines [24]	APEC Privacy Framework [26]	GAPP [29]
Data processing awareness	Specification of purpose	Notice	Notice

The most general goal for information transparency is set as a specification of purpose principle in the OECD guidelines: 'The purposes for which personal data is collected should be specified not later than at the time of data collection and the subsequent use limited to the fulfilment of those purposes or such others as are not incompatible with those purposes and as are specified on each occasion of change of purpose', which provides guidance regarding the type and quality of transparency or respective tools, setting the first categorization criteria for requirement engineering.

The concept of transparency implies two dimensions: visibility, i.e. the degree of completeness of information and the possibility of finding it, and inferability, the degree to which information can be used to make the right decisions [30]. So, effective transparency tools should aim at meeting a high degree of both dimensions of transparency to ensure that information asymmetry is reduced, ensuring a multi-faceted means for 'providing necessary information', as the first and 'providing quality mechanisms', as the second initial or root factor. This is also recognized by APEC, which has set out in more detail the principle of privacy of notification notices, referring to the availability and comprehensibility of data processing statements, as well as the main requirements in informativeness, ie. the transfer of good quality information.

Transparency prerequisites and requirements in the NIST privacy framework are targeted as a data processing awareness category in the communicate function section of the document, generally defined as a rule that 'individuals and organizations have reliable knowledge of data processing practices and associated privacy risks', implying that mechanisms for communicating this knowledge are established and in place.

For these principles, in the GAPP measurement criteria are presented in more detail, giving the most detailed set of requirements in privacy engineering. Notice principle, defined in a separate section as prerequisite in privacy policies, extends its criteria also to other principles describing more detailed requirements for achieving transparency goals.

6.3.2 Transparency requirements mining

In the detailed requirement-mining process from framework documents the formulation of the identified requirements was kept close to the original documents to ease the overlap distinguishment. Some of the requirements represent a refinement of another requirement, adding further details on how (applying 'providing quality mechanisms' factor, noted with M) or which possibilities have to exist (applying 'providing necessary information' factor, noted with I) in order to maximize the quality of information transparency.

The analysis started with provide notice principle as root principle of providing information about policies and procedures (I1), following principles related to the mechanism requirements regarding the notice.

I1 Provide notice about privacy policies and procedures [27].

M1 Provide clear and easily accessible notices about practices and policies with respect to personal information [26].

M2 Provide notice at the time of, or before information about them is collected [24, 26].

M3 Notice is conspicuous and uses plain and simple language [29].

M4 Notice is appropriately labelled and easy to use [29].

Requirements M1 and M2 are the refinement of the principle requirement I1 providing more specific demands on the notice such as a place (where it should be provided) and time (when notice should be provided). By defining the notice criteria as easily accessible, it is suggested that transparency should be attained considering best media for notice dissemination. This requirement can be further refined with M4, as transparency increases with appropriate label of notice and simplicity in use and endorsed with M3 that emphasizes the demand of visibility and details the ease of use with a plain and simple language requirement.

Providing information of data processing purpose is a principle used to define transparency requirements of informativeness, starting with I2 as the most generic one.

I2 Identify the purposes for which personal information is collected, used, retained and disclosed [24, 26, 29].

I3 Describe the personal information collected, sources and methods used to collect it and purposes for which it is collected [29].

I4 Provide the purpose for collecting sensitive personal information (if applicable) and whether such purpose is part of a legal requirement [29].

I5 Inform data subjects that information is collected only for the purposes identified in the notice [29].

I6 Inform that personal information not essential to the purposes need not be provided [29].

I7 Describe the consequences, if any, of not providing the requested information [29].

I2 defines the data processing activities (collection, usage, retention and disclosure) across the information flow and I3 is the refinement of the collection phase. I4 places emphasis on providing explanations whenever sensitive data is used and hence refines the previous requirement I3.

As the purpose of data processing is the key element of transparency, on which data subjects can base their decision about (not) sharing their personal data, requirements I5–I7 explicitly mandate that.

I12 Indicate that certain information about individuals may be developed [29].

I12 is another refinement of I2 considering that collection of information is not strictly constricted directly from the first party but, considering contemporary technology, it can be aggregated from other sources.

I10 Describe the practices relating to sharing of personal information (if any) with third parties and the reasons for information sharing [29].

I11 Identify third parties or classes of third parties to whom personal information is disclosed [29].

I10 and I11 reference disclosure phase of data flow, while I11 is a detailed refinement of I10.

I15 Provide information that personal information is retained for no longer than necessary to fulfil the stated purposes or for a period specifically required by law or regulation [29].

I16 Provide information that personal information is disposed of in a manner that prevents loss, theft, misuse or unauthorized access [29].

I17 Inform about precautions taken to protect personal information [29].

I18 Describe the general types of security measures used to protect personal information [29].

I15 and I16 focus on the retention phase of the data flow and disposal of data, while I17 and I18 refer to security measures applied.

Finally, the principle of user control and participation in data processing derived requirements that can emancipate user intervenability and contribution.

I8 Inform that implicit or explicit consent is required to collect, use and disclose personal information, unless a law or a regulation specifically requires or allows otherwise [29].

I9 Inform that preferences may be changed and consent may be withdrawn at a later time, subject to legal or contractual restrictions and a reasonable notice [29].

Consent is a major principle in data processing legitimacy. If there isn't any regulatory legal basis for collecting, using and disclosing personal information that would imply implicit consent, it is required for the data controller to ensure an explicit one and inform the user about that (I8) as well as to imply that consent is not indefinite, but subject to change (I9). In terms of explicitness, the quality of being clear and exact in consenting, I9 is a refinement of I8.

I14 Notice is clearly dated to allow individuals to determine whether it has changed since the last time they read it or since the last time they submitted their personal information to the entity [29].

To address currentness of notice, requirement I14 is defined to improve transparency.

I13 Provide information about the identity and location of the personal information controller, including information on how to contact them about their practices and handling of personal information [29].

I13 is a prerequisite requirement for intervenability of data subjects that can be refined with succeeding requirements.

I20 Explain how disagreements related to personal information may be resolved [29].

I21 Provide information about choices and means available for limiting the use and disclosure of personal information, accessing and correcting them [29].
I22 Explain the process of how the data subject may gain access to personal information and any cost associated with gaining such access [29].
I23 Outline the means by which data subjects may update and correct their personal information [29].

6.3.3 Transparency requirements metamodel

The structure of identified transparency requirements for effective TETs can be modelled by using a UML class diagram (figure 6.1). Requirements are mapped to reflect their relations, using standardized notation to signal the relationship strength, mutual association and/or dependence.

6.3.4 Transparency requirements classification

Developing from the described relations in figure 6.1, metamodel, requirements can be mapped in taxonomy, showed in table 6.2, according to the goals they achieve. In

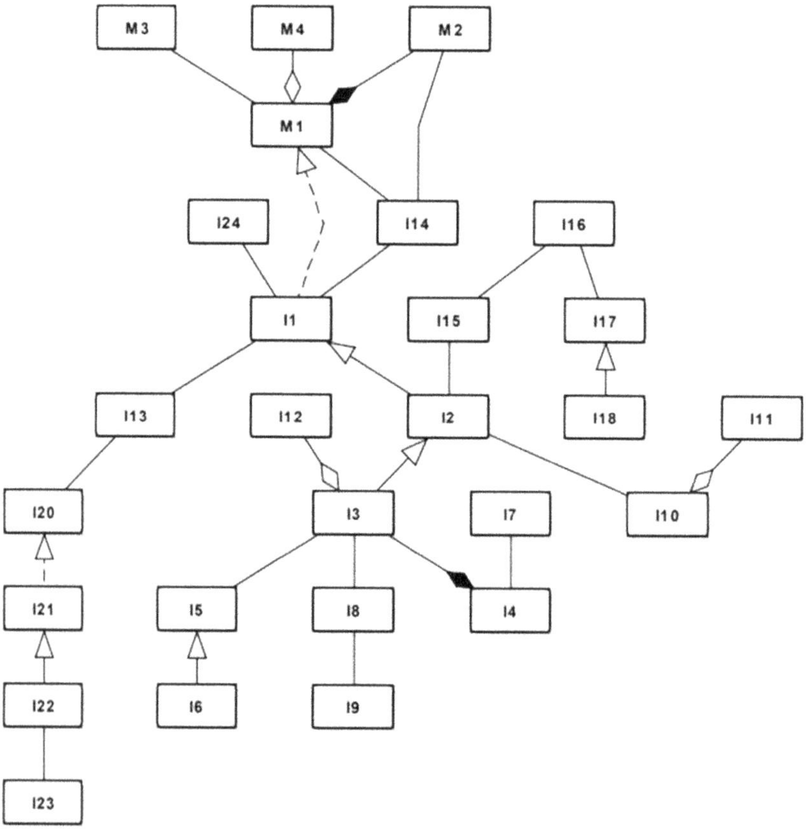

Figure 6.1. A metamodel of TET requirements.

Table 6.2. Alignment of privacy frameworks in transparency terminology.

Goal	Attribute	
Transparency	notice	I1, I14
	controller	I13
	legal	I8, I9
Mechanism	mechanism	M1–M4
Processing	purpose	I2, I4, I5, I6
	collection	I3, I12
	retention	I15, I16
	disclosure	I10, I11
	security	I16, I17, I18
Control	choice	I14, I20, I21
	information quality	I22, I23

requirements engineering, the goal-driven approaches focus on why the systems are constructed, expressing the rationale and justification for the proposed system [31]. To 'target' them more specifically to the operationalization goals of the system, requirements are further classified by attributes.

On the top-level element of hierarchy there is the general transparency goal which corresponds to the initial requirement I1. It has three attributes that instantiate requirements more specifically. The attribute notice relates to requirements that are related to the notice itself—its existence (I1) and its currentness or accuracy in providing information about the real process of the system (I14). I14 is an informativeness requirement as it provides the date of notice as a criterion establishing the currentness of the document, as opposed to other possible methods of stating accuracy of notice within the mechanisms of media (for example, setting automatic date of publishing the document on electronic media). The Controller attribute is used to single out the requirement about the personal data controller, their identity, location and contact information (I13). Lastly, to separate requirements which are contextual to legal regulations, attribute legal is used. If a legal basis for data processing is consent, it is required to inform the data subjects about that (I8), as well as mention 'conditions' of such consent (I9). In the model, these instances are associated to more generalized I3 which describes methods, sources and collected information specifying how it can be used by data subjects for decision-making about (non)consenting to the data processing.

To address requirements which are subject to mechanism qualities, mechanism goal is defined with instances, accordingly annotated, from M1 to M4. As appropriate labelling of mechanism (M4) is a prerequisite for providing 'easily accessible notices' (M1) the relationship is defined as an aggregation to indicate that labelling is a part of privacy notices. Composition, a stronger form of association is used to define the relationship between M1 and M2 which defines the timeliness of the notice as an important part of transparency that refers to the time expected for accessibility and availability of information. Finally, comprehensibility of the language for the targeted audience is required in order for it to enhance transparency by using 'plain and simple language' (M3) which is associated with the mechanism quality.

The processing goal presents requirements grounded in I2 and contains properties of data processing practices and its purposes along the data flow. It has five attributes, with the purpose attribute used to provide a set of statements (I4 to I6) that could consist of declarative requirements: fulfilment of what cause the personal data of the data subject is needed for. It is also considered in the I3 requirement, as its specialization within the collection requirements. Since providing purpose for collecting sensitive information is a conditional instance and it is only required if applicable, so I4 is set as a composition of I3—collection description, while I5 and I6 are more specialized instances of I2 and I3 as a proxy requirement. I12 describes collection methods in case certain information may be developed about individuals and, as such, it is aggregated part of I3.

The retention attribute represents requirements which inform the data subject about the set retention periods and criteria for its determination (I15) as well as methods of its disposal 'in a manner that prevents loss, theft, misuse or unauthorized access' (I16). The means described in I16 are related also to the security requirements investigated by I17—to 'inform about precautions taken to protect personal information' and I18 as its more specialized requirement of describing data security types of measures. And although these requirements are not part of the data flow, security is its integral part and an inevitable layer in privacy engineering, so its requirements are attributed accordingly and put under the processing goal.

The requirements of control goal are essential to managing the data subject's rights. They are represented with the choice and information quality attributes. Although I14 requirement, which says that 'notice is clearly dated to allow individuals to determine whether the notice has changed since the last time they read it or since the last time they submitted personal information to the entity' is subject to transparency goal, it can also be a decisive element for the data subject consent, therefore it is also sorted under the choice cohort, alongside requirements I20 'explain how disagreements related to the personal information may be resolved' and providing 'information about choices and means available for limiting the use and disclosure of personal information, accessing and correcting them' (I21), where I21 can be interpreted as a realization of I20.

To distinguish the more specific requirements to I21, an information quality attribute is introduced to refine requirements I22 and I23 as detailed representations of explaining 'the process of how the data subject may gain access to the personal information and any cost associated with gaining such access' and 'the means by which data subjects may update and correct their personal information'.

6.4 Leveraging privacy principles

Since the appearance of the General Data Protection Regulation (GDPR) [32] in European Union (EU) member countries, the majority of privacy engineering literature has focused on explaining requirements aligned with this legislative document.

But privacy engineering, voluntary or regulatory, is not a new concept. The Council of Europe's 1981 Convention has had a greater influence than the OECD Guidelines in the legislation of the European Union Member States. It has continued in the EU's data protection Directive 95/46/EC which has now been superseded by the GDPR. With minor, but important changes of wording, the Directive replicated the Convention Articles and added important changes of wording, as the Directive depicted the Convention Articles, adding further rules about the legitimacy of processing and the transfer of personal data to third countries [33].

Meanwhile, as OECD guidelines have become globally very influential, which is reflected in the countries' adoption of their own data protection legislation, it was the report from United States of America's Federal Trade Commission in 1998 that led to modernization of privacy endeavours. By having reduced prior collections of principles down to five, it stated that most of them, except for security, are procedural, as substantive obligations concerning fairness and data quality were ignored in favour of procedural requirements concerning notice, choice, access and enforcement.

It was the APEC Privacy Framework in 2005 that put a conscious effort into building on the OECD guidelines and modernizing them, escalating demand for standards that facilitate multinational data flows [34].

While the numbers and formulations of the principles vary in compliance frameworks, a consensus has existed since the 1970s. Any public or private organization that deals with PI should be accountable for all of the PI in its possession. It should also identify the purposes for which the information is processed at or before the time of collection. Data gathering should also be processed lawfully and transparently by collecting only PI with the knowledge and consent of the individual (except under specified circumstances). The collection of PI should be limited to what is necessary for pursuing the identified purposes and collected personal data should not be used or disclosed for purposes other than those identified (except with the individual's consent). Information should be retained only as long as necessary; while ensuring that PI is kept accurate, complete, up to date and protected with appropriate security safeguards. Organizations also need to be transparent about their policies and practices and maintain no secret information systems, allowing the data subjects access to their PI, with an ability to amend it if it is inaccurate, incomplete or obsolete [33].

But the most significant privacy protection 'textbook' is an ISO 29100 international standard for privacy principles, published by the International Organization for Standardization in 2011, deriving from the existing principles developed by various states, countries and international organizations. These standards for voluntary compliance are defined in 11 privacy principles which are a superset of the OECD principles and the US fair information practices (FIPs).

6.5 Research findings and limitations within the scope of the goal-based requirements analysis method

6.5.1 Major research findings and contributions

Since privacy goals in all frameworks are evolutionary, they provide a common language for all participants in the process, regardless of whether they observe them from the technical and/or organizational perspective.

The Goal-Based Requirement Analysis Method (GBRAM) [31, 35] is a straightforward methodical approach in identifying and refining the goals that software systems must achieve, converting them into operational requirements. As transparency is one notion of privacy management, it is generally perceived simply as a notice about data governing practices, but, as a derived taxonomy clearly shows, tools for ensuring effective transparency require quality of mechanism properties to be assured. And this is, in most cases within contemporary environment of digital economy, a functional requirement of engineering software systems.

The GBRAM method suggests goal identification and refinement strategies and techniques through the inclusion of a set of heuristics as a form of knowledge and reasoning: identification heuristics, classification heuristics, refinement heuristics, elaboration heuristics and modelling heuristics.

Identification of requirements as well as their refinement is a preliminary step used towards achieving the set goals, as they are formulated at different levels of abstraction in respective documents.

As a result, the proposed taxonomy suggests aggregation of requirements with different granularity of functionalities in frameworks, from GAPP being the most granular and represented, to NIST as the most aggregated and set as fundamental (I1), with irrelevant concerns disregarded and ‘overlaps’ managed.

Subsequently, by characterizing the requirements and distributing them by respective attributes to the set taxonomy, qualitative values that can be used to ensure requirement pertinence to a specified goal representing a precise criterion for achieving the goal completeness are given.

Finally, derived entity-relationship metamodel can be used as a basis for further modelling heuristics in software and privacy policies engineering.

6.5.2 Limitations of research

Elaboration, as a significant part of GBRAM method, refers to analysing the set goals with consideration of possible obstacles and a detailed operationalization. Although the research lacks these heuristics to complete the goal-based requirement analysis, nevertheless, the proposed requirements accompanied with a detailed metamodel of their relationships of mutual association and/or dependence, can serve as a prerequisite for the development of transparency system functionalities through the use case scenarios. Further goal validation, alongside with taxonomy validation is in order.

6.6 Conclusion

Building effective transparency mechanisms in comprehensive environments of digital economy can be very challenging. It goes beyond efficient root factors of ‘providing necessary information’ and ‘providing quality mechanisms’, as effectiveness and efficiency are two separate terms. While efficiency is the state of achieving maximum productivity, with the least amount of effort expended, effectiveness is the extent to which something is successful in delivering the desired result. So, in the long term, effectiveness is a strategic choice and transparency in the context of privacy engineering should be considered as such.

By modelling an effective TET metamodel based on heuristics-based approach abstracted statements about PI management were associated with the specific problem solutions or features that characterize a solution in the system application. Derived goals can be used as a cornerstone in the development of such systems: transparency goal—to stipulate general requirements in achieving transparency, the mechanism goal—that specifies requirements to realize quality of transparency mechanisms, the processing goal—that emerges from informing about personal information data flow, and the control goal—as a result of data subjects' rights to intervenability.

Subsequently, the resulting goals and applied methods can be used for a wider scope of research in directions that are related to scalability in terms of TET system quality as privacy management practices evolve to ensure more data security and risk management requirements in the prospects of new ePrivacy regulation.

References

[1] Sweeney L 2013 Discrimination in online ad delivery *Commun. ACM* **56** 44–54

[2] Datta A, Tschantz M C and Datta A 2015 Automated experiments on ad privacy settings *Proc. Priv. Enhancing Technol.* **2015** 92–112

[3] Calo R 2011 The boundaries of privacy harm *Indiana Law J.* **86** 1132–61

[4] Ranzini G, Etter M and Vermeulen I E 2017 Privacy in the sharing economy: european perspectives *SSRN Electron. J.*

[5] Bednar K, Spiekermann S and Langheinrich M *et al* 2019 Engineering privacy by design: are engineers ready to live up to the challenge? *Inf. Soc.* **35** 122–42

[6] do Prato, Leite J C S and Cappelli C 2010 Software transparency *Bus. Inf. Syst. Eng.* **2** 127–39

[7] Chung L, Nixon B A and Yu E 2000 *Non-Functional Requirements in Software Engineering* (Cham: Springer)

[8] Yu E S 1995 Modelling strategic relationships for process *PhD Thesis* University of Toronto

[9] do Orato, Leite J C S and Cappelli C 2008 Exploring i* characteristics that support software transparency *iStar'08, 3rd Int. i* Workshop* eds J Castro, X Franch, A Perini and E Yu https://ceur-ws.org/Vol-322/paper13.pdf

[10] Dabbish L, Stuart H C and Tsay J *et al* 2012 Social coding in GitHub: transparency and collaboration in an open software repository *Proc. ACM 2012 Conf Comput Support Coop Work* 1277–86

[11] Dabbish L, Stuart C and Tsay J *et al* 2013 Leveraging transparency *IEEE Softw.* **30** 37–43

[12] Serrano M and Do Prado Leite J C S 2011 Capturing transparency-related requirements patterns through argumentation *2011 1st Int. Work Requir. Patterns, RePa'11* 00 32–41

[13] Hosseini M, Shahri A and Phalp K *et al* 2015 Towards engineering transparency as a requirement in socio-technical systems *2015 IEEE 23rd Int. Requir. Eng. Conf. RE* 268–73

[14] Hosseini M, Shahri A and Phalp K *et al* 2016 Foundations for transparency requirements engineering *Lect. Notes Comput. Sci.* **9619** 225–31

[15] Hosseini M, Shahri A and Phalp K *et al* 2016 A modelling language for transparency requirements in business information systems *Lect. Notes Comput. Sci.* **9694** 239–54

[16] Hosseini M, Shahri A and Phalp K *et al* 2018 Four reference models for transparency requirements in information systems *Requir. Eng.* **23** 251–75
[17] Koehlinger J S 1990 Substantive due process analysis and the lockean liberal tradition: rethinking the modern privacy cases substantive due process analysis and the lockean liberal tradition: rethinking the modern privacy cases *Indiana Law J.* **65** 8
[18] Ponesse J 2014 The ties that bind: conceptualizing anonymity *J. Soc. Philos.* **45** 304–22
[19] Schermer B W 2011 The limits of privacy in automated profiling and data mining Comput. Law Secur. Rev. **27** 45–52
[20] Karegar F 2018 Towards Improving Transparency, Intervenability and Consent in HCI *Licentiate thesis* Karlstad University
[21] Zimmermann C 2015 A categorization of transparency-enhancing technologies arXiv:1507.04914
[22] Zimmermann C, Accorsi R and Müller G 2014 Privacy dashboards: reconciling data-driven business models and privacy *Int. Conf. on Availability, Reliability and Security*
[23] Dennedy M F, Fox J and Finneran T R 2014 *The Privacy Engineer's Manifesto* (Cham: Springer)
[24] OECD 2013 *The OECD Privacy Guidelines*
[25] Gellman R 2014 Fair information practices: a basic history *SSRN Electron J.*
[26] Asia Pacific Economic Cooperation 2015 APEC Privacy Framework
[27] National Institute of Standards and Technology 2020 NIST Privacy Framework - a tool for improving privacy through enterprise risk management
[28] Barrett M N 2018 Framework for improving critical infrastructure cybersecurity *Proc Annu ISA Anal Div Symp* **535** 9–25
[29] AICPA and Chartered Accountants of Canada 2009 Generally Accepted Privacy Principles
[30] Michener G and Bersch K 2013 Identifying transparency *Inf Polity* **18** 233–42
[31] Van Lamsweerde A 2001 Goal-oriented requirements engineering: a guided tour *Proc. IEEE Int. Conf. Requir. Eng.* 249–61
[32] European Commission 2016 General Data Protection Regulation
[33] Wright D and Raab C 2014 Privacy principles, risks and harms *Int. Rev. Law, Comput. Technol.* **28** 277–98
[34] Cate F H 2006 The failure of fair information practice principles *Consumer Protection in the Age of the Information Economy* (Aldershot: Ashgate Publishing)
[35] Anton A I and Potts C 1998 Use of goals to surface requirements for evolving systems *Proc. Int. Conf. on Software Engineering* 157–66

IOP Publishing

Human-Assisted Intelligent Computing
Modeling, simulations and applications
Mukhdeep Singh Manshahia, Igor S Litvinchev, Gerhard-Wilhelm Weber, J Joshua Thomas and Pandian Vasant

Chapter 7

A model of cells' regeneration towards smart healthcare

Hiroshi Yoshida

A log-periodic based model of leg-segment regeneration phenomena in multicells is here proposed towards smart healthcare. In this model, each cell is assumed to have a value of a log-periodic curve. A log-periodicity was originally introduced to model destruction phenomena, where cooperative behavior seems important [1]. In our previous work [2], a multicell was assumed to consist of some cells that have two attributes: left and right heterodimers, which stemmed from the *Dachsous/Fat* heterodimeric system and the steepness model [9]. According to differences between the left-right dimers, a cell is assumed to proliferate, move, and vanish (die). Using this framework, dimers were assumed to be redistributed in a manner of p left + $(1 - p)$ right $(0 < p < 1)$, which enables explanation of some leg-regeneration phenomena. It was, however, impossible to explain regeneration across leg segments, namely segment regeneration. In this work, on the other hand, each cell is assumed to have a value of a log-periodic curve, which gives an explanation of segment regeneration. I am going to also show and discuss some regenerating patterns and to give some turnover (under *dynamic equilibrium*) cell mass for smarter healthcare for future scope.

7.1 Introduction

Regeneration phenomena in cells' group will play an important role in healthcare. Legs of some life are sometimes able to regenerate even when their parts are amputated. Such regeneration has always been explained using the concept of positional information [3], where neighboring natural numbers are assigned to some parts in a leg, and regeneration is explained as recovery of numbers lost by amputation. It has further been long mentioned that regenerative cure will improve our health and life because of replenishment of lost parts.

doi:10.1088/978-0-7503-4801-0ch7

Crickets are able to regenerate lost parts of their legs [5]. Such regeneration has always been explained with the notion of continuous natural numbers in parts of legs—the positional-information model. There, however, have been some regeneration experiments that are not consistent with the positional-information model, especially when regeneration occurs across multiple segments [6, 7]. Instead of continuous natural numbers in positional-information, here log-periodic power-law curves are assigned to parts of legs, thereby segments regeneration can be described. A log-periodicity was inspired by critical phenomena such as tank destruction and has been applied to various crashes: stock-market crash or earthquakes [1]. These crashes are thought to derive from cooperative behavior of many elements. In multicellular organisms also, cooperative behavior seems to play an important role in development and regeneration of legs. This is why the log-periodic power law was here adopted as assigned values of legs.

7.2 Model

First, our previous model is briefly explained [2], where cells were assumed to have heterodimers on their boundary. In this model, during cell division, the left and right values (l and r) were redistributed to a newly created cell boundary with a value of $pl + (1 - p)$ $(0 < p < 1)$. Within this framework, values across the cells were calculated as illustrated in figure 7.1(a) and regeneration inside a segment was able to be well explained as in figure 7.1(b). On the other hand, regeneration across multiple segments has not been well explained with this framework because there are parts assigned to the same number (positional information) across segments.

To deal with segment regeneration, a log-periodic curve was used here. This curve can be described by the following equation:

$$p(x) = a[1 + b(x_c - x)m\{1 + c\cos(\omega \log(x_c - x) - ø)\}] \tag{7.1}$$

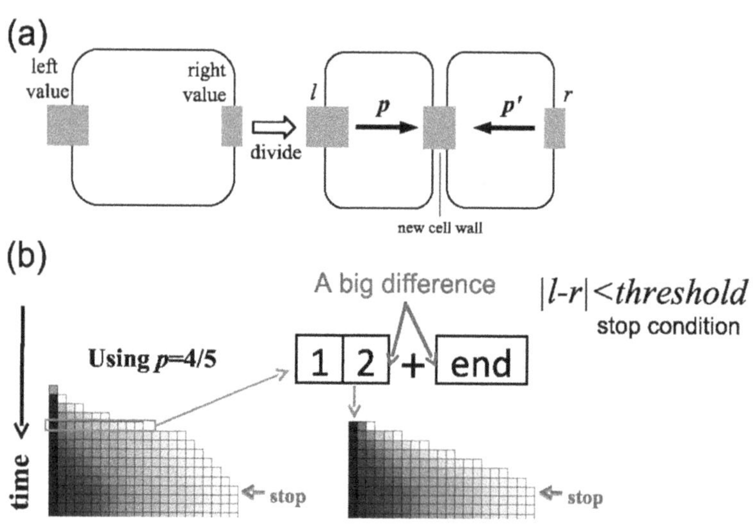

Figure 7.1. Proliferation of the cell.

where $p(x)$ denotes the positional value at x and a, b, c, m, x_c, ω, and $ø$ are parameters.

Note that in equation (7.1), x_c is a critical parameter that is here used to limit the cell number. In the same manner of the original model for cooperative crash, this equation was adopted for modeling cooperative behavior of cells.

7.3 Result and discussion

Using log-periodic curves described by equation (7.1), some characteristic segments were produced. In this case, we adopt a model starting with two cells inspired by the early embryo [8] where the existence of animal and vegetable poles plays an important role in development. Figure 7.2(a) shows a wave-like positional information produced with parameters: $a = 7$, $b = 0.2$, $c = 3$, $m = 0.6$, $\omega = 6.2$, $\varphi = 5$, $x_c = 150$.

Further figure 7.2(b) illustrates an intercalary (inserting) regeneration occurred after a third of the leg was amputated.

Next, we investigated segment regeneration that means regeneration across multiple segments. Figure 7.3 denotes two kinds of regeneration: insert and distal regenerations across segments. Please notice that in these experiments, reset of positional values was not necessary, which played an essential rule in previous models. Further, we show non-segmental regeneration in figure 7.3, where cancer-like monoclonal structures appeared. This may mean destruction of cell-group cooperation.

So far, some segment regenerations were shown with the aid of log-periodic power low (LPPL) models [1]. It might be remarkable that LPPL models enabled regeneration without reset of the end value.

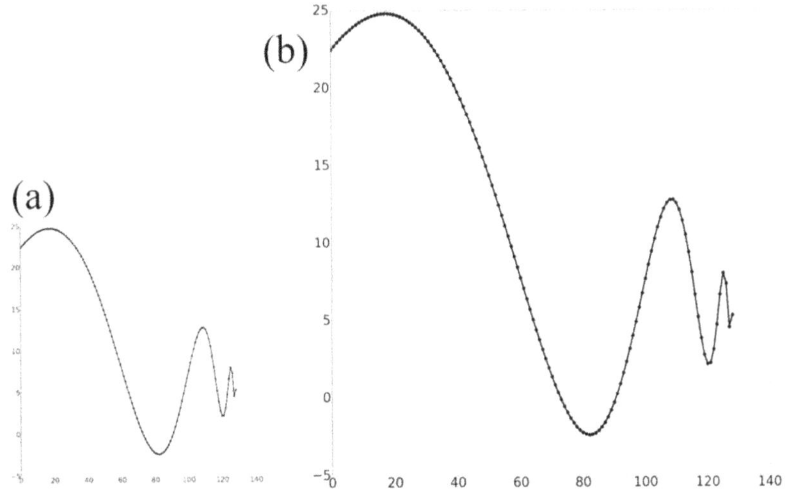

Figure 7.2. (a) Wave-like positional information to produce a segment. (b) Intercalary regeneration after amputation, where in this example, the new multicells were the same as the original one because of complete regeneration.

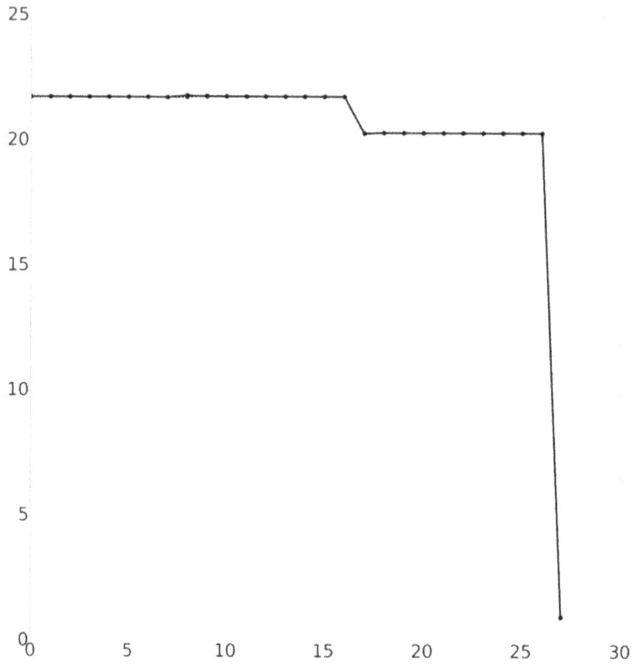

Figure 7.3. Cancer-like 'mono' cell mass.

7.4 Conclusion and highlight

In this paper we briefly showed segment regeneration without reset of positional values with the aid of LPPL models. Monoclonal cancer-like structures further appeared in the cell group, which may lead to a new concept of smart healthcare in the near future, as seen in the section below.

7.5 Future scope and literature review

In the Results section, one-type-only cell mass was seen in figure 7.3. This type of regeneration is dangerous to the body because it may provide the right cell mass in the body with serious destruction like cancer. It is, however, not very serious in plants because one-type cell mass just leads to a ball in the skin. Here we have a Lindenmayer system (an L-system) with a grammar: $L = (\Sigma, P, S)$ [4, 10, 12], where Σ is a set of letters, P is a rewriting rule, S is a starting symbol (sometimes called *axiom*).

An example of L-system is ({X,F,[,],+,-},{X→F[-X]FF[-X]+X,F→FF},X). The first application of this system is X→ F[-X]FF[-X]+X. The seventh application of the rewriting rule P makes a picture figure 7.4 when read as a turtle graphics with an angle 53 [14].

Another growth example of the plant is ({F,[,],+,-},{F→FF-[-F+F-F]+[+F-F-F]},F). Angle 37 turtle graphics of the fourth application gets us to figure 7.5. Using this L-system, we further made a turnover experiment for future scope. The turnover

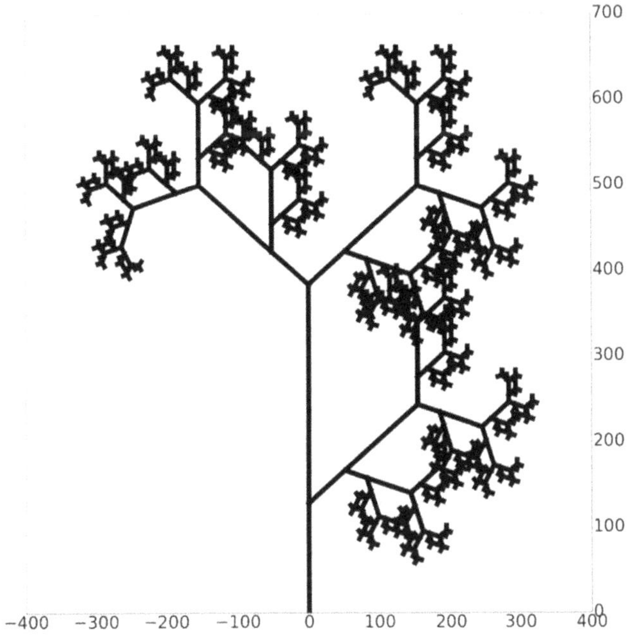

Figure 7.4. An example of L-system.

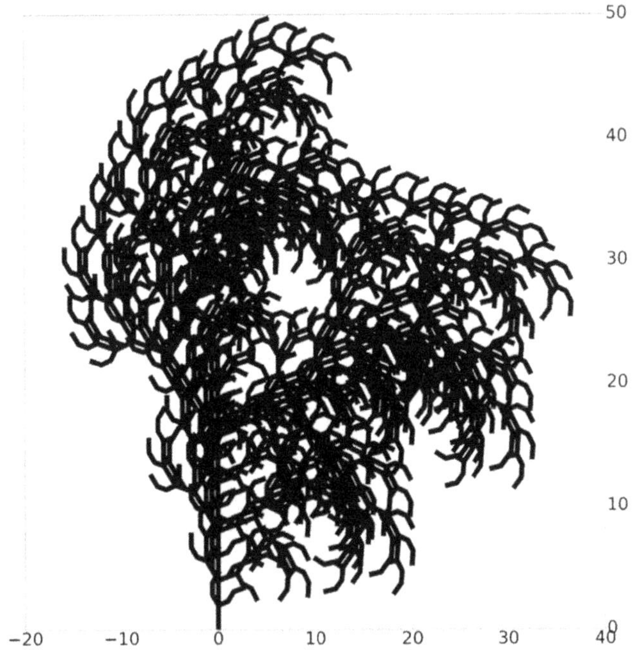

Figure 7.5. Another example of L-system.

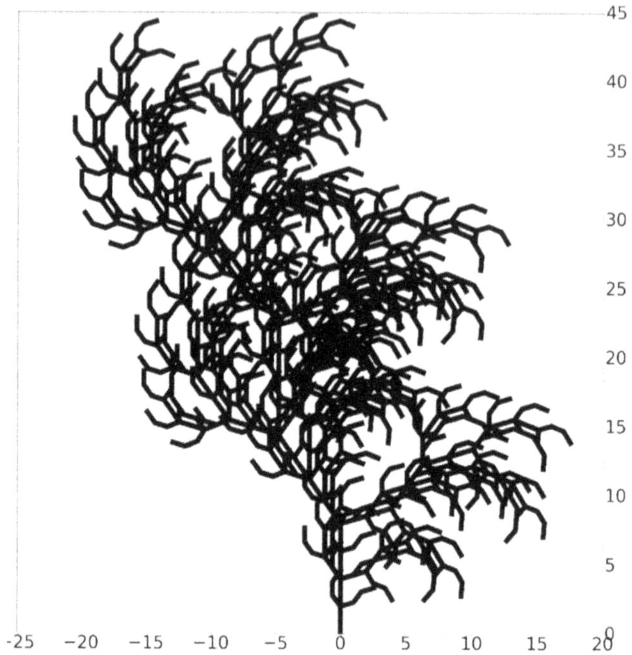

Figure 7.6. Turnover experiment for the L-system of figure 7.5.

phenomenon has been investigated [11, 12, 14] because it plays an essential role in maintenance of cells' good health in plants as well as animals. Fukuoka has recently submitted an idea that such turnover corresponds to the concept 'dynamic equilibrium,' where a little faster removal of cells and production of cells are essential to maintenance of life itself as well as healthcare [15]. We hence continued cutting in the ends of figure 7.5 similarly to old skin removal in animals. As seen in figure 7.6 we got similar and turnover cell mass for smart health.

Acknowledgements

This work was supported by MEXT KAKENHI Grant number (18K12036).

References

[1] Sornette D 2002 *Why Stock Markets Crash: Critical Events in Complex Financial Systems* (Princeton, NJ: Princeton University Press)

[2] Yoshida H 2012 A pattern to regenerate through turnover *Biosystems* **110** 43–50

[3] Wolpert L 1994 Positional information and pattern formation in development *Dev. Genet.* **15** 485–90

[4] Koshy T 2001 *Fibonacci and Lucas Numbers with Applications(Pure and Applied Mathematics: A Wiley Series of Texts, Monographs and Tracts)* (New York: Wiley-Interscience)

[5] Yoshida H, Bando T, Mito T, Ohuchi H and Noji S 2014 An extended steepness model for leg-size determination based on Dachsous/fat trans-dimer system *Sci. Rep.* **4** 4335

[6] Mittenthal J E and Trevarrow W W 1983 Intercalary regeneration in legs of crayfish: central segments *J. Exp. Zool.* **225** 15–31

[7] Palmeirim I, Henrique D, Ish-Horowicz D and Pourquie O 1997 Avian hairy gene expression identifies a molecular clock linked to vertebrate segmentation and somitogenesis *Cell* **91** 639–48

[8] Yoshida H, Furusawa C and Kaneko K 2005 Selection of initial conditions for recursive production of multicellular organisms *J. Theor. Biol.* **233** 501–14

[9] Lawrence P A, Struhl G and Casal J 2008 Do the protocadherins fat and dachsous link up to determine both planar cell polarity and the dimensions of organs? *Nat. Cell Biol.* **10** 1379–82

[10] Henke H, Sarlikioti V, Kurth W, Buck-Sorlin G H and Pagès L 2014 Exploring root developmental plasticity to nitrogen with a three-dimensional architectural model *Plant Soil* **385** 49–62

[11] Fernández M P 2008 Functional-structural model for radiata pine (*Pinus radiata* D. Don) *Thesis* Pontificia Universidad Catolica de Chile Escuela de Ingenieria

[12] Lindenmayer A 1968 Mathematical models for cellular interaction in development I. Filaments with one-sided inputs *J. Theor. Biol.* **18** 280–99

[13] Lindenmayer A 1968 Mathematical models for cellular interactions in development. II. Simple and branching filaments with two-sided inputs *J. Theor. Biol.* **18** 300–15

[14] Prusinkiewicz P and Lindenmayer A 1990 *The Algorithmic Beauty of Plants* (Berlin: Springer)

[15] Maynard S K 2022 Empty self and empty place in Japanese studies *Exploring the self, subjectivity, and character across Japanese and translation texts* (Leiden: Brill) pp 101–16

IOP Publishing

Human-Assisted Intelligent Computing
Modeling, simulations and applications
Mukhdeep Singh Manshahia, Igor S Litvinchev, Gerhard-Wilhelm Weber, J Joshua Thomas and Pandian Vasant

Chapter 8

Anomaly detection in location-based services

Jane Rubel Angelina Jeyaraj, Subhashini Sottallu Janakiram, Gayathri Narayana Yegnanarayanan and Yegnanarayanan Venkataraman

The increasing use of smartphones and the internet expose the real-time location information of users with or without the consent of the user or provider. This geographic information is used to provide location-based services and information to the users. This chapter attempts to discuss various location-based services available and also to highlight the various anomaly detection techniques available for those services. Mapping and navigation services that provide maps, features, attribute data, positioning information, navigation and route guidance accessible to client applications are discussed. Tracking services that focus on vehicle tracking, traffic prediction and traffic monitoring are reviewed. Finally, several anomaly detection techniques such as route anomalies, user behavior anomalies, fake check-in anomalies are discussed in the context of location-based services. This chapter also highlights the limitations that exist in location-based services and suggests ways to improve systems using these services.

8.1 Introduction

Combining technological breakthroughs in location sensing, mobile computing, and wireless networking opens up new and intriguing potential in the field of location-aware computing. The rise of location-aware computing and mobile Geographic Information System (GIS) is transforming the way we interact with data, our physical environment, and one another (Wilson 2012). Location knowledge is the use of information about a person's actual location to provide that individual with more specific information and services. The integration of three distinct technological capabilities makes position-aware computing possible: position and orientation sensing, wireless networking, and mobile computing systems.

Location-based services are among the most widely used and beneficial location-aware services (LBS). Location-based service providers (LSPs) leverage people's

doi:10.1088/978-0-7503-4801-0ch8

location data to give desired information (Almusaylim and Jhanjhi 2020). Location-based services (LBS) have become prevalent in a range of businesses and in our daily lives as a result of significant improvements in mobile information technology. LBS include applications that rely on the location of the user to provide a service or information at that location that is important to the user. Normally, LBS use mobile devices with positioning capabilities to provide the consumer with service or information.

The evolution and dissemination of smartphones is undeniably one of the most impressive advances in the last few decades in information and communication technologies (Arnaiz *et al* 2010). Location-based services are prevalent among the different applications of mobile platforms, as they mainly operate in positioning and navigation, helping numerous applications communicate with users on a real-time basis.

When we try to navigate and find places of interest in an unfamiliar area, region, state, or tourist location, a lot of challenges emerge because obstacles could vary from language norms to cultural practises and lifestyle obligations. Therefore, asking for directions may not always evoke a favourable reaction. When reaching the intended destination, we appear to get lost briefly, get embarrassed, irritated, and even depressed. However, since the evolution of maps and navigation, incorporated into smartphones, while travelling outside, it is uncommon for people to lose their way (Joseph *et al* 2020).

Tracking based on location refers to systems that physically identify, monitor, and track the movement of individuals or items electronically. With Global Positioning System (GPS) navigation, positions located on digital images, and searching for companies nearby using popular applications, location tracking technology are in use every day.

The GPS is a satellite-based navigation system that uses data from 24 earth-orbiting satellites to determine where you are. The GPS satellite measures the position by timing how long a radio signal travels to reach either a fixed or mobile earth tracking system, such as a GPS navigation device installed in your vehicle or a GPS chip smartphone. A GPS system may determine its position by longitude and latitude using multiple satellites and show the information to the person using the device or send the information to a software app or program (Dafallah 2014).

Information services are services offered through a cell phone, and consider the gadget's topographical area. They commonly give data or diversion. Since location-based services are dependent on the portable client's area, the essential target of the specialist co-op's framework is to figure out where the client is based on information services. There are numerous procedures to accomplish this.

The goal of this chapter is to give an overview of location-based services, as well as the ongoing evolution of such services and certain anomaly detection strategies. Section 8.2 is about maps and navigation services, which help with object location, navigation, and route assistance. Section 8.3 discusses location-based tracking services such as vehicle tracking, traffic forecasting, and traffic monitoring. Section 8.4 discusses several anomaly detection strategies such as route anomaly detection, user behaviour anomaly detection, and false check-in anomaly detection.

The limits of maps and navigation services, location-based tracking services, and anomaly detection approaches are discussed in section 8.5. The final section deals with the conclusion and future improvements.

8.2 Maps and navigation services

This section covers the maps and navigation services subcategory of LBS. Mapping and navigation services are depicted separately in this section.

8.2.1 Navigation system

Although early navigation was limited to following landmarks and remembering routes, navigation has a long history in human history. Various navigation technologies have been tried over the years (Ahmadpoor and Smith 2020).

A navigation system is a computing system that aids in navigating. Navigation systems can be run wholly on board the vehicle or vessel that is powered by the system (for example, on the ship's bridge), or they can be run elsewhere and lead the vehicle or vessel using a radio or other signal transmission device. In other cases, a combination of these procedures is used.

A modern navigation device is a system that combines position and orientation sensors, as well as computer and communication hardware and software, to make transporting people, cars, and other moving objects from one location to another as simple as possible. This includes methods for determining the destination, route, and distance travelled (Guerrero-Ibáñez *et al* 2018). From land-based vehicles to space-based satellites, the platform might be anything. Navigation systems are the hardware and software components that allow for automatic and intelligent navigation, according to Manulis *et al* (2021) while navigation is the process of guiding an object's movement between two points in space. As a result, navigation systems encompass a broad range of integrated technologies that allow the precise determination of geographical coordinates, velocity, and height of moving objects.

LBS are only possible because of this ability to accurately determine the position of moving objects. To analyse the location of a moving object, LBS use precise and real-time positioning technologies, as well as GIS. There are two types of positioning system technologies: outdoor (Zhao and Chen 2010) and inside (Qing-gui *et al* 2012) positioning. Yi *et al* (2013) used GPS, which is the most widely used and well-proven outdoor positioning system. The most recent indoor locating system technologies include WiFi, Radio Frequency Identification (RFID), laser, infrared, and ultra-sound. Modern localization systems include a variety of methodologies and algorithms, including Sakpere *et al* (2017)'s received signal strength indicator (RSSI), arrival time (TOA), arrival time difference (TDOA), and arrival angle (AOA). Aside from a gadget to place on the resource for service tracking, GPS is a solution that does not require any technology installation on a construction site (Zhao and Chen 2010).

- GPS—The Global Positioning System is an array of satellites that only work to help locate stuff all over the world. The satellites can be pinged to that receiver by any computer with a GPS receiver (which includes most smartphones) (Joseph *et al* 2020). This will allow it to communicate with at least four satellites, and the signal delay can be compared by the satellites to determine where the signal originated. This makes it possible for your phone to know exactly where you are and have turn-by-turn navigation.

- GIS—Geographic Information System is a system for collecting, storing, analysing, and managing data and related qualities that are spatially referred to the Earth. Geospatial information system is another name for it. GIS are software applications that offer and manage base map data such as man-made structures (streets, buildings) and topography (mountains, rivers) (Jovanović 2016). Information on points of interest, such as gas station locations, restaurants, nightclubs, and so on, is frequently handled using GIS. Finally, GIS data can be used to determine the radio frequency characteristics of a mobile network. This allows the gadget to determine the user's serving cell position.
- Wi-Fi—Tracking the Wi-Fi position is a bit different from other approaches. A system can usually connect to only one Wi-Fi network at a time. This removes the triangulation risk. For this method of location monitoring, IP addresses are used instead. Each network has a physical IP address that helps the Internet understand where it is. This is important in order to transmit data correctly through the Internet infrastructure. When your handset connects to a Wi-Fi network, it is combined with the network's physical IP. That enables your current address to be known by location services. The Wi-Fi Positioning System (WPS) is a geolocation system that uses the features of nearby Wi-Fi hotspots and other wireless access points to find where a device is located (Jones and Liu 2007). It is used where satellite navigation such as GPS is ineffective for numerous reasons, including indoor multipath and signal blockage, or where it would take too long to obtain a satellite fix.
- Cellular—Cellular monitoring operates a lot like GPS. However, the system connects to cellular towers instead of satellites. In general, you're going to be in the range of at least two buildings, and that's enough for the machine to locate your location using triangulation.
- QR codes—QR monitoring is closer to Wi-Fi. It logs information relevant to the scan when a dynamic QR code is scanned. Its physical location can be documented when the QR code is created (Eken and Sayar 2014). Anytime the code is scanned, the location can then be tagged. Users can install a QR code reader app and scan the created code to access positional information as well as other pieces of data. The positions of users can be determined using either GPS or the approach QR code. Due to the availability of GPS signals, GPS for outdoor localisation is recommended, while QR codes are used for interiors. To localise themselves, users can search for and use QR codes. The best route can be determined after identifying the user's location using GPS for outdoors and QR code positioning for indoors and outdoors, and the navigational instructions attaching text and photos of the nearest landmark on the way are given to the user. Landmarks can be located both indoors and outdoors, so this technique can seamlessly provide navigation facilities, and

pedestrians can also see a picture of the nearest landmark so that they can enjoy exploring the campus while travelling by collecting information about each structure.

- RFID—RFID belongs to a category of technologies known as Data Capture and Automatic Recognition (AIDC). AIDC methods automatically classify, collect, and enter items directly into computer systems with little to no human interaction, gathering data about them (Abdelhalim and Ei-Khayat 2013). To do this, RFID techniques use radio waves. At a basic level, RFID systems contain three components: an RFID tag or smart mark, an RFID reader, and an antenna. RFID tags provide an integrated circuit and an antenna for the transmission of data to the RFID reader (also called an interrogator). The reader then transforms the radio waves into a form of data that is more accessible. The information obtained from the tags is then passed to a host computer system via a communication interface, where the data can be stored in a database and evaluated at a later time.

8.2.2 Mapping services

Within several types of client applications, a map service makes charts, features, and attribute data available. One common use of a map service is to display business data from ArcGIS Online, Bing Maps, or Google Maps on top of base map tiles.

Google Maps is a free online mapping service from Google that provides a wealth of geographic data. On February 8, 2005, Googlemaps was originally revealed on GoogleBlog, and on June 20 of that year, the map coverage was expanded from the United States, United Kingdom, and Canada to the entire world. Google Maps, formerly GoogleLocal, is a global online map service that contains landmarks, route lines, area shapes, vector maps, satellite maps, and topographic maps, among other features.

Hu and Dai (2013), for example, developed an online map application using Google Maps APIs, SQL database, and ASP.NET, and a trip guide teaching platform using GoogleStreetView. Ibrahim and Mohsen (2014) created an online location-based service for Android phones utilising Google Maps.

Other companies continued to market both satellite and road map views. The BingTM Maps REST Services Application Programming Interface (API) provides a Representational State Transfer (REST) interface for operations such as establishing a path, geocoding an address, extracting metadata from photos, and generating a static map with pushpins. A hybrid view is provided by the BingTM Maps REST Services Application Programming Interface (API), which combines a road network with satellite views. It is possible to obtain latitude and longitude coordinates for a location by entering values such as locality, postal code, and street address. The position information can also be included as a query string. Local businesses, natural points of interest, and a reverse geocoded address for a given latitude and longitude coordinate can also be collected. Elevation data can be gathered for a variety of sites, polylines, or regions on the Earth.

To view a route, you can also get a static map. It is possible to design a path that connects two or more locations, as well as routes from main highways. Routes for driving or walking can be established. Driving routes can benefit from traffic statistics. The 'Bird's Eye View' integrated into Bing Maps was an early innovation, in addition to the standard map, satellite, and hybrid views.

In April 2005, Paul Rademacher, a 3D graphic artist, created the first map mash-up by combining Craigslist housing data with the newly accessible Google Maps. This ushered in a new era of Web mapping, controlled by so-called 'programmer-mapmakers'. Quick and appealing

Speeds and memory have substantially improved, and it is now possible to generate large amounts of vector data in an acceptable amount of time. Fast mobile broadband networks and low prices have also made mobile mapping access applications pervasive and affordable. A recent version of Google Maps for Mobile changed this paradigm by delivering vector maps that were accessible offline and could also be redirected offline.

8.3 Location-based tracking services

This section covers the location-based tracking services such as vehicle tracking services and traffic tracking services.

8.3.1 Vehicle tracking services

The use of automatic vehicle position in individual vehicles is combined by a vehicle tracking device with software that gathers certain fleet data for a detailed image of vehicle locations (Bloom *et al* 2017). A vehicle tracking system allows vehicles to be tracked and monitored 24/7 through an online computer, mobile phone, tablet, etc.

The device employs a camera to track vehicles as they pass through traffic analysis tracking systems, allowing for the calculation of their route, category, speed, changes in lanes, and other relevant data. Some tracking solutions employ computer vision in conjunction with traffic surveillance cameras as a placement strategy to identify cameras in critical locations (Sochor *et al* 2017). Other options use radio frequency identification (RFID) readers at transit vehicle stops (bus terminals or bus stops) for deployment (Prinsloo and Malekian 2016). Despite the fact that this technique does not allow for continuous surveillance or precise location, it is adequate for meeting the needs of travellers at a reasonable cost. To track cars, a few solutions combine long-range (LoRa) and radio frequency (RF) transceivers. GPS solutions remain the most popular positioning technology (O'Connor *et al* 2019), despite the fact that various other alternatives have emerged.

To connect the vehicle's system to the data-gathering cloud server, GSM, GPRS, 3G, and LTE communication networks can be employed. Communication between the vehicle device and the gateway bus stop can be established using LoRa technology (Salazar-Cabrera *et al* 2019). Computer vision remote control employing traffic security cameras does not track the vehicle in real time and instead uses technologies like RFID to identify the vehicle passing through the bus stop. Solutions that do not directly provide data to a cloud server rely on an indirect link between the bus stops and the cloud server, which is often accomplished via WiFi or a wired Internet connection (Kumar *et al* 2020).

Vehicle monitoring provides passengers with information such as the position of transit buses, the estimated arrival time at a specific station, and vehicle occupancy. Vehicle monitoring also provides services such as traffic detection, pollutant emission measurement, transportation company information, traffic information, vehicle specific identification, and vehicle theft.

Regions or blobs can be described in region-based vehicle tracking as linked image components with distinctive common properties, such as statistics on strength, colour, or texture. Regional or blob-based monitoring seeks to screen cars based on the differences in the image regions (Datondji *et al* 2016). A whole region associated with a specific vehicle is tracked over time using appearance, geometry features, and mobility signals. In free-flowing traffic, region-based tracking is computationally efficient and effective.

Contour-based vehicle tracking algorithms describe objects by their contours, which are simply their limits, and dynamically update these contours at each phase. In reality, powerful image intensity shifts typically occur in contours, making them ideal for tracking purposes (Cai *et al* 2017).

Feature-based vehicle tracking uses the idea that a group of features, rather than an entire entity, should reflect vehicles. This refers to the group of techniques that track features in individual images by first extracting them and then mapping the features across the frames. Features such as corners, lines, and standard shapes can be chosen as representative sections of the vehicle (Sharma 2018).

The model-based approach to vehicle tracking entails matching a predicted model to the image frame by frame as the vehicle moves. This allows trajectories and models to be retrieved, as well as the location of the vehicle with greater precision.

Artificial intelligence is utilised to estimate the arrival timings of buses at stations (Chen 2018). When the vehicle-to-terminal communication system fails or there is a problem with availability, these techniques can be used to calculate an approximate arrival time and not leave the user in the dark. Other AI uses include traffic jam avoidance utilising licence plate recognition and route planning for a trip.

8.3.2 Traffic tracking services

Vehicle tracking on roads and analysis of vehicle data from an ongoing vehicle can be used to improve traffic safety and provide drivers with information about nearby vehicles and warning signs about dangerous situations. It can also be used to distinguish traveller origin and feature-based vehicle tracking uses the idea that a group of features, rather than an entire entity, should reflect vehicles. This refers to the group of techniques that track features in individual images by first extracting them and then mapping the features across the frames. Features such as corners, lines, and standard shapes can be chosen as representative sections of the vehicle (Sharma 2018) destination trends, driver destinations over a period of time using a certain off ramp and whom. It can also be used to find out the percentage of travellers who go from one place to another along a given path. Traffic engineers may also use the data generated by the platforms in order to recommend better-informed detours for moving traffic during road construction projects.

Sensors with a fixed location are commonly utilised. By monitoring the shift in the magnetic field, inductive loop sensors are installed in roads to identify the presence of a conductive metal component (Marszalek and Duda 2018). By producing a magnetic anomaly in the Earth's magnetic field, magnetic sensors detect the presence of ferrous metal materials. Video image processors analyse video images from surveillance cameras on the road and calculate multi-lane traffic flow. In active mode, microwave radar sensors transmit electromagnetic signals and collect echoes from targets. Low-power infrared energy is used to illuminate detecting zones emitted by laser diodes, and the reflected energy is then used to detect automobiles. In a passive mode, these sensors detect electricity produced by automobiles or energy emitted by the surroundings and reflected by vehicles.

Recently, the introduction of smartphones and automobiles equipped with GPS has spawned a new type of data source (Geetha *et al* 2017) that could replace presence-type sensors by collecting more precise data or acquiring road data not yet covered by presence sensors. It is possible to build better and better traffic flow predictions for advanced traffic management system (ATMS) and intelligent transportation system (ITS) by using real-time and historical traffic trajectories from GPS sources. These trajectories can also be obtained from cell phones in cars and pedestrians using mobile crowd-sensing methods, providing us with relevant data on car and pedestrian traffic trajectories.

8.3.2.1 Traffic prediction

Predictability of traffic flow denotes the probability of prediction over a desired prediction time period to satisfy certain accuracy requirements. The expected value is calculated by combining the deterministic and predictable incertitude components.

Some methods of prediction use only simple statistical assumptions and are unable to use any external traffic characteristics to minimise the uncertainty of the prediction. The Instantaneous Travel Times (ITT) method, developed by Kwak and Geroliminis (2020), uses the actual calculated value as the measurement to be estimated next. This procedure is very quick since there is no need for calculation. Yet, in most situations, the accuracy of the forecast is poor. The arithmetical average of prior values is used to calculate the historical average (HA). It is more accurate than ITT and can outperform some more complex prediction models over longer time horizons, but it cannot handle rapid changes in traffic flow. This is a common misconception.

Some prediction systems rely on a limited set of known traffic flow factors. One of the key advantages of these prediction algorithms is the requirement of less training data. Simulation methods aid in the planning and design of transportation networks. These models simulate traffic in the place of historical data and traffic in real-time data because no historical data is available during the development process of a road network. It's worth noting that traffic simulation models can be used to assess future traffic levels in order to verify the viability of a transportation system design. CellularAutomata (CA) is a common microscopic simulation technology that divides highways into cells that can either be vacant or filled with a vehicle (Chen *et al* 2020). Only global features of a simulated road network, such as density, speed, or traffic count, are handled in the macroscopic simulation approach, where these variables are generated for each road segment of the road network (Mazloumian *et al* 2010).

To forecast the next traffic scenario, certain prediction systems employ historical and real-time traffic data. The Autoregressive (AR) component predicts the variable of interest by combining past values in a linear fashion, whereas the Moving Average (MA) components in a regression-like model use prior forecast mistakes (Nagy and Simon 2018).

Some traffic flow prediction systems do not rely on a fixed set of known parameters because vast amounts of data must be analysed and model training or forecast can be a computationally difficult effort. These methods may necessitate the employment of Bayesian network predictor variations by Chen *et al* (2019), which divide flow of traffic into groups such as unrestricted flow and overcrowding. These methods may also use regression algorithms that use the real and nearest k (based on distance measurement) flow states previously calculated to predict the next traffic flow states. Because they are incredibly expandable and capable of modelling non-linear, stationary, or non-stationary behaviour, neural networks (NNs) are presently the most often utilised prediction models for traffic flow prediction (Khajeh Hosseini and Talebpour 2019).

8.3.2.2 Traffic monitoring

The goal of road traffic surveillance is to collect data on all of the people involved in the surveillance process. Such data is important to provide numerous services that make transport easier, safer, and more eco-friendly.

Cameras are commonly used at intersections for traffic control and provide rich visual details. With the camera, objects become apparent because of the light reflection on the vision sensor from their surface. A projection matrix transforms a 3D world reference point into a 2D point on the picture plane's reference. For daytime activities, visible light cameras can be used. A visible light camera, on the other hand, is unlikely to meet performance standards at night or in bad weather for long periods of time. Infrared cameras can provide a good night vision option (Kansal and Mukherjee 2019).

Roadside intersection detection systems (Zhao *et al* 2019) provide automated intersection monitoring algorithms and local analysis of individual vehicle activity based on local analysis. This technique has been demonstrated to be resilient enough in the face of light shifts, tree leaf movement and slow moving objects. However, the output is generally impacted by shadows.

Stereo-vision systems situated in front of the car are the most common monitoring devices for in-vehicle intersections (Datondji *et al* 2016). After time-to-contact computation, stereo-vision will empower detection of vehicles with up to 10 command alerts to the driver. Several methods for monitoring and tracking roadside intersections are based on region and rely on expectable vehicle motions. Feature-based techniques can be utilised to manage incomplete occlusions in junctions.

It is possible to detect and track moving objects using a visible light sensor (Hoang *et al* 2017). Variations in infrared radiation detected by a passive-infrared sensor when a vehicle or a human travels close to the sensor have been employed in a wake-up device, which allows sensor nodes to be placed in sleep mode until they are needed. The shadows cast by objects were detected using near-infrared sensors.

Many attempts have been made to explore the possibility of using wireless communication networks to track road traffic (Bernas *et al* 2018). Analyzing information on the channel state, the signal strength indicator obtained, the connection quality indicator, and the rate of packet loss can be used to conduct vehicle detection and localization tasks. Wireless transmitters and receivers are used in some road traffic control systems (Bhatt *et al* 2010). In some systems, WiFi access points and WiFi-enabled laptops are employed for vehicle detection and speed estimation (Kassem *et al* 2012).

8.4 Anomaly detection in LBS

The difficulty of discovering designs in data that do not follow the rules to expected behaviour is known as 'anomaly detection' (Ahmed *et al* 2016). In various application sectors, these nonconforming patterns are referred to as anomalies, outliers, discordant observations, exceptions, aberrations, surprises, oddities, or contaminants. The purpose of anomaly detection is to find out-of-the-ordinary cases within seemingly comparable data. Anomaly detection is a valuable tool for detecting fraud, network intrusion, and other odd events that are important but hard to notice. In the context of LBS, this chapter examines anomaly detection approaches such as route anomalies, user behaviour anomalies, and phoney check-in anomalies.

8.4.1 Route anomaly detection

The GPS feature of smartphones, according to Wen-chen Hu *et al* (2012), provides mobile users with location information. Mobile users' journey routes, such as walking routes between households and schools or salesmen's delivery routes, can be visualised using location data. Any variations in the path are detected using location data. The authors look into several sorts of route anomalies and suggest different detection methodologies. It is divided into five sections: (i) path data collecting; (ii) path data preparation; (iii) path pattern discovery; (iv) path pattern analysis and visualisation; and (v) route anomaly detection. Linear route representation and incremental location searches, which locate matched routes by entering the search route place by place, are the most prevalent methods. As soon as the first location in the search path is input, it begins searching. Location by location, one or more probable route matches are found and displayed.

Wang *et al* (2013) have extensively investigated road traffic patterns or anomaly detections during the last few decades (Zheng *et al* 2015). Many traditional technologies have been developed, including video surveillance by Wen *et al* (2015), sensor networks by Zheng *et al* (2016), and RFID technology by Khan *et al* (2009). With the proliferation of GPS-enabled location-based methodologies, the spatio-temporal data has made road anomaly detection in road data a difficult topic to solve, attracting a lot of research.

Individual questionable cars, such as those that meander around aimlessly, can be identified using GPS tracking, according to one kind of anomaly detection technique developed by Sun *et al* (2015). The other type of anomaly detection is based on road traffic, with the goal of monitoring the inflows and outflows of road segments and extrapolating possible occurrences based on the number of vehicles that remain parked. For example, the formation of unusual or unexpected traffic behaviour using GPS data from taxi cabs has been investigated.

Detecting anomalies in road traffic from GPS sample data is becoming more significant in urban computing, according to Wang *et al* (2017), because they typically hint at underlying occurrences. To address these concerns, the authors propose a two-stage strategy that includes two components: a Collaborative Path Inference (CPI) model and a Road Anomaly Test (RAT) model. Rather than relying solely on static features for path inference, the author proposes that the CPI model learns dynamic properties jointly via a tensor decomposition technique. Collaborative path inference is performed using the CPI model, which incorporates both static and dynamic variables into a Conditional Random Field (CRF) before reconstructing sparse GPS snippets into fine-grained trajectories. Dynamic feature learning uses a tensor decomposition technique to learn dynamic context characteristics from data in a cooperative manner. They use two strong normalisation factors to overcome the data sparsity problem in the GPS snippets dataset while avoiding over-fitting.

8.4.2 User behavior anomaly detection

Human mobility is pervasive in modern society, and it is an intrinsic element of our daily activities. User behaviour anomaly detection can be used to predict the possibility of cyber attacks. According to Alejandro *et al* the session fingerprint must be supplied first. To enable the anomaly detection procedure, relevant and descriptive qualities must be chosen and included in the fingerprint. The anomalous behaviours of users are extracted from their fingerprints. To detect an anomaly, outlier detection techniques based on machine learning techniques focusing on distance or similarities between behavioural fingerprints are applied.

According to several studies, the device can be used to obtain up-to-date and precise human behaviour traits. The most frequent devices are personal computers (Ikuesan and Venter 2019) or cell phones (Meng *et al* 2018), although any device that can extract behavioural data could be employed (e.g., smartwatches or tablets). Keystrokes or mouse dynamics are often used to show behaviour when using home computers. However, when employing portable devices, sensor information (Shahid *et al* 2018), such as touchscreens, accelerometers, and gyroscopes, can be chosen.

User behaviour anomaly detection can be used to learn the daily patterns of the user and to proactively detect unusual situations such as loss of consciousness and mobility. Novák *et al* (2013) presented a smart home solution that can learn the user's behavioural patterns by observing and detecting abnormalities in such patterns. A caregiver, relative, or friend who can react quickly can use detected abnormalities as an informative input. Self-organizing maps (SOMs) are used in the presented system. According to Bhatti *et al* (2020), an outlier identification methodology known as iF Ensemble is utilised to analyse RSSs utilising a combination of supervised, unsupervised, and ensemble machine learning algorithms in the Wi-Fi indoor localization environment. An isolation forest (iForest) is employed as an unsupervised learning strategy in this work. Support vector machine (SVM), K-nearest neighbour (KNN), and random forest (RF) classifiers with stacking are included in the supervised learning technique, which is an ensemble learning method.

Deep neural networks (DNNs) now have a high probability of detecting any item, thanks to advances in computing power and processing capacity, ushering in a new era of machine learning. According to Lu *et al* (2018), they used deep learning to examine human behavior recognition using the YOLOv3 model. Gonzalez *et al* (2021) developed an innovative approach using auto encoders for monitoring everyday activities in nursing facilities for the elderly. The consumption of power by various household appliances is studied in order to model typical or normal behaviour in a person's daily activities.

8.4.3 Fake check-in anomaly detection

The expanding popularity of LBS has spawned an economy in which users advertise their location to their friends, thereby indirectly advertising particular businesses. Customers are attracted to venues by incentives and discounts for users of such services. Unfortunately, this economy may become a target for attackers seeking to disrupt the system for the sake of amusement or profit. This concern has piqued the interest of LBS, which has devoted resources to preventing bogus check-ins.

Based on empirical data, Liu *et al* (2014) review spatial interaction and distance decay in the context of human movement patterns and spatially embedded networks. The exponential trip displacement distribution is accurately reproduced by the gravity model. Individual mobility, on the other hand, may not experience the same distance degradation as group mobility, resulting in an ecological fallacy. In addition, we establish a geographical network with edge weights that represent the strength of interactions. The communities in the network are spatially consistent, closely according to province borders. The fact that intra-province and inter-province journeys have different distance decay parameters explains this trend.

Rizwan and Wan (2018) used location-based social networks (LBSN) data to monitor individual-level check-in behaviour and check-in intensity over time in a city. Using ArcGIS, the overall geographical patterns are examined using kernel density estimation (KDE). Check-in data from LBSN is well known for its ability to forecast human movement. However, because users can easily spoof their location in LBSN, there are substantial differences between check-in statistics and actual user mobility. Location spoofing is the deliberate creation of a false location, which has a negative impact on the trustworthiness of LBSN as well as the accuracy of spatial-temporal data. Lim *et al* (2019) show that location spoofing assaults, such as the sybil attack, may be identified quickly using unique advanced driver assistance system (ADAS) sensor data, such as fingerprints, without the need for infrastructure or a third-party trusted authority. A method was proposed for detecting behavioural patterns that makes use of the gyroscope and accelerometer included in most mobile devices. The authors checked the accuracy of the GPS data by comparing the travel direction to the facing direction calculated from the gyroscope's orientation data.

8.5 Limitations

The development of maps and navigation services based on modern technologies such as GPS, GIS, Wi-Fi, cellular codes, and RIFD has resulted in substantial changes in the way people and vehicles move from one site to another, deciding on the location, route, and distance to be travelled. However, such systems' accuracy has to be enhanced (Bang *et al* 2016). Some geographical characteristics can hinder communication between GPS satellites and devices that are equipped with the technology. Signals may not be able to pass through solid things such as high-rise buildings or mountains etc.

When known traffic flow parameters and past real-time traffic data are available, traffic prediction systems will be effective (Chen *et al* 2018). However, most cases only provide simulated data, making traffic prediction systems impractical. Driver-assist technology can be provided via traffic monitoring systems, which can help cars stay in their lanes, keep up with traffic, and even respond to traffic signs and signals (Pulugurtha and Gouribhatla 2022). This feature has the potential to make driving more enjoyable. It can, however, contribute to distracted driving, which can be fatal.

Nowadays, the GPS system tracking technology improves anomaly detection in recognizing abnormalities in road traffic (Alizadeh *et al* 2021). However, the noisy and sparse nature of GPS monitoring data has introduced a plethora of challenges, making it incredibly difficult to spot road traffic abnormalities. Privacy is the biggest issue in LBS since they allow unknown people to track the user's location (Asuquo *et al* 2018).

8.6 Conclusion and future enhancement

This chapter presented an overview of LB and illustrated the evolution of maps and navigation services. This chapter depicted the tracking technology based on location with a focus on vehicle tracking and traffic tracking. This chapter also focused on anomaly detection in location-based services. Thus, this chapter introduced location-aware computing illustrating various location-based services available and highlighted some of the anomaly detection techniques available.

There is a lot of scope to improve the location-based services and the systems using these services. Maps and navigation services can be improved by increasing the accuracy of such systems in determining route discovery, predicting the distance to be travelled, the duration of the journey, and possible alternative routes. The issue of GPS-enabled devices' signal strength can be addressed by focusing on research that enables the device to automatically configure and select which GPS satellite to connect to. Tracking and monitoring services, which have seen significant advancements, may result in the leakage of users' personal data. As a result, research aimed at improving the security and privacy of users' personal information can be conducted. Traffic monitoring services providing driver-assist technologies may contribute to distraction in driving. Driver distractions can be improved by research focusing on driver-alerting mechanisms.

References

Abdelhalim E A and Ei-Khayat G A 2013 A survey on analytical approaches used in RFID based applications *2013 Int. Conf. on Computer Applications Technology (ICCAT)* (Piscataway, NJ: IEEE) pp 1–6

Ahmadpoor N and Smith A D 2020 Spatial knowledge acquisition and mobile maps: the role of environmental legibility *Cities* **101** 102700

Ahmed M, Mahmood A N and Hu J 2016 A survey of network anomaly detection techniques *J. Netw. Comput. Appl.* **60** 19–31

Almusaylim Z A and Jhanjhi N Z 2020 Comprehensive review: privacy protection of user in location-aware services of mobile cloud computing *Wirel. Pers. Commun.* **111** 541–64

Alizadeh M, Hamilton M, Jones P, Ma J and Jaradat R 2021 Vehicle operating state anomaly detection and results virtual reality interpretation *Expert Syst. Appl.* **177** 114928

Arnaiz A, Iung B, Adgar A, Naks T, Tohver A, Tommingas T and Levrat E 2010 Information and communication technologies within E-maintenance *E-maintenance* (London: Springer) pp 39–60

Asuquo P, Cruickshank H, Morley J, Ogah C P A, Lei A, Hathal W, Bao S and Sun Z 2018 Security and privacy in location-based services for vehicular and mobile communications: an overview, challenges, and countermeasures *IEEE Internet Things J.* **5** 4778–802

Bang Y, Kim J and Yu K 2016 An improved map-matching technique based on the Fréchet distance approach for pedestrian navigation services *Sensors* **16** 1768

Bernas M, Płaczek B, Korski W, Loska P, Smyła J and Szymała P 2018 A survey and comparison of low-cost sensing technologies for road traffic monitoring *Sensors* **18** 3243

Bhatt V D, Khati S S, Pandey D and Pant H C 2010 Wireless traffic system with speed control *2010 The 2nd Int. Conf. on Computer and Automation Engineering (ICCAE)* vol 1 (Piscataway, NJ: IEEE) pp 413–7

Bhatti M A, Riaz R, Rizvi S S, Shokat S, Riaz F and Kwon S J 2020 Outlier detection in indoor localization and internet of things (IoT) using machine learning *J. Commun. Netw.* **22** 236–43

Bloom C, Tan J, Ramjohn J and Bauer L 2017 Self-driving cars and data collection: privacy perceptions of networked autonomous vehicles *Thirteenth Symp. on Usable Privacy and Security (SOUPS 2017)* 357–75

Cai L, Wang L, Li B, Zhang L and Lv W 2017 A novel vehicle tracking algorithm based on mean shift and active contour model in complex environment *Proc. SPIE Automated Visual Inspection and Machine Vision II* **10334** 161–7

Chen C H 2018 An arrival time prediction method for bus system *IEEE Internet Things J.* **5** 4231–2

Chen K, Chen F, Li K, Liu J, Zhang F, Mei L and Zhai J 2019 An early warning method for highway traffic accidents based on bayesian networks *Proc. of the 2019 Int. Conf. on Artificial Intelligence and Computer Science* 111–6

Chen M, Chen Q, Gao L, Chen Y and Wang Z 2020 Predicting geographic information with neural cellular automata *arXiv preprint* arXiv:2009.09347

Chen Y, Guizani M, Zhang Y, Wang L, Crespi N, Lee G M and Wu T 2018 When traffic flow prediction and wireless big data analytics meet *IEEE Netw.* **33** 161–7

Dafallah H A A 2014 Design and implementation of an accurate real time GPS tracking system *The Third Int. Conf. on e-Technologies and Networks for Development (ICeND2014)* (Piscataway, NJ: IEEE) pp 183–8

Datondji S R E, Dupuis Y, Subirats P and Vasseur P 2016 A survey of vision-based traffic monitoring of road intersections *IEEE Trans. Intell. Transp. Syst.* **17** 2681–98

Eken S and Sayar A 2014 A smart bus tracking system based on location-aware services and QR codes *2014 IEEE Int. Symp. on Innovations in Intelligent Systems and Applications (INISTA) Proc.* (Piscataway, NJ: IEEE) pp 299–303

Geetha M, Priyadarshini T, Sangeetha B and Sanjana S 2017 Anti-theft and tracking mechanism for vehicles using GSM and GPS *2017 Third Int. Conf. on Science Technology Engineering and Management (ICONSTEM)* (Piscataway, NJ: IEEE) pp 252–5

Gonzalez D, Patricio M A, Berlanga A and Molina J M 2021 Variational autoencoders for anomaly detection in the behaviour of the elderly using electricity consumption data *Expert Syst.* **39** e12744

Guerrero-Ibáñez J, Zeadally S and Contreras-Castillo J 2018 Sensor technologies for intelligent transportation systems *Sensors* **18** 1212

Hoang T M, Baek N R, Cho S W, Kim K W and Park K R 2017 Road lane detection robust to shadows based on a fuzzy system using a visible light camera sensor *Sensors* **17** 2475

Hu S and Dai T 2013 Online map application development using google maps API, SQL database, and ASP .NET *Int. J. Inform. Commun. Technol. Res.* **3** 102–10

Hu W C, Kaabouch N, Yang H J and Mousavinezhad S H 2012 Route anomaly detection using a linear route representation *J. Comput. Netw. Commun.* **2012** 675605

Huang H, Gartner G, Krisp J M, Raubal M and Van de Weghe N 2018 Location based services: ongoing evolution and research agenda *J. Loc. Based Serv.* **12** 63–93

Ibrahim O A and Mohsen K J 2014 Design and implementation an online location based services using google maps for android mobile *Int. J. Comput. Netw. Commun. Sec.(CNCS)* **2** 113–8

Ikuesan A R and Venter H S 2019 Digital behavioral-fingerprint for user attribution in digital forensics: are we there yet? *Dig. Investig.* **30** 73–89

Jones K and Liu L 2007 What where wi: an analysis of millions of wi-fi access points *2007 IEEE Int. Conf. on Portable Information Devices* (Piscataway, NJ: IEEE) pp 1–4

Joseph L, Neven A, Martens K, Kweka O, Wets G and Janssens D 2020 Measuring individuals' travel behaviour by use of a GPS-based smartphone application in Dar es Salaam, Tanzania *J. Trans. Geog.* **88** 102477

Jovanović V 2016 The application of GIS and its components in tourism *Yugoslav J. Oper. Res.* **18** 261–72

Kansal S and Mukherjee S 2019 Automatic single-view monocular camera calibration-based object manipulation using novel dexterous multi-fingered delta robot *Neur. Comput. Applic.* **31** 2661–78

Kassem N, Kosba A E and Youssef M 2012 RF-based vehicle detection and speed estimation *2012 IEEE 75th Vehicular Technology Conf. (VTC Spring)* (Piscataway, NJ: IEEE) pp 1–5

Khan F, Akhtar N and Qadeer M A 2009 RFID enhancement in road traffic analysis by augmenting reciever with telegraphc *2009 Int. Workshop on Knowledge Discovery and Data Mining* (Piscataway, NJ: IEEE) pp 331–4

Khajeh Hosseini M and Talebpour A 2019 Traffic prediction using time-space diagram: a convolutional neural network approach *Transp. Res. Rec.* **2673** 425–35

Kumar H, Singh M K, Gupta M P and Madaan J 2020 Moving towards smart cities: solutions that lead to the smart city transformation framework *Technol. Forecast. Soc. Change* **153** 119281

Kwak S and Geroliminis N 2020 Travel time prediction for congested freeways with a dynamic linear model *IEEE Trans. Intell. Transp. Syst.* **22** 7667–77

Lim K, Tuladhar K M and Kim H 2019 Detecting location spoofing using ADAS sensors in VANETs *2019 16th IEEE Annual Consumer Communications and Networking Conf. (CCNC)* (Piscataway, NJ: IEEE) pp 1–4

Liu Y, Sui Z, Kang C and Gao Y 2014 Uncovering patterns of inter-urban trip and spatial interaction from social media check-in data *PLoS One* **9** e86026

Lu J, Yan W Q and Nguyen M 2018 Human behaviour recognition using deep learning *2018 15th IEEE Int. Conf. on Advanced Video and Signal Based Surveillance (AVSS)* (Piscataway, NJ: IEEE) pp 1–6

Manulis M, Bridges C P, Harrison R, Sekar V and Davis A 2021 Cyber security in new space *Int. J. Inf. Secur.* **20** 287–311

Marszalek Z and Duda K 2018 Vehicle magnetic signature compatibility for inductive loop sensor with various signal conditioning systems *2018 Int. Conf. on Signals and Electronic Systems (ICSES)* (Piscataway, NJ: IEEE) pp 33–6

Mazloumian A, Geroliminis N and Helbing D 2010 The spatial variability of vehicle densities as determinant of urban network capacity *Phil. Trans. R. Soc. A* **368** 4627–47

Meng W, Wang Y, Wong D S, Wen S and Xiang Y 2018 TouchWB: touch behavioral user authentication based on web browsing on smartphones *J. Netw. Comput. Appl.* **117** 1–9

Nagy A M and Simon V 2018 Survey on traffic prediction in smart cities *Pervasive Mob. Comput.* **50** 148–63

Novák M, Jakab F and Lain L 2013 Anomaly detection in user daily patterns in smart-home environment *J. Sel. Areas Health Inform* **3** 1–11

O'Connor A C, Gallaher M P, Clark-Sutton K, Lapidus D, Oliver Z T, Scott T J, Wood D W, Gonzalez M A, Brown E G and Fletcher J 2019 Economic benefits of the global positioning system (GPS) *RTI Report Number 0215471* Gaithersburg, MD: NIST

Prinsloo J and Malekian R 2016 Accurate vehicle location system using RFID, an internet of things approach *Sensors* **16** 825

Pulugurtha S S and Gouribhatla R 2022 Drivers' response to scenarios when driving connected and automated vehicles compared to vehicles with and without driver assist technology *MTI Report* Mineta Transportation Institute Publications

Qing-gui C, Kai L, Ye-jiao L, Qi-hua S and Jian Z 2012 Risk management and workers' safety behavior control in coal mine *Saf. Sci.* **50** 909–13

Rizwan M and Wan W 2018 Big data analysis to observe check-in behavior using location-based social media data *Information* **9** 257

Sakpere W, Adeyeye-Oshin M and Mlitwa N B 2017 A state-of-the-art survey of indoor positioning and navigation systems and technologies *S. Afr. Comput. J.* **29** 145–97

Salazar-Cabrera R, Pachón de la Cruz Á and Madrid Molina J M 2019 Proof of concept of an iot-based public vehicle tracking system, using lora (long range) and intelligent transportation system (its) services *J. Comput. Netw. Commun.* **2019** 9198157

Shahid M R, Blanc G, Zhang Z and Debar H 2018 IoT devices recognition through network traffic analysis *2018 IEEE Int. Conf. on Big Data (Big Data)* (Piscataway, NJ: IEEE) pp 5187–92

Sharma K 2018 Feature-based efficient vehicle tracking for a traffic surveillance system *Comput. Electr. Eng.* **70** 690–701

Sochor J, Juránek R and Herout A 2017 Traffic surveillance camera calibration by 3d model bounding box alignment for accurate vehicle speed measurement *Comput. Vision Image Understanding* **161** 87–98

Sun Y, Zhu H, Liao Y and Sun L 2015 Vehicle anomaly detection based on trajectory data of ANPR system *2015 IEEE Global Communications Conf. (GLOBECOM)* (Piscataway, NJ: IEEE) pp 1–6

Wang H, Wen H, Yi F, Zhu H and Sun L 2017 Road traffic anomaly detection via collaborative path inference from GPS snippets *Sensors* **17** 550

Wang X, Guo L, Ai C, Li J and Cai Z 2013 An urban area-oriented traffic information query strategy in VANETs *International Conference on Wireless Algorithms, Systems, and Applications* (Berlin: Springer) pp 313–24

Wen H, Ge S, Chen S, Wang H and Sun L 2015 Abnormal event detection via adaptive cascade dictionary learning *2015 IEEE Int. Conf. on Image Processing (ICIP)* (Piscataway, NJ: IEEE) pp 847–51

Wilson M W 2012 Location-based services, conspicuous mobility, and the location-aware future *Geoforum* **43** 1266–75

Yi T H, Li H N and Sun H M 2013 Multi-stage structural damage diagnosis method based on *Smart Struct. Syst.* **12** 345–61

Zhao J, Xu H, Liu H, Wu J, Zheng Y and Wu D 2019 Detection and tracking of pedestrians and vehicles using roadside LiDAR sensors *Transport. Res. C: Emerg. Technol.* **00** 68–87

Zheng X, Cai Z, Li J and Gao H 2015 An application-aware scheduling policy for real-time traffic *2015 IEEE 35th Int. Conf. on Distributed Computing Systems* (Piscataway, NJ: IEEE) pp 421–30

Zheng X, Cai Z, Li J and Gao H 2016 A study on application-aware scheduling in wireless networks *IEEE Trans. Mob. Comput.* **16** 1787–801

Zhao S F and Chen L C 2010 The application of the integrated indicators based on BP neural network in colliery equipment safety monitoring *2010 Int. Conf. on E-Product E-Service and E-Entertainment* (Piscataway, NJ: IEEE) pp 1–4

IOP Publishing

Human-Assisted Intelligent Computing
Modeling, simulations and applications
Mukhdeep Singh Manshahia, Igor S Litvinchev, Gerhard-Wilhelm Weber, J Joshua Thomas and Pandian Vasant

Chapter 9

Optimized packing soft ellipses

T Romanova, Yu Stoyan, A Pankratov, I Litvinchev, O Kravchenko, Z Duryagina, O Melashenko and A Chugai

Packing soft ellipses in a minimal convex rectangle domain is presented. The ellipses are soft in the sense that their shapes are not fixed *a priori* and can vary in a certain range subject to their individual areas' conservation. Free translation and rotation of ellipses is permitted. The objective is minimizing the container's height. New mathematical tools to state analytically layout constraints are introduced based on the phi-function approach. Packing soft ellipses is stated as a nonconvex optimization problem, a solution technique is developed, and results of a numerical experiment are discussed. Soft packing problems are motivated by modeling porous media under pressure and arise in the oil and gas extracting industry.

9.1 Introduction

Packing ellipses is NP-hard [1] and one can find various applications of this problem in molecular dynamics and powder metallurgy, logistics and transportation, robotics and manufacturing [2–6].

Different settings of ellipse packing are known. In [4] a set of given ellipses must be produced from a minimal area rectangular plate. Both width and length of the rectangular plate are bounded, while free translation and rotation of ellipses is permitted. To state the layout conditions separating lines are used. The global optimal solutions were obtained for a small number of ellipses. For larger problem instances the so- called polylithic approach was used. The ellipses were added in each step in a strip-packing manner and the area of the rectangle was minimized by a greedy technique.

Packing freely moving ellipses in a minimized rectangular container was studied in [7]. The quasi-phi-functions approach was used to state analytical layout conditions.

doi:10.1088/978-0-7503-4801-0ch9

A minimized regular polygon was considered for packing ellipses in [8]. The solution approach is based on embedded Lagrange multipliers, while Lipschitz-continuous global optimizer (LGO) solver was used to solve arising nonlinear optimization problems.

Optimized packing ellipses (ellipsoids) are presented in [6]. The dimension of the arising model is linear with respect to the number of objects. The layout constraints are derived similar to the transformation-based model presented in [5].

Approximating the container by a regular grid is used in [9, 10] to state the optimal packing as a linear integer optimization problem. Different regular objects are considered (circles, ellipses, rhombuses, rectangles, octagons, etc). Recursive packing, i.e., packing objects inside one another is also permitted.

Packing freely rotating and translating ellipses in a minimal convex scaling polygon is considered in [11]. To obtain a corresponding scaling parameter for the polygonal container the phi-function approach is used. Novel (quasi) phi-functions are used to state layout conditions and formulate a continuous nonlinear optimization problem. The decomposition procedure [7] is combined with the starting point algorithm to get locally optimal solutions.

Packing a fixed number of ellipses in a minimal rectangle is studied in [12] using the (quasi) phi-function approach to state the placement constraints. Two algorithms are proposed to get feasible starting points for equal and different ellipses, correspondingly. A decomposition algorithm is used to reduce the problem dimension and find local optimal solutions.

Packing optimized ellipses in a (disconnected) polygonal domain to maximize the packing factor is presented in [13]. The problem arises in designing parts for 'support-free' 3D printing under constraints for parts static/dynamic strength. In this problem the shapes and the number of ellipses can vary subject to certain constraints. By the phi-function approach the optimized layout is reduced to nonlinear programming subproblems.

In this work packing different freely translated and rotated ellipses within a rectangle of minimal height is presented. The shapes of ellipses can vary in a certain range subject to preserving their individual areas. In what follows we refer to this case as packing soft ellipses.

Our interest in this kind of packing problems is motivated by modeling porous media under pressure [14–20]. These problems arise frequently in the oil and gas extracting industry [21–27]. Elements of porous media can be deformed by external force, however, the mass of each individual element remains unchanged. In a 2D setting this is equivalent to area conservation.

To the best of our knowledge packing problems for soft ellipses were not considered before. A novel mathematical model is provided for minimizing the height of the container filled by a number of soft ellipses and a multistart solution strategy is proposed. Two related problems are solved successively. First, an optimized circle packing problem is considered for the circles having the same area as individual ellipses. The layout obtained this way is used as a feasible starting point for packing soft ellipses.

The organization of the remaining part of the chapter is as follows. The general formulation for packing soft ellipses is stated in section 9.2. layout constraints are derived in section 9.3 using the phi-functions approach. The next section presents an optimization problem for packing soft ellipses, while details of the multistart solution approach are given in section 9.5. Results of numerical experiments are discussed in section 9.6 and the next section concludes. Definitions and properties of the phi-functions are given in appendix A.

9.2 The main problem

Let a container Ω be a convex rectangle defined by its fixed length l and variable height h in the fixed coordinate system XOY.

We also define a family of ellipses $\{E_i, i \in I_n\}$, $I_n = \{1, 2, \dots, n\}$. An ellipse E_i is given by the equation $\frac{x_i^2}{a_i^2} + \frac{y_i^2}{a_i^2} = 1$, where a_i and b_i are variable parameters (semi-axes) of the ellipse. With each ellipse we associate a circle S_i of radius r_i such that $a_i = \lambda_i r_i$ and $b_i = \frac{1}{\lambda_i} r_i$, where λ_i is a variable, $1 \leqslant \lambda_i \leqslant \lambda_{\text{upper}}$. Note that the area of ellipse E_i for any horizontal stretching by λ_i while vertical shrinking by $\frac{1}{\lambda_i}$ remains equal to the area of the circle S_i since $\text{Area}(E_i(\lambda_i)) = \pi a_i \cdot b_i = \pi r_i^2$.

Let us denote the variable motion vector of each ellipse E_i by $u_i = (v_i, \theta_i)$, where $v_i = (x_i, y_i)$ and θ_i are its shift vector and rotation parameter.

Let λ_i be a variable horizontal stretching ratio of E_i while $\frac{1}{\lambda_i}$ is its vertical shrinking ratio.

Each ellipse E_i rotating by an angle θ_i, shifting by a vector v_i, horizontally streaching by λ_i and vertically shrinking by $\frac{1}{\lambda_i}$ is described as $E_i(u_i, \lambda_i) = \{p \in R^2 : p = v_i + M(\theta_i) \cdot \Lambda(\lambda_i) \cdot p^{0T}, \forall p^0 \in E_i^0\}$. Here E_i^0 denotes the non-translating, non-rotating, non-streaching and non-shrinking ellipse E_i (circle S_i) with $a_i = r_i$ and $b_i = r_i$ corresponding to $\lambda_i = 1$, $\Lambda(\lambda_i) = \begin{pmatrix} \lambda_i & 0 \\ 0 & \frac{1}{\lambda_i} \end{pmatrix}$, $M(\theta_i) = \begin{pmatrix} \cos\theta_i & \sin\theta_i \\ -\sin\theta_i & \cos\theta_i \end{pmatrix}$.

Packing problem of soft ellipses. Arrange the set of non-overlapping soft ellipses $E_i(u_i, \lambda_i)$, $i \in I_n$, within a rectangular domain $\Omega(h)$ of the minimum height.

In the ellipse packing problem the following placement constraints must be satisfied:

$\text{int}\, E_i(u_i, \lambda_i) \cap \text{int}\, E_j(u_j, \lambda_j) = \varnothing$, for $i > j \in I_n$,

$E_i(u_i, \lambda_i) \subset \Omega(h)$ for $i \in I_n$.

The first equation presents the interior non-overlapping conditions for each pair of ellipses while the second equation provides arrangement of each ellipse fully inside $\Omega(h)$ (containment conditions).

In some applications (see, e.g., [18]) containment constraints can be relaxed to containment for the centers of ellipses, i.e.

$v_i \in \Omega(h)$ for each $i \in I_n$.

9.3 Geometric tools

The phi-function approach is used for an analytical description of the stated packing constraints (see, e.g. [28–30]).

In what follows, the phi-functions used to formulate containment conditions and the quasi-phi-functions used to state non-overlapping are presented for packing soft ellipses. These geometric tools allow considering continuously moving and stretching ellipses.

Basic definitions and characteristics of (quasi) phi-functions one can find, e.g., in [8, 28–31].

9.3.1 Formulation of containment conditions

The phi-function to state analytically the containment $E_i(u_i, \lambda_i) \subset \Omega(h) \Leftrightarrow \text{int } E_i(u_i, \lambda_i) \cap \Omega^*(h) = \varnothing, \Omega^*(h) = R^2 \backslash int\Omega(h)$ can be constructed as follows.

The function defined by

$$\Phi^{E_i\Omega^*}(u_i, \lambda_i, h) = \min_{k=1,\dots,4} \varphi_k(u_i, \lambda_i, h) \tag{9.1}$$

is the phi-function of $E_i(u_i, \lambda_i)$ and $\Omega^*(h)$, where

$$\varphi_1(u_i, \lambda_i, h) = x_i - \frac{r_i}{\lambda_i}\sqrt{1 + (\lambda_i^4 - 1)\cos\theta_i},$$

$$\varphi_2(u_i, \lambda_i, h) = y_i - \frac{r}{\lambda_i}\sqrt{1 + (\lambda_i^4 - 1)\sin\theta_i},$$

$$\varphi_3(u_i, \lambda_i, h) = l - x_i - \frac{r_i}{\lambda_i}\sqrt{1 + (\lambda_i^4 - 1)\cos\theta_i},$$

$$\varphi_4(u_i, \lambda_i, h) = h - y_i - \frac{r_i}{\lambda_i}\sqrt{1 + (\lambda_i^4 - 1)\sin\theta_i}.$$

Therefore, according to (9.1), the inequality $\Phi^{E_i\Omega^*}(u_i, \lambda_i, h) \geqslant 0$ insures the complete containment condition $(E_i(u_i, \lambda_i) \subset \Omega) \Leftrightarrow \text{int } E_i(u_i, \lambda_i) \cap \text{int } \Omega^*(h) = \varnothing$.

For the relaxed containment constraints $v_i \in \Omega(h)$ the following function can be used

$$\varphi^{E_i\Omega^*}(v_i, h) = \min_{k=1,\dots,4} \varphi_k(v_i, h),$$

$$\varphi_1(v_i, h) = x_i, \varphi_2(v_i, h) = y_i, \varphi_3(v_i, h) = l - x_i, \varphi_4(v_i, h) = h - y_i.$$

9.3.2 Formulation of non-overlapping constraints

For a pair of soft ellipses $E_i(u_i, \lambda_i)$, $E_j(u_j, \lambda_j)$ the quasi-phi-function is constructed similar to [11].

The function defined by

$$\Phi'^{E_iE_j}\left(v_i, v_j, \theta_i, \theta_j, \lambda_i, \lambda_j, \phi_{ij}\right) = f'_{ij}\left(v_i, \phi_{ij}\right) - f'_{ji}\left(v_j, \phi_{ij}\right) - \left(g_{ij}\left(\theta_i, \lambda_i, \phi_{ij}\right) + g_{ji}\left(\theta_j, \lambda_i, \phi_{ij}\right)\right) \quad (9.2)$$

is the quasi-phi-function for $E_i(u_i, \lambda_i)$ and $E_j(u_j, \lambda_j)$, where

$f'_{ij}(v_i, \phi_{ij}) = x_i\cos\phi_{ij} - y_i\sin\phi_{ij}$, $f'_{ji}(v_j, \phi_{ij}) = x_j\cos\phi_{ij} - y_j\sin\phi_{ij}$,

$$g_{ij}\left(\theta_i, \lambda_i, \phi_{ij}\right) = \frac{r_i}{\lambda_i}\sqrt{1 + (\lambda_i^4 - 1)\cos^2\left(\theta_i - \phi_{ij}\right)},$$

$$g_{ji}\left(\theta_j, \lambda_i, \phi_{ij}\right) = \frac{r_j}{\lambda_j}\sqrt{1 + \left(\lambda_j^4 - 1\right)\cos^2\left(\theta_j - \phi_{ij}\right)}$$

Here ϕ_{ij} is the auxiliary variable angle generating by axis OX of the fixed coordinate system OXY and the perpendicular line to a separating line between two ellipses $E_i(u_i, \lambda_i)$ and $E_j(u_j, \lambda_j)$.

The following characteristic of the quasi-phi-function [7] is used: if $\Phi'^{E_iE_j}(u_i, u_j, \phi_{ij}, \lambda_i, \lambda_j) \geqslant 0$ for some ϕ_{ij}, then $\text{int}\, E_i(u_i, \lambda_i) \cap \text{int}\, E_j(u_j, \lambda_j) = \varnothing$.

9.4 Mathematical model

We collect the decision variables of the problem in the vector: $t = (v, \theta, \lambda)$, where $v = (v_1, v_2, \ldots, v_n)$, $\theta = (\theta_1, \theta_2, \ldots, \theta_n)$, $\lambda = (\lambda_1, \lambda_2, \ldots, \lambda_n)$, $\phi = (\phi_{ij}, (i, j) \in \Xi = \{(i, j): i > j \in I_n\})$,

Packing soft ellipses in the rectangle Ω of the minimal height is stated as follows:

$$\min h, \ s.\ t.\ (t, \phi, \lambda) \in V \subset R^\sigma \quad (9.3)$$

$$V = \left\{(t, \phi, \lambda) \in R^\sigma: \Phi'^{E_iE_j}(u_i, u_j, \lambda_i, \lambda_j, \phi_{ij}) \geq 0, (i, j) \in \Xi, \ \Phi^{E_i\Omega^*}(u_i, \lambda_i, h) \geq 0, i \in I_n, 1 \leq \lambda_i \leq \lambda_{\text{upper}}\right\}, \quad (9.4)$$

where $\Phi'^{E_iE_j}(u_i, u_j, \lambda_i, \lambda_j, \phi_{ij})$ is defined in (9.2), $\Phi^{E_i\Omega^*}(u_i, \lambda_i, h)$ is defined in (9.1), $u_i = (v_i, \theta_i)$, $v_i = (x_i, y_i)$, $\sigma = 4n + \dfrac{(n^2 - n)}{2} + 1$.

For relaxed containment constraints the phi-function $\Phi^{E_i\Omega^*}(u_i, \lambda_i, h)$ in (9.4) is replaced by the function $\varphi^{E_i\Omega^*}(v_i, h)$.

The auxiliary variables in (9.2) generate $O(n^2)$ nonlinear inequalities and variables in the nonlinear programming model (9.3) and (9.4).

9.5 Solution strategy

To find local solutions of the problem (9.3) and (9.4) a multistart strategy is used. It combines a starting point algorithm using a circular packing problem and an optimization procedure for packing ellipses in a minimal rectangle introduced in [7]. In most cases this approach results in reducing the problem to smaller nonlinear programming problems with dimensions linear to the number of ellipses.

The main solution approach consists in the following principal stages:

Stage 1. Generate a set of feasible solutions to the problem (9.3) and (9.4) by solving the circular packing problem corresponding to $\lambda_i = 1$ for all i (see section 9.5.1).

Stage 2. Using a compaction algorithm described in section 9.5.2 get local minima of the problem (9.3) and (9.4) starting from each feasible point obtained at *Stage* 1.

Stage 3. Choose the best local minimum from those found at *Stage* 2.

9.5.1 Finding a feasible starting point

To find feasible starting points of (9.3) and (9.4) a circular packing problem is used as follows.

Let $S_i, i = 1, 2, \ldots, n$ be a given collection of circles having their radii r_i. Let Ω be a rectangular container centred at origin and having fixed length l and variable height h. Denote by (x_i, y_i) an (unknown) centre of the circle S_i and let $(x, y) = ((x_1, y_1), (x_2, y_2), \ldots, (x_n, y_n))$.

The problem of packing the circles S_i, $i \in I_n$ in the minimal height rectangular domain Ω is stated as the following continuous optimization problem in R^{2n+1}:

$$h^* = \min_{h,x,y} h, \text{ s.t.} \tag{9.5}$$

$$\Phi_{ij}(x_i, x_j, y_i, y_j) = (x_i - x_j)^2 + (y_i - y_j)^2 - (r_i + r_j)^2 \geq 0, i > j \in I_n, \tag{9.6}$$

$$\Phi_i(x_i, y_i, h) = \min_{k=1,\ldots,4} \varphi_k(x_i, y_i, h) \geqslant 0, \tag{9.7}$$

where

$$\varphi_1(x_i, y_i, h) = x_i - r_i, \ \varphi_2(x_i, y_i, h) = y_i - r_i,$$

$$\varphi_3(x_i, y_i, h) = -x_i + l - r_i, \ \varphi_4(x_i, y_i, h) = -y_i + h - r_i.$$

Constraints (9.6) assure the circles S_i and S_j, $i > j \in I_n$, are non-overlapping, while constraints (9.7) guarantee the containment of a circle S_i inside the rectangular container Ω, $i \in I_n$. For solving problem (9.5)–(9.7) the homothetic transformations of the circles are used to generate feasible stating points and the decomposition method [7] is applied to find local optimal solutions. Different methods for packing circles can also be employed (see, e.g., [8–10]).

If relaxed containment constraints are used, then the phi-function $\Phi_i(x_i, y_i, h)$ (9.7) is replaced by the function $\varphi^{E_i\Omega^*}(v_i, h)$ in (9.7).

This algorithm returns a vector (h^0, x^0, y^0) to be used in finding local a minimum of the problem (9.3) and (9.4).

9.5.2 Compression algorithm

The compression algorithm is an iterative procedure that substitutes the original large-scale problem (9.3) and (9.4) by several smaller problems having dimensions growing linearly with the number of ellipses. The main idea of the algorithm is as follows. Fixed individual rectangular ε-containers housing all ellipses are constructed with respect to each vector of placement parameters. An ellipse can be freely moved in the corresponding rectangular ε-container. A system of four ε-inequalities defines the movement of each ellipse. Then a subset of W is formed: $4n$ ε-inequalities are added to constraints (9.4) and phi-functions inequalities for pairs of ellipses with non-overlapping ε-containers are cancelled. Some extra containment conditions are also eliminated.

This way $O(n^2)$ auxiliary variables are eliminated thus reducing the size of each subproblem. The subproblems with $O(n)$ variables and constraints are locally optimized. The local optimal solution is used as a feasible starting point in the next iteration. A local optimum of (9.3) and (9.4) is found at the last iteration of the local optimization procedure. The detailed algorithm is presented below.

Let u^1 be a point found by the circular packing algorithm. Set the decomposition step of the algorithm $\varepsilon = \frac{1}{n} \cdot \sum_{i=1}^{n} r_i$.

The compression algorithm works as follows:

Step 1. Set $k = 1$.

Step 2. For each $i \in I_n$ define an individual container $\Omega_i^k \supset E_i(u_i^k, \lambda_i^k)$ having dimensions $2(\lambda_i^k \cdot r_i + \varepsilon)$, $2\left(\frac{1}{\lambda_i^k} \cdot r_i + \varepsilon\right)$ and centered at the point v_i^k.

Step 3. Construct a system of 'artificial' inequalities for (u_i, λ_i^k) corresponding to each ellipse E_i as follows: $\Phi^{\widehat{E_i}\Omega_i^{k*}}(u_i, \lambda_i^k) \geqslant 0$, $i \in I_n$, where

$$\Phi^{\widehat{E_i}\Omega_i^{k*}}(u_i, \lambda_i^k) = \min\left\{f_{i1}^k(u_i, \lambda_i^k), f_{i2}^k(u_i, \lambda_i^k), f_{i3}^k(u_i, \lambda_i^k), f_{i4}^k(u_i, \lambda_i^k)\right\}.$$

The single inequality $\Phi^{\widehat{E_i}\Omega_i^{k*}}(u_i, \lambda_i^k) \geqslant 0$ is described by the following inequality system

$$\begin{cases} f_{i1}^k(u_i, \lambda_i^k) \geqslant 0 \\ f_{i2}^k(u_i, \lambda_i^k) \geqslant 0 \\ f_{i3}^k(u_i, \lambda_i^k) \geqslant 0 \\ f_{i4}^k(u_i, \lambda_i^k) \geqslant 0 \end{cases},$$

where

$$f_{i1}^k(u_i, \lambda_i^k) = x_i - \frac{r_i}{\lambda_i}\sqrt{1 + (\lambda_i^4 - 1)\cos\theta_i} - (x_i^k - r_i\lambda_i^k - \varepsilon),$$

$$f_{i2}^{k}(u_i, \lambda_i^k) = y_i - \frac{r_i}{\lambda_i}\sqrt{1 + (\lambda_i^4 - 1)\sin\theta_i} - \left(y_i^k - r_i\lambda_i^k - \varepsilon\right),$$

$$f_{i3}^{k}(u_i, \lambda_i^k) = -x_i - \frac{r_i}{\lambda_i}\sqrt{1 + (\lambda_i^4 - 1)\cos\theta_i} + (x_i^k + r_i\lambda_i^k + \varepsilon),$$

$$f_{i4}^{k}(u_i, \lambda_i^k) = -y_i - \frac{r_i}{\lambda_i}\sqrt{1 + (\lambda_i^4 - 1)\sin\theta_i} + \left(y_i^k + r_i\lambda_i^k + \varepsilon\right).$$

Step 4. Define a set of indexes

$$\Xi^k = \left\{(i, j)\colon \Phi^{\Omega_i^k\Omega_j^k}\left(u_i^k, u_j^k, \lambda_i^k, \lambda_j^k\right) < 0,\ i > j \in I_n\right\},$$

where $\Phi^{\Omega_i^k\Omega_j^k}(u_i^k, u_j^k, \lambda_i^k, \lambda_j^k)$ is a phi-function for polygonal objects $\Omega_i^k(u_i^k, \lambda_i^k)$ and $\Omega_j^k(u_j^k, \lambda_j^k)$.

Step 5. Define an 'artificial' subset of the space $R^{\sigma-\sigma_k}$:

$$\Lambda_k^\varepsilon = \left\{(t, \phi_{w_k}) \in R^{\sigma-\sigma_k}\colon f_{i1}^k(u_i, \lambda_i^k) \geq 0, f_{i2}^k(u_i, \lambda_i^k) \geq 0,\right.$$
$$\left. f_{i3}^k(u_i, \lambda_i^k) \geq 0, f_{i4}^k(u_i, \lambda_i^k) \geq 0,\ i \in I_n\right\},$$

where $\sigma_k = card(\Xi \backslash \Xi^k)$.

Step 6. Define an index set

$$\Xi^{*k} = \left\{(i, s)\colon \Phi^{\Omega_i^k\Omega^*}(u_i^k, \lambda_i^k, h) < 0,\ i \in I_n\right\},$$

where $\Phi^{\Omega_i^k\Omega^*}(u_i^k, \lambda_i^k, h)$ is a phi-function for objects $\Omega_i^k(u_i^k, \lambda_i^k)$ and Ω^*.

Step 7. Get a vector $\phi_{w_k}^k = (\phi_{ij}^k, (i, j) \in \Xi^k)$ of starting feasible values of auxiliary variables.

For a pair $(i, j) \in \Xi^k$ the maximal value of $\phi_{ij}$is obtained by the following continuous optimization problem:

$$\phi_{ij}^k = \arg \max_{\phi_{ij} \in [0,2\pi] \subset R^1} \Phi'^{\widehat{E_i}\widehat{E_j}}\left(u_i^k, u_j^k, \lambda_i^k, \lambda_j^k, \phi_{ij}\right),$$

whereu_i^k, u_j^k, λ_i^k, λ_j^k are fixed.

Step 8. Solve the kth subproblem, using feasible starting point $(u^k, \phi_{w_k}^k, \lambda^k) = (v^k, \theta^k, \lambda^k, \phi_{w_k}^k)$:

$$\min_{\left(u^k, \phi_{w_k}^k, \lambda^k\right) \in W_k} h, \tag{9.8}$$

$$W_k = \left\{(u^k, \phi_{w_k}^k, \lambda^k) \in R^{\sigma-\sigma_k}\colon \Phi'^{\widehat{E_i}\widehat{E_j}}(u_i, u_j, \lambda_i, \lambda_j, \phi_{ij}) \geq 0,\right. \tag{9.9}$$

$$\left.(i, j) \in \Xi_k,\ \Phi_i^*(u_i, \lambda_i, h) \geq 0,\ (i, s) \in \Xi_k^*,\ \Phi^{E_i\Omega_i^{k*}}(u_i, \lambda_i) \geq 0,\ i \in I_n\right\},$$

where $(u, \phi_{w_k}) = (v, \theta, \lambda, \phi_{w_k})$,$\Phi'^{E_iE_j}(u_i, u_j, \lambda_i, \lambda_j, \phi_{ij})$ is defined in (9.2), $\Phi_{is}^*(u_i, \lambda_i)$ is defined by (9.1); $\Phi^{E_i\Omega_i^{k*}}(u_i, \lambda_i)$, Ξ_k, σ_k, Ξ_k^* are defined at Steps 3–6, correspondingly.

If relaxed containment constraints are applied, the phi-function $\Phi_i^*(u_i, \lambda_i, h)$ in (9.9) is replaced by the function $\varphi^{E_i\Omega^*}(v_i, h)$.

Step 9. If the local minimum point $(u^{k*}, \lambda^{k*}, \phi^*_{w_k})$of the k-th subproblem (9.8) and (9.9) is on the frontier of Λ_k^ε, then set $u^{k+1} = u^{k*}$, update $k = k + 1$ and go to Step 2. Otherwise set $u^*=u^{k*}$ and stop algorithm.

The algorithm involves only $O(n)$ from the total $O(n^2)$ pairs of ellipses, since only 'ε-neighbours' have to be compared for each ellipse. The efficiency of this approach considerably depends on the value of ε representing an intelligent compromise between the number of constraints in each subproblem and the number of the subproblems (9.8) and (9.9) solved to get a local solution of the problem (9.3) and (9.4).

9.6 Computational results

In this section two problem instances corresponding to generating digital and artificial rock cores are considered. In the first case the mathematical model of (9.3) and (9.4) with the strong containment constraints is used, while the second is related to the relaxed containment constraints. Computational experiments for the circular and ellipse packing problems were running on an AMD Athlon 64×2 5200+ computer. To solve nonlinear programming subproblems the free solver IPOPT is used [32].

The radii $r_i$of the circles S_i, $i = 1, \dots, 99$ are given in table 9.1. The rectangular domain has its length $l = 15.000\,000$, $\lambda_{\text{upper}} = 1.6$.

Table 9.1. Radii of circles (input data).

$r_i, i = 1, \dots, 20$	$r_i, i = 21, \dots, 40$	$r_i, i = 41, \dots, 60$	$r_i, i = 61, \dots, 80$	$r_i, i = 81, \dots, 99$
1.3	0.7	0.9	1.1	0.7
1.3	0.8	0.9	1.1	1.2
1.3	0.8	0.8	1.1	1.2
1.2	0.8	0.8	1.0	1.2
1.2	0.7	0.8	1.0	1.1
1.2	0.7	0.7	1.0	1.1
1.1	0.7	0.7	0.9	1.1
1.1	1.3	0.7	0.9	1.0
1.1	1.3	0.8	0.9	1.0
1.0	1.3	0.8	0.8	1.0
1.0	1.2	0.8	0.8	0.9
1.0	1.2	0.7	0.8	0.9
0.9	1.2	0.7	0.7	0.9
0.9	1.1	0.7	0.7	0.8
0.9	1.1	1.3	0.7	0.8
0.8	1.1	1.3	0.8	0.8
0.8	1.0	1.3	0.8	0.7
0.8	1.0	1.2	0.8	0.7
0.7	1.0	1.2	0.7	0.7
0.7	0.9	1.2	0.7	

Table 9.2. Optimized values of $\lambda_i, i = 1, \ldots, 99$ (output data) in example 1.

$\lambda_i, i = 1, \ldots, 20$	$\lambda_i, i = 21, \ldots, 40$	$\lambda_i, i = 41, \ldots, 60$	$\lambda_i, i = 61, \ldots, 80$	$\lambda_i, i = 81, \ldots, 99$
1.600 000	1.238 246	1.073 697	1.021 217	1.087 430
1.169 567	1.211 077	1.034 266	1.029 903	1.000 000
1.000 000	1.600 000	1.338 715	1.558 570	1.000 000
1.054 764	1.600 000	1.025 922	1.434 337	1.265 302
1.154 923	1.163 516	1.246 098	1.000 000	1.492 651
1.000 000	1.021 501	1.095 246	1.080 063	1.000 000
1.217 561	1.188 102	1.000 000	1.364 761	1.255 289
1.328 241	1.336 447	1.600 000	1.577 950	1.065 210
1.000 000	1.040 036	1.148 606	1.020 223	1.110 722
1.122 089	1.406 624	1.333 850	1.600 000	1.005 521
1.131 219	1.209 588	1.563 150	1.497 485	1.000 000
1.600 000	1.265 747	1.270 826	1.542 977	1.000 000
1.222 052	1.000 000	1.000 000	1.054 630	1.391 685
1.533 235	1.004 030	1.377 397	1.041 552	1.075 272
1.385 594	1.044 324	1.120 170	1.248 836	1.252 279
1.329 926	1.192 657	1.118 187	1.305 322	1.359 913
1.122 956	1.171 632	1.004 898	1.000 000	1.511 465
1.130 747	1.074 297	1.038 363	1.152 958	1.039 370
1.000 000	1.267 236	1.272 215	1.000 000	1.000 000
1.488 019	1.309 100	1.222 507	1.000 000	

Example 1. The total number of ellipses is $n = 99$. The complete containment constraints are used. The optimized values of $\lambda_i$and ellipses' semi-axes are given in tables 9.2 and 9.3. The locally optimal layouts are presented in figure 9.1. The best objective value in the circular packing problem obtained for 77 s is $h = 23.979\ 470$. The height h in the soft ellipse packing problem found for 505 s is 22.070 149. The total area of all 99 circles (ellipses) in the container is 290.471 657. The areas of the optimized rectangular containers are 359.692 05 for circles and 331.052 235 for ellipses. The corresponding porosities (in %) are 19.244 348 881 217 for circles and 12.258 058 913 271 for soft ellipses.

Example 2. In this case relaxed containment constraints are used requiring containing only for centers of the circles for the same values of r_i as in example 1. The locally optimal arrangements are presented in figure 9.2. The best objective value in the circular packing problem obtained for 68 s is $h = 18.989\ 839$. The height in the soft ellipse packing problem found for 255 s is $h = 16.834\ 254$. The optimized values of λ_i for soft ellipses are given in table 9.4. The corresponding porosities (in %) are 17.68 for circles and 11.21 for soft ellipses.

Table 9.3. Optimized semi-axes of soft ellipses (output data) in example 1.

a_i, $b_i i = 1, \ldots, 33$	a_i, $b_i i = 34, \ldots, 66$	a_i, $b_i i = 67, \ldots, 99$
2.080 000, 0.812 500	1.104 433, 1.095 584	1.228 284, 0.659 456
1.520 437, 1.111 523	1.148 756, 1.053 313	1.420 155, 0.570 360
1.300 000, 1.300 000	1.311 923, 0.922 310	0.918 201, 0.882 160
1.265 717, 1.137 695	1.171 632, 0.853 510	1.280 000, 0.500 000
1.385 908, 1.039 030	1.074 297, 0.930 841	1.197 988, 0.534 229
1.200 000, 1.200 000	1.267 237, 0.789 119	1.234 381, 0.518 478
1.339 317, 0.903 446	1.178 190, 0.687 495	0.738 241, 0.663 740
1.461 065, 0.828 163	0.966 327, 0.838 225	0.729 086, 0.672 074
1.100 000, 1.100 000	0.930 839, 0.870 182	0.874 185, 0.560 522
1.122 089, 0.891 195	1.070 972, 0.597 588	1.044 258, 0.612 876
1.131 219, 0.884 002	0.820 738, 0.779 786	0.800 000, 0.800 000
1.600 000, 0.625 000	0.996 878, 0.642 004	0.922 366, 0.693 867
1.099 847, 0.736 466	0.766 672, 0.639 126	0.700 000, 0.700 000
1.379 912, 0.586 994	0.700 000, 0.700 000	0.700 000, 0.700 000
1.247 034, 0.649 541	1.120 000, 0.437 500	0.761 201, 0.643 720
1.063 940, 0.601 537	0.918 885, 0.696 496	1.200 000, 1.200 000
0.898 365, 0.712 405	1.067 080, 0.599 768	1.200 000, 1.200 000
0.904 598, 0.707 497	1.250 519, 0.511 787	1.518 362, 0.948 390
0.700 000, 0.700 000	0.889 578, 0.550 823	1.641 917, 0.736 944
1.041 613, 0.470 424	0.700 000, 0.700 000	1.100 000, 1.100 000
0.866 772, 0.565 316	0.964 178, 0.508 205	1.380 818, 0.876 292
0.968 862, 0.660 569	1.456 221, 1.160 538	1.065 210, 0.938 782
1.280 000, 0.500 000	1.453 644, 1.162 596	1.110 722, 0.900 315
1.280 000, 0.500 000	1.306 367, 1.293 664	1.005 521, 0.994 509
0.814 461, 0.601 625	1.246 036, 1.155 665	0.900 000, 0.900 000
0.715 051, 0.685 266	1.526 658, 0.943 237	0.900 000, 0.900 000
0.831 671, 0.589 175	1.467 008, 0.981 590	1.252 517, 0.646 698
1.737 381, 0.972 729	1.123 339, 1.077 146	0.860 218, 0.743 998
1.352 047, 1.249 956	1.132 893, 1.068 062	1.001 823, 0.638 835
1.828 611, 0.924 199	1.714 427, 0.705 775	1.087 930, 0.588 273
1.451 506, 0.992 073	1.434 337, 0.697 186	1.058 026, 0.463 127
1.518 896, 0.948 057	1.000 000, 1.000 000	0.727 559, 0.673 485
1.200 000, 1.200 000	1.080 063, 0.925 872	0.700 000, 0.700 000

9.7 Conclusions

The new problem of packing soft ellipses in a rectangle of minimum height is studied. Each ellipse has variable metric characteristics and placement parameters. Affine transformations of translation, rotation and stretching ellipses are allowed. The limits for stretching (shrinking) ratio of the half-axes of ellipses are assigned. The phi-functions are used for analytical presentation of placement conditions (non-intersection of ellipses and layout (complete or relaxed) of ellipses in a container).

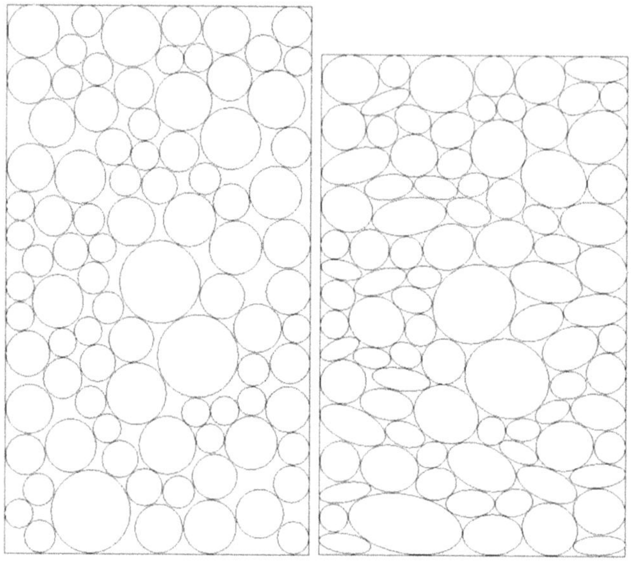

(a) (b)

Figure 9.1. Local optimal packings: (a) for circles, (b) for soft ellipses.

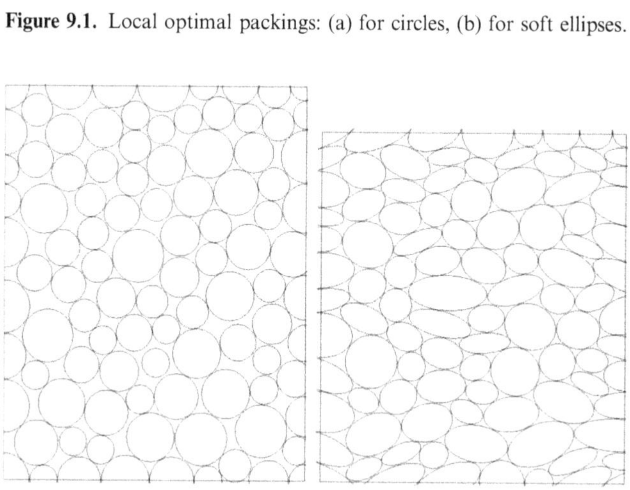

(a) (b)

Figure 9.2. Local optimal arrangements: (a) for circles, (b) for soft ellipses.

A mathematical model is formulated as a continuous nonlinear optimization problem. To find local solutions of the optimized soft ellipse packing problem, a combined methodology is proposed. It is based on a multistart strategy, a method of constructing feasible starting points (using homothetic transformations of circles) and a decomposition approach to reduce the large original problem to several smaller subproblems.

Packing soft ellipses is motivated by modelling porous media under pressure and arise in the oil and gas extracting industry. In this paper we have considered only

Table 9.4. Optimized values of $\lambda_i, i = 1, \ldots, 99$ (output data) in example 2.

$\lambda_i, i = 1, \ldots, 20$	$\lambda_i, i = 21, \ldots, 40$	$\lambda_i, i = 41, \ldots, 60$	$\lambda_i, i = 61, \ldots, 80$	$\lambda_i, i = 81, \ldots, 99$
1.517 169	1.062 562	1.072 921	1.242 176	1.157 478
1.005 029	1.600 000	1.600 000	1.262 902	1.499 393
1.416 681	1.600 000	1.163 405	1.291 465	1.385 243
1.085 674	1.153 589	1.115 928	1.330 618	1.311 607
1.478 218	1.600 000	1.398 650	1.230 496	1.033 483
1.078 025	1.355 733	1.000 000	1.600 000	1.329 723
1.586 077	1.278 614	1.171 693	1.077 594	1.600 000
1.174 016	1.600 000	1.454 726	1.000 000	1.086 975
1.600 000	1.600 000	1.600 000	1.211 654	1.025 205
1.167 057	1.000 000	1.261 125	1.098 015	1.176 879
1.082 358	1.167 999	1.000 000	1.264 127	1.384 828
1.541 502	1.036 398	1.189 410	1.000 000	1.193 612
1.600 000	1.576 794	1.575 759	1.600 000	1.281 696
1.000 000	1.259 704	1.476 423	1.421 499	1.000 000
1.148 892	1.000 000	1.325 771	1.013 554	1.600 000
1.108 551	1.521 165	1.326 103	1.000 000	1.408 711
1.600 000	1.450 186	1.199 771	1.254 422	1.257 947
1.000 000	1.515 776	1.197 457	1.600 000	1.130 390
1.000 000	1.600 000	1.600 000	1.600 000	1.600 000
1.543 119	1.282 057	1.326 576	1.016 950	

circular/ellipsoidal objects. Meanwhile, in applications polygonal objects arise frequently. Thus, developing models and solution techniques for packing soft convex polygons needs further research. Some results on packing 2D and 3D soft polygonal objects are on the way. The results of [33–38] and the experimental data applied in the technology are used. To cope with large-scale problems arising in different steps of the algorithmic approach Lagrangian heuristics [39] can be used. Alternatively, decomposition or aggregation techniques [40, 41] can also be applied.

Acknowledgements

This research is partially funded by National Research Foundation of Ukraine (grant no. 2020.02/0128).

Appendix A

Let A and B be 2D objects. The object A is defined by a vector $u_A = (v_A, \theta_A)$, where: $v_A = (x_A, y_A)$ is its translation vector and θ_A is its rotation angle. The object A translated by the vector v_A and rotated by the angle θ_A is denoted by $A(u_A)$.

The *Phi*-function distinguishes the following three cases: $A(u_A)$ and $B(u_B)$ are intersecting ($A(u_A)$ and $B(u_B)$ have common interior points); $A(u_A)$ and $B(u_B)$ do not intersect ($A(u_A)$ and $B(u_B)$ do not have common points); $A(u_A)$ and $B(u_B)$ are tangent ($A(u_A)$ and $B(u_B)$ have only common frontier points).

Definition [28]. A continuous function $\Phi^{AB}(u_A, u_B)$ is called a phi-function for objects $A(u_A)$ and $B(u_B)$ if

$$\Phi^{AB}(u_A, u_B) < 0, \text{int } A(u_A) \bigcap \text{ int } B(u_B) \neq \varnothing;$$

if and

$$\Phi^{AB}(u_A, u_B) = 0, \text{ int } A(u_A) \bigcap \text{ int } B(u_B) = \varnothing frA(u_A) \bigcap frB(u_B) \neq \varnothing;$$

if

$$\Phi^{AB}(u_A, u_B) > 0, A(u_A) \bigcap B(u_B) = \varnothing.$$

The inequality $\Phi^{AB}(u_A, u_B) \geqslant 0$ gives the non-overlapping, i.e., $\text{int } A(u_A) \cap \text{ int } B(u_B) = \varnothing$, and inequality $\Phi^{AB^*}(u_A, u_B) \geqslant 0$ assures the containment $A(u_A) \subset B(u_B)$, i.e. $\text{int } A(u_A) \cap \text{ int } B^*(u_B) = \varnothing$, where $B^* = R^2 \backslash \text{ int } B$.

Definition [7]. A continuous function $\Phi'^{AB}(u_A, u_B, u')$ is called a quasi-phi-function for $A(u_A), B(u_B)$ if $\max_{u'} \Phi'^{AB}(u_A, u_B, u')$ is a phi-function for these objects.

Here u' denotes a vector of auxiliary continuous variables.

By the properties of a quasi-phi-function [7] the non-overlapping constraint can be described in the form: if $\Phi'^{AB}(u_A, u_B, u') \geqslant 0$ for some u', then $\text{int } A(u_A) \cap \text{ int } B(u_B) = \varnothing$.

References

[1] Chazelle B, Edelsbrunner H and Guibas L J 1989 The complexity of cutting complexes *Discrete Comput. Geom.* **4** 139–81

[2] Donev A, Cisse I, Sachs D, Variano E, Stillinger F H, Connelly R, Torquato S and Chaikin P M 2004 Improving the density of jammed disordered packings using ellipsoids *Science* **303** 990–3

[3] Kallrath J 2017 Packing ellipsoids into volume-minimizing rectangular boxes *J. Global Optim.* **67** 151–85

[4] Kallrath J and Rebennack S 2014 Cutting ellipses from area-minimizing rectangles *J. Global Optim.* **59** 405–37

[5] Birgin E G, Lobato R D and Martinez J M 2016 Packing ellipsoids by nonlinear optimization *J. Global Optim.* **65** 709–43

[6] Birgin E G, Lobato R D and Martínez J M 2017 A nonlinear programming model with implicit variables for packing ellipsoids *J. Global Optim.* **68** 467–99

[7] Stoyan Y, Pankratov A and Romanova T 2016 Quasi-phi-functions and optimal packing of ellipses *J. Global Optim.* **65** 283–307

[8] Kampas F J, Castillo I and Pintér J D 2016 General ellipse packings in optimized regular polygons, to appear http://optimization-online.org/DB_FILE/2016/03/5348.pdf

[9] Litvinchev I, Infante L and Ozuna L 2015 Packing circular like objects in a rectangular container *J. Comput. Syst. Sci. Int.* **54** 259–67

[10] Litvinchev I, Infante L and Ozuna L 2015 Approximate packing: integer programming models, valid inequalities and nesting *Optimized Packings and Their Applications, SOIA* vol 105 (Berlin: Springer) pp 117–35

[11] Pankratov A, Romanova T and Litvinchev I 2019 Packing ellipses in an optimized convex polygon *J. Global Optim.* **75** 495–522

[12] Pankratov A, Romanova T and Litvinchev I 2018 Packing ellipses in an optimized rectangular container *Wirel. Netw.* **26** 4869–79

[13] Romanova T, Stoyan Y, Pankratov A, Litvinchev I, Avramov K, Chernobryvko M, Yanchevskyi I, Mozgova I and Bennell J 2021 Optimal layout of ellipses and its application for additive manufacturing *Int. J. Prod. Res.* **59** 560–75

[14] Tkachenko R, Duriagina Z, Lemishka I, Izonin I and Trostianchyn A 2018 Development of machine learning method of titanium alloy properties identification in additive technologies *Eastern-Eur. J. Enterprise Technol.* **3** 23–31

[15] Fang T T and Murty K L 1983 Grain-size-dependent creep of stainless steel *Mater. Sci. Eng.* **61** 7–10

[16] Duryahina Z A, Kovbasyuk T M and Bespalov S A *et al* 2016 Micromechanical and electrophysical properties of Al_2O_3 nanostructured dielectric coatings on plane heating elements *Mater. Sci.* **52** 50–5

[17] Duriagina Z, Lemishka I and Litvinchev I *et al* 2020 Optimized filling of a given cuboid with spherical powders for additive manufacturing *J. Oper. Res. Soc. China* **9** 853–68

[18] Blunt M J 2017 *Multiphase Flow in Permeable Media: A Pore-Scale Perspective* (Cambridge: Cambridge University Press) p 500

[19] Gerke K M, Korost D V, Karsanina M V, Korost S P, Vasiliev R V, Lavrukhin V R and Gafurova D R 2021 Modern approaches to pore space scale digital modeling of core structure and multiphase flow *Georesursy* **23** 197–213

[20] Sedaghat M H, Gerke K, Azizmohammadi S and Matthai S K 2016 Simulation-based determination of relative permeability in laminated rocks *Energy Procedia* **97** 433–9

[21] Eichheimer P, Thielmann M, Popov A, Golabek G J, Fujita W, Kottwitz M O and Kaus B J P 2019 Pore-scale permeability prediction for Newtonian and non-Newtonian fluids *Solid Earth* **10** 1717–31

[22] Dong X, Liu H, Hou J, Zhang Z and Chen Z (J) 2015 Multi-thermal fluid assisted gravity drainage process: a new improved-oil-recovery technique for thick heavy oil reservoir *J. Petrol. Sci. Eng.* **133** 1–11

[23] Al-Nakhli A, Tariq Z, Mahmoud M, Abdulraheem A and Al Shehri D 2019 A novel thermochemical fracturing approach to reduce fracturing pressure of high strength rocks *Abu Dhabi Int. Petroleum Exhibition & Conf., SPE-197593-MS*

[24] Kravchenko O, Velighotskiy D, Avramenko A and Habibullin R 2014 An improved technology of a complex influence on productive layers of oil and gas wells *Eastern-Eur. J. Enterprise Technol.* **6** 4–9

[25] Kravchenko O, Veligotskyi D, Bashtovyi A and Veligotska Y 2019 Improving the controllability and effectiveness of the chemical-technological process of the technology for hydrogen thermobaric chemical stimulation of hydrocarbon recovery *Eastern-Eur. Enterprise Technol.* **6** 57–86

[26] Kravchenko O, Suvorova I, Baranov I and Goman V 2017 Hydrocavitational activation in the technologies of production and combustion of composite fuels *Eastern-Eur.J. Enterprise Technol.* 33–42

[27] Ebert-Uphoff I, Gosselin C M, Rosen D W and Laliberte T 2005 Rapid prototyping for robotics *Cutting Edge Robotics* ed V Kordic, A Lazinca and M Merdan (Rijeka: InTech) pp 17–46

[28] Stoyan Y and Romanova T 2013 Mathematical models of placement optimization: two- and three-dimensional problems and applications Modeling and Optimization in Space Engineering, *SOIA* vol 73 (Berlin: Springer) pp 363–88

[29] Stoyan Y, Pankratov A, Romanova T and Chugay A 2015 Optimized object packings using quasi-phi-functions Optimized Packings and Their Applications, *SOIA* vol 105 (Berlin: Springer) pp 265–91

[30] Stoyan Y, Pankratov A and Romanova T 2017 Placement problems for irregular objects: mathematical modeling, optimization and applications *Optimization Methods and Applications, SOIA* vol 130 (Berlin: Springer) pp 521–59

[31] Stoyan Y, Pankratov A and Romanova T 2016 Cutting and packing problems for irregular objects with continuous rotations: mathematical modeling and nonlinear optimization *J. Oper. Res. Soc.* **67** 786–800

[32] Wachter A and Biegler L T 2006 On the implementation of an interior-point filter line-search algorithm for large-scale nonlinear programming *Math. Program.* **106** 25–57

[33] Romanova T, Litvinchev I and Pankratov A 2020 Packing ellipsoids in an optimized cylinder *Eur. J. Oper. Res.* **285** 429–43

[34] Stoyan Y G, Romanova T E, Pankratov O V, Stetsyuk P I and Maximov S V 2021 Sparse balanced layout of ellipsoids *Cybernetics and Systems Analysis* **57** 864–73

[35] Stoyan Y, Pankratov A, Romanova T, Fasano G, Pintér J D, Stoian Y E and Chugay A 2019 Optimized packings in space engineering applications: Part I *Modeling and Optimization in Space Engineering, SOIA* vol 144 (Berlin: Springer) pp 395–437

[36] Romanova T, Bennell J, Stoyan Y and Pankratov A 2018 Packing of concave polyhedra with continuous rotations using nonlinear optimization *Eur. J. Oper. Res.* **268** 37–53

[37] Romanova T, Stoyan Y, Pankratov A, Litvinchev I and Marmolejo J A 2019 Decomposition algorithm for irregular placement problems *Intelligent Computing and Optimization, AISC* vol 1072 (Berlin: Springer) pp 214–21

[38] Kallrath J 2021 Cutting & packing beyond and within mathematical programming *Business Optimisation Using Mathematical Programming* 2nd Edn (Berlin: Springer) pp 495–526

[39] Litvinchev I, Mata M, Rangel S and Saucedo J 2010 Lagrangian heuristic for a class of the generalized assignment problems *Comput. Math. Appl.* **60** 1115–23

[40] Litvinchev I 1991 Decomposition-aggregation method for convex programming problems *Optimization* **22** 47–56

[41] Litvinchev I and Rangel S 1999 Localization of the optimal solution and *a posteriori* bounds for aggregation *Comput. Oper. Res.* **26** 967–88

IOP Publishing

Human-Assisted Intelligent Computing
Modeling, simulations and applications
Mukhdeep Singh Manshahia, Igor S Litvinchev, Gerhard-Wilhelm Weber, J Joshua Thomas and Pandian Vasant

Chapter 10

Analysis of phishing attacks

Ladislav Burita, Kamil Halouzka and Pavel Kozak

This chapter deals with the analysis of phishing emails and modelling of phishing attacks. The introduction explains the definition of phishing, the classification of messages in the content of a phishing email, and techniques of phishing email threats and attacks. The research includes some experiments processed during the calendar year. Data collection was made from email accounts of one of the authors in the time interval of one month at beginning, middle, and end of the period. Data are included in tables, which allow better statistical processing and frequency analysis. Segmentation of emails according to the content of the message resulting in segments business, fund, transfer, charity, and others is explained, characterized by keywords, and a sample of an email message is introduced. Text analytical software (SW) Tovek is used for analysis and extraction entities (name, email address, phone numbers, geographic data, etc) from the text of emails. This intelligent function of the SW Tovek in the entity's extraction was tested and evaluated. The research results, their limits, and further orientation are included.

10.1 Introduction

A phishing email is an attempt by hackers to deceive you into providing them with personal data. This can include your name, address, phone numbers, date of birth, occupation, age, or other sensitive personal information such as an identification card, passport, or letter of recommendation. Even more dangerous to disclose are passwords, credit card details, or bank account numbers.

Users are prone to succumb to attacks because phishing emails look like legitimate ones. One study [1] represents that people have problems recognizing phishing emails, although they are warned in advance of a possible attack. Phishing emails are targeted or untargeted attacks where hackers use social engineering techniques to try to convince the addressed person to perform actions,

doi:10.1088/978-0-7503-4801-0ch10

for example opening an attachment or link, with a virus, and enter sensitive personal information [2].

The structure of this paper is as follows. The introduction explains phishing. The literature review analyses the theme of phishing threats, attacks, their prediction, and detection. This is followed by methodology and used tools, then phishing email analysis (statistics and classification) and a description of the segments business, charity, fund, transfer, and other. Next is the part of the phishing emails content analysis and testing of the intelligent function of SW Tovek in the automatic extraction of entities (names, email addresses, geographic information, etc). The last parts are on research results, their limits, further orientation, and discussion and conclusion.

10.2 Literature review

Many authors available on Scopus and Web of Science (WoS) describe the problem of phishing attack analysis and phishing attack detection modelling. Many papers are devoted to prediction and defence against phishing attacks. Also, articles are specifically devoted to phishing email detection, where for example in [3], neural network (NN) concepts and ways to test data are described, which provides a brief idea about the use of NNs in network security. Features such as feed-forward backpropagation, gradient descent moment for training purposes, sigmoid transfer, and other features, and a supervised learning model were used to train the model for predicting fraudulent attacks.

Publication [4] deals with the prediction and prevention of phishing attacks in securing online transactions. The authors are focused on the data mining tool due to its simplicity and also its capability to mine large amounts of data in a short time and guarantee accurate results. To determine if an email is phishing or legitimate, the authors used machine learning (ML) techniques such as random forest, NN, decision tree, and a linear model. Furthermore, the authors here focus on the analysis of phishing attacks on Internet of Things (IoT) devices. ML algorithms random forest classifier, support vector machine, and logistic regression were used here.

ML for analysing the characteristics of phishing attacks and techniques for detecting them using models is also described in another article [5]. It describes three main ways of an attack using phishing: Uniform Resource Locator (URL), phishing email, and phishing website. In this paper, ML models are used to find out phishing attacks. The accuracy was evaluated using a reliable model. XGBoost classifier provides higher accuracy and takes less time. A more accurate model for checking phishing emails was proposed. ML methods for detecting phishing attacks and solutions for phishing website detection are also described here [6, 7]. An automated approach to find phishing attacks using the fuzzy method is discussed in [8].

A fuzzy system is a rule-based system that uses fuzzy sets and fuzzy logic concepts to solve problems, but it is not easy to achieve an optimal solution when applied to a complex problem where the process of identifying the fuzzy parameter becomes more complex. An optimization method that automatically identifies the fuzzy parameter is needed. The optimization method derives from the metaheuristic algorithm.

In another paper [9], the authors focused on evaluating the percentage accuracy of phishing filtering capabilities by reviewing more than 500 phishing emails received on Gmail, Yahoo, and mailboxes of specific end users. The authors are oriented on the 16 most prominent phishing elements and analysed the quality of 20 phishing detection filters. They then compared the results with internal phishing detection systems such as rules in an antispam system, filtering on an Exchange server, and user-defined Outlook rules.

The goal of the paper [10] is to analyse the effectiveness of different deep learning (DL) techniques in detecting phishing activities. The analysis is intended to help in selecting an appropriate solution while respecting the needs and technological capabilities against phishing scams.

DL algorithms [11–13] are an effective tool in cybersecurity in general and therefore have relevance in phishing detection. A study was prepared using the following DL algorithms: Convolutional Neural Network (CNN), Deep Neural Network (DNN), Gated Recurrent Unit (GRU), and Long Short-Term Memory (LSTM). To analyse the behaviour of DL architectures, many experiments were conducted to investigate the result of input parameters on the accuracy and performance of DL solutions. The research was oriented on the specification of parameter settings in NN architectures, the hyper-parameter optimization process for DL algorithms, and effectiveness metrics for proving the phishing finding model. The DL method has many advantages, but one of its main disadvantages is the necessity of manual parameter tuning. Currently, there is no standard and complete algorithm for selecting appropriate hyper-parameters to achieve the best performance.

In a similar study [14], a solution is proposed to detect phishing attacks using a combined model. The study is based on two well-known DL techniques, LSTM and CNN. The defined model applies techniques to recognize phishing attacks using Hypertext Markup Language (HTML) and URL-based features. 1D CNN and LSTM recognize abstract-level in URLs and applications without manual extraction of features.

The information from the NN is combined with an activation layer to find the final prediction. The suggested solution shows an accuracy of about 98.3% in alerting the user of a phishing attack and it has good accuracy recorded for an implemented model. The contribution is a suggestion of a network for recognizing phishing attacks with optimal accuracy.

Another principle protecting against phishing emails uses game theory. Game theory is used for the prevention of phishing attacks but also for cybersecurity in general [15]. Principles of game theory can be used to model interactions involving different actors and to seek consequences resulting from the ongoing interactions [16, 17].

Game theory is used to define strategic interactions between the attacker during different attack phases. Game theory provides the defender with guidance to improve strategy and deceive the attacker. The potential victim is the target of the attacks that the attacker tries to force into a communication error at different stages. The attack may succeed if the user receives the first email (in the case of a naive victim). The attack may not succeed if the user is cautious. Adapting defence tactics and changing attack techniques during an exchange between both players can be modelled using game theory and combined to strengthen existing anti-phishing programs. The attacker changes attack strategies over time while the victim behaves differently on their level of knowledge.

Papers [18, 18] describe a model for classifying and detecting phishing sites. Phishing websites have certain features and patterns and identifying these features can help to detect them. Identifying these features is a classification task and can be solved using data mining techniques. Phishing is realized in several directions, but they all use a common set of features. One approach is directed at maintaining a blacklist and checking the requested URLs, but with low effectiveness. The second technique uses a heuristic phishing website and then uses approaches that identify features of these features to categorize the requested URL as phishing or legitimate; the effect of this technique depends on the features that can distinguish between phish or legal ones. Feature selection is done by analysing web pages and examining the patterns and features used by phishing websites. The experimental results showed that the proposed hybrid model achieves better results, is accurate, and has less error rate.

The last paper [19] reviewed discusses in detail several mobile anti-phishing models to help users avoid phishing attacks. The article explains dangerous operational situations typical only for mobile devices. No effective technique has yet been invented or adopted against mobile phishing that can accurately distinguish between authentic and fraudulent websites. With the increasing use of smartphones, it is convenient for users to store their sensitive data on their mobile phones, allowing phishers to use mobile devices to collect valuable data. The limitation lies in the small screen size and lower computing power which makes mobile phone security more vulnerable to phishing attacks compared to desktop computers. Mobile phone users tend to stay online, increasing the number of situations in which they will be victims of phishing. Finally, experimental results based on model evaluation are presented, and based on these facts a model is proposed which can detect effectively and accurately.

10.3 Methodology and used tools

The research of phishing email attacks started last year and includes three experiments, in which were collected the emails sent into email accounts by one of the authors. The first experiment was carried out in November 2020 (77 emails), the second in May 2021 (84 emails), and the third in November 2021 (82 emails). Data from the three experiments are a source for the frequency analysis, the statistical surveys, and the classification methods.

Classification analysis of emails was prepared using the text analytical SW Tovek and manually corrected upon the phishing emails characteristics. The typical words from phishing emails were applied for classification algorithms, and the result *n* is already influenced by previous research, which was divided into five segments of emails (by the email message): business, fund, charity, transfer, and other. The results of all research experiments are summarized, compared, and depicted in tables and graphs.

The last analysis was oriented to entities, extracted from the emails using the intelligent abilities of SW Tovek (name, email address, geographic data, phone number, etc).

10.3.1 The text analytical SW Tovek

The text analytical SW Tovek [20] is used to easily find information in the text of phishing emails. Tovek includes five modules (Index Manager, Tovek Agent, Query Editor, Info Rating, and Harvester). The start of data processing is the indexing of data by Index Manager; Tovek Agent provides a search using a single or complex query. This module is able to automatically extract entities from the text (name, URL address, date, phone number, geographic information, etc). That intelligent function is based on the ML approach (part of AI-artificial intelligence). Info Rating is the context analysis module that allows finding a context in documents concerning context queries. The group of test documents can be exported to the module Harvester for content analysis processing. It can find various forms of word connections, use the word frequency analysis or graphs of words context.

10.4 Statistical analysis of phishing emails

The first result of the statistical survey of the email attacks is the frequency analysis (see figure 10.1) that shows how many emails were sent in any experiment to the mail account.

The outcome of the frequency analysis is simple: the number of phishing attacks was during a year nearly the same. This means that the number of attackers did not probably change either, only the content of the reports changed, as evidenced by the research carried out in the classification section.

The parameters of the emails are depicted in the statistical survey (see table 10.1). Parameter 'Personal email' means that the sender is a person, while any company or organization sent 'Corporate mail'. The parameter 'Contains the sender's name' means that the names of senders are in the email mentioned— personal or corporate.

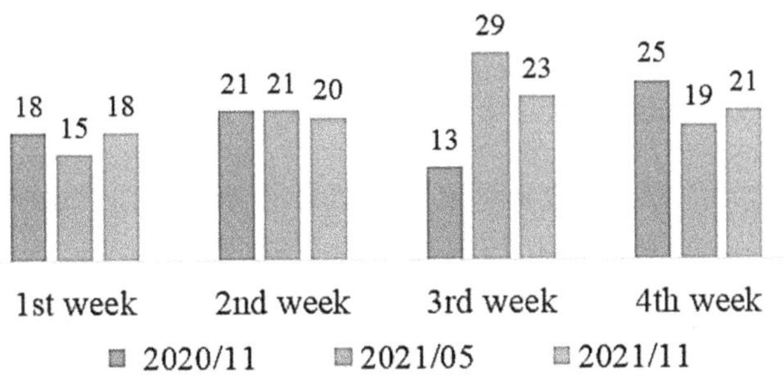

Figure 10.1. Frequency analysis of the phishing attacks [source own].

Table 10.1. General parameters of phishing emails [source own].

Message (77–2020/11; 84–2021/05; 82–2021/11)		2020/11		2021/05		2021/11	
		Sum	%	Sum	%	Sum	%
1	Personal mail	54	70	54	61	50	61
2	Corporate mail	23	30	33	39	32	39
3	Contains the sender's name	73	95	77	92	71	87
4	Required basic pers-info	6	8	4	5	6	7
5	Required detailed pers-info	13	17	9	11	18	22
6	Required pers-info fill in form	3	4	0	0	3	4
7	Required pers-identification	5	6	2	2	9	11
8	Required account number	3	4	4	5	1	1.
9	Required a quick response	71	92	32	38	30	37
10	Other language than English	5	6	10	12	6	7
11	Money in mil. USD	826		510		438	

The personal information is mostly required in the mail: 'Required basic pers-info' applies to name, phone, and address information. 'Required detailed pers-info' requires even more data, such as occupation, sex, nationality, date of birth, etc. 'Required pers-info fill in the form' aims to fill personal information into the submitted form, and 'Required pers-identification' is a requirement for disclosing the number of personal documents, passports, or letters of recommendation.

Nearly all emails are in English, but there are some exceptions, see the experiment:

- One (6—Czech or Slovak).
- Two (10—Czech four, Germany three; Slovenia, Spain and Portugal one).
- Three (6—Czech three, France two, Germany one).

The last parameter of table 10.1 is the sum of money promised in phishing emails of a particular experiment. This is such a huge amount of money that none of the authors can imagine and could not earn it in their whole life. This figure confirms that no one can be serious about distributing such a large amount of money, so it is really a fraud.

10.5 Classification of phishing emails

The phishing emails are classified into five segments:

(1) Business, (2) Charity, (3) Fund, (4) Transfer, and (5) Other (see table 10.2).

The following sections briefly explain all segments and are characterized by keywords. A typical mail message is introduced, including spelling and stylistic errors, the typical characteristics of phishing messages.

The distribution of segments by phishing emails is different in experiments. In the first experiment, the Transfer segment predominates (28%), in the second, it is Business (29%), and in the third, it is Fund (37%), see figure 10.2. Attackers seem to respond to the success of their actions by changing messages.

Table 10.2. Categorization of the message in email [source own].

Message Content	2020/11 Sum	2020/11 %	2021/05 Sum	2021/05 %	2021/11 Sum	2021/11 %
BUSINESS	**21**	**27**	**25**	**29**	**21**	**26**
Project, contract or investment	15	19	12	14	12	15
Trading offer	2	3	10	12	8	10
Job offer	4	5	2	2	1	1
Payment for services	0	0	1	1	0	0
CHARITY	**17**	**22**	**6**	**8**	**5**	**6**
Charity due to a fatal illness	15	19	6	8	3	4
Charity project	2	3	0	0	2	2
FUND	**14**	**18**	**22**	**26**	**30**	**37**
Gift prize	4	5	2	2	8	10
Fund of bank, compensation fund	3	4	11	13	16	20
Contractor of the fund, to share fund	4	5	7	9	1	1
Inheritans	3	4	2	2	5	6
TRANSFER	**21**	**28**	**15**	**18**	**15**	**18**
Money from bank account to receiver account	19	25	15	18	11	13
The pick-up shipment	2	3	0	0	4	5
OTHER	**4**	**5**	**16**	**19**	**11**	**13**
Loan offer	3	4	2	2	0	0
Incoming mail blocked	0	0	0	0	1	1
Reminder of the previous message	1	1	6	8	4	5
Offer friendship, (erotica too)	0	0	2	2	0	0
Unblocking a bank account; actualize account	0	0	2	2	0	0
Unspecified message, call to communicate	0	0	4	5	6	7

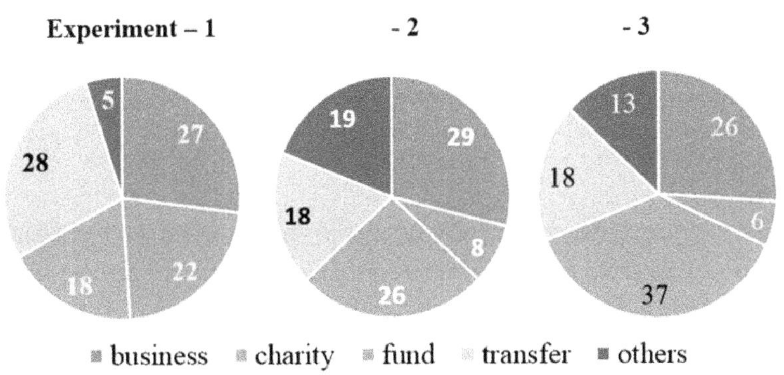

Figure 10.2. Percentage distribution of phishing emails in segments [source own].

10.5.1 Segment business

The Business segment includes many types of emails, in which cooperation on a project, investment, execution of a contract, or realization of a business opportunity is offered. Furthermore, a potential partner offers any product or service, possibly employment in various areas with high salary and lucrative benefits.

Keywords:

Business, investment, project, contract, intention, export, product, service, inquiry, partner, relationship, cooperation, opportunity, employment, recruit, benefit, salary.

Example of a mail (used in education):

Hello

I got your contact from (Linkedin) India directory. Please allow me to introduce myself, I am (Dr. Akira Morita) and I am writing to you on behalf of my Company (Kyowa Kirin Co., Ltd.) is a Japan-based Global Specialty Pharmaceutical Company, contributing to health worldwide through innovative drug research driven by progressive technologies, in the core areas of neurology, oncology, and immunology.

The company oriented in the production of rhythm devices, electrophysiological, ablations, surgical, and intervention goods. Presently we would like establish in India for purchase of a raw material COMANITE with our company.

Therefore, we want to know if you are capable of representing our company in India for five years when your interest will be protected, and this may not be in line with your current business. Kindly answer your interest for more details. I'm expecting to read from you soon.

Dr. Akira Morita, (Director) Kyowa Kirin Co. Ltd.

10.5.2 Segment fund

The Fund segment contains phishing emails in which is promised the opportunity to obtain money or other assets from the various funds within a wide variety of grounds, such as scams or fraud, compensation, Covid-19, etc. The next message in the email is a financial gift or inheritance.

Keywords:

Fund, gift, price, bank, deposit, fraud, scam, credit, compensation, investigation, court, Homeland Security, FBI, contract, inheritance.

Email example (used in education):

Mr John Desmond <luckm2043@gmail.com>

Your Funds

Attn, Beneficiary

We are to Notify you about the latest development concerning your payment that is left in our custody, besides,you are given a bill of Sum in order to receive your payment $10.8 Million usd which We haven't heard from you for some time now. Hence,we are now offering a Special BONUS to help all our customers that are having their payment in our custody due to high prices. We offer you should pay only the sum of $100 to receive your funds payment abandoned by online transfer or ATM card. so you are *asked to send the fee $100 only by Bitcoin, or Google Play CARD, amazon's Steam Wallet is also ACCEPTED. I send you the account with details to enable you to access online and proceed on transfer to your bank account in any part of the world Or Tracking Number Of Your ATM Card Delivery to enable you to Monitor the Arrives of your ATM without any further delay as soon as you update us with a copy of the required Fee $100 to take note.*

Yours Mr John Desmond

10.5.3 Segment charity

The often-used story of the charity segment tells that an old woman, mostly a widow without children, has a large fortune (millions USD) left to her by her deceased husband, which she wants to donate to charity. She complains of a fatal illness (cancer) with the sad fact that she only has a few months left to live. The author of the phish is mostly referring to Christian love. The next reason for the phishing mail of the charity segment is an offer of the charity project.

Keywords:

Charity, project, fund, money, donate, Christ, God, sister, brother, motherless baby, promise, illness, disease, hospital, cancer, orphanage home, widow, husband, inheritance.

The email sample (used in education):

Dear,

My name is Justine Yao I am 52, suffering on cancer. From doctors information, my condition is not good and the cancer stage is coming to an end stage. My husband died last four years, and during the time of our marriage, we were very wealthy. I inherited all business and money. The doctors have advised me that I may not live for more than three months due to my present predicament. So, I now decided to divide the part of this wealth to contribute to the development of the God work to your country. I suppose to donate the sum of 1,900.000.00 UD Dollars to use as the fund to support the less privileged in your country, I hope you to fulfil this dream to come true and I will the fund transfer to you in your country.

I honestly pray that this money when transferred to your country and it will be used for the charity purpose.

Your sister, Mrs. Justine Yao.

10.5.4 Segment transfer

The segment includes phishing emails about cooperation in money or assets transfer. The commission for transfer is from 30% to 60% of transferred amounts. The initiator is usually a bank clerk who discovered a free money account and claims it as a completely risk-free operation. The next reason for the transfer, mentioned in the segment, is the pick-up of any shipment.

Keywords:

Transfer, money, bank, property, gold, diamonds, box, contract, cooperation, packet, shipment, airport.

Example of a mail (used in education):

my apology dear friend

Mrs. Aisha Gaddafi <aishagaddaf95@gmail.com>

Dear Partner,

I am Mrs. Aisha Gaddafi, the biological daughter of Former President of Libya Col. Muammar Gaddafi. I got your contact while searching for a trustworthy someone who will understand my present condition and come to my rescue here in Oman where I have been granted asylum, I have passed through pains and sorrowful moment since the death of beloved, all accounts have been locked and we are not possible to realize transfer money from any or source.

I received an urgent email from Oman government stated that the new Libya government are tracing hidden deposit of our account which was deposited Eco Bank, though this particular funds, the sum of £73.9 Million GBP was deposited in Eco Bank. Your assistance is needed to me, kindly get back email to me with all your details and contact address of the Eco Bank, to enable you the final release of the funds to your onward accredited account in your Country.

I offer to reward you bountifully with 40% while I myself will also share 60% ratio, Please kindly contact me immediately via *my private email; below (mrs.aisha-muhammed-gaddafi@munich.com) for more details.*

May Allah bless you

Mrs. Aisha Gaddafi.

10.5.5 Segment other

The segment contains phishing emails of marginal significance, for example, unspecific offers, repeatedly notified contact, undelivered packages, loan offer, etc.

Keywords:

Offer, loan, communicate, message, response, contact, friendship, undelivered package.

Example of a mail (used in education):

French:

Cher Bénéficiaire

Je suis inquiet de n'avoir reçu aucune réponse de votre part jusqu'à ce jour, j'espère que vous et votre famille êtes en bonne santé aujourd'hui. J'espère recevoir votre réponse urgente car j'ai un message important pour vous.

Cordialement,

Mme Roux Jeannette Muller (Assistant personnel)

Siège de la Cedeao

English:

Dear Beneficiary

Florence ROUX Clement <bigeorgeanderson204@gmail.com>

I am afraid that I have not received an answer from you until this day, I hope you are OK and healthy today. Hope to receive soon your immediately response.

Regards,

Ms. Roux Jeannette Muller, (Personal assistant), ECOWAS Headquarters

Email: mrsanitaanitageorge@gmail.com

10.6 Content analysis of phishing emails

The content analysis of the emails in an experiment focused on entity extraction using SW Tovek, an intelligent function that applies ML. The attention was oriented on comparing the quality and accuracy of the machine-extracted data with the subsequent manual analysis. In total, 82 phishing emails were compared between machine and manual analysis, oriented to entity person, phone number, city, country, email, and website.

The aim was to extract the required data not only from the email headers/footers, but the entire emails that were analysed to obtain relevant information. The sub-charts summarise the information on summarization of emails, the result of the SW analysis, and manually found entities. The errors of the machine-extracted entity data (number of SW errors), and the total number of entities that were not machine detected (by using SW was not found).

10.6.1 Person entity

This first analysis shows the biggest weakness of machine data mining. From all emails, 80 person entities were found using Tovek SW and 76 person entities were found manually. Behind the seemingly similar occurrences of person entities, however, there were 27 incorrectly found person entities and 31 person entities were not found by the SW at all (error rate 34%), see figure 10.3.

10.6.2 Phone number entity

The second comparison shows the machine's ability to extract phone numbers from phishing emails. From all emails, only six phone numbers were machine retrieved (error rate 33%). Twelve phone numbers were found manually. The relatively large error in the machine retrieval of the phone number entity was due not only to the incorrect format of the listed numbers but also to the correct filter settings on the entity's tel. phone, and phone. The results are shown in figure 10.4.

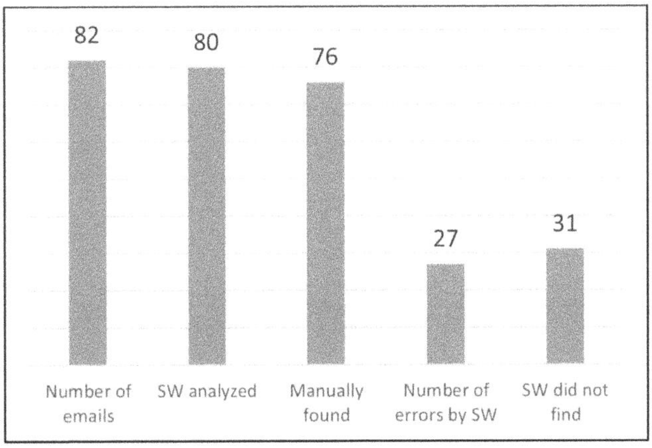

Figure 10.3. Entity person analysis [source own].

10.6.3 City and country entity

The third and fourth comparisons of the SW and manual data extraction were used on the entity city and the entity country. For entity city (figure 10.5), only 26 entity data were correctly matched out of 48 SW retrieved cities (error rate 42%). 31 city entities were manually found. Some errors for the machine determination of the entity city were the word Mobile assigned as the entity city in seven cases. In four cases, a girl's or boy's name was incorrectly assigned as the entity city (Sofia, Nancy, 2*x* George). The state entity designation was more accurate than the city entity designation. There were 44 occurrences of the state entity found by the machine (error rate 11%), and of this number, 39 city entities were determined correctly. The manual analysis found 50 country entities (figure 10.6).

Figure 10.4. Entity phone number analysis [source own].

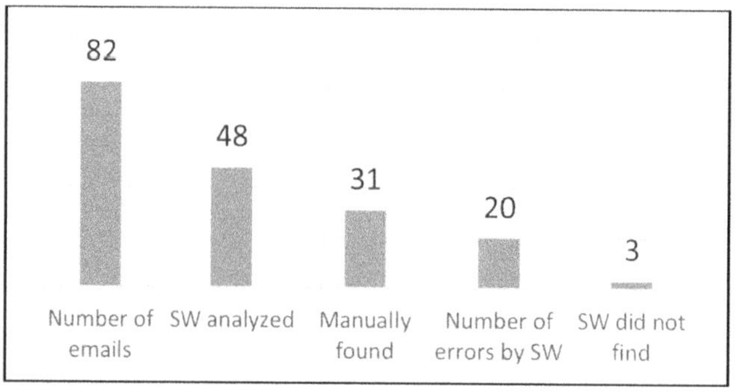

Figure 10.5. Entity city analysis [source own].

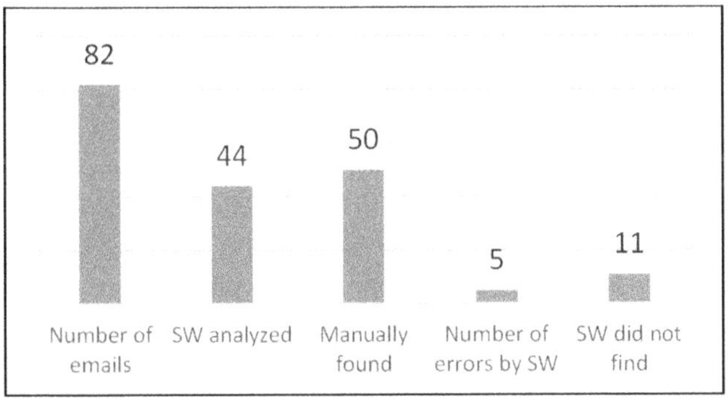

Figure 10.6. Entity country analysis [source own].

10.6.4 Email and website entity

The absolute most accurate determinations were the entity of email account and entity website. In both cases, we can speak of a well-set filter for the machine analysis of emails, where no errors were found. All occurrences were found correctly.

10.7 Research results, their limits, and further research orientation

The major findings of the research:

- Phishing attacks analysis, addressed to one person and their long-term research.
- Detailed knowledge of attacks, collected set of emails for cyber defence, education and training; classification, and categorization of emails.
- Content analysis of emails and its use to improve the AI functions of SW Tovek for text-mining.
- Based on the analysis of the phishing emails' content, other emails can be better assessed whether or not they are phishing emails.

Research limits:

- Analysis of phishing attacks addressed to only one person and use of only one analytical SW Tovek.
- The quality of the data obtained for the analysis of emails can never be 100%.
- Impossibility of accurate analysis of phishing attacks for a larger group of people or companies.
- Protection against phishing attacks will always lag behind hackers' attacks. The behaviour of the attackers is constantly improving and the ability to imitate official websites and legal emails is improving.

Suggestions for the future orientation of research:

- Increase volume of analysed mail accounts that are goals of phishing attacks; application of multiple analytical tools and comparison of research results.
- Finding the causes of inaccuracies in the Tovek analytical SW in extracting entities from phishing emails.

- Capturing and correctly assigning the required values, for use in the filter settings (user requirements) for the phishing mail search SW (reduction of search error rate).
- Monitoring of the development of phishing attacks. Analysis of the variability of the attacker's behaviour on the subject of the attack.
- Analysis of the most suitable time for sending phishing emails (the initial research revealed the frequency of sending on individual days of the week).
- Create materials for education in the field of phishing attack evaluation. How to distinguish useful mail from malicious mail (analysis of mail headers and contents). Targeted focus on school teaching and education for companies and organizations, young and older people.
- Comparison of the annual reports of The National Security Agency (NSA) of the EU member states in terms of the development of phishing attacks.
- Use of research results for the protection of email communication based on ML.

10.8 Discussion and conclusion

Three experiments conducted over one year confirmed the somewhat steady-state of phishing attacks (in terms of number) into the corporate email account of one of the authors. But their composition/classification changed. The greatest number of detected emails was reached in Experiment 3 in the Fund segment (37%); overall, however, emails in the Fund and Business segments were almost as numerous.

The result of the analysis of phishing emails is their perfect knowledge, which can be used by education and training in defence against phishing attacks.

The great advantage of machine data acquisition using TOVEK SW is the possibility of processing a huge amount of data, which it analyses, arranges according to the user's requirements, and then evaluates. For machine analysis, you need to set up search filters that capture and correctly assign as many desired values as possible.

As the content analysis of the phishing emails showed, the accuracy of the machine retrieval was dependent not only on finding the desired entity but also on the subsequent correct identification of the desired entity. For example, a large error rate was observed when searching for person entities, where 22 entities were not found, which is a really large number for 82 phishing emails. Similarly, 18 wrongly found person entities is also a lot for the number of emails. Great emphasis should be directed on the quality of the data obtained because correct research of the received mails can then correctly classify the mails into useful and phishing ones with great accuracy.

References

[1] Dhamija R, Tygar J D and Hearst M 2006 Why phishing works *Proceedings of the SIGCHI Conference on Human Factors in Computing Systems (CHI '06) (Montréal, April 22–27, 2006)* (New York: ACM Press)

[2] Hong J 2012 The situation of phishing attacks *Commun. ACM* **55** 74–81

[3] Archana P, Divyabharathi P, Joshua Camry Y and Sudha 2021 Artificial neural network model for predicting fraudulent attacks *J. Phys.: Conf. Ser.* 1979 012016

[4] Naaz S and Hamdard J 2021 Detection of phishing in the internet of things using machine learning approach *Int. J. Dig. Crime Forensics* **13** 1

[5] Ripa S P, Islam F and Arifuzzaman M 2021 The emergence threat of phishing attack and the detection techniques using machine learning models *2021 Int. Conf. on Automation, Control and Mechatronics for Industry 4.0 (ACMI)*

[6] Basit A, Zafar M, Javed A R and Jalil Z 2020 A novel ensemble machine learning method to detect phishing attack *2020 IEEE 23rd Int. Multitopic Conf. (INMIC)* 1–5

[7] Tang L and Mahmoud Q H 2021 A survey of machine learning-based solutions for phishing website detection *Machine Learning and Knowledge Extraction.* **3** 672–94

[8] Noor Syahirah N, Arfian Mohd I, Tole S, Shahreen K, Rohayanti H, Zalmiyah Z and Saberi Mohd M 2021 A comparative analysis of metaheuristic algorithms in fuzzy modeling for phishing attack detection *Indonesian J. Elec. Eng. Comput. Sci.* **23** 1146–58

[9] Akashdeep B, Fadi A-T, Varun S, Manoj K and Thompson S 2021 Privacy-aware detection framework to mitigate new-age phishing attacks *Comput. Electr. Eng.* **96** 107546

[10] Nguyet D Q, Ali S, Ondrej K, Takeru Y and Hamido F 2021 The phishing webpage classification by deep learning algorithms: a study, advances in AI: machine learning *Data Mining Data Sci.* **2021** 9210

[11] Guan Y, Zou F, Yao Y, Wang W and Zhu T 2018 Web phishing detection using a deep learning framework *Wirel. Commun.Mob. Comput.* **2018** 4678746

[12] Adebowale M A, Lwin K T and Hossain M A 2020 Intelligent phishing detection scheme using deep learning algorithms *J. Enterprise Inform. Manage.*

[13] Somesha M, Pais A R, Rao R S and Rathour V S 2020 Efficient deep learning techniques for the detection of phishing websites *Sādhanā* **45** 165

[14] Subhash A, Subha F and Shantha F 2020 Detecting phishing attacks using a combined model of LSTM and CNN *Int. J. Adv. Appl. Sci.* **7** 55–67

[15] Bhosale D V, Mitkal P K and Lonkar Y S 2016 Cyber security using game theory *Int. J. Innov. Sci. Eng. Technol.* **3**

[16] Tchakounte F, Nyassi V S, Danga D E H, Udagepola K P and Atemkeng M 2020 A game theoretical model for anticipating email spear-phishing strategies *European Union Digital Library* available at https://eudl.eu/doi/10.4108/eai.26–5-2020.166354

[17] Kamran S A, Sengupta S and Tavakkoli A 2021 Semi-supervised Conditional GAN for Simultaneous Generation and Detection of Phishing URLs: A Game theoretic Perspective. arXiv preprint arXiv:2108.01852

[18] Tahir M A U H, Asghar S, Zafara A and Gillani S 2016 A hybrid model to detect phishing-sites using supervised learning algorithms *2016 Int. Conf. on Computational Science and Computational Intelligence (CSCI)* 1126–33

[19] Javaria K, Rabiya J, Myda K, Maliha M, Aatif S M and Wajid R 2019 Anti-phishing Models for Mobile Application Development: A Review Paper, Intelligent Technologies, and Applications *Intap 2018*

[20] Tovek software, available at https://tovek.cz/cs/

Chapter 11

Human-assisted intelligent computing and ecological modeling (drought early warning system)

Asmae Zbiri and Azeddine Hachmi

Abbreviaitons

VITO	Vlaamse Instelling voor Technologisch Onderzoek Flemish Institute for Technological Research
SWI	Soil water index
NDVI	Normalized Difference Vegetation Index
CGLS	Copernicus Global Land Service
ArcGIS	Geographic Information System
SPIRITS	Software for the Processing and Interpretation of Remotely sensed Image Time Series
JMP	JMP Powerful and interactive data visualization and statistical analysis tool
TaylorFit	Statistical software for Multivariate Polynomial Regression MPR
MPR	Multivariate Polynomial Regression
MARA	Ministry of Agriculture and Agrarian Reform WMO World Meteorological Organization
r	Coefficient of correlation
eMODIS	Moderate Resolution Imaging Spectroradiometer
DMP	Dry Matter Productivity
FAPAR	Fraction of Absorbed Photosynthetically Active Radiation
SPOT-VEGETATION	Multi-spectral scanning radiometer
PROBA-V	Project for on-board autonomy—Vegetation instrument

Technology and algorithms are fast factors to understand soil–climate–vegetation interaction in arid and semi-arid rangelands. During the last decades, rangelands

doi:10.1088/978-0-7503-4801-0ch11

have experienced several severe and prolonged periods of drought that have severely affected forage production. Our goal is to predict drought by remote sensing, which is an important step in the design and implementation of the spatio-temporal drought management plan. Overall, we are interested in the interaction between natural vegetation and climate algorithms (ecological modeling or human-assisted intelligent computing (HAIC)), particularly in the development of a drought early warning system that would identify drought risk levels from remote sensing. We are working in particular on Morocco rangelands where access is difficult, in these regions the majority of household income is based on livestock.

11.1 Introduction

11.1.1 Rangelands

On a global scale, food security in arid and semi-arid areas will be compromised, due to climate change, with two challenges: meeting basic needs of populations whose numbers are continuously increasing; and strategies for adaptation and mitigation of the impact of diminishing water resources.

Future investments must consider natural resources as an indispensable capital in any improvement of rational use of water resources and in a better management of risks related to water in rangelands [1].

Drylands are predominantly rangelands and croplands supporting an integrated agro-pastoral way of life, occupying 41% of the 6.2 billion hectares of land area [2]. These areas supported crops, pastures and domestic animals for one third of the human population, or 2 billion people in the year 2000. But this production of crops, forage, wood and other services provided by these ecosystems is limited by water scarcity. According to Puigdefabregas and Mendizabal, rangelands link humans and natural resources in a single system [3]. Any disturbance of this system leads to its imbalance and the appearance of numerous climatic and socio-economic concerns. Among climatic disturbances are frequent droughts, severe floods, etc, in addition to temporal climatic fluctuations. Socio-economic disturbances involve changes in demography, grazing, cultivated land, etc and in the long run all these phenomena weigh negatively on natural resources.

Any disturbance of this system leads to its imbalance and the appearance of numerous climatic and socio-economic concerns. Among climatic disturbances: frequent droughts, severe floods, etc, in addition to temporal climatic fluctuations. While socio-economic disturbances involve changes in demography, grazing, cultivated land, etc and at long run all these phenomena weigh negatively on natural resources.

Rangeland is a source of many global environmental problems and deserves more attention from policy makers because its degradation leads to a loss of vegetation cover and biomass productivity, which is a threat to survival of local populations [4].

In India and the United States, periods of drought have resulted in reduced forage and livestock production [5–7].

In North African pastures in particular, drought is the most important natural phenomenon related to climate change. It permanently affects large areas of rangelands and is responsible for severe impacts on life expectancy of pastoral populations and their economic performance as a result of repetitive droughts, causing drastic drops in forage production.

In Africa, rangelands occupy more than 40% of the land, with large variations between countries. Livestock and related activities, contribute at least 50% to production and livelihood of pastoral communities [8].

In Morocco, rangelands are located in arid and semi-arid areas. Thus, dryland pastures are ecologically, economically, and socially important because they provide livelihoods for thousands of people and protect a country from rapid pasture drought [9]. According to Global Land Cover classification we considered three types of rangelands. For simplicity, 'rangelands' in this study represents a combination of degraded rangeland sparse vegetation, and shrub rangeland covering, respectively, 68%, 25%, and 7% of total rangelands areas [10]. In this rangeland, climate change scenarios suggest changes in rainfall patterns related to increased variability of precipitation responsible for recurrent droughts, for example the coefficient of variation of annual rainfall varies between 25% and 100%.

Drought remains one of the most costly natural disasters for policy makers and politicians. This phenomenon can lead to a reduction in water supply, deterioration of water quality and ultimately the reduction of forage production [11]. In pastures, the effects of drought on vegetation have serious consequences for people's livelihoods and socio-economic development. Human life is dependent on rangelands as they form ecosystems that are habitats for wildlife; also, they provide boreholes for livestock and livestock production [12].

According to Ministry of Agriculture and Agrarian Reform of Morocco, 15% of these ecosystems are severely degraded and concentrated in the East and South of the country [13].

Overall aerial cover during 2014 was variable while phytomass remained stable. This is due to presence of some species, with low phytomass but high seed productions, which colonize open spaces and contribute to increase of cover rate in these rangelands. Degradation of Eastern Morocco rangelands is another obstacle to development in these areas [14].

The degradation of rangelands is a threat to biodiversity. The sedentarization linked to the reduction of herd movements have only accelerated this degradation process to which are added socio-economic and environmental problems. The arid rangelands of the eastern highlands have a well-documented biological potential, however, the resilience potential of these rangelands has not been investigated. These lands are highly subject to excessive exploitation of their resources and thus their inevitable degradation. Figure 11.1 shows this degradation during 2016. Compared to the year 2011, these lands appear to be highly degraded and desertified.

Due to all these reasons that we mention, many scientific contributions, national and international, have been made on the search for an efficient monitoring system capable of providing timely drought alerts. Such a system, opted for by the authorizers, could contribute to early and appropriate decisions in response to rangelands drought. Among the timely parameters of such monitoring systems is precipitation as it provides crucial information on water availability and therefore potential drought occurrence [15].

Figure 11.1. Degraded Eastern Morocco rangelands between 2011 and 2016 (field sampling; potential of arid rangelands in Morocco: towards a sustainable management system sustainable, case of the eastern highlands [14].

Typically, drought monitoring is based on observations provided by weather stations. Unfortunately, in these sparsely populated areas, there is no continuous spatial coverage needed to characterize drought conditions.

11.1.2 Ecological modeling and early warning (theory)

Thus, lack of reliable monitoring information based on rigorous empirical data, adequate methodologies and concrete assessments of these rangelands, all hinder monitoring of any climate change and implementation of effective programs in drought mitigation. Conventional drought monitoring methods are not adapted to spatial scale of these phenomena.

In the last decades, several studies [16–19] using remote sensing data to monitor various land dynamic processes have emerged. For example, satellite remote sensing provides a general view of earth and a spatial context for measuring drought impacts. Remote sensing techniques are currently widely regarded as a time- and cost-efficient alternative for estimating climate change and the recurrent drought events that accompany it [20–22].

Remote sensing could play a critical role in detecting environmental change on regional and global scales. It can be used to improve monitoring efforts as well as provide valuable information on dryland pasture drought. However, the low vegetation cover and heterogeneity of arid rangelands is a major obstacle in using these remote sensing techniques to predict and estimate drought in these regions [23].

11.1.3 Ecological modeling and early warning (applications)

Currently, the exceptional growth of remote sensing data has allowed an adequate assessment of arid and semi-arid rangelands around the world at different spatial scales. However, in the study of arid rangelands, the use of remote sensing alone shows some limitations and does not provide reliable information for drought monitoring, especially when the vegetation is sparse. Indeed, the vegetation cover is formed by a mixture of dry plants, without foliage, whose reflectance is similar to that of bare soil, and plants that are still green.

Therefore, monitoring these rangelands by remote sensing, especially in Morocco, requires a more appropriate approach using remote sensing coupled with biophysical indicators capable of providing accurate information of drought risk in these rangelands.

The objective of our study is to develop drought monitoring methods, in Moroccan rangelands, based on climatic, hydrological and vegetation indicators. To achieve this, four specific objectives will be developed which are to:

- Provide an overview of drought in arid and semi-arid rangelands in Morocco.
- Provide a detailed land use map of Moroccan rangelands, including Saharan and pre-Saharan domain.
- Study efficiency of remote sensing data used in monitoring of rangeland drought.
- Develop a specific drought early warning system for arid and semi-arid rangelands

Figure 11.2 shows severe drought and reduction of forage production in Eastern, High atlas and Saharan rangelands. Given lack of reliable information of the current state in Moroccan rangelands, most development projects have been implemented in these areas based primarily on expert opinion or auxiliary sources. Severe NDVI anomalies were observed for north Moroccan rangelands during drought year in 2015 (figure 11.2).

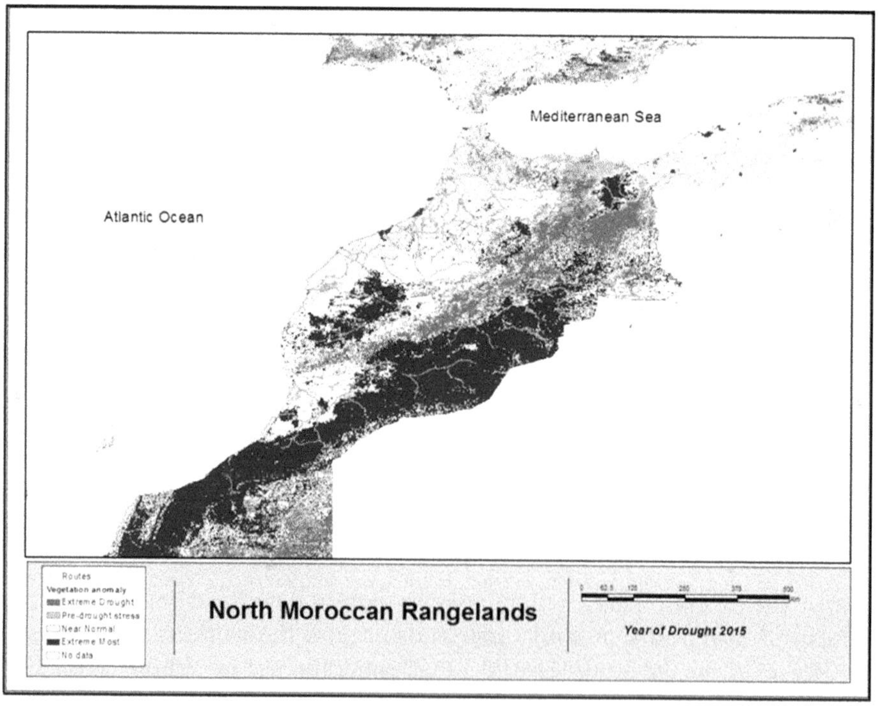

Figure 11.2. Vegetation index anomaly detection map in North Moroccan rangelands during drought year in 2015 (drought monitoring using soil water index and normalized difference vegetation index time series in Moroccan rangelands) [24].

11.2 Contribution of ecological modeling

Our results can be grouped into three probable contributions to drought prevention in Moroccan rangelands (figure 11.3).

11.2.1 Efficiency and algorithm theoretical to calibration of remote sensing data

Ensuring reliability of the raw data base is an important step, especially in studies that exploit remotely sensed data.

Our data concerning fraction of photosynthetically active radiation absorbed: FAPAR and productivity of dry matter: DMP, emanating from two satellites SPOT-VEGETATION and PROBA-V, were evaluated by NDVI method of eMODIS, which has shown its validity in numerous studies on rangelands.

Theoretical algorithms for calibration of these data in a larger scale for all Moroccan rangelands are made with two hypotheses [24]. Provision of pixel quality and validation information greatly facilitated use of these products. With recent research efforts focusing on product consistency. Validation framework can act synergistically to further refine accuracy and precision of these products over the long term.

After this step of verification of two phenological indices: FAPAR and DMP, correlations, of linear and polynomial type, were established between these two variables and NDVI according to the correlation coefficients: $r^2 = 0.98$ and $r^2 = 0.91$. Following this correlation we could show that our two phenological indices would be reliable in such a drought forecast.

11.2.2 Spatial and temporal analysis and polynomial regression

Our analysis of spatial and temporal variability of soil moisture, rainfall and vegetation in semi-arid or arid rangelands of Morocco have allowed us to show

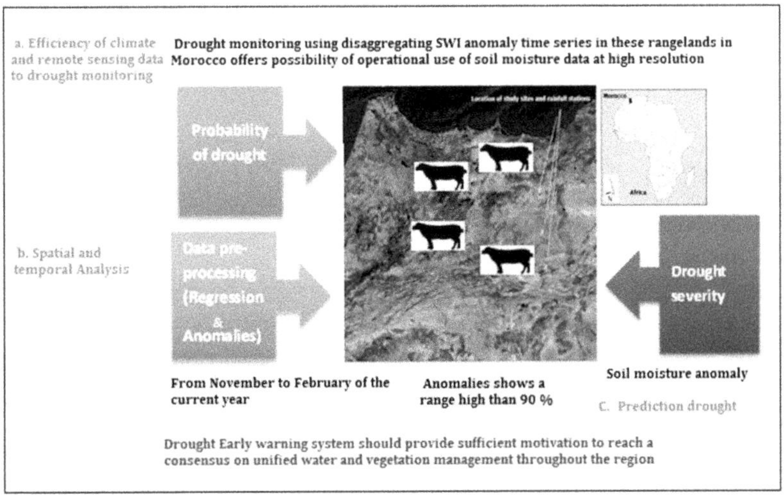

Figure 11.3. Ecological modeling and key steps to preparing drought early warning in Moroccan rangelands.

relevance of seasonal averages such as soil moisture index, rainfall and vegetation index: NDVI and phenological indices: FAPAR and DMP in the interpretation of these variables in our rangelands.

Polynomial correlation between NDVI (from February to April) and SWI (from November to February) was high for all rangeland types. The Pearson coefficients $r^2 = 0.93$ and $r^2 = 0.92$ that were estimated in this polynomial regression meant that vegetation index could be estimated from the soil moisture index (SWI) is vis towards that [10].

It should be added that polynomial correlation observed in all Morocco's rangelands was not observed at scale of the three stations studied. Soil moisture index SWI is significant and proves that it depends on nature of soil and presence of vegetation; it is sensitive to absence of vegetation in degraded areas. Based on spatial and temporal analysis of remote sensing data, we have retained advantages and disadvantages from the perspective of this study on the use of spatial data in arid and semi-arid grazing areas.

Also, the relationship established between cumulative rainfall, from September to February, and NDVI means, from February to April, from polynomial regression where $r^2 = 0.87$ and linear one with $r^2 = 0.75$ is significant in our three stations. This supports the possibility of estimating vegetation index in these regional rangelands from stationary rainfall.

11.2.3 Spatial disaggregation and anomalies

Correlations between SWI, precipitation and vegetation indices, from ten years of studies, allowed us to estimate anomalies. Spatial disaggregation of SWI from vegetation index would be necessary to characterize drought across Moroccan rangelands.

The estimation of vegetation index anomaly would be more reliable from precipitation anomalies at three regional stations. And, for all types of rangeland: shrub, herbaceous and degraded, the relationship between anomaly of disaggregated SWI and NDVI is estimated to be 90% and thus anomaly of SWI could appreciate that of vegetation index or other phenological indices.

11.3 Conclusion

In conclusion, our results show that soil moisture is dependent on rainfall, soil characteristics and vegetation abundance.

Our results on soil moisture anomaly would lead us to conclude that a deficit in this index would lead to a decrease in NDVI vegetation index, photosynthetic fraction FAPAR and dry matter productivity DMP; and that this anomaly analysis process would be in favor of its application in prevention of drought in Moroccan rangelands.

Following our work, we can suggest that an early warning of drought in Moroccan rangelands should be based on potential warning indicators such as SWI, NDVI, FAPAR, DMP, and rainfall, whose analysis would allow the establishment of an effective system, in the short and medium term, in prediction of this phenomenon.

The choice of these indicators was based on our bibliographic analysis and contribution of these indicators in early warning of drought in countries where the climatic conditions are similar to ours.

We also used many indices derived from remote sensing, such as those related to hydrology and crop production, which allowed us to save time that would be required for field data collection.

This system proposes simple and/or composite indicators at national and regional scales corresponding to two functions: early warning and medium-term monitoring that will be able to provide useful information on state and evolution of pastoral areas. This will simplify interpretation of results, facilitate decision making by decision makers and improve targeting of interventions.

Appendix A: Prospects

Following our study, it appears that in order to make operational an effective early warning system applicable to drought in our arid and semi-arid zones, some considerations should be taken into account in future studies such as:

- Early warning system must ensure, in addition to monitoring drought in the rangelands, an effective action in the fight against food insecurity of rural populations.
- Early warning system should help decision makers to better protect rangelands, in particular against excessive degradation caused by the sedentarization of nomadic families.
- Early warning system should allow action to be taken when necessary to prevent an economic crisis in the livestock market.
- Early warning system based solely on estimation of climatic indices, such as rainfall, can lead to a failure in protocol of such a system. This is because a delay or disruption of rainfall events may be due to global climate change.
- Until now the existing warning systems show a deficiency in their historical data and specific indicators that are responsible for anticipating and managing the recurrent droughts experienced by pastoral areas.

In this context, the institutions in charge of piloting early warning systems to this phenomenon should seize the opportunity of these new warning systems that would be judicious to:

- Update the existing warning systems with this new specific model for arid and semi-arid lands.
- Use new software for processing and interpretation of remote sensing data.
- Use data with a good resolution to forecast of drought in arid and semi-arid rangelands.
- Train the persons in institutions in charge of this field of forecasting and early warning of drought in arid and semi-arid rangelands.

- To look for positive international collaborations for more exchange and expertise in the field of drought early warning in arid and semi-arid rangelands, and sustainable protection of their ecosystems.

Appendix B: Ecological modeling

Benefits of modeling can be summarized in four principles:
- Use a lot of reliable data;
- Save time;
- Fast analysis;
- Generate a clear idea on a large spatio-temporal scale.

Manual methods have proven to be very difficult to apply to seemingly simple tasks such as object recognition in images. Data from the real world—samples of a sound or pixels of an image—are complex, variable and fraught with noise.

To a machine, an image is an array of numbers indicating the brightness (or color) of each pixel, and a sound signal is a sequence of numbers indicating the air pressure at each instant. But like any powerful technology, HAIC can be used for the benefit of all humanity.

Emergence of HAIC will undoubtedly displace jobs. But it will also save lives (through food, road, environmental, climate and medical safety). It will most likely be accompanied by an increase in production of wealth per capita.

Appendix C: Questions for the governing bodies

How to distribute this new wealth? and how to train displaced workers for new jobs created by technological progress?

This is a political question, not a technological one. It is not a new question: the effect of technological progress on the labor market has been around since the industrial revolution. The emergence of HAIC is just a symptom of accelerating technological progress.

So, we are grateful to companies such as Copernicus, CGLS or other free software developers like SPIRITS (Software for the Processing and Interpretation of Remotely sensed Image Time Series); fully developed by VITO because they help reseach.

Also, statistical software SAS or JMP is more or less used compared to the new generation of programs like *TaylorFi*t. Multivariate Polynomial Regression (MPR) modeling approach is very useful in our work. MPR in free online software (*TaylorFit*) makes MPR models very easy to develop [25]. *TaylorFit* incorporates polynomial terms with user-defined exponents, including negative exponents to test for ratios among variables. MPR can capture data features with comparable accuracy to artificial neural networks but produces representational models that are easier to use and communicate.

Our goal is to make this software known and to share its use with a network of interested researchers.

As experts, we still have a chance to make our marks in the universe of science 'The real investment in the world is not where you make money; scientific research is future investment'.

Funding

This research received no external funding.

Acknowledgments

This chapter was collaborated by two research couples in natural sciences and technology. The authors are grateful to the editors and the anonymous reviewers for their comments and suggestions.

References

[1] WMO 2006 Drought monitoring and early warning principles, *progress and future challenges* (Geneva: World Meteorological Organization) p 28

[2] Safriel U and Adeel Z 2005 *Dryland systems.Ecosystems and human well-being: Current state and trends.* (Washington, D.C: Island Press) p 948

[3] Puigdefabregas J and Mendizabal T 2004 Prospects for desertification impacts in Southern Europe *Environmental Challenges in the Mediterranean 2000-50NATO Science Series: IV, Earth and Environmental Sciences* section III 37 (Cham: Springer) pp 155–72

[4] Prince S D, Becker-Reshef I and Rishmawi K 2009 Detection and mapping of long-term land degradation using local net production scaling: Application to Zimbabwe *Remote Sens. Environ.* **113** 1046–57

[5] Dutta D, Kundu A, Patel N R, Saha S K and Siddiqui A R 2015 Assessment of agricultural drought in Rajasthan (India) using remote sensing derived vegetation condition index (VCI) and Standardized Precipitation Index (SPI) *Egypt. J. Remote Sens. Space Sci.* **18** 53–63

[6] Derner J D and Augustine D J 2016 Adaptive management for drought on rangelands *Rangelands* **38** 211–5

[7] Knutson C and Fuchs B 2016 New tools for assessing drought conditions for rangeland management *Rangelands* **38** 177–82

[8] International Work Group for Indigenous Peoples 2010 *A Policy Framework for Pastoralism in Africa: Securing, Protecting and Improving the Lives, Livelihoods and Rights of Pastoralist Communities* (Addis Ababa: African Union. Econ. Rur. and Agri.)

[9] Bounejmate M, Mahyou H and Bechchari A 2001 Rangeland degradation in Morocco: A concern for all *ICARDA Caravan* **15h** 33–6

[10] Zbiri A, Haesen D, El Alaoui-faris F E and Mahyou H 2019 Drought monitoring using soil water index and normalized difference vegetation index time series in Moroccan rangelands *WSEAS Trans. Environ. Dev.* **15** 261–78

[11] Riebsame W E, Changnon S A and Karl T 1991 *Drought and Natural Resources Management in the United States: Impacts and Implications of the 1987–89 Drought* (Boulder, CO: Westview Press Inc.)

[12] Brunson M W, Huntsinger L, Kreuter U P and Ritten J P 2016 Usable socio-economic science for Rangelands *Rangelands* **38** 85–9

[13] MARA 1992 Ministry of agriculture and agrarian reform *Stratégie de Développement des Terres de Parcours au Maroc* vol 1 (Rabat: Situation Actuelle des Terres de Parcours) pp 1–103

[14] Hachmi A 2019 Potential of arid rangelands in morocco: towards a sustainable management system sustainable, case of the eastern highlands *Thesis* Mohamed V University Rabat

[15] Velpuri N M, Senay G B and Morisette J T 2016 Evaluating New SMAP soil moisture for drought monitoring in the rangelands of the US high plains *Rangelands* **38** 183–90

[16] Reed B C, Brown J F, VanderZee D and Loveland T R 1994 Measuring phenological variability from satellite imagery *J. Veg. Sci.* 703–14

[17] Yang Z L, Dickinson R E, Shuttleworth W J and Shaikh M 1998 Treatment of soil, vegetation and snow in land surface models: a test of the biosphere-atmosphere transfer scheme with the hapex-mobilhy, abracos and Russian data *J. Hydrol.* **212–213** 109–27

[18] Peters A J, Walter-Shea E A, Ji L, Vina A, Hayes M and Svoboda M D 2002 Drought monitoring with NDVI-based standardized vegetation index *Photogramm. Eng. Remote Sens.* **68** 71–5

[19] Anderson M C, Norman J M, Mecikalski J R, Otkin J A and Kustas W P 2007 A climatological study of evapotranspiration and moisture stress across the continental United States based on thermal remote sensing surface moisture climatology *J. Geophys. Res.* **D11** 13

[20] Escadafal R 2007 Les bases de la surveillance de la désertification par satellites *Sécheresse* **4** 263–70

[21] Hill J, Stellmes M, Udelhoven T, Röder A and Sommer S 2008 Mediterranean desertification and land degradation: mapping related land use change syndromes based on satellite observations *Global Planet. Change* **64** 146–57

[22] Lambin E F, Geist H, Reynolds J F and Stafford-Smith D M 2009 Coupled humanenvironment system approaches to desertification: Linking people to pixels *Recent Advances in Remote Sensing and Geoinformation Processing for Land Degradation Assessment* ed A Roder and J Hill (London: CRC Press, Taylor and Francis) pp 3–14

[23] Okin G S, Roberts D A, Murraya B and Okin W J 2001 Practical limits on hyperspectral vegetation discrimination in arid and semiarid environments *Remote Sens. Environ.* **77** 212–5

[24] Zbiri A, Haesen D, El Alaoui-faris F E, Hachmi A and Vaccari D A 2021 Algorithm theoretical for FAPAR and DMP calibration using remote sensing and field data in moroccan arid areas *Int. J. Environ. Sci.* **6** 11–22

[25] Vaccari D A 2021 *TaylorFit Users' Manual*, www.TaylorFit-RSA.com

IOP Publishing

Human-Assisted Intelligent Computing
Modeling, simulations and applications
Mukhdeep Singh Manshahia, Igor S Litvinchev, Gerhard-Wilhelm Weber, J Joshua Thomas and Pandian Vasant

Chapter 12

Attention mechanisms in machine vision: a survey of the state of the art

Abdul Mueed Hafiz

With the advent of state-of-the-art Nature-inspired pure attention-based models, i.e. transformers, and their success in natural language processing (NLP), their extension to machine vision (MV) tasks was inevitable and much welcomed. Subsequently, vision transformers (ViTs) were introduced which are giving quite a challenge to the established deep learning-based machine vision techniques. However, pure attention- based models/architectures like transformers require huge data, large training times and large computational resources. Some recent works suggest that combinations of these two varied fields can prove to build systems which have the advantages of both these fields. Accordingly, it is hoped that introducing this state-of-the-art survey chapter will help readers get useful information about this interesting and potential research area. A gentle introduction to attention mechanisms is given, followed by a discussion of the popular attention-based deep architectures. Subsequently, the major categories of the intersection of attention mechanisms and deep learning for MV-based tasks are discussed. Afterwards, the major algorithms, issues and trends within the scope of the paper are discussed.

12.1 Introduction

In this section we discuss the attention mechanism on top of which transformers are built. The important types of attention mechanisms are discussed. This is followed by section 12.2 wherein the attention-based deep learning architectures are discussed. Next, in section 12.3 the broad categories of attention and deep learning in MV are discussed. This is followed by section 12.4 which discusses trends and limitations present in the area. We conclude in section 12.5.

Recently, attention-based mechanisms like transformers [85] have been successfully applied to various MV tasks by using them as vision transformers (ViTs) [18] in

doi:10.1088/978-0-7503-4801-0ch12

image recognition [83], object detection [8, 111], segmentation [104], image super-resolution [101], video understanding [24, 79], image generation [10], text–image synthesis [70] and visual question answering [78, 80], among others [17, 45, 89, 103] achieving at par as well as even better results as compared to the established convolutional neural networks (CNN) models [40]. However, transformers have various issues like being 'data-hungry' and requiring large training times. Deep learning [25, 50, 75] based CNNs [30, 49, 51] on the other hand do not have such problems significantly. Accordingly, techniques have emerged which are at the intersection of pure attention-based models and the established pure CNNs which have best of the both features. MV has also benefitted from this merger of the two important vision models viz. ViTs and CNNs. In the this section we will discuss the source of power of ViTs and transformers in general, i.e. attention and its types [40] briefly for readers to have an idea of the new type of MV models, i.e. ViTs.

12.1.1 Self-attention

For a given sequence of elements, the self-attention process gives a measurable estimate of the relevance of one element to others. For example, which elements like words can come together in a sequence like a sentence. The self-attention process is an important unit of attention-based models like transformers, that model the dependencies among all elements of the sequence for formal or structured prediction applications. Plainly stated, a self-attention model layer assigns a value to every element in a structure or sequence by combining information globally from the input vector or sequence.

Denoting a sequence of n entities ($\mathbf{x}_1$, $\mathbf{x}_2$, $\cdots$ $\mathbf{x}_n$) by $\mathbf{X} \in \mathbb{R}^{n \times d}$, d being the dimension which embeds dependency of every element, the purpose of self-attention is capturing the dependency between all n elements after encoding every element inside the overall contextual knowledge. This process is achieved by the definition of three weight matrices which have to be learnt for transforming: Queries ($\mathbf{W}^Q \in \mathbb{R}^{n \times d_q}$), Keys ($\mathbf{W}^K \in \mathbb{R}^{n \times d_k}$) and Values ($\mathbf{W}^V \in \mathbb{R}^{n \times d_v}$). First the input vector $\mathbf{X}$ is projected to the three weight matrices for obtaining $\mathbf{Q} = \mathbf{X}\mathbf{W}^Q$, $\mathbf{K} = \mathbf{X}\mathbf{W}^K$ and $\mathbf{V} = \mathbf{X}\mathbf{W}^V$. The output $\mathbf{Z} \in \mathbb{R}^{n \times d_v}$ in the self-attention layer is next expressed as,

$$Z = \text{softmax}\left(\frac{\mathbf{QK}^T}{\sqrt{d_q}}\right)\mathbf{V} \tag{12.1}$$

For a certain element in the vector or sequence, the self-attention mechanism fundamentally finds the dot product of query with all the keys, this product being subsequently normalized by the softmax function for obtaining the attention-map scores. Every element now assumes the value of the weighted summation for all elements inside the vector or sequence, wherein all weights are equal to the attention map scores.

12.1.2 Masked self-attention

The self-attention layer applies to every element or entity. For the transformer [85] having been trained for prediction of the next entity in the vector or sequence, the self-attention units inside the decoder are then masked for prevention of their application to the entities coming in future. This technique is achieved by calculating the element-wise product with a mask $\mathbf{M} \in \mathbb{R}^{n \times n}$, where $\mathbf{M}$ is the upper triangular matrix. Thus masked self-attention is calculated as:

$$\text{softmax}\left(\frac{\mathbf{QK}^T}{\sqrt{d_q}} \circ \mathbf{M}\right) \tag{12.2}$$

where $\circ$ is the Hadamard product. During prediction of an element in the vector or sequence, the attention map scores of the future elements are set to 0 in the masked self-attention.

12.1.3 Multi-head attention

For encapsulation of various complicated dependencies between various elements or entities in the vector or sequence, the multi-head attention structure consists of h self-attention units. $h = 8$ was used inside the original transformer architecture [85]. Every unit contains its own learnable weight matrices $\{\mathbf{W}^{Q_i}, \mathbf{W}^{K_i}, \mathbf{W}^{V_i}\}$, where $i = 0, 1, 2, \ldots, (h - 1)$. For a particular input $\mathbf{X}$, outputs of h self-attention units in the multi-head attention process are combined into one matrix $[\mathbf{Z}_0, \mathbf{Z}_1, \ldots \mathbf{Z}_{h-1}] \in \mathbb{R}^{n \times h \times d_v}$ and are subsequently projected to another weight matrix $\mathbf{W} \in \mathbb{R}^{h \cdot d_v \times d}$.

The notable difference between the self-attention process and the convolutional process is that in the former every weight is dynamically computed, whereas in the latter there are static weights for various inputs. Also, the self-attention process is invariable to permutation and change for different numbers of inputs with the result that it has a convenient operation over irregularity as against the convolutional operator which needs a grid array. See figure 12.1 for illustration of these concepts.

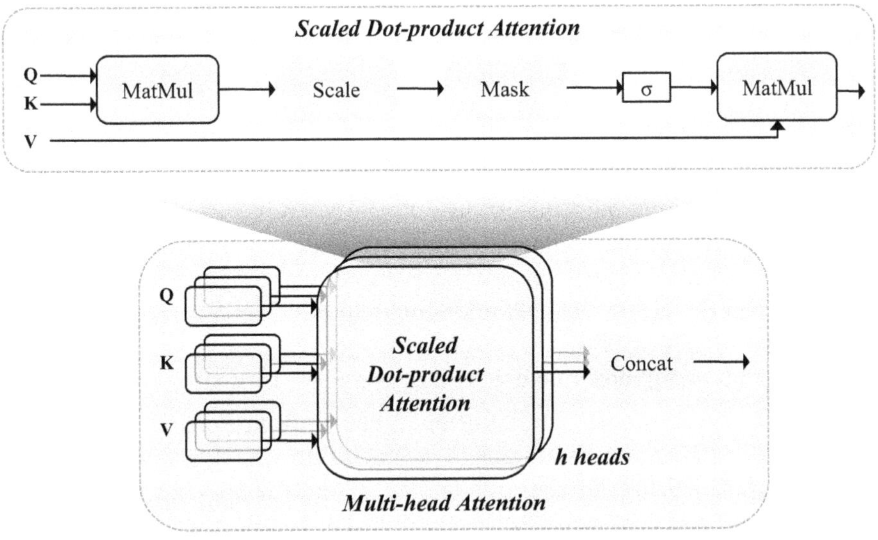

Figure 12.1. Illustration of various attention mechanisms. Adapted with permission from [40] CC BY-SA 4.0.

12.2 Attention-based deep learning architectures

In this section, some common architectures of deep attention models are discussed [88]. The architectures of the prevalent deep attention-based models are categorized into the following important classes:

1. Single-channel model;
2. Multi-channel model feeding on multi-scale data;
3. Skip-layer model;
4. Bottom-up or top-down model;
5. Skip-layer model with multi-scale saliency single network.

12.2.1 Single-channel model

The single-channel model is the predominant configuration of various CNN-based attention models and also is used by many attention-based models [38, 43, 44, 67]. Almost all the other types of CNN configurations can be considered as variants of the single-channel model. It has been demonstrated that cues on various levels and scales are vital for attention [100]. Using multi-scale features of CNNs in attention-based models is an obvious choice. In the next type of single-channel model, namely multi-channel model, the changes are done along this line.

12.2.2 Multi-channel model

Some implementations of this model include [37, 56, 62, 108]. This model learns multi-scale attention information by training multiple models with multi-scale data inputs. The multiple model channels are used in parallel and can have varying configurations with different scales. As shown in [97], input data is fed via multiple channels, and then the features are fused and fed into a unified output layer for producing the final attention map. We observe that in the multi-channel model, multi-scale learning takes place outside the individual models. As discussed in the next configuration, multi-scale learning is used inside the model, and this is achieved by combining feature maps from various convolutional layer hierarchies.

12.2.3 Skip-layer model

A common skip-layer model is used in [14, 46, 47]. Instead of learning from many parallel channels on multiple-scale images, the skip-layer model learns multi-scale feature maps inside a primary channel. Multi-scale outputs are learned from various layers with increasingly larger reception fields and down-sampling ratios. Next, these outputs are fused for giving the final attention map.

12.2.4 Bottom-up or top-down model

This relatively newer model configuration called bottom-up or top-down model has been used in attention-based object segmentation [102] and also in instance segmentation [27, 29, 68]. In the architecture of the model segmentation feature maps are first obtained by common bottom-up convolution techniques, and next top-down refinement is done for fusing the data from deep to shallow layers into the mask. The main motivation behind this configuration is to produce high-fidelity segmentation masks because deep CNN layers lose fine image detail. The bottom-up or top-down model is like a type of skip-layer model since different layers are connected to each other.

12.2.5 Skip-layer model with multi-scale saliency network

This model [88] is inspired by the model in [97] and also by the deep-supervised model in [52]. It uses multi-scale and multi-level attention-based information from various layers, and learns via the deep-supervised technique. An important difference between this model and the previous models is that the former provides combined straightforward supervision of the hidden layers while the latter uses supervision in only the last output layer and propagation of the output back to the previous layers. It uses the merit of the skip-layer model which does not learn from multiple model channels with multi-scale input data. Also, it is lighter than the multi-channel model and bottom-up/top-down model. It has been found that the bottom-up/top-down model faces training difficulties while the deeply supervised model shows high training efficiency.

In the next section we turn to the categorization of various attention mechanisms and deep learning in MV, and discuss each category in detail.

12.3 Attention and deep learning in machine vision: broad categories

In this section, we discuss category-wise the various techniques of attention mechanisms and deep learning applied to MV. The three broad categories are:

1. Attention-based CNNs;
2. CNN transformer pipelines;
3. Hybrid transformers.

First we discuss the attention-based CNNs in the following subsection.

12.3.1 Attention-based CNNs

Recently attention mechanisms have been applied in deep learning for MV applications, e.g. object detection [5, 71, 76], image captioning [3, 98, 105] and action recognition [74]. The central idea of the attention mechanisms is to locate the salient components of the feature maps in CNNs in such a manner that the redundancy is removed. Generally, attention is embedded into the CNN by using attention maps. Particularly, the attention-based maps in [71, 74, 76, 98] yield in a self-learned manner. Weak supervision of the attention maps is used. Other techniques cited in literature [99, 105] proceed by utilization of human attention data or guidance of the CNNs by focusing on the regions of interest (ROIs). In the following subsections, we discuss some noteworthy techniques in MV which use attention-based CNNs, e.g. in image classification or retrieval, object detection, sign language recognition, denoising and facial expression recognition.

12.3.1.1 Image classification or retrieval and object detection

It is well established that attention contributes to human perception [13, 42, 72]. One important characteristic of human vision is that it does not attempt to address the whole visual scene in one go. Instead, a sequence of partial glimpses is exploited and focusing is done selectively for capturing the visual structure in a better manner [48]. Recently, several attempts have been made [35, 87] for incorporation of attention processing mechanisms in order to improve the classification accuracy of CNNs on large-scale classification tasks. Wang *et al* [87] have proposed a residual attention network having an encoder–decoder based attention mechanism. By refinement of the features, the network gives good accuracy as well as showing robustness to noise. Without directly computing the three-dimensional (3D) attention map, the process is decomposed such that it learns channel-attention and spatial-attention exclusively. The exclusive attention map generation technique for 3D features is computationally inexpensive and parameter restricted, and hence can be used as a plug and play unit for existing CNN networks. In their work [35], the authors have introduced a compact unit for exploitation of the relationship between various channels. In this 'Squeeze and Excitation' unit, the authors have used global average-pooling of feature maps for computation of each channel's attention. However, the authors of [93] show that the features used in [35] are suboptimal for inferring fine-channel attention. Accordingly, the authors of [93] use max-pooled feature maps. According to [35, 93], spatial attention is missed which contributes in an important manner for deciding the focusing [11]. The authors of [93] thus propose the convolutional block attention module (CBAM) for exploitation of both the spatial attention as well as channel attention with the help of a robust network and proceed to verify that exploitation of both these mechanisms is better than use of only the channel-wise attention mechanism [35]. They use it on the ImageNet-1K dataset [15]. The authors of [93] experimentally demonstrate that their module is also effective for object detection tasks by using two popular datasets viz. MS-COCO [61] and VOC [21]. They achieve impressive results by inserting their module into the pre-existing one-shot object detector [92] in the VOC2007 testing set. Figure 12.2 shows the CBAM for both channel and spatial-attention processes. Here we attempt to briefly explain the attention mechanism in CBAM.

For a given input feature map $\mathbf{F} \in \mathbb{R}^{C\times H\times W}$, CBAM [93] produces a 1D attention map $\mathbf{M}_c \in \mathbb{R}^{C\times 1\times 1}$ and a 2D spatial attention map $\mathbf{M}_s \in \mathbb{R}^{1\times H\times W}$ as shown in figure 12.2. This operation can be put as:

$$\mathbf{F}' = \mathbf{M}_c(\mathbf{F}) \otimes \mathbf{F} \tag{12.3}$$

$$\mathbf{F}'' = \mathbf{M}_s(\mathbf{F}') \otimes \mathbf{F}' \tag{12.4}$$

where $\otimes$ is the multiplication operator for elements.

Channel attention is mathematically computed as:

$$\begin{aligned}\mathbf{M}_c(\mathbf{F}) &= \sigma(MLP(\mathrm{AvgPool}(\mathbf{F})) + MLP(\mathrm{MaxPool}(\mathbf{F}))) \\ &= \sigma\left(\mathbf{W}_1\left(\mathbf{W}_0\left(\mathbf{F}^c_{\mathrm{avg}}\right)\right) + \mathbf{W}_1(\mathbf{W}_0(\mathbf{F}^c_{\mathrm{max}}))\right)\end{aligned} \tag{12.5}$$

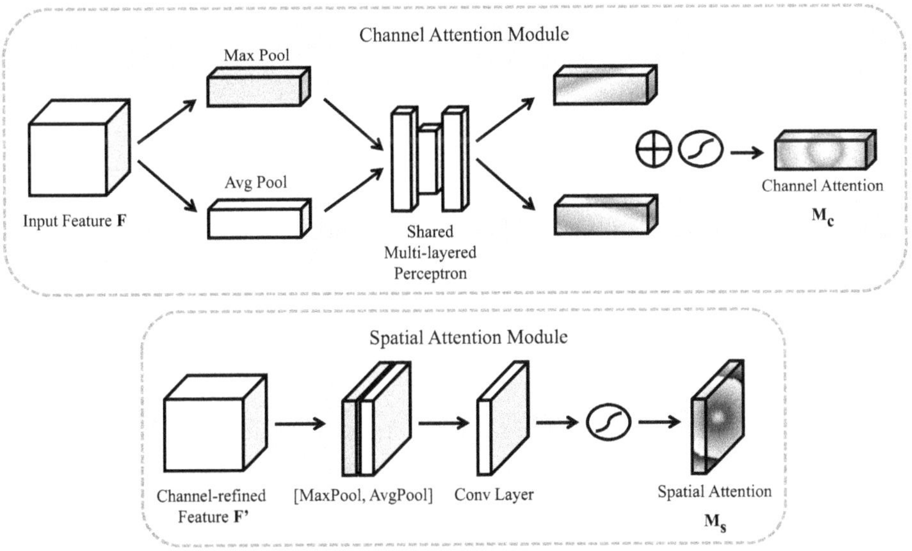

Figure 12.2. Illustration of attention modules in CBAM [93]. As shown, the channel-wise module utilizes max-pooling as well as average-pooling. On the other hand, the spatial-wise sub-module uses two identical feature outputs by pooling them along their channel axes and then forwarding them to the convolutional layer. Adapted from [93], copyright 2018, Springer Nature Switzerland AG, with permission of Springer.

where σ is the sigmoid function, $\mathbf{W}_0 \in \mathbb{R}^{C/r \times C}$ and $\mathbf{W}_1 \in \mathbb{R}^{C \times C/r}$. The multi-layer perceptron (MLP) weights, $\mathbf{W}_0$ and $\mathbf{W}_1$, are shared for both the inputs. $\mathbf{W}_0$ comes after the ReLU activation function.

$$\mathbf{M}_s(\mathbf{F}) = \sigma\left(f^{7\times7}([\text{AvgPool}(\mathbf{F}); \text{MaxPool}(\mathbf{F})])\right) = \sigma\left(f^{7\times7}\left(\left[\mathbf{F}^s_{\text{avg}}; \mathbf{F}^s_{\text{max}}\right]\right)\right) \quad (12.6)$$

where σ is the sigmoid function and $f^{7\times7}$ is the convolutional operator with a 7×7 filter.

The authors of [93] have used their technique for both image classification or retrieval on the ImageNet-1K dataset and object detection on both MS-COCO and VOC2007 datasets. The results obtained using their CBAM integrated networks outperform other contemporary ones.

Another novel work in the area of image classification or retrieval by using attention-based CNNs is given by the authors of [58] for glaucoma detection in medical image analysis [28]. They call their network attention-based CNN for glaucoma detection AG-CNN. It includes a novel attention-prediction subnet along with other subnets. They achieve 'end-to-end' training on an attention-based CNN architecture by supervision of the training through three separate loss functions based on: (i) attention-prediction, (ii) feature-visualization, and (iii) glaucoma-classification. Based on the work of authors in [37], the authors use the Kullback–Leibler (KL) divergence function as an equivalent of the nature-inspired attention-loss Loss_a given by:

$$\text{Loss}_a = \frac{1}{I \cdot J} \sum_{i=1}^{I} \sum_{j=1}^{J} A_{ij} \log\left(\frac{A_{ij}}{\hat{A}_{ij}}\right) \tag{12.7}$$

where $\hat{A}$ (with its elements $\hat{A}_{ij} \in [0, 1]$) is the attention map, and, I and J are the attention-map length and width, respectively. By incorporating these novel features, the authors of [58] demonstrate that their proposed AG-CNN technique significantly improves the state of the art in glaucoma detection.

For more interesting techniques on image classification or retrieval using attention-based CNNs, readers may refer to some of the recent outstanding works in this area as given in [22, 31], etc.

12.3.1.2 Sign language recognition

Sign language recognition (SLR) is a valuable and challenging research area in MV. Conventionally, SLR relies on handcrafted features with low performance. In their novel work [36], the authors use attention-based 3D CNNs for SLR. Their model has two advantages. First, it learns spatial and temporal features from video frames without any pre-processing or prior knowledge. Attention mechanisms help the model to select the clues. During training, spatial attention is used in the model for focusing on the ROIs. After this, temporal attention is used for selection of the important motions in the action-class. Their method has been benchmarked on a self-made large Chinese SL dataset having 500 classes, and also on the ChaLearn14 dataset [20]. The authors demonstrate that their technique outperforms other state-of-the-art techniques on the datasets used. We discuss this interesting technique in more detail below.

The spatial attention map is calculated as follows. They use an attention-based mask for denotation of the value of each image pixel. Let $x_{i,k} \in \mathbb{R}^2$ denote the position of a viewpoint k in an image i, the value of the location $p \in \mathbb{R}^2$ inside the attention map $M_{i,k} \in \mathbb{R}^{w\times h}$ for k is given by:

$$M_{i,k}(p) = \exp\left(-\frac{\|p - x_{i,k}\|_2^2}{\sigma}\right), \tag{12.8}$$

where σ is experimentally chosen, and w and h are the image dimensions. The attention mask is formed by aggregating the peaks of various viewpoints obtained previously with the help of a max operator:

$$M_i(p) = \max_k M_{i,k}(p). \tag{12.9}$$

Consequently the ith attention weighed image I_i is the element-wise product and is given by:

$$I_i(p) = I_i(p) \times M_i(p). \tag{12.10}$$

Based on the video feature obtained above, they use a support vector machine (SVM)-based classifier [84] for classification by clubbing it to another temporal attention-based pipeline. As done earlier in [19], the features are fed to a bi-directional long short term memory (LSTM) for generation of an attention vector $s \in \mathbb{R}^{8192}$. The features are also fed to a one-layer MLP which gives the hidden vector $H = \{h_1, h_2, \dots, h_n\}$, $h_i \in \mathbb{R}^{8192}$. This vector is an integration of the sequence of clip features by attention pooling. This technique measures the value of each clip feature by determining its relation with the attention vector s. Finally, they combine the video and trajectory features and use softmax based classification. Although an effective technique, the authors still admit that the work focuses on isolated SLR. For dealing with continuous SLR, which translates a clip into a sentence, recurrent neural network (RNN)-based methods are going to give better results as admitted by the authors.

12.3.1.3 Image denoising

Image denoising is a low-level MV task. Deep CNNs are quite popular in low-level MV. Research has been done to improve performance by using very deep networks. However, as the network depth increases, the effects of the shallow layers on deep layers decrease. Accordingly, the authors of [82] have proposed an attention-based denoising CNN named ADNet featuring an attention block (AB). The AB has been used for fine extraction of the noise data hidden in complex backgrounds. This technique has been proved by the authors of [82] to be very effective for denoising images with complex noise, e.g. real noise-induced images. Various experiments demonstrate that ADNet delivers very good performance for three tasks viz. denoising of synthetic images, denoising of real noisy images, and also blind denoising. Here, the AB guides the previous network section by using the current network section in order to learn the noise nature. This is particularly useful for unknown images having noise, i.e. real noisy images and blind denoising. The AB uses two successive steps for incorporating attention. First a 1x1 convolution is done on the output from the 17th CNN layer output in order to compress the feature map into a weight vector for adjustment of the previous section. Next, the weights thus obtained are used to multiply the feature map of the 16th CNN layer for extraction of more refined noise feature maps. It should be noted that inspired by this work, more complex attention mechanisms can be used along with more dedicated 'denoising' deep CNNs. The code of ADNet is available online at: https://github.com/hellloxiaotian/ADNet.

12.3.1.4 Facial expression recognition

One hot topic in MV is facial expression recognition (FER) which can be used in various MV fields like human–computer interaction (HCI), affective computing, etc. In their work [57], the authors have proposed an end-to-end CNN network featuring an attention mechanism for auto FER. It has four main parts viz. feature extraction unit, attention unit, reconstruction unit and classification unit. The attention mechanism guides the CNN for paying more attention to important features extracted from earlier units. The authors combine their local binary pattern (LBP) features and their attention mechanism for enhancing the attention mechanism for obtaining better performance. They have applied their technique to their own dataset and four others, i.e., JAFFE [65], CK+ [64], FER2013 [1] and Oulu-CASIA

[107], and demonstrate that their technique performs better than other contemporary techniques. The attention mechanism used in the work has been proved to be valuable in pixelwise MV tasks. Their attention unit consists of two branches. The first is used to obtain feature map F_p, and the second combines the LBP feature maps to obtain the attention maps F_m. The element-wise multiplication is done for the attention maps F_m and the feature maps F_p to obtain the final feature maps F_m as:

$$F_{\text{final}} = F_p F_m \tag{12.11}$$

Suppose that the input of previous layer in the second branch is f_m, then the attention maps F_m are given by:

$$F_m = \text{sigmoid}\left(Wf_m + b\right) \tag{12.12}$$

where W and b are denotations for weights and bias of the Conv. layer, respectively. The technique is suitable for 2D images and its architecture needs to be modified to extend it for video, 3D facial data, depth-image data, etc. The authors also state that they are considering using more robust and efficient machine learning techniques for enhancement of the architecture.

In another work in FER as given in [60],the authors state that in spite of the fact that conventional FER systems are almost perfect for analyzing constrained poses, they cannot perform well for partially occluded poses which are common in the real world. Accordingly, they have proposed an attention-based CNN (ACNN) for perception of facial occlusion which focuses on the highly discriminative unoccluded parts. Learning in their model is end to end. For various ROIs, they have introduced two types of ACNN viz. patch-based type and global–local-based type. The first uses attention for local patches in face regions. The second combines local features at the patch level with global features at the image-level. Evaluation is done on their own face expression dataset having in-the-wild occlusions, two of the largest in-the-wild face expression datasets viz. RAF-DB [59] and AffectNet [66], and others. They show experimentally that using ACNNs improves the FER performance wherein the ACNNs shift attention from occluded facial regions to others. They also show that their ACNN outperforms other state-of-the-art techniques on several important FER datasets. However, the technique relies on landmarks. The authors intend to address this issue. Hence ACNNs have to be made more robust for generation of attention maps without landmarks, and this is an open area for research.

In the next subsection, we turn to another important category of techniques of attention mechanisms and deep learning in machine vision, namely CNN transformer pipelines.

12.3.2 CNN transformer pipelines

In this subsection, we discuss another important category of attention and deep learning in MV, namely the CNN transformer pipeline. Here a CNN is used to feed feature maps to a transformer, and acts like a teacher to the transformer. The notable works in this category for MV have been discussed below.

12.3.2.1 Image recognition

Transformers are 'data-hungry.' For example a large-scale dataset like ImageNet [15] is not sufficient to train a vision transformer from scratch. To address this issue, Touvron *et al* [83] propose to distill information from a teacher CNN to a student transformer in order to train the transformer only on ImageNet sans additional data. This data-efficient image transformer (DeiT) [83] is a first in large-scale image classification or retrieval without using a large-scale dataset like JFT [2]. DeiT shows that transformers can also be trained on medium-sized datasets (e.g., 1.2M images as against 100M+ images used in ViT [18]) with shorter training times. An important contribution of DeiT is its novel native distillation technique [33] which uses a teacher CNN (RegNetY-16GF [69]) whose output is fed to the transformer for training. The feature-map output of the teacher CNN helps the transformer (DeiT) in finding important representations of the input images. The representations learned by DeiT are as good as top-performing CNNs like EfficientNet [81] and also are efficiently applicable to various downstream image recognition tasks.

12.3.2.2 Object detection

Like image classification or retrieval, transformers can be applied to image feature maps obtained from CNNs for precise object detection. This involves prediction of object bounding boxes (BBoxes) and their corresponding category labels. In detection transformer (DETR) [8], for spatial features obtained from a CNN backbone, the transformer encoder flattens the spatial axes along a single axis as shown in figure 12.3 which is feature map flattening from 3D to 1D. A sequence of features ($d \times n$) is obtained where d= feature dimension, and $n = h \times w$ ([h, w] = size of the feature map). Next, the 1D flattened features are encoded and decoded by the multi-head self-attention units, as given in [85].

12.3.2.3 Multi-modal machine vision tasks

The MV tasks in this category include vision–language tasks like visual question-answering (VQA) [4], visual commonsense-reasoning (VSR) [106], crossmodal retrieval [53] and image-captioning [86]. There is a body of work for these areas within the scope of this paper, and the notable works have been mentioned here. In their work [78], the authors propose VL-BERT [78], one such technique for learning features which can be generalized to multi-modal MV downstream tasks like VSR and VQA. This technique involves aligning both visual as well as linguistic cues for

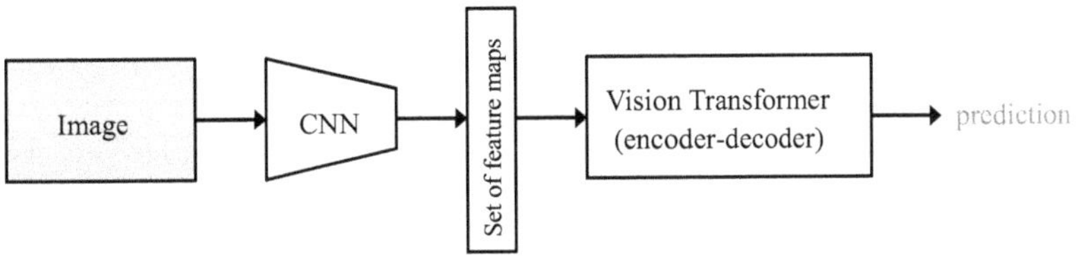

Figure 12.3. Overview of the DETR pipeline. Adapted from [8], copyright 2020, Springer Nature Switzerland AG), with permission of Springer.

learning effectively. For this, Su *et al* [78] use the BERT (bi-directional encoder representations from transformers) [16] architecture, and feed it with the features obtained from both visual and language domains. The language features are the tokens in the input text sequences and the visual features are the ROIs obtained from the input image by using a faster R-CNN model [71]. Their performance on various multi-modal MV tasks shows the advantage of the proposed technique over conventional 'language only' pre-training as done in BERT [16].

12.3.2.4 Video understanding

Videos are audio-visual data which are abundantly found. In spite of this, the contemporary techniques learn from short videos (up to a few seconds) allowing them to interpret short-range relationships [34, 85]. Long-range relationship learning is needed in different uni-modal and multi-modal MV tasks like activity recognition [9, 23, 39, 73, 91]. In this section, we highlight some recent techniques from the CNN transformer pipeline domain which address this issue better than transformers.

In their work [110], the authors study the problem of dense-video captioning with transformers. This requires producing language data for every event occurring in the video. The earlier techniques used for the same usually proceed sequentially, i.e. event-detection followed by caption-generation inside distinct sub-blocks. The authors of [110] propose a unified transformer architecture which learns one model for tackling both the aforementioned tasks jointly. Thus the proposed technique combines both the multi-modal MV tasks of event-detection and caption-generation. In the first stage, a video-encoder has been used to obtain frame- wise features, which is followed by two decoder units which propose relevant events and related captions. As a matter of fact, [110] is the first technique for dense-video captioning without using recurrent models. It uses the self-attention-based encoder which is fed CNN output features. Experimentation on ActivityNet Captions [41] and YouCookII [109] datasets reports valuable improvement over earlier RNN and double-staged techniques.

In their work [54], the authors note that in multi-modal MV task learning techniques like VideoBERT [79], ViLBERT [63], etc the language-processing part is generally kept fixed for a pre-trained model like BERT [16] for reducing the training complexity. As an alternative, they propose PEMT, a multi-modal bi-directional transformer which can learn end-to-end video data. In their model, short-term dependencies are first learnt using CNNs, and this is followed by a long-term dependency learning unit. The technique uses CNN features learned during its training for selection of negative samples which are similar to positive ones. The results obtained show that the concept has good performance on multi-modal tasks.

Traditionally, CNN-based techniques for video classification performed 3D spatio-temporal manipulation on relatively small intervals for video understanding. In their work [7], the authors have proposed the video transformer network (VTN) which first obtains frame features from a 2D CNN then applies a transformer encoder for learning temporal relationships. There are two advantages of using transformer encoder for the spatial features: (i) the whole video is processed in a

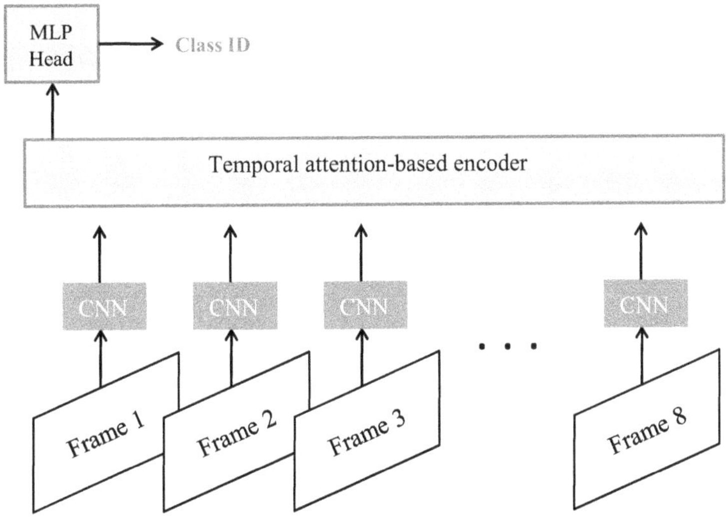

Figure 12.4. Video transformer network (VTN) architecture [7].

single pass, and (ii) training and efficiency are improved considerably by avoiding expensive 3D convolution.

These feats make VTN suitable for learning from long videos in which inter-entity interactions are spread length-wise. The experiments of the authors on the Kinetics-400 dataset [39] with various CNN, and non-CNN backbones, e.g. ResNet [32], ViT [18] and DeiT [83], show good performance. Figure 12.4 shows the overall schematic of the proposed model.

In the next subsection, we turn to the third category of techniques of attention mechanisms and deep learning, i.e. hybrid transformers.

12.3.3 Hybrid transformers

Transformers used to be exclusively attention-based networks. However, some recent works have introduced two new variants, i.e. convolutional vision transformers (CvTs) and hybrid CNN-transformer models. These variants are discussed below.

12.3.3.1 Convolutional vision transformers

In NLP and Speech recognition (SR), convolutional operations were used for modification of the transformer unit. This was done by changing the multi-head attention blocks with convolutional layers [94], or by adding more parallel convolutional layers [96] or more sequential convolutional layers [26] in order to capture local dependencies. Earlier research [90] proposed propagation of the attention maps to following layers by residual connections.

Convolutional vision transformers (CvTs) [95] improve the ViT both in terms of performance and efficiency with the introduction of convolutions into ViT for yielding the best of both architectures. This has been achieved through two important modifications. First, a range of transformers with a novel convolutional token-embedding is used, and second, a convolutional transformer unit giving convolutional projections is used. The authors propose introduction of convolutional operations to two primary parts of the ViT by replacing 'linear projection' used for every position in the attention mechanism with their novel 'convolutional projection', and using their hierarchical multistage architecture for enabling variable resolution of 2D reshaped tokens just like CNNs. These fundamental changes have introduced the desirable properties of CNNs to ViTs, i.e., shift-, scale-, and distortion-invariance. At the same time they have maintained the merits of transformers, i.e. global context, dynamic attention, and higher level of generalization. The authors validate CvT through extensive experimentation showing that their technique achieves state-of-the-art performance as compared to other ViTs and ResNets on the ImageNet-1k dataset, with lesser parameters and lesser floating-point operations per second (FLOPs). Also, the performance gains stay when CvT is pre-trained on larger datasets like ImageNet-22k [15] and is subsequently fine-tuned for downstream tasks. Pre-training on ImageNet-22k leads to top-1 accuracy of 87.7% for the ImageNet-1k validation set. Lastly, their results demonstrate that positional encoding, which is an important component in existing ViT's, can be suitably removed in CvT, thus simplifying its architecture for higher resolution MV tasks.

12.3.3.2 Hybrid CNN-transformer models

A wide range of recent developments in handcrafted neural network models for MV tasks have asserted the important need for exploration of hybrid models which consist of diverse building blocks. At the same time neural network parameter searching techniques are surging with expectations of reduction in human effort. In evidence brought out by some works [6, 18, 77] it is stated that hybrids of CNNs and transformers can perform better that both pure CNNs and pure transformers. In spite of this, the question of whether neural architecture search (NAS) methods can handle different search spaces with different candidates like CNNs and transformers, effectively and efficiently, leads to an open research area. In their work [55], the authors propose the 'block-wise self-supervised neural architecture search' (BossNAS) which is an unsupervised NAS technique which addresses the issue of inaccurate model rating due to large weight-sharing space and supervision with bias. Going into specifics, they factorize the search-space into smaller blocks and also utilize a new self-supervision-based training technique called 'ensemble bootstrapping', for training every block individually prior to search. Also, they propose a search-space called HyTra which is like a hybrid search-space fabric of CNNs and transformers. The fabric of the search-space consists of model architectures similar to the common ViTs [12, 18, 83], CNNs [32, 35] and hybrid CNN-transformers [77] at various scales. Over this difficult search-space, their hybrid model viz. BossNet-T yields 82.2% accuracy for ImageNet, going beyond EfficientNet by a margin of 2.1% with similar computation time. Also, they report that their technique achieves better accuracy on the MBConv search-space for ImageNet and on NATS-Bench size search-space for CIFAR-100 as compared to the state of the art techniques. The code and the pre-trained models are available online at: https://github.com/changlin31/BossNAS.

In the next section, we discuss the major research algorithms, trends and limitations of attention and deep learning in MV.

12.4 Major research algorithms, trends, and limitations

In the field of MV, attention-based mechanisms are generating a lot of interest. Pure attention-based architectures or models are slowly and steadily loosening the grip of deep learning over MV as more efficient attention-based models are coming to the fore. However, pure attention-based models come with their own set of issues. They are quite 'data-hungry' as they require huge amounts of data to pre-train before being applied to MV downstream tasks after fine-tuning. For example, vision transformers have to be pre-trained on the JFT dataset [2] which consists of 300 million images, and subsequently have to be fine-tuned on ImageNet-1K [15] before they can be used for tasks like image classification or retrieval. Also, the training times are exceedingly long for pre-training in transformers. Hence, reducing the 'hunger or appetite' of transformers is an open research area. Also, reducing the training time of transformers by using efficient architectures and training techniques is also an open research area. Reducing the computational load for training of ViTs is also an open research area. Finding novel ways to port them to limited hardware resource platforms is another research area. A large body of research work is present on deep learning and CNN-based architectures and transformers can benefit from the same, as CNN-based models have taken a foothold in MV. The industrial footprint of deep learning and CNN-based models is also large. Attention-based models can benefit from the work done and industrial footprint of deep learning-based models. Some works [6, 18, 77] state that hybrids of CNNs and transformers can perform better that both pure CNNs and pure transformers.

Currently, the algorithms applicable to transformers benefitting from deep learning and CNN architecture are present in three main categories as discussed earlier. The first category is attention-based CNNs. The algorithms in this category augment the performance of classical CNN architectures by plugging into them attention-based units in order to refine the features. Attention-based CNN plugins like CBAM have been used successfully in various CNN models in order to boost their performance with relatively small computational overhead. In spite of this, the amount of attention available in this category is limited and CNNs use the attention-based mechanisms sparingly. Deeper integration and merger of attention-based mechanisms and CNNs are required before record breaking performances can be achieved. Coming to the second category of CNN transformer pipelines as discussed, the pipeline is just like the hybrid two-stage classifiers wherein a feature map generated by a 'teacher' CNN is fed to a 'student' classifier which operates on this feature map. In this two-stage model, it is safe to say that the performance of the second-stage model depends on the image or video interpretation capability of the CNN. As such, the design of the first-stage CNN is in question regarding its design-based efficacy at interpreting the image or video data. It is also known that there is currently a large number of CNN architectures and making the correct choice is an open research field. Coming to the third category of hybrid CNN-transformers, the merger of these two different techniques is a difficult one. NAS has been used to search through the hybrid CNN-transformer search-space fabric. However, given its exhaustive nature requiring large computational resources and careful fabric design, the optimization of the same is also an open research area. In spite of the limitations and issues mentioned above, attention-based mechanisms like vision transformers (ViTs) are considered to have an impact on the MV research and industry. Combined with the power and experience of deep learning, the merger of the two techniques can prove to be revolutionary for both the existing and also the upcoming MV tasks, as larger and more efficient computational hardware and software are developed.

12.5 Conclusion

In this chapter, the merger of attention-based mechanisms and deep learning for various MV tasks has been discussed. Firstly, various types of attention mechanism were briefly discussed. Next, various attention-based architectures were discussed. This was followed by discussion of various categories of combinations of attention mechanisms and deep learning techniques for MV. The various architectures and their associated MV tasks were discussed. Afterwards, major research algorithms, trends and limitations within the scope of the chapter were discussed. By using 110+ papers as reference, the readers of this survey chapter are expected to form a knowledge base and get a head-start in the area of attention-based mechanisms and deep learning for MV. Coming to the future scope, attention mechanism-based technologies are ripe with options. Integration of attention mechanism into deep learning has been experimented with to a limited degree. However, attention-based deep networks are still an open area. Developing attention-based hardware is another interesting area. Applying ViTs to advanced MV tasks, in particular real-time technologies, is a research area which is unfolding gradually. Implementing parallelization for transformers, ViTs, etc by imbibing Nature's powerful parallelized data processing is also an interesting area. Also, integration of transformers into statistical machine learning techniques also remains to be seen.

Conflict of interest

The authors declare no conflict of interest.

Funding acknowledgement

The authors declare that this project has received no funding.

References

[1] https://http://www.kaggle.com/c/challenges-in-representation-learning-facial-expression-recognition-challenge/data

[2] Revisiting the unreasonable effectiveness of data, https://ai.googleblog.com/2017/07/revisiting-unreasonable-effectiveness.html

[3] Anderson P, He X, Buehler C, Teney D, Johnson M, Gould S and Zhang L 2018 Bottom-up and top-down attention for image captioning and visual question answering *2018 IEEE/CVF Conf. on Computer Vision and Pattern Recognition* 6077–86

[4] Antol S, Agrawal A, Lu J, Mitchell M, Batra D, Zitnick C L and Parikh D 2015 VQA: visual question answering *2015 IEEE Int. Conf. on Computer Vision (ICCV)* 2425–33

[5] Ba J, Mnih V and Kavukcuoglu K 2015 Multiple object recognition with visual attention arXiv:1412.7755

[6] Irwan B 2021 Lambda networks: modeling long-range interactions without attention *Int. Conf. on Learning Representations*

[7] Berg A, O'Connor M and Cruz M T 2021 Keyword transformer: A self-attention model for keyword spotting arXiv:2104.00769

[8] Carion N, Massa F, Synnaeve G, Usunier N, Kirillov A and Zagoruyko S End-to-end object detection with transformers *Computer Vision–ECCV 2020* ed A Vedaldi, H Bischof, T Brox and J-M Frahm (Cham: Springer Int. Publishing) pp 213–29

[9] Carreira J, Noland E, Hillier C and Zisserman A 2019 A short note on the kinetics-700 human action dataset arXiv:1907.06987

[10] Chen H, Wang Y, Guo T, Xu C, Deng Y, Liu Z, Ma S, Xu C, Xu C and Gao W 2020 Pre-trained image processing transformer arXiv:2012.00364

[11] Chen L, Zhang H, Xiao J, Nie L, Shao J, Liu W and Chua T-S 2017 SCA-CNN: Spatial and channel-wise attention in convolutional networks for image captioning *2017 IEEE Conf. on Computer Vision and Pattern Recognition (CVPR)* 6298–306

[12] Chu X, Tian Z, Zhang B, Wang X, Wei X, Xia H and Shen C 2021 Conditional positional encodings for vision transformers arXiv:2102.10882

[13] Corbetta M and Shulman G L 2002 Control of goal-directed and stimulus-driven attention in the brain *Nat. Rev. Neurosci.* **3** 201–15

[14] Cornia L, Baraldi G, Serra G and Cucchiara R 2016 A deep multi-level network for saliency prediction *2016 23rd Int. Conf. on Pattern Recognition (ICPR)* 3488–93

[15] Deng J, Dong W, Socher R, Li L-J, Li K and Fei-Fei L 2009 Imagenet: a large-scale hierarchical image database *2009 IEEE Conf. on Computer Vision and Pattern Recognition* 248–55

[16] Devlin J, Chang M-W, Lee K and Toutanova K 2019 BERT: pre-training of deep bidirectional transformers for language understanding *Proc. 2019 Conf. of the North American Chapter of the : Human Language Technologies, Volume 1 (Long and Short Papers)Association for Computational Linguistics* (Association for Computational Linguistics: Minneapolis, Minnesota) 4171–86

[17] Doersch C, Gupta A and Zisserman A 2021 Crosstransformers: spatially-aware few-shot transfer arXiv:2007.11498

[18] Dosovitskiy A, Beyer L and Kolesnikov A *et al* 2020 An image is worth 16 x 16 words: Transformers for image recognition at scale arXiv:2010.11929

[19] Er M J, Zhang Y, Wang N and Pratama M 2016 Attention pooling-based convolutional neural network for sentence modelling *Inf. Sci.* **373** 388–403

[20] Escalera S, Baró S and Gonzàlez J *et al* 2015 Chalearn looking at people challenge 2014: Dataset and results *Computer Vision—ECCV 2014 Workshops* ed L Agapito, M M Bronstein and C Rother (Cham: Springer Int. Publishing) pp 459–73

[21] Everingham M and Williams C K I 2007 *The PASCAL visual object classes challenge 2007 (voc2007) results*

[22] Gessert N, Sentker T, Madesta F, Schmitz R, Kniep H, Baltruschat I, Werner R and Schlaefer A 2020 Skin lesion classification using cnns with patch-based attention and diagnosis-guided loss weighting *IEEE Trans. Biomed. Eng.* **67** 495–503

[23] Ging S, Zolfaghari M, Pirsiavash H and Brox T 2020 Cooperative hierarchical transformer for video-text representation learning arXiv:2011.00597

[24] Girdhar R, Carreira J J, Doersch C and Zisserman A 2019 Video action transformer network *2019 IEEE/CVF Conf. on Computer Vision and Pattern Recognition (CVPR)* 244–53

[25] Goodfellow I, Bengio Y and Aaron Courville 2016 *Deep Learning* (Cambridge, MA: MIT Press)

[26] Gulati A, Qin J and Chiu C-C *et al* 2020 *Conformer: convolution-augmented transformer for speech recognition Proc. Interspeech 2020* pp 5036–40

[27] Guo Y, Liu Y, Georgiou T and Michael S L 2018 A review of semantic segmentation using deep neural networks *Int. J. Multimed. Inform. Retr.* **7** 87–93

[28] Hafiz A M and Bhat G M 2020 A survey of deep learning techniques for medical diagnosis *Information and Communication Technology for Sustainable Development* ed M Tuba, S Akashe and A Joshi (Singapore: Springer) pp 161–70

[29] Hafiz A M and Bhat G M 2020 A survey on instance segmentation: state of the art *Int. J. Multimed. Inform. Retr.* **9** 171–89

[30] Hafiz A M, Bhat R A and Hassaballah M 2022 Image classification using convolutional neural network tree ensembles *Multimedia Tools Appl.* https://doi.org/10.1007/s11042-022-13604-6

[31] Hang R, Li Z, Liu Q, Ghamisi P and Bhattacharyya S S 2021 Hyperspectral image classification with attention-aided CNNs *IEEE Trans. Geosci. Remote Sens.* **59** 2281–93

[32] He K, Zhang X, Ren S and Sun J 2016 Deep residual learning for image recognition *Proc. IEEE Conf. on Computer Vision and Pattern Recognition (CVPR)* 770–8

[33] Hinton G, Vinyals O and Dean J 2015 Distilling the knowledge in a neural network arXiv:1503.02531

[34] Hochreiter S and Schmidhuber J 1997 Long short-term memory *Neural Comput.* **9** 1735–80

[35] Hu J, Shen L, Albanie S, Sun G and Wu E 2020 Squeeze-and-excitation networks *IEEE Trans. Pattern Anal. Mach. Intell.* **42** 2011–23

[36] Huang J, Zhou W, Li H and Weiping Li 2019 Attention-based 3D-CNNs for large-vocabulary sign language recognition *IEEE Trans. Circuits Syst. Video Technol.* **29** 2822–32

[37] Huang X, Shen C, Boix X and Zhao Q 2015 Salicon: Reducing the semantic gap in saliency prediction by adapting deep neural networks *2015 IEEE Int. Conf. on Computer Vision (ICCV)* 262–70

[38] Jetley S, Murray N and Vig E 2016 End-to-end saliency mapping via probability distribution prediction *2016 IEEE Conf. on Computer Vision and Pattern Recognition (CVPR)* 5753–61

[39] Kay W, Carreira J and Simonyan K *et al* 2017 The kinetics human action video dataset arXiv:1705.06950

[40] Khan S, Naseer M, Hayat M, Zamir S W, Khan F S and Shah M 2021 Transformers in vision: A survey arXiv:2101.01169

[41] Krishna R, Hata K, Ren F, Fei-Fei L and Niebles J C Dense-captioning events in videos *2017 IEEE Int. Conf. on Computer Vision (ICCV)* pp 706–15

[42] Alex Krizhevsky *et al* 2009 Learning multiple layers of features from tiny images https://www.cs.toronto.edu/~kriz/learning-features-2009-TR.pdf

[43] Kruthiventi S S S, Kumar Ayush and Venkatesh Babu R 2017 Deepfix: a fully convolutional neural network for predicting human eye fixations *IEEE Trans. Image Process.* **26** 4446–56
[44] Kruthiventi S S S, Gudisa V, Dholakiya J H and Venkatesh Babu R 2016 Saliency unified: a deep architecture for simultaneous eye fixation prediction and salient object segmentation *2016 IEEE Conf. on Computer Vision and Pattern Recognition (CVPR)* 5781–90
[45] Kumar M, Weissenborn D and Kalchbrenner N 2021 Colorization transformer arXiv:2102.04432
[46] Kümmerer M, Theis L and Bethge M 2015 Deep gaze I: Boosting saliency prediction with feature maps trained on imagenet arXiv:1411.1045
[47] Kümmerer M, Wallis T S A and Bethge M 2016 Deepgaze II: Reading fixations from deep features trained on object recognition arXiv:1610.01563
[48] Larochelle H and Hinton G 2010 Learning to combine foveal glimpses with a third-order Boltzmann machine *Proc. 23rd Int. Conf. on Neural Information Processing Systems—Volume 1, NIPS'10* pp 1243–51
[49] Lecun Y, Bottou L, Bengio Y and Haffner P 1998 Gradient-based learning applied to document recognition *Proc. IEEE* **86** 2278–324
[50] LeCun Y, Bengio Y and Hinton G 2015 Deep learning *Nature* **521** 436–44
[51] LeCun Y, Kavukcuoglu K and Farabet C 2010 Convolutional networks and applications in vision *Proc. 2010 IEEE Int. Symp. on Circuits and Systems* 253–6
[52] Lee C-Y, Xie S, Gallagher P, Zhang Z and Tu Z May 2015 Deeply-supervised nets *Proc. 18th Int. Conf. on Artificial Intelligence and Statistics vol 38 of Proc. Machine Learning Research* G Lebanon and S V N Vishwanathan 562–70
[53] Lee K-H, Chen X, Hua G, Hu H and He X 2018 Stacked cross attention for image-text matching *Proc. European Conf. on Computer Vision (ECCV)*
[54] Lee S, Yu Y, Kim G, Breuel T, Kautz J and Song Y 2020 Parameter efficient multimodal transformers for video representation learning arXiv:2012.04124
[55] Li C, Tang T, Wang G, Peng J, Wang B, Liang X and Chang X 2021 Bossnas: Exploring hybrid cnn-transformers with block-wisely self-supervised neural architecture search arXiv:2103.12424
[56] Li G and Yu Y 2015 Visual saliency based on multiscale deep features *2015 IEEE Conf. on Computer Vision and Pattern Recognition (CVPR)* pp 5455–63
[57] Li J, Jin K, Zhou D, Kubota N and Ju Z 2020 Attention mechanism-based cnn for facial expression recognition *Neurocomputing* **411** 340–50
[58] Li L, Xu M, Wang X, Jiang L and Liu H 2019 Attention based glaucoma detection: a large-scale database and cnn model *2019 IEEE/CVF Conf. on Computer Vision and Pattern Recognition (CVPR)* 10563–72
[59] Li S, Deng W and Du J 2017 Reliable crowdsourcing and deep locality-preserving learning for expression recognition in the wild *Proc. IEEE Conf. on Computer Vision and Pattern Recognition (CVPR)*
[60] Li Y, Zeng J, Shan S and Chen X 2019 Occlusion aware facial expression recognition using cnn with attention mechanism *IEEE Trans. Image Process.* **28** 2439–50
[61] Lin T-Y, Maire M, Belongie S, Hays J, Perona P, Ramanan D, Dollár D and Zitnick C L 2014 Microsoft coco: common objects in context *Computer Vision–ECCV 2014* ed D Fleet, T Pajdla, B Schiele and T Tuytelaars (Cham: Springer) pp 740–55

[62] Liu N, Han J, Liu T and Li X 2018 Learning to predict eye fixations via multiresolution convolutional neural networks *IEEE Trans. Neur. Netw. Learn. Syst.* **29** 392–404
[63] Lu J, Batra D, Parikh D and Lee S 2019 Vilbert, pretraining task-agnostic visiolinguistic representations for vision-and-language tasks arXiv:1908.02265
[64] Lucey P, Cohn J F, Kanade T, Saragih J, Ambadar Z and Matthews I 2010 The extended Cohn–Kanade dataset (ck+): a complete dataset for action unit and emotion-specified expression *2010 IEEE Computer Society Conf. on Computer Vision and Pattern Recognition —Workshops* 94–101
[65] Lyons M, Akamatsu S, Kamachi M and Gyoba J 1998 Coding facial expressions with gabor wavelets *Proc. 3rd IEEE Int. Conf. on Automatic Face and Gesture Recognition* 200–5
[66] Mollahosseini A, Hasani B and Mahoor M H 2019 Affectnet: a database for facial expression, valence, and arousal computing in the wild *IEEE Trans. Affect. Comput.* **0** 18–31
[67] Pan J, Sayrol E, Xavier G-I-N, McGuinness K and O'Connor N E 2016 Shallow and deep convolutional networks for saliency prediction *2016 IEEE Conf. on Computer Vision and Pattern Recognition (CVPR)* 598–606
[68] Pinheiro P O, Lin T-Y, Collobert R and Dollár P 2016 Learning to refine object segments *Computer Vision–ECCV 2016* ed B Leibe, J Matas, N Sebe and M Welling (Cham: Springer) pp 75–91
[69] Radosavovic I, Kosaraju R P, Girshick R, He K and Dollar P 2020 Designing network design spaces *2020 IEEE/CVF Conf. on Computer Vision and Pattern Recognition (CVPR)* 10425–33
[70] Ramesh A *et al* 2021 Dalle: creating images from text. OpenAI blog https://openai.com/blog/dall-e
[71] Ren S, He K, Girshick R and Sun J 2017 Faster R-CNN: towards real-time object detection with region proposal networks *IEEE Trans. Pattern Anal. Mach. Intell.* **39** 1137–49
[72] Rensink A R 2000 The dynamic representation of scenes *Vis. Cogn.* **7** 17–42
[73] Seong H, Hyun J and Kim E 2019 Video multitask transformer network *2019 IEEE/CVF Int. Conf. on Computer Vision Workshop (ICCVW)* 1553–61
[74] Sharma S, Kiros R and Salakhutdinov R 2016 Action recognition using visual attention *Int. Conf. on Learning Representations (ICLR) Workshop*
[75] Shrestha A and Mahmood A 2019 Review of deep learning algorithms and architectures *IEEE Access* **7** 53040–65
[76] Simonyan K and Zisserman A 2015 Very deep convolutional networks for largescale image recognition arXiv:1409.1556
[77] Srinivas A, Lin T-Y, Parmar N, Shlens J, Abbeel P and Vaswani A 2021 Bottleneck transformers for visual recognition arXiv:2101.11605
[78] Su W, Zhu X, Cao Y, Li B, Lu L, Wei F and Dai J 2020 Vl-bert: pre-training of generic visual-linguistic representations *Int. Conf. on Learning Representations*
[79] Sun C, Myers A, Vondrick C, Murphy K and Schmid C 2019 *2019 IEEE/CVF Int. Conf. on Computer Vision (ICCV)* 7463–72
[80] Tan H and Bansal M 2019 LXMERT: learning cross-modality encoder representations from transformers *Proc. 2019 Conf. on Empirical Methods in Natural Language Processing and the 9th Int. Joint Conf. on Natural Language Processing (EMNLP-IJCNLP) Association for Computational Linguistics (Hong Kong)* pp 5100–11

[81] Tan M and Le Q 2019 EfficientNet: rethinking model scaling for convolutional neural networks *Proc. 36th Int. Conf. on Machine Learning, volume 97 of Proc. Machine Learning Research PMLR (London)*K Chaudhuri and R Salakhutdinov pp 6105–14

[82] Tian C, Xu Y, Li Z, Zuo W, Fei L and Liu H 2020 Attention-guided CNN for image denoising *Neural Netw.* **124** 117–29

[83] Touvron H, Cord M, Douze M, Massa F, Sablayrolles A and Jégou H 2021 Training data-efficient image transformers and distillation through attention arXiv:2012.12877

[84] Tran D, Bourdev L, Fergus R, Torresani L and Paluri M 2015 Learning spatiotemporal features with 3d convolutional networks *Proc. IEEE Int. Conf. on Computer Vision (ICCV)*

[85] Vaswani A, Shazeer N, Parmar N, Uszkoreit J, Jones L, Gomez A N, Kaiser U and Polosukhin I 2017 Attention is all you need *Proc. 31st Int. Conf. on Neural Information Processing Systems, NIPS'17* (Red Hook, NY: Curran Associates Inc) 6000–10

[86] Vinyals O, Toshev A, Bengio S and Erhan D 2015 Show and tell: a neural image caption generator *2015 IEEE Conf. on Computer Vision and Pattern Recognition (CVPR)* 3156–64

[87] Wang F, Jiang M, Qian C, Yang S, Li C, Zhang H, Wang X and Tang X 2017 Residual attention network for image classification *2017 IEEE Conf. on Computer Vision and Pattern Recognition (CVPR)* 6450–8

[88] Wang W and Shen J 2018 Deep visual attention prediction *IEEE Trans. Image Process.* **27** 2368–78

[89] Wang X, Yeshwanth C and Niebner M 2021 Sceneformer: Indoor scene generation with transformers arXiv:2012.09793

[90] Wang Y, Yang Y, Bai J, Zhang M, Bai J, Yu J, Zhang C, Huang G and Tong Y 2021 Evolving attention with residual convolutions arXiv:2102.12895

[91] Wang Y, Xu Z, Wang X, Shen C, Cheng B, Shen H and Xia H 2021 End-to-end video instance segmentation with transformers arXiv:2011.14503

[92] Woo S, Hwang S and Kweon I S 2018 Stairnet: top-down semantic aggregation for accurate one shot detection *2018 IEEE Winter Conf. on Alications of Computer Vision (WACV)pp* 1093–102

[93] Woo S, Park J, Lee J-Y and Kweon I S 2018 Cbam: convolutional block attention module *Computer Vision–ECCV 2018* ed V Ferrari, M Hebert, C Sminchisescu and Y Weiss (Cham: Springer Int. Publishing) pp 3–19

[94] Wu F, Fan A, Baevski A, Dauphin Y N and Auli M 2019 Pay less attention with lightweight and dynamic convolutions arXiv:1901.10430

[95] Wu H, Xiao B, Codella N, Liu M, Dai X, Yuan L and Zhang L 2021 CvT: Introducing convolutions to vision transformers arXiv:2103.15808

[96] Wu Z, Liu Z, Lin J, Lin Y and Han S 2020 Lite transformer with long-short range attention arXiv:2004.11886

[97] Xie S and Tu Z 2015 Holistically-nested edge detection *2015 IEEE Int. Conf. on Computer Vision (ICCV)* 1395–403 pp

[98] Xu K, Ba J, Kiros R, Cho K, Courville A, Salakhudinov R, Zemel R and Bengio Y 2015 Show, attend and tell: neural image caption generation with visual attention *Proc. 32nd Int. Conf. on Machine Learning, vol 37 of Proc. Machine Learning Research PMLR (London)* ed F Bach and D Blei 2048–57

[99] Xu M, Li C, Liu Y, Deng X and Lu J 2017 A subjective visual quality assessment method of panoramic videos *2017 IEEE Int. Conf. on Multimedia and Expo (ICME)* 517–22

[100] Yang C, Zhang L, Lu H, Ruan X and Yang M-H 2013 Saliency detection via graph-based manifold ranking *2013 IEEE Conf. on Computer Vision and Pattern Recognition* pp 3166–73
[101] Yang F, Yang H, Fu J, Lu H and Guo B 2020 Learning texture transformer network for image super-resolution *2020 IEEE/CVF Conf. on Computer Vision and Pattern Recognition (CVPR)* 5790–9
[102] Yao X, Han J, Zhang D and Nie F 2017 Revisiting co-saliency detection: a novel approach based on two-stage multi-view spectral rotation co-clustering *IEEE Trans. Image Process.* **26** 3196–209
[103] Ye H-J, Hu H, Zhan D-C and Sha F 2020 Few-shot learning via embedding adaptation with set-to-set functions *2020 IEEE/CVF Conf. on Computer Vision and Pattern Recognition (CVPR)* 8805–14
[104] Ye L, Rochan M, Liu Z and Wang Y 2019 Cross-modal self-attention network for referring image segmentation *2019 IEEE/CVF Conf. on Computer Vision and Pattern Recognition (CVPR* 10494–503
[105] Yu Y, Choi J, Kim Y, Yoo K, Lee S-H and Kim G 2017 Supervising neural attention models for video captioning by human gaze data *2017 IEEE Conf. on Computer Vision and Pattern Recognition (CVPR)* 6119–27
[106] Zellers R, Bisk Y, Farhadi A and Choi Y 2019 From recognition to cognition: Visual commonsense reasoning *2019 IEEE/CVF Conf. on Computer Vision and Pattern Recognition (CVPR)* 6713–24
[107] Zhao G, Huang X, Taini M, Li S Z and Pietikäinen M 2011 Facial expression recognition from near-infrared videos *Image Vis. Comput.* **29** 607–19
[108] Zhao R, Ouyang W, Li H and Wang X 2015 Saliency detection by multi-context deep learning *2015 IEEE Conf. on Computer Vision and Pattern Recognition (CVPR)* 1265–74
[109] Zhou L, Xu C and Corso J 2018 Towards automatic learning of procedures from web instructional videos *Proc. AAAI Conf. on Artificial Intelligence* 32
[110] Zhou L, Zhou Y, Corso J J, Socher R and Xiong C 2018 End-to-end dense video captioning with masked transformer *2018 IEEE/CVF Conf. on Computer Vision and Pattern Recognition* 8739–48
[111] Zhu X, Su W, Lu L, Li B, Wang X and Dai J 2021 Deformable DETR: deformable transformers for end-to-end object detection arXiv:2010.04159

Chapter 13

Sparse 2D packing in thermal deburring with shock waves acting effects

Sergiy Plankovskyy, Tatiana Romanova, Alexander Pankratov, Igor S Litvinchev, Yevgen Tsegelnyk, Olga Shypul and Pandian Vasant

Optimized sparse balance packing is considered. The problem is related to removing burrs by thermal deburring—an intelligent technology of processing parts by combusting gas mixtures. To ensure stable quality, especially when shock waves act, it is desirable to have thermal and pressure characteristics uniformly distributed over the surfaces of the part. The location of parts (objects) should be optimal with respect to themselves as well as to the border of the working volume (chamber or container). The problem can be considered as a two-dimensional optimized sparse layout under balancing restrictions. Applying commercial software ANSYS CFX, numerical modeling of the heat transfer between the objects and the heat field was performed and distributions of temperature and pressure in the chamber were obtained. Two cases are compared: the sparse layout with and without balancing conditions. The balance layout gives the most effective distribution of the heat flows.

13.1 Introduction

Packing problems are NP-hard [1]. Along with non-overlapping and containments constraints, different variants of packing problems may consider special requirements, e.g., weight distribution, balance conditions, cargo stability, 3D printing standards [2–10]. Optimal packing objects for a convex container are studied in [11] under constraints on the location of the gravity center.

There are numerous references on regular packing, see [12–16]. Packing circles within a container of circular form is considered in [17] to optimize distribution of heat fluxes in the presence of shock waves.

The concept of sparse packing was proposed in [18–21]. The objects in the sparse packing must be allocated distantly in the container. The concept of sparse packing

doi:10.1088/978-0-7503-4801-0ch13

is suitable for various problems, especially where the influence of thermal effects is considered in the form of constraints on the location of objects. For example, sparse packing arises in materials sheet cutting using thermal energy sources, such as plasma, flame, laser [22–26]. In this case the parts on the sheet must be arranged considering the zones of thermal influence. Minimizing overheating in thermal influence zones corresponding to adjacent parts may be achieved using a special S-curve acceleration/deceleration algorithm [27, 28]. In the electronics industry sparse packing corresponds to optimizing location of components on printed circuit boards to achieve a lower temperature of devices [29, 30]. In designing power electrical cables [31–33] an important aspect is the correspondence between layout of wires and the cable harnesses. Sparse packing helps finding a suitable multi-wire circuit with minimized maximal temperature. The search for the optimal arrangement of tube sheets to increase the efficiency of tubular heat exchanger designs also applies to sparse packing [34–36]. The problem, in this case, is formulated as locating circles at an equal distance from each other in a region of a simple shape.

The concept of sparse packing can be applied for determining locations of parts in a group heat treatment. In this method the parts are processed in a closed working volume filled with a fuel/gas mixture. After ignition of the mixture, high-temperature gases act on all surfaces of the parts, thus removing the burrs [37–39] from edges and cleaning surfaces of the complex shaped parts.

Several processing methods using the energy of combustion of gas mixtures are known, while the most used is the TEM (Thermal Energy Method). The main characteristic of TEM is the combustion of gas mixture in oxygen excess [40–43]. Having a higher ratio (surface area)/(volume), the burrs burned out first. This allows heat entering the burrs faster than into other parts. Gases are removed from the chamber when their temperature drops down to a certain level. The machining process usually takes 15 s to 40 s and in some cases can lead to overheating the parts and depositing metal oxides on their surfaces [44, 45].

The Impulse Thermal Energy Method (ITEM) is an improvement of TEM. The principal difference is the controlled exhaust of hot combustion products [46, 47]. Obviously, for ITEM one of the most significant parameters is the processing time. Due to this feature, the scope of the ITEM method is expanded. More specifically, the ability to work with parts made from low melting point materials, e.g., thermoplastics, is added [48].

When the shock waves arise, generated by detonation or volumetric explosion, the greatest effect on the heat transfer has the velocity of gas movement. Such combustion leads to an increase in heat fluxes by 10–100 times compared to deflagration combustion of the same mixture [49]. This effect underlies the ITEMSW (Impulse Thermal Energy Method with Shock Wave) generation having various applications in finishing cleaning precision parts. ITEMSW with different treatment modes can be used for cleaning from microparticles as well as for removing laps [47]. ITEMSW is one of the most promising methods for cleaning 3D-printed parts of non-sintered powder after 3D printing technologies [50]. As noted above, the explosive combustion of gas mixtures in the working camera varies significantly in the values of heat fluxes [51]. Thus, when determining the optimal location of processing objects, a related problem of balancing geometric / mechanical and thermal conditions must be solved. In this chapter the optimized packing in a circular deburring chamber (container) is studied. The aim is to develop a method of optimizing the uniformity of heat fluxes while shock waves are acting.

The chapter is structured as follows. Section 13.2 gives the formulation of the sparse packing problem taking into account balancing constraints, presents a solutions approach to solve the corresponding nonconvex optimization problem and summarized results of computational experiment. Section 13.3 provides the problem formulation of finding optimal layout of parts in the heat treatment. Numerical results of the balanced layout of 2D objects with shock waves acting effect are given in section 13.4, while section 13.5 concludes and offers future scope of research.

13.2 Sparse packing

In this section the sparse packing problem is formulated, the numerical optimization approach is described and numerical examples are provided.

13.2.1 The main problem and mathematical model

Denote by $A_i \subset R^2$, $i \in I_n = \{1,..., n\}$ a set of objects limited by circular arcs and line segments. It is assumed that each object A is composed by simple basic objects B_j, $j=1, \ldots, m$. Let $B_j = \bigcap_{k=1}^{m_j} B_{\mathrm{kj}}$, where $B_{\mathrm{jk}}, k = 1,..., m_j$, are primitive objects (a half-plane or a circle or the complement to a circle). Thus $A = \bigcup_{j=1}^{m} \bigcap_{k=1}^{m_j} B_{\mathrm{kj}}$. Each object A may be discribed analytically. We describe the object B_j by inequality $f_j(t) \leqslant 0$, where $f_j(t) = \max\{f_{\mathrm{jk}}(t),\ k = 1,..., m_j\}$, $j=1, \ldots, m$, $f_{\mathrm{jk}}(t)$ is a differentiable function associated with the primitive object B_{kj}. Each object$A$ is defined in the following way: $A = \left\{t \in R^2\colon \min_{j=1,\ldots,m} f_j(t) \leq 0\right\}$, i.e. $A = \left\{t \in R^2\colon \min_{j=1,\ldots,m} \max_{k=1,\ldots,m_j} f_{jk} \leq 0\right\}$. We take $\min_{j=1,\ldots,m} f_j(t)$ since A is a union of basic objects B_j and take $\max_{k=1,\ldots,m_j} f_{\mathrm{jk}}$ since B_j is an intersection of primitive objects.

A circular domain (container) D centered at the origin (0,0) and having radius r is defined by inequality $x^2 + y^2 - r^2 \geqslant 0$.

The objects A_i, $i \in I_n$, are allowed freely shifted by vector $v_i = (x_i, y_i)$ and rotated through angle θ_i. Denote the vector of variable parameters of A_i by $u_i = (v_i, \theta_i)$, $i \in I_n$. Therefore, the moving object A_i can be presented in the form $A_i(u_i) = \{(x, y) \in R^2\colon (x, y) = v_i + \Xi(\theta_i) \cdot (x^0, y^0)^T, \forall\, (x^0, y^0) \in A_i^0\}$, where A_i^0 means non-moved object A_i, $\Xi(\theta_i) = \begin{pmatrix} \cos\theta_i & \sin\theta_i \\ -\sin\theta_i & \cos\theta_i \end{pmatrix}$ is the standard rotation matrix.

In addition, the weight w_i, of each object A_i is given for , $i \in I_n$, while the weight of D is denoted by w_0. We set the gravity center of $A_i(u_i)$ at the point v_i and place the gravity center of D at the point (0,0).

For the container D, the allowable deviation from its center (0,0) is defined in the form

$$g(v) = \min\{g_1(v), g_2(v)\} \geqslant 0, \tag{13.1}$$

where

$$g_1(v) = \min\{x_c + \varepsilon^0, -x_c + \varepsilon^0\}, g_2(v) = \min\{y_c + \varepsilon^0, -y_c + \varepsilon^0\},$$

$$x_c(v) = \sum_{i=1}^{n} \frac{w_i}{M} x_i, \; y_c(v) = \sum_{i=1}^{n} \frac{w_i}{M} y_i, \; M = \sum_{i=0}^{n} w_i,$$

$v_c = (x_c, y_c)$ is the gravity center of the objects A_i, $i \in I_n$ and $\varepsilon^0 \geqslant 0$ is a given threshold.

Let $\operatorname{dist}(A_i(u_i), A_j(u_j)) = \min_{a_i \in A_i(u_i), a_j \in A_j(u_j)} \| a_i - a_j \|$ denote the Euclidean distance between the objects $A_i(u_i)$ and $A_j(u_j)$, while $\operatorname{dist}(A_i(u_i), D^*) = \min_{a_i \in A_i(u_i), a \in D^*} \| a_i - a \|$ is used to denote the Euclidean distance between the object $A_i(u_i)$ and the boundary of the container D, where $D^* = R^2 \setminus \operatorname{int} D$.

Packing is related to a sparse packing if it maximizes the minimal of pairwise Euclidean distances between all objects as well as Euclidean distances between each pair of objects A_i and D^* for $i \in I_n$, i.e., maximizes

$$\rho = \min\{\operatorname{dist}(A_i(u_i), A_j(u_j)), i < j = 1, \ldots, n, \operatorname{dist}(A_i(u_i), D^*), i = 1, \ldots, n\} \tag{13.2}$$

Sparse packing problem with balancing condition. Find the sparse layout of the objects A_i, $i \in I_n$ in the circle D subject to balancing condition (13.1).

For describing distance constraints $\operatorname{dist}(A_i(u_i), A_j(u_j)) \geqslant \rho$ and $\operatorname{dist}(A_i(u_i), D^*) \geqslant \rho$ the phi-function approach [52–56] is used.

Now we formulate the sparse balance packing problem as a continuous non-convex optimization problem

$$\max_{(u,\tau,\rho) \in W} \rho \tag{13.3}$$

$$W = \{(u, \tau, \rho) \colon \Phi_i(u_i, \rho) \geq 0, i \in I_n, g(v) \geq 0,$$

$$\Phi'_{ij}(u_i, u_j, \tau_{ij}, \rho) \geq 0, i < j \in I_n, \rho > 0\} \tag{13.4}$$

where ρ is the objective function defined in (13.2), $u = (u_1, \ldots, u_n)$ is the vector that defines a layout of the family of objects $A_i(u_i)$, $i \in I_n$, in R^2, $u_i = (x_i, y_i, \theta_i)$ for $i \in I_n$; $\tau = (\tau_{11}, \tau_{12}, \ldots, \tau_{ij}, \ldots, \tau_{(n-1), n})$, τ_{ij} is the vector of the extra variables for $i < j \in I_n$; $\Phi'_{ij}(u_i, u_j, \tau_{ij}, \rho)$ is the adjusted quasi-phi-function describing distance constraints of the objects $A_i(u_i)$ and $A_j(u_j)$ while $\Phi_i(u_i, \rho)$ is the adjusted phi-function providing the distance constraints of the objects $A_i(u_i)$ and D^* in (13.2); $g(v) \geqslant 0$ serves the balancing condition (13.1).

Based on the characteristics of adjusted phi-functions and adjusted quasi-phi-functions we can conclude that for

$$\Phi_i(u_i, \rho) \geqslant 0 \Leftrightarrow \mathrm{dist}(A_i(u_i), D^*) \geqslant \rho \quad \text{for } i \in I_n;$$

$$\Phi'_{\mathrm{ij}}(u_i, u_j, \tau_{\mathrm{ij}}, \rho) \geqslant 0 \Rightarrow \mathrm{dist}(A_i(u_i), A_j(u_j)) \geqslant \rho,\ i < j \in I_n.$$

The solution space W (13.4) is given by non-smooth inequalities. The later can be transformed to inequalities with smooth functions. Problems (13.3) and (13.4) are a continuous optimization problem with $\sigma = 1{+}3n + 2\sum_{i=1}^{n-1}\sum_{j=2}^{n} n_i n_j$ variables, where n_i is the number of convex components in $A_i(u_i)$, $i \in I_n$. Models (13.3) and (13.4) have $O(n^2)$ constraints and variables.

13.2.2 Solution approach and computational results

The following strategy is proposed to get local-optimal solutions of (13.3) and (13.4).

The approach consists of the following steps.

Step 1. Form a random point $v^{(0)} = (v_i^{(0)},\ i \in I_n)$, such that $v_i^{(0)} \in D$ for $i \in I_n$.

Step 2. Solve the following optimization subproblem: s.t.

$$\min \varepsilon \text{ s.t. } (v, \varepsilon) \in W_\varepsilon \subset R^{2n+1}, \tag{13.5}$$

$$W_\varepsilon = \{(v, \varepsilon): \phi_i(v) \geqslant 0,\ g(v, \varepsilon) \geqslant 0,\ i \in I_n\}, \tag{13.6}$$

starting from the point v^0. In the problems (13.5) and (13.6) $v = (v_1, \ldots, v_n)$ denotes the vector of variable translation parameters of $A_i(u_i)$, $i \in I_n$; $\phi_i(v) = x_i^2 + y_i^2 - r_i^2 \geqslant 0$ ensures that $v_i \in D$. Search for a local-optimal point $v^{(1)} = (v_1^{(1)}, \ldots, v_n^{(1)})$of the problems (13.5) and (13.6).

Step 3. For each quasi-phi-function $\Phi'_{\mathrm{ij}}(u_i, u_j, \tau_{\mathrm{ij}})$ calculate starting values of extra variables τ_{ij} used to define the lines separating pairs $v_i^{(1)}$ and $v_j^{(1)}$, $i < j \in I_n$. Find $\tau^{(1)} = (\tau_{\mathrm{ij}}^{(1)}, i < j \in I_n)$.

Step 4. Define the vector $(u^{(1)}, \tau^{(1)})$, where $u^{(1)} = (v^{(1)}, \theta^{(1)})$, $\theta^{(1)} = (\theta_1^{(1)}, \ldots, \theta_n^{(1)})$ is the vector of rotation angles generated randomly.

Step 5. Solve the optimization problem: s.t.

$$\max \beta \text{ s.t. } (u, \tau, \beta) \in V_\beta, \tag{13.7}$$

$$V\beta = \{(u, \tau, \beta): \Phi_i(u_i, \beta) \geq 0,\ i \in I_n,$$

$$\Phi'ij(u_i, u_j, \tau_{ij}, \beta) \geq 0,\ i < j \in I_n,\ g(u) \geq 0,\ \beta \geq 0\}, \tag{13.8}$$

using the point $(u^{(1)}, \tau^{(1)}, \beta^{(1)} = 0)$ to start.

The variable β in the problems (13.7) and (13.8) is a homothetic ratio of $A_i(u_i)$, $i \in I_n$, $\Phi_i(u_i, \beta)$ is a phi-function for $\beta A_i(u_i)$ and D^*, while $\Phi'_{ij}(u_i, u_j, \tau_{ij}, \beta)$ is a quasi-phi-function of $\beta A_i(u_i)$ and $\beta A_j(u_j)$.

Find a local optimum $(u^{(2)}, \tau^{(2)}, \beta^{(2)})$ of the problems (13.7) and (13.8). If $\beta^{(2)} = 1$ then go to Step 6, if $\beta^{(2)} < 1$ then go to Step 1.

Step 6. Get

$$\rho^{(2)} = \min\{\Phi'_{ij}(u_i^{(2)}, u_j^{(2)}, \tau_{ij}^{(2)}),\ \ i < j \in I_n,\ \Phi_i(u_i^{(2)}, \beta^{(2)}),\ i \in I_n\}.$$

Step 7. Resolve problems (13.3) and (13.4), starting from the point $(u^{(2)}, \tau^{(2)}, \rho^{(2)})$.

Find a local maximum point of (13.3) and (13.4) that involves the optimized objective function value $\rho^*$and the corresponding vector $u^*$of placement parameters $u_1^*, \ldots, u_n^*$ of the objects A_i, $i \in I_n$.

Figure 13.1 shows local-optimal unbalanced sparse packing (the first colomn) and sparse packing under balancing conditions (the second colomn). The interior point optimizer code reported in [57] is used for the local optimization under default options.

For multidimensional sparse problems we apply the decomposition approach [58].

13.3 Thermal problem formulation

For the problem of finding optimal layout of parts in the heat treatment it was conjectured that such an arrangement corresponds to the sparsest balance layout of parts [11]. To test this hypothesis numerical simulations were performed. A simplified formulation was considered corresponding to heating 2D objects in a circular region. Simulations were performed under the following assumptions.

1. The heat exchange between cylindrical objects with a constant temperature 25 °C and a gas having an initial temperature 1000 °C is analyzed. The validity of this assumption is due to the short interaction time of the gas and the walls of the cylinders ($\sim 10^{-3}$ s). As shown by numerous experiments, the surface of the parts is practically not heated during this short time.
2. The conditions of the adiabatic wall are established for the boundary of the location area (container). This is since the distribution of heat fluxes on the boundary is irrelevant for the problem under consideration. On the other hand, the decrease in gas temperature caused by heat loss through this wall can be omitted due to the short heat transfer time.
3. The computational time does not exceed the attenuation time of the shock waves generated by the high pressure in the container.

For numerical simulations a software ANSYS CFX is used. The characteristics of the gases were determined using the approach described in [47, 51].

Let us define first the effective stress tensor as follows:

$$\tau_{\text{eff}} = (\mu + \mu_t)[\nabla \mathbf{u} + (\nabla \mathbf{u})^T - 2/3\ \mathbf{I} \cdot (\nabla \mathbf{u})],$$

where μ_t is the turbulent viscosity, μ is the viscosity; $\mathbf{I}$ is the unit tensor, $\mathbf{u}$ is the velocity vector; t is the time.

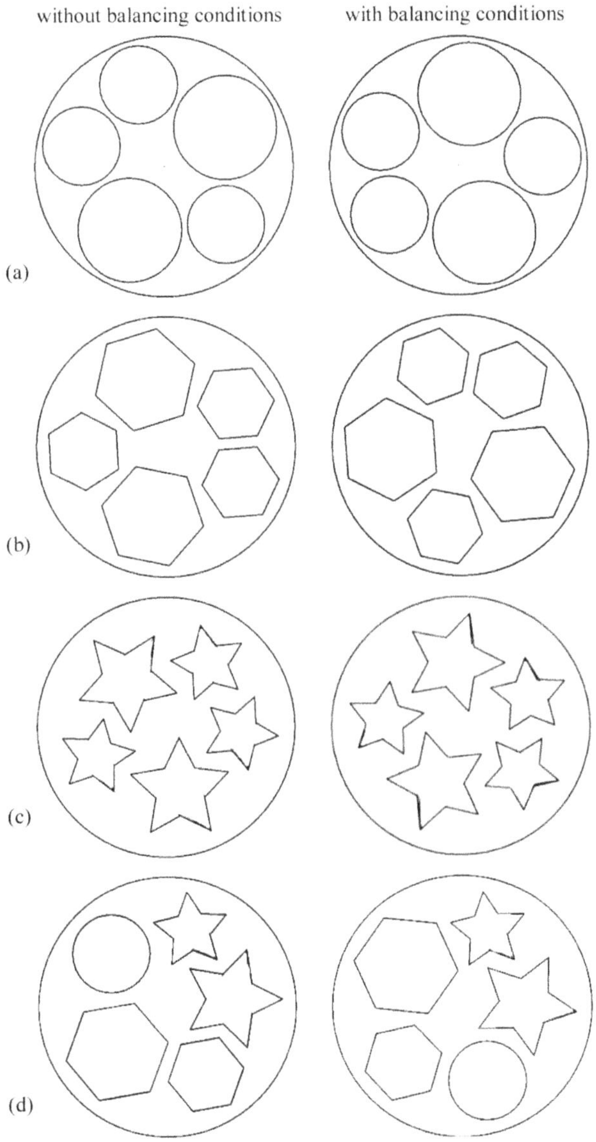

Figure 13.1. Local-optimal sparse packings for circles (a), convex polygons (b), nonconvex polygons (c), mix of objects (d), unbalanced and with balancing conditions.

Omitting the effects of radiation, diffusion and gravity the corresponding equation system has the form

$$\frac{\partial \rho}{\partial t} + \nabla \cdot (\rho \cdot \mathbf{u}) = 0,$$

$$\frac{\partial (\rho \cdot \mathbf{u})}{\partial t} + \nabla \cdot (\rho \cdot \mathbf{u} \cdot \mathbf{u}) = -\nabla P + \nabla \cdot \tau_{\text{eff}},$$

$$\frac{\partial(\rho h)}{\partial t} + \nabla \cdot (\mathbf{u} \cdot \rho h) = \frac{\partial P}{\partial t} + \mathbf{u} \cdot \nabla P + \nabla(\lambda_{\text{eff}} \nabla T + \tau_{\text{eff}} \cdot \mathbf{u}),$$

where ρ means the density while P denotes the pressure, notation h is used for the enthalpy of the gas, $\lambda_{\text{eff}} = \lambda + \lambda_t$ is the effective thermal conductivity, λ is the laminar and $\lambda_t = C_p \mu_t \text{Pr}_t^{-1}$ is the turbulent heat conductivity, C_p is the specific heat of the gas, Pr_t is turbulent Prandtl number, T is the temperature.

The SAS SST turbulence model was used for the calculation [59]. For calculations of convective heat flux, Kader's solution is used [60]:

$$T^+ = \text{Pr} \cdot \tilde{y}^+ \exp(-\Gamma) + [2.12 \ln(1 + \tilde{y}^+) + \beta] \exp(-1/\Gamma),$$

$$\beta = (3.85\, \text{Pr}^{1/3} - 1.3)^2 + 2.12 \ln(\text{Pr}),\ \Gamma = 0.01(\text{Pr} \cdot \tilde{y}^+)^4/(1+5\, \text{Pr} \cdot \tilde{y}^+).$$

Dimensional temperature T^+ is defined as

$$T^+ = \frac{\rho C_p \tilde{u}_{\tan}(T_w - T_f)}{q_w},$$

where T_f is the gas temperature outside the boundary layer, T_w is the wall temperature, $\tilde{u}_{\tan} = [(\tilde{u}_{\tan}^{\text{vis}})^4 + (\tilde{u}_{\tan}^{\log})^4]^{0.25}$ is the velocity profile in the boundary layer, $\tilde{u}_{\tan}^{\text{vis}} = \frac{U_1}{\tilde{y}^+}$ is the velocity in the viscous sublayer, U_1 is the flow rate at the node that is the closest to the wall, $\tilde{y}^+ = \max(y^+,\ 11.067)$, where 11.067 is the limit value, corresponding to the intersection of logarithmic and linear profiles, y^+ is the dimensionless distance from the first grid node to the wall, $\tilde{u}_{\tan}^{\log} = \frac{U_1}{(1/k \cdot \ln(\tilde{y}^+) + c)}$ is the velocity in the logarithmic sublayer, q_w is the heat flow into the wall.

Thus, the value of heat flux in numerical experiments was calculated as follows:

$$q_w = \frac{\rho c_p \tilde{u}_{\tan}}{T^+}(T_w - T_f).$$

In this setting several test problems were solved for packing objects of different shapes and sizes (circles, convex and nonconvex polygons) in a circular area.

To define the pressure pulse, its initial distribution in the calculation area can be derived as follows:

$$P_0 = 3\,[\text{atm}]*\text{step}\left(\left(\frac{r}{1\,[\text{mm}]}\right)^2 - \left(\frac{x}{1\,[\text{mm}]}\right)^2 - \left(\frac{y}{1\,[\text{mm}]}\right)^2\right) + 1\,[\text{atm}]$$

where step means the Heavyside function record received by ANSYS CFX, r is the radius of the circle centered at the origin, which is a region with high pressure ($r = 3$ mm is taken).

The expression above specifies the following distribution of initial pressure:

$$P_0 = \begin{cases} 4\,[\text{atm}], \text{ if } r^2 - x^2 - y^2 > 0 \\ 1\,[\text{atm}], \text{ if } r^2 - x^2 - y^2 < 0 \end{cases}.$$

The calculated finite element grid and the solver settings correspond to the recommendations on numerical modeling of heat transfer problems in the case of shock waves provided in [61]. The finite element sizes are chosen providing the value $y^+ \approx 1$ in a wall zone where objects are located. The finite element grid is additionally fine-meshed in the zone where the high pressure is set at the initial moment (figure 13.2). Relations between of the maximum (y^+_{max}) and averaged (y^+_{av}) value of y^+ on the surfaces where objects placed on the shock waves attenuation time are shown in figure 13.3.

The solution time discretization step is taken to guarantee that the Courant number is below 5. A high-resolution advection scheme and a second-order Euler transient scheme are used to adjust the solver. The condition $P_{max}/P_{min} \leqslant 1.05$ was used as a stopping criterion for calculations.

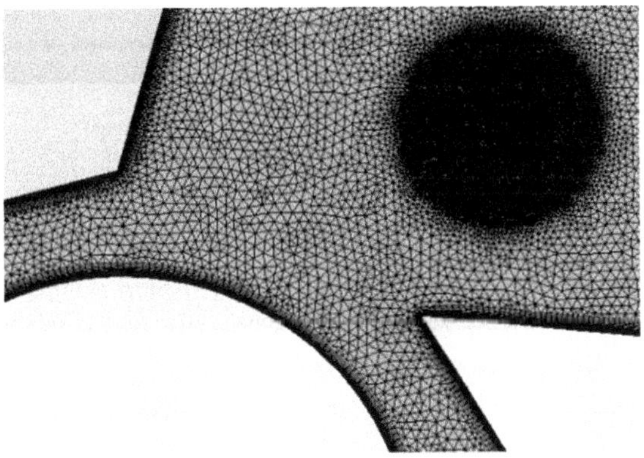

Figure 13.2. A fragment of the calculation grid for the layout on figure 13.1(d) with thickening of the elements in the initial pressure and in the wall area.

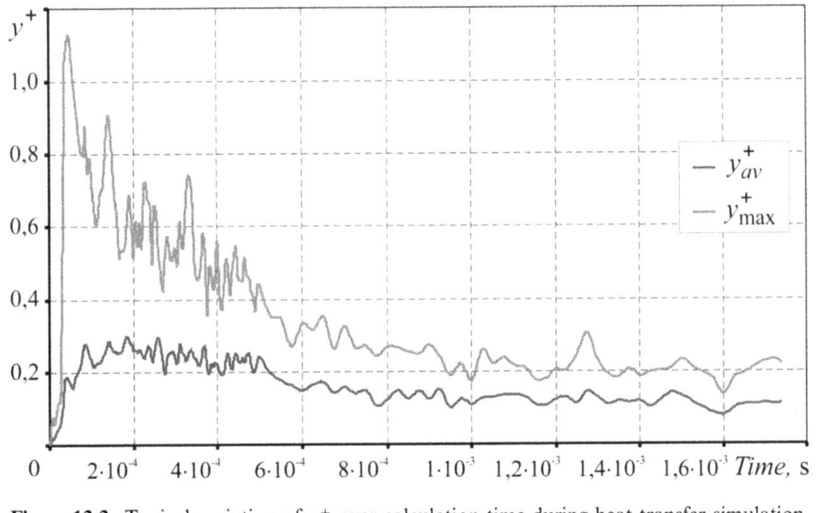

Figure 13.3. Typical variation of y^+ over calculation time during heat transfer simulation.

13.4 The balanced layout of 2D objects with shock waves action

Four problems were considered in numerical experiments corresponding to balanced layouts and layouts without balancing conditions shown in figure 13.1. The average value of the specific heat flux $\bar{q}_i$ at the boundary $\partial\Omega_i$ of the object Ω_i,

$$\bar{q}_i = \int_{\partial\Omega_i} q \; d(\partial\Omega_i) \Big/ \int_{\partial\Omega_i} d(\partial\Omega_i),$$

was calculated.

Figures 13.4 and 13.5 present built dependences $\bar{q}_i$ for the examples with circular objects (figure 13.1(a)) and convex polygonal objects (figure 13.1(b)). Moreover, the figures show the distribution of pressure gradients in the container for $t = 0.00013$ s.

Additionally, the relative error of the averaged specific heat flux $\bar{q}_i$ for each object,

$$\delta = \left|(\bar{q}_i - \bar{q})/\bar{q}\right|,$$

was calculated.

The relative error for balanced and unbalanced layouts for circles (figure 13.1(a)) and convex polygons (figure 13.1(b)) are shown in figures 13.6–13.9. For both examples the distribution of errors in symmetrically located objects of the same size was almost the same. Therefore, the data are presented for three objects only. In both cases the balanced layout provided a more uniform distribution of heat fluxes. Estimating the total amount of heat absorbed by the surfaces of objects during the attenuation of shock waves, we note that for circular objects the relative error for the balanced layout was 1.02% while for the unbalanced layout it was 1.81%.

For hexagonal objects the relative error corresponding to the balanced layout was 1.75%, while for the unbalanced layout it was 2.56%. We may assume that the loss of

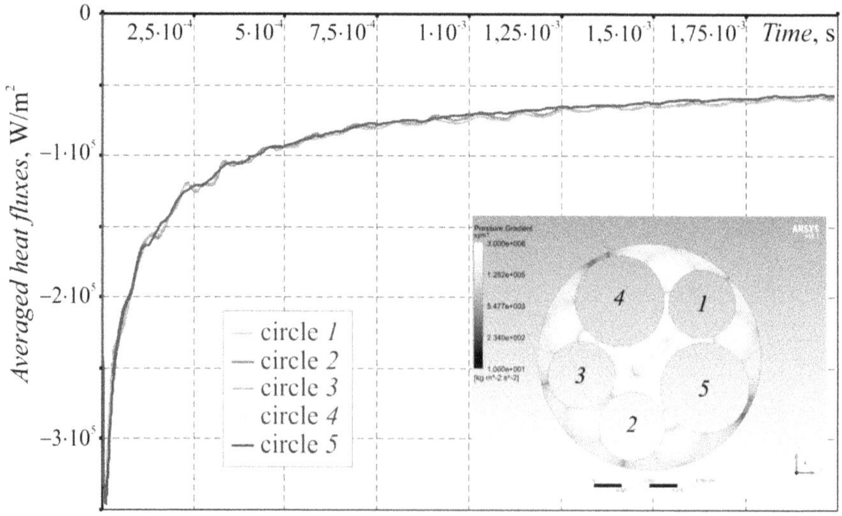

Figure 13.4. Averaged heat fluxes for balanced layout of circles and the distribution of the pressure gradient at $t = 1.3{\cdot}10^{-4}$ s.

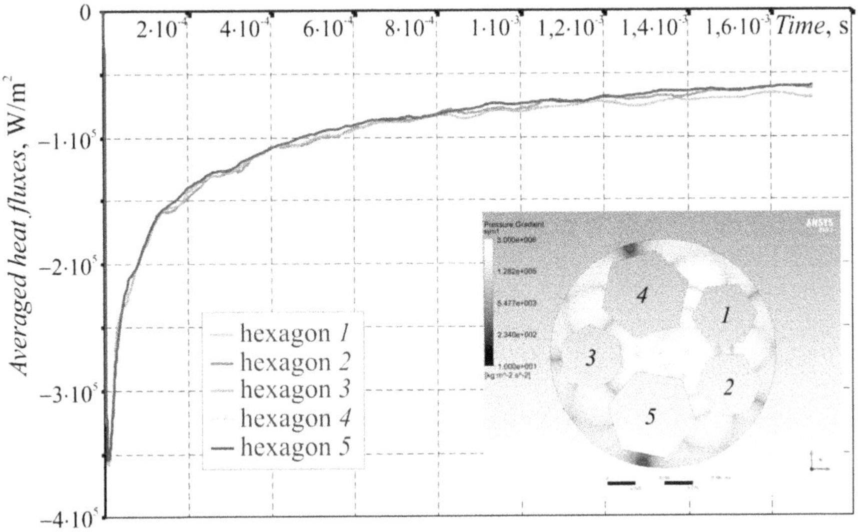

Figure 13.5. The averaged heat fluxes for the balanced layout of convex polygons and the distribution of the pressure gradient at $t = 1.3\cdot10^{-4}$ s.

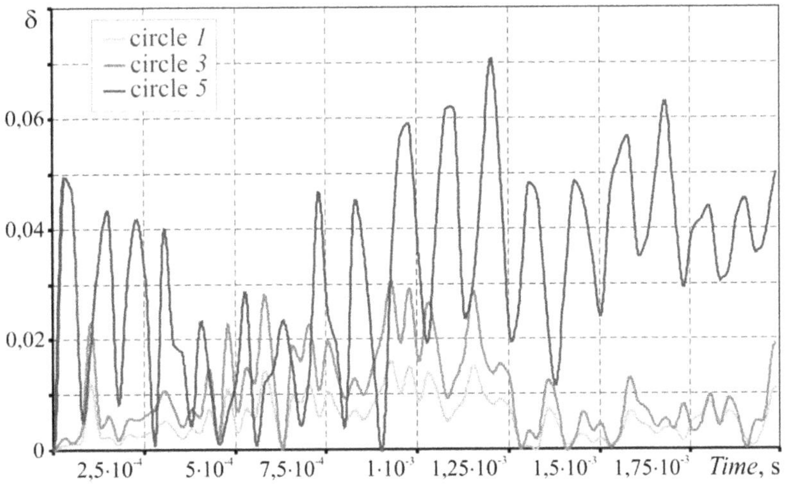

Figure 13.6. Variation in the relative error of the averaged heat fluxes for balanced layout of circles.

uniformity in heat flux distribution for more complex shapes is caused by more complex wave patterns and wave interferences.

This assumption was confirmed for nonconvex polygons (figure 13.1(c)) and for different shapes of objects (figure 13.1(d)). These cases are presented in figures 13.10 and 13.11.

The relative errors for nonconvex polygons and different shapes objects are shown in figures 13.12–13.15. For nonconvex polygons (figure 13.1(c)) the layout

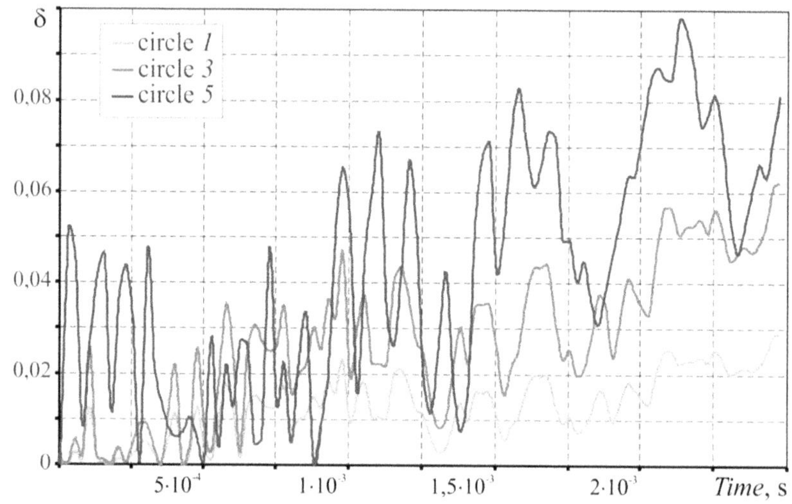

Figure 13.7. Variation in the relative error of the averaged heat fluxes for layout without balance conditions of circles.

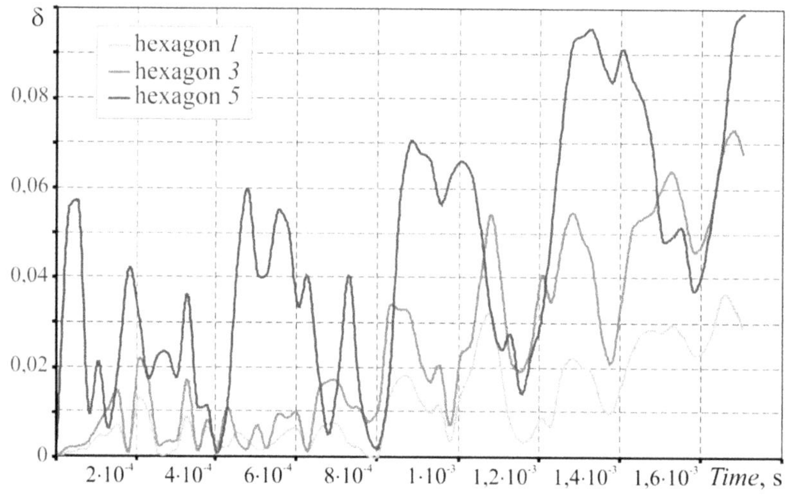

Figure 13.8. Variation in the relative error of the averaged heat fluxes for balanced layout of convex polygons.

without balance conditions provided a more uniform distribution of heat fluxes along the boundaries of the objects. The relative error for the balanced layout was 2.05%, while for unbalanced layout it was 0.99%. The worst results in terms of uniformity of heat flows were observed for different shapes objects. In this case the relative error was 5.54% for the balanced layout and 6.13% for the unbalanced.

The simulation shows that the sparse balanced layout in most cases provides the most atractive results in terms of uniformity of heat fluxes and heat transfer under the shock waves. Note the center of the high-pressure region that formed the shock

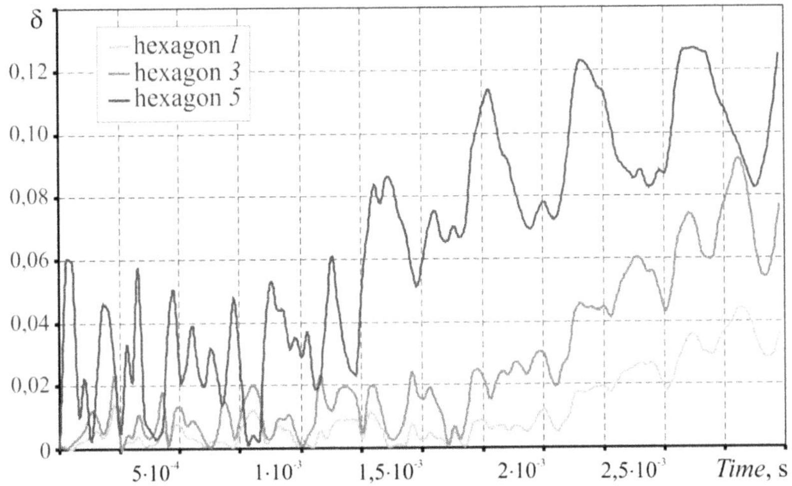

Figure 13.9. Variation in the relative error of the averaged heat fluxes for layout without balance conditions of convex polygons.

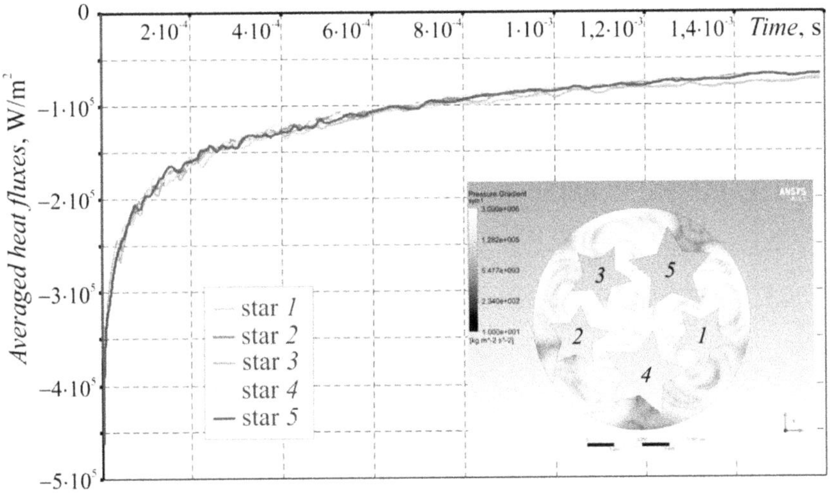

Figure 13.10. Averaged heat fluxes for balanced layout of nonconvex polygons and the distribution of the pressure gradient at time $t = 1.3{\cdot}10^{-4}$ s.

waves coincided with the center of balance of the objects. Simultaneous processing of different shapes and/or sizes increases the averaged heat fluxes. However, using the method of sparse balanced layout for identical objects results in more stable processing conditions.

For the group TEM treatment, the following can be recommended to ensure uniformity of heat distribution on the surfaces of the parts:

- arrange the processed details on shelves of the device [43] on the basis of sparse balanced layout;

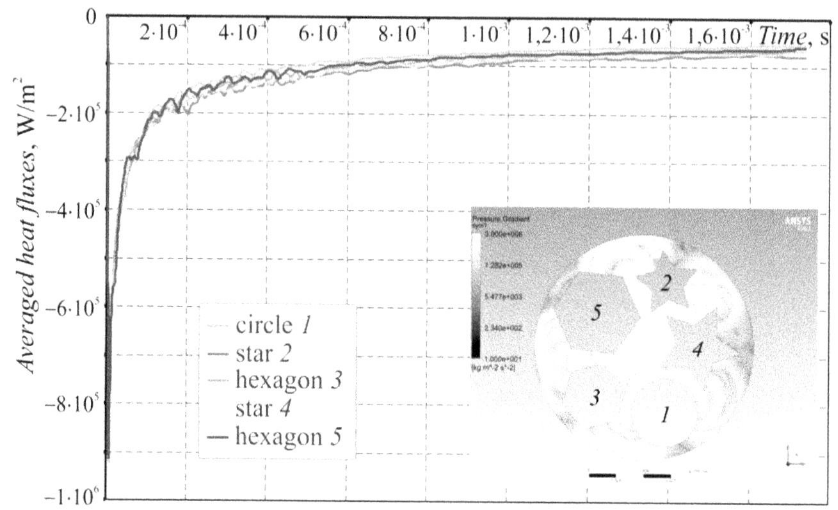

Figure 13.11. Averaged heat fluxes for balanced layout of different shape objects and the distribution of the pressure gradient at time $t = 1.3 \cdot 10^{-4}$ s.

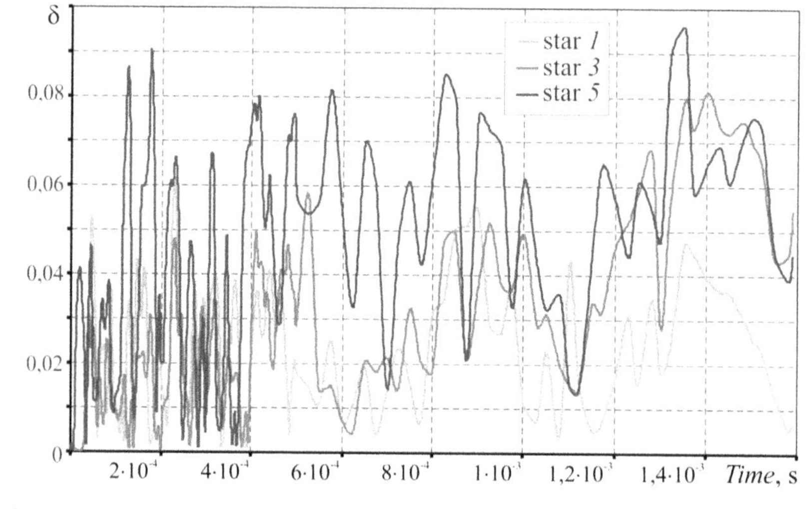

Figure 13.12. Variation in the relative error of the averaged heat fluxes for balanced layout of nonconvex polygons.

- process similar (shape and size) parts simultaneously during the group processing, especially with increased quality assurance requirements [62];
- locate zones of shock wave formation so that the gravity center of the zones would coincide with the point relative to which the layout of the workpieces is balanced.

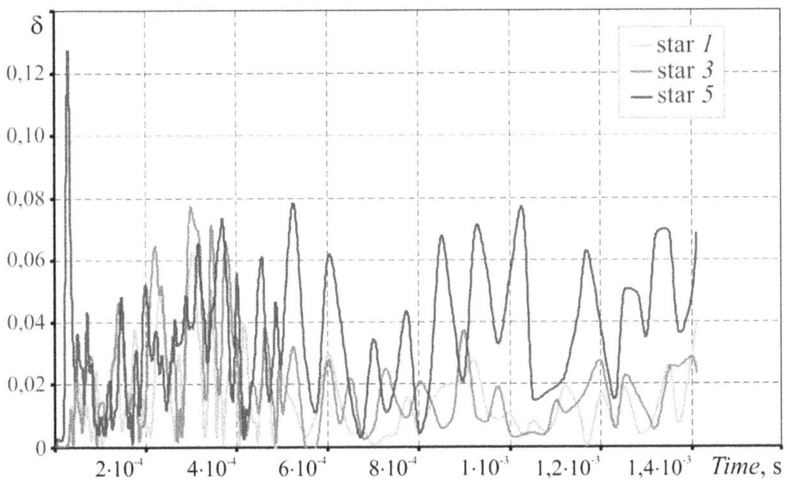

Figure 13.13. Variation in the relative error of the averaged heat fluxes for layout without balance conditions of nonconvex polygons.

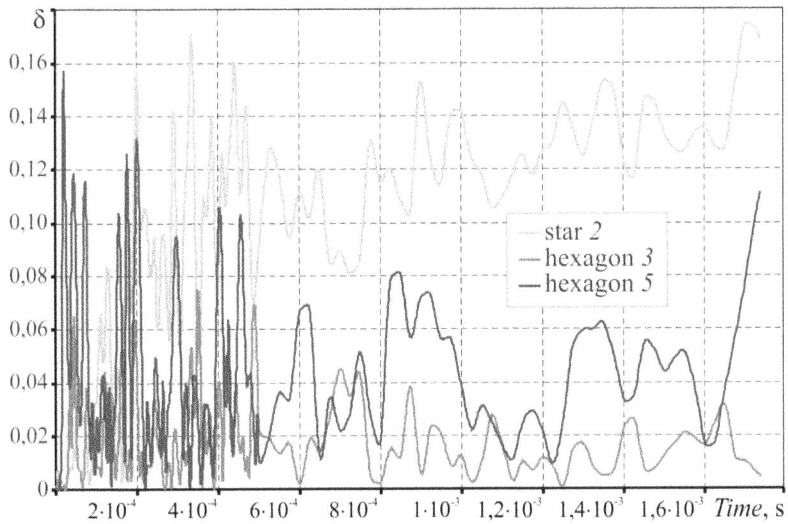

Figure 13.14. Variation in the relative error of the averaged heat fluxes for balanced layout of different shapes of objects.

13.5 Conclusions and future research

Sparse balanced layout can be used for determining the optimal arrangement of parts in the group thermal energy processing under shock waves. The uniformity of the heat flux distribution along the boundaries of the objects can be used as a criterion for optimal location during the time of attenuation of shock waves. This

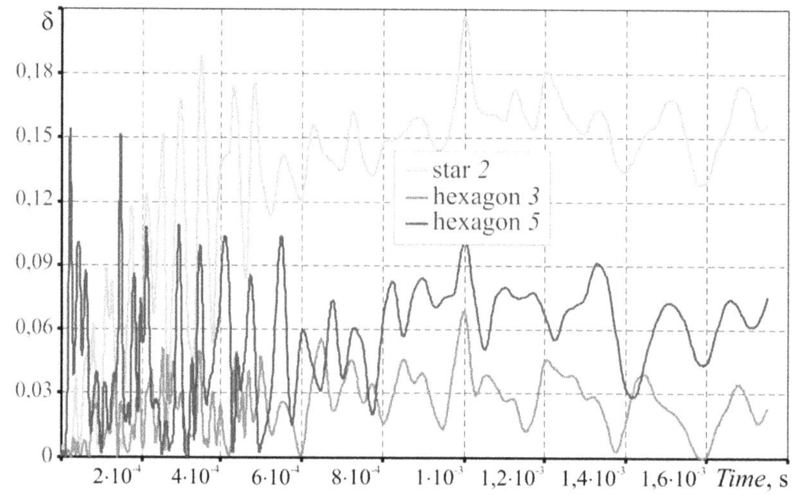

Figure 13.15. Variation in the relative error of the averaged heat fluxes for layout without balance conditions of different shapes of objects.

proposition was confirmed by solving several test problems formulated as heat transfer between hot gas and located 2D objects with a constant temperature. Numerical simulation was carried out using the ANSYS CFX software. It is shown that the phi-function approach can be effectively used for sparse balanced packing. In this study, only 2D objects were considered. However, in real technological problems, three-dimensional shapes of objects must be considered. Locating objects one above another (nesting) can also improve characteristics of technological processes [63, 64]. Large-scale optimizations problems arising in sparse packing require special decomposition and/or aggregation solution techniques [65]. Generalizing original models, solution methods and simulating for these cases is an interesting area for future research.

Despite the trend towards simplified simulation models, for instance, when building digital twins of technological processes, it is extremely necessary to have an analysis approach that describes it as adequately as possible. Therefore, the continuation of the investigation of the sparse packing in the 3D formulation is needed and justified.

Acknowledgments

This research is partially supported by National Research Foundation of Ukraine (grant No. 2020.02/0128) and by the Ministry of Education and Science of Ukraine (scientific research projects No. 0121U109639, 0121U109601)

References

[1] Chazelle B, Edelsbrunner H and Guibas L J 1989 The complexity of cutting complexes *Disc. Comput. Geom.* **4** 139–81

[2] Bortfeldt A and Gehring H 2001 A hybrid genetic algorithm for the container loading problem *Eur. J. Oper. Res.* **131** 143–61

[3] Gehring H and Bortfeldt A 2002 A parallel genetic algorithm for solving the container loading problem *Int. Trans. Oper. Res.* **9** 497–511

[4] Bortfeldt A and Wäscher G 2013 Constraints in container loading—a state-of-the-art review *Eur. J. Oper. Res.* **229** 1–20

[5] Mack D, Bortfeldt A and Gehring H 2004 A parallel hybrid local search algorithm for the container loading problem *Int. Trans. Oper. Res.* **11** 511–33

[6] Stoyan Y, Grebennik I, Romanova T and Kovalenko A 2019 Optimized packings in space engineering applications: part II *Modeling and Optimization in Space Engineering, SOIA* vol 144 (Cham: Springer) pp 439–57

[7] Grebennik I V, Kovalenko A A, Romanova T E, Urniaieva I A and Shekhovtsov S B 2018 Combinatorial configurations in balance layout optimization problems *Cybernet. Syst. Anal.* **54** 221–31

[8] Blyuss O, Koriashkina L, Kiseleva E and Molchanov R 2015 Optimal placement of irradiation sources in the planning of radiotherapy: mathematical models and methods of solving *Comput. Math. Methods Med.* **2015** 142987

[9] Romanova T, Stoyan Y, Pankratov A, Litvinchev I, Avramov K, Chernobryvko M, Yanchevskyi I, Mozgova I and Bennell J 2021 Optimal layout of ellipses and its application for additive manufacturing *Int. J. Prod. Res.* **59** 560–75

[10] Romanova T, Litvinchev I, Grebennik I, Kovalenko A, Urniaieva I and Shekhovtsov S 2020 Packing convex 3D objects with special geometric and balancing conditions *Intelligent Computing and Optimization, AISC* vol 1072 (Cham: Springer) pp 273–81

[11] Plankovskyy S, Nikolaev A, Shypul O, Litvinchev I, Pankratov A and Romanova T 2020 Balance layout problem with the optimized distances between objects *Data Analysis and Optimization for Engineering and Computing Problems, EAI/SICC* (Cham: Springer) pp 85–93

[12] Hifi M and M'hallah R 2009 A literature review on circle and sphere packing problems: models and methodologies *Adv. Oper. Res.* **2009** 150624

[13] Stoyan Y and Yaskov G 2012 Packing equal circles into a circle with circular prohibited areas *Int. J. Comp. Math.* **89** 1355–369

[14] Litvinchev I, Infante L and Ozuna E L 2014 Espinosa. Approximate circle packing in a rectangular container: integer programming formulations and valid inequalities *Computational Logistics, LNCS* vol 8750 (Cham: Springer) pp 47–60

[15] Kampas F G, Castillo I and Pintér J D 2019 Optimized ellipse packings in regular polygons *Optimiz. Lett.* **13** 1583–613

[16] Leao A A, Toledo F M, Oliveira J F, Carravilla M A and Alvarez-Valdés R 2020 Irregular packing problems: a review of mathematical models *Eur. J. Oper. Res.* **282** 803–22

[17] Plankovskyy S, Shypul O, Tsegelnyk Y, Pankratov A, Romanova T and Litvinchev I 2021 Circular layout in thermal deburring *Mathematical Modeling and Simulation of Systems (MODS'2020), AISC,* vol 1265 111–20 (Cham: Springer)

[18] Romanova T, Pankratov A, Litvinchev I, Plankovskyy S, Tsegelnyk Y and Shypul O 2021 Sparsest packing of two-dimensional objects *Int. J. Prod. Res.* **59** 3900–15

[19] Romanova T, Stoyan Y, Pankratov A, Litvinchev I, Plankovskyy S, Tsegelnyk Y and Shypul O 2021 Sparsest balanced packing of irregular 3D objects in a cylindrical container *Eur. J. Oper. Res.* **291** 84–100

[20] Stoyan Y G, Romanova T E, Pankratov O V, Stetsyuk P I and Maximov S V 2021 Sparse balanced layout of ellipsoids *Cybernet. Syst. Anal.* **57** 864–73
[21] Stoyan Y G, Romanova T E, Pankratov O V, Stetsyuk P I and Stoian Y E 2021 Sparse balanced layout of spherical voids in three-dimensional domains *Cybernet. Syst. Anal.* **57** 542–51
[22] Huang X, Xi F, Li J and Zhong Z 2009 Optimal layout and path planning for flame cutting of sheet metals *Int. J. Comput. Integ. Manu.* **22** 30–41
[23] Hajad M, Tangwarodomnukun V, Jaturanonda C and Dumkum C 2019 Laser cutting path optimization with minimum heat accumulation *The Int. J. Adv. Manu. Tech.* **105** 2569–79
[24] Plankovskyy S, Shypul O, Tsegelnyk Y, Tryfonov O and Golovin I 2016 Simulation of surface heating for arbitrary shape's moving bodies/sources by using R-functions *Acta Polytech.* **56** 472–77
[25] Plankovskyy S, Tsegelnyk Y, Shypul O, Pankratov A and Romanova T 2020 Cutting irregular objects from the rectangular metal sheet *Integrated Computer Technologies in Mechanical Engineering, AISC* vol 1113 (Cham: Springer) pp 150–7
[26] Anghel C, Gupta K and Jen T C 2020 Analysis and optimization of surface quality of stainless steel miniature gears manufactured by CO_2 laser cutting *Optik* **203** 164049
[27] Kombarov V, Sorokin V, Fojtů O, Aksonov Y and Kryzhyvets Y 2019 S-curve algorithm of acceleration/deceleration with smoothly-limited jerk in high-speed equipment control tasks *MM Sci. J.* **2019** 3264–70
[28] Kombarov V, Sorokin V, Tsegelnyk Y, Plankovskyy S, Aksonov Y and Fojtů O 2022 S-shape feedrate scheduling method with smoothly-limited jerk in cyber-physical systems *Int. Conf. on Reliable Systems Engineering (ICoRSE)—2021, LNNS* vol 305 (Cham: Springer) 54–68
[29] Alexandridis A, Paizis E, Chondrodima E and Stogiannos M 2017 A particle swarm optimization approach in printed circuit board thermal design *Integ. Comput.-Aided Eng.* **24** 143–55
[30] Wang L, Lu G and Yang K 2018 Thermal optimization of electronic devices on PCB based on the ant colony algorithm *Int. Conf. on Electronics Technology (ICET)* (Piscataway, NJ: IEEE) 55–9
[31] Harbrecht H and Loos F 2016 Optimization of current carrying multicables *Computational Optimization and Applications* **63** 237–71
[32] Yang Z, Lu Q, Yan J, Chen J and Yue Q 2018 Multidisciplinary optimization design for the section layout of umbilicals based on intelligent algorithm *J. Offshore Mech. Arc. Eng.* **140** 031702
[33] Pliuhin V, Sukhonos M and Bileckiy I 2020 Object oriented mathematical modeling of electrical machines *IEEE 4th Int. Conf. on Intelligent Energy and Power Systems (IEPS)* (Piscataway, NJ: IEEE) 267–72
[34] Baadache K and Bougriou C 2015 Optimisation of the design of shell and double concentric tubes heat exchanger using the genetic algorithm *Heat and Mass Transfer* **51** 1371–81
[35] Roetzel W, Luo X and Chen D 2019 Optimal design of heat exchangers *Design and Operation of Heat Exchangers and their Networks* (New York: Academic press) pp 191–229
[36] Tovazhnyanskyy L, Klemeš J J, Kapustenko P, Arsenyeva O, Perevertaylenko O and Arsenyev P 2020 Optimal design of welded plate heat exchanger for ammonia synthesis column: an experimental study with mathematical optimisation *Energies* **13** 2847
[37] Jin S Y, Pramanik A, Basak A K, Prakash C, Shankar S and Debnath S 2020 Burr formation and its treatments—a review *Int. J. Adv. Manu. Tech.* **107** 2189–210

[38] Aksonov Y, Kombarov V, Fojtů O, Sorokin V and Kryzhyvets Y 2019 Investigation of processes in high-speed equipment using CNC capabilities *MM Sci. J.* **2019** 3271–6

[39] Kombarov V, Sorokin V, Tsegelnyk Y, Plankovskyy S, Aksonov Y and Fojtů O 2021 Numerical control of machining parts from aluminum alloys with sticking minimization *Int. J. Mechatronics Appl. Mech.* **1** 209–16

[40] Geen H C and Rice E E 1969 Process for treating articles of manufacture to eliminate superfluous projections Patent 3475229

[41] Lamikiz A, Ukar E, Tabernero I and Martinez S 2011 Thermal advanced machining processes *Modern Machining Technology* (Cambridge: Woodhead Publishing) pp 335–72

[42] Fritz A, Sekol L, Koroskenyi J, Walch B, Minear J, Fernandez V and Liu L 2012 Experimental analysis of thermal energy deburring process by design of experiment *In ASME Int. Mechanical Engineering Congress and Exposition* vol 45196 (New York: American Society of Mechanical Engineers) pp 2035–41

[43] Struckmann J and Kieser A 2020 Thermal deburring. ATL anlagentechnik Luhden GmbH Luhden, Germany

[44] Konzok D 2013 Reinigen nach dem thermischen entgraten *JOT J. für Oberflächentechnik* **53** 48–50

[45] Lutz T 2019 Oxide nach thermischem entgraten effektiv entfernen *JOT J. für Oberflächentechnik* **59** 102–04

[46] Bozhko V P 1998 Determination of duration of the part edges melting under gas explosion deburring *Fizika i Khimiya Obrabotki Materialov* **3** 113–16

[47] Plankovskyy S, Popov V, Shypul O, Tsegelnyk Y, Tryfonov O and Brega D 2021 Advanced thermal energy method for finishing precision parts *In Advanced Machining and Finishing* (Amsterdam: Elsevier) pp 527–75

[48] Plankovskyy S, Shypul O, Tsegelnyk Y, Brega D, Tryfonov O and Malashenko V 2022 Basic principles for thermoplastic parts finishing with Impulse Thermal Energy Method *Handbook of Research on Advancements in the Processing, Characterization, and Application of Lightweight Materials* (Pennsylvania, PA: IGI Global) pp 49–87

[49] Plankovskyy S, Shypul O, Tsegelnyk Y, Pankratov A and Romanova T 2021 Amplification of heat transfer by shock waves for thermal energy method *Integrated Computer Technologies in Mechanical Engineering—2020, LNNS* vol 188 (Cham: Springer) pp 577–87

[50] Sibanda P S, Carr P, Ryan M and Bigot S 2019 State of the art in surface finish of metal additive manufactured parts *Advances in Manufacturing Technology XXXIII* **9** 221–5

[51] Plankovskyy S, Teodorczyk A, Shypul O, Tryfonov O and Brega D 2019 Determination of detonable gas mixture heat fluxes at thermal deburring *Acta Polytech.* **59** 162–9

[52] Stoyan Y G, Romanova T, Scheithauer G and Krivulya A 2011 Covering a polygonal region by rectangles *Comput. Optimiz. Appl.* **48** 675–95

[53] Stoyan Y, Pankratov A and Romanova T 2017 Placement problems for irregular objects: mathematical modeling, optimization and applications *Optimization Methods and Applications, SOIA* vol 130 (Cham: Springer) pp 521–9

[54] Stoyan Y, Pankratov A, Romanova T, Fasano G, Pintér J D, Stoian Y E and Chugay A 2019 Optimized packings in space engineering applications: part I *Modeling and Optimization in Space Engineering, SOIA* vol 144 (Cham: Springer) pp 395–437

[55] Pankratov A, Romanova T and Litvinchev I 2019 Packing ellipses in an optimized convex polygon *J. Global Optimiz.* **75** 495–522

[56] Duriagina Z, Lemishka I, Litvinchev I, Marmolejo J A, Pankratov A, Romanova T and Yaskov G 2021 Optimized filling of a given cuboid with spherical powders for additive manufacturing *J. Oper. Res. Soc. Chin.* **9** 853–68

[57] Wächter A and Biegler L T 2006 On the implementation of an interior-point filter line-search algorithm for large-scale nonlinear programming *Mathematical Programming* **106** 25–57

[58] Romanova T, Stoyan Y, Pankratov A, Litvinchev I and Marmolejo J A 2020 Decomposition algorithm for irregular placement problems *Intelligent Computing and Optimization, AISC* vol 1072 (Cham: Springer) pp 214–21

[59] Menter F R 1994 Two-equation eddy-viscosity turbulence models for engineering applications *AIAA J.* **32** 1598–605

[60] Kader B A 1981 Temperature and concentration profiles in fully turbulent boundary layers *Int. J. Heat Mass Trans.* **24** 1541–4

[61] Egorov Y, Menter F R, Lechner R and Cokljat D 2010 The scale-adaptive simulation method for unsteady turbulent flow predictions. part 2: application to complex flows *Flow Turbul. Combust.* **85** 139–65

[62] Kato Y, Ohmri K, Hatano E and Takazawa K 2007 The standardization for the edge quality of the precise machining products *Adv. Mater. Res.* **24** 83–90

[63] Litvinchev I and Ozuna E L 2014 Approximate packing circles in a rectangular container: valid inequalities and nesting *J. App. Res. and Techn.* **12** 716–23

[64] Torres-Escobar R, Marmolejo-Saucedo J A and Litvinchev I 2020 Binary monkey algorithm for approximate packing non-congruent circles in a rectangular container *Wireless Netw.* **26** 4743–52

[65] Litvinchev I S and Rangel S 1999 Localization of the optimal solution and *a posteriori* bounds for aggregation *Comput. Oper. Res.* **26** 967–88

IOP Publishing

Human-Assisted Intelligent Computing
Modeling, simulations and applications
Mukhdeep Singh Manshahia, Igor S Litvinchev, Gerhard-Wilhelm Weber, J Joshua Thomas and Pandian Vasant

Chapter 14

Implementation of smart manufacturing in small and medium-sized enterprises

Udai C Jhaa and Abhijeet A Shahadeb

In recent times, smart industry technology has emerged as the main research issue to increase productivity and efficiency, where smart machines collaborate with each other and with users and customers. Smart industry requires the use of information and communication technology (ICT) convergence for production resources as well as four zero factors, including zero waiting-time/inventory/defects/down-time. Smart manufacturing is the backbone of intelligent manufacturing with the involvement of process automation and automated machine tools, whereas data intelligence is related to data acquisition, storage and analysis for smart decision making. It is possible with the integration of the latest IoT gadgets, cloud computing and various ERP packages. The selection varies as per the diversified requirements of the manufacturing units. Quality consultancy is required for the selection of tools and techniques in order to excel in business performance. It is followed by the critical phase of deployment with the requirement of high-level expertise. This chapter proposes a framework for the implementation of smart manufacturing in small and medium-sized enterprises (SMEs). This framework will be the guiding tool for those SMEs who want to apply smart manufacturing (SM) to their units.

14.1 Introduction

14.1.1 Need for smart manufacturing

In today's technologically advanced world, normal life is dominated by smart technology driven gadgets and applications which force manufacturing companies to deploy a high degree of automation along with data-driven technologies in order to excel in quality standards of products or processes. The essential part of SM is to upgrade the manufacturing units with the latest automated tools coupled with automation for handling materials at different stages of manufacturing. With

doi:10.1088/978-0-7503-4801-0ch14

existing machine tools, if the changeover is not possible, it is required to go for automation with automated data acquisition at various stages in order to support the intelligent decision-making process. SM makes possible the availability of analysis required for decision making on touchscreen devices like a smartphone, tablet, etc.

14.1.2 Electronic hardware with machine and software interface

IoT devices are quite popular and can be integrated with various ERP packages in order to collect the data during different stages of manufacturing. Cloud computing enables the sharing of various resources over a wide variety of platforms. Various technologies like RFID, Bluetooth, Wifi, GSM and infrared enabled devices are available for real-time data capturing from different manufacturing stages which in turn can be directly interfaced with various ERP packages. With the revolution in the Industrial Internet of Things (IIoT) many big players are emerging as IIoT device suppliers; one such name which has been gaining momentum recently is Mazak Smartbox. This smart box can be connected to the manufacturing equipment for data collection and can be interfaced with ERP systems using the MTConnect protocol. With these advancements in technology, deployment of SM can be done to meet the requirements of the Industrial Revolution 4.0. Most of the modern machine tools have built-in interface ports for the connectivity of the various devices. If machine tools do not have the interface, sensor-enabled devices can be attached to them which in turn can be interfaced with the computer systems.

14.1.3 Management information system

The integration of these technology-enabled devices with the management systems for collecting real-time data will enable the units to make smart decisions in the better interests of the organization. Analyzing the causes of failure will become easier. The main goal of every enterprise is to improve its performance. The various parameters which are an integral part of performance can be employee performance, market share, equipment performance, customer satisfaction, profit levels, etc. Visualization of analysis for effective decision making is possible only when the system is updated with real-time data. Deployment of SM facilitates the development of the system with the input of real-time data from all sections of the SME working environment. Various open source ERPs available are helpful to those SMEs that cannot afford professionally developed software. These open source ERPs have full functionality to satisfy the needs of small-to-medium sector organizations.

14.2 Literature review

Zhang *et al* (2014) extended IoT to the Internet of Manufacturing Things (IoMT) by integrating sensors with machines, pallets, and materials, etc for capturing real-time data. This would make the information readily available and allow a reduction in personnel for collecting and storing data manually. They provided the architecture for IoMT for capturing real-time information. Coronado (2018) developed a shop floor digital twin by implementing a smartphone app with data entry from operator to supervisor on the shop floor and various personnel of the manufacturing unit. He attached smart devices to modern machine tools for collecting real-time data. Data from both the smartphone app and machine tools are stored in the cloud database servers from where it is accessible to management, clients and providers. His work as part of a cyber-physical system (CPS) is a step forward for implementing Industry 4.0. Dirican (2015) has written a conceptual and hypothetical paper elaborating the scope of artificial intelligence, robots, and mechatronics in the coming future. David and Bogle (2017) explored smart manufacturing for process system engineering. In their opinion, a smart process industry is entirely different from other manufacturing units. Tao *et al* (2018) discussed the role played by big data in SM and proposed a conceptual framework for it. They developed an application covering various aspects of the SM unit which are driven by the stored data. Their study is supported by a case study on a silicon wafers production line. Their research contributes to SM from three perspectives namely historical, development and envisaging future data in manufacturing. Wang *et al* (2018) have done a survey on deep learning algorithms and their application for SM. They proposed an analytical framework based on deep learning, especially for SM. They discussed several deep learning architectures to explore manufacturing intelligence as a part of SM. Finally, they elaborated the future development trends for data matter, model selection, model visualization, generic model and incremental learning. Peschi *et al* (2013) developed manufactronic network architecture. The architecture can be applied from a single machine to the entire production process. The main subject which was part of their research was the production configuration system (PCS). They demonstrated the validity of their concept with three case studies from different industrial sectors. Munguía *et al* (2009) developed a model for showing different alternatives by rapid manufacturing. The suggested method fills the gap between the knowledge of conventional manufacturing and rapid manufacturing. Wang *et al* (2018) proposed a framework for correlating wireless networks and clouds with machine tools, products, and conveyors. Their proposed framework makes possible the communication between available resources, which is in turn integrated with the information system. They expressed the need for smart software and hardware in order to meet the challenges of Industry 4.0. Zhong *et al* (2017) have provided a review of intelligent manufacturing, IoT, cloud manufacturing and technologies like cloud computing, CPSs, and big data analytics. May and Member (2004) have covered a review on system-on-package (SOP), which is dependent on manufacturers of various electronic devices. In their opinion, the research article has the potential for the deployment of techniques like artificial intelligence (AI) and genetic algorithms (GAs) in the manufacturing facilities of SOP. Sethi and Sarangi (2017) have proposed a taxonomy for IoT technologies that can make considerable contributions in the betterment of human life. Shen *et al* (2005) have presented the iShopFloor concept for manufacturing products intelligently. They proposed a reference architecture for implementing intelligent manufacturing on different kinds of shop floor. The prototype developed was tested offline on a network of PCs. Li *et al* (2017) have developed an architecture based on AI plus Internet. The architecture was divided into five layers. They elaborated the development of intelligent manufacturing in the context of global development. Watson *et al* (2018) described the development and implementation of manufacturing execution system (MES)-enabled Android devices along with an interface for collecting data directly from the machine tools. His research work was supported by a case study. A shop floor digital twin concept based on the utilization of MES and MTConnect enabled machines was presented. Bao *et al* (2018) used modeling in the form of virtual physical convergence for the manufacturing factory. They used automation markup language for building the model. Three kinds of digital twin for product, process, and operation were developed in order to optimize the production process. Shafiq *et al* (2016) proposed an experience and knowledge-based virtual manufacturing environment which in turn forms the basis for a virtual engineering factory (VEF). He validated the proposed concept in a case study. The VEF is subdivided into virtual engineering object (VEO) and virtual engineering process (VEP) for easy implementation across the factory level.

14.3 Levels of data for intelligent SME

This section provides details of various objects involved in the entire operations of SME followed by the framework which depicts the communication between these objects. The following subsections explain various parameters associated with SMEs in general and the goal of an intelligent system to optimize them. While carrying out the discussion with many SMEs in the context of the framework proposed and developed by the other researchers, it was observed that the key personnel from these units were not familiar with the terms used in the framework. It is a big challenge to provide a framework that will best suit the needs of most of the SMEs. They expected a neat and simple framework which they can understand easily and implement. Our effort is to provide a framework that will work as a guide for aspiring and existing SMEs who wish to implement SM in their organizations.

14.3.1 Resources for SME

Various resources which are an integral part of any organization are employees, machines, materials, tools, etc. There is data associated with each and every resource which as part of the intelligent system is stored and retrieved for decision making. There are various means for collecting data and it varies from one resource to another. For example, employee data consists of recruitment data, entered manually in the software system, daily attendance captured with the help of a biometric scanner, leave related data is facilitated by web or app on the smartphone, auto calculation of salary on the basis of daily attendance and leave data forms the basis for smart calculations. Figure 14.1 shows how an employee-centric intelligent database can be generated.

The second important resource for any smart unit is machine tools. Each individual machine tool is characterized by its specifications which are provided by the manufacturer. Most of the advanced machine tools have an interface for collecting data, IoT devices can be attached to the machine tools which do not have the inbuilt interface. Figure 14.2 shows a machine specific database.

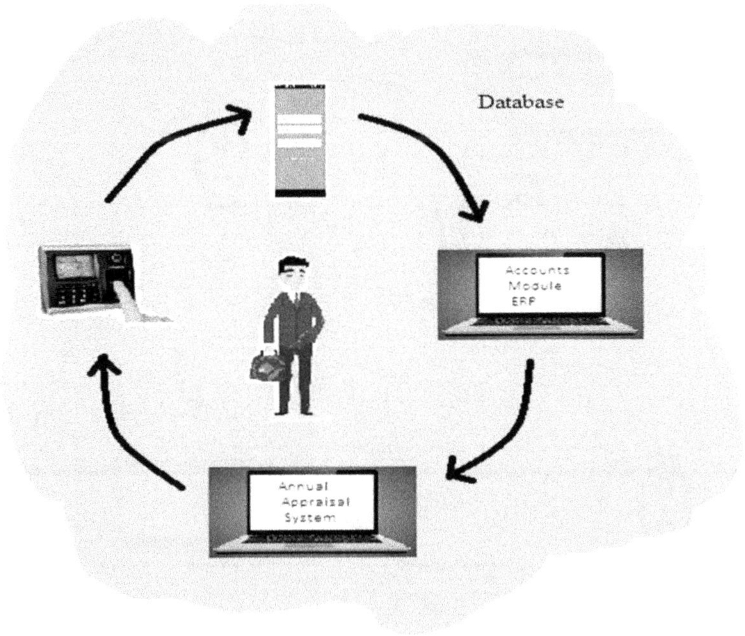

Figure 14.1. Employee centric database.

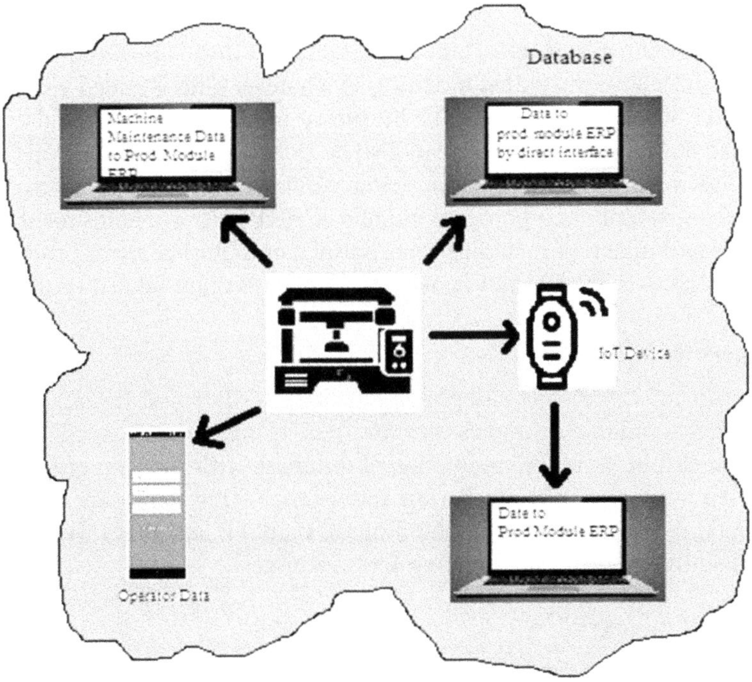

Figure 14.2. Machine specific database.

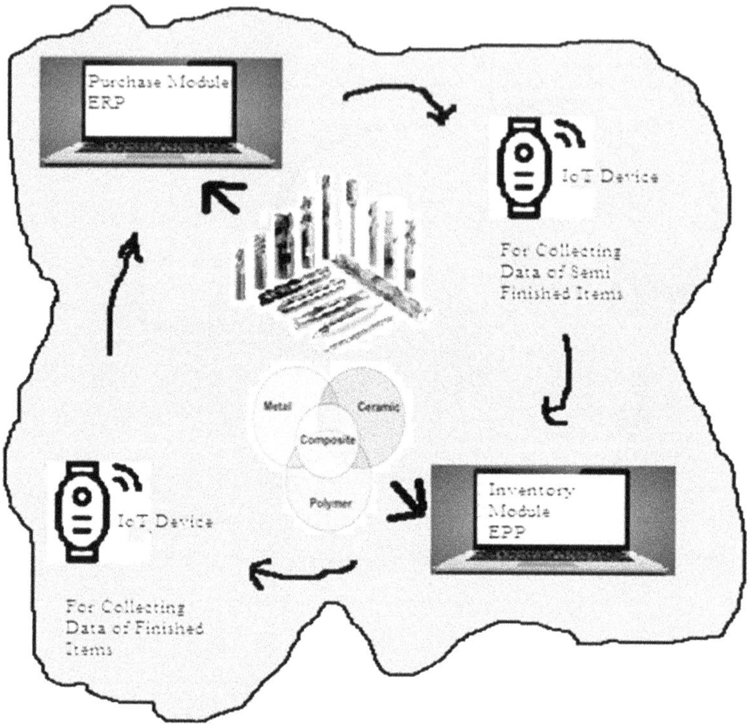

Figure 14.3. Materials and tools specific database.

A third important resource for any manufacturing unit is materials and tools. As most of the ERPs have integrated modules, so whatever data is issued in the form of a purchase order will become part of the inventory module after due validation on the receipt of the material. Direct entry can also be done for existing materials and tools. Figure 14.3 shows a materials and tools specific database. It is clearly evident from the figure that the inventory and purchase module of ERP software holds the database for various tools and materials including semi-finished and finished items produced in any particular SMEs. IoT devices can be used for data collection related to process items.

14.3.2 Inputs for SMEs

The inputs for any SMEs are categorized as direct orders and revenue is generated by outsourcing available resources that are free. There is data associated with both and this data can be stored in an intelligent database with the help of freeware ERP software. As a part of manufacturing intelligence, this data can be utilized for decision making pertaining to the planning of available resources for executing the orders and simultaneously outsourcing free resources.

14.3.3 Outputs for SMEs

Processed products, semi-finished products, and revenue generated by outsourcing become an integral part of outputs produced by any industry. On the basis of data collected for these various outputs, intelligent decisions can be taken for production scheduling on various machines and processes with due consideration to the requirements of the clients.

14.3.4 Flow diagram

Refer to figure 14.4 for levels of data.

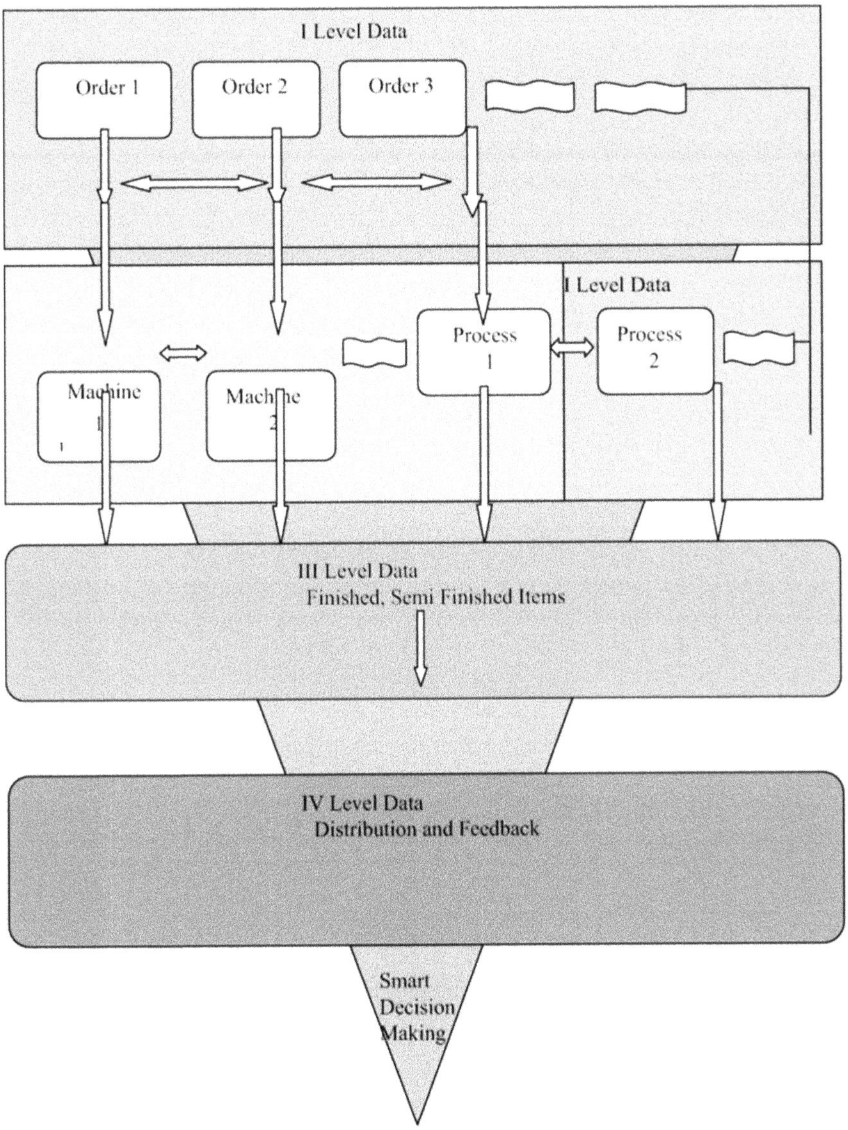

Figure 14.4. Levels of data.

14.3.5 Data collection

It is essential to understand the tools and techniques used for collecting data during various stages of manufacturing. The two factors which play a crucial role in data collection are selection of IoT devices and selection of ERP software and database.

14.3.5.1 Selection of IoT devices

The following factors should be carefully considered while selecting the IoT devices:

- It should have a ready interface with the machines available;
- There should be ease in installation of such a device;
- The interface driver should be easily upgradable so as to provide the interface for maximum resources;
- It should allow an interface for newly installed equipment.

14.3.5.2 Selection of ERP Software

The following list provides open source ERP software available for small businesses:

- Dolibarr ERP;
- ERPNext;
- Idempiere;
- MixERP;
- Odoo.

There are many more available that can be easily downloaded from the internet. Most of them provide professional services for customization.

14.3.6 Applications for analysis and decision making

14.3.6.1 Resource availability

This application provides insight about the resources which are free and the duration for which they can be outsourced for revenue generation.

14.3.6.2 Production schedule

This application can be utilized in those industries especially where batch production takes place. It really is a hectic job to plan the orders to meet the diversified requirements of different clients. This tool enhances the ability of the management to take better decisions.

14.3.6.3 Execution

This tool provides real-time monitoring of the actual work being processed at various stages of manufacturing so that uncertainties can be avoided for the timely execution of the orders.

14.3.6.4 Billing

In order to have your balance sheet at the end of the financial year, it is essential to have a database of all transactions where money is involved. With the help of such tools, it can be generated in real time and with one click financial statements can be generated at any point in time.

14.3.6.5 Distribution and transportation

This tool takes care of generating and maintaining data related to managing the distribution network and transactions carried out with the external transportation agency.

14.4 Proposed architectural framework for intelligent SMEs

The proposed architectural framework is mainly divided into four components:

- Preparing blueprint;
- System deployment;
- Measuring business performance;
- Smart decision making.

With these major actions, data is collected from various sections of the manufacturing unit. The centre of all is the manufacturing intelligence that supports smart decision making (figure 14.5).

14.5 Case study

The practical aspects of the above-proposed framework are illustrated on the basis of a case study conducted at one of the plastic molding companies located in India. The plastic molding company produces around 45 various two-wheel and four-wheel components for the automobile industry. Managing batch production of 45 components on the 15 different capacity plastic molding machines is a difficult task and with the existing manual data collection, the time frame required for decision making for the switchover is cumbersome and requires a high level of expertise. With the proposed architectural framework the majority of the data can be collected with the help of an overhanging smart box which is available on the market that is in its initial stage. Remaining data can be collected with the help of a ready interface available on the machines for desktop connectivity. With the proposed framework it is possible to plot a graph for the energy consumption of various machines coupled with the maintenance expenditure. The same can be compared with the newly available high-efficiency plastic molding machines in order to support the smart decision making for replacing the existing machine with the new one (table 14.1).

EC—Energy Consumption, EB—Energy Bill, ME—Maintenance Expenditure.

The data for the existing machine M1 is collected by attaching an energy meter to it. The data for the new machine is provided by the manufacturer with testing of part A for one day. The comparison clearly shows that there are annual savings of Rs. 197 901 if the management decides to replace the existing machine M1 with the new machine M2. The same concept can be applied across all horizontals and verticals in any manufacturing unit. The proposed architecture will serve as a guiding template to those SMEs who are ready for the deployment of SM.

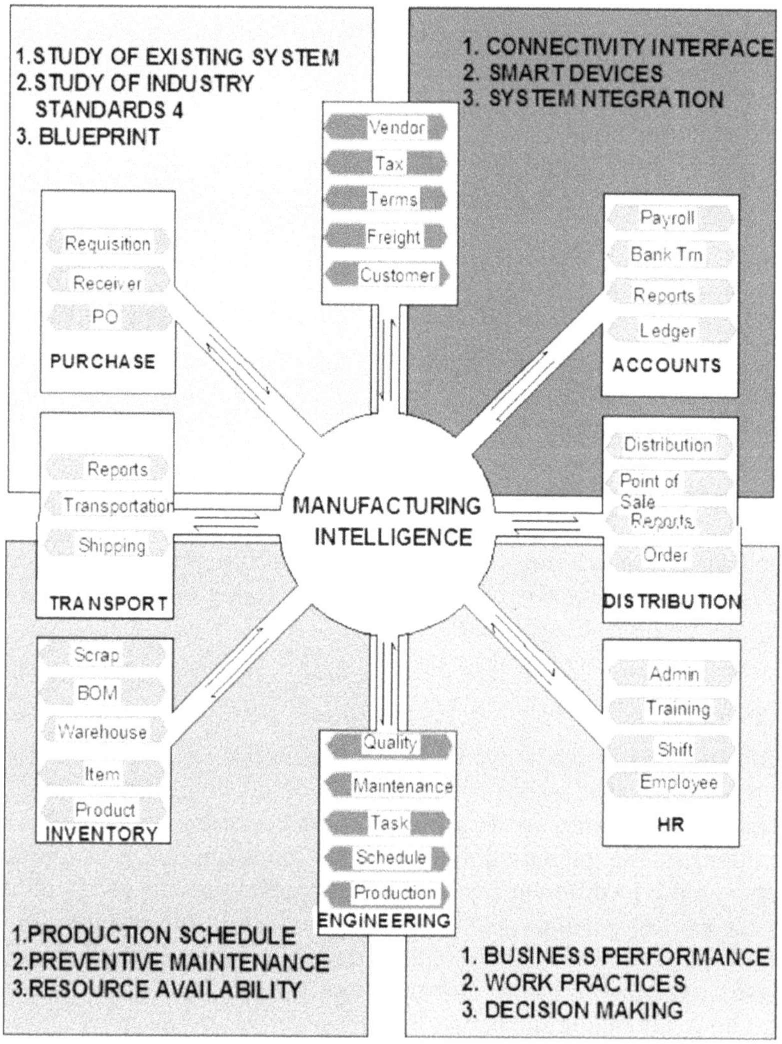

Figure 14.5. Architectural framework for an intelligent SME.

Table 14.1. EC comparison.

	200 Ton Existing Machine (M1) for Part A				200 Ton New Machine (M2) for Part A			
Month	**EC for M1**	**EB for M1**	**ME for M1**	**Total for M1**	**EC for M2**	**EB for M2**	**ME for M2**	**Total for M2**
Jan	4800	72 646	4000	76 646	3200	47 481	3000	50 481
Feb	3700	55 345	6000	61 345	3200	47 481	3000	50 481
March	4200	63 209	3500	66 709	3200	47 481	3000	50 481
April	3900	58 491	4700	63 191	3200	47 481	3000	50 481
			Total M1	267 891			**Total M2**	201 924

14.6 Conclusions and future scope

Smart decisions are based on the data collected from various functional departments of the manufacturing unit and these decisions, in turn, improve the business performance of the unit. This chapter provides insight into the means for collecting data in future-ready SM units and elaborates details of various freeware tools available for collecting and analyzing data in SMEs. An architectural framework is proposed for efficient deployment of intelligent systems in the manufacturing units, especially in SMEs. A case study was conducted in a plastic molding company for making smart decisions regarding the replacement of energy inefficient machines. The future economy of any nation is based on the network of such SM units. There is huge scope for developing simulated factories in order to provide a ready solution for the deployment of SM.

References

Bao J, Guo D, Li J and Zhang J 2018 *The modelling and operations for the digital twin in the context of manufacturing* **7575**

Coronado P D U 2018 Part data integration in the Shop Floor Digital Twin: Mobile and cloud technologies to enable a manufacturing execution system *J. Manu. Syst.* **48 Part C** 25–33

David I and Bogle L 2017 A perspective on smart process manufacturing research challenges for process systems engineers *Engineering* **3** 161–5

Dirican C 2015 The impacts of robotics, artificial intelligence on business and economics *Procedia - Soc. Behav. Sci.* **195** 564–73

Li B, Hou B, Yu W, Lu X and Yang C 2017 Applications of artificial intelligence in intelligent manufacturing: a review *Front. Inform. Technol. Electron. Eng.* **18** 86–96

May G S 2004 Intelligent SOP manufacturing *IEEE Trans. Adv. Packaging* **27** 426–37

Munguía J, Lloveras J, Llorens S and Laoui T 2009 Development of an AI-based rapid manufacturing advice system *Int. J. Prod. Res.* **48** 2261–78

Peschi M, Link N, Hoffmeister M, Goncalves G and Fenrando L F 2013 Designing and implementation of an intelligent manufacturing system *J. Indust. Eng. Manage.* **4** 718–45

Shafiq M, Yu X, Laghari A A, Yao L, Karn N K and Abdessamia F 2016 Network traffic classification techniques and comparative analysis using machine learning algorithms *2016 2nd IEEE Int. Conf. on Computer and Communications (ICCC)* 2451–5

Sethi P and Sarangi S R 2017 Internet of things: architectures, protocols, and applications *J. Elec. Comput. Eng.* **2017** 9324035

Shen W, Member S, Lang S Y T and Wang L 2005 iShopFloor: an Internet-enabled agent-based intelligent shop floor *IEEE Trans. Syst. Manage. Cybernet. C* **35** 371–81

Swan E 2008 All electric injection molding machines: how much energy can you save

Tao F, Qi Q, Liu A and Kusiak A 2018 Data-driven smart manufacturing *J. Manuf. Syst.* **48** 157–69

Wang J, Ma Y, Zhang L, Gao R X and Wu D 2018 Deep learning for smart manufacturing: methods and applications *J. Manuf. Syst.* 1–13

Watson R N M, Woodruff J, Roe M, Moore S W and Neumann P G 2018 Capability hardware enhanced RISC instructions (CHERI): notes on the Meltdown and Spectre attacks *Technical Report 916* (University of Cambridge)

Zhang Z H 2014 A comparative study of techniques for differential expression analysis on RNA-Seq data *PLoS One* **9** e103207

Zhong R Y, Xu X, Klotz E and Newman S T 2017 Intelligent manufacturing in the Context of Industry 4.0 a review *Engineering* **3** 616–30

IOP Publishing

Human-Assisted Intelligent Computing
Modeling, simulations and applications
Mukhdeep Singh Manshahia, Igor S Litvinchev, Gerhard-Wilhelm Weber, J Joshua Thomas and Pandian Vasant

Chapter 15

Performance analysis of fractal image compression methods for medical images: a review

Parijata Majumdar, Sanjoy Mitra, Sayan Kumar Das and Pallavi Majumdar

Medical imaging techniques aid clinicians in assessing clinical staging and surgical range, which is considerable. A significant number of these medical images necessitate a substantial quantity of storage space and transmission bandwidth. As a result, high-quality medical image compression is particularly research-oriented. The major goal is to study fractal image compression (FIC) algorithms to replicate the same information content in the decompressed image as the original image. The reasearchers consider a 3D image to determine spatiotemporal similarity and find range and domain blocks which are reduced in the matching pool by leveraging self-similarity, to improve the matching speed. By comparing compression reduction time factor and decompression quality assessment, a review of literature demonstrates the importance of each fractal image compression algorithm. It has also been observed how these algorithms exceed other standard techniques in terms of peak signal-to-noise ratio (PSNR), compression time, and quality to avoid information loss about lesions, that may lead to misdiagnosis.

15.1 Introduction

A large volume of data quantities when transmitted in real-time are challenging to achieve under current bandwidth conditions. It is not only necessary to increase memory capacity and transmission bandwidth, but also crucial to research how to compress medical data efficiently. As a result, an image compression technique must be used to accomplish effective size reduction of various medical images. Lossless compression and lossy compression are the two types of picture compression used in medicine. Medical diagnostics benefit from lossless compression since image data is of the same standard as the original image. The temporal and spatial correlations of

doi:10.1088/978-0-7503-4801-0ch15

medical images are extensive. The spatiotemporal correlation describes the high similarity between adjacent areas of a single pixel in a layer of an image and the pixel in a medical image slice. Because of this spatiotemporal association, medical image scans contain a lot of (local) self-similar information. Fractal image compression exploits an iterated function system (IFS) to complete data compression by replacing the image data and keeping only the self-similarity characteristics of the current image. Contractive transformations are utilized to locate an IFS utilizing fractal theorems [1]. The following theorems are used to find IFSs where the final modified picture blocks or attractors look similar to the original image after a proper union or collage:

1. Contractive mapping—according to contractive mapping, something that is naturally contractive can be retrieved by repeatedly applying subparts with the same starting point and joining them to form a single fixed point. If A: $Z \to Z$ is contractive and Z is an entire metric space, then A has a distinct fixed point $|Z|$. Where metric space has no breaks and distances are calculated by connecting any two points.
2. Theorem of collage—it is necessary for the FIC methodology to work. It states that to obtain IFS close or best comparable in a given set, to find a set of transform mappings whose union, or collage, replicates the original set. Fisher's equation uses a fixed point to express it.

$$d(z, zf) \leqslant \frac{1}{1 - s} d(z, f(z)) \tag{15.1}$$

where z is a point in Z's complete metric space, $f: Z \to Z$ is a contractive transform, and zf is Z's fixed point. A fractal can be mathematically expressed by the equation

$$w\begin{pmatrix} x \\ y \end{pmatrix} = \begin{pmatrix} ab \\ cd \end{pmatrix}\begin{pmatrix} x \\ y \end{pmatrix} + \begin{pmatrix} s \\ o \end{pmatrix} \tag{15.2}$$

where z is a point in Z's complete metric space, f: Z is a contractive transform, and zf is Z's fixed point. And, x and y are the beginning values, s and o signify relocation, and a, b, c, and d signify operations of rotation and skewing, respectively. Recursively iterating the equation produces fractals. The set $\{W\}$ is known as affine transformation, and it is represented by a set of contractive transforms given by P_n, which indicates their relative importance. The code for the IFS is shown below.

$$w_n, p_n, \text{ where, } n = 1,2,3,\ldots N \tag{15.3}$$

P_n denotes their individual importance. Equation (15.3) represents IFS code.

The basic steps of FIC are as follows: partition an image into subimages or subblocks so that the lesser number of subblocks behaves similarly to other image components when subjected to specified modifications. In a statistical manner, look for fractals or sections of images that are self-similar. Apply modifications to alter position and contrast brightness once the match has been found in the picture subparts. Finally, create an IFS that closely resembles the original image.

FIC has the advantage of storing fractal parts of images in mathematical form rather than bit maps. As a result, the original image's decompression can have high or low resolutions. When compared to JPEG, FIC can scale images without causing distortion. Because FIC relies on self-similarity, medical images having random content do not compress well. Within varied picture sizes, the randomness element of the image exhibits extremely few commonalities, thus distorting the compressed image. Because of the intensive search between image blocks, the encoding difficulty is higher than the decoding complexity, resulting in a longer compression time. To address these limitations, a comprehensive literature review was conducted in order to improve performance metrics and obtain high-quality medical images, such as computer-assisted tomography (CT), computer-assisted x-ray (CR), digital subtraction angiography (DSA), magnetic resonance imaging (MRI), and ultrasound (US), among others. The next section discusses relevant literature. Figure 15.1 shows the steps in FIC for medical images.

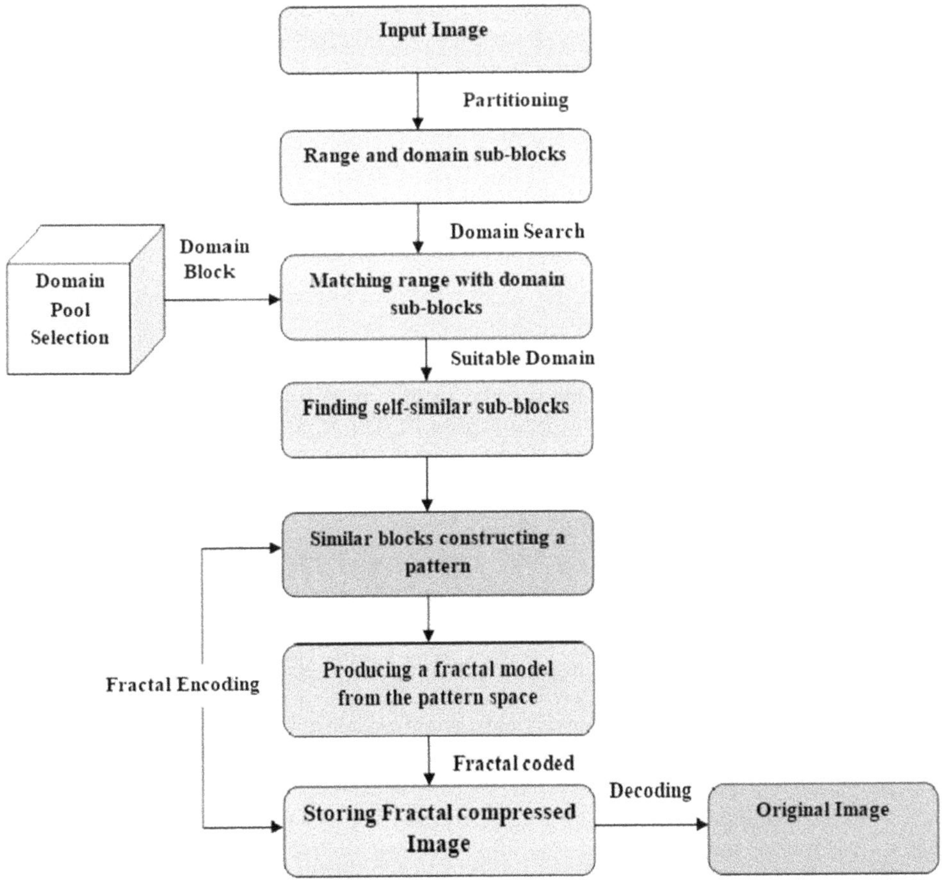

Figure 15.1. FIC process for medical image compression.

15.1.1 Self-similarity in fractals

A self-similar image is identical to or nearly identical to a section of itself. Many real-world phenomena, are statistically self-similar, meaning that parts of them exhibit the same statistical traits at several sizes. Fractals are known for their self-similarity. Scale invariance is an accurate self-similarity in which a smaller component of the thing is similar to the total at any magnification. When the numerical value of a certain observable quantity $f(x,t)$ recorded at successive times differs, but the corresponding dimensionless quantity at a given value of x/t^z is constant, a time evolving phenomena is said to exhibit self-similarity. It occurs when the quantity $f(x,t)$ is dynamically scaled. It's worth noting that two triangles are comparable if their sides have different numerical values but their associated dimensionless quantities, such as angles, are the same. According to Peitgen *et al* [3], the concept is as follows.

A figure is said to be self-similar if parts of it are miniature duplicates of the total. If a figure can be broken down into components that are precise duplicates of the whole, it is rigorously self-similar. An exact reproduction of the entire figure can be found in any random part. It is impossible to duplicate this physically because a fractal can display self-similarity under limitless magnification mathematically. Approximations are suggested by Peitgen *et al* [3], for researching self-similarity where we are forced to deal with limited approximations of the limit figure in order to give the attribute of self-similarity an operational meaning. This is accomplished via a technique known as box self-similarity, in which measurements are taken on finite stages of the image using different sizes of grids.

15.2 Motivation of the survey

With the constant demand for larger data rates and improved deployment of image processing applications, attempts for image compression with better picture metrics appear to be infinite. To address these difficulties, effective and modern solutions are required. By indicating the self-similarity found in photographs, FIC provides a potential answer to most of these challenges. The FIC approach achieves greater compression ratios, regardless of resolution, and allows for faster decoding, but it takes longer to encode. As a result, with better image compression metrics, there is room for improvement in terms of reduced compression time and reduced search complexity. Performance metrics like compression reduction time factor and decompression quality assessment are particularly important for medical images to avoid missing important information and to detect sharp edges (lesions) present in the medical image related to the patient for better diagnosis and appropriate treatment modalities.

15.3 Relevant literature

Due to its excellent compression ratio and quality preservation, FIC has emerged as one of the most promising picture encoding techniques. Its origins were in the 1990s, when Jacquin presented image compression, which divides the image into squares domain pieces [4, 5]. The designed compression principle is to find the most closely resembled domain block for a corresponding range block, calculate the justified transform of contraction, and save their data. The concept seemed intriguing, but as it has time constraints, it can only be used in household settings. Since then, experts have come up with various approaches to help minimize the lengthy encoding process. With the use of the region-growing method, integrating range blocks and making them more adaptable to image data is a solution given by Thomas and Deravi [6].

Cardinal [7] offered a similar concept based on geometrically partitioning the greyscale image block attributes space. When compared to previously published methodologies, the experimental results show a considerable increase in velocity with no degradation in the original image. One-norm of normalized block in block matching is used to reduce wasteful search as proposed by He *et al* [8]. Other studies presented novel concepts to increase search quality, such as Fourier transform encoding [9], discrete cosine transform (DCT) inner product [11], specific image features [10].

The majority of methods relied on a matching error threshold to narrow the search space. A search approach to sharp changes was shown to be effective as suggested by Lin and Wu [12].

A genetic approach to enhance the computing time of FIC while maintaining acceptable image quality is proposed by Chakrapani and Soundara Rajan [13]. The results reveal that in the instance of fractal picture compression, the genetic algorithm outperforms standard exhaustive search. A genetic algorithm based on spatial correlation with fractal having partitioned IFSs was proposed by Xing-yuan *et al* [14]. It entails using spatial correlation in pictures to leverage local optima in both the range and domain pools. If it does not satisfy the local optima, it uses simulated annealing genetic method to explore the global optima. In FIC, the particle swarm optimization (PSO) technique is used [15].

The search is made first using PSO for a closest optimal match to encode a given block. PSO demonstrates it's capability of quickly locating suitable domain blocks. When compared to the complete evaluation of FIC, the recovered image quality can be kept temporarily. Using a fitting plane, the grey-level transform is adjusted by Wang *et al* [16].

Improved grey-level transforms can lower the minimum resembling error between a range and its corresponding domain, increasing the scope of domain-range matching. A new fractal image reduction method that combines wavelet transforming and diamond searching for quick positioning is suggested [17].

The technique just needs to evaluate the domain blocks in the specified position surrounding the range, according to the search pattern and path of diamond. Bio-inspired heuristics are founded on the notion of communities of individuals that communicate and generate a common pattern, as seen in animal social behaviour such as bird swarms, ant colonies, and fish aggregation. Such methods appear to be a well-known paradigm that has been effectively employed as a potent tool for addressing complicated combinatorial problems with reasonable resource consumption [18].

Wolfpack algorithm (WPA) [19] is an algorithm which follows bio-inspired heuristics that can be used for optimization issues. WPA is a population-oriented where wolves' performs social hunting behaviour. It entails training wolves to hunt, finding prey, and the prey gets caught under the supervision of a main wolf. It is led by a wolf who is considered the most powerful and the most intelligent of all. It assumes command of all the wolves. The chief wolf makes decisions influenced by the surrounding situation, which includes prey, pack wolves, and other predators. The wolves in the pack are separated into two groups: calm and furious. The first class wanders through the surroundings on its own and regulates its path based on the *s* smell of the prey. When a prey is tracked, the wolves belonging to this clan cry and use sound to communicate the information to the leader, who evaluates the distance spatially, summons the furious wolves, and travels speedily toward the loud crying. Subsequent capturing of the prey is done and delivered to others in order of strength. Feeble wolves may die in future due to a shortage of food. This is how the pack maintains its dynamic and strong nature at all times. First, 3D MRI scans are turned into a 2D image sequence, compressed using the fractal compression approach to make the image sequence easier to read. Then, based on the underlying spatiotemporal similarity of 3D objects, range and domain are classified. Reduction in number of blocks in matching pool is done by leveraging self-similarity, which improves the suggested method's matching speed. Finally, a residual compensation mechanism is used to accomplish high-quality decompression of MRI images [20]. Other significant literature was also studied.

Table 15.1 shows the contribution, merits and demerits identified for different FIC algorithms.

Table 15.2 describes improved performance metrics of different FICs.

Table 15.1. Review of different FIC techniques.

Author	Algorithm used	Advantages	Disadvantages
Biswas *et al* 2020 [21]	Fractal dimension based on quadtree partition.	PSNR, compression ratio, and less encoding time.	Need for fractal encoding based on fractal dimension using quadtree to achieve better compression.
Magar *et al* 2019 [22]	Oscillation concept and quasi fractal compression.	Acceptable PSNR and compression ratio.	Limited user interface.
Menassel *et al* 2017 [23]	FIC using WPA.	Fast convergence and reducing of complexity.	It has to be more robust to design complex problems.
Padmashree *et al* 2015 [24]	Embedded block coding optimization truncation encoding (EBCOT).	Better PSNR is achieved along with high compression ratio.	It should be made more robust by implementing it on bigger image sizes.
Khalili *et al* 2013 [25]	Quadtree FIC.	Greater range reduces calculation time while maintaining quality.	Exploited partitioning scheme blocky output causes decompressed image.

Bulkunde *et al* 2019 [26]	FIC.	High compression, low encoding and decoding time.	It has to be more robust to design complex problems.
Biswas *et al* 2015 [27]	Fractal dimension to reduce complexity and fuzzy logic for processing.	Decreased encoding time, and increased compression ratio.	Best domain block to find the best matching while lessening computation is needed.
Yang shou-yi *et al* 2002 [28]	Quadtree partition multi-threshold FIC algorithm	Better decoding quality less compression time, high compression ratio.	Need to improve the quality using affine transformation.
Shuai liu *et al* 2019 [29]	Compression using spatiotemporal similarity.	Fast compression, better quality.	Need to incorporate statistical test using new features.
Rahman *et al* 2020 [30]	FIC using sum of absolute difference (SAD) correlation coefficient.	Good quality output and fast retrieving time.	Need to improve accuracy.
Devadoss *et al* 2019 [31]	Burrows–Wheeler transform (BWT) and Huffman encoding using MTF.	Good compression capability, and space saving.	Long execution time.
Panjavarnam *et al* 2017 [32]	Quadtree decomposition and contractive affine transformation.	Higher compression ratio, low transmission bandwidth.	Low quality compared to set partitioning in hierarchical trees (SPIHT) compression.

15.4 Comparative survey results and discussion

It is seen from figure 15.2 that WPA followed by FIC using spatiotemporal similarity obtains better compression ratio, whereas oscillation concept and quasi-fractals obtain least compression ratio.

It is seen from figure 15.3 that WPA followed by FIC using spatiotemporal similarity requires comparatively less encoding time, whereas fractal dimension for quadtree partition requires high encoding time.

It is seen from figure 15.4 that the fractal dimension for quadtree partition followed by FIC using BWT and move to front (MTF) with hybrid fractal encoding obtains higher PSNR values, whereas quadtree partition using multi-threshold FIC obtains lower PSNR values comparatively.

15.5 Improvements on existing algorithms

WPA suffers from slow convergence and a proclivity for sliding into local optimum. In [33], opposition-based learning is used to retain the initial population's diversity

Table 15.2. Improved performance metrics of different FIC techniques.

Author	Contribution	Improved performance metrics
Biswas *et al* 2020 [19]	Comparative analysis for grayscale medical images using fixed partition of quadtree.	Average PSNR is 37.64 dB and encoding time is 39.01 s
Magar *et al* 2019 [20]	PSNR is lowered using adaptive thresholding and morphological band pass filter.	Compression ratio is 24.61, PSNR is 33.51 dB.
Menassel *et al* 2017 [21]	Reduced encoding time of lengthy data and obtained better compression ratio.	Compression ratio is 1.655. Encoding time is 2.04.
Padmashree *et al* 2015 [22]	Comparative analysis of EBCOT and quadtree partitioning without EBCOT.	Compression ratio is 19.9. PSNR is 28 dB.
Khalili *et al* 2013 [23]	Computing costs is reduced with improved compression accuracy, with different range sizes assigned to a particular segment.	Compression ratio is 5.3 (chest x-ray) 5.9 (head x-ray). NMSE is 8.6e−3% (chest x-ray) 1.03e−2% (head x-ray).
Bulkunde *et al* 2019 [24]	Consecutive and parallel adaptation of fractal image pressure calculations.	Lossless and high compression.
Biswas *et al* 2015 [25]	Fractal dimension and fuzzy logic are used for different medical image texture analysis.	Encoding time is 13.59, and PSNR is 34.77.
Yang shou-yi *et al* 2002 [26]	Image compression method based on regions of interest.	PSNR is 18.73, compression and encoding time are 21.21, 9.91.
Shuai liu *et al* 2019 [27]	Increased compression speed and PSNR values.	Compression ratio is 4.79, PSNR is 26.68.
Rahman *et al* 2020 [28]	Radiography medical image compression.	PSNR is 27.48, compression time is 4.51, compression ratio is 15.96.
Devadoss *et al* 2019 [29]	Ultrasound and MRI medical FIC.	For USG and MRI images having average value of 36.166 dB and 34.097 dB. Space saving is 84.18%.
Panjavarnam *et al* 2017 [30]	Comparative analysis of FIC and SPIHT using compression ratio and quality of image.	PSNR values varying from 29 dB. Encoding time is 15 s.

during the global search. Meanwhile, to avoid slipping into a local optimum, genetic algorithm is used to select the leader wolf, and Levy's flight optimizes the round-up behavior to synchronize global exploration and local development capabilities. In [34], it is possible to generalize the pixel intensity approximation and construct significantly better approximations. Here, a fractal-based image compression

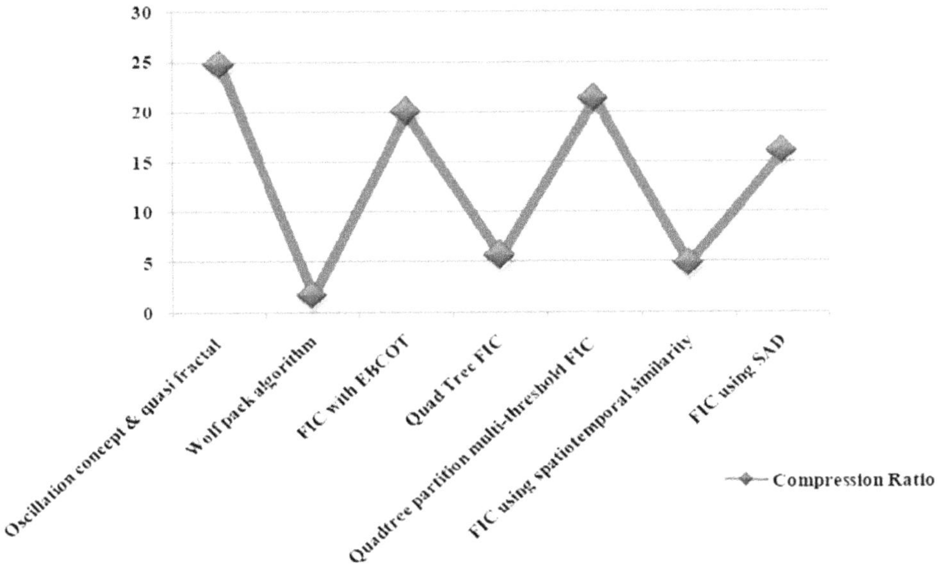

Figure 15.2. Evaluation of compression ratios of different FIC techniques.

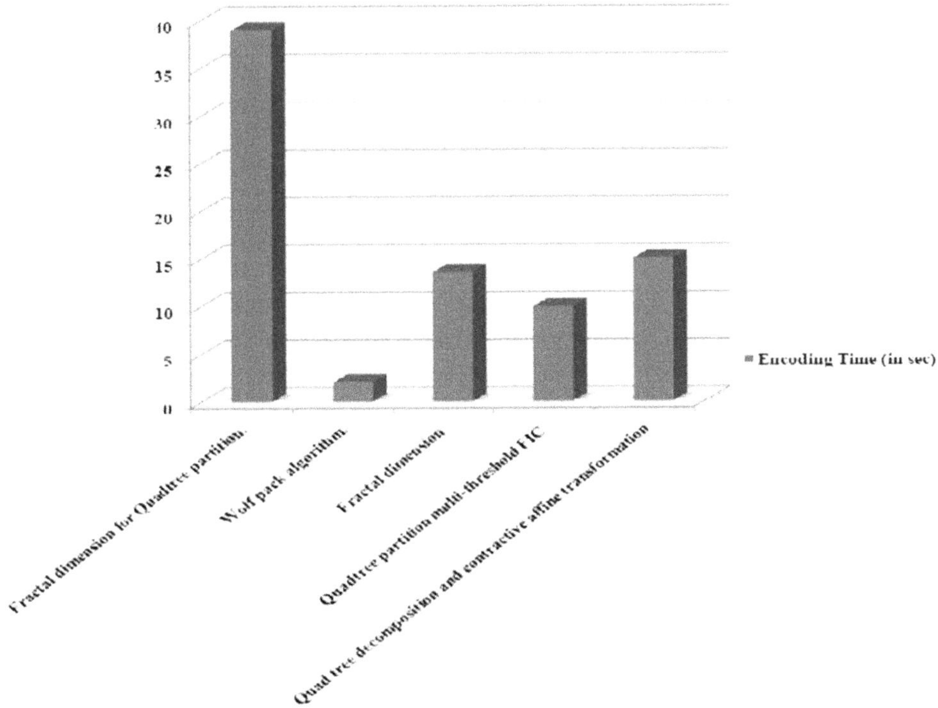

Figure 15.3. Evaluation of encoding time of different FIC algorithms.

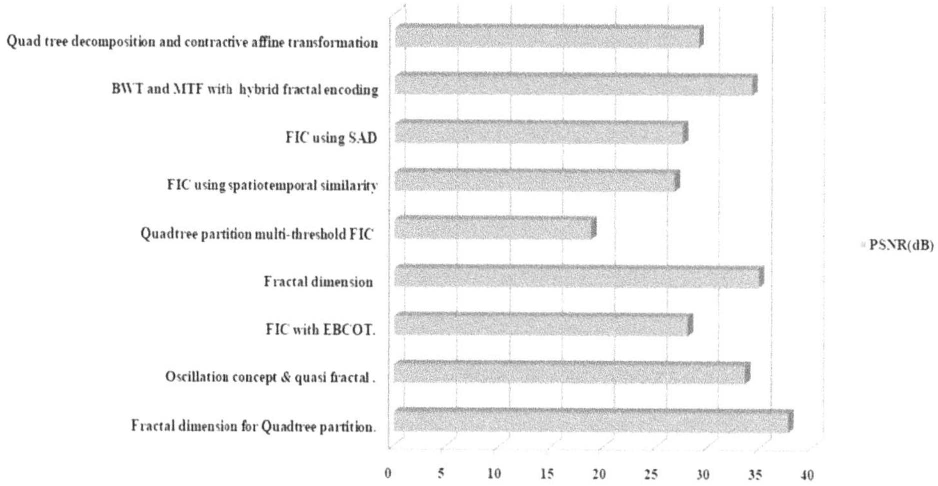

Figure 15.4. Evaluation of PSNR values of different FIC algorithms.

technique based on nonlinear contractive affine maps is described, which uses adaptive quadtree partitioning to split images in a context-dependent manner to improve decoded image quality. The technique divides the image to be compressed twice to generate a collection of ranges and domains, then determines the nonlinear affine converted domain of each range that matches the highest. The compressed file also includes the affine parameters. In the event that there are not enough matching domains, a range can be divided into subranges via adaptive quadtree partitioning, and the process repeated. This process ensures better image decoding and maintains high compression ratios. In [35], multi-population parallel WPA is used which divides the wolf population into numerous sub-populations that optimize separately at the same time, reducing the size of the wolf population. Using a rough estimate, the population is divided into a number of equal mass sub-populations using the average division method. A sub-population of better candidates is considered elite. The distribution of the elite-mass population can be seen through the elite-mass population distribution. The elite sub-population and mass sub-populations both optimize those who are better. It has the potential to hasten convergence. Population diversity must be preserved in order to maintain population diversity. It is suggested that pretreatment be used. Sub-populations migrate using a fixed migration probability and re-dividing the confluent population is equal to the migration of sub-populations.

15.6 Conclusion and future work

A large amount of 3D medical data, such as three-dimensional ultrasound, CT, and MRI, is generated due to the rapid growth of medical imaging technologies. The huge size of 3D medical images causes significant network traffic loading and communication expenses during diagnosis and treatment. Medical image compression decreases the quantity of data sent. After that, compressed data is loaded and transferred. It not only saves memory need, but also maximizes communication performance and reduces remote diagnosis communication and ensures timely delivery of important information. Raising the compression ratio and preserving vital information in medical images are two benefits of increasing the compression ratio. Therefore, to get better quality medical images, different FIC techniques are explored in this chapter that maximize PSNR, and increase compression ratio while preserving quality of medical images for early and accurate disease detection. Comparative analysis is drawn based on PSNR values, encoding time and compression ratio to ascertain better performing techniques in a specific scenario. In future, based on the survey results obtained, encoding time needs to be reduced while outperforming other compression algorithms in terms of the rest of the performance metrics.

References

[1] Fisher Y 1994 Fractal image compression with quadtrees *Fractal Image Compression: Theory and Applications to Digital Images* (New York: Springer)

[2] Hassan M K, Hassan M Z and Pavel N I 2011 Dynamic scaling, data-collapse and self-similarity in Barabási–Albert networks *J. Phys. A: Math. Theor.* **44** 175101

[3] Peitgen H O, Jürgens H, Saupe D, Maletsky E, Perciante T and Yunker L 2013 *Fractals for the Classroom: Strategic Activities, Volume Two* (Berlin: Springer Science & Business Media)

[4] Jacquin A E 1992 Image coding based on a fractal theory of iterated contractive image transformations *IEEE Trans. Image Process.* **1** 18–30

[5] Jacquin A E 1993 Fractal image coding: a review *Proc. of IEEE* **81** 1451–65

[6] Thomas L and Deravi F 1995 Region-based fractal image compression using heuristic search *IEEE Trans. Image Process.* **4** 832–8

[7] Cardinal J 2001 Fast fractal compression of greyscale images *IEEE Trans. Image Process.* **10** 159–64

[8] He C, Xu X and Yang J 2006 Fast fractal image encoding using one-norm of normalized block *Chaos Solitons Fractals* **27** 1178–86

[9] Hartenstein H and Saupe D 2000 Lossless acceleration of fractal image encoding via the fast Fourier transform *Signal Process. Image Commun.* **16** 383–94

[10] Zhang C, Zhou Y and Zhang Z 2007 Fast fractal image encoding based on special image features *Tsinghua Sci. Technol.* **12** 58–62

[11] Truong T K, Jeng J H and Reed I S *et al* 2000 A fast encoding algorithm for fractal image compression using the DCT inner product *IEEE Trans. Image Process.* **9** 529–35

[12] Lin Y L and Wu M S 2011 An edge property-based neighborhood region search strategy for fractal image compression *Comput. Math. Appl.* **62** 310–8

[13] Chakrapani Y and Soundararajan K 2009 Genetic algorithm applied to fractal image compression *ARPN J. Eng. Applic. Sci.* **4** 53–8

[14] Xing-yuan W, Fan-ping L and Shu-guo W 2009 Fractal image compression based on spatial correlation and hybrid genetic algorithm *J. Visual Commun. Image Represent.* **20** 505–10

[15] Chakrapani Y and Soundararajan K 2010 Implementation of fractal image compression employing particle swarm optimization *World J. Model. Simul.* **6** 40–6

[16] Wang X-Y, Zhang D-D and Wei N 2015 Fractal image coding algorithm using particle swarm optimization and hybrid quadtree partition scheme *IET Image Proc.* **9** 153–61

[17] Wang Y X and Yun J J 2010 An improved no-search fractal image coding method based on a fitting plane *Image Vision Comput.* **28** 1303–8
[18] Zhang Y and Wang X Y 2012 Fractal compression coding based on wavelet transform with diamond search *J. Nonlin. Anal.-B: Real World Applic.* **13** 106–12
[19] Gandomi A H and Alavi A H 2011 Multi-stage genetic programming: a new strategy to nonlinear system modeling *Inform. Sci. (NY)* **181** 5227–39
[20] Wu H S and Zhang F M 2014 Wolf pack algorithm for unconstrained global optimization *Math. Probl.Eng.* **2014** 465082
[21] Liu S, Bai W, Zeng N and Wang S 2019 A fast fractal based compression for MRI images *IEEE Access* **7** 62412–20
[22] Biswas A K, Karmakar S and Sharma S 2021 Performance analysis of a new fractal compression method for medical images based on fixed partition *Int. J. Inf. Technol.* **14** 411–9
[23] Magar S S and Sridharan B 2019 Hybrid image compression technique using oscillation concept & quasi fractal *Health Technol.* **10** 313–20
[24] Menassel R, Nini B and Mekhaznia T 2018 An improved fractal image compression using wolf pack algorithm *J. Exp. Theor. Artif. Intell.* **30** 429–39
[25] Padmashree S and Nagapadma R 2015 Statistical analysis of objective measures using fractal image compression for medical images *IEEE Int. Conf. on Signal and Image Processing Applications (ICSIPA)*, 563–8
[26] Khalili F, Celenk M and Akinlar M 2013 A Medical image compression using quad-tree fractals and segmentation *Proc. of the Int. Conf. on Image Processing, Computer Vision, and Pattern Recognition (IPCV)* The Steering Committee of The World Congress in Computer Science, Computer Engineering and Applied Computing (WorldComp) 1
[27] Bulkunde M V V, Bodne M N P and Kumar S 2019 Implementation of fractal image compression on medical images by different approach *Int. J. Trend Sci. Res. Dev.* **3** 398–400
[28] Biswas A K, Karmakar S, Sharma S and Kowar M K 2015 Performance of fractal image compression for medical images: a comprehensive literature review *Int. J. Appl. Inform. Syst. (IJAIS)* **8** 14–24
[29] Shou-Yi Y and Luo W X 2002 Multithreshold fractal image compression of medical images based on regions of interest *Second Int. Conf. on Image and Graphics* 4875 55–60
[30] Rahman N A Z, Ismail R C, Shapri A H M and Isa M N 2020 Enhancing fractal image compression speed using peer adjacent mapping with sum of absolute difference for computed radiography images *AIP Conf. Proc.* 2203 020011
[31] Devadoss C P and Sankaragomathi B 2019 Near lossless medical image compression using block BWT–MTF and hybrid fractal compression techniques *Cluster Computing* **22** 12929–37
[32] Panjavamam B and Bhuvaneswari P T V 2017 Suitability analysis of fractal compression technique for medical image *IEEE Ninth Int. Conf. on Advanced Computing (ICoAC)* 127–33
[33] Chen X, Cheng F, Liu C, Cheng L and Mao Y 2021 An improved wolf pack algorithm for optimization problems: design and evaluation *PLoS One. 16* **8** e0254239
[34] Nandi U 2020 Fractal image compression with adaptive quadtree partitioning and non-linear affine map *Multimedia Tools Appl.* **79** 26345–68
[35] Lu Y, Ma Y and Wang J Multi-population parallel Wolf Pack algorithm for task assignment of UAV swarm *Appl. Sci.* **11** 11996

IOP Publishing

Human-Assisted Intelligent Computing
Modeling, simulations and applications
Mukhdeep Singh Manshahia, Igor S Litvinchev, Gerhard-Wilhelm Weber, J Joshua Thomas and Pandian Vasant

Chapter 16

Mobile edge computing for efficient energy management systems

Padmanayaki Selvarajan, Betty Elezebeth Samuel, Krishnamoorthy Ranganathan, Arvind Kumar Shukla, M Amina Begum and Sundaram Arun

Due to the growth of various devices which are connected and work along with the internet, the Internet of Things (IoT) has emerged. These applications involve numerous factors that need to be addressed for generalizing more sophisticated systems. The major two factors are latency and efficiency of energy or lifetime of device which need to be taken as primary considerations. Hence as a solution, the edge computing environment provides an optimal solution and it is been integrated with other techniques such as networks and other computing paradigms. Initially, the system needs to be standardized using the most common strategy called cloud computing. But the complexity of the technique is very high such that it has to be maintained and integrated in a timely manner and should be monitored. Thus edge computing will be considered as the next step in developing applications in the IoT environment to maintain the benefits. Utilization of energy can be understood efficiently in this chapter for how it influences devices. There are overheads that occur in computation at the edges and each of the edge nodes will directly or indirectly influence the battery life, that is, energy consumption which is maintained by batteries. Apart from the regular constraints, edge computing needs to focus on privacy and data reduction methods, which is then compared with other computational systems. The chapter further addresses the future challenges to be considered in this particular area which could give rise to future research.

16.1 Introduction

Computing includes a variety of formulation of things that are emerging in all different fields. When considering the term mobile edge computing (MEC) it is essential in resolving application and computation problems by enabling users to have feasibility of storage and computational facilities [1]. Due to numerous conditions, the cloud is not that capable of providing the requirements and this might be due to various reasons such as latency, mobility support etc. Hence in accordance with these issues it has given rise to other ways of computing such as fog, mobile edge computing and mobile cloud computing. The concept of mobile edge computing is emerging in multi-dimensional aspects in terms of research. But the challenging fact is that no specific exploration is carried out in terms of security, and that paves way for researchers to enable this under different categories. Previously we had noticed that the cloud was the only source of computing platform. The focus was towards the concepts of centralization, storage and management of resources that can be connected with multiple places by multiple users [2]. This reflects networks like cellular and refers to different centers of data from where data is collected. The enormous amount of data and resources available in the cloud specifies the development of various computational techniques, thereby enabling end-user devices. This can be justified by different case studies; in the current scenario if we consider the most profitable cloud then we can quote Amazon, which has greater demand and is highly dependable. But due to many developments, the change is from cloud functioning towards edge computing in networks. In a rough estimation, it is said that more than 10 billions edges will be developed and utilized in the future, which will increase the speed of processing. This chapter includes firstly an understanding of the concepts of mobile edge computing holistically, and then finding out the security challenges, threats and other related features related to this.

Concerning the increase of IoT and mobile internet, there are a variety of emerging applications and techniques. Although these many applications are evolving, they are still not high in terms of performance [3, 4]. An application consistent in one field is said to be different in others, for example, recognition, healthcare and augmented reality. Developing applications and deploying them locally is highly difficult and we need to check for quality, which can be taken from users and usage of resources. The above-stated facts make the concept of MEC a suitable solution for the problems. To exploit this advantage the applications developed through MEC help the applications by enabling operations to take place at nodes that are present at the edge of the network. This helps in reducing the consumption of energy and latency thereby bringing nodes closer to the device-based applications [5]. Various research has progressed by creating multiple mobile edge computing models with different tier architectures. The single side model is developed by consumption of data at a rapid rate, thereby enabling binary computations. The model comprises an offloading mechanism which will be helpful in doing the process as a whole task application and will split and deploy on a task basis. Due to the functionality of this model, the partial way of executing and offloading was introduced as shown in figure 16.1.

The task allocated will be divided and one of the tasks will be deployed and loaded, which will reduce the consumption of energy. The urging of different tasks that happen at edge nodes will be computed in the way of minimizing the consumption of energy and also in terms of latency [6, 7]. Various other models such as Lyapunov optimization-based dynamic computations also fall under this

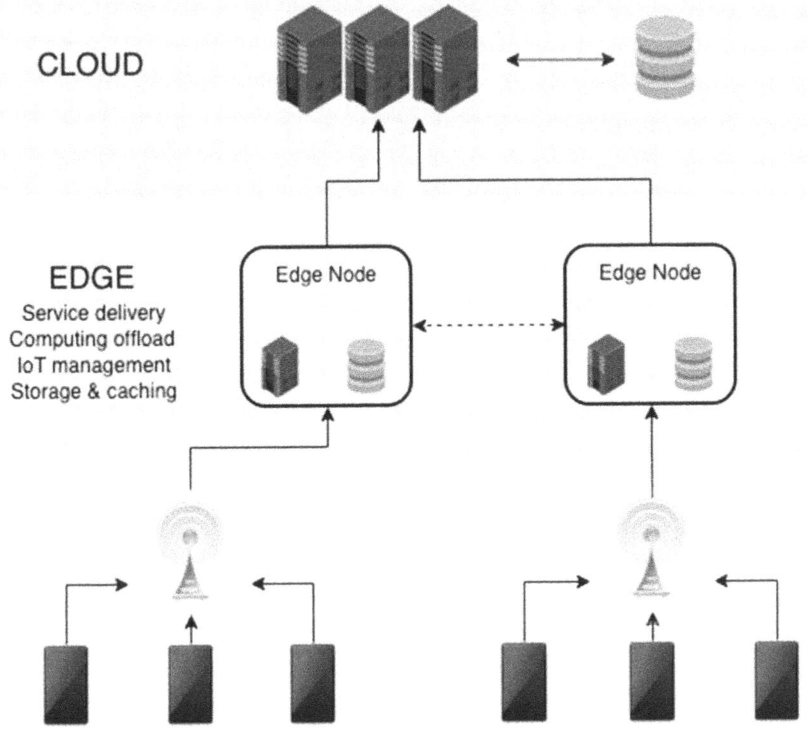

Figure 16.1. Overall concept of mobile edge computing.

category. When compared to the single side model we consider the multiserver models, the advantages and execution of tasks along with energy consumption differ. For the model comprised of multiusers, the offloading mechanism should be of multiusers through which the tasks can be carried out. Apart from these things the consumption of energy and other executions of tasks are carried out by a proper allocation mechanism. The reduction of executing the same task again and again repeatedly will also consume energy and resources which can be minimized by utilizing the base station resources. Introduction of user experience and quality made through wireless power was included in the multiserver model, providing a particular aim to minimize energy use.

Apart from these basic mechanisms, edge cloud architectures started with a rapid development and were differentiated into flat edge and hierarchical edge architectures [8, 9]. In the various-leveled edge cloud designs, MEC servers are situated at various levels. What's more, MEC servers in various levels have particular calculation and capacity abilities. For level edge cloud engineering, topography data of smart mobile devices (SMDs) and MEC servers was utilized to decrease the assignment execution delays. Considering boosting the income of specialist organizations, assets from various specialist co-ops were unified to make an asset pool and the income was designated by utilizing center and Shapley esteems. To limit the correspondence idleness, a cloudlet determination model dependent on a blended number of straight writing computer programs was created. Besides, by using the inactive processing assets of vehicles, a decentralized system named autonomous vehicular edge was created to build the computational capacities of vehicles. For progressive edge cloud engineering, a three-level MEC model was based on an long-term evolution (LTE)-progressed versatile backhaul network. For working on the expense proficiency of organization administrators, one should consider the expense difference of the edge levels.

Under a three-level MEC model, the Stackelberg game was utilized to distribute the restricted processing assets of edge cuts to the information administration endorsers. Joined with heterogeneous organizations, a various-leveled MEC was additionally contemplated. The little base station (SBS) and large-scale base station (MBS) are furnished with MEC servers to serve SMDs. Especially, offloading choices and radio assets were advanced together for limiting the framework energy cost. Then, at that point, the structure was grown further. SBSs were enriched with registering abilities. What's more, an asset allotment issue for limiting the energy utilization of portable clients and MEC waiters was designed. In light of the heterogeneous organization fueled by mixture energy, client affiliation and asset designation were upgraded for boosting the organization utility. Thinking about the inconsistency of cell phones' abilities and client inclinations, offloading choices and asset portions were enhanced for augmenting framework utility. Also, an original data driven heterogeneous organization system was planned and a virtual asset portion issue was detailed.

The chapter is organized as follows. Section 16.2 focuses on the paradigm of edge computing which provides an overview on centralized architecture and decentralized architecture in the perspective of mobile edge computing, data dealing with difficulties, edge example, edge or cloud, benefits, skills required for edges, edge enabler and model. Section 16.3 describes the role of factors in the energy consumption model. Section 16.4 provides the importance of energy efficient systems integration. Section 16.5 focuses on research findings and limitations, and section 16.6 discusses future research challenges in the healthcare domain, big data management, privacy of data and integrated applications. Finally, the chapter concludes with section 16.7 summarizing the essence of the chapter, presenting the conclusion and future work.

16.2 Paradigm of edge computing

Data processing in edge systems are moved towards the edges of a network in a closer fashion which takes the time of response between devices to a faster rate, thereby increasing the efficiency of energy, as opposed to transmitting the information to the cloud each time, increasing the cost of energy, and each time data has to be mined and processed between the server and edge devices. Hence data handled by edge devices enables the latency to be at lower rate allowing response on time. Despite its advantages, it is still challenging to process a large amount of data as it is sent to and from the cloud, which deals with security and privacy issues. By using edge nodes in a network, privacy can be sustained and easy usability can be implemented. This also will result in accurate transmissions as each time the communication is recorded [10].

The beginning phase of IoT arrangements depended on restrictive applications settling explicit errands they were intended for. Be that as it may, these arrangements could not associate with one another as the assumptions for a framework developed over the long run, which finally led to the prerequisite of more unique methodologies. Thus, the pattern has moved from explicitly situated tight-coupled applications to more open and inexactly coupled IoT joining stages [11, 12]. The main influx of IoT stages has been driven by the distributed computing WorldView with the trademark element of putting the entire rationale in the cloud. Amazon Web Services1, Microsoft Azure2, and Bluemix3 are just a few instances of famous cloud stages that have made their mark. While the unified engineering of these stages is basic and clear, it additionally implies the need of uploading all information to the actual cloud prior to settling on any choice cycle, in the long run prompting overheads. A superior methodology might be to move a piece of the dynamic abilities from the cloud to the edge of the organization, for example to a passage or even to end hubs themselves. The circulation of rationale can significantly decrease the volume of moved information, further developing the organization traffic and bringing down the necessities for cloud administrations, as shown in figure 16.2. The following flood of IoT stages will be driven by the edge registering WorldView, empowering constant investigation and independent direction. Be that as it may, the decentralized engineering additionally builds the intricacy of the executive's interaction, provoking an exorbitant interest for the proficient design plan [13].

Therefore, there is a compromise between the underlying intricacy and the acquired advantages. While concentrated engineering enjoys a benefit in simple set-up and execution, a decentralized design can offer more proficient correspondence, as shown in figure 16.3. There are trademark elements to facilitate the determination interaction of the right design for an IoT stage in a specific climate [14, 15]. At the point when we need to associate a lower number of gadgets with less regular sending rates, the organization network is solid, cloud assets are not limited, and the reaction rate can be in many ms, a basic and direct concentrated design

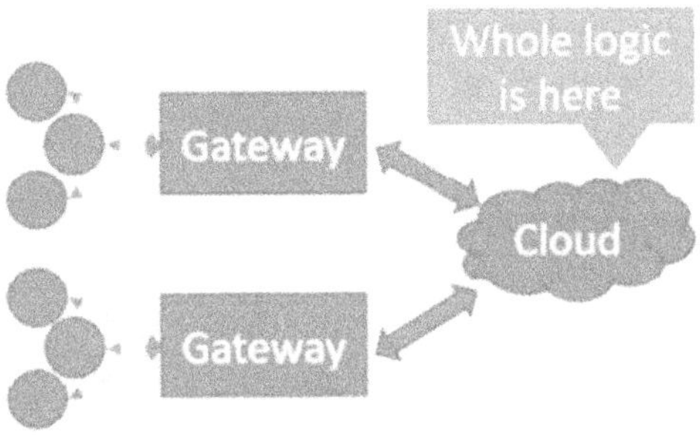

Figure 16.2. Centralized architecture.

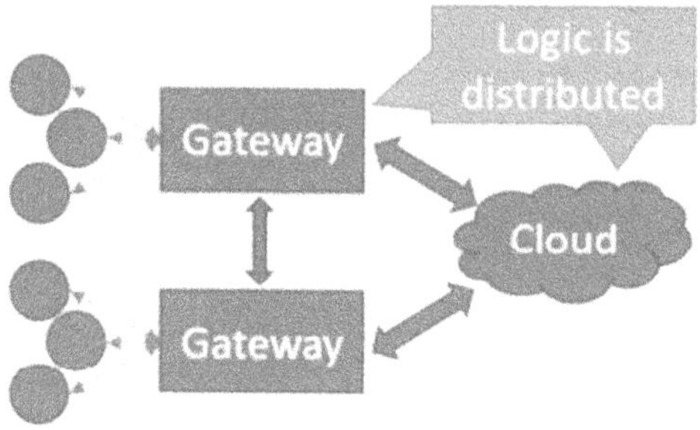

Figure 16.3. Decentralized architecture.

might be a reasonable decision. Unexpectedly, in circumstances where we really want to productively use the accessible organization and cloud assets, and the reaction is needed in many ms, a decentralized design with calculation at the edge will be ideal. All things considered, these two methodologies do not reject one another. Indeed, an entire arrangement can be the blend of the two of them. As the intricacy of IoT arrangements rises, we can expect various administrations utilizing diverse rationale dissemination to accomplish the ideal objective. Real execution will be a utilization case ward and IoT stages ought to be adequately dynamic to adjust to these changing necessities as needs be.

To summarize the examination, the edge-featuring WorldView can bring a few benefits, for example, network traffic decrease, quicker reaction rate, lower necessities of organization association of unwavering quality, more proficient usage of cloud administrations, and so forth. The underlying intricacy of arrangements dependent on edge design is higher, however, the acquired advantages will in the end take care of the contributed exertion [16, 17]. Until now, we portrayed edge design just from an entirety framework perspective. Notwithstanding, consider one more viewpoint—what the edge registering means for IoT gadgets themselves. End gadgets in IoT networks are directed commonly. The registering abilities are low, and the energy assets can be restricted. In particular, application regions with troublesome availability to IoT gadgets are extremely intense on the life expectancy of gadgets, since supplanting them may not be a simple task. At the factor while we examine the layout each one of the facts this is made through matters are dispatched straightforwardly to the cloud and dealing with it will start from right here. Sending the facts to the cloud will be examined through dissecting it and making bits of knowledge to be viewed continuously [18]. The data challenge: for example, a connected automobile can create 4 TB of facts every day as every automobile has in excess of 200 sensors. Likewise, weather facts may be as much as 5 PB/day, aircraft will generate 2.5 TB/Day of facts that are added through personal cloud or 1/2 of cloud.

(a) ***Data dealing with difficulties:***

1. Discontinuous affiliation is a problem.
2. Insufficient records switching capability is a further problem if matters are distant.

3. Terabytes of data. Information will not be dispatched to customers on schedule and data can be lost.
4. Security and consistency also are issues. The placement right here is shipped or disbursed in the processing of facet/fog computing. In comparison to preceding fashions, complicated data arrives immediately from the cloud. We are presently sending the chosen facts to the cloud. The link is a prepared device already linked to the web. The route method determines the complex data and then determines the quantity of data it desires to ship from the cloud and the quantity of data it is able to process locally [19, 20]. Transition hubs include haze hubs and facet hubs. This is how data processing is initiated through the edge hub itself, some data is finished through edge, some through Nebel, and the rest is retrieved from the cloud. In a given diagram, edge collects all of the data from devices, edge takes over the fundamental elements throughout the operation, and then takes over the fog that can be in enterprise manipulate increase. For Ex-Fog, that can be your organization's migration center. Whatever data is processed idle, you could devote it to the cloud, and what you want to keep permanently is saved within the cloud. In edge, critical insights are streamed locally and the area is constrained, so now no longer may all the recorded data be saved. The subsequent layer is the cloud that can switch all data processed idle to the cloud [21, 22]. You can ship permanent data to the cloud. Haze and edges are not that difficult a task. The edges are topographically visible, very near objects, and the rims are nearly out of stock, making them the maximum critical node for critical information to pass through. Edges can preserve data for a finite number of days, so edges can enjoy this constrained data.

(b) ***Edge example:***

- Primary facet device.
- Power grid, mobile network power matrix has its very own strength distribution organization. There are diverse factors of presence hubs that businesses screen from the cloud to data sources.
- They may be used as fog/edges. Brilliant city—all acquainted programs are topographically dispersed.
- Industrial plants, oil rigs, ships, planes. These are overseen through neighborhood businesses and no longer have instantaneous right of entry to the transition organization's hub locally.

(c) ***Edge or cloud:***
The facet isn't a substitute for the cloud. To put together an AI application, we want a package deal of recorded data, which makes the cloud a key factor of data, so edge no longer updates the cloud and is a dependable complement.

(d) ***Benefits***

- Converts huge data into greater conservative data.
- The narrowest wide variety is used.
- Processes data very near the edge.
- The idle velocity is slow.
- Information remains on the supply and optimum flows.
- Investment choices are needed.

(e) ***Skills required for edges:***

- Compactness—devices that carry out facet registration are available in a whole lot of sizes.
- Edge devices are robust in extreme environmental conditions (impact, vibration, excessive ambient temperature, pressure, etc).
- Security is a chief problem given the great geography of IoT devices.
- Remote organization, monitoring, and manipulation are required due to the fact that more gadgets are communicating remotely and need to be shipped or updated in a coordinated manner.
- Modularity for clean substitute and overhaul of the subsystem.

(f) ***Edge enabler:***

To meet the brink requirements, a smaller, excellent interconnect association is required. Some of them are processors and accelerators; there are diverse processing gadgets. Some of the fashions are examples. Atom16 calls for low strength and excessive procedure. Xeon E5 is a device that calls for excessive overall performance and has a huge wide variety of registrations. Accelerator pedal: computational strength cannot be included through the processor alone [23, 24].

(g) ***Model:***

1) FPGA-field programmable gate array:
    - Reprogrammable for the newest subjects from ever-converting improvements and movement plans.
    - Up to 1500 GFLOP, even much less energy consumption.
    - Intel self-driving car, used at level.
    - Supports execution of neural tissue for Bing and Baidu searches.
2) ASIC-Google's tensor processing unit (TPU)
    - A low-overall performance, 15× to several× quicker neural organization.
    - 15 new server farm Google price savings.
    - Expensive, very long lasting and now no longer programmable.
    - Google and Facebook want to have AI chips on gadgets close to their houses.

16.3 Role of factors in energy consumption

Consumption of energy is becoming such an important field that so many have started researching in that area. Devices are employed in conditions where there are so many constraints that tend to arrive in which optimization is the main concrn [25]. Mostly we come across various IoT devices which are driven by batteries and are inaccessible. Extending battery life seems to be very challenging and difficult to implement. So the implementation of this feature is crucial. But when taking into account wireless sensor networks, the communication medium paves a major way in implementation of concepts of IoT that have provided various concepts of conservation of energy in previous researches. The architecture has proved that various techniques such as algorithms can be used to retain energy that helps in providing better performance in terms of energy. Apart from offering wireless concepts there are many ways in MEC to make this possible. In implementation of IoT it provides a way that makes the architecture dynamic, which will be suitable in making devices move on to sleep state when not in use [26, 27]. This mode can be implemented by taking into consideration various parameters like offloading, conflict factor, variation coefficient, information quality and existing power of battery. Apart from this, different machine learning algorithms can be used to train the devices so that they will be able to react and sustain in changing environments, giving way to an optimization solution in power consumption. But the concepts include keeping the server centralized in one particular area. The nodes' distance from the servers will be a major influencing factor in energy efficiency [28, 29].

As far as offering power and reaction time, present day and cutting-edge medical care gives a large number of administrations another arrangement of prerequisites, as shown in figure 16.4. To work at the pinnacle of their capacity, these newer

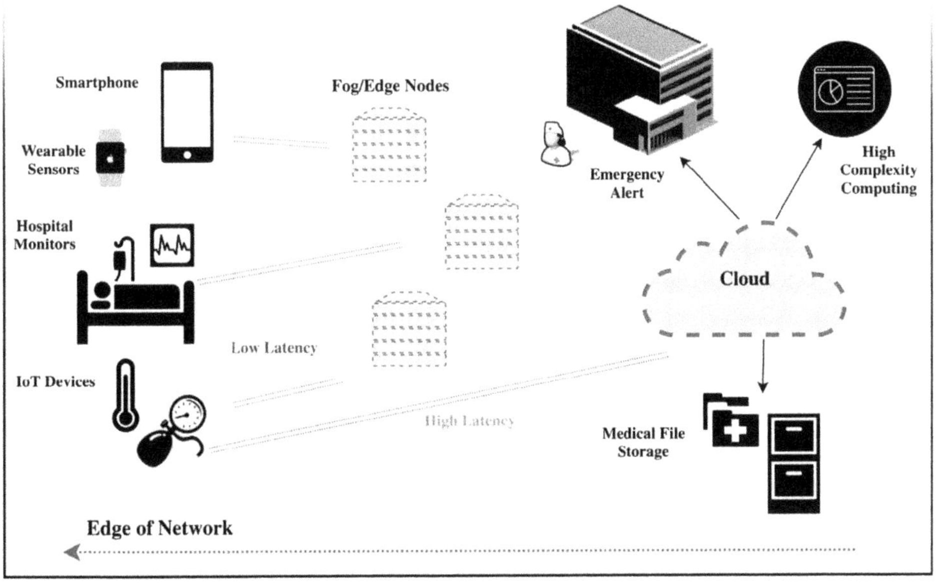

Figure 16.4. Sample edge architecture for the healthcare domain.

gadgets require quick and energy-proficient registering, more noteworthy stockpiling limit, and area awareness that conventional distributed computing cannot adapt to. Maybe the most encouraging innovation is mist figuring, which is at times named 'edge processing' because of mist alluding to the development of registering to the edge of the organization [30]. The archetype of edge registering, portable distributed computing or mobile cloud computing (MCC), is portrayed by high information transmission costs, long reaction times, and restricted inclusion. Two comparable processing strategies, cloudlet and neighborhood cloud, offer subpar nature of administration for new gadgets. The significant expenses related with information transmission come from the high organization traffic, which influences the transmission times. Although cloudlet-based arrangements have lower dormancy than MCC, they actually neglect to get the required versatility for gadgets due to restricted Wi-Fi inclusion. Many works have analyzed the presentation of cloud-based and edge-based design and found that main edge-based processing can satisfy current necessities for idleness, portability and energy proficiency [31].

In one case, the utilization of the cloud-just registering in video investigation brought about a multiplied reaction time contrasted and customer just processing. The further developed exhibition of edge designed contrasted and conventional distributed computing can be used particularly by the medical services area for some applications. Edge-based arrangements give the structure to decreased dormancy for time-subordinate arrangements, for example, important bodily function observation or fall recognition for the elderly. They can likewise give clients added security contrasted with conventional registering, which takes into consideration circulatory strain, pulse, glucose, and wellbeing history information to be sent to guardians through an associated framework [32]. Because of progress in following and portability that accompanies edge registering frameworks, wellbeing suppliers can really focus on individuals with constant diseases in their own homes utilizing surrounding sensors set around their homes related to wearable indispensable sign sensors. These sensors can gather area subordinate information, both indoors and in the open air, which permits medical services laborers to decide if a patient is at serious risk. Medical care would now be able to turn into a customized administration, custom-made explicitly to every person and their requirements. To appropriately offer continuous quality assistance to patients, the edge gadgets and hubs need information activities to perform with low inertness, energy effectiveness, area awareness, and a significant degree of safety. The recognizable proof of explicit information activity methods that take into account quality execution of an edge-based medical care framework is the fundamental objective of this review. Thus, this data can be utilized to give the ideal order, confirmation, encryption, and information decrease strategies for the arrangement of an edge gadget [33].

16.4 Energy efficient systems

Increasingly, IoT applications have uncovered the possible benefits in moving some of activities from the cloud to the edge resulting in study papers about the vision and potential increases of disseminating activities across the organization, but emphasised the issues that need overcoming. It is important to call attention to the fact that edge registering carries extra calculations to the edge, which can add some overheads. Nonetheless, the greatest energy consumer in a gadget is the handset, not the CPU. Thus, we can accept that edge features can in any case be energy consuming, yet we want to know the size of the overheads right away [34]. All of the previously mentioned papers manage energy conservation in compelled conditions. Notwithstanding, as far as we could possibly know, there is no basic contextual investigation estimating the specific overheads brought about by the edge design WorldView and what it means for the battery life of IoT gadgets. Therefore, we have chosen to compose this chapter to dissect the effect of edge registering on energy utilization of IoT gadgets.

Reaping the tremendous measure of the inactive calculation power and extra space disseminated at the organization edges can yield adequate capacities with respect to performing calculations concentrated and idleness basic assignments in cell phones. This WorldView is called MEC [35]. While long spread postponements remain a vital disadvantage for cloud computing, for MEC, with its general access, there is broad consent that it is a critical innovation for acknowledging different dreams for cutting-edge internet applications, like tactile internet (with millisecond-scale response time), IoT, and Internet of Me. By and by, analysts from both the scholarly world and industry have been effectively advancing MEC innovation by seeking the combination of strategies and hypotheses from the two disciplines of registering and remote correspondence. This chapter gives a review of key exploration progress in this youthful field. We will likewise introduce an examination viewpoint containing a troupe of promising exploration bearings for MEC.

We concentrate on energy-effective asset allotment plans for various-leveled MEC design in heterogeneous organizations, as shown in figure 16.5. In this engineering, both SBS and MBS are outfitted with MEC servers and assist with harnessing cell phones to perform errands. Each errand can be divided into three sections. These techniques each perform a piece of the undertaking and structure a three-level processing structure. In view of this processing structure, an advancement issue is detailed to limit the energy utilization of all subjects to the dormancy imperatives, where radio and calculation assets are thought about mutually [36].

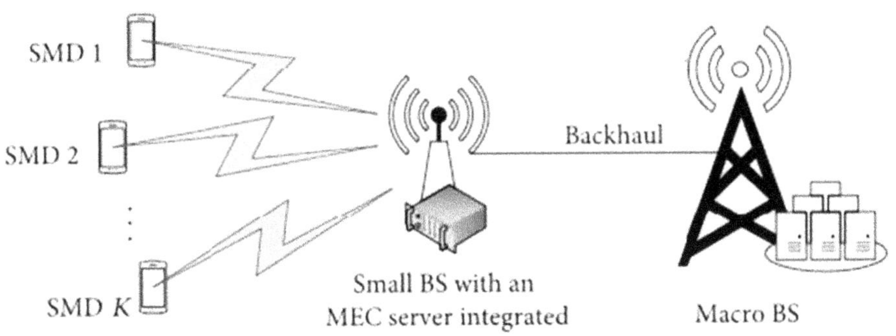

Figure 16.5. Energy efficient mobile edge computing.

Then, at that point, a component dependent on the variable replacement procedure is intended to ascertain the ideal responsibility appropriation, edge calculation ability assignment, and devices sending power. Finally, mathematical reproduction results show the energy productivity improvement of the proposed system over the standard plans. In actuality, the inaccurately anticipated worth will make the end gadget reproduce the expectation display and send the new boundaries α also, β along with the right value. Thus, two states can occur:

(i) The model predicts a value accurately—the end gadget will adopt a self-operating mode without sending any value.
(ii) The model predicts a value mistakenly—the end gadget will reproduce the expectation display and send new boundaries along with the right value to the entryway. Then, at that point, it adopts rest mode.

Clearly, the model increases energy utilization with the first choice, but the second option has higher costs. Presently, the inquiry is the extent of the costs and under what conditions we ought to consider carrying out edge activities even on the most applicable gadgets [37]. In any case, rather than just sending all information to the cloud, we have carried out a useful expectation model dependent on a direct relapse that addresses the dynamic cycle at the edge. The model is available in both the end gadget and the entryway that gathers information from the organization. Since we utilized straightforward direct relapse, the forecast cycle is characterized by:

$$Y = \alpha + \beta^* X \tag{16.1}$$

where, X is considered to be a variable which takes values that are independent and Y will be the dependent variable. As stated earlier, α is the Y-intercept of the regression line and β will be considered to be the slope of the regression line

16.5 Research findings and limitations

Edge designed WorldView can bring a few benefits such as network traffic decrease, quicker reaction rate, lower necessities of organization association unwavering quality, more proficient usage of cloud administration, and so forth. The underlying intricacy of arrangements dependent on edge design is higher, however, the acquired advantages will in the end take care of the contributed exertion. Edge-based arrangements give structure to decreased dormancy for time-subordinate arrangements, for example, important bodily functions observation or fall recognition for the elderly. Many works have analyzed the presentation of cloud-based and edge-based features and found that main edge-based processing can satisfy current necessities for idleness, portability and energy proficiency. For IoT gadget progression, there is still a lot of work to be done in further developing the energy proficiency part of exceptionally complex AI strategies. Specifically, the compromise among execution and information computational effectiveness should be proactively overseen. Analysts should zero in on growing low-idleness decentralized preparing models on the edge gadgets that can utilize assorted information from wellbeing sensors and yield precise individualized inductions.

16.6 Future research challenges

Making upcoming networks support these types of computing in various applications will brings in more benefits to society. But there are various constraints which need to be sorted out to make this happen. This section deals with various research challenges which are prevailing in MEC.

16.6.1 The healthcare domain

Healthcare is becoming the competitive field of invention. Numerous solutions are developed and deployed in small-scale environments [38]. Developing a model that is taking up decisions based on the environment would help users to come up with great understanding about various things happening around which may be either in terms of diseases, medicines or other trends in spreading the diseases. There are other techniques which help around 1000 users and usage of more than 50 clouds. But even though these many nodes are utilized, there are still many requirements that need to be addressed. When we think of healthcare systems there are many numbers patients that are taking up treatments in hospital. By using edge devices we will be able to lessen the inequality between devices present in the system and future requirements in the case of storage and monitoring.

16.6.2 Big data management

Managing data at large scale is very important because a healthcare system needs to be combined with real-time data as it needs to be analyzed and secured. These types of issue can be implemented using mobile edge techniques which help in reducing the data amount passed to the cloud. Even though this has been implemented, the mechanism of reduction still needs to be done for a longer period of time since the data received will be continuous. Sometimes data will be large and won't be reduced, hence the need to be analyzed [39]. Due to these techniques, having much experience needs to be developed that holds analysis features.

16.6.3 Privacy of data

While developing systems with large data in various different fields of applications, the privacy of data needs to be maintained. In healthcare the patient systems need to be preserved privately without being disclosed to anyone else. Currently, there are some applications that are developed on edge enabled healthcare, but they are insufficient to preserve the data. Also, if data is leaked then so many legal problems may arise for both parties. Hence systems with privacy protocols need to be developed to safeguard the data in all aspects.

16.6.4 Integrated applications

Current organization arrangements do not have the ability to deal with the huge scope of dispersed sensor-based clinical observing and revealing. Uniting broadcast communications and IT administrations from the concentrated cloud stage to the edge is fundamental, but subject to the achievement of different empowering advancements. One of the key empowering influences is virtualization procedures including virtual machines and compartments [40]. While virtual machines give clients a completely useful machine, paying little heed to the fundamental equipment engineering, compartment conditions, for example, Docker works with edge-featured gadgets by offering lightweight virtualization arrangements at client gadgets. Likewise, network work virtualization decouples network capacities and administrations from restrictive equipment, permitting collocation of various support occurrences over a similar virtual mode and significantly saving in the administrator's capital and functional uses. In an MEC-based medical services climate, this gives the administrator the capacity to move framework processes starting with one edge stage then onto the next when needed, for example, when there is clog because of blaze swarm occasions. Another pivotal empowering innovation is programming characterized networks. The fundamental head behind is the decoupling of control and information plane, and presentation of an intelligent concentrated control through which different virtual organization occurrences can be started and offered by means of edge to the clients. Coordination of dynamic provisioning of appropriated administrations at the organization edge is a test with existing organization designs. Programming characterized networks are relied upon to assume a critical part in giving organization availability and administration of the board across heterogeneous MEC stages. Also, network cutting permits dividing of one organization into various events, each streamlined for a specific application/use case.

Like its application in a self-arranging network-empowered 5G remote organizations, the utilization of man-made reasoning in medical services frameworks is normal in writing, as illustrated in the past area on order and forecast. Man-made reasoning can take in a few information sources, for example, patient factors, and utilize these to give more bits of knowledge on unusual qualities for arrangement, as specialists do when diagnosing a patient. This guarantees a setting mindful wellbeing framework, which is significant for customized results. Man-made consciousness procedures in writing have demonstrated to be more valuable than basic limit based techniques. One of these portrayed an assignment including the determination of cellular breakdown in the lungs where IBM Watson accomplished a higher accuracy in analysis than the normal emergency clinic. Essentially, different works for shrewd medical care utilizing edge processing have exhibited higher accuracy for a voice issue evaluation and high forecast of pain feeling location to permit the control features to proactively take care of patients' requirements. Regardless of all the examination and IoT gadget progressions, there is still a lot of work to be done in further developing the energy proficiency part of exceptionally complex AI strategies. Specifically, the compromise among execution and information computational effectiveness should be proactively overseen. Analysts should zero in on growing low-idleness decentralized preparing models on the edge gadgets that can utilize assorted information from wellbeing sensors and yield precise individualized inductions. Furthermore, numerous social worries about the utilization of computerized reasoning, particularly including medical services choices, should be tended to.

16.7 Conclusion

MEC is emerging in such a way that it keeps satisfying and creating demands in the quality of computation from the end-user. The focus tends towards attaining storage of resources and energy thereby giving way to improving the capabilities of IT and cloud storage. This is implemented by moving the resources towards the edges of the network which is the actual methodology of MEC. Communication between devices and edge servers is done by a wireless medium, which brings solutions for supporting various applications that need latency at a lower rate and preserving energy for a longer period. These applications will keep evolving at new different dimensions and design in which we need to consider the uniqueness and challenges for each of them. The recognizable proof of explicit information activity methods that take into account quality execution of an edge-based medical care framework is the fundamental objective of this review. Thus, this data can be utilized to give the ideal order, confirmation, encryption, and information decrease strategies for the arrangement of an edge gadget. This chapter helps in understanding what MEC actually is and what are the challenges, and how unique it as differentiated from other computing techniques. Along with this, various modeling techniques that help in communication, computation with edges and servers were described. These features help to understand the concepts of latency and the performance of energy in mobile edge systems. The management of resources was exploited with the understanding of offloading, resource allocation and its deployment. Further, there are some securities and privacy constraints which are addressed that help in stabilizing the implementation of mobile edge systems. Also, this chapter will further provide deeper insights for users to investigate valuable guidelines in this area.

References

[1] Eleonora C *et al* 2016 Efficient exploitation of mobile edge computing for virtualized 5G in EPC architectures *4th IEEE international conference on mobile cloud computing services and engineering (MobileCloud)*

[2] Kai K, Cong W and Tao L 2016 Fog computing for vehicular ad hoc networks: paradigms scenarios and issues *J. Chin. Univ. Posts Telecommun.* **23** 56–96

[3] Orsini G, Bade D and Lamersdorf W 2015 Computing at the mobile edge: Designing elastic android applications for computation offloading *8th IFIP wireless and mobile networking conference (WMNC)*

[4] Marotta M A *et al* 2015 Managing mobile cloud computing considering objective and subjective perspectives *Comput. Netw.* **93** 531–42

[5] Eleonora B *et al* 2016 Mobile edge clouds for information-centric IoT services *IEEE symposium on computers and communication (ISCC)*

[6] Milan P *et al* 2014 Mobile-edge computing introductory technical white paper *White paper mobile-edge computing (MEC) industry initiative* 1089–7801

[7] Hu Y C *et al* 2015 Mobile edge computing-A key technology towards 5G *ETSI white paper* **11.11** 1–16

[8] Heidenreich P A *et al* 2011 Forecasting the future of cardiovascular disease in the United States: a policy statement from the American Heart Association *Circulation* **123** 933–44

[9] Yu C *et al* 2015 FAST: a fog computing assisted distributed analytics system to monitor fall for stroke mitigation *IEEE international conference on networking architecture and storage (NAS)*

[10] Misra R, Panda B and Tiwary M 2016 Big data and ICT applications: a study *Proc. of the Second Int. Conf. on Information and Communication Technology for Competitive Strategies*

[11] Datta S K, Bonnet C and Haerri J 2015 Fog computing architecture to enable consumer centric internet of things services *Int. Symp. on Consumer Electronics (ISCE)*

[12] ETSI, 'Mobile-edge computing introductory technical white paper,' White paper, Mobile-edge Computing Industry Initiative. [Online] Available https://portal.etsi.org/portals/0/tbpages/mec/docs/mobile-edge computing-introductory technical white paper v1

[13] Fuqaha A A, Guizani M, Mohammadi M, Aledhari M and Ayyash M 2015 Internet of Things: a survey on enabling technologies, protocols, and applications *IEEE Commun. Surveys Tuts.* **17** 2347–76

[14] Fettweis G P 2014 The tactile Internet: Applications and challenges *IEEE Veh. Techn. Mag.* **9** 64–70

[15] Armbrust M, Fox R G A, Joseph A D, Katz R H, Konwinski A, Lee G, Patterson D A, Rabkin A, Stoica I and Zaharia M 2012 *Above the clouds: A Berkeley view of cloud computing* [Online]. Available: https://www2.eecs.berkeley.edu/Pubs/TechRpts/2009/EECS-2009-28.pd

[16] Zhang Q, Cheng L and Boutaba R 2010 Cloud computing: state-of-theart and research challenges *J. Internet Serv. Appl.* **1** 7–18

[17] Salman O, Elhajj I, Kayssi A and Chehab A 2015 Edge computing enabling the internet of things *Proc. IEEE World Forum Internet of Things (WFIOT)* 603–8

[18] Ahmed A and Ahmed E 2016 A survey on mobile edge computing *Proc. IEEE Int. Conf. Intell. Syst. Control (ISCO) (Coimbatore, India)* 1–8

[19] Sabella D, Vaillant A, Kuure P, Rauschenbach U and Giust F 2016 Mobile-edge computing architecture: the role of MEC in the internet of things. *IEEE Consum. Electron. Mag.* **5** 84–91

[20] Beck M T, Werner M, Feld S and Schimper S 2014 Mobile edge computing: a taxonomy *Proc. Int. Conf. Advances Future Internet (AFIN) (Lisbon, Portugal)* 48–54

[21] Gorantla M C, Boyd C and Nieto J M G*(2010)* Attribute-based authenticated key exchange *in Proc. Australian Conf. Info. Security and Privacy (ACISP) (Sydney, Australia)* 1–25

[22] Pimentel H M, Kopp S, Jr. M A S, Silveira R M and Bressan G 2015 OCP: a protocol for secure communication in federated content networks *Compt. Commun.* **68** 47–60

[23] Liyanage M, Abro A B, Ylianttila M and Gurtov A 2016 Opportunities and challenges of software-defined mobile networks in network security *IEEE Security Privacy* **14** 34–44

[24] Yang W and Fung C 2016 A survey on security in network functions virtualization *in Proc. IEEE NetSoft Conf. Workshops (NetSoft) (Seoul, Korea)* 15–9

[25] Liang B *Mobile edge computing.* [Online]. Available: http://www.comm.utoronto.ca/~liang/publications/Chapter MEC 2016.pdf

[26] Alcatel-Lucent, 'Providing security in NFV: Challenges and opportunities.' [Online]. Available http://tmcnet.com/tmc/whitepapers/documents/whitepapers/2014/10172-providing-security-nfv.pdf

[27] Wang C, Ren K and Wang J 2016 Secure optimization computation outsourcing in cloud computing: a case study of linear programming *IEEE Trans. Comput.* **65** 216–29

[28] Gennaro R, Craig G and Bryan P 2010 Non-interactive verifiable computing: outsourcing computation to untrusted workers *Annu. Conf. Adv. Cryptol. (Santa Barbara, CA)* 465–82

[29] ETSI, 'Executive briefing – mobile edge computing (MEC) initiative.' [Online] Available https://portal.etsi.org/portals/0/tbpages/mec/docs/mec%20executive% 20brief %20v1%2028-09-14.pdf

[30] 'Mobile-edge computing (MEC): Terminology.' [Online]. Available http://etsi.org/deliver/etsigs/MEC/001 099/001/01. 01.01 60/gs MEC001v010101p.pdf

[31] Han Z, Tan H, Chen G, Wang R, Chen Y and Lau F C M 2016 Dynamic virtual machine management via approximate Markov decision process *in Proc. IEEE Int. Conf. Comput. Commun. (INFOCOM) (San Francisco, CA)* 1–9

[32] Sudevalayam S and Kulkarni P 2011 Energy harvesting sensor nodes: survey and implications *IEEE Commun. Surveys Tuts.* **13** 443–61

[33] Ulukus S, Yener A, Erkip E, Simeone O, Zorzi M, Grover P and Huang K 2015 Energy harvesting wireless communications: a review of recent advances *IEEE J. Sel. Areas Commun.* **33** 360–81

[34] Lee K and Shin I 2015 User mobility model based computation offloading decision for mobile cloud *J. Comput. Sci. Eng.* **9** 155–62

[35] Mao Y, Zhang J and Letaief K B 2016 Dynamic computation offloading for mobile-edge computing with energy harvesting devices *IEEE J. Sel. Areas Commun.* **34** 3590–605

[36] Mao Y, Zhang J and Letaief K B May 2016 Grid energy consumption and QoS tradeoff in hybrid energy supply wireless networks *IEEE Trans. Wireless Commun.* **15** 3573–86

[37] Doppler K, Rinne M, Wijting C, Ribeiro C B and Hugl K 2009 Device-to-device communication as an underlay to LTE-advanced networks *IEEE Commun. Mag.* **47** 42–9

[38] Suryaprakash V, Møller J and Fettweis G 2015 On the modeling and analysis of heterogeneous radio access networks using a poisson cluster process *IEEE Trans. Wireless Commun.* **14** 1035–47

[39] Kirby G, Dearle A, Macdonald A and Fernandes A *An approach to ad hoc cloud computing.* [Online]. Available: https://arxiv.org/pdf/1002.4738v1.pdf

[40] Wang C, Li Y and Jin D 2014 Mobility-assisted opportunistic computation offloading *IEEE Commun. Lett.* **18** 1779–82

IOP Publishing

Human-Assisted Intelligent Computing
Modeling, simulations and applications
Mukhdeep Singh Manshahia, Igor S Litvinchev, Gerhard-Wilhelm Weber, J Joshua Thomas and Pandian Vasant

Chapter 17

Modeling 3D nanocomposites with multi-spherical inclusions by optimized packing

E Strelnikova, T Romanova, A Pankratov, I Litvinchev and K Degtyariov

Computational models for a class of 3D nanomaterials and nanocomposites are proposed. The main aim is to simulate elastic properties of nanostructures with ordered and stochastic distribution of non-classical inclusions. The representative volume elements approach is used. The nanosize cubes are considered as matrices, while conglomerates of spheres with different diameters are used as inclusions. Modeling nanocomposites is reduced to packing one-connected multi-spherical objects in an optimized container. The nonlinear programming problem is formulated by the phi-function technique. A multistart solution strategy is proposed and illustrated by numerical examples. Effective mechanical characteristics of 3D nanocomposites for different structural parameters are estimated.

17.1 Introduction

Theory and practice of modern engineering of multifunctional materials requires developing theoretically justified computer tools and software for adequately simulating elastic properties of nanocomposite and composite materials of 3D configuration with general material and geometric diversity of nanoparticles both of ordered and stochastic distribution. Computational experiment gives a wide perspective for such study due to its ability to ensure the elastic properties unified parameterization for composites and nanocomposites in a wide range of their geometric, surface, and material characteristics.

If research is focused on molecular reactions or atom interactions in nanocomposites, then the simulations based on molecular dynamics or quantum mechanics should be involved. However, when the aim of simulation is investigating the global mechanical characteristics, in particular, deformations, effective stiffness or elastic modules of nanocomposites and metamaterials, then the approaches of

doi:10.1088/978-0-7503-4801-0ch17

continuum mechanics may be applied safely to provide such information efficiently, [1–3]. For this purpose, the approach based on the concept of representative volume elements (RVEs) is often used in recent simulations [4, 5]. For instance, in publications [6, 7] devoted to estimating the average mechanical properties of nanomaterials, the influence of interaction surfaces [8] is studied, which substantially affects average elastic modules of composites and nanomaterials as well as elastic fields.

So, it is topical to elaborate new analytical and numerical methods for studying effective properties of nanomaterials in all their variety of material components, peculiar nanoparticle distribution, the connection quality, the order and shapes of nanofibers and nano-inclusions. Especially important is investigation of the wave processes and transformation on the interfacial surfaces of inhomogeneous material under longitudinal and transverse waves. This requires elaboration of effective numerical methods that are able to simulate the nonlinear dynamic processes adequately [9–11]. It should be noted that advanced technological and innovative materials are effectively used in practical applications as responsible covering elements in modern engineering structures and systems. The structures made of such materials are able to withstand intense thermopower dynamic loads. So, the computational models for studying three-dimensional nanocomposites are needed to be elaborated, that will adequately describe the elastic properties of nanostructures and will be suitable for capable numerical simulations. Such models are usually based on using the concept of RVE. These volume elements include matrices and inclusions.

A lot of research is devoted to studying RVEs with single inclusions such as spheres, cylinders, rounded cylinders [12–14]. But non-canonical inclusions are insufficiently studied despite their obvious widespread prevalence. In real composites and nanocomposites there are sets of disordered inclusions with different shapes; among these inclusions most likely are stuck together nanoparticles, or conglomerates of particles with different shapes and sizes. It is also of great interest to study interacting ordered or stochastic distributed systems of inclusions in RVEs.

This chapter is concerned with the topical issue of numerical simulations of effective elastic modules for an RVE with ordered and stochastic distribution of nano-inclusions in the form of different diameter spheres stuck together. To this aim, an optimization problem of packing spheres is used.

In many applications, packing spheres in a bounded domain (volume) have been studied [15–17]. A lot of publications address sphere packing problems (see, e.g., [18–23]). Sphere packing is an NP-hard problem [24] and thus heuristic approaches are widely used to obtain good approximate solutions in a reasonable computational time. Packing spheres as nonlinear optimization problems are considered, e.g., in [25–29] using the phi-function technique for modeling placement conditions. Then global/local optimizers combined with multistart or decomposition techniques [30] were used to solve arising optimization problems.

The rest of the paper is organized as follows. Problem statement and concept of the representative volume element are introduced in section 17.2. The next section 'Packing problem' is devoted to the solution strategy for the packing problem. Results of computational experiments for four instances of packing objects, to illustrate the work of the algorithm for a packing problem are described in section 17.4, 'Computational results'. These results became the basis for numerical estimations of mechanical properties of nanocomposites that are discussed in the section 'Numerical estimation of effective modulus'. Finally, the main outcomes and future scope of research are given in the Conclusion.

17.2 Problem statement

Consider an elastic parallelepiped (matrix) with a set of inhomogeneities (inclusions) of different shapes, figure 17.1. Denote the matrix outer boundary as S^M and its region as Ω^M. The inclusion's external boundaries and their volumes are denoted as S^I and Ω^I, and $\Omega^I = \cup\Omega^I_k$, $S^I = \cup\partial\Omega^I_k = \cup S^I_k$, $k = 1, 2,\ldots,K$. The boundary surface of the matrix body $S^M = \partial\Omega^M$ includes boundary S^I of the inclusion set.

Let $S^I = S_{\text{int}}$ be the interface surface. The material of the matrix Ω^M is given by the shear modulus G^M and the Poisson ratio ν^M, while the inclusion' material (Ω^I) is designated by the elastic constants G^I and ν^I, the same for all inclusions Ω^I_k, $k = 1, 2, \ldots, K$. This parallelepiped with inclusions is considered as the RVE for estimating the mechanical characteristics of composites and nanocomposites.

The equations of elastostatics for the matrix and inclusion are as follows:

$$\nabla \cdot \boldsymbol{\sigma}^D = 0,\ \boldsymbol{\sigma}^D = 2G^D[\nu^D/(1-2\nu^D)tr(\boldsymbol{e}^D)\boldsymbol{I} + \boldsymbol{e}^D], \tag{17.1}$$

$2\boldsymbol{e}^D = \nabla\boldsymbol{u}^D + (\nabla\boldsymbol{u}^D)$, $\text{tr}(\boldsymbol{e}^D) = e^D_{\text{ii}}$, $G^D = E^D 0.5 / (1 + \nu^D)$,where $\boldsymbol{\sigma}^D$, $\mathbf{e}^D$ are the stress and strain tensors, $\boldsymbol{u}^D$ is the displacement vector, E^D is Young's modulus, ν^D is Poisson's ratio. Here and after $D = M, I$.

Assume that the boundary of the volume is $\partial\Omega^M = \Sigma_1\cup\Sigma_2\cup\Sigma_3$. Here $\Sigma_1\subset\partial\Omega^M$ is the boundary with given displacements, whereas $\Sigma_2 \subset\partial\Omega^M$ is the boundary with given tractions, $\Sigma_3 = S_{\text{int}} = \partial\Omega^I$ is the interface surface.

Both in classical and in the Gurtin–Murdoch boundary conditions [7], the continuity of displacements along the interface surface S_{int} needs to be fulfilled

$$\boldsymbol{U}^M_{\text{int}} = \boldsymbol{U}^I_{\text{int}}. \tag{17.2}$$

Considering an ideal contact, for tractions on the interface surface S_{int} we have

$$\boldsymbol{T}^M_{\text{int}} = \boldsymbol{T}^I_{\text{int}}. \tag{17.3}$$

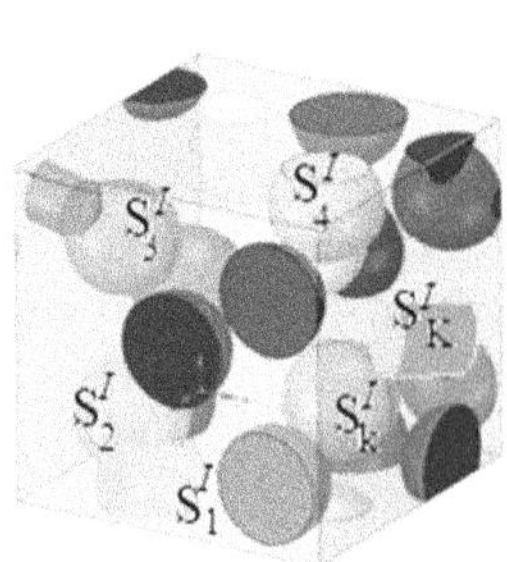

Figure 17.1. Sketch of representative volume element with K inclusions.

The Gurtin–Murdoch theory [8] is used to study the influence of nanosizes. It allows us to describe the interaction between the matrix and inclusions at the nanoscale. So, the non-classical traction boundary conditions at the interface S_{int} are applied. The surface S_{int} is the elastic membrane with own Lame constants λ^S and G^S, as well as the surface tension τ_0. For evaluating the displacements $\mathbf{u}^S$, strains $\boldsymbol{\varepsilon}^S$ and stresses $\boldsymbol{\sigma}^S$ the following equations are involved [8]:

$$\text{div}_S\boldsymbol{\sigma}^S = \boldsymbol{\sigma} \cdot \boldsymbol{n},\ \boldsymbol{\sigma}^S = \tau_0\boldsymbol{I}_\tau + 2(G^S - \tau_0)\boldsymbol{\varepsilon}^S + (\lambda^S - \tau_0)(tr\boldsymbol{\varepsilon}^s)\boldsymbol{I}_\tau + \tau_0\nabla_S\boldsymbol{u}^S,$$

where $\boldsymbol{I}_\tau$ is the unit tangent tensor, ∇_S,div_S are the surface gradient and divergence.

It is supposed that along the interface the next condition is valid:

$$\boldsymbol{U}_3^M = \boldsymbol{U}_3^I = \boldsymbol{U}_3^S. \tag{17.4}$$

Considering the Gurtin–Murdoch conditions for tractions, we use equation (17.4) with an additional differential relation from [4, 8]

$$\boldsymbol{T}_3^I - \boldsymbol{T}_3^M = \mathbf{G}\boldsymbol{U}_3^S. \tag{17.5}$$

Here, the Laplace–Young equation at nanoscale is used for receiving the differential operator $\mathbf{G}$ [4]

$$\boldsymbol{G} = \nabla_S\boldsymbol{\sigma}^s = [\boldsymbol{\sigma}]\boldsymbol{n},\ [\boldsymbol{\sigma}] = \boldsymbol{\sigma}^I - \boldsymbol{\sigma}^M, \quad [\sigma_{ij}]n_i n_j = \sigma^S_{\alpha\beta}\chi_{\alpha\beta}.$$

Here $\{\chi_{\alpha\beta}\}$ is the tensor of curvature.

After solving boundary value problems (17.1), (17.3), (17.4) and (17.1), (17.3), (17.5) with finite element methods [14], the surface tension effect is estimated. The initial data were taken from [31, 32]. It has been demonstrated, that accounting for the surface tension effect increases the effective elastic modulus E_z by about 10%. Thus, if the surface tension is neglected, under the ideal contact conditions, the lower estimates will be obtained for efficient modules.

Next, as in [14] the simplified formulas for estimating the effective elastic modulus E_i $(i = 1,2,3)$ and comparing the results of [14] and [31] obtained by finite and boundary element methods were used

$$E_i = (F \cdot H_i)/(\Delta H_i \cdot S_b).$$

Here F is the uniform axial load, H_i is the numerical value of axial deformation, S^b is the area of the RVE base.

In [33, 34] modeling nanocomposites with spherical, cylindrical, spherocylindrical, ellipsoidal and conical inclusions by optimized packing were introduced.

In this chapter as matrices, the nanosize cubes are considered and the spheres stuck together with different diameters are chosen as inclusions. The effective elastic characteristics are received numerically in the ideal contact suppositions.

17.3 Packing problem

Let a collection of objects $\mathbf{S}_i(u_i)$ be given. Each object is a one-connected object composed by a union of different spheres S_{ik} of radius r_{ik}, $k = 1, \ldots, m_i$, i.e.,

$\mathbf{S}_i(u_i) = \bigcup\limits_{k=1}^{m_i} \mathrm{S}_{ik}(u_i)$, where $u_i = (v_i, \theta_i)$, $i \in I_n = \{1,\cdots,n\}$ are variable placement parameters, $\mathrm{v_i}$ and $\mathrm{v_j}$ are translation vectors, $\theta_i = (\theta_i^1, \theta_i^2, \theta_i^3)$ are rotation angles. Further we call the objects $\mathbf{S}_i(u_i)$ multi-spherical.

In addition, let a cuboid container Ω of variable sizes l, w, h be given.

The optimization packing problem is aimed at arranging a set of multi-spherical objects $\mathbf{S}_i$, $i \in I_n$, in a cuboid Ω of minimal volume providing the following placement (non-overlapping and containment) constraints:

$$\mathrm{int}\, \mathbf{S}_i(v_i, \theta_i) \bigcap \mathrm{int}\, \mathbf{S}_j(v_j, \theta_j) = \varnothing,\ i < j,\ i, j \in I_n, \tag{17.6}$$

$$\mathbf{S}_i(v_i, \theta_i) \subset \Omega \Leftrightarrow \mathrm{int}\, \mathbf{S}_i(v_i, \theta_i) \bigcap \Omega^* = \varnothing,\ i \in I_n, \tag{17.7}$$

where $\Omega^* = R^3 \backslash \mathrm{int}\, \Omega$.

Note that each sphere S_{ik}, of the object $\mathbf{S}_i$ is 'rigid' for $k = 1, \ldots, m_i$, therefore holds the same position for all motions of $\mathbf{S}_i$ for $i \in I_n$.

For analytical description of conditions (17.6) and (17.7) the phi-function technique is employed.

Non-overlapping of objects $\mathbf{S}_i(u_i)$ *and* $\mathbf{S}_j(u_j)$

Let $\mathbf{S}_i(u_i) = \mathrm{S}_{il} \cup \ldots \mathrm{S}_{ik} \cup \ldots \cup \mathrm{S}_{im_i}$ and $\mathbf{S}_j(u_j) = \mathrm{S}_{jl} \cup \ldots \mathrm{S}_{jl} \cup \ldots \cup \mathrm{S}_{jm_j}$.

We define a phi-function for $S_{ik}(u_i)$ and $S_{jl}(u_j)$ in the form

$$\begin{aligned}\Phi_{ij}^{kl}(u_i, u_j) = {} & (x_{ik}(u_i) - x_{jl}(u_j))^2 + (y_{ik}(u_i) - y_{jl}(u_j))^2 + \\ & (z_{ik}(u_i) - z_{jl}(u_j))^2 - (r_{ik} - r_{jl})^2,\end{aligned} \tag{17.8}$$

where

$$x_{ik}(u_i)y_{ik}(u_i)z_{ik}(u_i) = (x_i, y_i, z_i) + (x_{ik}^0, 0{,}0) \cdot A(\theta_i),$$
$$x_{jl}(u_j)y_{jl}(u_j)z_{jl}(u_j) = (x_j, y_j, z_j) + (x_{jl}^0, 0{,}0) \cdot A(\theta_j).$$

In (17.8) $A(\theta_i)$ is a rotation matrix

$$\begin{pmatrix} \cos\theta_i^1 \cos\theta_i^3 - \sin\theta_i^1 \cos\theta_i^2 \sin\theta_i^3 & -\cos\theta_i^1 \sin\theta_i^3 - \sin\theta_i^1 \cos\theta_i^2 \cos\theta_i^3 & \sin\theta_i^1 \sin\theta_i^2 \\ \sin\theta_i^1 \cos\theta_i^3 + \cos\theta_i^1 \cos\theta_i^2 \sin\theta_i^3 & -\sin\theta_i^1 \sin\theta_i^3 + \cos\theta_i^1 \cos\theta_i^2 \cos\theta_i^3 & -\cos\theta_i^1 \sin\theta_i^2 \\ \sin\theta_i^2 \sin\theta_i^3 & \sin\theta_i^2 \cos\theta_i^3 & \cos\theta_i^2 \end{pmatrix}.$$

Then a continuous function

$$\mathbf{\Phi}_{ij}(u_i, u_j) = \min_{k = 1,\ldots,m_i, l = 1,\ldots,m_j} \Phi_{ij}^{kl}(u_i, u_j), \tag{17.9}$$

is the phi-function for $\mathbf{S}_i(u_i)$ and $\mathbf{S}_j(u_j)$.

Thus the inequality $\mathbf{\Phi}_{ij}(u_i, u_j) \geqslant 0$ describes constraint (17.6) that is equivalent to the system of inequalities $\Phi_{ij}^{kl}(u_i, u_j) \geqslant 0$ for $k = 1,..., m_i$, $l = 1,..., m_j$, where $\Phi_{ij}^{kl}(u_i, u_j)$ and $\mathbf{\Phi}_{ij}(u_i, u_j)$ are defined in (17.8) and (17.9).

Containment of object $\mathbf{S}_i(u_i)$ *into cuboid* Ω.

Let $\Phi_i^k(u_i, h, w, l)$ be a phi-function for a sphere $S_{ik}(u_i)$ and the object Ω^*, $k = 1,..., m_i$, where

$$\Phi_i^k(u_i, l, w, h) = \min\{\varphi_{si}^k(u_i, l, w, h), s = 1,....,6\},$$

$$\varphi_{1i}^k(u_i, l, w, h) = x_{ik}(u_i) - r_{ik}, \varphi_{2i}^k(u_i, l, w, h) = -x_{ik}(u_i) + l - r_{ik},$$

$$\varphi_{3i}^k(u_i, l, w, h) = y_{ik}(u_i) - r_{ik}, \varphi_{4i}^k(u_i, l, w, h) = -y_{ik}(u_i) + w - r_{ik},$$

$$\varphi_{5i}^k(u_i, l, w, h) = z_{ik}(u_i) - r_{ik}, \varphi_{6i}^k(u_i, l, w, h) = -z_{ik}(u_i) + h - r_{ik}.$$

Then a continuous function

$$\mathbf{\Phi}_i(u_i, l, w, h) = \min_{k = 1,...,m_i} \Phi_i^k(u_i, l, w, h), \tag{17.10}$$

is a phi-function for objects $\mathbf{S}_i(u_i)$ and Ω^*.

The inequality $\mathbf{\Phi}_i(u_i, h, w, l) \geqslant 0$ guarantees containing $\mathbf{S}_i(u_i)$ in Ω.

The packing problem can be formulated as the following optimization problem, s.t.

$$\min_{u \in W \subset \mathbb{R}^\sigma} f(u), \text{ s.t. } u \in W \subset \mathbb{R}^\sigma \tag{17.11}$$

$$W = \{u \in \mathbb{R}^\sigma: \mathbf{\Phi}_{ij}(u_i, u_j) \geqslant 0, i < j \in I_n, \tag{17.12}$$

$$\mathbf{\Phi}_i(u_i, l, w, h) \geqslant 0, i \in I_n, l \geqslant 0, w \geqslant 0, h \geqslant 0\},$$

where $\sigma = 3+6n$, $u = (p, u_1, ..., u_n)$, $p = (l, w, h)$, $f(u) = l \cdot w \cdot h$ is the volume of cuboid Ω, $\mathbf{\Phi}_{ij}(u_i, u_j)$ is the phi-function (17.9) for multi-spheres $\mathbf{S}_i(u_i)$ and $\mathbf{S}_j(u_j)$, $\mathbf{\Phi}_i(u_i, l, w, h)$ is the phi-function (17.10) for objects $\mathbf{S}_i(u_i)$ and Ω^*.

In (17.12) the number of non-overlapping constraints is $\sum_{i=1}^{n-1} \sum_{j=i+1}^{n} m_i \cdot m_j$ and the number of containment conditions is $6 \cdot \sum_{i=1}^{n} m_i$.

The solution strategy for the packing problem includes the sequence of the following stages.

Stage 1. Generating feasible starting arrangements of objects.

Stage 2. Finding a local extremum to problems (17.11) and (17.12) based on the procedure presented in [25], for each starting arrangement.

Stage 3. Choosing the minimum local extremum from those found at the previous stage.

The algorithm of finding starting feasible motion vectors for $\mathbf{S}_i(u_i)$, $i \in I_n$, has the following steps.

Step 1. Set $R_i = d_i + \varepsilon^*$, $\varepsilon^* = \max_{i=1,\ldots,n} \varepsilon_i$, $d_i = \sum_{k=1}^{m_i} r_i^k$, $i \in I_n$ and circumscribe each scaled object $\lambda \mathbf{S}_i(v_i)$ by the sphere $\widehat{\mathbf{S}}_i(v_i)$ of radius λR_i.

Step 2. Generate randomly a set of centers $v_i^0 = (x_i^0, y_i^0, z_i^0)$ of $\widehat{\mathbf{S}}_i(v_i)$, $i \in I_n$, inside the cuboid Ω^0 of sufficiently large sizes l^0, w^0 and h^0.

Step 3. Grow the spheres $\widehat{\mathbf{S}}_i(v_i)$, $i \in I_n$, to the full size (from $\lambda = 0$ to $\lambda^* = 1$), solving the problem

$$\max_{v \in W_\lambda} \lambda, \quad s.\ t. \quad v \in W_\lambda \subset \mathbb{R}^{3n+1} \tag{17.13}$$

$$W_\lambda = \Big\{ v \in \mathbb{R}^{3n+1}\colon \Phi^{\widehat{S}_i\widehat{S}_j}(v_i, v_j, \lambda) \geqslant 0, \\ \Phi^{\widehat{S}_i\Omega^*}v_i, \lambda) \geqslant 0,\ i < j \in I_n,\ 1 - \lambda \geqslant 0,\ \lambda \geqslant 0 \Big\}, \tag{17.14}$$

starting from the point $v^0 = (x_1^0, y_1^0, z_1^0, \ldots, x_n^0, y_n^0, z_n^0, \lambda^0 = 0)$.

In problems (17.13) and (17.14)

$v = (v_1, \ldots, v_n, \lambda)$ is the decision vector,

$$\Phi^{\widehat{S}_i\widehat{S}_j}(v_i, v_j, \lambda) = \left\| v_i - v_j \right\|^2 - \lambda^2 (R_i + R_j)^2,$$

is a phi-function for two scaled spheres $\widehat{\mathbf{S}}_i(v_i)$ and $\widehat{\mathbf{S}}_j(v_j)$ of radii λR_i and λR_j,

$$\Phi^{\widehat{S}_i\Omega^*}(v_i, \lambda) = \min\{\varphi_{1i}(v_i, \lambda), \varphi_{2i}(v_i, \lambda), \varphi_{3i}(v_i, \lambda), \\ \varphi_{4i}(v_i, \lambda), \varphi_{5i}(v_i, \lambda), \varphi_{6i}(v_i, \lambda)\}$$

is a phi-function for a scaled sphere $\lambda \widehat{\mathbf{S}}_i(v_i)$ of radius λR_i and the object Ω^*, where

$$\varphi_{1i}(v_i, \lambda) = x_i - \lambda R_i,\ \varphi_{2i}(v_i, \lambda) = -x_i + l^0 - \lambda R_i,$$

$$\varphi_{3i}(v_i, \lambda) = y_i - \lambda R_i,\ \varphi_{4i}(v_i, \lambda) = -y_i + w^0 - \lambda R_i,$$

$$\varphi_{5i}(v_i, \lambda) = z_i - \lambda R_i,\ \varphi_{6i}(v_i, \lambda) = -z_i + h^0 - \lambda R_i.$$

A point of the global maximum of problems (17.13) and (17.14) we denote by $v^* = (v_1^*, \ldots, v_n^*, \lambda^*)$, where $\lambda^* = 1$.

Step 4. Form a feasible shift vector v_i^0 for each $\mathbf{S}_i$ assuming $v_i^0 = v_i^*$, $i \in I_n$.

Step 5. Generate randomly rotation angles θ_i^0 for each $\mathbf{S}_i$, $i \in I_n$.

Step 6.Form a feasible point $u^0 = (l^0, w^0, h^0, u_1^0, \ldots, u_n^0)$ to problems (17.11) and (17.12), where $u_i^0 = (v_i^0, \theta_i^0)$.

An iterative procedure for searching for a local-optimal solution of problems (17.11) and (17.12) is used.

The optimization procedure allows reducing problems (17.11) and (17.12) with $O(\eta^2)$ nonlinear inequalities, to a sequence of problems with a smaller number of nonlinear inequalities (O(η)), where $\eta = \sum_{i=1}^{n} m_i$.

The sketch of the procedure involves the following main steps for each feasible shift vector of $\mathbf{S}_i$, $i \in I_n$:

- construct fixed cubic containers for all spheres that form multi-spherical objects;
- provide free moving each sphere within the corresponding cubic container;
- form a subset of feasible region (17.12);

substituting $O(\eta^2)$ nonlinear inequalities for the pairs of spheres having non-overlapping cubic containers by O(η) linear inequalities;

- search for a local extremum on the subregion defined by O(η) nonlinear inequalities.
- take found local extremum as a starting point for the next iteration.

17.4 Computational experiments

Four instances to illustrate the work of the solution algorithm are considered in this section. We use an AMD Athlon 64 × 2 5200 + computer for each experiment and interior point optimizer (IPOPT) [35] to solve nonlinear programing subproblems.

Packing $n = 20$ equal objects with the large sphere of the diameter 65 nm while the small sphere radius takes the value (a) $r = 1/2R$, (b) $r = 1/3R$, (c) $r = 1/4R$, (d) $r = 2/3R$.

CPU for 100 runs is: (a) 1344.41 s; (b) 1237.24 s; (c) 535.58 s; (d) 1553.09 s

The local-optimal solutions found by our algorithm:

(a) The value of the objective function is
$l^* \cdot w^* \cdot h^* = 194.953088 * 156.852473 * 194.905692 = f(u^*) = 5959996.5821$, the appropriate placement parameters of objects are given in table 17.1 (figure 17.2(a));

(b) The value of the objective function is
$l^* \cdot w^* \cdot h^* = 233.874954 * 121.291650 * 195.000000 = f(u^*) = 5531\ 580.4250$, the appropriate placement parameters of objects are given in table 17.2 (figure 17.2(b));

(c) The value of the objective function is
$l^* \cdot w^* \cdot h^* = 194.999999 * 121.291651 * 233.874954 = f(u^*) = 5531580.4417$, the appropriate placement parameters of objects are given in table 17.3 (figure 17.2(c));

Table 17.1. Placement parameters of objects for case (a) $r = 1/2R$.

#	x	y	z	R/r
1	159.971311	124.352473	162.405692	32.500000
	135.984538	139.852269	177.918301	16.250000
2	162.453088	124.352473	97.453088	32.500000
	178.703088	140.602473	120.434058	16.250000
3	97.481973	32.500000	32.500000	32.500000
	93.236421	61.717524	18.914657	16.250000
4	32.500000	124.352473	32.500000	32.500000
	22.334209	132.781716	62.196036	16.250000
5	32.500000	34.030729	32.500000	32.500000
	46.701243	19.806253	58.038970	16.250000
6	162.453088	32.500000	97.471114	32.500000
	178.701630	16.251381	74.488137	16.250000
7	162.453088	121.883384	32.500000	32.500000
	161.164989	92.666318	18.324182	16.250000
8	95.616621	32.500000	99.073301	32.500000
	116.492811	18.381659	78.552406	16.250000
9	95.136468	124.352473	98.564565	32.500000
	70.072231	138.274198	83.260330	16.250000
10	78.972395	124.352473	162.405692	32.500000
	102.936767	139.870440	177.934748	16.250000
11	162.443859	34.945407	32.501091	32.500000
	176.848329	61.444640	20.395230	16.250000
12	97.500000	124.352473	32.500000	32.500000
	117.961736	138.354041	53.512460	16.250000
13	121.371823	78.772285	136.763422	32.500000
	119.471853	111.159273	138.692966	16.250000
14	32.500000	124.352473	115.933297	32.500000
	52.289859	98.920533	120.155603	16.250000
15	80.569123	35.153326	162.405692	32.500000
	70.877470	16.250000	137.809226	16.250000
16	162.453088	35.415583	162.405692	32.500000
	168.574853	65.822542	172.110890	16.250000
17	32.500000	35.096525	114.388332	32.500000
	18.258533	47.172267	87.787447	16.250000
18	128.277430	78.420195	66.675658	32.500000
	126.288188	78.802128	34.238841	16.250000
19	32.500000	78.906720	162.405692	32.500000
	29.974747	46.590700	164.761096	16.250000
20	56.085967	79.191601	72.863322	32.500000
	60.786994	80.034751	40.716169	16.250000

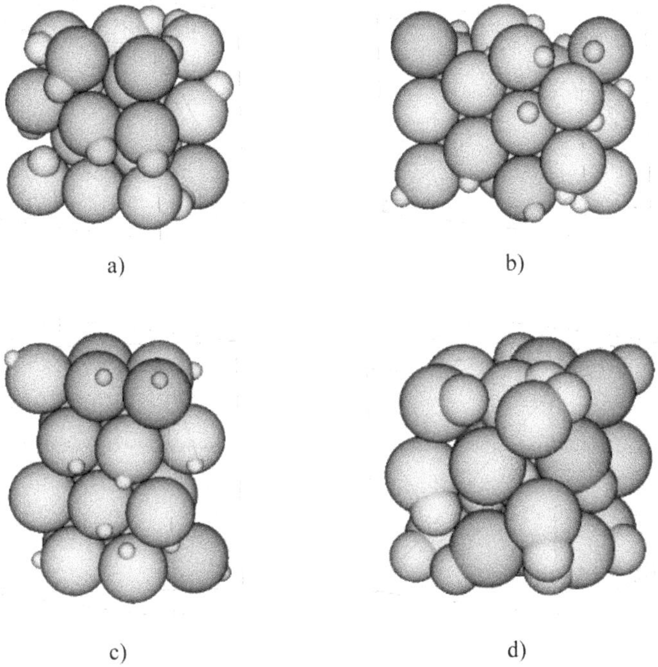

Figure 17.2. Optimized packings with different sizes representative volume elements: (a) $r = 1/2R$, (b) $r = 1/3R$, (c) $r = 1/4R$, (d) $r = 2/3R$.

(d) The value of the objective function is

$l^{*}{\cdot}w^{*}{\cdot}h^{*} = 181.727859*178.962807*190.289946 = f(u^{*}) = 6188710.0346,$
the appropriate placement parameters of objects are given in table 17.4 (figure 17.2(d)).

17.5 Numerical estimation of effective modulus

A number of nanocomposite materials with an aluminum matrix and rigid fillers in the shape of balls stuck together is considered.

It is supposed that the nanocomposite aluminum matrix has the following isotropic properties: elasticity modulus $E^M = 71$ GPa, density $\rho^M = 2770$ kg m^{-3}, bulk modulus 69.6 GPa, shear modulus 26.7 GPa, Poisson's coefficient $\nu^M = 0.35$. For all K inclusions it is supposed that $\rho^I = 2770$ kg m^{-3}, elasticity modulus $E^I = 710$ GPa, bulk modulus 696 GPa, shear modulus 267 GPa, Poisson's ratio $\nu^I = 0.35$.

The representative volume elements are presented in figures 17.2(a)–(d). The finite element method was in use to solve boundary value problems (17.1), (17.3), and (17.4). In calculations we use $K = 20$, and consider different ratios of sphere diameters.

The average mechanical characteristics of the new nanomaterials are clarified. Table 17.5 is shown the numerical simulation results.

It has been demonstrated that new composite materials are anisotropic. The insertion of isotropic inclusions into the nanoscale matrix leads to noticeable

Table 17.2. Placement parameters of objects for case (b) $r = 1/3R$.

#	x	y	z	R/r
1	201.374953	88.791650	32.500000	32.500000
	187.891030	64.496145	15.642888	10.833333
2	201.374955	32.499999	130.000000	32.500000
	219.363365	43.291002	105.176194	10.833333
3	145.083302	32.500000	97.500000	32.500000
	163.718678	12.004986	114.497859	10.833333
4	145.083304	32.500000	162.500001	32.500000
	175.670973	23.321179	168.532724	10.833333
5	88.791651	88.791649	32.499998	32.500000
	63.415869	106.443619	22.463678	10.833333
6	32.499999	88.791651	130.000002	32.500000
	29.604667	99.762510	160.455007	10.833333
7	88.791651	88.791650	97.500001	32.500000
	104.141699	108.551967	76.759801	10.833333
8	201.374954	88.791650	162.500000	32.500000
	212.270186	58.973486	169.458519	10.833333
9	201.374954	32.499999	65.000000	32.500000
	197.624876	21.725879	34.568023	10.833333
10	145.083302	88.791652	65.000000	32.500000
	169.997628	108.791438	59.038884	10.833333
11	88.791651	88.791651	162.500003	32.500000
	115.246246	103.244189	174.646135	10.833333
12	88.791651	32.499999	65.000000	32.500000
	87.136512	19.629326	35.203082	10.833333
13	32.499999	32.500000	32.499999	32.500000
	13.496794	13.346104	14.382150	10.833333
14	32.500000	88.791651	65.000000	32.500000
	21.861020	91.422716	34.403602	10.833333
15	145.083302	32.500000	32.500000	32.500000
	165.819849	13.679522	16.006510	10.833333
16	32.500000	32.499999	162.500001	32.500000
	17.684544	58.313564	175.554201	10.833333
17	145.083302	88.791651	130.000001	32.500000
	151.395139	102.012201	159.010823	10.833333
18	32.499999	32.500000	97.500001	32.500000
	13.243860	47.438920	75.999309	10.833333
19	201.374954	88.791651	97.500000	32.500000
	215.451473	106.561896	120.787765	10.833333
20	88.791652	32.499999	130.000002	32.500000
	103.348545	46.623506	155.394360	10.833333

Table 17.3. Placement parameters of objects for case (c) $r = 1/4R$.

#	x	y	z	R/r
1	130.000000	32.500000	32.499999	32.500000
	138.103112	10.070612	54.579676	8.125000
2	64.999999	32.500000	32.500000	32.500000
	35.777423	18.293535	33.183637	8.125000
3	130.000000	88.791651	201.374954	32.500000
	156.666347	107.055288	204.780173	8.125000
4	32.499999	32.500000	201.374954	32.500000
	13.315322	16.018252	221.784514	8.125000
5	97.500000	88.791651	32.499999	32.500000
	115.056764	109.006526	14.078032	8.125000
6	32.500000	88.791651	32.500000	32.500000
	12.882903	109.677186	17.163314	8.125000
7	97.500000	32.500000	201.374954	32.500000
	116.893129	11.421410	216.732349	8.125000
8	162.500000	88.791651	32.500000	32.500000
	179.825920	110.420665	15.522125	8.125000
9	162.500000	88.791651	145.083303	32.500000
	179.924183	67.526086	127.750571	8.125000
10	162.500000	32.500000	88.791651	32.500000
	169.529603	39.011772	57.736353	8.125000
11	130.000000	88.791652	88.791652	32.500000
	106.579238	110.139181	81.580488	8.125000
12	65.000000	88.791652	88.791651	32.500000
	37.875221	106.617700	87.139876	8.125000
13	65.000000	32.500000	145.083302	32.500000
	83.634938	11.124532	129.206324	8.125000
14	97.500000	88.791651	145.083303	32.500000
	75.623889	111.212630	153.742718	8.125000
15	64.999999	88.791651	201.374954	32.500000
	39.245056	107.273931	208.540024	8.125000
16	32.500000	88.791651	145.083302	32.500000
	14.391244	110.241774	161.460578	8.125000
17	162.500000	32.500000	201.374954	32.500000
	178.831906	12.166011	220.766904	8.125000
18	130.000000	32.500000	145.083302	32.500000
	135.546196	12.045549	120.443798	8.125000
19	32.499999	32.500001	88.791651	32.500000
	18.340734	61.748379	88.246133	8.125000
20	97.500000	32.500000	88.791651	32.500000
	113.864335	9.771732	72.302735	8.125000

Table 17.4. Placement parameters of objects for case (d) $r = 2/3R$.

#	x	y	z	R/r
1	32.499999	32.671691	94.895499	32.500000
	49.961167	21.666667	69.790777	21.666667
2	32.499999	95.861022	157.789947	32.500000
	22.260507	75.244714	134.847179	21.666667
3	32.499999	59.855999	35.575100	32.500000
	23.301749	30.290797	25.698814	21.666667
4	85.599697	97.260908	33.066143	32.500000
	81.732356	127.449409	21.666667	21.666667
5	149.227859	83.989265	32.500000	32.500000
	140.096626	54.661882	21.880434	21.666667
6	93.208311	33.000685	39.208845	32.500000
	68.307266	21.666667	21.666667	21.666667
7	82.472917	146.462807	75.426459	32.500000
	89.897780	157.296140	105.154566	21.666667
8	32.499999	146.462807	116.992160	32.500000
	23.022164	155.863209	87.360199	21.666667
9	95.041688	78.252634	155.923985	32.500000
	124.789514	81.421982	168.623280	21.666667
10	143.111818	32.500000	154.306755	32.500000
	160.061192	56.248807	168.623280	21.666667
11	95.777408	32.500000	109.759549	32.500000
	105.895749	57.996004	92.329031	21.666667
12	62.879346	89.847539	100.641602	32.500000
	67.479413	69.375670	75.822416	21.666667
13	131.281923	146.462807	32.500000	32.500000
	160.061192	135.944128	21.666667	21.666667
14	149.227860	146.462807	94.973541	32.500000
	124.047262	130.803821	108.277061	21.666667
15	149.227860	83.078787	112.998142	32.500000
	160.061192	94.427031	84.535775	21.666667
16	83.101783	146.462807	157.789947	32.500000
	53.197798	154.526741	167.637518	21.666667
17	146.001015	130.071145	157.789947	32.500000
	160.061192	157.296140	168.623280	21.666667
18	149.227859	32.500000	72.171848	32.500000
	159.606197	21.978767	43.226317	21.666667
19	32.500000	146.462807	33.860758	32.500000
	24.778053	118.448914	48.415598	21.666667
20	48.909111	32.500000	157.789946	32.500000
	79.036787	23.655540	166.177356	21.666667

Table 17.5. Effective elastic modulus.

	r/R			
Effective elastic characteristics	1/4	1/3	1/2	2/3
$E_{1,}$ GPa	132.97	181.05	198.02	227.49
$E_{2,}$ GPa	140.10	175.01	193.52	210.39
$E_{3,}$ GPa	130.67	187.60	213.23	221.17
$G_{12,}$ GPa	51.854	61.659	64.088	71.679
$G_{23,}$ GPa	44.940	59.543	66.355	69.778
$G_{31,}$ GPa	44.965	60.628	69.343	75.178
ν_{12}	0.27953	0.28798	0.26779	0.29057
ν_{13}	0.25178	0.25921	0.26798	0.2887
ν_{23}	0.24701	0.2509	0.25853	0.26088
ρ, kg m^{-3}	2771.4	2772.9	2770.3	2770.8

strengthening of new materials. These numerical data show the essential diversity in the effective elastic modulus via different r/R.

17.6 Conclusions

Mathematical models are elaborated for prediction of the effective properties of three-dimensional composites and nanocomposites with different structure parameters. The concept of representative volume element is accepted. The sets of non-classical inclusions are considered. The new nanocomposite materials are studied with more realistic inclusions. Shapes composed by the union of spheres are proposed for nanoinclusion simulations.

It should be noted that more sophisticated shapes used in the packing models, e.g. polyhedra [36, 37], may ensure more adequate results. The purpose of further research will be to analyze the strength characteristics of composites with more realistic inclusion systems. Combinations of stuck together spheres, cylinders, cones of different sizes will be considered as inclusions. This will lead to increasing the problem scale and will require the development of new efficient numerical algorithms. To cope with large-scale problems arising in different steps of the algorithmic approach, Lagrangian heuristics [38] can be used. Alternatively, decomposition or aggregation techniques [39, 40] can also be applied.

References

[1] Garg A, Chalak H D, Belarbi M-O, Zenkour A M and Sahoo R 2021 Estimation of carbon nanotubes and their applications as reinforcing composite materials—an engineering review *Compos. Struct.* **272** 114234

[2] Avramov K V 2018 Nonlinear vibrations characteristics of single-walled carbon nanotubes via nonlocal elasticity *Int. J. Nonlin. Mech.* **107** 149–60

[3] Sevostianov I, Mogilevskaya S G and Kushch V I 2019 Maxwell's methodology of estimating effective properties: alive and well *Int. J. Eng. Sci.* **140** 35–88

[4] Kushch V I 2018 Stress field and effective elastic moduli of periodic spheroidal particle composite with Gurtin–Murdoch interface *Int. J. Eng. Sci.* **132** 79–96

[5] Mykhas'kiv V V and Stasyuk B M 2017 Effective elastic properties of 3D composites with short curvilinear fibers: numerical simulation and experimental validation *Solid State Phenom.* **258** 452–5

[6] Tulskyi H H, Liashok L V, Shevchenko H S, Vasilchenko A V and Stelmakh O A 2019 Synthesis of functional nanocomposites based on aluminum oxides *Funct Mater* **26** 718–22

[7] Sierikova O, Koloskov V, Degtyarev K and Strelnikova O 2021 The deformable and strength characteristics of nanocomposites improvingMater. Sci. Forum **1038** 144–53

[8] Gurtin M E and Murdoch A I 1975 A continuum theory of elastic material surfaces *Arch. Ration. Mech. Anal.* **57** 291–323

[9] Strelnikova E, Kriutchenko D, Gnitko V and Degtyarev K 2020 Boundary element method in nonlinear sloshing analysis for shells of revolution under longitudinal excitations *Eng. Anal. Boundary Elem.* **111** 78–87

[10] Mirjavadi S S, Forsat M, Barati M R and Hamouda A M S 2020 Analysis of nonlinear vibrations of CNT- /fiberglass-reinforced multi-scale truncated conical shell segments *Mech. Based Des. Struct. Mach.* **50** 2067–83

[11] Smetankina N, Merkulova A, Merkulov D and Postnyi O 2021 Dynamic response of laminate composite shells with complex shape under low-velocity impact *Integrated Computer Technologies in Mechanical Engineering – 2020. ICTM 2020Lecture Notes in Networks and Systems* vol 188 ed M Nechyporuk, V Pavlikov and D Kritskiy (Cham: Springer)

[12] Surianinov M, Andronov V, Otrosh Y, Makovkina T and Vasiukov S 2020 Concrete and fiber concrete impact strengthMater. Sci. Forum **1006** 101–6

[13] Kushch V I 2018 Elastic fields and effective stiffness tensor of spheroidal particle composite with imperfect interface *Mech. Mater.* **124** 45–54

[14] Strelnikova O, Gnitko V, Degtyariov K and Tonkonozhenko A 2020 Advanced computational models and software on predicting the effective elastic properties for computer-simulated structures of nanocomposite *IEEE KhPI Week on Advanced Technology (KhPIWeek)* 171–6

[15] Ungson Y, Burtseva L, Garcia-Curiel E, Valdez-Salas B, Flores-Rios B L, Werner F and V. Petranovskii 2018 Filling of irregular channels with round cross-section: modeling aspects to study the properties of porous materials *Materials* **11** 1901

[16] Blyuss O, Koriashkina L, Kiseleva E and Molchanov R 2015 Optimal placement of irradiation sources in the planning of radiotherapy: mathematical models and methods of solving *Comput. Math. Methods Med.* **2015** 142987

[17] Halkarni S S, Sridharan A and Prabhu S V 2018 Experimental investigation on effect of random packing with uniform sized spheres inside concentric tube heat exchangers on heat transfer coefficient and using water as working medium *Int. J. Therm. Sci.* **133** 341–56

[18] Duriagina Z, Lemishka I, Litvinchev I, Marmolejo J, Pankratov A, Romanova T and Yaskov G 2020 Optimized filling a given cuboid with spherical powders for additive manufacturing *J. Oper. Res. Soc. Chin.* **9** 853–68

[19] Otaru A J and Kennedy A R 2016 The permeability of virtual macroporous structures generated by sphere packing models: comparison with analytical models *Scr. Mater.* **124** 30–3

[20] Zeng Z Z, Huang W Q, Xu R C and Fu Z H 2012 An algorithm to packing unequal spheres in a larger sphere *Adv. Mater. Res.* **546–547** 1464–9

[21] Hifi M and Yousef L 2019 A local search-based method for sphere packing problems *Eur. J. Oper. Res.* **274** 482–500

[22] Burtseva L, Valdez Salas B, Romero R and Werner F 2016 Recent advances on modelling of structures of multi-component mixtures using a sphere packing approach *Int. J. Nanotechnol.* **13** 44–59

[23] Burtseva L, Valdez Salas B, Werner F and Petranovskii V 2015 Packing of monosized spheres in a cylindrical container: models and approaches *Rev. Mex. Fís.* E **61** 20–7

[24] Chazelle B, Edelsbrunner H and Guibas L J 1989 The complexity of cutting complexes *Discr. Comput. Geom.* **4** 139–81

[25] Romanova T, Stoyan Y, Pankratov A, Litvinchev I, Avramov K and Chernobryvko M *et al* 2021 Optimal layout of ellipses and its application for additive manufacturing *Int. J. Prod. Res.* **59** 560–75

[26] Stoyan Y, Yaskov G, Romanova T, Litvinchev I, Yakovlev S and Cantú J M V 2020 Optimized packing multidimensional hyperspheres: a unified approach *Math. Biosci. Eng.* **7** 6601–30

[27] Romanova T, Litvinchev I and Pankratov A 2020 Packing ellipsoids in an optimized cylinder *Eur. J. Oper. Res.* **285** 429–43

[28] Pankratov A, Romanova T and Litvinchev I 2019 Packing ellipses in an optimized convex polygon *J. Global Optim.* **75** 495–522

[29] Stoyan Y G, Romanova T E, Pankratov O V, Stetsyuk P I and Stoian Y E 2021 Sparse balanced layout of spherical voids in three-dimensional domains *Cybernet. Syst. Anal.* **57** 542–51

[30] Romanova T, Stoyan Y, Pankratov A, Litvinchev I and Marmolejo J A 2020 Decomposition algorithm for irregular placement problems Intelligent Computing and Optimization. ICO 2019*Advances in Intelligent Systems and Computing book series AISC* vol 1072 ed P Vasant, I Zelinka and G W Weber (Berlin: Springer) pp 214–21

[31] Le M-T and Huang S-C 2014 Modeling and estimating the effective elastic properties of carbon nanotube reinforced composites by finite element method . *J. Eng. Technol. Educ.* **11** 145–58

[32] Miller R E and Shenoy V B 2000 Size-dependent elastic properties of nanosized structural elements *Nanotechnology* **11** 139–47

[33] Strelnikova E, Litvinchev I, Pankratov A, Duriagina Z, Romanova T, Lemishka I and Tonkonozhenko A 2020 Optimized packings in analysis of 3D nanocomposites with inclusion systems *KhPI week on advanced technology, KhPI Week 2020 - Conf. Proc.* 377–81

[34] Romanova T, Pankratov A, Litvinchev I and Strelnikova E 2021 Modeling nanocomposites with ellipsoidal and conical inclusions by optimized packing *Computer Science and Health Engineering in Health Services. COMPSE 2020 Lecture Notes of the Institute for Computer Sciences, Social-Informatics and Telecommunications Engineering, LNICST* vol 359 359 (Cham: Springer) pp 201–10

[35] Wächter A and Biegler L T 2006 On the implementation of a primal-dual interior point filter line search algorithm for large-scale nonlinear programming *Math. Program.* **106** 25–57

[36] Stoyan Y, Pankratov A, Romanova T, Fasano G, Pintér J D, Stoian Y E and Chugay A 2019 Optimized packings in space engineering applications: part I *Springer Optimization and Its Applications: Modeling and Optimization in Space Engineering Springer Optimization and Its Applications: Modeling and Optimization in Space Engineering* vol 144 ed G Fasano and J Pintér vol 144 (Cham: Springer) pp 395–437

[37] Romanova T, Bennell J, Stoyan Y and Pankratov A 2018 Packing of concave polyhedra with continuous rotations using nonlinear optimization *Eur. J. Oper. Res.* **268** 37–53

[38] Litvinchev I 1991 Decomposition-aggregation method for convex programming problems *J. Math. Program. Oper. Res.* **22** 47–56

[39] Litvinchev I and Rangel S 1999 Localization of the optimal solution and *a posteriori* bounds for aggregation *Comput. Oper. Res.* **26** 967–88 http://hdl.handle.net/11449/31830

[40] Litvinchev I, Mata M, Rangel S and Saucedo J 2010 Lagrangian heuristic for a class of the generalized assignment problems *Comput. Math. Appl.* **60** 1115–23

Chapter 18

Sentiment analysis for web series using deep learning techniques in the times of COVID-19

Muskan Dixit and Saravjeet Singh

Emotions and sentiments play a very important role in understanding user reactions, buying behaviour, and decision making. Sentiment analysis is concerned with determining the emotions and vehemence underlying the written material, while web series is the perception of emotion. Accelerated divergent opinions, ratings, recommendations, feedbacks are the key for future development and decision-taking units. This chapter deals with sentiment analysis for selected web series during the COVID-19 pandemic. In order to understand the impact and impression the web series makes on the audience, the contents from web platforms were collected and analysed using the natural language processing (NPL) technique. To analyse the viewers' sentiments, comments and utterances were collected and pre-processed to get a generalized vocabulary. The data of 63 578 mentions and reviews were collected and analysed using Brand24 software. The web series *Friends*, *Game of Thrones*, *Sherlock* and *Ragnarok* were found to have constrictive and pragmatic impact on viewers during COVID-19. However, web series *Cursed* was negatively reviewed by 61% during the same period. Overall, 54.53% of viewers have positive comments on web series.

18.1 Introduction

Sentiment analysis—known as automated text analysis/opinion mining—is quite a new and powerful tool in the field of data mining, which measures human activities and is being applied in fields where products and services are reviewed by customers and critics, utilizing social networking sites, newspapers, and blogs. We can extract an enormous amount of content and knowledge from the text comments, which encourage us if the comments are positive and at the same time help in further improvement of the content in the case of criticism. In both situations, it generates

doi:10.1088/978-0-7503-4801-0ch18

opportunities for advancement. This technique helps companies and organizations to know the current status to which a product or service is actually accepted in a particular segment; the present study deals with the web series segment. Web series review analysis is one of the segments to which the majority are connected, and its analysis gives us a compiled review of the sentiments of a large set of people. According to the data Netflix had set a very ambitious target of gaining more than 100 million viewers within five years. While adopting a premium pricing strategy and positioning themselves uniquely based on their international content [1]. This industry, therefore, targets a greater audience and is a huge industry where we have seen rapid growth in the past. To understand and appraise public views on movies and web series—a reliable and scalable assessment is required. We know that sample surveys of a representative population over time and space are expensive and time-consuming and hence, alternative technique(s) such as sentiment analysis are vital for extracting, processing, and seeking objective data (opinions, sentiments, and emotions) in text. There are many deep learning methodologies that are used to analyse comments and reviews. NLP is a combination of computer science, artificial intelligence, and linguistics. NLP is a tool through which we can do an intact study of reviews made in the time of the COVID-19 pandemic. As the COVID-19 lockdown time was very difficult, people staying at home tended to watch more web series. In March 2020, there was around a 28% rise in viewership over the previous months on the cinema streaming service MUBI (*Financial Express*, April 6, 2020). This use of time engaged more of the audience and played a significant role in the lives of many as it is a good source of entertainment and passes the time. Web series became one of the most viewed media channels. People expressed different views on web series using blogs, Twitter, Facebook, Instagram, media channels, etc. Over-the-top (OTT) platforms for web series succeeded in providing audiences with much-needed fresh content, interesting plots, and realistic presentations of characters and situations with which audiences tend to relate themselves [2]. In this chapter, we provide a sentiment analysis of users' comments on web series and identify factors affecting the future growth of the web series industry. The study will provide further insights for both viewers and production houses. A rise of fear and anxiety was probable during this pandemic but there was also a chance of increasing self-harming possibility among people with mental health issues [3]. In this chapter, linguistic processing using NPL set-up in the form of the toolkit of Brand24 software was used.

This chapter is organized as follows: the next section presents a brief review of recent studies on sentiment analysis. Section 18.3 provides the methodology used to perform the experiment, followed by analysis and discussion in the section 18.4. Finally, the paper is concluded with semantic, syntactic, and philosophical analyses of the web series.

18.2 Review of literature

NLP is rule-based modeling of sentiments in texts (i.e., detection and classification of human mood), using machine learning and deep learning techniques. It allows for the integration of language understanding and language generation, also used as multilinguistic event detection [4, 5]. The sentiments are being conveyed in different forms and types (in newspaper articles, blogs, reviews, forums, etc), which need to be dealt with using specialized methods [5]. NLP is done by two processing methods: NPL for speech recognition and NLP for speech synthesis. NLP for speech synthesis is a complex schema used for speech synthesis and extensively used for text-to-speech (TTS) processing. NLP approaches fall roughly into four categories: symbolic, statistical, connectionist, and hybrid [6]. The retrieval of information and dialogue through NLP (speech recognition)—known as the synchronic model of language—is the mainstay of sentimental analysis, which has advantages over the earlier sequential models [7]. In the pandemic time there have been major changes as we were under lockdown, which acted as an aid to media society as it got a boost in attracting audiences towards web series. In the first phase of lockdown (starting from March 1, 2020), the daily average users of OTT platforms were hiked by 83%, according to a Google trend report [8]. As the number of viewers has increased, there is a need for appraisal of the content and its sentimental impact on them. The sentiment of COVID-19 Tweets using deep learning models produced interesting results for further validation [9]. One more study revealed that the majority of the respondents (87%) are willing to continue with OTT services in the future while the remaining 13% want to keep away from OTT services in the future, which shows the interest of the audience in web series [10].

A brief review of recent works in India and abroad on the chosen topic is presented in table 18.1.

In summary of the reviews, web-based surveillance, YouTube, AssistDem were utilized to comprehend the COVID-19 situation and ML techniques, i.e., BERT, RNN provided better accuracy of the data analysed.

Table 18.1. Recent trends in sentiment analysis.

Reference No.	Data set used	Year	Purpose	Remarks
[9]	Indian tweets: 3090 (github.com)	2021	To comprehend the data for better understanding of public behaviour to fight against the pandemic and describing health-related problems. And to find a better machine learning (ML) model for accuracy.	The Bidirectional Encoder Representations from Transformers (BERT) model provided better accuracy of the data analysed. The data set collected gave public opinion regarding COVID-19.
[11]	Data set from blogs, forums, news, videos,	2021	To substantiate lower spread of propaganda	The usage of recurrent neural network (RNN) to analyze the impact

(*Continued*)

Table 18.1. (*Continued*)

Reference No.	Data set used	Year	Purpose	Remarks
	web, podcast and using hashtag tweets		using long-term memory algorithms.	of social media using hashtags to give the resonance of COVID-19 on the populace.
[12]	Twitter tweets and then scraping using Twitter API	2021	To do analysis and statistics of the data of users Twitter handles in the format of a positive and negative statement.	The emotional manifestations are articulated to specific classes and the overall outcome turns out to be positive. Classification of the emotional class was done using RNN.
[13]	Tweets from worldwide	2021	To analyze the state of mind and psychology of the public in the times of COVID-19 on the basis of tweets.	Integrated analysis of worldwide tweets resulted in a positive impact on the public and concludes that the overall usage of devices escalated.
[14]	Data of YouTube videos that have viewers more than 3 552 125 (SD 2 817 911).	2020	To study the trends and rapid changes in the contents of YouTube during COVID-19.	YouTube platform is considered to be one of the most used platforms and a comprehensive global platform to communicate the latest announcements. Understanding COVID behaviour protocols is the best methodology to reduce exposure to SARS-CoV-2 and improve the situation.
[15]	Data collected from global entertainment companies (i.e., Walt Disney World and Box Office).	2020	To do the assessment of pandemic and post-pandemic circumstances at different strands.	The implications of COVID-19 on the global entertainment companies and gaming industry. The devastating effect of the pandemic is discussed further in management minutes.

[16]	Data set on COVID-19 cases (official website, press and social media).	2020	(i) Surveillance of COVID-19 cases; (ii) Cognizance of the situation during the pandemic.	Using web-based surveillance and the cluster of cases and its spread in all the countries according to the frequency of traveling in different times of COVID-19.
[17]	Data collected from 93 participants in Spain through telephone calls and television-based assistive integrated technology (TV-AssistDem.)	2020	To study the effects of TV-AssistDem on health and social support	In times of pandemic, AssistDem helped to a great extent in providing COVID related information. The technology has the potential for intellectual stimulus.
[18]	Data set was collected from reports, documents, publications and videos of European Broadcasting Union (EBU) activities.	2020	To learn about the impact of COVID-19 in Europe and to emphasize the public value on and to observe the face of changes of audience behavior.	There is a change in trends of the informative and entertainment industry irrespective of the countries. During times of pandemic, the media has provided the essential support of spreading information. Moreover, media has also seen changes in demand in terms of preferences because of increased competition between traditional channels

18.3 Methodology

In this study, web series viewers' comments were collected and analysed using deep learning with the help of Brand24 software. The deep learning model has a hierarchical learning capability and the algorithms derived from the structure and functions of the brain are defined as artificial neutral networks. So, deep learning was used in eliminating pre-processing data. A methodology is required that guides attempts at providing or improving answer proposals [19]. Algorithms were used to ingest and process unstructured data, like text and images, and it automates feature extraction, removing some of the dependency on human experts. Deep learning has been used extensively on the data generated by IoT sensors in a smart city by several

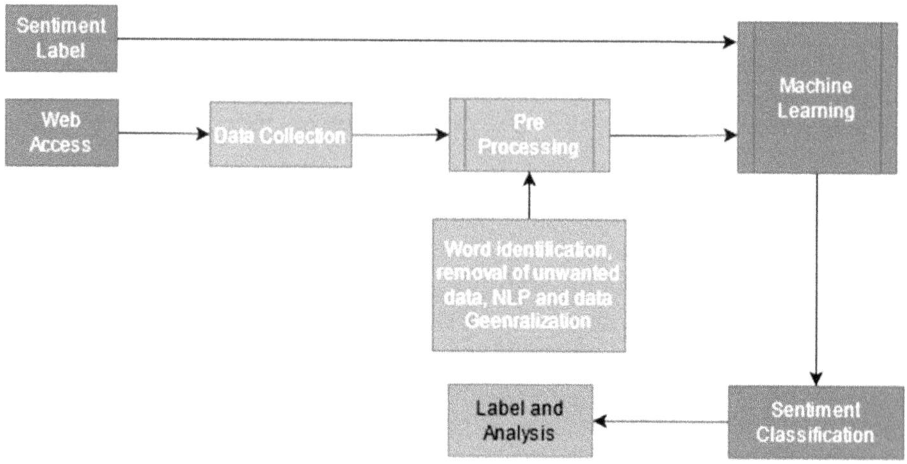

Figure 18.1. Procedure involved in sentiment analysis.

researchers [20]. Deep learning methodology is effective in sentiment analysis. Figure 18.1 exhibits the procedure involved in sentiment analysis.

18.4 Data collection and analysis

For this experiment, web series viewers' comments were collected from the web platforms NetFlix, Hot Star, Prime Video, Voot, Sony Liv, blogs, YouTube, and news using API access. The growth of social network sites has generated a slew of fields devoted to analysing these networks and their contents in order to extract necessary information [21]. Comments were considered for the peak lockdown period of the second wave of COVID-19 in India. Comments were considered from March 2021 to May 2021. Web APIs were used to collect comments or users' reactions on different media platforms. The individual project was created for collecting data from each web series. 63 578 mentions and reviews were collected for the analysis.

18.4.1 Pre-processing

Collected data contains complete reactions of users, which may include some unwanted words, wrong words, typing mistakes, local vocabulary, etc. Therefore, this collected data needs to be processed to filter unwanted information and to obtain the correct data. The pre-processing of a collection of comments and utterances was performed for the purpose of normalization and generation of the language to express a sentiment.

18.4.2 Data processing

Collected data were processed using a deep learning method to identify the sentiments. For this sentiment analysis, semantic tags were obtained and added to the model. A predefined model using Brand24 was used to identify the web series liking trends and linguistic processing was done. Model features were tuned as per the data requirement. It used the concept of an algorithm which is based on the manually created lexicon, ML, rule-based, and hybrid approaches. Usually, a lexicon-based approach performs entity level sentiment analysis and it gives high precision but low recall [22]. Furthermore, the lexicon (precompiled sentiment terms) is bifurcated into a dictionary-based approach and corpus-based approach to find the sentiment polarity of the text using semantic or statistical methods. Sentiment analysis is the first phase of our approach, which requires many tasks that help identify interesting information in reviews, which are the pre-processing and lexicon-based sentiment analysis [23]. The hybrid approach, i.e., the combination of rule-based approach and lexicon-based approach, provides more accuracy in aggregated results. Sentiment analysis was provided for the marked days. For processing, seven different projects with the same model were created.

18.4.3 Analysis

The processed data provided numerical summaries and infographics of individual projects. Based on the obtained results, an analysis of sentiment was provided.

18.5 Results and discussion

After collecting and processing the data as per NLP and the deep learning model, results were obtained in the form of numeric values. The analysis was done in steps firstly collecting the data of seven projects (based on different web series) that were compiled with the mention of individual web series. Then the mentions were critically studied and perused. The total number of mentions collected was 63 578.

In this project, the data of the *Friends* web series, which is a sitcom genre, was collected and had 12 125 mentions. Figure 18.2 is a graphical representation of the reviews obtained on a respective day. The linear graph gives us static data of the number of reviews on the day. This moreover gives us a key point that lockdown and night curfew was imposed in major areas in India from 24 April 2021 and we tend to see the major occurrence of the reviews at this time. The web series has impacted positively on the majority of the audience. Figure 18.3 gives us the analysis of the total number of volumes which is 12 125 and the total number of mentions, which are under the reach of social media, which is about 43 million. Then the sentimental analysis of the reviews is done directly on the positive and negative statement count. The positive reviews were to the tune of 76% which revealed that this web series impacted the audience with a constructive note.

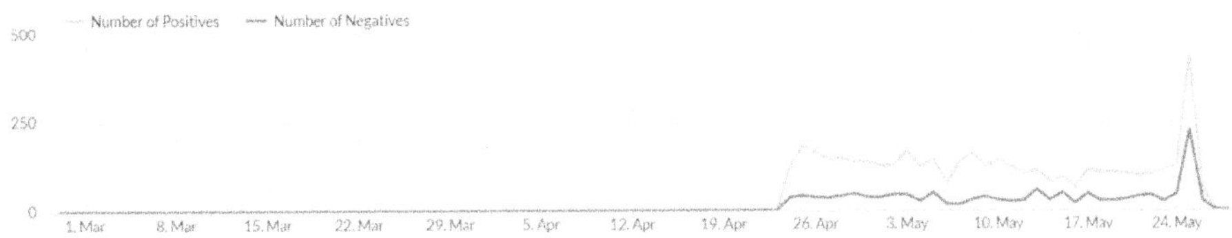

Figure 18.2. Day-wise analysis of mentions of web series *Friends*.

Figure 18.3. Summary of mentions of the web series *Friends*.

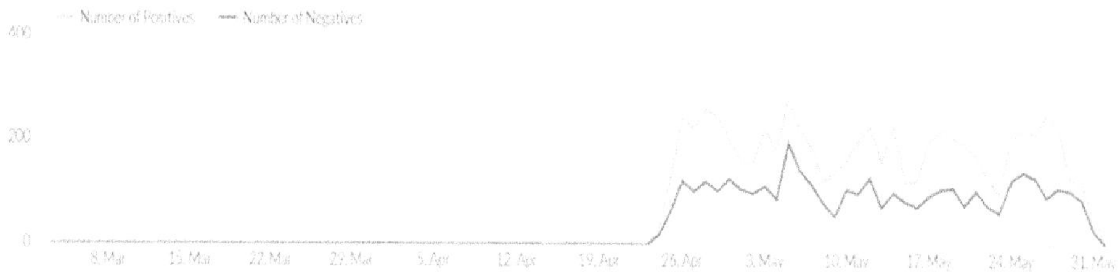

Figure 18.4. Day-wise analysis of mentions of the web series *Game of Thrones*.

Figure 18.5. Summary of mentions of the web series *Game of Thrones*.

In the second project, the data of the *Game of Thrones* web series whose genre is fantasy, serial drama, and tragedy has been collected, which has 15 962 mentions. Figure 18.4 shows the fluctuating reviews as the graph has many highs and lows on each day. The linear graph gives us static data of the number of reviews on the day. This web series has impacted positively the majority of the audience. Figure 18.5 gives us the analysis of the total number of volumes, which is 15 962, and the total number of mentions which were under the reach of social media (about 50 million). The numbers of positive reviews were 10 375 (i.e., 65% of the total reviews). This concludes that this web series has a positive impact on the viewers.

In the third project, the data of the *Money Heist* web series is been collected, which has 2604 mentions. The genre of this web series is drama, heist, and thriller. Figure 18.6 is a graphical representation that has slight review variations on the respective days. Figure 18.7 gives us the analysis of the total number of reviews, which is 2604, and the total number of mentions which are under the reach of social media which is about 37 million. The number of positive reviews is 1719 (66% of the total reviews). The number of negative reviews is 885 (34% of the total reviews). This concludes that there is an overall positive impact on viewers.

The data of the *Sherlock* web series has been collected, which has 150 mentions and its genre is crime mystery, comedy-drama. Figure 18.8 is a graphical

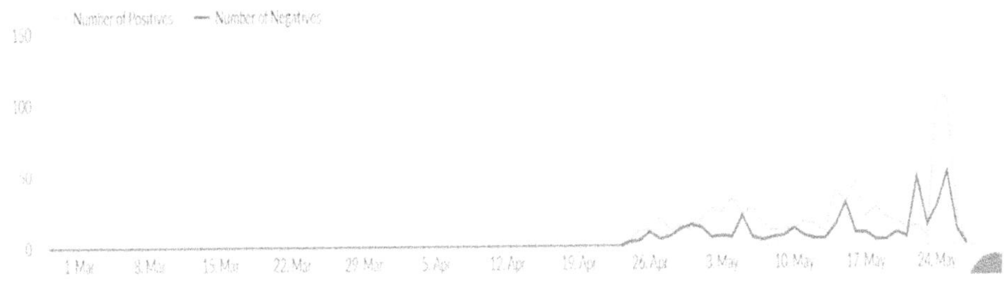

Figure 18.6. Day-wise analysis of mentions of web series *Money Heist*.

Figure 18.7. Summary of mentions of the web series *Money Heist*.

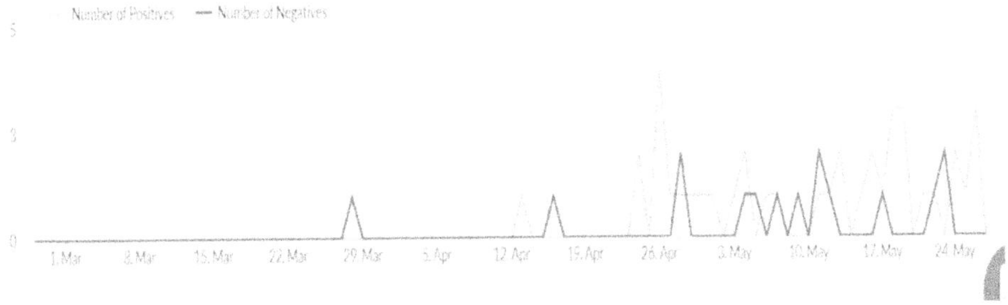

Figure 18.8. Day-wise analysis of mentions of the web series *Sherlock*.

Figure 18.9. Summary of mentions of the web series *Sherlock*.

representation of the reviews obtained on a respective day, which have sharp points with extreme variations. Figure 18.9 gives us the analysis of the total number of reviews, which is 150, and the total number of mentions which are under the reach of social media, which is 4350. The number of positive reviews were to the tune of 105 (70% of the total reviews), indicating positive impact on viewers.

In the fifth project, the data of the *Ragnarok* web series has been collected, which has 5258 mentions. The genre of this is fantasy and drama. Figure 18.10 also gives fluctuating reviews with almost the same pattern, but the number of positive reviews is more with each day. Figure 18.11 gives us the analysis of the total number of reviews, which is 5258 and the total number of mentions which are under the reach of social media which is 55 million. Positive reviews (3628 No) outweigh the number of negative reviews (1630 No). It can be said that there is a positive impact on the majority of viewers.

In the sixth project, the data of the *Cursed* web series has been collected, which has 22 216 mentions. The genre of this is fantasy, serial drama, adventure, and action. Figure 18.12 is a graphical representation that has fluctuating reviews as the graph has many highs and lows on each day and the overall impact on the audience is negative. While, figure 18.13 gives us the analysis of the total number of reviews (22 216) and the total number of mentions which are under the reach of social media (227 million). Around 61% of viewers had a negative perspective on web series *Cursed.*

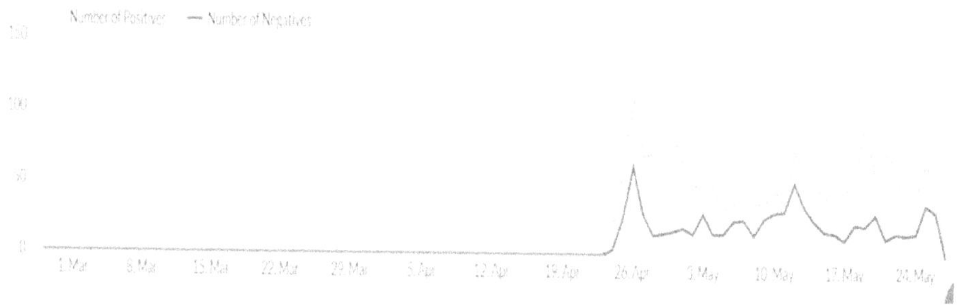

Figure 18.10. Day-wise analysis of mentions of the web series *Ragnarok*.

Figure 18.11. Summary of mentions of the web series *Ragnarok*.

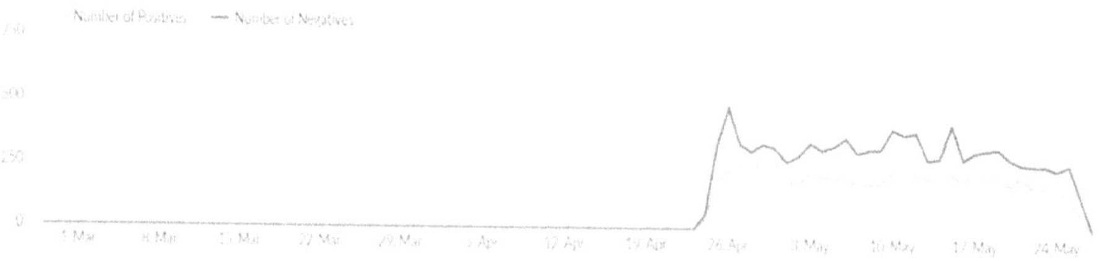

Figure 18.12. Day-wise analysis of mentions of web series *Cursed.*

Figure 18.13. Summary of mentions of the web series *Cursed.*

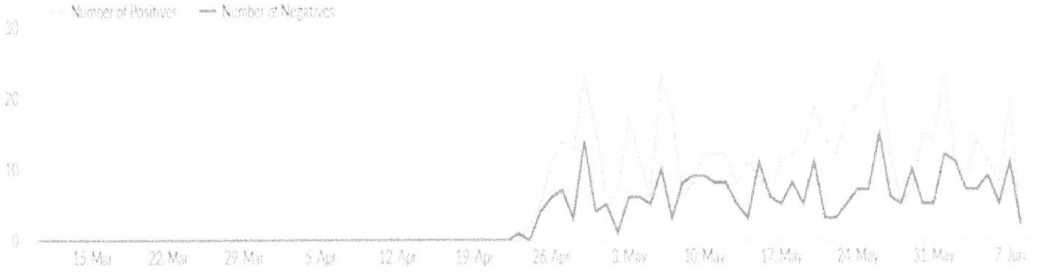

Figure 18.14. Day-wise analysis of mentions of web series *13 Reasons Why*.

Figure 18.15. Summary of mentions of the web series *13 Reasons Why*.

In this seventh project, the data of the *13 Reasons Why*, web series has been collected, which has 913 mentions. The genre of the series is teen drama, mystery, and psychological thriller. Figure 18.14 is a graphical representation with fluctuating reviews as the graph has many highs and lows on each day and the overall impact on the audience is negative. Figure 18.15 gives us the analysis of the total number of reviews, which is 1490, and the total number of mentions which are under the reach of social media, which is 18 million.

There are seven projects analysed and 63 578 comments were taken into consideration. It was taken into account that the rate of impact on the audience started in mid-April 2021 when the lockdown was again imposed. On an overall note, the positive impact on the viewers turns out to be 34 675 (54.53%) and negative reviews turn out to be 28 903 (45.46%), as shown in figure 18.16. The overall result has a slight difference, although the positivity rate is greater, there is still a lot to improve in terms of content, which will gradually provide more favourable results. The content, which is dominated by the viewers according to the genre, is sitcom, fantasy, and drama. The results recognised the sentiment challenges that have domain dependence.

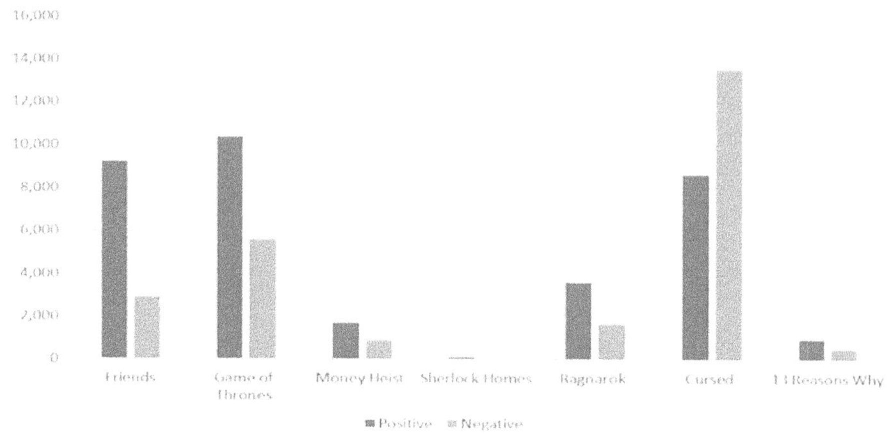

Figure 18.16. Overall impact of web series on the viewers.

18.5.1 Salient findings

The study perceived a positive impact of web series, although it varies according to viewers' interest and the content of series. Nonetheless, the improvement in content will improve the growth perspective.

18.6 Conclusion

Sentiment analysis associated with web series during the COVID-19 pandemic based on the contents clearly established constructive and positive impact on the audience. The entertainment sector is an integral part of the public sphere which boosts the sector as it affects the public mood and interests and the profitable aspects of investors' opinions. The majority of the viewers (54.53%) report a positive impact. The overall result has a slight difference, although the positivity rate is greater there is still a lot to improve in terms of content, which will gradually provide more favorable results. The capabilities of the tools enhance the depth analysis of the public interest which is important for the growth of the specific genre sectors. The content most favoured by the viewers, according to the genre, is sitcom, fantasy, and drama. There is a wide scope of web series as the audience is very keen on it. Future research in this field will include a greater number of head analyses and the angle to explore more genres for further growth perspective. The aim will be to see the growth of OTT platforms, which are the key platforms of web series in future research. Moreover, there will be a study to observe and analyse the interests of different age groups.

Acknowledgement

I extend my sincere thanks to Dr Saravjeet Sigh, Asstt. Professor, Chitakara University, Punjab and Dr Anil Kumar Dixit, Principal Scientist, ICAR-National

Dairy Research Institute, Karnal for their guidance and critical suggestions for improvement of the manuscript.

References

[1] Nafees L, Mehdi M, Gupta R, Kalia S and Kapoor S 2021 Netflix in India: expanding to success *Emerald Emerging Markets Case Studies* **11** 2

[2] Chattopadhyay A 2020 Web series and web movies and their psycho-sociological impact on netizens in India *Asian Think.* **7** 46–57

[3] Kundu B and Bhowmik D 202 Societal impact of novel corona virus (COVID- 19 pandemic) in India

[4] Khurana D, Koli A, Khatter K and Singh S 2017 Natural language processing: State of the art, current trends and challenges https://arxiv.org/ftp/arxiv/papers/1708/1708.05148.pdf

[5] Balahur A 2013 Sentiment analysis in social media texts Proc. 4th Workshop on Computational Approaches to Subjectivity, Sentiment and Social Media Analysis *(Atlanta, GA)* 120–8

[6] Liddy E D 2001 Natural language processing *Encyclopedia of Library and Information Science* 2nd Edn (New York: Marcel Decker, Inc) pp 1–15

[7] Reshamwala A, Mishra D and Pawar P 2013 Review on natural language processing *IRACST Eng. Sci. Technol.: Int. J. (ESTIJ)* **3** 113–16

[8] Patel M K, Awasya G and Khadia R A study: OTT viewership in 'lockdown' and viewer's dynamic watching experience *Int. J. Transform. Media Journal. Mass Commun.* **5** 10–22

[9] Chintalapudi N, Battineni G and Amenta F 2021 Sentimental analysis of COVID-19 tweets using deep learning models *Infect. Disease Rep.* **13** 329–39

[10] Kumari T 2020 A study on growth of over the top (OTT) video services in India *Int. J. Latest Res. Human. Soc. Sci. (IJLRHSS)* **3** 68–73

[11] Mugilan A, Kanmani R, Priya M D, Malar A C J and Suganya R 2021 Smart Sentimental analysis of the impact of social media on COVID-19 *Micro-Electronics and Telecommunication Engineering* (Singapore: Springer) pp 437–46

[12] Nemes L and Kiss A 2021 Social media sentiment analysis based on COVID-19 *J. Inform. Telecommun.* **5** 1–15

[13] Priyadarshini I, Mohanty P, Kumar R, Sharma R, Puri V and Singh P K 2021 A study on the sentiments and psychology of twitter users during COVID-19 lockdown period *Multimedia Tools Appl.* **81** 27009–31

[14] Basch C E, Basch C H, Hillyer G C and Jaime C 2020 The role of YouTube and the entertainment industry in saving lives by educating and mobilizing the public to adopt behaviors for community mitigation of COVID-19: successive sampling design study *JMIR Publ. Health Surveill.* **6** e19145

[15] Nhamo G, Dube K and Chikodzi D 2020 Implications of COVID-19 on gaming, leisure and entertainment industry *Counting the Cost of COVID-19 on the Global Tourism Industry* (Cham: Springer) pp 273–95

[16] Dawood F S, Ricks P, Njie G J, Daugherty M, Davis W, Fuller J A and Bennett S D 2020 Observations of the global epidemiology of COVID-19 from the prepandemic period using web-based surveillance: a cross-sectional analysis *Lancet Infect. Diseases* **20** 1255–62

[17] Goodman-Casanova J M, Dura-Perez E, Guzman-Parra J, Cuesta-Vargas A and Mayoral-Cleries F 2020 Telehealth home support during COVID-19 confinement for community-

dwelling older adults with mild cognitive impairment or mild dementia: survey study *J. Med. Internet Res.* **22** e19434

[18] Túñez-López M, Vaz-Álvarez M and Fieiras-Ceide C 2020 Covid-19 and public service media: impact of the pandemic on public television in Europe *Profes. Inform.* **29** 1–16

[19] Schlangen D 2020 Targeting the benchmark: on methodology in current natural language processing research arXiv preprint arXiv:2007.04792

[20] Bhattacharya S, Somayaji S R K, Gadekallu T R, Alazab M and Maddikunta P K R 2022 A review on deep learning for future smart cities *Internet Technol. Lett.* **5** e187

[21] Wankhade M, Rao A C S and Kulkarni C 2022 A survey on sentiment analysis methods, applications, and challenges *Artif. Intell. Rev.* **55** 5731–80

[22] Shinde G K, Lokhande V N, Kalyane R T, Gore V B and Raut U M 2021 Sentiment Analysis Using Hybrid Approach. Publication *Int. J. Res. Appl. Sci. Eng. Technol. (IJRASET)* **9** 282–5

[23] Sallam R M, Hussein M and Mousa H M 2022 Improving collaborative filtering using lexicon-based sentiment analysis *Int. Elec. Comput. Eng.* **12** 1744

Chapter 19

Generalized receiver: signal processing in DS-CDMA wireless communication systems over fading channels

Vyacheslav Tuzlukov

In this chapter, we consider employment of the generalized receiver in direct-sequence code-division multiple-access (DS-CDMA) wireless communication systems for several practical cases. Firstly, the blind generalized receiver in fading multipath channels, which utilizes the correlation information between consecutively received signals to generate the corresponding group constraint. In this case, the proposed generalized receiver can provide different performance gains in both the uplink and downlink environments. Compared with the well-known group-blind detectors, our new methods need only to estimate the multipath channel of the desired user and do not require the channel estimation of other users.

Secondly, the multicarrier (MC) DS-CDMA wireless communication using space-time spreading-assisted transmit diversity is investigated in the context of broadband wireless communications systems constructed based on the generalized approach to signal processing in noise over frequency-selective Rayleigh fading channels. We consider the issue of parameter design for the sake of achieving high-efficiency communications in various dispersive environments. In contrast to the conventional MC DS-CDMA wireless communication system employing the time-domain (T-domain) spreading only, the broadband MC DS-CDMA wireless communication schemes employ both the T-domain and frequency-domain (F-domain) spreading, i.e., employ the TF-domain spreading. The bit-error rate (BER) performance of the space-time spreading-assisted broadband MC DS-CDMA wireless communications system is investigated for downlink transmissions associated with the single-user and multiuser generalized detectors and is compared with that of the single-user correlation detector and the multiuser decorrelating detector. Our study demonstrates that with appropriately selecting the system parameters, the

doi:10.1088/978-0-7503-4801-0ch19

broadband MC DS-CDMA wireless communication system using the space-time spreading-assisted transmit diversity constitutes a promising downlink transmission scheme. This scheme is capable of supporting ubiquitous communications over diverse communication environments without *BER* performance degradation.

Thirdly, the capacity and error probability of orthogonal space-time block codes (STBCs) are considered for the pulse-amplitude modulation (PAM), phase-shift keying (PSK), and quadrature-amplitude modulation (QAM) in fading channels. The suggested approach is based on employment of the generalized approach to signal processing in noise over the equivalent scalar additive white Gaussian noise (AWGN) channel with a channel gain proportional to the Frobenius norm of the matrix channel for the STBC. Using this effective channel, the capacity and probability of error expressions are derived for the PSK, PAM, and QAM modulation with space-time block coding. The Rayleigh, Rician and Nakagami fading channels are considered. As an application, these results are extended to obtain the capacity and probability of error for a multiuser DS-CDMA wireless communication system employing the space-time block coding.

Fourthly, the parallel interference cancellation is considered as a simple yet effective multiuser detector for DS-CDMA wireless communication systems. However, the system performance can be deteriorated due to unreliable interference cancellation in the early stages. Thus, the generalized detector with partial parallel interference cancellation, in which partial cancellation factors are introduced to control the interference cancellation level, has been developed as a remedy. Although the partial cancellation factors are crucial, complete solutions for their optimal values are not available. We consider a two-stage decoupled generalized receiver with the partial parallel interference cancellation. Using the minimum *BER* criterion, we derive a complete set of optimal partial cancellation factors. This includes the optimal partial cancellation factors for periodic and aperiodic spreading codes in channels with the AWGN and multipath channels. The proposed two-stage generalized receiver with the partial parallel interference cancellation using the derived optimal partial cancellation factors outperforms not only a two-stage, but also a three-stage conventional generalized receiver with the full parallel interference cancellation.

19.1 Intersymbol detection in downlink DS-CDMA

19.1.1 Introduction

Multiuser detection for DS-CDMA wireless communication systems has been proposed to mitigate multiple-access interference (MAI) and enhance channel capacity. The concept of multiuser detection for DS-CDMA wireless communication systems was first started with the research published in [1], where an optimum multiuser detector for the multiple-access Gaussian channels was obtained. However, the optimum detection has never become the mainstream because of its unmanageable computational complexity. Therefore, a number of suboptimum detectors with good performance/complexity trade-off were developed during the several past decades. In [2] and [3] an adaptive linear decorrelating or zero-forcing detector was reported by using training sequences. The linear minimum mean square error (MMSE) detector was another popular suboptimum detector, as presented and analysed in [4] and [5]. In [6], the basic techniques for multiuser detection were summarized, depicting the evolution of this discipline over the past several years.

Some of the previously mentioned detectors require the information of active users, including the spreading waveform, the multipath channel, and the delay of each user. Unfortunately, such requirements are practically difficult to meet. Hence, the blind multiuser detection, which only requires the information of timing and spreading waveform of the desired user, has received much attention since it was first reported in [7]. Without considering multipath, the blind minimum output energy (MOE) detector was presented in [8–10] and then the canonical subspace representation of the decorrelating detector and the MMSE detector were reported in [11–13].

In [14], a reduced-rank MOE detector was proposed by using array processing techniques. However, these detectors cannot work properly when the intersymbol interference (ISI) cannot be ignored and the multipath channel is not known. In [15–19], several improved subspace approaches were developed based on the channel estimation. A reduced computational constrained optimization solution was proposed in [20–25] with a little sacrifice of the performance, i.e., inferior to the performance of MMSE detector.

In [26], several types of group-blind linear detectors were developed to provide substantial performance gains over the blind linear multiuser detection methods for uplink channels. The basic idea behind the group-blind detectors is to suppress the interference from the known users by using their spreading sequences to construct a useful group constraint and to suppress the interference from unknown users based on subspace-based blind methods. Since these detectors need to estimate the multipath channels and the time delays of all known users to obtain the group constraint, computational complexity has to be increased for the implementation of these detectors. In addition, the errors of channel estimation for each known user may cause the performance of these detectors to deteriorate.

The main focus of the present section is to develop improved blind detectors for DS-CDMA wireless communication systems based on the generalized approach to signal processing in noise [27–30] in fading multipath channels. It is noted that due to the existence of ISI, especially in asynchronous DS-CDMA wireless communication systems, the current received signal has indeed certain relationships with its preceeding and succeeding ones. Hence, a proper utilization of ISI would be beneficial for blind multiuser detection. The key idea of the proposed detectors is to construct a cross-correlation matrix by exploiting the correlation between the consecutive received signals. By utilizing this cross-correlation matrix, we generate an optimal constraint similar to the group constraint in [26] and then develop the improved blind generalized receiver.

Unlike the detectors in [26], our methods only require the channel estimation of the interested user. Although we mainly focus on the asynchronous DS-CDMA systems in the present section, it will be shown that for both asynchronous (uplink) and synchronous (downlink) cases, the proposed generalized receiver offers a superior performance to some extent over the conventional blind multiuser detection methods that do not utilize the optimal constraint. The performance improvement of the proposed generalized receiver is justified analytically.

19.1.2 Signal model

We consider a DS-CDMA wireless communication system with K users and a normalized spreading factor of N chips per symbol. The transmitted signal for the kth user is given by

$$x_k(t) = A_k \sum_{i=-\infty}^{\infty} b_k[i] s_k(t - iT), \tag{19.1}$$

where T is the symbol duration, and A_k and $b_k[i] \in [1, -1]$ are the amplitude and symbol stream of the kth user, respectively. The spreading waveform $s_k(t)$ can be presented in the following form

$$s_k(t) = \sum_{j=0}^{N-1} c_k[j] \psi(t - jT_c),\ 0 \leqslant t \leqslant T, \tag{19.2}$$

where $c_k[j] = \pm 1$, $(0 \leqslant j \leqslant N - 1)$ is the spreading sequence allocated to the kth user and $\psi(t)$ is the normalized chip waveform with the duration $T_c = T/N$. The discrete-time signal for user k generated by matched filtering and sampling at the chip rate is given by

$$x_k(n) = \sum_{i=-\infty}^{\infty} b_k(i) \bar{c}_k(n - iN), \tag{19.3}$$

where $\bar{c}_k(n) = A_k c_k(n)$, $n = 0, \ldots, N - 1$. By propagating through the asynchronous multipath channel that is assumed to have the maximum length of $M (M < N)$ in terms of chip duration, the received discrete-time signal $y_k(n)$ for user k is given by [31]

$$y_k(n) = \sum_{m=-\infty}^{\infty} x_k(m) g_k(n - d_k - m), \tag{19.4}$$

where $g_k(m) \neq 0, 0 \leqslant m \leqslant M$ is the mth complex channel gain for user k and $0 \leqslant d_k < N$ is the delay of user k in chip periods. Based on (19.3) and (19.4), we obtain

$$y_k(n) = \sum_{m=-\infty}^{\infty} b_k(m) h_k(n - d_k - mN), \tag{19.5}$$

$$h_k(n) = \sum_{j=-\infty}^{\infty} \bar{c}_k(j) g_k(n - j), \tag{19.6}$$

where $h_k(n)$ is the signature pulse of user k, which is the distorted version of the code $\bar{c}_k(n)$ due to the multipath gain $y_k(n)$. Finally, the received signal $y_k(n)$ is the superposition of the signals from all K users plus the AWGN $w(n)$ with the zero mean and variance σ_w^2, i.e.

$$y(n) = \sum_{k=1}^{K} y_k(n) + w(n). \tag{19.7}$$

From (19.6) and denoting

$$\mathbf{h}_{k,all} = [h_k(0), h_k(1), \ldots, h_k(N-1+M)]^H \tag{19.8}$$

as the signature sequence vector of user k, where $(\cdot)^H$ means the Hermitian transpose operator, we obtain

$$\mathbf{h}_{k,all} = \overline{\mathbf{C}}_k \mathbf{g}_k, \tag{19.9}$$

where

$$\overline{\mathbf{C}}_k = \begin{bmatrix} \bar{\mathbf{c}}_k(0) & \ddots & \mathbf{0} \\ \vdots & \ddots & \bar{\mathbf{c}}_k(0) \\ \bar{\mathbf{c}}_k(N-1) & \ddots & \vdots \\ \mathbf{0} & \ddots & \bar{\mathbf{c}}_k(N-1) \end{bmatrix}; \tag{19.10}$$

$$\mathbf{g}_k = \begin{bmatrix} g_k(0) \\ \vdots \\ g_k(M) \end{bmatrix}. \tag{19.11}$$

In (19.10), $\overline{\mathbf{C}}_k$ is the $(N+M) \times (M+1)$ matrix formed from the product of the spreading sequences and the amplitude of kth user, and $\mathbf{g}_k$ is the kth user's multipath channel vector. From (19.5)–(19.11), wc dcnotc

$$\mathbf{y}_k(n) = \begin{bmatrix} y_k(nN) \\ \vdots \\ y_k(nN+N-1) \end{bmatrix}; \tag{19.12}$$

$$\mathbf{h}_k = \begin{bmatrix} \mathbf{0} \\ h_k(0) \\ \vdots \\ h_k(N-d_k-1) \end{bmatrix}; \tag{19.13}$$

$$\bar{\mathbf{h}}_k = \begin{bmatrix} h_k(N-d_k) \\ \vdots \\ h_k(N+M-1) \\ \mathbf{0} \end{bmatrix}. \tag{19.14}$$

It is easy to obtain that

$$\mathbf{y}_k(n) = \mathbf{h}_k b_k(n) + \bar{\mathbf{h}}_k b_k(n-1), \tag{19.15}$$

where $\mathbf{y}_k(n)$ is the nth received signal vector of user k. Then, the total received user's signal vector

$$\mathbf{y}(n) = [y(nN), \ldots, y(nN+N-1)]^T, \tag{19.16}$$

where $(\cdot)^T$ means the transpose operator, is given by

$$\mathbf{y}(n) = \sum_{k=1}^{K} \mathbf{y}_k(n) + \mathbf{w}(n) = \mathbf{H}_0\mathbf{b}(n) + \mathbf{H}_1\mathbf{b}(n-1) + \mathbf{w}(n) = \mathbf{H}\bar{\mathbf{b}}(n) + \mathbf{w}(n), \quad (19.17)$$

where

$$\begin{cases} \mathbf{H}_0 = [\mathbf{h}_1, \ldots, \mathbf{h}_K]; \\ \mathbf{H}_1 = [\bar{\mathbf{h}}_1, \ldots, \bar{\mathbf{h}}_K]; \\ \mathbf{H} = [\mathbf{H}_0; \mathbf{H}_1]; \end{cases} \quad (19.18)$$

$\mathbf{H}_0$ is the signature matrix of the current bits of all users including MAI; $\mathbf{H}_1$ is the signature matrix of the previous bits of all users including MAI; $\mathbf{H}$ is the signature matrix of all users;

$$\begin{cases} \mathbf{b}(n) = [b_1(n), \ldots, b_K(n)]^T; \\ \mathbf{b}(n-1) = [b_1(n-1), \ldots, b_K(n-1)]^T; \\ \bar{\mathbf{b}}(n) = [\mathbf{b}^T(n); \mathbf{b}^T(n-1)]^T; \end{cases} \quad (19.19)$$

$\mathbf{b}(n)$ is the vector of current bits of all users; $\mathbf{b}(n-1)$ is the vector of previous bits of all users; $\bar{\mathbf{b}}(n)$ is the vector of bits of all users;

$$\mathbf{w}(n) = [w(nN), \ldots, w(nN + N - 1)]^T \quad (19.20)$$

is the independent AWGN vector.

In the asynchronous (uplink) DS-CDMA wireless communication systems, it is often assumed that the matrices $\mathbf{H}_0$ and $\mathbf{H}_1$ are mutually independent, and the matrix $\mathbf{H}$ is the tall matrix with full column rank $2K$ as the existence of the delays of different users [20, 26]. However, for the synchronous (downlink) DS-CDMA wireless communication systems, the full-rank condition on the matrix $\mathbf{H}$ is hardly satisfied as argued in [32]. It can be explained that in the synchronous DS-CDMA wireless communication systems ($d_k = 0$ for $k = 1, \ldots, K$), the nonzero elements in the matrix $\mathbf{H}_1$ are limited by the number of active users K and the multipath length M, i.e., only the $M \times K$ submatrix in the matrix $\mathbf{H}_1$ is nonzero. Hence the signature matrix $\mathbf{H}$ will not be full column rank unless K is less than M.

19.1.3 Conventional blind linear multiuser detectors

The canonical form of a linear detector for user k can be represented by the correlator characterized by the vector $\mathbf{v}_k \in C^N$ followed by the received signal vector $\mathbf{y}(n)$, such that the decision on user k takes the following form

$$\hat{b}_k[n] = \text{sgn}\{\mathcal{R}(\mathbf{v}_k^H \mathbf{y}(n))\}, \quad (19.21)$$

where sgn$(\cdot)$ is the signum operator. Based on (19.21), we next introduce the two most popular linear multiuser detectors.

19.1.3.1 Linear decorrelating detector

The linear decorrelating detector is known as the linear zero-forcing detector. The decorrelating detector is designed to eliminate the MAI and ISI completely at the expense of enhancing the ambient noise. It has the form as in (19.21) with the weight vector $\mathbf{d}_k = \mathbf{v}_k$, which is given by

$$\mathbf{d}_k = \arg\min_{\mathbf{d}} ||\mathbf{d}^H\mathbf{H}||^2, \text{ subject to: } \mathbf{d}^H\mathbf{h}_k = 1, \tag{19.22}$$

where the matrix $\mathbf{H}$ is defined in (19.17) and $\mathbf{h}_k$ is the signature vector of the desired user.

19.1.3.2 Linear MMSE detector

The linear MMSE detector has the form of (19.21) with the weight vector $\mathbf{m}_k = \mathbf{v}_k$, obtained by calculating the minimum output mean squared error, i.e.

$$\mathbf{m}_k = \arg\min_{\mathbf{d}} E\{|b_k[n] - \mathbf{m}^H\mathbf{y}[n]|^2\}. \tag{19.23}$$

The two detectors can be resolved by subspace methods. We denote the autocorrelation matrix of the received signal in (19.17) as

$$\mathbf{Y} = E\{\mathbf{y}(n)\mathbf{y}^H(n)\} = \mathbf{H}\mathbf{H}^H + \sigma^2\mathbf{I}_N. \tag{19.24}$$

By performing the eigendecomposition of the matrix $\mathbf{Y}$, we obtain

$$\mathbf{Y} = [\mathbf{U}_s\mathbf{U}_n]\begin{bmatrix}\mathbf{\Lambda}_s & \\ & \mathbf{\Lambda}_n\end{bmatrix}[\mathbf{U}_s\mathbf{U}_n]^H = \mathbf{U}_s\mathbf{\Lambda}_s\mathbf{U}_s^H + \mathbf{U}_n\mathbf{\Lambda}_n\mathbf{U}_n^H, \tag{19.25}$$

where

$$\mathbf{\Lambda}_s = diag(\lambda_1, \ldots, \lambda_L), \tag{19.26}$$

where $diag(\cdot)$ denotes the diagonal matrix, contains the L largest eigenvalues of the matrix $\mathbf{Y}$ and the matrix $\mathbf{U}_s$ contains the corresponding orthonormal eigenvectors of the signal subspace spanned by $\mathbf{HH}^H$. Both the vectors $\mathbf{\Lambda}_n = \sigma^2\mathbf{I}_{N-L}$ and the vectors $\mathbf{U}_n$ are the eigenvalues and orthonormal eigenvectors of the noise subspace, respectively. The numerical value of L depends on the column rank of the matrix $\mathbf{H}$ that has the maximum value $2K$ on the condition that the matrix $\mathbf{H}$ is the full column rank. By using the eigendecomposition in (19.25), the detectors in (19.22) and (19.23) can be expressed in terms of the subspace forms as described in [11], i.e.

$$\mathbf{d}_k = \mathbf{U}_s(\mathbf{\Lambda}_s - \sigma^2\mathbf{I}_L)^{-1}\mathbf{U}_s^H\mathbf{h}_k, \tag{19.27}$$

$$\mathbf{m}_k = \mathbf{U}_s\mathbf{\Lambda}_s^{-1}\mathbf{U}_s^H\mathbf{h}_k. \tag{19.28}$$

The signal subspace components $\mathbf{U}_s$ and $\mathbf{\Lambda}_s$ can be estimated from the eigendecomposition of the autocorrelation matrix of the received signal samples. For blind multiuser detection, the detector has only *a priori* knowledge of the spreading sequence of the desired user. The detectors in (19.27) and (19.28) need to estimate σ^2

and $\mathbf{h}_k$. By computing the average value of $N - L$ minimum eigenvalues of the matrix $\mathbf{Y}$, σ^2 can be easily obtained. Meanwhile, when the desired user is synchronized, its signature vector $\mathbf{h}_k$ can be estimated in terms of the received signal and the matrix $\overline{\mathbf{C}}_k$ in (19.11), [33]

$$\mathbf{g}_k = \text{Max-eigenvector}(\overline{\mathbf{C}}_{k,up}^H \mathbf{U}_s \mathbf{U}_s^H \overline{\mathbf{C}}_{k,up}), \tag{19.29}$$

$$\mathbf{h}_k = \overline{\mathbf{C}}_{k,up} \mathbf{g}_k, \tag{19.30}$$

where the matrix $\overline{\mathbf{C}}_{k,up}$ is composed of the first N rows of the matrix $\overline{\mathbf{C}}_k$. Table 19.1 summarizes the algorithms of the blind decorrelating detector and blind MMSE detector.

Table 19.1. Signal processing algorithms of subspace blind linear decorrelating and subspace blind linear MMSE detectors.

Signal frame: $\mathbf{y}(0), \mathbf{y}(1), \ldots, \mathbf{y}(P)$		
Step Number	**Operation**	**Formula**
STEP 1	Compute autocorrelation	$\mathbf{Y} = \frac{1}{P+1}\sum_{n=0}^{P} \mathbf{y}(n)\mathbf{y}^H(n)$
STEP 2	Compute eigendecomposition of the matrix $\mathbf{Y}$	$\mathbf{Y} = \mathbf{U}_s \mathbf{\Lambda}_s \mathbf{U}_s^H + \sigma^2 \mathbf{U}_n \mathbf{U}_n^H$
STEP 3	Parameter estimation	$\sigma^2 = \frac{1}{N-L}$ Sum of the min $N - L$ eigenvalues of the matrix$\mathbf{Y}$ $\mathbf{g}_k = \text{Max -eigenvector}(\overline{\mathbf{C}}_{k,up}^H \mathbf{U}_s \mathbf{U}_s^H \overline{\mathbf{C}}_{k,up})\mathbf{h}_k = \overline{\mathbf{C}}_{k,up}\mathbf{g}_k$
STEP 4	Form decorrelating and MMSE detectors	$\mathbf{d}_k = \mathbf{U}_s(\mathbf{\Lambda}_s - \sigma^2 \mathbf{I}_L)^{-1}\mathbf{U}_s^H \mathbf{h}_k \mathbf{m}_k = \mathbf{U}_s \mathbf{\Lambda}_s^{-1} \mathbf{U}_s^H \mathbf{h}_k$

19.1.4 Generalized receiver

The generalized receiver is constructed in accordance with the generalized approach to signal processing in noise [27–30]. The generalized approach to signal processing in noise introduces an additional noise source that does not carry any information about the parameters of desired transmitted signal with the purpose to improve the signal processing system performance. This additional noise can be considered as the reference noise without any information about the parameters of the signal to be detected.

The jointly sufficient statistics of the mean and variance of the likelihood function is obtained under the generalized approach to signal processing in noise employment, while the classical and modern signal processing theories can deliver only the sufficient statistics of the mean or variance of the likelihood function. Thus, the generalized approach to signal processing in noise implementation allows us to obtain more information about the parameters of the desired transmitted signal incoming at the generalized receiver input. Owing to this fact, the detectors constructed based on the generalized approach to signal processing in noise technology are able to improve the signal detection performance of signal processing systems in comparison with employment of other conventional detectors.

The generalized receiver (GR) consists of three channels (see figure 19.1): the GR correlation detector channel (GR CD)—the preliminary filter (PF), the multipliers 1 and 2, the model signal generator (MSG); the GR energy detector channel (GR ED)—the PF, the additional filter (AF), the multipliers 3 and 4, the summator 1; and the GR compensation channel (GR CC)—the summators 2 and 3, the accumulator 1. The threshold apparatus (THRA) device defines the GR threshold.

As we can see from figure 19.1, there are two bandpass filters, i.e., the linear systems, at the GR input, namely, the PF and AF. We assume for simplicity that these two filters or linear systems have the same amplitude–frequency characteristics or impulse responses. The AF central frequency is detuned relative to the PF central frequency. There is a need to note the PF bandwidth is matched with the transmitted signal bandwidth. If the detuning value between the PF and AF central frequencies is more than 4 or 5 times the transmitted signal bandwidth to be detected, i.e. 4–5Δf_s, where Δf_s is the transmitted signal bandwidth, we can believe that the processes at the PF and AF outputs are uncorrelated because the coefficient of correlation between them is negligible (not more than 0.05). This fact was confirmed independently by experiment in [34] and [35]. Thus, the transmitted signal plus noise can appear at the GR PF output and only the noise appears at the GR AF output. The stochastic processes at the GR AF and GR PF outputs present the input stochastic samples from two independent frequency-time regions. If the discrete-time noise $w_i[k]$ at the GR PF and GR AF inputs is Gaussian, the discrete-time noise $\zeta_i[k]$ at the GR PF output is Gaussian too, and the reference discrete-time noise $\eta_i[k]$ at the GR AF output is Gaussian owing to the fact that the GR PF and GR AF are the linear systems and we believe that these linear systems do not change the statistical parameters of the input process. Thus, the GR AF can be considered as a generator of the reference noise with *a priori* information a 'no' transmitted signal (the

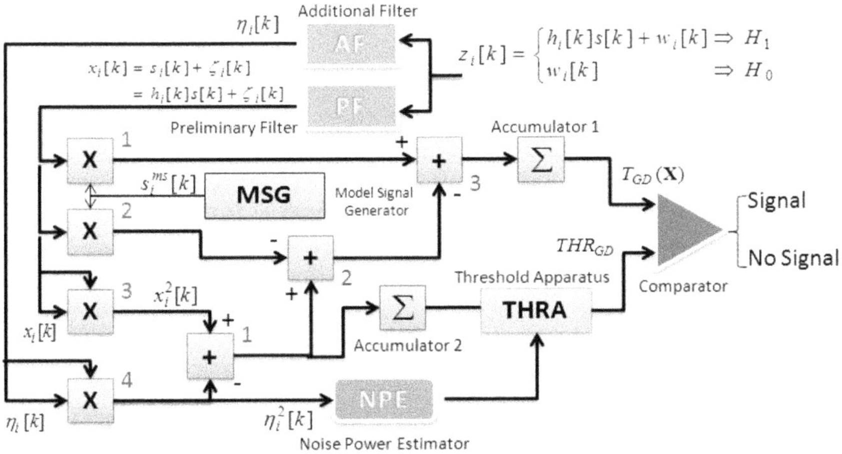

Figure 19.1. Generalized receiver.

reference noise sample) [28, chapter 5]. The noise at the GR PF and GR AF outputs can be presented as

$$\begin{cases} \zeta_i[k] = \sum_{m=-\infty}^{\infty} g_{PF}[m]w_i[k-m]; \\ \eta_i[k] = \sum_{m=-\infty}^{\infty} g_{AF}[m]w_i[k-m], \end{cases} \tag{19.31}$$

where $g_{PF}[m]$ and $g_{AF}[m]$ are the impulse responses of the GR PF and GR AF, respectively.

In general, under practical implementation of any detector in wireless communication system with sensor array, the bandwidth of the spectrum to be sensed is defined. Thus, the GR AF bandwidth and central frequency can be assigned, too (this bandwidth cannot be used by the transmitted signal because it is out of its spectrum). The case when there are interfering signals within the GR AF bandwidth, the action of this interference on the GR detection performance, and the case of non-ideal condition when the noise at the GR PF and GR AF outputs is not the same by statistical parameters are discussed in [36] and [37].

Under the hypothesis H_1 ('a yes' transmitted signal), the GR CD generates the signal component $s_i^m[k]s_i[k]$ caused by interaction between the model signal $s_i^m[k]$, forming at the MSG output, and the incoming signal $s_i[k]$, and the noise component $s_i^m[k]\zeta_i[k]$ caused by interaction between the model signal $s_i^m[k]$ and the noise $\zeta_i[k]$ at the PF output. GR ED generates the transmitted signal energy $s_i^2[k]$ and the random component $s_i[k]\zeta_i[k]$ caused by interaction between the transmitted signal $s_i[k]$ and the noise $\zeta_i[k]$ at the PF output. The main purpose of the GR CC is to cancel completely in the statistical sense the GR CD noise component $s_i^m[k]\zeta_i[k]$ and the GR ED random component $s_i[k]\zeta_i[k]$ based on the same nature of the noise $\zeta_i[k]$. The relation between the transmitted signal to be detected $s_i[k]$ and the model signal $s_i^m[k]$ is defined as:

$$s_i^m[k] = \mu s_i[k], \tag{19.32}$$

where μ is the coefficient of proportionality.

The main functioning condition under the GR employment in any signal processing system including the communication one with radar sensors is the equality between the parameters of the model signal $s_i^m[k]$ and the incoming signal $s_i[k]$, for example, by amplitude. Under this condition it is possible to cancel completely in the statistical sense the noise component $s_i^m[k]\zeta_i[k]$ of the GR CD and the random component $s_i[k]\zeta_i[k]$ of the GR ED. Satisfying the GR main functioning condition given by (19.32), $s_i^m[k] = s_i[k]$, $\mu = 1$, we are able to detect the transmitted signal with high probability of detection at a low signal-to-noise ratio (*SNR*) and define the transmitted signal parameters with the required high accuracy.

Practical realization of the condition (19.32) at $\mu \to 1$ requires increasing the complexity of GR structure and, consequently, leads us to increasing computation cost. For example, there is a need to employ an amplitude tracking system or to use off-line data samples processing. Under the hypothesis H_0 ('a no' transmitted signal), satisfying the main GR functioning condition (19.32) at $\mu \to 1$ we obtain only the background noise $\eta_i^2[k] - \zeta_i^2[k]$ at the GR output.

Under practical implementation, the real structure of GR depends on specificity of signal processing systems and their applications, for example, the radar sensor systems, adaptive wireless communication systems, cognitive radio systems, satellite communication systems, mobile communication systems and so on. In the present chapter the GR circuitry (figure 19.1) is demonstrated with the purpose to explain the main functioning principles. Because of this, the GR flowchart presented in the chapter should be considered under this viewpoint. Satisfying the GR main functioning condition (19.32) at $\mu \to 1$, the ideal case, for the wireless communication systems with radar sensor applications we are able to detect the transmitted signal with very high probability of detection and define accurately its parameters.

In the present section, we discuss the GR implementation in the broadband space-time spreading MC DS-CDMA wireless communication system. Since the presented GR test statistics is defined by the signal energy and noise power, the equality between the parameters of the model signal $s_i^m[k]$ and transmitted signal to be detected $s_i[k]$, in particular by amplitude, is required that leads us to high circuitry complexity in practice. For example, there is a need to employ the amplitude tracking system or off-line data sample processing. Detailed discussion about the main GR functioning principles if there is no *a priori* information and there is an uncertainty about the parameters of transmitted signal, i.e., the transmitted signal parameters are random, can be found in [27] and [28, chapter 6, pp 611–21 and chapter 7, pp 631–95].

The complete matching between the model signal $s_i^m[k]$ and the incoming signal $s_i[k]$, for example by amplitude, is a very hard problem in practice because the incoming signal $s_i[k]$ depends on both the fading and the transmitted signal parameters and it is impractical to estimate the fading gain at the low SNR. This matching is possible in the ideal case only. The GD detection performance will deteriorate under mismatching in parameters between the model signal $s_i^m[k]$ and the transmitted signal $s_i[k]$ and the importance of this problem is discussed in [38–41], where a complete analysis about the violation of the main GR functioning requirements is presented. The GR decision statistics requires an estimation of the noise variance σ_η^2 using the reference noise $\eta_i[k]$ at the AF output.

Under the hypothesis H_1, the signal at the GR PF output, see figure 19.1, can be defined as

$$x_i[k] = s_i[k] + \zeta_i[k], \tag{19.33}$$

where $\zeta_i[k]$ is the noise at the PF output and

$$s_i[k] = h_i[k]s[k], \tag{19.34}$$

where $h_i[k]$ are the channel coefficients. Under the hypothesis H_0 and for all i and k, the process $x_i[k] = \zeta_i[k]$ at the PF output is subjected to the complex Gaussian distribution and can be considered as the i.i.d. process.

In the ideal case, we can think that the signal at the GR AF output is the reference noise $\eta_i[k]$ with the same statistical parameters as the noise $\zeta_i[k]$. In practice, there is a difference between the statistical parameters of the noise $\eta_i[k]$ and $\zeta_i[k]$. How this difference impacts on the GR detection performance is discussed in detail in [28, chapter 7, pp 631–695] and in [42, 43].

The decision statistics at the GR output presented in [29] and [30, chapter 3] is extended for the case of antenna array when an adoption of multiple antennas and antenna arrays is effective to mitigate the negative attenuation and fading effects. The GR decision statistics can be presented in the following form:

$$T_{GR}(\mathbf{X}) = \sum_{k=0}^{N-1}\sum_{i=1}^{M} 2x_i[k]s_i^m[k] - \sum_{k=0}^{N-1}\sum_{i=1}^{M} x_i^2[k] + \sum_{k=0}^{N-1}\sum_{i=1}^{M} \eta_i^2[k] \underset{H_0}{\overset{H_1}{\gtrless}} THR_{GR}, \tag{19.35}$$

where

$$\mathbf{X} = [\mathbf{x}(0), \ldots, \mathbf{x}(N-1)] \tag{19.36}$$

is the vector of the random process at the GR PF output and THR_{GR} is the GR detection threshold.

Under the hypotheses H_1 and H_0 when the amplitude of the transmitted signal is equal to the amplitude of the model signal, $s_i^m[k] = s_i[k]$ i.e., $\mu = 1$, the GR decision statistics $T_{GD}(\mathbf{X})$ takes the following form in the statistical sense, respectively

$$\begin{cases} H_1\colon T_{GD}(\mathbf{X}) = \sum_{k=0}^{N-1}\sum_{i=1}^{M}\left\{s_i^2[k] + \eta_i^2[k] - \zeta_i^2[k]\right\}; \\ H_0\colon T_{GD}(\mathbf{X}) = \sum_{k=0}^{N-1}\sum_{i=1}^{M}\left\{\eta_i^2[k] - \zeta_i^2[k]\right\}. \end{cases} \tag{19.37}$$

In (19.37) the term $\sum_{k=0}^{N-1}\sum_{i=1}^{M} s_i^2[k] = E_s$ corresponds to the average transmitted signal energy, and the term $\sum_{k=0}^{N-1}\sum_{i=1}^{M}\eta_i^2[k] - \sum_{k=0}^{N-1}\sum_{i=1}^{M}\zeta_i^2[k]$ is the background noise at the GR output. The GR output background noise is a difference between the noise power at the GR PF and GR AF outputs. Practical implementation of the GR decision statistics requires an estimation of the noise variance using the reference noise $\eta_i[k]$ at the AF output.

19.1.5 Blind generalized receiver

The conventional generalized receiver discussed in section 19.1.4 only knows the spreading sequence of the desired user. However, some performance gains may be obtained if the generalized detector has the knowledge of the spreading sequences of a group of users. Such an expectation has been achieved in [26], where several group-blind linear multiuser detectors were presented. These detectors first exploit the known user spreading sequences to estimate their signature vectors based on the methods in (19.29) and (19.30). By using the estimated signal vectors, several group-blind generalized receivers can be developed with the following group constraint:

$$\mathbf{T}_k^H\widetilde{\mathbf{H}} = \mathbf{1}_{P,k}^T, \tag{19.38}$$

where P is the number of columns in the matrix $\widetilde{\mathbf{H}}$, $\mathbf{T}_k$ is the vector of decision statistics of the generalized receiver defined by (19.35) for user k, the matrix $\widetilde{\mathbf{H}}$ contains the estimated signature vectors of a group of known users, which is the subset of the matrix $\mathbf{H}$ in (19.17), and $\mathbf{1}_{P,k}$ is denoted as the P dimension column vector with all zero entries except for the kth entry. The constraint in (19.38) is the key idea of the group-blind zero-forcing generalized receiver and the group-blind hybrid detector in [26]. Equation (19.38) is equivalent to the following constraints:

$$\begin{cases} \mathbf{T}_k^H \mathbf{h}_k = 1\ ; \\ \mathbf{T}_k^H \hat{\mathbf{H}} = 0, \end{cases} \tag{19.39}$$

where the matrix $\hat{\mathbf{H}}$ contains the remaining column vectors of the matrix $\widetilde{\mathbf{H}}$ except for the vector $\mathbf{h}_k$. In (19.39), the first constraint is to ensure the existence of the desired user signal at the generalized receiver output, and the second constraint is used to zero force the interference of the known user's signal. Hence, the essence of the group-blind multiuser detection is to construct a group constraint, which exactly removes the influence of some interfering users, thereby achieving performance gains. Since the group constraint in [26] requires the known user's spreading sequences and the estimations of their multipath channels and delays, such techniques are only fit for the DS-CDMA uplink, where the base station knows the spreading sequences of the intracell users.

Inspired from the previously mentioned group methods, we develop two improved blind generalized receivers in this subsection. The basic idea for the proposed generalized receivers is to construct a new group constraint, which is similar to the group constraint in (19.39), by exploiting the intersymbol information of the received signals. In this method, we only need the channel estimation of the desired user. Therefore, our generalized receivers can provide performance gain over the blind linear decorrelating detector and the blind linear MMSE detector.

Let us assume without loss of generality that user 1 is the desired user, and the generalized receiver is synchronized to user 1, i.e., $d_1 = 0$. Then the signal in (19.17) can be rewritten in the following form:

$$\mathbf{y}(n) = \mathbf{h}_1 b_1(n) + \bar{\mathbf{h}}_1 b_1(n-1) + \breve{\mathbf{H}}\breve{\mathbf{b}}(n) + \mathbf{w}(n), \tag{19.40}$$

where

$$\breve{\mathbf{H}} = [\mathbf{h}_2, \ldots, \mathbf{h}_K, \bar{\mathbf{h}}_2, \ldots, \bar{\mathbf{h}}_K] \tag{19.41}$$

is the signature matrix and

$$\breve{\mathbf{b}}(n) = [b_2(n), \ldots, b_K(n), b_2(n-1), \ldots, b_K(n-1)]^T \tag{19.42}$$

is the vector of received signals of the interfering users. We next consider the channel estimation of $\mathbf{h}_1$, which is the signature vector of the desired signal $b_1(n)$. Meanwhile, we will also estimate the vector $\bar{\mathbf{h}}_1$ since it is required by the following derived detectors. With the assumption that the user 1 is synchronized, we denote

$$\overline{\mathbf{C}}_{1,up} = \begin{bmatrix} \bar{\mathbf{c}}_1(0) & \cdots & \mathbf{0} \\ \vdots & \ddots & \bar{\mathbf{c}}_1(\mathbf{0}) \\ \vdots & \ddots & \vdots \\ \bar{\mathbf{c}}_1(N-1) & \cdots & \bar{\mathbf{c}}_1(N-M-1) \end{bmatrix}, \tag{19.43}$$

$$\overline{\mathbf{C}}_{1,down} = \begin{bmatrix} \mathbf{0} & \bar{\mathbf{c}}_1(N-1) & \cdots & \bar{\mathbf{c}}_1(N-M) \\ \vdots & \vdots & \ddots & \\ \vdots & \mathbf{0} & \cdots & \bar{\mathbf{c}}_1(N-1) \\ \mathbf{0} & \cdots & \cdots & \mathbf{0} \end{bmatrix}, \tag{19.44}$$

where both $\overline{\mathbf{C}}_{1,up}$ and $\overline{\mathbf{C}}_{1,down}$ are the $N \times (M+1)$ matrices. The matrix $\overline{\mathbf{C}}_{1,up}$ is constructed by the first N rows of the matrix $\overline{\mathbf{C}}_1$ defined in (19.10), and the matrix $\overline{\mathbf{C}}_{1,down}$ is formed by the remaining M rows of the matrix $\overline{\mathbf{C}}_1$ plus the $(N-M) \times (M+1)$ zero matrix.

According to the definitions of the vectors $\mathbf{h}_1$ and $\bar{\mathbf{h}}_1$ in section 19.1.2 and the denotation in (19.43) and (19.44), it is easy to obtain that

$$\mathbf{h}_1 = \overline{\mathbf{C}}_{1,up}\mathbf{g}_1, \tag{19.45}$$

$$\bar{\mathbf{h}}_1 = \overline{\mathbf{C}}_{1,down}\mathbf{g}_1, \tag{19.46}$$

where the vector $\mathbf{g}_1$ is the multipath channel of user 1, which is defined in (19.11). Since the matrices $\overline{\mathbf{C}}_{1,up}$ and $\overline{\mathbf{C}}_{1,down}$ are easy to construct with the *a priori* knowledge of the spreading sequences of the desired user, we only need to consider the estimation of the vector $\mathbf{g}_1$. The multipath channel vector $\mathbf{g}_1$ can be estimated by exploiting the orthogonality between the signal subspace and the noise subspace. Since the vector $\mathbf{h}_1$ is the subspace of the matrix $\mathbf{U}_s$ in (19.25), and the subspace of the matrix $\mathbf{U}_s$ is orthogonal to the matrix $\mathbf{U}_n$, we have

$$\mathbf{U}_n^H\mathbf{h}_1 = \mathbf{U}_n^H\overline{\mathbf{C}}_{1,up}\mathbf{g}_1 = \mathbf{0}. \tag{19.47}$$

Hence, the estimation of the vector $\mathbf{g}_1$ can be uniquely determined by computing the principle eigenvector of the matrix $\overline{\mathbf{C}}_{1,up}^H\mathbf{U}_s\mathbf{U}_s^H\overline{\mathbf{C}}_{1,up}$[12, 28], i.e.

$$\hat{\mathbf{g}}_1 = \text{Max -eigenvector}(\overline{\mathbf{C}}_{1,up}^H\mathbf{U}_s\mathbf{U}_s^H\overline{\mathbf{C}}_{1,up}). \tag{19.48}$$

Based on (19.48), the signature vectors $\mathbf{h}_1$ and $\bar{\mathbf{h}}_1$ can be determined according to (19.45) and (19.46).

After the channel estimation, we construct the useful cross-correlation matrix $\overline{\mathbf{Y}}$ given by

$$\overline{\mathbf{Y}} = E\{\mathbf{y}(n)\mathbf{y}(n+1)^H\} + \text{E}\{\mathbf{y}(n)\mathbf{y}(n-1)^H\}^H = \mathbf{H}\begin{bmatrix} \mathbf{0} & \mathbf{I}_K \\ \mathbf{I}_K & \mathbf{0} \end{bmatrix}\mathbf{H}, \tag{19.49}$$

where the matrix $\overline{\mathbf{Y}}$ is generated by the cross-correlation of the received signal. It is seen that the matrix $\overline{\mathbf{Y}}$ is the $N \times N$ matrix, which is irrelevant to the background noise of the generalized receiver. This matrix plays an important role in the present section since it will be exploited to develop the proposed generalized receivers.

Recalling that the basic idea of the group-blind multiuser detection is to suppress the interference of some known users based on the group constraint, we, naturally, expect that the more subspace of the interfering users the constraint removes, the better performance improvement the detector achieves. Here we utilize the matrix $\overline{\mathbf{Y}}$ to develop a constraint similar to the group constraint in (19.38) for the desired user, which is given by

$$\mathbf{T}_1^H \overline{\mathbf{Y}} = \bar{\mathbf{h}}_1^H. \tag{19.50}$$

Let us now consider the properties of the above constraint with the following propositions to demonstrate analytically the performance improvement brought by the proposed constraint.

***Proposition* 1:** Based on the signal model given by (19.17) and the definition of the matrix $\overline{\mathbf{Y}}$ in (19.49), the constraint $\mathbf{T}_1^H \mathbf{H} = \mathbf{1}_{2K,1}^T$ implies the constraint $\mathbf{T}_1^H \overline{\mathbf{Y}} = \bar{\mathbf{h}}_1^H$, i.e.

$$\mathbf{T}_1^H \mathbf{H} = \mathbf{1}_{2K,1}^T \Rightarrow \mathbf{T}_1^H \overline{\mathbf{Y}} = \bar{\mathbf{h}}_1^H \tag{19.51}$$

Proof: The proof is straightforward by directly substituting the constraint $\mathbf{T}_1^H \mathbf{H} = \mathbf{1}_{2K,1}^T$ into the constraint $\mathbf{T}_1^H \overline{\mathbf{Y}}$, i.e.

$$\mathbf{T}_1^H \overline{\mathbf{Y}} = \mathbf{T}_1^H \mathbf{H} \begin{bmatrix} \mathbf{0} & \mathbf{I}_K \\ \mathbf{I}_K & \mathbf{0} \end{bmatrix} \mathbf{H}^H = \mathbf{1}_{2K,1}^T \begin{bmatrix} \mathbf{0} & \mathbf{I}_K \\ \mathbf{I}_K & \mathbf{0} \end{bmatrix} \mathbf{H}^H; \mathbf{1}_{2K,K+1}^T \mathbf{H}^H = \bar{\mathbf{h}}_1^H, \tag{19.52}$$

where the last equality follows from the definition of the matrix $\mathbf{H}$ in (19.17), i.e.

$$\mathbf{H}[:, K+1] = \bar{\mathbf{h}}_1. \tag{19.53}$$

The constraint $\mathbf{T}_1^H \mathbf{H} = \mathbf{1}_{2K,1}^T$ is the optimal group constraint for group-blind multiuser detection since it ensures that the decision statistics of the generalized receiver $\mathbf{T}_1$ is orthogonal to the subspace spanned by all interfering users except the desired user. The result of *Proposition* 1 demonstrates that the proposed constraint is the necessary condition of the optimal group constraint. It means that the proposed constraint $\mathbf{T}_1^H \overline{\mathbf{Y}} = \bar{\mathbf{h}}_1^H$ will not remove the subspace spanned by the desired user and it is possible to achieve the optimal group constraint based on this constraint. Therefore, we are interested in the feature of the proposed constraint and want to know if this constraint implies the optimal group constraint or to what extent it removes the subspace spanned by the interfering users. *Propositions* 2–4 summarize the proposed constraint's ability to resist the interference brought by the interfering users in different cases.

***Proposition* 2:** The constraint $\mathbf{T}_1^H \overline{\mathbf{Y}} = \bar{\mathbf{h}}_1^H$ implies the constraint $\mathbf{T}_1^H \mathbf{H} = \mathbf{1}_{2K,1}^T$ if the matrix $\mathbf{H}$ has the full column rank $2K$.

Proof: We proceed with a proof by contradiction. Assuming that $\mathbf{T}_1^H\overline{\mathbf{Y}} = \overline{\mathbf{h}}_1^H$ and $\mathbf{T}_1^H\mathbf{H} \neq \mathbf{1}_{2K,1}^T$, then the constraint $\mathbf{T}_1^H\mathbf{H}$ can be expressed in the following form

$$\mathbf{T}_1^H\mathbf{H} = \mathbf{1}_{2K,1}^T + \mathbf{f}^H, \tag{19.54}$$

where

$$\mathbf{f} = [\mathbf{f}_{up}^T, \mathbf{f}_{down}^T]^T \tag{19.55}$$

is the nonzero $2K$ dimensional column vector, and the vectors $\mathbf{f}_{up}$ and $\mathbf{f}_{down}$ are the first K entries and the last K entries of the vector $\mathbf{f}$, respectively. By denoting

$$\check{\mathbf{f}} = [\mathbf{f}_{down}^T, \mathbf{f}_{up}^T] \tag{19.56}$$

and substituting (19.54) into the constraint $\mathbf{T}_1^H\overline{\mathbf{Y}}$, we obtain

$$\mathbf{T}_1^H\overline{\mathbf{Y}} = \overline{\mathbf{h}}_1^H \Rightarrow \mathbf{T}_1^H\mathbf{H}\begin{bmatrix} \mathbf{0} & \mathbf{I}_K \\ \mathbf{I}_K & \mathbf{0} \end{bmatrix}\mathbf{H}^H = \overline{\mathbf{h}}_1^H \Rightarrow (\mathbf{1}_{2K,1}^T + \mathbf{f}^H)\begin{bmatrix} \mathbf{0} & \mathbf{I}_K \\ \mathbf{I}_K & \mathbf{0} \end{bmatrix}\mathbf{H}^H = \overline{\mathbf{h}}_1^H$$

$$\Rightarrow (\mathbf{1}_{2K,K+1}^T + \check{\mathbf{f}}^H)\mathbf{H}^H = \overline{\mathbf{h}}_1^H \Rightarrow \overline{\mathbf{h}}_1^H + \check{\mathbf{f}}^H\mathbf{H}^H = \overline{\mathbf{h}}_1^H \Rightarrow \check{\mathbf{f}} = 0 \Rightarrow \mathbf{f} = 0, \tag{19.57}$$

where the third right arrow follows from the fact that

$$\mathbf{f}^H\begin{bmatrix} \mathbf{0} & \mathbf{I}_K \\ \mathbf{I}_K & \mathbf{0} \end{bmatrix} = \check{\mathbf{f}}^H \tag{19.58}$$

and the fifth right arrow is based on the fact that the matrix $\mathbf{H}$ is of full column rank. Hence, equation (19.57) contradicts equation (19.54).

Proposition 2 shows that the proposed constraint is equivalent to the optimal group constraint, which removes all MAI and ISI on the condition that the matrix $\mathbf{H}$ is of full column rank. Recalling that the signature matrix $\mathbf{H}$ in the asynchronous (uplink) MC DS-CDMA wireless communication system model, which is given in section 19.1.2, is assumed to be full rank, we naturally expect that the proposed constraint provides the greatest performance gain on the uplink of MC DS-CDMA wireless communication system.

As mentioned before, the full-rank condition on the matrix $\mathbf{H}$ is hardly satisfied in the downlink of MC DS-CDMA wireless communication system, where the intracell users are transmitted synchronously and the intercell users are transmitted asynchronously. In this case, we divide the matrix $\mathbf{H}$ into the matrices $\mathbf{H}_0$ and $\mathbf{H}_1$ according to (19.17), where the matrix $\mathbf{H}_0$ contains the subspace spanned by the desired user and MAI, and the matrix $\mathbf{H}_1$ contains the subspace spanned by ISI. In the downlink of MC DS-CDMA wireless communication system, most treatments assume that the matrix $\mathbf{H}_0$ is the full rank matrix and independent of the matrix $\mathbf{H}_1$, while the matrix $\mathbf{H}_1$ is not the full rank matrix when the number of active users K exceeds the maximum length of the multipath channel M.

***Proposition* 3:** For the non-full-rank matrix $\mathbf{H}$, the constraint $\mathbf{T}_1^H\overline{\mathbf{Y}} = \overline{\mathbf{h}}_1^H$ implies $\mathbf{T}_1^H\mathbf{H}_1 = \mathbf{0}$ if the matrix $\mathbf{H}_0$ is independent of the matrix $\mathbf{H}_1$ with full column rank.

Proof: The proof is similar to the proof of *Proposition* 2, where

$$\mathbf{T}_1^H\bar{\mathbf{Y}} = \bar{\mathbf{h}}_1^H \Rightarrow \mathbf{T}_1^H\mathbf{H}\begin{bmatrix} \mathbf{0} & \mathbf{I}_K \\ \mathbf{I}_K & \mathbf{0} \end{bmatrix}\mathbf{H}^H = \bar{\mathbf{h}}_1^H \Rightarrow \mathbf{T}_1^H[\mathbf{H}_0 \quad \mathbf{H}_1]\begin{bmatrix} \mathbf{0} & \mathbf{I}_K \\ \mathbf{I}_K & \mathbf{0} \end{bmatrix}[\mathbf{H}_0 \quad \mathbf{H}_1]^H = \bar{\mathbf{h}}_1^H$$

$$\Rightarrow \mathbf{T}_1^H\mathbf{H}_0\mathbf{H}_1^H + \mathbf{T}_1^H\mathbf{H}_1\mathbf{H}_0^H = \bar{\mathbf{h}}_1^H \Rightarrow \mathbf{T}_1^H\mathbf{H}_1\mathbf{H}_0^H = \mathbf{0} \Rightarrow \mathbf{T}_1^H\mathbf{H}_1 = 0, \tag{19.59}$$

where the fourth arrow follows from the fact that the vector $\bar{\mathbf{h}}_1 \in$ the range $(\mathbf{H}_1)$ and the matrix $\mathbf{H}_0$ is independent of the matrix $\mathbf{H}_1$, and the last arrow is based on the fact that the matrix $\mathbf{H}_0$ is of full column rank.

Proposition 3 shows that the proposed constraint can totally remove the ISI with the non-full rank matrix $\mathbf{H}$ in the downlink of MC DS-CDMA wireless communication system. In particular, if we assumed that the vector $\bar{\mathbf{h}}_1$ is independent of other vectors in the matrix $\mathbf{H}_1$, a more satisfying result can be achieved by the proposed constraint.

***Proposition* 4:** For the non-full-rank matrix $\mathbf{H}$, the constraint $\mathbf{T}_1^H\bar{\mathbf{Y}} = \bar{\mathbf{h}}_1^H$ implies $\mathbf{T}_1^H\mathbf{H}_1 = \mathbf{1}_{2K,1}^T$ if the matrix $\mathbf{H}_0$ is independent of the matrix $\mathbf{H}_1$ and the vector $\bar{\mathbf{h}}_1$ is independent of the rest vectors in the matrix $\mathbf{H}_1$

Proof: The proof is similar to the proof of *Proposition* 3, i.e., we consider

$$\mathbf{T}_1^H\bar{\mathbf{Y}} = \bar{\mathbf{h}}_1^H \Rightarrow \mathbf{T}_1^H[\mathbf{H}_0 \quad \mathbf{H}_1]\begin{bmatrix} \mathbf{0} & \mathbf{I}_K \\ \mathbf{I}_K & \mathbf{0} \end{bmatrix}[\mathbf{H}_0\mathbf{H}_1]^H = \bar{\mathbf{h}}_1^H$$

$$\Rightarrow \mathbf{T}_1^H\mathbf{H}_0\mathbf{H}_1^H + \mathbf{T}_1^H\mathbf{H}_1\mathbf{H}_0^H = \bar{\mathbf{h}}_1^H \Rightarrow \mathbf{T}_1^H\mathbf{H}_1\mathbf{H}_0^H = \bar{\mathbf{h}}_1^H \Rightarrow \mathbf{T}_1^H\mathbf{H}_1 = \mathbf{1}_{2K,1}^T, \tag{19.60}$$

where the third arrow is derived from the independence between the matrices $\mathbf{H}_0$ and $\mathbf{H}_1$, and the last arrow is based on the fact that the vector $\bar{\mathbf{h}}_1$ cannot be constructed by the linear combination of other vectors in the matrix $\mathbf{H}_1$.

Proposition 4 shows that the proposed constraint can remove all MAI in the statistical sense if the signature vector of the desired user in the ISI matrix $\mathbf{H}_1$ is independent of the other signature vectors in ISI. In this case, we do not require the full rank $\mathbf{H}_0$. However, if we also assumed that the matrix $\mathbf{H}_0$ is of full rank, the constraint in the *Proposition* 4 can eliminate both MAI and ISI according to *proposition* 3, which means that our proposed constraint may achieve the optimal group constraint on certain conditions even without the full rank matrix $\mathbf{H}$.

The results discussed in *Propositions* 2–4 show that the proposed constraint $\mathbf{T}_1^H\bar{\mathbf{Y}} = \bar{\mathbf{h}}_1^H$ is able to remove the MAI and ISI in the statistical sense to different extents according to the properties of the signature matrix $\mathbf{H}$. In this case, we develop two improved blind generalized detectors by considering this constraint.

19.1.5.1 Improved blind generalized receiver with decorrelating

The improved blind generalized receiver with decorrelation considers the minimization of the following constraint cost function in the statistical sense

$$\mathbf{T}_{opt}^{d} = \arg\min_{\mathbf{T}} |\mathbf{T}^{H}\mathbf{H}|^{2},\ \mathbf{T} \in \text{range}(\mathbf{H}) \text{ subjected to: } \begin{cases} \mathbf{T}^{H}\mathbf{h}_{1} = \mathbf{1}, \\ \mathbf{T}^{H}\bar{\mathbf{Y}} = \bar{\mathbf{h}}_{1}^{H}, \end{cases} \tag{19.61}$$

where $\mathbf{T}_{opt}^{d}$ is the decision statistics matrix of the proposed generalized receiver. The first constraint in (19.61) is used to keep the information of the desired user, and the second constraint is used to suppress the MAI and ISI in the statistical sense. The two constraints compose an equivalent group-blind constraint to (19.39). As was shown in [38] and [39], the improved blind generalized receiver with decorrelating in (19.61) is equivalent to the decorrelating detector in (19.22) by physical sense, i.e. $\mathbf{T}_{opt}^{d} \approx \mathbf{d}_{1}$. *Proposition* 5 presents the resolution of the proposed blind generalized receiver with the decorrelating.

***Proposition* 5:** Based on the eigendecomposition in (19.25), the solution of the improved blind generalized receiver with decorrelating in (19.61) is given by

$$\mathbf{T}_{opt}^{d} = \mathbf{U}_{s}(\mathbf{\Lambda}_{s} - \sigma^{2}\mathbf{I}_{L})^{-1}\mathbf{U}_{s}^{H}(\boldsymbol{\lambda}_{1}\mathbf{h}_{1} + \boldsymbol{\lambda}_{2}\bar{\mathbf{Y}}), \tag{19.62}$$

where

$$\begin{cases} \boldsymbol{\lambda}_{2} = [\boldsymbol{\alpha}\bar{\mathbf{Y}}^{H}\mathbf{U}_{s}(\mathbf{\Lambda}_{s} - \sigma^{2}\mathbf{I}_{L})^{-1}\mathbf{U}_{s}^{H}\bar{\mathbf{Y}} - \boldsymbol{\theta}\boldsymbol{\theta}^{H}]^{\bar{*}}[\boldsymbol{\alpha}\bar{\mathbf{h}}_{1} - \boldsymbol{\theta}]; \\ \boldsymbol{\lambda}_{1} = \boldsymbol{\alpha}^{-1}[1 - \boldsymbol{\theta}^{H}\boldsymbol{\lambda}_{2}]; \\ \boldsymbol{\theta} = \bar{\mathbf{Y}}^{H}\mathbf{U}_{s}(\mathbf{\Lambda}_{s} - \sigma^{2}\mathbf{I}_{L})^{-1}\mathbf{U}_{s}^{H}\mathbf{h}_{1}; \\ \boldsymbol{\alpha} = \mathbf{h}_{1}^{H}\mathbf{U}_{s}(\mathbf{\Lambda}_{s} - \sigma^{2}\mathbf{I}_{L})^{-1}\mathbf{U}_{s}^{H}\mathbf{h}_{1}. \end{cases} \tag{19.63}$$

The symbol ($\bar{*}$) denotes the pseudo-inverse.

Proof: See appendix A.

19.1.5.2 Improved blind hybrid generalized receiver

The improved blind hybrid generalized receiver considers the following constrained optimization problem:

$$\mathbf{T}_{opt}^{m} = \arg\min_{\mathbf{m}} E\{|b_{1}(n) - \mathbf{T}^{H}\mathbf{y}_{1}(n)|^{2}\},$$
$$\mathbf{T} \in \text{range}(\mathbf{H}) \text{ subject to} \begin{cases} \mathbf{T}^{H}\mathbf{h}_{1} = \mathbf{1}; \\ \mathbf{T}^{H}\bar{\mathbf{Y}} = \bar{\mathbf{h}}_{1}^{H}, \end{cases} \tag{19.64}$$

where matrix $\mathbf{T}_{opt}^{m}$ is the decision statistics of the proposed blind hybrid generalized receiver.

Proposition* *6 gives us an implementation for the proposed blind hybrid generalized receiver.

$$\mathbf{T}_{opt}^{m} = \mathbf{U}_{s}(\mathbf{\Lambda}_{s}^{-1}\mathbf{U}_{s}^{H}(\bar{\boldsymbol{\lambda}}_{1}\mathbf{h}_{1} + \bar{\boldsymbol{\lambda}}_{2}\bar{\mathbf{Y}}), \tag{19.65}$$

where

$$\begin{cases} \bar{\lambda}_2 = [\bar{\alpha}\bar{\mathbf{Y}}^H\mathbf{U}_s(\mathbf{\Lambda}_s^{-1}\mathbf{U}_s^H\bar{\mathbf{Y}} - \bar{\theta}\bar{\theta}^H]^*[\bar{\alpha}\bar{\mathbf{h}}_1 - \bar{\theta}]; \\ \bar{\lambda}_1 = \bar{\alpha}^{-1}[1 - \bar{\theta}^H\lambda_2]\,; \\ \bar{\theta} = \bar{\mathbf{Y}}^H\mathbf{U}_s(\mathbf{\Lambda}_s - \sigma^2\mathbf{I}_L)^{-1}\mathbf{U}_s^H\mathbf{h}_1\,; \\ \bar{\alpha} = \mathbf{h}_1^H\mathbf{U}_s(\mathbf{\Lambda}_s - \sigma^2\mathbf{I}_L)^{-1}\mathbf{U}_s^H\mathbf{h}_1. \end{cases} \tag{19.66}$$

Proof: See appendix B.

In the above-mentioned results, two improved blind generalized receivers are expressed in subspace forms. In these detectors, the influence of interfering users is mitigated by the two constraints, which are constructed from the correlation matrix $\bar{\mathbf{Y}}$ and the channel estimation of the desired user. After suppressing the interfering signals, the signals of the desired user are identified by the transformation of the subspace based on the zero-forcing or the hybrid criteria. Unlike the group constraint in [26], our proposed constraints utilize the correlation matrix $\bar{\mathbf{Y}}$ to improve the performance of the detectors and then avoid the channel estimation of other users except the desired user. Therefore, our proposed detectors can be implemented blindly for both downlink and uplink of MC DS-CDMA wireless communication system channels, while the method in [26] is only suitable for uplink channels of MC DS-CDMA wireless communication system.

In addition, the performance gain provided by the proposed constraint depends on the property of the signature matrix $\mathbf{H}$. When the matrix $\mathbf{H}$ is of full column rank, i.e., the case of the uplink channel of MC DS-CDMA wireless communication system, the proposed constraint can totally remove MAI and ISI in the statistical sense to achieve the best performance gain. When the matrix $\mathbf{H}$ is not of full rank, i.e., the case of downlink channel of MC DS-CDMA wireless communication system, the proposed constraint can remove at least the influence of ISI. Table 19.2 summarizes the algorithms of the proposed receivers.

Table 19.2. Signal processing algorithms of the proposed receivers

		Signal frame: $\mathbf{y}(0), \mathbf{y}(1), \ldots, \mathbf{y}(P)$
Step Number	Operation	Formula
STEP 1	Compute autocorrelation and cross-correlation	$\mathbf{Y} = \frac{1}{P+1}\sum_{n=0}^{P}[2\mathbf{y}(n)\mathbf{x}^H(n) - \mathbf{y}(n)\mathbf{y}^H(n) + \boldsymbol{\eta}(n)\boldsymbol{\eta}^H(n)]$ $\bar{\mathbf{Y}} = \frac{1}{P+1}\sum_{n=0}^{P}[2\mathbf{y}(n)\mathbf{x}^H(n+1) - \mathbf{y}(n)\mathbf{y}^H(n+1) + \boldsymbol{\eta}(n)\boldsymbol{\eta}^H(n+1)]$
STEP 2	Compute eigendecomposition of the matrix $\mathbf{Y}$	$\mathbf{Y} = \mathbf{U}_s\mathbf{\Lambda}_s\mathbf{U}_s^H + \sigma^2\mathbf{U}_n\mathbf{U}_n^H$

(*Continued*)

Table 19.2. (*Continued*)

Step Number	Operation	Formula
		Signal frame: $\mathbf{y}(0), \mathbf{y}(1), \ldots, \mathbf{y}(P)$
STEP 3	Parameter estimation	$\sigma^2 = \frac{1}{N-L}$ Sum of the min $N - L$ eigenvalues of the matrix $\mathbf{Y}$ $\mathbf{g}_k = \text{Max} - \text{eigenvector}(\overline{\mathbf{C}}_{k,up}^H \mathbf{U}_s \mathbf{U}_s^H \overline{\mathbf{C}}_{k,up})$ $\mathbf{h}_1 = \overline{\mathbf{C}}_{1,up}\mathbf{g}_1$; $\overline{\mathbf{h}}_1 = \overline{\mathbf{C}}_{1k,down}\mathbf{g}_1$.
STEP 4	Compute $\boldsymbol{\alpha}, \overline{\boldsymbol{\alpha}}, \boldsymbol{\theta}, \overline{\boldsymbol{\theta}}, \boldsymbol{\lambda}_1, \overline{\boldsymbol{\lambda}}_1, \boldsymbol{\lambda}_2, \overline{\boldsymbol{\lambda}}_2$	$\boldsymbol{\alpha} = \mathbf{h}_1^H \mathbf{U}_s(\boldsymbol{\Lambda}_s - \sigma^2 \mathbf{I}_L)^{-1}\mathbf{U}_s^H \mathbf{h}_1$; $\overline{\boldsymbol{\alpha}} = \mathbf{h}_1^H \mathbf{U}_s \boldsymbol{\Lambda}_s^{-1} \mathbf{U}_s^H \mathbf{h}_1$; $\boldsymbol{\theta} = \overline{\mathbf{Y}}^H \mathbf{U}_s(\boldsymbol{\Lambda}_s - \sigma^2 \mathbf{I}_L)^{-1}\mathbf{U}_s^H \mathbf{h}_1$; $\overline{\boldsymbol{\theta}} = \overline{\mathbf{Y}}^H \mathbf{U}_s \boldsymbol{\Lambda}_s^{-1} \mathbf{U}_s^H \mathbf{h}_1$; $\boldsymbol{\lambda}_2 = [\boldsymbol{\alpha}\overline{\mathbf{Y}}^H \mathbf{U}_s(\boldsymbol{\Lambda}_s - \sigma^2 \mathbf{I}_L)^{-1}\mathbf{U}_s^H \overline{\mathbf{Y}} - \boldsymbol{\theta}\boldsymbol{\theta}^H]^*[\boldsymbol{\alpha}\overline{\mathbf{h}}_1 - \boldsymbol{\theta}]$; $\overline{\boldsymbol{\lambda}}_2 = [\overline{\boldsymbol{\alpha}}\overline{\mathbf{Y}}^H \mathbf{U}_s \boldsymbol{\Lambda}_s^{-1} \mathbf{U}_s^H \overline{\mathbf{Y}} - \overline{\boldsymbol{\theta}}\overline{\boldsymbol{\theta}}^H]^*[\overline{\boldsymbol{\alpha}}\overline{\mathbf{h}}_1 - \overline{\boldsymbol{\theta}}]$; $\boldsymbol{\lambda}_1 = \boldsymbol{\alpha}^{-1}[1 - \boldsymbol{\theta}^H \boldsymbol{\lambda}_2]$; $\overline{\boldsymbol{\lambda}}_1 = \overline{\boldsymbol{\alpha}}^{-1}[1 - \overline{\boldsymbol{\theta}}^H \overline{\boldsymbol{\lambda}}_2]$
STEP 5	Form the blind generalized receiver with decorrelating and the blind hybrid generalized receiver	$\mathbf{T}_{opt}^d = \mathbf{U}_s(\boldsymbol{\Lambda}_s - \sigma^2 \mathbf{I}_L)^{-1}\mathbf{U}_s^H(\boldsymbol{\lambda}_1 \mathbf{h}_1 + \boldsymbol{\lambda}_2 \overline{\mathbf{Y}})$ $\mathbf{T}_{opt}^m = \mathbf{U}_s(\boldsymbol{\Lambda}_s^{-1}\mathbf{U}_s^H)(\overline{\boldsymbol{\lambda}}_1 \mathbf{h}_1 + \overline{\boldsymbol{\lambda}}_2 \overline{\mathbf{Y}})$

19.1.6 Simulation results

In this subsection, simulation results are provided to demonstrate the performance of the improved blind generalized receivers and compare with the blind linear decorrelating detector and blind linear MMSE detector. We test the proposed methods in MC DS-CDMA wireless communication system with spreading gain $N = 31$. The spreading sequences for all users are generated by Gold codes. Both the asynchronous and synchronous cases are considered. In each case, user 1 is assumed to be the desired user which is synchronized, and each user has $M = 5$ multipath delays.

The multipath gains in each user's channel are randomly chosen and kept fixed, having been normalized with equal power. In addition, we simulate a severe near–far case in that the power of each interfering user is 10 dB more than that of the desired user. For each simulation case, an eigendecomposition is performed on the autocorrelation matrix of the received signals. The length of the signal frame is $P = 500$. The algorithmic details of the matrix operations and parameter estimation involved in computing the various detectors can be seen from tables 19.1 and 19.2.

19.1.6.1 Asynchronous MC DS-CDMA wireless communication systems

In the uplink of MC DS-CDMA wireless communication system the received signal at the base station is created by the asynchronous intercell and intracell users. For the asynchronous MC DS-CDMA wireless communication system, we assume that the delay of each interfering user is randomly distributed within the limits of the interval [0, T_c] where T_c is the chip period. Hence, the maximum delay spread is limited within one symbol interval. Meanwhile, it is also assumed that the signature matrix **H** in (19.17) is of full column rank as the existence of the delays of interfering users. We compare the performance of six receivers, i.e., the conventional blind decorrelating and MMSE detectors implemented by the algorithms in table 19.1, the group-blind zero-forcing and hybrid detectors investigated in [26, 40, 41] and the proposed improved blind generalized receiver with decorrelating and blind hybrid generalized receiver [42–44] implemented by the algorithm in table 19.2.

Figure 19.2 compares the *BER* of various detectors and receivers that only require us to estimate the channel of the desired user, in an asynchronous DS-CDMA wireless communication system with seven users. It shows that the proposed blind generalized receiver with decorrelating and blind hybrid generalized receiver provide substantial *BER* improvements over the conventional decorrelating and MMSE detectors. It is also observed that there exist trivial differences in performance between the proposed blind generalized receiver with decorrelating and blind hybrid generalized receiver. This is because the two receivers use the same constraint to suppress the ISI and MAI in the statistical sense. When the matrix **H** is of full rank, the proposed constraint totally removes the ISI and MAI in the statistical sense. Hence, both the proposed generalized receivers can zero force all signals from interfering users to achieve similar performance.

We next compare the performance of the group-blind detectors investigated in [26] with our proposed generalized receivers. The results of the simulation are presented in figures 19.3 and 19.4. In figure 19.3, a ten-user asynchronous

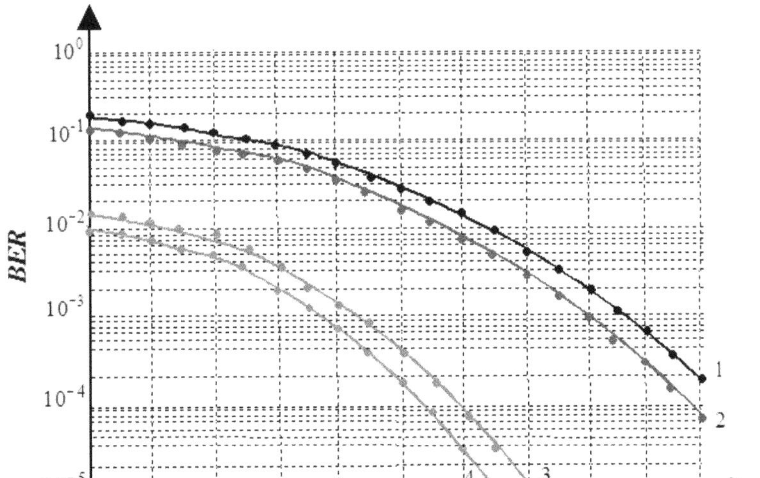

Figure 19.2. *BER* comparison of different detectors for asynchronous CDMA ($P = 500$; $K = 7$): 1—conventional decorrelating detector; 2—conventional MMSE detector; 3—proposed generalized receiver with decorrelating; 4—proposed hybrid generalized receiver; solid line—theoretical calculations; •—simulation results.

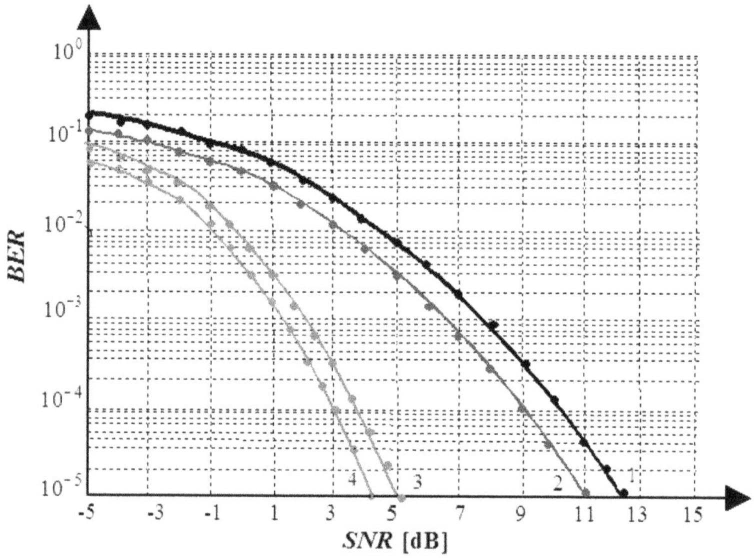

Figure 19.3. *BER* comparison of different detectors for asynchronous CDMA ($P = 500$; $K = 10$), eight known users for group detectors: 1—group-blind zero-forcing detector; 2—group-blind hybrid detector; 3—proposed generalized receiver with decorrelating; 4—proposed hybrid generalized receiver; solid line—theoretical calculations; •—simulation results.

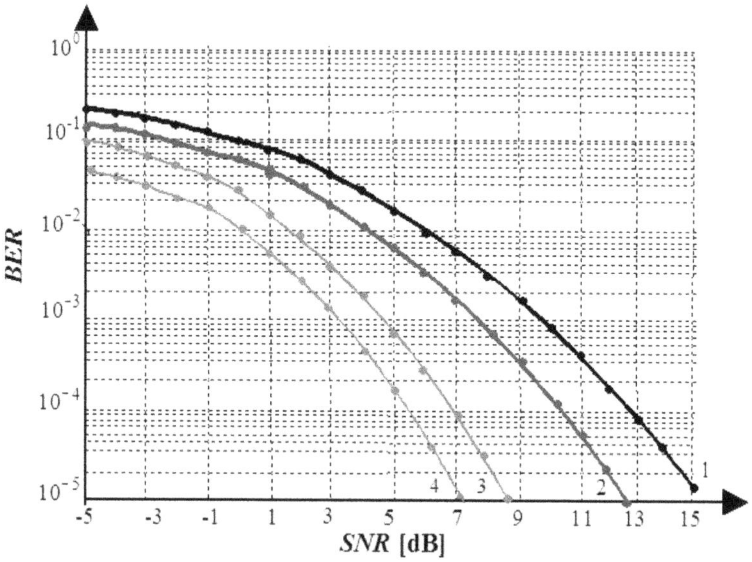

Figure 19.4. *BER* comparison of different detectors for asynchronous CDMA ($P = 500$; $K = 15$), eight known users for group detectors: 1—group-blind zero-forcing detector; 2—group-blind hybrid detector; 3—proposed generalized receiver with decorrelating; 4—proposed hybrid generalized receiver; solid line—theoretical calculations; •—simulation results.

DS-CDMA wireless communication system is considered. It is assumed that there are eight known intracell users and two unknown intercell users for the group-blind detectors. It is seen that the proposed blind generalized receiver with decorrelating has the better performance in comparison with the group-blind zero-forcing detector. The proposed blind hybrid generalized receiver has superiority over the conventional group-blind hybrid detector by performance. It should also be noted that the proposed blind generalized receiver with decorrelating and the blind hybrid generalized receiver only need the channel estimation of the desired user, while the conventional group-blind hybrid detectors require the channel estimation of all known users.

Figure 19.4 presents a consideration of CDMA wireless communication systems with 15 users including eight intracell known users and seven intercell unknown users. Such a situation may occur at the edge of the cell, where the number of the intracell users is close to the number of intercell users. It is observed that both the group-blind detectors and the proposed generalized receivers have deterioration by performance in comparison with the case presented in figure 19.3. In this case, the performances of the proposed blind generalized receiver with decorrelating and the blind hybrid generalized receiver are marginally better than that of the group-blind zero-forcing detector and the group-blind hybrid detector, respectively. It means that the group-blind detectors are very sensitive to the number of unknown users. This is because the group-blind detectors use the channel estimation of all known users to construct the group constraint to improve the performance. Hence, the more users the detectors know the better performance gain the detectors achieve. However, the proposed generalized receivers utilize the cross-correlation of the received symbols and the channel estimation of the desired user to construct the corresponding constraint. Such a constraint, which can remove both MAI and ISI in asynchronous DS-CDMA wireless communication systems, is irrelevant to the number of unknown users.

19.1.6.2 Performance of the proposed generalized receivers

Next, we consider the performance of the proposed generalized receivers in the downlink of DS-CDMA wireless communication system, i.e., in the synchronous DS-CDMA wireless communication system. In the downlink of DS-CDMA wireless communication system, the signal received by the desired user is made up of the synchronous intracell users and some asynchronous intercell users. In this case, the signature matrix $\mathbf{H}_1$, and hence the signature matrix $\mathbf{H}$, may not be of full rank when the number of synchronous intracell users surpasses the multipath length M.

It is noted from the above simulation results that the performance of the conventional blind MMSE detector and the proposed hybrid generalized receiver are close to the performance of the conventional blind decorrelating detector and the proposed blind generalized receiver with decorrelating, respectively. However, both the conventional blind decorrelating detector and the proposed blind generalized receiver with decorrelating require the estimate of the noise level. In addition, the group-blind detectors in [26] cannot be used for downlink channels of DS-CDMA wireless communication system because they need to know the spreading sequences of the other intracell users.

Therefore, we only compare three detectors for the synchronous DS-CDMA wireless communication system, i.e., the conventional MMSE detector, the proposed blind hybrid generalized receiver, and the true linear MMSE detector. The true linear MMSE detector is given by

$$\mathbf{T}_{true}^{m} = \mathbf{Y}^{-1}\mathbf{h}_1, \tag{19.67}$$

where the matrix $\mathbf{Y}$ is created by the average of 10^4 received samples at the high *SNR*.

Figure 19.5. demonstrates comparative analysis between the performance of the above three detectors. The DS-CDMA wireless communication system is assumed to have eight synchronous intracell users and two asynchronous intercell users. It is seen from this figure that the proposed hybrid generalized receiver still achieve the better performance in comparison with that of the conventional MMSE detector, and the performance of the conventional MMSE detector is inferior to the true linear MMSE detector one. The proposed hybrid generalized receiver is superior both the conventional MMSE detector and the true linear MMSE detector by performance in spite of the fact that because the constraint in the proposed hybrid generalized receiver can only remove the ISI in the statistical sense for synchronous DS-CDMA wireless communication system, while it can remove both the MAI and ISI in the case of asynchronous DS-CDMA wireless communication system in the statistical sense.

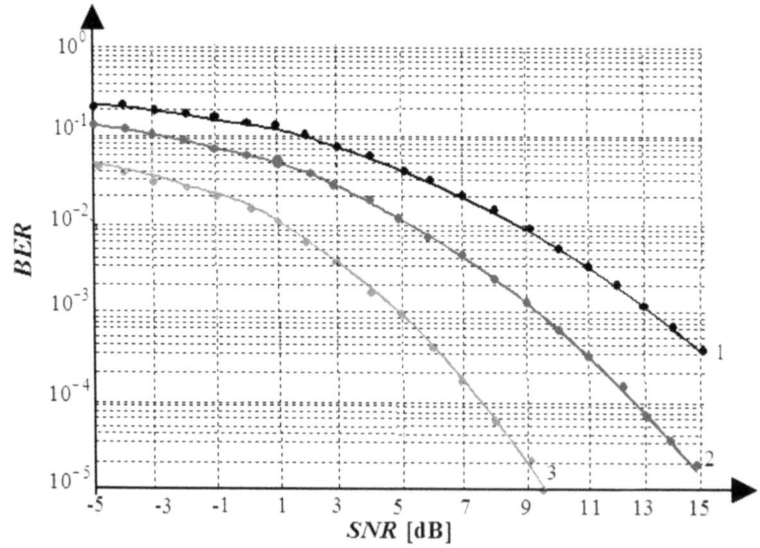

Figure 19.5. *BER* comparison of different detectors for synchronous CDMA ($P = 500$; $K = 10$) eight synchronous intracell users, seven asynchronous intercell users: 1—conventional MMSE; 2—true MMSE; 3—proposed hybrid generalized receiver; solid line—theoretical calculations; •—simulation results..

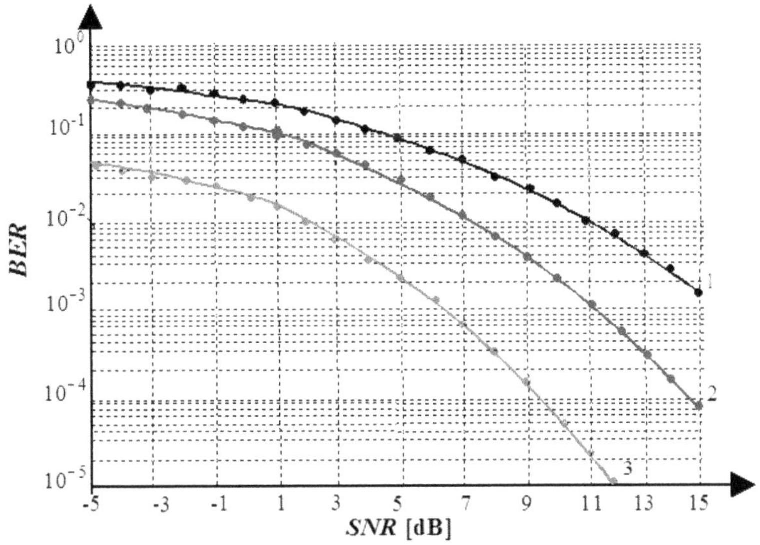

Figure 19.6. *BER* comparison of different detectors for synchronous CDMA ($P = 500$; $K = 15$) eight synchronous intracell users, 2 asynchronous intercell users: 1—conventional MMSE; 2—true MMSE; 3—proposed hybrid generalized receiver; solid line—theoretical calculations; •—simulation results.

In figure 19.6 the CDMA wireless communication system has seven asynchronous intercell users and eight synchronous intracell users. In this case, the signature matrix $\mathbf{H}_1$ has more column rank since the number of the asynchronous users is increased. It implies that the proposed constraint can remove more MAI. It is observed as expected that the proposed hybrid generalized receiver provides more performance gain over both the conventional MMSE detector and the true linear MMSE detector by performance in comparison with figure 19.5.

Theoretically, the conventional detectors converge to the true linear MMSE detector and the proposed generalized receivers converge to the true linear generalized receiver [42–44] at the high *SNR* when the signal frame length *P* is infinite. However, for a finite frame length *P*, the proposed generalized receiver significantly outperforms the conventional detectors no matter whether in the uplink or downlink of DS-CDMA wireless communication system. The reason for such performance improvement is that more multiuser environment information is incorporated in the derivation of the signal detection and signal processing.

19.2 Broadband multicarrier DS-CDMA system

19.2.1 Introduction

One of the basic requirements of the broadband DS-CDMA wireless communication systems is to support the expected high bit rates required by wireless internet service and for delivering high-speed multimedia services. However, the achievable capacity and data rate of the DS-CDMA wireless communication systems are limited by the time-varying characteristics of the dispersive fading channel. An efficient technique of combatting the time-varying effects of wireless channels is to employ diversity.

In recent years, the space-time coding has received much attention as an effective transmit diversity technique used for combatting fading in a DS-CDMA wireless communication system [45–48]. Inspired by the space-time codes, in [49] an attractive transmit diversity scheme based on the space-time spreading has been proposed for employment in the DS-CDMA wireless communication systems [50, 51]. A space-time spreading scheme designed for supporting two transmit antennas and one receive antenna has been included also in the CDMA2000 wideband CDMA (W-CDMA) standard [50–52]. In [48], the performance of the single-carrier DS-CDMA wireless communication systems using space-time spreading has been investigated, when the channel is modelled either as a flat or frequency-selective Rayleigh fading channel in the absence of multiuser interference.

In this section, we investigate the issues of parameter design and *BER* performance of the broadband MC DS-CDMA wireless communication systems constructed on the basis of the generalized approach to signal processing in noise [27–29] using the space-time spreading-assisted transmit diversity when communicating over frequency-selective Rayleigh fading channels. The reason to consider the broadband MC DS-CDMA wireless communication system is because it constitutes a generalized multiple-access scheme [6, 7, 12–16] which exhibits a high grade of design high flexibility.

The broadband MC DS-CDMA wireless communication system possesses a range of parameters that can be adjusted to satisfy the required design trade-off. Our objective in the context of parameter design is to configure broadband MC DS-CDMA wireless communication systems to achieve high efficiency communications in various propagation environments characterized by different grade of dispersion.

In the present section, specifically, the synchronous downlink (from the base station to moving platform) transmission of the user signals is considered and the *BER* performance is evaluated for a range of parameter values. Furthermore, in contrast to the family of conventional MC DS-CDMA wireless communication systems employing time-domain spreading only, in this contribution, we also investigate the broadband MC DS-CDMA wireless communication system performance when employing both the time-domain and frequency-domain spreading, i.e., employing the *TF*-domain spreading.

A typical advantage of using the *TF*-domain spreading in MC DS-CDMA wireless communication systems is that the maximum number of users supported is determined by the product of the time-domain spreading factor and the frequency-domain spreading factor. Therefore, the broadband MC DS-CDMA wireless communication system using the *TF*-domain spreading is capable of supporting a significantly higher number of users than in the case to use solely time-domain spreading, since in this case, the maximum number of users is supported by the time-domain spreading factor alone.

The performance of the space-time spreading-assisted broadband MC DS-CDMA wireless communication system using *TF*-domain spreading is investigated in conjunction with both the single-user and multiuser generalized detectors and is compared with the single-user correlation detector and multiuser decorrelating detector [6, 27–29, 50, 51, 56, 57]. Our study shows that a high number of users can be supported by broadband MC DS-CDMA wireless communication system using *TF*-spreading, without having to impose trade-off in terms of the achievable diversity order.

19.2.2 System model

19.2.2.1 Transmitter model

The wireless communication system considered in the present section is the orthogonal MC DS-CDMA wireless communication system and has a similar structure as discussed in [6, 50, 51, 54] using the $P \times G$ number of subcarriers, T the number of transmit antennas and one receive antenna. Furthermore, in this subsection, the synchronous broadband MC DS-CDMA wireless communication system is investigated where the K user signals are transmitted synchronously. The transmitter schematic of the kth user is shown in figure 19.7 where the real-valued data symbols using the binary phase-shift keying (BPSK) modulation and real-valued spreading [49–51] were considered. Figure 19.8 demonstrates the frequency arrangement of M subcarriers. As shown in figure 19.7, at the transmitter side the block of $P \times G$ data bits each having the bit duration of T_b is the serial-to-parallel (S-P) converted to P parallel subblocks. Each parallel subblock has G data bits, which are space-time spread using the schemes of [6, 49] with the aid of M orthogonal spreading codes [6]

$$\{a_{k,1}(t), a_{k,2}(t), \ldots, a_{k,M}(t)\},\ k = 1,2,\ldots,K \tag{19.68}$$

and mapped to T transmit antennas.

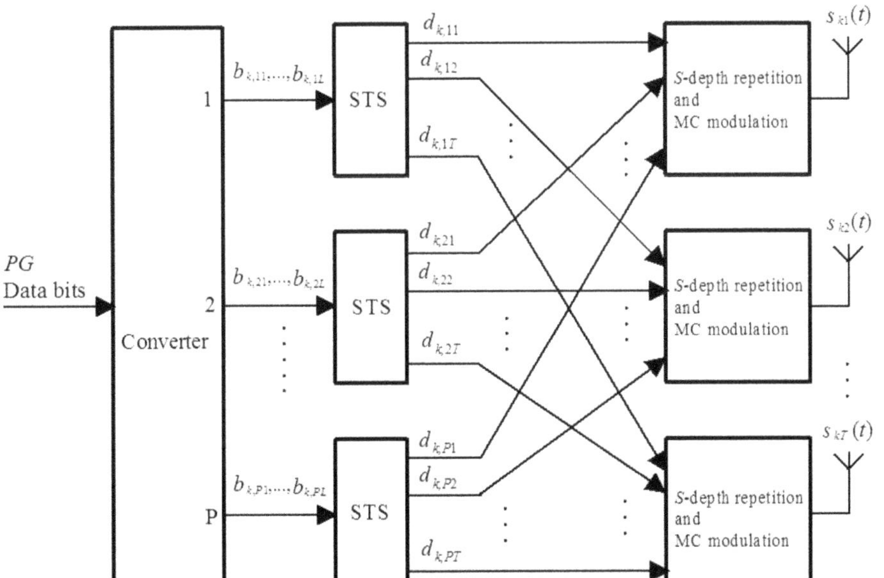

Figure 19.7. The transmitter schematic of the broadband MC DS-CDMA wireless communication system using space-time spreading.

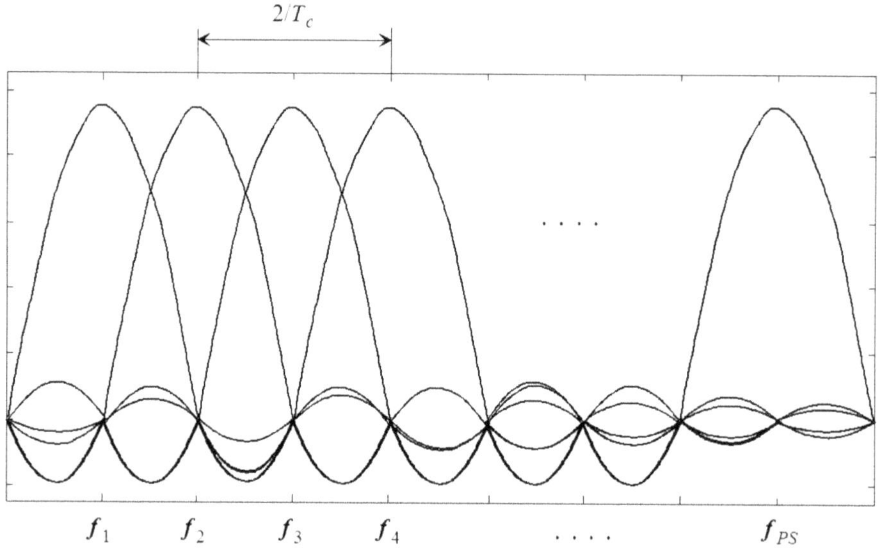

Figure 19.8. Spectrum of the orthogonal broadband MC DS-CDMA wireless communication system signals having a minimum subcarrier spacing of $1/T_c$, where the zero-to-zero bandwidth of each DS spread signal is $2/T_c$.

The symbol duration of the space-time spreading signals is PGT_b, and the discrete period of the orthogonal codes can be presented in the following form

$$\frac{PGT_b}{T_c} = PGN, \tag{19.69}$$

where $N = T_b/T_c$ and T_c represents the chip duration of the orthogonal spreading codes.

The orthogonal codes take the following form

$$a_{k,1}(t) = \sum_{j=0}^{PGN-1} a_{k,i}[j]P_{T_c}(t - jT_c), \tag{19.70}$$

where $a_{k,i}[j] \in \{+1, -1\}$ and obey the following relationship

$$\sum_{l=0}^{PGN-1} a_{i,m}[l]a_{j,n}[l] = 0 \tag{19.71}$$

whenever $i \neq j$ or $m \neq n$.

Furthermore, $P_{T_c}(t)$ represents the chip impulse waveform defined over the interval $[0, T_c)$. Since the total number of orthogonal codes having a discrete period of PGN is PGN and since each user requires M orthogonal codes for space-time spreading, the maximum number of users supported by these orthogonal codes is PGN/M. As seen in figure 19.7, the following space-time spreading, each space-time spreading block generates T parallel signals to be mapped to the T transmit antennas. For each transmit antenna, the specific P space-time spreading signals generated by the P space-time spreading blocks are the repeated S times, so that each space-time signal is transmitted on n subcarriers.

The corresponding number S of subcarriers is selected to guarantee that the same space-time spreading signal is transmitted by the specific S subcarriers having the maximum possible frequency spacing, so that they experience independent fading and, hence, achieve the maximum frequency diversity for a given S value. Specifically, let $\{f_1, f_2, \ldots, f_{PS}\}$ be the subcarrier frequencies, which are arranged according to figure 19.8. These subcarrier frequencies can be written in the following matrix form

$$\{f_i\} = \begin{pmatrix} f_1 & f_{P+1} & \cdots & f_{(S-1)P+1} \\ f_2 & f_{P+2} & \cdots & f_{(S-1)P+2} \\ \vdots & \vdots & \ddots & \vdots \\ f_P & f_{2P} & \cdots & f_{SP} \end{pmatrix}. \tag{19.72}$$

Then, the space-time spreading signal will be transmitted using the subcarrier frequencies from the same row of (19.72). Finally, as shown in figure 19.7, the inverse fast Fourier transform (IFFT) is invoked to carrying out multicarrier modulation, and the signal at the IFFT block output is transmitted using one of the transmit antenna.

The general form of the kth user's transmitted baseband signal corresponding to the T transmit antennas can be expressed in the following form

$$\mathbf{s}_k(t) = \mathrm{Re}\left\{\sqrt{\frac{2E_b}{PT_b} \times \frac{1}{SMT}}\mathbf{D}_k\mathbf{P}\boldsymbol{\omega}\right\}, \tag{19.73}$$

where E_b/PT_b represents the transmitted power per subcarrier expressed as

$$\frac{GE_b}{PGT_b} = \frac{E_b}{PT_b}, \tag{19.74}$$

the factor S in the denominator in (19.74) is due to the S-depth repetition, while the factor MT represents the same space-time spreading using M orthogonal codes and T transmit antennas.

In (19.73)

$$\mathbf{s}_k(t) = [s_{k1}(t)s_{k2}(t)\cdots s_{kT}(t)]^T, \tag{19.75}$$

where the superscript T denotes the vector or matrix transpose, represents the signal vector transmitted by T antennas, $\mathbf{P}$ represents the S-depth repetition operation, which is a $P \times PS$ matrix expressed as

$$\mathbf{P} = [\mathbf{I}_P\mathbf{I}_P\cdots\mathbf{I}_P] \tag{19.76}$$

with $\mathbf{I}_P$ being the unit matrix with the rank P.

Furthermore, in (19.73), $\mathbf{D}_k = \{d_{k,ij}\}$ is the $P \times T$-dimensional matrix representing the output of the space-time spreading. The space-time spreading invoked in the matrix $\mathbf{D}_k$ can be presented in the following form

$$\mathbf{D}_k = [\mathbf{C}_k\mathbf{B}_k]^T, \tag{19.77}$$

where $\mathbf{C}_k$ is the $P \times PM$-dimensional matrix constituted by orthogonal codes, which can be expressed in the following form

$$\mathbf{C}_k^T = \begin{pmatrix} a_{k,1}(t) & 0 & \cdots & 0 \\ a_{k,2}(t) & 0 & \cdots & 0 \\ \vdots & \vdots & \ddots & \vdots \\ a_{k,M}(t) & 0 & \cdots & 0 \\ 0 & a_{k,1}(t) & \cdots & 0 \\ 0 & a_{k,2}(t) & \cdots & 0 \\ \vdots & \vdots & \ddots & \vdots \\ 0 & a_{k,M}(t) & \cdots & 0 \\ \vdots & \vdots & \ddots & \vdots \\ 0 & 0 & \cdots & a_{k,1}(t) \\ 0 & 0 & \cdots & a_{k,2}(t) \\ \vdots & \vdots & \ddots & \vdots \\ 0 & 0 & \cdots & a_{k,M}(t) \end{pmatrix}. \tag{19.78}$$

In (19.77), $\mathbf{B}_k$ is the $PM \times T$ matrix mapped from the P subblock data bits, according to the requirements of the space-time spreading [49]. Specifically, the matrix $\mathbf{B}_k$ can be presented in the following form:

$$\mathbf{B}_k = [\mathbf{B}_{k1}^T \mathbf{B}_{k2}^T \cdots \mathbf{B}_{kP}^T]^T, \tag{19.79}$$

where $\mathbf{B}_{kp}$ is the $M \times T$ dimensional matrix obeying the following structure

$$\mathbf{B}_{kp} = \begin{pmatrix} a_{11}b'_{k,11} & a_{12}b'_{k,12} & \cdots & a_{1L}b'_{k,1T} \\ a_{11}b'_{k,11} & a_{12}b'_{k,12} & \cdots & a_{1L}b'_{k,1T} \\ \vdots & \vdots & \ddots & \vdots \\ a_{M1}b'_{k,M1} & a_{12}b'_{k,M2} & \cdots & a_{1L}b'_{k,MT} \end{pmatrix}, \tag{19.80}$$

where $p = 1,2, \ldots, P$; a_{ij} represents the sign of the element at the ith row and the jth column, which is determined by the space-time spreading design rule, while $b'_{k,ij}$ in $\mathbf{B}_{kp}$ is the data bit assigned to the (i, j)-th element, which is one of the G input data bits $\{b_{k,p1}, b_{k,p2}, \ldots, b_{k,pG}\}$ of user k. For example, at $G = M = T = 2$, the corresponding matrix $\mathbf{B}_{kp}$ is given by [49]

$$\begin{pmatrix} b_{k,p1} b_{k,p2} \\ b_{k,p2} - b_{k,p1} \end{pmatrix}, p = 1,2,\ldots, P. \tag{19.81}$$

Finally, in (19.73), $\boldsymbol{\omega}$ represents the multicarrier modulated vector of the length PS, which can be presented in the following form

$$\boldsymbol{\omega} = [\exp(j2\pi f_1 t), \exp(j2\pi f_2 t), \ldots, \exp(j2\pi f_{PS} t)]^T. \tag{19.82}$$

Equation (19.73) represents the general form of the transmitted space-time spreading signals, regardless of the values G, M, and T. However, the investigation carried out in [6, 49] has shown that space-time spreading schemes using $G = M = T$, i.e., those having an equal number of data bits, orthogonal space-time spreading related spreading sequences, as well as transmit antennas constitute the attractive schemes, since they are capable to prove the maximal transmit diversity without requiring extra space-time spreading codes. Therefore, in the present section, we investigate only these attractive space-time spreading schemes, and our results are mainly based on the broadband MC DS-CDMA wireless communication systems using two or four transmit antennas.

As an example, in the case $G = M = T = 2$, the signals employed by the broadband MC DS-CDMA wireless communication system and transmitted by antennas 1 and 2 can be simply expressed in the following form:

$$\mathbf{s}_k(t) = \begin{pmatrix} s_{k1}(t) \\ s_{k2}(t) \end{pmatrix} = \sqrt{\frac{2E_b}{4_b PST}} \begin{pmatrix} \sum_{p=1}^{P}\sum_{s=1}^{S}[a_{k,1}b_{k,p1} + a_{k,2}b_{k,p2}]\cos(2\pi f_{(s-1)P+p}t) \\ \sum_{p=1}^{P}\sum_{s=1}^{S}[a_{k,1}b_{k,p1} - a_{k,2}b_{k,p2}]\cos(2\pi f_{(s-1)P+p}t) \end{pmatrix}. \quad (19.83)$$

Note that in (19.83) the explicit notation indicating the time dependence of $a_{k,i(t)}$ has been omitted for notational convenience, since in the present section only synchronous transmissions are considered.

19.2.2.2 Channel model and system parameter design

The channels are assumed to be the slowly varying frequency-selective Rayleigh fading channels and the delay spreads are assumed to be limited to the range of $[T_m, T_M]$, where T_m corresponds to the environments having the shortest delay spread considered, for example, in an indoor environment, while T_M is associated with an environment having the highest possible delay spread, as in an urban area. Below, we impose some limitations on the set of parameters used by the space-time spreading-assisted broadband MC DS-CDMA wireless communication systems, in order to ensure that the broadband MC DS-CDMA wireless communication systems operate efficiently in different dispersive environments having a delay spread in the range of $[T_m, T_M]$.

In order to ensure that space-time spreading maintains the required frequency diversity order in different wireless communication environments, we configure the system such that each subcarrier signal is guaranteed to experience flat fading. The required frequency diversity is attained by combining the independently faded subcarrier signals, with the aid of F-domain repetition. Since the delay spread experienced in different wireless communication environments is assumed to be limited to the range of $[T_m, T_M]$ the flat fading condition of each subcarrier in these different wireless communication environments is satisfied, provided that $T_c > T_M$.

In order to achieve the highest possible grade of frequency diversity for a given number of combined subcarrier signals, the subcarrier signals combined must experience independent fading. This implies that the F-domain spacing between the specific subcarriers that are combined must be higher than the maximum coherence bandwidth of $(\Delta f)_{cM} \approx 1/T_m$ [56–58]. Let P be the number of subblocks after the S–P conversion stage of figure 19.7. Then, according to figures 19.8 and (19.72), the above condition is satisfied, if $P/T_c \geqslant 1/T_m$, i.e., $P \geqslant T_c/T_m$.

According to the above design philosophy, it can be shown that the broadband MC DS-CDMA wireless communication system having $T_c > T_m$ and $P \geqslant T_c/T_m$ is capable of achieving a constant frequency-selective diversity order, provided that the delay spread of the wireless channels encountered falls within the limits of the interval $[T_m, T_M]$.

Assuming that K user signals in the form of (19.73) are transmitted synchronously over the Rayleigh fading channels, the received complex low-pass equivalent signal can be expressed in the following form

$$r(t) = \sum_{k=1}^{K}\sum_{g=1}^{T}\sqrt{\frac{2E_b}{PT_b} \times \frac{1}{SM_xT}}(\mathbf{X}_k)_g\mathbf{H}\boldsymbol{\omega} + w(t), \tag{19.84}$$

where $(\mathbf{X}_k)_g = (\mathbf{D}_k\mathbf{P})_g$ represents the g-th row of the matrix $\mathbf{X}$; $w(t)$ is the complex valued low-pass equivalent AWGN having a double-sided spectral density of $\mathcal{N}_0$, while

$$\begin{aligned}\mathbf{H} = diag\{&h_{1g}\exp(j\psi_{1g}), h_{2g}\exp(j\psi_{1g}),\ldots, h_{(PS)_g}\exp(j\psi_{(PS)_g})\},\\ &g = 1,2,\ldots,T\end{aligned} \tag{19.85}$$

is the diagonal matrix with the rank PS, which represents the channel's complex impulse response in the context of the g-th antenna. The coefficients h_{ig}, $i = 1,2,\ldots,PS$; $g = 1,2,\ldots,T$ in the matrix $\mathbf{H}$ are i.i.d. random variables obeying the Rayleigh distribution law that can be presented in the following form

$$f_{h_{ig}}(y) = \frac{2y}{\sigma^2}\exp(-y^2/\sigma^2),\ y \geqslant 0 \tag{19.86}$$

where $\sigma^2 = E[(h_{ig})^2]$ and $E[\cdot]$ is the mathematical expectation. Furthermore, the phases ψ_{ig}, $i = 1,2,\ldots,PS$, $g = 1,2,\ldots,T$ are introduced by the fading channels and uniformly distributed within the limits of the interval $[0,2\pi)$. Specifically, in the case of $G = M = T = 2$, the received complex low-pass equivalent signal takes the following form

$$\begin{aligned}r(t) = &\\ &\sum_{k=1}^{K}\sum_{p=1}^{P}\sum_{s=1}^{S}\sqrt{\frac{2E_b}{4PST_b}}\\ &\times\Big\{h_{(ps)1}\exp\{j\psi_{(ps)1}\}[a_{k,1}(t)b_{k,p1} + a_{k,2}(t)b_{k,p2}] + h_{(ps)2}\exp\{j\psi_{(ps)2}\}\\ &[a_{k,1}(t)b_{k,p2} - a_{k,2}(t)b_{k,p1}]\Big\}\exp\{j2\pi f_{(s-1)P+p}t\} + w(t).\end{aligned} \tag{19.87}$$

19.2.2.3 Receiver model

Let the first user be the user of interest and consider a generalized receiver employing the fast Fourier transform (FFT)-based multicarrier demodulation, space-time dispreading, as well as diversity combining, as shown in figure 19.9. The receiver in figure 19.9 is constructed on the basis of the generalized receiver (see figure 19.1) and essentially carries out the inverse operations of those seen in figure 19.7. In figure 19.9, the received signal is first demodulated using FFT-based multicarrier demodulation, obtaining PS number of parallel streams corresponding to the signals transmitted on PS subcarriers. Then, each stream is the space-time dispread using the approach discussed in [49, 59, 60], in order to obtain G separate variables $\{Z_{p,1}, Z_{p,2},\ldots, Z_{p,G}\}_{p=1}^{PS}$ corresponding to the G data bits transmitted on the pth stream, where $p = 1,2,\ldots, PS$, respectively. Following the space-time despreading, a decision variable is formed for each of the transmitted data bits $\{b_{p1}, b_{p2},\ldots, b_{pG}\}_{p=1}^{P}$ that can be expressed in the following form:

$$Z_{pi} = \sum_{s=1}^{S} Z_{((s-1)P+p),\, i},\ p = 1,2,\ldots, P;\ i = 1,2,\ \ldots, G \tag{19.88}$$

Finally, the PG number of transmitted data bits can be decided based on the decision variables $\{Z_{pi}, p = 1,2,\ldots, P;\ i = 1,2,\ldots, G\}$ using the conventional decision rule of a BPSK scheme. Let us now investigate the achievable BER performance.

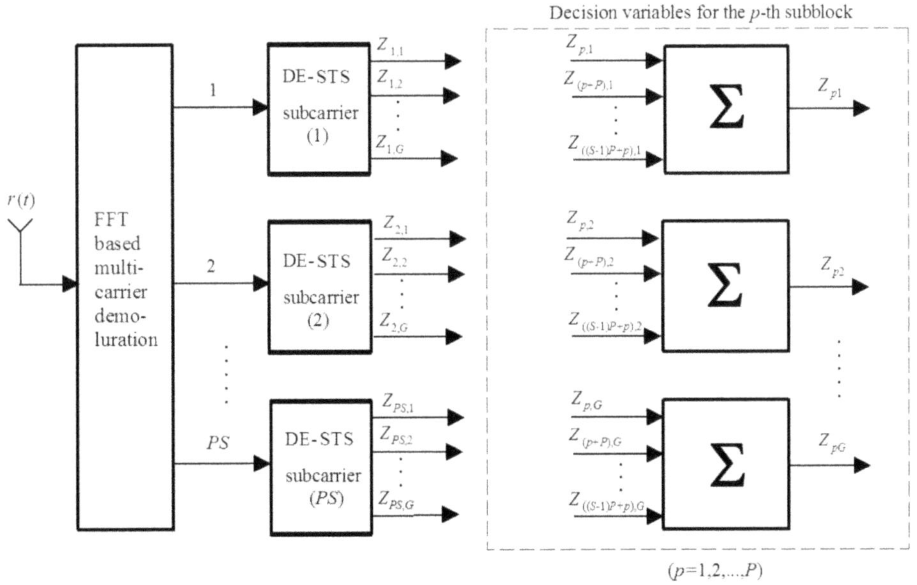

Figure 19.9. The receiver schematic of the broadband MC DS-CDMA wireless communication system using space-time spreading.

19.2.3 Bit-error rate analysis

In this subsection, we derive the *BER* performance expression of the broadband MC DS-CDMA wireless communication system using the space-time spreading, which was described above in the previous subsection. As an example, we derive the *BER* performance expression in detail for the space-time spreading based on the broadband MC DS-CDMA wireless communication system using the following parameters: $G = M = T = 2$. The generalized *BER* performance expression of the broadband MC DS-CDMA wireless communication system using the set of attractive space-time spreading schemes, i.e., using $G = M = T = 2,4,8, \ldots$ etc, is then derived from the case $G = M = T = 2$ without providing the detailed derivations, since the extension is relatively straightforward. In the case of $G = M = T = 2$, the analysis can be commenced from (19.87).

Let $y_{p,1}, y_{p,2}, p = 1,2, \ldots, PS$ represent the variables at the output of the generalized detector (figure 19.1) corresponding to the first two data bits transmitted on the pth subcarrier where

$$y_{p,1} = \int_0^{2PT_b} [2r(t)a_{1,1}(t) - r^2(t) + \eta_{1,1}^2(t)]\exp(-j2\pi f_p t)dt; \tag{19.89}$$

$$y_{p,2} = \int_0^{2PT_b} [2r(t)a_{1,2}(t) - r^2(t) + \eta_{1,2}^2(t)]\exp(-j2\pi f_p t)dt. \tag{19.90}$$

Since the orthogonal multicarrier signals, orthogonal space-time spreading codes, synchronous transmission of the K user signals, as well as slowly flat fading of each subcarrier are assumed, there is no interference between the different users and

$$y_{p,1} = \frac{4(P^2T_b^2 - 1)E_b}{PST_b}[h_{p1}\exp(j\psi_{p1})b_{1,\,p1} + h_{p2}\exp(j\psi_{p2})b_{1,\,p2}] + \varsigma_{p,1}\,; \tag{19.91}$$

$$y_{p,2} = \frac{4(P^2T_b^2 - 1)E_b}{PST_b}[h_{p1}\exp(j\psi_{p1})b_{1,\,p2} + h_{p2}\exp(j\psi_{p2})b_{1,\,p1}] + \varsigma_{p,2}\,; \tag{19.92}$$

where

$$\varsigma_{p,i} = \int_0^{2PT_b} [\eta_i^2(t) - \xi_i^2(t)]\exp(-j2\pi f_p t)dt, \; i = 1,2 \tag{19.93}$$

that can be approximated by the complex Gaussian variable distributed with the zero mean and variance equal to $8PT_b\mathcal{N}_0^2$.

Assuming that the generalized receiver has perfect knowledge with respect to the fading parameters $h_{pi}\exp(j\psi_{pi})$, $i = 1,2$, the decision variables corresponding to the data bits $b_{1,\,pi}$, $i = 1,2$ associated with the pth subcarrier can be expressed in the following form

$$\begin{aligned} Z_{p,1} &= \mathrm{Re}\{y_{p,1}h_{p1}\exp(-j\psi_{p1}) - y_{p,2}h_{p2}\exp(-j\psi_{p2})\} \\ &= \frac{4(P^2T_b^2 - 1)E_b}{PST_b}[h_{p1}^2 + h_{p2}^2]b_{1,p1} \\ &\quad + \mathrm{Re}\{\varsigma_{p,1}h_{p1}\exp(-j\psi_{p1}) - \varsigma_{p,2}h_{p2}\exp(-j\psi_{p2})\}; \end{aligned} \tag{19.94}$$

$$Z_{p,2} = \mathrm{Re}\{y_{p,1}h_{p2}\exp(-j\psi_{p2}) + y_{p,1}h_{p1}\exp(-j\psi_{p1})\}$$
$$= \frac{4(P^2T_b^2 - 1)E_b}{PST_b}[h_{p1}^2 + h_{p2}^2]b_{1,p2}$$
$$+ \mathrm{Re}\{\varsigma_{p,1}h_{p2}\exp(-j\psi_{p2}) - \varsigma_{p,2}h_{p1}\exp(-j\psi_{p1})\}, \tag{19.95}$$

where $p = 1,2,\ldots,PS$.

Finally, after combining the replicas of the same signal transmitted on the S subcarriers, the decision variables corresponding to the two bits in the pth subblock can be presented in the following form

$$Z_{p1} = \sum_{s=1}^{S} Z_{((s-1)P+p),1}, \tag{19.96}$$

$$Z_{p2} = \sum_{s=1}^{S} Z_{((s-1)P+p),2}, \tag{19.97}$$

where $p = 1,2,\ldots,P$. Since $Z_{((s-1)P+p),1}$ in (19.96) and $Z_{((s-1)P+p),2}$ in (19.97) are the i.i. d. random variables for different s values associated with the mean

$$E[Z] = \frac{4(P^2T_b^2 - 1)E_b}{PST_b}[h_{((s-1)P+p)1}^2 + h_{((s-1)P+p)2}^2] \tag{19.98}$$

and the variance

$$Var\{Z\} = 8PT_b\mathcal{N}_0^2[h_{((s-1)P+p)1}^2 + h_{((s-1)P+p)2}^2] \tag{19.99}$$

conditioned on $h_{((s-1)P+p)1}$ and $h_{((s-1)P+p)2}$, it is well recognized [61, 62] that the conditional BER can be presented in the following form

$$BER\{E|[h_{((s-1)P+p)1}, h_{((s-1)P+p)2}]\} = Q\left(\sqrt{2\sum_{s=1}^{S}\sum_{g=1}^{2}\gamma_{sg}}\right) \tag{19.100}$$

where $Q(x)$ is the Gaussian Q-function;

$$\gamma_{sg} = \bar{\gamma} \times \frac{[h_{((s-1)P+p)g}]^2}{\sigma^2}; \tag{19.101}$$

$$\bar{\gamma} = \frac{E_b\sigma^2}{2S\mathcal{N}_0^2}. \tag{19.102}$$

Finally, with the aid of (19.86) and [58], it can be readily shown that the average BER can be expressed in the following form

$$BER = 0.5(1 - \mu)^{2S} \sum_{k=0}^{2S-1} \binom{2S - 1 + k}{k} 0.5(1 + \mu)^k, \tag{19.103}$$

where

$$\mu = \sqrt{\frac{\bar{\gamma}}{1 + \bar{\gamma}}}. \tag{19.104}$$

In the general case $G = M = T = 2,4,8,\ldots$, the decision variable $Z_{p,1}$ corresponding to the first bit in the subblock p can also be expressed as in (19.96), but with $Z_{((s-1)P+p),1}$ given by [61]

$$Z_{((s-1)P+p),1} = \frac{4(P^2T_b^2 - 1)E_b}{PST_b} b_{1,p1} \sum_{g=1}^{G} h^2_{((s-1)P+p)g} \\ +\mathrm{Re}\{\varsigma'_{((s-1)P+p),1}\},\ s = 1,2,\ldots,S, \tag{19.105}$$

where $\mathrm{Re}\{\varsigma'_{((s-1)P+p),1}\}$ is the background noise with the zero mean and variance equal to

$$Var\{\mathrm{Re}[\varsigma'_{((s-1)P+p),1}] = 8PT_b\mathcal{N}_0^2 \sum_{g=1}^{G} h^2_{((s-1)P+p)g}. \tag{19.106}$$

The average BER performance in the case $G = M = T = 2,4,8,\ldots$ can be presented in the following form [63]

$$BER = 0.5(1 - \mu)^{TS} \sum_{k=0}^{TS-1} \binom{2S - 1 + k}{k} 0.5(1 + \mu)^k. \tag{19.107}$$

Note that according to (19.100) and (19.105) by using the space-time spreading and F-domain subcarrier repetition, the diversity order achieved is TS provided that T transmit antennas and S-depth F-domain repetition schemes were used. The resultant diversity order of TS can also be seen in (19.107).

Figure 19.10. demonstrates both the numerical and simulation results of the BER performance, which are drawn using the lines and markers, respectively, at $S = 1$, $T = 1,2,4$ as well as at $S = 3$, $T = 1,2,4$. From these results we observe that at the $BER = 0.01$ using two transmit antennas rather than one yields a gain of approximately 6.0 dB. Furthermore, when $T = 4$ the transmit antennas and the repetition depth $S = 3$ are considered instead of $S = 1$, $T = 1$, the diversity gain achieved is approximately 9.0 dB.

The BER performance presented in figure 19.10 can be achieved, provided that the number of orthogonal space-time spreading codes is sufficiently high for supporting the K number of users without reuse. Based on our arguments in the previous subsections, the number of orthogonal space-time spreading codes is given by $PGT_b/T_c = PGN$. Since each user requires M orthogonal space-time spreading

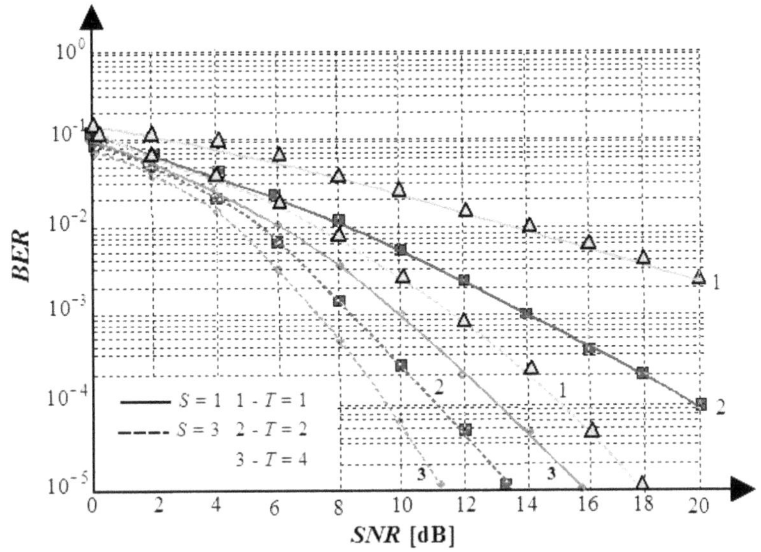

Figure 19.10. Numerical (lines) and simulated (markers) *BER* versus *SNR* per bit, $E_b/\mathcal{N}_0$, performance for the broadband MC DS-CDMA wireless communication system using space-time spreading based on the transmit diversity under the implementation of the generalized receiver when communicating over the frequency-selective Rayleigh fading channels evaluated by (19.47).

codes, the maximum number of users supported by the *PGN* orthogonal space-time spreading codes is given by $\mathscr{K}_{\max} = PGN/M$.

In other words, if the number of users supported by the synchronous broadband MC DS-CDMA wireless communication system designed according to the philosophy of the present section obeys $K < \mathscr{K}_{\max}$, the *BER* performance presented in figure 19.10 can be achieved for transmissions over the frequency-selective Rayleigh fading channels. For the attractive space-time spreading schemes using $G = M = T = 2,4,8,\ldots$, the maximum number of users supported by the orthogonal space-time spreading codes is defined as $\mathscr{K}_{\max} = PN$. It can be seen that, in this case, the number of users supported is independent of the number of transmit antennas, which emphasizes the advantages of the space-time spreading schemes using the specific values of $G = M = T = 2,4,8,\ldots$ [37].

Let $N = T_b/T_c$ and the total number of subcarriers *PS* be constant. Then, the maximum number of users supported by the broadband MC DS-CDMA wireless communication system depends only on the repetition depth *S*. Specifically, the maximum number of users supported decreases when increasing the subcarrier repetition depth *S*, i.e., when increasing the frequency diversity order. Consequently, the maximum number of users supported and the frequency diversity gain achieved have to obey the trade-off. This is not a desirable result. We would like to achieve the maximum transmit diversity gain as well as the required frequency diversity gain without having to accept any other trade-off, i.e., without decreasing the total number of users supported by the system. Let us now consider this issue in the next subsection.

19.2.4 Capacity extension using time-frequency-domain spreading

19.2.4.1 System description

In this subsection, we propose and investigate the broadband MC DS-CDMA wireless communication system, which employs both the time (T)-domain and frequency (F)-domain spreading, i.e., it employs TF-domain spreading. The transmitter schematic of the space-time spreading-assisted broadband MC DS-CDMA wireless communication system using the TF-domain spreading is similar to that seen in figure 19.7, except that the S-depth subcarrier repetition of figure 19.7 is now replaced by the F-domain spreading associated with an orthogonal spreading code of length S.

Specifically, let $\{c_k[0], c_k[1], \dots, c_k[S-1]\}$ be the kth user's orthogonal code in discrete form, which will be used for the F-domain spreading. By contrast, the kth user's T-domain orthogonal codes used for space-time spreading have been expressed in the previous subsection as $a_{k,i}(t)$, $i = 1,2,\dots,M$ in continuous form. In the broadband MC DS-CDMA wireless communication system using TF-domain spreading, the P subblock signals of user k after space-time spreading are now further spread over the F-domain using the above F-domain spreading codes. The signals transmitted from the T transmit antennas can be presented in the following form

$$\mathbf{s}_k(t) = \mathrm{Re}\left\{\sqrt{\frac{2E_b}{PT_bSMT}}\mathbf{D}_k\mathbf{Q}\boldsymbol{\omega}\right\}, \tag{19.108}$$

where all variables have the same interpretations as those in (19.73), except that the repetition matrix $\mathbf{P}$ in (19.73) is now replaced by the matrix $\mathbf{Q}$ in (19.108), which represents the F-domain spreading and is the $P \times PS$-dimensional matrix expressed as

$$\mathbf{Q} = \{\mathbf{C}_k[0], \mathbf{C}_k[1], \dots, \mathbf{C}_k[S-1]\}, \tag{19.109}$$

where $\mathbf{C}_k[s]$, $s = 0,1, \dots, S-1$ are the diagonal matrices of rank P which can be presented in the following form

$$\mathbf{C}_k[s] = diag\{c_k(s), c_k(s), \dots, c_k(s)\}. \tag{19.110}$$

Specifically, at $G = M = T = 2$, the TF-domain spread signals transmitted by the transmit antenna 1 and 2 of the broadband MC DS-CDMA wireless communication system can be simply presented in the following form

$$\mathbf{s}_k(t) = \begin{pmatrix} s_{k1}(t) \\ s_{k2}(t) \end{pmatrix} = \sqrt{\frac{E_b}{2PT_bS}} \times \begin{pmatrix} \sum_{p=1}^{P}\sum_{s=1}^{S}[a_{k,1}b_{k,p1} + a_{k,2}b_{k,p2}]c_k(s-1)\cos(2\pi f_{(s-1)P+p}t) \\ \sum_{p=1}^{P}\sum_{s=1}^{S}[a_{k,1}b_{k,p2} - a_{k,2}b_{k,p1}]c_k(s-1)\cos(2\pi f_{(s-1)P+p}t) \end{pmatrix}. \tag{19.111}$$

The total number of users supported by the broadband MC DS-CDMA wireless communication system using *TF*-domain spreading and the assignment of orthogonal codes to users is analysed as follows. According to our analysis in the previous subsections, the total number of orthogonal codes that can be used for the space-time spreading is equal to *PGN* and the maximum number of users supported by these orthogonal codes is defined as $\mathcal{K}_{\max} = PGN/M$. By contrast, the total number of orthogonal codes that can be used for *F*-domain spreading is equal to *S*. This implies that even if *S* that is the number of users shares the same set of space-time spreading codes, these *S* user signals might be distinguishable with the aid of the associated *S* number of the *F*-domain spreading codes.

Explicitly, the total number of users supported is equal to

$$\mathcal{K}_{\max} = \frac{SPGN}{M}. \tag{19.112}$$

Therefore, the orthogonal spreading codes can be assigned as follows. If the number of users is in the range of $0 \leqslant K \leqslant \mathcal{K}_{\max}$, these users will be assigned the required orthogonal space-time spreading codes and the same *F*-domain orthogonal spreading code. However, when the number of users is in the range of $s\mathcal{K}_{\max} \leqslant K \leqslant (s+1)\mathcal{K}_{\max}$, $s = 1,2,\ldots,S-1$, then the same set of the M space-time spreading orthogonal codes must be assigned to s or $(s+1)$ users, but these s or $(s+1)$ users are assigned to different *F*-domain spreading codes. These s or $(s+1)$ users employing the same set of space-time spreading orthogonal codes are identified by their corresponding *F*-domain spreading codes.

Since the subcarrier signals across which *F*-domain spreading takes place encounter independent fading, the orthogonality of the *F*-domain spreading codes cannot be retained. Hence, multiuser interference is inevitably introduced that degrades the *BER* performance when increasing the number of users sharing the same set of the M space-time spreading orthogonal codes.

Let $1 \leqslant K' \leqslant S$ be the number of users sharing the same set of space-time spreading orthogonal codes. We also assume that any set of the M space-time spreading orthogonal codes is shared by the same K' number of users. Then, when the $K' \times \mathcal{K}_{\max}$ signals expressed in the form of (19.108) are transmitted over the frequency-selective fading channels, the received complex low-pass equivalent signal can be expressed in the following form

$$\mathbf{r}(t) = \sum_{k=1}^{K'\mathcal{K}_{\max}} \sum_{g=1}^{T} \sqrt{\frac{2E_b}{PT_b} \times \frac{1}{SMT}} (\mathbf{D}_k\mathbf{Q})_g \mathbf{H}\boldsymbol{\omega} + \mathbf{w}(t), \tag{19.113}$$

where $(\mathbf{D}_k\mathbf{Q})_g$ and $\mathbf{w}(t)$ have the same interpretation as in (19.84). Specifically, in the

$$r(t) = \sum_{k=1}^{K'\mathcal{K}_{\max}} \sum_{p=1}^{P} \sum_{s=1}^{S} \sqrt{\frac{2E_b}{4PST_b}} \{h_{(ps)1} \exp(j\psi_{(ps)1})[a_{k,1}(t)b_{k,p1} + a_{k,2}(t)b_{k,p2}]c_k(s-1)$$

$$+ h_{(ps)2} \exp(j\psi_{(ps)2})[a_{k,1}(t)b_{k,p2} - a_{k,2}(t)b_{k,p1}]c_k(s-1)\}\exp(j2\pi f_{(s-1)P+p}t) + w(t). \tag{19.114}$$

The receiver schematic of the broadband MC DS-CDMA wireless communication system using the *TF*-domain spreading is similar to that of figure 19.9, excepting that the repetition operation seen in figure 19.9 is now replaced by the *F*-domain despreading. The signals at the output of the space-time-despreading block in figure 19.9 can be detected by invoking a range of single or multiuser detection schemes.

19.2.4.2 Signal detection

Following the derivations in the previous subsection, in the general case $G = M = T = 2,4,8, \ldots$, etc, the decision variable $Z_{((s-1)P+p),1}$ in terms of the first data bit in the subblock p and the subcarrier $(s-1)P+p$ can now be presented in the following form

$$Z_{((s-1)P+p),1} = \frac{4(P^2T_b^2-1)E_b}{PST_b}\sum_{k=1}^{K'}\sum_{g=1}^{T} h^2_{((s-1)P+p)g}c_k(s-1)b_{k,p1} + \mathrm{Re}\{\varsigma'_{((s-1)P+p),\, i}\},\ s = 1,2,\ \ldots,\ S, \tag{19.115}$$

where $\mathrm{Re}\{\varsigma'_{p,1}\}$ is the background noise having the zero mean and variance equal to $8PT_b\mathcal{N}_0^2 \times \sum_{g=1}^{T} h^2_{pg}$.

Let

$$\mathbf{z}_{p1} = [Z_{p,1}Z_{(P=P),1}\cdots Z_{((S-1)P+p),1}]^T; \tag{19.116}$$

$$\mathbf{A} = diag\left\{\sum_{g=1}^{T_x} h^2_{pg},\ \sum_{g=1}^{T_x} h^2_{(P+p)g},\ \ldots,\sum_{g=1}^{T_x} h^2_{((S-1)P+p)g}\right\}; \tag{19.117}$$

$$\mathbf{C} = \begin{pmatrix} c_1[0] & c_2[0] & \cdots & c_{K'}[0] \\ c_1[1] & c_2[1] & \cdots & c_{K'}[1] \\ \vdots & \vdots & \ddots & \vdots \\ c_1[S-1] & c_2[S-1] & \cdots & c_{K'}[S-1] \end{pmatrix}; \tag{19.118}$$

$$\mathbf{b} = [b_{1,p1}b_{2,p1}\cdots b_{K',p1}]^T; \tag{19.119}$$

$$\Xi = [\varsigma'_{p,1}\varsigma'_{(P+p),1}\cdots\varsigma'_{((S-1)P+p),1}]^T. \tag{19.120}$$

Then equation (19.115) can be written in the following matrix form

$$\mathbf{z}_{p1} = \frac{4(P^2T_b^2-1)E_b}{PST_b}\mathbf{ACb} + \Xi. \tag{19.121}$$

Detection of signals employed by the broadband MC DS-CDMA wireless communication system given in (19.121) is similar to the detection of signals employed by the conventional broadband MC DS-CDMA wireless communication system using the F-domain spreading, where the single-user detectors [42, 50, 51] or multiuser detectors [6, 7, 36–38, 61] can be implemented.

Detection of signals employed by the broadband MC DS-CDMA wireless communication system given in (19.121) is similar to the detection of signals employed by the conventional broadband MC DS-CDMA wireless communication system using the F-domain spreading, where the single-user detectors [42, 50, 51] or multiuser detectors [6, 7, 36–38, 61] can be implemented.

In the present subsection, we investigate two detection algorithms, namely, the single-user generalized detector [38, 61] and the multiuser generalized detector [44, 62] and compare them with the single-user correlation detector [6, 50, 51] and the multiuser decorrelating detector [50, 51, 59, 60].

In the context of the generalized detector or receiver, let

$$\mathbf{z} = [Z_{p,1} Z_{p,2} \cdots Z_{p,K'}]^T \tag{19.122}$$

represent the decision variables. Then, these decision variables are obtained by multiplying both sides of (19.121) with the matrix $\mathbf{C}^T$, which can be presented in the following form

$$\mathbf{z} = \frac{4(P^2 T_b^2 - 1)E_b}{PST_b} \sum_{s=1}^{S} \sum_{g=1}^{T} h^2_{((s-1)P+p)g} \times \mathbf{Rb} + \mathbf{C}^T \boldsymbol{\Xi}, \tag{19.123}$$

where

$$\mathbf{R} = \begin{pmatrix} 1 & \rho_{12} & \cdots & \rho_{1K'} \\ \rho_{21} & 1 & \cdots & \rho_{2K'} \\ \vdots & \vdots & \ddots & \vdots \\ \rho_{K'1} & \rho_{K'2} & \cdots & 1 \end{pmatrix} \tag{19.124}$$

is the correlation matrix among the K' user signals, while ρ_{ij} is the correlation factor between user i and user j that can be represented in the following form

$$\rho_{ij} = \frac{\sum_{s=1}^{S} \left\{ c_i[s-1] c_j[s-1] \sum_{g=1}^{T} h^2_{((s-1)P+p)g} \right\}}{\sum_{s=1}^{S} \sum_{g=1}^{T} h^2_{((s-1)P+p)g}}. \tag{19.125}$$

Equation (19.123) suggests that the diversity gain contributed both by the transmit diversity and frequency diversity can be retained, since we have a double sum of the components h^2 corresponding to the transmission and frequency diversity orders of S and T, respectively. However, the multiuser interference is introduced by the channel's time-varying characteristics. Finally, the corresponding data bits, $b_{k,p1}, k = 1,2,\ldots,K'$ are decided according to $\hat{b}_{k,p1} = \operatorname{sgn} \mathbf{z}_k, k = 1,2,\ldots,K'$, where $\mathbf{z}_k$ represents the kth row of $\mathbf{z}$, while sgn(·) is the sign function [6].

Note that the correlation factors $\{\rho_{ij}\}$ in (19.125) are time-variant due to the time-varying nature of the channel's fading envelope. However, since

$$\sum_{s=1}^{S} c_i[s-1]c_j[s-1] = 0, \tag{19.126}$$

it can be shown that $\rho_{ij} = 0$, provided that the sum of $\sum_{g=1}^{T} h^2_{((s-1)P+p)g}$ is identical for different values of s. Moreover, it can be shown that the correlation factors $\{\rho_{ij}\}$ are contributed by the differences of the sums $\sum_{g=1}^{T} h^2_{((s-1)P+p)g}$ experienced according to the different values of s, while the common part of $\sum_{g=1}^{T} h^2_{((s-1)P+p)g}$ in terms of different values of s can be successfully removed due to the orthogonality of the F-domain spreading codes.

Specifically, let

$$\sum_{g=1}^{T} h^2_{((s-1)P+p)g} = A_h + \Delta_s, \tag{19.127}$$

where A_h is the average value of $\sum_{g=1}^{T} h^2_{((s-1)P+p)g}$ in terms of s, while

$$\Delta_s = \sum_{g=1}^{T} h^2_{((s-1)P+p)g} - A_h. \tag{19.128}$$

Then, equation (19.125) can be written as

$$\rho_{ij} = \frac{\sum_{s=1}^{S} \{c_i[s-1]c_j[s-1]\Delta_s\}}{\sum_{s=1}^{S} (A_h + \Delta_s)}. \tag{19.129}$$

Figure 19.11 demonstrates the probability density function (pdf) of the correlation factor ρ_{12} between the signals of user 1 and user 2 for the two user broadband MC DS-CDMA wireless communication system employing the space-time spreading transmit diversity under communication over the frequency-selective Rayleigh fading channels. The curves in figure 19.11 show that the correlation factor using $T = 1,2$ and four transmit antennas is symmetrically distributed around $\rho_{12} = 0$.

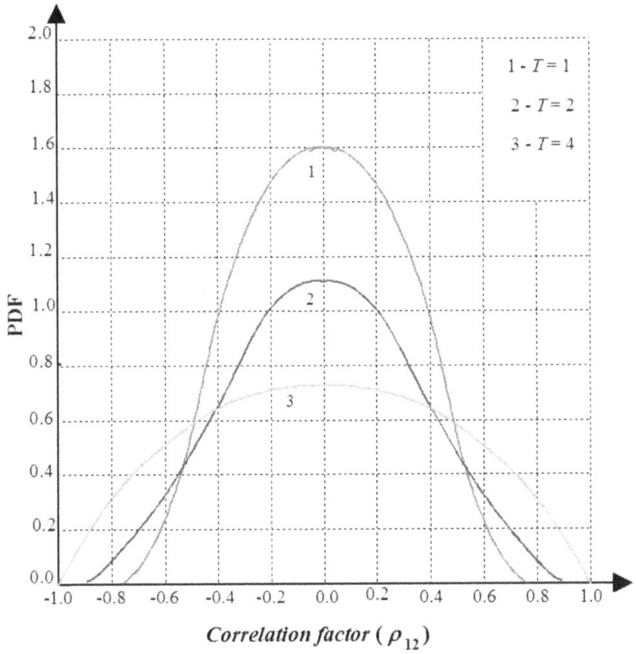

Figure 19.11. Simulated pdf of the correlation factor ρ_{12} for the two user broadband MC DS-CDMA communication system using $T = 1,2,4$ transmit antennas and the space-time spreading when communicating over the frequency-selective Rayleigh fading channels.

An important observation is that the correlation factor value is predominantly distributed in the vicinty of $\rho_{12} = 0$ and becomes similar to the truncated Gaussian random variable distributed within the limits of the interval [–1,1] having a relatively low variance, when increasing the number of transmit antennas. This observation implies that the space-time spreading using several transmit antennas has two-fold importance. Firstly, it is capable of providing the spatial diversity. Secondly, it is capable of suppressing the multiuser interference imposed by the *F*-domain despreading.

In the context of the multiuser generalized detector, the decision variables associated with $\{b_{k,p1}\}_{k=1}^{K'}$ are obtained by multiplying both sides of (19.123) with the inverse matrix **R**, i.e., with the matrix $\mathbf{R}^{-1}$ that can be presented in the following form

$$\mathbf{R}^{-1}\mathbf{z} = \sqrt{\frac{2E_bPT_b}{S}}\sum_{s=1}^{S}\sum_{g=1}^{T}h^2_{((s-1)P+p)g} \times \mathbf{b} + \mathbf{R}^{-1}\mathbf{C}^T\mathbf{w} \tag{19.130}$$

and the corresponding data bits $b_{k,p1}$, $k = 1,2,\ldots,K'$ are decided according to $\hat{b}_{k,p1} = \text{sgn}(\mathbf{R}^{-1} \times \mathbf{z})_k, k = 1,2,\ldots,K'$. Equation (19.130) shows that each user data can be decided independently of the other user data and the diversity order achieved is *TS*. Let us now provide a range of simulation results for the space-time spreading broadband MC DS-CDMA wireless communication system using the *TF*-domain spreading.

19.2.4.3 BER performance

The *BER* performance versus *SNR* per bit, $E_b/\mathcal{N}_0$, performance of the single-user and multiuser generalized detector in comparison with both the single-user correlation detector and the multiuser decorrelating detector is presented in figures 19.12 and 19.13 for the broadband MC DS-CDMA wireless communication system using the *TF*-domain spreading. In both figures we considered $T = 2$ transmit antennas and supporting $K = \mathcal{K}_{\max}, 2\mathcal{K}_{\max}, 3\mathcal{K}_{\max}, 4\mathcal{K}_{\max}$ users corresponding to $K' = 1,2,3,4$, where $K_{\max}$ represented the maximum number of users supported by the *T*-domain orthogonal spreading codes without imposing the multiuser interference. The condition $K' = 1$ corresponds to an absence of the multiuser interference. The difference between figures 19.12 and 19.13 is that in figure 19.12 the length of the *F*-domain spreading codes is $S = 4$, while in figure 19.13 it is $S = 8$.

As expected, we observe in both figures that the *BER* performance is significantly improved when both the correlation detector and the decorrelating detector are replaced by the generalized detector. For the generalized detector, correlation detector and the decorrelating detector the *BER* performance degrades with increasing the number of users sharing the same *T*-domain spreading code, i.e., with increasing the value of K'. However, the *BER* increase due to increasing the value of K' is significantly lower for the generalized detector in comparison with the correlation detector and decorrelating detector. Furthermore, upon comparing figures 19.12 and 19.13, we observe that the *BER* performance of the generalized

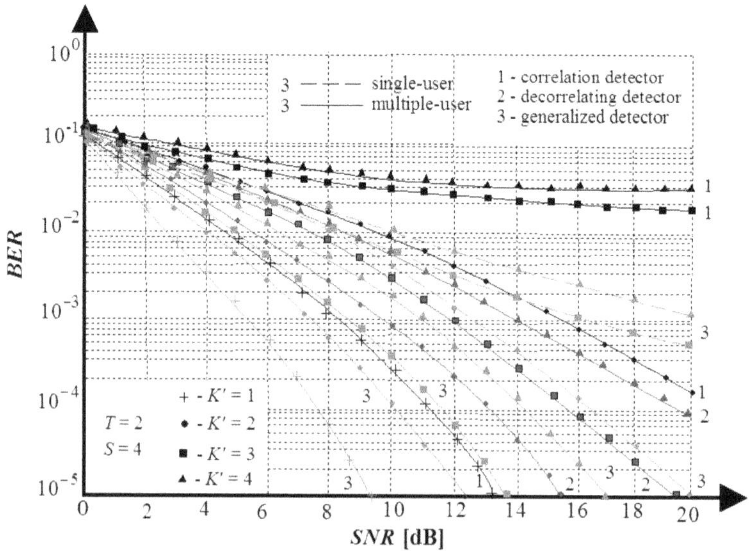

Figure 19.12. Simulation of the *BER* versus the *SNR* per bit, $E_b/\mathcal{N}_0$, performance of the correlation detector, decorrelating detector and generalized detector for the space-time spreading broadband MC DC-CDMA using *TF*-domain spreading when communicating over the frequency-selective Rayleigh fading channels.

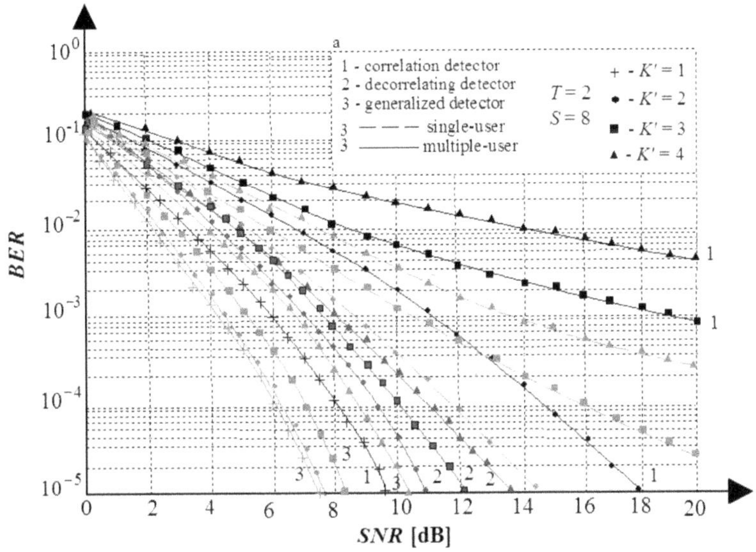

Figure 19.13. Simulation of the *BER* versus the *SNR* per bit, $E_b/\mathcal{N}_0$, performance of the correlation detector, decorrelating detector and generalized detector for the space-time spreading based broadband MC DC-CDMA using *TF*-domain spreading when communicating over the frequency-selective Rayleigh fading channels.

detector is closer to the *BER* performance without the multiuser interference, when using $S = 8$ (figure 19.13) instead of $S = 4$ (figure 19.12).

In figure 19.14 we investigated the *BER* performance of the generalized detector in comparison with both the correlation detector and the decorrelating detector at various numbers of the transmit antennas, namely, at $T = 1,2,4$ and $S = 8,4,2$ *F*-domain spreading codes, while maintaining a constant *TS* value of eight. In our experiments, we assumed that $K' = 2$, i.e., that each set of *T*-domain space-time spreading codes was shared by two users. Let the maximum number of users supported by the *T*-domain spreading codes be $\mathcal{K}_{\max}$, while using the parameters of $T = 4,\ S = 2$.

Then for the broadband MC DS-CDMA wireless communication system having a constant system bandwidth, the maximum number of users, $\mathcal{K}_{\max}$ supported by the *T*-domain codes and using the parameters $T = 1,\ S = 8$ or $T = 2,\ S = 4$ is equal to $0.25\mathcal{K}_{\max}$ or $0.5\mathcal{K}_{\max}$, respectively. In other words, there is a maximum of two, four or eight users sharing the same set of the orthogonal space-time spreading codes, corresponding to the cases of $T = 2,\ S = 4,\ T = 4,\ S = 2;\ T = 2,\ S = 4$ or $T = 1,\ S = 8$, respectively.

From the results we infer the following observations:

- All schemes achieve the same total diversity gain.
- The number of transmit antennas has the same effect on the *BER* performance as the length of the *F*-domain spreading codes, i.e., the same *BER* can be

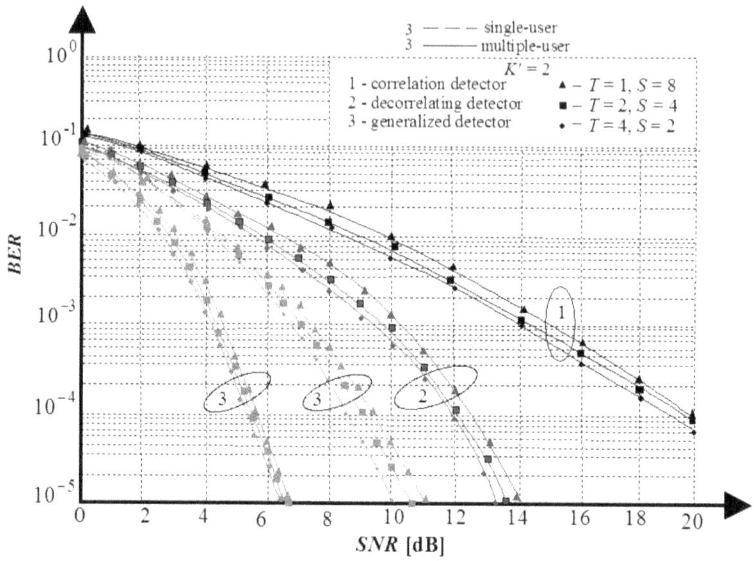

Figure 19.14. Simulation of the *BER* versus the *SNR* per bit, $E_b/\mathcal{N}_0$, performance of the correlation detector, decorrelating detector and generalized detector for the space-time spreading based broadband MC DC-CDMA using *TF*-domain spreading when communicating over the frequency-selective Rayleigh fading channels.

maintained, regardless of what values of T and S must be taken to provide that the product TS could be a constant.

- The generalized detector significantly outperforms the correlation detector and decorrelating detector. The gain achieved at the *BER* equal to 10^{-3} by using the multiuser generalized detector is 6–7 dB in comparison with the multiuser decorrelating detector and by using the single-user generalized detector is 8–9 dB in comparison with the correlation detector.
- The maximum number of users $K'_{\max}$ sharing the same set of space-time spreading orthogonal codes is two, four or eight, when we use the parameters $T = 4$, $S = 2$; $T = 2$, $S = 4$; $T = 1$, $S = 8$.

Furthermore, since, according to figures 19.12 and 19.13, the *BER* performance degrades upon increasing the number of users sharing the same set of the space-time spreading orthogonal codes, consequently, for a fully loaded system using the maximum values of $K'_{\max}$, we can surmise that the broadband MC DS-CDMA wireless communication system employing the parameters $T = 4$, $S = 2$ outperforms the one using the parameter combinations $T = 2$, $S = 4$ and $T = 1$, $S = 8$.

Furthermore, the broadband MC DS-CDMA wireless communication system using the parameters $T = 2$, $S = 4$ outperforms that employing the parameters $T = 1$, $S = 8$. The above arguments suggest that the best broadband MC DS-CDMA wireless communication system will only use the transmit diversity and no frequency diversity at all, i.e., use the parameters $T = 8$, $S = 1$, which simultaneously suggests that no multiuser detection is required.

19.3 DS-CDMA with STBC over fading channels

19.3.1 Introduction

The growing demand for high-rate date services through wireless communication channels experienced in recent years motivates the design of multiple antenna wireless communication systems to transmit increased data rates without substantial bandwidth expansion. In particular, the antenna diversity can be used to improve the performance of wireless communication systems such as the DS-CDMA. First presented in [46] for two transmitting antennas and generalized in [64] and [65] for an arbitrary number of transmitting antennas, orthogonal space-time block coding (STBC) is a remarkable technique which can provide full diversity gain with very low computational complexity.

However, a loss in capacity, characterized by the code rate and the number of receive antennas, is discussed in [66] and [67] for an arbitrary channel. Following the analysis in [65–67], a characterization based on the equivalent scalar AWGN channel multiplied by a coefficient, which is a function of the Frobenius norm of the channel matrix with multiple antennas, was given in [66] assuming a full code rate. The Shannon and outage capacity for the scalar AWGN channel were also given.

The Shannon capacity

$$C = W \log_2(1 + SNR), \tag{19.131}$$

where SNR is the signal-to-noise ratio and W is the channel bandwidth, predicts the channel capacity C for an AWGN channel with continuous-valued inputs and continuous-valued outputs. However, a channel employing the STBC with the pulse-amplitude modulation (PAM), phase-shift keying (PSK) or quadrature-amplitude modulation (QAM) has discrete-valued inputs and continuous-valued outputs, which imposes an additional constraint on the capacity calculation.

In this section, we generalize the effective channel representation in [66] for all rate orthogonal STBCs, including the rate 0.5 STBCs $\mathbf{G}_N$, $N > 2$ and the rate 0.75 STBCs $\mathbf{H}_3$ and $\mathbf{H}_4$, given in [64]. A new capacity calculation taking into account the constraint of discrete-valued inputs is presented here, as well as the capacity loss incurred by employing STBC.

In [68], an analysis of the bit error probability (BEP) performance of $\mathbf{G}_2$ for q-ary PSK was presented for the Rayleigh fading channel using the probability density function (pdf) of the received signal phase from [56]. However, the BEP for q-ary PSK ($q > 4$) is very complex using this approach. In [69], a union bound on the symbol error probability (SEP) for the STBC was presented. A general form for the exact pair-wise error probability of STBCs was obtained in [70] based on the moment generating function of the Gaussian tail function. In [71], the STBC was applied to the DS-CDMA downlink, and a novel decoding algorithm was presented. In [72], the exact expression for the pair-wise error probability in a flat Rayleigh fading channel was derived in terms of the symbol distance between two message vectors for quaternary phase-shift keying (QPSK),16-QAM, 64-QAM and 256-QAM. In [73], a unified approach to calculate the error rates of linearly modulated signals over generalized fading channels was presented. However, the results of both [72] and [73] are given in an open form that has to be evaluated via numerical integration.

In this section, we analyse the error probability of STBCs for PAM, PSK, QAM modulated signals as a function of an *SNR* perspective based upon the equivalent scalar channel induced by the STBC. Using the pdf of the *SNR*, the closed form *SEPs* are given for various combinations of modulation and fading channels. Furthermore, these results are extended to the multiuser DS-CDMA system with STBC employing the generalized receiver. Expressions for the capacity and error probability of the DS-CDMA wireless communication system with STBC are derived and analysed.

19.3.2 Channel model

19.3.2.1 General channel model

The channel model is the same as in [64–66]. Consider the wireless communication system with N transmitting and M receiving antennas. The channel is assumed to be quasistatic with flat fading, which means that the channel parameters are constant within one frame period, but are varied independently between frames. Furthermore, the perfect channel state information is assumed available at the receiver input, but the channel parameters are unknown at the transmitter.

Let T represents the number of time slots used to transmit S symbols. Hence, a general form for the transmission matrix of STBC is given as

$$\mathbf{G} = \begin{pmatrix} g_{11} & g_{21} & \cdots & g_{N1} \\ g_{12} & g_{22} & \cdots & g_{N2} \\ \cdots & \cdots & \cdots & \cdots \\ g_{1T} & g_{2T} & \cdots & g_{NT} \end{pmatrix}, \qquad (19.132)$$

where g_{ij} represent a linear combination of the signal constellation components and their conjugates, and are transmitted simultaneously by the ith transmitting antenna in the jth time slot for $i = 1 \ldots N$ and $j = 1 \ldots T$. Since there are S symbols transmitted over T time slots, the code rate of the STBC is given by

$$R = S/T. \qquad (19.133)$$

It is shown in [64], based on the theory of orthogonal designs, that full-rate STBCs exist for any number of transmitting antennas using an arbitrary real constellation such as PAM. For an arbitrary complex constellation such as PSK, QAM, half-rate STBCs exist for any number of transmitting antennas, while full-rate STBCs exist only for two transmitting antennas. As specific cases for two, three, and four transmitting antennas, the rate 1, 0.5, and 0.75 STBCs are given in [64], and are denoted as $\mathbf{G}_2$, $\mathbf{G}_3$, $\mathbf{G}_4$, $\mathbf{H}_3$, and $\mathbf{H}_4$, respectively.

At the particular time nT, the received signal corresponding to the nth input block spanning T time slots takes the form

$$\mathbf{Y}_{nT} = \mathbf{H}\mathbf{G}^T + \mathbf{W}_{nT}, \qquad (19.134)$$

where $\mathbf{Y}_{nT}$ is the $M \times T$ matrix; $\mathbf{H}$ is the $M \times N$ fading channel coefficient matrix with the independent identically distributed (i.i.d.) entries modelled as the circular complex Gaussian random variables; $\mathbf{G}^T$ is the transpose of $\mathbf{G}$ with the size $N \times T$, and $\mathbf{W}_{nT}$ is the $M \times N$ receiver noise matrix with the i.i.d. entries modelled as the circular complex Gaussian random variables with zero mean and variance $\sigma_W = \Delta f \times N_0/2$ in each dimension, where Δf is the bandwidth of linear system at the receiver input and $N_0/2$ is the AWGN power spectral density.

19.3.2.2 Effective scaled AWGN channel

In [66], an equivalent scaled AWGN channel induced by the STBC for the complex constellations was given as

$$\mathbf{y}_{nT} = ||\mathbf{H}||_F^2 \mathbf{x}_{nT} + \mathbf{w}_{nT}, \tag{19.135}$$

where $\mathbf{y}_{nT}$ is the $S \times 1$ complex matrix after STBC decoding from the received matrix $\mathbf{Y}_{nT}$; $\mathbf{x}_{nT}$ is the input $S \times 1$ complex input matrix with each entry having the energy E_s/N, E_s is the maximum total transmitted energy on the N transmitting antennas per symbol time; and $\mathbf{w}_{nT}$ is the complex Gaussian noise with the zero mean and variance $||\mathbf{H}||_F^2 N_0/2$ in each real dimension;

$$||\mathbf{H}||_F^2 = \sum_{i=1}^{N}\sum_{j=1}^{M} ||h_{ij}||^2 \tag{19.136}$$

is the squared Frobenius norm of $\mathbf{H}$; h_{ij} is the channel gain from the ith transmit antenna to the jth receiving antenna. Taking into account the code rate, the equivalent AWGN scaled channel with STBC is

$$\mathbf{y}_{nT} = (1/R)||\mathbf{H}||_F^2 \mathbf{x}_{nT} + \mathbf{w}_{nT}, \tag{19.137}$$

where $\mathbf{w}_{nT}$ is the complex Gaussian noise with the zero mean and variance given as

$$Var = (1/2R)||\mathbf{H}||_F^2 N_0 \tag{19.138}$$

in each real dimension. Therefore, the effective instantaneous SNR denoted as γ_s at the receiver input takes the following form

$$\gamma_s = \frac{E_s}{NRN_0}||\mathbf{H}||_F^2. \tag{19.139}$$

Let

$$h = \frac{1}{R}||\mathbf{H}||_F^2 = \sum_{i=1}^{N}\sum_{j=1}^{M} \frac{||h_{ij}||^2}{R}, \tag{19.140}$$

then the STBC channel model of (19.137) can be simplified to

$$\mathbf{y}_{nT} = h\mathbf{x}_{nT} + \mathbf{w}_{nT} \tag{19.141}$$

and γ_s can be written as

$$\gamma_s = \frac{E_s}{NN_0}h. \tag{19.142}$$

19.3.2.3 Distribution of the channel coefficients and SNR *for fading channels*

Rayleigh fading: With Rayleigh fading, the coefficients h_{ij} can be modelled as the complex Gaussian variable with the zero mean and variance σ_w^2 in each dimension. The pdf of the coefficient h is then the central chi-square distribution with 2 MN degrees of freedom

$$f_{\text{Rayleigh}}(h) = \frac{R^{MN}}{(2\sigma_w^2)^{MN}\Gamma(MN)}h^{MN-1}\exp\left\{-\frac{hR}{2\sigma_w^2}\right\},\ h \geqslant 0. \tag{19.143}$$

Consequently, the instantaneous SNR per symbol γ_s is also chi-square distributed. Using a change of variables, the pdf of γ_s is given by

$$f_{\text{Rayleigh}}(h) = \frac{R^{MN}}{\bar{\gamma}_{ch}^{MN}\Gamma(MN)}\gamma_s^{MN-1}\exp\left\{-\frac{\gamma_s}{\bar{\gamma}_{ch}}\right\},\ \gamma_s \geqslant 0 \tag{19.144}$$

where $\bar{\gamma}_{ch}$ is the average SNR per channel, which is assumed to be identical for all channels, i.e.

$$\bar{\gamma}_{ch} = \frac{E_s}{NR\mathcal{N}_0}E[||h_{ij}||^2] = \frac{2\sigma_w^2 E_s}{NR\mathcal{N}_0}, \tag{19.145}$$

where $E[\cdot]$ is the mathematical expectation. It can easily be shown that the instantaneous SNR per bit γ_b has the same pdf except that

$$\bar{\gamma}_{ch} = \frac{E_s}{NR\mathcal{N}_0\log_2 M} \tag{19.146}$$

for the M-ary signal constellation.

Rician fading: For Rician fading, the coefficients h_{ij} can be modelled as a complex Gaussian variable with the means μ_I and μ_Q for the real and imaginary parts, respectively, and the variance σ_w^2 in each dimension. In this case, $||\mathbf{H}||_F^2$ has a non-central chi-square distribution with $2MN$ degrees of freedom. The pdf of h is given by

$$f_{\text{Rician}}(h) = \frac{R}{2\sigma_w^2}\left[\frac{Rh}{s^2}\right]^{\frac{MN-1}{2}}\exp\left\{-\frac{s^2+Rh}{2\sigma_w^2}\right\}I_{MN-1}\left(\frac{\sqrt{Rh}\,s}{\sigma_w^2}\right),\ h \geqslant 0 \tag{19.147}$$

where

$$s^2 = MN(\mu_I^2 + \mu_Q^2) \tag{19.148}$$

is the non-centrality parameter, $I_\alpha(x)$ is the α-th order modified Bessel function of the first kind, which may be represented by the infinite series

$$I_\tau(x) = \sum_{k=0}^{\infty}\frac{(0.5x)^{n+2k}}{k!\Gamma(n+k+1)}. \tag{19.149}$$

Introducing the Rician parameter

$$\beta = \frac{\mu_I^2 + \mu_Q^2}{2\sigma_w^2}, \tag{19.150}$$

the pdf in (19.143) can be written in the following form

$$f_{\text{Rician}}(h) = \sum_{i=0}^{\infty} \frac{(MN\beta)^i \exp\{-MN\beta\} R^{MN+i}}{\Gamma(i+1)\Gamma(MN+i)(2\sigma_w^2)^{MN+i}} \times h^{MN+i-1} \exp\{-Rh/2\sigma_w^2\}, \quad h \geqslant 0. \tag{19.151}$$

Using a change of variables, the pdf of the instantaneous SNR takes the following form

$$f_{\text{Rician}}(h) = \sum_{i=0}^{\infty} \frac{(MN\beta)^i \exp\{-MN\beta\}\gamma_s^{MN+i-1} \exp\{-\gamma_s/\gamma_c\}}{\Gamma(i+1)\Gamma(MN+i)\bar{\gamma}_c^{MN+i}}, \; \gamma_s \geqslant 0 \tag{19.152}$$

where $\bar{\gamma}_c$ is the average SNR per channel, which is assumed to be identical for all channels, as given in (19.145).

Nakagami-m fading: For Nakagami-m fading with the integer m, $||h_{ij}||$ is the amplitude of the channel coefficient h_{ij} and has a Nakagami-m distribution with the variance σ_N^2 in each dimension. The random variable

$$y = R^{-1}||h_{ij}||^2 \tag{19.153}$$

then has the pdf

$$f(y) = \frac{R^m}{(2\sigma^2)^m\Gamma(m)} y^{m-1} \exp\left\{-\frac{Ry}{2\sigma^2}\right\}, \tag{19.154}$$

where $\sigma^2 = \sigma_N^2/m$. Observing that the pdf for Nakagami-m fading has the same form as the pdf for the Rayleigh fading but with 2 m degree in (19.143), a single Nakagami-m fading channel is equivalent to an m diversity system for the Rayleigh fading channel. It is then straightforward to show that the results for STBCs over the Nakagami-m fading channels can be obtained by considering the Rayleigh fading channels with the channel diversity order increased from MN to $m \times MN$. Consequently, the pdf of the instantaneous SNR per symbol γ_s can be obtained directly from (19.140) as

$$f_{\text{Nakagami}-m}(\gamma_s) = \frac{1}{\bar{\gamma}_c^{mMN}\Gamma(mMN)} \gamma_s^{mMN-1} \exp\{-\gamma_s/\bar{\gamma}_c\}, \tag{19.155}$$

where $\bar{\gamma}_c$ is the average SNR per channel, which is assumed to be identical for all channels, as in (19.145).

19.3.3 Capacity analysis of STBC

19.3.3.1 Shannon capacity over fading channels

The capacity of a multiple antenna wireless communication system over a fading channel with continuous-valued inputs and continuous-valued outputs is given in [74] in the following form:

$$C = E\left[\log_2 \det\left(\mathbf{I} + \frac{E_s}{\mathcal{N}_0}\mathbf{H}\mathbf{H}^{T*}\right)\right], \quad [(b/s)/Hz] \tag{19.156}$$

where $E[\cdot]$ is the mathematical expectation; $\mathbf{I}$ is the identity matrix with M dimension; det($\mathbf{x}$) denotes the determinant of the matrix $\mathbf{x}$, and the superscript $T*$ denotes the matrix transpose and conjugate. The capacity of the equivalent STBC channel in (19.134) with the continuous-valued inputs and continuous-valued outputs for complex signals is given in [66] and [67] as

$$\overline{C} = E\left[R\log_2 \det\left(1 + \frac{E_s}{RN\mathcal{N}_0}\|\mathbf{H}\|_F^2\right)\right] = E\left[R\log_2(1+\gamma_s)\right], [(b/s)/Hz]. \tag{19.157}$$

Given the pdf of γ_s, the capacity of the equivalent STBC channel can be obtained based on

$$\overline{C} = R\int_0^\infty \log_2(1+\gamma_s)f(\gamma_s)d\gamma_s, \quad [(b/s)/Hz]. \tag{19.158}$$

19.3.3.2 Capacity of M*-ary signal constellations over fading channels*

Both (19.156) and (19.157) were obtained assuming continuous-valued inputs. Here, we consider modulation channels with the discrete-valued multilevel phase inputs and continuous-valued outputs. Assuming maximum likelihood (ML) soft decoding with perfect channel state information at the receiver input, it is well known [75–77] that the capacity C^*_{STBC} of the STBC channel (19.137) can be obtained by averaging the corresponding conditional capacity $\widetilde{C}^*(\mathbf{H})$ with respect to the joint pdf of the channel matrix $\mathbf{H}$. By doing so, the following expression for the capacity C^*_{STBC} of the fading channel is obtained

$$C^*_{\mathrm{STBC}} = E[\widetilde{C}^*(\mathbf{H})] = \int \widetilde{C}^*(\mathbf{H})f(\mathbf{H})d\mathbf{H}[(b/s)/\mathrm{Hz}], \tag{19.159}$$

with

$$\widetilde{C}^*(\mathbf{H}) = R\left\{\log_2 q - \frac{1}{q\pi R^{-1}\|\mathbf{H}\|_F^2\mathcal{N}_0}\sum_{j=1}^{q}\int_{y\in C}\exp\left\{-\frac{\|y - R^{-1}\|\mathbf{H}\|_F^2\alpha_j\|^2}{R^{-1}\|\mathbf{H}\|_F^2\mathcal{N}_0}\right\}\right.$$

$$\times \log_2\left[\sum_{s=1}^{q} \exp\left\{\frac{||y - R^{-1}||\mathbf{H}||_F^2\alpha_j||^2}{R^{-1}||\mathbf{H}||_F^2\mathcal{N}_0} - \frac{||y - R^{-1}||\mathbf{H}||_F^2\alpha_s||^2}{R^{-1}||\mathbf{H}||_F^2\mathcal{N}_0}\right\}\right]dy\Bigg\}, \tag{19.160}$$

where α_j, $j = 1,\ldots, q$ is a real signal in the q-ary PAM constellation or complex in the q-ary PSK/QAM constellation, and $f(\mathbf{H})$ is the joint pdf of the $M \times N$ random elements of the channel matrix $\mathbf{H}$ for the fading channel.

Applying the channel model (19.141), (19.159) can be simplified to the one-dimensional integral containing the pdf of h

$$C^*_{\mathrm{STBC},\, R} = E[\widetilde{C}^*(h)] = \int \widetilde{C}^*(h)f(h)dh, \quad [(b/s)/Hz] \tag{19.161}$$

where

$$\widetilde{C}^*(h) = R\Bigg\{\log_2 q - \frac{1}{q\pi h\mathcal{N}_0}\sum_{j=1}^{q}\int_{y\in C} \exp\left\{-\frac{||\mathbf{y} - h\alpha_j||^2}{h\mathcal{N}_0}\right\}$$

$$\times \log_2\left[\sum_{s=1}^{q} \exp\left\{\frac{||\mathbf{y} - h\alpha_j||^2 - ||\mathbf{y} - h\alpha_s||^2}{h\mathcal{N}_0}\right\}\right]d\mathbf{y}\Bigg\}. \tag{19.162}$$

Note that (19.161) applies to both the real signal constellations such as PAM, and the complex signal constellations such as the PSK and QAM.

19.3.3.3 Capacity comparison

It is shown in [66] that the difference between (19.156) and (19.157) is the capacity loss incurred by using a STBC in the multiple-input multiple output (MIMO) wireless communication system over fading channel with the continued valued inputs. The capacity of MIMO fading channel with the PAM, PSK, QAM is given in [15] as

$$C^*_{M,\, N} = \int \widetilde{C}^*_{M,\, N}(\mathbf{H})f(\mathbf{H})d\mathbf{H}, \quad [(b/s)/Hz] \tag{19.163}$$

where

$$\begin{aligned}\widetilde{C}^*_{M,\, N}(\mathbf{H}) &= N \log_2 q - q^{-N}(\pi\mathcal{N}_0)^{-M} \\ &\times \sum_{\mathbf{x}\in(Ax)^N}\int_{\mathbf{y}\in C} \exp\left\{-\frac{||\mathbf{y} - \mathbf{Hx}||^2}{\mathcal{N}_0}\right\}\log_2 \\ &\times\left[\sum_{\mathbf{x}'\in(Ax)^N} \exp\left\{-\frac{||\mathbf{y} - \mathbf{Hx}||^2 - |\mathbf{y} - \mathbf{Hx}'||^2}{\mathcal{N}_0}\right\}\right]d\mathbf{y}.\end{aligned} \tag{19.164}$$

Here, N and M are the number of transmitting and receiving antennas, respectively;

$$Ax \equiv \{\alpha_1, \ldots, \alpha_q\} \tag{19.165}$$

is the q-ary complex signal constellation; $(Ax)^N$ is the N-fold Cartesian product of Ax with itself; the coded vector

$$\mathbf{x} \equiv [x_1, \ldots, x_N] \in (Ax)^N \tag{19.166}$$

is the q^N-variate random variable with outcomes taking values from the expanded signal constellation $(Ax)^N$; and

$$\mathbf{y} \equiv [y_1, \ldots, y_N]^T \tag{19.167}$$

is the M-dimensional output vector of the receive antennas. It can easily be shown that the second terms in (19.162) and (19.164) vanish as the *SNR* increases. This fact implies the capacity of a MIMO fading channel approaches $N \log_2 q$ bit/channel use while the capacity with STBC approaches only $R \log_2 q$ bit /channel use for the large *SNR*. While the capacity loss of $(N - R) \times \log_2 q$ bit/channel incurred by using STBC is fairly significant, it will be shown below that the *SNR* threshold for reliable data transmission is reduced because of the STBC diversity gain.

19.3.4 Analysis of error probability over fading channels

19.3.4.1 Error probability with Rayleigh fading

Let $P_q^{error}(\gamma_s)$ is the error probability of q-ary signal constellation with STBC in AWGN channel. The error probability with the Rayleigh fading can be obtained by averaging $P_q^{error}(\gamma_s)$ over the pdf of γ_s

$$P_{\text{STBC},\,q}^{error}(\gamma_s) = \int_0^{\infty} P_q^{error}(\gamma_s) f_{\text{Rayleigh}}(\gamma_s) d\gamma_s. \tag{19.168}$$

Note, $P_q^{error}(\gamma_s)$ can be *SEP* or *BEP*, respectively.

Error probability for PAM: Since full-rate STBCs exist for any number of transmitting antennas using the real PAM constellation [64], $R = 1$ for q-ary PAM. The average *SEP* for PAM over AWGN channel is [56]

$$P_q^{error}(\gamma_s) = 2(1 - q^{-1}) Q\left[\sqrt{6(q^2 - 1)^{-1}\gamma_s}\right], \tag{19.169}$$

where $Q(\cdot)$ is the Gaussian tail function. Substituting (19.144) and (19.169) into (19.168), the average *SEP* for PAM is

$$P_{\text{STBC, PAM},\,q}^{error}(\gamma_s) = \int_0^{\infty} 2(1 - q^{-1}) Q\left[\sqrt{6(q^2 - 1)^{-1}\gamma_s}\right] \frac{\gamma_s^{MN-1}}{\overline{\gamma}_c^{MN}\Gamma(MN)} \times \exp\{-\gamma_s/\overline{\gamma}_c\} d\gamma_s. \tag{19.170}$$

To evaluate the integral in (19.170), the following integral function can be employed:

$$g(L) = \int_0^\infty Q(\sqrt{ax})x^{L-1}\exp\{-x/u\}dx$$
$$= 0.5u^L\Gamma(L)\left[1 - \sum_{k=0}^{L-1}\mu\left(\frac{1-\mu^2}{4}\right)^k\binom{2k}{k}\right], \tag{19.171}$$

where

$$\mu = \sqrt{\frac{au}{2 + au}}. \tag{19.172}$$

The proof is given in appendix C. Closed form of the *SEP* for PAM is then given by

$$P^{error}_{\text{STBC, PAM}, q}(\gamma_s) = (1 - q^{-1})\left[1 - \sum_{k=0}^{MN-1}\mu\left(\frac{1-\mu^2}{4}\right)^k\binom{2k}{k}\right], \tag{19.173}$$

where

$$\mu = \sqrt{\frac{3\overline{\gamma}_c}{q^2 - 1+3\overline{\gamma}_c}}. \tag{19.174}$$

<u>*Error probability for PSK*</u>: Based on the equivalent scalar AWGN channel model presented before, the error probability for q-ary PSK is equivalent to the analysis in [56] and [78] for adaptive reception of multiphase signals in Rayleigh fading but with MN branch diversity. This approach was also employed in [68]. Following the same steps as in [78], the *SEP* is given by

$$P^{error}_{\text{STBC}, q} = \frac{(-1)^{MN-1}(1-\mu^2)^{MN}}{\pi\Gamma(MN)}$$
$$\times\left\{\frac{\partial^{MN-1}}{\partial s^{MN-1}}\left[\frac{1}{s-\mu^2}\left(\frac{\pi}{M}(M-1) - \frac{\mu\sin(\pi/M)}{\sqrt{s-\mu^2\cos^2(\pi/M)}}\cot^{-1}\left(-\frac{\mu\cos(\pi/M)}{\sqrt{s-\mu^2\cos^2(\pi/M)}}\right)\right)\right]\right\}, \tag{19.175}$$

where

$$\mu = \sqrt{\frac{\overline{\gamma}_c}{1 + \overline{\gamma}_c}}; \tag{19.176}$$

$$\left.\frac{\partial^{MN-1}}{\partial s^{MN-1}}f(s, \mu)\right|_{s=1}$$

denotes the $(MN - 1)$-th partial derivative of the function $f(s, \mu)$ evaluated at $s = 1$. Note that the coherent detection with perfect channel state information at the receiver input is assumed in (19.175). Following approach in [56, 78], performing the differentiation indicated in (19.175) and evaluating the resulting function at $s = 1$ for $q = 2$ and 4, we obtain the following closed form *BEP*s for the binary phase-shift keying (BPSK) and QPSK

$$P^{error}_{\mathrm{STBC},\,2} = 0.5\left[1 - \mu\sum_{k=0}^{MN-1}\binom{2k}{k}\left(\frac{1-\mu^2}{4}\right)^k\right], \tag{19.177}$$

$$P^{error}_{\mathrm{STBC},\,4} = 0.5\left[1 - \frac{\mu}{\sqrt{2-\mu^2}}\sum_{k=0}^{MN-1}\binom{2k}{k}\left(\frac{1+\mu^2}{4-2\mu^2}\right)^k\right], \tag{19.178}$$

respectively. Note that the Gray coding was assumed in the *BEP* calculation for QPSK. The same procedure can be applied to calculate the *SEP* for q-ary PSK at $q = 8,16,32$, however, the expressions are not as simple as in (19.177) and (19.178). In the remainder of this subsection we employ (19.168) in order to derive a simpler expression for the error probability.

It is well known [56] that the *BEP* for BPSK and QPSK over the additive white Gaussian noise channel are given as

$$P^{error}_{\mathrm{BPSK}}(\gamma_s) = Q(\sqrt{2\gamma_s}), \tag{19.179}$$

$$P^{error}_{\mathrm{QPSK}}(\gamma_s) = Q(\sqrt{\gamma_s}), \tag{19.180}$$

respectively. As shown in [79], the exact *SEP* of M-ary PSK for the AWGN channel can be presented in the following form

$$P^{error}_{\mathrm{PSK,\,AWGN},\,M}(\gamma_s) = 2Q\left[\sqrt{2\gamma_s}\,\sin(\pi/q)\right] - \frac{1}{\pi}\int_{\pi/2-\pi/q}^{\pi/2}\exp\left\{-\gamma_s\frac{\sin^2(\pi/q)}{\cos^2\theta}d\theta\right\}. \tag{19.181}$$

For large *SNR* and large values of q, the *SEP* of q-ary PSK in the AWGN channel can be approximated as

$$P^{error}_{\mathrm{PSK,\,AWGN},\,q}(\gamma_s) \approx 2Q[\sqrt{2\gamma_s}\,\sin(\pi/q)] \tag{19.182}$$

and the equivalent *BEP* is given by

$$P^{error}_{\mathrm{PSK,\,AWGN},\,q}(\gamma_s) \approx \frac{SEP_q}{\log q}, \tag{19.183}$$

where the Gray coding is assumed. This approximation is good for large values of q, however, for $q = 2$ there is a difference in the factor of 2 with the exact probability given in (19.177).

By substituting for $P^{error}_{\mathrm{PSK,\,AWGN},\,q}(\gamma_s)$ in (19.182) and using (19.171), (19.168) can be written in the following form

$$P^{error}_{\text{STBC, PSK, }q}(\gamma_s) \approx \int_0^\infty 2Q\left[\sqrt{2\gamma_s}\sin(\pi/q)\right]\frac{\gamma_s^{MN-1}}{\overline{\gamma}_c^{MN}\Gamma(MN)} \times \exp\{-\gamma_s/\overline{\gamma}_c\}d\gamma_s = 1 - \sum_{k=0}^{MN-1}\mu\left(\frac{1-\mu^2}{4}\right)^k\binom{2k}{k}, \tag{19.184}$$

where

$$\mu = \sqrt{\frac{\sin^2(\pi\gamma_c/q)}{1+\sin^2(\pi\gamma_c/q)}}. \tag{19.185}$$

Therefore, the *BEP* can be approximated as

$$P^{error}_{\text{STBC, PSK, }q}(\gamma_s) \approx \frac{1}{\log q}\left[1 - \sum_{k=0}^{MN-1}\mu\left(\frac{1-\mu^2}{4}\right)^k\binom{2k}{k}\right]. \tag{19.186}$$

By substituting for $P^{error}_{\text{BPSK}}(\gamma_s)$ or $P^{error}_{\text{QPSK}}(\gamma_s)$ in (19.179) and (19.180) and using (19.171), the exact *BEP* for BPSK and QPSK can be derived from (19.168) as

$$P^{error}_{\text{STBC, PSK, }q}(\gamma_s) = \frac{1}{2}\left[1 - \sum_{k=0}^{MN-1}\mu\left(\frac{1-\mu^2}{4}\right)^k\binom{2k}{k}\right], \tag{19.187}$$

where

$$\mu = \sqrt{\frac{\overline{\gamma}_c}{1+\overline{\gamma}_c}} \tag{19.188}$$

for BPSK and

$$\mu = \sqrt{\frac{\overline{\gamma}_c}{2+\overline{\gamma}_c}} \tag{19.189}$$

for QPSK, respectively. It can easily be shown that (19.187) is equivalent to (19.177) and (19.178). Using (19.186), approximations for the *BEP*s of BPSK and QPSK can be obtained as

$$P^{error}_{\text{STBC, BPSK, }2} \approx 1 - \sum_{k=0}^{MN-1}\mu\left(\frac{1-\mu^2}{4}\right)^k\binom{2k}{k} \tag{19.190}$$

with μ given by (19.188) and

$$P^{error}_{\text{STBC, QPSK, }4} \approx \frac{1}{2}\left[1 - \sum_{k=0}^{MN-1}\mu\left(\frac{1-\mu^2}{4}\right)^k\binom{2k}{k}\right] \tag{19.191}$$

with μ given by (19.189), respectively. As expected, this approximation is unsuitable for BPSK, but equation (19.191) brings us the exact *BEP* for QPSK. It is shown later that this approximation is very accurate for $q > 4$ and large *SNR*.

Error probability for QAM: Rectangular QAM signal constellations are frequently employed because they are equivalent to two PAM signals on quadrature carriers. For q-ary, $q = 2^k$ (k is even), rectangular QAM, the *SEP* is given in [56] as

$$P_q^{error} = 1 - [1 - P_{\sqrt{q}}^{error}(\gamma_s)]^2, \tag{19.192}$$

where

$$P_{\sqrt{q}}^{error}(\gamma_s) = 2(1 - q^{-0.5})Q\left(\sqrt{\frac{3}{q - 1}\gamma_s}\right). \tag{19.193}$$

By substituting for P_q^{error} in (19.193), (19.168) can be written as

$$P_{\text{STBC, PAM, }\sqrt{q}}^{error}(\gamma_s) = \int_0^{\infty} 2(1 - q^{-0.5})Q\left(\sqrt{\frac{3}{q - 1}\gamma_s}\right)\frac{\gamma_s^{MN-1}\exp\{\gamma_s/\overline{\gamma}_c\}}{\overline{\gamma}_c^{MN}\Gamma(MN)}d\gamma_s. \tag{19.194}$$

Using (19.171), the closed-form *SEP* for the rectangular q-ary QAM is then given by

$$P_{\text{STBC, QAM, }q}^{error}(\gamma_s) = 1 - [1 - P_{\text{STBC, PAM, }\sqrt{q}}^{error}(\gamma_s)]^2, \tag{19.195}$$

where

$$P_{\text{STBC, PAM, }\sqrt{q}}^{error}(\gamma_s) = (1 - q^{-0.5})\left[1 - \sum_{k=0}^{MN-1}\mu\left(\frac{1 - \mu^2}{4}\right)^k\binom{2k}{k}\right] \tag{19.196}$$

and

$$\mu = \sqrt{\frac{3\overline{\gamma}_c}{2q - 2+3\overline{\gamma}_c}}. \tag{19.197}$$

19.3.4.2 Error probability over Rician fading

Substituting $f_{\text{Rician}}(\gamma_s)$ given by (19.152) in (19.168) instead of $f_{\text{Rayleigh}}(\gamma_s)$ and following the same procedure used previously, the *SEP* over Rician fading channel can be presented in the following form

$$P_{\text{STBC, Rician, }q}^{error}(\gamma_s) = \sum_{n=0}^{\infty}\frac{(MN\beta)^n\exp\{-MN\beta\}\lambda}{\Gamma(n + 1)}\left[1 - \sum_{k=0}^{MN+n-1}\mu\left(\frac{1 - \mu^2}{4}\right)^k\binom{2k}{k}\right], \tag{19.198}$$

where

$$\mu = \sqrt{\frac{3\overline{\gamma}_c}{q^2 - 1+3\overline{\gamma}_c}} \text{ and } \lambda = 1 - q^{-1} \tag{19.199}$$

for q-ary PAM,

$$\mu = \sqrt{\frac{\sin^2(\pi\gamma_c/q)}{1 + \sin^2(\pi\gamma_c/q)}} \tag{19.200}$$

with $\lambda = 0.5$ at $q = 2$ and $\lambda = 1$ at $q > 2$ for q-ary PSK, and

$$\mu = \sqrt{\frac{3\bar{\gamma}_c}{2q - 2+3\bar{\gamma}_c}} \quad \text{and } \lambda = 1 - q^{-0.5} \tag{19.201}$$

for $\sqrt{q}$-ary PAM in q-ary rectangular QAM. The *SEP* of q-ary rectangular QAM can then be calculated using (19.195). Note that each term in the second part of (19.198) is a monotonically decreasing function of i, and is strictly smaller than 1 for all i. The truncation of the first L terms will introduce an error of at most

$$\text{Error} = \frac{\lambda\mu(1 - \mu^2)^{MN+L}}{1 - \sum_{k=0}^{L}\frac{(MNK)^k \exp\{-MNK\}}{\Gamma(k + 1)}} \tag{19.202}$$

in the probability of error. The proof is given in appendix D.

19.3.5 Error probability under Nakagami-*m* fading

The probability of error over Nakagami-m, m is the integer, can be obtained from the results presented in the previous subsection by increasing the diversity order from MN to $m \times MN$. The *SEP* for STBC over the Nakagami-m fading channel is given then

$$P^{error}_{\text{STBC, Nakagami, } q}(\gamma_s) = \lambda\left[1 - \sum_{k=0}^{MN+n-1} \mu\left(\frac{1 - \mu^2}{4}\right)^k \binom{2k}{k}\right], \tag{19.203}$$

where μ and λ for q-ary PAM, q-ary PAM, and $\sqrt{q}$-ary PAM in q-ary rectangular QAM are given by (19.199)–(19.201), respectively. The *SEP* of q-ary rectangular QAM can be calculated by (19.195).

19.3.6 Extension to STBC DS-CDMA

There is a great interest in the application of STBCs to practical wireless communication systems constructed based on the generalized approach to signal processing in noise and employing the generalized receiver.

19.3.6.1 System model

To facilitate the analysis, we generalize the DS-CDMA multiple-access interference model from [30] and [31] to accommodate multiple antennas. The system model is presented in figure 19.15. At the transmitter, S information symbols for K users are encoded by the respective STBC encoders, and then spread by each user's pseudo noise code, modulated and transmitted from N transmitting antennas over the symbol duration T, simultaneously. At the receivers, each user has M receive

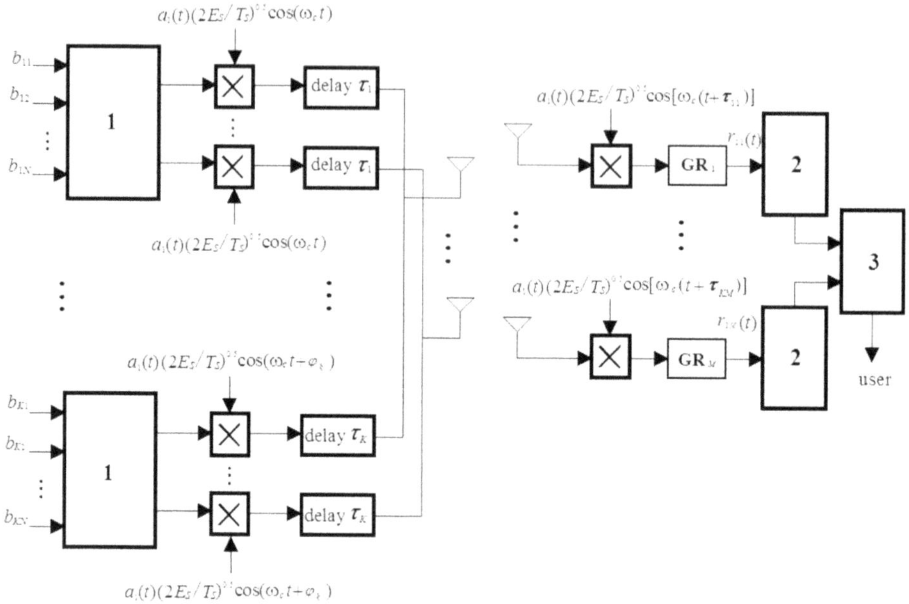

Figure 19.15. System model for STBC DS-CDMA with multiple antennas employing the generalized receiver: 1—STBC encoder; 2—STBC decoder; 3—decision device: GR—generalized receiver.

antennas, and the filtered signals are first dispread, and then sent to the STBC decoders. The symbol decisions are made based on the M outputs of the STBC decoder. The signal at the jth receive input antenna is given by

$$z_j(t) = \sum_{n=1}^{N}\sum_{k=1}^{K}\sqrt{2P_k}h_{knj}(t)a_k(t-\tau_{knj})b_{nk}(t-\tau_{knj})\cos[\omega_c(t-\tau_{knj})] + w(t), \quad (19.204)$$

where $h_{knj}(t)$ is the channel coefficient from the nth transmitting antenna to the jth receive antenna for the kth user; $P_k = E_s/T_s$ is the symbol power of the kth user; E_s is the symbol energy; T_s is the symbol duration; $a_k(t)$ is the PN spreading chip sequence with chip duration; $w(t)$ is the zero mean AWGN with the power spectral density $\mathcal{N}_0/2$ in each real dimension; τ_{knj} is the time delay from the nth transmitting antenna to the jth receive antenna; ω_c is the carrier frequency; $b_{nk}(t)$ is the encoded signal transmitted from the nth antenna of user k. Binary modulation is assumed in this model.

19.3.6.2 Channel model analysis

To facilitate the analysis, we assume the first user is the desired one, without loss of generality. The dispread signal input to the jth STBC decoder for the ith received symbol is defined as follows

$$\hat{z}_{1j}(t) = \sum_{q=1}^{N}\int_{(i-1)T_s}^{iT_s}\left[\sqrt{2P_k}\sum_{n=1}^{N}\sum_{k=1}^{K}h_{knj}(t)a_k(t-\tau_{knj})b_{nk}(t-\tau_{knj})\cos[\omega_c(t-\tau_{knj})] + w(t)\right]$$

$$\times a_1(t-\tau_{1qj})\cos[\omega_c(t-\tau_{1qj})]dt = \sqrt{\frac{P_1}{2}}T_s\sum_{n=1}^{N}h_{1nj}^{(i)}b_{n1}^{(i)}$$

$$+\int_{(i-1)T_s}^{iT_s}[\sqrt{2P_k}\sum_{n=1}^{N}\sum_{\substack{q=1\\q\neq n}}^{N}h_{1nj}(t)a_1(t-\tau_{1nj})b_{n1}(t-\tau_{1nj})\cos[\omega_c(t-\tau_{1nj})]]$$

$$\times a_1(t-\tau_{1nj})\cos[\omega_c(t-\tau_{1nj})]dt +$$

$$\sum_{q=1}^{N}\int_{(i-1)T_s}^{iT_s} w(t)a_1(t-\tau_{1nj})\cos[\omega_c(t-\tau_{1nj})]dt. \tag{19.205}$$

Note that only the first term of (19.205) is the desired signal; the second term of (19.205) is the MAI produced by the same user from different transmit antennas; the third term of (19.205) is the MAI produced by other users; the fourth term of (19.205) is the AWGN. Using the Gaussian approximation in [80], (19.205) can be presented in the following form

$$\hat{z}_{1j}(t) = \sqrt{0.5P_1}\,T_s\sum_{n=1}^{N}h_{1nj}b_{n1} + \eta_{1j} \tag{19.206}$$

where $\hat{z}_{1j}(t)$ is the Gaussian random variable; η_{1j} is the combination of the interference and noise. The expected mean and variance of η_{1j} are given by

$$\begin{cases} E[\eta_{1j}] = 0; \\ Var[\eta_{1j}] = N(N-1)\dfrac{T_s^2}{6G}\displaystyle\sum_{k=1}^{K}P_k + 4\sigma_w^4NT_s \end{cases} \tag{19.207}$$

respectively, where G is the processing gain of the DS-CDMA system. Note that (19.207) has the same form as (19.134). After STBC decoding is performed on $\hat{z}_{1j}(t)$ given in (19.206), the decision statistic for user 1 over T symbol durations takes the form

$$\hat{\mathbf{z}}_1(t) = R^{-1}\sqrt{0.5P_1}\,T_s||\mathbf{H}||_F^2\mathbf{b}_{1T} + \boldsymbol{\eta}_T, \tag{19.208}$$

where $\eta_{iT}(t)$ has the zero mean and the variance is defined as

$$Var\{\eta_{iT}(t)\} = \frac{1}{R}||\mathbf{H}||_F^2\left[\frac{N(N-1)T_s^2}{6G}\sum_{k=1}^{K}P_k + NT_s4\sigma_w^4\right]. \tag{19.209}$$

Therefore, the effective instantaneous SNR at the generalized receiver output is given by

$$\gamma_s = \left\{\frac{N(N-1)K}{3G} + \frac{4N\sigma_w^4}{E_s^2}\right\}^{-1}R^{-1}||\mathbf{H}||_F^2. \tag{19.210}$$

Note that the perfect power control is assumed in (19.210), i.e., $P_k = P_1$.

19.3.6.3 Capacity analysis of STBC-CDMA

To facilitate the capacity analysis, we first normalize the equivalent channel by $\sqrt{0.5T_s}$, then (19.208) can be written in the same form as (19.137)

$$\mathbf{y}_{nT} = R^{-1}||\mathbf{H}||_F^2\mathbf{x}_{nT} + \boldsymbol{\eta}_{nT}, \tag{19.211}$$

where $\mathbf{x}_{nT}$ is the $S \times 1$ complex input matrix with each entry having symbol energy E_s; the combination of the interference and noise $\boldsymbol{\eta}_{nT}$ has the zero mean and variance

$$\text{Var}\{\boldsymbol{\eta}_{nT}\} = R^{-1}\frac{||\mathbf{H}||_F^2 N(N-1)K}{3G} + 4\sigma_w^4 N. \tag{19.212}$$

The capacity of this STBC-CDMA wireless communication system constructed based on the generalized approach to signal processing in noise [27–29] and employing a q-ary signal constellation can be obtained directly from (19.163).

19.3.6.4 Probability of error for DS-CDMA with STBC

The average *SNR* per channel is determined as

$$\bar{\gamma}_c = \frac{E\{||h_{ij}||^2\}}{R\left\{\dfrac{N(N-1)K}{3G} + \dfrac{4N\sigma_w^4}{E_s^2}\right\}} = \frac{2\sigma^2}{R\left\{\dfrac{N(N-1)K}{3G} + \dfrac{4N\sigma_w^4}{E_s^2}\right\}} \tag{19.213}$$

and this can be used with the probability of error results in the previous subsection to obtain the performance in fading channels. In particular, the exact *BEP* of BPSK is given by

$$P^{error}_{\text{STBCCDMA, Rayleigh, }2b} = \frac{1}{2}\left[1 - \sum_{k=0}^{MN-1}\mu\left(\frac{1-\mu^2}{4}\right)^k\binom{2k}{k}\right] \tag{19.214}$$

for the Rayleigh fading channel;

$$P^{error}_{\text{STBCCDMA, Rician, }2b} = \sum_{n=0}^{\infty}\frac{(MN\beta)^n\exp\{-MN\beta\}}{2\Gamma(n+1)}\lambda\left[1 - \sum_{i=0}^{MN+n-1}\mu\left(\frac{1-\mu^2}{4}\right)^i\binom{2i}{i}\right] \tag{19.215}$$

for the Rician fading channel;

$$P^{error}_{\text{STBCCDMA, Naragami, }q} = \frac{\lambda}{2}\left[1 - \sum_{k=0}^{mMN-1}\mu\left(\frac{1-\mu^2}{4}\right)^k\binom{2k}{k}\right] \tag{19.216}$$

for the Nakagami-m fading channel, where μ is given by (19.188) and $\bar{\gamma}_c$ is defined in (19.213). Note that there are two factors in $\bar{\gamma}_c$, which determine the *BEP* of the DS-CDMA wireless communication system with STBC, $N(N-1)K/3G$ and $4\sigma_w^4 N$. The first term corresponds to the MAI from other users and the self-interference from the different transmitting antennas. The second term corresponds to the system noise, i.e., AWGN. At the high *SNR*, $\bar{\gamma}_c$ will be dominated on the MAI, i.e., the number of users limits the performance, as expected.

19.3.7 Numerical results

In this subsection, some numerical results are presented to illustrate and verify the capacity and probability of error results obtained before. Figure 19.16 demonstrates the capacity using SBTC $\mathbf{G}_2$ over Rician fading channel with one, two and four receive antennas for BPSK, QPSK, and 8-PSK. The Rician parameter is $\beta = 100$. Figure 19.16 shows that the capacity with STBC $\mathbf{G}_2$ is not increased as the number of receiving antennas increases. However, the *SNR* threshold required to achieve capacity improves as the number of receive antennas is increased. The capacity with a single antenna over Rician fading channel for PSK is included for reference.

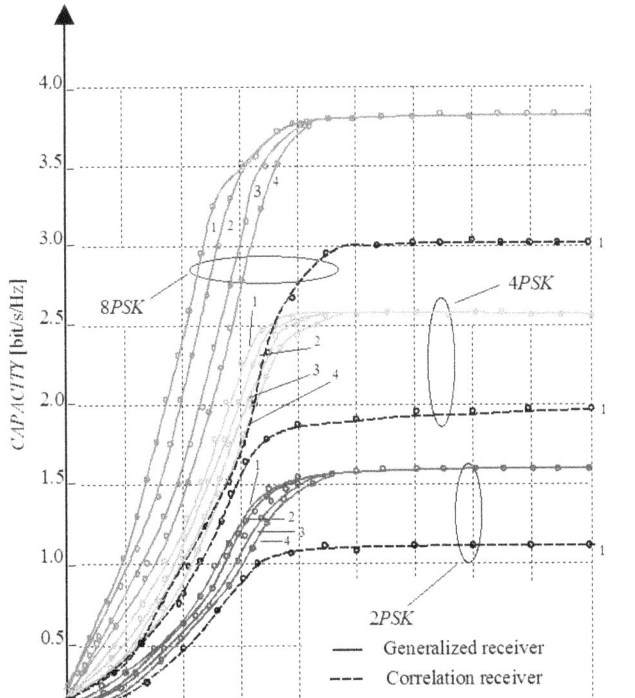

Figure 19.16. Capacity of DS-CDMA system employing STBC $\mathbf{G}_2$ over Rician fading channel with Rician parameter $\beta = 100$: 1—MIMO 4 × 2; 2—MIMO 2 × 2; 3—MIMO 1 × 2; 4—MIMO 1 × 1.

Additionally, figure 19.16 represents superiority of employment of the generalized receiver in DS-CDMA wireless communication system in comparison with the correlation one.

The capacity using several STBCs over Rayleigh fading channel is presented in figure 19.17. As expected, it shows that $\mathbf{G}_2$ is the optimal code from a capacity perspective, and $\mathbf{H}_4$ is more efficient in comparison with $\mathbf{G}_4$. Also, a demonstration of superiority to employ the generalized receiver in comparison with the correlation one in DS-CDMA wireless communication system with STBCs is shown in figure 19.17. Comparison between figures 19.16 and 19.17 demonstrates that the DS-CDMA wireless communication system with STBC codes achieves the capacity at a lower *SNR* over the Rician fading channel at $\beta = 100$ than the Rayleigh fading channel.

Figure 19.18 demonstrates the relationship between the Rician parameter β and the capacity if STBC code $\mathbf{G}_2$ is used. Note that the capacity is insensitive to the Rician parameter when $\beta > 15$ dB. Additionally, we can see a superiority of

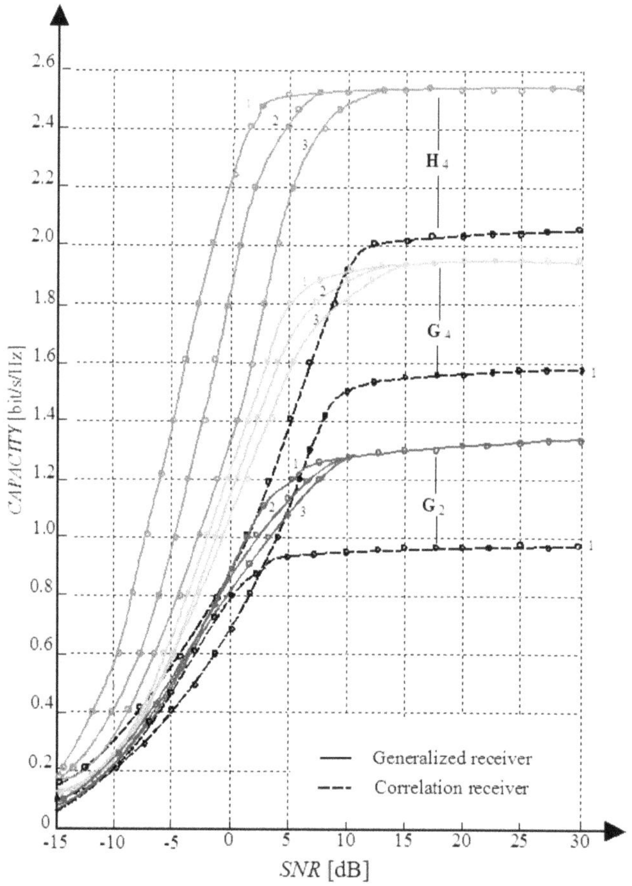

Figure 19.17. Capacity of DS-CDMA system employing various STBCs over Rayleigh fading channel: 1—MIMO 4 × 2; 2—MIMO 2 × 2; 3—MIMO 1 × 2.

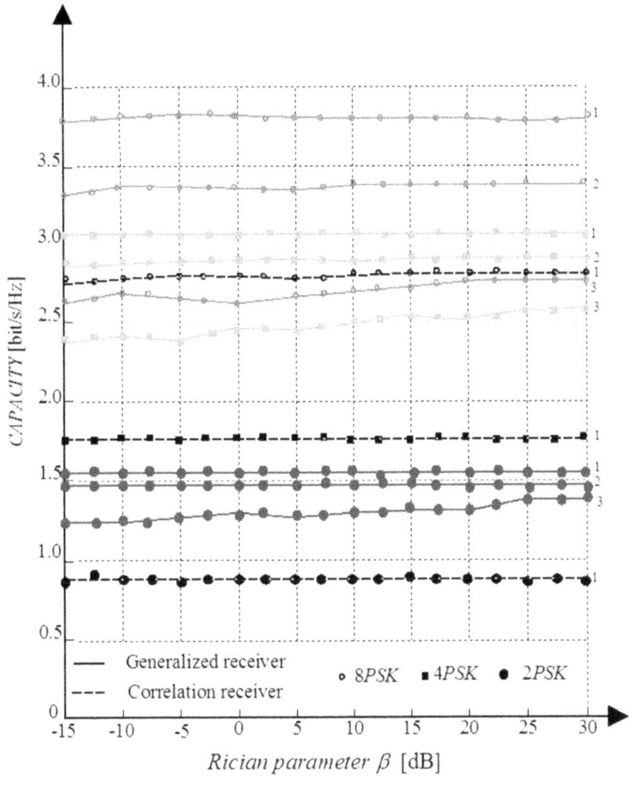

Figure 19.18. Capacity of DS-CDMA system with STBC $\mathbf{G}_2$ versus the Rician parameter β; $SNR = 5$ dB: 1—MIMO 4 x 2; 2—MIMO 2 x 2; 3—MIMO 1 x 2.

implementation of the generalized receiver over the correlation one in DS-CDMA wireless communication system with STBC codes.

Simulation was used to verify the exact and approximate error probabilities given in the previous subsection. In figure 19.19, the *BEP* performance of QPSK at STBCs $\mathbf{G}_2$, $\mathbf{G}_3$, $\mathbf{G}_4$, $\mathbf{H}_3$ and $\mathbf{H}_4$ with one and two receive antennas are presented, and these results are identical to those obtained using (19.178). Also, a superiority of employment of the generalized receiver in DS-CDMA wireless communication system with STBC in comparison with the correlation one is evident. Figure 19.20 shows a comparison between the approximate and exact (via simulation) *SEP* for the 8-PSK. Note that the approximation error is negligible. Figure 19.21 demonstrates the *SEP* for the 16-QAM with one and two receive antennas for different STBCs. Superiority of implementation of the generalized receiver in the DS-CDMA wireless communication system with STBC over the correlation one is presented, too. These results are identical to those obtained with (19.169).

In figure 19.21 the capacity of DS-CDMA wireless communication system based on the generalized approach to signal processing in noise [27–29] with several STBCs is demonstrated for the case of BPSK modulation over the Rayleigh fading channel. We can see that with the given number of users and signal processing gain, the

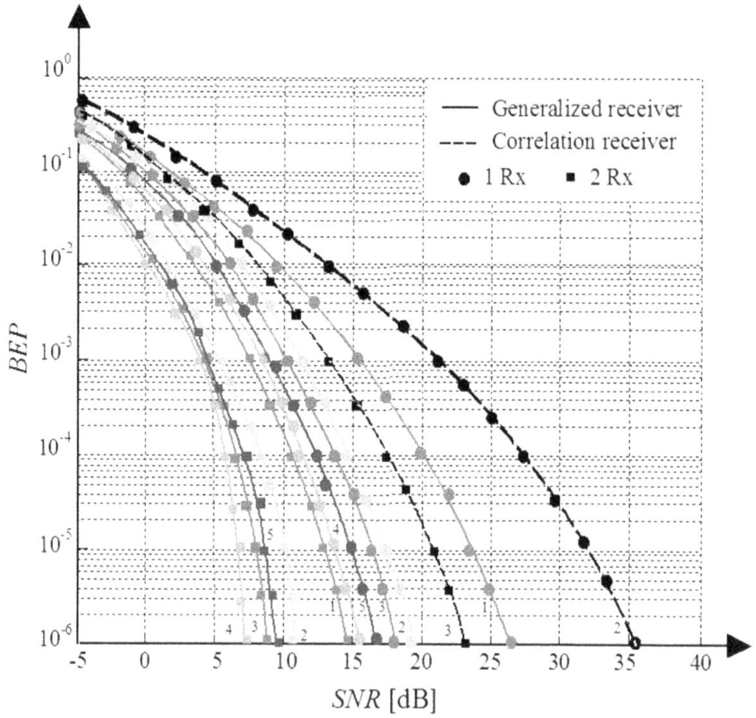

Figure 19.19. *BEP* of DS-CDMA system with QPSK for STBC using one and two receive antennas over Rayleigh fading channel:1—STBC $\mathbf{G}_2$; 2—STBC $\mathbf{G}_3$; 3—STBC $\mathbf{H}_3$; 4—STBC $\mathbf{G}_4$; 5—STBC $\mathbf{H}_4$.

system may not be able to achieve the full channel capacity even with infinite *SNR* due to the dominant MAI component. In this case, increasing the number of antennas will increase the achievable DS-CDMA wireless communication system capacity. Note that the DS-CDMA wireless communication system capacity increases significantly as the number of receive antennas increases for a given number of users and signal processing gain, as expected. However, it should be noted that if the DS-CDMA wireless communication system can already achieve the channel capacity for a given number of antennas, users and signal processing gain, increasing the number of antennas cannot increase the DS-CDMA wireless communication system capacity.

Figure 19.23 presents us the relationship between the DS-CDMA wireless communication system capacity and the number of users given the processing gain and *SNR* over the Rayleigh fading channel. It can be seen that the capacity decreases rapidly as the number of users is increased for one and two receive antennas. However, with four receive antennas increasing the number of users has much less effect on the DS-CDMA wireless communication capacity.

The *BEP* for DS-CDMA wireless communication system constructed on the basis of the generalized approach to signal processing in noise with STBC using BPSK modulated signals is presented in figure 19.24 for one, two, three, and four receive antennas. The signal processing gain is 64, the number of users is 20 and the

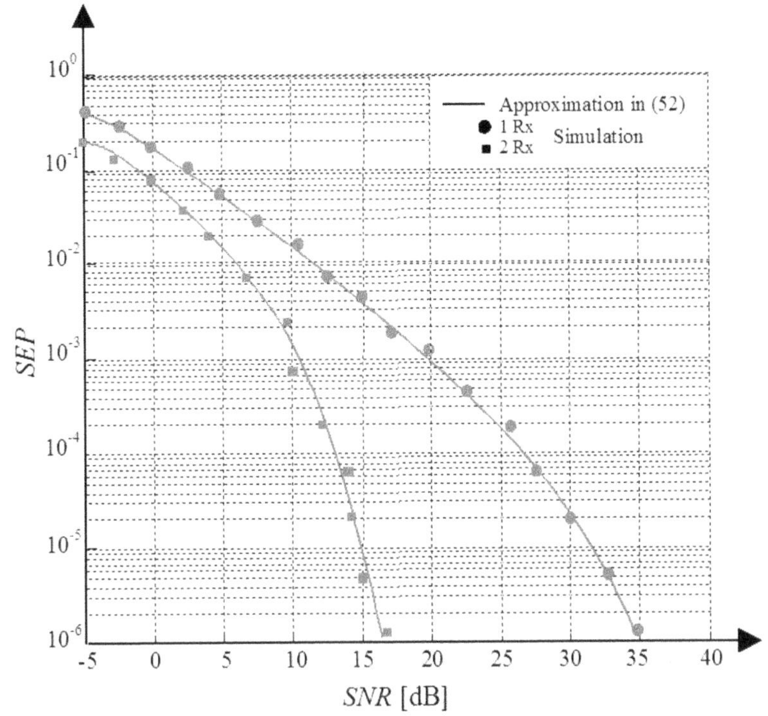

Figure 19.20. *SEP* of DS-CDMA system with QPSK for STBC using one and two receive antennas over Rayleigh fading channel:1—STBC $\mathbf{G}_2$; 2—STBC $\mathbf{G}_3$; 3—STBC $\mathbf{H}_3$; 4—STBC $\mathbf{G}_4$; 5—STBC $\mathbf{H}_4$.

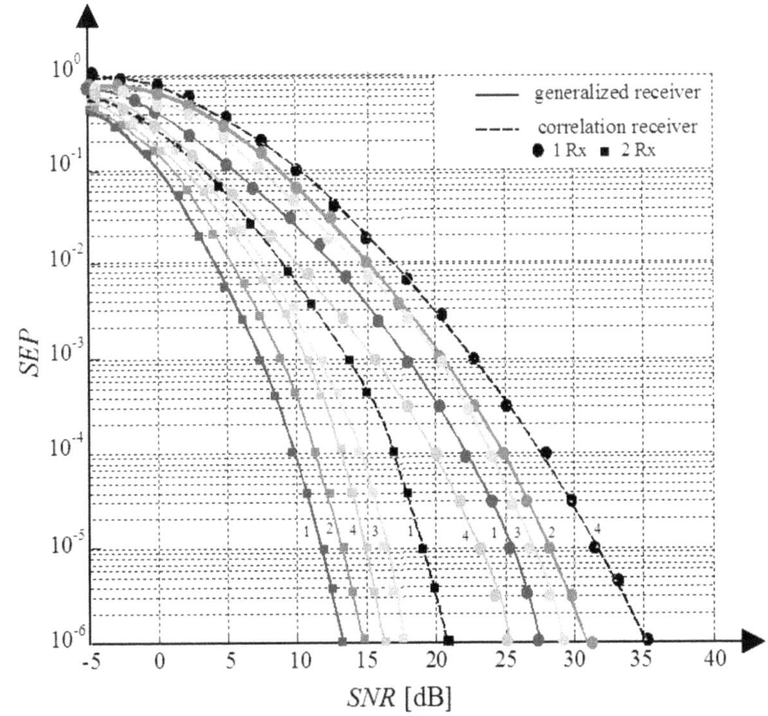

Figure 19.21. *SEP* of DS-CDMA system with 16-QAM for STBC using one and two receive antennas over Rayleigh fading channel:1—STBC $\mathbf{H}_4$; 2—STBC $\mathbf{H}_3$; 3—STBC $\mathbf{G}_3$; 4—STBC $\mathbf{G}_4$.

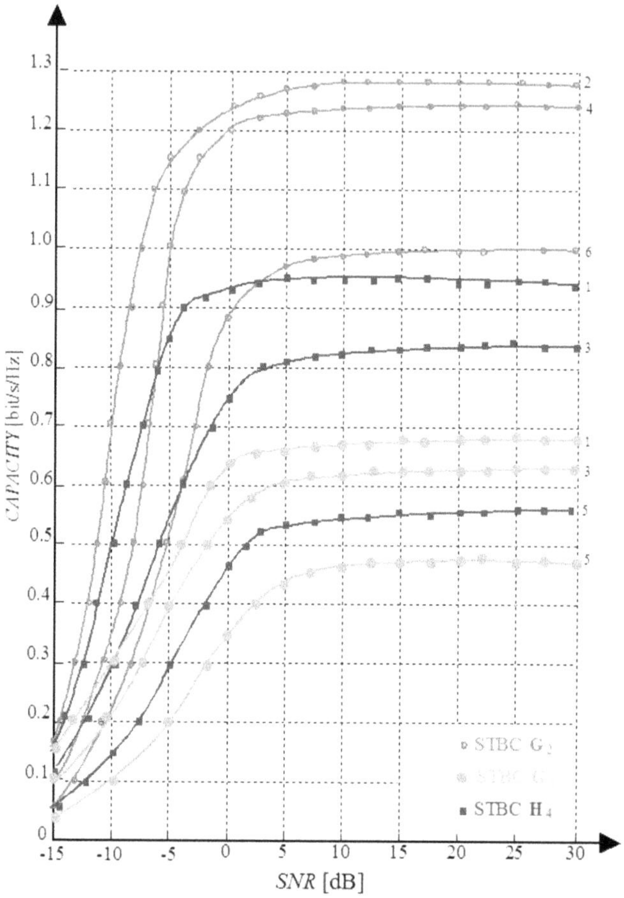

Figure 19.22. Capacity of DS-CDMA system with BPSK, STBC over Rayleigh fading channel $G = 32$, $K = 30$:1—MIMO 4 × 4; 2—MIMO 4 × 2; 3—MIMO 2 × 4; 4—MIMO 2 × 2; 5—MIMO 1 × 4; 6—MIMO 1 × 2.

Rayleigh fading is employed for all DS-CDMA wireless communication system figures. Figure 19.24 presents that the significant performance gain can be obtained with multiple receive antennas. The simulation results for the correlation receiver are presented, too, for comparison. We can see a great superiority of implementation of the generalized receiver in DS-CDMA wireless communication system with STBC over the correlation one.

Figure 19.25 demonstrates the relationship between the *BEP* and the number of users in the DS-CDMA wireless communication system at *SNR* equal to 7 dB with $\mathbf{G}_2$ and $\mathbf{G}_4$. As the number of users is increased, the performance degrades, but at the four receive antennas the DS-CDMA wireless communication system is capable of accommodating far more users than with one receive antenna. As is shown in figure 19.25, $\mathbf{G}_4$ provides better performance than $\mathbf{G}_2$, however, this is obtained at the price of the capacity loss as shown in figure 19.23.

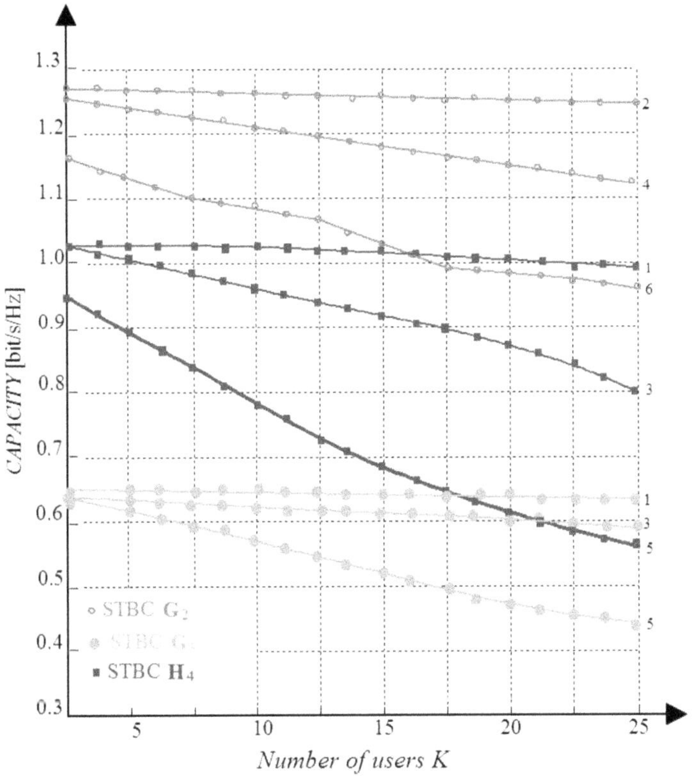

Figure 19.23. Capacity of DS-CDMA system with BPSK and STBC over Rayleigh fading channel $G = 32$, $SNR = 7$ dB:1—MIMO 4 × 4; 2—MIMO 4 × 2; 3—MIMO 2 × 4; 4—MIMO 2 × 2; 5—MIMO 1 × 4; 6—MIMO 1 × 2.

19.4 Parallel interference cancellation for multiuser detection

19.4.1 Introduction

DS-CDMA wireless communication system is considered as a promising technique in cellular and personal communications. Conventional matched-filter receivers suffer from MAI and the near–far effect. A maximum-likelihood multiuser detector was proposed in [82] to mitigate these problems. Unfortunately, the computational complexity of this approach grows exponentially with the user number, prohibiting its practical applications.

Suboptimum receivers were then considered in [83–87] to reduce the computational complexity. The decorrelator, being a linear receiver, can effectively eliminate the MAI. However, it may greatly enhance the noise [88]. The linear minimum mean square error (LMMSE) detector discussed in [88–91] is an improvement to the decorrelator and represents a compromise between interference suppression and noise enhancement. Although these suboptimal approaches are much simpler than the optimal solution, they require matrix inversion operations that are undesirable in practice.

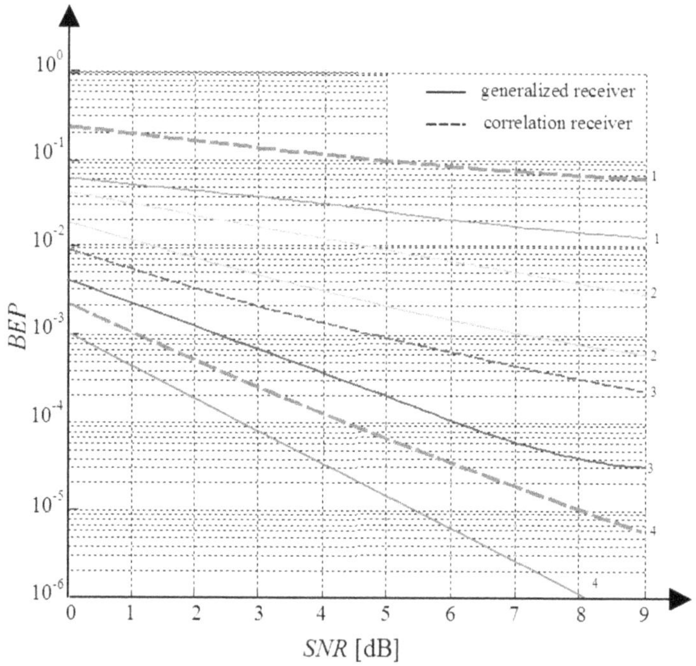

Figure 19.24. *BEP* of DS-CDMA system with BPSK and STBC $\mathbf{G}_2$ over Rayleigh fading channel $G = 64$, $K = 20$: 1—one receive antenna; 2—two receive antennas; 3—three receive antennas; 4—four receive antennas.

In addition to the aforementioned linear detectors, another category of interest is the subtractive-type interference cancellation method. Cancellation of this type involves only vector operations making it a good candidate for real-world implementation. For a particular desired user, the subtractive-type canceller estimates the interference from other users, regenerates it, and cancels it from the received signal. This cancellation process can be carried out for each interfering user either successively, i.e., successive interference cancellation [92–94] or in parallel, i.e. parallel interference cancellation [95–99]. Implementation of the successive interference cancellation allows us to estimate and cancel MAI one by one while under employment of parallel interference cancellation all interferences are cancelled simultaneously.

Using the successive interference cancellation, it is possible to reach better performance in comparison with parallel interference cancellation. However, its computational complexity is higher and processing delays are larger. There are two types of parallel interference cancellation classified according to the tentative decision devices used in each stage, namely, hard-decision parallel interference cancellation [95–102] and soft-decision parallel interference cancellation [96, 100, 103–105]. It has been observed that hard-decision parallel interference cancellation can provide better performance in comparison with soft-decision parallel interference cancellation [106].

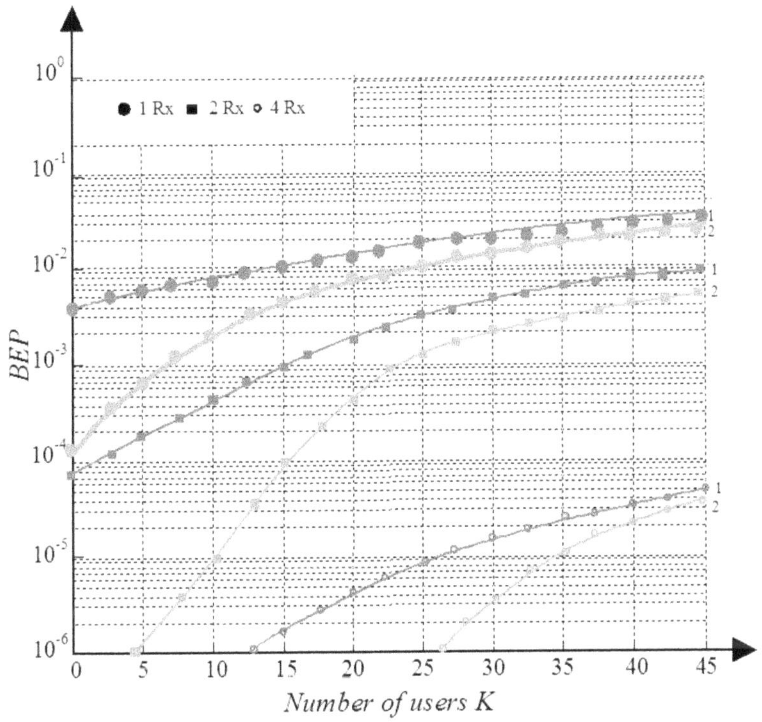

Figure 19.25. *BEP* versus the number of users for DS-CDMA system with BPSK, STBC $\mathbf{G}_2$ (the curve 1) and $\mathbf{G}_4$(the curve 2) over the Rayleigh fading channel with $G = 64$, $SNR = 7$ dB.

Conventional receivers with parallel interference cancellation permit us a full MAI cancellation. One problem associated with this approach is that the MAI estimate may not be reliable in the earlier cancelling stages. This makes parallel interference cancellation less effective when the number of users is large. A partial parallel interference cancellation detector has been proposed in which partial cancellation factors are introduced to control the interference cancellation level as a remedy [100, 101, 107]. However, theoretical analysis of the partial hard-decision parallel interference cancellation is difficult due to the nonlinear decision devices used in the receiver. Consequently, the optimal partial cancellation factors are usually obtained either by training via the least mean square adaptive algorithm [108] and [109] or theoretical derivation under some simplifying assumptions [110].

It is well known that the least mean square algorithm is simple but converges slowly. The approaches in [108–115] may not be adequate in fast fading environments. On the other hand, the optimal partial cancellation factors derived in [116] and [117] are only valid when the number of users is small. The optimal partial cancellation factors for soft-decision parallel interference cancellation are derived in [117]. However, these results can be applied only to a perfect power control scenario. As mentioned above, hard-decision parallel interference cancellation allows us to get better performance in comparison with partial soft-decision parallel interference cancellation. Although this seems intuitively reasonable, it may not be true. The previous investigation demonstrates that a two-stage canceller incorporated into the generalized receiver [114] with optimal partial soft-decision parallel interference cancellation can deliver performance similar to the generalized receiver based on optimal partial hard-decision parallel interference cancellation.

A complete partial parallel interference cancellation requires $K(K-1)$ partial cancellation factors, where K is the number of users and the computational complexity is high. Simplified partial parallel interference cancellation has been proposed, in which only K partial cancellation factors are needed. Two structures are commonly used for simplified partial parallel interference cancellation. We call them the coupled and decoupled structures. In the coupled structure, each user output is related to all K partial cancellation factors [108, 109] while in the decoupled structure, each user output is only related to a specific partial cancellation factor.

The hard-decision parallel interference cancellation mentioned above uses coupled structure. While partial soft-decision parallel interference cancellation described in [101] uses a decoupled structure, the optimal partial cancellation factors are not derived. A complete comparison of these two structures is not available in the literature. Our primary study [106] demonstrates that both receivers' structures employing the optimal partial cancellation factors have similar performance. Since optimizing one partial cancellation factor is much easier than optimizing K partial cancellation factors, it is preferable to deal with the decoupled structure.

In the present section, we focus on the generalized receiver constructed based on the generalized approach to signal processing in noise [27–30] with two-stage partial soft-decision parallel interference cancellation using a decoupled structure. Our motivation to use two-stage signal processing is that it requires a low computational complexity and is particularly suitable for real-world implementation. It is indicated in [101] that in higher stage processing, partial cancellation factors will approach unity for stages greater than two. In other words, partial cancellation factors in the second stage will dominate system performance.

We first consider the AWGN channel and derive the optimal partial cancellation factors for systems employing periodic codes. The criterion for optimization is the *BER* performance. We then extend the result to DS-CDMA wireless communication systems with aperiodic spreading codes. Finally, we consider the optimal partial cancellation factors with multipath channels. Simulation results show that the performance of the proposed theoretical optimal partial cancellation factors is close to that of empirical ones. In addition, optimal two-stage partial soft-decision parallel interference cancellation outperforms not only two-stage full soft-decision parallel interference cancellation, but also three-stage full soft-decision parallel interference cancellation.

19.4.2 System model

Consider a synchronous DS-CDMA wireless communication system accommodating K users. Let $x(t)$ denote the received signal for a certain bit interval, $s_k(t)$ is the kth user's transmitted signal, $w(t)$ is the AWGN. The equivalent baseband received signal can be presented in the following form:

$$x(t) = \sum_{k=1}^{K} s_k(t) + w(t) = \sum_{k=1}^{K} A_k b_k a_k(t) + w(t),\ t \in [0,\ T] \tag{19.229}$$

where A_k is the kth user's amplitude, b_k is the kth user's data bit, $a_k(t)$ denotes its signature waveform, and T is the bit period. The signature waveform can be expressed as

$$a_k(t) = \sum_{i=0}^{N-1} a_{k,i} \Pi_{T_c}(t - iT_c) \tag{19.230}$$

where $a_{k,i} \in \{1/\sqrt{N},\ -1/\sqrt{N}\}$ is the binary spreading chip sequence for user k; N is the processing gain; Π_{T_c} is the rectangular pulse waveform with support T_c; and unit amplitude; T_c is the chip period.

The first stage of the generalized receiver with the parallel interference cancellation is the conventional bank of generalized receivers. The output can be presented in the following form

$$y_k = \int_0^T [2x(t)a_k^m(t) - x^2(t)]dt = A_k b_k + \sum_{j \neq k} A_k b_k \rho_{jk} + \xi_k \tag{19.231}$$

where

$$\rho_{jk} = \int_0^T a_j(t) a_k(t) dt \tag{19.232}$$

is the coefficient of correlation and

$$\xi_k = \int_0^T [\eta_k^2(t) - \zeta_k^2(t)]dt \tag{19.233}$$

is the background noise forming at the generalized receiver output after dispreading (see the previous subsection). As was discussed previously, the GR CD noise component and the GR ED random component are cancelled in the statistical sense if the main functioning condition of the generalized receiver (19.32) is satisfied, for simplicity we assume that $\mu \to 1$.

It can be seen that the output metric in (19.231) consists of three components: the desired signal, the first term; the MAI, the second term; and the background noise ξ_k of the generalized receiver, the third term. The conventional generalized receiver makes a decision based on the statistics y_k given in (19.231). Thus, MAI is treated as another noise source. When the number of users is high, MAI will seriously degrade the system performance. A parallel interference cancellation, being a multiuser detection scheme, is proposed to alleviate this problem.

Let $\hat{x}_k(t)$ be the interference-subtracted signal for user k given by

$$\hat{x}_k(t) = x(t) - \sum_{j \neq k} \hat{s}_j(t), \tag{19.234}$$

where $\hat{s}_j(t)$ is the regenerated signal for user j. For soft-decision parallel interference cancellation this signal is obtained by

$$\hat{s}_j(t) = y_j a_j(t). \tag{19.235}$$

Thus, the output signal in the second stage is then

$$z_k = \int_0^T [2\hat{x}_k(t)a_k^m(t) - \hat{x}_k^2(t)]dt, \tag{19.236}$$

Finally, the symbol data is detected as $\hat{b}_k = \text{sgn}(z_k)$.

In principle, the interference cancellation procedure in (19.234)–(19.236) can be repeated with multiple stages to obtain better performance. It is apparent from (19.231) and (19.235) that the regenerated signal is noisy. Thus, fully cancelling the regenerated interference may not yield the best results. One solution to this problem is to partially cancel the interference. This idea is implemented by modifying (19.234) in the following form

$$\hat{x}_k(t) = x(t) - \sum_{j \neq k} C_{jk}\hat{s}_j(t). \tag{19.237}$$

The constants C_{jk} are called the partial cancellation factors for the user k and their amplitudes should reflect the fidelity of the interference estimate. The structure of the generalized receiver with three stages of partial soft-decision parallel interference cancellation with three users is presented in figure 19.26.

Generally, the $K \times (K - 1)$ partial cancellation factors are needed for a two-stage partial parallel interference cancellation. It is apparent that the computational complexity of the partial parallel interference cancellation is high when the number of users is large on the order of $O(K^2)$. Two simplified structures, whose complexities are on the order of $O(K)$, were investigated in [63]. The first one corresponds to the case that $C_{jk} = C_j$ in (19.231). In this case, all regenerated signals are first weighted and then summed. Thus, each regenerated interference signal in (19.237) has the individual partial cancellation factor and the signal to be estimated is a function of all partial cancellation factors. We call this structure the coupled structure.

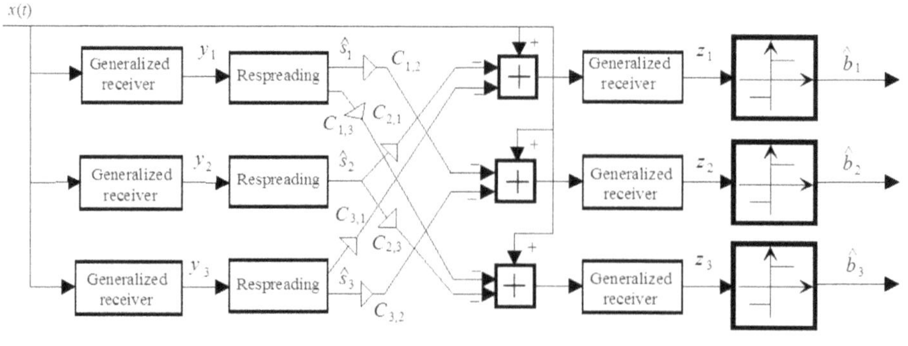

Figure 19.26. Generalized receiver structure with partial soft-decision parallel interference cancellation.

The other structure is one in which $C_{jk} = C_k$. In this case, all regenerated signals are summed first and then weighted. Thus, there is one partial cancellation factor for the signal to be estimated. We thus call this structure the decoupled structure. A thorough discussion of both structures is not available in the literature. Optimal partial cancellation factors have only been derived for the coupled structure under equal power scenarios [118, 119]. In what follows, we focus our attention on the generalized receiver with two-stage partial soft-decision parallel interference cancellation, which has decoupled structure. Primary simulation results demonstrate that both parallel interference cancellation structures with optimal partial cancellation factors have similar performance.

19.4.3 Optimal partial cancellation factors for AWGN channels

In this subsection, we derive optimal partial cancellation factors for two-stage partial soft-decision parallel interference cancellation under the AWGN channel. For simplicity of description, we only give the results associated with synchronous transmission. Periodic and aperiodic spreading codes are both considered.

19.4.3.1 Periodic code scenario

Assuming perfect chip synchronization, we first sample the received continuous time signal in (19.229) with the period T_c. Let

$$\mathbf{x} = [x(0),\ x(T_c),\ldots,x((N-1)T_c]^T \tag{19.238}$$

be the received signal sample vector;

$$\mathbf{a}_k = [a_{k,0},\ a_{k,1},\ \ldots,\ a_{k,N-1}]^T \tag{19.239}$$

be the kth user's spreading sequence vector, and

$$\mathbf{w} = [w(0),\ w(T_c),\ \ldots,\ w((N-1)T_c]^T \tag{19.240}$$

be the noise sample vector. Based on (19.229), we have

$$\mathbf{x} = \sum_k A_k b_k \mathbf{a_k} + \mathbf{w}, \tag{19.241}$$

$$\mathbf{y}_k = 2\mathbf{x}^T\mathbf{a}_k - \mathbf{x}\mathbf{x}^T = A_k b_k + \sum_{j\neq k} A_j b_j \mathbf{a}_j^T \mathbf{a}_k + \boldsymbol{\xi}_k. \tag{19.242}$$

Note that $\mathbf{a}_j^T\mathbf{a}_k$ is the discrete vector version of the correlation coefficient ρ_{jk} shown in (19.232) and $\boldsymbol{\xi}_k$ is the discrete-time vector version of the background noise (19.233) of the generalized receiver. Thus (19.242) can be rewritten in the following scalar form

$$y_k = A_k b_k + \sum_{j\neq k} A_k b_k \rho_{jk} + \xi_k. \tag{19.243}$$

For the second stage of partial soft-decision interference cancellation with the decoupled structure of the generalized receiver, the regenerated signal for the user k takes the following form

$$\hat{\mathbf{x}}_k = \mathbf{x} - C_k \sum_{j \neq k} \hat{\mathbf{s}}_j, \tag{19.244}$$

where $\hat{\mathbf{s}}_j = y_j \mathbf{a}_j$. The second stage output is then

$$\begin{aligned} z_k = \hat{\mathbf{x}}_k^T \mathbf{a}_k &= y_k - C_k \sum_{j \neq k} y_j \rho_{jk} \\ &= A_k b_k + \sum_{j \neq k} A_j b_j \rho_{jk} + \xi_k - C_k \sum_{j \neq k} \left[A_j b_j + \sum_{m \neq j} A_m b_m \rho_{\mathrm{mj}} + \xi_j \right] \rho_{jk} \\ &= A_k b_k \left[1 - C_k \sum_{j \neq k} \rho_{jk}^2 \right] + \xi_k - C_k \sum_{j \neq k} \xi_j \rho_{jk} \\ &\quad + \sum_{j \neq k} A_j b_j \left[\rho_{jk} - C_k \rho_{jk} - C_k \sum_{m \neq j,k} \rho_{jm} \rho_{mk} \right]. \end{aligned} \tag{19.245}$$

The BEP for the user k denoted as $P_{error}(z_k)$ can be written as

$$P_{error}(z_k) = 0.5[P(z_k|b_k = 1) + P(z_k|b_k = -1)] = P(z_k|b_k = 1). \tag{19.246}$$

In (19.246) we assume that the occurrence of the probabilities for $b_k = 1$ and $b_k = -1$ are equal, and the probabilities of error at $b_k = 1$ and $b_k = -1$ are also equal. As we can see, there are three terms in (19.244). The first term corresponds to the desired user bit. If we let $b_k = 1$, it is the deterministic value. The second term corresponds to the noise interference, which is Gaussian distributed. The third term corresponds to the interference from other users and each interference component is subjected to the binomial distribution. Note that the correlation coefficients in (19.245) are small and the DS-CDMA wireless communication systems are usually operated under low SNR environments. The variance of the third term is then much smaller than that of the second term. Thus, we can assume that z_k conditioned on $b_k = 1$ is subjected to Gaussian distribution. The BEP takes the following form:

$$P_{error}(z_k) = Q\left(\sqrt{\frac{M_k}{V_k}}\right), \tag{19.247}$$

where $Q\{\cdot\}$ is the Q-function and the mean and variance can be determined in the following form

$$M_k = \{E[z_k|b_k = 1]\}^2; \tag{19.248}$$

$$V_k = E(z_k^2) - M_k. \tag{19.249}$$

Note that the expectations in (19.248) and (19.249) are operated on interfering user bits and noise.

Let

$$E(\mathbf{w}\mathbf{w}^T) = \sigma_w^2 \mathbf{I}_N \tag{19.250}$$

and

$$SNR_j = A_j^2/\sigma_w^2. \tag{19.251}$$

Evaluating (19.248), we obtain

$$\mathcal{M}_k = A_k^2(1 - C_k\Lambda_k)^2, \tag{19.252}$$

where

$$\Lambda_k = \sum_{j\neq k} \rho_{jk}^2. \tag{19.253}$$

Similarly, we obtain the variance as

$$\mathcal{V}_k = \sigma_w^2(\Omega_{1,k}C_k^2 - 2\Omega_{2,k}C_k + \Omega_{3,k}), \tag{19.254}$$

where the coefficients of $\mathcal{V}_k$ are represented by

$$\Omega_{1,k} = \sum_{j\neq k} SNR_j \left[\rho_{jk} + \sum_{m\neq j,k} \rho_{jm}\rho_{mk}\right]^2 + \sum_{j\neq k}\left[\rho_{jk}^2 + \sum_{m\neq j,k} \rho_{jm}\rho_{mk}\rho_{jk}\right]; \tag{19.255}$$

$$\Omega_{2,k} = \sum_{j\neq k} SNR_j^2 \left[\rho_{jk}^2 + \sum_{m\neq j,k} \rho_{jm}\rho_{mk}\rho_{jk}\right] + \sum_{j\neq k}\rho_{jk}^2; \tag{19.256}$$

$$\Omega_{3,k} = \sum_{j\neq k} SNR_j^2\rho_{jk}^2 + 1. \tag{19.257}$$

The optimal partial cancellation factors for the user k can be determined as

$$C_k^{opt} = \arg\max_{C_k}\{\mathcal{M}_k/\mathcal{V}_k\} = \left\{C_k^{opt}: \mathcal{V}_k\frac{d\mathcal{M}_k}{dC_k} - M_k\frac{d\mathcal{V}_k}{dC_k} = 0\right\}. \tag{19.258}$$

Substituting (19.252) and (19.254) into (19.258) and simplifying the result, we have the following equation:

$$(1 - C_k^{opt}\Lambda_k)[C_k^{opt}(\Omega_{1,k} - \Lambda_{1,k}\Omega_{2,k}) + \Lambda_k\Omega_{3,k} - \Omega_{2,k}] = 0. \tag{19.259}$$

We have two possible solutions now. The first solution for the first parenthesis is trivial since it makes the squared mean value $\mathcal{M}_k$ in (19.252) equal to zero. The optimum partial cancellation factor takes the following form

$$C_k^{opt} = \frac{\Omega_{2,k} - \Omega_{3,k}\Lambda_k}{\Omega_{1,k} - \Omega_{2,k}\Lambda_k} \tag{19.260}$$

We also derive the optimal partial cancellation factors for the asynchronous DS-CDMA wireless communication system. The results are summarized in appendix E. In what follows, we discuss some special cases to give better understanding of the characteristics of the optimal partial cancellation factor. Let the correlations between any two user spreading codes be equal, i.e., $\rho_{jk} = \rho$ at $j \neq k$, and the power control be perfect, i.e., $A_k = A$ and $SNR_k = SNR$. The optimal partial cancellation factor can then be expressed as

$$C_k^{opt} = \frac{SNR}{1 + SNR[1 + \rho(K - 2)]}. \tag{19.261}$$

As we can see from (19.261), the optimal partial cancellation factor is smaller when ρ or K is larger, because when the correlations between the user codes are higher and the number of users is larger, the MAI is larger, and the regenerated signal is unreliable. As a result, the partial cancellation factor should be smaller. Also, when the user power is larger or the noise is smaller, the SNR is higher and the optimal partial cancellation factor is larger. If we assume that the noise is much smaller than the signal power, i.e., $SNR > > 1$, the optimal partial cancellation factor can be further simplified to

$$C_k^{opt} = \frac{1}{1 + \rho(K - 2)]}. \tag{19.262}$$

Now the optimal partial cancellation factor is independent of the transmission signal power. The BEP performance would also be saturated in this interference-limited region. From (19.261) we can also see that when the noise power is large, $SNR < < 1$, the optimal partial cancellation factor tends to be small, $C_k \to 0$. Note that the effect of the processing gain N is reflected in the receiving SNR. If N is larger, the receiving SNR will become smaller.

19.4.3.2 Aperiodic code scenario

In commercial DS-CDMA wireless communication systems, the users' spreading codes are often modulated with another code having a very long period. As far as the received signal is concerned, the spreading code is not periodic. In other words, there will be many possible spreading codes for each user. If we use the result derived above, we then have to calculate the optimum partial cancellation factors for each possible code and the computational complexity will become very high. Since the period of the modulating code is usually very long, we can treat the code chips as independent random variables and approximate the correlation coefficients ρ_{jk}, as the Gaussian random variable. As a result, the expectations in (19.248) and (19.249) can be further operated on ρ_{jk}. This greatly simplifies the optimal partial cancellation factor evaluation. We now rewrite (19.247) in the following form

$$P_{error}(z_k) = Q\left(\sqrt{\frac{E_{\mathscr{L}}\{\mathscr{M}_k^{(l)}\}}{E_{\mathscr{L}}\{\mathscr{V}_k^{(l)}\}}}\right), \tag{19.263}$$

where $E_{\mathscr{L}}\{\cdot\}$ denotes the expectation operator over the spreading code set $\mathscr{L}$ and $\mathscr{M}_k^{(l)}$ and $\mathscr{V}_k^{(l)}$ are the expected squared mean and variance of z_k, respectively, given the lth possible code in $\mathscr{L}$. Letting

$$I_k = \sum_{j \neq k} \mathrm{SNR}_j^2, \tag{19.264}$$

and considering ρ_{jk} as the Gaussian random variable, and evaluating (19.248) and (19.265), we obtain

$$E_{\mathscr{L}}\{\mathscr{M}_k^{(l)}\} = A_k^2[1 - C_k E_{\mathscr{L}}\{\Lambda_k^{(l)}\}]^2, \tag{19.265}$$

where

$$E_{\mathscr{L}}\{\Lambda_k^{(l)}\} = \frac{K-1}{N} \tag{19.266}$$

and

$$E_{\mathscr{L}}\{\mathscr{V}_k^{(l)}\} = \sigma_w^2[E_{\mathscr{L}}\{\Omega_{1,k}^{(l)}\}C_k^2 - 2E_{\mathscr{L}}\{\Omega_{2,k}^{(l)}\}C_k + E_{\mathscr{L}}\{\Omega_{3,k}^{(l)}\}], \tag{19.267}$$

where

$$\begin{aligned} E_{\mathscr{L}}\{\Omega_{1,k}^{(l)}\} = {} & I_k\left(\frac{1}{N} + \frac{3(K-2)}{N^2} + \frac{(K-2)(K-3)}{N^3}\right) + \frac{K-1}{N} \\ & + \frac{(K-1)(K-2)}{N^2}; \end{aligned} \tag{19.268}$$

$$E_{\mathscr{L}}\{\Omega_{2,k}^{(l)}\} = I_k\left(\frac{1}{N} + \frac{K-2}{N^2}\right) + \frac{K-1}{N}; \tag{19.269}$$

$$E_{\mathscr{L}}\{\Omega_{3,k}^{(l)}\} = \frac{I_k}{N} + 1. \tag{19.270}$$

In the above expressions, the notation $X^{(l)}$ denotes the value X given the lth possible spreading code in $\mathscr{L}$. Equation (19.258) can be rewritten in the following form:

$$\begin{aligned} C_k^{opt} = \arg\max_{C_k}\left\{\frac{E_{\mathscr{L}}\{\mathscr{M}_k^{(l)}\}}{E_{\mathscr{L}}\{\mathscr{V}_k^{(l)}\}}\right\} = \Bigg\{ & C_k^{opt}: E_{\mathscr{L}}\{\mathscr{V}_k^{(l)}\}\frac{dE_{\mathscr{L}}\{\mathscr{M}_k^{(l)}\}}{dC_k} \\ & - E_{\mathscr{L}}\{\mathscr{M}_k^{(l)}\}\frac{dE_{\mathscr{L}}\{\mathscr{V}_k^{(l)}\}}{dC_k} = 0\Bigg\}. \end{aligned} \tag{19.271}$$

Substituting (19.265)–(19.270) into (19.267) and simplifying the result, we finally obtain

$$C_k^{opt} = \frac{E_{\mathscr{L}}\{\Omega_{2,k}^{(l)}\} - E_{\mathscr{L}}\{\Omega_{3,k}^{(l)}\}E_{\mathscr{L}}\{\Lambda_k^{(l)}\}}{E_{\mathscr{L}}\{\Omega_{1,k}^{(l)}\} - E_{\mathscr{L}}\{\Omega_{2,k}^{(l)}\}E_{\mathscr{L}}\{\Lambda_k^{(l)}\}} \tag{19.272}$$

As we can see, equation (19.272) only involves equation (19.266) and equations (19.268)–(19.270) and these expressions are easy to work with. We further consider the case, in which the noise is small, $I_k > > K$. Equation (19.272) can be simplified to

$$C_k^{opt} = \frac{N}{N + 2K - 4}. \tag{19.273}$$

This result is remarkably simple. We only require N and K to calculate the optimal partial cancellation factors. This will be useful in real-world applications.

19.4.4 Optimal partial cancellation factors for multipath channels

19.4.4.1 Periodic code scenario

Let the transfer function for the user k's channel be

$$H_k(z) = \sum_{i=1}^{L} h_{k,i} z^{-\tau_{k,i}}. \tag{19.274}$$

As we can see from (19.274), the number of paths is L and the gain and delay for the ith channel path are $h_{k,i}$ and $\tau_{k,i}$, respectively. We use two vectors to represent these parameters

$$\mathbf{t}_k = [\tau_{k,1}, \tau_{k,2}, \dots, \tau_{k,L}]^T \tag{19.275}$$

and

$$\mathbf{h}_k = [h_{k,1}, h_{k,2}, \dots, h_{k,L}]^T. \tag{19.276}$$

Let $\tau_{k,1} \leqslant \tau_{k,2} \leqslant \cdots \leqslant \tau_{k,L}$ and the channel power is normalized, i.e. $\sum_{k,i} h_{k,i}^2 = 1$. Without loss of generality, we may assume that $\tau_{k,1} = 0$ for each user and L is the maximum possible number of paths. When a user's path number, say L', is less than L, we can let all elements in $\tau_{k,i}$ and $h_{k,i}$ be zero for $L' + 1 \leqslant i \leqslant L$. We may also assume that the maximum delay is much smaller than the processing gain N [54]. Before our formulation, we first define the $(2N - 1)L$ composite signature matrix $\mathbf{S}_k$ in the following form

$$\mathbf{S}_k = [\tilde{\mathbf{a}}_{k,1}, \tilde{\mathbf{a}}_{k,2}, \dots, \tilde{\mathbf{a}}_{k,L}], \tag{19.277}$$

where $\tilde{\mathbf{a}}_{k,i}$ is the vector containing ith delayed spreading code for the user k. It is defined as

$$\tilde{\mathbf{a}}_{k,i} = [\overbrace{0, \dots, 0}^{\tau_{k,i}}, \mathbf{a}_k^T, \overbrace{0, \dots, 0}^{N-\tau_{k,i}-1}]^T. \tag{19.278}$$

Since a multipath channel is involved, the current received bit signal will be interfered with by previous bit signals. As mentioned above, the maximum path delay is much smaller than the processing gain. The interference will not be severe and for simplicity, we may ignore this effect. Let

$$\mathbf{f}_k = \mathbf{S}_k\mathbf{h}_k. \tag{19.279}$$

As that in (19.241), we can obtain the received signal vector as

$$\mathbf{x} = \sum_k A_k b_k \mathbf{f}_k + \mathbf{w}. \tag{19.280}$$

To have the better results, we use the maximum ratio rake combining scheme in the generalized receiver. Let

$$\begin{cases} \rho_{jk} = \mathbf{f}_j^T\mathbf{f}_k \ ; \\ \rho_k = \rho_{kk} \ ; \end{cases} \tag{19.281}$$

the output of the generalized receiver takes the following form

$$\begin{aligned} y_k = 2\mathbf{x}^T\mathbf{f}_k - \mathbf{x}\mathbf{x}^T &= A_k b_k \mathbf{f}_k^T\mathbf{f}_k + \sum_{j\neq k} A_j b_j \mathbf{f}_j^T\mathbf{f}_k + \xi_k \\ &= A_k b_k \rho_k + \sum_{j\neq k} A_j b_j \rho_{jk} + \xi_k. \end{aligned} \tag{19.282}$$

This result is similar to that in (19.242) except that $a_j^T a_k$ is replaced by ρ_{jk}. For the second stage of the partial soft-decision parallel interference cancellation, the regenerated signal takes the following form

$$\hat{\mathbf{x}}_k = \mathbf{x} - C_k \sum_{j\neq k} \hat{\mathbf{s}}_j = \mathbf{x} - C_k \sum_{j\neq k} y_j \mathbf{f}_j. \tag{19.283}$$

We then have the output signal for the second stage as

$$\begin{aligned} z_k &= 2\mathbf{x}_k^T\mathbf{f}_k - \mathbf{x}_k\mathbf{x}_k^T \\ &= A_k b_k\left[\rho_k - C_k \sum_{j\neq k} \rho_{j,k}^2\right] + v_k - C_k \sum_{j\neq k} v_j \rho_{jk} \\ &\quad + \sum_{j\neq k} A_j b_j \left[\rho_{jk} - C_k \rho_{jk} - C_k \sum_{m\neq j,k} \rho_{jm}\rho_{mk}\right]. \end{aligned} \tag{19.284}$$

As previously, we assume that z_k is approximated by the Gaussian probability distribution density; the interfering bits and noise are random; and parameters N, K,$\mathbf{t}_k$, $\mathbf{h}_k$, SNR_k,ρ_{jk} are known beforehand. Thus, the output probability of error is expressed as in (19.247) where the squared mean for z_k, similar to that of (19.252) is obtained from (19.248) and (19.284) in the following form

$$\mathcal{M}_k = A_k^2(\rho_k - C_k\Gamma_k)^2, \tag{19.285}$$

where

$$\Gamma_k = \sum_{j \neq k} \rho_{jk}^2 \tag{19.286}$$

and the variance is obtained from (19.249) and (19.284) as

$$\mathcal{V}_k = \sigma_w^2(\Xi_{1,k}C_k^2 - 2\Xi_{2,k}C_k + \Xi_{3,k}), \tag{19.287}$$

where

$$\Xi_{1,k} = \sum_{j \neq k} SNR_j^2 \left[\rho_{jk}\rho_j + \sum_{m \neq j,k} \rho_{jm}\rho_{mk}\right]^2 + \sum_{j \neq k}\left[\rho_{jk}^2\rho_j + \sum_{m \neq j,k} \rho_{jm}\rho_{mk}\rho_{jk}\right]; \tag{19.288}$$

$$\Xi_{2,k} = \sum_{j \neq k} SNR_j^2 \left[\rho_{jk}^2\rho_j + \sum_{m \neq j,k} \rho_{jm}\rho_{mk}\rho_{jk}\right] + \sum_{j \neq k}\rho_{jk}^2; \tag{19.289}$$

$$\Xi_{3,k} = \sum_{j \neq k} SNR_j^2\rho_{jk}^2 + \rho_{jk}. \tag{19.290}$$

The optimal partial cancellation factor derivation for the multipath channels is similar to that in (19.258). Substituting (19.285) and (19.287) into (19.258), we then obtain

$$C_k^{opt} = \frac{\rho_k\Xi_{2,k} - \Xi_{3,k}\Gamma_k}{\rho_k\Xi_{1,k} - \Xi_{2,k}\Gamma_k}. \tag{19.291}$$

19.4.4.2 Aperiodic code scenario

If aperiodic codes are utilized, the correlation coefficients ρ_{jk} can be considered as the Gaussian random variables. Using the method discussed in the previous subsection we can obtain the corresponding optimal partial cancellation factors. From (19.285) we have the expected squared mean in the following form

$$E_{\mathcal{L}}\{\mathcal{M}_k^{(l)}\rho_k^{(l)}\} = A_k^2[E_{\mathcal{L}}\{\rho_k^{(l)} - C_kE_{\mathcal{L}}\{\Gamma_k^{(l)}\}]^2 = A_k^2[1 - C_kE_{\mathcal{L}}\{\Gamma_k^{(l)}\}]^2 \tag{19.292}$$

and the variance takes the form

$$E_{\mathcal{L}}\{\mathcal{V}_k^{(l)}\} = \sigma_w^2[E_{\mathcal{L}}\{\Xi_{1,k}^{(l)}\}C_k^2 - 2E_{\mathcal{L}}\{\Xi_{2,k}^{(l)}\}C_k + E_{\mathcal{L}}\{\Xi_{3,k}^{(l)}\}]. \tag{19.293}$$

Comparing (19.292) and (19.293) with (19.265)–(19.267), we see that the optimal partial cancellation factor here is similar to that in (19.271). We then have the partial cancellation factor in the following form

$$C_k^{opt} = \frac{E_{\mathcal{L}}\{\Xi_{2,k}^{(l)}\} - E_{\mathcal{L}}\{\Xi_{3,k}^{(l)}\}E_{\mathcal{L}}\{\Gamma_k^{(l)}\}}{E_{\mathcal{L}}\{\Xi_{1,k}^{(l)}\} - E_{\mathcal{L}}\{\Xi_{2,k}^{(l)}\}E_{\mathcal{L}}\{\Gamma_k^{(l)}\}}. \tag{19.294}$$

Unlike that in the AWGN channel, the result for the aperiodic code scenario is more difficult to obtain because there are more correlation terms in (19.286) and (19.288)–(19.290) to work with. Before evaluating expectation terms in (19.294), we define some functions as follows:

$$h_{jk}(p,q) = h_{j,p}h_{k,q}; \tag{19.295}$$

$$\tau_{jk}(p,q) = \tau_{j,p} - \tau_{k,q}; \tag{19.296}$$

$$\chi_{jk}(p,q) = \tilde{\mathbf{a}}_{j,p}^{T}\tilde{\mathbf{a}}_{k,q}. \tag{19.297}$$

Thus, (19.295)–(19.297) define some relative figures between the pth channel path of the jth user and qth channel path of the kth user. The notation $h_{jk}(p,q)$ denotes the path gain product, $\tau_{jk}(p,q)$ is the relative path delay, and $\chi_{jk}(p,q)$ is the code correlation with the relative delay $\tau_{jk}(p,q)$. Expanding (19.288)–(19.290), we have seven expectation terms to evaluate. For purpose of illustration, we show how to evaluate the first term $E_{\mathscr{L}}\{\rho_{jk}^{2}\}$ here. By definition, the correlation coefficient ρ_{jk} can be presented in the following form

$$\begin{aligned}\rho_{jk} &= \mathbf{f}_j^T\mathbf{f}_k = \left(\sum_{p=1}^{L}\tilde{\mathbf{a}}_{j,p}h_{j,p}\right)^T\left(\sum_{q=1}^{L}\tilde{\mathbf{a}}_{k,q}h_{k,q}\right) = \sum_{p=1}^{L}\sum_{q=1}^{L}h_{j,p}h_{k,q}\tilde{\mathbf{a}}_{j,p}^{T}\mathbf{a}_{k,q} \\ &= \sum_{p=1}^{L}\sum_{q=1}^{L}h_{jk}(p,q)\chi_{jk}(p,q).\end{aligned} \tag{19.298}$$

The mathematical expectation of the correlation coefficient ρ_{jk} over all possible codes is obtained in the following form:

$$\begin{aligned}E_{\mathscr{L}}\{\rho_{jk}^{2}\} &= E\left\{\sum_{p_1=1}^{L}\sum_{q_1=1}^{L}\sum_{p_2=1}^{L}\sum_{q_2=1}^{L}h_{jk}(p_1,q_1)\chi_{jk}(p_1,q_1)\,h_{jk}(p_2,q_2)\chi_{jk}(p_2,q_2)\right\} \\ &= \sum_{p_1=1}^{L}\sum_{q_1=1}^{L}\sum_{p_2=1}^{L}\sum_{q_2=1}^{L}h_{jk}(p_1,q_1)h_{jk}(p_2,q_2)E\{\chi_{jk}(p_1,q_1)\chi_{jk}(p_2,q_2)\}.\end{aligned} \tag{19.299}$$

Let

$$F_{jk}(p_1,\, q_1,\, p_2,\, q_2) = N^2E\{\chi_{jk}(p_1,\, q_1)\chi_{jk}(p_2,\, q_2)\}. \tag{19.300}$$

The coefficient N^2 in (19.300) is only the normalization constant. Since the spreading codes are seen as random, only, when $\tau_{jk}(p_1,q_1)$ is equal to $\tau_{jk}(p_2,q_2)$, the function $\mathscr{F}_{jk}(\cdot)$ will be nonzero. Consider the specific set of $\{p_1,q_1,p_2,q_2\}$ such that

$$\tau_{jk}(p_1,q_1) = \tau_{jk}(p_2,q_2) = \tau\ ,\ \ \tau \geqslant 0. \tag{19.301}$$

We then have

$$\mathscr{F}_{jk}(p_1,q_1,p_2,q_2) = N^2 \sum_{\upsilon=0}^{N-\tau-1} E\{a^2_{j,\upsilon+\tau}a^2_{k,\upsilon}\} = N - \tau. \tag{19.302}$$

For $\tau < 0$, we have the same result except that the sign of τ in (19.302) is plus. We then conclude that the function $\mathscr{F}_{jk}(\cdot)$ in (19.300) takes the following form:

$$\mathscr{F}_{jk}(p_1,q_1,p_2,q_2) = \begin{cases} N - |\tau| \text{ , if } \tau_{jk}(p_1,q_1) = \tau_{jk}(p_2,q_2) = \tau, \\ 0 \text{ , otherwise.} \end{cases} \tag{19.303}$$

Using (19.299), (19.300), and (19.303), we can evaluate $E_{\mathscr{L}}\{\rho^2_{jk}\}$ in (19.288)–(19.290). The general formulations for the other six mathematical expectations and variances are summarized in appendix F.

We now provide a simple example to show the multipath effect on the optimal partial cancellation factors. Let $\forall k$, $\alpha^2 + \beta^2 = 1$, then

$$\begin{cases} \mathbf{t}_k = [0, D]^T \text{ ;} \\ \mathbf{h}_k = [\alpha, \beta]^T \text{ ;} \end{cases} \tag{19.304}$$

$$\begin{cases} \mathscr{G}_a = (N - D)\alpha^2\beta^2 \text{ ;} \\ \mathscr{G}_b = (N - 2D)\alpha^4\beta^4. \end{cases} \tag{19.305}$$

In this case we can write

$$E_{\mathscr{L}}\{\Gamma_k^{(l)}\} = E_{\mathscr{L}}\{\Lambda_k^{(l)}\} + \frac{2\mathscr{G}_a(K-1)}{N^2}; \tag{19.306}$$

$$\begin{aligned} E_{\mathscr{L}}\{\Xi_{1,k}^{(l)}\} &= E_{\mathscr{L}}\{\Omega_{1,k}^{(l)}\} \\ &+ 2\mathscr{G}_a\left\{\frac{I_k}{N^4}[N^2 + 10N + 4\mathscr{G}_a + 2(K-2)(4N + 3K + \mathscr{G}_a + 1] \right. \\ &\left. + \frac{K-1}{N^3}(N + 3K - 2)\right\} \\ &+ \mathscr{G}_b\left\{\frac{I_k K}{N^4} + 6K - 12\right\} + \frac{I_k}{N^4}(6N - 10D)\alpha^4\beta^4; \end{aligned} \tag{19.307}$$

$$E_L\{\Xi_{2,k}^{(l)}\} = E_{\mathscr{L}}\{\Omega_{2,k}^{(l)}\} + 2\mathscr{G}_a\left[\frac{I_k}{N^3}(N + 3K - 2) + \frac{K-1}{N^2}\right]; \tag{19.308}$$

$$E_{\mathscr{L}}\{\Xi_{3,k}^{(l)}\} = E_{\mathscr{L}}\{\Omega_{3,k}^{(l)}\} + 2\mathscr{G}_a\frac{I_k}{N^2}. \tag{19.309}$$

Note that the first terms in (19.306)–(19.309) are those in (19.266) and (19.268)–(19.270) which correspond to the optimal partial cancellation factors in the AWGN channel of DS-CDMA wireless communication system. Other terms are due to the multipath channel effect. It is evident to see that if $\beta = 0$, $\mathcal{G}_a = \mathcal{G}_b = 0$ and the metrics above are then degenerated to (19.266) and (19.268)–(19.270).

19.4.5 Simulation results

19.4.5.1 Various partial parallel interference cancellations. Performance comparison

In this subsection, we provide the simulation results to verify the validity of our derived partial cancellation factors. Before we do that, we present some comparison results to justify the parallel interference cancellation structure we considered. First, we compare the performance of partial soft-decision parallel interference cancellation and that of partial hard-decision parallel cancellation. We used periodic codes of length 31 as spreading codes.

Let $E_b/\mathcal{N}_0 = 8$ dB, where $\sigma_w^2 = 0.5\mathcal{N}_0$, and assume a perfect power control scenario. It is straightforward to see that in the perfect power control case, the optimal partial cancellation factors are equal for the coupled and decoupled structures. Figure 19.27 demonstrates the *BER* performance versus the number of users *K*. Here, the optimal partial cancellation factors for the partial hard-decision

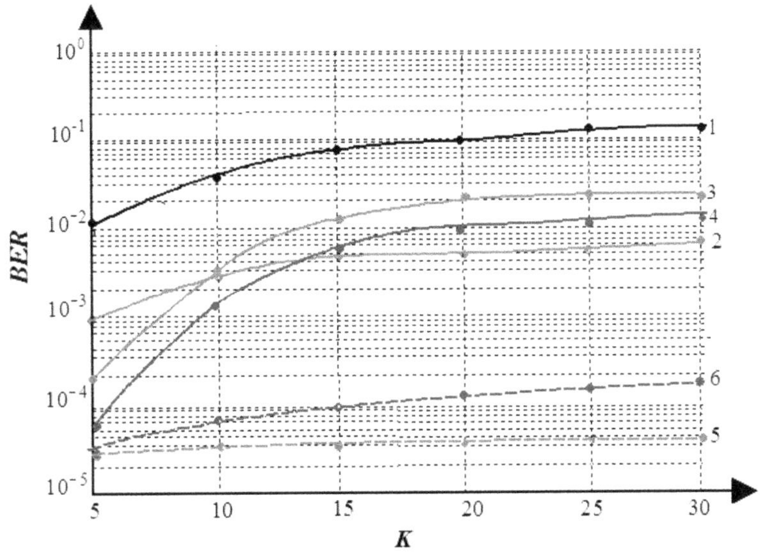

Figure 19.27. Performance comparison for hard- and soft-decision parallel interference cancellation ($N = 31$, $p = N^{-0.5}$, $E_b/\mathcal{N}_0 = 8$dB). Optimal partial cancellation factors for partial hard-decision parallel interference cancellation were obtained by trial and error and those for soft-decision parallel interference cancellation were obtained from (19.260): 1—conventional matched filter; 2—conventional generalized receiver; 3—full soft-decision parallel interference cancellation; 4—full hard-decision parallel interference cancellation; 5—partial soft-decision parallel interference cancellation; 6—partial hard-decision parallel interference cancellation.

parallel interference cancellation were determined empirically (trial and error with a resolution of 0.01). Surprisingly, we found that optimal partial soft-decision parallel interference cancellation outperforms optimal partial hard-decision parallel interference cancellation. This result differs from the result given in [36, 53–56] where full soft-decision partial interference cancellation was found to be inferior to full hard-decision parallel interference cancellation. Additionally, we made the performance comparison between the generalized receiver and matched filter. We see that generalized receiver outperforms the matched-filter receiver by performance.

In the second set of simulations, we made a comparison between the performance of the coupled and decoupled structures using partial soft-decision parallel interference cancellation. As mentioned above, the optimal partial cancellation factors are equal for both structures under perfect power control. Thus, we compared their performance in an imperfect power control scenario. The optimal partial cancellation factors for the coupled structure were determined empirically.

Let the number of users be three and the spreading code be aperiodic of length 31. We assume that the third user has the fixed SNR, i.e. $E_b/\mathcal{N}_0 = 8$ dB, and the other two users have variable SNR, for example, the first user has $E_b/\mathcal{N}_0 - \Delta SNR = 8 - \Delta SNR$ dB and the second user has $E_b/\mathcal{N}_0 - 2\Delta SNR = 8 - 2\Delta SNR$ dB, respectively. Figure 19.28 represents the BER performance as a function of ΔSNR for these three structures. As we can see, both structures, coupled and decoupled, possess similar BER performance.

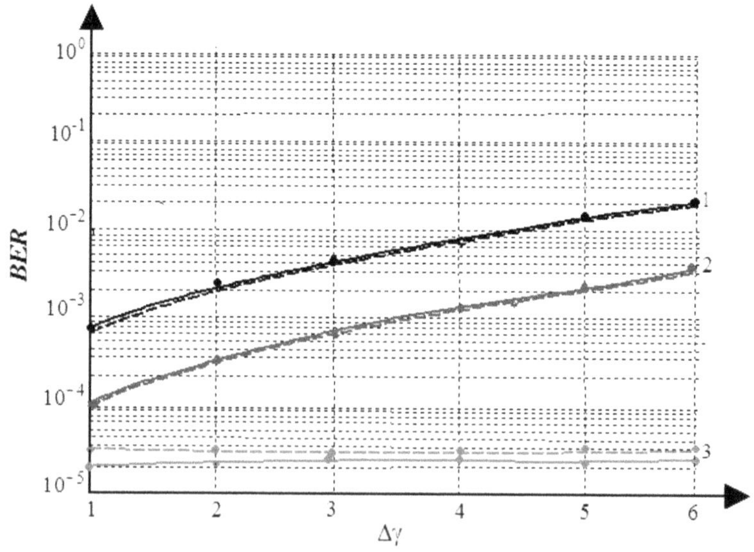

Figure 19.28. Performance comparison for the coupled (solid line) and decoupled (dashed line) structures (three users with $(E_b/\mathcal{N}_0) - \Delta SNR$ dB). Optimal partial cancellation factors for the coupled structure were obtained by trial and error, and those for the decoupled structure were obtained from (19.272); 1-user #1; 2-user #2; 3-user #3.

19.4.5.2 Validity of derived partial cancellation factors

In this subsubsection, we report simulation results demonstrating the accuracy of theoretical solutions carried out in previous subsections for optimal partial soft-decision parallel interference cancellation. A two-stage decoupled partial parallel interference cancellation is considered. For the simulations conducted, we used the Gold codes for periodic code systems and random codes for aperiodic code systems. Figure 19.29 gives the empirical and theoretical *BER* performances for the generalized receiver with optimal partial soft-decision parallel interference cancellation under the aperiodic code scenario. This figure shows the validity of the Gaussian approximation used in our derivation. As we can see, when the number of users is smaller and the $SNR = E_b/\mathcal{N}_0$ is higher, the Gaussian approximation is less valid.

Figure 19.30 demonstrates the optimal partial cancellation factors in (19.260) and the empirical optimal partial cancellation factors as a function of the number of users. The channel here is the asynchronous AWGN channel. The spreading codes are periodic and $E_b/\mathcal{N}_0 = 8$ dB for each user. We can see from this figure that the theoretical optimal partial cancellation factors are very close to the empirical ones in all cases.

We then consider the optimal partial cancellation factors for the multipath channel. The assumed multipath channel is the two-ray channel with the transfer function $H_k(z) = 0.762{+}0.648z^{-2}$ for all users. Theoretical optimal partial cancellation factors derived in (19.294) are compared with empirical partial cancellation factors and the results are presented in figure 19.31. We can observe that the theoretical results are also matched with the empirical ones satisfactorily. Note that when the number of users is smaller, the theoretical values are less accurate. This is

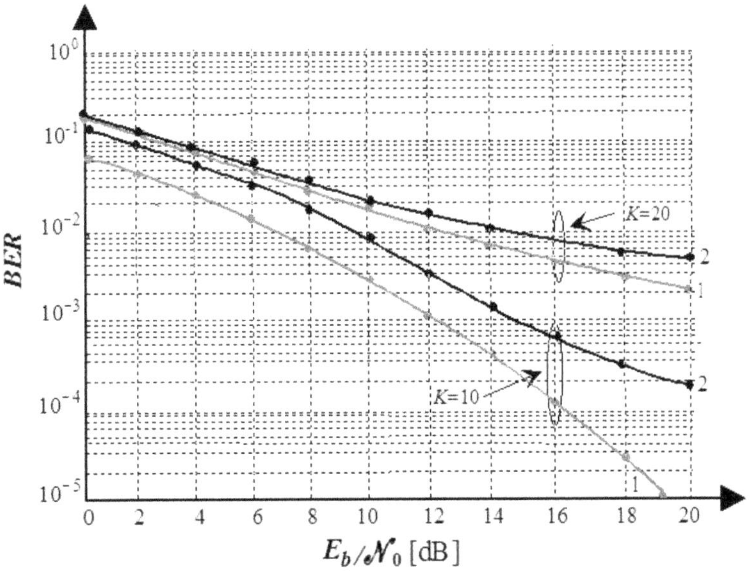

Figure 19.29. *BER* performance of the generalized receiver with partial soft-decision parallel interference cancellation as a function of $E_b/\mathcal{N}_0$(aperiodic AWGN channels and perfect power control): 1—theoretical curve; 2—empirical curve.

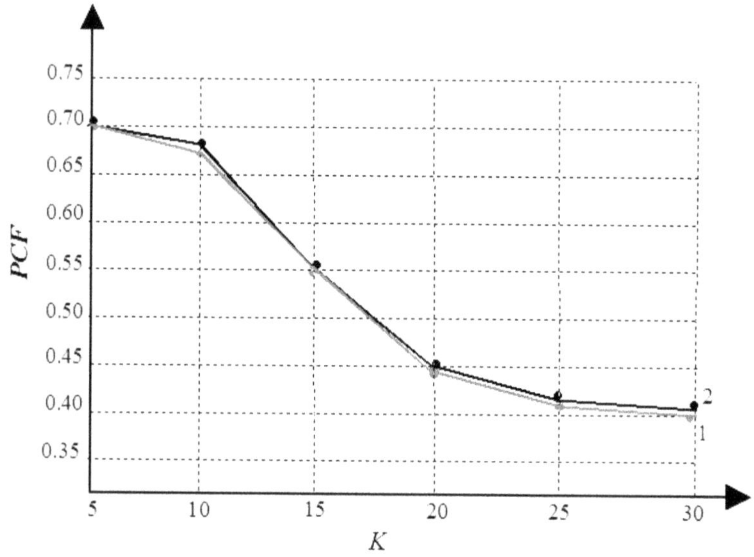

Figure 19.30 Optimal partial cancellation factor (PCF) versus the number of users (Gold codes, asynchronous AWGN channels, $E_b/\mathcal{N}_0 = 8$ dB, and perfect power control): 1—theoretical curve; 2—empirical curve.

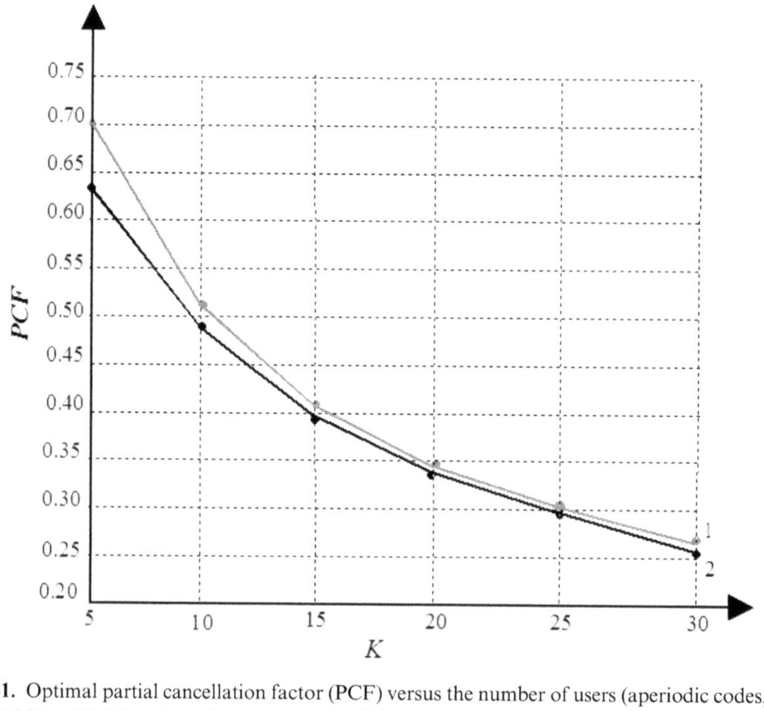

Figure 19.31. Optimal partial cancellation factor (PCF) versus the number of users (aperiodic codes, multipath channels, $E_b/\mathcal{N}_0 = 10$ dB, and perfect power control): 1—theoretical curve; 2—empirical curve.

because when the number of users is small, the Gaussian approximation in (19.263) is less valid. This is also consistent with the results observed in figure 19.29.

19.4.5.3 BER *performance comparison*

In what follows, we report the *BER* performance for the matched filter and generalized receivers with soft-decision parallel interference cancellation. Figure 19.32 demonstrates comparative analysis of performances between the conventional matched-filter receiver and generalized one in the case of optimal two-stage partial soft-decision parallel interference cancellation, namely, two-stage full soft-decision parallel interference cancellation, and three-stage full soft-decision parallel interference cancellation. From figure 19.32, we see that *BER* performance of the generalized receiver outperforms the matched-filter receiver performance. The spreading codes are periodic and the channel is the asynchronous channel with the AWGN, also $SNR = E_b/\mathcal{N}_0 = 10$ dB and perfect power control is assumed. From figure 19.32, we can see that optimal two-stage partial soft-decision parallel interference cancellation possesses better performance in comparison with other cases.

The performance of the generalized receiver with two-stage and three-stage soft-decision parallel interference cancellation is better than the performance of the conventional matched-filter receiver. The performances of the generalized receiver with two-stage and three-stage soft-decision parallel interference cancellation are worse in comparison with those of the conventional generalized receiver when the

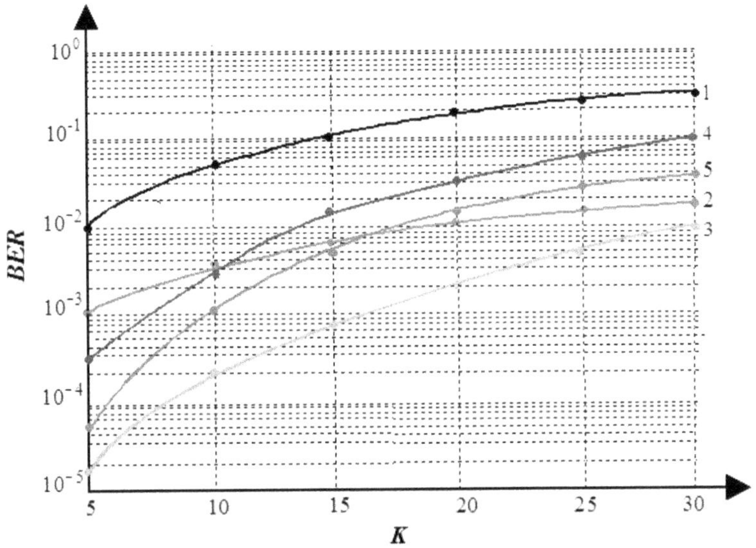

Figure 19.32. *BER* performance versus the number of users (Gold codes, asynchronous AWGN channels, $E_b/\mathcal{N}_0 = 10$ dB, and perfect power control): 1—the matched-filter receiver; 2—the generalized receiver; 3—the generalized receiver with two-stage partial soft-decision interference cancellation; 4—the generalized receiver with the two-stage full soft-decision interference cancellation; 5—the generalized receiver with three-stage full soft-decision interference cancellation.

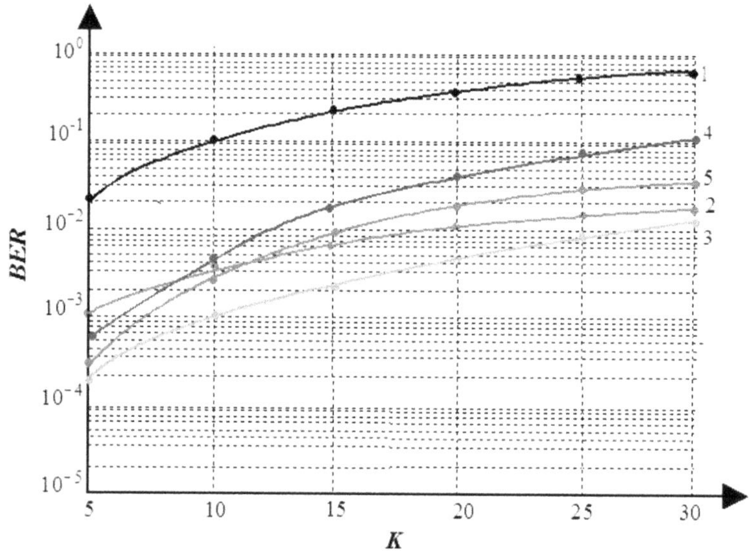

Figure 19.33. *BER* performance versus the number of users (aperiodic spreading codes, asynchronous multipath channels, $E_b/\mathcal{N}_0 = 10$ dB, and perfect power control): 1—the Rake receiver; 2—the generalized receiver; 3—the generalized receiver with the two-stage partial soft-decision interference cancellation; 4—the generalized receiver with the two-stage full soft-decision interference cancellation; 5—the generalized receiver with the three-stage full soft-decision interference cancellation.

number of users is large. Optimal two-stage partial soft-decision parallel interference cancellation always is better than the conventional generalized receiver performance.

Finally, figure 19.33 demonstrates the performance comparison for the generalized receiver and Rake detector considered in the previous sections for the case of the multipath channels. The simulation setup is identical to that in the previous cases except that the spreading code is aperiodic. The partial cancellation factors for optimal two-stage partial soft-decision parallel interference cancellation have been calculated using (19.294). As in the case of channel with the AWGN, the performance of the generalized receiver with optimal two-stage partial soft-decision parallel interference cancellation outperforms the performance of other types of the generalized detectors. Additionally, we see a great superiority of employment of the generalized receiver in comparison with the Rake one in the considered DS-CDMA wireless communication systems.

19.4.5.4 Effect of imperfect parameter estimation

In optimal partial cancellation factor formulation, we assume that the required parameters are perfectly known. In practice, this may not be always possible. Some parameters will have to be estimated for time-varying channels, which may introduce errors. The main parameters we need to know are the channel responses and the noise variance. Once the channel responses are known, A_k, ρ_{jk}, SNR_k can be calculated accordingly. We model the channel estimation error as follows. Let

$g_{k,i} = A_k h_{k,i}$ be the ith path channel of the user k, and $g'_{k,i} = g_{k,i} + \Delta g_{k,i}$, where $g'_{k,i}$ is the estimated channel response, $g_{k,i}$ is the actual response, and $\Delta g_{k,i}$ is the Gaussian random variable denoting the estimation error.

We first let the noise variance be exactly known and varied the channel estimation error. The performance impact is demonstrated in figure 19.34. The presented results correspond to the case in which the user number is six, the spreading code is aperiodic, the channel is the multipath channel, and $SNR = E_b/\mathcal{N}_0 = 10$ dB. In figure 19.34, σ_g^2 is the variance of $\Delta g_{k,i}$ that is the same for $\forall\ k,i$. Since the conventional generalized receiver and the generalized receiver with the full soft-decision parallel interference cancellation do not rely on channel information, the channel estimation error has no influence on their performance. The variations in the *BER* performance in figure 19.34 are caused by the random data used in differrent runs. Additionally, we see a great superiority of employment of the generalized receiver in comparison with the Rake one in the considered DS-CDMA wireless communication systems.

As we can see, the performance of the generalized receiver with the partial soft-decision parallel interference cancellation is not affected until $\sigma_g^2 = 0.09$. Note that the magnitude of the main path is 0.762. Thus, the estimation error is quite high in this case. The second case we consider is the noise variance estimation error. The simulation setup is identical to the previous one. We let the channel responses be known and varied the noise variance from $0.1 \times \sigma_w^2$ to $10 \times \sigma_w^2$, where σ_w^2 is the actual noise variance. We find that the optimal soft-decision parallel interference cancellation performance is almost unaffected. Thus, we conclude that the optimal partial

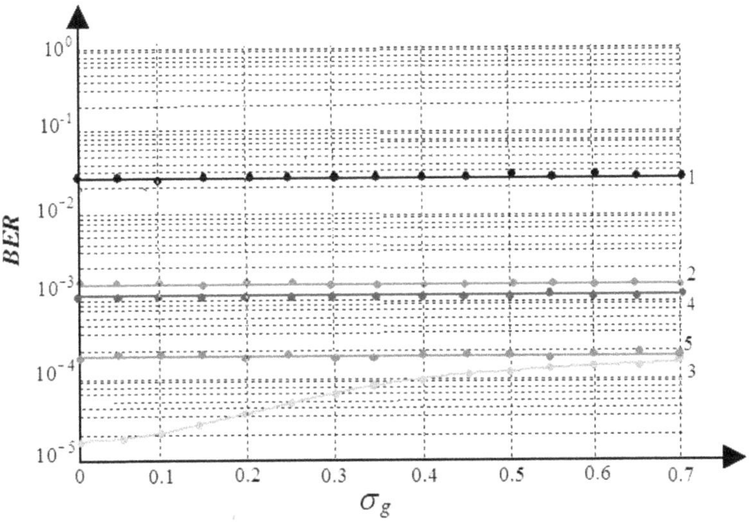

Figure 19.34. *BER* performance with channel estimation error (aperiodic spreading codes, multipath channels, $K = 6$, $E_b/\mathcal{N}_0 = 10$ dB, and perfect power control): 1—the Rake receiver; 2—the generalized receiver; 3—the generalized receiver with the two-stage partial soft-decision interference cancellation; 4—the generalized receiver with the two-stage full soft-decision interference cancellation; 5—the generalized receiver with the three-stage full soft-decision interference cancellation.

soft-decision parallel interference cancellation has good immunity to parameter estimation errors.

19.5 Conclusions

New improved blind multiuser detection techniques are proposed for both the downlink of the synchronous DS-CDMA wireless communication system and uplink of the asynchronous DS-CDMA wireless communication system. The new techniques make use of an important cross-correlation matrix between the adjacent symbols as a constraint to suppress the effect of interfering users. Two improved blind multiuser generalized receivers are developed based on different optimal criteria with the constraint constructed by the cross-correlation matrix. The proposed generalized receivers can be implemented blindly only with the channel estimation of the desired user. Simulation results show that the proposed improved blind generalized receivers provide a substantial performance gain over the conventional blind detectors.

We have investigated the performance of the broadband MC DS-CDMA wireless communication system using space-time spreading-assisted transmit diversity when the frequency-selective Rayleigh fading channels are considered. The issue of parameter design has been investigated motivated by the objective to ensure the same broadband MC DS-CDMA wireless communication system is equipped to provide efficient communications in various fading channels having different grade of frequency selectivity. The *BER* performance of the broadband MC DS-CDMA wireless communication system using space-time spreading has been evaluated both analytically and by simulation.

Furthermore, we have considered the capacity extension achievable by the space-time spreading-assisted broadband MC DS-CDMA wireless communication system with the aid of *TF*-domain spreading. The corresponding *BER* performance has been investigated in the context of the multiuser and single-user generalized detectors, single-user correlation detector and multiuser decorrelating detector for transmissions over the frequency-selective Rayleigh fading channels. In summary, the broadband MC DS-CDMA wireless communication system using space-time spreading-assisted transmit diversity has the following characteristics.

- By appropriately selecting the system parameters, the same broadband MC DS-CDMA wireless communication system using the space-time spreading-assisted transmit diversity is rendered capable of achieving similar *BER* performance in various communication environments characterized by different grades of frequency selectivity.
- It is capable of mitigating the peak-to-average power fluctuation experienced, since with the advent of direct-sequence spreading of the subcarriers, we require only a decreased number of subcarriers.
- Using multiple transmit antennas in the broadband MC DS-CDMA wireless communication system makes it capable of providing transmit diversity and, simultaneously, suppressing the multiuser interference. The associated space-time spreading transmit diversity scheme used in the broadband MC

DS-CDMA wireless communication system can be designed to maintain constant diversity gain in various fading channels having a different grade of frequency selectivity.

- When the space-time spreading-assisted broadband MC DS-CDMA wireless communication system employs both T-domain spreading and F-domain spreading, the maximum number of users supported becomes significantly higher than that employing solely T-domain spreading. The higher number of users supported is achieved without any trade-off imposed on the achievable diversity order.

The capacity and error probability of STBCs employed by DS-CDMA wireless communication system with STBC constructed on the basis of the generalized approach to signal processing in noise have been studied in fading channels for q-ary signal constellations. Rayleigh, Rician, and Nakagami-m fading channels were investigated for PAM, PSK, and QAM modulations. The closed form of the error probabilities under employment of the generalized receiver based on the generalized approach to signal processing in noise were derived for various fading and modulation combinations. This analysis has been employed to determine the performance of STBC multiuser DS-CDMA wireless communication system. Comparative analysis concerning implementation of the generalized receiver and correlation one in DS-CDMA wireless communication system with STBCs demonstrates a great superiority in favour of the first.

In DS-CDMA wireless communication systems, MAI is considered as the main factor in the system performance degradation. Among multiuser detection schemes, the generalized receiver with parallel interference cancellation is considered as a simple and effective approach. It has been shown that the performance of the generalized receiver with parallel interference cancellation can be further improved if interference is not fully cancelled. The performance of the generalized receiver with partial parallel interference cancellation depends totally on the partial cancellation factors. Thus, how to determine the partial cancellation factors optimally is then of great concern.

We have considered the generalized receiver with two-stage decoupled partial soft-decision interference cancellation and derived a set of closed-form solutions for the case of optimal partial cancellation factors. These partial cancellation factors are useful for periodic and aperiodic spreading codes in channels with the additive white Gaussian noise and those in multipath channels. Simulation results show that the derived optimal partial cancellation factors agree closely with empirical optimal partial cancellation factors. The performance of the generalized receiver with optimal two-stage partial soft-decision parallel interference cancellation outperforms the performance of the conventional generalized receiver when the number of users is more than 10 and has superiority in comparison with the generalized receiver with two-stage full soft-decision parallel interference cancellation and even with three-stage full soft-decision parallel interference cancellation.

We have also shown that the performance of the generalized receiver with derived partial cancellation factors is not sensitive to parameter estimation errors. The optimal partial cancellation factors for aperiodic spreading code systems in AWGN channel have a simple expression. This will be a great advantage for real- world applications since the optimal partial cancellation factors can be determined efficiently online in a time-varying environment.

We are mainly concerned with BPSK modulation. Note that the same result can be extended to accommodate QAM modulation. In this case, however, we have to take the interference between in-phase quadrature components into account. It turns out that for the in-phase or quadrature component of one user, we may treat the number of interfering users as $2K - 1$.

Appendix A

Proof of *Proposition* 5

Referring to the method in [26], we use the Lagrange multiplier to resolve the problem in *Proposition* 5. For the cost function in (19.61), we have

$$\begin{aligned}\mathbf{T}^{d}_{opt} &= \arg\min_{\mathbf{d}} |\mathbf{d}^H\mathbf{H}|^2 + \mathscr{R}\{\boldsymbol{\lambda}_1^*(\mathbf{h}_1^H\mathbf{d} - \mathbf{1}) + \boldsymbol{\lambda}_2^H(\overline{\mathbf{Y}}^H\mathbf{d} - \bar{\mathbf{h}}_1)\} \\ &= (\mathbf{H}\mathbf{H}^H)^{\bar{*}}(\boldsymbol{\lambda}_1\mathbf{h}_1 + \overline{\mathbf{Y}}\boldsymbol{\lambda}_2).\end{aligned} \tag{19.310}$$

Combining the constraint $\mathbf{h}_1^H\mathbf{d} = \mathbf{1}$ with (19.310), we obtain

$$\mathbf{h}_1^H(\mathbf{H}\mathbf{H}^H)^{\bar{*}}(\boldsymbol{\lambda}_1\mathbf{h}_1 + \overline{\mathbf{Y}}\boldsymbol{\lambda}_2) = \mathbf{1}. \tag{19.311}$$

Hence, it is easy to obtain

$$\boldsymbol{\lambda}_1 = \frac{\mathbf{1}}{\mathbf{h}_1^H(\mathbf{H}\mathbf{H}^H)^{\bar{*}}\mathbf{h}_1}[\mathbf{1} - \mathbf{h}_1^H(\mathbf{H}\mathbf{H}^H)^{\bar{*}}\overline{\mathbf{Y}}\boldsymbol{\lambda}_2]. \tag{19.312}$$

Substituting (19.312) into (19.310), we have

$$\mathbf{T}^{d}_{opt} = \frac{(\mathbf{H}\mathbf{H}^H)^{\bar{*}}}{\mathbf{h}_1^H(\mathbf{H}\mathbf{H}^H)^{\bar{*}}\mathbf{h}_1}[\mathbf{h}_1 - \mathbf{h}_1\mathbf{h}_1^H(\mathbf{H}\mathbf{H}^H)^{\bar{*}}\overline{\mathbf{Y}}\boldsymbol{\lambda}_2 + \mathbf{h}_1^H(\mathbf{H}\mathbf{H}^H)^{\bar{*}}\mathbf{h}_1\overline{\mathbf{Y}}\boldsymbol{\lambda}_2]. \tag{19.313}$$

Combining the constraint

$$(\mathbf{T}^{d}_{opt})^H\overline{\mathbf{Y}} = \bar{\mathbf{h}}_1^H \tag{19.314}$$

with (19.313) and denoting

$$\boldsymbol{\alpha} \cong \bar{\mathbf{h}}_1^H(\mathbf{H}\mathbf{H}^H)^{\bar{*}}\mathbf{h}_1, \tag{19.315}$$

we obtain

$$\boldsymbol{\lambda}_2 = [\boldsymbol{\alpha}\overline{\mathbf{Y}}^H(\mathbf{H}\mathbf{H}^H)^{\bar{*}}\overline{\mathbf{Y}} - \overline{\mathbf{Y}}^H(\mathbf{H}\mathbf{H}^H)^{\bar{*}}\mathbf{h}_1\mathbf{h}_1^H(\mathbf{H}\mathbf{H}^H)^{\bar{*}}\overline{\mathbf{Y}}]^{\bar{*}}[\boldsymbol{\alpha}\bar{\mathbf{h}}_1 - \overline{\mathbf{Y}}^H(\mathbf{H}\mathbf{H}^H)^{\bar{*}}\mathbf{h}_1]. \tag{19.316}$$

According to the eigendecomposition in (19.25), we can make the replacement

$$(\mathbf{H}\mathbf{H}^H)^{\bar{*}} = \mathbf{U}_s(\boldsymbol{\Lambda}_s - \sigma^2\mathbf{I}_L)^{-1}\mathbf{U}_s^H. \tag{19.317}$$

We then rewrite the vectors $\boldsymbol{\alpha}$ and $\boldsymbol{\lambda}_2$ in the following form

$$\boldsymbol{\alpha} = \mathbf{h}_1^H \mathbf{U}_s(\boldsymbol{\Lambda}_s - \sigma^2 \mathbf{I}_L)^{-1} \mathbf{U}_s^H \mathbf{h}_1; \tag{19.318}$$

$$\begin{aligned}\boldsymbol{\lambda}_2 = {} & [\boldsymbol{\alpha}\overline{\mathbf{Y}}^H \mathbf{U}_s(\boldsymbol{\Lambda}_s - \sigma^2 \mathbf{I}_L)^{-1} \mathbf{U}_s^H \overline{\mathbf{Y}} - \overline{\mathbf{Y}}^H \mathbf{U}_s(\boldsymbol{\Lambda}_s - \sigma^2 \mathbf{I}_L)^{-1} \mathbf{U}_s^H \mathbf{h}_1 \mathbf{h}_1^H \mathbf{U}_s(\boldsymbol{\Lambda}_s - \sigma^2 \mathbf{I}_L)^{-1} \mathbf{U}_s^H \overline{\mathbf{Y}}]^{\bar{*}} \\ & \times [\boldsymbol{\alpha}\overline{\mathbf{h}}_1 - \overline{\mathbf{Y}}^H \mathbf{U}_s(\boldsymbol{\Lambda}_s - \sigma^2 \mathbf{I}_L)^{-1} \mathbf{U}_s^H \mathbf{h}_1] \\ = {} & [\boldsymbol{\alpha}\overline{\mathbf{Y}}^H \mathbf{U}_s(\boldsymbol{\Lambda}_s - \sigma^2 \mathbf{I}_L)^{-1} \mathbf{U}_s^H \overline{\mathbf{Y}} - \boldsymbol{\theta}\boldsymbol{\theta}^H]^{\bar{*}} [\boldsymbol{\alpha}\overline{\mathbf{h}}_1 - \boldsymbol{\theta}],\end{aligned} \tag{19.319}$$

where

$$\boldsymbol{\theta} \cong \overline{\mathbf{Y}}^H \mathbf{U}_s(\boldsymbol{\Lambda}_s - \sigma^2 \mathbf{I}_L)^{-1} \mathbf{U}_s^H \mathbf{h}_1. \tag{19.320}$$

Substituting the vectors $\boldsymbol{\alpha}$ and $\boldsymbol{\theta}$ into (19.312), it is easy to obtain

$$\boldsymbol{\lambda}_1 = \frac{1}{\boldsymbol{\alpha}}[\mathbf{1} - \mathbf{h}_1^H \mathbf{U}_s(\boldsymbol{\Lambda}_s - \sigma^2 \mathbf{I}_L)^{-1} \mathbf{U}_s^H \overline{\mathbf{Y}} \boldsymbol{\lambda}_2] = \frac{1}{\boldsymbol{\alpha}}[\mathbf{1} - \boldsymbol{\theta}^H \boldsymbol{\lambda}_2]. \tag{19.321}$$

Finally, the proposed generalized receiver is given by

$$\mathbf{T}_{opt}^d = \mathbf{U}_s(\boldsymbol{\Lambda}_s - \sigma^2 \mathbf{I}_L)^{-1} \mathbf{U}_s^H (\boldsymbol{\lambda}_1 \mathbf{h}_1 + \overline{\mathbf{Y}} \boldsymbol{\lambda}_2). \tag{19.322}$$

Appendix B

Proof of *Proposition* 6

Similar to the proof of *Proposition* 5, we use the Lagrange multiplier to resolve the problem in *Proposition* 6. For the cost function in (19.64), we have

$$\begin{aligned}\mathbf{T}_{opt}^m &= \arg\min_{\mathbf{m}} E\{|\mathbf{b}_1(n) - \mathbf{m}^H \mathbf{y}_1(n)|^2\} + \mathscr{R}\{\boldsymbol{\lambda}_1^*(\mathbf{h}_1^H \mathbf{m} - \mathbf{1}) + \boldsymbol{\lambda}_2^H(\overline{\mathbf{Y}}^H \mathbf{m} - \overline{\mathbf{h}}_1)\} \\ &= \arg\min_{\mathbf{m}} \mathbf{m}^H \mathbf{Y} \mathbf{m} - 2\mathscr{R}\{\boldsymbol{\lambda}_1^*(\mathbf{h}_1^H \mathbf{m}\} + \mathscr{R}\{\boldsymbol{\lambda}_1^*(\mathbf{h}_1^H \mathbf{m} - \mathbf{1}) + \overline{\boldsymbol{\lambda}}_2^H(\overline{\mathbf{Y}}^H \mathbf{m} - \overline{\mathbf{h}}_1)\}.\end{aligned} \tag{19.323}$$

Denoting the vector $\overline{\boldsymbol{\lambda}}_1 = \boldsymbol{\lambda}_1 - \mathbf{2}$ and substituting the vector $\overline{\boldsymbol{\lambda}}_1$ into (19.323), we obtain

$$\begin{aligned}\mathbf{T}_{opt}^m &= \arg\min_{\mathbf{m}} \mathbf{m}^H \mathbf{Y} \mathbf{m} + \mathscr{R}\{\overline{\boldsymbol{\lambda}}_1^*(\mathbf{h}_1^H \mathbf{m} - \mathbf{1}) + \overline{\boldsymbol{\lambda}}_2^H(\overline{\mathbf{Y}}^H \mathbf{m} - \overline{\mathbf{h}}_1)\} \\ &= \mathbf{Y}^{-1}(\overline{\boldsymbol{\lambda}}_1 \mathbf{h}_1 + \overline{\mathbf{Y}} \overline{\boldsymbol{\lambda}}_2).\end{aligned} \tag{19.324}$$

Referring to (19.312)–(19.316) and denoting

$$\overline{\boldsymbol{\alpha}} \cong \mathbf{h}_1^H \mathbf{Y}^{-1} \mathbf{h}_1, \tag{19.325}$$

we have

$$\overline{\boldsymbol{\lambda}}_1 = \frac{1}{\boldsymbol{\alpha}}[\mathbf{1} - \mathbf{h}_1^H \mathbf{Y}^{-1} \overline{\mathbf{Y}} \overline{\boldsymbol{\lambda}}_2]; \tag{19.326}$$

$$\overline{\boldsymbol{\lambda}}_2 = [\boldsymbol{\alpha}\overline{\mathbf{Y}}^H \mathbf{Y}^{-1} \overline{\mathbf{Y}} - \overline{\mathbf{Y}}^H \mathbf{Y}^{-1} \mathbf{h}_1 \mathbf{h}_1^H \mathbf{Y}^{-1} \overline{\mathbf{Y}}]^{\bar{*}} [\overline{\boldsymbol{\alpha}} \overline{\mathbf{h}}_1 - \overline{\mathbf{Y}}^H \mathbf{Y}^{-1} \mathbf{h}_1]. \tag{19.327}$$

It is seen from (19.40) and (19.49) that the vector $\mathbf{h}_1$ and the matrix $\overline{\mathbf{Y}} \in$ range ($\mathbf{U}_s$), i.e.

$$\mathbf{h}_1^H \mathbf{U}_s = \mathbf{0} \text{ and } \overline{\mathbf{Y}}^H \mathbf{U}_s = \mathbf{0}. \tag{19.328}$$

Thus, by denoting

$$\overline{\boldsymbol{\theta}} \cong \overline{\mathbf{Y}}^H \mathbf{U}_s \boldsymbol{\Lambda}_s^{-1} \mathbf{U}_s^H \mathbf{h}_1, \tag{19.329}$$

we can rewrite the vectors $\overline{\boldsymbol{\alpha}}$, $\overline{\boldsymbol{\lambda}}_1$, and $\overline{\boldsymbol{\lambda}}_2$ in the following subspace form:

$$\overline{\boldsymbol{\alpha}} = \mathbf{h}_1^H \mathbf{U}_s \boldsymbol{\Lambda}_s^{-1} \mathbf{U}_s^H \mathbf{h}_1; \tag{19.330}$$

$$\begin{aligned} \overline{\boldsymbol{\lambda}}_2 &= [\overline{\boldsymbol{\alpha}} \overline{\mathbf{Y}}^H \mathbf{U}_s \boldsymbol{\Lambda}_s^{-1} \mathbf{U}_s^H \overline{\mathbf{Y}} - \overline{\mathbf{Y}}^H \mathbf{U}_s \boldsymbol{\Lambda}_s^{-1} \mathbf{U}_s^H \mathbf{h}_1 \mathbf{h}_1^H \mathbf{U}_s \boldsymbol{\Lambda}_s^{-1} \mathbf{U}_s^H \overline{\mathbf{Y}}]^{\ast} [\overline{\boldsymbol{\alpha}} \overline{\mathbf{h}}_1 - \overline{\mathbf{Y}}^H \mathbf{U}_s \boldsymbol{\Lambda}_s^{-1} \mathbf{U}_s^H \mathbf{h}_1] \\ &= [\overline{\boldsymbol{\alpha}} \overline{\mathbf{Y}}^H \mathbf{U}_s \boldsymbol{\Lambda}_s^{-1} \mathbf{U}_s^H \overline{\mathbf{Y}} - \overline{\boldsymbol{\theta}} \overline{\boldsymbol{\theta}}^H]^{\ast} [\overline{\boldsymbol{\alpha}} \overline{\mathbf{h}}_1 - \overline{\boldsymbol{\theta}}]; \end{aligned} \tag{19.331}$$

$$\overline{\boldsymbol{\lambda}}_1 = \frac{1}{\boldsymbol{\alpha}} [\mathbf{1} - \mathbf{h}_1^H \mathbf{U}_s \boldsymbol{\Lambda}_s^{-1} \mathbf{U}_s^H \overline{\mathbf{Y}} \overline{\boldsymbol{\lambda}}_2] = \frac{1}{\boldsymbol{\alpha}} [\mathbf{1} - \overline{\boldsymbol{\theta}}^H \overline{\boldsymbol{\lambda}}_2]. \tag{19.332}$$

Finally, the proposed detector can be given by

$$\mathbf{T}_{opt}^m = \mathbf{U}_s \boldsymbol{\Lambda}_s^{-1} \mathbf{U}_s^H (\overline{\boldsymbol{\lambda}}_1 \mathbf{h}_1 + \overline{\mathbf{Y}} \overline{\boldsymbol{\lambda}}_2). \tag{19.333}$$

Appendix C

Using integration by parts, the proof of (19.171) is as follows:

$$\begin{aligned} g(L) &= \int_0^\infty Q(\sqrt{ax}) x^{L-1} \exp\{-x/u\} dx \\ &= -\int_0^\infty Q(\sqrt{ax}) x^{L-1} u d\{\exp[-x/u]\} + \int_0^\infty \exp\{-x/u\} u [Q(\sqrt{ax}) x^{L-1}] dx \\ &= u(L-1) \int_0^\infty \exp\{-x/u\} Q(\sqrt{ax}) x^{L-2} dx - u\sqrt{a/8\pi} \int_0^\infty x^{L-3/2} \\ &\quad \times \exp\{-x/u\} \exp\{-ax/2\} dx \\ &= u(L-1) g(L-1) - \frac{1}{2} u^L \mu \left(\frac{1-\mu^2}{4} \right)^{L-1} \frac{(2L-2)!}{(L-1)!}, \end{aligned} \tag{19.334}$$

where

$$\mu = \sqrt{\frac{au}{2+au}}. \tag{19.335}$$

Repeating the process, we have

$$g(L) = u^{L-1} \Gamma(L) g(1) - \frac{1}{2} u^L \Gamma(L) \sum_{k=2}^{L} \mu \left(\frac{1-\mu^2}{4} \right)^{k-1} \binom{2k-2}{k-1}. \tag{19.336}$$

Now, using the fact that

$$g(1) = \int_0^\infty Q(\sqrt{ax})\exp\{-x/u\}dx = \frac{1}{2}u(1 - \mu), \tag{19.337}$$

we obtain (19.172)

$$g(L) = \frac{1}{2}u^L\Gamma(L)\left[1 - \sum_{k=0}^{L-1}\mu\left(\frac{1-\mu^2}{4}\right)^k\binom{2k}{k}\right]. \tag{19.338}$$

Appendix D

The truncation of (19.198) to the first L terms will introduce the error

$$\begin{aligned} \text{Error} = \lambda\sum_{i=L}^{\infty}\mu\left(\frac{1-\mu^2}{4}\right)^{MN+i}\binom{2(MN+i)}{MN+i} \\ \times\left[1 - \sum_{n=0}^{i}\frac{(MNK)^n\exp\{-MNK\}}{\Gamma(n+1)}\right]. \end{aligned} \tag{19.339}$$

Given the fact that

$$4^{-MN-i}\binom{2(MN+i)}{MN+i} < 1 \tag{19.340}$$

for all i, we have

$$\begin{aligned} &\lambda\sum_{i=L}^{\infty}\mu\left(\frac{1-\mu^2}{4}\right)^{MN+i}\binom{2(MN+i)}{MN+i}\left[1 - \sum_{n=0}^{i}\frac{(MNK)^n\exp\{-MNK\}}{\Gamma(n+1)}\right] \\ &<\lambda\mu\sum_{i=L}^{\infty}(1-\mu^2)^{MN+i}\left[1 - \sum_{n=0}^{L}\frac{(MNK)^n\exp\{-MNK\}}{\Gamma(n+1)}\right]. \end{aligned} \tag{19.341}$$

The right-hand side of (19.334) can be simplified to

$$\begin{aligned} &\lambda\mu\sum_{i=L}^{\infty}(1-\mu^2)^{MN+i}\left[1 - \sum_{n=0}^{L}\frac{(MNK)^n\exp\{-MNK\}}{\Gamma(n+1)}\right] \\ &= \lambda\mu\left[1 - \sum_{n=0}^{L}\frac{(MNK)^n\exp\{-MNK\}}{\Gamma(n+1)}\right](1-\mu^2)^{MN+L}\sum_{i=0}^{\infty}(1-\mu^2)^i. \end{aligned} \tag{19.342}$$

Given that

$$\sum_{i=0}^{\infty}q^i = \frac{1}{1-q}, \quad -1 \leqslant q \leqslant 1 \tag{19.343}$$

(19.70) can be written as

$$\lambda\sum_{i=L}^{\infty}\mu\left(\frac{1-\mu^2}{4}\right)^{MN+i}\binom{2(MN+i)}{MN+i}\left[1-\sum_{n=0}^{i}\frac{(MNK)^n\exp\{-MNK\}}{\Gamma(n+1)}\right]$$

$$<\lambda\frac{(1-\mu^2)^{MN+L}}{\mu}\left[1-\sum_{n=0}^{L}\frac{(MNK)^n\exp\{-MNK\}}{\Gamma(n+1)}\right]. \tag{19.344}$$

Thus, truncation of (19.198) to the first N terms will introduce the following error in the probability of error.

$$\text{Error}=\lambda\left[1-\sum_{n=0}^{L}\frac{(MNK)^n\exp\{-MNK\}}{\Gamma(n+1)}\right](1-\mu^2)^{MN+L}. \tag{19.345}$$

Appendix E

Periodic code system optimal PCFs for asynchronous AWGN channels

Let $b_{k,j}$ denote the ith bit for the kth user and τ_k is the user delay. Then the received signal for asynchronous channels can then be represented in the following form

$$x(t)=\sum_k\sum_i b_{k,i}a_k(t-iT-\tau_k)\Pi_T(t-iT-\tau_k)+w(t). \tag{19.346}$$

We further define the relative delay between the users j and k as $\tau_{j,k}=\tau_j-\tau_k$, and the cross-correlation functions are given by

$$\rho_{jk}(\tau_{jk})=\begin{cases}\displaystyle\int_{T+\tau_{jk}}^{T} a_j(t-\tau_{jk}-T)a_k(t)dt,\ \tau_{jk}<0,\\ \displaystyle\int_{\tau_{jk}}^{T} a_j(t-\tau_{jk})a_k(t)dt,\ \tau_{jk}\geqslant 0,\end{cases} \tag{19.347}$$

and

$$\hat{\rho}_{jk}(\tau_{jk})=\begin{cases}\displaystyle\int_{0}^{T+\tau_{jk}} a_j(t-\tau_{jk})a_k(t)dt,\ \tau_{jk}<0,\\ \displaystyle\int_{\tau_{jk}}^{T} a_j(t-\tau_{jk})a_k(t)dt,\ \tau_{jk}\geqslant 0.\end{cases} \tag{19.348}$$

For simplicity, we use ρ_{jk} and $\hat{\rho}_{jk}$ instead of $\rho_{jk}(\tau_{jk})$ and $\hat{\rho}_{jk}(\tau_{jk})$ in the sequel. The process at the output of the generalized receiver for the kth user's i—the bit is obtained in the following form

$$y_{k,i}=\int_{iT+\tau_k}^{(i+1)T+\tau_k}[2x(t)a_k(t-\tau_k)-x(t)x(t-\tau_k)+\eta_k(t)\eta_k(t-\tau_k)]dt$$

$$= A_j b_{k,i} + \sum_{j \neq k} A_j (b_{j,i-l_{jk}} \hat{\rho}_{jk} + b_{j,i-l_{jk}+1} \rho_{jk}) + \xi_{k,i}, \tag{19.349}$$

where the delay index and noise term are expressed as l_{jk} and ξ_{ki}. They are defined as

$$l_{jk} = \begin{cases} 1\,, & \tau_{jk} \geqslant 0 \\ 0\,, & \text{otherwise} \end{cases} \tag{19.350}$$

and (see figure 19.1 and (19.37))

$$\xi_{ki} = \int_{iT+\tau_k}^{(i+1)T+\tau_k} [\eta_k(t)\eta_k(t-\tau_k) - \zeta_k(t)\zeta_k(t-\tau_k)]dt \tag{19.351}$$

The regenerated received signal using partial soft-decision parallel interference cancellation is given by

$$\hat{x}_k(t) = x(t) - C_k \sum_{j \neq k} \sum_i y_{j,i} a_j(t - iT - \tau_j) \Pi_T(t - iT - \tau_j). \tag{19.352}$$

Thus, the second stage output can be presented in the following form

$$z_{k,i} = \int_{iT+\tau_k}^{(i+1)T+\tau_k} [2\hat{x}(t)a_k(t-\tau_k) - \hat{x}(t)\hat{x}(t-\tau_k) + \eta_k(t)\eta_k(t-\tau_k)]dt$$

$$= y_{k,i} - C_k \sum_{j \neq k} (y_{j,i-l_{jk}} \hat{\rho}_{jk} + y_{j,i-l_{jk}+1} \rho_{jk})$$

$$= A_k b_{k,i} + \sum_{j \neq k} A_j (b_{j,i-l_{jk}} \hat{\rho}_{jk} + b_{j,i-l_{jk}+1} \rho_{jk}) + \xi_{k,i} - C_k \sum_{j \neq k} \{ A_j (b_{j,i-l_{jk}} \hat{\rho}_{jk} + b_{j,i-l_{jk}+1} \rho_{jk})$$

$$+ \sum_{m \neq j} A_m (b_{m,i-l_{mj}-l_{jk}} \hat{\rho}_{mj} \hat{\rho}_{jk} + b_{m,i-l_{mj}-l_{jk}+1} \rho_{mj} \hat{\rho}_{jk} + b_{m,i-l_{mj}-l_{jk+1}} \hat{\rho}_{mj} \rho_{jk} + b_{m,i-l_{mj}-l_{jk}+2} \rho_{mj} \rho_{jk})$$

$$+ \xi_{j,i-l_{jk}} \hat{\rho}_{jk} + \xi_{j,i-l_{jk}+1} \rho_{jk} \}. \tag{19.353}$$

Without loss of generality, we may assume that $\tau_j \geqslant \tau_k$, $j \neq k$. Then $l_{jk} = 1$, $\forall j$ and the result can be simplified to

$$z_{k,i} = A_k b_{k,i} \left\{ 1 - C_k \sum_{j \neq k} (\hat{\rho}_{jk}^2 + \rho_{jk}^2) \right\} - A_k C_k \sum_{j \neq k} (b_{k,i-1} + b_{k,i+1}) \hat{\rho}_{jk} \rho_{jk}$$

$$- C_k \sum_{j \neq k} \sum_{m \neq j,k}^{\tau_m \leqslant \tau_j} A_j b_{j,i-2} \hat{\rho}_{jm} \hat{\rho}_{mk} - C_k \sum_{j \neq k} \sum_{m \neq j,k}^{\tau_m \leqslant \tau_j} A_j b_{j,i+1} \rho_{jm} \rho_{mk}$$

$$+ \sum_{j \neq k} A_j b_{j,i-1} \Phi_{jk} + \sum_{j \neq k} A_j b_{j,i} \Psi_{jk} + \xi_{k,i} - C_k \sum_{j \neq k} (\xi_{j,i-l_{jk}} \hat{\rho}_{jk} + \xi_{j,i-l_{jk}+1} \rho_{jk}), \tag{19.354}$$

where Φ_{jk} and Ψ_{jk} are defined in the following form

$$\Phi_{jk} = \hat{\rho}_{jk}(1 - C_k) - C_k\left\{\sum_{m\neq j,k}^{\tau_m>\tau_j} \hat{\rho}_{jm}\hat{\rho}_{mk} + \sum_{m\neq j,k}^{\tau_m\leqslant\tau_j} (\rho_{jm}\hat{\rho}_{mk} + \hat{\rho}_{jm}\rho_{mk})\right\}, \tag{19.355}$$

$$\Psi_{jk} = \rho_{jk}(1 - C_k) - C_k\left\{\sum_{m\neq j,k}^{\tau_m\leqslant\tau_j} \rho_{jm}\rho_{mk} + \sum_{m\neq j,k}^{\tau_m>\tau_j} (\rho_{jm}\hat{\rho}_{mk} + \hat{\rho}_{jm}\rho_{mk})\right\}, \tag{19.356}$$

The squared mean for $z_{k,i}$ is obtained from (19.248) and (19.354) in the following form

$$\mathscr{M}_k = A_k^2(1 - C_k\Lambda_k)^2, \tag{19.357}$$

where

$$\Lambda_k = \sum_{j\neq k}(\hat{\rho}_{jk}^2 + \rho_{jk}^2). \tag{19.358}$$

Similarly, the variance can also be obtained as

$$\mathscr{V}_k = \sigma_w^2(\Omega_{1,k}C_k^2 - 2\Omega_{2,k}C_k + \Omega_{3,k}), \tag{19.359}$$

where $\Omega_{i,k}$, $1 \leqslant i \leqslant 3$ are defined in the following form

$$\begin{aligned}\Omega_{1,k} = {} & 2SNR_k^2\sum_{j\neq k}\hat{\rho}_{jk}^2\rho_{jk}^2 + \sum_{j\neq k}SNR_j^2(\Phi_{jk}^2 + \Psi_{jk}^2)\\ & + \left(\sum_{j\neq k}\sum_{m\leqslant j,k}^{\tau_m\leqslant\tau_j} SNR_j^2\hat{\rho}_{jm}\hat{\rho}_{mk}\right)^2 + \left(\sum_{j\neq k}\sum_{m\leqslant j,k}^{\tau_m>\tau_j} SNR_j^2\rho_{jm}\rho_{mk}\right)^2 + \sum_{j\neq k}\hat{\rho}_{jk}^2 + \rho_{jk}^2\\ & + \sum_{j\neq k}\sum_{m\leqslant j,k}^{\tau_m\leqslant\tau_j} 2(\rho_{jm}\hat{\rho}_{jk}\hat{\rho}_{mk} + \rho_{jm}\rho_{jk}\rho_{mk} + \hat{\rho}_{jm}\hat{\rho}_{jk}\rho_{mk})\\ & + \sum_{j\neq k}\sum_{m\leqslant j,k}^{\tau_m\leqslant\tau_j} (\rho_{jm}\hat{\rho}_{jk}\hat{\rho}_{mk} + \rho_{jm}\rho_{jk}\rho_{mk});\end{aligned} \tag{19.360}$$

$$\Omega_{2,k} = \sum_{j\neq k}SNR_j^2(\hat{\rho}_{jk}\Phi_{jk} + \rho_{jk}\Psi_{jk}) + \sum_{j\neq k}(\hat{\rho}_{jk}^2 + \rho_{jk}^2); \tag{19.361}$$

$$\Omega_{3,k} = \sum_{j\neq k}SNR_j^2(\hat{\rho}_{jk}^2 + \rho_{jk}^2) + 1. \tag{19.362}$$

Thus, the optimal partial cancellation factor can be obtained by substituting (19.358) and (19.360)–(19.362) into (19.260).

Appendix F

Expressions for the expected terms in (19.288)–(19.290)

Extending the definition in (19.300) we have

$$\mathscr{F}_{jk}(p_1, q_1, \dots, p_i, q_i) = N^i E\{\chi_{jk}(p_1, q_1), \dots, \chi_{jk}(p_i, q_i)\} \tag{19.363}$$

where i is the integer. To make this expression simpler, we let $\mathbf{w}_i = \{p_i, q_i\}$. Then, (19.363) can be presented in the following form

$$\mathscr{F}_{jk}(\mathbf{w}_1, \dots, \mathbf{w}_i) = N^i E\{\chi_{jk}(\mathbf{w}_1), \dots, \chi_{jk}(\mathbf{w}_i)\}. \tag{19.364}$$

We further omit the subscript in $\mathscr{F}(\cdot)$ and use the following notational substitution:

$$\sum_{\mathbf{w}_i=0}^{L^2} \rightarrow \sum_{p_i=0}^{L} \sum_{q_i=0}^{L}. \tag{19.365}$$

In what follows, six expected terms are given without detailed derivation

$$E_{\mathscr{L}}(\rho_{jk}^2 \rho_j) = \frac{1}{N^3} \sum_{\mathbf{w}_1=1}^{L^2} \sum_{\mathbf{w}_2=1}^{L^2} \sum_{\mathbf{w}_4=1}^{L^2} h_{jk}(\mathbf{w}_1) h_{jk}(\mathbf{w}_2) h_{jj}(\mathbf{w}_3) \mathscr{F}(\mathbf{w}_1, \mathbf{w}_2, \mathbf{w}_3),$$

if $\tau_{jk}(\mathbf{w}_1) = \tau_{jk}(\mathbf{w}_2),\ \tau_{jj}(\mathbf{w}_3) = 0$,

$$\mathscr{F}(\mathbf{w}_1, \mathbf{w}_2, \mathbf{w}_3) = N(N - |\tau_{jk}(\mathbf{w}_1)|).$$

Else if $|\tau_{jk}(\mathbf{w}_1) - \tau_{jk}(\mathbf{w}_2)| = |\tau_{jj}(\mathbf{w}_3)|$,

$$\mathscr{F}(\mathbf{w}_1, \mathbf{w}_2, \mathbf{w}_3) = N - \max\{|\tau_{jk}(\mathbf{w}_1)|, |\tau_{jk}(\mathbf{w}_2)|, |\tau_{jj}(\mathbf{w}_3)|\}.$$

Else

$$\mathscr{F}(\mathbf{w}_1, \mathbf{w}_2, \mathbf{w}_3) = 0 \tag{19.366}$$

$$E_{\mathscr{L}}(\rho_{jk}^2 \rho_{jm} \rho_{mk}) = \frac{1}{N^3} \sum_{\mathbf{w}_1=1}^{L^2} \sum_{\mathbf{w}_2=1}^{L^2} \sum_{\mathbf{w}_3=1}^{L^2} h_{jk}(\mathbf{w}_1) h_{jm}(\mathbf{w}_2) h_{mk}(\mathbf{w}_3) \mathscr{F}(\mathbf{w}_1, \mathbf{w}_2, \mathbf{w}_3)$$

if $\tau_{jm}(\mathbf{w}_1) + \tau_{mk}(\mathbf{w}_2) = \tau_{jk}(\mathbf{w}_3)$,

$$\mathscr{F}(\mathbf{w}_1, \mathbf{w}_2, \mathbf{w}_3) = N - \max\{|\tau_{jk}(\mathbf{w}_1)|, |\tau_{jm}(\mathbf{w}_2)|, |\tau_{mk}(\mathbf{w}_3)|\}.$$

Else

$$\mathscr{F}(\mathbf{w}_1, \mathbf{w}_2, \mathbf{w}_3) = 0 \tag{19.367}$$

$$E_{\mathscr{L}}(\rho_{jk}^2 \rho_j) = \frac{1}{N^4} \sum_{\mathbf{w}_1=1}^{L^2} \sum_{\mathbf{w}_2=1}^{L^2} \sum_{\mathbf{w}_3=1}^{L^2} \sum_{\mathbf{w}_4=1}^{L^2} h_{jk}(\mathbf{w}_1) h_{jk}(\mathbf{w}_2) h_{jj}(\mathbf{w}_3) h_{jj}(\mathbf{w}_4) \mathscr{F}(\mathbf{w}_1, \mathbf{w}_2, \mathbf{w}_3, \mathbf{w}_4),$$

if $\tau_{jk}(\mathbf{w}_1) = \tau_{jk}(\mathbf{w}_2),\ \tau_{jj}(\mathbf{w}_3) = \tau_{jj}(\mathbf{w}_4) = 0$,

$$\mathscr{F}(\mathbf{w}_1,\mathbf{w}_2,\mathbf{w}_3,\mathbf{w}_4) = N^2(N - |\tau_{jk}(\mathbf{w}_1)|).$$

Else if $\tau_{jk}(\mathbf{w}_1) = \tau_{jk}(\mathbf{w}_2),\ \tau_{jj}(\mathbf{w}_3) = \tau_{jj}(\mathbf{w}_4)$,

$$\mathscr{F}(\mathbf{w}_1,\mathbf{w}_2,\mathbf{w}_3,\mathbf{w}_4) = (N - |\tau_{jk}(\mathbf{w}_1)|)(N - |\tau_{jj}(\mathbf{w}_3)|).$$

Else if $|\tau_{jk}(\mathbf{w}_1) - \tau_{jk}(\mathbf{w}_2)| = \tau_{jj}(\mathbf{w}_3),\ \tau_{jj}(\mathbf{w}_4) = 0$,
or $|\tau_{jk}(\mathbf{w}_1) - \tau_{jk}(\mathbf{w}_2)| = \tau_{jj}(\mathbf{w}_4),\ \tau_{jj}(\mathbf{w}_3) = 0$,

$$\mathscr{F}(\mathbf{w}_1,\mathbf{w}_2,\mathbf{w}_3,\mathbf{w}_4) = N - \max\{|\tau_{jk}(\mathbf{w}_1)|,|\tau_{jk}(\mathbf{w}_2)|,|\tau_{jj}(\mathbf{w}_3)|,|\tau_{jj}(\mathbf{w}_4)|\}.$$

Else if $|\tau_{jk}(\mathbf{w}_1) - \tau_{jk}(\mathbf{w}_2)| = |\tau_{jj}(\mathbf{w}_3) \pm \tau_{jj}(\mathbf{w}_4)|,\ \tau_{jk}(\mathbf{w}_1) \neq 0,\ \tau_{jk}(\mathbf{w}_2) \neq 0$,

$$\mathscr{F}(\mathbf{w}_1,\mathbf{w}_2,\mathbf{w}_3,\mathbf{w}_4) = N - \max\{|\tau_{jk}(\mathbf{w}_1)|,|\tau_{jk}(\mathbf{w}_2)|,|\tau_{jj}(\mathbf{w}_3)|,|\tau_{jj}(\mathbf{w}_4)|,$$

$$|\tau_{jk}(\mathbf{w}_1) - \tau_{jk}(\mathbf{w}_2)|,|\tau_{jk}(\mathbf{w}_1) \pm \tau_{jj}(\mathbf{w}_3)|,|\tau_{jk}(\mathbf{w}_1) \pm \tau_{jj}(\mathbf{w}_4)|\}.$$

Else if $|\tau_{jk}(\mathbf{w}_1) - \tau_{jk}(\mathbf{w}_2)| = |\tau_{jj}(\mathbf{w}_3) \pm \tau_{jj}(\mathbf{w}_4)|$,

$$\mathscr{F}(\mathbf{w}_1,\mathbf{w}_2,\mathbf{w}_3,\mathbf{w}_4) = N - \max\{|\tau_{jk}(\mathbf{w}_1)|,|\tau_{jk}(\mathbf{w}_2)|,|\tau_{jj}(\mathbf{w}_3)|,|\tau_{jj}(\mathbf{w}_4)|\}.$$

Else

$$\mathscr{F}(\mathbf{w}_1,\mathbf{w}_2,\mathbf{w}_3,\mathbf{w}_4) = 0. \tag{19.368}$$

$$E_{\mathscr{L}}(\rho_{jm}^2\rho_{mk}^2) = \frac{1}{N^4}\sum_{\mathbf{w}_1=1}^{L^2}\sum_{\mathbf{w}_2=1}^{L^2}\sum_{\mathbf{w}_3=1}^{L^2}\sum_{\mathbf{w}_4=1}^{L^2} h_{jm}(\mathbf{w}_1)h_{jm}(\mathbf{w}_2)h_{mk}(\mathbf{w}_3)h_{mk}(\mathbf{w}_4)\mathscr{F}(\mathbf{w}_1,\mathbf{w}_2,\mathbf{w}_3,\mathbf{w}_4),$$

if $\tau_{jm}(\mathbf{w}_1) = \tau_{jm}(\mathbf{w}_2),\ \tau_{mk}(\mathbf{w}_3) = \tau_{mk}(\mathbf{w}_4)$,

$$\mathscr{F}(\mathbf{w}_1,\mathbf{w}_2,\mathbf{w}_3,\mathbf{w}_4) = (N - |\tau_{jm}(\mathbf{w}_1)|)(N - |\tau_{mk}(\mathbf{w}_3)|).$$

Else, if

$$|\tau_{jm}(\mathbf{w}_1) - \tau_{jm}(\mathbf{w}_2)| = |\tau_{mk}(\mathbf{w}_3) - \tau_{mk}(\mathbf{w}_4)|,$$

$$\tau_{jm}(\mathbf{w}_1) \neq 0,\ \tau_{jm}(\mathbf{w}_2) \neq 0,\ \tau_{mk}(\mathbf{w}_3) \neq 0,\ \tau_{mk}(\mathbf{w}_4) \neq 0,$$

$$\mathscr{F}(\mathbf{w}_1,\mathbf{w}_2,\mathbf{w}_3,\mathbf{w}_4)$$

$$= N - \max\{|\tau_{jm}(\mathbf{w}_1)|,|\tau_{jm}(\mathbf{w}_2)|,|\tau_{mk}(\mathbf{w}_3)|,|\tau_{mk}(\mathbf{w}_4)|,|\tau_{jm}(\mathbf{w}_1) - \tau_{jm}(\mathbf{w}_2)|,|\tau_{jm}(\mathbf{w}_1) + \tau_{mk}(\mathbf{w}_3)|,$$

$$|\tau_{jm}(\mathbf{w}_1) + \tau_{mk}(\mathbf{w}_4)|\}.$$

Else if $|\tau_{jm}(\mathbf{w}_1) - \tau_{jm}(\mathbf{w}_2)| = |\tau_{mk}(\mathbf{w}_3) - \tau_{mk}(\mathbf{w}_4)|$,

$$\mathscr{F}(\mathbf{w}_1,\mathbf{w}_2,\mathbf{w}_3,\mathbf{w}_4) = N - \max\{|\tau_{jm}(\mathbf{w}_1)|,|\tau_{jm}(\mathbf{w}_2)|,|\tau_{mk}(\mathbf{w}_3)|,|\tau_{mk}(\mathbf{w}_4)|\}.$$

Else

$$\mathscr{F}(\mathbf{w}_1,\mathbf{w}_2,\mathbf{w}_3,\mathbf{w}_4) = 0. \tag{19.369}$$

$$E_{\mathscr{L}}(\rho_{jm}\rho_{mk}\rho_{jn}\rho_{nk}) = \frac{1}{N^4}\sum_{\mathbf{w}_1=1}^{L^2}\sum_{\mathbf{w}_2=1}^{L^2}\sum_{\mathbf{w}_3=1}^{L^2}\sum_{\mathbf{w}_4=1}^{L^2} h_{jm}(\mathbf{w}_1)h_{mk}(\mathbf{w}_2)h_{jn}(\mathbf{w}_3)h_{nk}(\mathbf{w}_4)\mathscr{F}(\mathbf{w}_1,\mathbf{w}_2,\mathbf{w}_3,\mathbf{w}_4),$$

if

$$\tau_{jm}(\mathbf{w}_1) + \tau_{mk}(\mathbf{w}_2) = \tau_{jn}(\mathbf{w}_3) + \tau_{nk}(\mathbf{w}_4),\ \tau_{jm}(\mathbf{w}_1) \neq 0,\ \tau_{mk}(\mathbf{w}_2) \neq 0,\ \tau_{jn}(\mathbf{w}_3) \neq 0,\ \tau_{nk}(\mathbf{w}_4) \neq 0,$$

$$\mathscr{F}(\mathbf{w}_1,\mathbf{w}_2,\mathbf{w}_3,\mathbf{w}_4)$$

$$= N - \max\{|\tau_{jm}(\mathbf{w}_1)|,|\tau_{mk}(\mathbf{w}_2)|,|\tau_{jn}(\mathbf{w}_3)|,|\tau_{nk}(\mathbf{w}_4)|,|\tau_{jm}(\mathbf{w}_1) + \tau_{mk}(\mathbf{w}_2)|,|\tau_{jm}(\mathbf{w}_1) - \tau_{jn}(\mathbf{w}_3)|\}.$$

Else if $\tau_{jm}(\mathbf{w}_1) + \tau_{mk}(\mathbf{w}_2) = \tau_{jn}(\mathbf{w}_3) + \tau_{nk}(\mathbf{w}_4)$,

$$\mathscr{F}(\mathbf{w}_1,\mathbf{w}_2,\mathbf{w}_3,\mathbf{w}_4) = N - \max\{|\tau_{jm}(\mathbf{w}_1)|,|\tau_{mk}(\mathbf{w}_2)|,|\tau_{jn}(\mathbf{w}_3)|,|\tau_{nk}(\mathbf{w}_4)|\}.$$

Else

$$\mathscr{F}(\mathbf{w}_1,\mathbf{w}_2,\mathbf{w}_3,\mathbf{w}_4) = 0 \tag{19.370}$$

$$E_{\mathscr{L}}(\rho_{jm}\rho_{mk}\rho_{jk}\rho_{jj}) = \frac{1}{N^4}\sum_{\mathbf{w}_1=1}^{L^2}\sum_{\mathbf{w}_2=1}^{L^2}\sum_{\mathbf{w}_3=1}^{L^2}\sum_{\mathbf{w}_4=1}^{L^2} h_{jm}(\mathbf{w}_1)h_{mk}(\mathbf{w}_2)h_{jk}(\mathbf{w}_3)h_{jj}(\mathbf{w}_4)\mathscr{F}(\mathbf{w}_1,\mathbf{w}_2,\mathbf{w}_3,\mathbf{w}_4),$$

if $\tau_{jm}(\mathbf{w}_1) + \tau_{mk}(\mathbf{w}_2) = \tau_{jk}(\mathbf{w}_3),\ \tau_{jj}(\mathbf{w}_4) = 0$,

$$\mathscr{F}(\mathbf{w}_1,\mathbf{w}_2,\mathbf{w}_3,\mathbf{w}_4) = N\{N - \max\{|\tau_{jm}(\mathbf{w}_1)|,|\tau_{mk}(\mathbf{w}_2)|,|\tau_{jk}(\mathbf{w}_3)|\}\}.$$

Else if

$$|\tau_{jm}(\mathbf{w}_1) + \tau_{mk}(\mathbf{w}_2) - \tau_{jk}(\mathbf{w}_3)| = |\tau_{jj}(\mathbf{w}_4)|, \tau_{jm}(\mathbf{w}_1) \neq 0,\ \tau_{mk}(\mathbf{w}_2) \neq 0,\ \tau_{jk}(\mathbf{w}_3) \neq 0,$$

$$\mathscr{F}(\mathbf{w}_1,\mathbf{w}_2,\mathbf{w}_3,\mathbf{w}_4)$$

$$= N - \max\{|\tau_{jm}(\mathbf{w}_1)|,|\tau_{mk}(\mathbf{w}_2)|,|\tau_{jk}(\mathbf{w}_3)|,|\tau_{jj}(\mathbf{w}_4)|,|\tau_{jm}(\mathbf{w}_1) + \tau_{mk}(\mathbf{w}_2)|,|\tau_{jm}(\mathbf{w}_1) \pm \tau_{jj}(\mathbf{w}_4)|\}.$$

Else if $|\tau_{jm}(\mathbf{w}_1) + \tau_{mk}(\mathbf{w}_2) - \tau_{jk}(\mathbf{w}_3)| = |\tau_{jj}(\mathbf{w}_4)|$,

$$\mathscr{F}(\mathbf{w}_1,\mathbf{w}_2,\mathbf{w}_3,\mathbf{w}_4) = N - \max\{|\tau_{jm}(\mathbf{w}_1)|,|\tau_{mk}(\mathbf{w}_2)|,|\tau_{jk}(\mathbf{w}_3)|,|\tau_{jj}(\mathbf{w}_4)|\}.$$

Else

$$\mathscr{F}(\mathbf{w}_1,\mathbf{w}_2,\mathbf{w}_3,\mathbf{w}_4) = 0. \tag{19.371}$$

The first term is (19.366). The second term is (19.367). The third term is (19.368). The fourth term is (19.369). The fifth term is (19.370). The sixth term is (19.371).

References

[1] Verdu S 1983 Minimum probability of error for asynchronous multiple access communication systems *Proc. of IEEE Military Communications Conf.* vol 1*(November 1983)* 213–9

[2] Chen D S and Roy S 1994 An adaptive multiuser receiver for CDMA systems *IEEE J. Sel. Areas Commun.* **12** 808–16

[3] Pados D A and Batalama S N 1997 Low-complexity blind detection of DS-CDMA signals: auxilary-vector receivers *IEEE Trans. Commun.* **41** 1586–94
[4] Madhow U and Honig M L 1994 MMSE interference suppression for direct-sequence spread spectrum CDMA *IEEE Trans. Commun.* **38** 3178–88
[5] Poor H V and Verdu S 1997 Probability error in MMSE multiuser detection *IEEE Transactions on Information Theory.* **43** 858–71
[6] Verdu S 1998 *Multiuser Detection* (Cambridge: Cambridge University Press) p 474
[7] Honig M, Madhow U and Verdu S 1995 Blind adaptive multiuser detection *IEEE Trans. Inform. Theory* **41** 944–60
[8] Xia X-G 2000 *Modulated Coding for Intersymbol Interference Channels* (Boca Raton, FL: CRC Press)
[9] Wang X 2000 Advanced signal processing for wireless multimedia communications *Signal Process.* **3** 23–30
[10] Wang X and Poor H V 2004 *Wireless Communication Systems: Advanced Techniques for Signal Reception* (Englewood Cliffs, NJ: Prentice-Hall Professional)
[11] Wang X and Poor H V 1998 Blind multiuser detection: a subspace approach *IEEE Trans. Inf. Theory* **44** 677–90
[12] Gelli G, Paura L and Verde F 2009 Blind direct multiuser detection for uplink MC-CDMA: performance analysis and robust implementation *EURASIP J. Wirel. Commun. Netw.* **1** 125–40
[13] Fahmy Y A, Mourad H-A M and Al-Hussainin E K 2006 A generalized blind adaptive multi-user detection algorithm for multipath Rayleigh fading channel employed in a MIMO system *J. Commun. Netw.* **8** 290–6
[14] Schodorf J B and Williams D B 1997 Array processing techniques for multiuser detection *IEEE Trans. Commun.* **41** 1375–8
[15] Chkeif A, Abed-Meraim K and Kawas Kaleh G 2000 Spatio-temporal blind adaptive multiuser detection *IEEE Trans. Comun.* **48** 729–32
[16] Meng Y, Meng L-M, Hua J-Y and Peng H 2009 Subspace-based MMSE group-blind multiuser detection algorithm *J. Syst. Eng. Electron.* **31** 1573–6
[17] Bouziane R and Killey R I 2015 Blind symbol synchronization for direct detection optical OFDM using a reduced number of virtual subcarriers *Opt. Express* **23** 6444–54
[18] Pinchas M 2016 Inspection of the output of a convolution and deconvolution process from the leading digit point of view—Benfold's law *J. Signal Inform. Process.* **7** 227–51
[19] Ruan X, Li C, Yang W, Cui G, Zhu H, Zhou Z, Dai Y and Shi X 2017 Blind sequence detection using reservoir computing *Dig. Signal Process.* **62** 81–90
[20] Tsatsanis M K and Xu Z 1998 Performance analysis of minimum variance CDMA receivers *IEEE Trans. Signal Process.* **49** 3014–22
[21] Yin J 2017 Blind adaptive multiuser detection for under acoustic communications with mobile interfering users *J. Acoust. Soc. Am.* **147**
[22] Zhou W and Nelson J K 2018 Blind sequential detection for sparse ISI channels *EURASIP J. Adv. Signal Process.* **2018** 6
[23] Sanchez J A H and Gomez P E J 2018 Effects of blind channel equalization using the regressive accelerator algorithm *Sist. Telemat.* **16** 9–20
[24] Scarano G, Petroni A, Biagi M and Cusani R 2019 Blind fractionally spaced channel equalization for shallow water PPM digital communication links *Sensors* **19** 4604

[25] Xu Z and Tsatsanis M K 2001 Blind adaptive algorithms for minimum variance CDMA receivers *IEEE Trans. Commun.* **49** 180–94

[26] Wang X and Host-Madsen A 1999 Group-blind multiuser detection for uplink CDMA *IEEE J. Select. Areas Commun.* **17** 1971–84

[27] Tuzlukov V 1998 A new approach to signal detection theory *Dig. Signal Process.* **8** 166–84

[28] Tuzlukov V 2001 *Signal Detection Theory* (New York: Springer)

[29] Tuzlukov V 2002 *Signal Processing Noise* (Boca Raton, FL: CRC Press)

[30] Tuzlukov V 2005 *Signal and Image Processing in Navigational Systems* (Boca Raton, FL: CRC Press)

[31] Tsatsanis M K and Giannakis G B 1996 Optimal decorrelating receivers for DS-CDMA systems: a signal processing framework *IEEE Trans. Signal Process.* **44** 3044–55

[32] Loubation P and Moulines E 2000 On blind multiuser forward link channel estimation by the subspace method: Identifiability results *IEEE Trans. Signal Process.* **48** 2366–76

[33] Wang X and Poor H V 1998 Blind equalization and multiuser detection in dispersive CDMA channels *IEEE Trans. Commun.* **46** 91–103

[34] Maximov M 1956 Joint correlation of fluctuative noise at outputs of frequency filters *Radio Eng.* **9** 28–38

[35] Chernyak Y 1960 Joint correlation of noise voltage at the outputs of amplifiers with no overlapping responses *Radio Phys. Electron.* **4** 551–61

[36] Tuzlukov V 2011 DS-CDMA downlink systems with fading channel employing the generalized detector *Digital Signal Process.* **21** 725–33

[37] Tuzlukov V 2011 Signal processing by generalized detector in DS-CDMA wireless communication systems with frequency-selective channels *Circuits Syst. Signal Process.* **30** 1197–230

[38] Shbat M and Tuzlukov V 2019 Primary signal detection algorithms for spectrum sensing at low SNR over fading channels in cognitive radio *Digital Signal Process.* **93** 187–207

[39] Shbat M and Tuzlukov V 2014 Evaluation of detection performance under employment of the generalized detector in radar sensor systems *Radioengineering* **23** 50–65

[40] Reynolds D, Wang X and Poor H V 2002 Blind adaptive space-time multiuser detection with multiple transmitter and receiver antennas *IEEE Trans. Signal Process.* **50** 1261–76

[41] Sajeed S, Chaiwongkhot P and Huang A *et al* 2021 An approach for security evaluation and certification of a complete quantum communication system *Sci. Rep.* **11** 5110

[42] Shbat M and Tuzlukov V 2014 Definition of adaptive detection threshold under employment of the generalized detector in radar sensor systems *IET Signal Proc.* **8** 622–32

[43] Shbat M and Tuzlukov V 2015 SNR wall effect alleviation by generalized detector employment in cognitive radio networks *Sensors* **15** 16105–35

[44] Tuzlukov V 2021 Signal processing by generalized receiver in wireless communications systems over fading channels *Advances Signal Processing* (Barcelona: IFSA Publishing Corp.) ch 2 pp 55–111

[45] Tarokh V, Seshadri N and Calderbank A R 1998 Space-time codes for high data rate wireless communication: performance criterion and code construction *IEEE Trans. Inf. Theory* **44** 744–65

[46] Alamouti S M 1998 A simple transmit diversity technique for wireless communications *IEEE J. Sel. Areas Commun.* **16** 1451–8

[47] Hanzo L, Liew T H and Yeap B L 2002 *Turbo Equalization and Space-Time Coding* (New York: Wiley)

[48] Yang L-L and Hanzo L 2005 Performance of broadband multicarrier DS-CDMA using space-time spreading-assisted transmit diversity *IEEE Trans. Wirel. Commun.* **4** 885–94

[49] Hochwald B, Marzetta T L and Papadias C B 2001 A transmitter diversity scheme for wideband CDMA systems based on space-time spreading *IEEE J. Sel. Areas Commun.* **19** 48–60

[50] Hanzo L, Yang L-L, Kuan E-L and Yen K 2003 *Single- and Multi-Carrier DS-CDMA: Multi-User Detection, Space-Time Spreading, Synchronization, Standards and Networking* (New York: IEEE Press/Wiley)

[51] Yang L-L and Hanzo L 2005 Adaptive space-time spreading-assisted wideband CDMA systems communicating over dispersive Nakagami-m fading channels *EURASIP J. Wirel. Commun. Netw.* **2005** 364197

[52] Telecomm. Industry Association (TIA) 2000 , TIA/EIA Interim Standard: Physical Layer Standard for CDMA2000 Standards for Spread Spectrum Systems

[53] Yang L-L and Hanzo L 2005 Performance of generalized multicarrier CDMA in a multi-path fading channels *IEEE Trans. Commun.* **4** 885–94

[54] Sourour E A and Nakagawa M 2005 Performance of orthogonal multicarrier CDMA in themultipath fading channels *IEEE Trans. Commun.* **4** 356–67

[55] Kondo S and Milstein L B 1996 Performance of multicarrier DS CDMA systems *IEEE Trans. Commun.* **44** 238–46

[56] Proakis J G and Salehi M 2007 *Digital Communications* 5th edn (New York: McGraw-Hill, USA)

[57] Feng J and Zhao X 2016 Asymptotic performance analysis of free-space optical links with transmit diversity *J. Opt. Soc. Korea* **20** 451–63

[58] Wen M, Beixiong Z, Kim K J, Di Renzo M, Tsiftsis T A, Chen K-C and Al-Dahir N 2019 A survey on spatial modulation in emerging wireless systems: research progress and applications *IEEE J. Sel. Areas Commun.* **37** 1949–72

[59] Tuzlukov V 2013 *Communication Systems: New Research* ed V Tuzlukov (New York: NOVA Science Publisher, Inc.)

[60] Tuzlukov V 2021 Interference cancellation for MIMO systems employing the generalized receiver with high spectral efficiency *WSEAS Trans. Signal Process.* **17** 1–15

[61] Minallah N, Ullah K, Fruda J, Cengiz K and Javed M A 2021 Transmit diversity gain technique aided irregular channel coding for mobile video transmission Entropy *(Basel)* **23** 235–43

[62] Minallah N, Ahmed I, Ijaz M, Khan A S, Hasan L and Rehman A 2021 On the performance of self-concatenated coding for wireless mobile video transmission using DSTS-SP-assisted smart antenna system *Wirel. Commun. Mobile Comput.* **2021** 8836808

[63] Shbat M and Tuzlukov V 2015 Generalized detector as a spectrum sensor in cognitive radio networks *Radioengineering* **24** 558–71

[64] Tarokh V, Jafarkhani H and Claderbank A R 1999 Space-time block codes from orthogonal designs *IEEE Trans. Inf. Theory* **45** 1456–67

[65] Tarokh V 1999 Space-time block coding for wireless communications: performance results *IEEE J.Sel. Areas Commun.* **16** 1452–8

[66] Sandhu S and Paulraj A 2000 Space-time block codes: a capacity perspective *IEEE Commun. Lett.* **4** 384–6

[67] Yue D W and Wang Q 2009 Capacity of orthogonal space-time block codes in MISO fading channels with co-channel interferences and noise *Sci. China. Ser. F: Inform. Sci.* **52** 1697–703

[68] Dai L, Sfar S and Lefaief K B 2006 Optimal antenna selection based on capacity maximization for MIMO systems in correlated channels *IEEE Trans. Commun.* **54** 563–73

[69] Li X, Luo T, Yue G and Yin C 2001 A squaring method to simplify the decoding of orthogonal space-time block codes *IEEE Trans. Commun.* **49** 1700–3

[70] Taricco G and Biglieri E 2002 Exact pair wise error probability of space-time codes *IEEE Trans. Inform. Theory* **48** 510–14

[71] Kshetrimayum R 2017 Advanced topics in MIMO wireless communications *Fundamentals of MIMO Wireless Communications* (Cambridge: Cambridge University Press) pp 270–308

[72] Martins C, Brandao M L and Brandani da Silva E 2019 New space-time block codes from spectral norm *PLoS One.* **14** e02227083

[73] Alouini M-S and Goldsmith A J 1999 A unified approach for calculating error rates of linearly-modulated signals over generalized fading channels *IEEE Trans. Commun.* **47** 1324–34

[74] Foschini G J and Gans M J 1998 On limits of wireless communications in a fading environment when using multiple antennas *Wirel. Pers. Commun.* **6** 311–35

[75] Ungerboeck G 1982 Channel coding with multiple-phase signals *IEEE Trans. Inform. Theory* **28** 55–67

[76] Baccarelli E and Fasano A 2000 Some simple bounds on the symmetric capacity and outage probability for QAM wireless channels with Rice and Nakagami fading *IEEE J. Sel. Areas Commun.* **18** 361–8

[77] Baccarelli E 2001 Evaluation of the reliable data rates supported by multiple-antenna coded wireless links for QAM transmissions *IEEE J. Sel. Areas Commun.* **19** 295–304

[78] Proakis G J 1968 Probabilities of error for adaptive reception of M-phase signals *IEEE Trans. Commun. Technol.* **16** 71–81

[79] Shayesteh M and Aghamohammadi A 1995 On the error probability of linearly modulated signals on frequency-flat Rician, Rayleigh, and AWGN channels *IEEE Trans. Commun.* **43** 1454–66

[80] Wei S X 1994 An alternative derivation for the signal-to-noise ratio of a SSMA system *IEEE Trans. Commun.* **42** 2224–6

[81] Rappaport T S 1996 *Wireless Communications: Principles and Practice.* (Englewood Cliffs, NJ: Prentice-Hall)

[82] Verdu S , 1986 Minimum probability of error for asynchronous Gaussian multiple-access channels *IEEE Trans. Inf. Theory* **IT-32,1** 85–96

[83] Moshavi S 1996 Multiuser detection for DS-CDMA communications *IEEE Commun. Mag.* **34** 124–36

[84] Duel-Hallen A, Holtzman J and Zvonar Z 1995 Multiuser detection for CDMA systems *IEEE Pers. Commun.* **2** 46–58

[85] Xie Z, Short R T and Ruthforth C K 1990 A family of suboptimum detector for coherent multi-user communications *IEEE J. Sel. Areas Commun.* **8** 683–90

[86] Burhrer R M, Correal-Mendoza N S and Woerner B D 2000 A simulation comparison of multiuser receivers for cellular CDMA *IEEE Trans. Veh. Technol.* **59** 1065–85

[87] Wu W, Su W S and Yu-Tao 2001 A two-stage MMSE partial PIC receiver for multiuser detection *Proc. 2001 IEEE Third Workshop on Signal Processing Advances in Wireless Communications (SPFWC'01) (Taipei, Taiwan, March 20–23)*

[88] Lupas R and Verdu S 1989 Linear multiuser detectors for asynchronous code-division multiple-access channels *IEEE Trans. Inf. Theory* **IT-35** 123–36

[89] Lupas R and Verdu S 1990 Near-far resistance of multiuser detectors in asynchronous channels *IEEE Trans. Commun.* **35** 496–508
[90] Viterbi A J 1990 Very low rate convolutional codes for maximum theoretical performance of spread-spectrum multiple-access channels *IEEE J. Sel. Areas Commun.* **8** 641–9
[91] Hong S-C, Choi J, Jung Y-H and Lee Y H 2004 Constrained MMSE receivers for CDMA systems in frequency-selective fading channels *IEEE Trans. Wirel. Commun.* **3** 1393–8
[92] Holtzman J M 1994 Successive interference cancellation for direct sequence code division multiple access *IEEE Trans. Commun.* **19** 793–9
[93] Patel P and Holtzman J M 1994 Analysis of simple successive interference cancellation scheme in DS-CDMA system *IEEE J. Sel. Areas Commun.* **12** 796–807
[94] Ghotbi M and Soleymani M R 2004 Multiuser detection of DS-CDMA signals using parallel interference cancellation in satellite communications *IEEE J. Sel. Areas Commun.* **22** 584–93
[95] Varanasi M K and Aazhang B 1994 Multistage detection in asynchronous code-division multiple-access communications *IEEE J. Sel. Areas Commun.* **12** 796–807
[96] Buehrer R M and Woerner B D 1996 Analysis of adaptive multistage interference cancellation for CDMA using an improved Gaussian approximation *IEEE J.Trans. Commun.* **44** 1308–20
[97] Kohno R, Imai H, Hatori M and Pasupathy S 1990 An adaptive canceller of co-channel interference for spread-spectrum multiple-access communication networks in a power line *IEEE J. Sel. Areas Commun.* **8** 691–9
[98] Yoon Y, Kohno R and Imai H 1993 A spread-spectrum multi-access system with co-channel interference cancellation *IEEE J. Sel. Areas Commun.* **11** 1067–75
[99] Hsien Y-N and Wu W-R 2008 Performance analysis of an adaptive two-stage PIC CDMA receiver in AWGN channels *Signal Process.* **88** 1413–27
[100] Divsalar D, Simon M K and Raphaeli D 1998 Improved parallel interference cancellation for CDMA *IEEE Trans. Commun.* **46** 258–68
[101] Correal N S, Buehrer R M and Worner B D 1999 A DSP-based DS-CDMA multiuser receiver employing partial parallel interference cancellation *IEEE J. Sel. Areas Commun.* **17** 613–30
[102] Wen J-H, Chang C-W and Hung H-L 2009 Multiuser detection using TGA-based partial parallel interference cancellation for CDMA systems *Int. J. Innov. Comput. Inform. Control* **5** 2745–67
[103] Juntti M J and Latvaaho M 2000 Multiuser receivers for CDMA systems in Rayleigh fading channels *IEEE Trans. Veh. Technol.* **49** 885–99
[104] Chaonech H and Bouallegue R 2012 Multiuser detection in asynchronous multibeam communications *Int. J. Wirel. Mobile Netw.* **4** 21–34
[105] Li Y, Chtn M and Cheng S 2000 Determination of cancellation factors for soft-decision partial PIC detector in DS-CDMA Systems *Electron. Lett.* **36** 154–62
[106] Tuzlukov V 2011 Signal processing by generalized receiver in DS-CDMA wireless communication systems with optimal combining and partial cancellation EURASIP *J. Adv. Signal Process.* **2011** 913189
[107] Chaonech H and Bonallegue R 2012 Multiuser detection and channel estimation for multibeam satellite communications *Int. J. Comput. Netw. Commun.* **4** 163–74
[108] Xue G, Weng J, Le-Ngoc T and Tahar S 1999 Adaptive multistage parallel interference cancellation for CDMA IEEE *J. Sel. Areas Commun.* **17** 1815–27

[109] Buehrer R M, Nicoloso S P and Gollamudi S 1999 Linear versus nonlinear interference cancellation *J. Commun. Netw.* **1** 118–33
[110] Ravindrababu J and Krishna E V 2019 Rao, Interference reduction in fading environment using multistage multiuser detection technique *WSEAS Trans. Signal Process.* **15** 39–46
[111] Ravindrababu J, Krishna Rao E V and Raja Rao Y 2014 Interference cancellation and complexity reduction in multistage multiuser detection *WSEAS Trans. Commun.* **13** 62–70
[112] Wang J, Zhang S, Chen W, Rjng D and Yu Z 2018 Convex optimization-based multiuser detection in underwater acoustic sensor networks *Int. J. Distrib. Sens. Netw.* **14** 1–11
[113] Gou D, Rasmussen L K, Sun S and Lim T J 2000 A matrix-algebraic approach to linear parallel interference cancellation in CDMA *IEEE Trans. Commun.* **48** 152–61
[114] Ren Y, Zhu C and Xiao S 2018 Deformable faster R-CNN with aggregating multilayer features for partially occluded object detection in optical remote sensing images *Remote Sens.* **10** 1470
[115] Mandayam N B and Verdu S 1998 Analysis of an approximate decorrelating detector *Wirel. Pers. Commun.* **6** 97–111
[116] Buehrer R B and Nicoloso S P 1999 Comments on partial parallel interference cancellation for CDMA *IEEE Trans. Commun.* **47** 658–61
[117] Renucci P G and Woerner B D 1998 Optimization of soft interference cancellation for DS-CDMA *Electron Lett.* **34** 731–3
[118] Brown D R, Matani M, Veeravalli V V, Poor Y V and Johnson C R 2001 On the performance of linear parallel interference cancellation *IEEE Trans. Inf. Theory* **47** 1957–70
[119] Gou D, Verdu S and Rasmussen L K 2002 Asymptotic normality of linear multiuser receiver outputs *IEEE Trans. Inf. Theory* **48** 3080–95
[120] Kim S R, Choi I, Rang S and Lee J G 1998 Adaptive weighted parallel interference cancellation for CDMA systems *Electron. Lett.* **34** 2085–6
[121] Tuzlukov V 2009 Optimal combining, partial cancellation and channel estimation and correlation in DS-CDMA systems employing the generalized detector *WSEAS Trans. Commun.* **8** 718–33

IOP Publishing

Human-Assisted Intelligent Computing
Modeling, simulations and applications
Mukhdeep Singh Manshahia, Igor S Litvinchev, Gerhard-Wilhelm Weber, J Joshua Thomas and Pandian Vasant

Chapter 20

Critical success factors for successfully implementation of smart manufacturing in the context of Industry 4.0

U C Jha

Considering the Industry 4.0 context, smart manufacturing (SM) highlights the convergence of traditional production methods and digital techniques for modeling and analyzing the production system. Basically, its main goal is to assist product lifecycle management and to enable the development, through improvements and maturity evolution, of all aspects related to factory and product design. It is noticed there is a significant amount of information related to SM concepts and technologies, however, its implementation process is not widely framed. This paper aims to propose a set of critical success factors (CSFs) for SM implementation. For mapping CSFs we apply a research strategy based on academic literature review and consulting reports. Therefore, interviews were conducted for assessing digital manufacturing CSF influences in an automotive assembly factory. The main result is a conceptual framework to assist organizations in developing a strategy for SM implementation, and map for that purpose all the required resources and capabilities. This research contributes for updating digital manufacturing CSF discussion in the new context of Industry 4.0 and it provides a guide to checking organizational readiness for SM.

20.1 Introduction

Industry 4.0, also known as the Fourth Industrial Revolution, is based on the following concepts: CPS—cyber-physical systems (a fusion of the physical and the virtual worlds), the Internet of Things (IoT) and the Internet of Services. This scenario is already changing several aspects of manufacturing companies [1].

SM is a subject that is becoming highly relevant in the global technological scenario as one of the areas of knowledge within the Industry 4.0 agenda. Industry

doi:10.1088/978-0-7503-4801-0ch20

4.0 technologies such as IoT data analysis, Big Data, integrated communication, smart machines and autonomous robots are variables that also directly affect the context of digital manufacturing. This change in production context is occurring due to the new technologies and it requires a new analysis approach. Thus, Industry 4.0 has been converting aspects and variables that were previously not relevant (or nonexistent) in crucial variables to companies that aim to reach world-class excellence

Previous studies [3] have shown that publications on the subject of digital manufacturing have grown, with several publications about technologies related [2, 4–9], some research regarding content models [10–13], a few case studies [14–17] and a lack of in-depth studies of the implementation process in companies. Some studies about CSFs for digital manufacturing have been conducted, but did not consider this new manufacturing context. Thus, many relevant variables, both for implementation and use, were not included in those analyses.

There is a relevant mass of information about SM concept, SM applied technologies, however, are still scarce information of how the implementation process should be conducted and, consequently, which are its CSFs in an Industry 4.0 scenario.

Thus, this chapter aims to identify and map the Industry 4.0 CSFs for the introduction of SM.

For mapping CSF a research strategy was applied based on academic literature review and consulting reports. Therefore, interviews with digital manufacturing users/deployers were conducted at an automotive company to verify if the problems currently encountered in SM implementation are on the list of CSF, thus giving greater reliability to the factors compilation.

20.2 Literature review

In the literature, there are several definitions for SM or the smart factory. All of them converges in the technical point of view of digital technologies combination to facilitate the integration of product, process and resources information. However, there is a divergence of scope on those studies.

Some authors include activities related to factory floor, production planning and supply chain management [10, 18–20], while others authors restrict the scope to product, process and resource development departments [21–23]. This study uses the extended concept of SM, which in addition to developing a product design in digital platforms, produces and simulates prototypes based on process analysis and resource planning, also involves the collection, processing, analysis and real-time reporting of production planning, plant planning and integration with stakeholders. Therefore, SM represents the data across the entire product lifecycle.

From the management point of view, unlike isolated conducts of planning activities in traditional enterprises, SM focuses on integrated planning that includes all stakeholders in the planning process.

The main gain of using SM is that all aspects of the plant can be developed and improved until the physical product manufacturing meets all the goals in terms of quality, time and cost. Only when the digital product successfully crosses the production line in the digital factory is the product released for physical manufacturing [24]. Since the cost and time of correction in the virtual environment is substantially lower than the corrections made in the physical environment, it is clear the gains of companies that stand out in SM implementation.

20.3 Methodology

This study is divided into four steps: (i) literature review seeking the CSF for SM in the context of Industry 4.0; (ii) interviews with an automotive company's employees that are participating on SM implementation process to map the difficulties experienced; (iii) improvement of the CSF list based on the difficulties cited during the interviews; and (iv) analysis of results.

In the first step, we conducted a literature review on academic journals and consulting reports developed by organization specialized in concepts of Industry 4.0. From this information, it was possible to compile a set of CSFs for SM implementation.

During the second step, we performed interviews in an automotive multinational organization, which has a digital transformation vision in the context of Industry 4.0. This company has been conducting the SM implementation process during the last two years. These interviews aim to map the main organization difficulties during this process and to verify which CSFs were not well developed, as well as identify new variables that directly affect the success of the implementation project.

Twelve interviews were carried out with employees from different departments, involving: product and process engineering, layout development, equipment development and IT. Several departments were consulted enabling a global view of the company situation in relation to digital manufacturing.

To mitigate the risk of external influence (anchoring) on the answers, only an open question was used, thus leading each interviewee to show the difficulties experienced in SM context that influence their daily work. The interview question was: *'Currently, which are the main difficulties you see on the smart manufacturing implementation in the company? From technical and organizational aspects to financial and innovation aspects'.*

In the third step, an improvement of the initial CSF list was made based on the answers obtained with the interviews. For that, the causes of the current difficulties were analyzed to transform them into CSF. This process resulted in an improved list of issues that companies need to be aware of for adaptation in the new competitive scenario.

Finally, in the fourth step, the CSFs were categorized and analyzed. For this categorization, we used the risk breakdown structure proposed by PMI [22]: (i) technical: includes aspects such as technical, technology, complexity and interfaces, performance and quality; (ii) organizational: includes aspects such as estimates, planning, control and communication; (iii) project management: includes aspects such as project dependencies, resources, financing and prioritization; (iv) External: includes aspects such as subcontractors and suppliers, regulations, market and customer.

20.4 Results

During the literature review 70 CSFs were initially mapped and after an analysis to refine the list it was possible to compile them in 27 CSFs that directly affect the success of SM in the context of Industry 4.0, as is shown in table 20.2. The interviews conducted resulted in 20 difficulties related to the daily work considering SM concepts and tools. In order to contextualize them in the CSF it was necessary to identify the root causes of the problems. Table 20.1 lists the difficulties and classifies them according to the risk breakdown structure proposed by PMI.

The available infrastructure suggests itself to be a key difficulty reported. The appropriate data network has been shown to be relevant being cited seven times by the interviewees. The need of a viable speed for transfer data is justified by the large amount of data received and sent by users. Low productivity was noticed due the large file size, especially when dealing with computer-aided design (CAD) files, generating a low added value in the process of loading, sharing and saving files. In addition to the network speed, the lack of appropriate hardware that supports SM tools is also related to the infrastructure issue.

The planning of training programs was also a critical problem in the company, as it was cited five times and it was the root cause of other difficulties reported, such as the lack of technical knowledge and the low productivity. The high time demanded for learning is influenced by the complexity of SM tools. To solve this problem the

Table 20.1. List of difficulties.

Difficulties	Freq.	Tech.	Org.	P.M.	Ext.
1 Data network does not meet the minimum requirements	7	X			
2 Lack of specialized training	5		X		
3 Hardware does not meet the minimum requirements	4	X			
4 Lack of tools integration	3	X			
5 Lack of technical knowledge	3		X	X	
6 Low productivity	3	X	X	X	
7 Poorly defined scope for SM project	3		X	X	
8 Lack of internal stakeholders integration	2			X	
9 Limited licenses	2		X		
10 High financial investment	2		X		
11 Learning process to use SM technologies demands a lot of time	2		X	X	
12 High workload does not allow innovation activities	2		X	X	
13 Cultural barriers	1		X		
14 Lack of tool support	1	X		X	
15 Bureaucracy for decision-making	1		X		
16 Governmental aspects	1			X	
17 Lack of collaborative tools with suppliers	1	X		X	
18 Data management	1	X			
19 Poorly communication	1		X	X	
20 Lack of standardization for new technologies utilization	1			X	

Table 20.2. Critical success factors for smart manufacturing implementation.

Categories		CSF for SM implementation in the context of Industry 4.0	Literature review	Interview
	1	Data management interoperability related to data management (data migration, information management, differentiated file extensions) and tools and systems integration	X	X
	2	Operating system speed and ease software configuration	X	X
	3	Real-time data	X	
	4	Infrastructure and facilities for the project (rooms, computers, networks)	X	X
	5	System architecture that support data from IoT	X	
Technical	6	Connectivity	X	
	7	Ability to transform large amounts of data (Big Data) into knowledge and decision-making	X	
	8	Advanced robotics	X	
	9	Cybersecurity	X	
	10	Traceability	X	
	11	Logistic automation	X	
	12	Technical support for SM tools	X	X
	13	Availability of collaborative tools	X	
	14	User knowledge	X	X
	15	Training programs (project team, support team and users)	X	X
	16	Decision-makers trained and authorized (agility in decisions)	X	X
	17	Support and continuous commitment of top management	X	
	18	Economic and profitability analysis	X	X
Organizational	19	Centralized management of products, processes and resources	X	X
	20	Dynamic design of business processes and engineering	X	
	21	Be an attractive company seeking the best available resources	X	
	22	Rapid responses to market technological developments		X
	23	Innovation-driven culture	X	X
	24	Workload management to enable innovation activities		X

(*Continued*)

Table 20.2. (*Continued*)

Categories	CSF for SM implementation in the context of Industry 4.0	Literature review	Interview
Project	25 Implementation strategy (communication, planning, scope, objectives, roles, responsibilities, change management and support)	X	X
Management	26 Employee adherence, commitment and participation	X	
	27 Collaborative organizations with self-training teams	X	
	28 Composition of the project team	X	X
	29 Internal and external communication	X	X
	30 Research and development model	X	
	31 Partners with knowledge and experience	X	
Extern	32 Governmental aspects		X
	33 Integration with external suppliers		X
	34 Greater customer focus	X	

managers need to better plan the employees' workload seeking to enable new technologies adaptation.

However, other variables can be the root cause for this low productivity. Some interviewees mentioned that the traditional method was simpler and faster to perform their work activities than using SM tools. Besides the specialized training and the technical problems, it was noticed that the employees working on SM scenario had not yet understood its real benefits and proposal. Thus, the project scope (also referred to as a difficulty) was not well defined, since it is clear the doubts among the users regarding the scope of SM within the company. In summary, the root causes of low productivity can be: (i) lack of specialized training; (ii) lack of communication of the project scope for all stakeholders; (iii) workload management to enable innovation activities; and (iv) lack of appropriate infrastructure.

Technical support was also listed as a problem by the interviewees. Training programs alone are not enough, constant technical support is required for the successful SM implementation.

Besides the above, the lack of systems and tools integration was likewise reported as a difficulty. There is a huge diversity of systems for each department within the organization. This aspect directly affects the SM and its root cause is related to interoperability of different systems.

SM implementation success also depends on the change of the organization project structure, once the phase of numerical analysis using SM tools demands more time than the conventional method while providing more quality and complexity for analysis. However, the gain is perceived in the implantation phase, which is performed faster and has less reworks, reducing cost and improving quality.

The CSF related to financial issues influences several difficulties listed. The lack of appropriated infrastructure, the need of specialized training, skilled people working in the project and the limited licenses reflect on organization financial planning.

Issues related to organizational strategic management are found in cultural barriers and decision-making bureaucracy. Culture needs to be innovation-driven and employees need to be engaged in this project. Moreover, decision-making needs to be agile to keep up with the constant technologies that come from the current scenario.

On external context, the supply chain integration is also an objective of SM. It is necessary to have collaborative tools integrating the factory and its suppliers. During the interviews, we noticed a difficulty of sharing project information with all stakeholders. Furthermore, the government environment also influences SM, as some countries have protectionist markets and hamper import of both software and hardware technologies.

From these aspects raised by the company's employees and literature review it was possible to develop table 20.2 with a set of CSFs that need to be considered before SM implementation project kickoff in the context of Industry 4.0.

Most of the difficulties pointed out during the interviews come from poorly implemented CSFs already found in the literature and consulting reports. Four factors were added to this list: rapid responses to market technological developments, workload management to enable innovation activities, governmental aspects and integration with external suppliers.

Although SM is considered a technical matter, the influence of organizational factors is critical. The difficulties related to understanding the project scope and workload planning evince this fact. However, technical issues also need attention because they directly affect user performance.

Even though not all CSFs mapped in the literature have been cited in the interviews, it is necessary to consider them on SM implantation strategy.

20.5 Conclusion

It has become evident during the interviews that most of the difficulties pointed out regarding digital manufacturing are related to basic implementation requirements, such as system understanding, training, workload and infrastructure. It was also clear that complex factors, such as architecture for IoT data, cybersecurity and integrated management were not mentioned because it is still far from the daily reality of the employees.

Thus, it is noticeable that there is a low maturity of SM implementation, although it started the process two years ago. One of the key difficulties found is the misunderstanding about the real purpose of digital manufacturing. A clear project scope definition, difficulties and benefits in each phase, besides specialized training in the early stages of the project have shown potential for a successful implementation.

This study fulfilled its objective by presenting the CSFs for SM implementation in the new context of Industry 4.0. We presented a set of CSFs found in the literature and consulting reports, besides confronting these results with the SM users' feedback within a multinational automotive company.

For further studies, we suggest an extension of this research in companies on the process of SM implementation, seeking to expand and improve the list of CSFs. It is also suggested to prioritize the CSF and develop an organizational maturity assessment tool for SM implementation. The purpose of this tool is to enable enhanced decision-making by prioritizing factors since the beginning of the project and which organizational aspects should be improved for no delays or demotivation of the project stakeholders.

This research contributes for updating smart manufacturing CSF discussion in the new context of Industry 4.0 and it provides a guide to checking the organizational readiness for SM.

References

[1] Almada-Lobo F 2015 The Industry 4.0 revolution and the future of manufacturing execution systems *J. Innov. Manage.* **3** 16–21

[2] Duarte Filho N, Botelho S C, Carvalho J T, Marcos P B, Maffei R Q, Oliveira R R, Oliveira R R and Hax V A 2010 An immersive and collaborative visualization system for digital manufacturing *Int. J. Adv. Manu. Technol.* **50** 1253–61

[3] Ribeiro Da Silva E H D, Shinohara A C, Rocha L M, Pinheiro De Lima E and Deschamps F 2015 Análise de estudos na área de manufatura digital: uma revisão da literatura *Proc. of the Production Engineering Symp.* November 9–11 (Bauru, Brazil)

[4] Butterfield J, Mcclean A, Yan Yin R, Curran R, Burke B W and Devenney C 2010 Use of DM to improve management learning in aerospace assembly *J. Aircr.* **47** 315–22

[5] Shariatzadeha N, Sivarda G and Chena D 2012 Software evaluation criteria for rapid factory layout planning, design and simulation *Procedia CIRP* **3** 299–304

[6] Dombrowski U and Ernst S 2013 Scenario-based simulation approach for layout planning *Procedia CIRP* **12** 354–9

[7] Hincapié M, Ramírez M J, Valenzuela A and Valdez J A 2014 Mixing real and virtual components in automated manufacturing systems using PLM tools *Int. J. Interact. Des. Manuf.* **8** 209–30

[8] Chen-Fu C, Mitsuo G, Yongjiang S and Chia-Yu H 2014 Manufacturing intelligence and innovation for digital manufacturing and operational excellence *J. Intell. Manuf.* **25** 845–7

[9] Dulina L and Bartanusova M 2015 CAVE design using in digital factory *Procedia Eng.* **100** 291–298

[10] Bracht U and Masurat T 2005 The digital factory between vision and reality *Comput. Ind.* **56** 325–33

[11] Yon-Iun X and Zhou-Ping Y 2006 Digital manufacturing – the development direction of the manufacturing technology in 21st century *Front. Mech. Eng. Chin.* **1** 125–30

[12] Rohrlack T 2008 The Digital Factory – From Concept to Reality. Bentley solution for automobile manufacturers. White Pater

[13] Stef I, Draghici G and Draghici A 2013 Product design process model in the digital factory context *Procedia Technol.* **9** 451–62

[14] Kim H, Lee J, Park J, Park B and Jang D 2002 Applying digital manufacturing technology to ship production and the maritime environment *Integr. Manuf. Syst.* **13** 295–305

[15] Vidal O C, Kaminski P C and Netto S N 2009 Exemplos de aplicação do conceito de fábrica digital no planejamento de instalações para armação de carroçarias na indústria automobilística brasileira *Produto & Produção* **10** 75–84

[16] Fonseca J C 2013 Fatores de risco na implementação de um projeto de fábrica digital—Um estudo de caso em organização multinacional do setor automotivo *B.Sc. Dissertation* Federal University of Parana

[17] Caggiano A, Caiazzo F and Teti R 2015 Digital factory approach for flexible and efficient manufacturing systems in the aerospace industry *Procedia CIRP* **37** 122–7

[18] Zuelch G and Stowasser S 2005 The digital factory: an instrument of the present and the future *Comput. Ind.* **56** 323–4

[19] Zulch G and Grieger T 2005 Modelling of occupational health and safety aspects in the digital factory *Comput. Ind.* **56** 384–92

[20] Woerner J and Woern H 2005 A security architecture integrated co-operative engineering platform for organized model exchange in a digital factory environment *Comput. Ind.* **56** 347–60

[21] Wohlke G and Schiller E 2005 Digital planning validation in automotive industry *Comput. Ind.* **56** 393–405

[22] Kühn W 2008 Paradigm shift in simulation methodology and practice separation of modelling the physical system behavior and control modelling *Proc. of the 10th Int. Conf. on Computer Modeling and Simulation* April 1–3 (Cambridge, UK) 380–5

[23] Matsuda M, Kashiwase K and Sudo Y 2012 Agent oriented construction of a digital factory for validation of a production scenario *45th CIRP Conf. on Manufacturing Systems*

[24] PM 2008 *A Guide to Project Management Body of Knowledge—PMBOK®* (Pennsylvania, PA: Project Management Institute) 4th edn

Chapter 21

An efficient heart disease diagnosis prediction model using decision tree classifiers: Streamlit

D Doreen Hephzibah Miriam, C R Rene Robin, Rachel Nallathamby and B Yamini

The delay in predicting heart diseases or cardiovascular disease has lead to a large number of deaths in the past in both developing and developed countries. However, monitoring a patient throughout the day is not possible, especially when the number of patients are high. This chapter develops a prediction model using Streamlit and evaluated it using benchmarked University of California, Irvine (UCI) repository dataset for heart disease diagnosis which consists of various heart attributes of the patient. Its detects impending heart disease for patients using three novel algorithms: the Genetic Tree based Heart Predictor (GDH), Random Forest Based Heart Predictor (RFH) and Bayesian tree based Heart Predictor (BDH). The results are further evaluated using confusion matrix and cross-validation. The early detection of cardiovascular diseases and the causes that lead to it can help doctors to easily detect high risk patients, help introduce diet and lifestyle changes for patients that would reduce complications and also treat patients early preventing death. The study achieved 99% accuracy in decision tree algorithms that correctly predicts the cause of heart disease.

21.1 Introduction

Cardiovascular disease, otherwise known as heart disease, refers to problems of the heart and the associated blood vessels. The disease causes a large number of deaths despite new advances for diagnosis and treatment. The people who are at risk of developing cardiac disease are those who smoke/consume alcohol and have other health conditions like high blood pressure, diabetes, hypertension, cholesterol and obesity. Several health conditions increase the risk of developing heart disease, such as hypertension, untreated diabetes in addition to age and family history. Early detection of cardiovascular disease can decrease the mortality rate and help patients improve the quality of life.

doi:10.1088/978-0-7503-4801-0ch21

Nowadays, artificial intelligence is playing a huge role in the medical industry, helping physicians and medical researchers in predicting, classifying and diagnosing various diseases [1]. Machine learning technologies complemented by the knowledge of doctors can help screen people at risk. Machine learning algorithms provide the advantage of faster prediction and help in the diagnosis of serious heart conditions. The primary focus of researchers is to provide insight and transform healthcare [2]. The potential to integrate medicine and artificial intelligence allows doctors to make informed decisions with regard to the patient's health. Computer algorithms that can automate the process of learning play a critical role in analyzing the massive and complex data of the healthcare industry. The models use existing data as training data, and create a model that can identify patterns and predict the presence of the disease in new data. Various hidden patterns can also be found that will provide accurate predictions in the future [3]. Decision trees prove to be a great predictive modelling tool as they allow any Boolean function to be represented on the discrete attributes. Supervised learning followed by decision trees allow one to solve both classification and regression problems.

The structure of the chapter is as follows. In section 21.2, we review literature that discusses various machine learning algorithms and models that helped synthesize the data to support cardiologists in the treatment of cardiac disease. In section 21.3, the framework of the heart predictor model is detailed: the data is pre-processed, three different algorithms are applied to study the accuracy of prediction and the parameters are tuned to improve the accuracy of the models. In section 21.4 the performance is evaluated using different metrics, and section 21.5 is the sample output done using Streamlit. Section 21.6 discusses the final outcome of the research and future directions of research.

21.2 Literature review

Various papers and techniques proposed to diagnose heart disease are reviewed below. The merits and demerits of previous work done for prediction of heart disease is reviewed in detail in order to explain the importance of the proposed work.

Zriqat *et al* (2016) [4] developed an effective intelligent medical decision support system and proposed various methodologies to help physicians reduce medical costs and errors and achieved accuracy of 99%. Nichenametla *et al* (2018) [5] discussed an algorithm to predict heart disease using the naive Bayes decision tree but the dataset used was small. Maheswari *et al* (2019) [6] used naive Bayes techniques to retrieve patient details. The various symptoms of a heart disease patient were used to make an intelligent prediction. Jindal *et al* (2020) [7] used K-Nearest Neighbor, Random Classifier and Logistic Regression models to predict if a patient was likely to get heart disease based on the medical history of the patient. The paper concluded that by using machine learning techniques, disease prediction could be easier and more cost-effective. Salhi *et al* (2021) [8] used data analytics to predict disease's patients and in the pre-processing phase they used the most relevant features. Three methods (namely neural networks, SVM and KNN) were used and it was found that neural networks were easier to configure, and they obtained a higher accuracy of 93% compared to the other methods.

In particular, investigations on the application of the decision tree techniques [9] for diagnosing heart ailments that cause death have had considerable success in previous work. Andreeva (2006) [10] achieved a 75.73% accuracy by using the C4.5 Decision Tree [11] for the diagnosis of heart problems in their model. Sitair-Taut *et al* (2009) [12] analyzed various risk factors from data to apply data mining techniques that classified high risk cardiovascular patients. The work used naive Bayes [13] techniques to classify the high risk patients based on gender [14]. In order to explore the advantages of the bagging algorithm, the authors used it for prediction. They combined a series of learned models and predicted the presence of heart disease with an accuracy of 81.41%.

Singh *et al* (2017) [15] used random forest classifier and cross-validated the model to achieve an accuracy of 85.81%. Maji *et al* (2019) [16] combined both decision trees and artificial neural networks method to detect heart disease at a very early stage. Their method showed that statistical methods were incapable of disease prediction when there were a large amount of missing values. Their algorithm also showed that a hybrid decision tree gave better results for heart disease prediction. Almustafa (2020) [17] analyzed the heart disease dataset with various classification algorithms. Feature extraction was done to estimate the accuracy of all the classifiers and it was found that heart disease could be predicted. The authors suggested the use of a minimal number of attributes instead of the complete dataset. Gupta *et al* (2020) [18] used six classification algorithms to predict coronary disease. The model reduced the number of attributes using the backward elimination [19] method and filter method for feature selection that used Pearson's correlation [20] to choose the factors for prediction and achieved an accuracy of 88.16%.

Yang *et al* (2020) [21] studied the risk of cardiovascular disease in eastern China based on the culture, lifestyle, and genetic background of the population. The prediction model was built using random forests and it was found to be more superior to AdaBoost, CART, naive Bayes and bagged trees.

Previous work have proved that decision trees have shown a better accuracy. But in the real world a higher accuracy of prediction is favorable and for this the proposed work aims to improve the accuracy achieved by previous models. The proposed work aims to explore the different variations of decision tree to achieve a higher prediction and classify the high risk cardiovascular patients.

21.3 Methodology

21.3.1 Data collection

The data presented in this paper is retrieved from the reputed UCI machine learning repository and is an extraction obtained from health records of four different databases. The subset of the dataset used has 13 medical attributes and one target field. The two different classes for the target column were encoded as follows: '1' indicated the presence of heart disease and target variable '0' indicates the absence of heart disease. The parameters of a patient with heart disease, the description of the medical parameters and the values acceptable are tabulated in table 21.1.

Table 21.1. Parameters of a patient with heart disease.

S No	Medical parameter	DESCRIPTION of medical parameter	VALUES acceptable
1.	PAge	Age of the patient	continuous
2.	PSex	Gender of the patient	(1 = male 0 = female)
3.	Pcp	Chest pain (cp)/chest discomfort	(0 = typical type, 1 = atypical angina, 2 = non-anginal pain 3 = asymptomatic)
4.	Prestbps	Resting Blood pressure	value in mm Hg
5.	Pchol	Serum cholesterol	Continuous value less than 170 mg dl^{-1}
6.	Prestecg	Electrocardiographic results at rest	0 indicates normal 1 indicates patient having ST–T wave abnormality 2 indicates patient with left ventricular hypertrophy
7.	Pfbs	Blood sugar fasting	1 120 mg dl^{-1} 0 120 mg dl^{-1}
8.	Pthalach	Maximum heart rate	Continuous value (minimum heart rate=200-patient age)
9.	Pexang	Exercise-induced angina (Angina symptom of heart disease)	0 = no 1 = yes
10.	Poldpeak	Depression induced by exercise	Continuous value
11.	Pslope	Peak exercise ST segment	0 = unsloping 1 = flat 2 = downsloping
12.	PCa	Capillaries colored by fluoroscopy	0–4 value
13.	Pthal	Thallasemia	(3 = normal 6 = fixed 7 = reversible defect)

21.4 Proposed framework

The heart disease predictor makes use of three variants of decision tree algorithms: Genetic Decision Tree Based Heart Predictor (GDH), Random Forest Based Heart Predictor (RFH), Bayesian Decision Tree Heart Predictor (BDH). The three algorithms are compared with different classification algorithms like Linear Support Vector and KNN algorithm. The performance analysis of the three tree based algorithms is evaluated and hyperparameter tuning is performed by varying the 1. maximum depth 2. minimum sample split 3. minimum sample Leaf. The chapter shows how decision trees help to effectively predict future heart disease. Figure 21.1 shows the processes involved in the developed system.

21.5 Exploratory data analysis

Exploratory data analysis was performed on the dataset. Data cleaning and integration was done. It was found that there were no missing/null values in the 14 attributes taken to build the prediction model. The exploratory data analysis techniques helped in data discovery to bring the important aspects of that data into focus for further analysis. However, it was found that the data was not distributed properly and various outliers were present. Feature selection was performed using the sci-kit library.

Figure 21.2 shows heart disease and ST depression caused due to exercise. Figure 21.3 shows the maximum heart rate achieved for patients with heart disease and is left skewed for few patients with a low heart rate. It shows that people without heart disease had a higher heart rate than for people with heart disease.

The heatmap in figure 21.4 shows that a positive correlation exists between chest pain (cp) and the target (predictor). Based on the amount of chest pain experienced

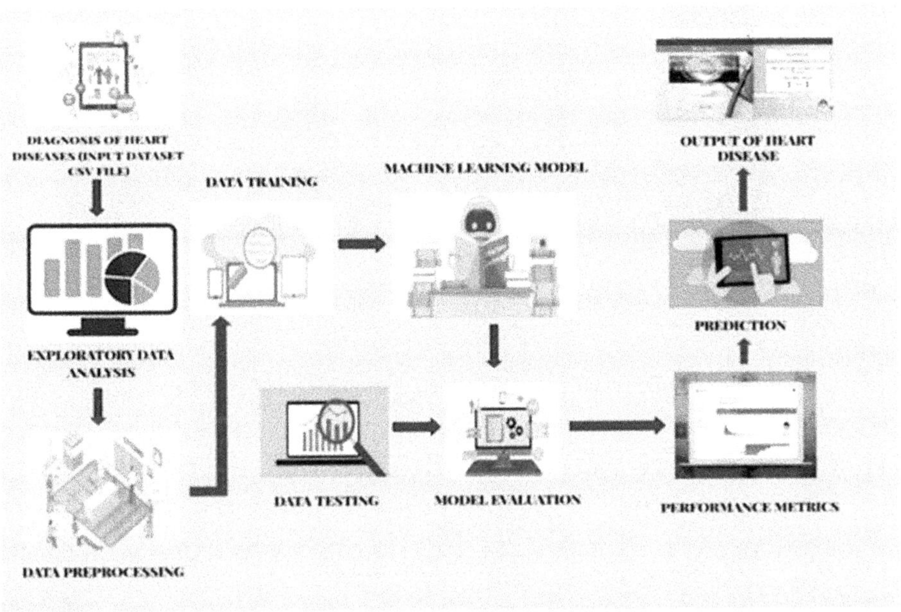

Figure 21.1. System model for heart disease diagnosis.

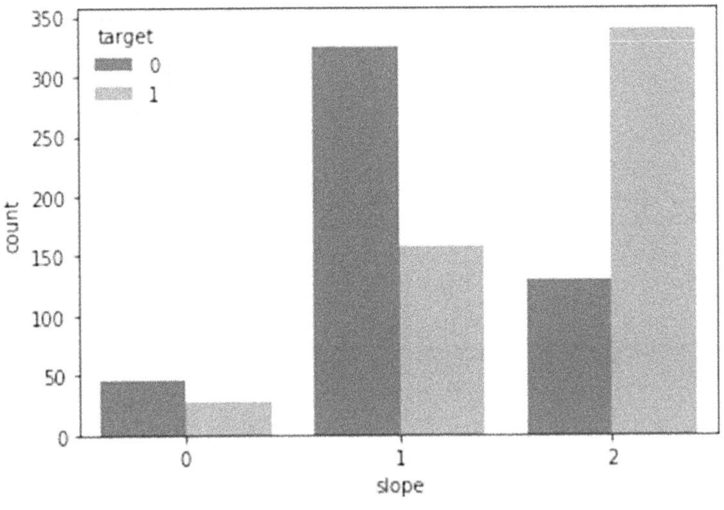

Figure 21.2. Target versus slope (ST depression induced by exercise relative to rest).

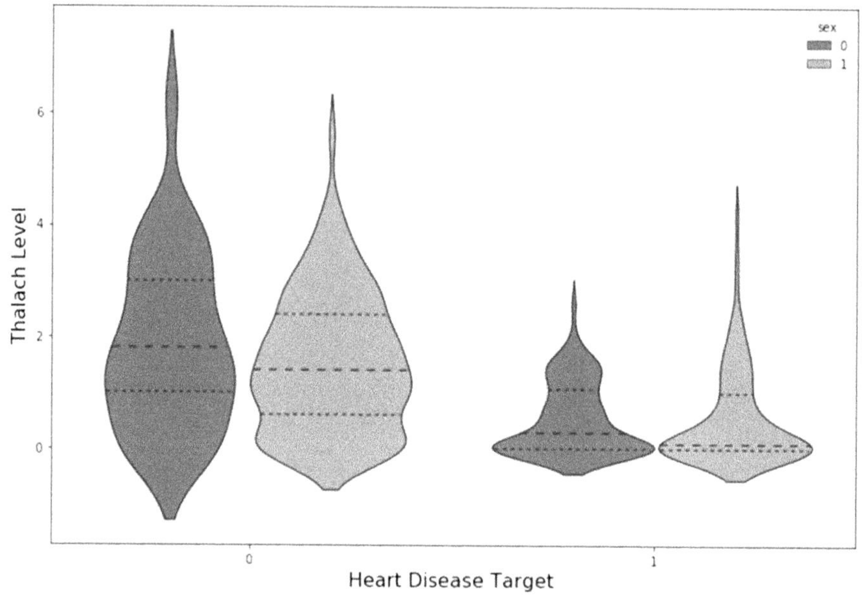

Figure 21.3. Target versus thalach (maximum heart rate achieved).

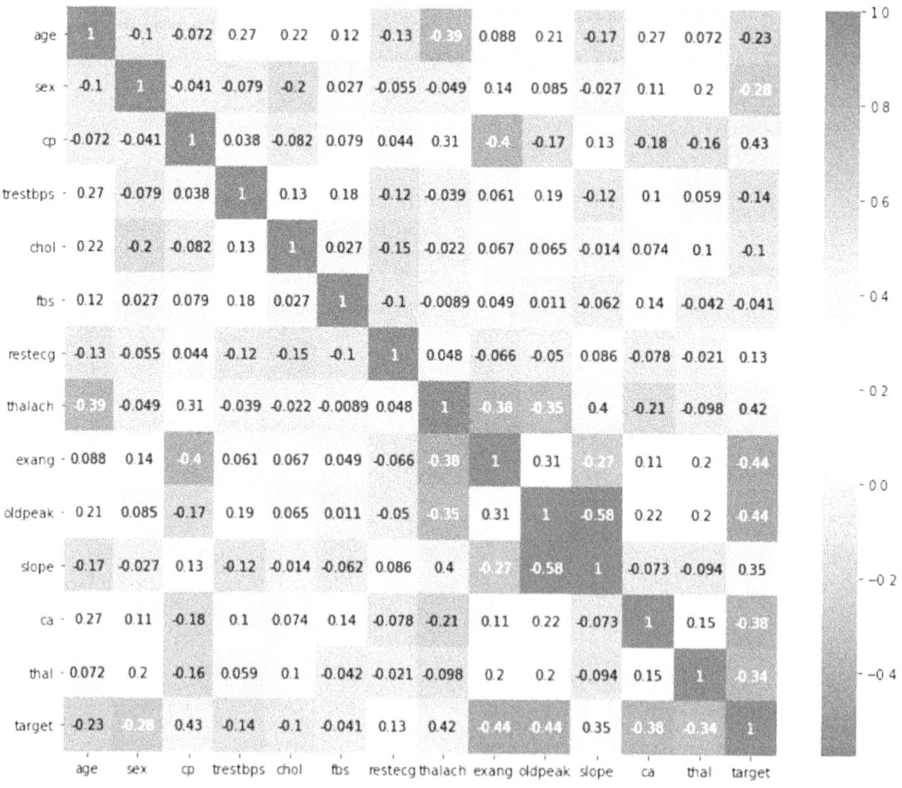

Figure 21.4. Correlation matrix plot of heart disease dataset.

by patients, the level of heart disease could be seen. cp, maximum heart rate (thalach), slope and resting values also have a positive correlation as seen. There is a negative correlation between exercise-induced angina (exang) and predictor indicating the need for more blood to the arteries when a person exercised. However, for patients who had narrowed arteries there was slowed down blood flow resulting in heart disease.

From figure 21.5, most patients who complained of cp had a non-anginal pain indicated by value 2. In figure 21.6, a comparison of patients who had heart disease was done based on the gender to see who was more likely to get cp. The values were encoded as follows: 0 specifies female patients who experienced cp and 1 specifies male patients. The graph shows that male patients were likely to be affected more with heart disease than female patients.

The exploratory analysis studied patients with three categories of cp: value 0 representing typical angina—a chest pain caused by physical exertion and emotional stress, value 1 representing atypical angina—a chest pain which resulted in insufficient oxygen and patients experienced discomfort; value 2 representing non-anginal pain faced by patients who did not have heart disease; and value 3 represents asymptomatic angina showing patients who faced a silent heart attack.

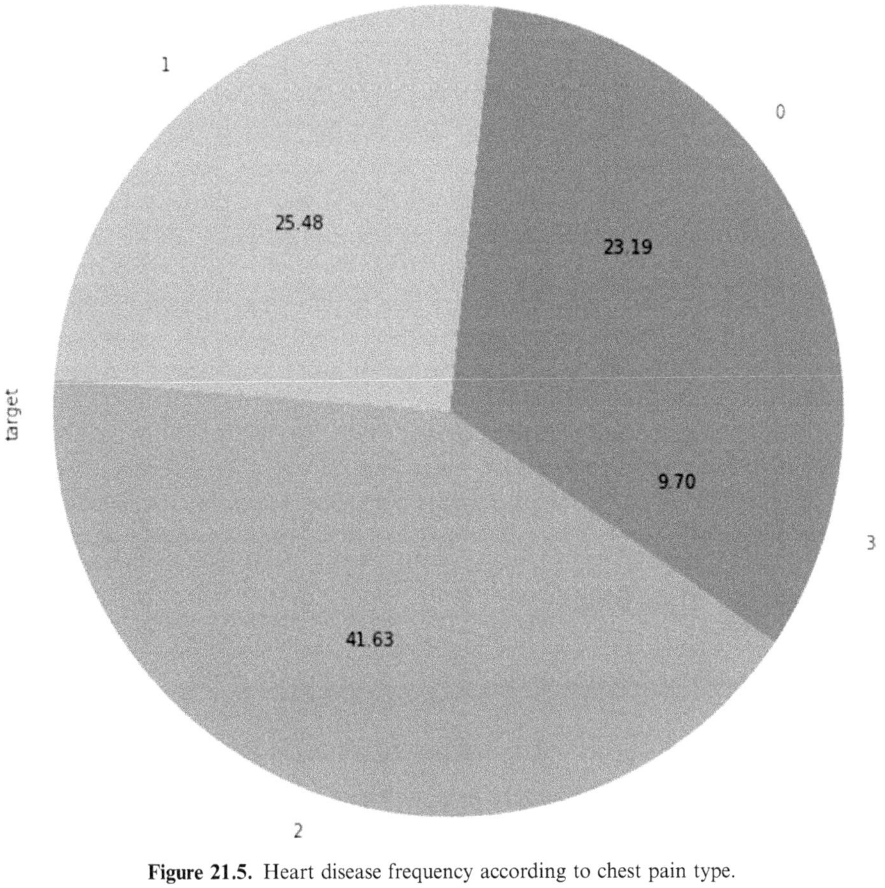

Figure 21.5. Heart disease frequency according to chest pain type.

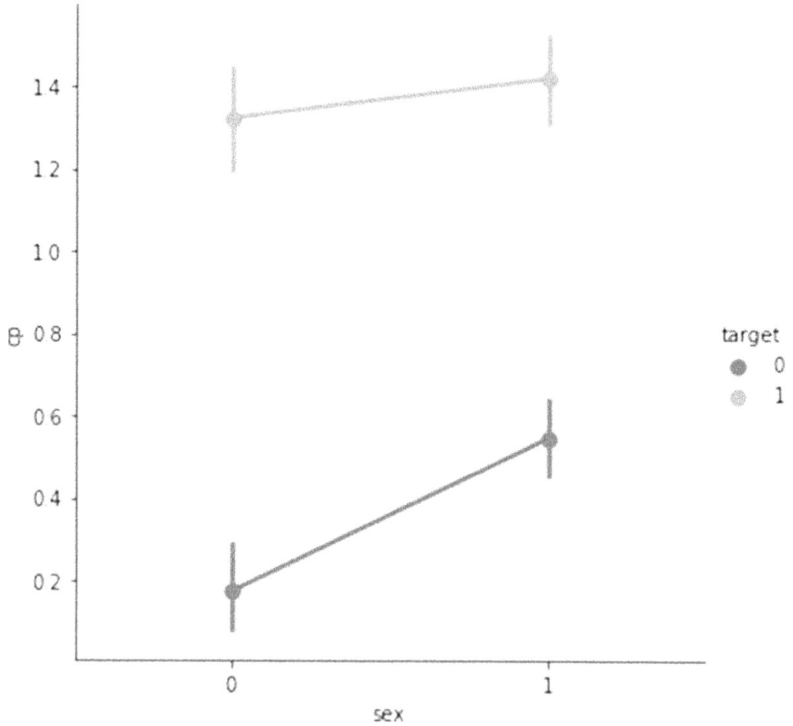

Figure 21.6. Gender versus cp (chest pain).

The exploratory analysis also highlighted three types of patients based on their resting electrocardiographic results: those represnting patients with normal values, patients having an ST–T wave abnormality that showed an increased risk of heart disease and finally patients with left ventricular hypertrophy caused by the thickening of the wall of the heart's pumping chamber. From figure 21.7, 0 represents the absence of risk of future heart disease (target 0) and 1 represents the presence of future risk of heart disease (target 1).

Figure 21.8 shows the thalach level under which age the patients were suffering from maximum heart rate. Figure 21.9 shows that 51% of the patients suffered from heart disease compared to 48.7% of patients who were not at risk of developing any heart ailments.

21.6 Proposed algorithms

In this chapter, various decision tree algorithms have been trained to get the best accuracy for predicting heart disease.

21.6.1 Model 1: GDH—genetic decision tree based heart predictor

Decision trees have been used widely in operations research and decision analysis. The impurity measures used by decision tree algorithms suffer from drawbacks like generating over-complex trees and leading to sub-optimal solutions. The Genetic

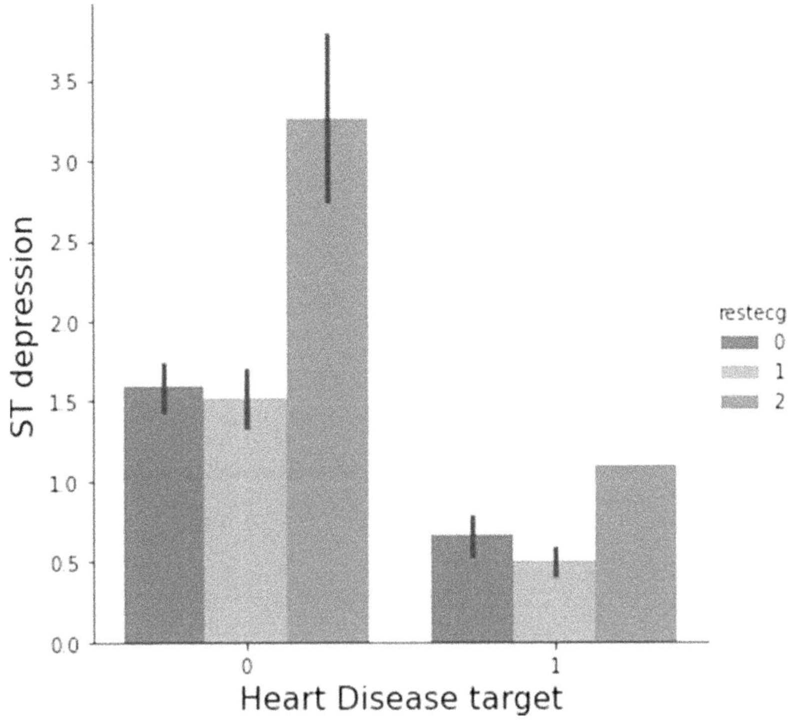

Figure 21.7. Target versus oldpeak (ST depression induced by exercise relative to rest).

Decision Tree based Heart (GDH) predictor algorithm performs a global search for candidate solutions to overcome this problem. GDH selects individuals based on fitness function where each individual is a tree. Selection is performed by choosing the individuals with the highest fitness. The GDH predictor proves very useful for determining the presence or absence of heart problems and whether or not it will lead to a heart attack in the future. The accuracy gained with this algorithm is 99%. Figure 21.12 shows the receiver operator characteristic (ROC) curve and precision–recall curve for GDH predictor.

The GDH predictor algorithm is explained in algorithm 1.

Algorithm 1: Heart disease diagnosis using genetic decision trees.

Data Heart disease dataset

Result Predict the number of patients with/without heart disease

- Step 1: Load dataset with parameters such as age, thalach, sex, cp type, chol, smoke, exang, fbs, oldpeak, slope, Ca, thal.
- Step 2: Compute fitness of patient p. Generate an initial random tree population rp with probability L.
- Step 3: Select the individuals based on fitness and apply crossover and mutation to generate new trees.

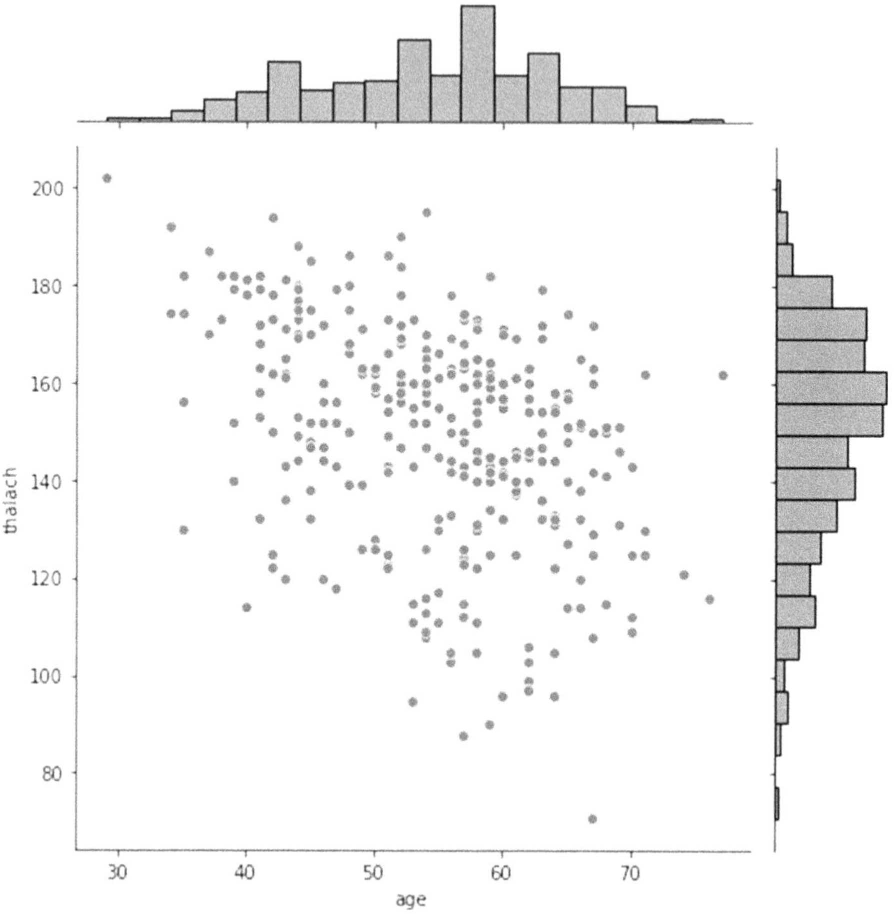

Figure 21.8. Age versus thalach (maximum heart rate achieved).

(Continued)

- Step 4: Fitness compute f = α1f1 + α2f2 where f1—training set accuracy, f2—penalty, α1 and α2 are the chosen parameters
- Step 5: Perform selection. Update the population with new individuals.
- Step 6: Perform mutation and crossover.
- Step 7: Generate decision tree and update till stopping criteria cs is reached.
- step 8: Evaluate the results of the algorithm.

21.6.2 Model 2: RBH-random forest based heart predictor

The RFH consists of a large number of individual decision trees that follow supervised learning. The RFH takes patient data such as cp, serum cholesterol, fasting blood sugar and gives higher accuracy for the prediction model. Random

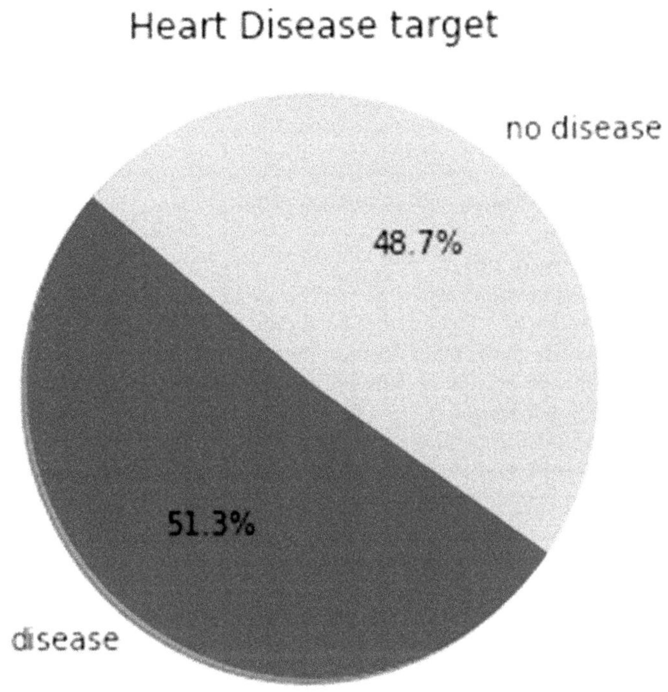

Figure 21.9. Diagnosis of heart diseases.

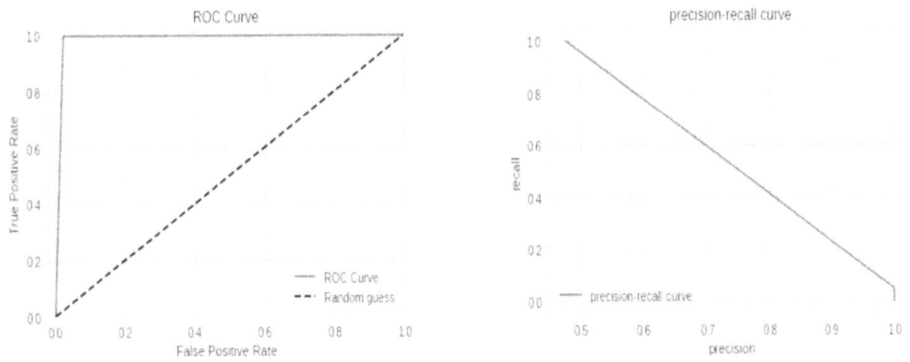

Figure 21.10. ROC curve and precision–recall curve for random forest using heart disease dataset.

forest works in two-phases: first it creates a random forest by combining *N* decision trees, and second it makes predictions for each tree created. The RFH recognizes the most important attributes to give a prediction. By using the random forest classifier, the developed model recorded an accuracy of 95%. The model used three parameters to increase the predictive power namely: *n* parameters, maxfeatures, minsampleleaf. *n* parameters refers to the number of trees built and by increasing the number of trees the model increased the accuracy of prediction. The maxfeatures which the random forest considers to split a node and minsampleleaf are the other two parameters that improve the predictive power of the model. Figure 21.10 shows us the ROC curve and the precision–recall curve for RFH.

The heart predictor based on random forests is explained in algorithm 2.

Algorithm 2: Heart disease diagnosis using random forest.

Data Heart disease dataset

Result Having heart disease or not

- Step 1: Import heart disease dataset.
- Step 2: Create a classifier by selecting random K data points from the training data (age, cp, thal, fasting blood sugar, chol). Build decision trees with all the selected data points.
- Step 3: Average all the selected data points and predict the risk for each patient.
- Step 4: Repeat Step 2 and Step 3.
- Step 5: Validate the model using cross-validation. Evaluate the random forest model.

21.6.3 Model 3: Bayesian decision tree based heart predictor

Bayesian models help define a prediction model based on probabilistic theory. BDH is based on assuming that the predictors in the dataset are independent and follows the 'Bayes theorem'. The Bayesian tree predictor combines prior information with observations and solves the greediness of classic decision trees. By combining Bayesian approaches with decision trees the algorithm is able to quantify the uncertainty and explore the tree space more. The prediction is generating tree based models which split patient data along explanatory variables. The accuracy recorded for the BDH is 79%. Figure 21.11 shows the ROC curve and precision–recall for BDH. The BDH algorithm is explained in algorithm 3 (figure 21.12).

For each algorithm, a classification report with precision, recall, and F1-score are also visualized as shown in figure 21.13.

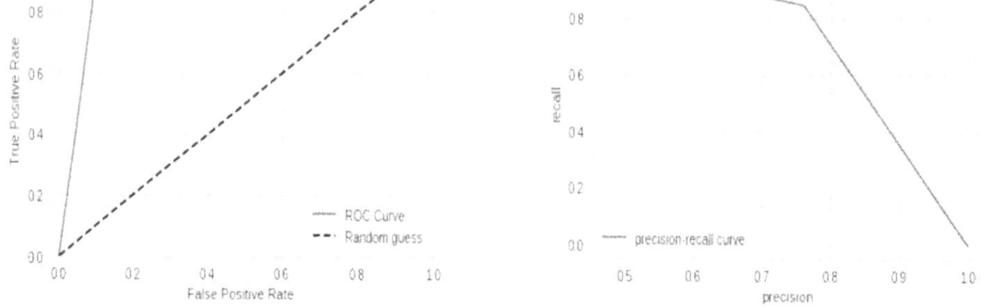

Figure 21.11. ROC curve and precision–recall curve for BDH.

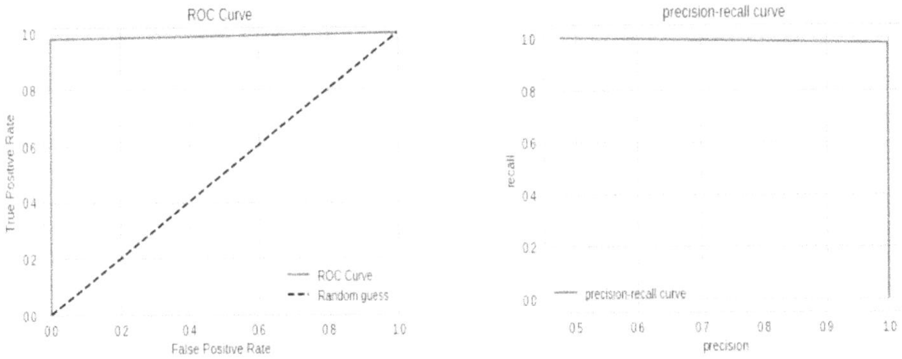

Figure 21.12. ROC curve and precision–recall curve for GDH predictor.

Algorithm 3: Heart disease using Bayesian decision trees.
Data Heart disease dataset
Result Having heart disease or not

- Step 1: Import heart disease dataset.
- Step 2: Create frequency tables.
- Step 3: Generate likelihood table
- Step 4: Starting from T, calculate the probability of splitting the node.
- Step 5: Calculate the posterior probability for each node in the tree
- Step 6: Predict based on the probability.

From comparing the five algorithms in the developed prediction model, it is concluded that GDH yields the highest accuracy and the accuracy value is 99%.

21.7 Performance evaluation

21.7.1 Metrics

21.7.1.1 Accuracy

For the performance evaluation, accuracy is taken by defining the following: Tp = showing the number of patients correctly predicted; Fp = showing number of patients incorrectly predicted; Tn = showing the number of patients correctly predicted but not required; and Fn = showing the number of patients incorrectly predicted but not required.

The accuracy of predicting if a patient has heart disease is given as A and is obtained as follows:

$$A = (Tp + Tn)/(Tp + Fp + Tn + Fn) \tag{21.1}$$

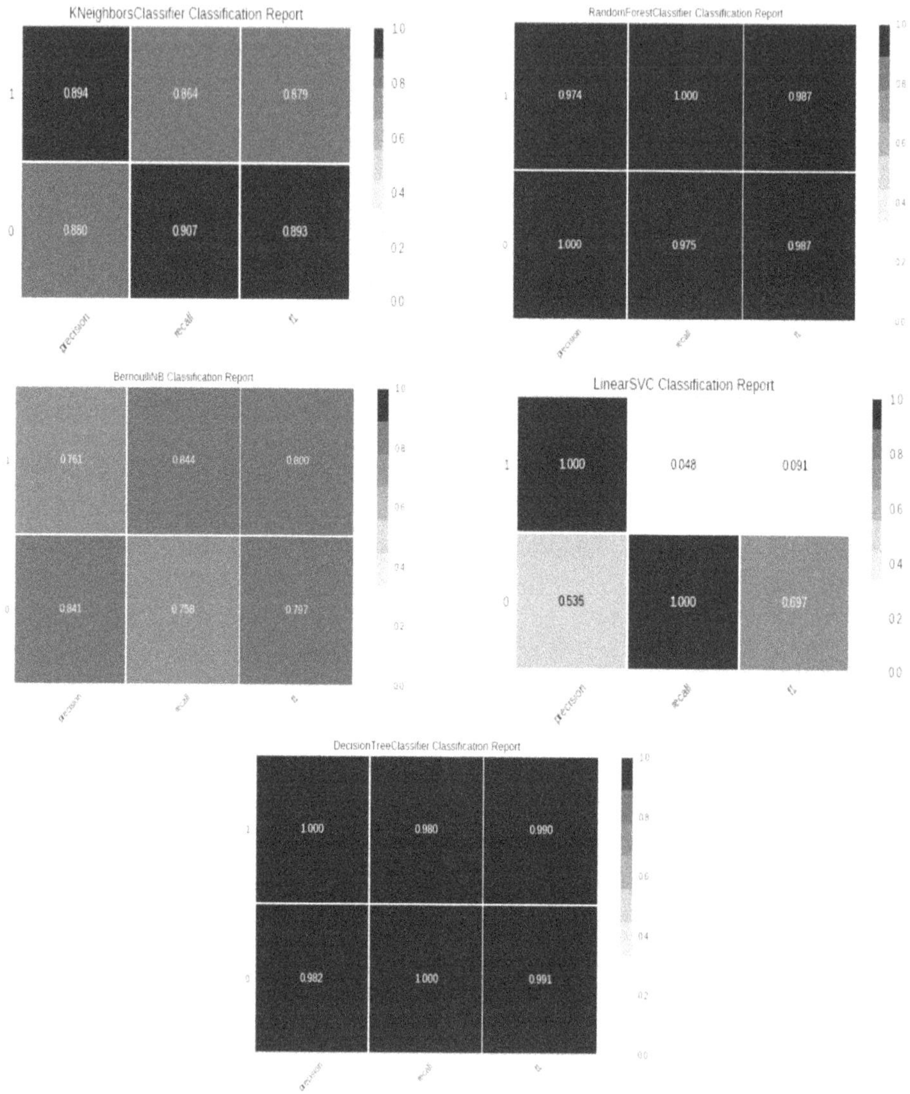

Figure 21.13. Classification report of five models: heart predictor using k-nearest neighbors (HKNN), random forests based heart predictor (RFH), Bayesian decision heart predictor (BDH), linear SVC based heart predictor (SVH) and genetic tree based heart predictor (GDH).

21.7.1.2 Precision

The precision, P, of the heart predictor shows the number of patients correctly classified within the class.

$$P = Tp/Tp + Fp \tag{21.2}$$

21.7.1.3 Recall

The recall, R, of the heart predictor shows the total number of correctly classified positive patients.

$$R = Tp/Tp + Fn \tag{21.3}$$

21.7.1.4 F1-score

The F1-score of the heart predictor is defined as the reciprocal of the average of the precision and recall values.

$$\text{F1-score} = (2 * (P * R)/(P + R)) \tag{21.4}$$

21.7.1.5 Confusion matrix

The confusion matrix for the heart predictor evaluates the performance of the classifiers, as shown in figure 21.14. It helps visualize the performance of each GDH, RFH, and BDH algorithm and identifies the confusion between classes.

21.7.1.6 Log-loss

Log-loss measure indicates how close the prediction was to the actual/true value by penalizing incorrect classifications. The log-loss favored the RFH classifier that distinguished more strongly the classes. The log-loss for the classifier was calculated using

$$[H_p(q) = -1/N \sum_{(i=1)}^{N} y_i \cdot \log(p(y_i)) + (1 - y_i) \cdot \log(1 - p(y_i))] \tag{21.5}$$

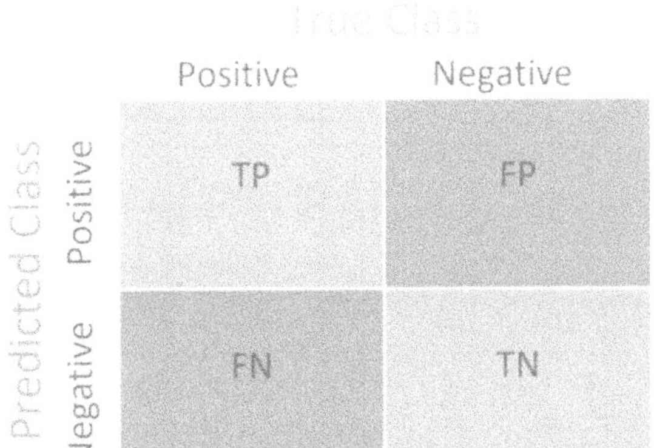

Figure 21.14. Confusion matrix.

21.7.1.7 ROC_AUC score

The ROC curve for the heart predictor model showed the probability at different threshold values. The area under the curve (AUC) for the heart predictor model distinguished between the classes. Figure 21.15 shows the ROC_AUC curve.

21.7.2 Performance measures

Trained machine learning algorithms and performance metrics for heart disease dataset are shown in figure 21.16.

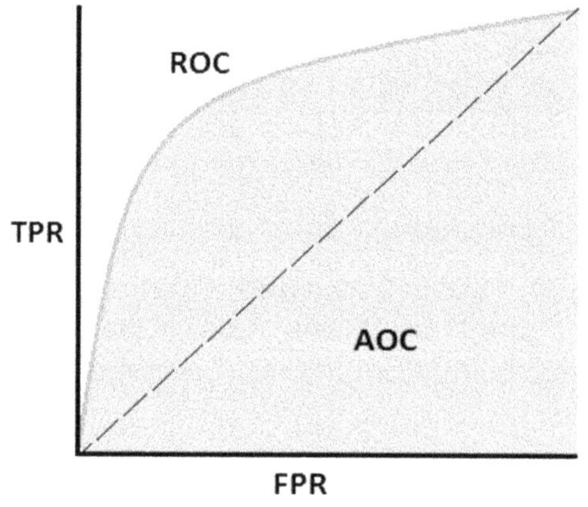

Figure 21.15. ROC_AUC curve.

ALGORITHM	Decision Tree	Random Forest	K-Nearest Neighbors	Bernoulli NB	Linear SVC
ACCURACY	0.99	0.98	0.88	0.79	0.54
LOG-LOSS	0.33	0.44	3.92	6.95	15.69
ROC_AUC SCORE	0.98	0.98	0.88	0.80	0.52
PRECISION SCORE	0.98	0.97	0.83	0.71	0.50
CONFUSION MATRIX	[[161 0] [3 144]]	[[157 4] [0 147]]	[[146 15] [20 127]]	[[122 39] [23 124]]	[[161 0] [140 7]]

Figure 21.16. Trained machine learning algorithms and performance metrics for heart disease dataset.

21.8 Experimental design

Streamlit provides an open-source Python library that makes it easy to implement various machine learning algorithms and share them as web applications. Streamlit is a front-end framework that updates the app live while coding.

By entering the various symptoms of the patients in the web application, the doctor can identify whether a patient would develop heart disease or not based on their symptoms and current health conditions, as shown in figure 21.17.

21.9 Conclusion and future enhancement

This work proved the advantages of using decision trees over other machine learning algorithms for heart disease prediction. Genetic decision trees optimize the performance of normal decision trees. The performance of the GDH proved superior based on the accuracy of prediction when compared to the BDH and RFH. The three classification models, namely GDH, BDH and RFH were trained and their performances was compared with seven performance metrics. An intelligent system

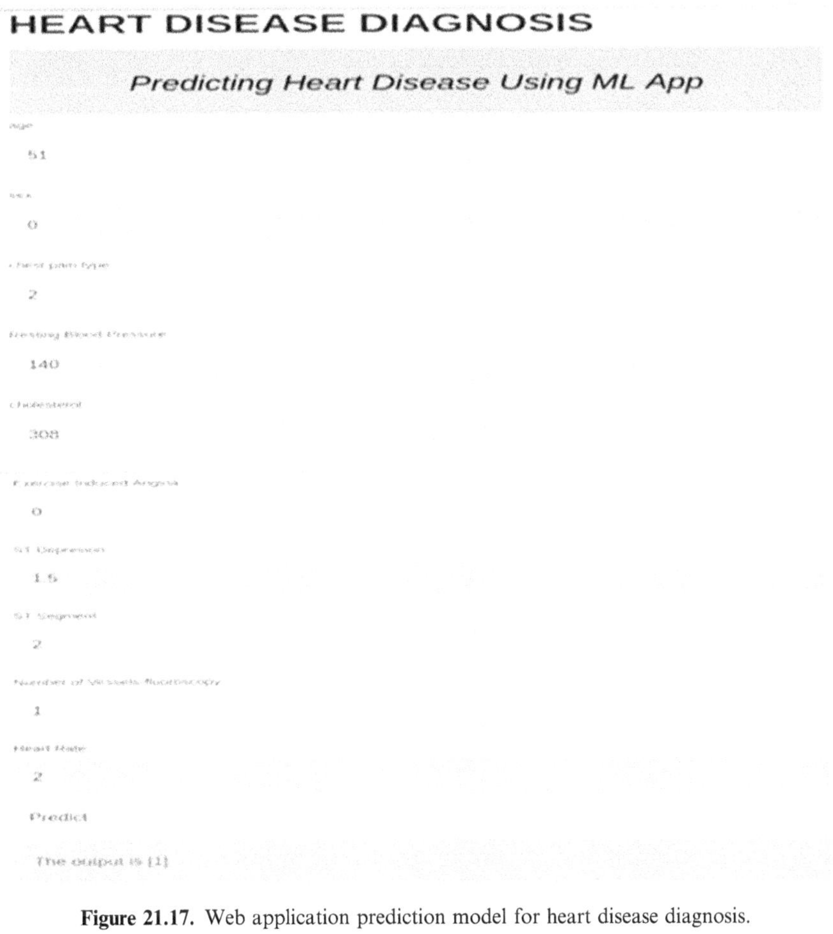

Figure 21.17. Web application prediction model for heart disease diagnosis.

was developed to check the risk of heart disease on the basis of assumed parameters and finally implemented as a web application.

For future work, the research described here can be extended to compare with other hybrid ensemble methods. The study achieved 99% accuracy in genetic decision tree algorithms that correctly predicted the cause of heart disease. By using this predictive model, it is noted that machine learning techniques help in faster and better prediction and can be applied to various healthcare scenarios.

References

[1] Nallathamby R, Rene Robin C R and Miriam D H 2021 Optimizing appointment scheduling for out patients and income analysis for hospitals using big data predictive analytics *J. Ambient Intell. Human Comput.* **12** 5783–95

[2] Vanitha N, Rene R and Doreen H M 2021 *A spatial temporal classification analysis and visualization of tropical cyclone tracks in Bay of Bengal using GIS*

[3] Jayanthi S and Rene Robin C R 2021 Analysis of microarray data by empirical wavelet transform for cancer classification using block by block method *J. Med. Imag. Health Inform.* **11** 697–702

[4] Zriqat I A, Altamimi A M and Azzeh M 2016 A comparative study for predicting heart diseases using data mining classification methods *Int. J. Comput. Sci. Inform. Sec. (IJCSIS)* **14** 868–79

[5] Nichenametla R, Maneesha T, Hafeez S and Krishna S 2018 Prediction of heart disease using machine learning algorithms *Int. J. Eng. Technol.* **7** 363–6

[6] Maheswari S and Pitchai R 2019 Heart disease prediction system using decision tree and naive Bayes algorithm *Curr. Med. Imaging. Rev.* **8** 712–7

[7] Jindal H, Agrawal S, Khera R, Jain R and Nagrath P 2021 Heart disease prediction using machine learning algorithms *IOP Conf. Series: Mater. Sci. Eng.* 12 012072

[8] Salhi D E, Tari A and Kechadi M 2021 Using machine learning for heart disease prediction *Advances in Computing Systems and Applications* 70–81

[9] Quinlan J R 1986 Induction of decision trees *Mach. Learn.* **1** 81–106

[10] Andreeva P 2006 Data modelling and specific rule generation via data mining techniques *Int. Conf. on Computer Systems and Technologies*

[11] Dalela P K *et al* 2018 C4.5 Decision tree machine learning algorithm based GIS route identification *2018 10th Int. Conf. on Ubiquitous and Future Networks (ICUFN)* 213–8

[12] Sitar-Taut V A and Zdrenghea D *et al* 2009 Using machine learning algorithms in cardiovascular disease risk evaluation *J. Appl. Comput.Sci. Math.*

[13] Webb G I 2011 Naïve Bayes *Encyclopedia of Machine Learning* ed C Sammut and G I Webb (Boston, MA: Springer)

[14] Tu M C and Shin D *et al* 2009 Effective diagnosis of heart disease through bagging approach *IEEE Biomedical Engineering and Informatics*

[15] Singh Y K, Sinha N and Singh S K 2017 Heart disease prediction system using random forest *Advances in Computing and Data Sciences. ICACDS 2016Communications in Computer and Information Science* vol 721 ed M Singh, P Gupta, V Tyagi, A Sharma, T Ören and W Grosky (Singapore: Springer)

[16] Maji S and Arora S 2019 Decision tree algorithms for prediction of heart disease *Information and Communication Technology for Competitive StrategiesLecture Notes in Networks and Systems* vol 40 ed S Fong, S Akashe and P Mahalle (Singapore: Springer) pp 447–54

[17] Almustafa K M 2020 Prediction of heart disease and classifiers' sensitivity analysis *BMC Bioinform.* **21** 1–18
[18] Gupta A, Kumar L, Jain R and Nagrath P 2020 Heart disease prediction using classification (naive Bayes) *Proc. 1st Int. Conf. on Computing, Communications, and Cyber-Security (IC4S 2019) Lecture Notes in Networks and Systems* vol 121 (Singapore: Springer)
[19] Karnan M and Kalyani P 2010 Attribute reduction using backward elimination algorithm *2010 IEEE Int. Conf. on Computational Intelligence and Computing Research* 1–4
[20] Bommert A 2020 Benchmark for filter methods for feature selection in high-dimensional classification data *Comput. Stat. Data Anal.* **143** 1–23
[21] Yang L, Wu H and Jin X *et al* 2020 Study of cardiovascular disease prediction model based on random forest in eastern *Chin. Sci. Rep.* **10** 5245

IOP Publishing

Human-Assisted Intelligent Computing
Modeling, simulations and applications
Mukhdeep Singh Manshahia, Igor S Litvinchev, Gerhard-Wilhelm Weber, J Joshua Thomas and Pandian Vasant

Chapter 22

Mathematical and informational support of decision-making in risk management of cross-border high technology projects

Marina Batova, Irina Baranova, Vyacheslav Baranov, Sergey Mayorov, Oleg Korobchenko and Kai Zhao

This research suggests a mechanism for choosing the optimal risk management strategy for the implementation of cross-border cooperation projects. It includes a step-by-step algorithm covering the identification of factors leading to the occurrence of undesirable events, determination of lost profits under risk conditions, a probabilistic assessment of the proposed strategies to counter project risks, identification of alternative losses of projects and assessment of the economic consequences of the proposed strategies to counter risks. It is proposed to use the criteria of Savage, Wald and Hurwitz as evaluation criteria. The solution of the practical problem of choosing the optimal risk management strategy by Russian companies in cross-border projects involving the use of innovative technologies for the repair of Chinese-made trucks has been obtained. The concept of creating and using information systems to support decision-making of risk management of cross-border cooperation projects of innovation-oriented cluster structures of the Kama agglomeration (Russia) is proposed.

22.1 Introduction

22.1.1 Research relevance

In modern conditions the dynamics and level of economic development of a country are, to a large extent, determined by high-tech manufacturing companies, the activities of which are characterised by in-depth diversification of production and development of breakthrough technological innovations competitive on the global markets. The projects implemented by high-tech companies are characterized by a greater level of uncertainty and risk as well as scientific and capital intensity of the final scientific and technical results obtained [8].

Such projects are associated with total robotisation and informatisation of production and management processes [9]. Therefore, these projects require significant amounts of material, intellectual and financial resources and go beyond the framework of national states. In the knowledge economy, project activity acquires a transboundary character, and the unified information space becomes the digital environment, which contributes to minimising the time costs of providing transboundary project activity with the necessary resources [10, 17].

22.1.2 Review of the chapter's structure

The chapter consists of six sections, four figures and 15 tables.

Section 22.1 acquaints the reader with the relevance of our research and the chapter's structure.

Section 22.2 discusses organizational tools for the formation of effective cross-border cooperation projects and represents:

- the experimental platform of our research, that are the enterprises of the Kama agglomeration of Russia;
- the subject of our research, which is innovative projects of cross-border cooperation and risk management of the projects;
- the purpose of our research, which is the development of mathematical apparatus and information tools of decision-making in the risk management during implementation of cross-border cooperation projects.

Section 22.3 presents the theoretical development and justification of the mathematical apparatus for selecting the optimal risk management strategy for cross-border cooperation projects. The presented theoretical problem solution contains:

- the developed algorithm of choosing the optimal risk management strategy under the conditions of environmental uncertainty;
- mathematical and economic assessment of project risk management strategies;
- justification of evaluation criteria for a choice of optimum strategy of counteraction to a project's risks.

Section 22.4 is dedicated to the practical application of the theoretical developments of section 22.2.

In section 22.3, the practical problem of selecting the best risk management strategy for a Russian company in implementing a cross-border Chinese truck repair project is solved step by step. To solve the problem of minimizing the risks of a cross-border project:

- the effectiveness of the initial version of a cross-border project for the Russian company 'Korib' is calculated;
- the factors shaping Korib's risks are revealed;
- the risk mitigation strategies for the company 'Korib' are developed;
- the assessments of strategy parameters, of the loss amount of Korib's benefit, of economic consequences of Korib's risk management strategies are carried out.

A discussion of the results, prospects and recommendations for the company 'Korib' based on the problem solution is presented.

Section 22.5 discusses the concept of creating and using an information system for decision-making support in risk management of cross-border projects. The key component of such an information system is considered, providing a high level of credibility of decisions aimed at countering the risks detected. This is an expert component (subsystem), its structure and description are given. This section also discusses promising areas for the development of information systems for decision support, prospects for the development of decision support systems tools, further research, new tasks.

Section 22.6 completes the chapter. This section compiles the findings of the study, summarizes the results and achievements of the research.

22.2 Organizational tools for the formation of effective cross-border cooperation of innovation-oriented cluster structures of the Kama agglomeration

22.2.1 Kama agglomeration (Russia)

In the global economy the most successful project activity is carried out not by separate companies, but by integrated formations, for example, innovation-oriented cluster structures. Such structures have a managing company, which regulates the processes of search for partners and interaction of cluster participants with different categories of stakeholders.

In the Russian Federation one of such formations is the Kama agglomeration of the Republic of Tatarstan, which unites a number of innovation-oriented clusters, including the machine-building cluster and the Kama innovative territorial-production cluster [1–5, 14, 15, 27, 28, 35]. Kama agglomeration is a polycentric territory and formed by four urbanized cores. These are cities: Naberezhnye Chelny, Nizhnekamsk, Yelabuga and Mendeleevsk. The centre of the territorial zone is Naberezhnye Chelny. At present, participants of these clusters are actively developing bilateral and multilateral cross-border partnerships, including cooperation with Chinese companies [10, 17, 20].

It concerns various areas, first of all, scientific, technical and industrial spheres, preparation of intellectual resources, etc [11, 12, 16]. The cooperation vector is largely focused on the innovative sphere of activity and contributes to the formation of global cooperative synergy effect both at the level of macroeconomic Russian–Chinese interaction and at the level of the megaproject of creating Greater Eurasia.

22.2.2 Improving the efficiency of high-tech cooperation projects

One of the strategically important tasks, the solution of which is of current interest, both for the processes of effective implementation of high-tech cooperation projects of individual entities, and for the processes of Eurasian integration of meso- and macroeconomic systems, is the improvement of risk management methodology with due account of the formation specifics of national and Eurasian dual identity of the cooperation participants.

In order to improve the efficiency of implementation of both individual high-tech projects, as well as cross-border cooperation as a whole, it is necessary to not simply enforce informatisation of business processes, but also to create an integrated project management system [7, 13, 15]. This system should have an applied nature and cover:

- firstly, the original mathematical provision of tasks solved in project management;
- secondly, the creation of information systems to support decision-making, including decisions in the field of risk management.

The efficiency of high-tech projects is achieved through various factors. Figure 22.1 shows the chart of basic factor groups of the efficiency of high-tech projects:

- firstly, by minimising the cost component of the project life cycle and reducing the running costs that form the cost price level of the product innovations produced;
- secondly, due to the positive dynamics of sales volume growth, which is largely facilitated by the expansion of contacts with consumers and their encouragement to purchase the manufactured product innovations by providing various discounts and preferences;
- thirdly, the implementation within the framework of project management of the risk mitigation strategy. First of all, it concerns counteraction to innovative project risks.

To activate the first two of the factors listed above, the innovation-oriented clusters of the Kama agglomeration of the Republic of Tatarstan actively use organisational tools, including the Eurasian technological platform 'Technologies of maintenance and repair of industrial equipment' [26] and the National subcontracting portal Innokam.pro [43].

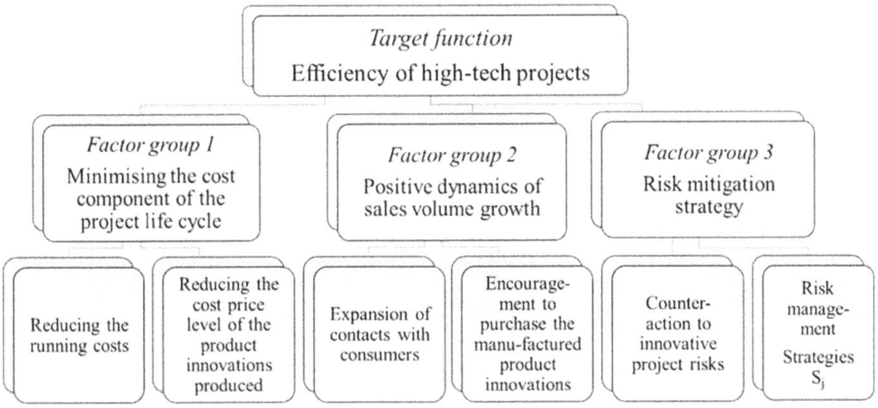

Figure 22.1. Chart of basic factor groups of the efficiency of high-tech projects. Source: authors' research.

22.2.2.1 The Eurasian Technology Platform

The Eurasian Technology Platform was formed in accordance with the decision of the Eurasian Intergovernmental Council in 2016. The activities of the Platform are aimed at solving such problems as the development and implementation of breakthrough high technologies, innovative modernisation of production and reengineering of obsolete equipment based on the development of industrial cross-border partnerships. As a full-cycle platform, the Eurasian Technology Platform contributes to solving technological problems and developing specialised Eurasian service centres.

Initially, the Platform provided technical support to companies of the Eurasian Union. Currently, other Eurasian states participate in the activities of the Eurasian Technology Platform, in particular China, with which a trade and economic cooperation agreement was signed in 2018. The platform integrates the best competences and solutions possessed by industrial enterprises and educational organisations, engineering centres, and expands the opportunities for platform participants to conduct research and development work.

As part of the Eurasian Technology Platform, 'Korib' and PJSC KAMAZ, which are part of the machine-building cluster of the Republic of Tatarstan, have developed an innovative technology for industrial repair of trucks. The technology makes it possible to fully restore the service life of automotive equipment to the condition that is characteristic of new vehicles coming off the assembly line. At the same time, customers save up to 50% of their financial resources [10].

The warranty for an overhauled vehicle is the same as for the manufacturer's vehicles and covers Russian KAMAZ and Ural trucks as well as Chinese companies including Great Wall Motors (Baoding, Hebei Province), Shanghai Automotive Industry Corporation—SAIC Motor (Shanghai), China International Marine Containers Group Ltd—CIMC, Dongfeng Motor Group—DFG, Jiangling Motors Corporation Limited—JMC, Beijing Automotive Industry Holding Co.—BAIC Motor, Guangzhou Automobile Group—GAC Motor, etc (Guangzhou, Guangdong) [10, 15, 20].

22.2.2.2 National subcontracting portal Innokam.pro

Another significant organisational tool used to develop Russian and cross-border cooperation of innovation-oriented cluster structures in Kama agglomeration is the national subcontracting portal Innokam.pro [43]. Created in 2017 in the form of an online platform, the portal allows organising effective interaction of participants of innovation activities by connecting customers and manufacturers of product and process innovations into a single chain. The portal provides access to orders from Russian and foreign companies for manufacturing complex scientific and technical products. The national subcontracting portal Innokam.pro is integrated with the State Industry Information System (gisp.info), which provides access to the markets of the Eurasian Economic Union (EAEU) and Shanghai Cooperation Organisation (SCO) member states.

The interaction of agents of innovation within the framework of the Innokam.pro national subcontracting portal allows:

- firstly, the integration of foreign and Russian companies' competences and resources into a single system as part of cross-border project management. The convergence of competences and knowledge has a positive effect on the minimisation process of the project's costs.

  This makes it possible to reduce the cost component of the life cycle of created technological innovations, including R&D, engineering, testing and certification of product innovations, facilitating cross-border cooperation;
- secondly, the contractor gets an opportunity to increase the level of utilisation of its production capacities, the structural component of which, as a rule, is unique and expensive equipment.

In 2020, a new version of the portal was launched, which is a radically redesigned automated information platform that fully automates the business processes of procurement, sales and marketing. The national subcontracting portal Innokam.pro is an open information system, which enables it to address the increasingly complex interaction tasks of the participants in innovative activities.

The development prospects of the national subcontracting portal Innokam.pro are connected:

- firstly, with its integration into the unified procurement system of large companies and automation of export operations;
- secondly, with the expansion of cross-border cooperation and improvement of the quality of high-tech cross-border projects that are being implemented. This concerns not only accessing markets in other countries, especially in the Asia-Pacific region, but also increasing the knowledge-intensive nature of orders for progressively more complex scientific and technical products.

22.3 Mechanism for selecting the optimal risk management strategy for cross-border cooperation projects

Risk management is an important tool for increasing the efficiency of implementation of high-tech cross-border projects. This management can be implemented as part of various strategies, each of which provides a different level of efficiency of the implemented project [38]. Therefore, the task of choosing the best risk management strategy arises. The results of solving this problem are influenced by a large number of factors, which can be taken into account with the help of game theory tools [25, 41, 42, 44, 56].

22.3.1 The factor of environmental uncertainty

One of the dominating factors which influence the efficiency of the project is the uncertainty factor of the environment. A detailed study of this factor was done by Savage [45]. Savage used terms such as 'world' and 'state of world' in his analysis of environmental uncertainty. Savage defined 'world' as 'an object to which the interests of project participants are connected'. The 'state of world' is not known in advance to project participants, and this uncertainty gives rise to various project risks. According to Savage's conclusions, the uncertainty of the project environment characterises the situation in which a project's costs and results, and therefore its net cash flows and net discounted income, depend on the 'state of world' [24, 48, 50].

The introduction of the integral 'state of world' factor into the project's performance evaluation model makes it possible to combine all decision-relevant but predetermined uncertain factors into a single system. This allows the scenario approach to be used correctly in project management. According to Bayes' rules for the behaviour of project participants and the rules for changes in the external environment, scenarios can be assigned a probability of occurrence [21, 36, 37, 49]. In this case it is possible to quantify the probabilistic evaluation of the effectiveness and efficiency of the project [21, 22, 29, 30, 52, 53, 55]. Such an assessment is carried out based on the values of the mathematical expectation of net discounted income, calculated at the interval of the project life cycle. Based on the theoretical framework proposed by Savage and Bayes, we propose a mechanism for selecting an efficient option for a high-tech cross-border project. The proposed mechanism is focused on projects implemented in the presence of environmental uncertainty. In our proposed mathematical models, the uncertainty factor is taken into account through the set of project risks that are generated by this factor.

22.3.2 Problem solution

22.3.2.1 The algorithm of solving the problem of choosing the optimal risk management strategy

Consider a situation where a high-tech cross-border project is implemented and various risks arise within it. Let's denote by i the number of risks arising within the project. Since these risks are different for the customer and the developer of complex scientific and technological products, it is advisable to consider the risk management problem separately for each project participant. In this case, we consider this task from the point of view of the developer of technological innovations.

We will assume that several variants of risk management strategies (S_1, S_2, …, S_j, …, S_n) have been developed to solve the task of minimising project risks. These strategies, while claiming the same limited resources of the project, are alternative. So, the problem arises of choosing the best strategy for counteracting the risks. We will make the assumption that there are sufficient resources to implement any (but only one) of the alternative strategies for counteracting the project risks.

The development and implementation of high-tech cross-border projects requires significant investment [10]. These investments are made through a variety of resources, including material, financial and information-intellectual components [15]. In order not to complicate the problem of choosing the optimal risk management strategy, in particular, not to increase its dimensionality, we will introduce an integral parameter (K). This parameter will reflect the cost estimate of the total costs of all types of resources of the project. Then each jth strategy of the totality of alternative strategies (n) will be characterised by its parameters, including the cost of resources for the implementation of measures to counteract the risks, as well as the results obtained from the implementation of these measures in practice.

Let us denote the total cost of resources of a high-tech cross-border project for the implementation of a set of measures to counteract risks within the framework of the jth strategy by the symbol K_j. This parameter includes the cost of resources to counteract each ith risk occurring within the project, i.e.

$$K_j = \sum K_{ij} \tag{22.1}$$

In the case of game theory tools, the process of implementing a high-tech cross-border project can be interpreted as a 'game with world', i.e., with an adversary whose actions are not known in advance. It is only possible to assume the range of possible actions, as well as to predict the result that will be obtained from the implementation of the project.

To solve this problem, we have proposed an algorithm comprising the following sequence of steps. Figure 22.2 shows basic steps the algorithm of solving the problem of choosing the optimal risk management strategy.

Step 1. The factors ($f_1, f_2, \ldots, f_k$) leading to the occurrence of undesirable events ($z_1, z_2, \ldots, z_m$) are identified. We will assume that any ith event is independent of the other events and its occurrence reduces the efficiency of project implementation.

Step 2. Determine the loss of benefit to the participant in the implementation of the project in the risk environment. The occurrence of each ith event ($z_1, z_2, \ldots, z_m$) results in a lost benefit Y_i ($Y_1, Y_2, \ldots, Y_m$). Let us assume that Y_i is uniquely related to the occurrence of the ith event.

Step 3. For each jth strategy (S_j) of counteraction to project risks we calculate

- total damage Y;
- total resource expenditure (in cost terms) on the implementation of the jth strategy K_j.

Step 4. A probabilistic assessment of each jth project risk management strategy is performed. To perform the estimation for each ith event ($z_1, z_2, \ldots, z_m$), the following parameters are introduced:

- intensity of the ith event—λ_i ($\lambda_1, \lambda_2, \ldots, \lambda_m$);
- probability of occurrence of the ith event—p_i ($p_1, p_2, \ldots, p_m$);
- loss of profits from the occurrence of an event—Y_i ($Y_1, Y_2, \ldots, Y_m$).

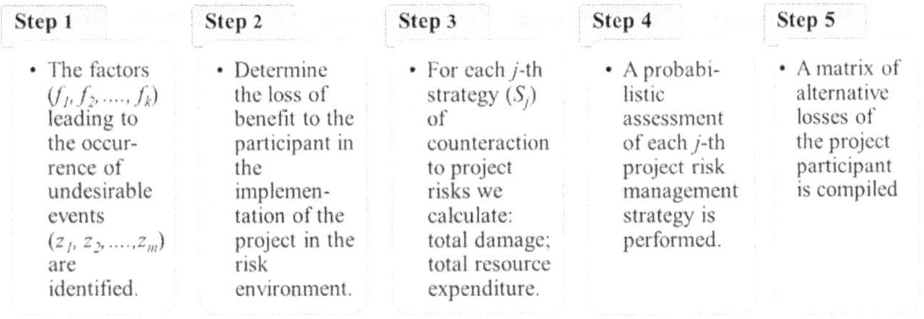

Figure 22.2. Algorithm of solving the problem of choosing the optimal risk management strategy. Source: authors' research.

Thus, the total lost profit of the project participant from the occurrence of all the risk events ($z_1, z_2, \ldots, z_m$) under the evaluated strategy of the project implementation will be

$$X_{j\Sigma} = \sum \lambda_i \cdot p_i \cdot Y_i \qquad (22.2)$$

Step 5. A matrix of alternative losses of the project participant is compiled. Table 22.1 shows this matrix. These losses are determined by the amount of lost profit of the participant.

The following notations are used in table 22.1:

S_0—strategy representing the initial state of the project, i.e. the state of the project before the beginning of the complex of risk management measures;

K_i—expenses of resources (in cost terms) of the project participant to counteract the *i*th risk;

X_{ij}—losses of the project participant from occurrence of *i*th risk within the *j*th risk management strategy.

22.3.2.2 *Mathematical and economic assessment of project risk management strategies*

Let us assume that we have developed a set of measures to counteract the risks of a high-tech cross-border project. Each of these sets will be in the form of a corresponding *j*th plan which is unambiguously linked to each *j*th strategy.

Assume that the implementation of each *j*th project risk management plan reduces the intensity of negative event flows (λ_i) and the risk of occurrence of events (p_i), while the damage (Y_i) from the occurrence of the *i*th event remains unchanged. On the basis of the assumptions made, let us describe the project risk management strategies in the new designations of these strategies. Table 22.2 describes project risk management strategies.

Then, the project participant's alternative loss matrix is generated in table 22.3.

Let us convert the loss matrix into a matrix of conditional gains of the project participant, which is shown in table 22.4. To do this, we will introduce a parameter M, which is the value of the marginal loss of profits that the participant could have

Table 22.1. Matrix of alternative losses of a project participant. Source: authors' research.

	Losses from the occurrence of an event						
Strategy	Event Z_1	Event Z_2	...	Event Z_i	...	Event Z_m	Total losses
S_0	X_{10}	X_{20}	...	X_{i0}	...	X_{m0}	ΣX_{i0}
S_1	$K_1 + X_{11}$	$K_1 + X_{21}$	...	$K_i + X_{i1}$	...	$K_1 + X_{m1}$	$K_1 + \Sigma X_{i1}$
S_2	$K_2 + X_{12}$	$K_2 + X_{22}$	...	$K_i + X_{i2}$	...	$K_2 + X_{m2}$	$K_2 + \Sigma X_{i2}$
...	...	...	...	...	...	...	...
S_j	$K_j + X_{1j}$	$K_j + X_{2j}$	....	$K_i + X_{ij}$	....	$K_j + X_{mj}$	$K_j + \Sigma X_{ij}$
...	...	...	...	...	...	...	...
S_n	$K_n + X_{1n}$	$K_n + X_{2n}$	...	$K_i + X_{3n}$	...	$K_n + X_{mn}$	$K_n + \Sigma X_{in}$

Table 22.2. Description of project risk management strategies. Source: authors' research.

Strategy	Costs of implementing the strategy	Intensity and risk of events occurrence after implementation of strategy							
		Event Z_1		…	Event Z_i		…	Event Z_m	
		Intens.	Risk	…	Intens.	Risk	…	Intens.	Risk
S_1	K_1	λ^*_{11}	p^*_{11}	…	λ^*_{i1}	p^*_{i1}	…	λ^*_{m1}	p^*_{m1}
S_2	K_2	λ^*_{12}	p^*_{12}	…	λ^*_{i2}	p^*_{i2}	…	λ^*_{m2}	p^*_{m2}
…	…	…	…	…	…	…	…	…	…
S_j	K_j	λ^*_{1j}	p^*_{1j}	…	λ^*_{ij}	p^*_{ij}	…	λ^*_{mj}	p^*_{mj}
…	…	…	…	…	…	…	…	…	…
S_n	K_n	λ^*_{1n}	p^*_{1n}	…	λ^*_{in}	p^*_{in}	…	λ^*_{mn}	p^*_{mn}

Table 22.3. Alternative loss matrix of the project participants. Source: authors' research.

Strategies	Value of alternative losses					Minimum value (Min)	Maximum value (Max)
	Event Z_1	…	Event Z_i	…	Event Z_m		
S_1	$K^*_1 + \lambda^*_1$ p^*_1 Y_1	…	$K^*_1 + \lambda^*_i$ p^*_i Y_i	…	$K^*_1 + \lambda^*_m$ p^*_m Y_m	min $\{K^*_1 + \lambda^*_i$ p^*_i $Y_i\}$	max $\{K^*_1 + \lambda^*_i$ p^*_i $Y_i\}$
S_2	$K^*_2 + \lambda^*_1$ p^*_1 Y_2	…	$K^*_2 + \lambda^*_i$ p^*_i Y_i	…	$K^*_2 + \lambda^*_m$ p^*_m Y_m	min $\{K^*_2 + \lambda^*_i$ p^*_i $Y_i\}$	max $\{K^*_2 + \lambda^*_i$ p^*_i $Y_i\}$
…	…	…		…	…	…	…
S_j	$K^*_j + \lambda^*_1$ p^*_1 Y_1		$K^*_j + \lambda^*_i$ p^*_i Y_i	…	…	min $\{K^*_i + \lambda^*_i$ p^*_i $Y_i\}$	max $\{K^*_i + \lambda^*_i$ p^*_i $Y_i\}$
…	…	…		…	…	…	…
S_n	$K^*_n + \lambda^*_1$ p_1 Y_1	…	$K^*_n + \lambda^*_i$ p^*_i Y_i	…	$K^*_n + \lambda^*_m$ p^*_m Y_m	min $\{K^*_n + \lambda^*_i$ p^*_i $Y_i\}$	max $\{K^*_n + \lambda^*_i$ p^*_i $Y_i\}$

gained from the project. This value can be defined as the difference between the positive values of the maximum and minimum expected net discounted income. Then the value of the project participant's conditional gain (D_j) for each jth risk management strategy (S_j) would be:

$$D_j = M - \left(K_j + \sum \lambda_i \cdot p_i \cdot Y_i\right) \quad (22.3)$$

Let us estimate the economic consequences of the risk of the occurrence of the ith event (ER_{ji}) in the jth project risk management strategy (S_j), considering these risks as the negative consequences of erroneous decisions. Let us assume that only events belonging to the set Z_i may occur when implementing strategy S_j. Then the difference between the gain which could be received by the participant of the project

Table 22.4. Matrix of project participant's conditional gains from implementing risk management strategies. Source: authors' research.

Strategies	Conditional gains of project participant: Event Z_1	... Event Z_i	... Event Z_m	Minimum value (Min)	Maximum value (Max)
S_1	$M - (K^*_1 + \lambda^*_1 p^*_1 Y_1)$	... $M - (K^*_1 + \lambda^*_i p^*_i Y_i)$	... $M - (K^*_1 + \lambda^*_m p^*_m Y_m)$	$\min \{M - (K^*_1 + \lambda^*_i p^*_i Y_i)\}$	$\max \{M - (K^*_1 + \lambda^*_i p^*_i Y_i)\}$
S_2	$M - (K^*_2 + \lambda^*_1 p^*_1 Y_2)$	... $M - (K^*_2 + \lambda^*_i p^*_i Y_i)$	... $M - (K^*_2 + \lambda^*_m p^*_m Y_m)$	$\min \{M - (K^*_2 + \lambda^*_i p^*_i Y_i)\}$	$\max \{M - (K^*_2 + \lambda^*_i p^*_i Y_i)\}$
...	...	...	... ...	...	...
S_j	$M - (K^*_j + \lambda^*_1 p^*_1 Y_1)$	$M - (K^*_j + \lambda^*_i p^*_i Y_i)$	$M - (K^*_j + \lambda^*_i p^*_i Y_i)$	$\min \{M - (K^*_j + \lambda^*_i p^*_i Y_i)\}$	$\max \{M - (K^*_j + \lambda^*_i p^*_i Y_i)\}$
...	...	... ...	... ...	...	...
S_n	$M - (K^*_n + \lambda^*_1 p_1 Y_1)$	... $M - (K^*_n + \lambda^*_i p^*_i Y_i)$	... $M - (K^*_n + \lambda^*_m p^*_m Y_m)$	$\min \{M - (K^*_n + \lambda^*_i p^*_i Y_i)\}$	$\max \{M - (K^*_n + \lambda^*_i p^*_i Y_i)\}$
b_i	$\max \{M - (K^*_j + \lambda^*_1 p^*_1 Y_1)\}$	... $\max \{M - (K^*_j + \lambda^*_i p^*_i Y_i)\}$	... $\max \{M - (K^*_n + \lambda^*_i p^*_i Y_i)\}$		

in the case of known conditions of occurrence of each event z_i of this set, and the gain which will be received by the participant, in a situation when these conditions are unknown, reflects economic consequences of risk (ER_{ji}) of occurrence in *j*th risk management strategy (S_j) of *i*th event. The following model can be used for quantitative risk magnitude assessment (ER_{ji}):

$$ER_{ij} = \max \left\{M - \left(K_j^* + \lambda_i^* \cdot p_i^* \cdot Y_i\right)\right\} - \left(M - \left(K_j^* + \lambda_i^* \cdot p_i^* \cdot Y_i\right)\right) \quad (22.4)$$

Based on the results of the calculations, a matrix reflecting the economic consequences of the project risks when implementing risk management strategies is compiled in table 22.5.

22.3.2.3 Evaluation criteria for a choice of optimum strategy of counteraction to project's risks

We use Savage's minimax risk criterion [24, 44, 45, 47–50] to evaluate strategies for dealing with the risks of the outsourced project. According to this criterion for counteracting the risks of the project, the strategy in which the greatest value of risk is minimal is chosen, i.e.:

Table 22.5. Matrix of economic consequences of project risks when implementing risk management strategies. Source: authors' research.

Strategies	Economic implications of risks of implementing the strategy					Maximum value (Max)
	Event Z_1	...	Event Z_i	...	Event Z_m	
S_1	ER_{11}	...	ER_{1i}	...	ER_{1m}	max $\{ER_{1i}\}$
S_2	ER_{21}	...	ER_{2i}	...	ER_{2m}	max $\{ER_{2i}\}$
...	...	...	...	...	...	...
S_j	ER_{j1}		ER_{ji}		ER_{jm}	max $\{ER_{ji}\}$
...	...	...	...	...	...	...
S_n	ER_{n1}	...	ER_{ni}	...	ER_{nm}	max $\{ER_{ni}\}$

$$S_{ji}^{S} = \min_i \max_j ER_{ji} \tag{22.5}$$

In practice, at a choice of optimum strategy of counteraction to risks of the project, except for Savage's criterion of the minimax risk, other criteria can be used. For example, these criteria can be the Wald or Hurwitz criteria [24, 31–33, 54, 57].

The maximin Wald criterion (criterion of extreme optimism) allows us to evaluate the results of 'playing' with the world as an intelligent and aggressive adversary. According to this criterion the optimal solution is the choice of such a strategy, which in the worst conditions of its implementation provides the maximum value of the win (W).

$$S_{\rm ji}^{W} = \min_i \max_j W_{\rm ji} = \min_i \max_j \left\{ M - \left(K_j^{*} + \lambda_i^{*} \cdot p_i^{*} \cdot Y_i \right) \right\} \tag{22.6}$$

The Hurwitz criterion implies that when deciding on the project risk counteraction strategy one should not be guided both by extreme pessimism (always count on the worst) and unjustified optimism (stick to the viewpoint that 'we'll be lucky' when deciding). When forming the Hurwitz criterion, either indicators of economic evaluation of risk consequences (ER_{ji}) or indicators of winning (W_{ji}) can be used.

If the Hurwitz criterion is oriented to the use of indicators of economic assessment of risk consequences (ER_{ji}), the optimum strategy of counteraction to project risks is chosen from the condition:

$$S_{\rm ji}^{H} = \max_i \left[x \cdot \min_j ER_{\rm ji} + (1 - x) \cdot \max_j ER_{\rm ji} \right] \tag{22.7}$$

When using gain measures (W_{ji}), the Hurwitz criterion would be a model of the following form:

$$S_{\rm ji}^{H} = \max_i \left[x \cdot \min_j W_{\rm ji} + (1 - x) \cdot \max_j W_{\rm ji} \right] \tag{22.8}$$

where: x is the 'pessimism factor' whose quantitative value is in the interval:

$$0 \leqslant x \leqslant 1 \tag{22.9}$$

Since there is an element of subjectivity in the considered criteria (Savage, Wald and Hurwitz) when assessing the risk management strategy of a high-tech cross-border project, in a practical situation it is advisable to use several criteria. At the same time assessments of a project's risk management strategy against these criteria may yield different results. However, focusing on a set of criterion assessments when choosing the optimal strategy for counteracting the risks of a project—an array of data, the processing of which provides information that influences the decision-making process.

This information, based on a set of economic evaluations of the project whose quantitative values vary, prompts the decision maker to subject the project risks to a more detailed analysis. The final decision on the choice of risk management strategy for a high-tech cross-border project, therefore, should take into account the extent to which the chosen strategy is characterised by the closeness of the estimates for most of the criteria [38].

The decision should take into account not only quantitative but also qualitative characteristics. This applies both to the project itself and to the proposed risk management strategies. It is especially useful to consider the readiness of the enterprise to implement a particular strategy. In practice, these qualitative assessments, using expert methods, are usually reduced to one or more quantitative assessments.

For example, in a digital environment, the readiness of a developer of complex scientific and technological products is largely determined by the availability of, firstly, highly qualified personnel (intellectual resources), and, secondly, modern information systems for decision support (information resources). Therefore, the information and intellectual resources of the company-developer of complex scientific and technological products become a significant factor in the effectiveness of the strategy to counteract the risks of a high-tech cross-border project. In this regard, the problem arises of the rational distribution of these resources in time according to the steps (business processes) of the strategy being implemented. It is advisable to use the theory of schedules and graph theory as a tool for solving such a problem [19].

22.4 Solving the practical problem of selecting the best risk management strategy by a Russian company in implementing a cross-border Chinese truck repair project

22.4.1 Calculating the effectiveness of the initial version of a cross-border project for the Russian company 'Korib'

In accordance with the results of the theoretical developments, let us consider solving the problem of selecting the best risk management strategy. A similar problem was solved by us with regard to the activities of the company 'Korib', which is a member of the machine-building cluster of the Kama agglomeration of the Republic of Tatarstan. The cross-border project we are considering involves the implementation of an innovative technology for industrial repairs of Chinese trucks

Table 22.6. Korib's risks of implementing a cross-border project. Source: authors' research.

No.	Type of risk	Risk assessment, %
1.	Reduced revenue figures	4,0
2.	Excess of the actual cost of repair services over the planned level	4,0
3.	Claims made by the customer because the quality of the work does not meet contractual requirements	4,5
4.	Deviations from environmental standards	2,5
Total risk value		15,0

operated by Russian companies. 'Korib', implementing innovative technology of industrial repair of automobiles, uses original sets of spare parts and process liquids, which are supplied by Chinese manufacturers.

For 'Korib', we calculated the effectiveness of the initial version of a cross-border project, the implementation period of which is 10 years. This option is characterised by the fact that it has no mechanisms to deal with project risks. In determining the value of the risk-free rate of return, emphasis was placed on stock market returns, in particular those of long-term government debt. According to the Central Bank of the Russian Federation (web-site: www.cbr.ru), the yield on government bonds as of 29 October 2021 (depending on maturity) is 8.21% per annum [6]. Therefore, the risk-free rate of return was assumed to be 8.0%. An expert method was used to assess the risks of the project. The confidence interval for each of the risks listed in table 22.6 was in the range of 0%–5%.

Using an expert valuation method, the total risk value of Korib's cross-border Chinese truck repair project is 15.0%. Then the value of the discount rate used to calculate the net discounted income of the project implemented by 'Korib' is 21.0%.

Calculations of the project's efficiency showed that the net discounted income that can be received by 'Korib' (in national currency) is 78 778 rubles (that is $1 012 344.30 at the current rate), and the amount of revenue in the initial year of the project implementation ($t = 0$), which is the basis for calculating the company's lost profits when evaluating various strategies to counter project risks amounted (in national currency) to 60 823 rubles (that is $781 611.8 at the current rate).

22.4.2 The factors shaping Korib's risks. The loss amount of Korib's benefit

The formation of the strategy to counteract the risks of the cross-border project was preceded by the identification of factors that lead to the occurrence of undesirable events ($z_1, z_2, \ldots, z_4$), i.e. the manifestation of project risks in the activities of 'Korib'. Table 22.7 systematizes these factors.

Next, using the parameters for the events in table 22.7, we determine the amount of benefit (Y_i) lost by 'Korib' in table 22.8. This loss of benefit is the consequence of the occurrence of undesirable events when the company implements a cross-border project involving the repair of Chinese-made cars.

Table 22.7. Factors and events shaping Korib's risks. Source: authors' research.

No. Factors leading to the occurrence of undesirable project events	Korib's risk events	Event designation
Factors influencing the risks of the first event	Revenue figure below the profitability threshold	Z_1
1.1. Reduced sales of repair services		
1.2. Reduced market prices for repair services		
1.3. Changes in the structure of repair customers		
Factors influencing the risks of the second event	Actual cost of repair services exceeded the standard level	Z_2
2.1. The actual labour input exceeds the normative value		
2.2. The occurrence of unexpected costs due to errors in order formation: a) the emergence of additional work during the execution of an order b) increased lead times		
2.3. Downtime due to Chinese counterparts failing to meet spare parts delivery conditions (price and delivery rhythm)		
Factors influencing the risks of the third event	Claims made by the customer because the quality of the work does not meet contractual requirements	Z_3
3.1. Outdated technologies for carrying out the work		
3.2. Obsolete technological and measurement equipment		
3.3. Replacement of original spare parts with counterfeit parts		
3.4. The qualifications of the personnel do not match the technological requirements of the order		
Factors influencing the risks of the fourth event	Deviations from environmental standards exceed permissible values	Z_4
4.1. Lack of environmental management mechanisms and internal environmental audits		
4.2. Non-compliance of production conditions with environmental standards		
4.3. Obsolete waste management technology		

Table 22.8. Calculating Korib's loss of benefit in the execution of project baseline case. Source: authors' research.

		Events that trigger the emergence of risk			
No.	Parameter name	Z_1	Z_2	Z_3	Z_4
1.	Intensity of occurrence of the *i*th event (λ_i)	5	2	3	2
2.	Probability of occurrence of the *i*th event (p_i)	0,008	0,02	0,015	0,0125
3.	Risk of the occurrence of the *i*th event (r_i)	0,04	0,04	0,045	0,025
4.	Basis for calculation of the company's lost profits, thousand rub.	60 823	60 823	60 823	60 823
4.	The benefit lost by the company due to a reduction in revenue as a result of the *i*th event (Y_i), thousand rub.	2 433	2 433	2 737	1 521

The baseline scenario for the cross-border project is one in which no risk management mechanism is in place. In calculating the lost benefit, 'Korib' uses the revenue generated by the company in the first year of the project ($t = 0$) as the baseline.

22.4.3 The risk mitigation strategies for the company 'Korib'

To solve the problem of minimising the risks of a cross-border project, 'Korib' has developed four options for risk mitigation strategies (S_1, S_2, S_3, S_4).

- The first strategy is the service strategy, which aims to improve the quality of repair work.
- The second strategy, being an infocommunication strategy, is focused on increasing the level of informatisation of the business processes implemented by the company.
- The third strategy is the innovation strategy. It is aimed at innovative developments and their integration into the cross-border project management system.
- As part of the fourth strategy, 'Korib' prioritizes environmental issues.

The characteristics and costs of these strategies are presented in table 22.9.

Table 22.10 calculates the parameters for alternative risk management strategies for the cross-border project implemented by 'Korib'.

22.4.4 Assessment of economic consequences of Korib's risk management strategies

Now, in table 22.11, let's form an alternative loss matrix for 'Korib', which implements a cross-border Chinese car repair project.

We then transform the loss matrix into a contingent benefit matrix for 'Korib', which implements a cross-border project to repair Chinese-made vehicles. The marginal benefit that the company could have gained from the cross-border project

Table 22.9. Characteristics of risk minimisation strategies for project under implementation. Source: authors' research.

Type of strategy	Characteristics of the strategy	Costs of implementation, thousand rub.	
		Events	Strategies
Strategy S_1 (service strategy)	Improving the functional marketing strategy, including the advertising component	1 275	5 250
	Acquisition and implementation of a CRM system	3 975	
Strategy S_2 (infocommunication strategy)	Development and implementation of an information system for the operational and calendar management of production resources	4 370	9 860
	Acquisition and implementation of a supply chain management information system	5 490	
Strategy S_3 (innovation strategy)	Formation and integration of the innovation subsystem into the project management system	2 630	4 130
	Training staff in innovative repair services	1 500	
Strategy S_4 (environmental strategy)	Development of environmental management systems and internal environmental audits	1 800	3 950
	Acquisition and implementation of innovative waste management technology	2150	

is the profitability threshold (*Prof.Thr.*) of the repair services provided by 'Korib' (the value of the vertical coordinate of the break-even point). This indicator reflects the revenue limit at which the company's operations remain break-even. The profitability threshold can be calculated using the following formula:

$$Prof.\ Thr = \frac{FRS}{RC - VRS} \cdot RC \tag{22.10}$$

where:

FRS—fixed costs attributable to Korib's cost of repair services;

RC—revenue of 'Korib', which is determined by the volume of payments received from the client;

VRS—the amount of variable costs of 'Korib', attributable to the cost of repair services.

The calculations show that for the first year ($t = 0$) of the cross-border project the profitability threshold in national currency is:

$$Prof.\ Thr = 30\,289 \text{ thousand rubles (that is \$389 231.7 at the current rate)} \tag{22.11}$$

Table 22.10. Calculation of the parameters for the risk management strategies of the project under implementation. Source: authors' research.

No.	Parameter name	Events that give rise to project risk			
		Z_1	Z_2	Z_3	Z_4
Strategy S_1 (service strategy)					
1.1.	Intensity of occurrence of the *i*th event (λ_i)	4	2	3	2
1.2.	Probability of occurrence of the *i*th event (p_i)	0,007	0,02	0,015	0,0125
1.3.	Risk of the occurrence of the *i*th event (r_i)	0,028	0,04	0,045	0,025
1.4.	The basis for calculating the company's lost profits, thousand rub.	60 823	60 823	60 823	60 823
1.5.	Benefit lost by the company due to a reduction in revenue as a result of the *i*th event (Y_i), thousand rub.	1 703	2 433	2 737	1 521
1.6.	Total loss of revenue by the company as a result of the strategy (Y_1), thousand rub.	8 394			
Strategy S_2 (infocommunication strategy)					
2.1.	Intensity of occurrence of the *i*th event (λ_i)	5	1	3	2
2.2.	Probability of occurrence of the *i*th event (p_i)	0,008	0,015	0,015	0,0125
2.3.	Risk of the occurrence of the *i*th event (r_i)	0,04	0,015	0,045	0,025
2.4.	Basis for calculation of company's loss of profit, thousand rub.	60 823	60 823	60 823	60 823
2.5.	The company's loss of revenue as a result of the occurrence of the *i*th event (Y_i), thousand rub.	2 433	912	2 737	1 521
2.6	Total loss of revenue by the company as a result of implementing the strategy (Y_2), thousand rub.	7 606			
Strategy S_3 (innovation strategy)					
3.1.	Intensity of occurrence of the *i*th event (λ_i)	5	2	2	2
3.2.	Probability of occurrence of the *i*th event (p_i)	0,008	0,02	0,01	0,0125
3.3.	Risk of the occurrence of the *i*th event (r_i)	0,04	0,04	0,02	0,025
3.4.	Basis for calculation of company's loss of profit, thousand rub.	60 823	60 823	60 823	60 823
3.5.	The company's loss of revenue as a result of the occurrence of the *i*-th event (Y_i), thousand rub.	2 433	2 433	1 216	1 521
3.6.	Total loss of revenue by the company as a result of implementing the strategy (Y_3), thousand rub.	7 603			
Strategy S_4 (environmental strategy)					
4.1	Intensity of occurrence of the *i*-th event (λ_i)	5	2	3	1
4.2.	Probability of occurrence of the *i*-th event (p_i)	0,008	0,02	0,015	0,01
4.3.	Risk of the occurrence of the *i*-th event (r_i)	0,04	0,04	0,045	0,01
4.4.	Basis for calculation of company's loss of profit, thousand rub.	60 823	60 823	60 823	60 823
4.5.	The company's loss of revenue as a result of the occurrence of the *i*-th event (Y_i), thousand rub.	2 433	2 433	2 737	608
4.6.	Total loss of revenue by the company as a result of the strategy (Y_4), thousand rub.	8 211			

Then the matrix of conditional benefits received by 'Korib' from the implementation of risk management strategies can be presented in the form of the table 22.12.

For each risk management strategy, let us estimate the economic impact of the risk of all the negative events from Korib's perspective, as shown in table 22.12. To do this, using the mathematical models we have obtained, we will perform the relevant calculations and, based on their results, compile a matrix in table 22.13.

Table 22.11. Alternative loss matrix for 'Korib'. Source: authors' research.

	Value of Korib's Alternative Losses					
Strategies	Event Z_1	Event Z_2	Event Z_3	Event Z_4	Minimum value (Min)	Maximum value (Max)
S_1	1 703	2 433	2 737	1 521	1 521	2 737
S_2	2 433	912	2 737	1 521	912	2 737
S_3	2 433	2 433	1 216	1 521	1 216	2 433
S_4	2 433	2 433	2 737	608	608	2 737

Table 22.12. Matrix of conditional benefits gained by 'Korib' from implementing risk management strategies. Source: authors' research.

	Conditional gains for 'Korib'					
Strategies	Event Z_1	Event Z_2	Event Z_3	Event Z_4	Minimum value (Min)	Maximum value (Max)
S_1	28 586	27 856	27 552	28 768	27 552	28 768
S_2	27 856	29 377	27 552	28 768	27 552	29 377
S_3	27 856	27 856	29 073	28 768	27 856	29 073
S_4	27 856	27 856	27 552	29 681	27 552	29 681
b_i	28 586	29 377	29 073	29 681		

Table 22.13. Matrix of economic consequences of risks in the course of implementation of Korib's risk management strategies. Source: authors' research.

	Economic consequences of the risks of implementing the strategy				
Strategies	Event Z_1	Event Z_2	Event Z_3	Event Z_4	Maximum value (Max)
S_1	0	1791	1521	913	1791
S_2	730	0	1521	913	1521
S_3	730	1791	0	913	1791
S_4	730	1791	1521	0	1791

22.4.5 Results and discussion

Using the criteria for evaluating cross-border project risk management strategies, let us evaluate the results. According to Savage's minimax risk criterion, the strategy with the highest value of risk is the one that is chosen to counteract the risks of a cross-border project. Table 22.13 shows that this strategy is the infocommunication strategy. The Wald criterion (criterion of extreme optimism) yields an ambiguous result for choosing the optimal strategy. According to this criterion, service, infocommunication and environmental strategies may be appropriate for 'Korib'.

The Hurwitz criterion, which recommends not going to extremes (both extreme pessimism and unwarranted optimism) in deciding the choice of strategy to counter project risk, relies heavily on the choice of the 'pessimism factor'. Table 22.14 shows the estimated characteristics of the risk management strategy for a cross-border project according to the Hurwitz criterion, obtained with different values of the 'pessimism factor'.

The calculations show that as the 'pessimism factor' increases, the preference for choosing the optimal strategy for dealing with risks shifts from an environmental strategy to an innovation strategy. The increase in the 'pessimism factor' is largely consistent with the reality of Korib's operations in an increasingly turbulent external environment.

Table 22.15 summarises the results recommended by various criteria for selecting the optimal risk management strategy for a cross-border project implemented by 'Korib'.

According to the Savage and Wald criteria, the infocommunication strategy should be preferred, while the Hurwitz criterion recommends focusing on the innovation strategy in a pessimistic evaluation. Therefore, not only quantitative but also qualitative factors should be taken into account, in particular the competitive strategy and the development prospects of 'Korib'. The company's development prospects are related to further development of innovation activities, creation of a common information space, and training of personnel in order to improve their competences. Therefore, in this situation, innovation and infocommunication strategies become the most appropriate.

Table 22.14. Estimated characteristics of the project risk management strategy according to the Hurwitz criterion for different values of the 'pessimism factor'. Source: authors' research.

	Hurwitz criterion scores			
Strategy	$x = 0{,}5$	$x = 0{,}7$	$x = 0{,}8$	$x = 0{,}9$
S_1	28 160	27 917	27 795	27 674
S_2	28 465	28 100	27 917	27 735
S_3	28 465	**28 227**	**28 099**	**27 998**
S_4	**28 617**	28 191	27 978	27 765
Recommended strategy	S_4	S_3	S_3	S_3

Table 22.15. Strategies recommended by the various criteria for dealing with the risks of the project implemented by 'Korib'. Source: authors' research.

No.	Strategy selection criterion	Recommended strategy
1	Savage criterion	Infocommunication strategy (S_2)
2	Wald criterion	Service (S_1), infocommunication (S_2) or environmental (S_4) strategies
3	Hurwitz criterion (for optimistic and medium assessments)	Environmental strategy (S_4)
	Hurwitz criterion (for pessimistic assessment)	Innovative strategy (S_3)

22.5 The concept of creating and using information systems for decision-making support in the field of risk management of cross-border projects

22.5.1 Promising areas for the development of information systems for decision support

Our studies have shown that one of the promising areas of development of information systems for decision support that ensure the control of heterogeneous risks is the enhancement of the intelligence of systems [7, 8, 13–15, 18, 19, 40]. This is achieved by giving the modelling processes of development and decision-making the properties characteristic of the situation when decisions, based on the use of heterogeneous data, are developed directly by a human being. This can be either an expert or a project manager (e.g., decision maker).

In doing so, the information model of the development and decision-making process, which is implemented according to the 'recognition-action' scheme characteristic of human action, is significantly extended. The extension of the information model involves the creation of new data sets and their integration into existing databases. And the types of these data may be different, differing in structural description, indexing and retrieval methods [39]. Orientation on the factor of intellectualisation in the construction of the decision support system provides the innovation-oriented cluster structures of the Kama agglomeration, implementing the projects of cross-border cooperation, with the flexibility of the system to counteract project risks. In its turn, the flexibility factor positively influences the effectiveness and efficiency of implemented cross-border projects. Figure 22.3 shows the pattern of the development of information system of decision-making support in the field of risk management for cross-border cooperation projects of innovation-oriented cluster structures of the Kama agglomeration.

The information system of decision-making support in the field of risk management of cross-border cooperation projects of innovation-oriented cluster structures of the Kama agglomeration should be attributed to the class of hybrid systems of calculation-logic type [7, 9, 15, 23]. This judgment is based on the fact that the

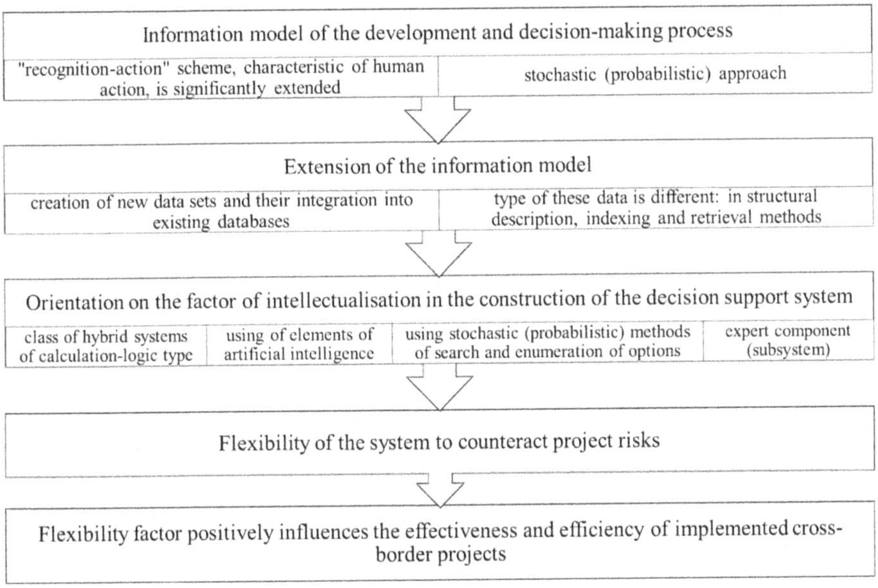

Figure 22.3. Pattern of the development of information system of decision-making support in the field of risk management for cross-border cooperation projects of innovation-oriented cluster structures of the Kama agglomeration. Source: author's research.

creation of the system is focused on the use of elements of artificial intelligence. In the construction of such systems, both strict mathematical rules of search for optimal solutions and various search methods, in particular, methods of expert evaluations are used [34, 46, 51]. For such systems one of the key tasks of designing is the task of choosing adequate tools, which are often based on the knowledge of experts.

In this case, the mathematical toolkit will contain the formal apparatus necessary for decision-making. For example, it may be productive models. Then in the information system the process of development and decision-making will be represented as a semantic network in the form of an oriented graph [14]. The tops of the graph will correspond to the objects of the subject area, and the arcs (edges of the graph) will set the relations between the objects. The decision-making process in the sphere of risk management of cross-border cooperation projects of innovation-oriented cluster structures of the Kama agglomeration will reflect the search for the best solution on the acceptable set of project states.

22.5.2 Prospects for the development of decision support systems tools

Prospects for the development of decision support systems tools are associated with the improvement of algorithms for the functioning of production systems. At present, almost all these algorithms are based on a deterministic treatment of the process of project implementation, and, consequently, of the process of systems' functioning [34]. However, the processes that take place within the implementation of high-tech projects of transboundary cooperation of innovation-oriented cluster structures of Kama agglomeration with Chinese partners have stochastic (probabilistic) nature and are characterized by incomplete information.

In such a case, the use of a deterministic approach to building a decision support system for risk management and describing the processes of functioning of the information system is ineffective. Therefore, when designing the information system, the emphasis was placed on the stochastic (probabilistic) approach. On this basis, the expert subsystem should play a key role in the structure of the established decision-making support system in the field of risk management of high-tech cross-border projects. When building such a subsystem, in addition to expert methods, it was proposed to use a combination of computational and logical methods.

22.5.3 The expert subsystem

The expert component, playing a key role in the structure of the created information system of decision-making support in the sphere of risk management of cross-border cooperation projects of innovation-oriented cluster structures of Kama agglomeration, provides the use of stochastic (probabilistic) methods of search and enumeration of options. This component is based on a set of expert knowledge, presented in a user-friendly form. The structure of the expert component of the decision-making support system in the sphere of risk management of cross-border cooperation projects of innovation-oriented cluster structures of the Kama agglomeration is based on the modular principle of construction. It is shown in figure 22.4. The set of

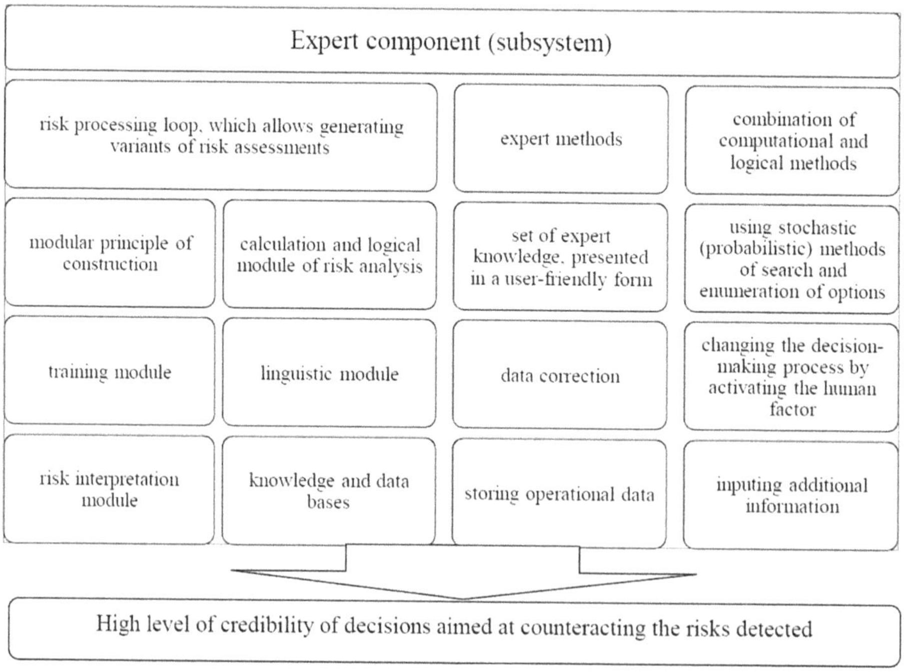

Figure 22.4. Diagram of expert component of the decision-making support system in the sphere of risk management. Source: author's research.

modules of the expert component of the system covers training and risk interpretation modules, calculation and logical module of risk analysis, and linguistic module. Additionally, the structure of the expert subsystem includes knowledge and databases, and also provides for storing operational data, which is ensured by a set of independent databases.

The proposed structure of the expert component of the decision-making support system in the field of risk management of cross-border cooperation projects of innovation-oriented cluster structures of the Kama agglomeration is new. This novelty is determined by the presence in the system of risk processing loop, which allows generating variants of risk assessments. Such assessments are formed with the help of search algorithms, implemented on the basis of local operational databases independent of each other.

The system can implement both standard algorithms and original ones developed to solve highly specialised problems of risk management. Such organization of the operational component of the expert component of the decision-making support system in the field of risk management of cross-border cooperation projects of innovation-oriented cluster structures of the Kama agglomeration allows using different strategies, cardinally different from each other, for the purpose of finding various risks. This guarantees a high level of credibility of decisions aimed at counteracting the risks detected.

Another feature of the expert subsystem is the possibility for innovation-oriented cluster structures of the Kama agglomeration to solve risk management tasks in the situation when the risk has already manifested itself. In this case, the decision support system in the field of risk management of cross-border cooperation projects performs data correction and inputs additional information. Such information makes it possible to change the decision-making process by activating the human factor. In this case, the effectiveness of the decision made will to a large extent be determined by the professional qualities of the system user (decision maker or expert). Therefore, the innovation-oriented cluster structures of the Kama agglomeration have a new task. The solution of this task is connected with the formation of a set of digital competences among the personnel involved in the development and implementation of high-tech cross-border projects [11, 12, 16, 20].

And quite often in the situation when the risk has already manifested itself and there are time constraints, it is necessary to obtain an acceptable (in terms of achieving the planned efficiency of the project implemented by the innovation-oriented cluster structures of Kama agglomeration in the sphere of cross-border cooperation with Chinese partners) solution. The complexity of the implemented high-tech cross-border projects and the presence of non-deterministic factors in the external environment do not allow using classical algorithmic methods and models of decision-making theory.

In particular, the lack of a theoretical and methodological framework for managing complex science-intensive cross-border projects that involve R&D in a highly uncertain environment generates additional risks. In this case, at the stages of mastering the created technological innovations, releasing an innovative product or rendering qualitatively new services, as well as transferring the results to the Chinese customer, ineffective decisions on the choice of risk counteraction strategy can be made.

Therefore, the expert component of the decision-making support system in the sphere of risk management of cross-border cooperation projects of innovation-oriented cluster structures of the Kama agglomeration should be built on the knowledge of highly qualified specialists. This can be the knowledge of specialists in the field of diagnostics of difficult-to-formalize problems, project management, risk management, etc. In this case, the solutions developed on the basis of expert knowledge in the field of risk management of cross-border cooperation projects of innovation-oriented cluster structures of the Kama agglomeration will be of high quality.

In this situation, for the innovation-oriented cluster structures of Kama agglomeration, it becomes relevant to solve a number of tasks:

- firstly, it concerns problems of developing expert models of problem situation representation (states of subject area);
- secondly, problems of designing means of organising dialog interaction of information system of decision-making support with a user (for example, a decision maker or an expert).

22.6 Conclusion

Thus, in the course of the study it has been found that in the implementation of innovation-oriented cluster structures of Kama agglomeration of high-tech projects implemented in the sphere of cross-border cooperation it is advisable to use such organizational mechanisms as Eurasian technological platform 'Technologies of maintenance and repair of industrial equipment' and National subcontracting portal Innokam.pro, which is an effective online communication platform.

The proposed mechanism for choosing the optimal risk management strategy for cross-border cooperation projects includes a step-by-step algorithm, covering:

- the identification of factors that lead to undesirable events;
- the definition of foregone benefits in the implementation of the project at risk;
- probabilistic assessment of the proposed strategies to counteract project risks;
- identification of alternative losses of project participants;
- assessment of the economic impact of risks in the implementation of the proposed risk management strategies.

As evaluation criteria, the use of Savage, Wald and Hurwitz criteria has been proposed.

The solution of the practical task of choosing optimal risk management strategy by a Russian company during the implementation of a transboundary project, which foresees the use of innovative technologies of repair of Chinese-made trucks, was obtained. For the company 'Korib', which is a member of the machine-building cluster of the Republic of Tatarstan, various risk management strategies have been evaluated. For such strategies the following are considered:

- firstly, service strategy, which is aimed at improving the quality of repair work;
- secondly, infocommunication strategy, focused on increasing the level of informatisation of business processes implemented by the company;

- thirdly, innovation strategy, which involves the implementation of innovative developments and their integration into the project management system:
- in the framework of the fourth strategy, the company 'Korib' gives priority to the solution of environmental problems.

The concept of creation and use of information systems for decision-making support in risk management of cross-border cooperation projects of innovation-oriented cluster structures of Kama agglomeration is proposed. The proposed concept of building the system is based on expert methods of risk assessment, reflecting the specifics of high-tech cross-border project management.

References

[1] Abashkin V, Boiarov A and Kutsenko E 2012 Cluster policy in Russia: from theory to practice *Foresight* **6** 16–27

[2] Abashkin V L, Artemov S V and Islankina E A *et al* 2017 *Methodological Materials for the Creation of Industrial Clusters* (Moscow: NRU HSE) (in Russian)

[3] Abdikeev N M and Malova D V 2012 Dynamic modeling and scenario analysis of the development of innovative clusters in the regions *Fin. Anal.: Prob.Sol.* **31** 12–23

[4] Abzalilova R L 2016 *On the Strategic Directions of Development of Innokam—Kama Innovative Territorial-Production Cluster* https://imemo.ru/files/File/ru/conf/2016/09122016/09122016-PRZ-ABZ.pdf [accessed 17 February 2022] (in Russian)

[5] Ashpina O 2015 Innokam—a territory of development *Chem. J.* **9** 36–42

[6] Bank of Russia 2021 *Banking Sector Liquidity and Financial Markets: Informational and Analytical Commentary* **10(68)** November 11, 2021. http://cbr.ru/Collection/Collection/File/39311/LB_2021-68.pdf (in Russian)

[7] Baranov V, Batova M and Baranova I 2020 Information tools for effective management of business processes of a high-technology enterprise *Thesis of Reports '2nd Scientific-Practical Conf. of Russian and Croatian Scientists in Dubrovnik' As Part of The Federal Target Program 'Research and Development in Priority Areas of Development of The Scientific and Technological Complex of Russia for 2014–2020' (Moscow-Dubrovnik Oct. 2020)*

[8] Baranov V V, Baranova I V and Zaitsev I V 2018 *Management of the High-Tech Enterprise Development in the Context of Information Society* (Moscow: Creative economy)) (in Russian)

[9] Baranova I V, Batova M M and Zhao K 2020 *Information Tools for Digital Transformation of High-Tech Enterprises* (Moscow: Creative Economy) (in Russian)

[10] Baranova I V, Batova M M and Zhao K 2021 Convergence as a factor of effective development of cross-border systems 'education-science production' (on the example of Russian-Chinese cooperation) *Vectors of Socio-Economic Development of Russia: Modern Challenges and Opportunities of Convergence of Theoretical, Methodological and Applied Research* ed O A Podkopaev *et al* (Samara: LLC SIC 'Volga Scientific Corporation') ch 3 pp 157–215 (in Russian)

[11] Batova M M 2021 *Digital Paradigm of Evolution of the System 'Education-Science-Production'* (Moscow: First Economic Publishing House)) (in Russian)

[12] Batova M M 2020 Formation of information and intellectual capital in the system 'education-science-production' *Prop. Rel. Russ. Fed.* **8** 7–13 (in Russian)

[13] Batova M M, Baranov V V, Korobchenko O V and Zhao K 2021 Informatization of risk management processes as one of the aspects of effective risk management in the field of international collaboration *Proc. of the Int. Scientific and Practical Conf. Vectors of development of the modern economy: problems of theory and practice (Moscow 23 November 2021)* (Moscow: Publishing House Moscow Polytech) pp 504–11
[14] Batova M, Baranov V and Mayorov S 2021 Automation of economic activity management of high-tech structures of innovation-oriented clusters *J. Ind. Integ. Manage.* **06** 15–30
[15] Batova M, Baranov V, Mayorov S and Zhao K 2021 Informatisation of project activities performed by innovation clusters of the Kamsky agglomeration in Russia *Conf. Proc. 2021 Asia-Pacific Conf. on Communications Technology and Computer Science (ACCTCS) (Shenyang January 2021)* 118–22
[16] Batova M M and Baranova I V 2019 Information technology knowledge management in the system of interaction of educational and scientific-production structures *WSEAS Trans. Bus. Econ.* **16** 545–51 http://wseas.org/wseas/cms.action?id=19913
[17] Batova M M, Baranova I V and Celiloglu Y T 2021 Int. technological exchange in the IT-sphere as a form of effective transfer of innovations *Proc. of the IV All-Russian Scientific and Practical Conf. with international participation 'Financial, economic and information support of innovative development of regions' (Yalta March 2021)* (Simferopol: Limited Liability Company 'Publishing House Printing House 'Arial') pp 289–93 (in Russian)
[18] Batova M, Baranova I, Baranov V and Celiloglu Y T 2020 Developing a system to support banks in making investment decisions when organizing project financing *WSEAS Trans. Syst. Control* **15** 613–26
[19] Batova M, Baranova I, Korobchenko O and Baranov V 2021 System theory for an information system for planning project activities in a high-tech enterprise *Int. J. Circ., Syst. Sign. Process.* **15** 187–96
[20] Batova M M, Baranova I V and Zhao K 2020 The development of digital competencies in the creation of the MES-system for the production of spare parts for Chinese automobiles brilliance auto by a Russian enterprise *Proceedings of International Conference 'Process Management and Scientific Developments' (Birmingham UK January 2020)* (Moscow: Scientific Publishing House Infinity)
[21] Berger J O 1985 *Statistical Decision Theory and Bayesian Analysis* (New York: Springer)
[22] Bradley R 2017 *Decision Theory with a Human Face* (Cambridge UK: Cambridge University Press)
[23] Brocke J vom and Mendling J 2018 *Business Process Management Cases: Digital Innovation and Business Transformation in Practice* (Cham: Springer)
[24] Dadashov Ch M 2016 *Game theory: Game with World. Educational and methodical textbook: 1st part* (Moscow: Moscow Aviation Institute) http://rstu.ru/metods/books/Dad.pdf (in Russia)
[25] Durlauf S N and Blume L E 2010 *Game Theory* (London: Palgrave Macmillan)
[26] Eurasian Technological Platform 'Technology of maintenance and repair of industrial equipment' [Electronic resource accessed 17 February 2022]. https://drive.google.com/drive/folders/1TZGBHt2C9qj1r3lPugS_rTycYfd4acu4?usp=sharing
[27] Gagarin G I and Arkhipova L S 2014 Innovative territorial clusters as a tool to increase the competitiveness of the Russian economy *Bull. Iaroslav Mudryi NSU* **82** 28–33 (in Russian)
[28] Gokhberg L M and Shadrina A E (ed) 2015 *Pilot Innovative Territorial Clusters in The Russian Federation: Directions of Implementation of Development Programs* (Moscow: NRU HSE) (in Russian)

[29] Heard N 2021 *An Introduction to Bayesian Inference, Methods and Computation* (Cham: Springer)
[30] Hey J D 1985 *Data in Doubt: An Introduction to Bayesian Statistical Inference for Economists* (Oxford: Basil Blackwell)
[31] Hurwitz A 1895 About the conditions under which an equation has only roots with negative real parts [Ueber die Bedingungen, unter welchen eine Gleichung nur Wurzeln mit negativen reellen Theilen besitzt] *Math. Annal.* **46** 273–84 (in German)
[32] Hurwitz A 1931 *Mathematical Works: Second Volume Number Theory Algebra and Geometry (German Edition)* 1st edn (Basel: Springer)) (in German)
[33] Hurwitz A and Pólya G *et al* 1933 *Mathematical Works: First Volume of Function Theory (German Edition)* 1st edn (Basel: Springer)) (in German)
[34] Kallrath J 2021 *Business Optimization Using Mathematical Programming: An Introduction with Case Studies and Solutions in Various Algebraic Modeling Languages* (Cham: Springer)
[35] Kutsenko E 2015 Pilot innovative territorial clusters of Russia: a sustainable development model *Foresight* **9** 32–55
[36] Kwon I-W 1978 *Statistical Decision Theory with Business and Economic Applications: A Bayesian Approach* (New York: Petrocelli/Charter)
[37] Laraki R, Renault J and Sorin S 2019 *Mathematical Foundations of Game Theory* (Cham: Springer)
[38] Laskina L Y and Silakova L V 2019 *Estimation and Risk Management in Innovation Activity* (Saint-Petersburg: ITMO University) (in Russian)
[39] Ma Y and Du H 2022 *Enterprise Data at Huawei: Methods and Practices of Enterprise Data Governance* (Singapore: Springer)
[40] Makarenko S I 2009 *Intelligent Information Systems* (Moscow-Stavropol: Sholokhov Moscow State University) (in Russian)
[41] Matsumoto A and Szidarovszky F 2016 *Game Theory and Its Applications* (Tokyo: Springer Japan)
[42] Munoz-Garcia F and Toro-Gonzalez D 2019 *Strategy and Game Theory. Practice Exercises with Answers* 2th edn (Cham: Springer Nature Switzerland AG)
[43] National Portal of Subcontracting Innokam.pro. [Electronic resource accessed 17 February 2022] https://innokam.pro
[44] Rass S and Schauer S 2018 *Game Theory for Security and Risk Management. From Theory to Practice* (Cham: Birkhäuser)
[45] Read C 2012 The Theory of Friedman and Savage *The Portfolio Theorists. Great Minds in Finance* (London: Palgrave Macmillan)
[46] Ren J (ed) 2021 *Multi-Criteria Decision Analysis for Risk Assessment and Management* (Cham: Springer)
[47] Savage L J 1951 The theory of statistical decision *J. Am. Stat. Assoc.* **46** 55–67
[48] Savage L J 1972 *Foundations of Statistics* 2th rev.edn. (New York: Dover)
[49] Savage L J 1975 *Studies in Bayesian econometrics and statistics* ed J Leonard Savage, E Stephen, S E Fienberg and A Zellner (New York: Elsevier)
[50] Savage L J and Dubins L E 2014 *How to Gamble If You Must: Inequalities for Stochastic Processes* ed W Sudderth and D Gilat (Mineola, NY: Dover)
[51] Skormin V A, Gorodetski V I and Popyack L J 2002 Data mining technology for failure prognostic of avionics *IEEE Trans. Aerosp. Electron. Syst.* **38** 388–403

[52] Smith J Q 2012 *Bayesian Decision Analysis: Principles and Practice* (Cambridge, UK: Cambridge University Press)

[53] Triantafyllopoulos K 2021 *Bayesian Inference of State Space Models: Kalman Filtering and Beyond* (Cham: Springer)

[54] Vertakova Y, Izmalkova I and Leontyev E 2019 Game theory for the formation of a cluster risk management strategy *E3S Web Conf.* **138** 02005

[55] Viertl R (ed) 1987 *Probability and Bayesian Statistics* (Boston MA: Springer)

[56] Vorob'ev N N 1977 *Game Theory. Lectures for Economists and Systems Scientists* (New York: Springer)

[57] Wald A 1945 Statistical decision functions which minimize the maximum risk *Ann. Math.* **46** 265–80

IOP Publishing

Human-Assisted Intelligent Computing
Modeling, simulations and applications
Mukhdeep Singh Manshahia, Igor S Litvinchev, Gerhard-Wilhelm Weber, J Joshua Thomas and Pandian Vasant

Chapter 23

Artificial intelligence (AI) in the era of precision medicine

Fathinul Fikri Ahmad Saad, Shazreen Shaharudin, Mohd Nawawi Abdullah, Rabiatul Adawiyah, Amirul Tajuddin, Ahmad Danial Ahmad Shahrir, Khairul Alif Khairumman and Syed Ejaz Shamim Syed Reyaz Uddin Ahmed

Artificial intelligence (AI) is the adoption of human intelligence processes by computer systems to enable the adaption of theory and development in machine-manned technology. The intuitive system has been largely used in data mining ability combining big-scaled data compiling information into theories to guide scientific innovations in material science fields. The considerable promise of AI has resulted in the improved efficacy of imaging system development through material science technology adoption. AI systems are now taking centre stage in the medical field to conduct tasks such as medical surveillance systems, diagnoses treatment, recommendations to cope with precision management in healthcare, known as precision medicine. An efficient medical imaging system and healthcare epidemiological data surveillance are essential in the era of precision medicine in ensuring specific treatment is tailored to the patients' problems. Colossal data usage and AI software development platforms are making an impact across the medical imaging workhorses, for example, RADIOMIC, MATLAB, PHYTON, AIME, REDINT which have tremendously increased patient throughput in daily medical imaging systems, expediting and improving the image processing and data categorization, which help the physician to provide personalized care to patients. Its utility potentially results in healthcare improvement whilst averting unnecessary toxic treatment or futile surgery, and helps reduce the workload of medical imaging personnel. This article documents various AI usage in methods and benefits in medical imaging systems and healthcare surveillance in disease outbreak via the emerging machine intelligence technologies.

doi:10.1088/978-0-7503-4801-0ch23

23.1 Introduction

AI is defined as an intelligence exhibited by machines, the opposite of human intellectual thinking. It is a system endowed with intellectual properties exhibited by humans, such as reasoning, discovering meaning, generalization, classification, and learning from the past. As technology advances, AI has become part of daily living in every aspect of human life. It is mentioned in many sectors such as the economy, military, education, healthcare and much more (Robert *et al* 2020).

AI consists of machine learning, and within it lies the core, which is deep learning. Machine learning or so-called supervised learning learns from the collection of data extracted and interpreted by a human. From there, the system improvises their task and applies what it learns to make an informed decision.

Deep learning is a subset of machine learning approach whereby the system analyzes and learns by itself from raw data provided without human assistance. A multilayer of the neural network is exposed to vast data and trains itself to perform tasks like speech and image recognition. Deep learning is an algorithm which has no theoretical limit of what it can learn. The greater the amount of data and time given, the better the outcome the system will provide.

In the era of precision medicine, physicians are looking at new techniques in achieving the best care for patients. In this regards, each disease is assigned a specific treatment planning based on the evidence-based data on genomic profiles; disease process and the drug targets are tailored to each other in ensuring good disease prognosis (Uddin *et al* 2019). Therefore, AI is bringing the medical industries to a higher level through its integration into the diagnostic imaging procedures involving epidemiological disease surveillance data mining, patient care, medical imaging diagnostic and therapeutics. A few models or signatures have been created as AI to help physicians in imaging, like RADIOMIC, MATLAB, AIME, REDINT AND PHYTON (Felix *et al* 2019, Aktolun 2019).

In dealing with the crucial emergency in a medical intervention such as the pandemic COVID-19 or dengue epidemics, a large-scale data mining processing platform utilizing an AI tool are of paramount importance. The system would generate results on the global database platform to predict the disease burden and help circumvent the disease outbreak.

In managing medical imaging procedures, AI can help the front desk plan patients' appointment needs and it is an enabler to anticipate data defaults or no-show patients which improve the healthcare standard in providing a cost-effective management system (Felix *et al* 2019). AI can improve image acquisition through maximum prediction of image construction by predicting the amount of correct activity and scatter removal with resultant better image interpretation and provides a precise diagnosis. Data collection and analysis by AI help the clinician compare with the same case from a vast database.

AI helps detect minor changes of the pathological processes from the previous imaging scan, thus detecting early disease—however, many challenges in devising a well-suited and comprehensive AI in aiding clinical diagnosis

The AI system can triage different solid-states in human composition, i.e. free fluid, air and fat through the deep learning of the database. Thus, the disease's prediction progresses on image results by comparing a series of images or databases; the accuracy of disease prediction is far better formulated than by a human clinician. This will reduce missed diagnosis among physicians due to multifactorial causes such as lack of experience. As AI is able to predict the amount of activity during image acquisition, thus lesion segmentation in an organ will be more accurate as a computer is able to remove the scatter and delineate the lesion more precisely (Hall 2019, Lee *et al* 2019).

The AI usage methods in the precision medicine era have great potential in expediting large data mining and processing in providing benefits to end-users in the healthcare system via machine intelligence technologies.

23.2 Artificial intelligence in medical imaging and challenges

In cancer disease, most of the cancer hallmarks can be quantified and imaged using hybrid imaging technology i.e. positron emission tomography–computed tomography (PET–CT). These cancers include cellular processes that correlate with cellular cascades of biological processes and altered molecular pathways which contribute to the development of tumour growth. Measurements of these cellular activities are essential in identifying the individual phenotypes that help to understand the mechanism of tumour behaviour regarding its effect on the normal that could predict and monitor the disease response to treatments (Hanahan and Weinberg 2011). The changes of biological processes that underpin the tumour metabolism can be measured by the unmanned machine-system through AI deep learning influence on the advanced analysis employing RADIOMIC methodology system (Sanduleanu *et al* 2018).

The utility of AI in medical imaging is to assimilate additional information obtained from a hybrid imaging technology system, i.e. PET–CT through AI algorithm data processing acceleration based on the deep learning theory of intratumoral and intertumoral genetic heterogeneity in patients and their genetic profile that contribute to the time and treatment changes. The immediate treatment decision can be given according to the molecular profiling heterogeneous individual tumours (Andor *et al* 2016).

Several studies have proved that by using PET radiopharmaceuticals there is a direct relationship between RADIOMIC signatures and treatment response and disease prognostication in certain tumour lineages. Study in murine cancers showed that the spatial distribution of 18F-fluorodeoxyglucose (FDG)—a molecular marker utilised in the PET–CT system showed changes and reflected the spatial distribution of necrosis, cellular density and stromal tissue. In murine pancreatic tumours, FDG spatial heterogeneity indicated the distribution of cellular glucose transporters and hexokinase activities (Henriksson *et al* 2007, Xu *et al* 2014). Using the RADIOMIC signatures from FDG, PET–CT images in humans have facilitated the physician's important observation in differentiating lung tumour subtypes, breast cancer and tumour cellular landscape, which results in changes in patient's management (Ma *et al* 2018).

The reports on the utility of the RADIOMIC software system in magnetic resonance imaging (MRI) have indicated that there is a strong correlation of the cellular expression of vascular endothelial growth factor with microvascular density in renal cell carcinoma on the MRI images (Yin *et al* 2017). A study on the datasets and textural features correlation exploiting AI of the LASSO methodology have paved the machine-manned system pathway into the prediction of the disease effects on the treatment institution (Ohri *et al* 2016, Arshad *et al* 2019).

In this regards, AI applications in a medical imaging system, i.e. PET–CT or MRI enables the adoption of the 'unseen' features from images into the characterisation of the disease processes which allows better treatment stratification, prediction and prognostication. An AI tool in neuroimaging has impacted on the adoption of the machine's deep learning on the human's attention mechanisms and a convolutional neural network of the neurodegenerative disease to accurately identify the well-known signs of Alzheimer's disease (AD) through the exhibition of the subtle linguistic patterns that are readily overlooked on clinical evaluation by a neurologist (figure 23.1). The use of an AI algorithm that analyses the theory of the verbal contents of healthy subjects has enabled the adoption of its digital characterisation in a unique numerical sequence representing a specific point in a 512-dimensional space to simulate the neurological deficits in AD subjects.

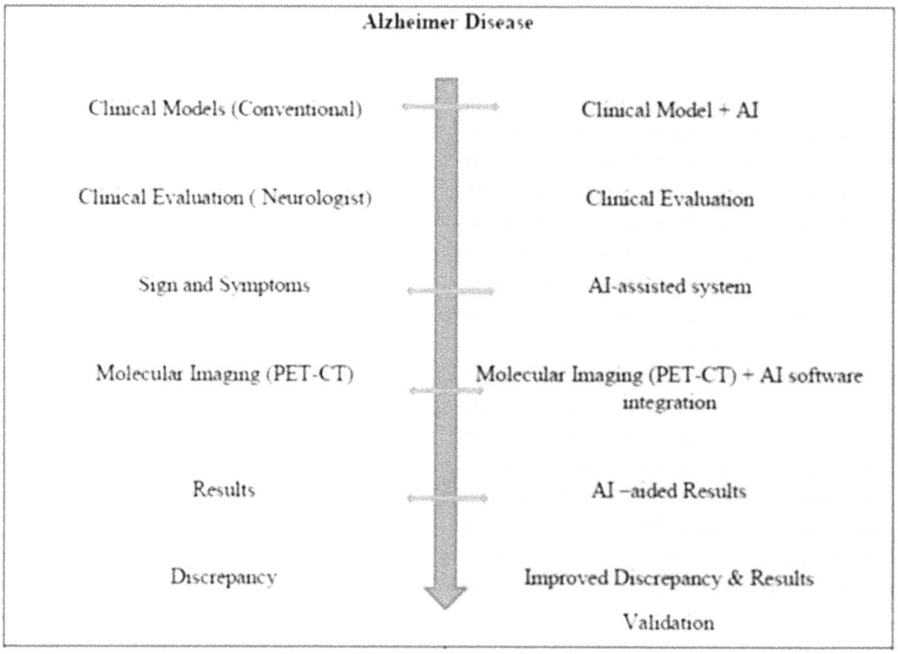

Figure 23.1. Concept of workflow with AI in medical imaging as compared to the conventional method in analyzing the results of a patient with Alzheimer's Disease.

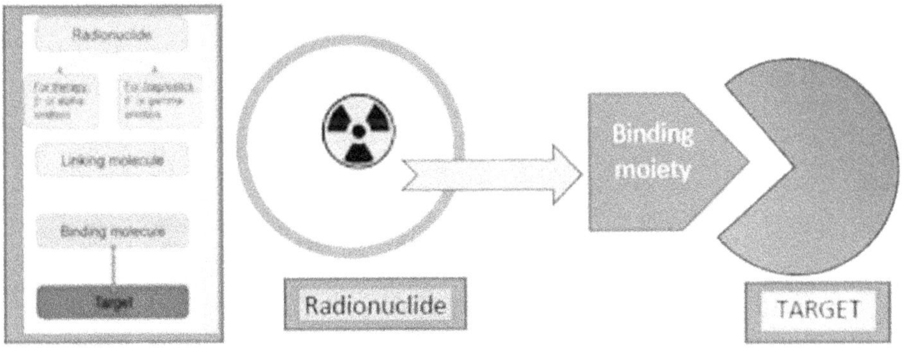

Figure 23.2. The theranostic principle in nuclear medicine.

Gradually, AI will enable identifying differences between the sentences of verbal content by healthy and unhealthy individuals and thence accelerate the prediction of potential individuals who may develop AD disease as they age (figure 23.2).

23.3 Artificial intelligence in therapeutics

AI is becoming popular and being applied in almost every field, including medical imaging and therapy. Its influence, particularly in the medical field, is rapidly growing, especially in the current era. Regardless of the specific technique, the main goal of AI in healthcare is to use a computer algorithm to collect optimum information data and help make diagnosis and treatment. Most developed countries adopted the AI system because it improves and specifies human capabilities and is directed towards healthcare accuracy (Jie *et al* 2019).

A computer-based diagnostic system has been established to enhance the precise accuracy of imaging, increasing consistency in interpretation of an image, help the prognostic evaluation and assist in deciding on the therapeutic field. Although these tools have an enormous impact, their role is still limited in clinical practice. With the emerging era of AI and big data, these limitations are being overcome and the use of computer-based diagnostic tools in routine practice can be explored (Mercel *et al* 2019).

In nuclear medicine, theranostic means use of the same targeting molecule for both diagnosis and therapy. The potential targets visible in diagnostic imaging can be positively predicted to get benefit from treatment (figure 23.3).

For example, differentiated thyroid cancer. Radiolabeled meta-iodobenzyl-guanidine (MIBG), a molecule that is analogue to noradrenaline, is used to detect neuroendocrine tumours like neuroblastoma, pheochromocytoma, paraganglioma etc. Radiolabeled phosphonates have high affinity to bones and can be used to imaging and palliate painful osseous metastasis. Radiolabeled somatostatin analogues are used in well-differentiated neuroendocrine neoplasia which overexpresses somatostatin receptors (SSTRs), like gastroenteropancreatic neuroendocrine tumours (GEP-NET). There are three routine SSA tracers labelled with gallium-68: DOTA-TATE, DOATA-TOC and DOTA-NOC. Radiolabeled prostate-specific

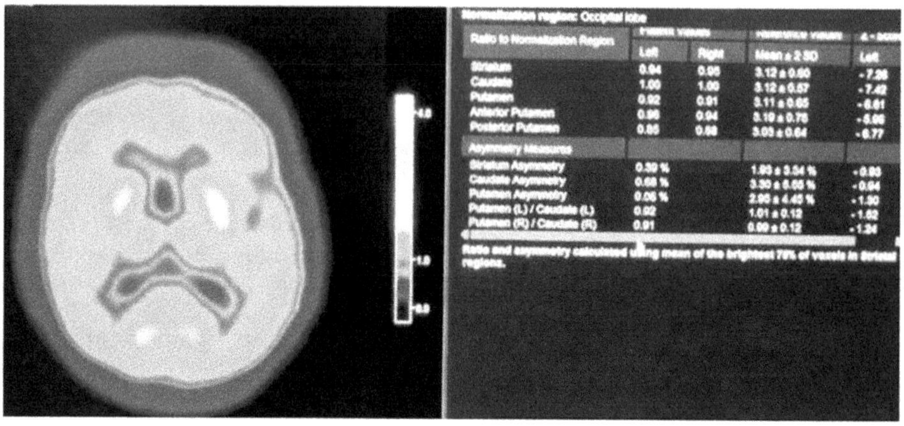

Figure 23.3. Medical imaging in Alzheimer's Disease.

membrane antigen (PSMA)-ligands are used in prostate cancer cells that overexpress PSMA on the cell surface, the radiopharmaceuticals that target PSMA gallium-68-PSMA 11 and gallium-68-PSMA 617 labelling with long half-life lutetium-177 for therapy (Yordanova *et al* 2017).

The imaging system's best advantage is that they are non-invasive and provide characterizations and quantifications of the pathophysiologic process in disease staging and monitoring. The arrival of hybrid imaging like PET–CT, single-photon emission computed tomography–computed tomography (SPECT–CT) and positron emission tomography–magnetic resonance imaging (PET–MRI) have brought a fantastic benefit to humanity. AI can perform tasks successfully by acquiring machines which usually require human intelligence (Francesco *et al* 2019).

23.4 Artificial intelligence in radiopharmaceutical discovery and development

Molecular imaging is highly dependent on radiopharmaceuticals' ability to target specific receptors or proteins of biological processes. The emergence of radiomics, which accelerates the imaging and reporting processes (Nensa *et al* 2019), further drives the need for new radiopharmaceuticals development and efficient preparation technology to improve the availability of targeted study and provides a reliable service.

Developing a new drug until it is marketable takes more than ten years and billions in expenses (Zimmermann 2013, Morgan *et al* 2011). The drug development processes include iodine as an example of theranostic agent albeit the gold standard for both the diagnosis and therapy in discovery and development, pre-clinical, clinical trials, regulatory review and post-marketing surveillance (US FDA 2020). The compound discovery and development phase consumes the longest time as researchers need to filter from thousands of compounds with drug-like characteristics looking for potential therapeutic value. Development of new radiotracers also needs to abide by these regulatory processes which impede the interest of pharmaceutical companies. Besides, the limited market group in nuclear medicine further hinders the development of new radiotracers (Chan *et al* 2019).

Various AI software has been utilized in conventional drug development which helps to expedite the discovery of unique compounds with therapeutic value and safe profiling. Currently, there are hundreds of AI start-ups focussing on various functions in drug discovery and development processes including primary drug screening (finding the compound of interest), secondary drug screening (predicting physical properties, bioactivity and toxicology profile of the compound), drug design (prediction of the 3D structure of a target protein and its interaction with drug), chemical synthesis (designing efficient synthesis pathway for high-yield production) and automation of chemical synthesis (ensuring standardization in production utilizing robotics) (Yordanova *et al* 2017).

On 30 January 2020, the BBC News reported the first AI-invented medicine approved to proceed with Phase I Clinical Trial for obsessive-compulsive disorder (OCD) in Japan. The fact that this drug passed to this stage within 12 months is astonishing because traditionally, it takes more than five years for a drug to get to trial. This was made possible by collaborating with AI start-up Exscientia and Japanese pharmaceutical company, Sumitomo Dainippon Pharma. The drug in the study, DSP-1181, was discovered by applying AI algorithm screening tools to go through big public databases such as ChEMBL and Puchem and other parameters for potential candidates.

Their AI drug discovery tools can gather, screen, and extract the potential drug candidates from the vast database in a short period, helping chemists decide which molecules to further research. Besides therapeutic potential, a machine learning algorithm that can filter out molecules with toxic profile and laborious manufacturing is equally crucial to ensure a successful clinical trial phase. Thus far, the British AI company has collaborated with nine giant corporations including six from pharmaceutical firms, e.g. GSK, Bayer, Sunovion, Sanofi, BMS and three biotechnology companies, e.g. Evotec, GT Apeiron Therapeutics and Rallybio. In October 2020, it initiated another collaboration with Blue Oak Pharmaceuticals aiming to combat brain diseases.

In nuclear medicine, personalized medicine and theranostics therapy has gained much hype, which requires particular targeting molecules to increase efficacy and reduces toxicity to other parts of the body (Hanahan and Weinberg 2011, Sanduleanu *et al* 2018). Machine learning tools such as PotentialNet can predict the ligand-binding affinity whilst DeepTox shows potential toxicity of the studied compounds (Jeelani *et al* 2014). The synergistic collaboration of multiple AI tools is believed to efficiently formulate the ideal radiotracer required in a shorter period compared to traditional drug development.

The advancement of machine learning software and the abundant amount of data in the field will accelerate the development of target-specific radiotracers with minimal or no toxicity. Hence, AI aiding the development of radiopharmaceuticals may be the future in this field.

23.5 Artificial intelligence in medical imaging data systems

Radiomics is a method that extracts qualitative and quantitative data from the clinical image to support evidence-based clinical decision-making (Gillies *et al* 2016). The qualitative and quantitative data from morphological and functional clinical images reflect the pathophysiology of a tissue. Tumour regions, metastatic lesions and normal tissues are tissues that can be analyzed using the radiomic method.

Qualitative and quantitative features are derived from clinical images. Qualitative features are used in radiology lexicon to describe lesions, while quantitative features are calculated using dedicated software. The software accepts medical images as input. Even though many tools are designed to assist this process, it is still a challenge to filter the input data's quality and choose the optimal parameters to guarantee a reliable and robust output.

Several factors affect the quality of features extracted, their association with clinical data and the model data derived from them. The factors are included by the type of image acquisition, post-processing, and segmentation (figure 23.4).

On the other hand, the quantitative features which affect the model data include shape, first- and second-order statistic and higher-order statistic. The shape feature defines the traced region of interest (ROI) and its geometric properties such as volume, maximum diameter of different orthogonal planes, tumour compactness, and sphericity. For example, a spiculated tumour will feature higher surface-to-volume ratio values as opposed to the round tumour of comparable volume (Lambin *et al* 2017).

The first-order statistic features evaluate on the distribution of individual voxel values without spatial relationships. The derived reports are measured for mean,

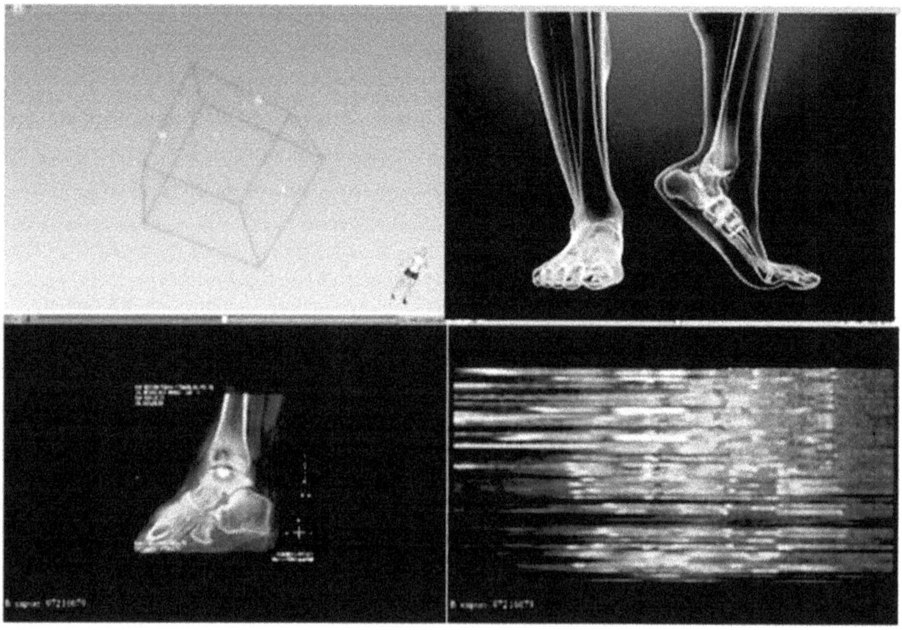

Figure 23.4. 3D slicer algorithm transforming the 3D PET–CT ankle into the segment of images in RADIOMIC medical images analysis.

median, maximum, minimum values of the voxel intensities on the image, as well as their skewness in the histogram-based configuration. Subsequent calculation evaluates the statistical inter-relationships of neighbouring voxels on the second-order statistics which derives the spatial arrangement of the voxel intensities and intra-lesion heterogeneity. The utility of the grey-level co-occurrence matrix (GLCM) is exploited via quantifying the incidence of voxels of the same intensities and the consecutive voxels along with fixed directions. The application of these quantitative methods of the model data exploiting voxels of pathological tumour configuration are being utilised in post- processing clinal imaging images of the picture archiving system (PACS) in (MRI, (CT), or PET–CT. This methodology predicts pathological types, gene expression status, treatment outcomes, prognosis, and other aspects that occupy an essential role in treating cancers (figure 23.5).

The higher-order statistics features are derived after applying filters or mathematical transforms to the images. For example, to identify repetitive or non-repetitive patterns, the software will suppress noise or highlight details. These include fractal analysis, Minkowski functionals, wavelet transform, and Laplacian transforms of Gaussian-filtered images, which can extract areas with increasingly coarse texture patterns (Rizzo *et al* 2018).

There are two main steps in radiomics analysis, the dimensionality reduction and the feature selection. These are obtained via unsupervised approaches. The unsupervised approaches used are cluster analysis and principal component analysis (PCA). Cluster analysis aims to create groups of similar features (clusters) with high intra-cluster redundancy and low intercluster correlation. A cluster heat map generally characterizes this analysis. A single feature may be selected from each cluster as representative and used in the following association analysis. PCA will create a smaller set of maximally uncorrelated variables from a large set of correlated variables. It will explain as much as possible of the total variation in

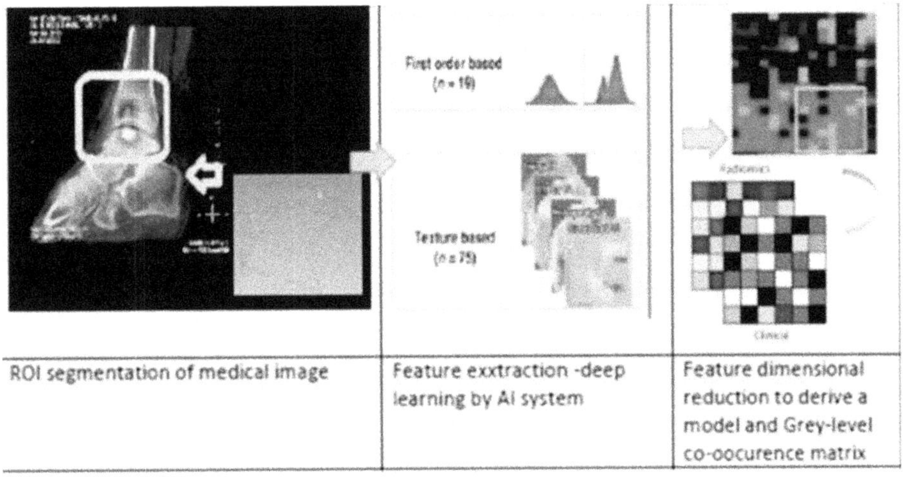

Figure 23.5. A Tumour lesion quantitative analysis in radiomics methodology to predict pathological type of tumour for treatment outcome via statistical voxel-intensity mapping and filtration.

the data set with the fewest possible principal components. The output of PCA consists of score plots, indicating grouping in the datasets for similarity. The second step is analysis with one or more specific outcomes via supervised approaches.

23.6 Artificial intelligence in disease outbreak

The emergence of disease outbreaks dengue fever epidemic or COVID-19 epidemic poses a significant challenge in manual surveillance, which is a profoundly a weak method to circumvent the fast spreading disease that results in pandemic scale. In developing countries with high density urbanised population such as Malaysia, dengue is perceived as a perennial public health concern in the year 2000. As a sequalae, in 2014, Malaysia had suffered a threefold increment in fatal infections after its first epidemic in Penang in 1901 (Skae 1902). The failure to curb the epidemic was the incompetent health officer's lack of vigilance and reporting which had resulted in the delay and lack of sensitivity for outbreak predictions (Ooi and Gubler 2009). This is essential in adopting a robust AI system in medical epidemiology (AIME) software package tool that is cabale of supporting data entry, retrieval, storage and analysis for dengue vector management. The pharmacovigilance and health vigilance system are hence integrated into the language programming to realize the system's machine learning and deep learning algorithm. Large-scale data information including entomological, epidemiological, spatial and temporal data are utilized and then georeferenced and stored in a data warehouse called REDINT (Remote Data Input Interface) figure 23.6. The resultant output of the analyses can be processed and predicted to produce maps, models and

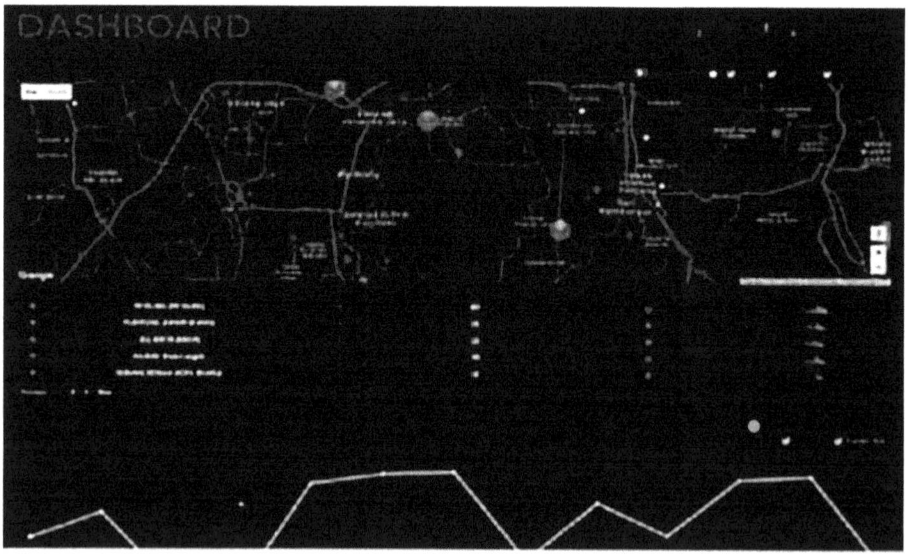

Figure 23.6. Georeferencing of data warehouse using machine learning in REDINT AI system. The geographical data on travellers with whom there is suspicion of spreading COVID-19 can be predicted through a machine learning algorithm.

tables based on the specified machine learning algorithm with supervised and unsupervised learning algorithm (Scott and Morrison 2008).

REDINT automatically searches through more than 90 different databases for 276 different variables. For this study, all of the 276 different variables collected by REDINT were used. These variables range from different categories, explicitly obtaining weather data, geographical data, socioeconomic data and historical epidemiological data (Bala *et al* 2019).

The COVID-19 outbreak that started in mid-December in China, 2019, was then transmitted globally as a pandemic disease. This highly contagious infection took the lives of more than 1000 people and infected over 43 000 people globally (World Health Organization 2020). At this juncture, there is no mature database processing system that can process large-scale data in providing information of the pandemic COVID-19 spreading pattern across the world. The BlueDot's algorithm uses machine learning (ML) and natural language processing (NLP) technology to detect signs of potential disease outbreaks from the collected information that becomes training data while developing such AI models (Niiler and An 2020). BlueDot's algorithm would galvanize us to process data from multiple outbreaks which could predict the expected time frame of a disease surge at different locations (Heaven 2020). It can create a prioritization index across the affected region, so insecticides, larvicides and human resources can be deployed most effectively (BlueDot 2020). This allows public health professionals to preempt outbreaks with the best course of preventative action. BlueDot uses an AI-driven algorithm that scours foreign-language news reports, animal and plant disease networks, and official proclamations to give its clients warning to avoid danger zones like Wuhan (Bowles 2020).

23.7 Artificial intelligence in patient care

The digitization of health records and advances in information analysis and data storage have made it possible to create sophisticated algorithms as AI. There are a series of possible repercussions from the usage of AI in medical treatment. Before this era, medical judgment was made entirely by a human, but it may pose concerns of consent, confidentiality, responsibility, and integrity with the use of the intelligent machine.

The biggest challenge to be tackled for current technologies is integrity. Concerning data privacy and security, responsibility and transparency for AI applications are the legal problems. Questions about who is solely accountable for a healthcare decision based on AI application or supported by it have yet to be addressed. AI programmes would certainly make errors in medical care, and it is impossible to establish responsibilities. Machine learning systems can also be algorithmically biased in healthcare. For example, they may predict an increased probability of disease based on gender or race when these are not causal factors (Skae 1902). Will healthcare professionals be kept ultimately accountable for actions that they cannot comprehend through algorithms? Will clinicians use a device that they cannot even understand? Will the developer be held to account? The issue is complicated because it is challenging, sometimes too complex, to grasp the logic in AI applications (Price 2017).

AI ventures mostly work under the garbage-in–garbage-out principle, which implies a great deal of appropriate and accurate data is required. High-quality data sources can be challenging to access healthcare because health data is often scattered and dispersed among multiple agencies with numerous data structures. After all, patients usually see different doctors and often change insurers. Many countries still have low data consistency and decentralized data structures that make consolidation and digitalization of health information impossible. Even in the United States, where medical systems' digitization is actively campaigned for, digitized information accuracy remains a concern (Obermeyer and Emanuel 2016). Medical recording is a tedious process that requires immense computing power and cooperation of the data owners to sort, consolidate and digitize records on their own. However, automated and improved recording devices make medicine more effective and more reliable. Healthcare stakeholders need to identify ways to enhance data consolidation and digitalization so that AI can process and analyze patient data adequately.

An additional obstacle is a need for quality healthcare data. Machine learning needs large quantities of data to ensure the algorithms perform correctly and are adequately implemented to their particular objectives. Sometimes machine learning needs millions of observations to attain reasonable standards of efficiency (Obermeyer and Emanuel 2016). Researchers and developers need the accessibility of thousands of patients for vast sets of health data. The effectiveness of AI application depends on the accuracy of the data used to create and train the framework. AI depends on data at its heart. If the data itself is missing, partial or otherwise corrupted, the AI system is in danger of not being correct (Hurd and Kelly 2018).

23.8 Conclusion

AI is useful in complementing the competency of medical imaging technique in the era of precision medicine as these methods are employed as a computer-aided diagnosis (CAD) system in clinical practice and play a crucial role in improving the accuracy of diagnostic yield whilst improving the standard of healthcare services. An efficient disease outbreak emergency response and efficient diagnostic imaging tools utilizing extensive data surveillance systems should become the impetus in the revolution of efficient data processing technologies in forecasting a global calamity to the fullest. It is important to note that while the development and adoption of AI in healthcare are happening rather quickly, its success will still require all stakeholders' full participation.

Compliance with ethical requirements

The write-up and the design of the study is an accordance with the Helsinki Declaration.

Conflict of interests

No funds, grants, or other support was received. All authors declare there is no conflict of interest.

Acknowledgements

On behalf of all authors, we acknowledge the contribution of the Centre for Diagnostic Nuclear Imaging in fascilitating the use of related resources.

References

Aktolun C 2019 Artificial intelligence and radiomics in nuclear medicine: potentials and challenges *Eur. J. Nucl. Med. Mol. Imaging* **46** 2731–6

Andor N, Graham T A, Jansen M, Xia L C, Aktipis C A and Petritsch C *et al* 2016 Pan- cancer analysis of the extent and consequences of intratumor heterogeneity *Nat. Med.* **22** 105–13

Arshad M A, Thornton A and Lu H *et al* 2019 Discovery of pre-therapy 2-deoxy-2-(18)F- fluoro-D-glucose positron emission tomography-based radiomics classifiers of survival outcome in non-small-cell lung cancer patients *Eur. J. Nucl. Med. Mol. Imaging* **46** 455–66

Bala M S, Dhesi B R, Fazilah M, Ting C Y, Yee K R and Fadzilah K 2019 Artificial intelligence model as predictor for dengue outbreaks *Malaysian J. Public Health Med.* **19** 103–8

BlueDot 2020 Better Public Health Surveillance for Infectious Diseases. Available online: https://bluedot.global/products/explorer/ (Accessed on 8 December)

Bowles J 2020 How Canadian AI Start-Up Bluedot Spotted Coronavirus Before Anyone Else Had a Clue. https://diginomica.com/how-canadian-ai-start-bluedot-spotted-coronavirus-any-one-else-had-clue. (Accessed on 8 December)

Chan H C S, Shan H, Dahoun T, Vogel H and Yuan S 2019 Advancing drug discovery via artificial intelligence *Trends Pharmacol. Sci.* **40** 592–604

Coronavirus Disease (COVID-2019) Situation Reports (World Health Organization, 2020) (Accessed on 6 November 2020)

Francesco G, Riemer H J A S and Pedro F C 2019 Two new theranostic series- spotlight on artificial intelligence and a specific platform for technologist *Eur. J. Hybr. Imaging* **3** 22

Gillies R J, Kinahan P E and Hricak H 2016 Radiomics: images are more than pictures, they are data *Radiology* **278** 563–77

Hall M 2019 Artificial intelligence and nuclear medicine *Nucl.Med. Commun.* **40** 1–2

Hanahan D and Weinberg R A 2011 Hallmarks of cancer: the next generation *Cell* **144** 646–74

Henriksson E, Kjellen E, Wahlberg P, Ohlsson T, Wennerberg J and Brun E 2007 2- Deoxy-2-[18F]fluoro-D-glucose uptake and correlation to intratumoral heterogeneity *Anticancer Res.* **27** 2155–9

Heaven W D 2020 AI Could Help With the Next Pandemic- but Not With This One. Available. https://technologyreview.com/2020/03/12/905352/ai-could-help-with-the-next- pandemicbut-not-with-this-one/. (Accessed on 8 December)

Hurd H and Kelly R 2018 Rise of the Machines. Artificial Intelligence and its Growing Impact on U.S. Policy. https://oversight.house.gov/wp-content/uploads/2018/09/AI-White- paper-.pdf: Subcommittee on Information Technology Committee on Oversight and Government Reform. (Accessed on 8 December 2020)

Jeelani S, Jagat Reddy R C and Maheswaran T *et al* 2014 Theranostics: a treasured tailor for tomorrow *J. Pharm. Bioallied Sci.* **6** S6–8

Jie X, Kanmin X and Kang Z 2019 Current status and future trends of clinical diagnosis via image-based deep learning *Theranostics* **9** 7556–65

Lambin P, Leijenaar R T H and Deist T *et al* 2017 Radiomics: the bridge between medical imaging and personalized medicine *Nat. Rev. Clin. Oncol.* **14** 749–62

Lee L I T, Kanthasamy S, Ayyalaraju R S and Ganatra R 2019 The current state of artificial intelligence in medical imaging and nuclear medicine *BJR Open.* **16** 20190037

Ma Y, Feng W, Wu Z, Liu M, Zhang F and Liang Z *et al* 2018 Intra-tumoural heterogeneity characterization through texture and colour analysis for differentiation of non- small cell lung carcinoma subtypes *Phys. Med. Biol.* **63** 165018

Mercel K S, Jose RF J, Danilo T W, Ariane PM T, Mercello HN B and Paulo M d A M 2019 Artificial intelligence, machine learning, computer-aided diagnosis and radiomics: advances in imaging towards the precision medicine *Radiol Bras.* **52** 387–96

Morgan S, Grootendorst P, Lexchin J, Cunningham C and Greyson D 2011 The cost of drug development: a systematic review *Health Policy.* **100** 4–17

Nensa F, Demircioglu A and Rischpler C 2019 Artificial intelligence in nuclear medicine *J. Nucl. Med.* **60** 29S–37S

Niiler E and An A I 2020 Epidemiologist Sent the First Warnings of the Wuhan Virus. Available online: https: //www.wired.com/story/ai-epidemiologist-wuhan-public-health-warnings/ (accessed on 6 November)

Obermeyer Z and Emanuel E J 2016 Predicting the future big data, machine learning, and clinical medicine *N. Engl. J. Med.* **375** 1216–9

Ohri N, Duan F and Snyder B S *et al* 2016 Pretreatment 18F-FDG PET textural features in locally advanced non-small cell lung cancer: secondary analysis of ACRIN 6668/RTOG 0235 *J. Nucl. Med.* **57** 842–8

Ooi E E and Gubler D J 2009 Global spread of epidemic dengue: the influence of environmental change *Future Virology.* **4** 571–80

Price N 2017 Artificial intelligence in health care: applications and legal issues *SciTech Lawyer* **14** 1

Rizzo S, Botta F and Raimondi S *et al* 2018 Radiomics: the facts and the challenges of image analysis *Eur Radiol Exp.* **2** 36

Sanduleanu S, Woodruff H C, de Jong E E C, van Timmeren J E, Jochems A and Dubois L *et al* 2018 Tracking tumor biology with radiomics: a systematic review utilizing a radiomics quality score *Radiother. Oncol.* **127** 349–60

Scott T W and Morrison A C 2008 Longitudinal field studies will guide a paradigm shift in dengue prevention', Vector-borne diseases: understanding the environmental, human health, and ecological connections *Workshop Summary* (Washington DC: The National Academies Press) pp 132–49

Seifert R, Weber M, Kocakavuk E, Rischpler C and Kersting D 2020 Artificial intelligence and machine learning in nuclear medicine: future perspectives *Semin. Nucl. Med.* **51** 170–7

Skae F M T 1902 Dengue fever in penang *Br. Med. J.* **2** 1581–2

Uddin M, Wang Y and Woodbury-Smith M 2019 Artificial intelligence for precision medicine in neurodevelopmental disorders *npj Digit. Med.* **2** 112

U.S. Food And Drugs (FDA) 2020 The Drug Development and Approval Process. 2020. https:// fda.gov/drugs/development-approval-process-drugs (Accessed on 6 November)

Xu R, Kido S, Suga K, Hirano Y, Tachibana R and Muramatsu K *et al* 2014 Texture analysis on 18F-FDG PET/CT images to differentiate malignant and benign bone and soft- tissue lesions *Ann. Nucl. Med.* **28** 926–35

Yin Q, Hung S C, Wang L, Lin W, Fielding J and Rathmell W K *et al* 2017 Associations between tumor vascularity, vascular endothelial growth factor expression and PET/MRI radiomic signatures in primary clear-cell-renal-cell-carcinoma: a proof-of-concept study *Sci Rep.* **7** 43356

Yordanova A, Eppard E, Kürpig S, Bundschuh R A, Schönberger S, Gonzalez-Caromona M, Feldmann G, Ahmadzadehfar H and Essler M 2017 Theranostics in nuclear medicine practice *OncoTarg. Ther.* **10** 4821–8

Zimmermann R G 2013 Why are investors not interested in my radiotracer? The industrial and regulatory constraints in the development of radiopharmaceuticals *Nucl. Med. Biol.* **40** 155–66

Chapter 24

Optimal choice for convenience store chain in Vietnam

Nguyen Thi Ngan and Bui Huy Khoi

This chapter explores factors influencing a decision to choose a convenience store chain in the Vietnam market. Data used in the study was collected by the author from highly reliable information sources and primary data collected through a survey of 210 consumers living in Vietnam. The results of exploratory factor analysis with independent and dependent variables all show high convergence of factors in the research model, the tests all give the value to achieve reliability. Factors extracted from the analysis of the independent variables include brand (BD), social influence (SI), quality perception (QP), price perception (PP), distribution density (DD), responsiveness (RE), and promotion perception (PPE). The results of regression analysis showed that factors in the research model could explain 63.73% of the variation in factors affecting shopping decisions at the convenience store chain in the area. A relatively high percentage shows that the suitability of the theoretical model with the actual data is quite good. This study uses optimal choice by the AIC algorithm for a decision to choose the convenience store chain in the Vietnam market.

24.1 Introduction

Vietnam has Southeast Asia's fastest-growing middle class, and the country's retail sector has boomed. Given its relatively young population's demographics and strong consumer purchasing habits, this trend is likely continue in the future. Indeed, the rise of e-commerce and digital retail channels is one of the most important trends to follow in Vietnam: by 2025, the country's e-commerce sector will be second only to Indonesia in Southeast Asia [1]. Along with the development of the economy in recent years, the modern distribution channel, especially the convenience store model, has positively contributed to promoting the consumption of goods [2]. People

doi:10.1088/978-0-7503-4801-0ch24

have a new choice in deciding where to buy food besides traditional markets or grocery stores. With the advantages of store size and convenient service hours, convenience stores are increasingly present in residential areas, near schools, to meet the needs of compact and economical shopping time, but still ensure the prime requirements for the quality of the goods [3]. Overcoming the disadvantages of traditional markets and supermarkets, convenience stores will probably dominate the retail market shortly. This is an extended arm of businesses and suppliers to bring goods closer to consumers, step- by-step changing the shopping habits of Vietnamese people [4]. Bui *et al* [5] investigated the elements that determine trademark choice behavior among retail chains in Vietnam, as well as the extent to which these elements affect client decision intentions. The eight criteria of shop image, price perception, risk perception, brand attitude, brand awareness, and brand familiarity were strong-minded, according to the research. In particular, this type of convenience store still has a lot of scope and great potential for development. It realizes the importance of how to give consumers more access to safe food products at convenience stores and how to help businesses run the modern retail system. In particular, the convenience store chain captures the key factors that are critical to customers' purchasing decisions scientifically to offer solutions to increase their capacity. Therefore, this chapter uses the AIC algorithm for a decision to choose the convenience store chain in the Vietnam market.

24.2 Literature review

24.2.1 Brand (BD)

Shopping trends of customers are often directed at reputable brands. With a reputable brand they believe that the product quality will be guaranteed and the quality of service is good [6]. Therefore, the selection of reputable and branded convenience stores to shop for customers is always important when shopping at convenience stores [7].

24.2.2 Social influence (SI)

The perception of a person, along with that individual's primary references as to whether the activity should or should not be done, is used to a degree along with the influence of the community on stakeholders with the consumer, as indicated by standard ideas about the behavior's expected performance and personal incentive to meet that expectation [8]. Social influence is a social determinant of the reflection of social pressure on behavior. These social influences can be cross-cultural and social influences on one's beliefs that others agree to shop for goods [9].

24.2.3 Quality perception (QP)

Product quality involves a customer's perception of a product's quality and superiority over competing products and services, as well as the product's intended use [10]. The perceived quality of the product will directly affect the purchase decision and customer loyalty for that product. So a quality product will always receive trust from customers [11]. Quality standards includes the degree of conformance to the quality specification and whether the product, in particular, is free from defects. This can be considered as one of the most important requirements of a product because a product with good quality is one that consumers can trust and are willing to use as well as being loyal to it and deciding to buy it [12].

24.2.4 Price perception (PP)

Price is one of the four key variables of the marketing mix [13]. Price is also one of the factors determining customers' behavior of choosing one item or another. As for convenience stores, it directly affects sales and profits. Therefore, the convenience store chain needs to consider carefully before offering a price for the product so that it is suitable for customers' ability to pay and can compete well with competitors and achieve the best profit [14].

24.2.5 Distribution density (DD)

The location of a store is a geographical indication of where a business places the convenience store chain to sell products/goods [15]. Customers care about the location as well as the distance and convenience of transportation when coming to the store [16]. Beautiful, well-positioned, well-located, easy-to-find shops often have an advantage over some in an alley area, difficult to see or located on the side of a one-way street. In some cases, this is sometimes critical. Store location has been reviewed by several studies.

24.2.6 Responsiveness (RE)

The convenience store chain provides complete, timely, and accurate information to customers to quickly solve problems, handle complaints effectively and respond to customer requests. During the transaction, when there is any change of information, the store will promptly notify the customer. The store provides complete and accurate information to customers, ready to respond to customers' questions. The store's staff is always attentive during peak hours and there are attentive service staff for all customers. This increases the store's responsiveness to customers [17].

24.2.7 Promotion perception (PP)

This type of impact affects the customer's purchasing decision through the customer's feelings and emotions for the promotion, for the selection of the promotion, even for the dropout (missing the chance to choose in that promotion) [18]. The first benefit is that buyers would feel more at ease and confident when making purchases during the campaign since they believe they are clever and wise 'shoppers' (because they can find cheaper goods than usual). Furthermore, the campaign encourages clients to expand and improve their life knowledge and experience (through trying new products and brands). The campaign itself is still regarded as fascinating, and many customers enjoy learning about promotions, participating in reward programs. And with the promotional image and promotional prices with different colors, promotions also make a difference with diversity and 'fun' in the product display [19].

24.2.8 Choosing decision (CD)

The choosing decision is the final stage of the consumer's choosing behavior [20]. It results from weighing options based totally on a balance of needs and abilities; between the overall advantage or cost a client gets from a service or products as opposed to the full fee they need to pay to attain the product or service; at the same time as additionally being influenced by others (relatives, friends, colleagues). Unforeseen events occur, and customers perceive risks before making purchasing judgments about whether the products or services delivered are worthy and satisfy their previous demands and expectations. They will continue to use that product or service in the future and they will advertise on behalf of the supplier to other customers [21].

24.3 Methodology

Bollen [22] states that for one parameter to be assessed, a minimum sample size of five samples is required. The sample size is 5:1 (five observations per one variable) [23]. Because there are 21 variables in this observation, the sample length ought to be computed as $n = 5 \times 21 = 105$. Although a minimal pattern size of one 105 surveys is required, the writer selected to put up 210 survey questions online in a roundabout way, using centers that aid Google Forms for customers so one can guarantee sample variety and representativeness. The statistics on sample characteristics are shown in table 24.1.

The information gathered is encrypted and inserted into table 24.2.

Table 24.1. Statistics of sample.

Characteristics		Amount	Percent (%)
Sex and Age	Male	135	64.3
	Female	75	35.7
	Below 20	6	2.9
	21–35	84	40.0
	35–50	98	46.7
	Above 50	22	10.5
Income/Month	Below 7 million VND	6	2.9
	7–15 million VND	103	49.0
	Over 15 million VND	101	48.1
Job	Stay-at-home parent	69	32.9
	Officer	89	42.4
	Student	6	2.9
	Business executive	46	21.9

Table 24.2. Factor and item.

Factor	Code	Item
Brand (BD)	BD1	The convenience store chain is a popular brand.
	BD2	The convenience store chain brand name is easy to read, remember, and easy to recognize.
	BD3	The convenience store chain is a reputable corporation with long-term operations in the industry.
	BD4	The convenience store chain brand makes you feel confident and secure when choosing to shop.
Social influence (SI)	SI1	Family members influence you when shopping at the convenience store chain.
	SI2	Friends and colleagues influence you when shopping at the convenience store chain.
	SI3	Advertising through television, newspapers, and the internet affects me when shopping at the convenience store chain.
Quality perception (QP)	QP1	The convenience store chain specializes in distributing products with reputable brands and clear origins.
	QP2	Products sold at the convenience store chain are preserved in sealed, eye-catching, safe, and hygienic packaging.
	QP3	The convenience store chain has a team of experts and a food preservation process that ensures product quality.
	QP4	All products sold at the convenience store chain are still valid.
	QP5	There are no counterfeits for products sold at the convenience store chain.
Price perception (PP)	PP1	The selling price of products at the convenience store chain is currently reasonable.
	PP2	The selling price of products at the convenience store chain is commensurate with the quality.
	PP3	The selling price of products at the convenience store chain is listed on the package.
	PP4	Selling prices at the convenience store chain are competitive compared to other stores
	PP5	The selling price of products at the convenience store chain is in line with my financial ability.
Distribution density (DD)	DD1	There are many points of sale, convenient and easy to search for me to buy products at the convenience store chain store.
	DD2	The convenience store chain's points of sale are in central, prime locations, populous places, and the center of the market
	DD3	The convenience store chain's chain of points of sale has certain similarities following the brand's image (color design, display, preservation ...).
Responsiveness (RE)	RE1	Choosing an essential product *at* the convenience store chain is easy.
	RE2	The convenience store chain meets a variety of items according to my needs.

(*Continued*)

Table 24.2. (*Continued*)

Factor	Code	Item
	RE3	Fast and convenient payment time.
	RE4	I am provided with all the information I need about the product at the store and on the packaging (production date, expiry date, weight, listing price ...) at the convenience store.
Promotion perception (PPE)	PPE1	The promotion applies to all customers who purchase at the convenience store.
	PPE2	The convenience store chain has many attractive promotions.
	PPE3	Practical promotions for customers.
Choosing decision (CD)	CD1	I feel satisfied when deciding to shop at the convenience store chain.
	CD2	I will choose to shop at the convenience store chain first when necessary.
	CD3	I will continue to shop at the convenience store chain in the future.
	CD4	I am always ready to recommend to friends and relatives to shop at the convenience store chain.

For the period of the research, all study bodies of workers and individuals were blinded. The participants in the study had no contact with anyone from the outside world in table 24.1.

24.4 Results

24.4.1 Optimal choice

To choose an excellent model, the *R* software employed AIC (Akaike's Information Criteria). In the theoretical setting, AIC has been used to choose models. When there is multicollinearity, the AIC approach can handle many independent variables. Using a regression model, AIC can estimate one or more dependent variables from one or more impartial variables. The AIC is an essential and beneficial metric for finding a whole and simple version. Based on the AIC facts preferred, a model with a lower AIC is picked. The best version will quit whilst the minimal AIC coast is where given [24–26]. *R* reports capture each phase of the search for the best model. With seven independent variables, the step comes to a halt with AIC = −489.36 for CD = f (QP + PP + RE + DD + BR + SI + PPE).

All variables have a *P*-value of less than 0.05 [27], so they are associated with choosing decision (CD) in table 24.3 influencing brand (BD), social influence (SI), quality perception (QP), price perception (PP), distribution density (DD), responsiveness (RE), and promotion perception (PPE).

24.4.2 Model evaluation

Multicollinearity occurs whilst the impartial variables in regression fashions have a high correlation. Gujarati and Porter [28] discovered some multicollinearity

Table 24.3. The coefficients.

CD	Estimate				
Intercept	0.283 18	Std. Error	t value	*P*-value	Decision
QP	0.172 83	0.031 36	5.511	0.000	Accepted
PP	0.100 09	0.034 21	2.926	0.003	Accepted
RE	0.125 14	0.030 08	4.161	0.000	Accepted
DD	0.114 98	0.031 37	3.666	0.000	Accepted
BR	0.160 27	0.032 42	4.943	0.000	Accepted
SI	0.153 54	0.034 01	4.515	0.000	Accepted
PPE	0.102 18	0.030 62	3.337	0.001	Accepted

Table 24.4. Model test.

VIF	QP	PP	RE	DD	BR	SI	PPE
	1.511 921	1.347 734	1.390 825	1.267 445	1.461 458	1.188 374	1.265 013
Auto correlation	Durbin–Watson = 1.7789				test for autocorrelation p-value = 0.042 97		
Model Evaluation	R-Squared 0.6373				F-statistic 50.69	p-value: 0.000 00	

indicators in the model. Table 24.4 demonstrates that the independent variables' variance inflation factor (VIF) is less than 10 [29], showing that there is no collinearity between them. Because the P-value = 0.042 97 is less than 0.05, the Durbin–Watson test shows that the model in table 24.4 has autocorrelation [30]. Table 24.4 yields the following conclusion: the impact of BD, SI, QP, PP, DD, RE and PPE on CD is 63.73%. According to the foregoing analysis, the regression equation has a substantial statistical significance [31].

CD = 0.283 18 + 0.17283QP + 0.10009PP + 0.12514RE + 0.11498DD + 0.16027BR + 0.15354SI + 0.10218PPE

24.5 Conclusions

This chapter showed the AIC algorithm for a decision to choose the convenience store chain in the Vietnam market. It brings convenience and quality products to the Vietnamese market with a completely new model—convenience store and petrol station. Open 24 h a day and 7 days a week with professional customer service style and a warm, fast, clean and safe environment, the convenience store chain brings to customers genuine and diversified products including cold drinks, beer, confectionery, snacks, phone cards, food, personal care products and more … This is an advanced business model that has been developed in many countries around the world, bringing added value to the business and the development and penetration of the convenience store chain brand in the Vietnamese market.

Acknowledgments

IUH is funding this study.

References

[1] Deloitte 2019 *Retail in Vietnam*. Available: https://www2.deloitte.com/content/dam/Deloitte/vn/Documents/consumer-business/vn-cb-vietnam-consumer-retail-2019.pdf

[2] Kim Y-E 2017 A study on performance of retail store: focused on convenience store *J. Distrib. Sci.* **15** 47–51

[3] Leonnard L 2017 Measuring grocery stores service quality in Indonesia: a retail service quality scale approach *Stud. Sci. Res. Econ. Ed.* 32–44

[4] Rowley C and Truong Q 2009 *The Changing Face of Vietnamese Management* (Milton Park: Routledge)

[5] Bui T T, Nguyen H T and Khuc L D 2021 Factors affecting consumer's choice of retail store chain: empirical evidence from Vietnam *J. Asian Fin., Econ. Bus.* **8** 571–80

[6] Aperia T and Persson C 2016 Why are Swedish retail corporate brands so reputable? a comparative study of sustainable brand equity in Sweden *2016 Global Marketing Conf. at Hong Kong, China, July 21–24* 1028–31

[7] TRAN V D and LE N M T 2020 Impact of service quality and perceived value on customer satisfaction and behavioral intentions: evidence from convenience stores in Vietnam *J. Asian Fin., Econ. Bus.* **7** 517–26

[8] Howard D J 2012 Introduction to special issue: social influence and consumer behavior *Soc. Influence* **7** 131–33

[9] Dressler W W 1994 Cross-cultural differences and social influences in social support and cardiovascular disease *Social Support and Cardiovascular Disease* (Berlin: Springer) pp 167–92

[10] Gani A and Oroh A N H 2021 The effect of product quality, service quality and price on customer satisfaction at Loki Store *KnE Soc. Sci.* 116–128- 116–28

[11] Suhaily L and Darmoyo S 2017 Effect of product quality, perceived price and brand image on purchase decision mediated by customer trust (study on japanese brand electronic product) *J. Manaje.* **21** 179–94

[12] Lee E-J and Shin S Y 2014 When do consumers buy online product reviews? effects of review quality, product type, and reviewer's photo *Comput. Hum. Behav.* **31** 356–66

[13] Mullins J W, Walker O C, Boyd H W and Larréché J-C 2013 *Marketing Management: A Strategic Decision-making Approach* (New York: McGraw-Hill)

[14] Anselmsson J, Bondesson N V and Johansson U 2014 Brand image and customers willingness to pay a price premium for food brands *J. Prod. Brand Manage.*

[15] Silver M 1989 Store choice, store location and market analysis *J. R. Stat.Soc. Ser.* A **152** 275–5

[16] Meng X 2008 An empirical research on selecting location of chain convenience store 2008 4th Int. Conf. on Wireless Communications, Networking and Mobile Computing 1–6

[17] Handayani R, Rachmawati M, Kurniawan R and Roespinoedji D 2020 Building of E-customers loyalty through image department store in digital Era (survey of department store in the city of bandung) *Int. J. Psychosoc. Rehab.* **24** 3078–86

[18] Sugiono E and Widiastutik S 2021 The effect of product, price and promotion on purchase decision-mediated by customer satisfaction of oriflame M3 network community *Open Access Indonesia J. Soc. Sci.* **4** 129–42

[19] Mullin R 2018 *Promotional Marketing* (Milton Park: Routledge)
[20] Solomon M R, Marshall G W and Stuart E W 2008 *Study Guide for Marketing: Real People, Real Choices* (Englewood Cliffs, NJ: Prentice-Hall)
[21] Zhang J K 2015 Do other customers matter? examining the impact of other customers in retail/service settings *Revolution in Marketing: Market Driving Changes* (Berlin: Springer) p 5
[22] Bollen K A 1990 Overall fit in covariance structure models: two types of sample size effects *Psychol. Bull.* **107** 256
[23] Hair J F, Black W C, Babin B J, Anderson R E and Tatham R L 2006 *Multivariate Data Analysis* vol 6 (Upper Saddle River, NJ: Pearson Prentice Hall)
[24] Burnham K P and Anderson D R 2004 Multimodel inference: understanding AIC and BIC in model selection *Sociol. Methods Res.* **33** 261–304
[25] Khoi B H 2021 Factors influencing on university reputation: model selection by AIC *Data Science for Financial Econometrics* (Berlin: Springer) pp 177–88
[26] Mai D S, Hai P H and Khoi B H 2021 Optimal model choice using AIC method and naive Bayes classification *IOP Conf. Series: Mater. Sci. Eng.* 1088 012001
[27] Hill R C, Griffiths W E and Lim G C 2018 *Principles of Econometrics* (New York: Wiley)
[28] Gujarati D N and Porter D 2009 *Basic Econometrics* (New York: McGraw-Hill)
[29] Miles J 2014 Tolerance and variance inflation factor *Encyclopedia of Statistics in Behavioral Science* (Hoboken, NJ: Wiley)
[30] Durbin J and Watson G S 1971 Testing for serial correlation in least squares regression. III *Biometrika* **58** 1–19
[31] Greene W H 2003 *Econometric Analysis* (Noida: Pearson Education)

IOP Publishing

Human-Assisted Intelligent Computing
Modeling, simulations and applications
Mukhdeep Singh Manshahia, Igor S Litvinchev, Gerhard-Wilhelm Weber, J Joshua Thomas and Pandian Vasant

Chapter 25

Study of groundwater using hydrodynamic models

Irina Polshkova

Mathematical modeling opportunities make it possible to move from the simplified calculation schemes, used in analytical calculations, to mathematical models in a multilayer system of real hydrogeological objects, and that is principally a new level of research into natural and anthropogenic processes. The model corresponds to the adequate reproduction in space and time state of the hydrodynamic underground water flow, gives a schematic description of the occurring processes, explains the mechanism of these processes by the interaction of clearly identified factors and, finally, provides the possibility of quantitative forecasting and development of the processes in space and time. Mathematical modeling is a natural-like technology and provides the most complete implementation of three basic objectives of science: description, explanation and forecasting.

25.1 Introduction

Water resources management and forecasting the consequences of man-made and natural stress on the underground hydrosphere is a complex system problem. The subterranean hydrosphere happens to be one of the most unprotected ecosystems where the main hydrogeological processes are developing in real time. Thus, the possibility of experimental study exists, both in field and laboratory experiments.

The contemporary level of hydrogeology development and computing application makes it possible to solve a number of scientific and applied tasks whose setting enables adequately reflecting real natural and anthropogenic processes.

The foundation of any study is a tool that allows you to implement the experiment. Mathematical modeling is the implementation of an experiment, the accuracy of which depends not only on the mathematical description, which is the basis of an abstract representation of the real object, but also on the method of the experiment.

doi:10.1088/978-0-7503-4801-0ch25

The result of the experiment is the reproduction of the real object properties and state using abstract ideas about it, and the goal is the process of knowledge, i.e. obtaining new knowledge on the basis of existing information.

As a rule, the concept of 'mathematical model' characterizes the way to describe a process or phenomenon, i.e., a mathematical equation and the corresponding set of characteristics of the process determined by the original equation.

In this particular case, the concept of 'model' corresponds to the adequate reproduction in space and time state of the hydrodynamic flow within the boundaries of the hydrogeological object. The mathematical model gives a schematic description of the processes occurring in it, explains the mechanism of these processes by the interaction of clearly identified factors and, finally, provides the possibility of quantitative forecasting and development of the processes in space and time.

In order to justify the proposed concept, the main components of the computational experiment are necessary: mathematical description of modeled process and software.

25.2 The main approaches used in the study of hydrogeological processes

The text presents a consistent transition from empirical concepts in the study of groundwater movement to a more rigorous mathematical description based on the law of groundwater dynamics. The proposed type of equation determines the peculiarity of the methodology of mathematical modeling of geofiltration processes, which is implemented in the software. The implementation of the technique provides the creation of a system of models for natural and disturbed geofiltration process and a model of mass transfer in the approximation of a rigid mass transfer regime. The possibilities of the applicability of modeling for solving real hydrogeological problems are considered. Some examples of visualizing the state of groundwater in time, as a result of real hydrogeological object modeling, are given.

The beginning of a systematic approach and mathematical analysis of underground water flow usually, and justly, is tied up with the name of the first hydrogeologist, French engineer Henry Darcy, who based on numerous field experiments formulated the principle law of filtration of underground waters in 1856 [1]. However, the discovery of the empirical practice of building transport, irrigation, drainage and ornamental water systems existed, as well as that of drilling water intake and saline wells long before the work of Darcy.

The first formulation of the law was extremely simple: underground water current discharge through a unit area in a unit time depends on the different of levels of underground water at a 1 m distance, as well as on the properties of the media through which it flows.

The mathematical description of homogeneous groundwater filtration based on Darcy's law connects the volumetric rate of filtration with a gradient of piezometric head of groundwater:

$$V_L = k_L \frac{\partial H}{\partial L} \tag{25.1}$$

where
V_L is the component of velocity in the direction L,
k_L is the filtration coefficient in the direction L,
H is piezometric head of groundwater,
$\frac{\partial H}{\partial L}$ is head gradient in the direction L.

As an approximation to the real conditions of existence of hydrodynamic flow, the concept of a multilayer water exchange system is implemented, when the simulated region Ω is schematized, as an alternation of aquifers $\{\Omega n\}$ separated by relatively low permeable layers.

The underground water current movement is called geofiltration, the main property of media is filtration rate and Darcy's law is a basic law of underground water dynamics.

Hydrogeology has developed as a fundamental branch of science which studies both geofiltration process and its dependency on the hydrosphere properties.

The simplest image of the geofiltration, which illustrates equation (25.1) is given in figure 25.1.

Figure 25.1 shows that, as a rule, the groundwater level is below the Earth's surface, in the aeration zone. A part of precipitation recharges groundwater through the aeration zone—the process of infiltration, the reverse process is evaporation. The movement direction of the hydrodynamic flow occurs from a high level to lower one at the discharge place in the river. The free surface level of groundwater depends on both the amount of precipitation and the level of surface water.

The vertical subterranean hydrosphere structure formed over millions of years. An example of a vertical section water-bearing stratum is shown in figure 25.2.

According to geological laws, the structure of the underground sediments was formed as an alternation of layers with different filtration properties, which are determined by the parameter k_L in equation (25.1). Layers with high values of the filtration coefficient—(0.1–30) m/day are aquifers, for lower values of the parameter, the

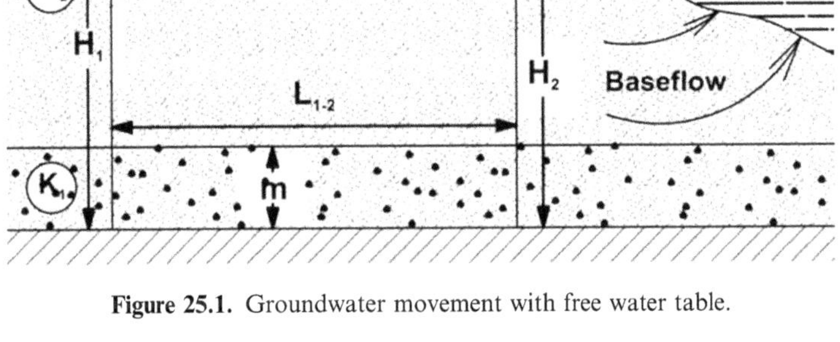

Figure 25.1. Groundwater movement with free water table.

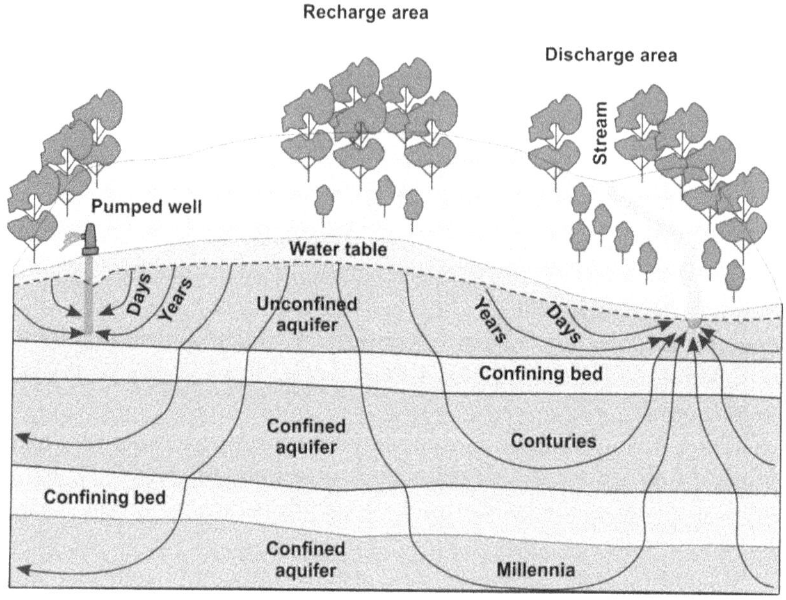

Figure 25.2. Scheme of the vertical structure of the underground hydrosphere.

layer can be considered as poorly permeable or separating (confining bed), as K_1 and K_2 in figure 25.1. The depth of the layers' bedding and their thickness are determined due to the absolute marks of top and bottom for each layer. In addition, aquifers are defined as confined or unconfined depending on the ratio of the absolute marks of the groundwater level and the top mark of the aquifer. If the groundwater level is higher than the top mark of the aquifer, it is considered as confined and vice versa.

It should be emphasized that the absolute marks of the groundwater levels of adjacent confined aquifers depend on the properties of the composing sediments, and water exchange between the horizons occurs depending on their ratio. Thus, the function of the head (level) of underground water is continuous within a separate aquifer and discontinuous in vertical.

The surface water network, in addition to rivers, includes swamps, lakes and springs and is usually an area of groundwater discharge. The main recharge of groundwater is carried out on watersheds, see [2].

Underground water is a conditionally renewable resource. The rate of renewal decreases significantly with the depth of the aquifer bedding. Therefore, the preservation of groundwater quality is an urgent problem of mankind.

25.3 Mathematical description of geofiltration process

The law of underground water dynamics describes a complex system of the interplay of underground and surface waters both in space and time. Some approximations are introduced that allow adapting real conditions to the capabilities of mathematical algorithms when studying the process:

- multilayer water exchange system in region Ω is schematized, as an alternation of aquifers $\{\Omega n\}$, separated by relatively poor permeable layers;
- the continuous space is replaced by a discrete one divided into quadrilaterals with node points in the corners;
- all parameters are set in the grid nodes of the modeled area and at the same points a discrete sought-for function is calculated;
- the resulting function is replaced by a continuous one after the iteration process ending.

In the general case, the law of groundwater movement at confined–unconfined geofiltration, can be described by the system of nonlinear differential equations. The system dimension is determined by the number of simulated aquifers and commonly for aquifer n can be written as:

$$\frac{\partial}{\partial x}\left(\widetilde{T}_{xn}\frac{\partial H_n}{\partial x}\right) + \frac{\partial}{\partial y}\left(\widetilde{T}_{yn}\frac{\partial H_n}{\partial y}\right) + \frac{K_{n-1}}{M_{n-1}}(H_{n-1} - H_n) + \frac{K_n}{M_n}(H_{n+1} - H_n)$$
$$+ Q_2 + Q_3\ W_n = =\widetilde{\mu}_n\frac{\partial H_n}{\partial t} \quad (25.2)$$

The basic equation is reduced to a kind having simple physical sense—the sum of flow rates in each point i of aquifer n equals 0 in natural conditions or difference in capacity in the broken:

$$\sum_i Q_{xi}^n + \sum_i Q_{yi}^n + \sum_i Q_{zi}^{n-1} + \sum_i Q_{zi}^{n+1} + \sum_i Q_{3i}^n + \sum_i Q_{wi}^n = \sum_i Q_{ci}^n \quad (25.3)$$

Where in each node point i of aquifer n, specific flow rates are calculated, [m/day]:

- $Q_{xi}^n = \frac{\partial}{\partial x}\left(T_{xi}^n\frac{\partial H_i^n}{\partial x}\right)$—lateral flow along axis x, T_{xi}^n- water conductivity along x,
- $Q_{yi}^n = \frac{\partial}{\partial y}\left(T_{yi}^n\frac{\partial H_i^n}{\partial y}\right)$—lateral flow along axis y, T_{yi}^n- water conductivity along y,

The water conductivity of the aquifer at grid points defined by absolute marks of aquifer top and bottom: $T_i^n = (H_i^t - H_i^b)\,K_f$.

- $Q_{zi}^{n-1} = \frac{k_{zi}^{n-1}}{m_{zi}^{n-1}}(H_i^{n-1} - H_i^n)$, $Q_{zi}^{n+1} = \frac{k_{zi}^n}{m_{zi}^n}(H_i^{n+1} - H_i^n)$ vertical flows from adjacent aquifers,
  k_{zi}^n—vertical filtration coefficient in semi permeable layer n,
  m_{zi}^n—thickness of semi permeable layer n,
  H_{n+1}- groundwater level in underlying aquifer,
  H_{n-1} —groundwater level in above lying aquifer;
- Q_{wi}^n—infiltration;
- Q_{2i}^n—intensity of groundwater extraction, this function may be time dependent;
- $Q_{3i}^n = (H_{si}^n - H_i^n)\,G_{si}^n$—specific flow rate of groundwater/surface interaction:

H_{si}^n —surface water level, G_{3i}^n - conductivity of river-bed deposits,
$G_{3i}^n = (\frac{k_f}{m})^{rd} * S_i$: k_f, m—filtration coefficient and thickness of river-bed deposit,
S_i—area of interaction in a grid block i,

- $Q_{ci}^n = \mu_i^n \frac{\partial H_i^n}{\partial t}$ —changes in the capacity for transient filtration process,
- μ_i^n —effective value of aquifer capacity (elastic or gravitational) has different values for confined and unconfined aquifers,
- H_i^n —function of water pressure head at point i of aquifer n.

The strict decision of the system of differential equations is possible given the approximation assuming that flows in water-bearing aquifer have lateral character while in relatively water-resisting layer they are vertical.

The applied form of equation (25.2) and its modification (25.3) is the result of many years studying real hydrogeological processes when creating the 'Aquasoft' modeling system.

The first four terms reproduce obviously on the model anisotropic properties of the water-bearing stratum defined by the parameter values of aquifers and separating layers.

All the others determine the interaction of the modeled object with the external environment along boundaries:

- infiltration is set on the model as a matrix in units of specific flow (mm/year);
- the flow rates of water intake wells are set by the boundary conditions of the second kind, taking into account the operating mode;
- a feature of setting boundary conditions of the thirrd kind as it is implemented in equation (25.2) is the possibility of studying nonlinear non steady filtration processes, see [3];
- in the hydrogeological literature, the boundary of the fourth kind is introduced between the two soils with sharply different parameters in the aquifer, see [4]. According to equation (25.2) this feature of sediments is realized by setting parameter values and does not require a separate kind of boundary conditions;
- boundary conditions of the first kind are as 'known' values of the seeking-for function so can't be used as boundary conditions, because in this case the iteration process is substituted by an interpolation one.

The mathematical software implements an algorithm for solving a system of differential equations which describes the laws of dynamics of fresh groundwater, as well as groundwater and surface water interaction with a high degree of mathematical and hydrogeological accuracy

For numerical solving, differential equation system (25.2) is reduced to the form of finite-difference equations when the all parameters are averaged for each block of the grid region and for each segment of the simulated time. The special algorithm to solve a system (25.2) ensures sustainability and a high speed of the iterative process convergence.

25.4 Methods of modeling geofiltration processes

The described setting of the underground water dynamic task and the methodology of mathematic modeling is realized in the author's software 'Aquasoft', see [5, 6].

The software implements the process of mathematical modeling based on interlinked digital and cartographic database input and output data. The bases are problem-oriented and generated under the specific hydrogeological object. Databases are supplemented as the new processes are modeled. The information subsystem provides numerous capabilities for data input, output, and conversion in a digital database. The original and resulting information is double-bind:in precise geographical coordinates, as well as in relative coordinates of the grid area.

The software system has a modular structure and performs separately in time informational and computing operations.

The information system ensures the interaction of all operations when creating a model. The structure of the digital database provides for the storage of matrices of parameters that determine the properties of the water-bearing thickness. The coordinates of the points are determined automatically by the number of the points in the matrix. Boundary conditions are set only at individual points in the grid area of the model and require specifying the coordinates of each point.

The structural unit of information storage in the digital database is the input data of one parameter for one layer of the model. The set of initial parameters is determined by the simulated process. It is possible to set no more than 9 aquifers on the model, respectively, 8 weakly permeable layers. The maximum size of the matrix is (300 × 300) nodal points. Each operation, in addition to the necessary information (model number, layer number, parameter name) has an individual data set that is recognized by the information system.

There are no restrictions on the length of recording boundary conditions in the information system. However, when creating a model, you need to specify the maximum record length in the control file.

The modeling results enable you to obtain new information and provide the visualization of unknown information about the condition of the underground hydrosphere, which may be submitted in the form of tables, graphs and hydrogeological maps (to 15) for all the simulated field or its fragment.

25.4.1 Stages of development of a permanent hydrodynamic model (PHM)

- Integration and systematization of geological and hydrogeological data on the formation of groundwater within the aquifer for the period preceding the modeling work in the form of a cartographic and digital base of the simulated area;
- Implementation of the water pressure-less geofiltration process in the spatio-temporal scale adopted in the study of this object, as well as the solution of the mass transfer problem;

- Visualization of the dynamics of the state of the hydrodynamic flow under the influence of a changing natural or technogenic load, which provides not only control of the state of the geological environment, but also constant updating of prognosis as a result of additional technogenic impact;
- Optimization of anthropogenic load intensity to prevent depletion and pollution of ground and surface water;
- Study and quantification of operational groundwater reserves within a simulated water exchange system;
- Assessment of the conditions of interrelation between surface water and groundwater during natural and disturbed filtration regimes.

Author's software 'Aquasoft' implements the process of mathematical modeling based on interlinked digital and cartographic database input and output data. The bases are problem-oriented and are generated under the specific hydrogeological object. Databases are supplemented as the new processes are modeled.

The main stage of the preparatory work is the creation of a digital database after the analysis and evaluation of the original factographic (stock and archive) data. A base of existing observational and exploratory wells is supposed to be available, as well as hydrogeological data from cartographic bases with the geographic coordinates of the objects.

The work is carried out in two stages:

- Filling in the cartographic database relaying on customer materials, for which topographic base maps of a scale of at least 1:100 000, all available geological and hydrogeological maps of any scale are required. An indispensable condition: the angles of all maps must be geographically referenced to a kilometer or degree coordinate system;
- Filling out the digital database as the model system is created;
- Based on the results of the study, the following preliminary maps are compiled in the graphical interface of the software system by accurate geographical coordinates, in relation with the discretization of the simulated area;
- distribution and thickness of aquifers and poorly permeable layers;
- a map of surface watercourses and reservoirs, indicating surface water levels at the nodal points of the simulated area;
- maps of filtration coefficients (water conductivity) of aquifers and poorly permeable layers;
- infiltration map;
- a map of the boundary conditions that determine the conditions of feeding and unloading along the boundaries of the model;
- map of the observational network;
- map of production wells.

This methodology allows efficiently analyzing the source data and clarifying the hydrogeological schematization in plan and vertically before starting to develop a model as well as making precise the program of work if necessary.

25.4.2 Creation of digital mathematical models and modeling

The complex of work on developing models includes:

Model of steady filtering condition:

- filling and control over the digital database;
- solving the inverse problem in order to clarify the main parameters;
- assessment of the sensitivity of the model relative to the parameters of the water-bearing stratum and the parameters of boundary conditions;
- compilation of hydroisogypsum maps for all studied aquifers for the natural filtration regime;
- compilation of water exchange processes of the simulated area maps;
- calculation of the balance components of the supply and discharge of groundwater flow.

Impaired filter mode model:

- updating the grid data base (display of the operating mode of water intakes, infiltration and surface water levels) in accordance with the selected time step;
- reproduction of the period of exploitation of water intakes followed by the control of regime observations;
- calculation of prognostic options to optimize the location and operation mode of planned water intakes;
- calculation of balance components to analyze the conditions of groundwater reserves formation;
- construction of hydroisogypsum maps for the required (calculated) time steps at the exploited aquifers;
- construction of maps of water exchange processes of the hydrogeological model to confirm the sources of reserve formation.

Model of stationary mass transfer mode:

- supplementing the digital database with porosity parameters and coordinates of pollution sources;
- assessment of the model sensitivity relative to the porosity parameter of aquifers and poorly permeable layers and further determination of the acceptable range of porosity;
- calculation on the model of sanitary protection zones for intakes operated;
- compilation of isochron maps in the zones of sanitary protection of water intakes,
- calculation of the pollution fronts advancing time for various modes of operation of water intakes;
- compilation of isochron maps for each of the pollution sources;
- risk assessment of pulling the front of substandard waters for aquifers exploited.

The most important characteristics of the functioning model are adaptability and adequacy.

The adaptability of the model means the possibility of continuous development of the model—from refining its numerical parameters to changing the schematization of the simulated object on the basis of new factual data obtained in additional field studies. It is the ability of the model to adapt that ensures the expediency of its operation for a long time.

The adequacy of the model to the real process can be provided under the following conditions:

- matching of model coordinates to the true location of production and observational wells;
- accurate time reproduction of each production well operating mode;
- organization of the observational network in all aquifers according to vertical schematization;
- inadmissibility of using nodal points or external border of the second kind boundary conditions in surface water;
- inadmissibility of using the first kind of boundary conditions;
- complying with strict requirements for the quality of underground and surface water monitoring

Thus, a permanent hydrodynamic model (PHM) is a universal opened system, connecting with bases of factual and cartographic information as of separate subsystems, and is an integral part of groundwater monitoring. These challenges require not only the creation, but also the long-term operation of regional mathematical models of hydrodynamic flows. It should be noted, however, that the principles of their adequacy of real processes require a more rigorous approach to the management of geological monitoring.

In particular, mathematical models can be used:

- to assess operational reserves and develop rational methods of groundwater extraction for drinking and household water supply;
- to optimize the observational network of the hydrodynamic regime and quality control of underground water;
- to prevent dewatering of surface waters because of intensive exploitation of aquifers;
- to calculate the regime drainage of quarries during the development of solid mineral deposits;
- to study and predict the processes of flooding and deterioration of underground water quality in urbanized areas;
- to establish sanitary protection zones for water intake structures, as well as protected, resort and recreational areas;
- to study and predict changes in the hydrodynamic regime and groundwater quality in areas of large reservoirs, canals or irrigation systems;
- for control and optimal using of transboundary underground waters because a single hydrodynamic stream exists independently of neighbouring state borders.

Suggested hydrogeological problems are of a practical nature and were solved earlier on mathematical models with varying degrees of detail [7–9].

It would be interesting to simulate the process of interaction of fresh groundwater and marine waters at the boundary of their interaction. Analytical formulas of the process are given in the hydrogeological literature, for example, [10]. However, to confirm the adequacy of the model, systematic observations of coastal groundwater levels throughout the vertical section at different points in time are necessary.

25.5 Examples of modeling results

25.5.1 Hydrogeological features of the model

As an example, some aspects of the described methodology are presented in relation to the model of the Trans-Ili Alatau, a region of the Republic of Kazakhstan.

The size of the simulated area is 92 km × 104 km, 241 × 269 nodal points in the layer. The grid steps are 250 m and 500 m, depending on the density of water intake wells.

The common thickness of the water-bearing stratum is assumed to be 450–500 m, which was uniformly divided for three aquifers in vertical. However, there are no clear weakly permeable layers within the model area. In this case, two conditionally separating layers are used, the capacity of which is equal to the half-sum of the capacities of adjacent aquifers.

Coordinates of nodal points depend on the location of water intakes, observation wells and surface waters. All points identified both the geographic and relative grid coordinates in the digital database.

At the south-eastern border there are underground water recharge sources: glaciers, the sources of the rivers, which are located at an altitude of about 3500–4000 m. At the northern border, discharge of groundwater is carried out in the Ili River whose level is about 450 m. The boundary conditions of the third kind are set at border and surface waters points; at water-intake wells—the boundary conditions of the second kind, respectively. The Western and Eastern boundaries coincide with the streamlines and are considered as impermeable. Figure 25.1 demonstrates all the accepted boundary conditions that are set at the model nodal points.

The main geological feature of the area is the existence of alluvial deposits which were formed due to hydrodynamic flow. Deposits are extended as in plan and vertically through three aquifers. Within the limits of alluvial deposits, high values of water conductivity are observed: T~1000[m^2/day]. Main water intake wells with total capacity up to 2.5 million [m^3/day] are located there. In the other parts of the simulated area water conductivity values are (100–400) [m^2/day].

The structure of water conductivity parameters for the second and third aquifers is similar to that of the first one, but with lower values of the filtration coefficient. The southern part of the territory is represented by quaternary deposits Q1 along the entire vertical section with low filtration properties. According to hydrogeological studies, the filtration coefficient was set for these deposits approximately of 1 m/day.

The map of water conductivity for the first aquifer is shown in figure 25.2.

25.5.2 Some modeling results

On the model of undisturbed conditions as of 1960, the following parameters were estimated:

- coefficients of the plane and a vertical filtering;
- conductivity of river-bed deposits;
- infiltration.

It was found that the amount of infiltration practically does not affect the levels of underground waters. Parameters of water-bearing stratum initially were set up as results of hydrogeological research and then were clarified at the model of non-stationary geofiltration process.

Figure 25.3 shows a map of groundwater levels with observed marks in wells for the first aquifer with region of alluvial deposits as the result decision. It can be seen that the coincidence is satisfactory, the model of the steady process is adequate.

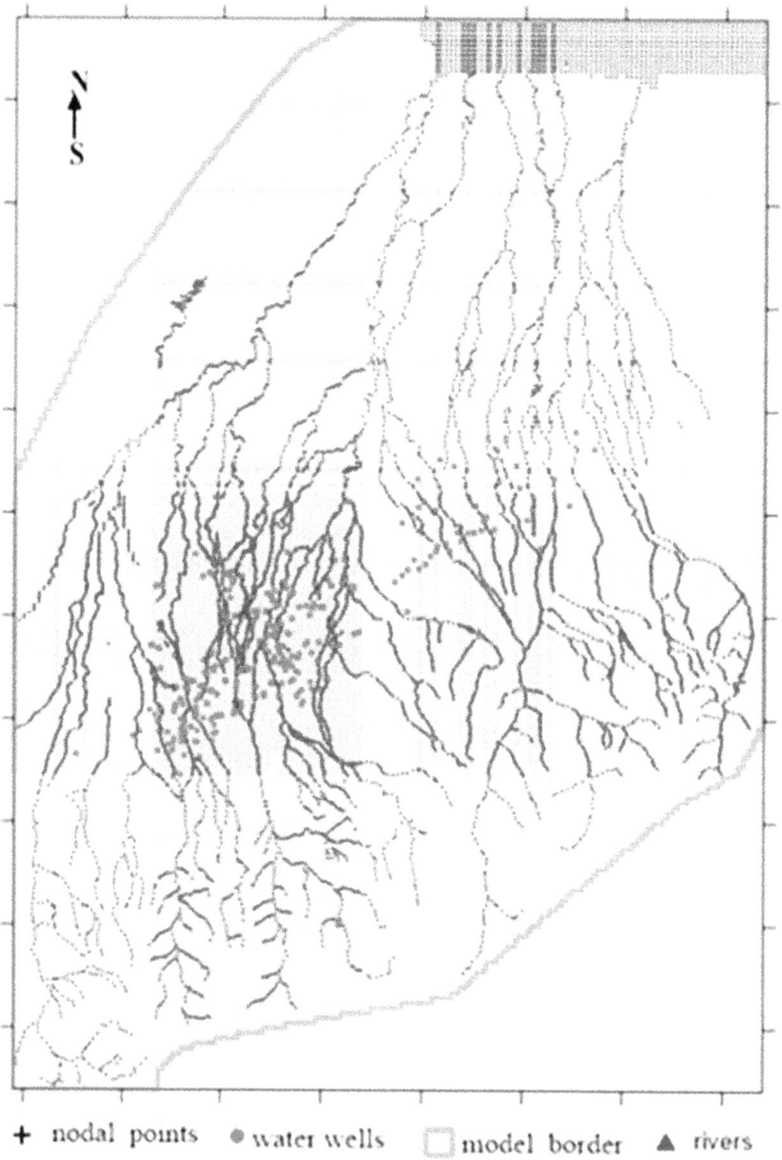

Figure 25.3. The model area with accepted boundary conditions.

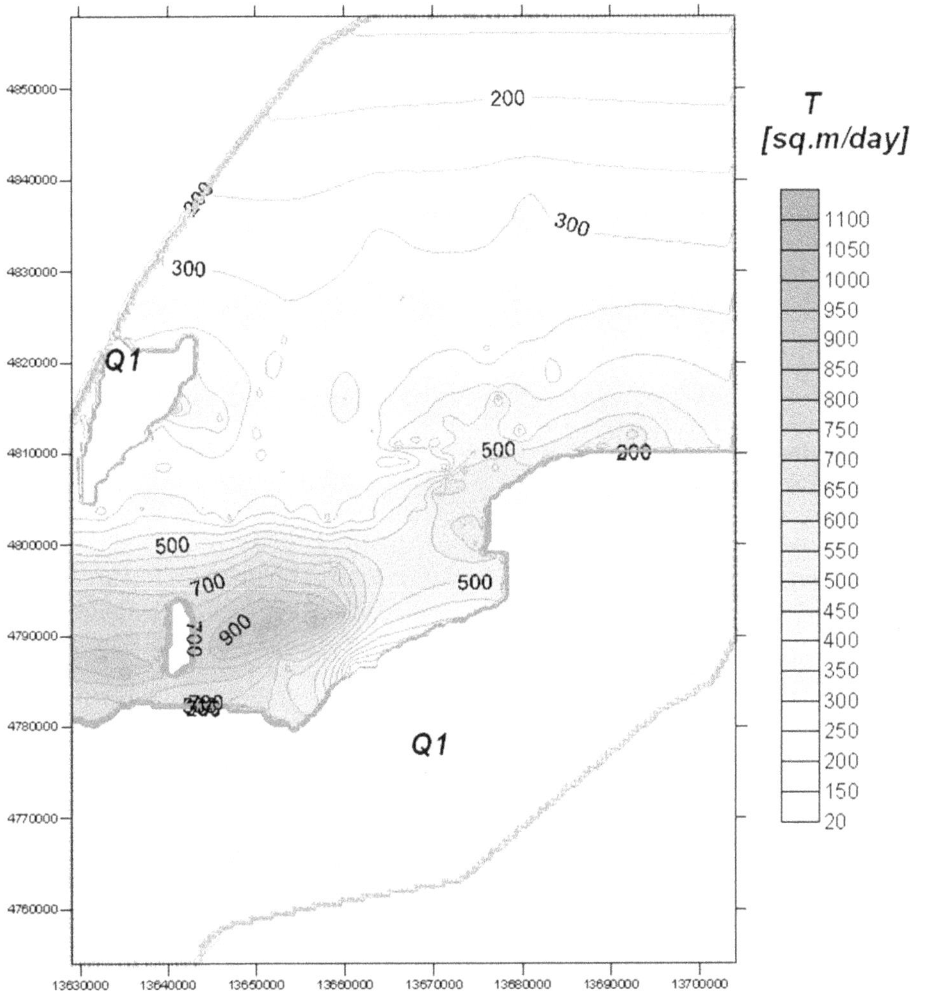

Figure 25.4. Map of water conductivity for first aquifer 1.

New information received as modeling results permit one to study the groundwater flow state in detail, for example, its quantitative water exchange between the aquifers (figure 25.4).

This map shows the numerical water exchange volumes through grid block which are calculated as inflow values from the underlying aquifer into the overlying one. Shades of brown indicate inflow from the underlying aquifer. Conversely, shades of green are the outflow from the overlying aquifer into the bottom, i.e. the alimentation of the lower aquifer.

The direction of water exchange is determined by the ratio of absolute values of groundwater levels in adjacent aquifers. The coordinates of the artesian wells shown on the map are located in the area where the values of the groundwater levels of the

Figure 25.5. The map of underground water levels for first aquifer.

underlying aquifer are higher than the levels of the upper. This fact is one of the signs of the model's adequacy.

Intensive exploitation of groundwater for more than 50 years has caused the depletion of the upper aquifer, since the groundwater level has decreased to 50–70 m with a depth of water wells of 100–150 m. Therefore, the modeling's main goal was to predict the state of groundwater flow for the next 25–30 years. The transfer of water intake wells to the underlying aquifer and the provision of underground water resources were simulated.

Figure 25.7A shows a map of the projected decrease in groundwater flow levels compared to undisturbed waters in the first aquifer. All water intake wells are located in the first layer. The second variant is accepted for practical mode of underground water withdrawal. The levels are reduced to 90 m in some water intake wells.

Figure 25.7B shows a map of the projected decrease of groundwater levels compared to natural geofiltration process in the first aquifer. Part of the water intake wells has been transferred to the second aquifer. At the maximum water intake, the levels are reduced only by 30 m. In parallel with this process, the levels are restored to 70 m.

Visualization of groundwater flow state changes in the process of water intake is realized on the model by calculating the balance components of the flow according

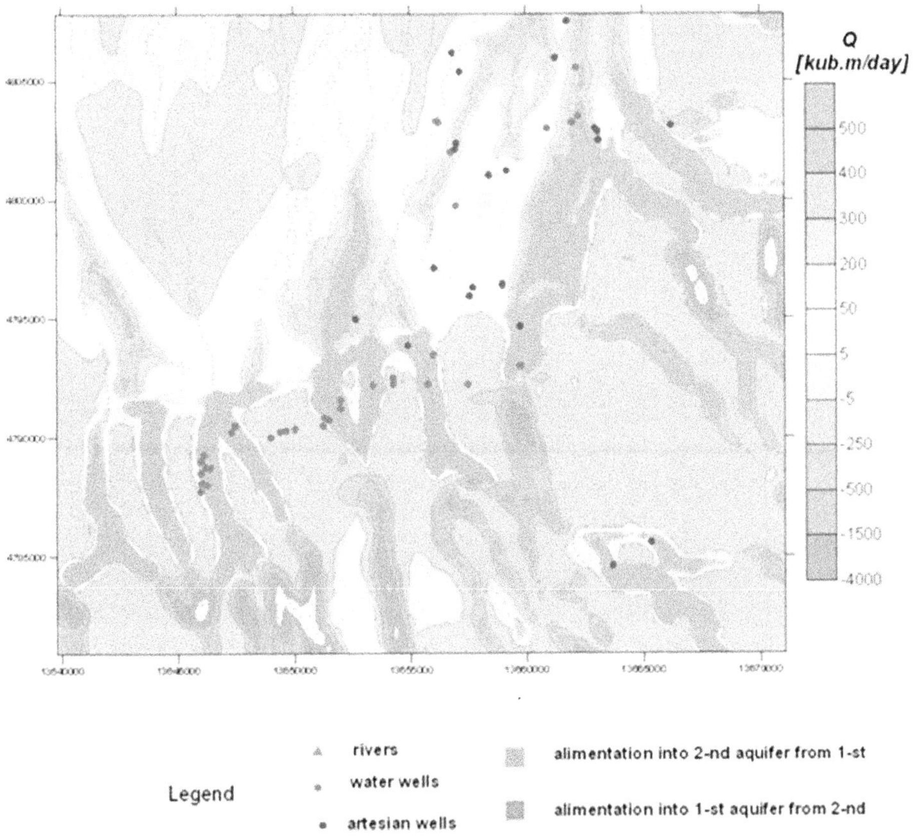

Figure 25.6. Map of numeical water exchange between aquifers 1 and 2.

to equation (25.3). Figure 25.8 shows graphs of the water-bearing stratum reaction to the anthropogenic load.

Graf '***river flow loss***' is calculated as the difference between the amount of ground-surface water exchange in natural and transient conditions of underground water states [9]. Capacity reserves account for about one percent from the total water intake and 'work' only with a sharp change in water intake in the well system. Capacity reserves account for about one percent from the total water intake and 'work' only with a sharp change in water intake in the well system.

Thus, total water withdrawal is provided with alimentation from surface waters.

25.6 Conclusions

Mathematical models as a tool of hydrogeological and ecological forecasting must be a general monitoring subsystem. In this case, hydrogeological services and government agencies get a real tool to assess the current and projected state of the underground hydrosphere, as well as for the effective management of anthropogenic impact.

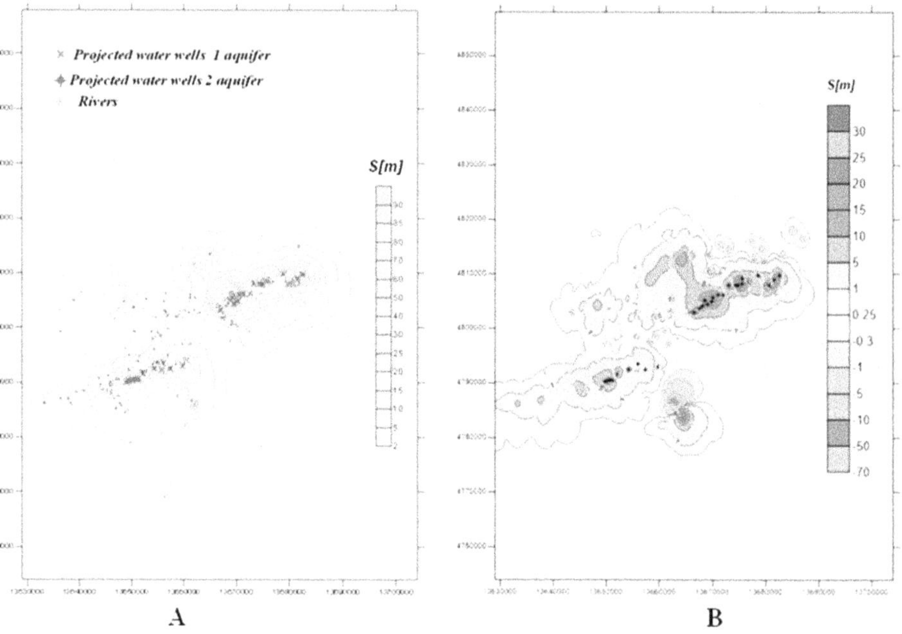

Figure 25.7. Forecast variants of water intakes placement for the year 2040.

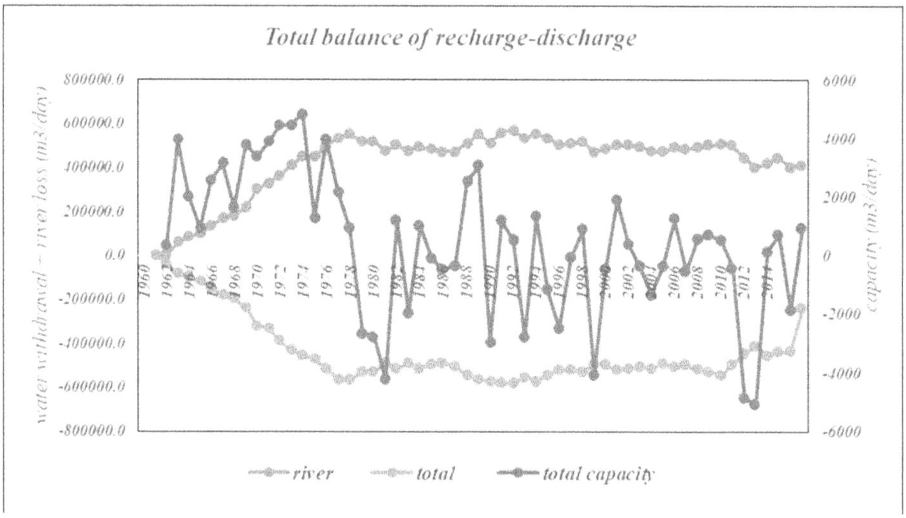

Figure 25.8. Change in structure of the underground water flow balance depending on the amount of water intake, as a modeling result.

As can be concluded from the above described methodology, the influence of water withdrawal destroys the natural process of ground and surface water interaction. The forecast of such a process is especially urgent for natural ecosystems such as swamps, lakes and springs, since their nourishment is ensured by ground waters. The mathematical modeling allows forecasting the distortion of geoecological equilibrium and estimating the anthropogenic load on groundwater including the damage of underground river component.

These challenges require not only the creation, but also the long-term operation of regional mathematical models of hydrodynamic flows. It should be noted, however, that the principles of model adequacy of real processes require a more rigorous approach to the management of geological monitoring.

References

[1] Darcy H 1856 Les fontaines publiques de la Ville Dijon, exposition et application des principes à suivre et des formules à employer dans les questions de distribution d'eau: ouvrage terminé par un appendice relative aux fournitures d'eau de plusieurs villes, au filtrage des eaux et à la fabrication des tuyaux de fonte, de plomb, de tôle et de bitum, Paris, V. Dalmont 647

[2] Devis S N and De Wiest. R J M 1966 *Hydrogeology* (New York: Wiley)

[3] Trihonov A N and Samarsky A A 1977 *Equations of Mathematical Physics* (Moscow: Science Press) (in Russian)

[4] Bear J, Zaslfvsky D and Irmey S 1968 *Physical Principles of Water Percolation and Seepage* (Paris: UNESCO)

[5] Polshkova I N 1994 Specifics of implementing of special math software system for grid models of basins and underground water deposits *Dr. Sci. Eng. Dissertation* Moscow (in Russian)

[6] Interoco. 22.12 2015 Certificate of Copyright № EU-1–000791. Computer programs: The system of special software for calculating flow and transport processes in groundwater 'AQUASOFT'.

[7] Polshkova I N 2011 *The importance of modelling as a tool for assessing transboundary groundwaters: Transboundary Groundwater Resources Management Multidisciplinary Approach* (Weinheim: WILEY-VCH) pp 101–9

[8] Polshkova I N 2012 Math modeling of underground water infiltration dynamics in exhausted gas deposit *J. Earth Sci. Eng.* **2** 77–83

[9] Polshkova I N 2015 Estimations of damage to underground component of rivers due to regional water withdrawals at mathematic models *Mod. Environ. Sci. Eng.* **1** 27–33

[10] Seelin-Bekchurin A I 1965 *Underground Water Dynamics* (Moscow: Moscow University Press) (in Russian)

Chapter 26

Long-term fatigue assessment of offshore monopile structure under corrosive environmental condition

Chana Sinsabvarodom, Wonsiri Punurai, Pornpong Asavadorndeja and Jin Wang

The purpose of this study is to develop an understanding of the fatigue behavior of offshore monopiles under corrosive environment through a numerical simulation framework. The concept of this study can be implemented in all kinds of fixed marine structures. The simulations were carried out using finite element analysis (FEA) to evaluate the dynamic responses of monopile structures employing shell elements. The foundation system consists of soil springs. For estimating the force spectrum, the hydrodynamic force from ocean waves is considered. The long-term sea state of monopile structures is simulated using a wave scatter diagram. The spectral analysis is used to determine the stress spectrum. Experimental *S–N* curves from previous research are used to assess the influence of a corrosive environment. These experimental curves are developed under corrosive environment, i.e., seawater. Three different cases are considered: in the air (ambient temperature), seawater (45 °C), and seawater (45 °C + diffused air). It was observed that higher amounts of diffused air in the seawater provide higher fatigue damage in the structure. The current study can be combined with decision support intelligent framework to develop a decision support tool for structural integrity assessment in the future.

	Nomenclature		
°C	Degree Celsius	PM	Pierson–Moskowitz spectrum
f	Wave frequency	S_{Force}	Wave force spectrum
f_P	Peak frequency	S_{PM}	PM spectrum
H_S	Significant wave height	S_{Stress}	Stress response spectrum
Hz	Frequency	TRF_{Stress}	Stress transfer response function

doi:10.1088/978-0-7503-4801-0ch26

26.1 Introduction

Offshore monopiles are employed as substructures for offshore wind turbines and substations in offshore wind farms. The design of safe and robust structures is a challenging issue because of the uncertain behavior of such structures and harsh ocean environments. New technologies are developed to improve the process in a convenient way, from both technical and economical points of view. However, there are still some concerns when the structures have been in operation for several years. The aging factors become a prominent issue that demonstrates the necessity to evaluate the lifetime of the structures. The evaluated life can be used as a benchmark for inspection and maintenance planning. When the structures are installed in the ocean, degradation of these offshore structures during the service life is a major concern. The underlying reasons are corrosion, fatigue, and effects of corrosion on fatigue accountable for reducing the service life of such offshore structures. Corrosion is a major hazard for offshore structures, especially for structures in the splash zone (Scott *et al* 1983).

Corrosion prediction models are used for ships and offshore structures in seawater including the splash zone (Garbatov *et al* 2007, Garbatov and Soares 2008). Environmental influences are briefly discussed by Soares *et al* (2009, 2011). The corrosion degradation process is highly relevant to aging offshore structures (Brennan and Tavares 2014). The aging of structures is a significant factor for safe operations in the offshore industry. Several offshore structures are still being operated, even though they are beyond their design life, such as those located at the Norwegian Continental Shelf (NCS) and in the United Kingdom Continental Shelf (UKCS) (Arshad and O'Kelly 2013). Corrosion is a natural process that changes a metal to a chemically active form. These active forms include its oxides, hydroxides, or sulfides, which are much more chemically operative. Corrosion causes gradual destruction of materials, most of which are metals. This destruction is due to the chemical or electrochemical reaction or both of metals with the environment. In the most common definition, electrochemical oxidation of metal in reaction with an oxidant is the main mechanism of corrosion. Rusting is the most common example of electrochemical corrosion caused by the formation of iron oxides. Rusting damages the original metal by changing it to its oxides or salts. Corrosion reduces useful properties of materials as well as degrading the entire structure by reducing the strength of materials and increases permeability to liquid and gases. In the case of the geometry of structural elements, corrosion decreases the cross-sectional properties, which affects the stiffness of local elements and hence influences stability on the global structure. Revie (2008) demonstrated corrosion and the influence of temperature in the corrosion process. Two different open and closed systems were considered in the study. It was illustrated and proved that the corrosion rate increases with the temperature.

In addition, fatigue life can be estimated using two approaches (DNV-RP-C203 2011): the fracture mechanics approach and the stress life approach. Many researchers explored both approaches based on the scope and objective of their study. Some researchers adopted the fracture mechanics approach to estimate fatigue life with the help of experimental data (Frost, 1959 1962, Frost and Denton 1964 1966, Frost and Dixon 1967) while, some other researchers focused on probabilistic crack growth (Madsen *et al* 1987, Ling and Mahadevan 2012). The present study deals with the stress life approach as per guidelines. The monopile is assumed as in perfect conditions with no visible crack. Miner's Rule is widely used for its simplicity as a linear accumulation for fatigue damage assessments (Miner 1945). The cumulative damage rule based on the knee point of the *S–N* curve was developed by Subramanyan (1976). Time-domain fatigue analysis is more accurate than spectral fatigue, however, the computation time and effort are very high. Though there are some purely practical reasons for less accuracy in spectral fatigue (Naess and Moan 2012, Mohammadi *et al* 2016), it can be used for the sake of assessment of the structures. Maddox *et al* (1975) first developed the spectral method for fatigue assessments for offshore jacket platforms. It was assumed that the ocean waves are a combination of several sea states, each of which is assumed to be a stationary, ergodic, narrow-banded, Gaussian process. The spectral fatigue method is feasible to consider the long-term distribution of sea states.

Environmental conditions such as air and seawater are some of the primary factors accountable for the initiation of corrosion. Adedipe *et al* (2016) demonstrated the challenges to reproduce the natural seawater environment in the laboratory. The effect of oxygen content, the salinity of water, and pH content are explored. It is observed that fatigue behavior is significantly affected by variations in temperature, pH, dissolved oxygen, and salinity. The pH of seawater ranges from 7.8 to 8.3 and is mildly alkaline (Thorpe *et al* 1983). Recent studies demonstrated corrosion fatigue behaviors of butt welds (Gkatzogiannis *et al* 2021) and T-welded joints (Liao *et al* 2021), and fatigue performances of corroded Q690 high-strength steel (Guo *et al* 2021) extensively. Micone and De Waele (2017) investigated the corrosion seawater environment effect in developing *S–N* curves of HSLA steel and it is equivalent to NVF460 steel. The *S–N* curve at 45 °C seawater temperature and with diffused air is found as the most critical environmental condition. *S–N* curves are developed for different seawater environmental conditions and load frequency. Both temperature and oxygen are reported to have a predominant role in damage processes in high-stress ranges. The addition of diffused air can have huge significance in low-stress cycles. It was also reported that the *S–N* curves are independent with respect to frequency. Arzaghi *et al* (2018) developed a methodology based on fracture mechanics for the prediction of pitting and the effect of corrosion on fatigue degradation of subsea pipelines through a probabilistic framework. The methodology can predict the fatigue life including corrosion. The corrosion effect in fatigue behavior is a complex phenomenon as illustrated above. It has already been found that corrosion accelerates the fatigue damage in structures, but predicting the relevant parameters is more complicated. Several studies depicted probabilistic models for different stages of damage. To perform probabilistic analysis, corrosion should be present in the model in any form, either a pit or small cracks. In this study, it is assumed that the monopile has a perfect cross-section during the installation. It is installed in seawater which will initiate corrosion during its service life. The effect of corrosion is considered by including it in the *S–N* curve.

A thoroughly conducted literature review indicates that no prior studies on fatigue assessments on monopile structures under corrosive environments have been conducted yet. This study aims to perform the fatigue assessment of offshore monopile structures considering corrosive environments. For ocean waves, the Pierson–Moskowitz spectrum (Pierson and Moskowitz 1964) has been generated from the data that is available in the wave scatter diagram over a year. The stress spectra are estimated from the load spectrum and the transfer function from the finite element method (FEM). Fatigue damage has been calculated for three different conditions. Three different *S–N* curves are adopted to evaluate the fatigue damage. *S–N* curves from the previous study have been adopted to conduct a comparative study. Different environmental conditions of air, seawater with 45 °C temperature, and seawater with 45 °C temperature (with diffused air) is adopted. The temperatures are chosen based on the experiments from Micone and De Waele (2017). 45 °C is the control temperature of the lab experiments of the above literature. These three conditions are considered as corrosive environments in this study.

26.2 Frequency domain approach

In the scope of this study, the frequency domain analysis of monopile structures modelled using the FEM is carried out. It is more feasible to compute the response in the frequency domain instead of the time-consuming time-domain analysis. The FEM-based frequency domain may reduce the complexity of this problem. A linear relation is established between the load and stress in the structure by combining the power spectral density (PSD) of the load with the transfer function of the unloaded structure. The stress response spectrum is the product of the stress TRF (transfer response function) and load spectrum. The flow chart of this research is presented in figure 26.1. The study starts with generating the wind and wave spectrum. After that, TRF is computed from harmonic analyses through finite element analysis in ANSYS. From the TRF and load spectra, stress response spectra are computed.

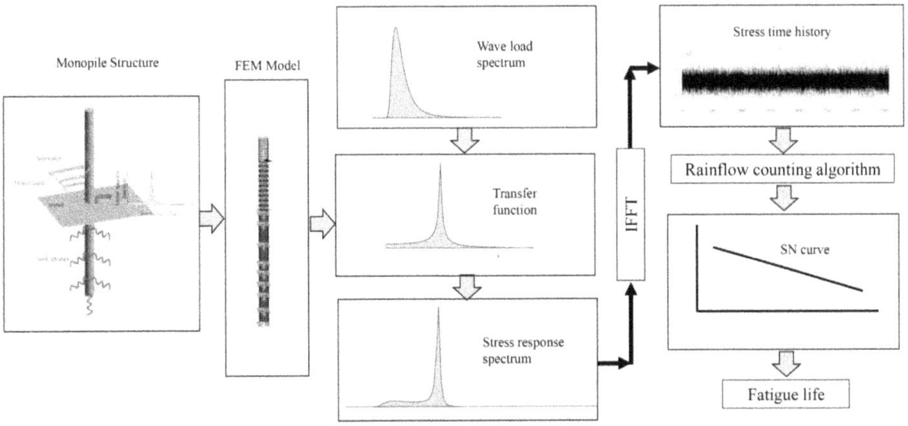

Figure 26.1. Flow diagram of the research.

The stress time histories are obtained from the stress spectra by implementing the inverse fast Fourier transform (IFFT). Finally, the fatigue damage is obtained from the Rainflow-counting algorithm and *S–N* curve applications. A separate MATLAB code is developed to compute the fatigue damage from the obtained stress response spectra.

26.3 Description of the model

A monopile support structure is the most used foundation type for a shallow water depth. In this analysis, the monopile substructure is designed to support a top mass of 480 Tons. This monopile is used for supporting a substation of a power supply. It consists of a single large diameter pile with a thick wall. The monopile is driven into the seabed with a hydraulic hammer. In this study, the diameter of the monopile is 4.5 m. The thickness of the monopile is 40 mm from top to seabed and 50 mm under the seabed. The depth of water is 20 m. The height of the monopile above the sea level is 10 m. The depth of penetration below the seabed is 46 m. The total length of the monopile is 76 m. The pile is constructed from welded roll plates. The weld is present in both longitudinal and circumferential directions. The welding detail was not available and as a result, the general effect of corrosion on fatigue will be demonstrated. Due to computational limitations, the adopted mesh size is 1 m × 1 m. A mesh convergence test was conducted in Azad (2019). Structural damping of 2% of the critical damping is applied in the monopile model (Yue *et al* 2009). It is assumed that the HSLA steel is used for constructing the monopile. The material property constant and fatigue design curves were added. The stress–strain curves used in the study are also added. The analysis was conducted within the linear-elastic range. The plastic properties are not considered in the simulation.

The offshore monopile is modeled in ANSYS 19.2 using the shell element. The SHELL181 element has been adopted which contains four nodes. Each node contains six degrees of freedom including three translations and three rotations. The monopile model in ANSYS is illustrated in figure 26.2. The top mass is assigned by using the MASS21 element. The top mass is distributed to all nodes equally at the top of the monopile. The added mass due to seawater is also calculated following the guideline of DNV (DNV-RP-C205 2010) and applied to each node at the water depth. Each mass and its dimensions are shown in figure 26.2. The application of mass is shown in figure 26.3.

The foundation of the monopile is designed as a driven pile. The design parameters include reaction due to self-weight, wind, and wave force. The guideline of API (API-RP-2A-WSD 2014) is used to design the foundation. The member strength has also been verified as per the criteria of AISC. The maximum vertical resistance is evaluated from the skin resistance and point bearing capacity. The soil report from Buacharoen (2010) has been adopted to evaluate the capacity. The lateral resistance is checked considering the wave force action.

For ease of modeling of the foundation, master node applications have been followed (Yeter *et al* 2018). Each master node is generated at the corresponding

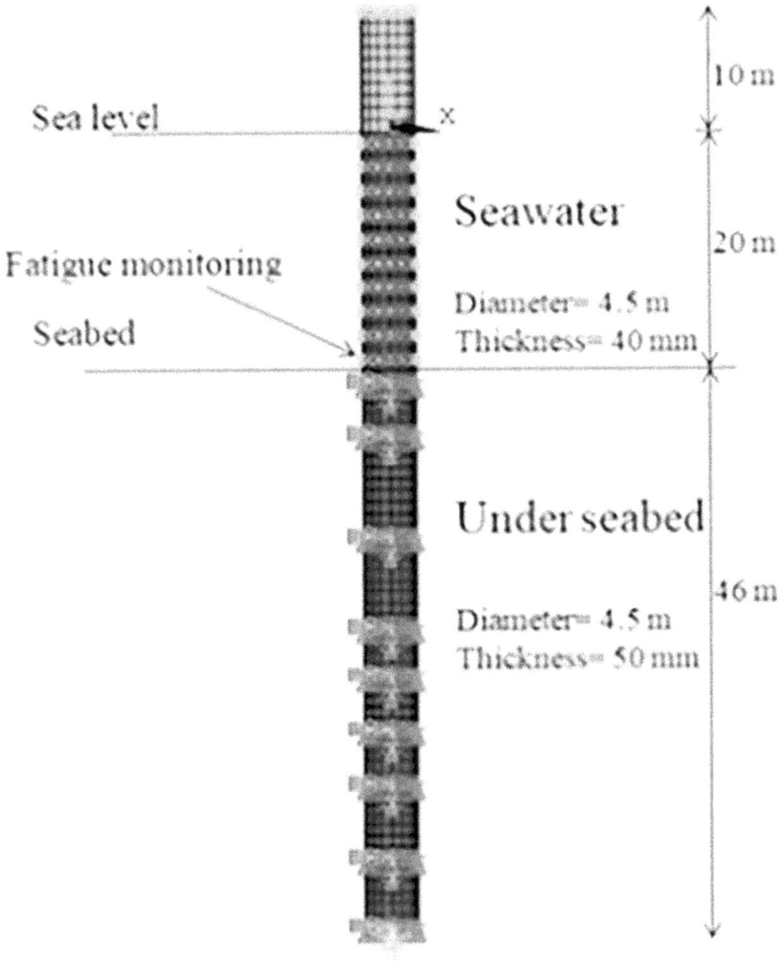

Figure 26.2. Monopile model in ANSYS.

nodes under the seabed. The master nodes are connected following the formulation of constraint equations (ANSYS User Manual 2019).

The other nodes are considered as slave nodes. All the slave nodes will follow the behavior of the master node equally. The massless soil springs are applied to each master node at each level. As shell elements are used in the ANSYS model along with coarse meshing, there are many nodes at each depth. To reduce computational time, the soil springs are only applied at the master nodes and will be followed by the surrounding slave nodes. The use of master nodes in the foundation is shown in figure 26.4. The properties of the monopile are illustrated in table 26.1. The wave load spectra are estimated, and the stress transfer function is computed from the FE model.

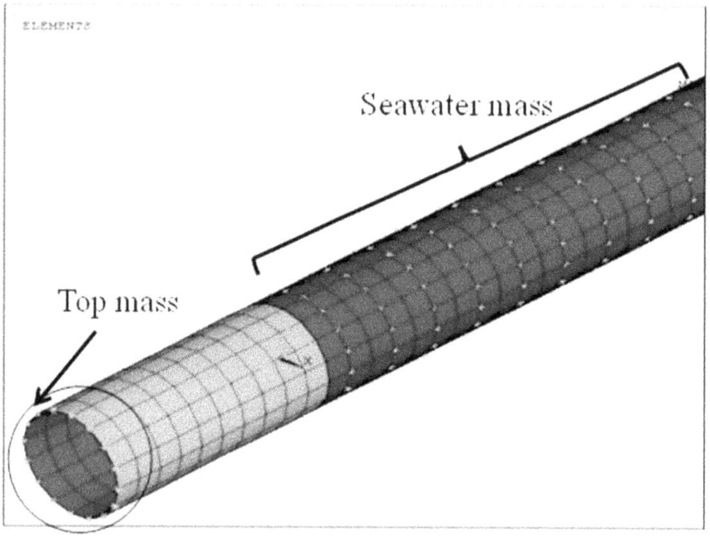

Figure 26.3. Application of MASS.

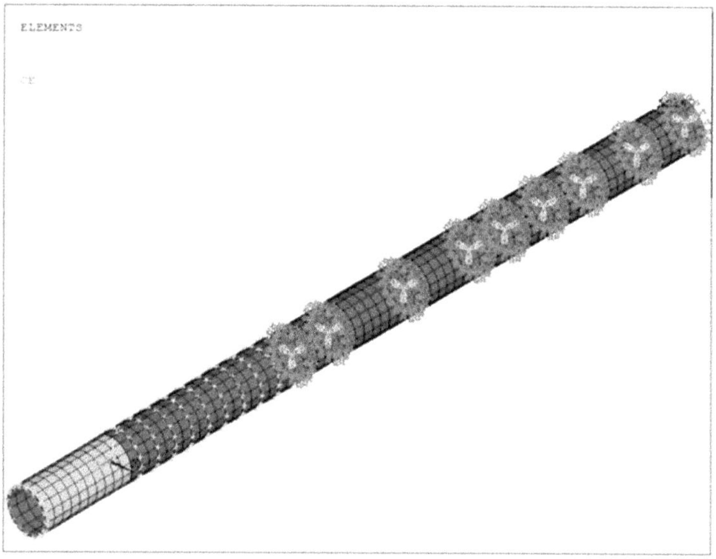

Figure 26.4. Master nodes in foundation levels.

26.4 Free vibration analysis

Free vibration analysis has been incorporated to compute the modal periods of the monopile. The reason for conducting free vibration analyses is to obtain the modal characteristics of natural frequencies and mode shapes of the structures. After conducting the free vibration analysis, the modal periods are illustrated in table 26.2.

Table 26.1. Properties of the offshore monopile (reprinted with permission from Azad 2019)

Contents	Properties
The total length of the monopile	76 m
Depth of water	20 m
Modulus of elasticity	2.05 × 1011 Pascal
Poisson ratio	0.3
Density of steel	7850 kg m^{-3}
Diameter	4.5 m
Thickness over seabed	40 mm
Thickness under seabed	50 mm

Table 26.2. Modal analysis.

Modes	Period (s)
Mode 1	0.892
Mode 2	0.892
Mode 3	0.791
Mode 4	0.791
Mode 5	0.427
Mode 6	0.427

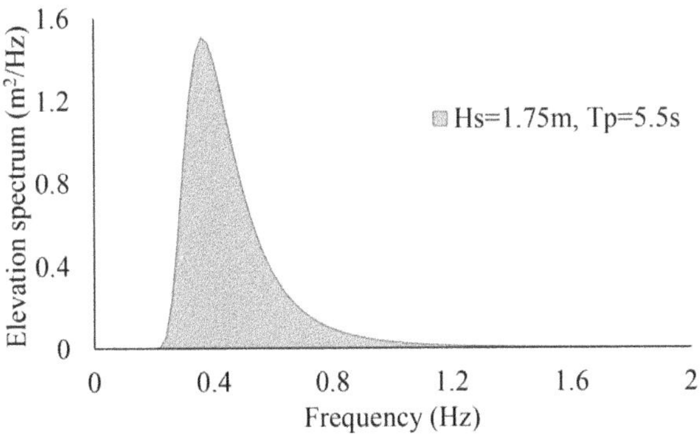

Figure 26.5. Wave elevation spectrum.

The first modal shape is illustrated in figure 26.5 that can be observed to be a translational mode. The first and second modal periods are 0.892 s.

The third and fourth modal periods are 0.791 s. The fifth and sixth modal periods are 0.427 s. The reasons for similar values in the first two modes are, (a) the top mass is applied as a lumped mass, and (b) the cross-section of the monopile is circular which initiates the same moment of inertia in both horizontal directions.

26.5 Wave load estimation

The monopile is a substructure of an offshore wind farm substation where wind does not have a significant effect on it. The current study only considers the wave loading conditions. Inherently, the behavior of an ocean wave is a stochastic and random process. In this research, the wave spectrum is used for designing the sea state of offshore structures to calculate the fluid–structure interaction. For long-term analysis, the two-dimensional wave scatter diagram has been adopted for simulation of the loading event of an ocean wave. For ocean waves, key parameters are defined for the correct representation of the sea state. The variables that specify a wave climate according to the standards are the significant wave height (H_s), which is considered as 1/3 of the highest amplitude of the wave, the spectral peak period (T_p), which is associated with the mean zero-crossing periods (T_z), and the depth of water. These values are assumed to be constant for a stationary wave condition, which is short-term and can be regarded as a three-hour period.

The most common wave spectra in the offshore sector are the Pierson–Moskowitz (PM) and JONSWAP ones. The JONSWAP (DNV 2010) spectrum is based on measurements from the North Sea. Since in the context of this study a site in the Gulf of Thailand is considered, the PM spectrum is used in the developed model. The illustration of the PM spectrum (DNV-RP-C205 2010) is shown in equation (26.1).

$$S_{PM}(f) = \frac{5}{16} H_S^2 f_P^4 f^{-5} \exp\left(-\frac{5}{4} \left(\frac{f}{f_P} \right)^{-4} \right) \tag{26.1}$$

where S_{PM} is the PM spectrum, H_s and f_p are the significant wave height and peak frequency.

The force spectrum is estimated following the procedure of Kaloritis (2016). The examples of wave elevation spectrum and load spectrum for a certain signification wave height of 1.75 m and peak period of 5.5 s are illustrated in figures 26.5 and 26.6, respectively.

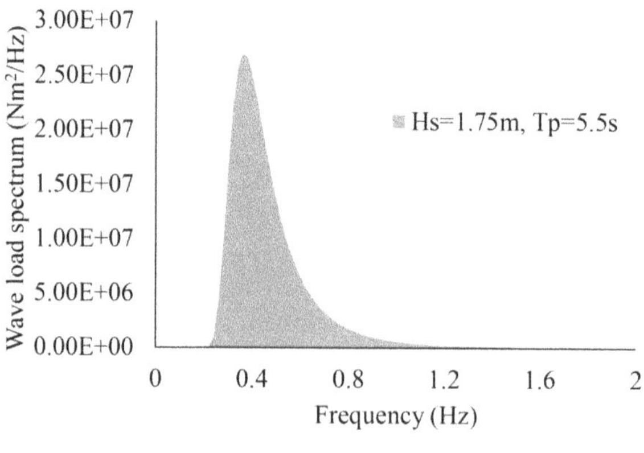

Figure 26.6. Wave force spectrum.

26.6 Stress transfer function and stress response spectrum

The research employs the harmonic module in ANSYS to determine the transfer function in the frequency domain. The analysis was run with a unit load at the frequency range between 0 Hz and 2 Hz to cover possible sea states of an ocean wave. The unit load is applied at every meter of the monopile from the top to the seabed level and global harmonic analysis is performed for the unit load at every meter. The hot spot stress transfer function is estimated from the global harmonic analysis conducted. The transfer function for Von-Mises stresses is obtained from the harmonic analysis. The application of harmonic load is delineated in figure 26.7. The harmonic analysis response is shown for the Von-Mises stress in figure 26.8. A typical stress contour plot from the global harmonic analysis is demonstrated in figure 26.9. After obtaining the harmonic responses as well as the transfer functions, the stress spectrum is evaluated using equation (26.2).

$$S_{\mathrm{Stress}} = S_{\mathrm{Force}} \times (\mathrm{TRF}_{\mathrm{Stress}})^2 \tag{26.2}$$

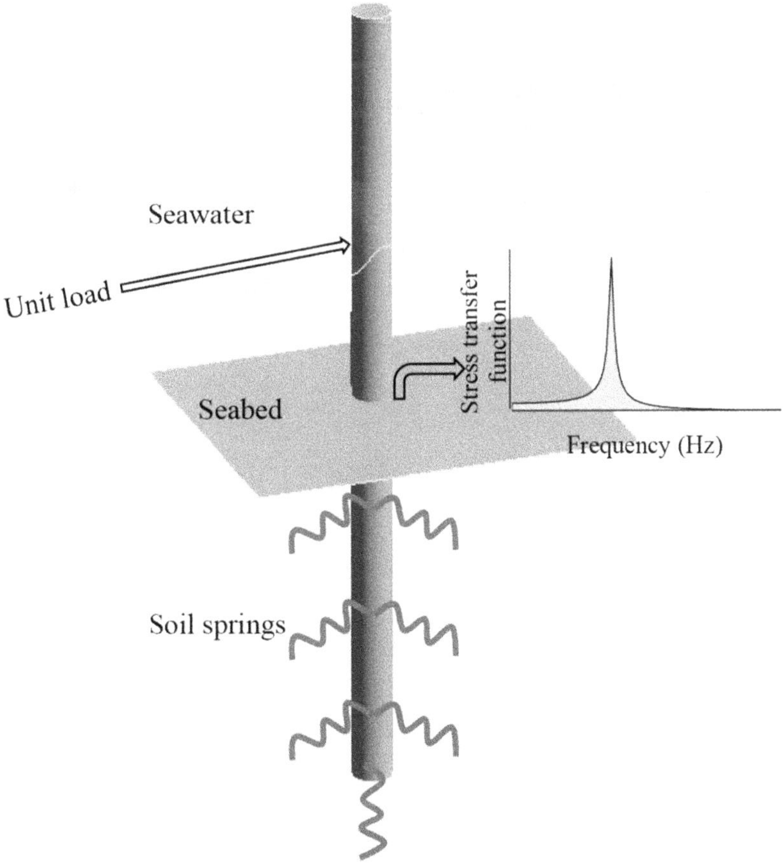

Figure 26.7. Harmonic load applied at sea level.

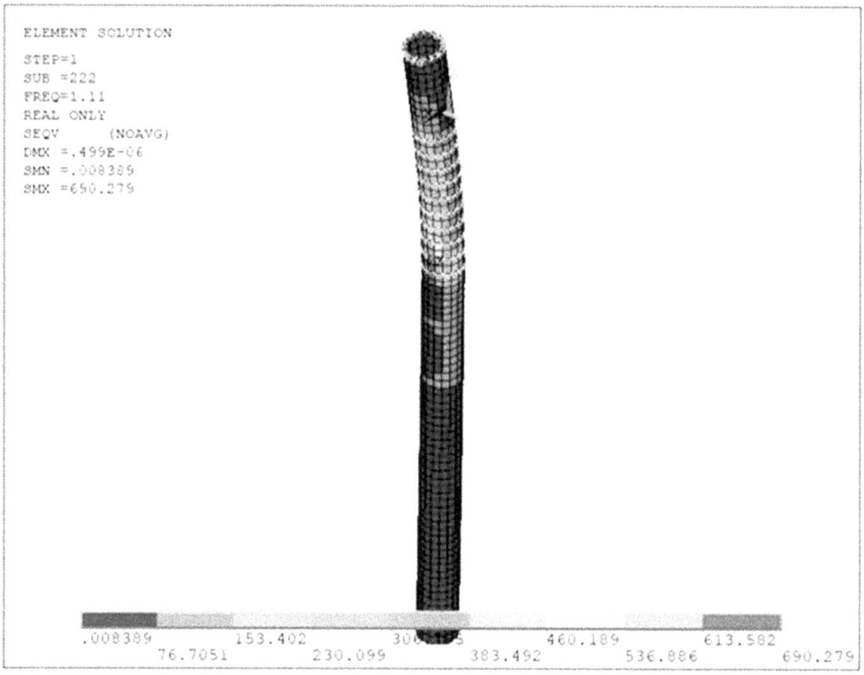

Figure 26.8. Harmonic response of monopile.

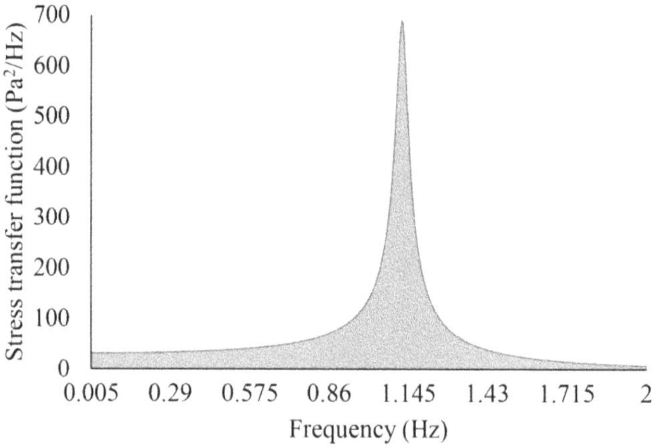

Figure 26.9. Stress transfer function at sea-level.

where S_{Stress} is the stress response spectrum, S_{Force} is the wind/wave force spectrum and $\mathrm{TRF}_{\mathrm{Stress}}$ is the stress transfer response function.

The stress response spectra corresponding to long-term wave conditions based on the wave scatter diagram as listed in table 26.3 are delineated in figure 26.10.

Table 26.3. Wave scatter diagram (reprinted with permission from Azad 2019).

Significant wave height (m)	Significant peak period (s)														
5.5-6.0	0.0-0.5	1.0-2.0	2.0-3.0	3.0-4.0	4.0-5.0	5.0-6.0	6.0-7.0	7.0-8.0	8.0-9.0	9.0-10.0	10.0-11.0	11.0-12.0	12.0-13.0	13.0-14.0	14.0-15.0	Total
5.0-5.5																0
4.5-5.0									4							4
4.0-4.5									27							27
3.5-4.0								2	109							111
3.0-3.5								94	149							242
2.5-3.0							66	965	29							1060
2.0-2.5						1	2643	2352	11	1						5008
1.5-2.0						2709	14909	1033	316	74						19041
1.0-1.5				7	7794	40207	16369	342	1778	225						66722
0.5-1.0				47319	93037	62000	24590	332	1491	930		76	119	3		229897
0.0-0.5			4849	57104	32622	21453	4309	152	87	806		146	148	97		121773
	0		4849	104430	133453	126370	62886	5272	4001	2036	0	222	267	100	0	443886

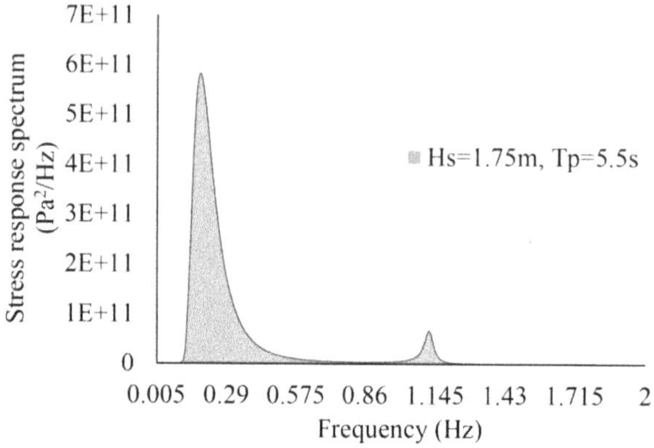

Figure 26.10. Stress response spectrum.

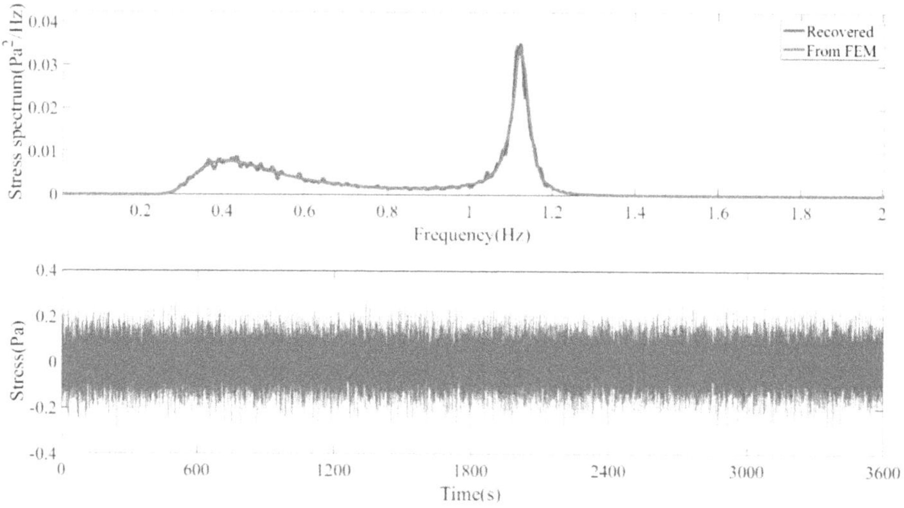

Figure 26.11. Application of IFFT to generate stress time history.

26.7 Fatigue life estimation

The fatigue damage is estimated from the stress response spectra. At first, the IFFT is implemented to convert the frequency domain signals or power spectral density (PSD) to time-domain signals. IFFT is a powerful tool to convert frequency domain signals to time-domain ones. Frequency domain signals do not have sufficient details on phases and hence random phase angles are considered in this study. The stress response spectra are converted into stress histories as illustrated in figure 26.11. After obtaining the time history of stress, the FFT is applied to recover the original PSD to check the estimation of scaling. Figure 26.11 illustrates the IFFT conversion and application of FFT to recover the original PSD. The represented case stands for a wave condition where H_s is 1.75 m and T_p is 5.5 s. The solid line illustrates the PSD

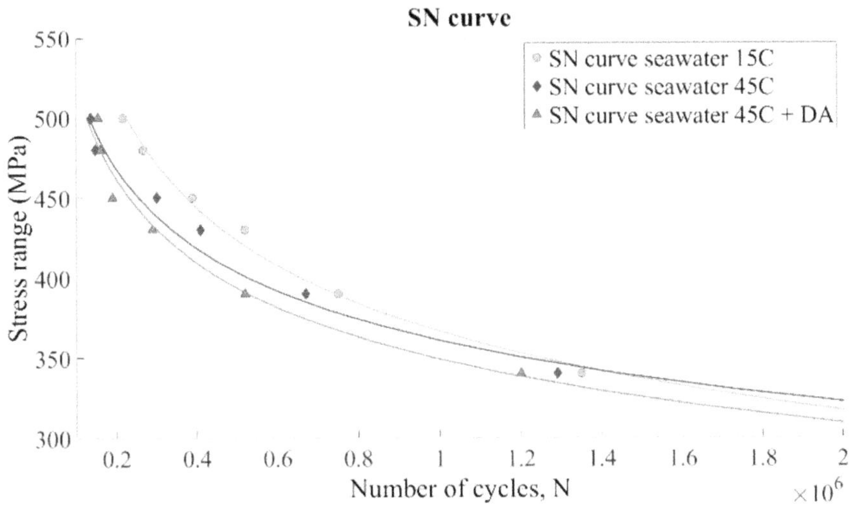

Figure 26.12. *S–N* curves at different conditions, from Micone and De Waele (2017).

from finite element analysis and the dotted line depicts the recovered PSD in the upper part of figure 26.11. The lower part of figure 26.11 delineates the generated stress time history. In this study, the length of each time history is considered as an hour. The minimum length of time histories is assumed as a minimum of 10 min. Since this study deals with long-term distribution of loading, one hour time histories are generated.

Rainflow counting algorithm is applied to estimate the number of cycles and stress range of the stress time history of the monopile substructure subjected to the wave loading. Then the accumulated fatigue damage is computed by employing Miner's linear damage rule (Miner 1945). As illustrated previously, the *S–N* curves from Micone and De Waele (2017) are employed in this study to evaluate the fatigue damage and the equivalent stress has a range of 300–500 MPa as shown in the *S–N* curves in figure 26.12. The estimation of the fatigue damage is based on the long-term response of the structure that includes all the sea states represented by the given scatter diagram. The service life of the monopile is 25 years and the fatigue damage is calculated accordingly.

Fatigue damage of a monopile during operation under ocean waves with corrosive conditions is investigated. In this research, the design life of the structure is 25 years. The damage index (D) is used to quantify the damage levels. If the D value is equal to one, it is specified as completely damaged. From the stress time series, the stress ranges are computed, and the fatigue damage and fatigue life are estimated. This study concerns three different environmental conditions as stated. The fatigue life of the monopile at different conditions are illustrated in figure 26.13. In air, the fatigue life is 94 429 years. At a higher temperature (45 °C), the fatigue life becomes 1274 years. The presence of air influences the fatigue behavior significantly. At 45 °C with diffused air, the fatigue life falls to a value of 487 years. The abrupt change due to the presence of air is noticeable.

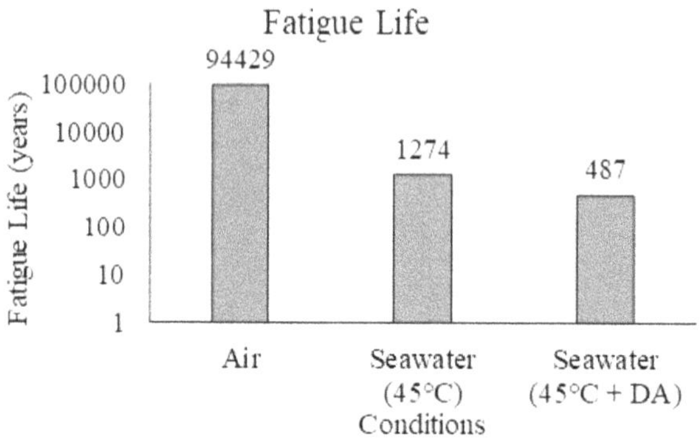

Figure 26.13. Fatigue life of the monopole.

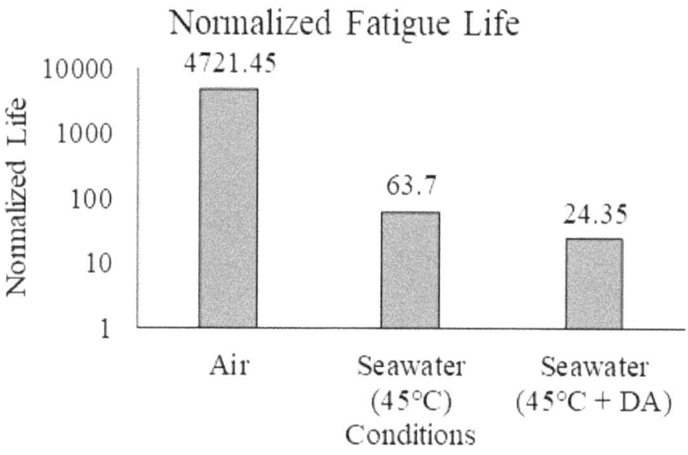

Figure 26.14. Normalized fatigue life.

The comparisons of the fatigue life prediction are represented with clarification in figure 26.14 in terms of normalized life ratio. The normalized values of fatigue life as shown in figure 26.14 are computed by dividing the fatigue life values by the design life of 25 years. There is a variation of the corrosive effects of fatigue life due to the presence of oxygen according to the proposed design life.

26.8 Conclusions and recommendations

The focus of this study is to analyze the structural behavior of an offshore monopile structure and obtain the fatigue life at different environmental conditions. Long-term distribution of wind–wave is considered to estimate the fatigue damage substantially over a year. The fatigue life is computed from fatigue damage per year as the relation between fatigue damage and fatigue life is reciprocal. There are 47 cases considered for wave load estimation and each case has a certain probability of occurrence. The fatigue damage is computed for each case and each instance of fatigue damage is multiplied with the probability of occurrence of the case. The quantities of damage for all cases are summed up to obtain the annual fatigue damage as well as the fatigue life. As stated, corrosion is taken into consideration in the *S–N* curves. The *S–N* curves were obtained from the experiments of the previous study. The analysis addresses the influence of corrosion on the fatigue degradation of materials. The governing factor is not only the temperature but also the presence of oxygen content. The mechanical properties of materials and interaction with the environment, salinity, and pH of the water are also important. The estimated fatigue life can be used as a baseline for inspection and maintenance planning. Since the weld profile detail is not available, the stress concentration cannot be simulated. The effect of general corrosion has been investigated and demonstrated. This effect can be elaborated once the welding profile has been implemented. The developed algorithm provides a solid basis for performing the fatigue assessment of any fixed offshore structure under a corrosive environment.

Acknowledgements

This project has received funding from the European Union's Horizon 2020 research and innovation under the Marie Skłodowska-Curie grant agreement No. 730888. The first and second authors would like to thank Pornpong Asavadorndeja, Synterra Co., Ltd., Bangkok, Thailand for supporting the ANSYS license throughout the research.

References

Adedipe O, Brennan F and Kolios A 2016 Review of corrosion fatigue in offshore structures: present status and challenges in the offshore wind sector *Renew. Sustain. Energy Rev.* **61** 141–54

ANSYS online user Manual. Available https://sharcnet.ca/Software/ANSYS/17.0/enus/help-/ans_ope/ [Accessed in 21 May, 2019]

API-RP-2A-WSD 2014 Planning, Designing, and Constructing Fixed Offshore Platforms—Working Stress Design, American Petroleum Institute.

Arshad M and O'Kelly B C 2013 Offshore wind-turbine structures: a review *Proc. of the Institution of Civil Engineers-Energy* 166 139–52

Arzaghi E, Abbassi R, Garaniya V, Binns J, Chin C, Khakzad N and Reniers G 2018 Developing a dynamic model for pitting and corrosion-fatigue damage of subsea pipelines *Ocean Eng.* **150** 391–96

Azad M S 2019 *Effect of corrosion on fatigue assessments of offshore monopile* (Thailand: Mahidol University)

Buacharoen J 2010 *Cost and practical: based concept for innovative Design of minimum offshore structures* (Thailand: Asian Institute of Technology)

Brennan F and Tavares I 2014 Fatigue design of offshore steel mono-pile wind substructures *Proc. of the Institution of Civil Engineers-Energy* **167** 196–202

DNV-RP-C203 2011 Fatigue Design of Offshore Steel Structures, Det Norske Veritas, Recommended Practice.

DNV-RP-C205 2010 Environmental Conditions and Environmental Loads, Det Norske Veritas, Recommended Practice.

Frost N E 1959 Propagation of fatigue cracks in various sheet materials *J. Mech. Eng. Sci.* **1** 151–70

Frost N E 1962 Effect of mean stress on the rate of growth of fatigue cracks in sheet materials *J. Mech. Eng. Sci.* **4** 22–35

Frost N E and Denton K 1964 The fatigue crack propagation characteristics of HS3OWP aluminium alloy *Department of Scientific and Industrial Research*

Frost N E and Denton K 1966 The rate of growth of fatigue cracks in various aluminium alloys

Frost N E and Dixon J R 1967 A theory of fatigue crack growth *Int. J. Fract.Mech.* **3** 301–16

Garbatov Y, Soares C G and Wang G 2007 Nonlinear time dependent corrosion wastage of deck plates of ballast and cargo tanks of tankers *J. Offshore Mech. Arct. Eng.* **129** 48–55

Garbatov Y and G Soares C 2008 Corrosion wastage modeling of deteriorated bulk carrier decks *Int. Shipbuilding Progress* **55** 109–25

Gkatzogiannis S, Weinert J, Engelhardt I, Knoedel P and Ummenhofer T 2021 Corrosion fatigue behaviour of HFMI-treated butt welds *Int. J. Fatigue* **145** 106079

Guo H, Wei H, Li G and Wang Y 2021 Experimental research on fatigue performance of corroded Q690 high-strength steel *J. Mater. Civ. Eng.* **33** 04021304

Kaloritis G 2016 Simplified fatigue assessment of offshore wind turbine full height lattice structures in the frequency domain *Nederland: Delft University of Technology*

Liao X, Qiang B, Wu J, Yao C, Wei X and Li Y 2021 An improved life prediction model of corrosion fatigue for T-welded joint *Int. J. Fatigue* **152** 106438

Ling Y and Mahadevan S 2012 Integration of structural health monitoring and fatigue damage prognosis *Mech. Syst. Sig. Process.* **28** 89–104

Maddox N, Roger and Roger W 1975 Wildenstein: A spectral fatigue analysis for offshore structures *Offshore Technology Conf.*

Madsen H O, Skjong R K and Tallin A G 1987 Probabilistic fatigue crack growth analysis of offshore structures, with reliability updating through inspection *Marine Structural Reliability Engineering Symp. (Arlington, VA)*

Miner M A 1945 Cumulative damage in fatigue *J. Appl. Mech.* **12** 159–64

Micone N and De Waele W 2017 Evaluation of methodologies to accelerate corrosion assisted fatigue experiments *Exp. Mech.* **57** 547–57

Mohammadi S F, Galgoul N S, Starossek U and Videiro P M 2016 An efficient time domain fatigue analysis and its comparison to spectral fatigue assessment for an offshore jacket structure *Mar. struct.* **49** 97–115

Naess A and Moan T 2012 *Stochastic dynamics of marine structures* (Cambridge: Cambridge University Press)

Pierson Willard J and Moskowitz Lionel 1964 A proposed spectral form for fully developed wind seas based on the similarity theory of SA Kitaigorodskii *J. Geophys. Res.* **69** 5181–90

Revie R W 2008 *Corrosion and corrosion control: an introduction to corrosion science and engineering* (New York: Wiley)

Scott P M, Thorpe T W and Silvester D R V 1983 Rate-determining processes for corrosion fatigue crack growth in ferritic steels in seawater *Corros. Sci.* **23** 559–75

Soares C G, Garbatov Y, Zayed A and Wang G 2009 Influence of environmental factors on corrosion of ship structures in marine atmosphere *Corros. Sci.* **51** 2014–26

Soares C G, Garbatov Y and Zayed A 2011 Effect of environmental factors on steel plate corrosion under marine immersion conditions *Corros. Eng. Sci. Technol.* **46** 524–41

Subramanyan S 1976 A cumulative damage rule based on the knee point of the *S–N* curve *J. Eng. Mater. Technol.* **98** 316–21

Thorpe T W, Scott P M, Rance A and Silvester D 1983 Corrosion fatigue of BS 4360: 50D structural steel in seawater *Int. J. Fatigue* **5** 123–33

Yeter B, Garbatov Y, Soares C G, Punurai W and Azad M S 2018 Response of monopile offshore wind turbine structure subjected to seismic loads and degradation *The 7th Asia Conf. on Earthquake Engineering (7ACEE 2018) (Bankok)*

Yue Q, Zhang L, Zhang W and Kärnä T 2009 Mitigating ice-induced jacket platform vibrations utilizing a TMD system *Cold Reg. Sci. Technol.* **56** 84–9

Chapter 27

Estimation of crop water use in agricultural systems

R Deepa and Mukhdeep Singh Manshahia

Irrigation scheduling is the process of determining when and how often water should be provided to a crop to keep it healthy. Evapotranspiration (ET)-based scheduling calculates daily crop rate demand using real-time crop and meteorological data. ET data or crop water use-based irrigation scheduling can lead to the optimum usage of water in agricultural systems and also determine the amount of water lost from the soil surface through evaporation as well as transpiration during crop development stages. ET-based irrigation is predicated on ET, which combines the impacts of soil evaporation and vegetation transpiration rates; and ET-related water loss from the root zone is replaced to fulfill plant water demands. With ET-based irrigation scheduling, a landowner will know the estimated quantity of water the crop will need for any given week to optimize the crop yields and also shows the actual water requirements of the crops.

27.1 Introduction

In many parts of the world, water is becoming an economically scarce resource. Agriculture is the world's largest consumer of groundwater, contributing to 70% of irrigation outflows [1]. To ensure a balance for agricultural production, municipal and industrial purposes, and ecological health, improving the effectiveness of water within the agricultural system is critical and an estimate of ETn provides a perspective of groundwater balance concerning the amount of precipitation and irrigation.

Irrigation is a critical activity in hot environments to ensure optimum agricultural productivity. It can also help to reduce production risks, especially in places with reasonable rainfall levels. Despite its advantages, irrigation should be handled appropriately to avoid using too much or too little water. Irrigation scheduling is

doi:10.1088/978-0-7503-4801-0ch27

important in this regard since it allows delivery of water to different crops based on their needs [2].

Irrigation scheduling refers to the time and duration of watering plants. ET-based irrigation scheduling combines the impacts of soil evaporation and plant transpiration rates and moisture lost from the root zone due to ET is replaced to fulfill crop water demands [3]. ET, canopy temperature [4], evaporation deficiency, soil water holding capacity and plant transpiration rate can all be used to evaluate water stress or irrigation schedule [5].

Increased yields in intensive farming operations are mostly dependent on timely and appropriate crop watering. Therefore, to acquire the best yield per unit area, it is critical to establish the period when plants are susceptible to water, in addition to the right estimation of plant water consumption and irrigation interval [6].

Irrigation scheduling can be carried out in various ways, but the most common method is to use reference evapotranspiration (ETo), which is often calculated using meteorological data [7–12]. ETo can be used to calculate ET for a wide range of crops. Thus, a crop coefficient (Kc) and a water stress coefficient (Ks) are employed to convert ETo to ET for a specific crop, taking into account the crop's growth phase and soil water availability.

Crop water use estimation aids in optimal irrigation water management, which in turn aids in conserving water, reduction of groundwater consumption, energy efficiency and crop quality preservation [13]. The soil moisture content estimated by the evaporation pan is similar to that of the measured gravimetric approach.

The technique by which an irrigation system is operated, maintained and monitored determines how effective it is. To aid the landowner in making irrigation decisions, it checks whether the irrigation system is evenly distributing water, whether the timing is linked to crop water need [14], and ensures that the state of the moisture present in the soil for an irrigated crop must be monitored regularly. Irrigation scheduling is usually done in one of two ways: (a) by using soil moisture sensors at various depths; and (b) scheduling based on the ET method.

ET, which integrates the processes of evaporation from the soil and transpiration from plants to describe the transfer of water vapor from the land to the atmosphere, is one of the most important surface land outflows. In farming practices, accurately calculating ET is critical for optimal use of groundwater sources and accurate irrigation management procedures that lead to enhanced water usage efficiency [15].

Crop water is determined by several factors [16]. These include the following.

1. Crop types;
2. Stages of development;
3. Environmental conditions and management;
4. Moisture in the soil, etc.

Environmental and plant factors influence how much water the crop use at different stages. Plant factors are related to the crop type, stages and vitality, while environmental factors are related to climate and weather. Cultural and site characteristics, such as irrigation scheduling, planting density and soil type all influence crop irrigation requirements. Climate and weather are examples of environmental elements. The amount of water essential for effective crop development is determined by temperature, wind speed, relative humidity and solar radiation. They can be computed as evaporation or measured directly using an evaporation pan (Epan).

ET irrigation management [18] is different based on irrigation purposes. The soil moisture storage capacity is important in scheduling irrigations for full coverage irrigation infrastructure such as furrow, sprinklers, drip and border flood. Water evaporates [19] from the surface through ETwhen irrigation is provided, the same way loss from an open pan evapometer occurs. It is the proportion of irrigation water (IW) supplied to cumulative pan evaporation (CPE). Daily, the pan evaporation data are added up until they equal a specified proportion of the amount of water used for irrigation.

The main objective of the present study: use an open pan evapometer which determines the most appropriate irrigation frequency for the crop by furrow irrigation and obtain the highest agricultural production and productivity.

The scope of this research work is to provide a detailed analysis of how water usage was reduced to the entire crop stages based on ET-based scheduling. The outline of the chapter is summarized as follows: an introduction and the role of water at different crop stages are presented followed by an experimental result analysis.

27.1.1 Role of water at different stages of crops

The role of water at different crop stages is summarized below:

1. As a solvent, water is used. When nutrients are exposed to water, plants can absorb them.
2. On a fresh weight basis, water makes up over 90% of the plant's body. They play an important role in the photosynthesis process for food production.
3. Water is required for seed germination, plant root growth and soil organisms.
4. Water aids in transpiration, which is essential to prolong nutrient absorption from the soil.
5. In soil, water aids chemical, physical, and biological reactions.

27.2 Experimental analysis

27.2.1 Experimental study site

Figure 27.1 represents an aerial view of the brinjal plant at the demo plot in Adhiparasakthi Agricultural College, Kalavai.

27.2.2 Experimental analysis of crop evapotranspiration based scheduling

ET is defined as a consumptive use of water. Consumptive water use (CU) is defined in equation (27.1),

$$\text{CU} = \text{Water lost through evaporation} + \text{Transpiration} \tag{27.1}$$

Figure 27.1. Aerial view of brinjal plant at demo plot.

The simplest technique for resembling ET-Pan evaporation method. Evaporation data was taken from the Open Pan Evapometer. The following equations (27.2) and (27.3) are calculations on ET data:

Calculation

$$ET_o = \text{Pan Value*Pan Factor} \tag{27.2}$$

= 6.00*0.7 = 4.2 mm

Crop coefficient

$$ET_{\text{CROP}} = ET_O{*}K_c \tag{27.3}$$

where K_c crop coefficient varies based on the various crop stages (four stages).

Crop water needed for the entire duration of eggplant: 400–800 mm. The details are as follows:

Duration: July 2017–October 2017
Soil type: Sandy Loam
Crop sowed: Eggplant/brinjal
Field capacity: 20% to 35%
Permanent wilting pPoint: 10% to 15%
Water holding capacity of sandy loam: 20%–25%

Water can be supplied to the crop either by rainfall or by irrigation. Sometimes due to less rainfall, a minimum amount of water is supplied to the crops as supplemental irrigation, during these days less irrigation is needed in addition to rainfall. It was noted that from July 7th to 17th, August 13th to 28th, September 1st to 7th and from 22nd to 28th there was an effective rainfall of a maximum of 75 mm of rainfall during this period.

Since a sufficient amount of water covers the root zone, manual irrigation is not needed on the scheduled day. Manual irrigation is done a maximum of 15 times

Table 27.1. Water requirement at each crop stage

Crop stages	Eggplant (days)	Water requirement at each stage (mm)
Initial growth stage	10	21
Mid-growth stage	30	133
Final growth stage	30	235
Maturity stage	82	367
Total	152	756

instead of 27 times based on 5 days watering interval for the entire period of crop stages. Due to the effective rainfall, usage of water is minimized.

Crop details:

The following represents the details of crop duration.

Crop sown: Eggplant (brinjal)

Crop duration: 152 days (Jun–Oct 2017)

Effective rainfall: 28 days (75 mm)

Area: 1 acre

Crop stages:

Table 27.1 represents the water requirement of eggplant at different crop stages namely initial, mid-growth, final-growth and maturity stage.

27.2.3 Irrigation interval based on conventional and ET

The following describes the irrigation scheduled based on conventional and ET-based.

Total irrigation: 15–18 times

Conventional method: 7 times

ET-based method: 4 times

Irrigation reduced to 7 from 10 times (figure 27.2).

Equation (27.4) defines the calculation on depth of water standing over an acre of land.

$$\text{Depth of water standing over an acre} = \text{No. of irrigation} * \text{depth of water at 5 cm} = 7*5 = 35\text{ mm} = >0.035\,m \tag{27.4}$$

The following analysis shows the difference between Conventional and ET – based scheduling and it was found that ET – based scheduling is effective. Conventional based = 20,00,000 liters of water ET based = 14,00,000 liters of water From the analysis, it was figured out that with ET – based scheduling, a landowner may know the estimated quantity of water the plant might require for any specific week to optimize the crop yields and also shows the precise irrigation requirements of the crops. A rainfall of 75 mm led to a hike in soil moisture (%) at various crop stages. Using ET – based scheduling total number of irrigation is reduced to 7 times

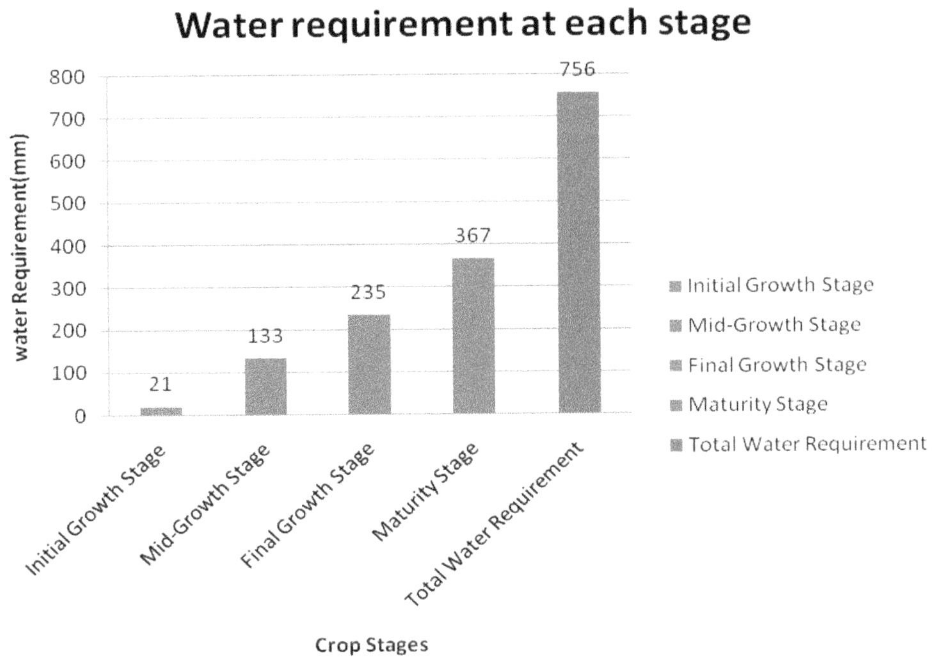

Figure 27.2. Crop ET of eggplant during 152 days of field cultivation.

Table 27.2. Planting details and crop growth stages.

S. No.	Crop used	Duration of crop stages	Critical stages	Root depth (inches)	Crop coefficient for four crop stages
1	Eggplant	152	Flowering and fruit development	18	0.45, 0.75,1.15,0.80

from 10 times. Thus, 60,000 liters of water were saved for the entire crop duration for the period from June 2017 – to Oct 2017.

Evapotranspiration (ET) data – based irrigation scheduling can lead to the optimum usage of water use and also determine the amount of water lost from the soil surface through evaporation as well as transpiration during various crop development stages.

The experiment was conducted from June to October 2017, in three experimental plots of nearly one acre of available land. Figure 2.1 represents the water requirement at each crop stage. Crop Co – efficient

$$ET_C = ET_0 * K \tag{27.5}$$

where, K_c crop coefficient varies based on the various crop stages (four stages) as given in table 27.2.

Table 27.3. Average monthly values and meteorological data during crop stages

Month/2017	No. of days	ET_{C1} (mm)	Max Temp (°C)	Min temp (°C)	Rainfall (mm)
June	30	3.89	37.7	26.76	50
July	31	10.4	39.5	28	84
August	31	13	37.7	26.9	75
September	30	4	36.3	26	135.7
October	31	4.8	35.4	26	71.7
November	05	4.9	33.8	26.3	99.7

ET data-based irrigation scheduling can lead to the optimum usage of water use [20] and also determine the amount of water lost from the soil surface through evaporation as well as transpiration during crop development stages.

Meteorological data:

The maximum and minimum air temperature and rainfall average in the region are collected from the nearby meteorological station. Additionally, soil moisture and ET data measured during the entire crop stages based on this irrigation schedule was prepared. In table 27.3, the values of meteorological data with crop ET are shown during the entire cultivation.

27.2.4 Advantage of using ET data

ET referred to as the water lost from the ground atmosphere due to a balance of direct soil evaporation and plant transpiration. The pan evaporation method is the simplest approach for simulating ET. A landowner may know the predicted volume of water the plant will require for any particular week with ET-based scheduling, as well as the exact water demands of the crops.

As a result, knowing ET rates can assist growers in fulfilling their cultivation goals, improving water use efficiency, increasing crop yields, reducing energy use, and lowering related environmental issues [17].

27.2.5 Research highlights

Pan evaporation is still frequently utilized across the world. This is due to the method's ease of use and simplicity, which attracts many farmers and experts. In underexposed areas, the evaporation pan performed well in terms of measuring evaporation and estimating ET.

Computation of ET data which shows the actual water requirements of the crops through an open pan evapometer to schedule irrigation using ET data, soil moisture and meteorological data.

ET data-based scheduling can lead to the optimum usage of water during crop development stages.

Thus, the estimation helps agricultural planners, landowners, environmental water resource planners, crop irrigation schedulers, etc to plan how to schedule irrigation and hence, attain maximum benefits. Thus, proper irrigation may maximize profit and optimizes water and energy use.

27.2.6 limitations

For appropriate use in ET computation and irrigation scheduling, pans must be properly designed, positioned, and managed. Every evaporation pan should be calibrated for its intended use.

Crop coefficient factors are determined by factors such as crop type, climate, soil evaporation and crop growth stages.

ETc gets affected due to factors such as climatic, soil water and irrigation methods.

27.3 Conclusion

ET-based irrigation scheduling can help track soil water deficiencies for predicting irrigation volume and frequency, based on a simple water balance principle. A landowner will know the predicted amount of water the crop will require for any given week with ET-based irrigation scheduling, as well as the actual water requirements of the crops. Based on the analysis, it was found that crop water requirement for eggplant ranges up to 800 mm. Based on ET data, a total of 44 mm of water usage was reduced at entire crop stages. Furthermore, accurate ET data creates significant prospects for agricultural applications that eliminate important trade-offs in the energy, water and food sectors. As ET is so inherently connected to moisture, plant biomass and heat, to develop a model in future research work, the following factors such as weather prediction, soil and vegetation factors produced that are precise and economical are taken into consideration. Finally, yield is a factor of frequency of irrigation as well as the amount of water provided. In terms of water management, irrigation scheduling based on data records is more efficient. In future work, ET-based scheduling can be used to forecast future trends in performance measurement on water systems under many scenarios including effect on global warming, population growth, etc.

References

[1] Awe G O, Akomolafe T N, Umam J and Ayuba M B 2020 Efficiency of small pan evaporimeter in monitoring evapotranspiration under poly-covered house and open-field conditions in a hot, tropical region of Nigeria *J. Hydrol.: Region.Stud.* **32** 100735

[2] Gu Z, Qi Z, Burghate R, Yuan S, Jiao X and Xu J 2020 Irrigation scheduling approaches and applications: a review *J. Irrig. Drain. Eng.* **146** 04020007

[3] http://edis.ifas.ufl.edu/topic_series_et-based_irrigation_scheduling_for_agriculture

[4] Mahan J R, Andrew W Y and Payton P 2015 Continuously monitored canopy temperature as a proxy for plant water status *Am. J. Plant Sci. 6* **6** 2287–302

[5] Laza *et al* 2021 Effect of elevated CO_2 on peanut performance in a semi-arid production region *Agric. For. Meteorol.* **308** 108599

[6] Ertek A, Şensoy S, Gedik I and Küçükyumuk C 2006 Irrigation scheduling based on pan evaporation values for cucumber (Cucumis sativus L.) grown under field conditions *Agricult. Water Manage.* **81** 159–72

[7] Pereira L S, Richard G A, Smith M and Raes D 2015 Crop evapotranspiration estimation with FAO56: past and future *Agric. Water Manage.* **147** 4–20

[8] Vellidis G, Liakos V, Perry C, Porter W, Tucker M, Boyd S, Huffman M and Robertson B 2016 Irrigation scheduling for cotton using soil moisture sensors, smartphone apps, and traditional methods *Proc. of the 2016 Beltwide Cotton Conf., New Orleans, LA. National Cotton Council (Memphis, TN)*

[9] Santos I, Silva E C, Mantovani L P, Venancio F F d, Cunha and Aleman C C 2020 Controlled water stress in agricultural crops in brazilian cerrado *Biosci. J.* **36** 886–95

[10] Ferreira L B, da Cunha F F, de Oliveira R A and Rodrigues T F 2020 A smartphone APP for weather-based irrigation scheduling using artificial neural networks *Pesq. Agrop. Bras.* **55**

[11] Pereira L S, Paredes P, Hunsaker D J, López-Urrea R and Mohammadi Shad Z 2021 Standard single and basal crop coefficients for field crops *Updates and advances to the FAO56 crop water requirements method. Agricultural Water Management* **243** 106466

[12] Ramadan K M, Oates M J, Molina-Martinez J M and Ruiz-Canales A 2018 Design and implementation of a low cost photovoltaic soil moisture monitoring station for irrigation scheduling with different frequency domain analysis probe structures *Comput. Electron. Agric.* **148** 148–59

[13] Johnson L F, Cahn M, Martin F, Melton F, Benzen S, Farrara B and Post K 2016 Evapotranspiration-based irrigation scheduling of head lettuce and broccoli *HortScience* **1** 935–40

[14] https://agric.wa.gov.au/water-management/evaporation-based-irrigation-scheduling

[15] Ghiat I, Hamish R M and Al-Ansari T 2021 A review of evapotranspiration measurement models, techniques and methods for open and closed agricultural field applications *Water* **13** 2523

[16] https://extension.umn.edu/irrigation/evapotranspiration-based-irrigation-scheduling-or-water-balance-method

[17] Maestre-Valero J F, Testi L, Jiménez-Bello M Á, Castel J R and Intrigliolo. D S 2017 Evapotranspiration and carbon exchange in a citrus orchard using eddy covariance *Irrig. Sci.* **35** 397–408

[18] https://ucmanagedrought.ucdavis.edu/Agriculture/Irrigation_Scheduling/Evapotranspiration_Scheduling_ET/How_to_Do_ET_Irrigiation_Scheduling/.

[19] http://ecoursesonline.iasri.res.in/mod/page/view.php?id=8936.

[20] Kisekka I, Migliaccio K W, Dukes M D, Schaffer B, Crane J H, Morgan K, Haimanote K, Bayabil and Guzman S M 2020 Evapotranspiration-based irrigation for agriculture: sources of evapotranspiration data for irrigation scheduling in Florida (University of Florida) article AE455 pp 1-4

IOP Publishing

Human-Assisted Intelligent Computing
Modeling, simulations and applications
Mukhdeep Singh Manshahia, Igor S Litvinchev, Gerhard-Wilhelm Weber, J Joshua Thomas and Pandian Vasant

Chapter 28

IOT based healthcare monitoring system for smart city applications

S C Dharmadhikari, Afshan Kausar, Mahendra Deore, Nilofer Shrenik Kittad, V S Bhagavan and R Krishnamoorthy

A remote health monitoring is initiated with the IoT (Internet of Things) to authorize the personal access data which stores up the data within the IOT platform. The IoT a has diverse set of applications where the applications get the data within healthcare such as diagnosis reports and types of diseases. The IoT can benefit patients, physicians and hospitals. The IoT applications are implied using a wearable type of device which monitors in the wired and wireless medium. These connected devices identify blood pressure, ECG (electrocardiogram), heart rate and other vital parameters of the human body. Remote monitoring allows physicians to adjust their medications and treatment of patients by regularly checking the status of their health. These smart health monitoring devices can determine the health conditions such as body temperature, ECG, EEG (electroencephalogram) and blood pressure. This health service system uses the different technology of wearable devices. IoT can connect devices using the internet to attain dynamic access to information, connect people and respond to the medical ecosystem structure. Smart cities use IoT devices that connect different sensors, meters and other light setups to collect and analyze the data. These IoT healthcare devices allow physicians to monitor patients to attain greater precision. Several clinical procedures are performed in an eco-friendly manner using the IoT. IoT improves accessibility in healthcare facilities using different growing technologies such as mobile computing, cloud infrastructure, big data and machine learning. Smart healthcare, which makes use of connection and sensors, plays a significant part in one's own care. Smart healthcare provides a better technique to achieve real-time diagnosis of healthcare data. IoT healthcare delivers a diverse set of computer resources in terms of a wirelessly connecting system that links patients to diagnose, track, monitor, and save crucial data on all such medical information. Healthcare is a big economic element when there is a lack of tools for communication, which replicates effective

doi:10.1088/978-0-7503-4801-0ch28

interoperability. The IoT enables individuals to remain better lives while also providing a smart item for automated IoT homes, facilitating automated operations and reducing effort and time.

28.1 Introduction

The IoT plays an important role in smart devices where it is used in various everyday aspects to provide information about services and for communication purpose. IoT is advanced in healthcare, being utilized to monitor and determine various healthcare parameters of the human body [1]. These focus on the healthcare condition of the patient's wellbeing. With constant feedback of statistical reports of vital parameters, stability over health condition can be determined. It is emphasized in the sensors to observe the different constraints of the human body. Independent living can be preserved in the elderly and patients with prolonged illness. Devices transmit signals as messages and alerts in the event of any uncommon vital signs. If there is any minor abnormality in health condition, then the IoT sends a message to the caregiver. The health monitoring response in the IoT requires less computational delay with the latency [2]. The information which is gathered can affect the overall performance. A smart city provides an intelligent way to arrange components such as energy, health and the environment. Smart healthcare provides, the utilities of IoT for alerting lifesaving telemedicine. Components are primarily generated by WSN (wireless sensor networks). This improves infrastructure service and the transport system. It reduces traffic congestion and provides waste management, as well as improving quality of life. What IoT contributes to health system sensors is transparency of the process, which optimizes the operation activities. IoT captures a different majority and revolutionary paradigm, which aims at an innovative framework. Smart healthcare monitoring provides improved and complete care for patients and especially elderly patients. Smart devices transmit the signals and need for best quality care. Healthcare creates better potential to progress, store and manage the healthcare related media content. Smart healthcare plays an important role on an individual's care using the connectivity and sensors. It offers a better way to attain real-time diagnosis of healthcare data [3, 4].

Smart instances encourage alertness in the hospital/doctor. IoT uses interconnectivity of devices, applications and sensors, which results in network connectivity where it gathers up information and data. IoT has important characteristics such as constant monitoring of patients where it infers a good attempt of results from the previous results of various parameters. Only at a time of emergency are the doctor/caretaker alerted using IoT devices. With a massive range of population in the city, a considerable range of IoT services are in health management services, which produce the appropriate range of solutions to each problem in a rapid manner [5]. Some of the related services require long time resources which administrate the system using innovative techniques. A healthcare service effectively reacts with the therapeutic treatment environment and advances interactions.

These intelligent healthcare services are operated in home services and other network medium resources. This technology has a role in healthcare to provide the sensory device as the communication and display. It monitors the medical parameters where IoT is termed as catalyst which plays a predominant role in identifying the healthcare vital parameters [6]. IoT generally consists of several objects that tend to be combined with the internet, which has control over the objects by remote monitoring. The IoT creates an invisible network which is controlled, sensed and programmed. These devices provide a better way of life, making it much safer with revolutionary healthcare. IoT stands with sensors, a gateway and other wireless network which enables communication and accesses applications. IoT provides new term life in the healthcare sector. A relevant set of information of patients can be quickly analyzed by the doctor without face-to-face interaction, i.e. where the old report can be also used to check stability in health condition. Some of the smart objects which consist of various sensors of other actuators are required to perform the various advanced actions. IoT has substantial influence over the healthcare system. It is used to preserve and identify health improvement by identifying the diagnosis, treatment and to promote prevention of diseases.

The raw data gathered by sensors is retained for later processing. Smart IoT modules, for instance, can be implemented inside network facilities, residences, and workplaces to effectively distribute and use energy. CSV (comma-separated values), tweets, database schemas, and text messages are among the formats used to capture diverse data [7]. IoT provides a wide array of services which are of considerable importance in terms of smart cities, both to improve the quality of human life, and to strengthen local management by lowering operating costs. As e-healthcare, IoT can be placed on a patient's body to measure health statistics such as temperature, pulse rate, and glucose level, enabling clinicians to continuously check their patients. The forms that have been collected are then analyzed using big data technologies to turn those into a standardized way.

Smart lighting, waste management, and water management are some of the major services provided [8]. While various research on IoT and smart cities has been undertaken, the confluence of these two domains allows for more educational attempts to be directed toward the development of IoT based pervasive computing. IoT's smart way of handling healthcare includes system management, medical sensor devices, different medical sensors, end user applications and other IoT medical services. IoT healthcare provides a heterogeneous way of using computing resources in a wirelessly communicating system, which connects patients to diagnosis, tracking, monitoring and storing up the vital statistics over all such medical information, as shown in figure 28.1. Telemedicine health is one of the healthcare services that carries the clinical information using two remote locations [9].

Patient data is collected using the IoT, which sends the data using a remote way of testing. Some of the tele-surgery methodology performs operations on the patient from a remote location. The health industry's major objective is to deliver quality treatment to every individual anywhere at any time across the globe [10]. Health surveillance is constantly developing as a consequence of a range of intelligent automation and technology that must continually monitor a patient's health indicators. Regarding the nature of health systems, numerous healthcare devices are made that use numerous methods and concepts including such remote

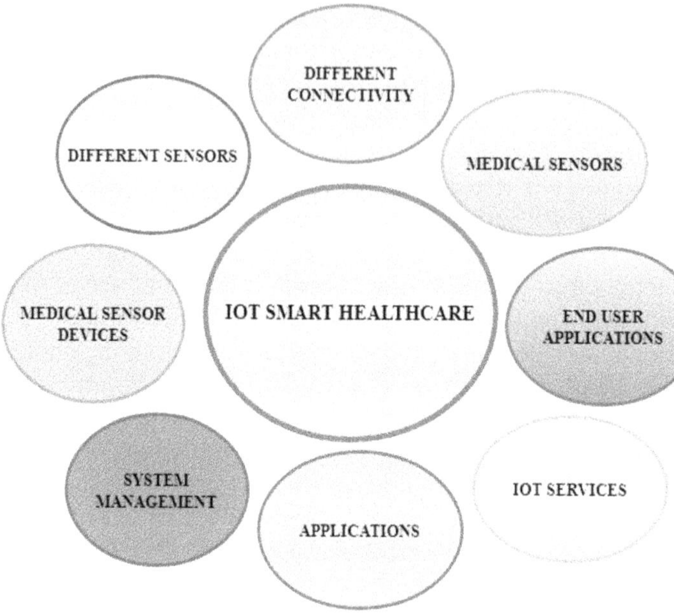

Figure 28.1. IoT in smart healthcare.

monitoring and even air ambulances, that have been initiated in many regions in strategies to succeed with rapidly increasing requirements of healthcare through crisis situations and speed up patients' recuperation. From this perspective, identifying the interaction procedure and framework design is a very challenging and interesting assignment [11]. Healthcare monitoring ought to be constant in order to monitor the patient's parameters as well as giving consistent and reliable data to the doctor or medical team for diagnosis. It should be accomplished in a patient-friendly and cost-effective way.

28.2 IoT contribution in healthcare

Healthcare plays a major role in terms of economical factors where there is a lack of tools for communication, which simulates functional interoperability. Some of the medical sensors use a group of transducers which sense in the electrical genetics and medium to evaluate the health state which comprises custom-based sensors. It sends out the information where the patient's complete health status can be checked within the IoT application [12, 13]. These types of empowered IoT use the physiological data of sensors over the patient's body using the cloud gateway which stores the data wirelessly. Each device factor receives data such as different vital parameters which can be used within the internet. It gets permanently stored in the server side which is permanent. By using this method, disease is identified early and diagnosis received without any delay. Specifically, elderly patients are saved from any chronic illness [14].

A smart way of handling healthcare is important as it addresses a specific way of demanding smart health characteristics. Each functional requirement over the specific task medium applied over healthcare is applied based on its application. In the health medium, it uses two different types of sensor devices. These standard types of sensor are placed internally or externally to attain the vital parameters. These computed devices are deployed using many IoT devices which are complex and assist advanced type devices which can communicate throughout the physical and wireless medium. IoT helps in defining the process using the remote type access, sharing the data and data connectivity faster [15, 16]. Some of the devices use time based upon the framework where these technologies provide medical assistance. IoT encourages automated industry across different types of platforms. IoT in smart healthcare uses sensors or actuators to provide the data of the healthcare parameter. Since smart healthcare handles the data in the internet medium, a password and exemption are required to avoid attacks, and security measures in smart healthcare provide an efficient way to handle the healthcare data. This achieves a flexible and friendly way to handle the patient's data along with the care. Transmission of the physiological data from the patient's body is to any location using GPS (global positioning system) [17, 18].

IoT allows individuals to live better lives, and smart technology for automated IoT homes is crucial for business, enabling automated processes and decreasing time and effort. For successful and safe transmission, users, patients, and the device work together. Physicians and healthcare providers utilize sophisticated technologies and IoT to analyze the vast health stream of data in order to keep their patients in good health, as shown in figure 28.2. As the data comes in, organizations must be able to detect any possible health risks and notify a physician to evaluate them. The primary objective of the stage is to transform the obtained heterogeneous data into a standard way. For successful and safe transmission, users, patients, and the communication unit work together. The majority of IoT applications include a user interface that serves as a dashboard for medical providers and allows user control, data visualization, and assessment. IoT helps the development of the health

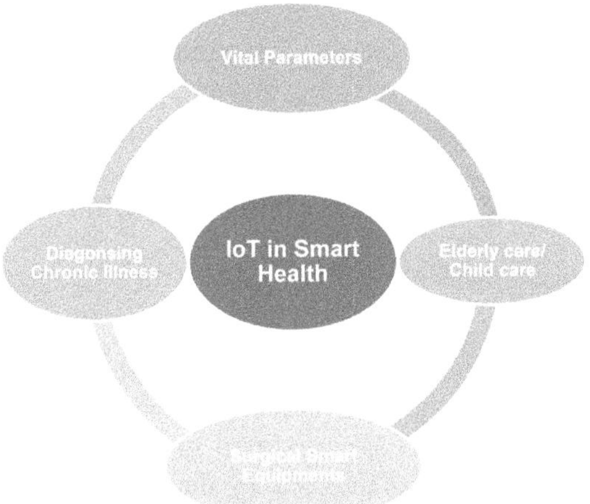

Figure 28.2. IoT in medical applications.

system and increases transparency in procedures and optimizes operations, which in turn serves to enhance patient care quality [19]. IOT analyzes the vital parameters, provides elderly patient care, remote monitoring of the patient and diagnosis of chronic illness.

28.3 Smart health architecture

28.3.1 Characteristics of smart healthcare

Smart health empowers manufacturing and aids remote monitoring. The medical devices are generally used to implement smart healthcare from on-body sensors. These are generally attached to the human body with the standard sterilization. Some of the efficient characteristics of using smart healthcare are low consumption power, quality of service, cost effectiveness, high efficiency, system reliability, ease amount of deployment and good internet connectivity in a wired/wireless medium [20, 21]. The prime motive of smart healthcare is to attain a prompt amount of medical service. This system needs the ambient range of intelligence to improve the quality of service.

Some of the components which are classified in smart healthcare based upon the actuators/sensors may vary according to their monitoring systems. Personalized range of computing devices is assigned to reduce the complexity. Data memory is used to store up the data in a reserved manner as it plays a major role in functioning of the system. Some of the data are stored in the broader range of the spectrum where it includes embedded sensing devices, memory and other big data analytics. Some of the network components such as routers, sensors, base stations, and switches are used to connect the devices through the internet medium. Some of the wireless technologies which are focused are Bluetooth, WIFI, RFID (radio frequency identification), which can easily exchange the information by configuring the healthcare network sector [22].

In general, the characteristics of architecture in smart healthcare indicate the application transmits the data in a personalized manner where the user's complexity devices are served. A large range of devices can be connected together using resource-constrained computing [23, 24]. To attain the location of device resources, they use location aware computing. To analyze the behavioral patterns of the necessary information they use a semantic oriented approach. This approach can create impact over efficiency with higher accuracy. Different physical systems are configured with the right use of sensors/actuators to attain the right value.

28.3.2 Attributes of smart healthcare

Some of the attributes in smart healthcare provide a multifunctional platform where it develops the platform, quality, connectivity, location tracking, sensing of the information and awareness of the environment with identification remarks [25]. The application environment is diversely computed using the frameworks of different sectors. These frameworks process the data by determining the health information using IoT where the attributes of different modeling frameworks are established. Many different services are available in the smart healthcare sector. In general, the assets of processing of some of the medical data are within the cloud and only during a period of emergency. Some of the WSN determines the healthcare monitoring in terms of local or neighborhood networks. It is generally energy efficient in terms of monitoring sectors. The main purpose of healthcare is to stimulate a healthy way of living; home care and actual level of care [26, 27].

28.3.3 Challenges faced in smart healthcare

Smart healthcare provides a better way of healthcare but can cause vulnerability. This is dynamic in nature, consisting of various factors where the security requirements vary with other key security requirements [28]. These can reduce the cost and save power but need additional security support. Some of the challenges faced in the vulnerability of smart healthcare are data service availability, data computability, data location sharing, data integrity, eavesdrop, identification [29].

A challenging task is presented with dynamic service security as updates. These can cause different vulnerability at any layer of the system. Attacks can target data transmitted over the network where it interrupts, forges and replays disruptive messages [30, 31].

Tampering of the data resources can even give incorrect data values which result in medical exploitation. Some of the possible vulnerable attacks in smart healthcare are active and passive methods. Passive networks can interrupt the communication over any medical method [32, 33]. Active attacks impersonate the remote control device over the medical device. One of the private ways of transmitting information is by using the user's confidentiality which is key security equipment. It needs two-level authentications to ensure the confidentiality over the data. Also, similar to confidentiality, integrity ensures user data is transmitted and received. This data gets breached if proper security guidance is not given [34].

28.3.4 Computational attacks on data

Some of the re-identification of attack involves healthcare. It causes a re-identification risk which can cause real exploitation over the health data. Some of the outdated technology can exploit risks in the hospital [35, 36]. Even user error can cause technology exploitation. Some of the health information exchanges can cause exploitation for health records. An unintentional action over healthcare exploits the vulnerability. Cyber attacks targeting the healthcare sector increase the vulnerability over the healthcare services. Data security over the healthcare sector plays a major concern. Some of the sabotage infrastructure and theft of medical research can cause ransomware type attacks where it is vulnerable to the cyber attacks. One of the critical infrastructures of the vulnerability where there is a critical threat is power failure of the server [37, 38].

28.3.5 Encryption standard in healthcare

Encryption is the best way to protect data protection system methods for healthcare organizations. Providers give encryption to data transit which deciphers the patient information to give access to their health data. Data encryption is an essential element with the layered approach to data security. Encryption prevents interference from any attacker. Healthcare data encryption converts the data into encoded text. To prevent unauthorized access to the applications, the data uses two-tier security mechanism aspects. Two-tier encryption standard improves the data integrity and the confidentiality with a pin or any other secured devices. All devices are monitored to avoid alteration of the device's settings along with different configurations. It encrypts the attachments and accounts which prevents any unauthorized access or malware infections. Multifactor authentication can cause strong improvisation where available patches should be updated.

28.3.6 IoT with smart healthcare

IoT devices are tagged along with the sensors which track the real-time location of each piece of medical equipment. As the patient's rate of recovery increases the smart way is very convenient for patient satisfaction; it can make faster recovery as it gives prior satisfaction. Data can also provide physicians who monitor patients with a greater range of precision. IoT is used to speed up healthcare delivery which saves the doctor's time. It can reduce transportation cost, diagnosing illness with a prior way of communicating with patients. Connected devices reinvent information for the caregiver and patiens in real time. This reliable connectivity is essential as it predicts the health state, as shown in figure 28.3. Smart healthcare updates in real time the patient's information and affords proactive measures of medical treatment [39]. These healthcare sectors allow the hospital to improve quality of standard in predicting diagnosis.

IoT Healthcare monitoring uses wearable gadgets to analyze the vital parameters of the human body. This vital parameter collects the data and stores it up for the statistical approach. The smart way of analyzing the vital parameters of the human body and elderly patients is cost friendly and highly effective.

28.3.6.1 Wearable watch

A wearable watch can track diet progress, health progress and other physiological activity of health data, which indicates the overall activity of the health. It monitors

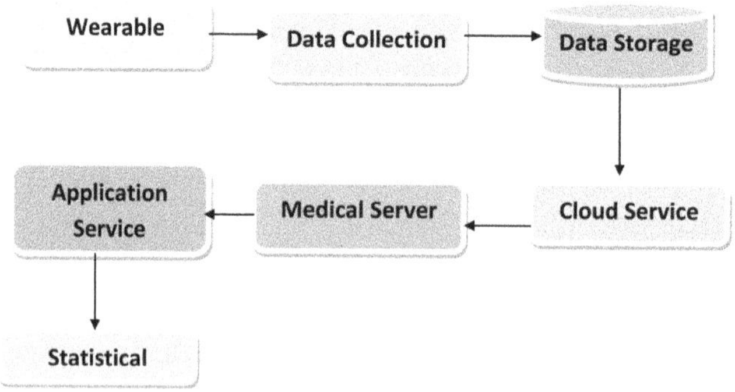

Figure 28.3. IoT healthcare monitoring.

and records heart related information, which can save lives. It can screen monitoring, treatment assistance, ongoing treatment and diagnosing treatment status. It can easily track data continuously by monitoring blood pressure level, heart rate level and other vital parameters of the human body.

28.3.6.2 Data collection

Data collection helps the health system to create personalized treatments, advancement in treatment, improves the communication between the patients and care providers. It develops an efficient way of communicating data and checks the overall quality over the patients' care providers. All these data are collected from different sources including medical records, surveys about patients and an administrative type database. By determining the *in vitro* and non-*in vitro* type sensors, the medical results can be analyzed.

28.3.6.3 Data storage

Data storage protects sensitive health information to analyze the growth in the threats. It physically safeguards the data by protecting sensitive information. Health Insurance Portability and Accountability Act (HIPAA) compliance safeguards the data compliance standards. The medical data are stored in a structured manner and specialized in the specific format according to their standardization. It collects the health data and there is efficient communication between the patients and doctors. It increases the overall quality over the patients' healthcare providers. By using encryption, the cloud providers get encrypted.

28.3.6.4 Medical server

Electronic health records (EHR) use software that serves according to their location. The physically securing of the servers performs backups. Patch-up checks the regular monitoring of the healthcare data within the server. Health data management provides advanced health conditions along with advanced treatment. It improves the health outcome of the track health status information. EHR is considered as the remote software program which maintains the health records in a remote server manner within the medical facility.

28.3.6.5 Statistical report

Statistical expertise assists in the collection of data, the application of appropriate analysis, as well as the efficient presentation of results. Analysis of the data is a strong tool that allows a researcher to derive relevant insights from data obtained by observation, survey, or trial. Such technologies may do sophisticated and predictive analyses on patient data and several patients or conditions inside a group. Statistical data analysis involves the process of executing different data analysis on data. This is a type of quantitative study that aims to organize information that usually employs any sort of data analysis. This is a type of statistical research that aims to record the results and usually employs a certain sort of statistical methods. The health information researcher analyses data pertaining to medical services, reimbursements, and restrictions.

28.4 IoT smart healthcare attribute

In IoT healthcare, some of the attributes are based on different attribute factors. The location services, identification of data, sensing over the data, connected devices like WIFI, Bluetooth, multi-functionality over data, platform dependency, environmental awareness, wearable type (invasive or non-invasive type) are determined in the IoT platform which is user-friendly, cost effective and highly reliable in nature, as shown in figure 28.4.

28.5 Security aspects of IoT in smart healthcare

Some of the key challenges of using healthcare are shown in figure 28.5. Some of the advantages of Iot in smart healthcare are as follows; improving the treatment outcomes; a better way of handling drugs; it can eliminate some of the system errors; it can decrease the operational cost; it enhances the patient's experience; and it identifies the disease management

28.5.1 Data care

The care of health data has to be improved as it is confidential. To avoid breaches over the medical data, the care of data tends to improve the quality of service over data. It includes clinical type metrics where it checks the behavioral information pertaining to wellness and health. Caregivers can analyze their check results and give

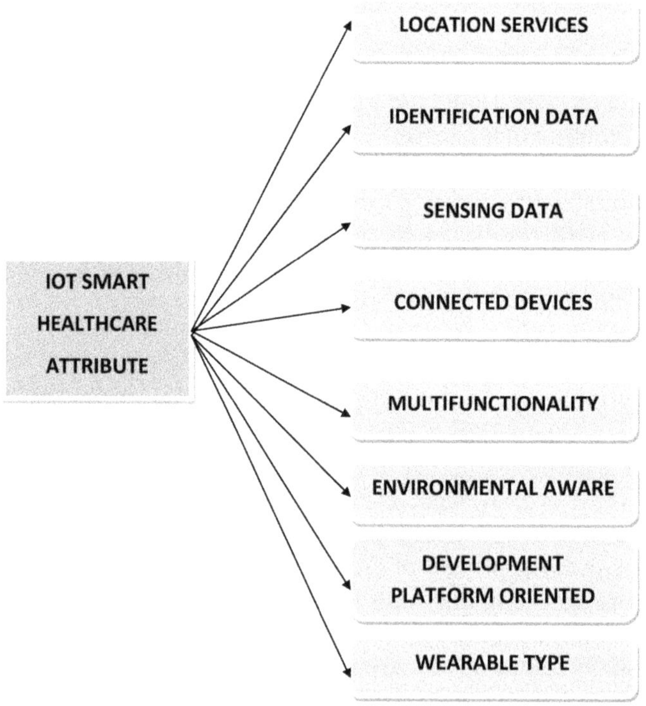

Figure 28.4. IoT in smart healthcare attributes.

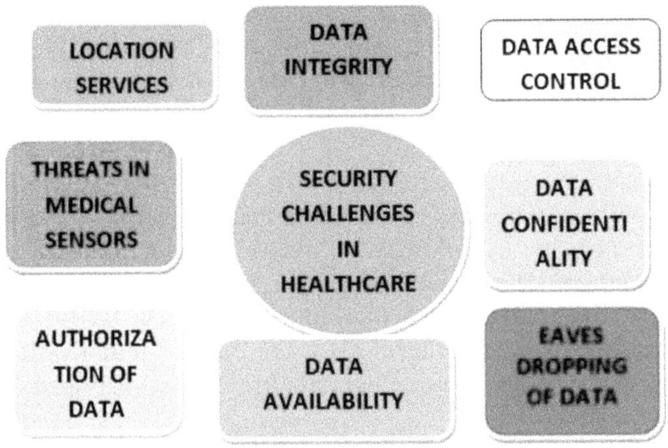

Figure 28.5. Security challenges in healthcare.

prior intervention of those treatments. They can provide efficient with personalized data care and higher quality. Patients can look over their health data and check their real-time monitoring. Healthcare is always data-driven which evaluates the patient's vital parameters by the doctors. The human body creates its own data points every second. It can alert the physicians to diagnose with a better way of alerting the customer. By encrypting the data, the data care can be efficiently handled. Data care ensures that the data are stored are in a confidential manner without any intervention. If any misconduct occurs within the data, then the data gets mishandled causing a personalized attack on patients.

28.5.2 Electronic record data

Electronic medicine records information about patients' health history. EHR is an electronic version of the patient's medical history with the key administrative clinical data. This allows access to evidence based tools where it provides necessary decisions about the patient's care. Health records are stored in a database of the health treatment for the patient. Easy access to the EHR can provide an update of real-time information. It streamlines sharing of the provider's information where the medical information can be accessed by patients and caregivers. EHR stores the data in a customized way, according to the patient's disease categorization. By using this methodology, the doctor is able to easily identify the current status of the patient. It can be used to analyze the statistical report analysis of the data of the patient's health status accordingly.

28.5.3 Security challenges in healthcare

28.5.3.1 Data integrity

To maintain proper accuracy, be reliable and with proper consistency over the data are the major roles of data integrity. Data integrity indicates the correctness of the data. If a data security breach occurs, the integrity tends to identify the accuracy by maintaining it. In terms of healthcare, the attribution over the patient's data is clearly demonstrated by recording and observing it. It records each and every patient's information. A proper transparency has to be preserved securely accordingly.

28.5.3.2 Data confidentiality

Here, it records all the necessary private data and gives access only to resourceful information. Correct use of information recorded in a physical and electronic manner is important since it is highly confidential. As the information analyzed in healthcare tends to be confidential in resource, the data has to be secured. To prevent any data breaches and other threats, the HIPAA initiated deep compliance over security events. These save potential data breaches which can cause damage to the health data centers.

28.5.3.3 Data availability

Data availability is used to attain the accessibility and usability of the patient information. If the patient's information is not present then the proper way of giving them treatment is difficult. It indicates the physical delivery or presence of giving minimum standard of utilization standard in the quality of the healthcare standard. Proper strategic planning tends to improve the exact motives of big data in the healthcare sector. These analyze the healthcare check-up results of people according to their health related information or any clinical trial part program.

28.5.3.4 Data access control

There is restricted access over the patient's information where the access control over the healthcare data is implemented. It allows the access of various entry points within the data. It requires data authentication ensuring only authorized users can access protected sets of information. It is capable of restricting and tracking information via vital healthcare equipment and other medical records. Data is easily available and quick enough to generate as the data quality is emphasized. It can be retrieved according to the data structure usage and can improve the accessibility over the data context.

28.5.3.5 Data eavesdropping

As the IoT is used, theft of information takes place, which is transmitted via a network which can cause exploitation over the data. Some of the attacks can take over unsecured network communications. Eavesdropping can discover the contents of confidential information. It can easily intercept personal communications or credentials of authorization. As the data is transmitted over the network, sometimes a man-in-the-middle attack can exploit the vulnerability and can cause interception over various methodologies.

28.5.3.6 Threats in medical sensors

From a medical perspective, medical risks are a common factor as medical data theft occurs. Data computation has major potential for the patient's treatment. It can cause damage to data privacy causing major disruption within the data format. Some of the common factors of security threats which occur are ransomware and web application attacks. If the hospital data is not updated regularly, the hackers can easily exploit the data. Security audits ensure that the data confidentiality is secured. Since the connectivity over IoT devices occurs in a network, a wireless and a wired medium the data connectivity should be ensured using an encryption standard. Regular conducting of audits ensures that the data is secured, as shown in figure 28.6.

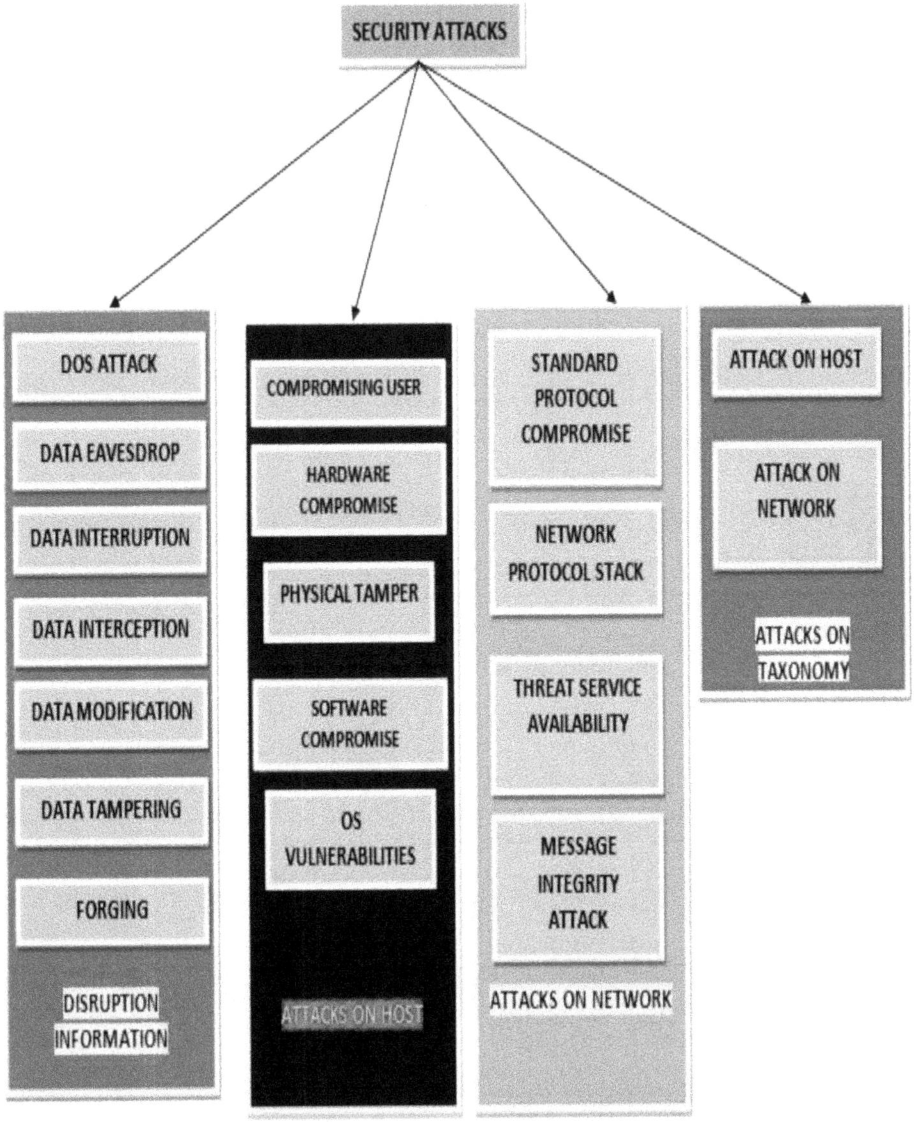

Figure 28.6. Security attacks in healthcare.

28.6 IoT healthcare in smart city applications

The smart city depends upon networking devices, which can have access over any device by everyone all over the world. This smart city completely depends upon every connected type device which are mostly automated. These significant access based technologies can use network connectivity which can control any accessibility within the period of time. These generally allow companies and sectors to work in a remote medium across anywhere in the world. In terms of smart technology, the smart city predicts in determining many smart facilities in deriving the data. Some of the smart ways of using the IoT in healthcare are progressive report analysis of the patient's health, smart surgical records and smart medical equipment, as shown in figure 28.7. As the technology is dramatically increasing, the world changes into a smarter way of evolution of medical data.

28.7 Applications of IoT in hospitals

Healthcare professionals can use monitors and remote technology to help patients acquire prescriptions and medicines, by use of their fingerprints. Some devices can also enable head communication over the internet. It can offer healthcare professionals information that is needed to establish care treatment for individuals on their

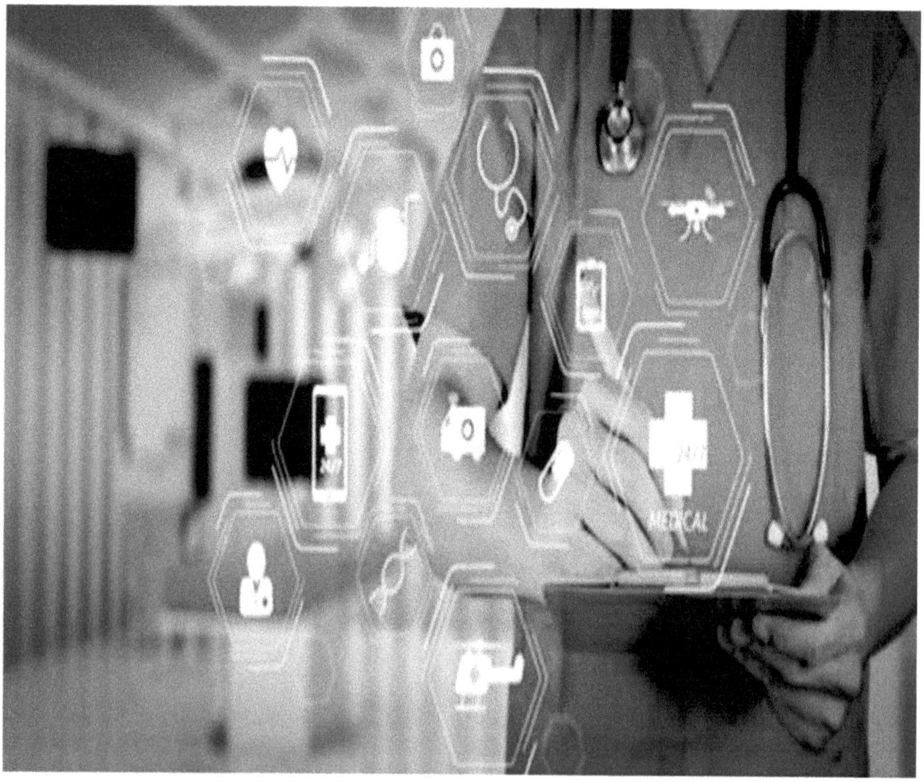

Figure 28.7. IoT healthcare in smart city applications.

route to the clinic. The results of emergency treatment are determined by timing, quality, and accessibility of relevant information. Furthermore, it is dependent on the level of the data acquired during an urgent situation where the gathered information of the patient has been transferred to the healthcare facilities for immediate care. Augmenting surgeries procedures focus on enhanced accuracy provided by automation surgeons. Moreover, linked devices and IoT apps can fully simplify the actions of medical personnel both before and after surgery. Virtual monitoring of critical hardware ensures that all advanced medical centers have cutting-edge hardware and software. IoT helps bring together the finest safety procedures and cutting-edge technologies to provide quicker drug delivery, better procedures, and improved quality of care. IoT clinics can provide increased productivity and competitiveness, medicine dispensing, security, and improved overall patient happiness. IoT has huge potential and could be extremely valuable to both healthcare patients and clinicians. It is also expected to improve both patient safety and organizational operations. Smart wearable devices that enable care providers to acquire a multitude of pieces of data on the patient's sleep habits, movement, heart rate, and temperature.

28.8 Encryption in IoT

Encryption prevents interference from any attacker. Healthcare data encryption converts the data into an encoded text. To prevent unauthorized access to applications, the data uses two- tier security mechanism aspects. Two-tier encryption standard improves the data integrity and the confidentiality with a pin or other means of securing devices. All devices should be monitored to secure their settings along with different configurations. Encryption of attachments and accounts prevents any unauthorized access or malware infections. IoT helps the health system sensors' accessibility of the process, which improves operation activities. The intelligent method of assessing the vital characteristics of the human body and geriatric patients is both cost effective and extremely successful. Smart health improves manufacturing and enables remote monitoring. Medical gadgets are commonly utilized to construct smart healthcare systems based on-body sensors.

28.9 Research limitations

IoT healthcare delivers a diverse set of computer resources in terms of a wirelessly connecting system that links patients to diagnose, track, monitor, and save crucial data on all such medical information. Healthcare is a big economic element when there is a lack of tools for communication, which replicates effective interoperability. The IoT enables people to live better lives while also providing smart items for automated IoT. The IoT enables individuals to have better lives while also providing smart items for automated IoT homes, facilitating automated operations and reducing effort and time. It is indeed important to identify and assess different IoT security and privacy aspects. Some of the smart ways of using the IoT in healthcare is progressive report analysis of patient's health, smart surgical records and smart medical equipment. Several medical uses, including remote health monitoring, fitness training, chronic illnesses, and elderly care, have the potential to be enabled by IOT.

28.10 Conclusion

Treatment and drug concordance are taken at home and by healthcare providers. This permits accessibility to the IoT infrastructure, including storage and receiving of medical information, and the usage of healthcare-specific connections. Diverse clinical devices, monitors, including diagnostic and therapeutic devices are seen as smart devices and appliances that are an essential component of the IoT network. Healthcare gadgets handle sensitive data. The data must be safeguarded against being divulged, altered, or fabricated. It is important to identify and assess different IoT security and privacy aspects. Some of the smart ways of using the IoT in healthcare are progressive report analysis of the patient's health, smart surgical records and smart medical equipment. Several medical uses, including remote health monitoring, fitness training, chronic illnesses, and elderly care, have potential to be enabled by IOT. Thus, the smart way of using the IoT empowers the technologies used in smart healthcare to maintain high accessibility for providers over the data.

References

[1] Misra S, Bishoyi P K and Sarkar S 2021 I-MAC: in-body sensor MAC in wireless body area networks for healthcare ioT *IEEE Syst. J.* **15** 4413–20

[2] Besher K M, Subah Z and Ali M Z 2021 IoT sensor initiated healthcare data security *IEEE Sensors J.* **21** 11977–82

[3] Bharadwaj H K *et al* 2021 A review on the role of machine learning in enabling IoT based healthcare applications *IEEE Access* **9** 38859–90

[4] Ray P P, Dash D, Salah K and Kumar N 2021 Blockchain for IoT-based healthcare: background, consensus, platforms, and use cases *IEEE Syst. J.* **15** 85–94

[5] Besher K M, Beitelspacher S, Nieto-Hipolito J I and Ali M Z 2021 Sensor initiated healthcare packet priority in congested IoT networks *IEEE Sensors J.* **21** 11704–11

[6] Bhuiyan M N, Rahman M M, Billah M M and Saha D 2021 Internet of things (IoT): a review of its enabling technologies in healthcare applications, standards protocols, security, and market opportunities *IEEE Internet Things J.* **8** 10474–98

[7] Gera S, Mridul M and Sharma S 2021 IoT based automated health care monitoring system for smart city *2021 5th Int. Conf. on Computing Methodologies and Communication (ICCMC)* 364–8

[8] Guleria C, Das K and Sahu A 2021 A survey on mobile edge computing: efficient energy management system *2021 Innovations in Energy Management and Renewable Resources (52042)* 1–4

[9] Pradhan B, Bhattacharyya S and Pal K 2021 IoT-based applications in healthcare devices *J. Healthc. Eng.* **2021** 6632599

[10] Li J *et al* 2020 A secured framework for SDN-based edge computing in IoT-enabled healthcare system *IEEE Access* **8** 135479–90

[11] Haghi M *et al* 2020 A flexible and pervasive ioT-based healthcare platform for physiological and environmental parameters monitoring *IEEE Internet Things J.* **7** 5628–47

[12] Kumar A, Krishnamurthi R, Nayyar A, Sharma K, Grover V and Hossain E 2020 A novel smart healthcare design, simulation, and implementation using healthcare 4.0 processes *IEEE Access* **8** 118433–71
[13] Islam M, Rahaman A and Rashedul I 2020 Development of smart healthcare monitoring system in IoT environment *SN Comput. Sci.* **1** 185
[14] Abdulrazaq, Mohammed, Faizah S, Al-Zubaidi S and Yusuf E 2020 An internet of things-based smart homes and healthcare monitoring and management system: review *J. Physics: Conf. Ser.* 1450 012079
[15] Rai P, Chatterjee J M, Kumar A and Balamurugan B (ed) 2020 *Internet of Things Use Cases for the Healthcare Industry* (Cham: Springer)
[16] Al-Mahmud O, Khan K, Roy R and Mashuque Alamgir F 2020 Internet of things (IoT) based smart health care medical box for elderly people *2020 Int. Conf. for Emerging Technology (INCET)* 1–6
[17] Min M *et al* 2019 Learning-based privacy-aware offloading for healthcare IoT with energy harvesting *IEEE Internet Things J.* **6** 4307–16
[18] Khattak H A, Farman H, Jan B and Din I U 2019 Toward integrating vehicular clouds with IoT for smart city services *IEEE Netw.* **33** 65–71
[19] Saha R, Kumar G, Rai M K, Thomas R and Lim S 2019 Privacy ensured e-healthcare for fog-enhanced IoT based applications *IEEE Access* **7** 44536–43
[20] Hossain M S, Muhammad G and Alamri A 2019 Smart healthcare monitoring: a voice pathology detection paradigm for smart cities *Multimedia Syst.* **25** 565–75
[21] Zouka H and Hosni M 2019 Secure IoT communications for smart healthcare monitoring system *Internet Things* 13
[22] Korra S and Sudarshan E 2019 Smart healthcare monitoring system using raspberry Pi on IoT platform *ARPN J. Eng. Appl. Sci.* **14** 872–76
[23] Sundaravadivel P, Kougianos E, Mohanty S P and Ganapathiraju M K 2018 Everything you wanted to know about smart health care: evaluating the different technologies and components of the internet of things for better health *IEEE Consum. Electron. Mag.* **7** 18–28
[24] Jaiswal K, Sobhanayak S, Turuk A K, Bibhudatta S L, Mohanta B K and Jena D 2018 An IoT-cloud based smart healthcare monitoring system using container based virtual environment in edge device *2018 Int. Conf. on Emerging Trends and Innovations In Engineering And Technological Research (ICETIETR)* 1–7
[25] Jangra P and Gupta M 2018 A design of real-time multilayered smart healthcare monitoring framework using IoT *2018 Int. Conf. on Intelligent and Advanced System (ICIAS)* 1–5
[26] Shaikh Y, Parvati V K and Biradar S R 2018 Survey of smart healthcare systems using internet of things (IoT) : (invited paper) *2018 Int. Conf. on Communication, Computing and Internet of Things (IC3IoT)* 508–13
[27] Mehmood Y, Ahmad F, Yaqoob I, Adnane A, Imran M and Guizani S 2017 Internet-of-things-based smart cities: recent advances and challenges *IEEE Commun. Mag.* **5** 16–24
[28] Budida D A M and Mangrulkar R S 2017 Design and implementation of smart healthCare system using IoT *2017 Int. Conf. on Innovations in Information, Embedded and Communication Systems (ICIIECS)* 1–7
[29] Saha H N, Paul D, Chaudhury S, Haldar S and Mukherjee R 2017 Internet of things based healthcare monitoring system *2017 8th IEEE Annual Information Technology, Electronics and Mobile Communication Conf. (IEMCON)* 531–5

[30] Shaikh S and Chitre V 2017 Healthcare monitoring system using IoT *2017 Int. Conf. on Trends in Electronics and Informatics (ICEI)* 374–7

[31] Dineshkumar P, SenthilKumar R, Sujatha K, Ponmagal R S and Rajavarman V N 2016 Big data analytics of IoT based health care monitoring system *2016 IEEE Uttar Pradesh section Int. Conf. on Electrical, Computer and Electronics Engineering (UPCON)* 55–60

[32] Gogate U and Bakal J W 2016 Smart healthcare monitoring system based on wireless sensor networks *2016 Int. Conf. on Computing, Analytics and Security Trends (CAST)* 594–9

[33] Vippalapalli V and Ananthula S 2016 Internet of things (IoT) based smart health care system *2016 Int. Conf. on Signal Processing, Communication, Power and Embedded System (SCOPES)* 1229–33

[34] Bhoomika B K and Muralidhara K N 2015 Secured smart healthcare monitoring system based on IoT *Int. J. Recent Innov. Trends Comput. Commun.* **3** 4958–61

[35] Gaur A, Scotney B, Parr, Gerard, McClean and Sally. 2015 Smart city architecture and its applications based on IoT . *Proced. Comput. Sci.* **52** 1089–94

[36] Catarinucci L *et al* 2015 An ioT-aware architecture for smart healthcare systems *EEE Internet Things J.* **2** 515–26

[37] He D and Zeadally S 2015 An analysis of RFID authentication schemes for internet of things in healthcare environment using elliptic curve cryptography *IEEE Internet Things J.* **2** 72–83

[38] Amendola S, Lodato R, Manzari S, Occhiuzzi C and Marrocco G 2014 RFID technology for IoT-based personal healthcare in smart spaces *IEEE Internet Things J.* **1** 144–52

[39] Zhang Y, Sun L, Song H and Cao X 2014 Ubiquitous WSN for healthcare: recent advances and future prospects *IEEE Internet Things J.* **1** 311–18

IOP Publishing

Human-Assisted Intelligent Computing
Modeling, simulations and applications
Mukhdeep Singh Manshahia, Igor S Litvinchev, Gerhard-Wilhelm Weber, J Joshua Thomas and Pandian Vasant

Chapter 29

Smart healthcare: the new digital revolution in medical management

Parameswaran Radhika Ravi and Ravi Ramaswamy

Abbreviations

AI—Artificial intelligence
AR—Augmented reality
BAN—Body area network
CAI—Confidentiality, accessibility, integrity
COTS—Commercial off-the-shelf
FDA—Food and drug administration
GDPR—General Data Protection Regulation
GRC—Governance, risk and compliance
GVC—Governance, visualization and risk based compliance
IEEE—Institute of Electrical and Electronics Engineers Academic and Science Electronics
IoT—Internet of Things (IoT)
LAN—Local area network
MAN—Metropolitan area network
MDP—Markov decision process
ML—Machine learning
RPM -Remote patient monitoring
UID—Unique identifier
VR—Virtual reality
VLSI—Very large-scale integration
WAN—Wide area network
Wi-Fi—Wireless fidelity

doi:10.1088/978-0-7503-4801-0ch29

Automation and digital transformation deploying advance technologies are becoming imperative for efficiency, accuracy and precision, and for building operations strategies for business transformations.

Automation is described as the automatic execution of process steps and tasks without interference, whereas digitalization is the conversion of analog information into text, photographs, and voice format as required.

The exponential upgrade and advent of new technologies, information management and scientific theories have brought in a paradigm shift in medical management which has introduced predictive and proactive patient care via connected systems and cybernetic devices. This automated system is called the 'smart healthcare' system.

The smart healthcare system deploys various platforms technologies and devices such as IoT, wearable devices, mobile, and computers. These are connected via internet technologies and are synchronized to work for a specific goal.

The breakthrough of smart healthcare systems has brought in reducing medical errors and improving diagnostic capabilities and better patient compliance. The recent connected technologies and medical devices have brought in controlled operation of diagnostic and therapeutic process

The wealth of information generated by smart healthcare systems has also benefited the clinical research institutions. A dramatic reduction is observed in the cost, research time, and redundancy in this connected environment.

The application of machine learning (ML) algorithms, artificial intelligence (AI) and other cognitive technologies in medical settings has introduced proactive and predictive care. ML helps in data-driven recommendations and suggestive decisions based on the patient health data or research information.

This chapter expounds the enabling technologies on the cloud that support smart healthcare service systems. The rest of the chapter is organized as follows: a preface which shares an introductory note to the subject, components of the system, attributes of smart health devices, contemporary technologies and frameworks that aid smart healthcare service, limitations of this research and a conclusion.

29.1 Limitations of this book chapter

This chapter examines the growth of new and novel technologies and underpinning research into advance technologies that catalyses better human lives. This study concentrates on some fundamental approaches used to investigate the impact of smart technologies in healthcare. It centers on comparative studies, real-time comparisons and attitudinal studies to illustrate the best use of technologies to build a connected world. The authors have taken possible measures to substantiate some of the claims made about the impact of technologies on the basis of some advanced research and experiences in the real world and statements from industry experts. This chapter deals with a highly dynamic technological world, which has exponential and connected novel innovations every day with changing perspectives and usage. Therefore, there are always debatable alternatives of any solutions discussed herein.

29.2 Preface

The Internet of Things (IoT) is the concept of connecting any device via an on/off switch to the internet and to other connected devices. IoT network of physical objects, referred as 'things' that are embedded with sensors, software, and networking and internet technologies. Therefore, these objects/things send data over the internet, allowing the device to communicate with people and other IoT-enabled things.

This IoT has also become a potential technology in connecting various health systems, medical devices, sensors, and healthcare professionals to provide quality medical services in any location. The advent of micro-sized, chiffon-thin, resilient, tensile and flexible, economical, user friendly, lightweight electronic chips, devices and systems has provided a platform for an exponential growth of smart healthcare systems.

The neologism of the phrase 'smart healthcare' was constituted from the concept —'smart planet' coined by IBM in 2009. Smart healthcare is a health provisioning system that combines technologies such as wearable devices, ingestible devices, IoT, and mobile internet to seamlessly draw and access information, connecting people, computer systems and medical devices and hospitals to offer the health ecosystem with a continuous dynamic stream of real-time data for seamless monitoring of care provisioning.

Smart healthcare refers to any digital healthcare solution which with the aid of futuristic software applications, protocol, algorithms and technological platforms connects and harmonises numerous networks, sensors, and electronic devices and medical networks and systems via the internet. Smart health mainly focuses on the mission to improve the quality and efficiency of healthcare by enabling self-care and complementing it with remote monitoring patient care.

Smart healthcare encapsulates, but is not limited to classifications such as radio transmissions, LSI and VLSI, embedded systems, big data analytics, ML, cloud computing, dynamic security and compliance, AI augmented reality (AR) and virtual reality (VR).

29.3 Components of a smart healthcare system

The topology of a smart healthcare system is the organization of different components of an IoT healthcare system/network that are lucidly connected in a healthcare environment. The smart healthcare devices integrate discrete components into a hybrid lattice network. Explicit purpose and related processes are dedicated to each component on the IoT network. Since the topology for smart healthcare devices depends on the patient condition and application, the frameworks are unique and it is complicated to frame a universal structure for smart healthcare devices.

The components of a smart healthcare system are classed and ranked based on the sensors, networks computational and information processing devices, data storage systems, application platforms, integration and harmonization and internet security. These components are classified under the following layered pattern: the IoT devices network, fog layer and the cloud layer. Moore's law has become a trajectory for the technological progress and profitability. It is observed that the number of transistors in a dense integrated circuit doubles about every two years while the cost of the devices gets halved. Smart devices are almost aligning to the Moore's law trajectory.

The IoT devices are the primary physical objects connected to the system. Here we can refer to the 'system' as a patient or a subject. For smart health systems, sensors are the components of the device connectivity layer. A sensor is an authorized node and an analytical device which syndicate with a biological element—the patient/subject—and create recognition of events. Morden techniques in semiconductor technology are quite skilled in producing microsmart sensors for various applications. These sensors are always in a remote location—with the patient living in some remote location.

Devices identification on the network abides by the process of getting assigned with a unique identifier (UID) to each authorized entity. Therefore, every component in the system is unique, easily identified, integrated, synchronized and data exchange is achieved unequivocally. In short, every entity associated with the smart healthcare system—the medical devices, hospitals, doctors, nurses, caregivers, pharma are assigned an electronic digital UID for seamless working.

These smart sensors continuously collect stipulated health data from the subject/patient and transmit the information to the next layer.

Figure 29.1 depicts a common framework and a basic structure of a smart healthcare device.

Smart healthcare architectures are designed to be interoperable across different technologies. For instance, the sensors used by the subject/patient interact amongst each other through a personal area network. The fog layer consists of fog nodes, which are essentially controllers, gateway computers, switches, and I/O devices that provide computing, storage, and connectivity services and exchange of data.

The smart healthcare IoT cloud is a high-performance network of servers which can perform high-speed data transfer, correlation and processing of myriads of devices and applications along with network traffic management. Interfacing, interoperability and data transfer happen via sophisticated communication technologies.

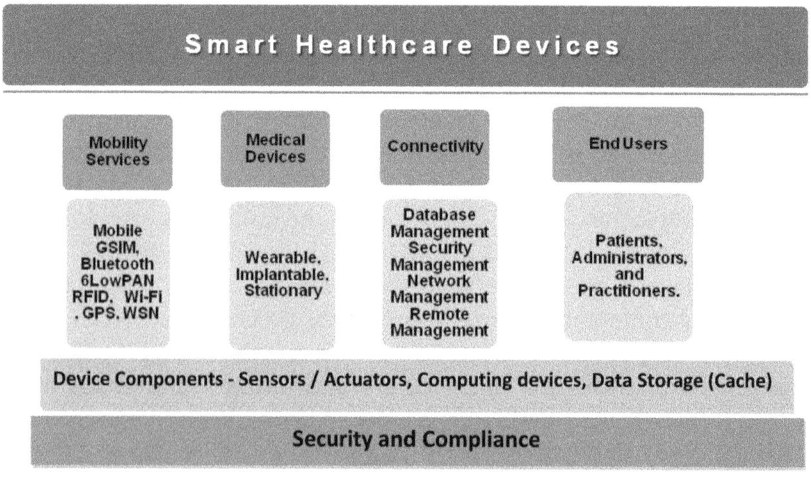

Figure 29.1. Components of smart healthcare devices.

The data is very specific and targeted and is transferred to a smartphone through a Bluetooth or Wi-Fi technology. This data further traverses on the network—which is high end sophisticated IoT cloud technology and applications. This layer is also called the fog layer.

Here we would like to mention some of the Vedic references on propagation of waves and information from TarkaSangraha written in Sanskrit by Sri Annambatta in the later years of 17th Century. Although the treatise falls under the category 'Indian Philosophy and Meta Physics', we are obliged to mention the verses on sound wave propagation and the ripple effects. The Vedic system also has explained the binary system '0 and 1' as existence and non-existence, which is the base of any form of transmission.

Back into the prevalent discussion: the data transfer can be broadly divided into short-range and medium-range technologies. The short-range communications are protocols that are used to establish connections between the objects within a finite range or within a body area network (BAN), whereas the medium-range communication devices generally support communication for a large distance. The standard short- and limited-region wireless communication technologies are UWB, Wi-Fi, ZigBee and Bluetooth. Please refer to figure 29.2 for more information on the wireless technologies.

Short-region wireless technology can communicate wirelessly within a smaller diameter region. IoT communication protocols are modes of communication that ensure secured data transfer between connected devices. The short-range, wireless standard (IEEE 802.15. 4), low power is generally employed using mesh topology to collect data individual sensors and devices over multiple assigned sensor nodes. Figure 29.2 depicts various communication devices.

Bluetooth technologies embrace the recent upgrades in wireless technologies that empower remote operation of mobile medical devices. Bluetooth Low Energy (BLE), released in 2010 focused on devising wireless applications in numerous fields

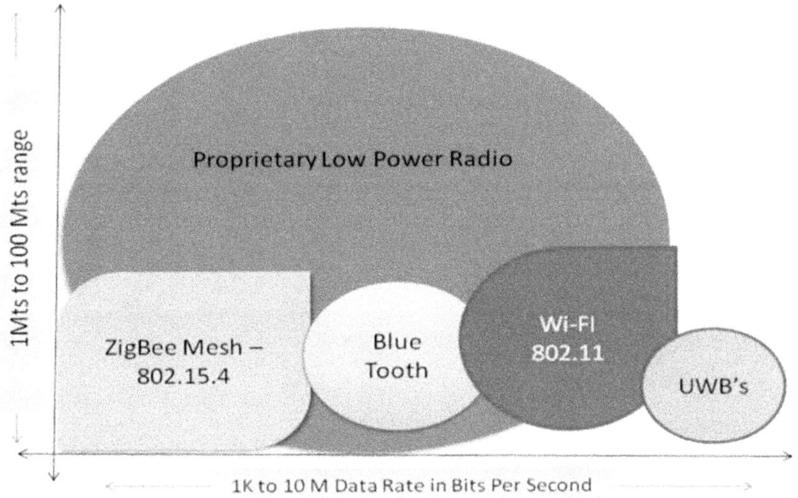

Figure 29.2. Short-range wireless technologies.

including healthcare systems (figure 29.3). The Bluetooth Mesh specification released in 2017 aims to enable an auxiliary and scalable deployment of BLE devices in smart health systems

Bluetooth Classic was originally invented with the intent to cater point-to-point or point-to-multipoint data exchange among multiple connected devices.

The open field transmission range, output power and power consumption are all companionable, which makes BLE a suitable wireless protocol for use in wireless mobile medical platforms. Meanwhile, the use of ANT, ZigBee, UEB and other wireless communications standards are also being explored for use in communications in connecting smart healthcare systems.

Wi-Fi belongs to a classification called the medium-range WLAN. This is a wired LAN but works without cables for connectivity. The intention of deploying Wi-Fi is to replace the Ethernet. Standard Wi-Fi is the obvious choice for IoT, but has limitations in both range and energy efficiency. Wi-Fi's major limitations when it comes to healthcare deployment are coverage, scalability and power consumption.

The IEEE addressed these shortcomings by publishing advance specification for the shortcomings to embrace new internet technologies. The evolution and publications from IEEE is continuous and they work to aid exponential growth and needs.

- PAN—personal area network—this is a computer network which connects together the computing devices used by one person only. The range of the PAN generally spans to a range of 10 m. Some devices on PAN are wireless mouse and keyboard, Bluetooth enabled head phones, remotes used for home appliances, car doors etc.
- LAN—local area network—is a computer network which links computing devices on one site located in utmost proximity—viz. the same building. Generally, a private ownership has designated control over the LAN.
- WAN—wide area network—is a network which links together computing devices across multiple sites. A WAN network comprises many LANs, CANs (CAN stands for the campus area network that joins two or more LANs together within a limited area, e.g. a network in a government office) and MANs—the metropolitan area network that spans over a larger geographical area such as a continent or even connects the entire world. Internet is the best common example to represent this network.

Parameter	Value	Unit
Open Field Transmission Range	150	m
Output Power	10	dBm
Max Current Draw	15	mA
Sleep Current	1.0	μA
Carrier Frequency	2.4	GHz
Data Throughput	1.0	Mbps

Figure 29.3. Source: Bluetooth 4.0: Low Energy—2010.

Figure 29.4 is a high level pictorial representation of various connecting networks.

The architecture framework for IoT-enabled smart healthcare systems, is described as an amalgamation of sensors, chips and devices, internet, software applications, frameworks, and programming languages which are integrated and described as components, applications and their interactions. IoT—the core of a smart health system is a highly correlated and securely harmonized ecosystem. There are ample new technologies thriving in the market that can connect and deliver complete, end-to-end smart solutions.

Figure 29.5 depicts one of the representations in the form of a simple block diagram architecture of smart health IOT systems.

Here the publisher is the device that sends the message and the client (subscriber) it is that receives the message. The publisher and the subscriber need not be in direct connection to establish contact. Publisher messages usually concern the patient health information.

IoT operations are the processes of provisioning and authenticating, configuring, maintaining, monitoring and diagnosing connected devices operating on the network.

Smart health device operations can be summarized as:

- Device and network connection;
- Seamless data collection and management;
- Data correlation and analytics;
- Collaboration.

Figure 29.4. A pictorial representation of various connecting networks.

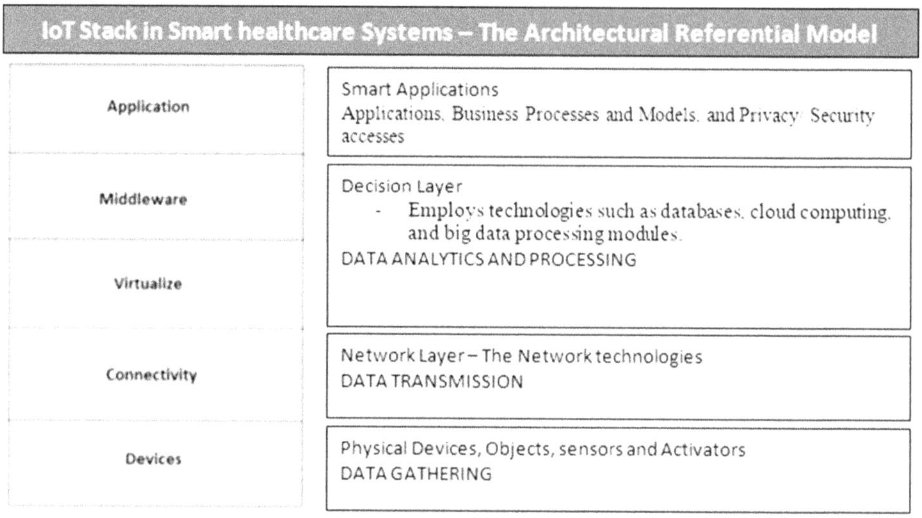

Figure 29.5. Architecture stack of smart health IOT systems.

29.4 Device and network connection

IoT, which is the base building block, is the interconnection of highly distributed physical objects, which have embedded electronics, computers, software and application, sensors or actuators, to the internet. The purpose of connectedness is collecting and exchanging data for monitoring and control. As more connected IoT devices are launched, the overall system has to deal with myriad arrays of software, firmware, connectivity issues, data structures and security capabilities. The focus of this function is related to how the device is connected to the ecosystem.

This connection layer manages the two-way data traffic between different networks and protocols. Another function of the connectivity layer is to translate different network protocols and ensure interoperability of the connected devices and sensors. Data security is maintained by higher order encryption protocols. Highly advanced data encryption methods, security protocols, and trust models will be established to help secure wireless medical instruments.

29.5 Seamless data collection and management

IoT middleware—this is a layer that connects the devices and information systems. The framework of this layer forms mechanisms and methodology for data collection, devices interoperability, security and data filtering processing by adopting standard protocols and framework accredited by standard development organizations (SDOs). There is also extensive compatible off-the-shelf (COTS) hardware across verticals to plug and use for this purpose.

The sensors in devices continuously collect data from the patient/environment and transmit the information to the next layer for processing. The data can be pushed or propelled from the sensor using applications and programs.

Figure 29.4 gives an enhanced understanding of smart health IoT operations. device management, data processing and management exist on this layer.

Smart health device management is the processes that assists in provisioning, configuration, authenticating, maintenance, monitoring and scrutinizing connected devices functioning as part of an IoT environment. The smart health IoT is a dynamic and a comprehensive network infrastructure, in which devices, individual physical and virtual elements are identifiable, autonomous, and self-configurable. Devices are designed to automatically communicate among themselves as designated and to interact with the environment subsystems responding to events and triggers.

Data visualization and action management both occur via a dta management service layer. The IoT data management system can be bifurcated and divided as an online, real-time frontend that interacts directly with the interconnected smart health devices—objects and sensors, and an offline backend that handles the mass storage with trillions of real-time data elements and in-depth analysis of the data; this in-depth analysis is performed using the theory and science called analytics and information management.

29.6 Data correlation and analytics

The focus of the data correlation function is to map the data to a requirement and a context and do correlation and limitations. This will create meaningful and succinct data sets that can be processed and be used to make informed decisions. The data transformation and co-relation requires information from multiple systems to be extracted transformed and processed. Therefore, the architecture supports high degree interoperability between the systems that hold the information. The data includes real-time data as well as historic data that are stored in the system.

The collection method of data from the device layer may be temporal or modal. Temporal data collection denotes collecting data from all devices that are connected at specified intervals as programmed, while modal collection involves collecting data belonging to specific devices and subsystems on specified timelines. An IoT ecosystem connects and interacts with more than one database schema to accommodate the possible data collection methodologies usually, the most advanced schemas are multi-layer IoT database schema with different nodes which organize and act to fetch/process data when there is a query to the database.

Analytics can be stated as the methodical computational analysis of data or information usually deploying statistical techniques. Analytics is used for the discovery, analysis, prediction, interpretation, and communication of meaningful patterns in data. It also entails applying data patterns towards effective predictions and decision making. The three main classes of smart health analytics are predictive analytics, real-time analytics and descriptive analytics.

Smart health analytics is performed by employing apt data analysis tools or procedures to the various types of data the devices and sensors generate. The analytics solution helps to analyze the historical data as well as real-time data. The advent of frameworks and applications using AI, ML algorithms and platform agnostic solutions are also capable of predicting the occurrence of a future event.

This is called predictive analytics, and helps a medical practitioner or a clinical researcher to gain insights to steer future action plans.

Some of the top smart healthcare IoT analytics tools are Google Cloud IoT Core, ThingSpeak, and AWS IoT Analytics, Datadog, AT&T IoT Platform, BellaDati, Oracle Internet of Things Cloud, ThingsBoard (*Ref: IDC.com/containerId=IDC_P33134*). These applications/tools explore intelligent healthcare and clinical decision support systems in smart health ecosystems and their implications for the real world, and automate the steps required to analyze data from these devices

29.7 Collaboration

The focus of this the federation layer is to enable the collaboration between the patient and the healthcare providers. IoT infrastructure often needs to incorporate cross-domain hardware and systems and connected and affiliated software applications.

The federation layer which is the epicentre of the smart health systems provides the glue that joins dispersed health IoT subsystems and data sources together to form a globalized view of the smart health system. It provides interoperability features for the diverse data types processed. The repositories that work in sync are harmonized together to perform a specific query to process indented data and to provide analytical insights for the end users. The smart healthcare systems are either location-agnostic or location-specific depending on the patient and disease requirements. IoT systems are projected to provide an ability to tap into diverse and multiple sources of data that may not be located on the same network environment. Therefore, a sources and location discovery mechanism is needed for the smart health system so that it can adhere to the service requirements and get responses from sources whose data can service these needs. Location-agnostic devices enable the different sources/subsystems to seamlessly connect and leave the coalition, while location-aware devices handle queries that have explicit location-specific requirements.

IoT interoperability entails effective data transfer to different users' application systems and servers. Open sourced messaging protocols like MQTT/CoAP and application programming interfaces (APIs) based on RESTful principles are some of the key drivers of cross-application/subsystems interoperability.

29.8 Attributes of smart healthcare devices

A smart health system or a device connects various products/applications, cross-platform technologies and services to work together by harmonizing an active engagement between them (figure 29.6).

Smart health IoT has its own technology stack that embarks on its networked journey from connecting things, capturing the data, fetching and communicating it and ends with applications—end-user nodes.

A spectrum of essential attributes needed is enlisted in the architecture (figure 29.7).

The above mentioned qualitative aspects are all essentials for continuous working and intelligent processing of information gathered. The data collected are analyzed for insights, predictions, proactive actions and other various purposes . Simulation frameworks and software application employing AI, ML and neural networks are deployed for prediction and foreseeing events.

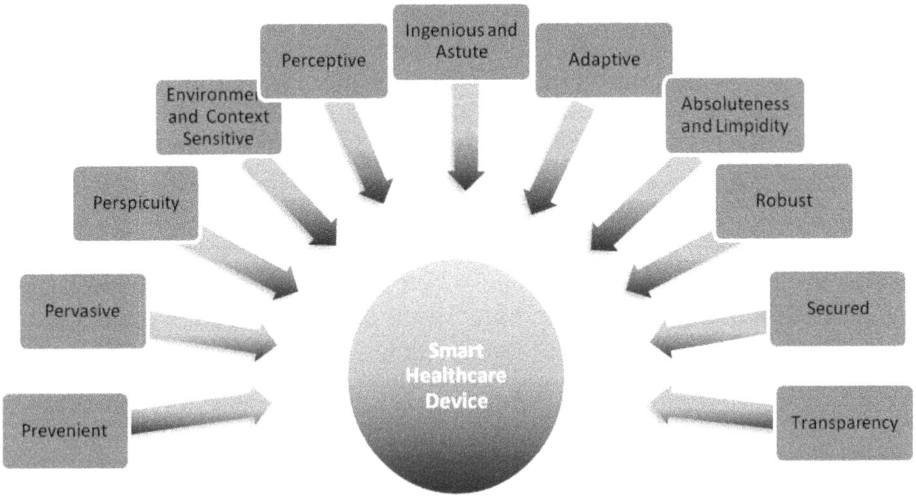

Figure 29.6. Essential attributes of a smart healthcare device.

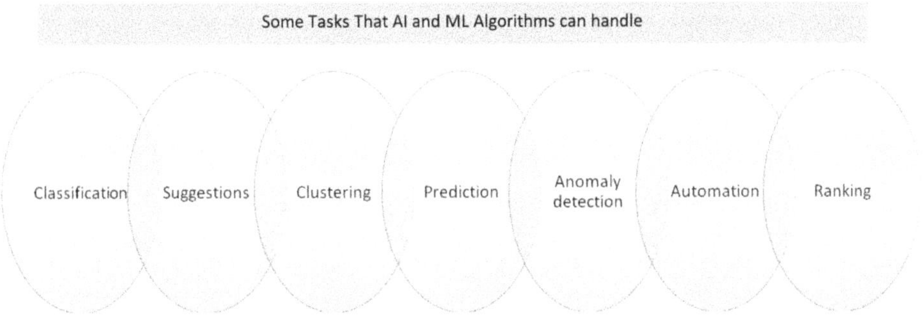

Figure 29.7. Tasks performed by AI and ML algorithms.

29.9 Contemporary technologies and frameworks that aid smart healthcare services

AI enabled smart health IoT is intelligent machines that simulate smart demeanour and support in predictions and decision making with minimum human interference. The IoT services inextricably follow five fundamental events viz. create, communicate, aggregate, analyze, and act. The AI applications aid predictive analysis and insights based action plans.

ML, which pertains to AI, is a process of development, analysis and implementation leading to establishing a systematic process. ML brings the ability to automatically identify patterns and detect anomalies in the data that smart health sensors and devices generate. The ML framework brings in operational predictions up to 20 times earlier than the traditional methods and with greater accuracy.

For data classification ML deploys decision trees—a graphical representation of all possible solutions to a decision under certain conditions. In general, clustering is performed using k-means clustering or a hierarchical clustering algorithm.

Prediction models are built using linear regression, which relates input variables and a single output variable. These models are built on the concept called reinforcement learning, which deploys the Markov decision process (MDP).

MDP is built on the Markov chain, which is a set of sequential events to automatically determine the ideal behaviour within a specific area and context. MDP is a mathematical framework which characterises the environment in reinforcement learning and building predictive models. This also can be extended in anomaly detection and complete automation.

AR and VR are two notable paradigms which are adapted to help treat a range of mental health problems like severe paranoid beliefs and fear of the real-world environment creating ignes fatui.

Deploying AR frameworks and applications, we can simulate virtual elements and environments as in the real world. In psychiatry, AR can be used to support experiential learning in relation to clinical change with treatment of a specific phobia, pharmacological treatments in stress management, driving delusions, hallucinations mental aberration.

VR induces the sense of 'presence' and creates an environment of 'being there'. The utilization of VR in controlled settings can help in effective management of persons with autistic spectrum disorder.

29.10 Vedic evidence of connected environments and VR

Indian epics have references to Maya (Sanskrit: माया)—which is nothing but 'illusion' or creation of delusions. The Vedic definition is a spiritual concept in Hinduism connoting 'That which exists, but is constantly changing and thus is spiritually unreal'.

The Rig Vedham, Arthvana Vedham and The Bhagawat Gita allude and ascribe references and hymns called Slokhams about—'Mayay'.

In the Hindu epic Ramayana, Maricha, or Mareecha (Sanskrit: मारीच, IAST: Mārīca) is referred to have practiced simulations and transformation similar to the theory and claims of the AR paradigm of today.

Chapter 42 of Aaranya Kandam in Srimad Valmiki Ramayanam has verses describing the transformation of a human being (The King Mareecha) into a golden deer with silver spots, which lure Seetha Devi and abduct her from the Ashramam in the Forest.

There is enormous evidence in scriptures on how the ancient Bharatiya (Indian) practices were sophisticated and innovative in day-to-day life.

29.11 Conclusion

Diagnostics, monitoring, and treatment systems have become portable, wearable, implantable and ingestible, which offers better and quick services when compared to traditional stationary non-connected, bulky medical instruments. This new era of connected healthcare has minimized patient discomfort and lowered costs for both healthcare providers and patients. This paradigm shift has transformed the healthcare industry by redefining a device's space and people's interaction in delivering the solutions.

Smart IoT healthcare solutions have the potential to significantly improve patient focus. The advent of remote patient monitoring (RPM) has helped in shrinking the rising healthcare costs and is beneficial to clinicians and patients.

Medical IoT devices transmit most sensitive personal information of patients. Since, the data management is persistent and unremitting, continuous visibility and control to keep devices compliant and current is imperative. The focus and emphasis is to also control network access in heterogeneous environments, to identify components in the system and assess risk and vulnerabilities for every smart healthcare device, IT endpoint, clinical devices, doctors, nurses and caregivers, identity management and building automation system in every location without disrupting care to strategize and plan for security and compliance.

Confidentiality, accessibility, integrity (CAI) of all electronic protected health information has to comply with privacy and security regulations. The standards and frameworks referenced are statutes of US FDA, MHRA, ISO/IEC series and groups of standards, GDPR, GxP guidelines and other Geo-specific regulations. Smart and secured applications are scrupulously built so as to achieve 'context aware and dynamic security' for the data being transferred, processed and analyzed. This is achieved by deploying GVC (Governance, Visualization and Risk) based compliance in place of GRC—governance, risk and compliance security paradigms.

Figure 29.8 depicts key market players working on smart device delivery, cost-containment in and accentuation on active patient engagement and patient-centric care delivery.

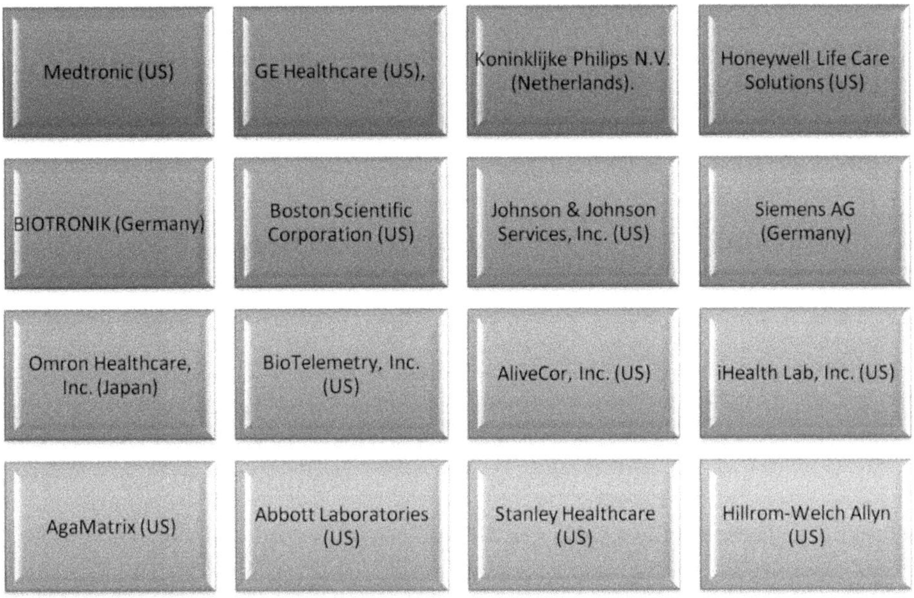

Figure 29.8. Some of the key market players in 2020–21.

Further reading

Ahmed E, Yaqoob I, Hashem I A T, Khan I, Ahmed A I A and Imran M *et al* 2017 The role of big data analytics in internet of things *Compute. Netw.* **129** 459–71

Amira A, Agoulmine N, Bensaali F, Bermak A and Dimitrakopoulos G 2018 Special Issue: Empowering eHealth with Smart Internet of Things (IoT) Medical Devices *J. Sens. Actuator Netw. 2019* **8** 33

Annambhaṭṭa and Ballantyne J R 1851 *The Tarka-sangraha, with a translation and notes in Hindí and English* (Presbyterian Mission Press) Retrieved 17 November 2016

Ananth S, Sathya P and Madhan Mohan P 2019 Smart health monitoring system through IOT *2019 Int. Conf. on Communication and Signal Processing (ICCSP)* 0968–70

CB Information Services 2016 64 healthcare IoT startups in patient monitoring, clinical efficiency, biometrics, and more https://cbinsights.com/research/iot-healthcare-market-map-company-list/

Frenzel L 2012 The fundamentals of short-range wireless technology *Electron. Design*

Kumar S P, Samson V R R, Sai U B, Rao P L S D M and Eswar K K 2017 Smart health monitoring system of patient through IoT *2017 Int. Conf. on I-SMAC (IoT in Social, Mobile, Analytics and Cloud) (I-SMAC)* 551–6

Handa T, Shoji S, Ike S, Takeda S and Sekiguchi T 1997 A very low-power consumption wireless ECG monitoring system using body as a signal transmission medium *Int. Solid State Sensor Actuators Conf.* 1003–6

https://sciencedirect.com/science/article/pii/S2414644719300508

https://ncbi.nlm.nih.gov/pmc/articles/PMC4156009/

https://researchgate.net/publication/342377536_Emerging_Biometrics_Deep_Inference_and_Other_Computational_Intelligence

https://researchgate.net/publication/277889178_Machine_learning_capabilities_in_medical_diagnosis_applications_Computational_results_for_hepatitis_disease

https://linkedin.com/pulse/digital-augmented-reality-maya-sanskrit-%E0%A4%AE%E0%A4%AF-tamil-%E0%AE%AE%E0%AE%AF%E0%AE%AE-connected-ravi

https://bakermckenzie.com/-/media/files/expertise/ma-resources/Compliance.pdf

https://sites.tufts.edu/eeseniordesignhandbook/2015/wireless-mobile-medical-devices/

IoT Healthcare Analytics 2016

Leffmann A 2000 Emerging technologies *Globalization and the Challenges of a New Century: A Reader* ed P O'Meara, H D Mehlinger and M Krain (Bloomington, IN: Indiana University Press) p 355

Mimansaka Y 1976 *Vaidika Siddhanta Mimansa, Sonipata* p 40

Mohan A 2014 Cyber security for personal medical devices internet of things *2014 IEEE Int. Conf. on Distributed Computing in Sensor Systems* 372–74

Mohan Roy R R 1999 *Vedic Physics, Scientific Origin of Hinduism* (Toronto: Golden Egg Publishing) p 6

Obaidat M A, Obeidat S, Holst J, Al Hayajneh A and Brown J A 2020 Comprehensive and systematic survey on the internet of things: security and privacy challenges, security frameworks, enabling technologies, threats, vulnerabilities and countermeasures *Computers* **9** 44

Pattnaik P K, Mohanty S and Mohanty S 2020 *Smart Healthcare Analytics in IoT Enabled Environment* (Cham: Springer)

Pradhan B, Bhattacharyya S and Pal K *et al* 2021 IoT applications in healthcare devices *J. Health. Eng.* **2021** 6632599 https://hindawi.com/journals/jhe/2021/6632599/fig1/

Pundit,Neil, and Anil Rewari

Ramayanam S V 2002 https://valmikiramayan.net/ © 1998–2008, Desiraju Hanumanta Rao and K M K Murthy

Scully P and Lueth K L 2016 Guide to IoT solution development *White paper* IoT Analytics

Subahi A and Theodorakopoulos G 2018 Ensuring compliance of IoT devices with their privacy policy agreement *2018 IEEE 6th Int. Conf. on Future Internet of Things and Cloud (FiCloud)* 100–7

Viswanathan H, Chen B and Pompili D 2012 Research challenges in computation, communication, and context awareness for ubiquitous healthcare *IEEE Commun. Mag.* **50** 92–9

Yu Y, Zheng L, Zhu J, Cao Y and Hu B 2018 Technology of short-distance wireless communication and its application based on equipment support *AIP Conf. Proc.* 1955 040135

1991 Narayanopanisat in Atharvaveda. Collection of Veda mantras (Mantra Puspam), Ramakrishna Math, Bombay

IOP Publishing

Human-Assisted Intelligent Computing
Modeling, simulations and applications
Mukhdeep Singh Manshahia, Igor S Litvinchev, Gerhard-Wilhelm Weber, J Joshua Thomas and Pandian Vasant

Chapter 30

Adequate implementation of simulation tools for enhancement performance on existing network infrastructure devices (OPNET)

Yakubu Ajiji Makeri

Acronyms and abbreviations

ACL: Access control list
ARP: Address resolution protocol
DHCP: Dynamic host configuration protocol
FDDI: Fiber distributed data interface
FTP: File transfer protocol
HTTP: Hypertext transfer protocol
HTTPS: Hypertext transfer protocol secure
ICT: Information and communications technology
IEEE: Institute of Electrical and Electronics Engineers
IP: Internet protocol
ITU: International telecommunication union
ISL: Inter-switch link
ISP: Internet service provider
LAN: Local area network
MAC: Media access control address
NOC: Network operations center
NO_VLAN: No virtual local area network
OPNET: Optimized network engineering tool
RIP: Routing information protocol
SPSS: Statistical Package for the Social Sciences

doi:10.1088/978-0-7503-4801-0ch30

TCP: Transmission control protocol
ULB: Université Lumière De Bujumbura
VLAN: Virtual local area network
VLT: Virtual local area network trunk

This research aimed to enhance an enterprise network performance through VLAN implementation by simulating an existing LAN and rectifying LAN using VLAN, in two different scenarios. Therefore, the study had the following objectives: to simulate and compare the new (VLAN) and existing (NO_VLAN) enterprise network performance. Broadly speaking, descriptive statistics were used to analyze the first objective while an interview guide was used to generate information from the structured interview in the second objective; also, OPNET was the tool used to get simulation results, measure and compare the network performance for both scenarios (NO_VLAN and VLAN). The simulated results for the fifth objective were a comparison for both scenarios NO_VLAN and VLAN. The statistics results and graphs showed that VLAN had lower traffic and response time compared to NO_VLAN due to segmentation of a single large broadcasting domain into three broadcasting domains to reduce and control traffic sent and received by the network. Hence, VLAN prohibits access to the network resources of other departments. Virtual LAN technology can also be used to mitigate vulnerability surface for hackers by reducing the traffic request to servers, network visualization leads to ease of administration. There were more benefits of network virtualization through the implementation of VLAN. Thus, VLANs improved bandwidth utilization, power, speed, and security.

30.1 Introduction

In a modern and global world, the importance and added values provided by network infrastructure are evident whether it is for government entities, business enterprises, or educational institutions, e.g., Universities in East Africa. This contributes to achieving important goals such as more efficiency, productivity, acquiring knowledge and collaboration. Increased use of information technologies in the business requires a robust technical infrastructure and adequate network architecture (Yoloye 2015). Computer networking enables the modern world to exchange information through an interconnection of systems regardless of the locality by implementing a certain set of rules which are defined within the system, different systems can connect in various ways to achieve certain objectives (Grandhi 2014).

Globally, academics including scientists and professors use the internet extensively and this explains why educational institutions were early adopters of the internet (Orike 2017). The strengths of the internet for academic work include currency of online information sources, accessibility to multimedia resources, and information that is not limited by distance or time constraints. With improved internet connectivity, academic institutions in developed countries for example the

USA, China, UK are tapping into the many opportunities offered by modern information societies (Neema-Abooki 2015). The increased use of the internet in worldwide academic institutions means that educational researchers recognize the significance and understand how and why students use it.

In developed countries, LAN infrastructure on the majority of campuses has been upgraded from 100 Mbps to a fully redundant and scalable 1 Gbps backbone (Kezar 2014). New models are being used to leverage existing infrastructure, add enhanced services and support the total infrastructure. Many new services have emerged to realize ubiquitous computing environments, owing to the increasing supply of mobile devices and more widespread internet and wireless network facilities (Kezar 2014). With effective availability of network infrastructure, users (students and lecturers) can get the information content whenever they want, in any media, over any facilities, anywhere, implying that research and education networks have been established. In Africa, the establishment of education networks started later with universities that introduced or pioneered access to the internet (using TCP/IP) in South Africa followed by Zambia in the University of Zambia establishing ZAMNET, the country's first ISP, and Mozambique by Eduardo Mondlane University (Penard 2015). According to Penard (2015), the lack of appropriate network infrastructure that allows for easy access to the information within institutions is a great limitation to the educational system in sub-Saharan countries.

The majority of these higher education institutions have limited access to connectivity due to their obsolete or lack of appropriate network design in place. According to ITU statistics on ICT penetration, while penetration of fixed broadband is growing at an average rate of 12% in developed countries, Africa stands at a less than 0.5%. Although the usage of internet resources in lesson preparation and learning is a necessity in improving the quality of teaching in higher education institutions in Uganda, the usage of these resources by lecturers and students and staff in higher education institutions in different private and public universities is low for enterprise network resources accessibility. This is due to several barriers that affect usage of the said resources such as slowness of the internet, network unreliability, lack of consistent technical support, poor network design which limits access to resources and old technology equipment (Adeleke 2016). The main factors of unreliability, slowness, and network congestion in higher education are related to poor network design, misuse of bandwidth, and it is based on these that this study will focus on the enhancement of enterprise network performance through VLAN implementation.

30.2 Statement of the problem

The world has undergone a technological revolution with the internet and the web has become an important part of lives since it provides many effective services in many fields of life (Walaa *et al* 2016). A university campus network (wired and wireless local area network) is an important instrument for communication and facilitating collaborative research, which is the key factor to building a strong knowledge culture and efficiently supporting academic mission (Martinez Rivera 2015). The implementation of the campus university network helps universities become more collaborative centers, which helps achieve their goals and provide development of a higher level of knowledge for the students (Rawat 2016).

Reliable internet connectivity has become a prerequisite for universities to provide quality education and undertake quality research works, despite these considerable investments, some universities continue to find themselves having slow and unreliable networks (Akpah *et al* 2017).

However, nowadays the high-speed network makes people sense that a network is a much more powerful tool to enhance any business enterprise and make the company run more efficiently.

The main purpose of the networkability in universities is to support learning, teaching, research, and sharing of information. Unfortunately, even though the capacity of the bandwidth is considered to be sufficient, the network can appear slow and inconsistent due to some factors like poor network design, the number of devices on the network, local network protocols (medium access control, MAC Protocol), and misuse of the bandwidth by accessing bandwidth-hungry websites and applications (Dhurgham 2018). Modern organizations are facing problems related to poor network design, which affects services in many fields that lead the responsible authorities to be interested in improving network local area performance by measuring the quality of services for the network (Walaa *et al* 2016).

Business is facing some challenges. Due to inconsistent and slow network, students and staff are being affected when unable to perform their daily activities for accessing books, doing their research, sharing information and other resources, which brings frustration to both sides; as long as the network is down nothing can be done. Behind this is poor network design and a lack of a VLAN to improve the existing network architecture.

The development of the VLAN led large organizations such as companies, universities, enterprises, etc, to build their network schemes depending on VLAN encapsulation method. VLAN is a data link layer aspect that allows the implementation of logical networks with respect to physical ones. This means, that computers, servers, and other network devices in a VLAN are connected logically regardless of their physical locations. Hence, even if these devices are located in different places, VLAN can logically group them into separate virtual networks. The purpose behind applying VLAN is to improve the security and traffic management, and make a network simpler. As an example, consider that there exists a three-story office building that contains computers belonging to certain departments mixed with computers belong to other departments on the same floor. Consider that the departments are identified by accounting, shipping, and management departments. All these computers in these three departments are all connected to a switch, so they all are on the same segment on the LAN. Thus, all the network broadcast traffic is mixed in with the other departments. Under this act, the departments can see other network traffic. Suppose that we wanted to separate the network broadcast traffic among these proposed departments such that the accounting department does not see any traffic from the shipping department and the management department does not see any traffic from the shipping department and so on by creating VLANs. VLANs can logically create several virtual networks to separate the network broadcast traffic through a VLAN switch. In this case, three VLANs must be created for the three departments (accounting, shipping, and management). By this action, the traffic among the three departments is isolated, so they won't see any traffic created from the other departments and they only see their own network traffic, even though all the computers from the different departments share the same cable and switch. In this proposed example, the VLANs are created on the switch which is done by designating specific ports on the switch and assigning those ports to specific VLANs. Hence, the switch incudes the VLAN of the management department, that is, the computers of that department are plugged into their corresponding ports in the switch, and then additional ports on the same switch are designated to plug the VLAN of the accounting department, and finally another additional setup port on the switch is designated for the VLAN of the shipping department. Thus, the network traffic is separated among three departments because of the VLANs. As stated before, there are several reasons for creating VLANs and the one main reason is for traffic management because as the LAN grows and more network devices are added, the frequency of the broadcast will increase accordingly and the network will get heavily congested with data. However, by creating VLANs which divide the network into smaller broadcast domains then the broadcast traffic will be eliminated.

30.2.1 Content scope

In this study, attention was focused on investigating the end-user satisfaction of the enterprise network performance and identifying the drawbacks of existing enterprise network performance. After data was collected, the researcher used the OPNET simulator to simulate the existing enterprise network and the new with the implementation of a VLAN for improving the network performance at Université Lumière de Bujumbura (ULB). The study was specifically concentrated on simulating and comparing the existing (NO_VLAN) and new (VLAN) enterprise network performance. Therefore, analyzing the network design of the infrastructure of the LAN identified the issues arising from the existence of a LAN to implement a VLAN for an effective and efficient network design for an improved enterprise network performance. Therefore, it is the only campus to which the research was confined and was known to be facing those challenges of the unstable network that triggered the research.

30.2.2 Significance of the study

The findings of this research was to enhance existing enterprise network or LAN performance, and the proposed VLAN was implemented in OPNET simulator for comparing the performance of the existing enterprise network with NO_VLAN and the other with VLAN for accessing and supporting learning, teaching, research and sharing of information at ULB's network.

The researcher in the same area of networking may use the findings of this research as background to solve the problems related to networking in different sectors.

The students and staff can benefit from this study for accessing a network of good quality that helps them to perform well in their daily campus activities like learning, teaching, research, and sharing of information.

30.3 Conceptual review

The computer network is composed of the computers in use and communication facilities, that is, the use of various means of communication, the geographical dispersion of the computers together to achieve mutual communication and sharing software, hardware and data resources, and other systems (Yunzhou *et al* 2018). The computer network according to its computer distribution range is usually divided into LANs and wide area networks (Yunzhou *et al* 2018). Enterprise network or LAN coverage of the geographical range is small, usually in the number of meters to tens of kilometers (Yunzhou *et al* 2018). VLAN is a set of users in different isolated logical LANs or broadcasting domains, they are communicated as the same LAN, i.e., same broadcasting domain (Dhurgham 2018). A LAN is a group of computers that are connected together in a small geographical area to communicate with one another through wired or wireless links and share resources such as printers and network storage (Hameed and Mian 2015). A LAN can be defined as a group of users or workstations that are located in the same physical area with the same broadcasting domain (Dhurgham 2018). the LAN is a group of computers and associated devices that share a common communication line or wireless link and typically share the resources of a single processor or server within a limited geographical area (Abid and Yousif 2016), interconnection of computers and network devices within a geographical area and providing shared access to printers, file servers, and other network devices (Grandhi 2014). A VLAN is defined as a local area network configured by software, not by physical wiring (Gyan and Sadhana 2013). According to Nweso (2015), A VLAN is a logical grouping of network users and resources connected to administratively defined ports on a switch.

A LAN is usually defined as a broadcast domain which means that all connected devices in the same physical LAN can communicate without the need for a router (Ali 2016). VLANs are regularly defined as a set of devices on different physical LAN segments which can communicate as if they have a common LAN segment. Switches are used in VLANs to divide the network into separate broadcast domains without having latency problems (AL khaffaf and D A J 2018).

An empirical review by Dhurgham (2018) tried to alleviate the end-to-end delay by using the VLAN technology to enhance the network performance, measuring key performance indicators such as traffic sent, traffic received, average delay, and throughput. By employing OPNET 17.5 Student Version, he found that there is more existing traffic without VLAN technology, hence, virtual area networks prohibit access to the network resources of other departments.

The objective of this research was to look at the benefits of network virtualization through the implementation of VLAN using a Cisco packet tracer to simulate the network architecture. The network was enhanced when the network broadcast domain was segmented into separate Layer 2 broadcast domains, because if a broadcast is not well contained in a network, it may lead to collision (Isiaka and Akeem 2015). Munam *et al* (2016) aimed to enhance network performance without incorporating additional hardware cost. OPNET Modeler 14.5 simulator was used to first implement the entire network infrastructure. They observed that the proposed design performs significantly better using VLANs. The research was interested in improving the quality of service using VLAN technology by overcoming delay problems using OPNET simulator. The simulated results show how to select a good way in designing a network to reduce the value delay for improving the quality of service (Walaa *et al* 2016).

In 2016 Ali (Ali 2016) divided one physical network into multiple broadcast domains where different scenarios were designed and simulated. A step-by-step procedure using the workspace of OPNET is given, the results obtained show a large reduction in traffic carried by the switch with more secure and efficient bandwidth utilization.

30.4 Overview of the enterprise network (LAN)

A LAN or enterprise network is a group of interconnected computers that interoperate and allow users to share resources, likely using no more than 1000 feet of cable. A LAN is generally a network of computers located in the same area. Today, LANs are defined as a single broadcast domain (Jayan and Kshama 2017). This means that if a user broadcasts information on an enterprise network or LAN, every user will receive the broadcast. In the local area, broadcasts are prohibited from leaving a LAN by using a router. The drawback of this technique is that the incoming data routers usually take more time to process compared to a switch or to a bridge. More significantly, the formation of broadcast domains depends on the physical connection of the devices in the network. VLANs were developed as another solution for using routers to contain broadcast traffic.

The increase in the number of devices on LANs become paramount as we populate the network with more switches and workstations. Since most workstations tend to be loaded with an existing operating system, it results in unavoidable broadcasts being sent occasionally on the network. Unfortunately, each host on such a network cannot escape from the effects generated by uncontrollable broadcasts that decrease network performance (Newest *et al* 2015). A LAN is a group of computers that are connected together in a small geographical area to communicate with one another through wired or wireless links and share resources such as printers and network storage (Hameed and Mian 2015).

30.4.1 Virtual LAN and NO_LAN with network protocols and design

To understand VLANs, firstly it is essential to have an understanding of LANs. A LAN can normally be defined as a broadcast domain. Hubs, bridges, or switches in the same physical segment (s) connect all end-node devices. End nodes can communicate with each other without the need for a router. Communications with devices on other LAN segments require the use of a router, as shown in figure 30.1.

VLANs can be viewed as a group of devices which are on different physical local area network segments which can communicate with each other as if they were all on the same physical LAN segment. Switches using VLANs create the same division of the network into isolated broadcast domains but do not have the latency problems of a router. Switches are an extra cost-effective solution, as shown in figures 30.2 and 30.3.

The most common protocol used nowadays to configure VLANs is IEEE 802.1Q. The committee of IEEE defined this technique of multiplexing VLANs to provide multivendor VLAN support. Prior to the introduction of the 802.1Q standard, several proprietary protocols existed, such as Cisco's ISL (Inter-Switch Link) and 3Com's VLT (VLAN Trunk). Cisco also implemented VLANs over FDDI by carrying VLAN information in an IEEE 802.10 frame header, opposing to the purpose of the IEEE 802.10 standard.

Both ISL and IEEE 802.1Q tagging is done by 'explicit tagging'—the frame itself is tagged with VLAN information. ISL uses an external tagging process that does not modify the existing ethernet frame, while 802.1Q uses a frame-internal field for tagging, and thus does change the ethernet frame. This internal tagging is what allows IEEE 802.1Q to work on both access and trunk links: frames are standard

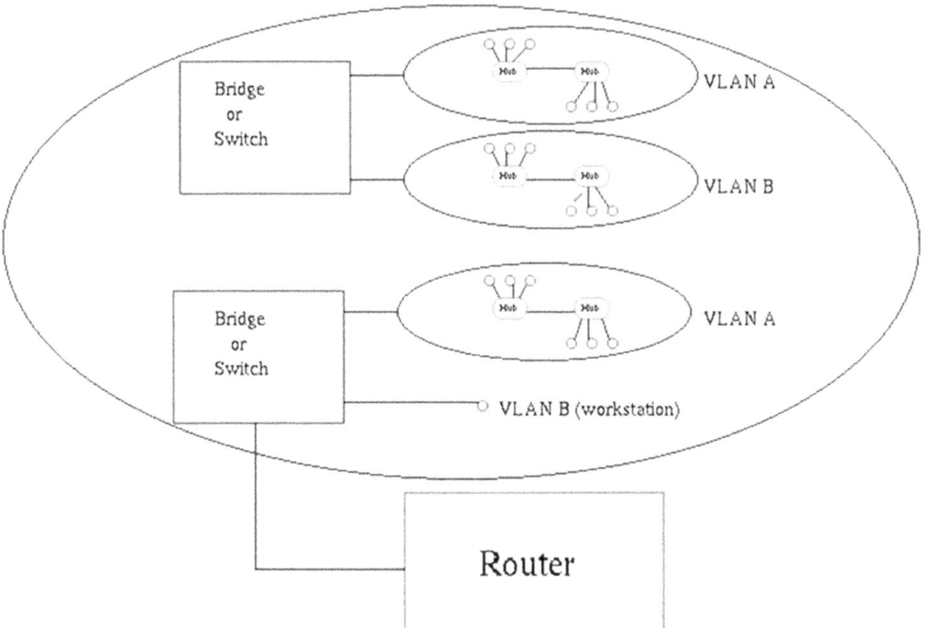

Figure 30.1. Physical view of a LAN.

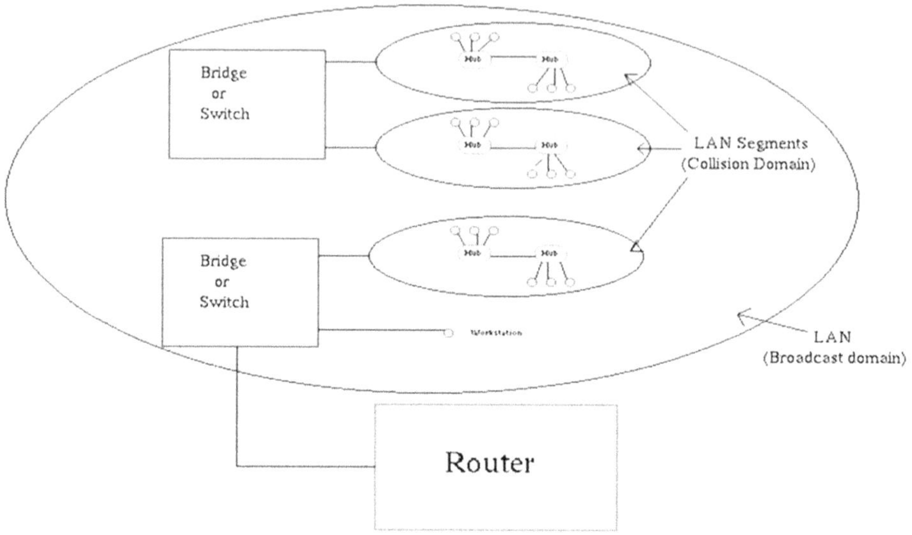

Figure 30.2. Logical view.

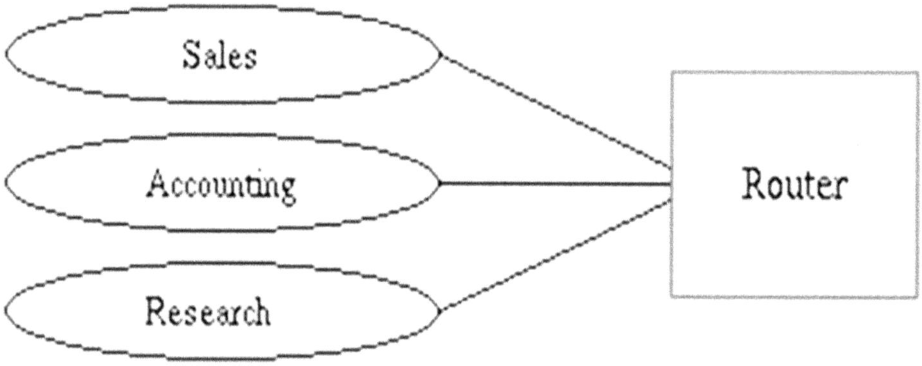

Figure 30.3. Physical and logical view of a VLAN.

ethernet, and so can be handled by product hardware. Under IEEE 802.1Q, the maximum number of VLANs on a given ethernet network is 4094. This does not impose the same limit on the number of IP subnets in such a network, meanwhile, a single VLAN can contain multiple IP subnets. The VLAN limit is expanded to 16 million with shortest path bridging (Rik 2014).

Primary network designers frequently configure virtual LANs to reduce the size of the collision domain in a large single ethernet segment and consequently improve performance. When ethernet switches made this a non-issue consideration turned to reducing the size of the broadcast domain at the MAC address layer. A VLAN can also serve to restrict access to network resources without regard to the physical topology of the network, although the strength of this method remains debatable as VLAN hopping (Rik 2014) is a means of bypassing such security measures. VLAN bouncing can be mitigated with proper switch port configuration.

30.4.2 Overview of virtual local area networks

A VLAN is the abstract design of the LAN; A VLAN might comprise a subset of the ports on a single switch or subsets of ports on multiple switches, by default, systems on one VLAN do not see the traffic associated with systems on other VLANs on the same network (Jayan and Kshama 2017).

Therefore, for improving network performance and scalability VLANs provide a broadcast control to eliminate unnecessary broadcast traffic. Security allows administrators to implement access lists to control traffic between VLANs by logically separating users and departments.

The VLANs allow a user or device to exist anywhere by removing the physical boundaries of the network. Often the user network can be separated from the server network using VLANs.

VLAN technologies are in a (main campus) network. Going by the normal flat LAN infrastructure where every user belongs to one broadcast domain, a diverse series of network insecurities exist. In the case of an enterprise network (LAN) having critical application servers, organizational databases, file servers, and other confidential information, this means that every user on the network would have equal access privileges to these resources. Segmentation of the existing network into different broadcast domains uses VLAN to successfully remove such situations from the operational network by restricting access at all levels of the network. A contrast to where all hosts are connected without segmentation is usually flat LAN architecture; a large broadcast domain into different sizes of broadcast domains is broken by creating VLANs. VLAN architecture is a logical grouping of network users and resources connected to organizationally defined ports on a switch, which if deployed in the ULB network would be of enormous benefit as outlined in the work.

In this work we thoroughly show the benefits of VLAN over enterprise network or LAN in managing and maintaining of networks.

To describe what a VLAN is and how VLAN memberships are used in a switched network, membership in a VLAN can be based on port members, MAC addresses, IP addresses, IP multicast addresses, and/or a combination of these features. VLANs are cost- and time-effective, and can reduce network traffic, and provide an extra measure of security (Gyan and Sadhana 2013). In this research, the LAN was studied to better understand and illustrate how VLANs are used in practice to improve the performance. This study of analyzing the LAN will indicate how VLANs will be used for many objectives that they were not originally intended for; the use of VLANs complicates network configuration management.

30.4.3 Virtual local area network usage in campus networks (LANs)

Enterprise network administrators use VLANs to achieve key policy objectives: limiting the scope of and simplifying access control policies, decentralized network management, broadcast traffic, supporting and enabling unified host mobility for wireless users. The network primarily runs IPv4, with the relatively limited experimental deployment of IPv6.

VLANs enable administrators to limit the scope of network-wide flooding and broadcast traffic, to reduce network overhead and enhance both privacy and security.

30.5 Limiting the flooding overhead/broadcast

End hosts broadcast dynamic host configuration protocol (DHCP) traffic when joining the LAN, and routinely broadcast address resolution protocol (ARP) requests to learn the MAC addresses of other hosts in the same IP subnet (Jayan and Kshama 2017).

It is not the only consummation of network bandwidth, but also bandwidth and energy resources on the end devices. Switches also flood packets to a destination MAC address without learning how to reach them. This consumes bandwidth resources, particularly if the switches forwarding tables are not big enough to store an entry for each MAC address on the LAN. Administrators often split large networks into multiple VLANs to limit the scope of flooding traffic and broadcast messages. broadcast domains might be small enough to limit the overhead on the switches and the end hosts.

30.5.1 Security and privacy

Flooding traffic and broadcast also increase privacy and security concerns. Sending extreme broadcast traffic is an effective denial-of-service attack on the network. In addition, a malicious host can purposely overload switch forwarding tables by spoofing many source MAC addresses forcing switches to flood legitimate traffic that can simply be monitored by the attacking host. ARP is similarly vulnerable to man-in-the-middle attacks, where a malicious host sends unsolicited ARP responses to impersonate another host on the LAN, thereby intercepting all traffic sent to the target. Network administrators can decrease these risks by constraining which users can belong to the same VLAN.

30.5.2 Benefits of virtual local area network

In networking, a LAN has a single broadcast domain and the traffic from a workstation reaches other workstations on the LAN through the broadcast. This is not desirable as certain classified information can be received by unauthorized parties. Also, if the broadcast is not well contained, it can lead to a collision in the network (Syed *et al* 2014).

Therefore, network administrators normally protect the broadcasts from leaving an enterprise network with the aid of routers.

However, routers usually take more time to process the incoming data compared to switches and are more expensive. The VLAN was developed as an alternative solution to using routers to contain broadcast traffic within a LAN, however, it is also for broadcast filtering, employed routers in the VLAN topologies and also addresses summarization for traffic flow management.

A VLAN is a switched network that is logically segmented based on features such as service requirement, workgroup, and protocol or application requirement rather than on a physical or geographical proximity (Isiaka and Akeem 2015). With the implementation of VLAN, geographically dispersed workstations, servers, and other peripheral devices used by a particular workgroup can be put on the same VLAN and communicate as if they are physically in the same location in the network (Alimi *et al* 2015). This enables the network administrators to manage the network without the need for running new cables or making major changes in the network infrastructure (Isiaka and Akeem 2015). Therefore, the VLAN is addressing the security, flexibility, scalability, and network management issues that are associated with the traditional method, as in figure 30.4.

Security: VLANs provide improved network security. In a virtual local network environment, in multiple broadcast domains, the network administrators

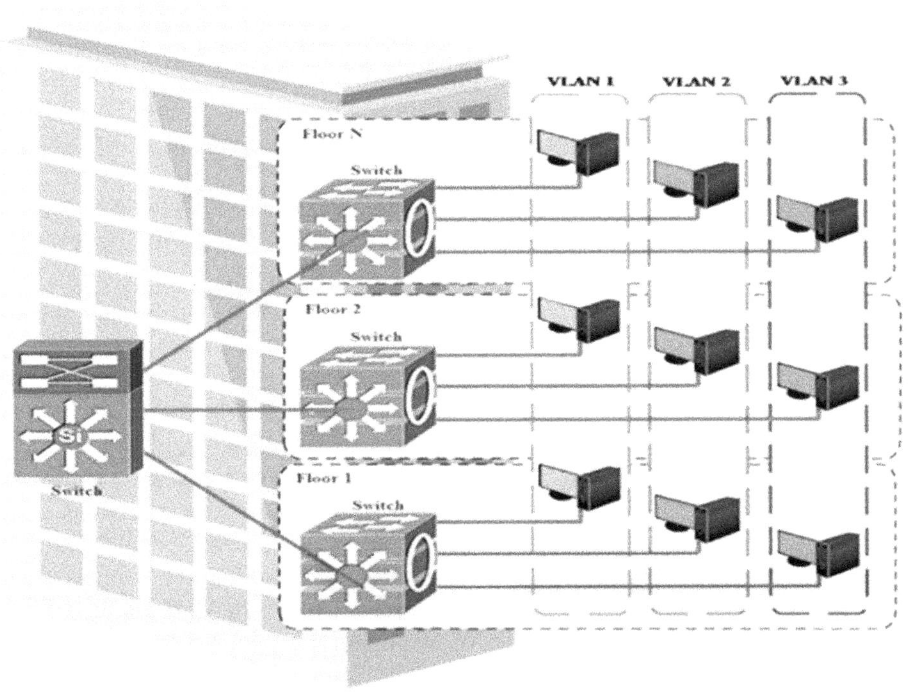

Figure 30.4. VLAN based LAN segmentation. Reprinted with permission from Jon (2018) CC BY-3.0.

have control over each port and user, as in figure 30.4. A malicious attacker can no longer just plug their workstation into any switch port and explore the network.

Creating workgroups: a group of users that need a remarkably high level of security can be put into its own VLAN so that users outside of that VLAN cannot communicate with it. This suggests that in an enterprise each department can be made independent from other departments.

Scalability: network moves, changes, and additions are achieved easily by just configuring a port into the appropriate VLAN and assigning hosts to the same VLAN traffic using a packet sniffer. The network administrator controls each port and all resources VLAN is allowed to use. VLANs help to restrict sensitive traffic originating from an organization department within itself.

Cost-effective: eliminating the need for additional expensive network equipment like switches and routers, can be cost savings to an organization. VLANs can also allow the network to work more efficiently by commanding a better use of bandwidth and resources.

Easy troubleshooting: by grouping the network users and resources into different VLANs, many problems in the network can be eliminated, and it is easy to identify and fix them by tracing which hosts groups belong to.

Integrity: users are logically grouped according to function, VLANs can be considered independent from their geographic or physical locations. Thus, university data can be handled without comprising only to the universities that have branches.

Broadcast control: the management of a broadcast network can be controlled by creating many VLANs, which always increases the number of broadcast domains while decreasing their size.

Benefits of network segmentation: running traditional flat networks is now an aging model and it is an outdated assumption that everything on the inside of an organization's network should be trusted (Julian 2018). By segmenting a network and applying appropriate controls, we can break a network into a multi-layer structure that hinders threat agents or actions from reaching hardened systems and restricts their movement across the network (Fort 2018).

While it should be understood that it is not possible to create the perfect IT network infrastructure defense, reducing the attack surface and eliminating unwanted access to network segments significantly reduces the risk of a system breach. Using the defense-in-depth security practice of network segmentation, an organization's network address space is subdivided into smaller subnets (Olzak 2018). The network can be physically segmented with routers, firewalls, or more commonly, logically separated by VLANs on network switches. These VLAN zones are interconnected with trunk links or switched virtual interfaces between them. There are numerous advantages to implementing this segmented network architecture (Julian 2018).

- This type of segmentation directly decreases the number of systems on the same network segment and reduces the broadcast domain, thus reducing device network processing and malicious reconnaissance. By limiting routed traffic to segments, the overall bandwidth usage in the LAN is reduced.
- The propagation of network worms such as WannaCry and NotPetya over a shared protocol such as SMB is not limited to a flat network as it would be on a segmented network.
- Segmentation aids compliance by separating zones that contain data with similar requirements whilst ensuring that systems holding sensitive data are kept isolated.
- Network segmentation enables segregation of systems by end-user category groups with facilitation of access control policy at the ingress/egress points. This granulation of security policy can be implemented over time with access control lists (ACLs) at the zone gateway or firewalls that control the flow for large segments.
- Further division of server systems, for example, protects against threat actors easily pivoting from one compromised server to another, such as performing the lateral movement with mimikatz pass-the-hash attacks (namely collecting hashed credential data for use on different machines).
- Often network segmentation projects can be run with current network equipment.
- Facilitate the addition of an untrusted VLAN for NAC Policy enforcement. NAC solutions allow network operators to define policies for enforcement, such as the types of computers or roles of users allowed to access areas of the network. This is then enforced using switches, routers, and firewalls. Implementing an untrusted VLAN segment can protect the network from non-compliant and/or unknown systems.

30.6 VLAN architecture

With the creation of VLANs, many problems can be forgotten. to create VLANs, a layer 2 switch is needed that can support such protocol (Agwu *et al* 2015). The misconception of many new people in the networking field that it is a matter of just installing additional software on the clients or switching, to 'enable' VLANs throughout the network, is completely incorrect. Rather, there should be VLAN-enabled switches like cisco catalysts switches for the cisco system. VLANs involve millions of mathematical calculations, they require special hardware which is built into the switch and your switch must therefore support VLANs at the time of purchase, otherwise, you cannot create VLANs on it (Newest *et al* 2015). A switch is a separated network on each VLAN created on it. By default, network broadcasts are filtered from all ports on a switch that are not members of the same VLAN. This is the reason why VLANs are very important in today's large networks where they can help segmentation, and poorly designed firewalls can extremely compound the problem already caused by these broadcast intensive applications (Ojiugwo *et al* 2015). A network design presents a lot of new

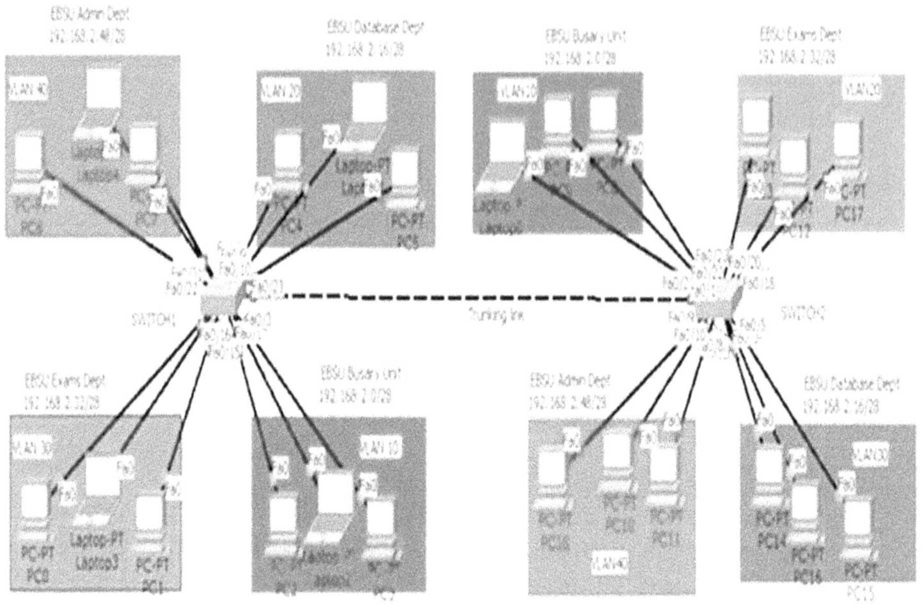

Figure 30.5. VLAN infrastructure.

challenges for administrators by using all these new dimensions of network design, as shown in figure 30.5.

30.7 Target population

The target population is the group of individuals that the intervention intends to conduct research in and draw conclusions from (Louise and Nghiem 2018). The unit of analysis of this research was the staff in the ICT, students, faculty and administration staff. The population of this study comprised 1864 students and staff, two ICT staff were collected on data using structured interview which were network and system administrators and questionnaires were on students and administration and faculty staff on sample size.

30.7.1 Sample size

Sample size is a count the of individual samples or observations in any statistical setting, such as a scientific experiment or a public opinion survey (Jon 2018).

Slovene's formula will be used to determine the minimum sample size of the study of the target population. The sample size will determine by using Slovene's (1960) formula which is as follows:

$n = N/\ 1+(Ne^2)$

n = sample size

N = population size

E = level of significance = $e^2 = 0.05$ $e = (0.05)^{\ 2} = 0.0025$

The sample size from students and staff: it was 1864/1+(1864*0.0025) = 329.

30.7.2 Sample technique

This is a primary concern in statistical sampling, the sample that was obtained from the population represented the same population. This was accomplished by using purposive non-random sampling method.

30.7.3 Data analysis

The choice of qualitative method emphasizes understanding the phenomena and it is verbal more than numerical in data collection generally referring to qualities over quantities. Data collection is based on analysis rather than a statistical form. It is important to remember pre-existing theory, previous empirical research or own expectations that may influence the choice of a qualitative study.

In order to avoid misunderstandings with the analysis of the interview data and questionnaire data the available recordings were wisely recorded into text. The purpose of recording into text minimized interpretation errors and allowed one to conclude afterward. Additionally, the data that was collected from the interviews and questionnaires was also linked in order to make overviews to the body of knowledge to construct theory. The data analysis was an iterative approach, where data collection and analysis occurred simultaneously in order to remain open to all options. This enables suggestions of new questions to ask in the interviews.

30.8 Data presentation, analysis and interpretation of the findings

30.8.1 Introduction

This chapter presents the response rate, demographic characteristics of the respondents, and the objectives results. The data accumulated from the field (questionnaire and structured interview guide) was captured and analyzed using SPSS software, and objective one was to investigate the end-user satisfaction of enterprise network at ULB, a descriptive analysis was conducted and the results were interpreted. In objective two the existing enterprise network was simulated using Reverbed modeler academic edition (OPNET) by measuring key performance indicators simulation. The interview guide was used to identify the drawbacks of the existing enterprise network at ULB in objective three. Objective four was to rectify the drawbacks of the existing enterprise network, VLAN was used to alleviate the end-to-end delay by using VLAN technology to enhance the network performance. In objective five, two different scenarios were presented to observe the performance of enterprise network (LAN) and VLAN networks. The simulation results illustrated that there was more existing traffic without VLAN technology. Therefore, VLANs prohibit the access of the network resources of other departments.

Table 30.1 showed that out of 219 responded questions there were 121 females participated in the respondents and 98 males. This implies that the majority of the respondents were female with 55.3% and males the minority with 44.7%, at ULB the majority of students are female which explains why among the students being corrected on data, the majority of respondents were female.

Table 30.1. Gender for the respondents.

		Frequency	Percent	Valid percent	Cumulative percent
Valid	Male	98	44.7	44.7	44.7
	Female	121	55.3	55.3	100.0
	Total	219	100.0	100.0	

Source: Primary data, 2020.

Table 30.2. What is the end-user role?

		Frequency	Percent	Valid percent	Cumulative percent
Valid	Student	210	95.9	95.9	95.9
	Faculty staff	6	2.7	2.7	98.6
	Administration staff	3	1.4	1.4	100.0
	Total	219	100.0	100.0	

Source: Primary data, 2020.

Table 30.3. How do you feel about the university network speed?

		Frequency	Percent	Valid percent	Cumulative percent
Valid	1–6 months	38	17.4	17.4	17.4
	6–12 months	11	5.0	5.0	22.4
	1–3 years	156	71.2	71.2	93.6
	over 3 years	14	6.4	6.4	100.0
	Total	219	100.0	100.0	

Source: Primary data, 2020.

According to table 30.2 most of the respondents were students (95.9%), followed by faculty staff (2.7%) and lastly administration staff (1.4%).

According to table 30.3 the majority of respondents had spent more than 1 to 3 years (71.2%), the respondents who had spent more than 1 to 6 months were (17.4%) followed by ones who had spent over 3 years (6.4%) and the last were the ones who had been there from 6 to 12 months (5.0%).

30.8.2 Descriptive statistics of the respondents responses

The study used cross-tabulation to identify the end-user satisfaction of campus network at ULB. Through the first objective, a Likert scale was used for statements regarding the satisfaction, availability and usage, as shown in the tables below.

Table 30.3 shows that the majority of respondents were very unsatisfied with the campus network: (65) students, (1) faculty staff and there are no administrative staff, which makes a total of 66 respondents who were very unsatisfied with the university network performance, therefore there are (41) students who were unsatisfied, with (2) faculty staff and (1) administrative staff.

In the case of the network satisfaction the majority of the respondents (110) out of 219 were unhappy with the ULB network performance, (48) students did not say anything about the network, thus, (50) students and (3) faculty staff with (1) administrative staff were satisfied with the network. (6) students were very satisfied and (1) with the campus network, which means that the minority end-users at ULB were happy with the network, with only 61 out of 219 respondents happy with this network at ULB.

This implies that students and staff cannot fully access the resources provided by the university network as they want, due to inconsistent and poor network. This could be caused by the poor network structure of the existing enterprise network of the university which causes more traffic on the LAN which is a single broadcast domain network (table 30.5).

Table 30.4 presents the majority of (83) students with (1) faculty and no administration staff who said that they were never content with the availability of the network at ULB, (49) students and (1) faculty staff member were rarely content with availability. (42) students with (4) faculty staff member and (1) administration staff member said that they were sometimes content with the availability. (24) students were often content with the availability and (12) students with only (1) administration staff member were always content with the availability of the network at ULB. Due to the inconsistent network at ULB end users cannot effectively do their daily activities on the campus LAN. This is probably because for the many end-users who had accessed the network, which is a single broadcast

Table 30.4. How do you feel about the university network speed?

		Very unsatisfied	Unsatisfied	Neutral	Satisfied	Very satisfied	
What is the end-user role?	Student	65	41	48	50	6	210
	Faculty staff	1	2	0	3	0	6
	Administration staff	0	1	0	1	1	3
Total		66	44	48	54	7	219

Source: Primary data, 2020.

Table 30.5. Are you content with the availability of the campus network?

		Never	Rarely	Sometimes	Often	Always	Total
What is the end-user role?	Student	83	49	42	24	12	210
	Faculty staff	1	1	4	0	0	6
	Administration staff	1	0	1	0	1	3
Total		85	50	47	24	13	219

Source: Primary data, 2020.

domain in this case, there occur many collision domains because of much traffic on the network and the network becomes unstable.

Table 30.5 shows that the majority of respondents (73) were using the university network searching to access resources on the network, (55) respondents used the network to download, while (42) respondents were doing everything they wanted with the campus network. Among 219 respondents (28) were uploading while (12) were chatting, and the minority were both (downloading and uploading) (table 30.6). This implies that what the respondent is doing might affect the network speed for others who are accessing the same network, because they are all accessing the single domain network where some make it slow for others depending on what they are doing on the network, which means network performance might be affected. This could be due to the fact that there are no user access policies enforced, which allows users to download or upload personal media files during peak hours, which could cause a lack of bandwidth for a user.

In table 30.7 a large number of the respondents (99) were accessing social media, followed by the respondents (47) most likely to be accessing streaming websites. (26) respondents were accessing torrents and (13) were doing research, with (3) respondents accessing all. Depending on which website the respondents are accessing, this might affect the network speed because there are some hungry websites that can affect the network easily.

In table 30.8 the highest number of respondents (124) were using the network in the morning, while (52) respondents were accessing in the afternoon and the minority of the respondents (43) were using the network in the evening. This shows that the higher the number of respondents accessing the network the more more

Table 30.6. What do you likely do with the campus network?

		Download	Upload	Both	Chat	Search	All	Total
What is the end-user role?	Student	55	28	9	12	70	36	210
	Faculty staff	0	0	0	0	1	5	6
	Administration staff	0	0	0	0	2	1	3
Total		55	28	9	12	73	42	219

Source: Primary data, 2020.

Table 30.7. What are the most likely websites you often access?

		Social media	Torrent	Commercial	Streaming websites	Research	All	
What is the end-user role?	Student	99	26	22	47	13	3	210
	faculty staff	0	0	0	0	4	2	6
	administration staff	0	0	0	0	3	0	3
Total		99	26	22	47	20	5	219

Source: Primary data, 2020.

Table 30.8. At what time do you most likely use the campus network?

		Morning time	Afternoon time	Evening time	Total
What is the end-user role?	Student	121	48	41	210
	Faculty staff	3	2	1	6
	Administration staff	0	2	1	3
Total		124	52	43	219

Source: Primary data, 2020.

Table 30.9. What devices do you mostly use for accessing the campus network?

		Phone	Tablet	Laptop	Campus desktop	Total
What is the end-user role?	Student	118	19	26	47	210
	Faculty staff	1	0	1	4	6
	Administration staff	1	0	1	1	3
Total		120	19	28	52	219

Source: Primary data, 2020.

Table 30.10. What type of campus network do you use to access the network?

		Wireless	Wired	Both	Total
What is the end-user role?	Student	154	45	11	210
	Faculty staff	1	4	1	6
	Administration staff	2	1	0	3
Total		157	50	12	219

traffic there is. At this point, the network can be affected at this time because of the number of respondents accessing the network, therefore, at the time that there are few respondents the network should be less affected than when there were many users on the network. Therefore, the network could be affected when there are a large number of end users on the network at the same time.

In table 30.9 one hundred and twenty (120) respondents were mostly using their phone to access the university network, while fifty two (52) respondents were using a campus desktop, (28) were using laptops and (19) were using tablets. This implies that respondents using phones to access the network could easily affect the network because by leaving the Wi-Fi on they could be connected without even using the phone. This is also a factor that affects the network by having much traffic even when the end user is not using the device.

In table 30.10 the majority of end users (respondents) (157) were using wireless to connect to the network of the university, while (50) were using wired and (12) were on both (wired and wireless). This makes wireless the most common form of network access.

30.9 Objective one: to investigate the end-user satisfaction of the enterprise network at ULB

This study sought to investigate the end-user satisfaction of the enterprise network. Questions on this aspect was asked based on the Likert scale and descriptive statistics on this aspect were established. Results are presented basing on the means and standard deviations of the statement asked in table 30.10.

In order to analyze the satisfaction of the campus network performance, a Likert scale was used to measure the level of end user satisfaction (figure 30.6). Therefore, the mean average is given in the following tables.

Source: Primary data, 2020.

Tables 30.11, 30.12 and figure 30.6 present the responses (from the respondents) on the level of agreement regarding the level of end-user satisfaction. The most frequently occurring value in the data set about the level of end-user satisfaction represented the respondents who were very unsatisfied with the enterprise network performance at ULB that was the model of the end-user satisfaction with the existing network performance without VLAN. The median had a value of two which is in the middle of the ordered data set in the second position which is unsatisfied with the enterprise network. 30.1% were very unsatisfied, 20.1% were unsatisfied, 21.9% were neutral, 24.7% were satisfied and 3.2% were very satisfied.

The central tendency of ordinal data set is where most values lie mode and median are most commonly used to measure the central tendency of ordinal data for measuring the level of end-user satisfaction with the existing enterprise network performance using VLAN implementation. The bar chart in figure 30.6 represents

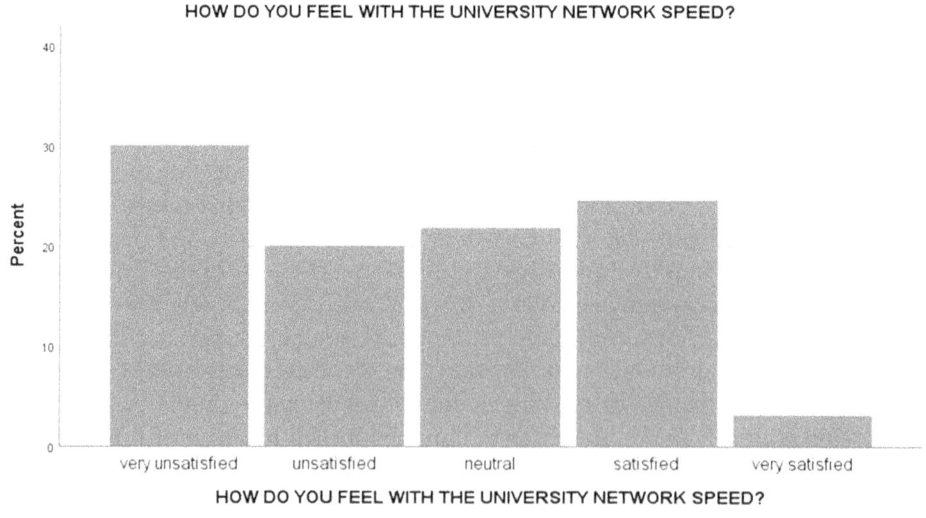

Figure 30.6. Bar chart.

the percentage of how respondents responded to the questionnaire that was given out to find out the level of end-user satisfaction of the existing enterprise network performance.

The highest value was for the respondents who were very unsatisfied with network performance and is easily seen as the highest bar in the chart.

There were 219 respondents to the questionnaire of the objective, about of the level of end-user satisfaction on the enterprise network performance. From the data that was collected at ULB, the majority of respondents were not satisfied with the network, which was very important to implement a VLAN in the existing network.

Hence, there is a need of analyzing the existing enterprise network performance with VLAN implementation.

A response rates study comprised 329 respondents with structured interviews and questionnaires. Out of 324 (100%) questionnaires distributed to students and staff, only 219 (68%) responded sufficiently for meaningful data analysis.

The interviews were only for ICT technical staff; the rest of the respondents (students and other staff) were given questionnaires to offer their opinion on end-user satisfaction. Five respondents consisting of ICT personnel were purposively selected because they were knowledgeable in ICT technical issues from a network perspective. Of these, only two responded; system and network administrators were made available by the ICT directorate for interviews.

30.10 Demographic characteristics of respondents

The demographic data of the respondents were deemed vital for internalizing study information. These are examined and presented in this section.

30.11 Ethical considerations

The entire research was conducted with respect to ethical considerations in research. The research obtained the consent of respondents to participate in the study. Ethics are very significant in the conduct of research and research is always under examination. There is a need to make sure the relevant issues are perceived while doing the research. In general, a high degree of openness regarding the purpose and nature of the research was observed in this study.

30.11.1 The simulation methodology

**

30.12 The three-tiered OPNET hierarchy

Three domains: network, node and process:

- Node model specifies object in network domain;
- Process model specifies object in node domain;
- Process model specifies object in network domain (figure 30.8).

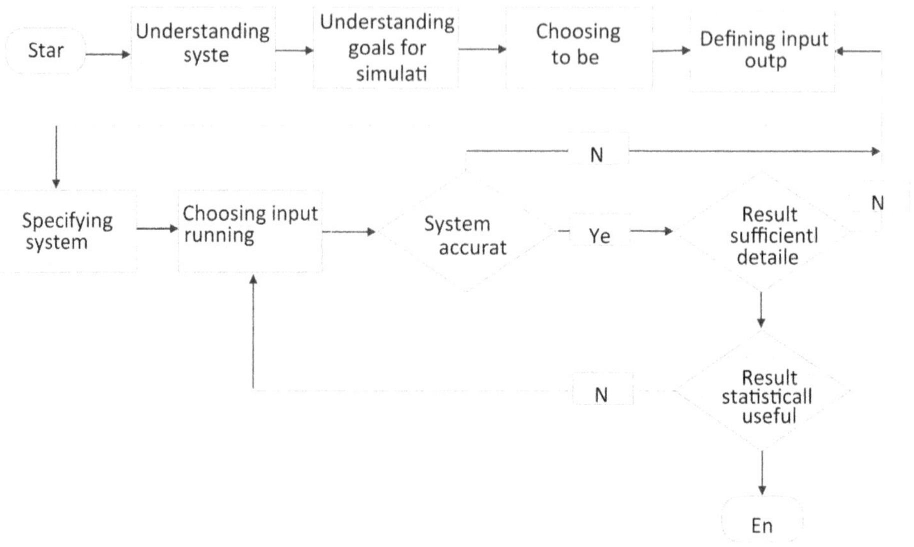

Figure 30.7. The simulation architecture.

30.12.1 Simulation of LAN (NO_VLAN) network or enterprise network

The first scenario was designed to visualize an enterprise network (NO_VLAN). However, in two buildings there were four main switching devices, student switches for student LAN with three labs in building A, and in building B there were department switches for department LAN and lecturers room LAN, administration switch for administration LAN and the servers switch in the server room that also connect all three switches (students, departments and administration LANs). A switch forwards the incoming packet to the output ports based on the destination address. In this scenario, there was a single broadcasting domain network only. Therefore, users were allowed access to confidential servers and shared all resources. All nodes were communicating with each other because there were no restrictions. Therefore, there were many traffic requests on servers.

The enterprise network description for creating a subnetwork with all the requirements:

- The entire network has four subnets—students, departments, and administration;
- Students' subnet, in building A there are three labs connected to a switch (students switch);
- Department's subnet which is in building B, there are two LANs, one is for all student departments and another for lecturers' room, which are all connected to departments switch;
- The administration subnet located in building B is connected to the administration switch;
- All three servers are located in the server room in building B, all those are connected to the server switch which connects all the three subnets and also connects to the firewall to the gateway through the IP Cloud.

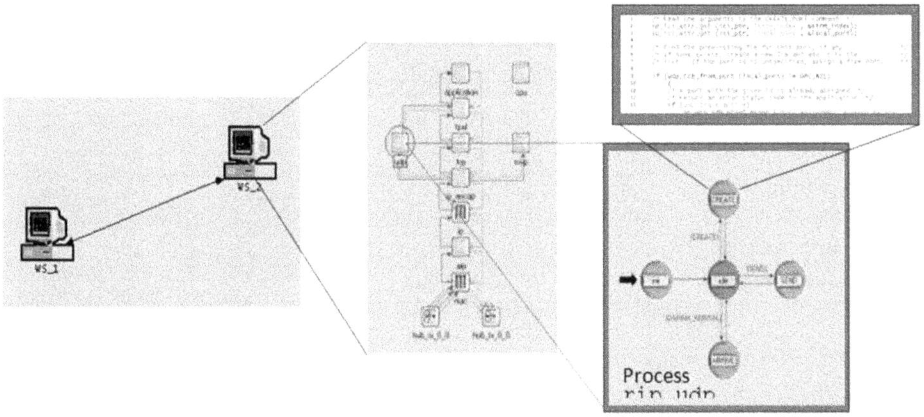

Figure 30.8. The three-tiered OPNET hierarchy.

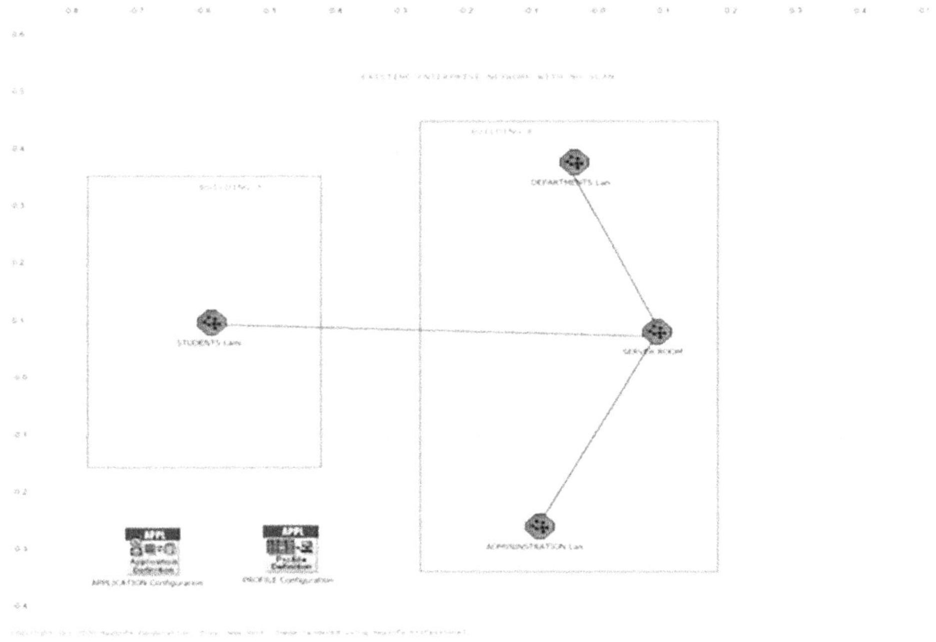

Figure 30.9. The entire ULB enhancement enterprise network with NO_VLAN.

Figure 30.9 shows that there were two buildings A and B, with different hosts classified, but all had a wireless access point as students LAN which had three labs and wireless access point in building A, and departments LAN had two subnet-works, lecturers room LAN and departments LAN, and a wireless access point, administration LAN and wireless access point in building B had one subnet in administration and server room which was in building B had three servers with the server switch which connected all the subnets in building A and B

Table 30.11. Percentage from the responses about the user satisfaction of the campus network speed.

		Frequency	Percent	Valid percent	Cumulative percent
Valid	Very unsatisfied	66	30.1	30.1	30.1
	Unsatisfied	44	20.1	20.1	50.2
	Neutral	48	21.9	21.9	72.1
	Satisfied	54	24.7	24.7	96.8
	Very satisfied	7	3.2	3.2	100.0
	Total	219	100.0	100.0	

Table 30.12. Median, mode and range of responses about the user satisfaction of the campus network.

N		Valid	219
		Missing	0
	Median		2.00
	Mode		1
	Range		4

Source: Primary data, 2020.

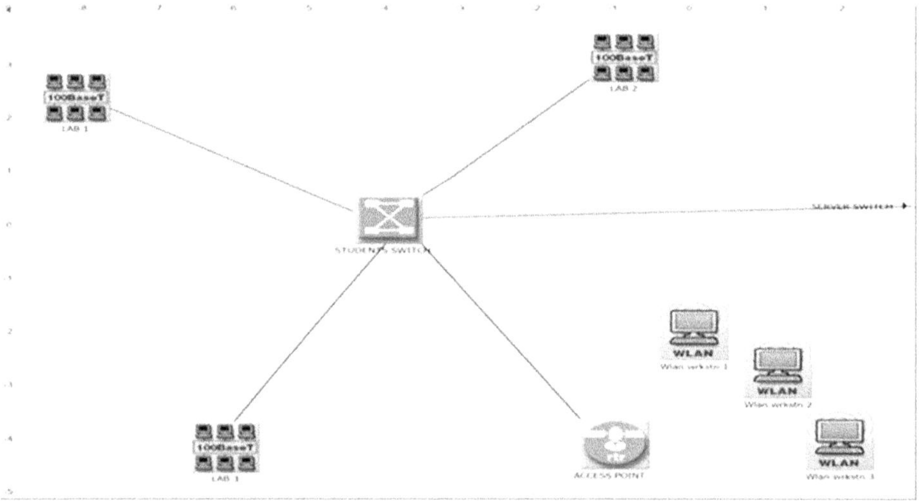

Figure 30.10. Students LAN subnet with NO_VLAN.

Four LANs created in Students LAN -LAB 1, LAB 2, LAB 3 and wireless access point of enterprise network configured the network elements as described in table 30.12 (figure 30.10).

Table 30.13. Students LAN subnet with NO_VLAN network elements.

Students LAN subnet	workstation	Link to SWITCH/WLAN Router	Central node for the LAN
LAB 1	100BaseT LAN	100BaseT	Ethernet64_switch
LAB 2	100BaseT LAN	100BaseT	
LAB 3	100BaseT LAN	100BaseT	
Wireless access point	WLAN workstation Mobile Node	Wireless link	WLAN_ethernet_router

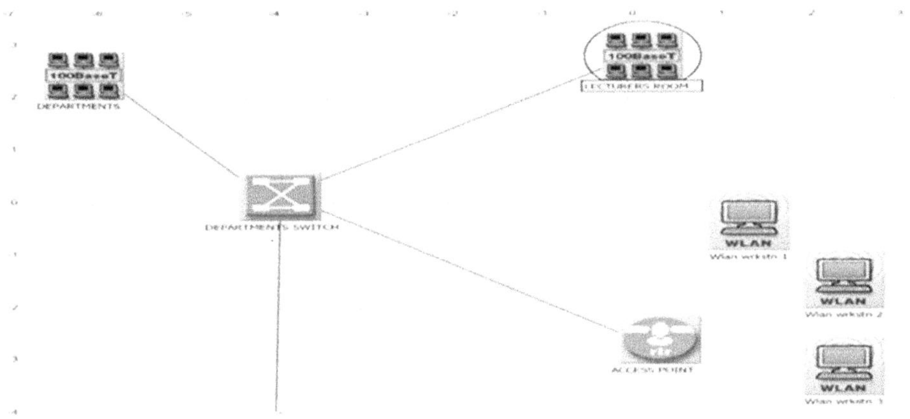

Figure 30.11. Departments LAN subnet with NO_VLAN.

Three LANs were created in Departments LAN subnet—Departments LAN, Lecturers' Room and a wireless access point of enterprise network configured the network elements, as shown in table 30.13 (figure 30.11).

Two LANs were created in Administration LAN subnet—Administration LAN and wireless access point of enterprise network configured the network elements as shown in tables 30.14–30.17 (figure 30.12).

The figures and tables above show the entire enterprise network at ULB. As described above, it had four subnets with four LANs in the subnet of students LAN with three labs and a wireless access point in building A, and three LANs in departments subnet which was departments LAN, lecturers room LAN and wireless access point, in administration LAN subnet had two LANs; both administration and departments subnets are located in building B and in both subnets there were wireless access points. The server room was also located in building B, it had a subnet of three servers (WEB, FILE, and Database) with were connected to the core ethernet64_switch to firewall and gateway connected to an IP cloud. The CISCO router was used to router information for the entire ULB network used to store and forward routing. The router is connected to the firewall and to the IP cloud with the help of a PP28 link.

Table 30.14. Departments LAN subnet with NO_VLAN network elements.

Departments LAN subnet	Workstation	Link to SWITCH/WLAN router	Central node for the LAN
Departments LAN	100BaseT LAN	100BaseT	Ethernet64_switch
Lecturers' room	100BaseT LAN	100BaseT	
Wireless access point	WLAN workstation (Mobile Node)	Wireless link	WLAN_ethernet_router

Table 30.15. Administration Lan subnet with NO_VLAN network elements.

Administration LAN subnet	Workstation	Link to SWITCH/ WLAN router	Central node for the LAN
Administration LAN	100BaseT LAN	100BaseT	Ethernet64_switch
Wireless access point	WLAN workstation (Mobile Node)	Wireless link	WLAN_ethernet_router

Table 30.16. Server Room Lan subnet with NO_VLAN network elements.

Server room subnet	Link to SWITCH/Router/ firewall/ IP cloud		Central node for the LAN	Connected to firewall to gateway to IP cloud
WEB server	100BaseT	PPP_28 K	Ethernet64_switch	
FILE server	100BaseT			
Database server	100BaseT			

Table 30.17. Database entry and query with NO_VLAN global statistic data.

Global statistics	Minimum	Maximum	Average time
1. DB Entry response time (s)	0.048 598 506 2868	0.069 479 173 4469	0.051 194 583 4623
2. DB Query response time (s)	0.044 410 189 2368	0.070 126 919 1489	0.047 952 866 3348
3. DB Entry traffic sent(bytes/s)	0.0	24,035.555 5556	13,164.088 8889
4. DB Query traffic sent(bytes/s)	0.0	24,960	13,182.577 7778
5. DB Entry traffic Received (bytes/s)	0.0	24,035.555 5556	13,164.088 8889
6. DB Query traffic Received(bytes/s)	0.0	24,960	13,182.577 7778

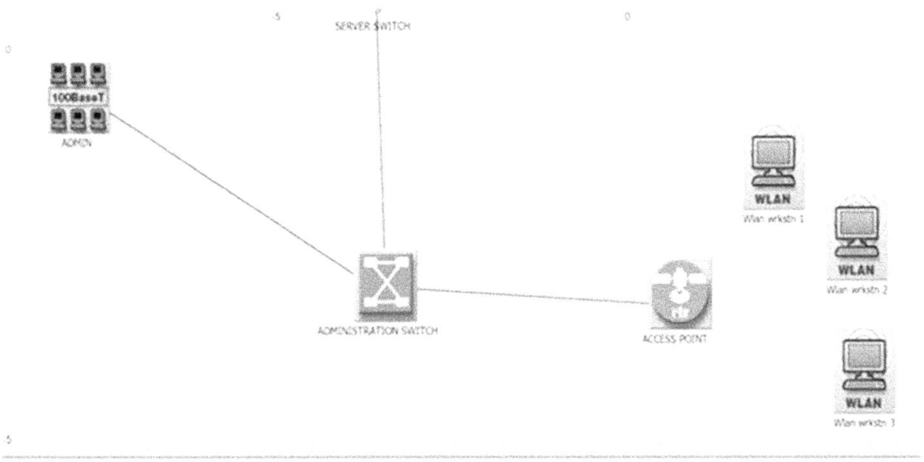

Figure 30.12. Administration LAN with NO_VLAN.

30.13 Application configuration parameters

In the model, every object (application, profile, node, and server) had a different and specific set of parameters. Generally, the application parameter was an application attribute definition that was used to specify the required application among the available applications such as FTP, HTTP, DATABASE. applications attribute that was created to produce the traffic on this ULB network, there were three applications in both scenarios as FTP (File Transfer Protocol), HTTP (Hypertext Transfer Protocol), and DATABASE application. Applications performance was used with both NO_VLAN and VLAN scenarios (figure 30.13).

30.13.1 Profile configuration parameters

Profile parameter was used to create user profiles/clients, these profiles were specified on different nodes/LANs in the network designed to generate the application traffic, profile configuration described as the activity of application for users throughout a time period. Student clients, department clients, and administration clients were used as profiles on HTTP, FTP, DATABASE as applications, they were used in sever (web, file, and database) parameters, respectively, to support the services that are requested by the clients. All profiles were configured to run together to allow more than one application to work at the same time (figure 30.14).

30.13.2 Servers configuration parameters

Server parameters in each server supported service are based on the user profiles that support HTTP, FTP and DATABASE, as in figure 30.16. The profile configuration was defined in clients as students, departments, administration clients, this configuration profiles helps the clients to receive the services from the servers that are being requested by the clients.

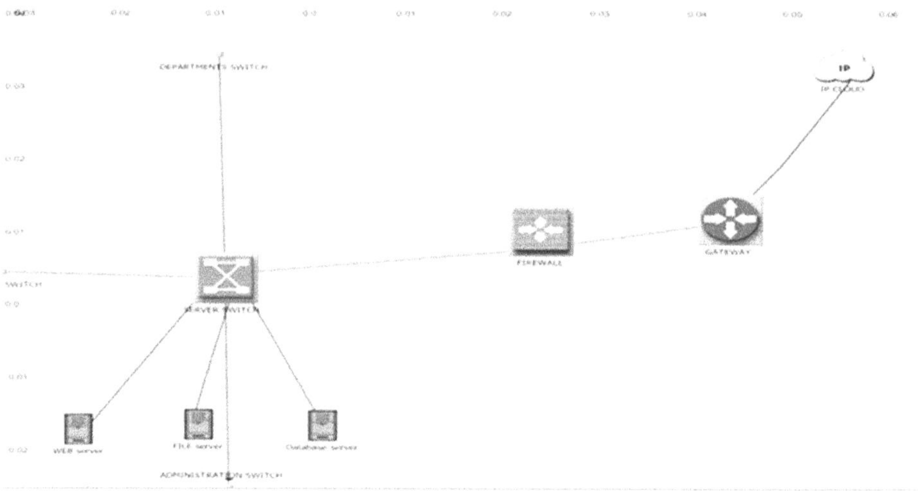

Figure 30.13. Server room with NO_VLAN.

Figure 30.14. Application configuration.

The WEB server was configured to run the HTTP services by right-clicking on the server model and choosing: edit attributes-application supported services-HTTP server. the web server was running both heavy and light web browsing traffic, as illustrated in figure 30.16.

FILE server was configured to run the FTP services by right-clicking on the server model and choosing: edit attributes-application supported services-FTP server. The file server was running both heavy and light file transfer traffic, which is illustrated in figure 30.17.

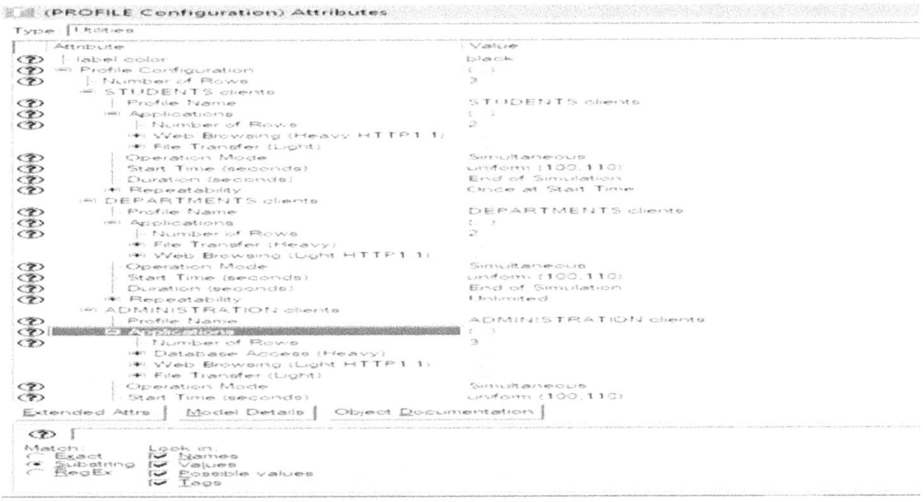

Figure 30.15. Profile configuration.

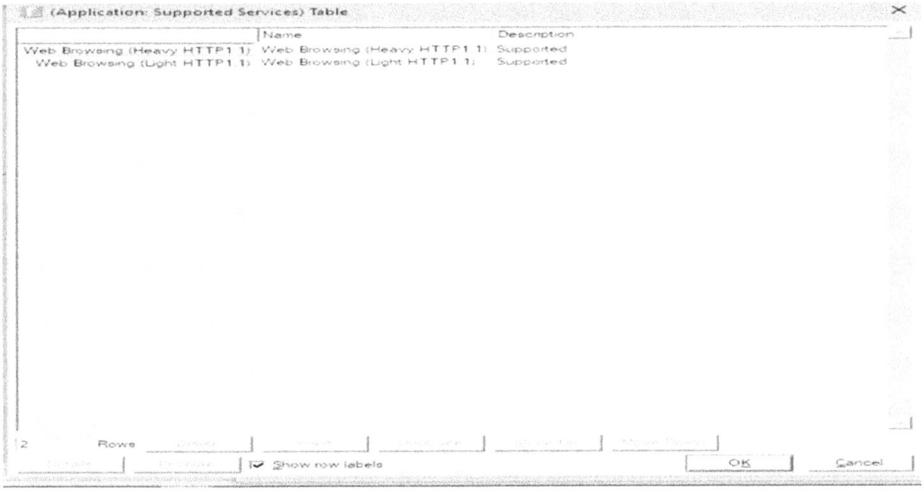

Figure 30.16. Web server configuration.

30.14 Results and graphs

After configuration in the enterprise network with NO_VLAN, the chosen program for the global statistics and individual statistics and ethernet with parameters like traffic sent/received for DATABASE, HTTP, and FTP. Page response time was for HTTP, this is the time the page takes to bring the results for the server; therefore, the download/upload response time was used for FTP and others downloads and response time for the database. The queuing delay for forwarded and received traffic was used for object statistics (figures 30.18 and 30.19)

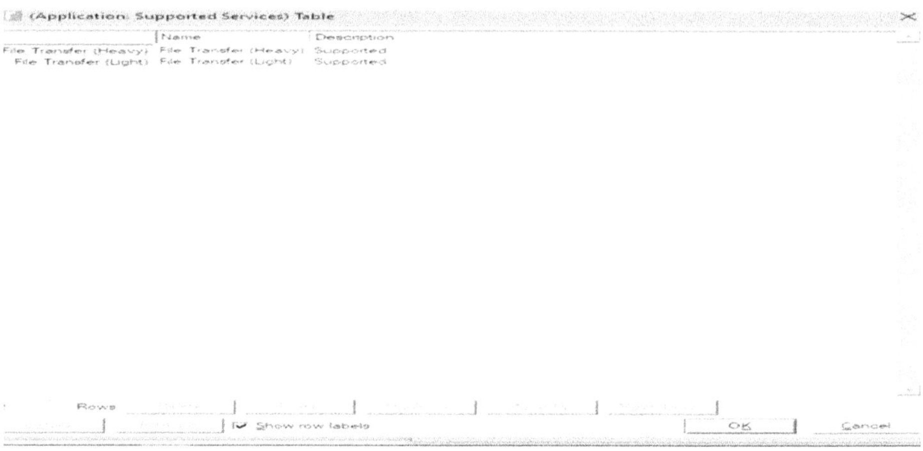

Figure 30.17. File server configuration.

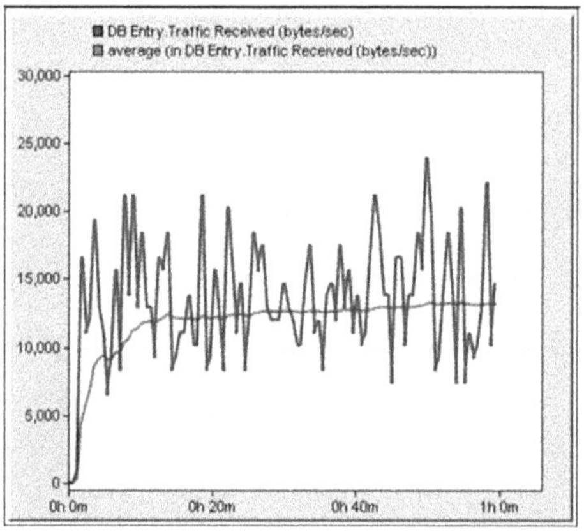

Figure 30.18. Database entry traffic received (bytes/s).

30.15 Global statistics simulation results for enhancement enterprise network with NO_VLAN

Table 30.18 explains the simulation results of global statistics at ULB enterprise network, it shows that traffic sent and received in database query and entry were the same but the response time for database entry and query were different. In database entry response time, the minimum and average time results were higher than database query response time, but maximum database query response time was higher than the entry response time.

Figure 30.20 shows the global statistics simulation results of universities enterprise network performance for all applications on this entire network. the red curve shows average time delay and the blue curve showed the ethernet delay which is measured in second, the ethernet delay showed the performance of the time delay of the global statistics for ULB enterprise network (see table 30.19).

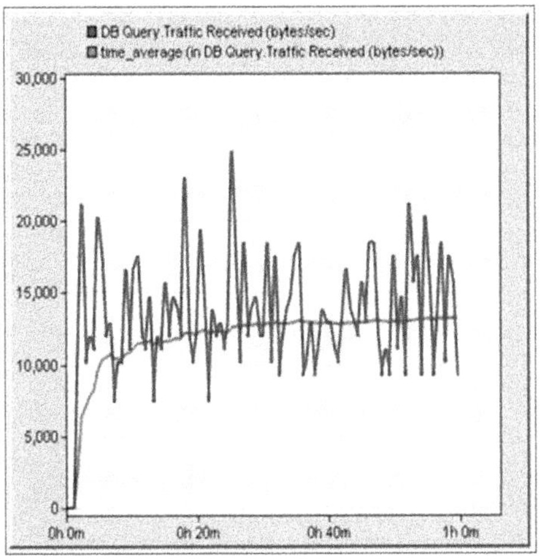

Figure 30.19. Database query traffic received (bytes/s).

Table 30.18. Ethernet delay with NO_VLAN global statistic data.

Global statistics	Minimum	Maximum	Average time
7. Ethernet delay (s)	0.000 606 854 684 32	0.001 036 593 645 66	0.000 850 873 310 869

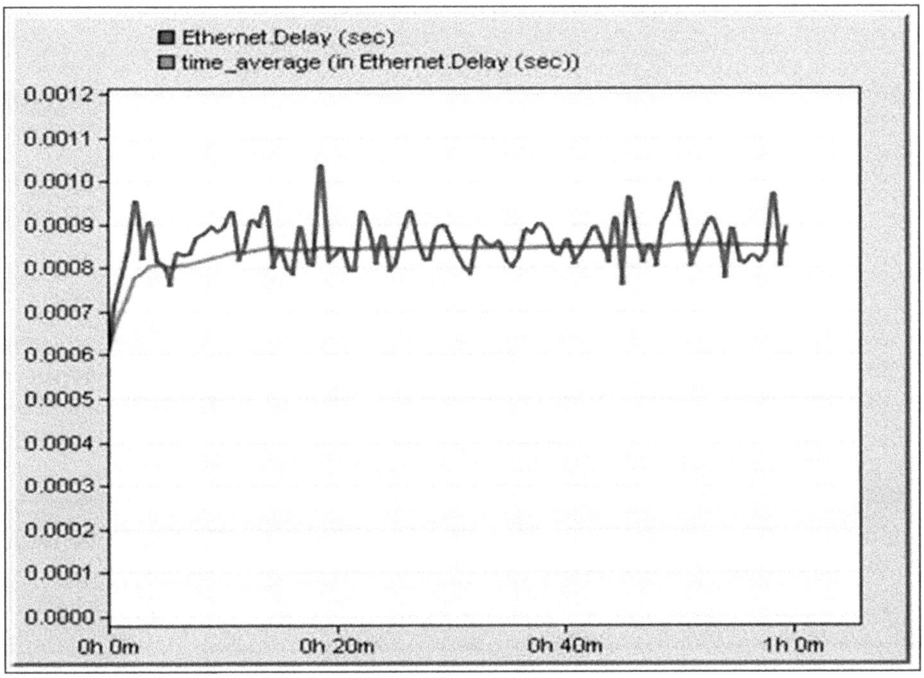

Figure 30.20. Ethernet delay (s).

Table 30.19. Ethernet delay with NO_VLAN global statistic data.

Global statistics	Minimum	Maximum	Average time
7. Ethernet delay (s)	0.000 606 854 684 32	0.001 036 593 645 66	0.000 850 873 310 869

Table 30.20. FTP global statistic data with NO_VLAN.

Global statistics	Minimum	Maximum	Average time
8. FTP traffic sent (bytes/s)	0.0	17 408.222 2222	1280.937 777 78
9. FTP traffic received (bytes/s)	0.0	17 408.222 2222	1280.937 777 78
10. FTP download response time(s)	0.025 378 399 6459	0.270 075 329 652	0.100 908 252 47
11. FTP upload response time(s)	0.030 872 854 9885	0.295 512 491 191	0.165 057 092 442

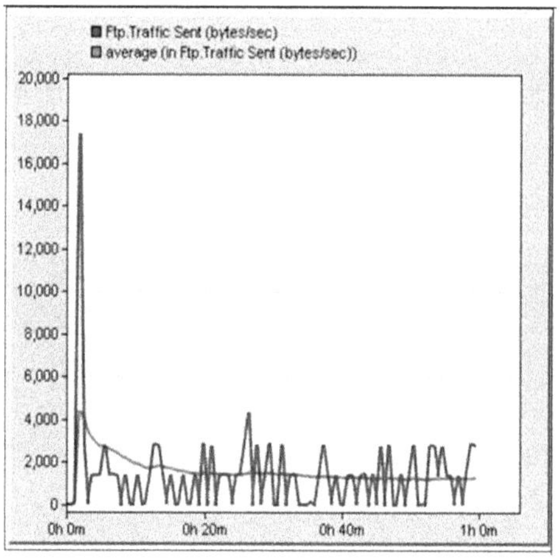

Figure 30.21. FTP traffic sent (bytes/s).

Global statistics results presented in table 30.20 traffic sent and received (bytes/sec) show the same results in the minimum, maximum and average for both sent and received traffic. However, FTP upload response time (s) took higher response time than FTP download response time (see figures 30.21–30.24).

Figures 30.25–30.26 show HTTP page response time (s).

In table 30.21 the global statistics simulation results of the HTTP response time (s) from minimum to maximum has taken almost twice that of the response time (table 30.22). The traffic sent (bytes/s) was higher than traffic received in HTTP and traffic received and sent has almost the same simulation statistic data, they all started form zero (figures 30.27–30.29).

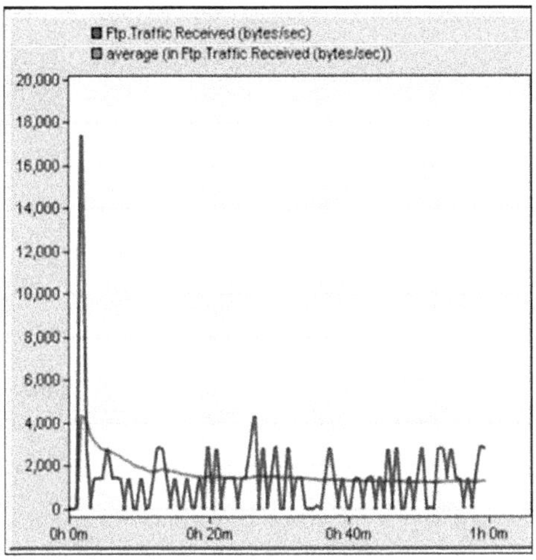

Figure 30.22. FTP traffic received (bytes/s).

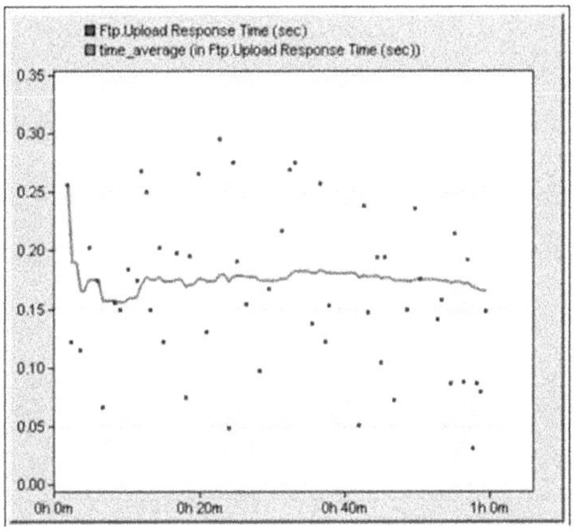

Figure 30.23. FTP upload response time(s).

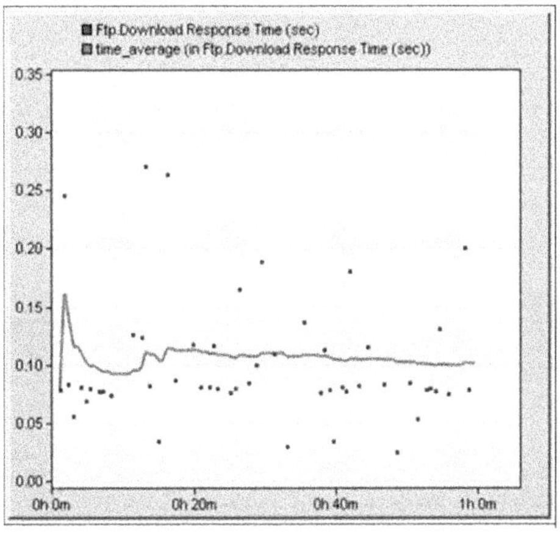

Figure 30.24. FTP download response time (s).

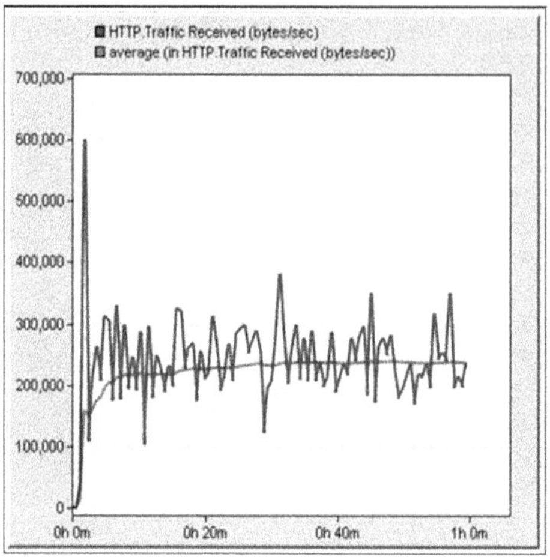

Figure 30.25. HTTP traffic received (bytes/s).

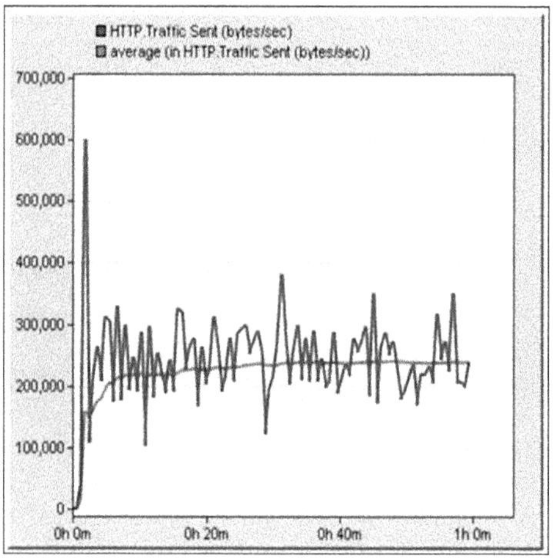

Figure 30.26. HTTP traffic sent (bytes/s).

Table 30.21. HTTP with NO_VLAN global statistics data.

Global statistics	Minimum	Maximum	Average time
12. HTTP page response time(s)	0.299 969 619 033	0.578 671 187 558	0.374 898 135 245
13. HTTP traffic received (bytes/s)	0.0	599 544.472 222 222	237 261.350 555 556
14. HTTP traffic sent (bytes/s)	0.0	599 626.583 333 333	237 663.281 944 444

Table 30.22. Queuing delay → (forwarded traffic) object statistics data.

Object statistics	Minimum	Maximum	Average time
1. Students queuing delay (s)→	0.000 406 039 687 747	0.000 678 808 086 534	0.000 618 223 996 928
2. Departments queuing delay (s)→	0.000 307 575 550 157	0.000 957 151 456 589	0.000 652 453 623 063
3. Administration queuing delay → (s)→	0.000 354 892 995 59	0.001 820 034 520 83	0.001 232 894 517 76

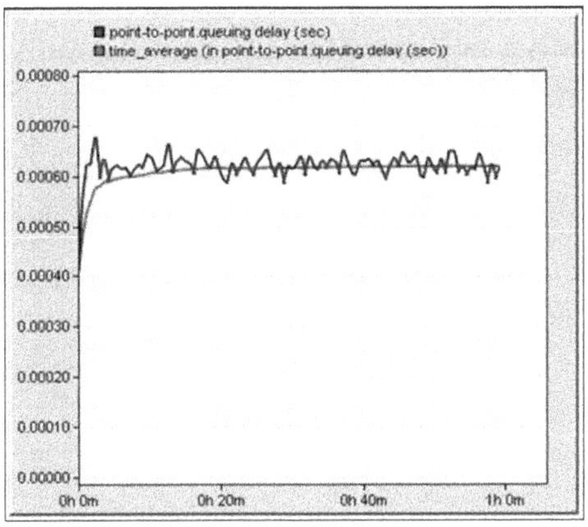

Figure 30.27. Departments queuing delay (s) →

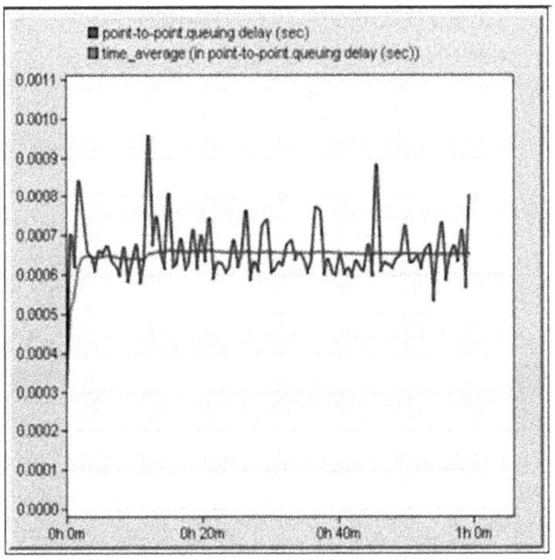

Figure 30.28. Students queuing delay (s) →

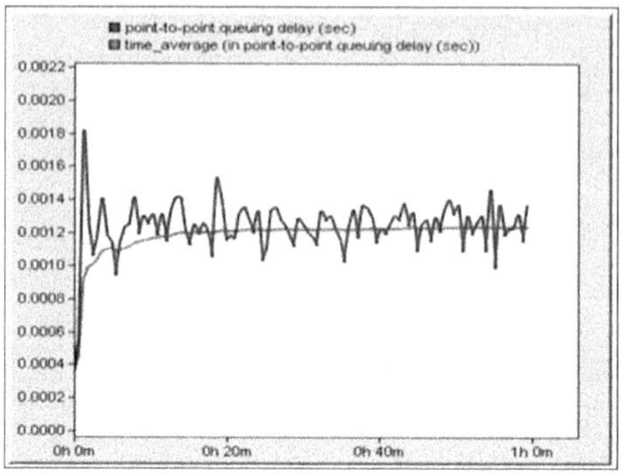

Figure 30.29. Administration queuing delay (s).→

30.16 Object statistics simulation results for enhancement enterprise network with NO_VLAN

In the object statistics for the outgoing data students' queuing delay took minimal time on the entire network followed by administration queuing delay and lastly departments subnetwork queuing delay, however, the administration subnetwork had higher queuing delay, the next is departments subnetwork and students had the lowest queuing delay. Therefore, average queuing delay time is, respectively, as the previews of maximum queuing delay, starting with administration, departments and students queuing delay (figures 30.30–30.32).

For the incoming data for the object statistics data, the departments queuing delay had the highest minimum time, the administration queuing delay came second for the higher number and the last is students queuing delay for incoming or received statistics data. For the maximum, students queuing delay took much time followed by departments queuing delay and the lowest maximum queuing delay was for administration, but the average time object statistics data the students took more average time than the others. The departments had the second highest and the lowest was the administration queuing delay time, when there is more data traffic on maximum object statistics there should be a higher queuing delay.

Simulation of VLAN or enterprise network with VLAN implementation second scenario was designed to visualize the VLAN implementation in the network (figures 30.33–30.37).

The VLAN scenario was the duplication scenario from NO_VLAN scenario (IEEE802.3 protocol) which was added in VLANs (IEEE802.1Q protocol) configuration considered with three logical groups of users, which were found in those two different buildings (A and B). These users (students, departments, and administration) were logically segmented for the purpose of network performance and security reasons by using the IEEE802.1Q VLAN protocol. Therefore, the results visualize the influence of different protocols on traffic sent and received, queuing delay, response time, average time, and application performance. Different VLANs such as students, departments, and administration LAN subnetworks, VLAN scenario has segregated a single large broadcasting domain into three broadcasting domains in

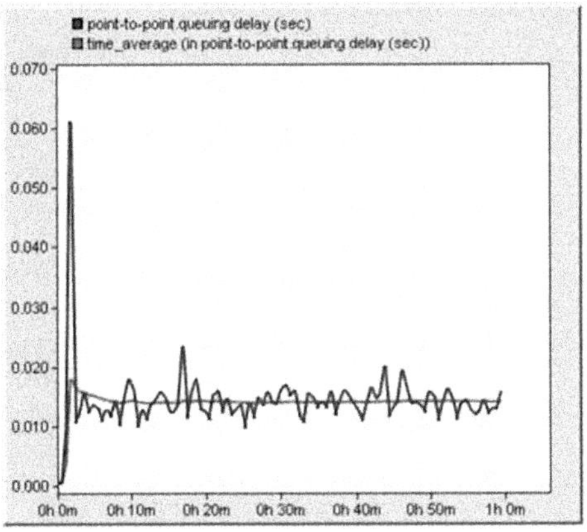

Figure 30.30. Students queuing delay (s). →

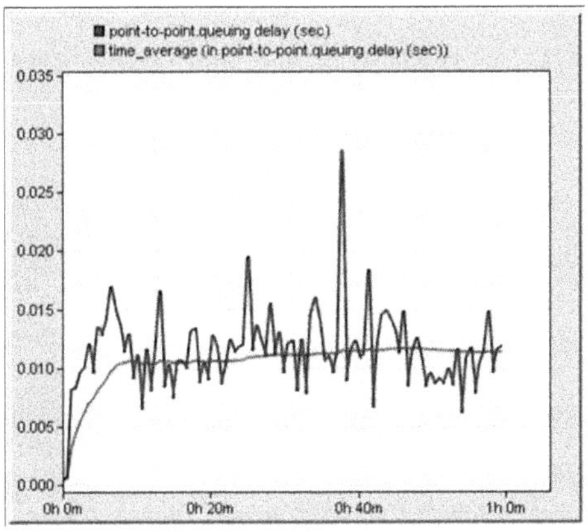

Figure 30.31. Departments queuing delay (s). →

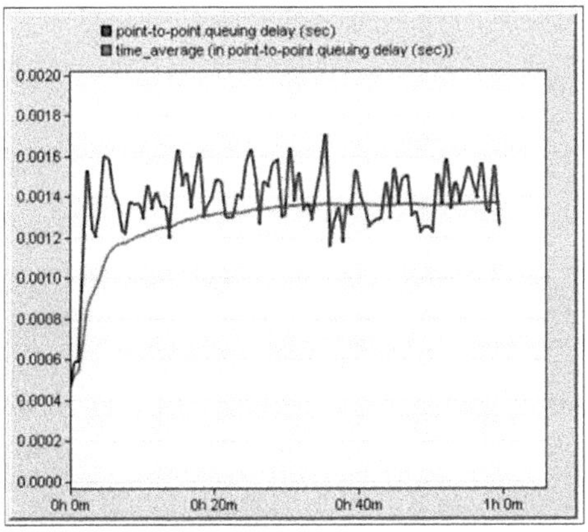

Figure 30.32. Administration queuing delay (s). →

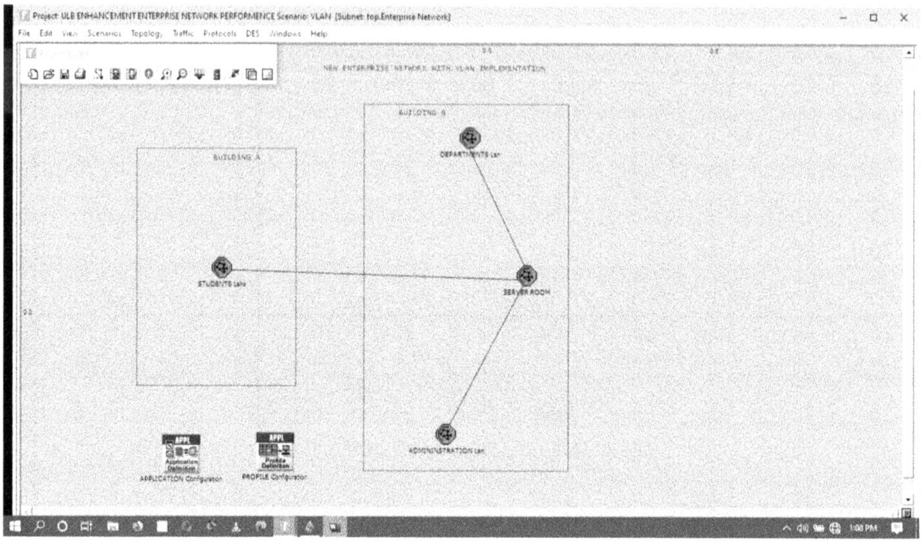

Figure 30.33. New enterprise network with VLAN implementation.

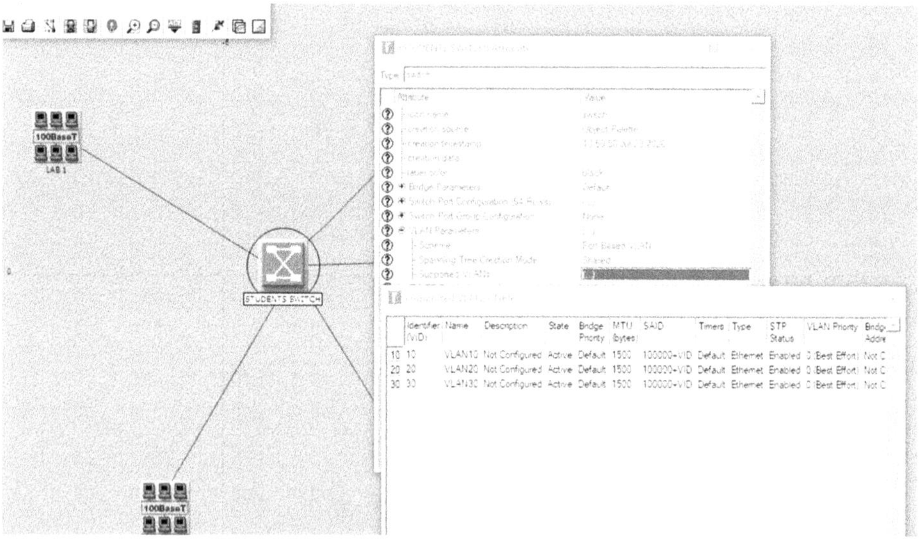

Figure 30.34. Students LANs subnet VLAN configuration.

order to reduce congestion and control traffic sent and received over the network. VLAN network technology was used to improve vulnerability surfaces for hackers by reducing the traffic request to servers, which are defined in the scenario as shown in table 30.23.

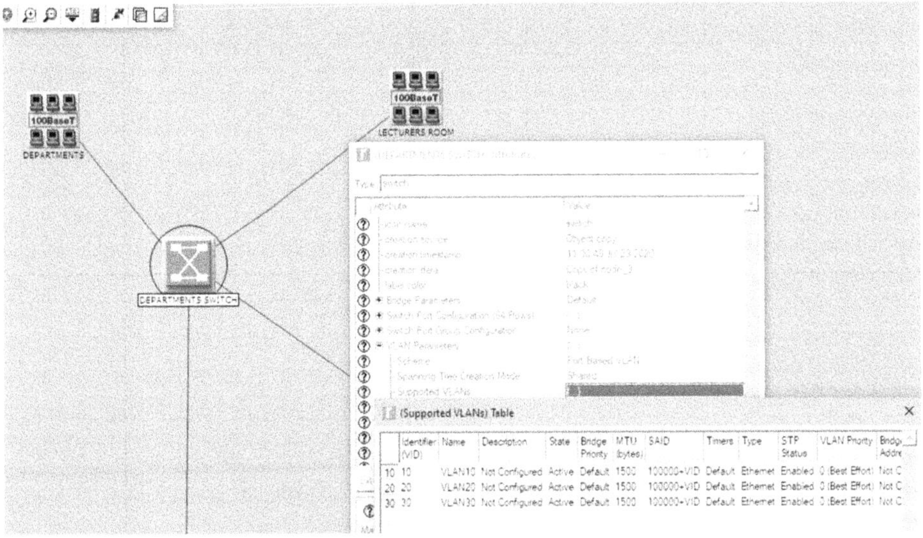

Figure 30.35. Departments LANs subnet VLAN configuration.

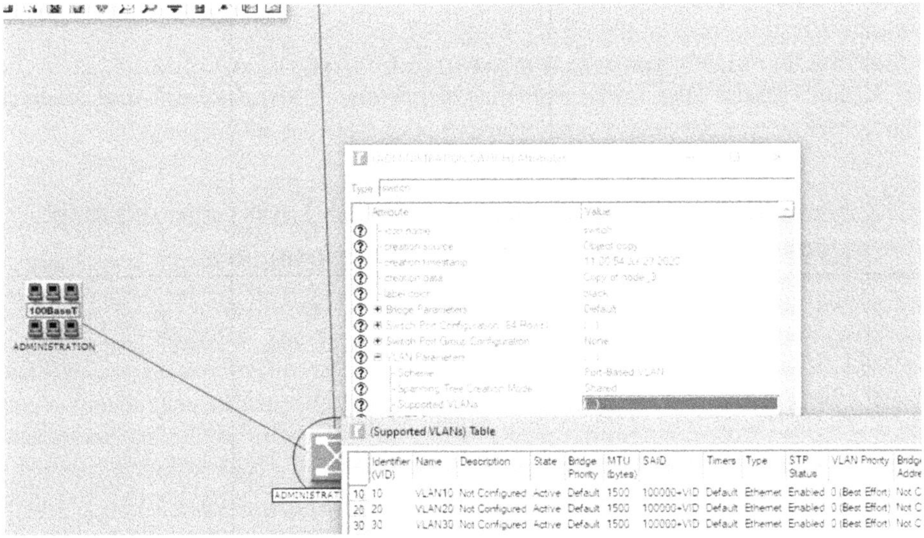

Figure 30.36. Administration LAN subnet VLAN configuration.

30.17 Global statistics simulation results for enhancement enterprise network performance with VLAN

The network was executed using VLAN to rectify the drawbacks for the existing enterprise network performance. The performance parameters that were considered in this research were average delay analysis, traffic sent and received, queuing delay for both (received and forwarded traffic), and application performance. The

Table 30.23. Queuing delay → (received traffic) object statistics data for NO_VLAN

Object statistics	Minimum	Maximum	Average time
4 Students queuing delay (s)→	0.000 415 082 581 562	0.061 160 342 9427	0.014 055 816 9895
5 Departments queuing delay (s)→	0.000 497 926 177 654	0.028 634 165 6191	0.011 311 225 3334
6 Administration queuing delay (s)→	0.000 461 776 637 034	0.001 707 059 051 03	0.001 368 600 7295

Table 30.24. VLANs group configuration.

Subnets	Server	VLAN Name	VLAN ID
Students LANs	Web server	VLAN 10	10
Departments LANs	File server	VLAN 20	20
Administration LAN	Database server	VLAN 30	30

simulation results were obtained by using the riverbed modeler academic Edition 17.5 (OPNET). VLAN scenario was used IEEE802.1Q VLAN protocol (VLAN). The results visualize the impact of VLAN protocol on traffic sent and received, queuing delay, response time, and application performance (table 30.24).

30.18 Simulating and comparing the new (VLAN) and existing (NO_VLAN) enterprise network performance

The simulation and comparison between new (VLAN) and existing (NO_VLAN) enterprise network performance using riverbed modeler academic Edition 17.5 (OPNET) were important in this research to know the different network performance for both scenarios. The VLAN scenario had lower traffic sent and received, queuing delay, download and upload response time than NO_VLAN scenario because VLAN scenario has segmented a single large broadcasting domain into three broadcasting domains in order to reduce and control traffic sent and received of the network. VLAN technology can be used to mitigate vulnerability surfaces for hackers by reducing the traffic request to servers. Moreover, VLAN can achieve power reduction in switches by reducing the required power to forwarding and receiving unnecessary traffic. This has affected the bandwidth utilization. VLAN (red curve in the above figures) had lower values of traffic sent and received than the NO_VLAN curve (blue curve in the above figures) across all nodes/LANs in two buildings. However, the traffic sent and received had reduced with VLAN technology compared with NO_VLAN because the network broadcasting domain has divided into three logical networks in order to distribute users. NO_VLAN scenario has higher traffic than VLAN scenario due to a single broadcast domain

Table 30.25. Server switch VLANs group configuration.

Server	VLAN Name	VLAN ID
Web server	VLAN 10	10
File server	VLAN 20	20
Database server	VLAN 30	30

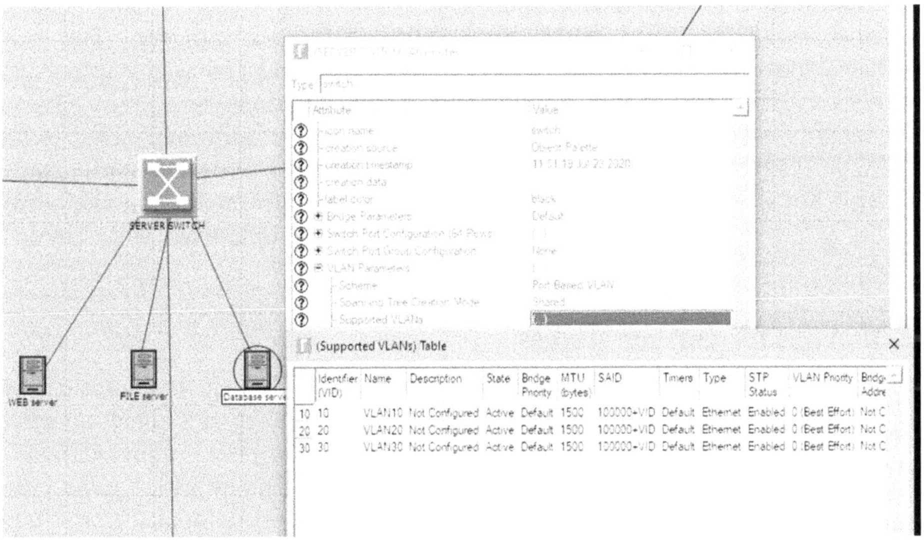

Figure 30.37. Server switch subnet VLAN configuration.

but VLAN works better by segmenting a single large network domain into three broadcast domains to achieve higher utilization of bandwidth with less traffic level (table 30.25).

Thus, the VLAN scenario divides the total users by three; VLAN mitigates the risk of a broadcasting storm by reducing the attacking surface. Under the VLAN scenario, students' LANs were prohibited from accessing the administration LAN. Therefore, a VLAN can reduce the congestion level in networks with more bandwidth utilization.

Queuing delay, traffic sent and received, response time and the average time for links and applications were the key performance indicators. VLAN proved that it has limited access to the confidential server database by controlling traffic and achieving better security and having a lower level of congestion. The comparison results for both existing (NO_VLAN) and new (VLAN) enterprise network performance gave a clear picture about the selection of VLAN techniques for heavy load applications giving a significant result for the performance of the network. This research aimed to enhance existing enterprise network performance by implementing VLAN technology, which has many advantages in terms of power, delay, and bandwidth utilization. It helps also for cost-effectiveness because it does not require a more additional component to improve the performance.

30.19 Conclusion

The study further identified threats, vulnerabilities facing the enterprises and universities and developed the Cyber Security Management and Threat Control (CSRM-TC) model. The model is believed to assist IT officials and policymakers in understanding challenges facing their information assets. This would further assist them to make appropriate decisions when developing cyber security policies, standards, guidelines, and procedures according to best practice. The study concluded that the best way to achieve a substantial and enduring improvement in cyber security is not only by embracing technical solutions but also by ensuring that human management and regulatory directives are addressed. This is true because in general security systems may be upgraded and physical security can be tightened but if employees at different levels are not informed about the correct procedures of handling such systems, those security initiatives will remain a challenge.

30.20 Area for further studies

As supported by the finding of this study, methods used from the literature, and conclusions are drawn, the researcher found it suitable to suggest a follow-up survey to be prepared. This will help for further and appropriate minimization of unnecessary network traffic and make available more bandwidth to the entire university community. It is also proposed that the network administrators should make adequate use of the proxy server and application server. Improvement of enterprise network performance could be made by managing bandwidth utilization with squidGuard.

References

Adeleke D S 2016 Relationship Between Information Literacy and Use of Electronic Information Resources by Postgraduate Students of the University of Ibadan Library Philosophy and Practice

Ajeeli A A and Al-Bastaki Y 2016 Designing a resilient and high performance network *Int. J. Business Data Commu. Netw.* **2** 18

Akpah S, Mireku-Gyimah D and L Aryeh F 2017 Improving the performance of a network by managing the utilisation with squidGuard

Ali A S 2016 Simulation of virtual LANs (VLANs) using OPNET *IOSR J. Electron. Commun. Eng. (IOSR-JECE)* **11** 67–80

Alimi I A, Mufutau A O and Ebinowen T D 2015 Cost-effective and resilient large-sized campus network design *Am. J. Inform. Sci. Comput. Eng.* **1** 21-32

Creswell J W 2007 *Qualitative Inquiry and Research Design: Choosing Among Five Approaches 3rd edn* (Thousand Oaks, CA: Sage)

Creswell J W 2016 *Research design: Qualitative, quantitative, and mixed method approaches* (London: Sage)

Eastlake D, Huawei, Perlman R, Intel Labs and Cisco 2014 Transparent interconnection of lots of links (TRILL) *RFC* **7177** [Online]. Available

Distribution of Network Services *Int. J. Science and Research (IJSR)* 2608–15

Dhurgham A J-K 2018 Improving LAN performance based on IEEE802.1Q VLAN switching techniques *J. Uni. Babylon* **26** 286–97

Fancy C and Mishal Mohammed Thanveer L 2017 An evaluation of alternative protocols-based virtual private LAN service (VPLS) *Int. Conference on IoT and Application (ICIOT)* (Nagapattinam, India: IEEE) 1–6 pp

Fort J 2018 Cyberpedia https://www.paloaltonetworks.com/solutions/initiatives/network-segmentation

Grandhi S A 2014 Method and system for improving responsiveness in exchanging frames in a wireless local area network *U.S. Patent* 8,830,846

Gyan P P and Sadhana P 2013 Virtual local area network (VLAN) *Int. J. Sci. Res. Eng. Technol. (IJSRET)* 006-010

Gyan and Sadhana 2018 *Virtual Local Area Network (VLAN).* greater noida: Int. J. Scientific Research Engineering and Technology (IJSRET). Retrieved from www.ijsret.org

Hameed A and A N 2015 Finding efficient VLAN topology for better broadcast containment *Int. Conf. on the Network of the Future* 1-6

Hameed A and Mian A N 2015 Finding efficient VLAN topology for better broadcast containment *Int. Conf. on the Network of the Future* 1–6

Hameed A and Mian A N 2012 Finding efficient VLAN topology for better broadcast containment *Third Int. Conf. on The Network of the Future (NOF), Gammarth, Tunisia, IEEEpp* 1–6

IEEE Computer Society 2012 Media Access Control (MAC) Bridges and Virtual Bridged Local Area Networks–Amendment 20: Shortest Path Bridging IEEE Std. 802.1aq. Institute of Electrical and Electronics Engineers

IEEE Computer Society 2014 IEEE Standard for Local and metropolitan area networks–Bridges and Bridged Networks. IEEE Std. Std 802.1Q-2014 (Revision of IEEE Std 802.1Q-2011). Institute of Electrical and Electronics EngineersIEEE Standard for Local and metropolitan area networks–Bridges and Bridged Networks. IEEE Std. Std 802.1Q- (Revision of IEEE Std 802.1Q-2011). Institute of Electrical and Electronics Engineers2014

Inamdar M S and Tekeoglu A 2018 Security analysis of open source network access control in virtual networks *pp32nd Int. Conf. on Advanced Information Networking and Alications Workshops (WAINA)pp (Krakow, Poland, IEEE)* 475–80

Isiaka A A and Akeem O M 2015 Enhancement of network performance of an enterprises network with VLAN *Am. J. Mob. Syst.* 82–93

Jasani H and Kulgachev V 2010 802.11 networks performance evaluation using OPNET *ACM Conf. on Information technology education (SIGITE '10)* 149–52

Jayan I and Kshama S B 2017 Study on virtual lan usage in campus networks *Int. J. Res. Comput. Inform.* 8–12

Jon Z 2018 What is the meaning of sample size? https://sciencing.com/meaning-sample-size-5988804.html

Julian F 2018 Jisc community *The advantages of network segmentation*

Kezar A 2014 Higher education change and social networks: a review of research *J. Higher Educ.* **85** 91–125

Kodama S, Nakagawa R, Tanouchi T and Kameyama S 2016 Management system by using embedded packet for hierarchical local area network *IEEE 7th Annual Ubiquitous Computing, Electronics and Mobile Communication Conf.* (New York: IEEE) 1–4

Louise B and Nghiem S 2018 Cost-effectiveness *Mechanical Circulatory and Respiratory Support*

Martinez Rivera D 2015 *Between theory and practice: the importance of ICT in Higher Education as a tool for collaborative learning* (London: Procedia-Social and Behavioral Sciences)

Minlan Y, Rexford J, Xin S, Sanjay R and Fe N 2011 A survey of virtual LAN usage in campus networks *IEEE Commu. Magazine* 98–103

Mohamed E M 2008 *Factors Affecting LAN Performance*

Munam A S, Khurram S and Carsten M 2016 Network performance optimization: a case study of enterprise network simulated in OPNET *2011 Frontiers of Information Technology* 57–62

Neema-Abooki P A-A 2015 Usability of computers in teaching and learning at tertiary-level institutions in Uganda *African J. Teach. Educ.* **4** 1

Northforge Innovations 2015 *OPNET Modeler (currently, Riverbed Modeler).* Retrieved 2019, from https://gonorthforge.com/opnet-modeler-currently-riverbed-modeler/

Odi A C *et al* 2015 The proposed roles of VLAN and inter-VLAN routing in effective distribution of network services *Int. J. Sci. Res. (IJSR)* **4** 2608–15

Olzak T 2018 *infosec* Retrieved from infosecinstitute.com https://resources.infosecinstitute.com/vlan-network-chapter-5/

Orike K U 2017 *Competency of Business Education Students in Information Communication Technology (ICT) for Learning in Tertiary Institutions in Rivers State*

Penard T P 2015 Internet adoption and usage patterns in Africa: evidence from Cameroon. technology in society *Technol. Soc.* **42** 71–80

Perlman R, Labs I, Eastlake D and Cisco 2011 Routing bridges (RBridges): base protocol specification *RFC* 6325

Perlman R and Touch J May 2009 Transparent Interconnection of lots of links (TRILL): problem and applicability statement *RFC* **5556**

Rawat D B 2016 Recent advances on software defined wireless networking *SoutheastCon: IEEE*

Rik F 2014 *rikfarrow.com.* Retrieved from VLAN INSECURITY" http://rikfarrow.com/Network/net0103.html

Saul M 2018 *Questionnaire.* simplypsychology. Retrieved from https://www.simplypsychology.org/questionnaires.html

Saunders M, Lewis P and Thornhill A 2015 *Research Methods for Business Students* (New York: Pearson)

Sehgal U, Anu and Prity. 2012 Virtual local area networks technologies implementation and developments in last few years classified by port, MAC address and LAN based protocol *Int. J. Adv. Eng. Res.* 82-93

Sekaran U and Bougie R 2010 *Research Methods for Business: A Skill-building Approach 5th edn* (Haddington: Wiley)

Smith A and Bluck C 2010 Multiuser collaborative practical learning using packet tracer *Sixth International Conference on Networking and Services (Cancun)* (Piscataway, NJ: IEEE) 356–62

Syed Z, Joshi S, Vikram R R and Kuriakose J 2014 A novel approach to naval architecture using 1G VLAN with RSTP *11th Int. Conf. on Wireless and Optical Commu. Networks* 1-5

Xinzhan L and Chuanqing C 2009 Discuss on VLAN stacking in packet network *Int. Symposium on Intelligent Ubiquitous Computing and Education (Chengdu)* (Piscataway, NJ: IEEE) 389–92

Zichao L, Ziwei H, Geng Z and Yan M 2014 Ethernet topology discovery for virtual local area networks with incomplete information *4th IEEE Int. Conference on Network Infrastructure and Digital Content (Beijing)* (Piscataway, NJ: IEEE) 252–6

IOP Publishing

Human-Assisted Intelligent Computing
Modeling, simulations and applications
Mukhdeep Singh Manshahia, Igor S Litvinchev, Gerhard-Wilhelm Weber, J Joshua Thomas and Pandian Vasant

Chapter 31

Artificial intelligence-based garbage monitoring system for garbage management using integrated sensors

C Gomathi, A Adaikalam and T Kavitha

Garbage management is one of the crucial mechanisms in real-world scenarios. The major issue of garbage management remains that garbage containers in public places overflow and cause difficulties in handling the garbage. Garbage overflow can spread harmful diseases such as dengue fever, pneumonia, etc. It can be avoided through the proposed garbage monitoring system. An objective of this investigation is to advance a garbage monitoring system for proper garbage management. The proposed method detects the range (low, medium, high) of the garbage filling a refuse container with the support of an ultrasonic sensor and sends an alert message to the authorities through a web service. The following equipment is integrated into the proposed system: 1) IR (infrared) sensor to identify the dry and wet garbage; 2) biosensor to detect hazardous gas; 3) LED (light emitting diode) indicates whether harmful disease can spread to the environment or not. After receiving notification through the web application, the authorities will then make a decision according to the harmfulness of the garbage.

The goal of this work is to avoid harmful effects and clean the city to develop a clean environment. The artificial intelligence based garbage monitoring system detects harmful diseases in wet garbage or dry garbage using a fuzzy inference system with fuzzy rules.

31.1 Introduction

Internet of Things (IoT) stands as a trending technology in many fields exclusively in industries like production or manufacturing, automation, healthcare and transport etc. Through artificial intelligence many developments have been proposed, especially in garbage monitoring systems.

doi:10.1088/978-0-7503-4801-0ch31

In recent years, garbage handling has been difficult in many environments because different procedures and strategies are applied in various places to solve the problem. Garbage management is the process of garbage collection, garbage transport, clearance, managing different types of material like wet, dry, medical waste, recycling and non-recycling waste etc, and monitoring of garbage. Most of the garbage management procedures are carried out in a public or semi-public place. This usually concerns garbage management organizational members, supervisor(s) of that organization, other stakeholders and also volunteers from the public.

Some locations have the least possible volume for garbage assimilation, hence this threshold volume may be exceeded and it creates pressure on managing the large capacity of garbage and it can cause environmental pollution [1]. Moreover, when there are dreadful conditions for managing the garbage, authorities will decrease their burden to handle harmful garbage through the proposed work.

Garbage contains unwanted materials discarded in public places, schools etc. Garbage can spread various diseases such as dengue fever, pneumonia, etc, which are important to avoid to maintain public hygiene, and health. The investigated results are connected with a smart garbage monitoring system. This study will help to improve an artificial intelligence-based garbage monitoring system using sensors for proper garbage management. In this system, the range (low, medium, high) of garbage in a dustbin is detected with the help of ultrasonic sensors that send the sensed information messages to the authorities concerned via a web server, and another method is by using proximity sensors which detect dry garbage and moisture sensors to detect wet garbage. Daily garbage increase can overflow (figure 31.1), affecting human beings, so this work can predict to what extent harmful diseases might spread to human beings. It will keep our environment green and also it can support the Indian national scheme called the Swatch Bharat Mission.

31.1.1 Working principle

The hardware components of such wireless sensors as ultrasonic sensors, biosensors, IR sensors, LED monitors and microcontrollers must be properly connected and

Figure 31.1. Overflowing garbage in a public place.

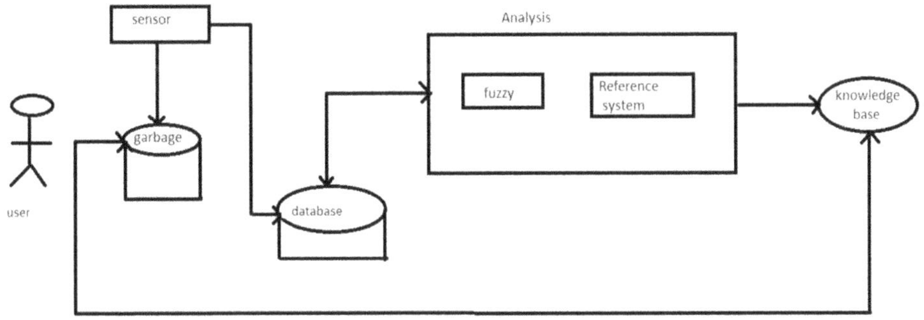

Figure 31.2. Block diagram of the garbage monitoring system.

one must ensure that the SIM card is placed correctly in the GSM module. A block diagram of a garbage monitoring system is shown in figure 31.2, and illustrates the working principle of the proposed system.

Smart garbage management is an idea where the end user can monitor and control a lot of issues that expose society to pollution and disease. It is strongly compatible with the concept of smart cities. Garbage monitoring management consists of:

1. Providing intelligent technology for garbage systems;
2. Avoiding human involvement;
3. Reducing human time and energy;
4. Resulting in a healthy and garbage controlled environment.

31.2 Related work

In many urban areas, the garbage management and monitoring method has been feasibly and successfully implemented. Many suggestions are executed and some of the suggested methods are authoritatively represented. Therefore, research article surveys have been done that incorporate adequate knowledge of among various garbage administration systems in urban areas.

In [2], the suggested system was powered by a solar cell and battery and also they used organic LED screens to present the status of the garbage collected range in the dustbin. The authors proposed a system that detects the garbage range continuously and sends that information to the corresponding authorities through web pages and mobile applications. The ultrasonic sensors are used to detect the level of garbage in the garbage bin. This will support efforts to keep our environment clean. This article adopts a GPS (global positioning service) link that will assist in finding the shortest path of that garbage bin.

In [3], the authors tried to reduce the unhealthy environment using the ESP8266 version of firmware. They found the level of a garbage bin through the ESP8266 firmware. Garbage is added to the garbage container/bin and the filled notification is sent to a particular control room. To identify [4] the status and to get more valuable output from the bin, ultrasonic sensors and other types of sensors are used. The garbage monitoring system module sends an SMS (smart message service) using an Arduino Uno which controls the system operation. It sends notification messages to the authorities concerned via SMS when the garbage is full or almost full so the garbage can be collected immediately. Also, the authors recommended adding a camera to the system to capture the image of the surroundings where people try to drop garbage outside the bin.

The authors of [5], proposed improving the garbage monitoring system using wireless sensors. This survey article is related to a 'Smart garbage monitoring system using Internet of Things (IoT)'. Using IoT helps us eradicate the garbage disposal problem, using microcontrollers, and transceivers for digital communication that will be able to communicate with one another. One of the approaches is by using ultrasonic sensors that are used to detect the level of the garbage in the bin, and another is by using biosensors that detect hazardous gases. Cities will become cleaner and garbage collectors will be many fewer, and this will keep our environment green and the can support the Swatch Bharat Mission. Therefore, in future work an android application will be developed via which the user can find a nearby bin in which to discard the garbage.

In [6], the authors used an Arduino based system consisting of an ultrasonic sensor to detect the garbage level along with a central system showing the current status of garbage, and a web browser HTML page, and a Wi-Fi module has been utilized to prove the result. A system proposed by [7] has an efficient method that can support sorting dry and wet garbage using moisturized sensors and ultrasonic sensors to detect the garbage bin level. The end user can also receive notifications through the mobile application.

An invention presented in [8] provides a smart garbage monitoring system that enables a cleaner, healthier, safer and disease-free environment. In the future, they will investigate how diseases are caused through a genetic algorithm. Cities develop rough algorithms for minimizing the cost of various municipal services [9–11] such as collecting trash. Rough algorithms can easily find the minimum cost. Various researchers adopt this algorithm for different feature extraction.

The authors of [12–14] developed a smart garbage monitoring system using IoT that has been used to avoid accumulation of garbage on the roadside, they tried to prevent the wide spread of many diseases. In that proposed system, the authors used different sensors, but these will not provide information about the level (low, medium, or high) in a garbage container.

31.3 Workflow

Figure 31.3 shows the workflow of the proposed work. The status of the bin is sensed by the ultrasonic sensor. The sensed data is checked through the coding and simultaneously it sends the status to the authorities. If the condition is true the server sends the message to the corresponding authorities and the subsequent process is carried out by supporting members. The following requirement analysis (table 31.1) is done for real-time implementation.

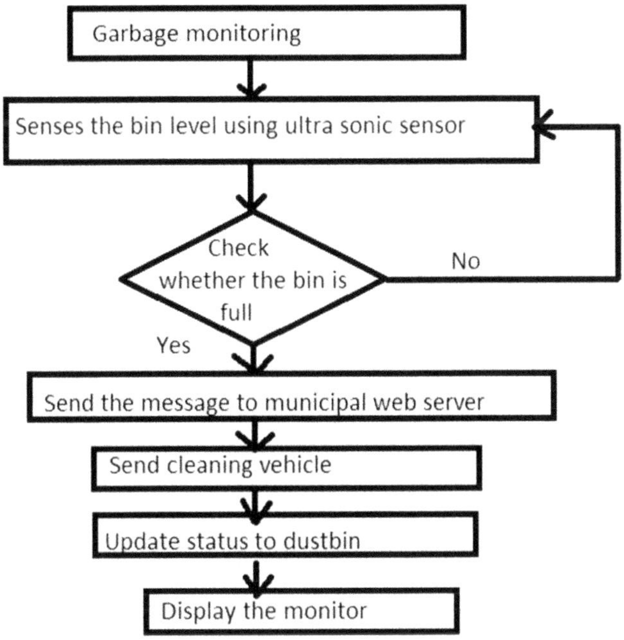

Figure 31.3. Garbage monitoring system for garbage management using integrated sensors.

Table 31.1. Requirement specification.

S. No.	Hardware name	Uses	Working principle
1	Ultrasonic sensor	It is used to detect the garbage level in garbage bin.	The modules consist of ultrasonic transmit, receivers and control units. This sensor is used to illustrate the most complex activities. For example, to find a crowded location with maximum accuracy.
2	Arduino Uno	Utilized as one of the mandatory equipment for IoT based tasks.	The working principle is very simple, called 'Plug and play', that is, an SD card inserted on the board acts as the drive for the Arduino. It is driven by Universal Serial Bus (USB) video output, and can be linked with a traditional TV, or digital monitor to view the results or output.

(*Continued*)

Table 31.1. (*Continued*)

S. No.	Hardware name	Uses	Working principle
3	Power supply	Used to provide a supply to the required circuit.	12 V power supply is required. It produces DC voltage to the sectors on board. 3.3 V is required for LPC 2138 and 4.2 V required for Wi-Fi. To transfer digital data, 5 V is required from the control unit. A solar panel acts as a power bank for the entire unit.
4	GSM (global system for mobile communications)	GSM modem for sending data and showing the status to the user via SMS. Here SMS is related to the garbage container.	GSM is used to transmit the audio message and data at a range of frequencies: 850 MHz, 900 MHz, 1800 MHz and 1900 MHz.
5	GPRS (general packet radio service is a packet-switching) technology	GPRS is used to detect the location of the garbage container.	GPRS permits the sensed data to be stored in the form of packets. The stored data is transmitted across the mobile network.
6	LCD Display	Used to monitor the output screen	LCD screen mechanism is blocking light rather than emitting light.
7	Mobile app	Used to send a notification to the municipal web server	It can get information from the Arduino and send it as a notification to the municipal web server.

31.3.1 Architecture

Figure 31.4 represents the working principle of the garbage monitoring system. It clearly illustrates the sensing data and forwarding data. Fuzzy logic is used to process the data and to predict the result. The following section elucidates the fuzzy logic concepts.

31.3.2 Fuzzy logic

The term fuzzy refers to the uncertainty condition. In the real-world scenario: any event or process, or function change occurring continuously means it cannot always be defined as either a true or false event. Therefore, it needs to define uncertain activities as fuzzy. A fuzzy logic (FL) method provides good perception that resembles human perception. This technique emulates the decision making that involves all intermediate possibilities between the digital values ‘0’ and ‘1’.

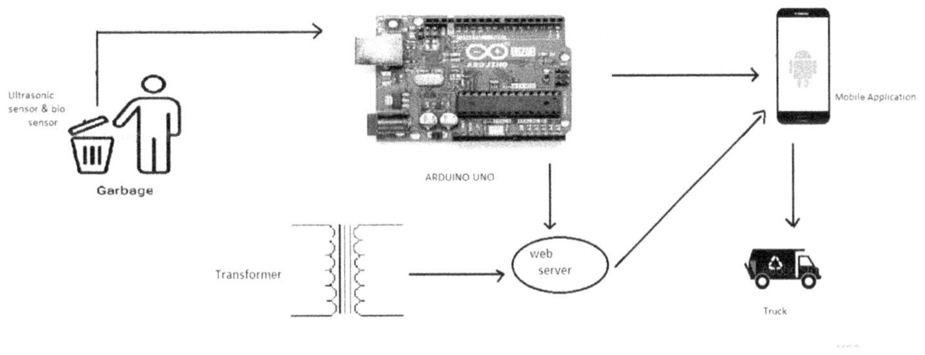

Figure 31.4. Garbage monitoring system architecture diagram.

31.3.3 Fuzzy logic system components

Fuzzification module: This is the first module in a fuzzy system. It converts crisp values into fuzzy values. This involves a domain transformation where crisp inputs are transformed into fuzzy input using the membership function. The assumed crisp value and fuzzy value of this proposed work are given below.

Defuzzification module: It is the process of converting a fuzzy output of interferences engine into crisp output by using a membership function.

Crisp value	Fuzzy value
High	0.75–1.0
Medium	0.4–0.74
Low	0.0–0.39

Knowledge base: It is the database used to store predefined IF–THEN rules. For example, if a person's problem-solving skills are excellent then they will become a good programmer.

Inference engine: It simulates the reasoning process by making fuzzy interferences on the inputs and IF–THEN rules.

Example:

If(GVH = low)AND(LIP = low)AND(CHG = low)AND(AAC = low)AND (ALM1 = low)AND (ALM2 = low)THEN class distribution is CP.

If(GVH = low)AND(LIP = low)AND(CHG = high)AND(AAC = low)AND (ALM1 = low)AND(ALM2 = low)THEN class distribution is PP.

31.3.4 Advantage

1. Time consumption is good.
2. Cleaning process is easy.

3. To avoid harmful diseases spreading via the garbage bin.
4. Communication process is easy between garbage bins through mobile application to the control room.

31.4 Results

For analysis, an *E. coli* dataset used. To find the harmfulness of *E. coli* present in the garbage bin, a MATLAB simulator is used (by using FUZZY RULES). The fuzzy rules have been simulated and are shown in figures 31.5 and 31.6.

Garbage can overflow in cities day by day, and can cause very harmful diseases. To avoid all such harmful disease and garbage overflow, an artificial

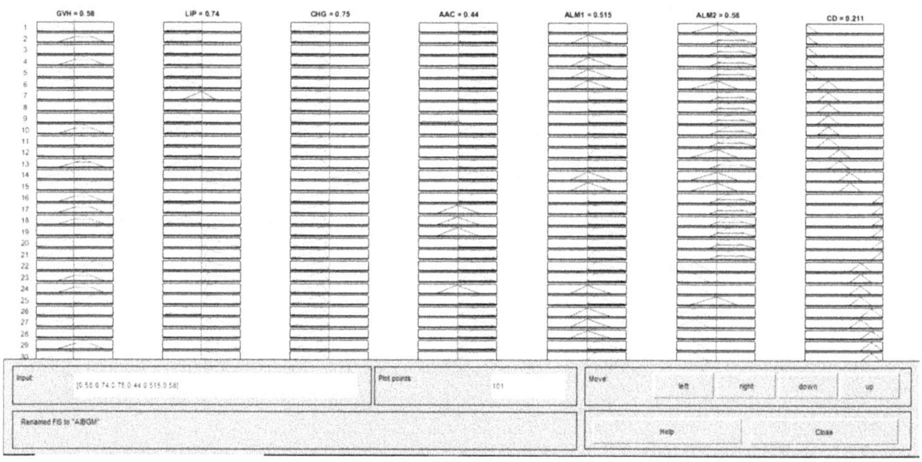

Figure 31.5. Matlab output-1.

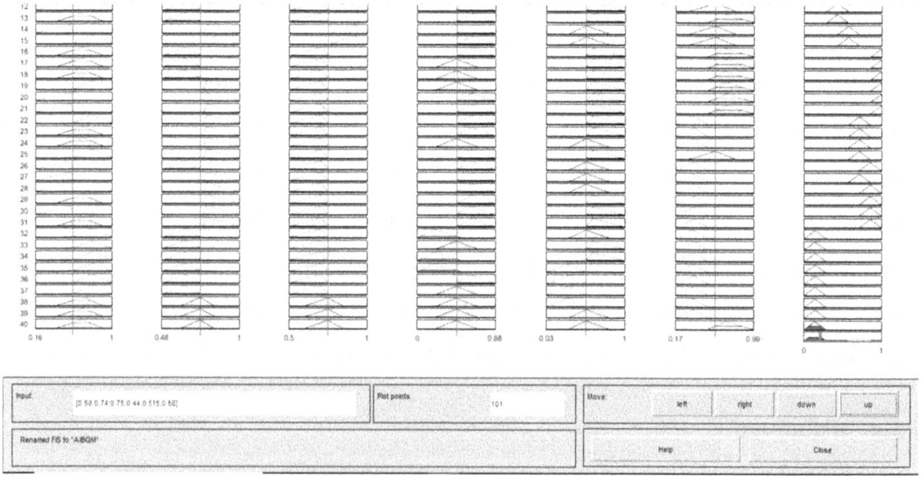

Figure 31.6. Matlab output-2.

intelligence-based garbage monitoring system used. This method is used to avoid all such problems and also a garbage overflow notification is sent to the municipal web server through the mobile application. After getting notification they can collect the garbage and clean properly. This is used to avoid harmful effects and clean the city to develop a clean environment. This system provides the advantage that people need not have to check all the bins manually, but instead receive notification when the bin is full.

31.5 Conclusion and future work

In this chapter, an artificial intelligence-based garbage monitoring and management system using integrated sensors has been proposed. It provides a simple way to remove old garbage. The essential aim, improving the efficiency of a garbage monitoring system, is to identify harmful garbage when it piles up in the container. Uncertainties exist in the system that continuously monitors the garbage level in the garbage container and alerts the authorities for immediate action. To optimize the uncertainties, fuzzy rules are raised in the suggested system. The proposed system is suitable to be implemented in all cities, residential areas, hospital waste management areas, industrial waste management areas etc, and is fast, reliable and reasonably inexpensive. Also, it is responsible for reducing health-related issues because of detecting harmful waste.

The limitations of this work are: (i) lack of the method in the proposed work because it provides only the detail about the monitoring system; (ii) lack of a real-time dataset; (iii) lack of real-time implementation. But the proposed method has been simulated successfully and it provides the expected results.

SQL query

```
Select SEQUENCE_NAME, (Count(SEQUENCE_NAME)* 100/(Select Count(*)
From ecolli)) as CLASS_DISTRIBUTION
   From ecolli WHERE MCG = 0
   AND GVH = 0 AND LIP = 0 AND CHG = 1 AND AAC = 1 AND ALM1 =
1 AND ALM2 = 1Group By CLASS_DISTRIBUTION = 'IM'
   UNION
   Select SEQUENCE_NAME,(Count(SEQUENCE_NAME)* 100/(Select Count
(*) From ecolli)) as CLASS_DISTRIBUTION
   From ecolli WHERE MCG = 4
   AND GVH = 6 AND LIP = 7 AND CHG = 8 AND AAC = 8 AND ALM1 =
7 AND ALM2 = 0 Group By CLASS_DISTRIBUTION
   UNION
   Select SEQUENCE_NAME,(Count(SEQUENCE_NAME)* 100/(Select Count
(*) From ecolli)) as CLASS_DISTRIBUTION
   From ecolli WHERE MCG = 0
   AND GVH = 0 AND LIP = 0 AND CHG = 1 AND AAC = 1 AND ALM1 =
1 AND ALM2 = 1 Group By CLASS_DISTRIBUTION
   UNION
```

```
Select SEQUENCE_NAME,(Count(SEQUENCE_NAME)* 100/(Select Count
(*) From ecolli)) as CLASS_DISTRIBUTION
From ecolli WHERE MCG = 1
AND GVH = 1 AND LIP = 1 AND CHG = 1 AND AAC = 1 AND ALM1 =
1 AND ALM2 = 1 Group By CLASS_DISTRIBUTION
UNION
Select SEQUENCE_NAME, (Count (SEQUENCE_NAME)* 100/(Select Count
(*) from ecolli)) as CLASS_DISTRIBUTION
From ecolli WHERE MCG = 0
AND GVH = 0 AND LIP = 1 AND CHG = 1 AND AAC = 1 AND ALM1 =
1 AND ALM2 = 1 Group by CLASS_DISTRIBUTION
UNION
Select SEQUENCE_NAME, (Count (SEQUENCE_NAME)* 100/(Select Count
(*) from ecolli)) as CLASS_DISTRIBUTION
From ecolli WHERE MCG = 0
AND GVH = 0 AND LIP = 0 AND CHG = 1 AND AAC = 1 AND ALM1 =
1 AND ALM2 = 1 Group By CLASS_DISTRIBUTION
UNION
Select SEQUENCE_NAME,(Count(SEQUENCE_NAME)* 100/(Select Count
(*) From ecolli)) as CLASS_DISTRIBUTION
From ecolli WHERE MCG = 1
AND GVH = 1 AND LIP = 1 AND CHG = 1 AND AAC = 1 AND ALM1 =
1 AND ALM2 = 1 Group By CLASS_DISTRIBUTION
UNION
Select SEQUENCE_NAME,(Count(SEQUENCE_NAME)* 100/(Select Count
(*) From ecolli)) as CLASS_DISTRIBUTION
From ecolli WHERE MCG = 1
AND GVH = 1 AND LIP = 0 AND CHG = 0 AND AAC = 1 AND ALM1 =
1 AND ALM2 = 1 Group By CLASS_DISTRIBUTION
UNION
Select SEQUENCE_NAME, (Count (SEQUENCE_NAME)* 100/(Select Count
(*) From ecolli)) as CLASS_DISTRIBUTION
From ecolli WHERE MCG = 1
AND GVH = 1 AND LIP = 1 AND CHG = 0 AND AAC = 1 AND ALM1 =
0 AND ALM2 = 1 Group By CLASS_DISTRIBUTION
UNION
Select SEQUENCE_NAME, (Count (SEQUENCE_NAME)* 100/(Select Count
(*) From ecolli)) as CLASS_DISTRIBUTION
From ecolli WHERE MCG = 1
AND GVH = 0 AND LIP = 0 AND CHG = 0 AND AAC = 1 AND ALM1 =
1 AND ALM2 = 1 Group By CLASS_DISTRIBUTION
UNION
Select SEQUENCE_NAME,(Count(SEQUENCE_NAME)* 100/(Select Count
(*) From ecolli)) as CLASS_DISTRIBUTION
From ecolli WHERE MCG = 1
```

```
AND GVH = 0 AND LIP = 0 AND CHG = 1 AND AAC = 1 AND ALM1 =
0 AND ALM2 = 1 Group By CLASS_DISTRIBUTION
UNION
Select SEQUENCE_NAME,(Count(SEQUENCE_NAME)* 100/(Select Count
(*) From ecolli)) as CLASS_DISTRIBUTION
From ecolli WHERE MCG = 0
AND GVH = 1 AND LIP = 1 AND CHG = 0 AND AAC = 1 AND ALM1 =
1 AND ALM2 = 1 Group By CLASS_DISTRIBUTION
UNION
Select SEQUENCE_NAME, (Count (SEQUENCE_NAME)* 100/(Select Count
(*) From ecolli)) as CLASS_DISTRIBUTION
From ecolli WHERE MCG = 1
AND GVH = 1 AND LIP = 1 AND CHG = 0 AND AAC = 1 AND ALM1 =
1 AND ALM2 = 1 Group by CLASS_DISTRIBUTION
UNION
Select SEQUENCE_NAME,(Count(SEQUENCE_NAME)* 100/(Select Count
(*) From ecolli)) as CLASS_DISTRIBUTION
From ecolli WHERE MCG = 1
AND GVH = 1 AND LIP = 1 AND CHG = 0 AND AAC = 0 AND ALM1 =
1 AND ALM2 = 0 Group By CLASS_DISTRIBUTION
UNION
Select SEQUENCE_NAME,(Count(SEQUENCE_NAME)* 100/(Select Count
(*) From ecolli)) as CLASS_DISTRIBUTION
From ecolli WHERE MCG = 0
AND GVH = 1 AND LIP = 0 AND CHG = 1 AND AAC = 0 AND ALM1 =
1 AND ALM2 = 1 Group By CLASS_DISTRIBUTION
UNION
Select SEQUENCE_NAME,(Count(SEQUENCE_NAME)* 100/(Select Count
(*) From ecolli)) as CLASS_DISTRIBUTION
From ecolli WHERE MCG = 1
AND GVH = 1 AND LIP = 1 AND CHG = 1 AND AAC = 0 AND ALM1 =
0 AND ALM2 = 0 Group By CLASS_DISTRIBUTION
UNION
Select SEQUENCE_NAME,(Count(SEQUENCE_NAME)* 100/(Select Count
(*) From ecolli)) as CLASS_DISTRIBUTION
From ecolli WHERE MCG = 1
AND GVH = 0 AND LIP = 0 AND CHG = 0 AND AAC = 1 AND ALM1 =
1 AND ALM2 = 1 Group By CLASS_DISTRIBUTION
UNION
Select SEQUENCE_NAME,(Count(SEQUENCE_NAME)* 100/(Select Count
(*) From ecolli)) as CLASS_DISTRIBUTION
From ecolli WHERE MCG = 0
AND GVH = 1 AND LIP = 0 AND CHG = 1 AND AAC = 0 AND ALM1 =
0 AND ALM2 = 1 Group By CLASS_DISTRIBUTION
```

Fuzzy rules

1. If(GVH = low)AND(LIP = low)AND(CHG = low)AND(AAC = low) AND(ALM1 = low)AND(ALM2 = low)THEN class distribution is CP.
2. If(GVH = medium)AND(LIP = low)AND(CHG = low)AND(AAC = high)AND(ALM1 = medium)AND(ALM2 = high)THEN class distribution is CP.
3. If(GVH = low)AND(LIP = low)AND(CHG = low)AND(AAC = high) AND(ALM1 = high)AND(ALM2 = high)THEN class distribution is CP.
4. If(GVH = medium)AND(LIP = low)AND(CHG = low)AND(AAC = high)AND(ALM1 = medium)AND(ALM2 = high)THEN class distribution is CP.
5. If(GVH = low)AND(LIP = low)AND(CHG = low)AND(AAC = high) AND(ALM1 = medium)AND(ALM2 = high)THEN class distribution is CP.
6. If(GVH = low)AND(LIP = low)AND(CHG = low)AND(AAC = high) AND(ALM1 = medium)AND(ALM2 = medium)THEN class distribution is IM.
7. If(GVH = low)AND(LIP = medium)AND(CHG = low)AND(AAC = high)AND(ALM1 = high)AND(ALM2 = high)THEN class distribution is IM.
8. If(GVH = high)AND(LIP = low)AND(CHG = low)AND(AAC = high) AND(ALM1 = high)AND(ALM2 = high)THEN class distribution is IM.
9. If(GVH = high)AND(LIP = low)AND(CHG = low)AND(AAC = low) AND(ALM1 = high)AND(ALM2 = high)THEN class distribution is IM.
10. If(GVH = medium)AND(LIP = low)AND(CHG = low)AND(AAC = high)AND(ALM1 = high)AND(ALM2 = high)THEN class distribution is IM.
11. If(GVH = low)AND(LIP = low)AND(CHG = low)AND(AAC = high) AND(ALM1 = medium)AND(ALM2 = high)THEN class distribution is IM.
12. If(GVH = medium)AND(LIP = low)AND(CHG = low)AND(AAC = high)AND(ALM1 = high)AND(ALM2 = high)THEN class distribution is IMS.
13. If(GVH = low)AND(LIP = high)AND(CHG = high)AND(AAC = high) AND(ALM1 = medium)AND(ALM2 = medium)THEN class distribution is IML.
14. If(GVH = high)AND(LIP = low)AND(CHG = low)AND(AAC = high) AND(ALM1 = medium)AND(ALM2 = medium)THEN class distribution is IML.
15. If(GVH = medium)AND(LIP = low)AND(CHG = low)AND(AAC = medium)AND (ALM1 = high) AND(ALM2 = high)THEN class distribution is IMU.

16. If(GVH = medium)AND(LIP = low)AND(CHG = low)AND(AAC = high)AND(ALM1 = medium) AND(ALM2 = high)THEN class distribution is IMU.
17. If(GVH = high)AND(LIP = high)AND(CHG = low)AND(AAC = medium)AND(ALM1 = high) AND(ALM2 = high)THEN class distribution is IMU.
18. If(GVH = low)AND(LIP = high)AND(CHG = low)AND(AAC = medium)AND(ALM1 = high)AND(ALM2 = high)THEN class distribution is IMU.
19. If(GVH = low)AND(LIP = high)AND(CHG = low)AND(AAC = high) AND(ALM1 = medium)AND(ALM2 = medium)THEN class distribution is IMU.
20. If(GVH = low)AND(LIP = low)AND(CHG = high)AND(AAC = low) AND(ALM1 = low)AND(ALM2 = high)THEN class distribution is OM.
21. If(GVH = medium)AND(LIP = high)AND(CHG = low)AND(AAC = low)AND(ALM1 = high)AND(ALM2 = low)THEN class distribution is OM.
22. If(GVH = medium)AND(LIP = high)AND(CHG = low)AND(AAC = medium)AND(ALM1 = medium)AND(ALM2 = high)THEN class distribution is OM.
23. If(GVH = high)AND(LIP = high)AND(CHG = low)AND(AAC = high) AND(ALM1 = high)
    AND (ALM2 = medium) THEN class distribution is OM.
24. If(GVH = low)AND(LIP = low)AND(CHG = low)AND(AAC = high) AND(ALM1 = medium)AND(ALM2 = low)THEN class distribution is OM.
25. If(GVH = low)AND(LIP = high)AND(CHG = low)AND(AAC = high) AND(ALM1 = medium) AND(ALM2 = low)THEN class distribution is OM.
26. If(GVH = low)AND(LIP = high)AND(CHG = low)AND(AAC = high) AND(ALM1 = medium)AND(ALM2 = high)THEN class distribution is OML.
27. If(GVH = low)AND(LIP = high)AND(CHG = low)AND(AAC = high)AND (ALM1 = high)AND(ALM2 = medium)THEN class distribution is OML.
28. If(GVH = high)AND(LIP = high)AND(CHG = low)AND(AAC = high)AND (ALM1 = medium)AND(ALM2 = high)THEN class distribution is OML.
29. If(GVH = medium)AND(LIP = high)AND(CHG = low)AND(AAC = high) AND(ALM1 = high)AND(ALM2 = low)THEN class distribution is OML.
30. If(GVH = high)AND(LIP = low)AND(CHG = low)AND(AAC = low) AND(ALM1 = medium)AND(ALM2 = low)THEN class distribution is PP.
31. If(GVH = high)AND(LIP = low)AND(CHG = low)AND(AAC = medium) AND(ALM1 = high)AND(ALM2 = low)THEN class distribution is pp.
32. If(GVH = high)AND(LIP = low)AND(CHG = low)AND(AAC = low) AND(ALM1 = high)AND(ALM2 = low)THEN class distribution is PP.

33. If(GVH = high)AND(LIP = low)AND(CHG = low)AND(AAC = low) AND(ALM1 = low)AND(ALM2 = low)THEN class distribution is PP.
34. If(GVH = high)AND(LIP = low)AND(CHG = low)AND(AAC = high) AND(ALM1 = low)AND(ALM2 = low)THEN class distribution is PP.
35. If(GVH = high)AND(LIP = low)AND(CHG = low)AND(AAC = medium)AND(ALM1 = low)AND(ALM2 = low)THEN class distribution is PP.
36. If(GVH = medium)AND(LIP = medium)AND(CHG = medium)AND (AAC = medium)AND(ALM1 = low)AND(ALM2 = low)THEN class distribution is PP.
37. If(GVH = medium)AND(LIP = medium)AND(CHG = medium)AND (AAC = medium)AND(ALM1 = medium)AND(ALM2 = low) THEN class distribution is PP.
38. If (GVH = medium) AND (LIP = medium) AND (CHG = medium) AND (AAC = medium) AND (ALM1 = medium) AND (ALM2 = high) THEN class distribution is PP.
39. If (GVH = high) AND (LIP = medium) AND (CHG = medium) AND (AAC = medium) AND (ALM1 = medium) AND (ALM2 = high) THEN class distribution is PP.
40. If (GVH = medium) AND (LIP = medium) AND (CHG = medium) AND (AAC = high) AND (ALM1 = medium) AND (ALM2 = high) THEN class distribution is PP.

References

[1] Medvedev A, Fedchenkov P, Zaslavsky A, Theodoros and Khoruzhnikov S 2015 Garbage management as an IoT-enabled service in smart cities *Int. J. Eng. and Comp. Sci.*

[2] Alicemary, Perreddy M, Apsurrunisha A, Sreekanth C and Kumar G P 2017 IOT based garbage monitoring system *Int. J. Scient. and Eng. Res. (IJSER)* 8

[3] Muhammad Fachrurrozi, Saparudin and Erwin 2017 Real time monitoring system of pollution waste on Musi River using support vector machine method *IOP Conf. Ser.: Mater. Sci. Eng.* **190** 012014

[4] Tarone A V, Aakanksha, Katgube A, Harsha, Shendre H, Ghugal R P and Bobade N P 2018 Internet of Things (IoT) based garbage monitoring system using ESP 8266 with GPS link *Int. Research J. Eng. and Tech. (IRJET)* **5**

[5] Abdurrahman F and Aweke S 2018 Automated garbage monitoring system using Arduino *IOSR J. Com. Eng. (IOSR-JCE)* **20**

[6] Mungara J, shobha, keerthana, kanakambika R G and kokila 2018 Survey on smart garbage monitoring system using IOT *Int. J. Inn. Res. in Com. and Comm. Eng. (IJIRCCE)* **6**

[7] Pranjali, channe P, Rasika, Butlekar M and Pohare. D B 2018 IOT based monitoring system and sorting system *Int. Res. J. Eng. and Tech. (IRJET)* **5**

[8] Ravichandran S 2017 Intelligent garbage monitoring system using IOT *Indian J. Sci. and Tech.* **10**

[9] Suryawanshi S, Blues R, Gite M and Hande D 2018 Garbage management system based on IOT *Int. Research J. Eng. and Tech. (IRJET)* **5**

[10] Sandeep, chaware M, Dighe S, Joshi A, Bajare N and orke R 2017 Smart garbage monitoring system using IOT *Int. J. Innovative Research in Electrical, Electronics, Instrumentation and Control Engineering (IJIREEICE)* **5**

[11] Pokalekar K, Ashvinisalunkhe P, Kachare and Yadav N C 2018 IOT based garbage monitoring system *Int. Research J. Eng. & Tech. (IRJET)* **5**

[12] Sharma N, Mishra N and Gupta P 2018 Internet of things(IoT) based garbage monitoring system *Int. J. Advance Rese. Ideas and Inn. in Tech. (IJARIIT)* **4**

[13] Navghane S, Killedar M S and Rohokale D V M 2016 IoT based garbage and garbage collection bin *Int. J. Advanced Res. in Elect. and Commu. Eng.*

[14] Bhor V, Morajkar P, Gurav M and Pandya D 2015 Smart garbage management system *Int. J. Engineering Research and Technology in Smart Cities Utilizing Internet of Things*

IOP Publishing

Human-Assisted Intelligent Computing
Modeling, simulations and applications
Mukhdeep Singh Manshahia, Igor S Litvinchev, Gerhard-Wilhelm Weber, J Joshua Thomas and Pandian Vasant

Chapter 32

Use of Internet of Things technology in the medical field during the pandemic era

Ashish Verma and Sherry N Siddiqui

32.1 Introduction

The system we propose can act as a tele-clinic in itself. The embedded system for health monitoring, along with GSM/GPRS module can also enable remote health monitoring. As we know, in severe times of pandemic, the ratio of doctors to patients becomes much less and hence, in such critical situations, developing countries like India require the technology of tele-clinics.

Designing an IoT based embedded system for monitoring rural health can also use a real-time monitoring system, with the help of which doctors and the paramedical staff can get real-time data of health parameters of patients from remote areas.

Covid-19 is a disease caused by severe acute respiratory syndrome virus. This pandemic proved to be very devastating for human life and the economy in the year 2020. There have been several attempts to save lives in different ways during the pandemic. The main responsibility was on the people from the field of medicine. Undoubtedly human efforts are the most important in this regard. It would be of great value if electronic gadgets assisted health workers. IoT is a very innovative and significant technology deploying embedded systems to communicate wirelessly so that data can be communicated with high accuracy in a short span of time. This technology can prove tremendously helpful in an emergency period like a pandemic.

IoT is the system of physical objects or 'things' installed with electronic gadgets, programming *n* different high level languages, sensors, which promotes communication between these objects and exchanges information. This technology connects nodes (including sensors and micro-controllers) wirelessly through WSN technology. Embedded systems based on IoT find application in monitoring of EGC, blood

doi:10.1088/978-0-7503-4801-0ch32

pressure, heart rate, body temperature, etc. IoT technology enables the monitoring of a patient from distant areas as well. This feature of such embedded systems can be used for monitoring of remote areas, such as villages.

Improvement in health facilities is the need of the hour, particularly in developing nations like India, because the ratio of number of doctors to the number of residents is much less than 1. Also, high rates of poverty in India do not allow poor people easy access to high quality of healthcare facilities. The use of smart devices based on IoT can prove very useful in this regard. Across the globe, the health status of people living in rural areas is generally worse as compared to the health status in urban areas. Particularly in India, there are different schemes to facilitate good health services, but the available resources are too little and too late at times. The largest number of maternity deaths are noted in India, a majority of which are noted in the rural areas of the country. Indian Government schemes like Ayushman Bharat Yojana and Gram Vani are continuously proving their potential to improve health facilities, especially in rural areas of India. Technology can assist the telehealth field to a great extent.

The proposed system can act as a tele-clinic in itself. The embedded system for health monitoring, along with GSM/GPRS modules can enable remote health monitoring. As we know, in severe times of pandemic, the ratio of doctors to patients becomes much lower and hence, in such critical situations, developing countries like India require the technology of tele-clinics.

Designing an IoT based embedded system for monitoring rural health can also use a real-time monitoring system, with the help of which doctors and paramedic staff can get real-time data of health parameters of patients from remote areas.

The preference of most doctors is accurate and precise information about the patients in minimum time. The application of smart IoT devices in rural areas can help a lot in this direction. The electronic machines used to monitor the conditions of patients can be operated by the paramedic staff or even by local residents of the area and the information collected through these systems can be communicated to doctors, who are a distance away. This system will also help to reduce human error.

This technology can prove tremendously helpful in anemergency period like a pandemic. IoT can prove very helpful to fight the situation of a pandemic like Covid-19. It finds applications in many ways.

32.2 IoT based system to check the entry of covid-19 infected patients arriving in a city

It was observed that the spread of Covid-19 pandemic was very rapid and it was through direct contact of people so an embedded system could be placed at the entry point of any city say, airports, railway stations, bus stands or metro stations. This embedded system could identify a Covid-19 infected patient and through the collected data the authorities concerned can take required decisions at an appropriate time.

There are many advances in industrial automation, automotive technology, remote sensing, etc. In many embedded systems image processing takes centre stage. Nowadays, image processing tasks in an embedded system, where there is no direct connection with a desktop, server, or the cloud is possible by the help of newer hardware modules specialized with GPUs. The appropriate board for interfacing these hardware modules is required for these types of embedded systems. Embedded systems used for advanced image processing applications, specifically for applications involving machine-learning or artificial intelligence models, require significant processing power and memory. Ideally, these capabilities integrated into a single package having a small form factor and huge amount of onboard memory for storing data with network or wireless connectivity, constitute a powerful machine-learning-based image processing system.

Plenty of work has been done using Raspberry Pi boards in the field of digital image processing. For example, image capturing technique is used in an embedded system, using Raspberry Pi 1 Model B, the biometric access systems, speaker recognition, password key systems, standalone face recognition system, etc, which make use of Raspberry Pi Model B or B+.

There can be more options too but Raspberry Pi 2 model B can be a good option for that embedded system which has been proposed in this chapter, as there are many interfaces on the Raspberry Pi board, which includes two USB ports by which a keyboard, mouse and pen-drive can also be connected. By the help of HDMI output, HD TVs and monitors can be connected. Input modules can be connected using the HDMI port or an HDMI to DVI lead can be used for monitors having DVI input. This system can also include Standard RCA composite video lead. The ethernet port can be used for the purpose of networking. An audio lead will be available in the system to get the stereo audio in case HDMI is not in use for the system, otherwise HDMI will get a digital audio facility with it.

Image processing in embedded systems includes steps like image identification, image segmentation and image classification, which can be stored for later use.

For medical and industrial purposes, radiography is an imaging technique by the use of x-rays. During the examination of patients, digital radiography uses x-ray-sensitive plates to capture images and immediately transfers it to a computer system. Because of many technological advancements in digital radiography, many companies and medical practitioners prefer to invest in digital and portable x-ray systems.

In this proposed embedded system design, embedded systems can be deployed at different places and thereafter communicate wirelessly to provide the necessary data to a defined database or a cloud. After uploading the data to the internet, collected data can be accessed anywhere globally. This would reduce a lot of time and quick actions can be taken.

The embedded system form comprises:

1. Micro-controller board: Raspberry Pi 2 model B (figure 32.1) acts as the brains of the embedded system. Its main parts include processing chip, ethernet port, USB port, HDMI out and Micro SD card for storing data. The main signal processing chip is Broadcom BCM 2836 900 MHz Quad Core cortex A7.

Figure 32.1. Raspberry Pi 2 (model B).

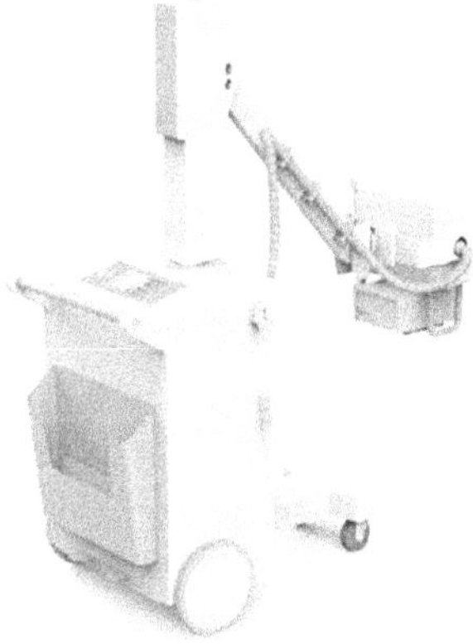

Figure 32.2. Portable x-ray device.

2. Output devices: the micro-controller is interfaced with a display monitor via HDMI output or data can be transferred interfaced using WiFi module with the micro-controller.
3. Input devices: a portable x-ray device (figure 32.2) can be used for the proposed system which can take x-rays of travelers as input and provide them to the micro-controller of the embedded system for further processing. The result that is obtained from the proposed embedded system can be helpful in the diagnosis of lung infection in Covid-19 patients at the entry point of railway stations, metro stations and airports, which are main sources of spread of the pandemic and therefore the system works as a computed tomography device, used for the diagnosis of Covid-19. This chapter proposes a very economical and technically updated method for x-ray analysis for the detection of Covid-19 patients. As the contents of the system are very lightweight, less power consuming and very efficient, it is easier to apply, and the use of the Raspberry Pi board makes it an efficient system. It is useful for getting optimized results.

This embedded system comprising micro-controller interfaced with input and output devices constitutes sensor nodes. These sensor nodes can be placed at different locations at the entry point of airports, railway stations, metro stations etc. Different sensor nodes communicate wirelessly to a master collector forming a cluster as a whole. Data from these clusters can further be uploaded to the cloud and can thereafter be distributed to concerned devices. This architecture of IoT enables wireless communication over long distances in short span of time and provides a direct communication between non-living 'things' or objects. This technology has immense application and scope in research.

32.3 Use of IoT to improve health conditions in rural areas of developing countries like India

Healthcare of a nation should be as effective and efficient as possible. IoT technologies have immense power to address some of the challenges faced by developing countries like India in providing affordable, accessible, high-quality healthcare services to each and every individual of the nation. The presented chapter proposes an embedded system design using IoT technology to provide a wide range of services in telehealth clinics which can enhance the quality of medical facilities in remote areas from a distance. We propose to design a system of nodes, comprising sensors and a micro-controller, implemented for collecting data and process them to extract useful information about health of the patients in remote areas. Sensors are interfaced with a micro-controller (the Arduino Uno board (figure 32.3) is suited for the purpose) at analog pins, the written software in the control board (in embedded C language) processes and analyses the data and the processed results are then sent to a central node using a WiFi module, and this information is uploaded to the web portal, which can be accessed globally. This IoT platform can be used to monitor health parameters remotely, like live ECG signal, heart rate, SPO2 (blood oxygen level), and the body temperature of patients. The proposed embedded system

Figure 32.3. Arduino UNO board.

working on IoT technology can collect data at different nodes which can be placed at health centers of a village which communicate to a central node present in the village and thereafter the health details of patients in villages can be uploaded to the internet which can be accessed by doctors in cities. Another approach of IoT that could prove helpful during the Covid-19 pandemic era can be designing of embedded systems for monitoring the health status of patients in rural areas, especially for developing countries like India. Mortality rate in hospitals of villages of developing countries like India is noted to be higher than in urban areas. IoT provides technology which can enhance health monitoring system diagnosis of the patient and thereafter necessary treatment for people in villages and remote areas who do not have direct access to the medical facilities of urban areas. The sensor node comprises an embedded system with a micro-controller and sensors to collect the data of various health parameters like blood pressure, blood oxygen level, heart rate etc. Data from the sensor nodes can be communicated wirelessly to a master collector forming a cluster and using the IoT technology this data can be communicated to the internet from where even doctors abroad can get health related data of people in villages or remote areas. In order to ensure data connectivity in rural areas, especially in developing countries like India, use of satellite phone can be made to avoid loss in data connectivity. Operation of embedded system deployed in IoT technology is quite easy and feasible and even paramedic staff can take the necessary actions upon the advice of doctors who are continuously getting updates of the patients.

Components of the embedded system:

Arduino Uno board: It is a micro-controller having AtMega 328 P. It acts as the brains of the embedded system. The Arduino Uno board has 14 output and input pins, six of which can be used as digital output and six are used as analog input. 16 MHz quartz crystals are also present on it, along with USB ports, power jack, ICSP header and a reset button as well. It can be supplied with power using an AC to DC adapter or battery [2].

SENSORS: Sensors act as the sense organs for an embedded system. These are interfaced with the micro-controller board via input pins to gather data from the physical environment.

The sensors proposed for the system are as follows:

Temperature Sensor (Lm-35): Linear output and low output impedance are the characteristics of this sensor. Only single power is needed to operate this sensor [1] (figure 32.4).

Heartbeat Sensor (KY039): An optical sensor and an infrared light emitting diode (IR LED) are present in these sensors, which are used to measure heartbeats in beats per minute (BPM) [3] (figure 32.5).

ECG Sensor module (Ad-8232): This sensor is used to measure the electrical activity of the heart. It is a single lead Heart Rate Monitor, which provides a cost-effective solution for monitoring ECG of a patient [4] (figure 32.6).

The proposed embedded system is designed using the sensor technology, which senses the physical parameters like body temperature, heart beat and ECG on receiving instructions from the micro-controller board Arduino Uno, followed by

Figure 32.4. Lm-35 temperature sensor.

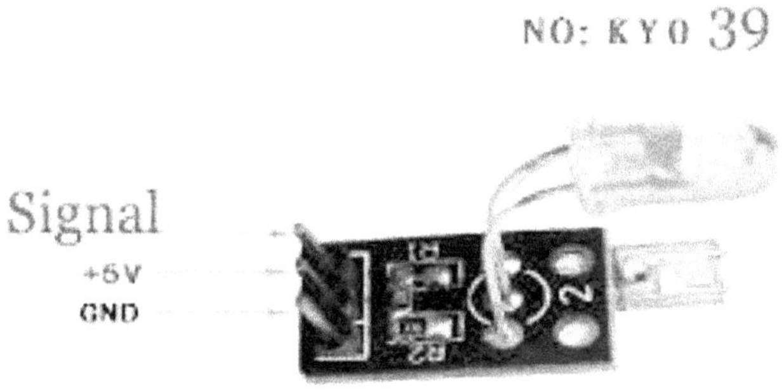

Figure 32.5. Heart beat sensor KY039.

Figure 32.6. ECG Sensor Module (Ad-8232).

processing and analysis of this data. Thereafter, this sensor node uses GSM/GPRS module to transfer the processed data to remote doctors. This technology enables doctors to monitor the health condition of patients in remote areas, specially in villages of developing countries like India [5].

This system can prove to be cost effective because the prices of health related sensors and micro-controllers forming a sensor node are calculated to be less than 2000 rupees. This lifesaving cost effective and easy to handle system could prove to be a revolution in the health sector, especially in times of emergency like the Covid-19 pandemic situation.

32.4 Live monitoring of patients in ICU using IoT technology

Another significant role that IoT technology can play in the medical field is enabling live monitoring of patient specially in ICU. It is often observed that the families of patients are not allowed in the ICU and IICU. This is a medical protocol and cannot be breached. But an electronic instrument can be present and can provide communication between patients and their families. This can provide live updates of the patients to their family members and also the morale and strength of the patients can be boosted. Along with the bedside monitors of patients in ICU, sensor nodes can be placed which can communicate wirelessly to a master collector; thereafter this data can be uploaded to the base station and from there this data can be uploaded to a desired database on the internet for further distribution of data.

For the purpose of enabling live monitoring, an Arduino Yún micro-controller board (figure 32.7) can be used as it is compatible with a web camera and it has an SD card slot which improves the memory of the system (figures 32.8).

Use of IoT technology in the medical field can prove effective for doctors, patients, their families, the paramedical staff and the whole of human society. In addition, the technology can also be used in the veterinary hospital to ensure the safety and good health of animals.

The electronics industry has immense applications and it would be wonderful if this innovative technology were used in the medical field to save lives, especially in extreme situations like the Covid-19 era.

Arduino Yun Micro-controller Board

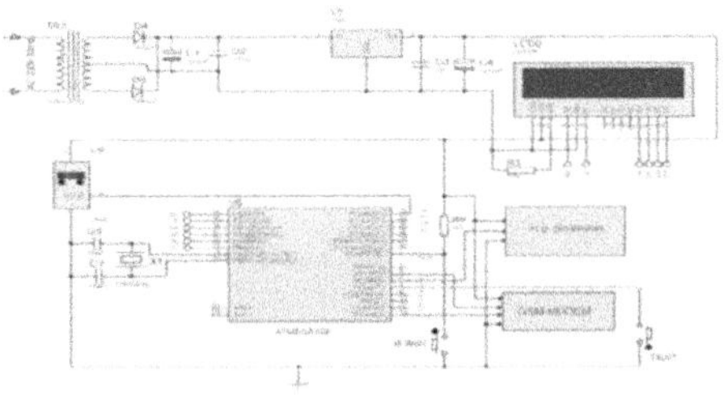

Arduino Yun board interfaced with GSM module for live broadcast

Figure 32.7. Arduino Yún board interfaced with GSM module for live broadcast.

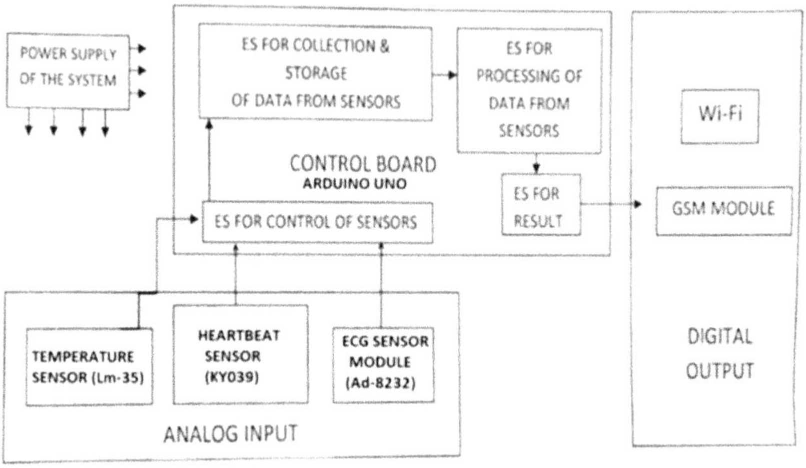

Figure 32.8. Arduino Yún Micro-controller board.

32.5 Conclusion

As already discussed, IoT is a technology that was introduced in the early 2000s. It has entered the health sector and has also attained common usage in new forms such as smart fitness bands. Awareness for maintaining good health and a fit body is rapidly increasing in society, which is also the need of the hour. As it is said that necessity is the mother of invention, this era of pandemic has paved way for a wide range of electronic devices like thermal scanners, biosensors, etc.

32.6 Future aspects

The era of the Covid-19 pandemic has given rise to many alternatives to the offline system and IoT can be used in the future in different sectors like distance learning, online entertainment, contact tracing applications like that developed in India named Aarogya Setu, the stock market, robotics, orchestration, fitness and health apps.

Although the Covid-19 era has proved very hazardous, it has made people strong enough to be well prepared in advance for any kind of crisis at individual and collective level. Covid-19 has brought a sudden change in the life of human society and has taught human beings to make their lives sustainable in this environment as well. We have found that the Arduino Yún board interfaced with GSM module for live broadcast electronic gadgets could replace the traditional methods. One of the key technologies from the field of electronics is IoT which can enhance different sectors with minimal human intervention in a cost-effective way.

References

[1] Ethelbhert D, Yu C, Danielle K, Yu S and Tan R R 2020 Implications of the pandemic-induced electronic equipment demand surge on essential technology metals *Clean. Respons. Consumpt.* **1** 100005

[2] Nasir S and Verma A 2021 Designing of WSN based embedded system using wearable sports sensors: a theoretical approach *J. Multi., Eng., Sci. Tech.*
[3] Verma S S 2021 Role Of electronics In combating Covid-19 *Electon Foru.com*
[4] Bhavana P N 2020 Role of Technology in the Era of COVID-19 Pandemic *ClearTax Chronicles*
[5] Nasir S and Verma A 2021 Designing and embedded system for analysis of x-ray results for covid-19 patients as x-ray computed tomography device for lungs diagnosis *Int. J Multi. Edu. and Res.* **10** 28–32

Chapter 33

Performance comparison of data security algorithms

M Sumathi, R Narmadha and G D Anbarasi Jebaselvi

This paper provides an overview of data security algorithms in network security and its performance evaluation. AES, RC5 and SHA algorithms have been taken for this study. AES (advanced encryption standard) is one of the mostly used security algorithms in network security. Due to the presence of brutal force attack, there is a chance of hacking the data during transmission and reception. It is based on the interleaving technique so as to reduce the logic elements used in encryption and decryption. The total number of logic elements of 38 386 in the existing AES is reduced drastically to 6386. In addition, this study discusses the hiding of data in an image after encryption and then improving data security and performance. The image is processed using MATLAB version R2009b. The software implementation of AES has been made using Verilog HDL and ModelSim 6.3g_p1. The performance factors of throughput, power consumption and operating frequency have been observed using Quartus II software. Implementation of this proposed AES, RC5 and SHA increases the throughput and reduces the power as well.

33.1 Introduction

The vulnerable risks found in digital communication systems are unauthorized access, denial of service, data corruption, leakage, monitoring attacks, authentication and trashing etc. These problems occur while executing different electronic operations such as video/text transfer, communications, online trade etc. Many procedures/algorithms have come out to reduce these risks by employing firewalls, detection systems, security via cryptographic algorithms and others [1–6]. The increasing need for secured data communication is a must due to the increased development of cryptographic algorithms such as DES, 3DES, AES, RSA, SHA,

doi:10.1088/978-0-7503-4801-0ch33

RC5 etc. The basic idea of a crypto algorithm is to secure the data while transmitting in the network. The data to be transmitted from sender to receiver in the network must be encrypted first using the encryption algorithm. By using decryption technique, the receiver can view the original data. The AES algorithm has proved in much of the literature [4, 7–9] that it works well both in hardware and software implementations. It can utilize data of different lengths say, for example 128, 192 or 256-bits for processing with a private key of the same length. Sub-byte, shift row, mixed column and add round key are the four basic operations carried out in 10, 12 or 14 rounds/iterations. The mixed column operation will not be carried out in the last round.

Further, hash functions are cryptographic elements used to provide solutions of data integrity and authentication issues. They perform operation in iterative fashion and map the binary digits of arbitrary length with the same fixed length. The existing algorithms for performing hash functions are MD5, SHA-1, SHA-2, Whirlpool, Haval and Ripe MD-160 and so on. Although many hardware and software implementations using hash function algorithms are reported, there is still a research gap in retrieving the data secured, which is a challenge both in academia and industry. The hardware architectures are reported to achieve better performance by customizing hardware elements that compute specific functions by using different techniques like carry save adders, embedded memories, pipelining, unrolling techniques etc. Currently, SHA-256 algorithm is becoming more popular in performance evaluation because it reduces the critical path by reordering the operations in each iteration. It is implemented and validated using FPGAVirtex-2Xc2VP-7 embedded on-boards. The performance of the hardware implementation of SHA-256 exhibits high throughput and efficiency.

RC5 is also a fast symmetric cryptography algorithm that uses the same key for encryption and decryption. The plain text and cipher text are fixed-length bit sequences, so it is named as block cipher. It uses two's complement addition and subtraction operation, bitwise exclusive-or operation and left-right rotation as primitives. It effectively works for real-time image encryption by partitioning the image into macro blocks and obtaining the resultant histogram of the cipher image. The key feature of RC5 is the usage of data-dependent rotations and evaluation of cryptographic primitives. It is fast and adaptable to any types of processors of different word-lengths. It provides high security.

33.2 AES algorithm

The National Institute of Standards and Technology (NIST) issued an open call for an AES algorithm which could overcome the drawbacks of 3DES in the year 1997. In the span of five years NIST received 15 algorithms. In the year 2001, NIST selected Rijndeal as the proposed AES algorithm. Rijndael was proposed by the team of Joan Daemen and Vincent Rijmen. Both of them are cryptographers from Belgium. The AES algorithm has a block length of 128-bits with different key sizes viz. 128-bits, 192-bits and 256-bits. The 128 bits requires 10 rounds of operation, 192-bits requires 12 rounds of operation and 256-bits requires 14 rounds of operations. AES uses a symmetric key and a block cipher. The symmetric key is the key which is the same for encryption and decryption. The block cipher takes a number of bits and encrypts them as a single unit. AES is not a Feistel structure. In a Feistel structure, half of the data is used to modify the other half and then the halves are swapped. The overall AES structure is shown in figure 33.1.

The rows have been shifted in Substitute byte transformation method as in figure 33.2. The first row will remain unchanged. The second row will be shifted one byte circularly in the left direction, the third row will be shifted two bytes circularly in the left direction, and the fourth row will be shifted three bytes circularly in the left direction. It is shown in figure 33.3.

With reverse shifting rows, individual rows are relocated in the opposite direction in a circular pattern. The first column will remain unchanged. The second row is circularly shifted in the correct direction by one byte. A two-byte circular right shift is applied to the third row. A client cyclical right shift is applied to the middle row [6–10].

In mix column, the transformation is performed on columns of the matrix. The first column will not be changed. The remaining columns will be changed in the following format. It is shown in figure 33.4.

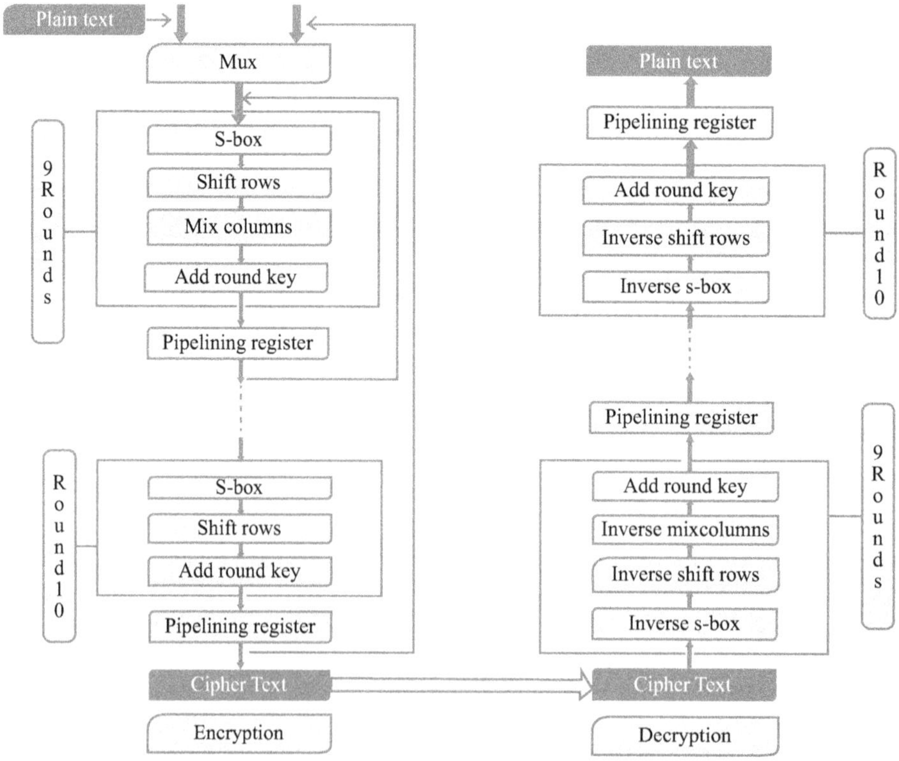

Figure 33.1. AES structure.

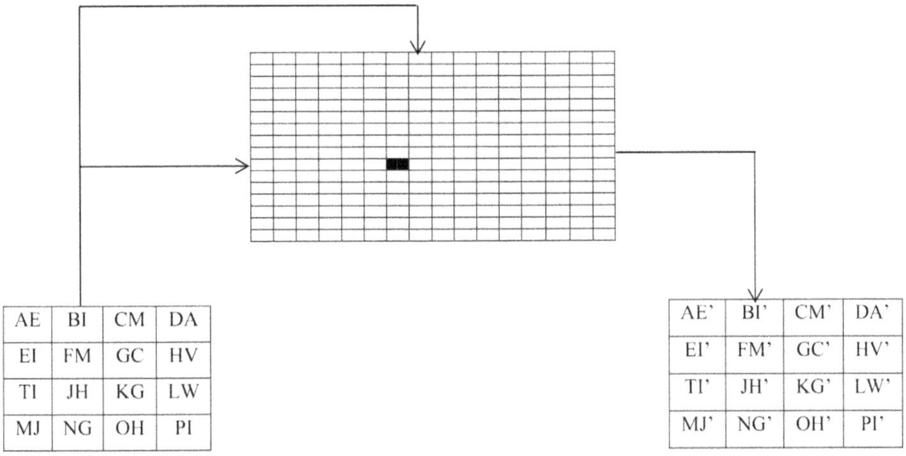

Figure 33.2. Substitute byte transformation.

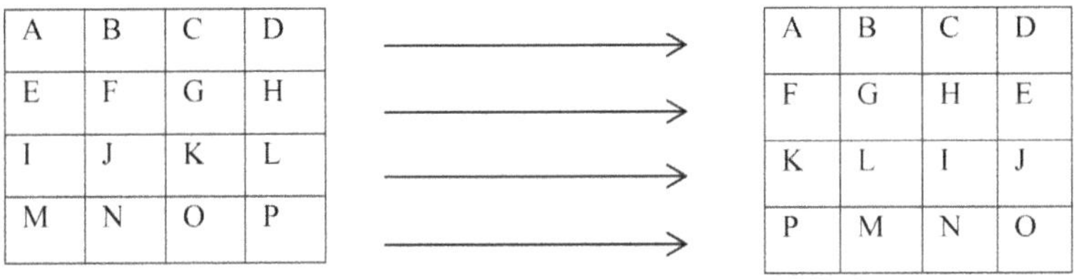

Figure 33.3. Shift row transformation.

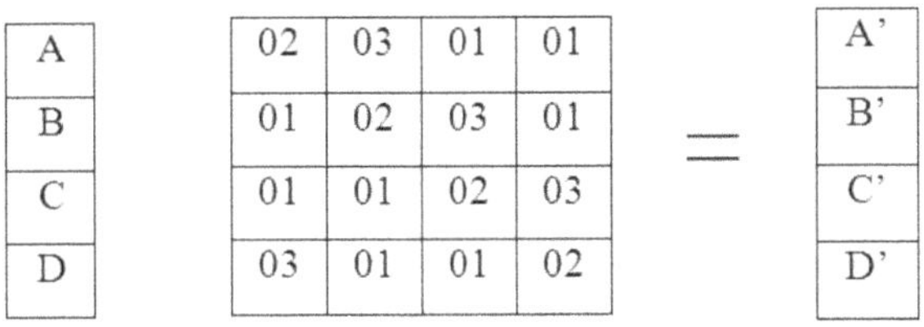

Figure 33.4. Mix columns transformation.

$$A' = (A*02)\text{xor}(B*03)\text{xor}(C*01)\text{xor}(D*01)$$

$$B' = (A*01)\text{xor}(B*02)\text{xor}(C*03)\text{xor}(D*01)$$

$$C' = (A*01)\text{xor}(B*01)\text{xor}(C*02)\text{xor}(D*03)$$

$$D' = (A*03)\text{xor}(B*01)\text{xor}(C*01)\text{xor}(D*02)$$

The bitwise opcode operation with (02) can be accomplished as follows: 1-bit left shift of a given 8-bit information, followed by a bitwise xor operation with (02). (0001 1011). Only conduct a bitwise xor operation if the leftmost bit of the original

$$\begin{bmatrix} A \\ B \\ C \\ D \end{bmatrix} \quad \begin{bmatrix} 0E & 0B & 0D & 09 \\ 09 & 0E & 0B & 0D \\ 0D & 09 & 0E & 0B \\ 0B & 0D & 09 & 0E \end{bmatrix} = \begin{bmatrix} A' \\ B' \\ C' \\ D' \end{bmatrix}$$

Figure 33.5. Inverse mix column transformation.

value is 1 well before shift. If the value is not 1 before the shift, it should be left unchanged after the shift. x xor (x*02) is the formula for multiplying x with (03). The opposite mix pilasters are achieved by means of the following formulations. An inverse mix column transformation is shown in figure 33.5.

$$A' = (A*0B)\text{xor}(B*0B)\text{xor}(C*09)\text{xor}(D*0E)$$

In add round key transformation, the 128 bits are XORed with 128 bits of the round key.

S′ = S xor R

S′ = state after adding round key

S = state before adding round key

R = round key

AES uses a symmetric block cipher for cryptography derived data. The block cipher obtains an extra-large quantity of bits and encodes them as a solitary unit. In the existing methodology hardware implementation of AES has been done. The architecture of the existing methodology is shown in figure 33.6.

In the proposed methodology, an interleaver has been used instead of the look-up table in the substitute box. Interleaver is the technique of interchanging the data. Use of an interleaver increases the performance of the substitute box. Use of interleaving technique decreases the power consumption. AES is a secured algorithm, but with the effect of attacks like brute force attack and dictionary attack there are chances of hacking the data. If the length of the key is small then one can hack the data using brute force attack. If the length of key is large then the data can be hacked using dictionary attack. So, in order to make the AES more secure, a new method has been used in this study. The method is to hide the cipher text in an image. By mixing the data with an image it will be difficult to identify which one is data and which one is pixel. By doing this security will be increased. The diagrammatical representation of the proposed methodology is shown in figure 33.7.

The output from the multiplexer is provided to the s-box, which functions using an interleaver, as represented in the figure. Shift rows accept the output from the s-box. Mix columns accept the result from shift rows. The add round key is given the output from mixing columns. The final output from the add round key has been given to pipelining registers. This completes the first round. Likewise, nine more rounds will be performed. Last round will not have mix column transformation. Thus, the cipher text which has been obtained from encryption is hidden in an image. After hiding the cipher in the image, it is extracted and is given for

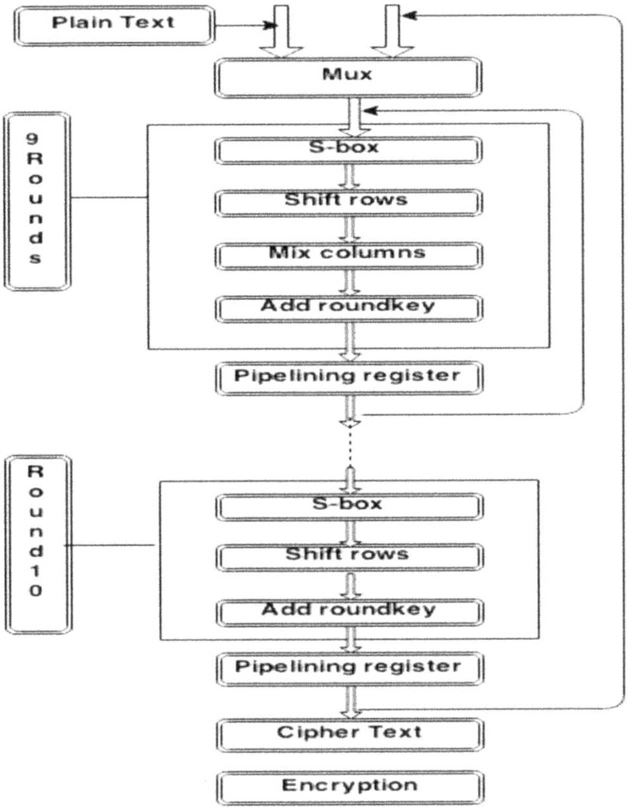

Figure 33.6. Pipelined architecture of AES.

decryption. In decryption the inverse of s-box, converse of modification rows, converse of mix pilasters and add smooth-edged key procedure will be accomplished.

Model sim 6.3g is used to simulate the AES algorithm, which again is written in Verilog. It was able to model 128-bit AES encryption and decryption. AESALGORITHM is a 128-bit data interchange format that is classified as plain text. It is decided to use a 128-bit key. The encryption technique takes both clear text and the key as input. Figure 33.8 depicts the simulation graph.

The output of the encryption procedure, cipher text is hided in an image to increase the security. The image in which the data is hidden is shown in figure 33.9. It is done using MATLAB.

The decipherment remains realized by means of Verilog HDL and prototypical sim. The cipher text which is extracted from the image is given as input to the decryption. The decryption simulation is shown in figure 33.10.

The performance strictures like area, influence feasting, occurrence quantity are observed using Quartus software. It is tabulated in table 33.1.

Quantity of the projected AES is more developed than the prevailing AES which is shown in table 33.1. It is calculated using the formula

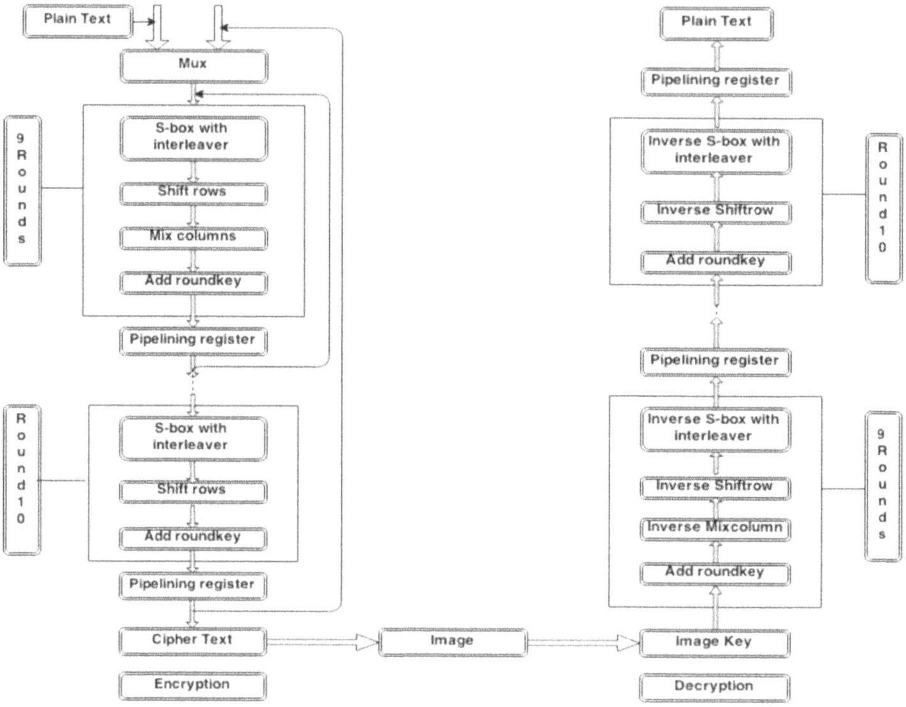

Figure 33.7. AES encryption and decryption with interleaver.

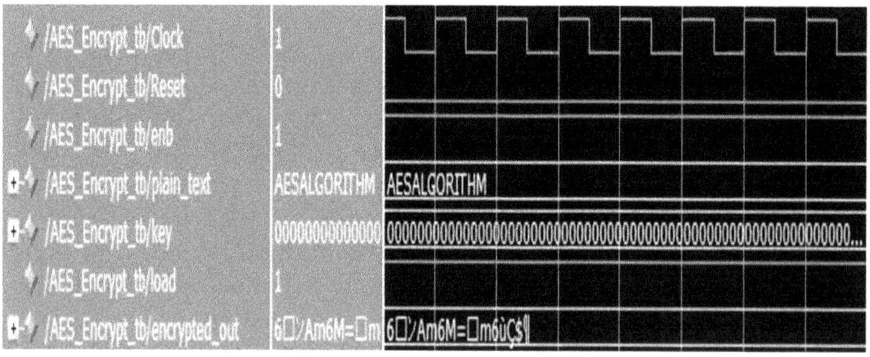

Figure 33.8. Encryption simulation.

$$\text{Throughput} = \frac{\text{Number of bits} * \text{Clock frenquency}}{\text{Clock cycle}}$$

When compared to reference paper [7] and existing AES, the proposed AES utilised more frequency. It indicates that operation requires less time for simulation. Throughput is also high for the proposed AES when compared with the existing AES. The graphical representation is shown in figures 33.11 and 33.12.

Figure 33.9. Data hidden image.

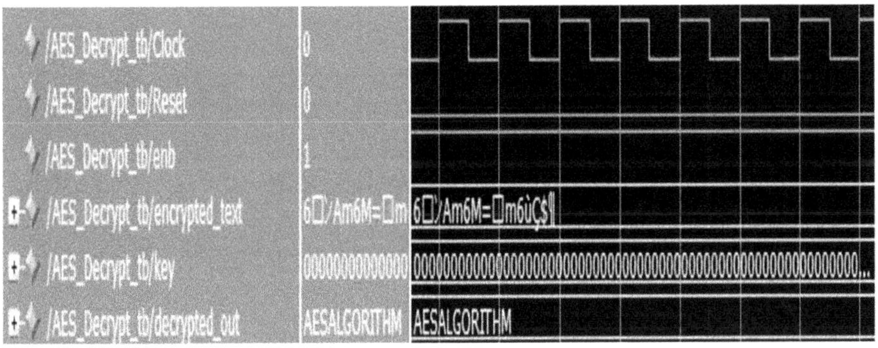

Figure 33.10. Decryption simulation.

Table 33.1. Performance parameters

Performance parameters	Existing AES	Proposed AES
Total logical elements	38,386	6386
Power dissipation	1074.11 mW	225.38 Mw
Frequency	194.74 Mhz	460.41 Mhz
Throughput	800 Mbytes sec^{-1}	980 Mbytes sec^{-1}

RC5 algorithm

The RC5 AES is a symmetric block cypher. It makes use of a variable number of rounds, keys, and data bytes. The very same secret key is used for encryption and decryption in encryption algorithm. As a consequence, the different keys should not be used. Encryption refers to a method by which plain text is converted into an incomprehensible sequence using a key. The Rc5 algorithm requires a two-word input and produces a 64-bit word encrypted message, and also plain text. A block diagram of Rc5 encryption and decryption is shown in figures 33.13 and 33.14.

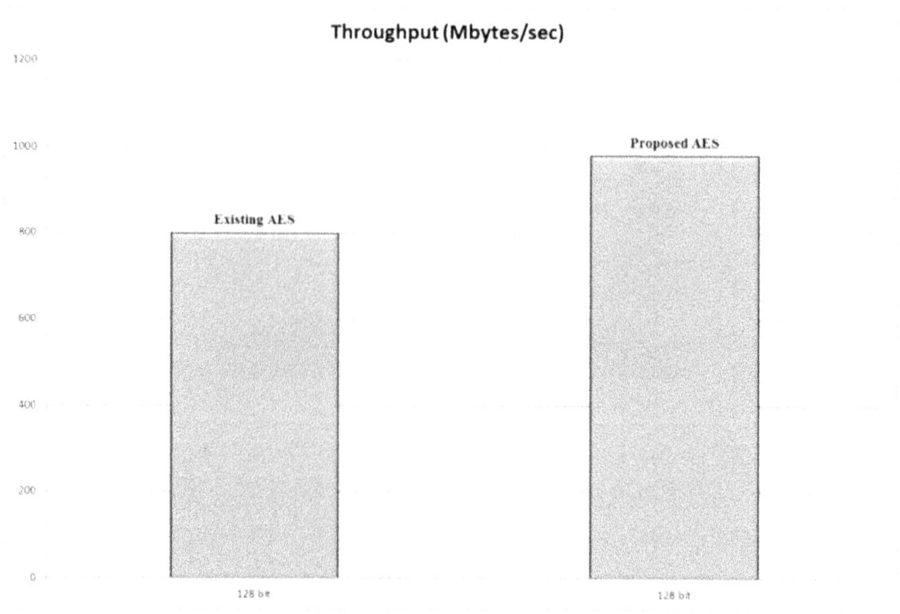

Figure 33.11. Comparison of throughput.

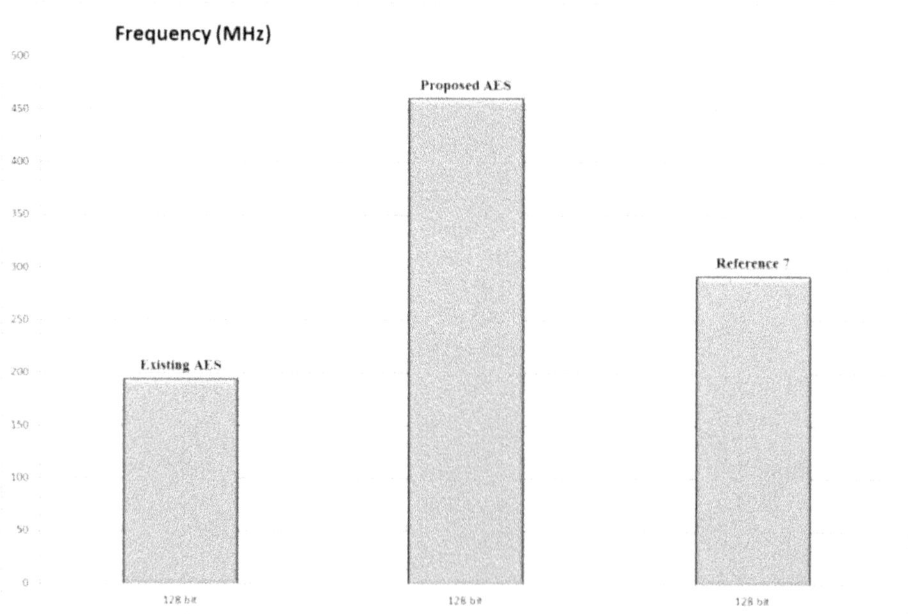

Figure 33.12. Comparison of frequency.

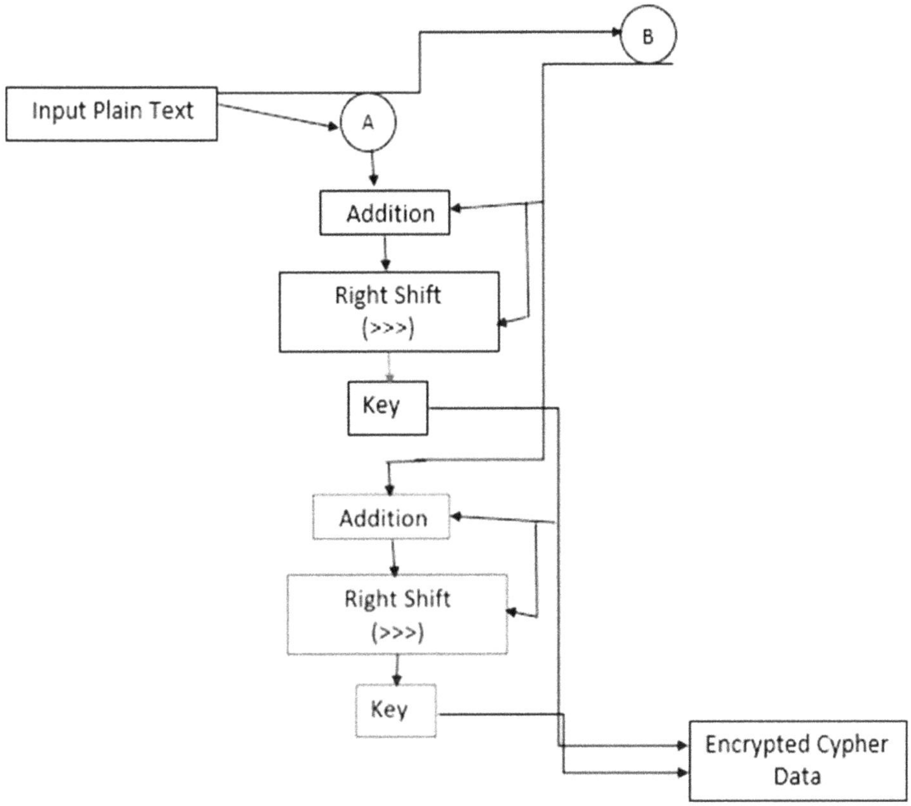

Figure 33.13. Architecture of RC5 encryption.

SHA algorithm

Cryptography basically means secure writing. It never discloses the content of a message to the intervener or the hacker while transmitting it from the sender to the recipient. Cryptography refers to the science of encompassing the method of converting a graspable message into one that is ungraspable and reconverting the message back to its original form. In this modern era, electronic gadgets like mobile phones, computer systems include operations like sending e-mails, transactions through net banking, document transfer, online shopping, and cryptography has occupied a vital role for safeguarding data conversion. Hash task mapping is one tool which uses mapping of message with erratic length to a string of fixed length called hash or digest. In 2002, NIST again published the advanced SHA algorithm with a few modifications, which specified three new secure hash algorithms SHA-224, SHA-256, SHA-384 and SHA-512. Hash function (or) task promotes many algorithms with cryptography approaches in digital signature standard (DSS), message authentication codes (MACs) with a secrete key encryption. Other utilization of hash task includes random noise generation (RNG), fastest encryption and password depot and verification. These are widely spread into HiperLAN and

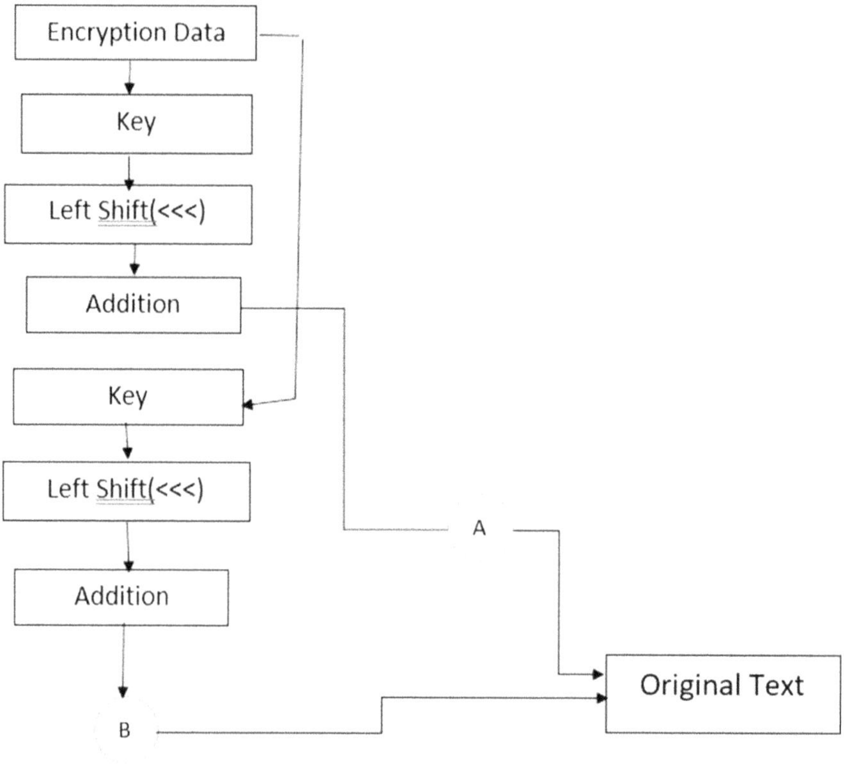

Figure 33.14. RC5 decryption.

wireless protocols (WAP) which use many security layers and various cryptographic schemes. Hash tasks are mainly used to guard the function of purity. They also provide the guard of authentication, when they are used in combination with digital signature and MAC algorithms. These algorithms are constant and of one-way functions that input message and output message digest. They process the data in different stages: (i) message filler (or) padding, (ii) message extension and (iii) message squeezing.

(i) Message filler (or) padding:

While processing the message, the binary message to be processed, is appended with a '1s' and padded with zeros up to its length of 448 modulo 512 named as M (M = 512 or 1024). The hash computation uses data as variable, constant and applies algebraic operations. SHA-2 algorithm with bits 224, 256 and 512. It differs mostly in the size of operands using 64-bit words instead of 32-bit.

Optimization techniques:

CSA(Expansion) algorithm separates the sum and carry root, the carry propagation technique is caused by minimizing the delay.

The techniques are unrolling and pipelining.

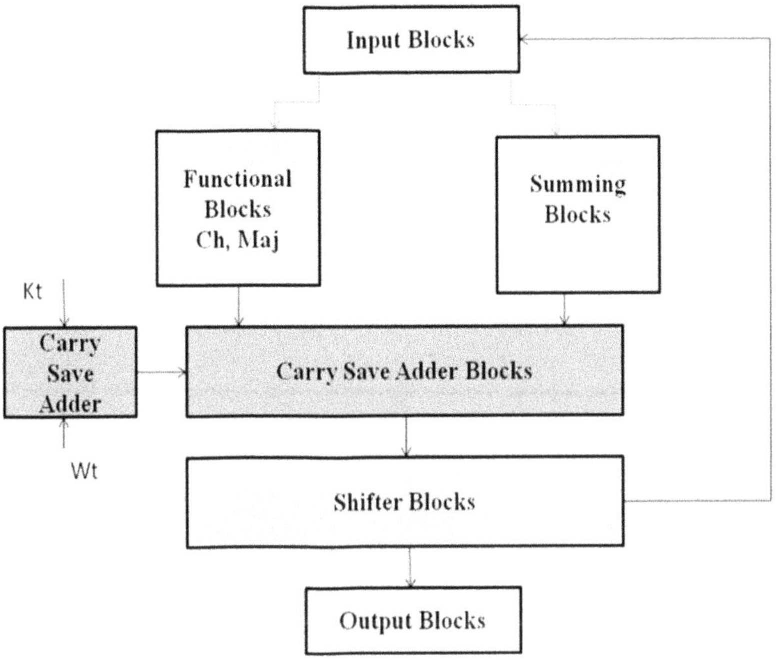

Figure 33.15. Block diagram depicting SHA algorithm.

Unrolling:

This unrolling technique performs multiple rounds of the squeezing function in combinational logic for computing the hash function, it will take a lower no. of clock cycles. Ex: core was unrolled once, the hash should be calculated in half of the clock cycles, it decreases the clock frequency.

Pipelining:

Fast pipelining can be used for registers to break the long critical path within the SHA core. External control circuitry is required to allow registers to save the data correctly. Pipelined designs achieve very short critical paths, allowing message hashes to be calculated at high frequencies and high data throughputs. It is shown in figure 33.15.

The acquired digital image is subjected to segmentation, where the pixels of highest intensity values are isolated and highlighted. The pixel details are then extracted and are used for recognition of the input signal, by comparing the particular feature with already stored database. This database is accessible by end users and any sorts of inputs can be classified based on the threshold values saved in the database.

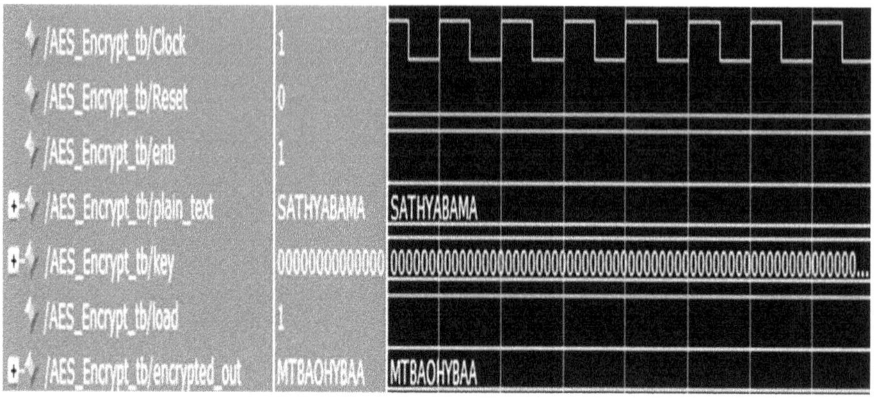

Figure 33.16. AES encryption result.

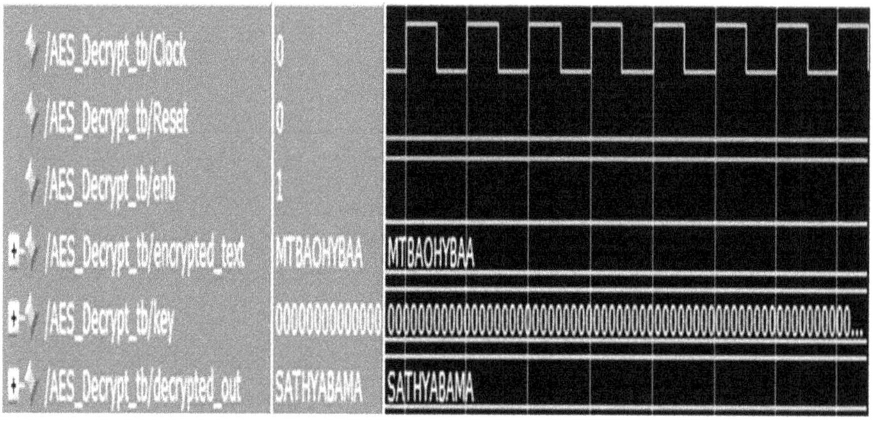

Figure 33.17. AES decryption result.

33.3 Results and discussions

The proposed AES algorithm is applied using Verilog HDL and simulated using the tool box ModelSim 6.3g. The AES encryption and decryption is carried out for 128-bit data and has been done. The data is SATHYABAMA word of 128-bit data as the plain text in this simulation. A 128-bit key is used for this simulation study. Both the plain text and key are treated as input to the encryption procedure. The simulated wave window for encryption of AES algorithm is shown in figure 33.16.

The received encrypted data is MTBAOHYBAA. This text is applied as input to the decryption algorithm along with 128-bit data. The original text is received after applying the decryption algorithm. From this study, it is understood that using pipelined registers increases the speed of the AES algorithm. It automatically reduces the power consumption. It is shown in figure 33.17. Similarly, the encryption

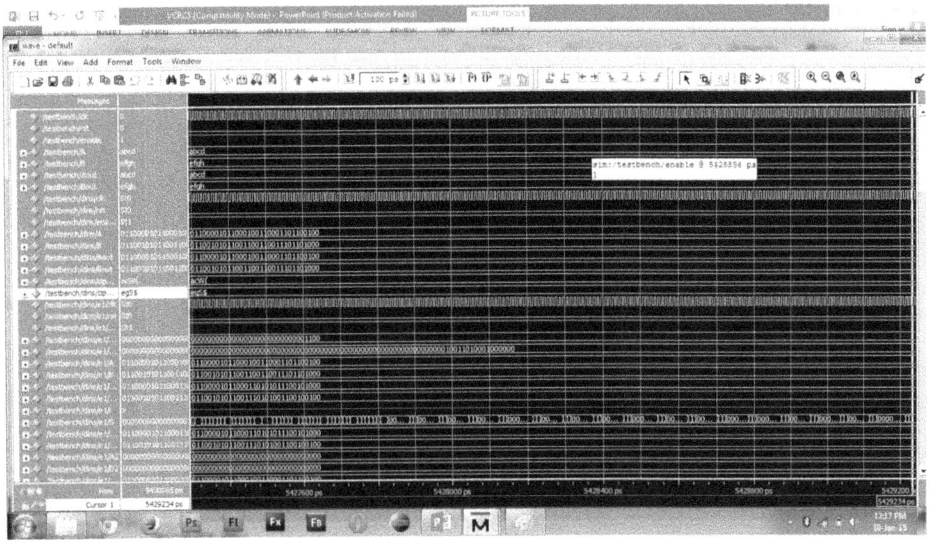

Figure 33.18. Encryption and decryption result of RC5.

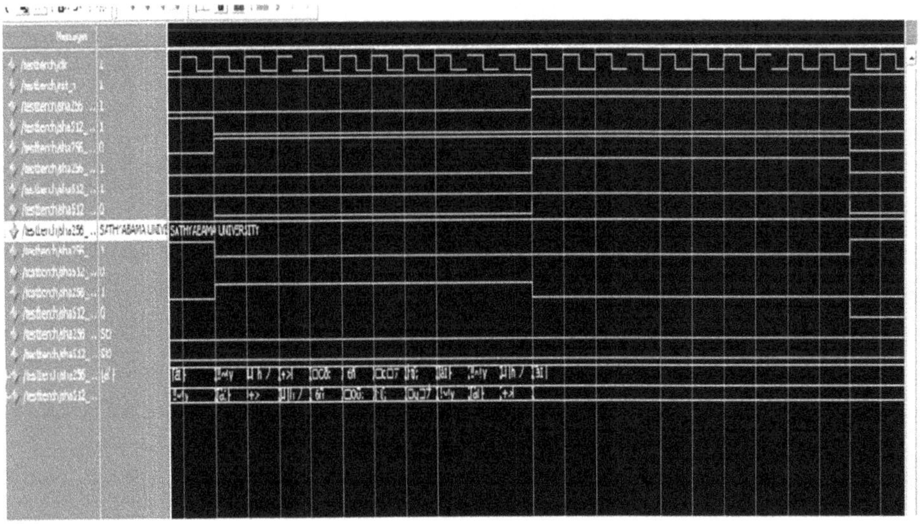

Figure 33.19. Encryption and decryption result of SHA-256.

and decryption of RC5 and SHA-256 algorithm is verified for the particular data and the results are shown in figures 33.18 and 33.19.

33.4 Conclusion

In this paper, the performance study of data security algorithms is implemented as a software framework is described. Three algorithms' AES, RC5 and SHA-256 have been taken in this study and its implementations are carried out in Quartus II software. The coding of encryption and decryption are written using Verilog HDL and simulation study is performed using ModelSim. The existing and proposed algorithm study and performance of architectures is analyzed in terms of efficiency, throughput and frequency. The system procedure satisfies all the requirements and the results prove its reliability for data transmission.

References

[1] Vanitha M and Sakthivel R 2012 Highly secured high throughput VLSI architecture for AES algorithm *2012 Int. Conf. on Devices, Circuits and Systems (ICDCS)* 403–7

[2] Zhang X, Parhi K K and VLSI H-S 2004 Architectures for the AES algorithm *Trans. VLSI Syst.* **12** 957–67

[3] Santhi B, Ravichandran K S, Arun A P and Chakkrapani L 2012 A novel cryptographic key generation method using image features *Res. J. Inform. Technol.* **4** 88–92

[4] Yadav K and Rajput S 2016 Data hiding in image using least significant bit with cryptography *Int. J. Eng. Appl. Sci. Technol.* **1** 80–5

[5] Pahal R and Kumar V 2013 Efficient implementation of AES *Int. J. Adv. Res. Comput. Sci. Softw. Eng.* **3** 290–5

[6] Abd-El-Barr M and Al-Farhan A 2014 A highly parallel area efficient S-box architecture for AES byte-substitution *IACSIT Int. J. Eng.Technol.* **6** 346–50

[7] Narasimhulu M, Mahaboob Basha S and Chandra Sekhar P 2014 Hardware implementation of high performance AES using minimal resources *Int. J. Eng. Res.* **3** 68–72

[8] Shelke R B, Patil A P and Patil S B 2015 VLSI based implementation of single round AES algorithm *IOSR-JECE* 63–7

[9] Kawle P, Hiwase A, Bagde G, Tekam E and Kalbande R 2014 Modified advanced encryption standard *Int. J. Soft Comput. Eng.* **4** 105–9

[10] Manjesh K N and Karunavathi R K 2013 Secured high throughput implementation of AES algorithm *Int. J. Manage. Inform. Technol.* **9** 152–60

[11] Rahman T, Pan S and Zhang Q 2010 Design of a high throughput 128-bit AES (Rijndeal Block Cipher) *Proc. Int. Multiconference of Engineers and Computer Scientists* vol II 3–7

[12] Shtewi A M 2010 An efficient modified advanced encryption standard adapted for image cryptosystems *7th Int. Conf. on Electrical Engineering ICEENG 2010* 71–8

[13] Stallings W 2003 *Cryptography and Network Security* 3rd edn (Upper Saddle River, NJ: Pearson Education)

[14] Julia J, Ramlan M, Salasiah S and Jazrin R 2012 Enhancing AES s-box generation based on round key *Int. J. Cyber-Secur. Dig. Forens.* **1** 183–8

[15] Gnanambika M, Adilakshmi S and Noorbasha F 2013 AES-128 bit algorithm using fully pipelined architecture for secret communication *Int. J. Eng. Res. Applic.* **3** 166–9

[16] Algredo-Badillo, Feregrino-Uribe C, Cumplido R and Morales-Sandoval M 2013 FPGA-based implementation alternatives for the inner loop of the secure Hash algorithm SHA-256 *J. Microproc. Microsyst.* **37** 750–7

[17] Zehid M, Bouallegue B, Machhout M, Baganne A and Tourki R 2008 Architectural design features of a programmable high throughput reconfigurable SHA-2 processor *J. Inform Assur. Secur.* **2** 147–58

[18] Koufopavlou O 2005 Implementation of the SHA-2 hash family standard using FPGA's *J. Supercomput.* **31**(3) 227–48